GREAT BOOKS OF THE WESTERN WORLD

28. GILBERT
    GALILEO
    HARVEY

29. CERVANTES

30. FRANCIS BACON

31. DESCARTES
    SPINOZA

32. MILTON

33. PASCAL

34. NEWTON
    HUYGENS

35. LOCKE
    BERKELEY
    HUME

36. SWIFT
    STERNE

37. FIELDING

38. MONTESQUIEU
    ROUSSEAU

39. ADAM SMITH

40. GIBBON I

41. GIBBON II

42. KANT

43. AMERICAN STATE
    PAPERS
    THE FEDERALIST
    J. S. MILL

44. BOSWELL

45. LAVOISIER
    FOURIER
    FARADAY

46. HEGEL

47. GOETHE

48. MELVILLE

49. DARWIN

50. MARX
    ENGELS

51. TOLSTOY

52. DOSTOEVSKY

53. WILLIAM JAMES

54. FREUD

AC
1
G7
V.8

61-848

Great books of the Western
    world; vol. 8

ST. LOUIS BAPTIST COLLEGE LIBRARY

GREAT BOOKS
OF THE WESTERN WORLD

ROBERT MAYNARD HUTCHINS, EDITOR IN CHIEF

8.

ARISTOTLE: I

MORTIMER J. ADLER, *Associate Editor*
Members of the Advisory Board: STRINGFELLOW BARR, SCOTT BUCHANAN, JOHN ERSKINE,
CLARENCE H. FAUST, ALEXANDER MEIKLEJOHN, JOSEPH J. SCHWAB, MARK VAN DOREN.
Editorial Consultants: A. F. B. CLARK, F. L. LUCAS, WALTER MURDOCH.
WALLACE BROCKWAY, *Executive Editor*

ST. LOUIS BAPTIST COLLEGE LIBRARY

888.8
G786
v.8

61-848

THE WORKS OF ARISTOTLE

VOLUME I

WILLIAM BENTON, *Publisher*

ENCYCLOPÆDIA BRITANNICA, INC.

CHICAGO · LONDON · TORONTO

The text and annotations of this edition are reprinted from
The Works of Aristotle, translated into English under the editorship
of W. D. Ross, by arrangement with OXFORD UNIVERSITY PRESS.

COPYRIGHT IN THE UNITED STATES OF AMERICA, 1952,
BY ENCYCLOPÆDIA BRITANNICA, INC.

COPYRIGHT 1952. COPYRIGHT UNDER INTERNATIONAL COPYRIGHT UNION BY
ENCYCLOPÆDIA BRITANNICA, INC. ALL RIGHTS RESERVED UNDER PAN AMERICAN
COPYRIGHT CONVENTIONS BY ENCYCLOPÆDIA BRITANNICA, INC.

BIOGRAPHICAL NOTE
Aristotle, 384–322 b.c.

Aristotle was born in 384 at Stagira, a Greek colonial town on the Aegean near the Macedonian border and somewhat east of the modern city of Salonica. Both of his parents were Ionian in origin. His mother was a native of Chalcis, from which Stagira had been colonized. His father, Nicomachus, belonged to the guild of the "sons of Aesculapius" and was court physician to Amyntas II, the father of Philip of Macedon. Aristotle, who seems to have remained with his parents during his first seventeen years, may have studied medicine with his father, and it was sometimes claimed in antiquity that he practised medicine when he first went to Athens.

In 367 Aristotle entered the Academy at Athens. Plato was then sixty-one and just entering upon his intervention in the politics of Syracuse. The Academy was giving particular attention to the problems of politics and legislation and, in addition to its more general philosophic interests, was increasingly preoccupied with mathematics and astronomy. Few details have survived of the life Aristotle led at the Academy for twenty years. He is said to have been called by Plato the intellect of the school. There is also a tradition that he taught rhetoric. He is known to have written numerous dialogues modeled after those of his master, which were famed in antiquity for their lucidity and the easy flow of their style. There is little evidence of any serious disagreement between master and pupil during these years, and on Plato's death in 347 Aristotle wrote an elegy for an altar of friendship to Plato in which he praised him as "the man whom it is not lawful for bad men even to praise, who alone or first of mortals clearly revealed, by his own life and by the methods of his words, how to be happy is to be good."

When Speusippus became head of the Academy in 347, Aristotle and another of Plato's pupils, Xenocrates, left Athens for Assus, in the Troiad, where two former members of the Academy were teaching. The "tyrant," or ruler, of the territory, Hermias, had become their pupil and, out of gratitude, had bestowed upon them the town of Assus. The four set up something like a colonial Academy. Through his teaching Aristotle apparently became the intimate friend of Hermias, and he married the ruler's adopted daughter. Theophrastus from the neighboring island of Lesbos was also among his pupils, and it may have been on his suggestion that Aristotle moved about 344 to Mytilene on Lesbos, where for two years he was engaged largely in the study of natural history, particularly marine biology.

In 342 Aristotle returned to Macedonia to act as tutor to the young Alexander. Although he had been in early youth close to the Macedonian court and already enjoyed some reputation for his dialogues, the deciding factor in the appointment may have been Aristotle's connection with Hermias, who at this time was apparently negotiating with Philip regarding an expedition against Persia. Aristotle stayed in Macedonia for seven years. The tradition is that he taught politics and rhetoric, and he is said to have prepared an edition of Homer for the use of Alexander, who was thirteen at the time of his coming. In 340, after Philip went to war, Alexander directed political affairs at home as regent, and it is likely that Aristotle set up a school and gave the greater part of his time to his own studies. He induced Alexander to restore Stagira, which had been destroyed a few years before, and is said to have provided it with a constitution. Perhaps at Alexander's request, he wrote the two political treatises or pamphlets, no longer extant, *On Kingship* and *On Colonies*. Although Aristotle could have seen but little of his royal pupil during the latter years of his Macedonian sojourn, there is evidence that Alexander did not forget his master. When he made his expedition to the East, he took Aristotle's nephew, Callisthenes, as his historian, and to further Aristotle's scientific researches, he appointed men to collect materials and specimens.

After the accession of Alexander in 336, Aristotle returned to Athens, where his friend, Xenocrates, had become head of the Academy. He established the Lycaeum, which came to be known as the Peripatetic School from the path in its garden where he walked and talked with his pupils. The Lycaeum was an organized institution for the "cult of the Muses." It possessed extensive equipment, including maps and the largest library then collected in Europe. It had its regular dinners and even its plate, and Aristotle himself wrote rules for holding *symposia*. The staff of lecturers included Theophrastus and Eudemus, and there was a fixed schedule for the lectures. Aristotle, according to tradition, devoted the mornings to the more difficult parts of philosophy and in the afternoon addressed a wider audience on rhetoric and dialectic.

The great body of the extant Aristotelian treatises probably represents the lectures which Aristotle delivered at the Lyceum. It is not likely that all were written at this time; they had probably been growing since he first began teaching. His various works of compilation almost certainly belong to these last years. He drew up lists of the victors in the Pythian and Olympic games and a chronology of the Athenian drama, later the basis for dating the Greek plays. He organized the collection of one hundred and fifty-eight Greek constitutions, and his work *On the Athenian Constitution,* the only extant treatise of this collection, is thought to have provided the model for this research. He also drew up an account of the "customs of the barbarians" and a treatise on "cases of constitutional law." The results of his investigations in natural history are evident in his biological works, particularly the *History of Animals.*

With the death of Alexander in 323, Aristotle's life at the Lyceum came to an abrupt end. Although Aristotle apparently had little relation with Alexander, especially after his nephew had been put to death for refusing to render oriental obeisance to him, the philosopher enjoyed the friendship and protection of Antipater, who governed Alexander's Greek affairs from Athens. The revolt of the Athenian party, following the news of Alexander's death, was directed against Antipater and through him it involved Aristotle. Charged with impiety for the elegy he had written to Hermias twenty years before, Aristotle recalled the fate of Socrates and fled to his mother's property in Chalcis, declaring, "I will not let the Athenians offend twice against philosophy."

Aristotle lived in Chalcis for only a few months. Writing to Antipater, he noted, "The more I am by myself, and alone, the fonder I have become of myths." He died in 322. His will discloses the care with which he put his affairs in order; he provided for his children and the disposition of his property in Stagira and Chalcis, left bequests for his household servants and directions for their freedom, directed that his body should be buried with that of his wife, as she had desired, and, as one of the arrangements for the observance of familial piety, ordered his executors to "set up in Stagira statues of life-size to Zeus and Athena the Saviours."

GENERAL CONTENTS, VOLUME I

Biographical Note, p. v

LOGIC (Organon)
  Categories (Categoriae), *translated by* E. M. Edghill, p. 5
  On Interpretation (De interpretatione), *translated by* E. M. Edghill, p. 25
  Prior Analytics (Analytica priora), *translated by* A. J. Jenkinson, p. 39
  Posterior Analytics (Analytica posteriora), *translated by* G. R. G. Mure, p. 97
  Topics (Topica), *translated by* W. A. Pickard-Cambridge, p. 143
  On Sophistical Refutations (De sophisticis elenchis), *translated by* W. A. Pickard-Cambridge, p. 227

PHYSICAL TREATISES
  Physics (Physica), *translated by* R. P. Hardie and R. K. Gaye, p. 259
  On the Heavens (De caelo), *translated by* J. L. Stocks, p. 359
  On Generation and Corruption (De generatione et corruptione), *translated by* H. H. Joachim, p. 409
  Meteorology (Meteorologica), *translated by* E. W. Webster, p. 445

METAPHYSICS (Metaphysica), *translated by* W. D. Ross, p. 499

ON THE SOUL (De anima), *translated by* J. A. Smith, p. 631

SHORT PHYSICAL TREATISES (Parva naturalia)
  On Sense and the Sensible (De sensu et sensibili), *translated by* J. I. Beare, p. 673
  On Memory and Reminiscence (De memoria et reminiscentia), *translated by* J. I. Beare, p. 690
  On Sleep and Sleeplessness (De somno et vigilia), *translated by* J. I. Beare, p. 696
  On Dreams (De somniis), *translated by* J. I. Beare, p. 702
  On Prophesying by Dreams (De divinatione per somnum), *translated by* J. I. Beare, p. 707
  On Longevity and Shortness of Life (De longitudine et brevitate vitae), *translated by* G. R. T. Ross, p. 710
  On Youth and Old Age, On Life and Death, On Breathing (De iuventate et senectute, De vita et morte, De respiratione), *translated by* G. R. T. Ross, p. 714

LOGIC (ORGANON)

CONTENTS: CATEGORIES

CHAP.	BERLIN NOS.
1. Homonyms, synonyms, and derivatives	1a 1
2. (1) Simple and composite expressions	1a 16

(2) Things (*a*) predicable of a subject, (*b*) present in a subject, (*c*) both predicable of, and present in, a subject, (*d*) neither predicable of, nor present in, a subject

3. (1) That which is predicable of the predicate is predicable of the subject   1b 10
(2) The differentiae of species in one genus are not the same as those in another, unless one genus is included in the other

4. The eight categories of the objects of thought   1b 25

5. Substance   2a 11
(1) Primary and secondary substance
(2) Difference in the relation subsisting between essential and accidental attributes and their subject
(3) All that which is not primary substance is either an essential or an accidental attribute of primary substance
(4) Of secondary substances, species are more truly substance than genera
(5) All species, which are not genera, are substance in the same degree, and all primary substances are substance in the same degree.
(6) Nothing except species and genera is secondary substance
(7) The relation of primary substance to secondary substance and to all other predicates is the same as that of secondary substance to all other predicates
(8) Substance is never an accidental attribute
(9) The differentiae of species are not accidental attributes
(10) Species, genus, and differentiae, as predicates, are 'univocal' with their subject
(11) Primary substance is individual; secondary substance is the qualification of that which is individual
(12) No substance has a contrary
(13) No substance can be what it is in varying degrees
(14) The particular mark of substance is that contrary qualities can be predicated of it
(15) Contrary qualities cannot be predicated of anything other than substances, not even of propositions and judgements

6. Quantity   4b 20
(1) Discrete and continuous quantity
(2) Division of quantities, i.e. number, the spoken word, the line, the surface, the solid, time, place, into these two classes
(3) The parts of some quantities have a relative position, those of others have not. Division of quantities into these two classes
(4) Quantitative terms are applied to things other than quantity, in view of their relation to one of the aforesaid quantities
(5) Quantities have no contraries
(6) Terms such as 'great' and 'small' are relative, not quantitative, and moreover cannot be contrary to each other
(7) That which is most reasonably supposed to contain a contrary is space
(8) No quantity can be what it is in varying degrees
(9) The peculiar mark of quantity is that equality and inequality can be predicated of it

7. Relation   6a 36
(1) First definition of relatives
(2) Some relatives have contraries
(3) Some relatives are what they are in varying degrees
(4) A relative term has always its correlative, and the two are interdependent
(5) The correlative is only clear when the relative is given its proper name, and in some cases words must be coined for this purpose
(6) Most relatives come into existence simultaneously; but the objects of knowledge and perception are prior to knowledge and perception
(7) No primary substance or part of a primary substance is relative
(8) Revised definition of relatives, excluding secondary substances
(9) It is impossible to know that a thing is relative, unless we know that to which it is relative

8. Quality   8b 25
(1) Definition of qualities
(2) Different kinds of quality: (*a*) habits and dispositions, (*b*) capacities, (*c*) affective qualities [Distinction between affective qualities and affections], (*d*) shape, &c. [Rarity, density, &c., are not qualities]
(3) Adjectives are generally formed derivatively from the names of the corresponding qualities
(4) Most qualities have contraries
(5) If of two contraries one is a quality, the other is also a quality
(6) A quality can in most cases be what it is in varying degrees, and subjects can possess most qualities in varying degrees; qualities of shape are an exception to this rule
(7) The peculiar mark of quality is that likeness and unlikeness is predicable of things in respect of it

3

- (8) Habits and dispositions as genera are relative; as individual, qualitative
- 9. Action and affection and the other categories described   11^b 1
- 10. Four classes of 'opposites': (*a*) Correlatives, (*b*) Contraries [Some contraries have an intermediate, and some have not], (*c*) Positives and privatives   11^b 15

  The terms expressing possession and privation are not the positive and privative, though the former are opposed each to each in the same sense as the latter

  Similarly the facts which form the basis of an affirmation or a denial are opposed each to each in the same sense as the affirmation and denial themselves

  Positives and privatives are not opposed in the sense in which correlatives are opposed

  Positives and privatives are not opposed in the same sense in which contraries are opposed

  For (i) they are not of the class which has no intermediate, nor of the class which has intermediates

  (ii) There can be no change from one state (privation) to its opposite

  (*d*) Affirmation and negation; these are distinguished from other contraries by the fact that one is always false and the other true [Opposite affirmations seem to possess this mark, but they do not]

- 11. Contraries further discussed   13^b 36

  Evil is generally the contrary of good, but sometimes two evils are contrary

  When one contrary exists, the other need not exist

  Contrary attributes are applicable within the same species or genus

  Contraries must themselves be within the same genus, or within opposite genera, or be themselves genera

- 12. The word 'prior' is applicable: (*a*) to that which is previous in time, (*b*) to that on which something else depends, but which is not itself dependent on it, (*c*) to that which is prior in arrangement, (*d*) to that which is better or more honourable, (*e*) to that one of two interdependent things which is the cause of the other.   14^a 26

- 13. The word 'simultaneous' is used: (*a*) of those things which come into being at the same time, (*b*) of those things which are interdependent, but neither of which is the cause of the other (*c*) of the different species of the same genus   14^b 24

- 14. Motion is of six kinds   15^a 13

  Alteration is distinct from other kinds of motion

  Definition of the contrary of motion and of the various kinds of motion

- 15. The meanings of the term 'to have'   15^b 16

CATEGORIES

1

1ᵃ Things are said to be named 'equivocally' when, though they have a common name, the definition corresponding with the name differs for each. Thus, a real man and a figure in a picture can both lay claim to the name 'animal'; yet these are equivocally so named, for, though they have a common name, the definition corresponding with the name differs for each. For [5] should any one define in what sense each is an animal, his definition in the one case will be appropriate to that case only.

On the other hand, things are said to be named 'univocally' which have both the name and the definition answering to the name in common. A man and an ox are both 'animal', and these are univocally so named, inasmuch as not only the name, but also the definition, is the [10] same in both cases: for if a man should state in what sense each is an animal, the statement in the one case would be identical with that in the other.

Things are said to be named 'derivatively', which derive their name from some other name, but differ from it in termination. Thus the grammarian derives his name from the [15] word 'grammar', and the courageous man from the word 'courage'.

2

Forms of speech are either simple or composite. Examples of the latter are such expressions as 'the man runs', 'the man wins'; of the former 'man', 'ox', 'runs', 'wins'.

[20] Of things themselves some are predicable of a subject, and are never present in a subject. Thus 'man' is predicable of the individual man, and is never present in a subject.

By being 'present in a subject' I do not mean present as parts are present in a whole, but being incapable of existence apart from the said subject.

Some things, again, are present in a subject, [25] but are never predicable of a subject. For instance, a certain point of grammatical knowledge is present in the mind, but is not predicable of any subject; or again, a certain whiteness may be present in the body (for colour requires a material basis), yet it is never predicable of anything.

Other things, again, are both predicable of a **1ᵇ** subject and present in a subject. Thus while knowledge is present in the human mind, it is predicable of grammar.

There is, lastly, a class of things which are neither present in a subject nor predicable of a [5] subject, such as the individual man or the individual horse. But, to speak more generally, that which is individual and has the character of a unit is never predicable of a subject. Yet in some cases there is nothing to prevent such being present in a subject. Thus a certain point of grammatical knowledge is present in a subject.

3

[10] When one thing is predicated of another, all that which is predicable of the predicate will be predicable also of the subject. Thus, 'man' is predicated of the individual man; but 'animal' is predicated of 'man'; it will, therefore, [15] be predicable of the individual man also: for the individual man is both 'man' and 'animal'.

If genera are different and co-ordinate, their differentiae are themselves different in kind. Take as an instance the genus 'animal' and the genus 'knowledge'. 'With feet', 'two-footed', 'winged', 'aquatic', are differentiae of 'animal'; the species of knowledge are not distinguished by the same differentiae. One species of knowledge does not differ from another in being 'two-footed'.

[20] But where one genus is subordinate to another, there is nothing to prevent their having the same differentiae: for the greater class is predicated of the lesser, so that all the differentiae of the predicate will be differentiae also of the subject.

4

[25] Expressions which are in no way composite signify substance, quantity, quality, relation, place, time, position, state, action, or affection. To sketch my meaning roughly, examples

---

Note: The bold face numbers and letters are approximate indications of the pages and columns of the standard Berlin Greek text; the bracketed numbers, of the lines in the Greek text; they are here assigned as they are assigned in the Oxford translation.

of substance are 'man' or 'the horse', of quantity, such terms as 'two cubits long' or 'three cubits long', of quality, such attributes as 'white', 'grammatical'. 'Double', 'half', 'great-[2a] er', fall under the category of relation; 'in the market place', 'in the Lyceum', under that of place; 'yesterday', 'last year', under that of time. 'Lying', 'sitting', are terms indicating position, 'shod', 'armed', state; 'to lance', 'to cauterize', action; 'to be lanced', 'to be cauterized', affection.

No one of these terms, in and by itself, in-[5] volves an affirmation; it is by the combination of such terms that positive or negative statements arise. For every assertion must, as is admitted, be either true or false, whereas expressions which are not in any way composite, [10] such as 'man', 'white', 'runs', 'wins', cannot be either true or false.

5

Substance, in the truest and primary and most definite sense of the word, is that which is neither predicable of a subject nor present in a subject; for instance, the individual man or horse. But in a secondary sense those things are called substances within which, as species, [15] the primary substances are included; also those which, as genera, include the species. For instance, the individual man is included in the species 'man', and the genus to which the species belongs is 'animal'; these, therefore—that is to say, the species 'man' and the genus 'animal'—are termed secondary substances.

It is plain from what has been said that both [20] the name and the definition of the predicate must be predicable of the subject. For instance, 'man' is predicated of the individual man. Now in this case the name of the species 'man' is applied to the individual, for we use the term 'man' in describing the individual; and the definition of 'man' will also be predicated of the individual man, for the individual [25] man is both man and animal. Thus, both the name and the definition of the species are predicable of the individual.

With regard, on the other hand, to those things which are present in a subject, it is generally the case that neither their name nor their definition is predicable of that in which they are present. Though, however, the definition is [30] never predicable, there is nothing in certain cases to prevent the name being used. For instance, 'white' being present in a body is predicated of that in which it is present, for a body is called white: the definition, however, of the colour 'white' is never predicable of the body.

Everything except primary substances is either predicable of a primary substance or present in a primary substance. This becomes [35] evident by reference to particular instances which occur. 'Animal' is predicated of the species 'man', therefore of the individual man, for if there were no individual man of whom it could be predicated, it could not be [2b] predicated of the species 'man' at all. Again, colour is present in body, therefore in individual bodies, for if there were no individual body in which it was present, it could not be present in body at all. Thus everything except primary substances is either predicated of primary sub-[5] stances, or is present in them, and if these last did not exist, it would be impossible for anything else to exist.

Of secondary substances, the species is more truly substance than the genus, being more nearly related to primary substance. For if any one should render an account of what a primary substance is, he would render a more instructive account, and one more proper to the sub-[10] ject, by stating the species than by stating the genus. Thus, he would give a more instructive account of an individual man by stating that he was man than by stating that he was animal, for the former description is peculiar to the individual in a greater degree, while the latter is too general. Again, the man who gives an account of the nature of an individual tree will give a more instructive account by mentioning the species 'tree' than by mentioning the genus 'plant'.

[15] Moreover, primary substances are most properly called substances in virtue of the fact that they are the entities which underlie everything else, and that everything else is either predicated of them or present in them. Now the same relation which subsists between primary substance and everything else subsists also between the species and the genus: for the species is to the genus as subject is to predicate, [20] since the genus is predicated of the species, whereas the species cannot be predicated of the genus. Thus we have a second ground for asserting that the species is more truly substance than the genus.

Of species themselves, except in the case of such as are genera, no one is more truly substance than another. We should not give a more appropriate account of the individual man by [25] stating the species to which he belonged, than we should of an individual horse by adopting the same method of definition. In the same way, of primary substances, no one is more truly substance than another; an individual man is not more truly substance than an individual ox.

It is, then, with good reason that of all that remains, when we exclude primary substances, [30] we concede to species and genera alone the name 'secondary substance', for these alone of all the predicates convey a knowledge of primary substance. For it is by stating the species or the genus that we appropriately define any individual man; and we shall make our definition more exact by stating the former than by stating the latter. All other things that [35] we state, such as that he is white, that he runs, and so on, are irrelevant to the definition. Thus it is just that these alone, apart from primary substances, should be called substances.

Further, primary substances are most properly so called, because they underlie and are the subjects of everything else. Now the same relation that subsists between primary substance and everything else subsists also between the species and the genus to which the primary substance belongs, on the one hand, and every attribute which is not included within these, on the other. For these are the subjects of all such. If we call an individual man 'skilled in grammar', the predicate is applicable [5] also to the species and to the genus to which he belongs. This law holds good in all cases.

It is a common characteristic of all substance that it is never present in a subject. For primary substance is neither present in a subject nor predicated of a subject; while, with regard to secondary substances, it is clear from the following arguments (apart from others) that they are not present in a subject. For [10] 'man' is predicated of the individual man, but is not present in any subject: for manhood is not present in the individual man. In the same way, 'animal' is also predicated of the individual man, but is not present in him. Again, [15] when a thing is present in a subject, though the name may quite well be applied to that in which it is present, the definition cannot be applied. Yet of secondary substances, not only the name, but also the definition, applies to the subject: we should use both the definition of the species and that of the genus [20] with reference to the individual man. Thus substance cannot be present in a subject.

Yet this is not peculiar to substance, for it is also the case that differentiae cannot be present in subjects. The characteristics 'terrestrial' and 'two-footed' are predicated of the species 'man', but not present in it. For they are not *in* man. [25] Moreover, the definition of the differentia may be predicated of that of which the differentia itself is predicated. For instance, if the characteristic 'terrestrial' is predicated of the species 'man', the definition also of that characteristic may be used to form the predicate of the species 'man': for 'man' is terrestrial.

The fact that the parts of substances appear to be present in the whole, as in a subject, should not make us apprehensive lest we [30] should have to admit that such parts are not substances: for in explaining the phrase 'being present in a subject', we stated[1] that we meant 'otherwise than as parts in a whole'.

It is the mark of substances and of differentiae that, in all propositions of which they form the predicate, they are predicated univocally. For all such propositions have for [35] their subject either the individual or the species. It is true that, inasmuch as primary substance is not predicable of anything, it can never form the predicate of any proposition. But of secondary substances, the species is predicated of the individual, the genus both of the species and of the individual. Similarly the differentiae are predicated of the species and of the individuals. Moreover, the definition of the species and that of the genus are applicable to the primary substance, and that of the genus to the species. For all that is predicated of the predicate will be predicated also of [5] the subject. Similarly, the definition of the differentiae will be applicable to the species and to the individuals. But it was stated above[2] that the word 'univocal' was applied to those things which had both name and definition in common. It is, therefore, established that in every proposition, of which either substance or a differentia forms the predicate, these are predicated univocally.

[10] All substance appears to signify that which is individual. In the case of primary substance this is indisputably true, for the thing is a unit. In the case of secondary substances, when we speak, for instance, of 'man' or 'animal', our form of speech gives the impression that we are here also indicating that which is [15] individual, but the impression is not strictly true; for a secondary substance is not an individual, but a class with a certain qualification; for it is not one and single as a primary substance is; the words 'man', 'animal', are predicable of more than one subject.

[1] 1ª24.   [2] 1ª6.

Yet species and genus do not merely indicate quality, like the term 'white'; 'white' indicates quality and nothing further, but species and genus determine the quality with reference to [20] a substance: they signify substance qualitatively differentiated. The determinate qualification covers a larger field in the case of the genus that in that of the species: he who uses the word 'animal' is herein using a word of wider extension than he who uses the word 'man'.

Another mark of substance is that it has no [25] contrary. What could be the contrary of any primary substance, such as the individual man or animal? It has none. Nor can the species or the genus have a contrary. Yet this characteristic is not peculiar to substance, but is true of many other things, such as quantity. There is nothing that forms the contrary of 'two cubits long' or of 'three cubits long', or of 'ten', [30] or of any such term. A man may contend that 'much' is the contrary of 'little', or 'great' of 'small', but of definite quantitative terms no contrary exists.

Substance, again, does not appear to admit of variation of degree. I do not mean by this that one substance cannot be more or less truly substance than another, for it has already been [35] stated[1] that this is the case; but that no single substance admits of varying degrees within itself. For instance, one particular substance, 'man', cannot be more or less man either than himself at some other time or than some other man. One man cannot be more man than another, as that which is white may be more or less white than some other white object, or as that which is beautiful may be more or less beautiful than some other beautiful object. The same quality, moreover, is said to subsist in a thing in varying degrees at different times. A body, being white, is said to be whiter at one time than it was before, or, being warm, is said to be warmer or less warm than at some [5] other time. But substance is not said to be more or less that which it is: a man is not more truly a man at one time than he was before, nor is anything, if it is substance, more or less what it is. Substance, then, does not admit of variation of degree.

[10] The most distinctive mark of substance appears to be that, while remaining numerically one and the same, it is capable of admitting contrary qualities. From among things other than substance, we should find ourselves unable to bring forward any which possessed this [15] mark. Thus, one and the same colour cannot be white and black. Nor can the same one action be good and bad: this law holds good with everything that is not substance. But one and the selfsame substance, while retaining its identity, is yet capable of admitting contrary qualities. The same individual person is at one [20] time white, at another black, at one time warm, at another cold, at one time good, at another bad. This capacity is found nowhere else, though it might be maintained that a statement or opinion was an exception to the rule. The same statement, it is agreed, can be both true [25] and false. For if the statement 'he is sitting' is true, yet, when the person in question has risen, the same statement will be false. The same applies to opinions. For if any one thinks truly that a person is sitting, yet, when that person has risen, this same opinion, if still held, will be false. Yet although this exception may be allowed, there is, nevertheless, a difference in the manner in which the thing takes place. [30] It is by themselves changing that substances admit contrary qualities. It is thus that that which was hot becomes cold, for it has entered into a different state. Similarly that which was white becomes black, and that which was bad good, by a process of change; and in the same way in all other cases it is by changing that substances are capable of admitting contrary qualities. But statements and opinions [35] themselves remain unaltered in all respects: it is by the alteration in the facts of the case that the contrary quality comes to be theirs. The statement 'he is sitting' remains unaltered, but it is at one time true, at another false, according to circumstances. What has been said of statements applies also to opinions. Thus, in respect of the manner in which the thing takes place, it is the peculiar mark of substance that it should be capable of admitting contrary qualities; for it is by itself changing that it does so.

If, then, a man should make this exception and contend that statements and opinions are [5] capable of admitting contrary qualities, his contention is unsound. For statements and opinions are said to have this capacity, not because they themselves undergo modification, but because this modification occurs in the case of something else. The truth or falsity of a statement depends on facts, and not on any power on the part of the statement itself of ad- [10] mitting contrary qualities. In short, there is nothing which can alter the nature of statements and opinions. As, then, no change takes

---
[1] 2ª 11–ᵇ 22.

place in themselves, these cannot be said to be capable of admitting contrary qualities.

But it is by reason of the modification which takes place within the substance itself that a substance is said to be capable of admitting contrary qualities; for a substance admits within itself either disease or health, whiteness or [15] blackness. It is in this sense that it is said to be capable of admitting contrary qualities.

To sum up, it is a distinctive mark of substance, that, while remaining numerically one and the same, it is capable of admitting contrary qualities, the modification taking place through a change in the substance itself.

Let these remarks suffice on the subject of substance.

6

[20] Quantity is either discrete or continuous. Moreover, some quantities are such that each part of the whole has a relative position to the other parts: others have within them no such relation of part to part.

Instances of discrete quantities are number and speech; of continuous, lines, surfaces, solids, and, besides these, time and place.
[25] In the case of the parts of a number, there is no common boundary at which they join. For example: two fives make ten, but the two fives have no common boundary, but are separate; the parts three and seven also do not join at any boundary. Nor, to generalize, would it ever be possible in the case of number that there should be a common boundary among [30] the parts; they are always separate. Number, therefore, is a discrete quantity.

The same is true of speech. That speech is a quantity is evident: for it is measured in long and short syllables. I mean here that speech which is vocal. Moreover, it is a discrete quantity, for its parts have no common boundary. [35] There is no common boundary at which the syllables join, but each is separate and distinct from the rest.

5ª A line, on the other hand, is a continuous quantity, for it is possible to find a common boundary at which its parts join. In the case of the line, this common boundary is the point; in the case of the plane, it is the line: for the parts of the plane have also a common boundary. Similarly you can find a common bound-[5]ary in the case of the parts of a solid, namely either a line or a plane.

Space and time also belong to this class of quantities. Time, past, present, and future, forms a continuous whole. Space, likewise, is a continuous quantity; for the parts of a solid occupy a certain space, and these have a com-[10]mon boundary; it follows that the parts of space also, which are occupied by the parts of the solid, have the same common boundary as the parts of the solid. Thus, not only time, but space also, is a continuous quantity, for its parts have a common boundary.
[15] Quantities consist either of parts which bear a relative position each to each, or of parts which do not. The parts of a line bear a relative position to each other, for each lies somewhere, and it would be possible to distinguish each, and to state the position of each on the plane and to explain to what sort of part among the [20] rest each was contiguous. Similarly the parts of a plane have position, for it could similarly be stated what was the position of each and what sort of parts were contiguous. The same is true with regard to the solid and to space. But it would be impossible to show that the parts of a number had a relative position [25] each to each, or a particular position, or to state what parts were contiguous. Nor could this be done in the case of time, for none of the parts of time has an abiding existence, and that which does not abide can hardly have position. It would be better to say that such parts had a relative order, in virtue of one being prior to [30] another. Similarly with number: in counting, 'one' is prior to 'two', and 'two' to 'three', and thus the parts of number may be said to possess a relative order, though it would be impossible to discover any distinct position for each. This holds good also in the case of speech. None of its parts has an abiding existence: when once a syllable is pronounced, it is not [35] possible to retain it, so that, naturally, as the parts do not abide, they cannot have position. Thus, some quantities consist of parts which have position, and some of those which have not.

Strictly speaking, only the things which I have mentioned belong to the category of quantity: everything else that is called quantitative is a quantity in a secondary sense. It is because we have in mind some one of these quantities, properly so called, that we apply quantitative 5ᵇ terms to other things. We speak of what is white as large, because the surface over which the white extends is large; we speak of an action or a process as lengthy, because the time covered is long; these things cannot in their own right claim the quantitative epithet. For [5] instance, should any one explain how long an action was, his statement would be made in terms of the time taken, to the effect that it lasted a year, or something of that sort. In the same way, he would explain the size of a white object in terms of surface, for he would state the area which it covered. Thus the things already mentioned, and these alone, are in their intrinsic nature quantities; nothing else can [10] claim the name in its own right, but, if at all, only in a secondary sense.

Quantities have no contraries. In the case of definite quantities this is obvious; thus, there is nothing that is the contrary of 'two cubits long' or of 'three cubits long', or of a surface, or of any such quantities. A man might, indeed, argue that 'much' was the contrary of 'little', and 'great' of 'small'. But these are not [15] quantitative, but relative; things are not great or small absolutely, they are so called rather as the result of an act of comparison. For instance, a mountain is called small, a grain large, in virtue of the fact that the latter is greater than others of its kind, the former [20] less. Thus there is a reference here to an external standard, for if the terms 'great' and 'small' were used absolutely, a mountain would never be called small or a grain large. Again, we say that there are many people in a village, and few in Athens, although those in the city are many times as numerous as those in [25] the village: or we say that a house has many in it, and a theatre few, though those in the theatre far outnumber those in the house. The terms 'two cubits long,' 'three cubits long,' and so on indicate quantity, the terms 'great' and 'small' indicate relation, for they have reference to an external standard. It is, therefore, plain that these are to be classed as relative. [30] Again, whether we define them as quantitative or not, they have no contraries: for how can there be a contrary of an attribute which is not to be apprehended in or by itself, but only by reference to something external? Again, if 'great' and 'small' are contraries, it will come about that the same subject can admit contrary qualities at one and the same time, and that things will themselves be contrary to them- [35] selves. For it happens at times that the same thing is both small and great. For the same thing may be small in comparison with one thing, and great in comparison with another, so that the same thing comes to be both small and great at one and the same time, and is of such a nature as to admit contrary qualities at one and the same moment. Yet it was agreed, when substance was being discussed, that nothing admits contrary qualities at one 6ᵃ and the same moment. For though sub-stance is capable of admitting contrary qualities, yet no one is at the same time both sick and healthy, nothing is at the same time both white and black. Nor is there anything which is qualified in contrary ways at one and the same time.

Moreover, if these were contraries, they would themselves be contrary to themselves. [5] For if 'great' is the contrary of 'small', and the same thing is both great and small at the same time, then 'small' or 'great' is the contrary of itself. But this is impossible. The term 'great', therefore, is not the contrary of the term 'small', nor 'much' of 'little'. And even though a man should call these terms not rela- [10] tive but quantitative, they would not have contraries.

It is in the case of space that quantity most plausibly appears to admit of a contrary. For men define the term 'above' as the contrary of 'below', when it is the region at the centre they mean by 'below'; and this is so, because nothing is farther from the extremities of the uni- [15] verse than the region at the centre. Indeed, it seems that in defining contraries of every kind men have recourse to a spatial metaphor, for they say that those things are contraries which, within the same class, are separated *by the greatest possible distance*.

Quantity does not, it appears, admit of varia- [20] tion of degree. One thing cannot be two cubits long in a greater degree than another. Similarly with regard to number: what is 'three' is not more truly three than what is 'five' is five; nor is one set of three more truly three than another set. Again, one period of time is not said to be more truly time than another. Nor is there any other kind of quantity, of all that have been mentioned, with regard to [25] which variation of degree can be predicated. The category of quantity, therefore, does not admit of variation of degree.

The most distinctive mark of quantity is that equality and inequality are predicated of it. Each of the aforesaid quantities is said to be equal or unequal. For instance, one solid is said to be equal or unequal to another; number, too, and time can have these terms applied to them, [30] as indeed can all those kinds of quantity that have been mentioned.

That which is not a quantity can by no means, it would seem, be termed equal or unequal to anything else. One particular disposition or one particular quality, such as whiteness, is by no means compared with another in terms of equality and inequality but rather in terms of similarity. Thus it is the distinctive [35] mark of quantity that it can be called equal and unequal.

7

Those things are called relative, which, being either said to be *of* something else or *related to* something else, are explained by reference to that other thing. For instance, the word 'superior' is explained by reference to something else, for it is superiority *over something else* that is meant. Similarly, the expression 'double' has this external reference, for it is the double of *something else* that is meant. So it is with 6^b everything else of this kind. There are, moreover, other relatives, e.g. habit, disposition, perception, knowledge, and attitude. The significance of all these is explained by a reference to something else and in no other way. Thus, a [5] habit is a habit of *something,* knowledge is knowledge *of something,* attitude is the attitude *of something*. So it is with all other relatives that have been mentioned. Those terms, then, are called relative, the nature of which is explained by reference to something else, the preposition 'of' or some other preposition being used to indicate the relation. Thus, one mountain is called great *in comparison with another;* for the mountain claims this attribute *by comparison with* something. Again, that which is called [10] similar must be similar *to something else,* and all other such attributes have this external reference. It is to be noted that lying and standing and sitting are particular attitudes, but attitude is itself a relative term. To lie, to stand, to be seated, are not themselves attitudes, but take their name from the aforesaid attitudes.

[15] It is possible for relatives to have contraries. Thus virtue has a contrary, vice, these both being relatives; knowledge, too, has a contrary, ignorance. But this is not the mark of all relatives; 'double' and 'triple' have no contrary, nor indeed has any such term.

[20] It also appears that relatives can admit of variation of degree. For 'like' and 'unlike', 'equal' and 'unequal', have the modifications 'more' and 'less' applied to them, and each of these is relative in character: for the terms 'like' and 'unequal' bear a reference to something external. Yet, again, it is not every relative term that admits of variation of degree. No term [25] such as 'double' admits of this modification. All relatives have correlatives: by the term 'slave' we mean the slave *of a master;* by the [30] term 'master', the master *of a slave;* by 'double', the double *of its half;* by 'half', the half *of its double;* by 'greater', greater *than that which is less;* by 'less,' less *than that which is greater.*

So it is with every other relative term; but the case we use to express the correlation differs in some instances. Thus, by knowledge we mean knowledge *of* the knowable; by the knowable, that which is to be apprehended *by* [35] knowledge; by perception, perception *of* the perceptible; by the perceptible, that which is apprehended *by* perception.

Sometimes, however, reciprocity of correlation does not appear to exist. This comes about when a blunder is made, and that to which the relative is related is not accurately stated. If a man states that a wing is necessarily relative to a bird, the connexion between these two will not be reciprocal, for it will not be possible to say that a bird is a bird by reason of its wings. The reason is that the original statement was 7^a inaccurate, for the wing is not said to be relative to the bird *qua* bird, since many creatures besides birds have wings, but *qua* winged creature. If, then, the statement is made accurate, the connexion will be reciprocal, for we can speak of a wing having reference necessarily to a winged creature, and of a winged creature as being such because of its wings.

[5] Occasionally, perhaps, it is necessary to coin words, if no word exists by which a correlation can adequately be explained. If we define a rudder as necessarily having reference to a boat, our definition will not be appropriate, for the rudder does not have this reference to a [10] boat *qua* boat, as there are boats which have no rudders. Thus we cannot use the terms reciprocally, for the word 'boat' cannot be said to find its explanation in the word 'rudder'. As there is no existing word, our definition would perhaps be more accurate if we coined some word like 'ruddered' as the correlative of 'rudder'. If we express ourselves thus accurately, at any rate the terms are reciprocally connected, for the 'ruddered' thing is 'ruddered' in virtue [15] of its rudder. So it is in all other cases. A head will be more accurately defined as the correlative of that which is 'headed', than as that of an animal, for the animal does not have a head *qua* animal, since many animals have no head.

Thus we may perhaps most easily comprehend that to which a thing is related, when a name does not exist, if, from that which has a name, we derive a new name, and apply it to that with which the first is reciprocally con- [20] nected, as in the aforesaid instances, when we derived the word 'winged' from 'wing' and 'ruddered' from 'rudder'.

All relatives, then, if properly defined, have a correlative. I add this condition because, if that to which they are related is stated as haphazard and not accurately, the two are not [25] found to be interdependent. Let me state what I mean more clearly. Even in the case of acknowledged correlatives, and where names exist for each, there will be no interdependence if one of the two is denoted, not by that name which expresses the correlative notion, but by one of irrelevant significance. The term 'slave,' if defined as related, not to a master, but to a man, or a biped, or anything of that sort, is not reciprocally connected with that in relation to [30] which it is defined, for the statement is not exact. Further, if one thing is said to be correlative with another, and the terminology used is correct, then, though all irrelevant attributes should be removed, and only that one attribute left in virtue of which it was correctly stated to be correlative with that other, the stated correlation will still exist. If the correlative of 'the slave' is said to be 'the master', then, though all [35] irrelevant attributes of the said 'master', such as 'biped', 'receptive of knowledge', 'human', should be removed, and the attribute 'master' alone left, the stated correlation existing between him and the slave will remain the same, for it is *of a master* that a slave is said to be the slave. On the other hand, if, of two cor-
7ᵇ relatives, one is not correctly termed, then, when all other attributes are removed and that alone is left in virtue of which it was stated to be correlative, the stated correlation will be found to have disappeared.

For suppose the correlative of 'the slave' should be said to be 'the man', or the correlative of 'the wing' 'the bird'; if the attribute 'master' [5] be withdrawn from 'the man', the correlation between 'the man' and 'the slave' will cease to exist, for if the man is not a master, the slave is not a slave. Similarly, if the attribute 'winged' be withdrawn from 'the bird', 'the wing' will no longer be relative; for if the so-called correlative is not winged, it follows that 'the wing' has no correlative.

[10] Thus it is essential that the correlated terms should be exactly designated; if there is a name existing, the statement will be easy; if not, it is doubtless our duty to construct names. When the terminology is thus correct, it is evident that all correlatives are interdependent.

[15] Correlatives are thought to come into existence simultaneously. This is for the most part true, as in the case of the double and the half. The existence of the half necessitates the existence of that of which it is a half. Similarly the existence of a master necessitates the existence of a slave, and that of a slave implies that of a master; these are merely instances of a general rule. Moreover, they cancel one another; [20] for if there is no double it follows that there is no half, and vice versa; this rule also applies to all such correlatives. Yet it does not appear to be true in all cases that correlatives come into existence simultaneously. The object of knowledge would appear to exist before knowledge itself, for it is usually the case that we acquire knowledge of objects already exist- [25] ing; it would be difficult, if not impossible, to find a branch of knowledge the beginning of the existence of which was contemporaneous with that of its object.

Again, while the object of knowledge, if it ceases to exist, cancels at the same time the knowledge which was its correlative, the converse of this is not true. It is true that if the object of knowledge does not exist there can be no knowledge: for there will no longer be anything to know. Yet it is equally true that, if [30] the knowledge of a certain object does not exist, the object may nevertheless quite well exist. Thus, in the case of the squaring of the circle, if indeed that process is an object of knowledge, though it itself exists as an object of knowledge, yet the knowledge of it has not yet come into existence. Again, if all animals ceased to exist, there would be no knowledge, but there might yet be many objects of knowledge.

[35] This is likewise the case with regard to perception: for the object of perception is, it appears, prior to the act of perception. If the perceptible is annihilated, perception also will cease to exist; but the annihilation of perception does not cancel the existence of the perceptible. For perception implies a body perceived and a body in which perception takes place. Now if that which is perceptible is annihilated, it follows that the body is annihilated, for the body is a perceptible thing; and if the body 8ᵃ does not exist, it follows that perception also ceases to exist. Thus the annihilation of the perceptible involves that of perception.

But the annihilation of perception does not involve that of the perceptible. For if the animal is annihilated, it follows that perception [5] also is annihilated, but perceptibles such as body, heat, sweetness, bitterness, and so on, will remain.

Again, perception is generated at the same time as the perceiving subject, for it comes into existence at the same time as the animal. But the perceptible surely exists before perception; for fire and water and such elements, out of [10] which the animal is itself composed, exist before the animal is an animal at all, and before perception. Thus it would seem that the perceptible exists before perception.

It may be questioned whether it is true that no substance is relative, as seems to be the case, or whether exception is to be made in the case of certain secondary substances. With regard [15] to primary substances, it is quite true that there is no such possibility, for neither wholes nor parts of primary substances are relative. The individual man or ox is not defined with reference to something external. Similarly with [20] the parts: a particular hand or head is not defined as a particular hand or head of a particular person, but as the hand or head of a particular person. It is true also, for the most part at least, in the case of secondary substances; the species 'man' and the species 'ox' are not defined with reference to anything outside themselves. Wood, again, is only relative in so far as it is some one's property, not in so far as it is wood. It is plain, then, that in the cases mentioned substance is not relative. But with [25] regard to some secondary substances there is a difference of opinion; thus, such terms as 'head' and 'hand' are defined with reference to that of which the things indicated are a part, and so it comes about that these appear to have a relative character. Indeed, if our definition of that which is relative was complete, it is very [30] difficult, if not impossible, to prove that no substance is relative. If, however, our definition was not complete, if those things only are properly called relative in the case of which relation to an external object is a necessary condition of existence, perhaps some explanation of the dilemma may be found.

The former definition does indeed apply to all relatives, but the fact that a thing is explained with reference to something else does not make it essentially relative.
[35] From this it is plain that, if a man definitely apprehends a relative thing, he will also definitely apprehend that to which it is relative. Indeed this is self-evident: for if a man knows that some particular thing is relative, assuming that we call that a relative in the case of which relation to something is a necessary condition 8ᵇ of existence, he knows that also to which it is related. For if he does not know at all that to which it is related, he will not know whether or not it is relative. This is clear, moreover, in particular instances. If a man knows definitely that such and such a thing is 'double', he will [5] also forthwith know definitely that of which it is the double. For if there is nothing definite of which he knows it to be the double, he does not know at all that it is double. Again, if he knows that a thing is more beautiful, it follows necessarily that he will forthwith definitely know that also than which it is more beautiful. He will not merely know indefinitely [10] that it is more beautiful than something which is less beautiful, for this would be supposition, not knowledge. For if he does not know definitely that than which it is more beautiful, he can no longer claim to know definitely that it is more beautiful than something else which is less beautiful: for it might be that nothing was less beautiful. It is, therefore, evident that if a man apprehends some relative thing definitely, he necessarily knows that also definitely to which it is related.

[15] Now the head, the hand, and such things are substances, and it is possible to know their essential character definitely, but it does not necessarily follow that we should know that to which they are related. It is not possible to know forthwith whose head or hand is meant. Thus these are not relatives, and, this being the [20] case, it would be true to say that no substance is relative in character. It is perhaps a difficult matter, in such cases, to make a positive statement without more exhaustive examination, but to have raised questions with regard to details is not without advantage.

8

[25] By 'quality' I mean that in virtue of which people are said to be such and such.

Quality is a term that is used in many senses. One sort of quality let us call 'habit' or 'disposition'. Habit differs from disposition in being more lasting and more firmly established. The various kinds of knowledge and of virtue are habits, for knowledge, even when acquired only in a moderate degree, is, it is agreed, abid- [30] ing in its character and difficult to displace, unless some great mental upheaval takes place, through disease or any such cause. The virtues, also, such as justice, self-restraint, and so on, are not easily dislodged or dismissed, so as to give place to vice.

[35] By a disposition, on the other hand, we mean a condition that is easily changed and quickly gives place to its opposite. Thus, heat,

cold, disease, health, and so on are dispositions. For a man is disposed in one way or another with reference to these, but quickly changes, becoming cold instead of warm, ill instead of well. So it is with all other dispositions also, unless through lapse of time a disposition has itself become inveterate and almost impossible to dislodge: in which case we should perhaps go so far as to call it a habit.

It is evident that men incline to call those conditions habits which are of a more or less permanent type and difficult to displace; for [5] those who are not retentive of knowledge, but volatile, are not said to have such and such a 'habit' as regards knowledge, yet they are *disposed,* we may say, either better or worse, towards knowledge. Thus habit differs from disposition in this, that while the latter in ephemeral, the former is permanent and difficult to alter.

[10] Habits are at the same time dispositions, but dispositions are not necessarily habits. For those who have some specific habit may be said also, in virtue of that habit, to be thus or thus disposed; but those who are disposed in some specific way have not in all cases the corresponding habit.

Another sort of quality is that in virtue of which, for example, we call men good boxers or runners, or healthy or sickly: in fact it in- [15] cludes all those terms which refer to inborn capacity or incapacity. Such things are not predicated of a person in virtue of his disposition, but in virtue of his inborn capacity or incapacity to do something with ease or to avoid defeat of any kind. Persons are called good boxers or good runners, not in virtue of such and [20] such a disposition, but in virtue of an inborn capacity to accomplish something with ease. Men are called healthy in virtue of the inborn capacity of easy resistance to those unhealthy influences that may ordinarily arise; unhealthy, in virtue of the lack of this capacity. Similarly with regard to softness and hardness. [25] Hardness is predicated of a thing because it has that capacity of resistance which enables it to withstand disintegration; softness, again, is predicated of a thing by reason of the lack of that capacity.

A third class within this category is that of affective qualities and affections. Sweetness, bitterness, sourness, are examples of this sort of quality, together with all that is akin to these; [30] heat, moreover, and cold, whiteness, and blackness are affective qualities. It is evident that these are qualities, for those things that possess them are themselves said to be such and such by reason of their presence. Honey is called sweet because it contains sweetness; the body is called white because it contains whiteness; and so in all other cases.

[35] The term 'affective quality' is not used as indicating that those things which admit these qualities are affected in any way. Honey is not called sweet because it is affected in a specific way, nor is this what is meant in any other instance. Similarly heat and cold are called affective qualities, not because those things which admit them are affected. What is meant is that [5] these said qualities are capable of producing an 'affection' in the way of perception. For sweetness has the power of affecting the sense of taste; heat, that of touch; and so it is with the rest of these qualities.

Whiteness and blackness, however, and the other colours, are not said to be affective quali- [10] ties in this sense, but because they themselves are the results of an affection. It is plain that many changes of colour take place because of affections. When a man is ashamed, he blushes; when he is afraid, he becomes pale, and so on. So true is this, that when a man is [15] by nature liable to such affections, arising from some concomitance of elements in his constitution, it is a probable inference that he has the corresponding complexion of skin. For the same disposition of bodily elements, which in the former instance was momentarily present in the case of an access of shame, might be a result of a man's natural temperament, so as to produce the corresponding colouring also as a natural characteristic. All conditions, therefore, of this [20] kind, if caused by certain permanent and lasting affections, are called affective qualities. For pallor and duskiness of complexion are called qualities, inasmuch as we are said to be such and such in virtue of them, not only if they originate in natural constitution, but also if they come about through long disease or sun- [25] burn, and are difficult to remove, or indeed remain throughout life. For in the same way we are said to be such and such because of these.

Those conditions, however, which arise from causes which may easily be rendered ineffective or speedily removed, are called, not qualities, but affections: for we are not said to be such [30] and such in virtue of them. The man who blushes through shame is not said to be a constitutional blusher, nor is the man who becomes pale through fear said to be constitutionally pale. He is said rather to have been affected.

Thus such conditions are called affections, not qualities.

In like manner there are affective qualities and affections of the soul. That temper with [35] which a man is born and which has its origin in certain deep-seated affections is called a quality. I mean such conditions as insanity, irascibility, and so on: for people are said to be mad or irascible in virtue of these. Similarly those abnormal psychic states which are not inborn, but arise from the concomitance of certain other elements, and are difficult to re- [5] move, or altogether permanent, are called qualities, for in virtue of them men are said to be such and such.

Those, however, which arise from causes easily rendered ineffective are called affections, not qualities. Suppose that a man is irritable when vexed: he is not even spoken of as a bad-tempered man, when in such circumstances he loses his temper somewhat, but rather is said to be affected. Such conditions are therefore [10] termed, not qualities, but affections.

The fourth sort of quality is figure and the shape that belongs to a thing; and besides this, straightness and curvedness and any other qualities of this type; each of these defines a thing as being such and such. Because it is triangular or quadrangular a thing is said to have a specific character, or again because it is straight or [15] curved; in fact a thing's shape in every case gives rise to a qualification of it.

Rarity and density, roughness and smoothness, seem to be terms indicating quality: yet these, it would appear, really belong to a class different from that of quality. For it is rather a certain relative position of the parts composing the thing thus qualified which, it appears, is indicated by each of these terms. A thing is dense, [20] owing to the fact that its parts are closely combined with one another; rare, because there are interstices between the parts; smooth, because its parts lie, so to speak, evenly; rough, because some parts project beyond others. [25] There may be other sorts of quality, but those that are most properly so called have, we may safely say, been enumerated.

These, then, are qualities, and the things that take their name from them as derivatives, or are in some other way dependent on them, are said to be qualified in some specific way. In most, indeed in almost all cases, the name of that which is qualified is derived from that of [30] the quality. Thus the terms 'whiteness', 'grammar', 'justice', give us the adjectives 'white', 'grammatical', 'just', and so on.

There are some cases, however, in which, as the quality under consideration has no name, it is impossible that those possessed of it should have a name that is derivative. For instance, the name given to the runner or boxer, who is [35] so called in virtue of an inborn capacity, is not derived from that of any quality; for those capacities have no name assigned to them. In this, the inborn capacity is distinct from the science, with reference to which men are called, e.g. boxers or wrestlers. Such a science is classed as a disposition; it has a name, and is called 'boxing' or 'wrestling' as the case may be, and the name given to those disposed in this way is derived from that of the science. [5] Sometimes, even though a name exists for the quality, that which takes its character from the quality has a name that is not a derivative. For instance, the upright man takes his character from the possession of the quality of integrity, but the name given him is not derived from the word 'integrity'. Yet this does not occur often.

We may therefore state that those things are said to be possessed of some specific quality [10] which have a name derived from that of the aforesaid quality, or which are in some other way dependent on it.

One quality may be the contrary of another; thus justice is the contrary of injustice, whiteness of blackness, and so on. The things, also, which are said to be such and such in virtue of these qualities, may be contrary the one to the other; for that which is unjust is contrary to that which is just, that which is white to that [15] which is black. This, however, is not always the case. Red, yellow, and such colours, though qualities, have no contraries.

If one of two contraries is a quality, the other will also be a quality. This will be evident from particular instances, if we apply the names used to denote the other categories; for instance, granted that justice is the contrary of injustice [20] and justice is a quality, injustice will also be a quality: neither quantity, nor relation, nor place, nor indeed any other category but that of quality, will be applicable properly to injustice. So it is with all other contraries falling under [25] the category of quality.

Qualities admit of variation of degree. Whiteness is predicated of one thing in a greater or less degree than of another. This is also the case with reference to justice. Moreover, one and the same thing may exhibit a quality in a greater degree than it did before: if a thing is white, it may become whiter.

Though this is generally the case, there are exceptions. For if we should say that justice ad-[30] mitted of variation of degree, difficulties might ensue, and this is true with regard to all those qualities which are dispositions. There are some, indeed, who dispute the possibility of variation here. They maintain that justice and health cannot very well admit of variation [35] of degree themselves, but that people vary in the degree in which they possess these qualities, and that this is the case with grammatical 11a learning and all those qualities which are classed as dispositions. However that may be, it is an incontrovertible fact that the things which in virtue of these qualities are said to be what they are vary in the degree in which they possess them; for one man is said to be better versed in grammar, or more healthy or just, than another, and so on.

[5] The qualities expressed by the terms 'triangular' and 'quadrangular' do not appear to admit of variation of degree, nor indeed do any that have to do with figure. For those things to which the definition of the triangle or circle is applicable are all equally triangular or circular. Those, on the other hand, to which the same definition is not applicable, cannot be said to differ from one another in degree; the square [10] is no more a circle than the rectangle, for to neither is the definition of the circle appropriate. In short, if the definition of the term proposed is not applicable to both objects, they cannot be compared. Thus it is not all qualities which admit of variation of degree.

[15] Whereas none of the characteristics I have mentioned are peculiar to quality, the fact that likeness and unlikeness can be predicated with reference to quality only, gives to that category its distinctive feature. One thing is like another only with reference to that in virtue of which it is such and such; thus this forms the peculiar mark of quality.

[20] We must not be disturbed because it may be argued that, though proposing to discuss the category of quality, we have included in it many relative terms. We did say that habits and dispositions were relative. In practically all such cases the genus is relative, the individual not. Thus knowledge, as a genus, is explained by reference to something else, for we mean a [25] knowledge *of something*. But particular branches of knowledge are not thus explained. The knowledge of grammar is not relative to anything external, nor is the knowledge of music, but these, if relative at all, are relative only in virtue of their genera; thus grammar is said [30] to be the *knowledge* of something, not the grammar of something; similarly music is the *knowledge* of something, not the music of something.

Thus individual branches of knowledge are not relative. And it is because we possess these individual branches of knowledge that we are said to be such and such. It is these that we actually possess: we are called experts because we possess knowledge in some particular branch. Those particular branches, therefore, of knowl-[35] edge, in virtue of which we are sometimes said to be such and such, are themselves qualities, and are not relative. Further, if anything should happen to fall within both the category of quality and that of relation, there would be nothing extraordinary in classing it under both these heads.

9

11b Action and affection both admit of contraries and also of variation of degree. Heating is the contrary of cooling, being heated of being cooled, being glad of being vexed. Thus they admit of contraries. They also admit of [5] variation of degree: for it is possible to heat in a greater or less degree; also to be heated in a greater or less degree. Thus action and affection also admit of variation of degree. So much, then, is stated with regard to these categories.

We spoke, moreover, of the category of position when we were dealing with that of relation, and stated that such terms derived their names from those of the corresponding attitudes.

[10] As for the rest, time, place, state, since they are easily intelligible, I say no more about them than was said at the beginning, that in the category of state are included such states as 'shod', 'armed', in that of place 'in the Lyceum' and so on, as was explained before.

10

[15] The proposed categories have, then, been adequately dealt with.

We must next explain the various senses in which the term 'opposite' is used. Things are said to be opposed in four senses: (i) as correlatives to one another, (ii) as contraries to one another, (iii) as privatives to positives, (iv) as affirmatives to negatives.

Let me sketch my meaning in outline. An instance of the use of the word 'opposite' with reference to correlatives is afforded by the ex-[20] pressions 'double' and 'half'; with reference to contraries by 'bad' and 'good'. Opposites in the sense of 'privatives' and 'positives' are 'blindness' and 'sight'; in the sense of affirmatives and negatives, the propositions 'he sits', 'he does not sit'.

(i) Pairs of opposites which fall under the category of relation are explained by a reference of the one to the other, the reference be-[25]ing indicated by the preposition 'of' or by some other preposition. Thus, double is a relative term, for that which is double is explained as the double *of something*. Knowledge, again, is the opposite of the thing known, in the same sense; and the thing known also is explained [30] by its relation to its opposite, knowledge. For the thing known is explained as that which is known *by something;* that is, by knowledge. Such things, then, as are opposite the one to the other in the sense of being correlatives are explained by a reference of the one to the other.

(ii) Pairs of opposites which are contraries are not in any way interdependent, but are contrary the one to the other. The good is not [35] spoken of as the good *of the bad,* but as *the contrary of the bad,* nor is white spoken of as the white *of the black,* but as *the contrary of the black*. These two types of opposition are 12ᵃ therefore distinct. Those contraries which are such that the subjects in which they are naturally present, or of which they are predicated, must necessarily contain either the one or the other of them, have no intermediate, but those in the case of which no such necessity obtains, always have an intermediate. Thus disease and [5] health are naturally present in the body of an animal, and it is necessary that either the one or the other should be present in the body of an animal. Odd and even, again, are predicated of number, and it is necessary that the one or the other should be present in numbers. Now there is no intermediate between the terms of either of these two pairs. On the other hand, in those contraries with regard to which [10] no such necessity obtains, we find an intermediate. Blackness and whiteness are naturally present in the body, but it is not necessary that either the one or the other should be present in the body, inasmuch as it is not true to say that everybody must be white or black. Badness and goodness, again, are predicated of [15] man, and of many other things, but it is not necessary that either the one quality or the other should be present in that of which they are predicated: it is not true to say that everything that may be good or bad must be either good or bad. These pairs of contraries have intermediates: the intermediates between white and black are grey, sallow, and all the other colours that come between; the intermediate between good and bad is that which is neither the one nor the other.

[20] Some intermediate qualities have names, such as grey and sallow and all the other colours that come between white and black; in other cases, however, it is not easy to name the intermediate, but we must define it as that which is *not* either extreme, as in the case of that which is neither good nor bad, neither [25] just nor unjust.

(iii) 'Privatives' and 'positives' have reference to the same subject. Thus, sight and blindness have reference to the eye. It is a universal rule that each of a pair of opposites of this type has reference to that to which the particular 'positive' is natural. We say that that which is capable of some particular faculty or possession has suffered privation when the faculty or pos-[30]session in question is in no way present in that in which, and at the time at which, it should naturally be present. We do not call that toothless which has not teeth, or that blind which has not sight, but rather that which has not teeth or sight at the time when by nature it should. For there are some creatures which from birth are without sight, or without teeth, but these are not called toothless or blind.

[35] To be without some faculty or to possess it is not the same as the corresponding 'privative' or 'positive'. 'Sight' is a 'positive', 'blindness' a 'privative', but 'to possess sight' is not equivalent to 'sight', 'to be blind' is not equivalent to 'blindness'. Blindness is a 'privative', to be blind is to be in a state of privation, but is not a 'privative'. Moreover, if 'blindness' were equivalent to 'being blind', both would be [40] predicated of the same subject; but though a man is said to be blind, he is by no means said to be blindness.

To be in a state of 'possession' is, it appears, the opposite of being in a state of 'privation', just as 'positives' and 'privatives' themselves are opposite. There is the same type of antithesis in both cases; for just as blindness is [5] opposed to sight, so is being blind opposed to having sight.

That which is affirmed or denied is not itself affirmation or denial. By 'affirmation' we mean an affirmative proposition, by 'denial' a negative. Now, those facts which form the matter of the affirmation or denial are not proposi-[10]tions; yet these two are said to be opposed in the same sense as the affirmation and denial, for in this case also the type of antithesis is the same. For as the affirmation is opposed to the denial, as in the two propositions 'he sits', 'he does not sit', so also the fact which constitutes the matter of the proposition in one case is opposed to that in the other, his sitting, that is [*15*] to say, to his not sitting.

It is evident that 'positives' and 'privatives' are not opposed each to each in the same sense as relatives. The one is not explained by reference to the other; sight is not sight *of blindness*, nor is any other preposition used to indicate the relation. Similarly blindness is not said to be [*20*] blindness *of sight,* but rather, privation of sight. Relatives, moreover, reciprocate; if blindness, therefore, were a relative, there would be a reciprocity of relation between it and that with which it was correlative. But this is not [*25*] the case. Sight is not called the sight *of blindness.*

That those terms which fall under the heads of 'positives' and 'privatives' are not opposed each to each as contraries, either, is plain from the following facts: Of a pair of contraries such that they have *no* intermediate, one or the other must needs be present in the subject in which [*30*] they naturally subsist, or of which they are predicated; for it is those, as we proved,[1] in the case of which this necessity obtains, that have no intermediate. Moreover, we cited health and disease, odd and even, as instances. But those contraries which *have* an intermediate are not subject to any such necessity. It is not necessary that every substance, receptive of such qualities, should be either black or white, cold or hot, for something intermediate between these con- [*35*] traries may very well be present in the subject. We proved, moreover, that those contraries have an intermediate in the case of which the said necessity does not obtain. Yet when one of the two contraries is a constitutive property of the subject, as it is a constitutive property of fire to be hot, of snow to be white, it is necessary determinately that one of the two contraries, not one *or* the other, should be pres- [*40*] ent in the subject; for fire cannot be cold, or snow black. Thus, it is not the case here that one of the two must needs be present in every subject receptive of these qualities, but only in 13ª that subject of which the one forms a constitutive property. Moreover, in such cases it is one member of the pair determinately, and not either the one or the other, which must be present.

In the case of 'positives' and 'privatives', on the other hand, neither of the aforesaid statements holds good. For it is not necessary that a subject receptive of the qualities should always [*5*] have either the one or the other; that which has not yet advanced to the state when sight is natural is not said either to be blind or to see. Thus 'positives' and 'privatives' do not belong to that class of contraries which consists of those which have no intermediate. On the other hand, they do not belong either to that class which consists of contraries which have an intermediate. For under certain conditions it is necessary that either the one or the other should form part of the constitution of every appropriate subject. For when a thing has reached [*10*] the stage when it is by nature capable of sight, it will be said either to see or to be blind, and that in an indeterminate sense, signifying that the capacity may be either present or absent; for it is not necessary either that it should see or that it should be blind, but that it should be either in the one state or in the other. Yet in the case of those contraries which have an intermediate we found that it was never necessary that either the one or the other should be present in every appropriate subject, but only that in certain subjects one of the pair should be present, and that in a determinate sense. It is, [*15*] therefore, plain that 'positives' and 'privatives' are not opposed each to each in either of the senses in which contraries are opposed.

Again, in the case of contraries, it is possible that there should be changes from either into the other, while the subject retains its identity, unless indeed one of the contraries is a constitutive property of that subject, as heat is of fire. [*20*] For it is possible that that which is healthy should become diseased, that which is white, black, that which is cold, hot, that which is good, bad, that which is bad, good. The bad man, if he is being brought into a better way of life and thought, may make some advance, [*25*] however slight, and if he should once improve, even ever so little, it is plain that he might change completely, or at any rate make very great progress; for a man becomes more and more easily moved to virtue, however small the improvement was at first. It is, therefore, natural to suppose that he will make yet greater progress than he has made in the past; and as this process goes on, it will change him completely and establish him in the contrary [*30*] state, provided he is not hindered by lack of time. In the case of 'positives' and 'privatives', however, change in both directions is impossible. There may be a change from possession to privation, but not from privation to possession. The man who has become blind does

---
[1] Cf. 11ᵇ 38.

[35] not regain his sight; the man who has become bald does not regain his hair; the man who has lost his teeth does not grow a new set. 13^b (iv) Statements opposed as affirmation and negation belong manifestly to a class which is distinct, for in this case, and in this case only, it is necessary for the one opposite to be true and the other false.

Neither in the case of contraries, nor in the case of correlatives, nor in the case of 'positives' and 'privatives', is it necessary for one to be true and the other false. Health and disease are [5] contraries: neither of them is true or false. 'Double' and 'half' are opposed to each other as correlatives: neither of them is true or false. The case is the same, of course, with regard to 'positives' and 'privatives' such as 'sight' and [10] 'blindness'. In short, where there is no sort of combination of words, truth and falsity have no place, and all the opposites we have mentioned so far consist of simple words.

At the same time, when the words which enter into opposed statements are contraries, these, more than any other set of opposites, would seem to claim this characteristic. 'Socrates is ill' is the contrary of 'Socrates is well', [15] but not even of such composite expressions is it true to say that one of the pair must always be true and the other false. For if Socrates exists, one will be true and the other false, but if he does not exist, both will be false; for neither 'Socrates is ill' nor 'Socrates is well' is true, if Socrates does not exist at all.

[20] In the case of 'positives' and 'privatives', if the subject does not exist at all, neither proposition is true, but even if the subject exists, it is not always the fact that one is true and the other false. For 'Socrates has sight' is the opposite of 'Socrates is blind' in the sense of the word 'opposite' which applies to possession and privation. Now if Socrates exists, it is not necessary that one should be true and the other false, for when he is not yet able to acquire the [25] power of vision, both are false, as also if Socrates is altogether non-existent.

But in the case of affirmation and negation, whether the subject exists or not, one is always false and the other true. For manifestly, if Socrates exists, one of the two propositions 'Soc- [30] rates is ill', 'Socrates is not ill', is true, and the other false. This is likewise the case if he does not exist; for if he does not exist, to say that he is ill is false, to say that he is not ill is true. Thus it is in the case of those opposites only, which are opposite in the sense in which the term is used with reference to affirmation and negation, that the rule holds good, that one [35] of the pair must be true and the other false.

11

That the contrary of a good is an evil is shown by induction: the contrary of health is disease, of courage, cowardice, and so on. But 14^a the contrary of an evil is sometimes a good, sometimes an evil. For defect, which is an evil, has excess for its contrary, this also being an evil, and the mean, which is a good, is equally the contrary of the one and of the other. It is only in a few cases, however, that [5] we see instances of this: in most, the contrary of an evil is a good.

In the case of contraries, it is not always necessary that if one exists the other should also exist: for if all become healthy there will be health and no disease, and again, if everything turns white, there will be white, but no black. [10] Again, since the fact that Socrates is ill is the contrary of the fact that Socrates is well, and two contrary conditions cannot both obtain in one and the same individual at the same time, both these contraries could not exist at once: for if that Socrates was well was a fact, then that Socrates was ill could not possibly be one.

[15] It is plain that contrary attributes must needs be present in subjects which belong to the same species or genus. Disease and health require as their subject the body of an animal; white and black require a body, without further qualification; justice and injustice require as their subject the human soul.

Moreover, it is necessary that pairs of contraries should in all cases either belong to the same genus or belong to contrary genera or be [20] themselves genera. White and black belong to the same genus, colour; justice and injustice, to contrary genera, virtue and vice; while good and evil do not belong to genera, but are themselves actual genera, with terms [25] under them.

12

There are four senses in which one thing can be said to be 'prior' to another. Primarily and most properly the term has reference to time: in this sense the word is used to indicate that one thing is older or more ancient than another, for the expressions 'older' and 'more ancient' imply greater length of time.

Secondly, one thing is said to be 'prior' to [30] another when the sequence of their being cannot be reversed. In this sense 'one' is 'prior' to 'two'. For if 'two' exists, it follows directly that 'one' must exist, but if 'one' exists, it does not follow necessarily that 'two' exists: thus the sequence subsisting cannot be reversed. It is agreed, then, that when the sequence of two things cannot be reversed, then that one on which the other depends is called 'prior' to [35] that other.

In the third place, the term 'prior' is used with reference to any order, as in the case of science and of oratory. For in sciences which use demonstration there is that which is prior and that which is posterior in order; in geom- 14[b] etry, the elements are prior to the propositions; in reading and writing, the letters of the alphabet are prior to the syllables. Similarly, in the case of speeches, the exordium is prior in order to the narrative.

Besides these senses of the word, there is a fourth. That which is better and more honourable is said to have a natural priority. In com- [5] mon parlance men speak of those whom they honour and love as 'coming first' with them. This sense of the word is perhaps the most far-fetched.

Such, then, are the different senses in which the term 'prior' is used. [10] Yet it would seem that besides those mentioned there is yet another. For in those things, the being of each of which implies that of the other, that which is in any way the cause may reasonably be said to be by nature 'prior' to the effect. It is plain that there are instances of this. The fact of the being of a man carries with it [15] the truth of the proposition that he is, and the implication is reciprocal: for if a man is, the proposition wherein we allege that he is is true, and conversely, if the proposition wherein we allege that he is is true, then he is. The true proposition, however, is in no way the cause of the being of the man, but the fact of the man's [20] being does seem somehow to be the cause of the truth of the proposition, for the truth or falsity of the proposition depends on the fact of the man's being or not being.

Thus the word 'prior' may be used in five senses.

13

The term 'simultaneous' is primarily and most appropriately applied to those things the genesis of the one of which is simultaneous [25] with that of the other; for in such cases neither is prior or posterior to the other. Such things are said to be simultaneous in point of time. Those things, again, are 'simultaneous' in point of nature, the being of each of which involves that of the other, while at the same time neither is the cause of the other's being. This is the case with regard to the double and the half, [30] for these are reciprocally dependent, since, if there is a double, there is also a half, and if there is a half, there is also a double, while at the same time neither is the cause of the being of the other.

Again, those species which are distinguished one from another and opposed one to another within the same genus are said to be 'simultaneous' in nature. I mean those species which are distinguished each from each by one and the [35] same method of division. Thus the 'winged' species is simultaneous with the 'terrestrial' and the 'water' species. These are distinguished within the same genus, and are opposed each to each; for the genus 'animal' has the 'winged', the 'terrestrial', and the 'water' species, and no one of these is prior or posterior to another; on the contrary, all such things ap- 15[a] pear to be 'simultaneous' in nature. Each of these also, the terrestrial, the winged, and the water species, can be divided again into subspecies. Those species, then, also will be 'simultaneous' in point of nature, which, belonging to the same genus, are distinguished each from each by one and the same method of differentiation.

[5] But genera are prior to species, for the sequence of their being cannot be reversed. If there is the species 'water-animal', there will be the genus 'animal', but granted the being of the genus 'animal', it does not follow necessarily that there will be the species 'water-animal'.

Those things, therefore, are said to be 'simultaneous' in nature, the being of each of which involves that of the other, while at the same time neither is in any way the cause of the [10] other's being; those species, also, which are distinguished each from each and opposed within the same genus. Those things, moreover, are 'simultaneous' in the unqualified sense of the word which come into being at the same time.

14

There are six sorts of movement: generation, destruction, increase, diminution, alteration, and change of place.
[15] It is evident in all but one case that all these sorts of movement are distinct each from each. Generation is distinct from destruction, increase and change of place from diminution, and so on. But in the case of alteration it may be argued that the process necessarily implies one or other of the other five sorts of mo- [20] tion. This is not true, for we may say that

all affections, or nearly all, produce in us an alteration which is distinct from all other sorts of motion, for that which is affected need not suffer either increase or diminution or any of the other sorts of motion. Thus alteration is a [25] distinct sort of motion; for, if it were not, the thing altered would not only be altered, but would forthwith necessarily suffer increase or diminution or some one of the other sorts of motion in addition; which as a matter of fact is not the case. Similarly that which was undergoing the process of increase or was subject to some other sort of motion would, if alteration were not a distinct form of motion, necessarily be subject to alteration also. But there are some things which undergo increase but yet not al-[30] teration. The square, for instance, if a gnomon is applied to it, undergoes increase but not alteration, and so it is with all other figures of this sort. Alteration and increase, therefore, are distinct.

15b Speaking generally, rest is the contrary of motion. But the different forms of motion have their own contraries in other forms; thus destruction is the contrary of generation, diminution of increase, rest in a place, of change of place. As for this last, change in the reverse direction would seem to be most truly its con-[5] trary; thus motion upwards is the contrary of motion downwards and vice versa.

In the case of that sort of motion which yet remains, of those that have been enumerated, it is not easy to state what is its contrary. It appears to have no contrary, unless one should define the contrary here also either as 'rest in its quality' or as 'change in the direction of the [10] contrary quality', just as we defined the contrary of change of place either as rest in a place or as change in the reverse direction. For a thing is altered when change of quality takes place; therefore either rest in its quality or change in the direction of the contrary quality may be called the contrary of this qualitative form of motion. In this way becoming white is [15] the contrary of becoming black; there is alteration in the contrary direction, since a change of a qualitative nature takes place.

15

The term 'to have' is used in various senses. In the first place it is used with reference to habit or disposition or any other quality, for we are said to 'have' a piece of knowledge or a virtue. Then, again, it has reference to quan-[20] tity, as, for instance, in the case of a man's height; for he is said to 'have' a height of three or four cubits. It is used, moreover, with regard to apparel, a man being said to 'have' a coat or tunic; or in respect of something which we have on a part of ourselves, as a ring on the hand: or in respect of something which is a part of us, as hand or foot. The term refers also to content, as in the case of a vessel and wheat, or of a jar and wine; a jar is said to 'have' [25] wine, and a corn-measure wheat. The expression in such cases has reference to content. Or it refers to that which has been acquired; we are said to 'have' a house or a field. A man is also said to 'have' a wife, and a wife a husband, and this appears to be the most remote [30] meaning of the term, for by the use of it we mean simply that the husband lives with the wife.

Other senses of the word might perhaps be found, but the most ordinary ones have all been enumerated.

CONTENTS: ON INTERPRETATION

CHAP.		BERLIN NOS.
1.	(1) The spoken word is a symbol of thought	16a 1
	(2) Isolated thoughts or expressions are neither true nor false	
	(3) Truth and falsehood are only attributable to certain combinations of thoughts or of words	
2.	(1) Definition of a noun	16a 18
	(2) Simple and composite nouns	
	(3) Indefinite nouns	
	(4) Cases of a noun	
3.	(1) Definition of a verb	16b 6
	(2) Indefinite verbs	
	(3) Tenses of a verb	
	(4) Verbal nouns and adjectives	
4.	Definition of a sentence	16b 26
5.	Simple and compound propositions	17a 8
6.	Contradictory propositions	17a 25
7.	(1) Universal, indefinite, and particular affirmations and denials	17a 36
	(2) Contrary as opposed to contradictory propositions	
	(3) In contrary propositions, of which the subject is universal or particular, the truth of the one proposition implies the falsity of the other, but this is not the case in indefinite propositions	
8.	Definition of single propositions	18a 12
9.	Propositions which refer to present or past time must be either true or false: propositions which refer to future time must be either true or false, but it is not determined which must be true and which false.	18a 27
10.	(1) Diagrammatic arrangement of pairs of affirmations and denials, (a) without the complement of the verb 'to be,' (b) with the complement of the verb 'to be,' (c) with an indefinite noun for subject	19b 5
	(2) The right position of the negative	
	(3) Contraries can never both be true, but subcontraries may both be true	
	(4) In particular propositions, if the affirmative is false, the contrary is true; in universal propositions, if the affirmative is false, the contradictory is true	
	(5) Propositions consisting of an indefinite noun and an indefinite verb are not denials	
	(6) The relation to other propositions of those which have an indefinite noun as subject	
	(7) The transposition of nouns and verbs makes no difference to the sense of the proposition	
11.	(1) Some seemingly simple propositions are really compound	20b 11
	(2) Similarly some dialectical questions are really compound	
	(3) The nature of a dialectical question	
	(4) When two simple propositions having the same subject are true, it is not necessarily the case that the proposition resulting from the combination of the predicates is true	
	(5) A plurality of predicates which individually belong to the same subject can only be combined to form a simple proposition when they are essentially predicable of the subject, and when one is not implicit in another	
	(6) A compound predicate cannot be resolved into simple predicates when the compound predicate has within it a contradiction in terms, or when one of the predicates is used in a secondary sense	
12.	(1) Propositions concerning possibility, impossibility, contingency, and necessity	21a 34
	(2) Determination of the proper contradictories of such propositions	
13.	(1) Scheme to show the relation subsisting between such propositions	22a 14
	(2) Illogical character of this scheme proved	
	(3) Revised scheme	
	(4) That which is said to be possible may be (a) always actual, (b) sometimes actual and sometimes not, (c) never actual	
14.	Discussion as to whether a contrary affirmation or a denial is the proper contrary of an affirmation, either universal or particular	23a 26

ON INTERPRETATION

1

16ª First we must define the terms 'noun' and 'verb', then the terms 'denial' and 'affirmation', then 'proposition' and 'sentence.'

Spoken words are the symbols of mental ex-[5] perience and written words are the symbols of spoken words. Just as all men have not the same writing, so all men have not the same speech sounds, but the mental experiences, which these directly symbolize, are the same for all, as also are those things of which our experiences are the images. This matter has, however, been discussed in my treatise about the soul, for it belongs to an investigation distinct from that which lies before us.

As there are in the mind thoughts which do [10] not involve truth or falsity, and also those which must be either true or false, so it is in speech. For truth and falsity imply combination and separation. Nouns and verbs, provided nothing is added, are like thoughts without combination or separation; 'man' and [15] 'white', as isolated terms, are not yet either true or false. In proof of this, consider the word 'goat-stag.' It has significance, but there is no truth or falsity about it, unless 'is' or 'is not' is added, either in the present or in some other tense.

2

By a noun we mean a sound significant by con-[20] vention, which has no reference to time, and of which no part is significant apart from the rest. In the noun 'Fairsteed,' the part 'steed' has no significance in and by itself, as in the phrase 'fair steed.' Yet there is a difference between simple and composite nouns; for in [25] the former the part is in no way significant, in the latter it contributes to the meaning of the whole, although it has not an independent meaning. Thus in the word 'pirate-boat' the word 'boat' has no meaning except as part of the whole word.

The limitation 'by convention' was intro-

NOTE: The bold face numbers and letters are approximate indications of the pages and columns of the standard Berlin Greek text; the bracketed numbers, of the lines in the Greek text; they are here assigned as they are assigned in the Oxford translation.

duced because nothing is by nature a noun or name—it is only so when it becomes a symbol; inarticulate sounds, such as those which brutes produce, are significant, yet none of these constitutes a noun.

[30] The expression 'not-man' is not a noun. There is indeed no recognized term by which we may denote such an expression, for it is not a sentence or a denial. Let it then be called an indefinite noun.

The expressions 'of Philo', 'to Philo', and so 16ᵇ on, constitute not nouns, but cases of a noun. The definition of these cases of a noun is in other respects the same as that of the noun proper, but, when coupled with 'is', 'was', or 'will be', they do not, as they are, form a proposition either true or false, and this the noun proper always does, under these conditions. Take the words 'of Philo is' or 'of Philo is not'; these words do not, as they stand, form either [5] a true or a false proposition.

3

A verb is that which, in addition to its proper meaning, carries with it the notion of time. No part of it has any independent meaning, and it is a sign of something said of something else.

I will explain what I mean by saying that it carries with it the notion of time. 'Health' is a noun, but 'is healthy' is a verb; for besides its proper meaning it indicates the present existence of the state in question.

[10] Moreover, a verb is always a sign of something said of something else, i.e. of something either predicable of or present in some other thing.

Such expressions as 'is not-healthy', 'is not-ill', I do not describe as verbs; for though they carry the additional note of time, and always form a predicate, there is no specified name for this variety; but let them be called indefinite [15] verbs, since they apply equally well to that which exists and to that which does not.

Similarly 'he was healthy', 'he will be healthy', are not verbs, but tenses of a verb; the difference lies in the fact that the verb indicates present time, while the tenses of the verb indicate those times which lie outside the present.

Verbs in and by themselves are substantival

[20] and have significance, for he who uses such expressions arrests the hearer's mind, and fixes his attention; but they do not, as they stand, express any judgement, either positive or negative. For neither are 'to be' and 'not to be' and the participle 'being' significant of any fact, unless something is added; for they do not themselves indicate anything, but imply a copu- [25] lation, of which we cannot form a conception apart from the things coupled.

4

A sentence is a significant portion of speech, some parts of which have an independent meaning, that is to say, as an utterance, though not as the expression of any positive judgement. Let me explain. The word 'human' has meaning, but does not constitute a proposition, either positive or negative. It is only when other words are added that the whole will form an [30] affirmation or denial. But if we separate one syllable of the word 'human' from the other, it has no meaning; similarly in the word 'mouse', the part '-ouse' has no meaning in itself, but is merely a sound. In composite words, indeed, the parts contribute to the meaning of the whole; yet, as has been pointed out,[1] they have not an independent meaning.

17ᵃ Every sentence has meaning, not as being the natural means by which a physical faculty is realized, but, as we have said, by convention. Yet every sentence is not a proposition; only such are propositions as have in them either truth or falsity. Thus a prayer is a sentence, but is neither true nor false.

[5] Let us therefore dismiss all other types of sentence but the proposition, for this last concerns our present inquiry, whereas the investigation of the others belongs rather to the study of rhetoric or of poetry.[2]

5

The first class of simple propositions is the simple affirmation, the next, the simple denial; all others are only one by conjunction.

[10] Every proposition must contain a verb or the tense of a verb. The phrase which defines the species 'man', if no verb in present, past, or future time be added, is not a proposition. It may be asked how the expression 'a footed animal with two feet' can be called single; for it is not the circumstance that the words follow in unbroken succession that effects the unity. This inquiry, however, finds its place in an investigation foreign to that before us.[3]

[15] We call those propositions single which indicate a single fact, or the conjunction of the parts of which results in unity: those propositions, on the other hand, are separate and many in number, which indicate many facts, or whose parts have no conjunction.

Let us, moreover, consent to call a noun or a verb an expression only, and not a proposition, since it is not possible for a man to speak in this way when he is expressing something, in such a way as to make a statement, whether his utterance is an answer to a question or an act of his own initiation.

[20] To return: of propositions one kind is simple, i.e. that which asserts or denies something of something, the other composite, i.e. that which is compounded of simple propositions. A simple proposition is a statement, with meaning, as to the presence of something in a subject or its absence, in the present, past, or future, according to the divisions of time.

6

[25] An affirmation is a positive assertion of something about something, a denial a negative assertion.

Now it is possible both to affirm and to deny the presence of something which is present or of something which is not, and since these same affirmations and denials are possible with reference to those times which lie outside the pres- [30] ent, it would be possible to contradict any affirmation or denial. Thus it is plain that every affirmation has an opposite denial, and similarly every denial an opposite affirmation.

We will call such a pair of propositions a pair of contradictories. Those positive and negative propositions are said to be contradictory which have the same subject and predicate. The [35] identity of subject and of predicate must not be 'equivocal'. Indeed there are definitive qualifications besides this, which we make to meet the casuistries of sophists.

7

Some things are universal, others individual. By the term 'universal' I mean that which is of such a nature as to be predicated of many subjects, by 'individual' that which is not thus [40] predicated. Thus 'man' is a universal, 'Callias' an individual.

17ᵇ Our propositions necessarily sometimes concern a universal subject, sometimes an individual.

---

[1] Cf. 16ᵃ 22–26
[2] Cf. *On Poetics*, 1456ᵇ 11.
[3] Cf. *Metaphysics*, VII. 12, VIII. 6.

If, then, a man states a positive and a negative proposition of universal character with regard to a universal, these two propositions are 'contrary'. By the expression 'a proposition of universal character with regard to a universal', such propositions as 'every man is white', 'no man is white' are meant. When, on the other hand, the positive and negative propositions, though they have regard to a universal, are yet not of universal character, they will not be contrary, albeit the meaning intended is sometimes contrary. As instances of propositions made with regard to a universal, but not of universal character, we may take the propositions 'man is white', 'man is not white'. 'Man' is a universal, but the proposition is not made as of universal character; for the word 'every' does not make the subject a universal, but rather gives the proposition a universal character. If, however, both predicate and subject are distributed, the proposition thus constituted is contrary to truth; no affirmation will, under such circumstances, be true. The proposition 'every man is every animal' is an example of this type.

An affirmation is opposed to a denial in the sense which I denote by the term 'contradictory', when, while the subject remains the same, the affirmation is of universal character and the denial is not. The affirmation 'every man is white' is the *contradictory* of the denial 'not every man is white', or again, the proposition 'no man is white' is the *contradictory* of the proposition 'some men are white'. But propositions are opposed as *contraries* when both the affirmation and the denial are universal, as in the sentences 'every man is white', 'no man is white', 'every man is just', 'no man is just'.

We see that in a pair of this sort both propositions cannot be true, but the contradictories of a pair of contraries can sometimes both be true with reference to the same subject; for instance 'not every man is white' and 'some men are white' are both true. Of such corresponding positive and negative propositions as refer to universals and have a universal character, one must be true and the other false. This is the case also when the reference is to individuals, as in the propositions 'Socrates is white', 'Socrates is not white'. When, on the other hand, the reference is to universals, but the propositions are not universal, it is not always the case that one is true and the other false, for it is possible to state truly that man is white and that man is not white and that man is beautiful and that man is not beautiful; for if a man is deformed he is the reverse of beautiful, also if he is progressing towards beauty he is not yet beautiful.

This statement might seem at first sight to carry with it a contradiction, owing to the fact that the proposition 'man is not white' appears to be equivalent to the proposition 'no man is white'. This, however, is not the case, nor are they necessarily at the same time true or false.

It is evident also that the denial corresponding to a single affirmation is itself single; for the denial must deny just that which the affirmation affirms concerning the same subject, and must correspond with the affirmation both in the universal or particular character of the subject and in the distributed or undistributed sense in which it is understood.

For instance, the affirmation 'Socrates is white' has its proper denial in the proposition 'Socrates is not white'. If anything else be negatively predicated of the subject or if anything else be the subject though the predicate remain the same, the denial will not be the denial proper to that affirmation, but on that is distinct.

The denial proper to the affirmation 'every man is white' is 'not every man is white'; that proper to the affirmation 'some men are white' is 'no man is white', while that proper to the affirmation 'man is white' is 'man is not white'.

We have shown further that a single denial is contradictorily opposite to a single affirmation and we have explained which these are; we have also stated that contrary are distinct from contradictory propositions and which the contrary are; also that with regard to a pair of opposite propositions it is not always the case that one is true and the other false. We have pointed out, moreover, what the reason of this is and under what circumstances the truth of the one involves the falsity of the other.

8

An affirmation or denial is single, if it indicates some one fact about some one subject; it matters not whether the subject is universal and whether the statement has a universal character, or whether this is not so. Such single propositions are: 'every man is white', 'not every man is white'; 'man is white', 'man is not white'; 'no man is white', 'some men are white'; provided the word 'white' has one meaning. If, on the other hand, one word has two meanings which do not combine to form one, the affirmation is not single. For instance, if a man should establish the symbol 'garment' as significant both of a horse and of a man, [20] the proposition 'garment is white' would not be a single affirmation, nor its opposite a single denial. For it is equivalent to the proposition 'horse and man are white', which, again, is equivalent to the two propositions 'horse is white', 'man is white'. If, then, these two propositions have more than a single significance, and do not form a single proposition, it is plain that the first proposition either has more than [25] one significance or else has none; for a particular man is not a horse.

This, then, is another instance of those propositions of which both the positive and the negative forms may be true or false simultaneously.

9

In the case of that which is or which has taken place, propositions, whether positive or negative, must be true or false. Again, in the case of a pair of contradictories, either when the subject is universal and the propositions [30] are of a universal character, or when it is individual, as has been said,[1] one of the two must be true and the other false; whereas when the subject is universal, but the propositions are not of a universal character, there is no such necessity. We have discussed this type also in a previous chapter.[2]

When the subject, however, is individual, and that which is predicated of it relates to the future, the case is altered. For if all propositions whether positive or negative are either [35] true or false, then any given predicate must either belong to the subject or not, so that if one man affirms that an event of a given character will take place and another denies it, it is plain that the statement of the one will correspond with reality and that of the other will not. For the predicate cannot both belong and not belong to the subject at one and the same time with regard to the future.

18ᵇ Thus, if it is true to say that a thing is white, it must necessarily be white; if the reverse proposition is true, it will of necessity not be white. Again, if it is white, the proposition stating that it is white was true; if it is not white, the proposition to the opposite effect was true. And if it is not white, the man who states that it is is making a false statement; and if the man who states that it is white is making a false

[1] Cf. 17ᵇ 26–9.   [2] Cf. 17ᵇ 29–37.

statement, it follows that it is not white. It may therefore be argued that it is necessary that affirmations or denials must be either true or false.

[5] Now if this be so, nothing is or takes place fortuitously, either in the present or in the future, and there are no real alternatives; everything takes place of necessity and is fixed. For either he that affirms that it will take place or he that denies this is in correspondence with fact, whereas if things did not take place of necessity, an event might just as easily not happen as happen; for the meaning of the word 'fortuitous' with regard to present or future events is that reality is so constituted that it may issue in either of two opposite directions. [10] Again, if a thing is white now, it was true before to say that it would be white, so that of anything that has taken place it was always true to say 'it is' or 'it will be'. But if it was always true to say that a thing is or will be, it is not possible that it should not be or not be about to be, and when a thing cannot not come to be, it is impossible that it should not come to be, and when it is impossible that it should not come to be, it must come to be. All, then, that is about to [15] be must of necessity take place. It results from this that nothing is uncertain or fortuitous, for if it were fortuitous it would not be necessary.

Again, to say that neither the affirmation nor the denial is true, maintaining, let us say, that an event neither will take place nor will not take place, is to take up a position impossible to defend. In the first place, though facts should prove the one proposition false, the op- [20] posite would still be untrue. Secondly, if it was true to say that a thing was both white and large, both these qualities must necessarily belong to it; and if they will belong to it the next day, they must necessarily belong to it the next day. But if an event is neither to take place nor not to take place the next day, the element of chance will be eliminated. For example, it would be necessary that a sea-fight should [25] neither take place nor fail to take place on the next day.

These awkward results and others of the same kind follow, if it is an irrefragable law that of every pair of contradictory propositions, whether they have regard to universals and are stated as universally applicable, or whether they have regard to individuals, one must be true [30] and the other false, and that there are no real alternatives, but that all that is or takes place is the outcome of necessity. There would be no need to deliberate or to take trouble, on the supposition that if we should adopt a certain course, a certain result would follow, while, if we did not, the result would not follow. For a man may predict an event ten thousand years beforehand, and another may pre- [35] dict the reverse; that which was truly predicted at the moment in the past will of necessity take place in the fullness of time.

Further, it makes no difference whether people have or have not actually made the contradictory statements. For it is manifest that the circumstances are not influenced by the fact of an affirmation or denial on the part of anyone. For events will not take place or fail to take place because it was stated that they would or would not take place, nor is this any more the case if the prediction dates back ten thousand 19ᵃ years or any other space of time. Wherefore, if through all time the nature of things was so constituted that a prediction about an event was true, then through all time it was necessary that that prediction should find fulfilment; and with regard to all events, circumstances have always been such that their occurrence is a matter of necessity. For that of which someone has said truly that it will be, cannot [5] fail to take place; and of that which takes place, it was always true to say that it would be.

Yet this view leads to an impossible conclusion; for we see that both deliberation and action are causative with regard to the future, and that, to speak more generally, in those things which are not continuously actual there is a [10] potentiality in either direction. Such things may either be or not be; events also therefore may either take place or not take place. There are many obvious instances of this. It is possible that this coat may be cut in half, and yet it may not be cut in half, but wear out first. In the same way, it is possible that it [15] should not be cut in half; unless this were so, it would not be possible that it should wear out first. So it is therefore with all other events which possess this kind of potentiality. It is therefore plain that it is not of necessity that everything is or takes place; but in some instances there are real alternatives, in which case the affirmation is no more true and no more [20] false than the denial; while some exhibit a predisposition and general tendency in one direction or the other, and yet can issue in the opposite direction by exception.

Now that which is must needs be when it is, and that which is not must needs not be when it is not. Yet it cannot be said without qualification that all existence and non-existence is the outcome of necessity. For there is a difference [25] between saying that that which is, when it is, must needs be, and simply saying that all that is must needs be, and similarly in the case of that which is not. In the case, also, of two contradictory propositions this holds good. Everything must either be or not be, whether in the present or in the future, but it is not always possible to distinguish and state determinately which of these alternatives must necessarily come about.

[30] Let me illustrate. A sea-fight must either take place to-morrow or not, but it is not necessary that it should take place to-morrow, neither is it necessary that it should not take place, yet it is necessary that it either should or should not take place to-morrow. Since propositions correspond with facts, it is evident that when in future events there is a real alternative, and a potentiality in contrary directions, the corresponding affirmation and denial have the same character.

[35] This is the case with regard to that which is not always existent or not always non-existent. One of the two propositions in such instances must be true and the other false, but we cannot say determinately that this or that is false, but must leave the alternative undecided. One may indeed be more likely to be true than the other, but it cannot be either actually true or actually false. It is therefore plain that it is 19ᵇ not necessary that of an affirmation and a denial one should be true and the other false. For in the case of that which exists potentially, but not actually, the rule which applies to that which exists actually does not hold good. The case is rather as we have indicated.

10

[5] An affirmation is the statement of a fact with regard to a subject, and this subject is either a noun or that which has no name; the subject and predicate in an affirmation must each denote a single thing. I have already explained[1] what is meant by a noun and by that which has no name; for I stated that the expression 'not-man' was not a noun, in the proper sense of the word, but an indefinite noun, denoting as it does in a certain sense a single thing. Similarly the expression 'does not enjoy health' is not a verb proper, but an in- [10] definite verb. Every affirmation, then, and every denial, will consist of a noun and a verb, either definite or indefinite.

[1] Cf. 16ᵃ 19, 30.

There can be no affirmation or denial without a verb; for the expressions 'is', 'will be', 'was', 'is coming to be', and the like are verbs according to our definition, since besides their specific meaning they convey the notion of time.

Thus the primary affirmation and denial are [15] as follows: 'man is', 'man is not'. Next to these, there are the propositions: 'not-man is', 'not-man is not'. Again we have the propositions: 'every man is', 'every man is not', 'all that is not-man is', 'all that is not-man is not'. The same classification holds good with regard to such periods of time as lie outside the present.

When the verb 'is' is used as a third element in the sentence, there can be positive and negative propositions of two sorts. Thus in the sentence [20] 'man is just' the verb 'is' is used as a third element, call it verb or noun, which you will. Four propositions, therefore, instead of two can be formed with these materials. Two of the four, as regards their affirmation and denial, correspond in their logical sequence with the propositions which deal with a condition of privation; the other two do not correspond with these.

I mean that the verb 'is' is added either to the [25] term 'just' or to the term 'not-just', and two negative propositions are formed in the same way. Thus we have the four propositions. Reference to the subjoined table will make matters clear:

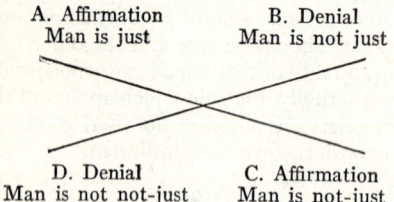

A. Affirmation   B. Denial
Man is just   Man is not just

D. Denial   C. Affirmation
Man is not not-just Man is not-just

Here 'is' and 'is not' are added either to 'just' [30] or to 'not-just'. This then is the proper scheme for these propositions, as has been said in the *Analytics*.[1] The same rule holds good, if the subject is distributed. Thus we have the table:

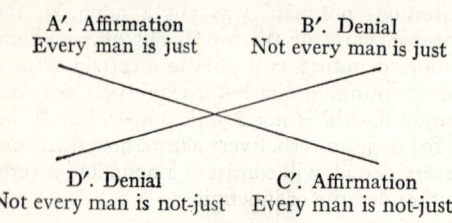

A'. Affirmation   B'. Denial
Every man is just   Not every man is just

D'. Denial   C'. Affirmation
Not every man is not-just Every man is not-just

[1] *Prior Analytics*, 51[b] 36–52[a] 17.

[35] Yet here it is not possible, in the same way as in the former case, that the propositions joined in the table by a diagonal line should both be true; though under certain circumstances this is the case.

We have thus set out two pairs of opposite propositions; there are moreover two other pairs, if a term be conjoined with 'not-man', the latter forming a kind of subject. Thus:

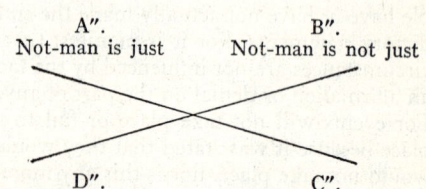

A''.   B''.
Not-man is just   Not-man is not just

D''.   C''.
Not-man is not not-just   Not-man is not-just

This is an exhaustive enumeration of all the pairs of opposite propositions that can possibly be framed. This last group should remain distinct from those which preceded it, since it employs as its subject the expression 'not-man'.

When the verb 'is' does not fit the structure of the sentence (for instance, when the verbs 'walks', 'enjoys health' are used), that scheme applies, which applied when the word 'is' was added.

[5] Thus we have the propositions: 'every man enjoys health', 'every man does-not-enjoy-health', 'all that is not-man enjoys health', 'all that is not-man does-not-enjoy-health'.

We must not in these propositions use the expression 'not every man'. The negative must be attached to the word 'man', for the word 'every' does not give to the subject a universal significance, but implies that, as a subject, it is [10] distributed. This is plain from the following pairs: 'man enjoys health', 'man does not enjoy health'; 'not-man enjoys health', 'not-man does not enjoy health'. These propositions differ from the former in being indefinite and not universal in character. Thus the adjectives 'every' and 'no' have no additional significance except that the subject, whether in a positive or in a negative sentence, is distributed. The rest of the sentence, therefore, will in each case be [15] the same.

Since the contrary of the proposition 'every animal is just' is 'no animal is just', it is plain that these two propositions will never both be true at the same time or with reference to the same subject. Sometimes, however, the contradictories of these contraries will both be true, as in the instance before us: the propositions 'not

every animal is just' and 'some animals are just' are both true.
[20] Further, the proposition 'no man is just' follows from the proposition 'every man is not-just' and the proposition 'not every man is not-just', which is the opposite of 'every man is not-just', follows from the proposition 'some men are just'; for if this be true, there must be some just men.

It is evident, also, that when the subject is individual, if a question is asked and the negative answer is the true one, a certain positive propo- [25] sition is also true. Thus, if the question were asked 'Is Socrates wise?' and the negative answer were the true one, the positive inference 'Then Socrates is unwise' is correct. But no such inference is correct in the case of universals, but rather a negative proposition. For instance, if to the question 'Is every man wise?' the answer is 'no', the inference 'Then every man is unwise' is false. But under these circumstances the inference 'Not every man is wise' is [30] correct. This last is the contradictory, the former the contrary. Negative expressions, which consist of an indefinite noun or predicate, such as 'not-man' or 'not-just', may seem to be denials containing neither noun nor verb in the proper sense of the words. But they are not. For a denial must always be either true or [35] false, and he that uses the expression 'not-man', if nothing more be added, is not nearer but rather further from making a true or a false statement than he who uses the expression 'man'.

The propositions 'everything that is not man is just', and the contradictory of this, are not equivalent to any of the other propositions; on the other hand, the proposition 'everything that is not man is not just' is equivalent to the prop- [40] osition 'nothing that is not man is just'.
20ᵇ The conversion of the position of subject and predicate in a sentence involves no difference in its meaning. Thus we say 'man is white' and 'white is man'. If these were not equivalent, there would be more than one contradictory to the same proposition, whereas it has been demonstrated[1] that each proposition has one proper contradictory and one only. For of the proposition 'man is white' the appropriate [5] contradictory is 'man is not white', and of the proposition 'white is man', if its meaning be different, the contradictory will either be 'white is not not-man' or 'white is not man'. Now the former of these is the contradictory of the proposition 'white is not-man', and the latter of these is the contradictory of the proposition 'man is white'; thus there will be two contradictories to one proposition.
[10] It is evident, therefore, that the inversion of the relative position of subject and predicate does not affect the sense of affirmations and denials.

11

There is no unity about an affirmation or denial which, either positively or negatively, predicates one thing of many subjects, or many things of the same subject, unless that which is indicated by the many is really some one thing. [15] I do not apply this word 'one' to those things which, though they have a single recognized name, yet do not combine to form a unity. Thus, man may be an animal, and biped, and domesticated, but these three predicates combine to form a unity. On the other hand, the predicates 'white', 'man', and 'walking' do not thus combine. Neither, therefore, if these three form the subject of an affirmation, nor if [20] they form its predicate, is there any unity about that affirmation. In both cases the unity is linguistic, but not real.

If therefore the dialectical question is a request for an answer, i.e. either for the admission of a premiss or for the admission of one of two contradictories—and the premiss is itself always one of two contradictories—the answer to such a question as contains the above predicates cannot be a single proposition. For as I [25] have explained in the *Topics*,[2] the question is not a single one, even if the answer asked for is true.

At the same time it is plain that a question of the form 'what is it?' is not a dialectical question, for a dialectical questioner must by the form of his question give his opponent the chance of announcing one of two alternatives, whichever he wishes. He must therefore put [30] the question into a more definite form, and inquire, e.g. whether man has such and such a characteristic or not.

Some combinations of predicates are such that the separate predicates unite to form a single predicate. Let us consider under what conditions this is and is not possible. We may either state in two separate propositions that man is an animal and that man is a biped, or we may combine the two, and state that man is an animal with two feet. Similarly we may use 'man' and 'white' as separate predicates, or unite them [35] into one. Yet if a man is a shoemaker and

---
[1] Cf. 17ᵇ 38.
[2] *Topics*, VIII. 7; *On Sophistical Refutations*, 169ᵃ 6, 175ᵇ 39 sqq., 181ᵃ 36 sqq.

is also good, we cannot construct a composite proposition and say that he is a good shoemaker. For if, whenever two separate predicates truly belong to a subject, it follows that the predicate resulting from their combination also truly belongs to the subject, many absurd results ensue. For instance, a man is man and white. Therefore, if predicates may always be combined, he is a white man. Again, if the predicate 'white' belongs to him, then the combination of that predicate with the former composite predicate will be permissible. Thus it will be right to say that he is a white white man [40] and so on indefinitely. Or, again, we may combine the predicates 'musical', 'white', and 'walking', and these may be combined many 21ᵃ times. Similarly we may say that Socrates is Socrates and a man, and that therefore he is the man Socrates, or that Socrates is a man and a biped, and that therefore he is a two-footed [5] man. Thus it is manifest that if a man states unconditionally that predicates can always be combined, many absurd consequences ensue.

We will now explain what ought to be laid down.

Those predicates, and terms forming the subject of predication, which are accidental either to the same subject or to one another, do not [10] combine to form a unity. Take the proposition 'man is white of complexion and musical'. Whiteness and being musical do not coalesce to form a unity, for they belong only accidentally to the same subject. Nor yet, if it were true to say that that which is white is musical, would the terms 'musical' and 'white' form a unity, for it is only incidentally that that which is musical is white; the combination of the two will, therefore, not form a unity.

Thus, again, whereas, if a man is both good and a shoemaker, we cannot combine the two propositions and say simply that he is a good shoemaker, we are, at the same time, able to combine the predicates 'animal' and 'biped' [15] and say that a man is an animal with two feet, for these predicates are not accidental.

Those predicates, again, cannot form a unity, of which the one is implicit in the other: thus we cannot combine the predicate 'white' again and again with that which already contains the notion 'white', nor is it right to call a man an animal-man or a two-footed man; for the notions 'animal' and 'biped' are implicit in the word 'man'. On the other hand, it is possible to predicate a term simply of any one instance, and to say that some one particular man is a [20] man or that some one white man is a white man.

Yet this is not always possible: indeed, when in the adjunct there is some opposite which involves a contradiction, the predication of the simple term is impossible. Thus it is not right to call a dead man a man. When, however, this is not the case, it is not impossible.

Yet the facts of the case might rather be stated thus: when some such opposite elements are present, resolution is never possible, but [25] when they are not present, resolution is nevertheless not always possible. Take the proposition 'Homer is so-and-so', say 'a poet'; does it follow that Homer is, or does it not? The verb 'is' is here used of Homer only incidentally, the proposition being that Homer is a poet, not that he is, in the independent sense of the word.

Thus, in the case of those predications which have within them no contradiction when the [30] nouns are expanded into definitions, and wherein the predicates belong to the subject in their own proper sense and not in any indirect way, the individual may be the subject of the simple propositions as well as of the composite. But in the case of that which is not, it is not true to say that because it is the object of opinion, it is; for the opinion held about it is that it is not, not that it is.

12

As these distinctions have been made, we must [35] consider the mutual relation of those affirmations and denials which assert or deny possibility or contingency, impossibility or necessity: for the subject is not without difficulty.

We admit that of composite expressions those are contradictory each to each which have the verb 'to be' in its positive and negative form respectively. Thus the contradictory of the proposition 'man is' is 'man is not', not 'not-man is', and the contradictory of 'man is white' is 'man is not white', not 'man is not-white'. For otherwise, since either the positive or the negative proposition is true of any subject, it will turn out true to say that a piece of wood is a man that is not white.

[5] Now if this is the case, in those propositions which do not contain the verb 'to be' the verb which takes its place will exercise the same function. Thus the contradictory of 'man walks' is 'man does not walk', not 'not-man walks'; for to say 'man walks' is merely equivalent to saying 'man is walking'.

[10] If then this rule is universal, the contradictory of 'it may be' is 'it may *not* be', not 'it cannot be'.

Now it appears that the same thing both may and may not be; for instance, everything that may be cut or may walk may also escape cutting and refrain from walking; and the reason is that those things that have potentiality in [15] this sense are not always actual. In such cases, both the positive and the negative propositions will be true; for that which is capable of walking or of being seen has also a potentiality in the opposite direction.

But since it is impossible that contradictory propositions should both be true of the same subject, it follows that 'it may *not* be' is not the contradictory of 'it may be'. For it is a logical consequence of what we have said, either that the same predicate can be both applicable and inapplicable to one and the same sub- [20] ject at the same time, or that it is not by the addition of the verbs 'be' and 'not be', respectively, that positive and negative propositions are formed. If the former of these alternatives must be rejected, we must choose the latter.

The contradictory, then, of 'it may be' is 'it cannot be'. The same rule applies to the proposition 'it is contingent that it should be'; the contradictory of this is 'it is not contingent that [25] it should be'. The similar propositions, such as 'it is necessary' and 'it is impossible', may be dealt with in the same manner. For it comes about that just as in the former instances the verbs 'is' and 'is not' were added to the subject-matter of the sentence 'white' and 'man', so here 'that it should be' and 'that it should not be' are the subject-matter and 'is [30] possible', 'is contingent', are added. These indicate that a certain thing is or is not possible, just as in the former instances 'is' and 'is not' indicated that certain things were or were not the case.

The contradictory, then, of 'it may *not* be' is not 'it cannot be', but 'it cannot not be', and the contradictory of 'it may be' is not 'it may *not* be', but 'it cannot be'. Thus the propositions 'it [35] may be' and 'it may *not* be' appear each to imply the other: for, since these two propositions are not contradictory, the same thing both may and may *not* be. But the propositions 'it may be' and 'it cannot be' can never be true of the same subject at the same time, for they are 22ᵃ contradictory. Nor can the propositions 'it may not be' and 'it cannot not be' be at once true of the same subject.

The propositions which have to do with necessity are governed by the same principle. The contradictory of 'it is necessary that it should be', is not 'it is necessary that it should not be,' but 'it is not necessary that it should be', and [5] the contradictory of 'it is necessary that it should not be' is 'it is not necessary that it should not be'.

Again, the contradictory of 'it is impossible that it should be' is not 'it is impossible that it should not be' but 'it is not impossible that it should be', and the contradictory of 'it is impossible that it should not be' is 'it is not impossible that it should not be'.

To generalize, we must, as has been stated, define the clauses 'that it should be' and 'that it should not be' as the subject-matter of the propositions, and in making these terms into [10] affirmations and denials we must combine them with 'that it should be' and 'that it should not be' respectively.

We must consider the following pairs as contradictory propositions:

It may be.	It cannot be.
It is contingent.	It is not contingent.
It is impossible.	It is not impossible.
It is necessary.	It is not necessary.
It is true.	It is not true.

13

Logical sequences follow in due course when we have arranged the propositions thus. From [15] the proposition 'it may be' it follows that it is contingent, and the relation is reciprocal. It follows also that it is not impossible and not necessary.

From the proposition 'it may *not* be' or 'it is contingent that it should not be' it follows that it is not necessary that it should not be and that it is not impossible that it should not be. From the proposition 'it cannot be' or 'it is not contingent' it follows that it is necessary that it should not be and that it is impossible that it [20] should be. From the proposition 'it cannot not be' or 'it is not contingent that it should not be' it follows that it is necessary that it should be and that it is impossible that it should not be.

Let us consider these statements by the help of a table:

A.	B.
It may be.	It cannot be.
[25] It is contingent.	It is not contingent.
It is not impossible that it should be.	It is impossible that it should be.
It is not necessary that it should be.	It is necessary that it should not be.

C.	D.
It may not be.	It cannot not be.
It is contingent that it should not be.	It is not contingent that it should not be.
[30] It is not impossible that it should not be.	It is impossible that it should not be.
It is not necessary that it should not be.	It is necessary that it should be.

Now the propositions 'it is impossible that it should be' and 'it is not impossible that it should be' are consequent upon the propositions 'it may be', 'it is contingent', and 'it cannot be', 'it is not contingent', the contradictories upon the contradictories. But there is inversion. The negative of the proposition 'it is impossible' is consequent upon the proposition 'it may [35] be' and the corresponding positive in the first case upon the negative in the second. For 'it is impossible' is a positive proposition and 'it is not impossible' is negative.

We must investigate the relation subsisting between these propositions and those which predicate necessity. That there is a distinction is clear. In this case, contrary propositions follow respectively from contradictory propositions, and the contradictory propositions belong to separate sequences. For the proposition 'it is not necessary that it should be' is not the negative of 'it is necessary that it should not be', for both these propositions may be true of the same subject; for when it is necessary that a thing should not be, it is not necessary that it should be. The reason why the propositions predicating necessity do not follow in the same kind of sequence as the rest, lies in the fact that the proposition 'it is impossible' is equivalent, when used with a contrary subject, to the proposition 'it is necessary'. For when it [5] is impossible that a thing should be, it is necessary, not that it should be, but that it should not be, and when it is impossible that a thing should not be, it is necessary that it should be. Thus, if the propositions predicating impossibility or non-impossibility follow without change of subject from those predicating possibility or non-possibility, those predicating necessity must follow with the contrary subject; for the propositions 'it is impossible' and 'it is necessary' are not equivalent, but, as has been said, inversely connected.
[10] Yet perhaps it is impossible that the contradictory propositions predicating necessity should be thus arranged. For when it is necessary that a thing should be, it is possible that it should be. (For if not, the opposite follows, since one or the other must follow; so, if it is not possible, it is impossible, and it is thus impossible that a thing should be, which must necessarily be; which is absurd.)

Yet from the proposition 'it may be' it follows that it is not impossible, and from that it [15] follows that it is not necessary; it comes about therefore that the thing which must necessarily be need not be; which is absurd. But again, the proposition 'it is necessary that it should be' does not follow from the proposition 'it may be', nor does the proposition 'it is necessary that it should not be'. For the proposition 'it may be' implies a twofold possibility, while, if either of the two former propositions is true, the twofold possibility vanishes. For if [20] a thing may be, it may also not be, but if it is necessary that it should be or that it should not be, one of the two alternatives will be excluded. It remains, therefore, that the proposition 'it is not necessary that it should not be' follows from the proposition 'it may be'. For this is true also of that which must necessarily be.

Moreover the proposition 'it is not necessary that it should not be' is the contradictory of that which follows from the proposition 'it can- [25] not be'; for 'it cannot be' is followed by 'it is impossible that it should be' and by 'it is necessary that it should not be', and the contradictory of this is the proposition 'it is not necessary that it should not be'. Thus in this case also contradictory propositions follow contradictory in the way indicated, and no logical impossibilities occur when they are thus arranged.

It may be questioned whether the proposition 'it may be' follows from the proposition 'it is necessary that it should be'. If not, the con- [30] tradictory must follow, namely that it cannot be, or, if a man should maintain that this is not the contradictory, then the proposition 'it may not be'.

Now both of these are false of that which necessarily is. At the same time, it is thought that if a thing may be cut it may also not be cut, if a thing may be it may also not be, and thus it would follow that a thing which must neces- [35] sarily be may possibly not be; which is false. It is evident, then, that it is not always the case that that which may be or may walk possesses also a potentiality in the other direction. There are exceptions. In the first place we must except those things which possess a potentiality not in accordance with a rational principle, as fire possesses the potentiality of giving out heat, that is, an irrational capacity. Those potentialities which involve a rational principle are potentialities of more than one result, that is, of 23ᵃ contrary results; those that are irrational are not always thus constituted. As I have said, fire cannot both heat and not heat, neither has anything that is always actual any twofold potentiality. Yet some even of those potentialities which are irrational admit of opposite results. [5] However, thus much has been said to emphasize the truth that it is not every potentiality which admits of opposite results, even where the word is used always in the same sense.

But in some cases the word is used equivocally. For the term 'possible' is ambiguous, being used in the one case with reference to facts, to that which is actualized, as when a man is said to find walking possible because he is actually walking, and generally when a capacity is predicated because it is actually realized; in the [10] other case, with reference to a state in which realization is conditionally practicable, as when a man is said to find walking possible because under certain conditions he would walk. This last sort of potentiality belongs only to that which can be in motion, the former can exist also in the case of that which has not this power. Both of that which is walking and is actual, and of that which has the capacity though not necessarily realized, it is true to say that it is not impossible that it should walk (or, in the other case, that it should be), but while [15] we cannot predicate this latter kind of potentiality of that which is necessary in the unqualified sense of the word, we can predicate the former.

Our conclusion, then, is this: that since the universal is consequent upon the particular, that which is necessary is also possible, though not in every sense in which the word may be used.

We may perhaps state that necessity and its absence are the initial principles of existence and non-existence, and that all else must be [20] regarded as posterior to these.

It is plain from what has been said that that which is of necessity is actual. Thus, if that which is eternal is prior, actuality also is prior to potentiality. Some things are actualities without potentiality, namely, the primary substances; a second class consists of those things which are actual but also potential, whose actuality is in nature prior to their potentiality, [25] though posterior in time; a third class comprises those things which are never actualized, but are pure potentialities.

14

The question arises whether an affirmation finds its contrary in a denial or in another affirmation; whether the proposition 'every man is just' finds its contrary in the proposition 'no man is just', or in the proposition 'every man [30] is unjust'. Take the propositions 'Callias is just', 'Callias is not just', 'Callias is unjust'; we have to discover which of these form contraries.

Now if the spoken word corresponds with the judgement of the mind, and if, in thought, that judgement is the contrary of another, which pronounces a contrary fact, in the way, for instance, in which the judgement 'every man is just' pronounces a contrary to that pronounced by the judgement 'every man is un- [35] just', the same must needs hold good with regard to spoken affirmations.

But if, in thought, it is not the judgement which pronounces a contrary fact that is the contrary of another, then one affirmation will not find its contrary in another, but rather in the corresponding denial. We must therefore consider which true judgement is the contrary of the false, that which forms the denial of the false judgement or that which affirms the contrary fact.

[40] Let me illustrate. There is a true judgement concerning that which is good, that it is good; another, a false judgement, that it is not good; and a third, which is distinct, that it is 23ᵇ bad. Which of these two is contrary to the true? And if they are one and the same, which mode of expression forms the contrary?

It is an error to suppose that judgements are to be defined as contrary in virtue of the fact that they have contrary subjects; for the judgement concerning a good thing, that it is good, and that concerning a bad thing, that it is bad, [5] may be one and the same, and whether they are so or not, they both represent the truth. Yet the subjects here are contrary. But judgements are not contrary because they have contrary subjects, but because they are to the contrary effect.

Now if we take the judgement that that which is good is good, and another that it is not good, and if there are at the same time other attributes, which do not and cannot belong to the good, we must nevertheless refuse to treat as the contraries of the true judgement those which opine that some other attribute subsists which does not subsist, as also those [10] that opine that some other attribute does not subsist which does subsist, for both these classes of judgement are of unlimited content.

Those judgements must rather be termed contrary to the true judgements, in which error is present. Now these judgements are those which are concerned with the starting points of generation, and generation is the passing from one extreme to its opposite; therefore error is a like transition.

[15] Now that which is good is both good and not bad. The first quality is part of its essence, the second accidental; for it is by accident that it is not bad. But if that true judgement is most really true, which concerns the subject's intrinsic nature, then that false judgement likewise is most really false, which concerns its intrinsic nature. Now the judgement that that which is good is not good is a false judgement concerning its intrinsic nature, the judgement that it is bad is one concerning that which is accidental. Thus the judgement which denies [20] the truth of the true judgement is more really false than that which positively asserts the presence of the contrary quality. But it is the man who forms that judgement which is contrary to the true who is most thoroughly deceived, for contraries are among the things which differ most widely within the same class. If then of the two judgements one is contrary to the true judgement, but that which is contradictory is the more truly contrary, then the latter, it seems, is the real contrary. The judge- [25] ment that that which is good is bad is composite. For presumably the man who forms that judgement must at the same time understand that that which is good is not good.

Further, the contradictory is either always the contrary or never; therefore, if it must necessarily be so in all other cases, our conclusion in the case just dealt with would seem to be [30] correct. Now where terms have no contrary, that judgement is false, which forms the negative of the true; for instance, he who thinks a man is not a man forms a false judgement. If then in these cases the negative is the contrary, then the principle is universal in its application.

Again, the judgement that that which is not good is not good is parallel with the judgement that that which is good is good. Besides these there is the judgement that that which is good is not good, parallel with the judgement that [35] that which is not good is good. Let us consider, therefore, what would form the contrary of the true judgement that that which is not good is not good. The judgement that it is bad would, of course, fail to meet the case, since two true judgements are never contrary and this judgement might be true at the same time as that with which it is connected. For since some things which are not good are bad, both judgements may be true. Nor is the judgement that it is not bad the contrary, for this too might be true, since both qualities might be predicated of the same subject. It remains, [40] therefore, that of the judgement concerning that which is not good, that it is not good, the contrary judgement is that it is good; for 24ᵃ this is false. In the same way, moreover, the judgement concerning that which is good, that it is not good, is the contrary of the judgement that it is good.

It is evident that it will make no difference if we universalize the positive judgement, for the universal negative judgement will form the [5] contrary. For instance, the contrary of the judgement that everything that is good is good is that nothing that is good is good. For the judgement that that which is good is good, if the subject be understood in a universal sense, is equivalent to the judgement that whatever is good is good, and this is identical with the judgement that everything that is good is good. We may deal similarly with judgements concerning that which is not good.

24ᵇ If therefore this is the rule with judgements, and if spoken affirmations and denials are judgements expressed in words, it is plain that the universal denial is the contrary of the affirmation about the same subject. Thus the propositions 'everything good is good', 'every man is good', have for their contraries the propositions 'nothing good is good', 'no man [5] is good'. The contradictory propositions, on the other hand, are 'not everything good is good', 'not every man is good'.

It is evident, also, that neither true judgements nor true propositions can be contrary the one to the other. For whereas, when two propositions are true, a man may state both at the same time without inconsistency, contrary propositions are those which state contrary conditions, and contrary conditions cannot subsist at one and the same time in the same subject.

CONTENTS: PRIOR ANALYTICS

BOOK I
A. Structure of the Syllogism
1. *Preliminary Discussions*

CHAP.		BERLIN NOS.
1.	Subject and scope of the Analytics; certain definitions and divisions	24ª 10
2.	Conversion of pure propositions	25ª 1
3.	Conversion of necessary and contingent propositions	25ª 26

2. *Exposition of the Three Figures*

4.	Pure syllogisms in the first figure	25ᵇ 26
5.	Pure syllogisms in the second figure	26ᵇ 34
6.	Pure syllogisms in the third figure	28ª 10
7.	Common properties of the three figures	29ª 19
8.	Syllogisms with two necessary premisses	29ᵇ 29
9.	Syllogisms with one pure and one necessary premiss in the first figure	30ª 15
10.	Syllogisms with one pure and one necessary premiss in the second figure	30ᵇ 7
11.	Syllogisms with one pure and one necessary premiss in the third figure	31ª 18
12.	Comparison of pure and necessary conclusions	32ª 6
13.	Preliminary discussion of the contingent	32ª 15
14.	Syllogisms in the first figure with two contingent premisses	32ᵇ 38
15.	Syllogisms in the first figure with one contingent and one pure premiss	33ᵇ 25
16.	Syllogisms in the first figure with one contingent and one necessary premiss	35ᵇ 23
17.	Syllogisms in the second figure with two contingent premisses	36ᵇ 26
18.	Syllogisms in the second figure with one contingent and one pure premiss	37ᵇ 19
19.	Syllogisms in the second figure with one contingent and one necessary premiss	38ª 13
20.	Syllogisms in the third figure with two contingent premisses	39ª 3
21.	Syllogisms in the third figure with one contingent and one pure premiss	39ᵇ 8
22.	Syllogisms in the third figure with one contingent and one necessary premiss	40ª 3

3. *Supplementary Discussions*

23.	Every syllogism is in one of the three figures, is completed through the first figure, and reducible to a universal mood of the first figure	40ᵇ 17
24.	Quality and quantity of the premisses of the syllogism	41ᵇ 6
25.	Number of the terms, propositions, and conclusions	41ᵇ 36
26.	The kinds of proposition to be established or disproved in each figure	42ᵇ 26

B. Mode of discovery of arguments
1. *General*

27.	Rules for categorical syllogisms, applicable to all problems	43ª 20
28.	Rules for categorical syllogisms, peculiar to different problems	43ᵇ 39
29.	Rules for *reductio ad impossibile*, hypothetical syllogisms, and modal syllogisms	45ª 23

2. *Proper to the several Sciences and Arts*

30.		46ª 3

3. *Division*

31.		46ª 31

C. Analysis (1) of arguments into figures and moods of syllogism

32.	Rules for the choice of premisses, terms, middle term, figure	46ᵇ 39
33.	Quantity of the premisses	47ᵇ 15
34.	Concrete and abstract terms	48ª 1
35.	Expressions for which there is no one word	48ª 29
36.	The nominative and the oblique cases	48ª 40
37.	The various kinds of attribution	49ª 6
38.	Repetition of the same term	49ª 11
39.	Substitution of equivalent expressions	49ᵇ 3
40.	The definite article	49ᵇ 10
41.	Interpretation of certain expressions	49ᵇ 15
42.	Analysis of composite syllogisms	50ª 5
43.	Analysis of definitions	50ª 11
44.	Analysis of arguments *per impossibile* and of other hypothetical syllogisms	50ª 16

D. Analysis (2) of syllogisms in one figure into another

45.		50ᵇ 5
46.	'Is not A' and 'is not-A'	51ᵇ 5

BOOK II
Properties and defects of syllogism; arguments akin to syllogism

A. Properties

1.	The drawing of more than one conclusion from the same premisses	52ᵇ 38
2.	The drawing of true conclusions from false premisses; the first figure	53ᵇ 4
3.	The drawing of true conclusions from false premisses; the second figure	55ᵇ 2
4.	The drawing of true conclusions from false premisses; the third figure	56ᵇ 3
5.	Circular proof; the first figure	57ᵇ 18
6.	Circular proof; the second figure	58ᵇ 13
7.	Circular proof; the third figure	58ᵇ 39
8.	Conversion; the first figure	59ᵇ 1
9.	Conversion; the second figure	60ª 15

37

CONTENTS

10. Conversion; the third figure — 60^b 6
11. *Reductio ad impossibile;* the first figure — 61^a 17
12. *Reductio ad impossibile;* the second figure — 62^a 20
13. *Reductio ad impossibile;* the third figure — 62^b 5
14. Comparison of *reductio ad impossibile* and ostensive proof — 62^b 29
15. Reasoning from opposites — 63^b 21

B. Defects

16. *Petitio principii* — 64^b 28
17. False Cause — 65^a 38
18. Falsity of conclusion due to falsity in one or more premisses — 66^a 16
19. How to impede opposing arguments and conceal one's own — 66^a 25
20. When refutation is possible — 66^b 3
21. Error — 66^b 18

C. Arguments akin to Syllogism

22. Rules for conversion and for the comparison of desirable and undesirable objects — 67^b 26
23. Induction — 68^b 8
24. Example — 68^b 37
25. Reduction — 69^a 20
26. Objection — 69^a 37
27. Enthymeme — 70^a 3

PRIOR ANALYTICS

BOOK I

1

24ᵃ [10] WE must first state the subject of our inquiry and the faculty to which it belongs: its subject is demonstration and the faculty that carries it out demonstrative science. We must next define a premiss, a term, and a syllogism, and the nature of a perfect and of an imperfect syllogism; and after that, the inclusion or non-inclusion of one term in another as in a whole, and what we mean by predicating one term of [15] all, or none, of another.

A premiss then is a sentence affirming or denying one thing of another. This is either universal or particular or indefinite. By universal I mean the statement that something belongs to all or none of something else; by particular that it belongs to some or not to some or not to all; by indefinite that it does or does not belong, without any mark to show whether [20] it is universal or particular, e.g. 'contraries are subjects of the same science', or 'pleasure is not good'. The demonstrative premiss differs from the dialectical, because the demonstrative premiss is the assertion of one of two contradictory statements (the demonstrator does not ask for his premiss, but lays it down), whereas the dialectical premiss de-[25] pends on the adversary's choice between two contradictories. But this will make no difference to the production of a syllogism in either case; for both the demonstrator and the dialectician argue syllogistically after stating that something does or does not belong to something else. Therefore a syllogistic premiss without qualification will be an affirmation or denial of something concerning something else in the way we have described; it will be [30] demonstrative, if it is true and obtained through the first principles of its science; while a dialectical premiss is the giving of a choice between two contradictories, when a man is proceeding by question, but when he is syl-24ᵇ [10] logizing it is the assertion of that which is apparent and generally admitted, as has been said in the *Topics*.[1] The nature then of a premiss and the difference between syllogistic, demonstrative, and dialectical premisses, may be taken as sufficiently defined by us in [15] relation to our present need, but will be stated accurately in the sequel.

I call that a term into which the premiss is resolved, i. e. both the predicate and that of which it is predicated, 'being' being added and 'not being' removed, or vice versa.

A syllogism is discourse in which, certain things being stated, something other than what [20] is stated follows of necessity from their being so. I mean by the last phrase that they produce the consequence, and by this, that no further term is required from without in order to make the consequence necessary.

I call that a perfect syllogism which needs nothing other than what has been stated to make plain what necessarily follows; a syllogism is imperfect, if it needs either one or more [25] propositions, which are indeed the necessary consequences of the terms set down, but have not been expressly stated as premisses.

That one term should be included in another as in a whole is the same as for the other to be predicated of all of the first. And we say that one term is predicated of all of another, whenever no instance of the subject can be found of which the other term cannot be asserted: 'to [30] be predicated of none' must be understood in the same way.

2

25ᵃ Every premiss states that something either is or must be or may be the attribute of something else; of premisses of these three kinds some are affirmative, others negative, in respect of each of the three modes of attribution; again some affirmative and negative premisses are [5] universal, others particular, others indefinite. It is necessary then that in universal attribution the terms of the negative premiss should be convertible, e.g. if no pleasure is good, then no good will be pleasure; the terms of the affirmative must be convertible, not however universally, but in part, e.g. if every pleasure is good, some good must be pleasure; the [10] particular affirmative must convert in part

---

NOTE: The bold face numbers and letters are approximate indications of the pages and columns of the standard Berlin Greek text; the bracketed numbers, of the lines in the Greek text; they are here assigned as they are assigned in the Oxford translation.

[1] 100ᵃ 29, 104ᵃ 8.

(for if some pleasure is good, then some good will be pleasure); but the particular negative need not convert, for if some animal is not man, it does not follow that some man is not animal.

First then take a universal negative with the [15] terms A and B. If no B is A, neither can any A be B. For if some A (say C) were B, it would not be true that no B is A; for C is a B. But if every B is A, then some A is B. For if no A were B, then no B could be A. But we as- [20] sumed that every B is A. Similarly too, if the premiss is particular. For if some B is A, then some of the As must be B. For if none were, then no B would be A. But if some B is not A, there is no necessity that some of the As should not be B; e.g. let B stand for animal [25] and A for man. Not every animal is a man; but every man is an animal.

3

The same manner of conversion will hold good also in respect of necessary premisses. The universal negative converts universally; each of the affirmatives converts into a particular. If [30] it is necessary that no B is A, it is necessary also that no A is B. For if it is possible that some A is B, it would be possible also that some B is A. If all or some B is A of necessity, it is necessary also that some A is B: for if there were no necessity, neither would some of [35] the Bs be A necessarily. But the particular negative does not convert, for the same reason which we have already stated.[1]

In respect of possible premisses, since possibility is used in several senses (for we say that what is necessary and what is not necessary and what is potential is possible), affirmative state- [40] ments will all convert in a manner similar to those described.[2] For if it is possible that all or some B is A, it will be possible 25[b] that some A is B. For if that were not possible, then no B could possibly be A. This has been already proved.[3] But in negative statements the case is different. Whatever is said to be possible, either because B necessarily is A, or because B is not necessarily [5] A, admits of conversion like other negative statements, e.g. if one should say, it is possible that man is not horse, or that no garment is white. For in the former case the one term necessarily does not belong to the other; in the latter there is no necessity that it should: and the premiss converts like other negative statements. For if it is possible for no man to be a [10] horse, it is also admissible for no horse to be a man; and if it is admissible for no garment to be white, it is also admissible for nothing white to be a garment. For if any white thing must be a garment, then some garment will necessarily be white. This has been already proved.[4] The particular negative also must be treated like those dealt with above.[5] But if anything is said to be possible because it is the gen- [15] eral rule and natural (and it is in this way we define the possible), the negative premisses can no longer be converted like the simple negatives; the universal negative premiss does not convert, and the particular does. This will be plain when we speak about the possible.[6] At present we may take this much as clear in addi- [20] tion to what has been said: the statement that it is possible that no B is A or some B is not A is affirmative in form: for the expression 'is possible' ranks along with 'is', and 'is' makes an affirmation always and in every case, whatever the terms to which it is added, in predication, e.g. 'it is not-good' or 'it is not-white' or in a word 'it is not-this'. But this also will be [25] proved in the sequel.[7] In conversion these premisses will behave like the other affirmative propositions.

4

After these distinctions we now state by what means, when, and how every syllogism is produced; subsequently[8] we must speak of demonstration. Syllogism should be discussed before demonstration, because syllogism is the [30] more general: the demonstration is a sort of syllogism, but not every syllogism is a demonstration.

Whenever three terms are so related to one another that the last is contained in the middle as in a whole, and the middle is either contained in, or excluded from, the first as in or from a whole, the extremes must be related by [35] a perfect syllogism. I call that term middle which is itself contained in another and contains another in itself: in position also this comes in the middle. By extremes I mean both that term which is itself contained in another and that in which another is contained. If A is predicated of all B, and B of all C, A must [40] be predicated of all C: we have already explained[9] what we mean by 'predicated of all'. 26[a] Similarly also, if A is predicated of no B,

---

[1] ll. 12, 22-6. [2] In ll. 7-13. [3] [a]20-2.
[4] [a] 14-17. [5] In [a] 12. [6] cc. 13, 17.
[7] c. 46.
[8] In the *Posterior Analytics*.
[9] 24[b] 28.

and B of all C, it is necessary that no C will be A.

But if the first term belongs to all the middle, but the middle to none of the last term, there will be no syllogism in respect of the extremes; for nothing necessary follows from the terms being so related; for it is possible that the [5] first should belong either to all or to none of the last, so that neither a particular nor a universal conclusion is necessary. But if there is no necessary consequence, there cannot be a syllogism by means of these premisses. As an example of a universal affirmative relation between the extremes we may take the terms animal, man, horse; of a universal negative relation, the terms animal, man, stone. Nor again can a syllogism be formed when neither the [10] first term belongs to any of the middle, nor the middle to any of the last. As an example of a positive relation between the extremes take the terms science, line, medicine: of a negative relation science, line, unit.

If then the terms are universally related, it is clear in this figure when a syllogism will be possible and when not, and that if a syllogism [15] is possible the terms must be related as described, and if they are so related there will be a syllogism.

But if one term is related universally, the other in part only, to its subject, there must be a perfect syllogism whenever universality is posited with reference to the major term either affirmatively or negatively, and particularity [20] with reference to the minor term affirmatively: but whenever the universality is posited in relation to the minor term, or the terms are related in any other way, a syllogism is impossible. I call that term the major in which the middle is contained and that term the minor which comes under the middle. Let all B be A and some C be B. Then if 'predicated of all' means what was said above,[1] it is neces-[25]sary that some C is A. And if no B is A, but some C is B, it is necessary that some C is not A. (The meaning of 'predicated of none' has also been defined.[2]) So there will be a perfect syllogism. This holds good also if the premiss BC should be indefinite, provided that it is affirmative: for we shall have the same syllogism whether the premiss is indefinite or particular.

[30] But if the universality is posited with respect to the minor term either affirmatively or negatively, a syllogism will not be possible, whether the major premiss is positive or negative, indefinite or particular: e.g. if some B is or is not A, and all C is B. As an example of a positive relation between the extremes take the [35] terms good, state, wisdom: of a negative relation, good, state, ignorance. Again if no C is B, but some B is or is not A, or not every B is A, there cannot be a syllogism. Take the terms white, horse, swan: white, horse, raven. The same terms may be taken also if the premiss BA is indefinite.

26ᵇ Nor when the major premiss is universal, whether affirmative or negative, and the minor premiss is negative and particular, can there be a syllogism, whether the minor premiss be indefinite or particular: e.g. if all B is A, and some C is not B, or if not all C is B. For the major term may be predicable both of all and of none of the minor, to some of which the [5] middle term cannot be attributed. Suppose the terms are animal, man, white: next take some of the white things of which man is not predicated—swan and snow: animal is predicated of all of the one, but of none of the other. Consequently there cannot be a syllo-[10]gism. Again let no B be A, but let some C not be B. Take the terms inanimate, man, white: then take some white things of which man is not predicated—swan and snow: the term inanimate is predicated of all of the one, of none of the other.

Further since it is indefinite to say some C [15] is not B, and it is true that some C is not B, whether no C is B, or not all C is B, and since if terms are assumed such that no C is B, no syllogism follows (this has already been stated[3]), it is clear that this arrangement of terms will not afford a syllogism: otherwise one would have been possible with a *universal* [20] negative minor premiss. A similar proof may also be given if the universal premiss is negative.

Nor can there in any way be a syllogism if both the relations of subject and predicate are particular, either positively or negatively, or the one negative and the other affirmative, or one indefinite and the other definite, or both [25] indefinite. Terms common to all the above are animal, white, horse: animal, white, stone.

It is clear then from what has been said that if there is a syllogism in this figure with a particular conclusion, the terms must be related as we have stated: if they are related otherwise, no syllogism is possible anyhow. It is evident also that all the syllogisms in this figure are

---
[1] 24ᵇ 28. [2] 24ᵇ 30. [3] a 2.

[30] perfect (for they are all completed by means of the premisses originally taken) and that all conclusions are proved by this figure, viz. universal and particular, affirmative and negative. Such a figure I call the first.

5

Whenever the same thing belongs to all of one [35] subject, and to none of another, or to all of each subject or to none of either, I call such a figure the second; by middle term in it I mean that which is predicated of both subjects, by extremes the terms of which this is said, by major extreme that which lies near the middle, by minor that which is further away from the middle. The middle term stands outside the extremes, and is first in position. A syllogism cannot be perfect anyhow in this figure, but it may be valid whether the terms are related universally or not.

If then the terms are related universally a syllogism will be possible, whenever the middle belongs to all of one subject and to none of another (it does not matter which has the [5] negative relation), but in no other way. Let M be predicated of no N, but of all O. Since, then, the negative relation is convertible, N will belong to no M: but M was assumed to belong to all O: consequently N will belong to no O. This has already been proved.[1] Again if [10] M belongs to all N, but to no O, then N will belong to no O. For if M belongs to no O, O belongs to no M: but M (as was said) belongs to all N: O then will belong to no N: for the first figure has again been formed. But since the negative relation is convertible, N will belong to no O. Thus it will be the same syllogism that proves both conclusions.

[15] It is possible to prove these results also by reduction *ad impossibile*.

It is clear then that a syllogism is formed when the terms are so related, but not a perfect syllogism; for necessity is not perfectly established merely from the original premisses; others also are needed.

But if M is predicated of every N and O, there cannot be a syllogism. Terms to illustrate a positive relation between the extremes are substance, animal, man; a negative relation, [20] substance, animal, number—substance being the middle term.

Nor is a syllogism possible when M is predicated neither of any N nor of any O. Terms to illustrate a positive relation are line, animal, man: a negative relation, line, animal, stone.

[1] 25^b 40.

It is clear then that if a syllogism is formed when the terms are universally related, the terms must be related as we stated at the outset:[2] for if they are otherwise related no [25] necessary consequence follows.

If the middle term is related universally to one of the extremes, a particular negative syllogism must result whenever the middle term is related universally to the major whether positively or negatively, and particularly to the minor and in a manner opposite to that of the universal statement: by 'an opposite manner' I mean, if the universal statement is negative, [30] the particular is affirmative: if the universal is affirmative, the particular is negative. For if M belongs to no N, but to some O, it is necessary that N does not belong to some O. For since the negative statement is convertible, N will belong to no M: but M was admitted to [35] belong to some O: therefore N will not belong to some O: for the result is reached by means of the first figure. Again if M belongs to all N, but not to some O, it is necessary that N does not belong to some O: for if N belongs to all O, and M is predicated also of all N, M must belong to all O: but we assumed that M does not belong to some O. And if M belongs to all N but not to all O, we shall conclude that N does not belong to all O: the proof is the same as the above. But if M is predicated of all O, but not of all N, there will be no syllogism. Take the terms animal, substance, raven; [5] animal, white, raven. Nor will there be a conclusion when M is predicated of no O, but of some N. Terms to illustrate a positive relation between the extremes are animal, substance, unit: a negative relation, animal, substance, science.

If then the universal statement is opposed to [10] the particular, we have stated when a syllogism will be possible and when not: but if the premisses are similar in form, I mean both negative or both affirmative, a syllogism will not be possible anyhow. First let them be negative, and let the major premiss be universal, e.g. let M belong to no N, and not to some [15] O. It is possible then for N to belong either to all O or to no O. Terms to illustrate the negative relation are black, snow, animal. But it is not possible to find terms of which the extremes are related positively and universally, if M belongs to some O, and does not belong to some O. For if N belonged to all O, but M to no N, then M would belong to no O: but we assumed that it belongs to some O. In this way

[2] l. 3.

[20] then it is not admissible to take terms: our point must be proved from the indefinite nature of the particular statement. For since it is true that M does not belong to some O, even if it belongs to no O, and since if it belongs to no O a syllogism is (as we have seen[1]) not possible, clearly it will not be possible now either.

Again let the premisses be affirmative, and let the major premiss as before be universal, [25] e.g. let M belong to all N and to some O. It is possible then for N to belong to all O or to no O. Terms to illustrate the negative relation are white, swan, stone. But it is not possible to take terms to illustrate the universal affirmative relation, for the reason already stated:[2] the point must be proved from the indefinite nature of the particular statement. [30] But if the *minor* premiss is universal, and M belongs to no O, and not to some N, it is possible for N to belong either to all O or to no O. Terms for the positive relation are white, animal, raven: for the negative relation, white, stone, raven. If the premisses are affirmative, terms for the negative relation are white, animal, snow; for the positive relation, white, animal, swan. Evidently then, whenever the premisses are similar in form, and one is univer- [35] sal, the other particular, a syllogism cannot be formed anyhow. Nor is one possible if the middle term belongs to some of each of the extremes, or does not belong to some of either, or belongs to some of the one, not to some of the other, or belongs to neither universally, or is related to them indefinitely. Common terms for all the above are white, animal, man: white, animal, inanimate.

28ª It is clear then from what has been said that if the terms are related to one another in the way stated, a syllogism results of necessity; and if there is a syllogism, the terms must be so related. But it is evident also that all the syllogisms in this figure are imperfect: for all are [5] made perfect by certain supplementary statements, which either are contained in the terms of necessity or are assumed as hypotheses, i.e. when we prove *per impossibile*. And it is evident that an affirmative conclusion is not attained by means of this figure, but all are negative, whether universal or particular.

6

[10] But if one term belongs to all, and another to none, of a third, or if both belong to all, or to none, of it, I call such a figure the third; by middle term in it I mean that of

[1] a 21.   [2] l. 18.

which both the predicates are predicated, by extremes I mean the predicates, by the major extreme that which is further from the middle, by the minor that which is nearer to it. The [15] middle term stands outside the extremes, and is last in position. A syllogism cannot be perfect in this figure either, but it may be valid whether the terms are related universally or not to the middle term.

If they are universal, whenever both P and R belong to S, it follows that P will necessarily belong to some R. For, since the affirmative statement is convertible, S will belong to some R: [20] consequently since P belongs to all S, and S to some R, P must belong to some R: for a syllogism in the first figure is produced. It is possible to demonstrate this also *per impossibile* and by exposition. For if both P and R belong to all S, should one of the Ss, e.g. N, be [25] taken, both P and R will belong to this, and thus P will belong to some R.

If R belongs to all S, and P to no S, there will be a syllogism to prove that P will necessarily not belong to some R. This may be demonstrated in the same way as before by converting the premiss RS. It might be proved also [30] *per impossibile*, as in the former cases. But if R belongs to no S, P to all S, there will be no syllogism. Terms for the positive relation are animal, horse, man: for the negative relation animal, inanimate, man.

Nor can there be a syllogism when both terms are asserted of no S. Terms for the positive relation are animal, horse, inanimate; for [35] the negative relation man, horse, inanimate—inanimate being the middle term.

It is clear then in this figure also when a syllogism will be possible and when not, if the terms are related universally. For whenever both the terms are affirmative, there will be a syllogism to prove that one extreme belongs to some of the other; but when they are negative, 28ᵇ no syllogism will be possible. But when one is negative, the other affirmative, if the major is negative, the minor affirmative, there will be a syllogism to prove that the one extreme does not belong to some of the other: but if the relation is reversed, no syllogism will be possible.

[5] If one term is related universally to the middle, the other in part only, when both are affirmative there must be a syllogism, no matter which of the premisses is universal. For if R belongs to all S, P to some S, P must belong to some R. For since the affirmative statement [10] is convertible S will belong to some P: consequently since R belongs to all S, and S to

some P, R must also belong to some P: therefore P must belong to some R.

Again if R belongs to some S, and P to all S, P must belong to some R. This may be demonstrated in the same way as the preceding. And it is possible to demonstrate it also *per impossibile* and by exposition, as in the former cases. [15] But if one term is affirmative, the other negative, and if the affirmative is universal, a syllogism will be possible whenever the minor term is affirmative. For if R belongs to all S, but P does not belong to some S, it is necessary that P does not belong to some R. For if P belongs to all R, and R belongs to all S, then P [20] will belong to all S: but we assumed that it did not. Proof is possible also without reduction *ad impossibile*, if one of the Ss be taken to which P does not belong.

But whenever the major is affirmative, no syllogism will be possible, e.g. if P belongs to all S, and R does not belong to some S. Terms for the universal affirmative relation are animate, man, animal. For the universal negative [25] relation it is not possible to get terms, if R belongs to some S, and does not belong to some S. For if P belongs to all S, and R to some S, then P will belong to some R: but we assumed that it belongs to no R. We must put the matter as before.[1] Since the expression 'it does not belong to some' is indefinite, it may be used truly of that also which belongs to none. But [30] if R belongs to no S, no syllogism is possible, as has been shown.[2] Clearly then no syllogism will be possible here.

But if the negative term is universal, whenever the major is negative and the minor affirmative there will be a syllogism. For if P belongs to no S, and R belongs to some S, P will not belong to some R: for we shall have [35] the first figure again, if the premiss RS is converted.

But when the minor is negative, there will be no syllogism. Terms for the positive relation are animal, man, wild: for the negative relation, animal, science, wild—the middle in both being the term wild.

Nor is a syllogism possible when both are stated in the negative, but one is universal, the other particular. When the *minor* is related universally to the middle, take the terms animal, science, wild; animal, man, wild. When the *major* is related universally to the middle, take as terms for a negative relation raven, snow, white. For a positive relation terms cannot be found, if R belongs to some S,

[1] 27[b] 20. [2] 28[a] 30.

[5] and does not belong to some S. For if P belongs to all R, and R to some S, then P belongs to some S: but we assumed that it belongs to no S. Our point, then, must be proved from the indefinite nature of the particular statement.

Nor is a syllogism possible anyhow, if each of the extremes belongs to some of the middle, or does not belong, or one belongs and the other does not to some of the middle, or one belongs to some of the middle, the other not to all, or if the premisses are indefinite. Common [10] terms for all are animal, man, white: animal, inanimate, white.

It is clear then in this figure also when a syllogism will be possible, and when not; and that if the terms are as stated, a syllogism results of necessity, and if there is a syllogism, the terms must be so related. It is clear also that [15] all the syllogisms in this figure are imperfect (for all are made perfect by certain supplementary assumptions), and that it will not be possible to reach a universal conclusion by means of this figure, whether negative or affirmative.

7

It is evident also that in all the figures, whenever [20] a proper syllogism does not result, if both the terms are affirmative or negative nothing necessary follows at all, but if one is affirmative, the other negative, and if the negative is stated universally, a syllogism always results relating the minor to the major term, e.g. if A belongs to all or some B, and B belongs to no C: for if the premisses are converted it is necessary [25] that C does not belong to some A. Similarly also in the other figures: a syllogism always results by means of conversion. It is evident also that the substitution of an indefinite for a particular affirmative will effect the same syllogism in all the figures.

[30] It is clear too that all the imperfect syllogisms are made perfect by means of the first figure. For all are brought to a conclusion either ostensively or *per impossibile*. In both ways the first figure is formed: if they are made perfect ostensively, because (as we saw) all are brought to a conclusion by means of conversion, and conversion produces the first figure: [35] if they are proved *per impossibile*, because on the assumption of the false statement the syllogism comes about by means of the first figure, e.g. in the last figure, if A and B belong to all C, it follows that A belongs to some B: for if A belonged to no B, and B belongs to all C,

A would belong to no C: but (as we stated) it belongs to all C. Similarly also with the rest.

29ᵇ It is possible also to reduce all syllogisms to the *universal* syllogisms in the first figure. Those in the second figure are clearly made perfect by these, though not all in the same way; the universal syllogisms are made perfect [5] by converting the negative premiss, each of the particular syllogisms by reduction *ad impossibile*. In the first figure particular syllogisms are indeed made perfect by themselves, but it is possible also to prove them by means of the second figure, reducing them *ad impossibile*, e.g. if A belongs to all B, and B to some C, it follows that A belongs to some C. For if it belonged to no C, and belongs to all B, then B [10] will belong to no C: this we know by means of the second figure. Similarly also demonstration will be possible in the case of the negative. For if A belongs to no B, and B belongs to some C, A will not belong to some C: for if it belonged to all C, and belongs to no B, then B will belong to no C: and this (as we [15] saw) is the middle figure. Consequently, since all syllogisms in the middle figure can be reduced to universal syllogisms in the first figure, and since particular syllogisms in the first figure can be reduced to syllogisms in the middle figure, it is clear that particular syllogisms can be reduced to universal syllogisms in the first figure. Syllogisms in the third figure, if the [20] terms are universal, are directly made perfect by means of those syllogisms; but, when one of the premisses is particular, by means of the *particular* syllogisms in the first figure: and these (we have seen) may be reduced to the universal syllogisms in the first figure: consequently also the particular syllogisms in the third figure may be so reduced. It is clear then that all syllogisms may be reduced to the uni- [25] versal syllogisms in the first figure.

We have stated then how syllogisms which prove that something belongs or does not belong to something else are constituted, both how syllogisms of the same figure are constituted in themselves, and how syllogisms of different figures are related to one another.

8

Since there is a difference according as some- [30] thing belongs, necessarily belongs, or may belong to something else (for many things belong indeed, but not necessarily, others neither necessarily nor indeed at all, but it is possible for them to belong), it is clear that there will be different syllogisms to prove each of these relations, and syllogisms with differently related terms, one syllogism concluding from what is necessary, another from what is, a third from [35] what is possible.

There is hardly any difference between syllogisms from necessary premisses and syllogisms from premisses which merely assert. When the terms are put in the same way, then, whether something belongs or necessarily belongs (or does not belong) to something else, a syllogism will or will not result alike in both cases, the only difference being the addition of the ex- 30ᵃ pression 'necessarily' to the terms. For the negative statement is convertible alike in both cases, and we should give the same account of the expressions 'to be contained in something as in a whole' and 'to be predicated of all of something'. With the exceptions to be made below, the conclusion will be proved to be necessary by means of conversion, in the same [5] manner as in the case of simple predication. But in the middle figure when the universal statement is affirmative, and the particular negative, and again in the third figure when the universal is affirmative and the particular negative, the demonstration will not take the same form, but it is necessary by the 'exposition' of a part of the subject of the particular negative [10] proposition, to which the predicate does not belong, to make the syllogism in reference to this: with terms so chosen the conclusion will necessarily follow. But if the relation is necessary in respect of the part taken, it must hold of some of that term in which this part is included: for the part taken is just some of that. And each of the resulting syllogisms is in the appropriate figure.

9

[15] It happens sometimes also that when *one* premiss is necessary the conclusion is necessary, not however when either premiss is necessary, but only when the major is, e.g. if A is taken as necessarily belonging or not belonging to B, but B is taken as simply belonging to C: for if [20] the premisses are taken in this way, A will necessarily belong or not belong to C. For since A necessarily belongs, or does not belong, to every B, and since C is one of the Bs, it is clear that for C also the positive or the negative relation to A will hold necessarily. But if the major premiss is not necessary, but the minor is necessary, the conclusion will not be neces- [25] sary. For if it were, it would result both through the first figure and through the third that A belongs necessarily to some B. But this

is false; for *B* may be such that it is possible that *A* should belong to none of it. Further, an example also makes it clear that the conclusion [30] will not be necessary, e.g. if *A* were movement, *B* animal, *C* man: man is an animal necessarily, but an animal does not move necessarily, nor does man. Similarly also if the major premiss is negative; for the proof is the same.

In particular syllogisms, if the universal [35] premiss is necessary, then the conclusion will be necessary; but if the particular, the conclusion will not be necessary, whether the universal premiss is negative or affirmative. First let the *universal* be necessary, and let *A* belong to all *B* necessarily, but let *B* simply belong to some *C*: it is necessary then that *A* belongs to [40] some *C* necessarily: for *C* falls under *B*, 30^b and *A* was assumed to belong necessarily to all *B*. Similarly also if the syllogism should be negative: for the proof will be the same. But if the *particular* premiss is necessary, the conclusion will not be necessary: for from the denial of such a conclusion nothing impossible results, just as it does not in the universal syl- [5] logisms. The same is true of negative syllogisms. Try the terms movement, animal, white.

10

In the *second* figure, if the negative premiss is necessary, then the conclusion will be necessary, but if the affirmative, not necessary. First let the *negative* be necessary; let *A* be possible [10] of no *B*, and simply belong to *C*. Since then the negative statement is convertible, *B* is possible of no *A*. But *A* belongs to all *C*; consequently *B* is possible of no *C*. For *C* falls under *A*. The same result would be obtained if the *minor* premiss were negative: for if *A* is possi- [15] ble be of no *C*, *C* is possible of no *A*: but *A* belongs to all *B*, consequently *C* is possible of none of the *B*s: for again we have obtained the first figure. Neither then is *B* possible of *C*: for conversion is possible without modifying the relation.

But if the *affirmative* premiss is necessary, the conclusion will not be necessary. Let *A* be- [20] long to all *B* necessarily, but to no *C* simply. If then the negative premiss is converted, the first figure results. But it has been proved[1] in the case of the first figure that if the negative major premiss is not necessary the conclusion will not be necessary either. Therefore the same result will obtain here. Further, if the [25] conclusion is necessary, it follows that *C* necessarily does not belong to some *A*. For if *B* necessarily belongs to no *C*, *C* will necessarily belong to no *B*. But *B* at any rate must belong to some *A*, if it is true (as was assumed) that *A* necessarily belongs to all *B*. Consequently it is [30] necessary that *C* does not belong to some *A*. But nothing prevents such an *A* being taken that it is possible for *C* to belong to all of it. Further one might show by an exposition of terms that the conclusion is not necessary without qualification, though it is a necessary conclusion from the premisses. For example let *A* be animal, *B* man, *C* white, and let the premisses be assumed to correspond to what we had before:[2] it is possible that animal should belong [35] to nothing white. Man then will not belong to anything white, but not necessarily: for it is possible for man to be born white, not however so long as animal belongs to nothing white. Consequently under these conditions the conclusion will be necessary, but it is not necessary without qualification.

31^a Similar results will obtain also in particular syllogisms. For whenever the negative premiss is both universal and necessary, then the conclusion will be necessary: but whenever the affirmative premiss is universal, the negative particular, the conclusion will not be nec- [5] essary. First then let the *negative* premiss be both universal and necessary: let it be possible for no *B* that *A* should belong to it, and let *A* simply belong to some *C*. Since the negative statement is convertible, it will be possible for no *A* that *B* should belong to it: but *A* belongs to some *C*; consequently *B* necessarily [10] does not belong to some of the *C*s. Again let the *affirmative* premiss be both universal and necessary, and let the *major* premiss be affirmative. If then *A* necessarily belongs to all *B*, but does not belong to some *C*, it is clear that *B* will not belong to some *C*, but not necessarily. For the same terms can be used to demonstrate the point, which were used in the [15] universal syllogisms.[3] Nor again, if the negative statement is necessary but particular, will the conclusion be necessary. The point can be demonstrated by means of the same terms.

11

In the *last* figure when the terms are related universally to the middle, and both premisses are affirmative, if one of the two is necessary, [20] then the conclusion will be necessary. But if one is negative, the other affirmative, whenever the negative is necessary the conclusion

---

[1] ^{a} 23-33. [2] l. 20. [3] 30^b 33-40.

also will be necessary, but whenever the affirmative is necessary the conclusion will not be necessary. First let both the premisses be affirmative, and let A and B belong to all C, and let [25] AC be necessary. Since then B belongs to all C, C also will belong to some B, because the universal is convertible into the particular: consequently if A belongs necessarily to all C, and C belongs to some B, it is necessary that A should belong to some B also. For B is under [30] C. The first figure then is formed. A similar proof will be given also if BC is necessary. For C is convertible with some A: consequently if B belongs necessarily to all C, it will belong necessarily also to some A.

Again let AC be negative, BC affirmative, and let the *negative* premiss be necessary. Since [35] then C is convertible with some B, but A necessarily belongs to no C, A will necessarily not belong to some B either: for B is under C. But if the *affirmative* is necessary, the conclusion will not be necessary. For suppose BC is affirmative and necessary, while AC is negative and not necessary. Since then the affirmative is [40] convertible, C also will belong to some B necessarily: consequently if A belongs to none of the Cs, while C belongs to some of the Bs, 31[b] A will not belong to some of the Bs—but not of necessity; for it has been proved, in the case of the first figure, that if the negative premiss is not necessary, neither will the conclusion be necessary. Further, the point may be made clear by considering the terms. Let [5] the term A be 'good', let that which B signifies be 'animal', let the term C be 'horse'. It is possible then that the term good should belong to no horse, and it is necessary that the term animal should belong to every horse: but it is not necessary that some animal should not be good, since it is possible for every animal to be good. Or if that is not possible, take as the term 'awake' or 'asleep': for every animal can [10] accept these.

If, then, the premisses are universal, we have stated when the conclusion will be necessary. But if one premiss is universal, the other particular, and if both are affirmative, whenever the universal is necessary the conclusion also [15] must be necessary. The demonstration is the same as before;[1] for the particular affirmative also is convertible. If then it is necessary that B should belong to all C, and A falls under C, it is necessary that B should belong to some A. But if B must belong to some A, then A must belong to some B: for conversion is possible. Similarly also if AC should be necessary [20] and universal: for B falls under C. But if the *particular* premiss is necessary, the conclusion will not be necessary. Let the premiss BC be both particular and necessary, and let A belong to all C, not however necessarily. If the proposition BC is converted the first figure is [25] formed, and the universal premiss is not necessary, but the particular is necessary. But when the premisses were thus, the conclusion (as we proved[2]) was not necessary: consequently it is not here either. Further, the point is clear if we look at the terms. Let A be waking, B biped, and C animal. It is necessary that B should belong to some C, but it is possible for [30] A to belong to C, and that A should belong to B is not necessary. For there is no necessity that some biped should be asleep or awake. Similarly and by means of the same terms proof can be made, should the proposition AC be both particular and necessary.

But if one premiss is affirmative, the other negative, whenever the universal is both negative and necessary the conclusion also will be [35] necessary. For if it is not possible that A should belong to any C, but B belongs to some C, it is necessary that A should not belong to some B. But whenever the affirmative proposition is necessary, whether universal or particular, or the negative is particular, the conclusion will not be necessary. The proof of this by re- [40] duction will be the same as before;[3] but if terms are wanted, when the universal affirmative is necessary, take the terms 'waking'—'animal'—'man', 'man' being middle, and when 32[a] the affirmative is particular and necessary, take the terms 'waking'—'animal'—'white': for it is necessary that animal should belong to some white thing, but it is possible that waking should belong to none, and it is not necessary that waking should not belong to some animal. But when the negative proposition being par- [5] ticular is necessary, take the terms 'biped', 'moving', 'animal', 'animal' being middle.

12

It is clear then that a simple conclusion is not reached unless both premisses are simple assertions, but a necessary conclusion is possible although one only of the premisses is necessary. But in both cases, whether the syllogisms are [10] affirmative or negative, it is necessary that one premiss should be similar to the conclusion. I mean by 'similar', if the conclusion is a simple assertion, the premiss must be simple; if

---

[1] [a]24-33. [2] 30[a] 35-7, [b] 1-5. [3] Cf. [a] 37-[b] 4, [b] 20-7.

the conclusion is necessary, the premiss must be necessary. Consequently this also is clear, that the conclusion will be neither necessary nor simple unless a necessary or simple premiss is assumed.

13

[*15*] Perhaps enough has been said about the proof of necessity, how it comes about and how it differs from the proof of a simple statement. We proceed to discuss that which is possible, when and how and by what means it can be proved. I use the terms 'to be possible' and 'the possible' of that which is not necessary but, being assumed, results in nothing impossible. We [*20*] say indeed ambiguously of the necessary that it is possible. But that my definition of the possible is correct is clear from the phrases by which we deny or on the contrary affirm possibility. For the expressions 'it is not possible to belong', 'it is impossible to belong', and 'it is necessary not to belong' are either identical or follow from one another; consequently their [*25*] opposites also, 'it is possible to belong', 'it is not impossible to belong', and 'it is not necessary not to belong', will either be identical or follow from one another. For of everything the affirmation or the denial holds good. That which is possible then will be not necessary and that which is not necessary will be possible. It results that all premisses in the mode of possi- [*30*] bility are convertible into one another. I mean not that the affirmative are convertible into the negative, but that those which are affirmative in form admit of conversion by opposition, e.g. 'it is possible to belong' may be converted into 'it is possible not to belong', and 'it is possible for A to belong to all B' into 'it is possible for A to belong to no B' or 'not to all B', and 'it is possible for A to belong to some B' [*35*] into 'it is possible for A not to belong to some B'. And similarly the other propositions in this mode can be converted. For since that which is possible is not necessary, and that which is not necessary may possibly not belong, it is clear that if it is possible that A should belong to B, it is possible also that it should not belong to B: and if it is possible that it should belong to all, it is also possible that it should not belong to all. The same holds good in the case of particular affirmations: for the proof is 32b identical. And such premisses are affirmative and not negative; for 'to be possible' is in the same rank as 'to be', as was said above.[1]

Having made these distinctions we next point out that the expression 'to be possible' is [*5*] used in two ways. In one it means to happen generally and fall short of necessity, e.g. man's turning grey or growing or decaying, or generally what naturally belongs to a thing (for this has not its necessity unbroken, since man's existence is not continuous for ever, although if a man does exist, it comes about ei- [*10*] ther necessarily or generally). In another sense the expression means the indefinite, which can be both thus and not thus, e.g. an animal's walking or an earthquake's taking place while it is walking, or generally what happens by chance: for none of these inclines by nature in the one way more than in the opposite.

That which is possible in each of its two senses is convertible into its opposite, not how- [*15*] ever in the same way: but what is natural is convertible because it does not necessarily belong (for in this sense it is possible that a man should not grow grey) and what is indefinite is convertible because it inclines this way no more than that. Science and demonstrative syllogism are not concerned with things which are indefinite, because the middle term is uncertain; but they are concerned with things [*20*] that are natural, and as a rule arguments and inquiries are made about things which are possible in this sense. Syllogisms indeed can be made about the former, but it is unusual at any rate to inquire about them.

These matters will be treated more definitely in the sequel;[2] our business at present is to state the moods and nature of the syllogism made from possible premisses. The expression [*25*] 'it is possible for this to belong to that' may be understood in two senses: 'that' may mean either that to which 'that' belongs or that to which it may belong; for the expression 'A is possible of the subject of B' means that it is possible either of that of which B is stated or of that of which B may possibly be stated. It makes no difference whether we say, A is pos- [*30*] sible of the subject of B, or all B admits of A. It is clear then that the expression 'A may possibly belong to all B' might be used in two senses. First then we must state the nature and characteristics of the syllogism which arises if B is possible of the subject of C, and A is possible of the subject of B. For thus both premisses [*35*] are assumed in the mode of possibility; but whenever A is possible of that of which B is true, one premiss is a simple assertion, the other a problematic. Consequently we must

[1] 25b 21.
[2] *Posterior Analytics*, I. 8.

14

Whenever A may possibly belong to all B, and B to all C, there will be a perfect syllogism to prove that A may possibly belong to all C. [40] This is clear from the definition: for it was in this way that we explained 'to be possible for one term to belong to all of another'.[1] Similarly if it is possible for A to belong to no B, and for B to belong to all C, then it is possible for A to belong to no C. For the statement that it is possible for A not to belong to that of which B may be true means (as we saw) that none of those things which can possibly fall [5] under the term B is left out of account. But whenever A may belong to all B, and B may belong to no C, then indeed no syllogism results from the premisses assumed, but if the premiss BC is converted after the manner of problematic propositions, the same syllogism results as before.[2] For since it is possible that B [10] should belong to no C, it is possible also that it should belong to all C. This has been stated above.[3] Consequently if B is possible for all C, and A is possible for all B, the same syllogism again results. Similarly if in both the premisses the negative is joined with 'it is possible': e.g. if A may belong to none of the Bs, [15] and B to none of the Cs. No syllogism results from the assumed premisses, but if they are converted we shall have the same syllogism as before. It is clear then that if the minor premiss is negative, or if both premisses are negative, either no syllogism results, or if one [20] does it is not perfect. For the necessity results from the conversion.

But if one of the premisses is universal, the other particular, when the major premiss is *universal* there will be a perfect syllogism. For if A is possible for all B, and B for some C, then A is possible for some C. This is clear from the [25] definition of being possible.[4] Again if A may belong to no B, and B may belong to some of the Cs, it is necessary that A may possibly not belong to some of the Cs. The proof is the same as above. But if the particular premiss is negative, and the universal is affirmative, the major still being universal and the minor particular, e.g. A is possible for all B, B may possi- [30] bly not belong to some C, then a clear syllogism does not result from the assumed premisses, but if the particular premiss is converted and it is laid down that B possibly may belong to some C, we shall have the same conclusion as before,[5] as in the cases given at the beginning.[6]

[35] But if the major premiss is *particular*, the minor universal, whether both are affirmative, or negative, or different in quality, or if both are indefinite or particular, in no way will a syllogism be possible. For nothing prevents B from reaching beyond A, so that as predicates they cover unequal areas. Let C be that [40] by which B extends beyond A. To C it is not possible that A should belong—either to all or to none or to some or not to some, since premisses in the mode of possibility are convertible and it is possible for B to belong to more things than A can. Further, this is obvious if we take terms; for if the premisses are as assumed, the major term is both possible for [5] none of the minor and must belong to all of it. Take as terms common to all the cases under consideration 'animal'—'white'—'man', where the major belongs necessarily to the minor; 'animal'—'white'—'garment', where it is not possible that the major should belong to the minor. It is clear then that if the terms are related in this manner, no syllogism results. For [10] every syllogism proves that something belongs either simply or necessarily or possibly. It is clear that there is no proof of the first or of the second. For the affirmative is destroyed by the negative, and the negative by the affirmative. There remains the proof of possibility. But this is impossible. For it has been proved [15] that if the terms are related in this manner it is both necessary that the major should belong to all the minor and not possible that it should belong to any. Consequently there cannot be a syllogism to prove the possibility; for the necessary (as we stated) is not possible.[7]

It is clear that if the terms are universal in possible premisses a syllogism always results in the first figure, whether they are affirmative or [20] negative, only a perfect syllogism results in the first case, an imperfect in the second. But possibility must be understood according to the definition laid down,[8] not as covering necessity. This is sometimes forgotten.

15

[25] If one premiss is a simple proposition, the other a problematic, whenever the major premiss indicates possibility all the syllogisms will be perfect and establish possibility in the sense

---

[1] 32^b 25-37.   [2] In 32^b 38-40.   [3] 32^a 34.   [5] l. 24.   [6] ll. 5-17.   [7] 32^a 28.
[4] 32^b 25-37.   [8] 32^a 18.

defined;[1] but whenever the minor premiss indicates possibility all the syllogisms will be imperfect, and those which are negative will es- [30] tablish not possibility according to the definition, but that the major does not necessarily belong to any, or to all, of the minor. For if this is so, we say it is possible that it should belong to none or not to all. Let A be possible for all B, and let B belong to all C. Since C falls under B, and A is possible for all B, clearly it is [35] possible for all C also. So a perfect syllogism results. Likewise if the premiss AB is negative, and the premiss BC is affirmative, the former stating possible, the latter simple attribution, a perfect syllogism results proving that [40] A possibly belongs to no C.

34[a] It is clear that perfect syllogisms result if the minor premiss states simple belonging: but that syllogisms will result if the modality of the premisses is reversed, must be proved *per impossibile*. At the same time it will be evident that they are imperfect: for the proof proceeds [5] not from the premisses assumed. First we must state that if B's being follows necessarily from A's being, B's possibility will follow necessarily from A's possibility. Suppose, the terms being so related, that A is possible, and B is impossible. If then that which is possible, when it is possible for it to be, might happen, and if that which is impossible, when it is impossible, [10] could not happen, and if at the same time A is possible and B impossible, it would be possible for A to happen without B, and if to happen, then to be. For that which has happened, when it has happened, is. But we must take the impossible and the possible not only in the sphere of becoming, but also in the spheres of truth and predicability, and the various other spheres in which we speak of the possible: for [15] it will be alike in all. Further we must understand the statement that B's being depends on A's being, not as meaning that if some single thing A is, B will be: for nothing follows of necessity from the being of some one thing, but from two at least, i.e. when the premisses are related in the manner stated to be that of the syllogism. For if C is predicated [20] of D, and D of F, then C is necessarily predicated of F. And if each is possible, the conclusion also is possible. If then, for example, one should indicate the premisses by A, and the conclusion by B, it would not only result that if A is necessary B is necessary, but also that if A is possible, B is possible.

[25] Since this is proved it is evident that if a false and not impossible assumption is made, the consequence of the assumption will also be false and not impossible: e.g. if A is false, but not impossible, and if B is the consequence of A, B also will be false but not impossible. For since it has been proved that if B's being is the consequence of A's being, then B's possibility [30] will follow from A's possibility (and A is assumed to be possible), consequently B will be possible: for if it were impossible, the same thing would at the same time be possible and impossible.

Since we have defined these points, let A belong to all B, and B be possible for all C: it is [35] necessary then that A should be a possible attribute for all C. Suppose that it is not possible, but assume that B belongs to all C: this is false but not impossible. If then A is not possible for C but B belongs to all C, then A is not possible for all B: for a syllogism is formed [40] in the third degree. But it was assumed that A is a possible attribute for all B. It is necessary then that A is possible for all C. For 34[b] though the assumption we made is false and not impossible, the conclusion is impossible. It is possible also in the first figure to bring about the impossibility, by assuming that B belongs to C. For if B belongs to all C, and A is possible for all B, then A would be possible for [5] all C. But the assumption was made that A is not possible for all C.

We must understand 'that which belongs to all' with no limitation in respect of time, e.g. to the present or to a particular period, but simply without qualification. For it is by the help of such premisses that we make syllo- [10] gisms, since if the premiss is understood with reference to the present moment, there cannot be a syllogism. For nothing perhaps prevents 'man' belonging at a particular time to everything that is moving, i.e. if nothing else were moving: but 'moving' is possible for every horse; yet 'man' is possible for no horse. Further let the major term be 'animal', the middle [15] 'moving', the minor 'man'. The premisses then will be as before, but the conclusion necessary, not possible. For man is necessarily animal. It is clear then that the universal must be understood simply, without limitation in respect of time.

Again let the premiss AB be universal and negative, and assume that A belongs to no B, [20] but B possibly belongs to all C. These propositions being laid down, it is necessary that A possibly belongs to no C. Suppose that it cannot belong, and that B belongs to C, as

[1] 32[a] 18.

above.[1] It is necessary then that A belongs to some B: for we have a syllogism in the third [25] figure: but this is impossible. Thus it will be possible for A to belong to no C; for if that is supposed false, the consequence is an impossible one. This syllogism then does not establish that which is possible according to the definition,[2] but that which does not necessarily belong to any part of the subject (for this is the contradictory of the assumption which was made: for it was supposed that A necessarily [30] belongs to some C, but the syllogism *per impossibile* establishes the contradictory which is opposed to this). Further, it is clear also from an example that the conclusion will not establish possibility. Let A be 'raven', B 'intelligent', and C 'man'. A then belongs to no B: for no [35] intelligent thing is a raven. But B is possible for all C: for every man may possibly be intelligent. But A necessarily belongs to no C: so the conclusion does not establish possibility. But neither is it always necessary. Let A be 'moving', B 'science', C 'man'. A then will belong to no B; but B is possible for all C. And the conclusion will not be necessary. For it is [40] not necessary that no man should move; 35ª rather it is not necessary that any man should move. Clearly then the conclusion establishes that one term does not necessarily belong to any instance of another term. But we must take our terms better.

If the minor premiss is negative and indicates possibility, from the actual premisses taken there can be no syllogism, but if the problematic premiss is converted, a syllogism [5] will be possible, as before.[3] Let A belong to all B, and let B possibly belong to no C. If the terms are arranged thus, nothing necessarily follows: but if the proposition BC is converted and it is assumed that B is possible for all C, a [10] syllogism results as before:[4] for the terms are in the same relative positions. Likewise if both the relations are negative, if the major premiss states that A does not belong to B, and the minor premiss indicates that B may possibly belong to no C. Through the premisses actually taken nothing necessary results in any way; but if the problematic premiss is con-[15] verted, we shall have a syllogism. Suppose that A belongs to no B, and B may possibly belong to no C. Through these comes nothing necessary. But if B is assumed to be possible for all C (and this is true) and if the premiss AB remains as before, we shall again have [20] the same syllogism. But if it be assumed that B *does* not belong to any C, instead of possibly not belonging, there cannot be a syllogism anyhow, whether the premiss AB is negative or affirmative. As common instances of a necessary and positive relation we may take the terms white—animal—snow: of a necessary and negative relation, white—animal—pitch.

[25] Clearly then if the terms are universal, and one of the premisses is assertoric, the other problematic, whenever the minor premiss is problematic a syllogism always results, only sometimes it results from the premisses that are taken, sometimes it requires the conversion of one premiss. We have stated when each of [30] these happens and the reason why. But if one of the relations is universal, the other particular, then whenever the major premiss is universal and problematic, whether affirmative or negative, and the particular is affirmative and assertoric, there will be a perfect syllogism, just as when the terms are universal. The [35] demonstration is the same as before.[5] But whenever the major premiss is universal, but assertoric, not problematic, and the minor is particular and problematic, whether both premisses are negative or affirmative, or one is negative, the other affirmative, in all cases there will be an imperfect syllogism. Only [40] some of them will be proved *per impossi-* 35ᵇ *bile*, others by the conversion of the problematic premiss, as has been shown above.[6] And a syllogism will be possible by means of conversion when the major premiss is universal and assertoric, whether positive or negative, and the minor particular, negative, and prob-[5] lematic, e.g. if A belongs to all B or to no B, and B may possibly not belong to some C. For if the premiss BC is converted in respect of possibility, a syllogism results. But whenever the particular premiss is assertoric and negative, there cannot be a syllogism. As instances of the positive relation we may take the [10] terms white—animal—snow; of the negative, white—animal—pitch. For the demonstration must be made through the indefinite nature of the particular premiss. But if the minor premiss is universal, and the major particular, whether either premiss is negative or affirmative, problematic or assertoric, nohow is a syllogism possible. Nor is a syllogism possible [15] when the premisses are particular or indefinite, whether problematic or assertoric, or the one problematic, the other assertoric. The demonstration is the same as above.[7] As in-

---

[1] ª 36. [2] Cf. 32ª 18. [3] 33ª 7.
[4] 34ª 34.
[5] Cf. 33ᵇ 33-40. [6] ª 14. [7] 33ª 34-ᵇ 17.

stances of the necessary and positive relation we may take the terms animal—white—man; of the necessary and negative relation, animal—white—garment. It is evident then that if [20] the major premiss is universal, a syllogism always results, but if the minor is universal nothing at all can ever be proved.

16

Whenever one premiss is necessary, the other problematic, there will be a syllogism when the terms are related as before;[1] and a perfect [25] syllogism when the minor premiss is necessary. If the premisses are affirmative the conclusion will be problematic, not assertoric, whether the premisses are universal or not: but if one is affirmative, the other negative, when the affirmative is necessary the conclusion will be problematic, not negative asser-[30] toric; but when the negative is necessary the conclusion will be problematic negative, and assertoric negative, whether the premisses are universal or not. Possibility in the conclusion must be understood in the same manner as before.[2] There cannot be an inference to the necessary negative proposition: for 'not neces-[35] sarily to belong' is different from 'necessarily not to belong'.

If the premisses are affirmative, clearly the conclusion which follows is not necessary. Suppose A necessarily belongs to all B, and let B be possible for all C. We shall have an imperfect syllogism to prove that A may belong to all C. That it is imperfect is clear from the [40] proof: for it will be proved in the same **36ᵃ** manner as above.[3] Again, let A be possible for all B, and let B necessarily belong to all C. We shall then have a syllogism to prove that A may belong to all C, not that A does belong [5] to all C: and it is perfect, not imperfect: for it is completed directly through the original premisses.

But if the premisses are not similar in quality, suppose first that the *negative* premiss is necessary, and let A necessarily not be possible for any B, but let B be possible for all C. It is [10] necessary then that A belongs to no C. For suppose A to belong to all C or to some C. Now we assumed that A is not possible for any B. Since then the negative proposition is convertible, B is not possible for any A. But A is supposed to belong to all C or to some C. Consequently B will not be possible for any C or [15] for all C. But it was originally laid down that B is possible for all C. And it is clear that the possibility of not belonging can be inferred, since the fact of not belonging is inferred. Again, let the *affirmative* premiss be necessary, and let A possibly not belong to any B, and let B necessarily belong to all C. The syllogism [20] will be perfect, but it will establish a problematic negative, not an assertoric negative. For the major premiss was problematic, and further it is not possible to prove the assertoric conclusion *per impossibile*. For if it were supposed that A belongs to some C, and it is laid down that A possibly does not belong to any B, no impossible relation between B and C follows from these premisses. But if the minor [25] premiss is negative, when it is problematic a syllogism is possible by conversion, as above;[4] but when it is necessary no syllogism can be formed. Nor again when both premisses are negative, and the minor is necessary. The same terms as before[5] serve both for the posi-[30] tive relation—white—animal—snow, and for the negative relation—white—animal—pitch.

The same relation will obtain in particular syllogisms. Whenever the negative proposition is necessary, the conclusion will be negative assertoric: e.g. if it is not possible that A should [35] belong to any B, but B may belong to some of the Cs, it is necessary that A should not belong to some of the Cs. For if A belongs to all C, but cannot belong to any B, neither can B belong to any A. So if A belongs to all C, to none of the Cs can B belong. But it was laid down that B may belong to some C. But when [40] the particular affirmative in the negative syllogism, e.g. BC the minor premiss, or the universal proposition in the affirmative syllo-**36ᵇ** gism, e.g. AB the major premiss, is necessary, there will not be an assertoric conclusion. The demonstration is the same as before.[6] But if the minor premiss is universal, and problematic, whether affirmative or negative, and the [5] major premiss is particular and necessary, there cannot be a syllogism. Premisses of this kind are possible both where the relation is positive and necessary, e.g. animal—white—man, and where it is necessary and negative, e.g. animal—white—garment. But when the universal is necessary, the particular problematic, if the universal is negative we may take the terms animal—white—raven to illustrate [10] the positive relation, or animal—white—pitch to illustrate the negative; and if the universal is affirmative we may take the terms ani-

---

[1] Cf. ᵃ25-ᵇ 8. [2] 33ᵇ 29, 34ᵇ 27.
[3] 34ᵃ 34-ᵇ 6. [4] 35ᵇ 7. [5] 35ᵇ 10. [6] ᵃ 19-25.

mal—white—swan to illustrate the positive relation, and animal—white—snow to illustrate the negative and necessary relation. Nor again is a syllogism possible when the premisses are indefinite, or both particular. Terms applicable in either case to illustrate the positive relation are animal—white—man: to illustrate the negative, animal—white—inanimate. For the relation of animal to some white, and of white to some inanimate, is both necessary and positive and necessary and negative. Similarly if the relation is problematic: so the terms may be used for all cases.

Clearly then from what has been said a syllogism results or not from similar relations of the terms whether we are dealing with simple existence or necessity, with this exception, that if the negative premiss is assertoric the conclusion is problematic, but if the negative premiss is necessary the conclusion is both problematic and negative assertoric. [It is clear also that all the syllogisms are imperfect and are perfected by means of the figures above mentioned.]

17

In the second figure whenever both premisses are problematic, no syllogism is possible, whether the premisses are affirmative or negative, universal or particular. But when one premiss is assertoric, the other problematic, if the affirmative is assertoric no syllogism is possible, but if the universal negative is assertoric a conclusion can always be drawn. Similarly when one premiss is necessary, the other problematic. Here also we must understand the term 'possible' in the conclusion, in the same sense as before.[1]

First we must point out that the negative problematic proposition is not convertible, e.g. if A may belong to no B, it does not follow that B may belong to no A. For suppose it to follow and assume that B may belong to no A. Since then problematic affirmations are convertible with negations, whether they are contraries or contradictories, and since B may belong to no A, it is clear that B may belong to all A. But this is false: for if all this can be that, it does not follow that all that can be this: consequently the negative proposition is not convertible. Further, these propositions are not incompatible, 'A may belong to no B', 'B necessarily does not belong to some of the As'; e.g. it is possible that no man should be white (for it is also possible that every man should be white), but it is not true to say that it is possible that no white thing should be a man: for many white things are necessarily not men, and the necessary (as we saw[2]) is other than the possible.

Moreover it is not possible to prove the convertibility of these propositions by a *reductio ad absurdum*, i.e. by claiming assent to the following argument: 'since it is false that B may belong to no A, it is true that it cannot belong to no A, for the one statement is the contradictory of the other. But if this is so, it is true that B necessarily belongs to some of the As: consequently A necessarily belongs to some of the Bs. But this is impossible.' The argument cannot be admitted, for it does not follow that some A is necessarily B, if it is not possible that no A should be B. For the latter expression is used in two senses, one if some A is necessarily B, another if some A is necessarily not B. For it is not true to say that that which necessarily does not belong to some of the As may possibly not belong to any A, just as it is not true to say that what necessarily belongs to some A may possibly belong to all A. If any one then should claim that because it is not possible for C to belong to all D, it necessarily does not belong to some D, he would make a false assumption: for it does belong to all D, but because in some cases it belongs necessarily, therefore we say that it is not *possible* for it to belong to all. Hence both the propositions 'A necessarily belongs to some B' and 'A necessarily does not belong to some B' are opposed to the proposition 'A may belong to all B'. Similarly also they are opposed to the proposition 'A may belong to no B'. It is clear then that in relation to what is possible and not possible, in the sense originally defined,[3] we must assume, not that A necessarily belongs to some B, but that A necessarily does not belong to some B. But if this is assumed, no absurdity results: consequently no syllogism. It is clear from what has been said that the negative proposition is not convertible.

This being proved, suppose it possible that A may belong to no B and to all C. By means of conversion no syllogism will result: for the major premiss, as has been said, is not convertible. Nor can a proof be obtained by a *reductio ad absurdum*: for if it is assumed that B can belong to all C, no false consequence results: for A may belong both to all C and to no C. In general, if there is a syllogism, it is clear

[1] 33[b] 29, 34[b] 27.   [2] 32[a] 28.   [3] 32[a] 18.

that its conclusion will be problematic because neither of the premisses is assertoric; and this must be either affirmative or negative. But neither is possible. Suppose the conclusion is affirmative: it will be proved by an example that the predicate cannot belong to the subject. Suppose the conclusion is negative: it will be proved that it is not problematic but necessary. Let A be white, B man, C horse. It is possible then for A to belong to all of the one and to none of the other. But it is not possible for B to belong nor not to belong to C. That it is not possible for it to belong, is clear. For no horse is a man. Neither is it possible for it not to belong. For it is necessary that no horse should be a man, but the necessary we found to be different from the possible.[1] No syllogism then results. A similar proof can be given if the major premiss is negative, the minor affirmative, or if both are affirmative or negative. The demonstration can be made by means of the same terms. And whenever one premiss is universal, the other particular, or both are particular or indefinite, or in whatever other way the premisses can be altered, the proof will always proceed through the same terms. Clearly then, if both the premisses are problematic, no syllogism results.

18

But if one premiss is assertoric, the other problematic, if the affirmative is assertoric and the negative problematic no syllogism will be possible, whether the premisses are universal or particular. The proof is the same as above, and by means of the same terms. But when the affirmative premiss is problematic, and the negative assertoric, we shall have a syllogism. Suppose A belongs to no B, but can belong to all C. If the negative proposition is converted, B will belong to no A. But A ex hypothesi can belong to all C: so a syllogism is made, proving by means of the first figure that B may belong to no C. Similarly also if the *minor* premiss is negative. But if both premisses are negative, one being assertoric, the other problematic, nothing follows necessarily from these premisses as they stand, but if the problematic premiss is converted into its complementary affirmative a syllogism is formed to prove that B may belong to no C, as before: for we shall again have the first figure. But if both premisses are affirmative, no syllogism will be possible. This arrangement of terms is possible both when the relation is positive, e.g. health,

[1] 32ª 28.

animal, man, and when it is negative, e.g. health, horse, man.

The same will hold good if the syllogisms are particular. Whenever the affirmative proposition is assertoric, whether universal or particular, no syllogism is possible (this is proved similarly and by the same examples as above), but when the negative proposition is assertoric, a conclusion can be drawn by means of conversion, as before. Again if both the relations are negative, and the assertoric proposition is universal, although no conclusion follows from the actual premisses, a syllogism can be obtained by converting the problematic premiss into its complementary affirmative as before. But if the negative proposition is assertoric, but particular, no syllogism is possible, whether the other premiss is affirmative or negative. Nor can a conclusion be drawn when both premisses are indefinite, whether affirmative or negative, or particular. The proof is the same and by the same terms.

19

If one of the premisses is necessary, the other problematic, then if the negative is necessary a syllogistic conclusion can be drawn, not merely a negative problematic but also a negative assertoric conclusion; but if the affirmative premiss is necessary, no conclusion is possible. Suppose that A necessarily belongs to no B, but may belong to all C. If the negative premiss is converted B will belong to no A: but A ex hypothesi is capable of belonging to all C: so once more a conclusion is drawn by the first figure that B may belong to no C. But at the same time it is clear that B *will* not belong to any C. For assume that it does: then if A cannot belong to any B, and B belongs to some of the Cs, A cannot belong to some of the Cs: but ex hypothesi it may belong to all. A similar proof can be given if the *minor* premiss is negative. Again let the affirmative proposition be necessary, and the other problematic; i.e. suppose that A may belong to no B, but necessarily belongs to all C. When the terms are arranged in this way, no syllogism is possible. For (1) it sometimes turns out that B necessarily does not belong to C. Let A be white, B man, C swan. White then necessarily belongs to swan, but may belong to no man; and man necessarily belongs to no swan. Clearly then we cannot draw a problematic conclusion; for that which is necessary is admittedly distinct from that which is possible. (2) Nor again can we draw a necessary conclusion: for that presupposes that both premisses are necessary, or at any rate the negative premiss. (3) Further it is possible also, when the terms are so arranged, that B should belong to C: for nothing prevents C falling under B, A being [40] possible for all B, and necessarily belonging to C; e.g. if C stands for 'awake', B for 'animal', A for 'motion'. For motion necessarily belongs to what is awake, and is possible for every animal: and everything that is awake is animal. Clearly then the conclusion cannot be the negative assertion, if the relation must be positive when the terms are related as above. Nor can the opposite affirmations be established: consequently no syllogism is possible. [5] A similar proof is possible if the *major* premiss is affirmative.

But if the premisses are similar in quality, when they are negative a syllogism can always be formed by converting the problematic premiss into its complementary affirmative as before. Suppose A necessarily does not belong to [10] B, and possibly may not belong to C: if the premisses are converted B belongs to no A, and A may possibly belong to all C: thus we have the first figure. Similarly if the minor premiss is negative. But if the premisses are affirmative there cannot be a syllogism. Clearly [15] the conclusion cannot be a negative assertoric or a negative necessary proposition because no negative premiss has been laid down either in the assertoric or in the necessary mode. Nor can the conclusion be a problematic negative proposition. For if the terms are so related, there are cases in which B necessarily [20] will not belong to C; e.g. suppose that A is white, B swan, C man. Nor can the opposite affirmations be established, since we have shown a case in which B necessarily does not belong to C. A syllogism then is not possible at all.

Similar relations will obtain in particular [25] syllogisms. For whenever the negative proposition is universal and necessary, a syllogism will always be possible to prove both a problematic and a negative assertoric proposition (the proof proceeds by conversion); but when the affirmative proposition is universal and necessary, no syllogistic conclusion can be drawn. This can be proved in the same way as for universal propositions, and by the same [30] terms.[1] Nor is a syllogistic conclusion possible when both premisses are affirmative: this also may be proved as above.[2] But when both premisses are negative, and the premiss that definitely disconnects two terms is universal and necessary, though nothing follows necessarily from the premisses as they are stated, a conclusion can be drawn as above[3] if the problematic [35] premiss is converted into its complementary affirmative. But if both are indefinite or particular, no syllogism can be formed The same proof will serve, and the same terms.[4]

It is clear then from what has been said that if the universal and negative premiss is necessary, [40] a syllogism is always possible, proving not merely a negative problematic, but also a negative assertoric proposition; but if the affirmative premiss is necessary no conclusion can be drawn. It is clear too that a syllogism is possible or not under the same conditions whether the mode of the premisses is assertoric or necessary. And it is clear that all the syllogisms are imperfect, and are completed by means of the figures mentioned.

20

In the last figure a syllogism is possible whether [5] both or only one of the premisses is problematic. When the premisses are problematic the conclusion will be problematic; and also when one premiss is problematic, the other assertoric. But when the other premiss is necessary, if it is affirmative the conclusion will be neither necessary or assertoric; but if it is negative [10] the syllogism will result in a negative assertoric proposition, as above.[5] In these also we must understand the expression 'possible' in the conclusion in the same way as before.

First let the premisses be problematic and [15] suppose that both A and B may possibly belong to every C. Since then the affirmative proposition is convertible into a particular, and B may possibly belong to every C, it follows that C may possibly belong to some B. So, if A is possible for every C, and C is possible for some of the Bs, then A is possible for some of the Bs. For we have got the first figure. And [20] if A may possibly belong to no C, but B may possibly belong to all C, it follows that A may possibly not belong to some B: for we shall have the first figure again by conversion. But if both premisses should be negative no necessary consequence will follow from them as they are [25] stated, but if the premisses are converted into their corresponding affirmatives there will be a syllogism as before. For if A and B may possibly not belong to C, if 'may possibly belong' is substituted we shall again have the first figure by means of conversion. But if one of

---

[1] Cf. a 26.-b 5. [2] ll. 12-23. [3] ll. 25-7. [4] Cf. 36b 12-18. [5] 38a 14.

the premisses is universal, the other particular, a syllogism will be possible, or not, under the [30] same arrangement of the terms as in the case of assertoric propositions. Suppose that A may possibly belong to all C, and B to some C. We shall have the first figure again if the particular premiss is converted. For if A is possible for all C, and C for some of the Bs, then [35] A is possible for some of the Bs. Similarly if the proposition BC is universal. Likewise also if the proposition AC is negative, and the proposition BC affirmative: for we shall again have the first figure by conversion. But if both premisses should be negative—the one universal and the other particular—although no syllogistic conclusion will follow from the premisses as they are put, it will follow if they are converted, as above. But when both premisses are indefinite or particular, no syllogism can be formed: for A must belong sometimes to all B and sometimes to no B. To illustrate the affirm- [5] ative relation take the terms animal—man—white; to illustrate the negative, take the terms horse—man—white—white being the middle term.

21

If one premiss is pure, the other problematic, the conclusion will be problematic, not pure; and a syllogism will be possible under the same [10] arrangement of the terms as before. First let the premisses be affirmative: suppose that A belongs to all C, and B may possibly belong to all C. If the proposition BC is converted, we shall have the first figure, and the conclusion that A may possibly belong to some [15] of the Bs. For when one of the premisses in the first figure is problematic, the conclusion also (as we saw[1]) is problematic. Similarly if the proposition BC is pure, AC problematic; or if AC is negative, BC affirmative, no matter which of the two is pure; in both cases the con- [20] clusion will be problematic: for the first figure is obtained once more, and it has been proved that if one premiss is problematic in that figure the conclusion also will be problematic. But if the minor premiss BC is negative, or if both premisses are negative, no syllogistic conclusion can be drawn from the premisses as they stand, but if they are converted a syllogism [25] is obtained as before.

If one of the premisses is universal, the other particular, then when both are affirmative, or when the universal is negative, the particular affirmative, we shall have the same sort of syllogisms: for all are completed by means of the [30] first figure. So it is clear that we shall have not a pure but a problematic syllogistic conclusion. But if the affirmative premiss is universal, the negative particular, the proof will proceed by a *reductio ad impossibile*. Suppose that B belongs to all C, and A may possibly not belong to [35] some C: it follows that A may possibly not belong to some B. For if A necessarily belongs to all B, and B (as has been assumed) belongs to all C, A will necessarily belong to all C: for this has been proved before.[2] But it was assumed at the outset that A may possibly not belong to some C.

Whenever both premisses are indefinite or particular, no syllogism will be possible. The demonstration is the same as was given in the case of universal premisses, and proceeds by means of the same terms.

22

If one of the premisses is necessary, the other [5] problematic, when the premisses are affirmative a problematic affirmative conclusion can always be drawn; when one proposition is affirmative, the other negative, if the affirmative is necessary a problematic negative can be inferred; but if the negative proposition is necessary both a problematic and a pure negative conclusion are possible. But a necessary nega- [10] tive conclusion will not be possible, any more than in the other figures. Suppose first that the premisses are affirmative, i.e. that A necessarily belongs to all C, and B may possibly belong to all C. Since then A must belong to all C, and C may belong to some B, it follows that [15] A may (not does) belong to some B: for so it resulted[3] in the first figure. A similar proof may be given if the proposition BC is necessary, and AC is problematic. Again suppose one proposition is affirmative, the other negative, the *affirmative* being necessary: i.e. suppose A may possibly belong to no C, but B necessarily [20] belongs to all C. We shall have the first figure once more: and—since the negative premiss is problematic—it is clear that the conclusion will be problematic: for when the premisses stand thus in the first figure, the conclusion (as we found[4]) is problematic. But if the [25] *negative* premiss is necessary, the conclusion will be not only that A may possibly not belong to some B but also that it does not belong to some B. For suppose that A necessarily does not belong to C, but B may belong to all C. If the affirmative proposition BC is con-

---
[1] 33^b 25-40.   [2] 30^a 15-23.   [3] 35^a 26-8.   [4] 36^a 17-25.

verted, we shall have the first figure, and the negative premiss is necessary. But when the [30] premisses stood thus, it resulted[1] that A might possibly not belong to some C, and that it did not belong to some C; consequently here it follows that A does not belong to some B. But when the minor premiss is negative, if it is problematic we shall have a syllogism by alter- [35] ing the premiss into its complementary affirmative, as before; but if it is necessary no syllogism can be formed. For A sometimes necessarily belongs to all B, and sometimes cannot possibly belong to any B. To illustrate the former take the terms sleep—sleeping horse —man; to illustrate the latter take the terms sleep—waking horse—man.

Similar results will obtain if one of the terms [40] is related universally to the middle, the other in part. If both premisses are affirmative, the conclusion will be problematic, not pure; and also when one premiss is negative, the other affirmative, the latter being necessary. But when the negative premiss is necessary, the conclusion also will be a pure negative proposi- [5] tion; for the same kind of proof can be given whether the terms are universal or not. For the syllogisms must be made perfect by means of the first figure, so that a result which follows in the first figure follows also in the third. But when the minor premiss is negative [10] and universal, if it is problematic a syllogism can be formed by means of conversion; but if it is necessary a syllogism is not possible. The proof will follow the same course as where the premisses are universal; and the same terms may be used.

It is clear then in this figure also when and how a syllogism can be formed, and when the conclusion is problematic, and when it is pure. It is evident also that all syllogisms in this fig- [15] ure are imperfect, and that they are made perfect by means of the first figure.

23

It is clear from what has been said that the syllogisms in these figures are made perfect by means of universal syllogisms in the first figure and are reduced to them. That every syllogism [20] without qualification can be so treated, will be clear presently, when it has been proved that every syllogism is formed through one or other of these figures.

It is necessary that every demonstration and every syllogism should prove either that something belongs or that it does not, and this either [25] universally or in part, and further either ostensively or hypothetically. One sort of hypothetical proof is the *reductio ad impossibile*. Let us speak first of ostensive syllogisms: for after these have been pointed out the truth of our contention will be clear with regard to those which are proved *per impossibile*, and in general hypothetically.

[30] If then one wants to prove syllogistically A of B, either as an attribute of it or as not an attribute of it, one must assert something of something else. If now A should be asserted of B, the proposition originally in question will have been assumed. But if A should be asserted of C, but C should not be asserted of anything, nor anything of it, nor anything else of A, no syllogism will be possible. For nothing neces- [35] sarily follows from the assertion of some one thing concerning some other single thing. Thus we must take another premiss as well. If then A be asserted of something else, or something else of A, or something different of C, nothing prevents a syllogism being formed, but it will not be in relation to B through the prem- [40] isses taken. Nor when C belongs to something else, and that to something else and so on, no connexion however being made with B, will a syllogism be possible concerning A in its relation to B. For in general we stated[2] that no syllogism can establish the attribution of one thing to another, unless some middle term is taken, which is somehow related to each by way of predication. For the syllogism [5] in general is made out of premisses, and a syllogism referring to *this* out of premisses with the same reference, and a syllogism relating *this* to *that* proceeds through premisses which relate this to that. But it is impossible to take a premiss in reference to B, if we neither affirm nor deny anything of it; or again to take a premiss relating A to B, if we take nothing [10] common, but affirm or deny peculiar attributes of each. So we must take something midway between the two, which will connect the predications, if we are to have a syllogism relating this to that. If then we must take something common in relation to both, and this is [15] possible in three ways (either by predicating A of C, and C of B, or C of both, or both of C), and these are the figures of which we have spoken, it is clear that every syllogism must be made in one or other of these figures. The argument is the same if several middle terms should be necessary to establish the relation to B; for the figure will be the same whether

---
[1] 36ᵃ 32-9
[2] Cf. 25ᵇ 32.

[20] there is one middle term or many.

It is clear then that the ostensive syllogisms are effected by means of the aforesaid figures; these considerations will show that *reductiones ad impossibile* also are effected in the same way. For all who effect an argument *per impossibile* infer syllogistically what is false, and [25] prove the original conclusion hypothetically when something impossible results from the assumption of its contradictory; e.g. that the diagonal of the square is incommensurate with the side, because odd numbers are equal to evens if it is supposed to be commensurate. One infers syllogistically that odd numbers come out equal to evens, and one proves hypothetically the incommensurability of the diag- [30] onal, since a falsehood results through contradicting this. For this we found to be reasoning *per impossibile*, viz. proving something impossible by means of an hypothesis conceded at the beginning. Consequently, since the falsehood is established in reductions *ad impossibile* by an ostensive syllogism, and the original conclusion is proved hypothetically, and we have [35] already stated that ostensive syllogisms are effected by means of these figures, it is evident that syllogisms *per impossibile* also will be made through these figures. Likewise all the other hypothetical syllogisms: for in every case the syllogism leads up to the proposition that [40] is substituted for the original thesis; but the original thesis is reached by means of a concession or some other hypothesis. But if this 41^b is true, every demonstration and every syllogism must be formed by means of the three figures mentioned above. But when this has been shown it is clear that every syllogism is perfected by means of the first figure and is re- [5] ducible to the universal syllogisms in this figure.

24

Further in every syllogism one of the premisses must be affirmative, and universality must be present: unless one of the premisses is universal either a syllogism will not be possible, or it will not refer to the subject proposed, or the original position will be begged. Suppose we [10] have to prove that pleasure in music is good. If one should claim as a premiss that pleasure is good without adding 'all', no syllogism will be possible; if one should claim that some pleasure is good, then if it is different from pleasure in music, it is not relevant to the subject proposed; if it is this very pleasure, one is assuming that which was proposed at the outset to be proved. This is more obvious in geometrical proofs, e.g. that the angles at the [15] base of an isosceles triangle are equal. Suppose the lines A and B have been drawn to the centre. If then one should assume that the angle AC is equal to the angle BD, without claiming generally that angles of semicircles are equal; and again if one should assume that the angle C is equal to the angle D, without the additional assumption that every angle of a segment is equal to every other angle of the same segment; and further if one should assume that when equal angles are taken from the whole angles, which are themselves equal, [20] the remainders E and F are equal, he will beg the thing to be proved, unless he also states that when equals are taken from equals the remainders are equal.

It is clear then that in every syllogism there must be a universal premiss, and that a universal statement is proved only when all the premisses are universal, while a particular statement is proved both from two universal premisses and from one only: consequently if the [25] conclusion is universal, the premisses also must be universal, but if the premisses are universal it is possible that the conclusion may not be universal. And it is clear also that in every syllogism either both or one of the premisses must be like the conclusion. I mean not only in being affirmative or negative, but also in be- [30] ing necessary, pure, problematic. We must consider also the other forms of predication.

It is clear also when a syllogism in general can be made and when it cannot; and when a valid, when a perfect syllogism can be formed; and that if a syllogism is formed the terms must be arranged in one of the ways that have [35] been mentioned.

25

It is clear too that every demonstration will proceed through three terms and no more, unless the same conclusion is established by different pairs of propositions; e.g. the conclusion E may be established through the propositions A and B, and through the propositions C and D, or through the propositions A and B, or A and C, or B and C. For nothing prevents there be- [40] ing several middles for the same terms. But in that case there is not one but several syllogisms. Or again when each of the propositions A and B is obtained by syllogistic inference, e.g. A by means of D and E, and again B by means of F and G. Or one may be obtained by syllogistic, the other by inductive inference. But thus also the syllogisms are many; [5] for the conclusions are many, e.g. A and B and C. But if this can be called one syllogism, not many, the same conclusion may be reached by more than three terms in this way, but it cannot be reached as C is established by means of A and B. Suppose that the proposition E is inferred from the premisses A, B, C, and D. It is necessary then that of these one should be [10] related to another as whole to part: for it has already been proved that if a syllogism is formed some of its terms must be related in this way.[1] Suppose then that A stands in this relation to B. Some conclusion then follows from them. It must either be E or one or other of C and D, or something other than these. [15] (1) If it is E the syllogism will have A and B for its sole premisses. But if C and D are so related that one is whole, the other part, some conclusion will follow from them also; and it must be either E, or one or other of the propositions A and B, or something other than these. And if it is (i) E, or (ii) A or B, either (i) the syllogisms will be more than one, or (ii) the same thing happens to be inferred by means of several terms only in the sense which we saw [20] to be possible.[2] But if (iii) the conclusion is other than E or A or B, the syllogisms will be many, and unconnected with one another. But if C is not so related to D as to make a syllogism, the propositions will have been assumed to no purpose, unless for the sake of induction or of obscuring the argument or something of the sort.

(2) But if from the propositions A and B [25] there follows not E but some other conclusion, and if from C and D either A or B follows or something else, then there are several syllogisms, and they do not establish the conclusion proposed: for we assumed that the syllogism proved E. And if no conclusion follows from C and D, it turns out that these propositions have been assumed to no purpose, [30] and the syllogism does not prove the original proposition.

So it is clear that every demonstration and every syllogism will proceed through three terms only.

This being evident, it is clear that a syllogistic conclusion follows from two premisses and not from more than two. For the three terms make two premisses, unless a new premiss is assumed, as was said at the beginning,[3] [35] to perfect the syllogisms. It is clear therefore that in whatever syllogistic argument the premisses through which the main conclusion follows (for some of the preceding conclusions must be premisses) are not even in number, this argument either has not been drawn syllogistically or it has assumed more than was [40] necessary to establish its thesis.

If then syllogisms are taken with respect to their main premisses, every syllogism will consist of an even number of premisses and an odd number of terms (for the terms exceed the premisses by one), and the conclusions will be [5] half the number of the premisses. But whenever a conclusion is reached by means of prosyllogisms or by means of several continuous middle terms, e.g. the proposition AB by means of the middle terms C and D, the number of the terms will similarly exceed that of the premisses by one (for the extra term must either be added outside or inserted: but in either case it follows that the relations of predication are one fewer than the terms related), [10] and the premisses will be equal in number to the relations of predication. The premisses however will not always be even, the terms odd; but they will alternate—when the premisses are even, the terms must be odd; when the terms are even, the premisses must be odd: for along with one term one premiss is added, if a term is added from any quarter. Consequently since the premisses were (as we [15] saw) even, and the terms odd, we must make them alternately even and odd at each addition. But the conclusions will not follow the same arrangement either in respect to the terms or to the premisses. For if one term is added, conclusions will be added less by one than the pre-existing terms: for the conclusion is drawn not in relation to the single term last [20] added, but in relation to all the rest, e.g. if to ABC the term D is added, two conclusions are thereby added, one in relation to A, the other in relation to B. Similarly with any further additions. And similarly too if the term is inserted in the middle: for in relation to one term only, a syllogism will not be constructed. [25] Consequently the conclusions will be much more numerous than the terms or the premisses.

26

Since we understand the subjects with which syllogisms are concerned, what sort of conclusion is established in each figure, and in how many moods this is done, it is evident to us both what sort of problem is difficult and what

---

[1] 40[b] 30. [2] l. 6. [3] Cf. 24[b] 24.

[30] sort is easy to prove. For that which is concluded in many figures and through many moods is easier; that which is concluded in few figures and through few moods is more difficult to attempt. The universal affirmative is proved by means of the first figure only and by this in only one mood; the universal negative is proved both through the first figure and [35] through the second, through the first in one mood, through the second in two. The particular affirmative is proved through the first and through the last figure, in one mood through the first, in three moods through the last. The particular negative is proved in all the figures, but once in the first, in two moods [40] in the second, in three moods in the third. It is clear then that the universal affirmative is most difficult to establish, most easy to overthrow. In general, universals are easier game for the destroyer than particulars: for whether the predicate belongs to none or not to some, they are destroyed: and the particular negative is proved in all the figures, the [5] universal negative in two. Similarly with universal negatives: the original statement is destroyed, whether the predicate belongs to all or to some: and this we found possible in two figures. But particular statements can be refuted in one way only—by proving that the predicate belongs either to all or to none. But particular statements are easier to *establish*: [10] for proof is possible in more figures and through more moods. And in general we must not forget that it is possible to refute statements by means of one another, I mean, universal statements by means of particular, and particular statements by means of universal: but it is not possible to establish universal statements by means of particular, though it is possible to establish particular statements by means of universal. At the same time it is evident that it is [15] easier to refute than to establish.

The manner in which every syllogism is produced, the number of the terms and premisses through which it proceeds, the relation of the premisses to one another, the character of the problem proved in each figure, and the number of the figures appropriate to each problem, all these matters are clear from what has been said.

27

We must now state how we may ourselves al- [20] ways have a supply of syllogisms in reference to the problem proposed and by what road we may reach the principles relative to the problem: for perhaps we ought not only to investigate the construction of syllogisms, but also to have the power of making them.
[25] Of all the things which exist some are such that they cannot be predicated of anything else truly and universally, e.g. Cleon and Callias, i.e. the individual and sensible, but other things may be predicated of them (for each of these is both man and animal); and [30] some things are themselves predicated of others, but nothing prior is predicated of them; and some are predicated of others, and yet others of them, e.g. man of Callias and animal of man. It is clear then that some things are naturally not stated of anything: for as a rule each sensible thing is such that it cannot be predicated of anything, save incidentally: for [35] we sometimes say that that white object is Socrates, or that that which approaches is Callias. We shall explain in another place[1] that there is an upward limit also to the process of predicating: for the present we must assume this. Of these ultimate predicates it is not possible to demonstrate another predicate, save as a matter of opinion, but these may be predicated of other things. Neither can individuals be [40] predicated of other things, though other things can be predicated of them. Whatever lies between these limits can be spoken of in both ways: they may be stated of others, and others stated of them. And as a rule arguments and inquiries are concerned with these things. We must select the premisses suitable to each problem in this manner: first we must lay down the subject and the definitions and the properties of the thing; next we must lay down those attributes which follow the thing, and again those which the thing follows, and those [5] which cannot belong to it. But those to which it cannot belong need not be selected, because the negative statement implied above is convertible. Of the attributes which follow we must distinguish those which fall within the definition, those which are predicated as properties, and those which are predicated as accidents, and of the latter those which apparently and those which really belong. The larger the [10] supply a man has of these, the more quickly will he reach a conclusion; and in proportion as he apprehends those which are truer, the more cogently will he demonstrate. But he must select not those which follow some particular but those which follow the thing as a whole, e.g. not what follows a particular man but what follows every man: for

[1] *Posterior Analytics*, i. 19-22.

the syllogism proceeds through universal prem-
[15] isses. If the statement is indefinite, it is uncertain whether the premiss is universal, but if the statement is definite, the matter is clear. Similarly one must select those attributes which the subject follows as wholes, for the reason given. But that which follows one must not suppose to follow as a whole, e.g. that every animal follows man or every science music, but only that it follows, without qualification, as [20] indeed we state it in a proposition: for the other statement is useless and impossible, e.g. that every man is every animal or justice is all good. But that which something follows receives the mark 'every'. Whenever the subject, for which we must obtain the attributes that follow, is contained by something else, what follows or does not follow the highest term universally must not be selected in dealing with [25] the subordinate term (for these attributes have been taken in dealing with the superior term; for what follows animal also follows man, and what does not belong to animal does not belong to man); but we must choose those attributes which are peculiar to each subject. For some things are peculiar to the species as distinct from the genus; for species being distinct there must be attributes peculiar to each. Nor must we take as things which the superior term follows, those things which the inferior [30] term follows, e.g. take as subjects of the predicate 'animal' what are really subjects of the predicate 'man'. It is necessary indeed, if animal follows man, that it should follow all these also. But these belong more properly to the choice of what concerns man. One must apprehend also normal consequents and normal antecedents: for propositions which obtain normally are established syllogistically from prem-
[35] isses which obtain normally, some if not all of them having this character of normality. For the conclusion of each syllogism resembles its principles. We must not however choose attributes which are consequent upon all the terms: for no syllogism can be made out of such premisses. The reason why this is so will be clear in the sequel.[1]

28

If men wish to establish something about some [40] whole, they must look to the *subjects* of that which is being established (the subjects of which it happens to be asserted), and the *attributes* which follow that of which it is to be predicated. For if any of these subjects is the same as any of these attributes, the attribute originally in question must belong to the subject originally in question. But if the purpose is to establish not a universal but a particular proposition, they must look for the terms of which the terms in question are predicable: for if any of these are identical, the attribute in question must belong to some of the subject in question. Whenever the one term has to belong to none of the other, one must look to the consequents of the subject, and to those attributes which cannot possibly be present in the predicate in question: or conversely to the attributes which cannot possibly be present in [5] the subject, and to the consequents of the predicate. If any members of these groups are identical, one of the terms in question cannot possibly belong to any of the other. For sometimes a syllogism in the first figure results, sometimes a syllogism in the second. But if the object is to establish a particular negative proposition, we must find antecedents of the subject in question and attributes which cannot [10] possibly belong to the predicate in question. If any members of these two groups are identical, it follows that one of the terms in question does not belong to some of the other. Perhaps each of these statements will become clearer in the following way. Suppose the consequents of A are designated by B, the antecedents of A by C, attributes which cannot [15] possibly belong to A by D. Suppose again that the attributes of E are designated by F, the antecedents of E by G, and attributes which cannot belong to E by H. If then one of the Cs should be identical with one of the Fs, A must belong to all E: for F belongs to all E, and A to all C, consequently A belongs to all E. If C and [20] G are identical, A must belong to some of the Es: for A follows C, and E follows all G. If F and D are identical, A will belong to none of the Es by a prosyllogism: for since the negative proposition is convertible, and F is identical with D, A will belong to none of the Fs, but F belongs to all E. Again, if B and H are [25] identical, A will belong to none of the Es: for B will belong to all A, but to no E: for it was assumed to be identical with H, and H belonged to none of the Es. If D and G are identical, A will not belong to some of the Es: for it will not belong to G, because it does not [30] belong to D: but G falls under E: consequently A will not belong to some of the Es. If B is identical with G, there will be a converted syllogism: for E will belong to all A, since B belongs to A and E to B (for B was

[1] 44[b] 20.

found to be identical with G): but that A should belong to all E is not necessary, but it must belong to some E because it is possible to [35] convert the universal statement into a particular.

It is clear then that in every proposition which requires proof we must look to the aforesaid relations of the subject and predicate in question: for all syllogisms proceed through these. But if we are seeking consequents and antecedents we must look for those which are primary and most universal, e.g. in [40] reference to E we must look to KF rather than to F alone, and in reference to A we must look to KC rather than to C alone. For if A be-
44ᵇ longs to KF, it belongs both to F and to E: but if it does not follow KF, it may yet follow F. Similarly we must consider the antecedents of A itself: for if a term follows the primary antecedents, it will follow those also which are subordinate, but if it does not follow [5] the former, it may yet follow the latter.

It is clear too that the inquiry proceeds through the three terms and the two premisses, and that all the syllogisms proceed through the aforesaid figures. For it is proved that A belongs to *all* E, whenever an identical term is found among the Cs and Fs. This will be the [10] middle term; A and E will be the extremes. So the first figure is formed. And A will belong to *some* E, whenever C and G are apprehended to be the same. This is the last figure: for G becomes the middle term. And A will belong to *no* E, when D and F are identical. Thus we have both the first figure and the middle figure; the first, because A belongs to [15] no F, since the negative statement is convertible, and F belongs to all E: the middle figure because D belongs to no A, and to all E. And A will *not* belong to *some* E, whenever D and G are identical. This is the last figure: for A will belong to no G, and E will belong to all [20] G. Clearly then all syllogisms proceed through the aforesaid figures, and we must not select consequents of all the terms, because no syllogism is produced from them. For (as we saw)[1] it is not possible at all to establish a proposition from consequents, and it is not possible to refute by means of a consequent of both the terms in question: for the middle term must belong to the one, and not belong to the other.

[25] It is clear too that other methods of inquiry by selection of middle terms are useless to produce a syllogism, e.g. if the consequents

[1] 27ᵃ 18-20, ᵇ 23-8.

of the terms in question are identical, or if the antecedents of A are identical with those attributes which cannot possibly belong to E, or if those attributes are identical which cannot belong to either term: for no syllogism is produced by means of these. For if the conse-[30] quents are identical, e.g. B and F, we have the middle figure with both premisses affirmative: if the antecedents of A are identical with attributes which cannot belong to E, e.g. C with H, we have the first figure with its minor premiss negative. If attributes which [35] cannot belong to either term are identical, e.g. C and H, both premisses are negative, either in the first or in the middle figure. But no syllogism is possible in this way.

It is evident too that we must find out which terms in this inquiry are identical, not which are different or contrary, first because the ob-[40] ject of our investigation is the middle term, and the middle term must be not diverse **45ᵃ** but identical. Secondly, wherever it happens that a syllogism results from taking contraries or terms which cannot belong to the same thing, all arguments can be reduced to the aforesaid moods, e.g. if B and F are contraries or cannot belong to the same thing. For [5] if these are taken, a syllogism will be formed to prove that A belongs to none of the Es, not however from the premisses taken but in the aforesaid mood. For B will belong to all A and to no E. Consequently B must be identical with one of the Hs. Again, if B and G can-[10] not belong to the same thing, it follows that A will not belong to some of the Es: for then too we shall have the middle figure: for B will belong to all A and to no G. Consequently B must be identical with some of the Hs. For the fact that B and G cannot belong to the same thing differs in no way from the fact [15] that B is identical with some of the Hs: for that includes everything which cannot belong to E.

It is clear then that from the inquiries taken by themselves no syllogism results; but if B and F are contraries B must be identical with one of the Hs, and the syllogism results [20] through these terms. It turns out then that those who inquire in this manner are looking gratuitously for some other way than the necessary way because they have failed to observe the identity of the Bs with the Hs.

29

Syllogisms which lead to impossible conclusions are similar to ostensive syllogisms; they also are formed by means of the consequents [25] and antecedents of the terms in question. In both cases the same inquiry is involved. For what is proved ostensively may also be concluded syllogistically *per impossibile* by means of the same terms; and what is proved *per impossibile* may also be proved ostensively, e.g. that A belongs to none of the Es. For suppose A to belong to some E: then since B belongs to [30] all A and A to some of the Es, B will belong to some of the Es: but it was assumed that it belongs to none. Again we may prove that A belongs to some E: for if A belonged to none of the Es, and E belongs to all G, A will belong to none of the Gs: but it was assumed to belong to all. Similarly with the other propositions requiring proof. The proof *per impos-* [35] *sibile* will always and in all cases be from the consequents and antecedents of the terms in question. Whatever the problem the same inquiry is necessary whether one wishes to use an ostensive syllogism or a reduction to impossibility. For both the demonstrations start from the same terms, e.g. suppose it has been proved that A belongs to no E, because it turns out that otherwise B belongs to some of the Es and this is impossible—if now it is assumed that B belongs to no E and to all A, it is clear that A will 45[b] belong to no E. Again if it has been proved by an ostensive syllogism that A belongs to no E, assume that A belongs to some E and it will be proved *per impossibile* to belong to no E. Similarly with the rest. In all cases it is necessary to find some common term other than the sub- [5] jects of inquiry, to which the syllogism establishing the false conclusion may relate, so that if this premiss is converted, and the other remains as it is, the syllogism will be ostensive by means of the same terms. For the ostensive syllogism differs from the *reductio ad impossibile* in this: in the ostensive syllogism both premisses are laid down in accordance with the [10] truth, in the *reductio ad impossibile* one of the premisses is assumed falsely.

These points will be made clearer by the sequel,[1] when we discuss the reduction to impossibility: at present this much must be clear, that we must look to terms of the kinds mentioned whether we wish to use an ostensive syllogism [15] or a reduction to impossibility. In the other hypothetical syllogisms, I mean those which proceed by substitution, or by positing a certain quality, the inquiry will be directed to the terms of the problem to be proved—not the terms of the original problem, but the new

[1] II, 14.

terms introduced; and the method of the inquiry will be the same as before. But we must [20] consider and determine in how many ways hypothetical syllogisms are possible.

Each of the problems then can be proved in the manner described; but it is possible to establish some of them syllogistically in another way, e.g. universal problems by the inquiry which leads up to a particular conclusion, with the addition of an hypothesis. For if the Cs and the Gs should be identical, but E should be assumed to belong to the Gs only, then A would [25] belong to every E: and again if the Ds and the Gs should be identical, but E should be predicated of the Gs only, it follows that A will belong to none of the Es. Clearly then we must consider the matter in this way also. The method is the same whether the relation is necessary or possible. For the inquiry will be the same, and the syllogism will proceed through [30] terms arranged in the same order whether a possible or a pure proposition is proved. We must find in the case of possible relations, as well as terms that belong, terms which can belong though they actually do not: for we have proved that the syllogism which establishes a possible relation proceeds through these terms [35] as well. Similarly also with the other modes of predication.

It is clear then from what has been said not only that all syllogisms can be formed in this way, but also that they cannot be formed in any other. For every syllogism has been proved to be formed through one of the aforementioned [40] figures, and these cannot be composed through other terms than the consequents and antecedents of the terms in question: for from 46[a] these we obtain the premisses and find the middle term. Consequently a syllogism cannot be formed by means of other terms.

30

The method is the same in all cases, in philosophy, in any art or study. We must look for the attributes and the subjects of both our [5] terms, and we must supply ourselves with as many of these as possible, and consider them by means of the three terms, refuting statements in one way, confirming them in another, in the pursuit of truth starting from premisses in which the arrangement of the terms is in accordance with truth, while if we look for dialectical syllogisms we must start from probable [10] premisses. The principles of syllogisms have been stated in general terms, both how they are characterized and how we must hunt for them, so as not to look to everything that is said about the terms of the problem or to the same points whether we are confirming or refuting, or again whether we are confirming of [15] all or of some, and whether we are refuting of all or some; we must look to fewer points and they must be definite. We have also stated how we must select with reference to everything that is, e.g. about good or knowledge. But in each science the principles which are peculiar are the most numerous. Consequently it is the business of experience to give the principles which belong to each subject. I mean for example that astronomical experi- [20] ence supplies the principles of astronomical science: for once the phenomena were adequately apprehended, the demonstrations of astronomy were discovered. Similarly with any other art or science. Consequently, if the attributes of the thing are apprehended, our business will then be to exhibit readily the demonstrations. For if none of the true attributes of [25] things had been omitted in the historical survey, we should be able to discover the proof and demonstrate everything which admitted of proof, and to make that clear, whose nature does not admit of proof.

In general then we have explained fairly well how we must select premises: we have discussed the matter accurately in the treatise [30] concerning dialectic.[1]

31

It is easy to see that division into classes is a small part of the method we have described: for division is, so to speak, a weak syllogism; for what it ought to prove, it begs, and it always establishes something more general than the attribute in question. First, this very point [35] had escaped all those who used the method of division; and they attempted to persuade men that it was possible to make a demonstration of substance and essence. Consequently they did not understand what it is possible to prove syllogistically by division, nor did they understand that it was possible to prove syllogistically in the manner we have described.[2] In demonstrations, when there is a need to prove [40] a positive statement, the middle term 46ᵇ through which the syllogism is formed must always be inferior to and not comprehend the first of the extremes. But division has a contrary intention: for it takes the universal as middle. Let animal be the term signified by A,

[1] *Topics*, especially I. 14.   [2] In cc. 1-30.

mortal by B, and immortal by C, and let man, whose definition is to be got, be signified by [5] D. The man who divides assumes that every animal is either mortal or immortal: i.e. whatever is A is all either B or C. Again, always dividing, he lays it down that man is an animal, so he assumes A of D as belonging to it. Now the true conclusion is that every D is [10] either B or C, consequently man must be either mortal or immortal, but it is not necessary that man should be a mortal animal—this is begged: and this is what ought to have been proved syllogistically. And again, taking A as mortal animal, B as footed, C as footless, and D as man, he assumes in the same way that A in- [15] heres either in B or in C (for every mortal animal is either footed or footless), and he assumes A of D (for he assumed man, as we saw, to be a mortal animal); consequently it is necessary that man should be either a footed or a footless animal; but it is not necessary that man should be footed: this he assumes: and it is just this again which he ought to have demonstrated. Always dividing then in this way it [20] turns out that these logicians assume as middle the universal term, and as extremes that which ought to have been the subject of demonstration and the *differentiae*. In conclusion, they do not make it clear, and show it to be necessary, that this is man or whatever the subject of inquiry may be: for they pursue the [25] other method altogether, never even suspecting the presence of the rich supply of evidence which might be used. It is clear that it is neither possible to refute a statement by this method of division, nor to draw a conclusion about an accident or property of a thing, nor about its genus, nor in cases in which it is unknown whether it is thus or thus, e.g. whether the diagonal is incommensurate. For if he assumes that every length is either commensu- [30] rate or incommensurate, and the diagonal is a length, he has proved that the diagonal is either incommensurate or commensurate. But if he should assume that it is incommensurate, he will have assumed what he ought to have proved. He cannot then prove it: for this is his method, but proof is not possible by this method. Let A stand for 'incommensurate or commensurate', B for 'length', C for 'diagonal'. It [35] is clear then that this method of investigation is not suitable for every inquiry, nor is it useful in those cases in which it is thought to be most suitable.

From what has been said it is clear from

what elements demonstrations are formed and in what manner, and to what points we must look in each problem.

32

Our next business is to state how we can reduce syllogisms to the aforementioned figures: for this part of the inquiry still remains. If we should investigate the production of the syllogisms and had the power of discovering them, and further if we could resolve the syllogisms produced into the aforementioned fig- [5] ures, our original problem would be brought to a conclusion. It will happen at the same time that what has been already said will be confirmed and its truth made clearer by what we are about to say. For everything that is true must in every respect agree with itself. [10] First then we must attempt to select the two premisses of the syllogism (for it is easier to divide into large parts than into small, and the composite parts are larger than the elements out of which they are made); next we must inquire which are universal and which particular, and if both premisses have not been stated, we must ourselves assume the one which is missing. For sometimes men put for- [15] ward the universal premiss, but do not posit the premiss which is contained in it, either in writing or in discussion: or men put forward the premisses of the principal syllogism, but omit those through which they are inferred, and invite the concession of others to no purpose. We must inquire then whether anything unnecessary has been assumed, or anything necessary has been omitted, and we must [20] posit the one and take away the other, until we have reached the two premisses: for unless we have these, we cannot reduce arguments put forward in the way described. In some arguments it is easy to see what is wanting, but some escape us, and appear to be syllogisms, because something necessary results from what has been laid down, e.g. if the assumptions were made that substance is not an- [25] nihilated by the annihilation of what is not substance, and that if the elements out of which a thing is made are annihilated, then that which is made out of them is destroyed: these propositions being laid down, it is necessary that any part of substance is substance; this has not however been drawn by syllogism from the propositions assumed, but premisses are wanting. Again if it is necessary that animal should exist, if man does, and that substance should exist, if animal does, it is necessary that substance should exist if man does: [30] but as yet the conclusion has not been drawn syllogistically: for the premisses are not in the shape we required. We are deceived in such cases because something necessary results from what is assumed, since the syllogism also is necessary. But that which is necessary is wider than the syllogism: for every syllogism is [35] necessary, but not everything which is necessary is a syllogism. Consequently, though something results when certain propositions are assumed, we must not try to reduce it directly, but must first state the two premisses, then divide them into their terms. We must take that term as middle which is stated in both the premisses: for it is necessary that the mid- [40] dle should be found in both premisses in all the figures.

If then the middle term is a predicate and a subject of predication, or if it is a predicate, and something else is denied of it, we shall have the first figure: if it both is a predicate and is denied of something, the middle figure: if other things are predicated of it, or one is [5] denied, the other predicated, the last figure. For it was thus that we found the middle term placed in each figure. It is placed similarly too if the premisses are not universal: for the middle term is determined in the same way. Clearly then, if the same term is not stated more than once in the course of an argument, a syllogism cannot be made: for a middle term has not been taken. Since we know what sort of thesis is established in each figure, and in [10] which the universal, in what sort the particular is described, clearly we must not look for all the figures, but for that which is appropriate to the thesis in hand. If the thesis is established in more figures than one, we shall recognize the figure by the position of the middle term.

33

[15] Men are frequently deceived about syllogisms because the inference is necessary, as has been said above;[1] sometimes they are deceived by the similarity in the positing of the terms; and this ought not to escape our notice. E.g. if *A* is stated of *B,* and *B* of *C:* it would seem that a syllogism is possible since the terms stand thus: but nothing necessary results, nor does a [20] syllogism. Let *A* represent the term 'being eternal', *B* 'Aristomenes as an object of

[1] a 31.

thought', *C* 'Aristomenes'. It is true then that *A* belongs to *B*. For Aristomenes as an object of thought is eternal. But *B* also belongs to *C*: for Aristomenes is Aristomenes as an object of [25] thought. But *A* does not belong to *C*: for Aristomenes is perishable. For no syllogism was made although the terms stood thus: that required that the premiss *AB* should be stated universally. But this is false, that every Aristomenes who is an object of thought is eternal, since Aristomenes is perishable. Again let *C* [30] stand for 'Miccalus', *B* for 'musical Miccalus', *A* for 'perishing to-morrow'. It is true to predicate *B* of *C*: for Miccalus is musical Miccalus. Also *A* can be predicated of *B*: for musical Miccalus might perish to-morrow. But to state *A* of *C* is false at any rate. This argument then is identical with the former; for it is not [35] true universally that musical Miccalus perishes to-morrow: but unless this is assumed, no syllogism (as we have shown) is possible.

This deception then arises through ignoring a small distinction. For if we accept the conclusion as though it made no difference whether we said 'This belong to that' or 'This belongs to all of that'.

34

48a Men will frequently fall into fallacies through not setting out the terms of the premiss well, e.g. suppose *A* to be health, *B* disease, *C* man. It is true to say that *A* cannot belong to any *B* (for health belongs to no disease) and [5] again that *B* belongs to every *C* (for every man is capable of disease). It would seem to follow that health cannot belong to any man. The reason for this is that the terms are not set out well in the statement, since if the things which are in the conditions are substituted, no [10] syllogism can be made, e.g. if 'healthy' is substituted for 'health' and 'diseased' for 'disease'. For it is not true to say that being healthy cannot belong to one who is diseased. But unless this is assumed no conclusion results, save in respect of possibility: but such a conclusion is not impossible: for it is possible that health [15] should belong to no man. Again the fallacy may occur in a similar way in the middle figure: 'it is not possible that health should belong to any disease, but it is possible that health should belong to every man, consequently it is not possible that disease should belong to any man'. In the third figure the fallacy results in reference to possibility. For health and disease, [20] and knowledge and ignorance, and in general contraries, may possibly belong to the same thing, but cannot belong to one another. This is not in agreement with what was said before: for we stated[1] that when several things could belong to the same thing, they could belong to one another.

It is evident then that in all these cases the [25] fallacy arises from the setting out of the terms: for if the things that are in the conditions are substituted, no fallacy arises. It is clear then that in such premisses what possesses the condition ought always to be substituted for the condition and taken as the term.

35

We must not always seek to set out the terms [30] in a single word: for we shall often have complexes of words to which a single name is not given. Hence it is difficult to reduce syllogisms with such terms. Sometimes too fallacies will result from such a search, e.g. the belief that syllogism can establish that which has no mean. Let *A* stand for two right angles, *B* for triangle, *C* for isosceles triangle. *A* then be-[35]longs to *C* because of *B*: but *A* belongs to *B* without the mediation of another term: for the triangle in virtue of its own nature contains two right angles, consequently there will be no middle term for the proposition *AB*, although it is demonstrable. For it is clear that the middle must not always be assumed to be an individual thing, but sometimes a complex of words, as happens in the case mentioned.

36

[40] That the first term belongs to the middle, and the middle to the extreme, must not be understood in the sense that they can always be predicated of one another or that the first term **48b** will be predicated of the middle in the same way as the middle is predicated of the last term. The same holds if the premisses are negative. But we must suppose the verb 'to belong' to have as many meanings as the senses in which the verb 'to be' is used, and in which the assertion that a thing 'is' may be said to be [5] true. Take for example the statement that there is a single science of contraries. Let *A* stand for 'there being a single science', and *B* for things which are contrary to one another. Then *A* belongs to *B*, not in the sense that contraries are the fact of there being a single science of them, but in the sense that it is true to say of the contraries that there is a single science of them.

[10] It happens sometimes that the first term

---
[1] 39ᵃ 14-19.

is stated of the middle, but the middle is not stated of the third term, e.g. if wisdom is knowledge, and wisdom is of the good, the conclusion is that there is knowledge of the good. The good then is not knowledge, though wisdom is knowledge. Sometimes the middle [15] term is stated of the third, but the first is not stated of the middle, e.g. if there is a science of everything that has a quality, or is a contrary, and the good both is a contrary and has a quality, the conclusion is that there is a science of the good, but the good is not science, nor is that which has a quality or is a contrary, though the good is both of these. Sometimes [20] neither the first term is stated of the middle, nor the middle of the third, while the first is sometimes stated of the third, and sometimes not: e.g. if there is a genus of that of which there is a science, and if there is a science of the good, we conclude that there is a genus of the good. But nothing is predicated of anything. And if that of which there is a [25] science is a genus, and if there is a science of the good, we conclude that the good is a genus. The first term then is predicated of the extreme, but in the premisses one thing is not stated of another.

The same holds good where the relation is negative. For 'that does not belong to this' does [30] not always mean that 'this is not that', but sometimes that 'this is not of that' or 'for that', e.g. 'there is not a motion of a motion or a becoming of a becoming, but there is a becoming of pleasure: so pleasure is not a becoming.' Or again it may be said that there is a sign of laughter, but there is not a sign of a sign, consequently laughter is not a sign. This holds in the other cases too, in which the thesis is refuted [35] because the genus is asserted in a particular way, in relation to the terms of the thesis. Again take the inference 'opportunity is not the right time: for opportunity belongs to God, but the right time does not, since nothing is useful to God'. We must take as terms opportunity—right time—God: but the premiss must be understood according to the case of the noun. For we state this universally without [40] qualification, that the terms ought always to be stated in the nominative, e.g. man, good, contraries, not in oblique cases, e.g. of man, of good, of contraries, but the premisses ought to be understood with reference to the cases of each term—either the dative, e.g. 'equal to this', or the genitive, e.g. 'double of this', or the accusative, e.g. 'that which strikes or sees this', or the nominative, e.g. 'man is an ani- [5] mal', or in whatever other way the word falls in the premiss.

37

The expressions 'this belongs to that' and 'this holds true of that' must be understood in as many ways as there are different categories, and these categories must be taken either with or without qualification, and further as simple or compound: the same holds good of the corresponding negative expressions. We must [10] consider these points and define them better.

38

A term which is repeated in the premisses ought to be joined to the first extreme, not to the middle. I mean for example that if a syllogism should be made proving that there is knowledge of justice, that it is good, the expression 'that it is good (or '*quâ* good') should be joined to the first term. Let A stand for [15] 'knowledge that it is good', B for good, C for justice. It is true to predicate A of B. For of the good there is knowledge that it is good. Also it is true to predicate B of C. For justice is identical with a good. In this way an analysis of the argument can be made. But if the expression 'that it is good' were added to B, the [20] conclusion will not follow: for A will be true of B, but B will not be true of C. For to predicate of justice the term 'good that it is good' is false and not intelligible. Similarly if it should be proved that the healthy is an object of knowledge *quâ* good, of goat-stag an object of knowledge *quâ* not existing, or man perishable *quâ* an object of sense: in every case in which an addition is made to the predicate, [25] the addition must be joined to the extreme.

The position of the terms is not the same when something is established without qualification and when it is qualified by some attribute or condition, e.g. when the good is proved to be an object of knowledge and when it is proved to be an object of knowledge that it is good. If it has been proved to be an object [30] of knowledge without qualification, we must put as middle term 'that which is', but if we add the qualification 'that it is good', the middle term must be 'that which is something'. Let A stand for 'knowledge that it is something', B stand for 'something', and C stand for 'good'. It is true to predicate A of B: for *ex hypothesi* there is a science of that which is something, that it is something. B too is true of C: for that which C represents is something. Consequently A is true of C: there will then be knowledge of the good, that it is good: for *ex hypothesi* the term 'something' indicates the thing's special nature. But if 'being' were taken as middle and 'being' simply were joined to the extreme, not 'being something', we should not have had a syllogism proving that there is knowledge of the good, that it is good, but that it is; e.g. let A stand for knowledge that it is, B for being, C for good. Clearly then in syllogisms which are thus limited we must take the terms in the way stated.

39

We ought also to exchange terms which have the same value, word for word, and phrase for phrase, and word and phrase, and always take a word in preference to a phrase: for thus the setting out of the terms will be easier. For example if it makes no difference whether we say that the supposable is not the genus of the opinable or that the opinable is not identical with a particular kind of supposable (for what is meant is the same in both statements), it is better to take as the terms the supposable and the opinable in preference to the phrase suggested.

40

Since the expressions 'pleasure is good' and 'pleasure is the good' are not identical, we must not set out the terms in the same way; but if the syllogism is to prove that pleasure is the good, the term must be 'the good', but if the object is to prove that pleasure is good, the term will be 'good'. Similarly in all other cases.

41

It is not the same, either in fact or in speech, that A belongs to all of that to which B belongs, and that A belongs to all of that to all of which B belongs: for nothing prevents B from belonging to C, though not to all C: e.g. let B stand for beautiful, and C for white. If beauty belongs to something white, it is true to say that beauty belongs to that which is white; but not perhaps to everything that is white. If then A belongs to B, but not to everything of which B is predicated, then whether B belongs to all C or merely belongs to C, it is not necessary that A should belong, I do not say to all C, but even to C at all. But if A belongs to everything of which B is truly stated, it will follow that A can be said of *all* of that of *all* of which B is said. If however A is said of that of *all* of which B may be said, nothing prevents B belonging to C, and yet A not belonging to all C or to any C at all. If then we take three terms it is clear that the expression 'A is said of all of which B is said' means this, 'A is said of all the things of which B is said'. And if B is said of all of a third term, so also is A: but if B is not said of all of the third term, there is no necessity that A should be said of all of it.

We must not suppose that something absurd results through setting out the terms: for we do not use the existence of this particular thing, but imitate the geometrician who says that 'this line a foot long' or 'this straight line' or 'this line without breadth' exists although it does not, but does not use the diagrams in the sense that he reasons from them. For in general, if two things are not related as whole to part and part to whole, the prover does not prove from them, and so no syllogism is formed. We (I mean the learner) use the process of setting out terms like perception by sense, not as though it were impossible to demonstrate without these illustrative terms, as it is to demonstrate without the premisses of the syllogism.

42

We should not forget that in the same syllogism not all conclusions are reached through one figure, but one through one figure, another through another. Clearly then we must analyse arguments in accordance with this. Since not every problem is proved in every figure, but certain problems in each figure, it is clear from the conclusion in what figure the premisses should be sought.

43

In reference to those arguments aiming at a definition which have been directed to prove some part of the definition, we must take as a term the point to which the argument has been directed, not the whole definition: for so we shall be less likely to be disturbed by the length of the term: e.g. if a man proves that water is a drinkable liquid, we must take as terms drinkable and water.

44

Further we must not try to reduce hypothetical syllogisms; for with the given premisses it is not possible to reduce them. For they have not been proved by syllogism, but assented to by agreement. For instance if a man should sup-[20] pose that unless there is one faculty of contraries, there cannot be one science, and should then argue that not every faculty is of contraries, e.g. of what is healthy and what is sickly: for the same thing will then be at the same time healthy and sickly. He has shown that there is not one faculty of all contraries, but he has not proved that there is not a sci-[25] ence. And yet one must agree. But the agreement does not come from a syllogism, but from an hypothesis. This argument cannot be reduced: but the proof that there is not a single faculty can. The latter argument perhaps was a syllogism: but the former was an hypothesis.

The same holds good of arguments which [30] are brought to a conclusion *per impossibile*. These cannot be analysed either; but the reduction to what is impossible can be analysed since it is proved by syllogism, though the rest of the argument cannot, because the conclusion is reached from an hypothesis. But these differ from the previous arguments: for in the former a preliminary agreement must be reached if one is to accept the conclusion; e.g. an agreement that if there is proved to be one faculty of contraries, then contraries fall under [35] the same science; whereas in the latter, even if no preliminary agreement has been made, men still accept the reasoning, because the falsity is patent, e.g. the falsity of what follows from the assumption that the diagonal is commensurate, viz. that then odd numbers are equal to evens.

Many other arguments are brought to a con-[40] clusion by the help of an hypothesis; these we ought to consider and mark out clearly. We shall describe in the sequel their differ-50b ences, and the various ways in which hypothetical arguments are formed: but at present this much must be clear, that it is not possible to resolve such arguments into the figures. And we have explained the reason.

45

[5] Whatever problems are proved in more than one figure, if they have been established in one figure by syllogism, can be reduced to another figure, e.g. a negative syllogism in the first figure can be reduced to the second, and a syllogism in the middle figure to the first, not all however but some only. The point will be clear in the sequel. If A belongs to no B, and B to [10] all C, then A belongs to no C. Thus the first figure; but if the negative statement is converted, we shall have the middle figure. For B belongs to no A, and to all C. Similarly if the syllogism is not universal but particular, e.g. if A belongs to no B, and B to some C. [15] Convert the negative statement and you will have the middle figure.

The universal syllogisms in the second figure can be reduced to the first, but only one of the two particular syllogisms. Let A belong to no B and to all C. Convert the negative state-[20] ment, and you will have the first figure. For B will belong to no A, and A to all C. But if the affirmative statement concerns B, and the negative C, C must be made first term. For C belongs to no A, and A to all B: therefore C belongs to no B. B then belongs to no C: for [25] the negative statement is convertible.

But if the syllogism is particular, whenever the *negative* statement concerns the major extreme, reduction to the first figure will be possible, e.g. if A belongs to no B and to some C: convert the negative statement and you will have the first figure. For B will belong to no A, [30] and A to some C. But when the *affirmative* statement concerns the major extreme, no resolution will be possible, e.g. if A belongs to all B, but not to all C: for the statement AB does not admit of conversion, nor would there be a syllogism if it did.

[35] Again syllogisms in the third figure cannot all be resolved into the first, though all syllogisms in the first figure can be resolved into the third. Let A belong to all B and B to some C. Since the particular affirmative is convertible, C will belong to some B: but A belonged to all B: so that the third figure is formed. Similarly if the syllogism is negative: for the particular affirmative is convertible: therefore [40] A will belong to no B, and to some C.

Of the syllogisms in the last figure one only cannot be resolved into the first, viz. when the negative statement is not universal: all the rest can be resolved. Let A and B be affirmed of all C: then C can be converted partially with [5] either A or B: C then belongs to some B. Consequently we shall get the first figure, if A belongs to all C, and C to some of the Bs. If A belongs to all C and B to some C, the argument is the same: for B is convertible in reference to C. But if B belongs to all C and A to [10] some C, the first term must be B: for B belongs to all C, and C to some A, therefore B belongs to some A. But since the particular statement is convertible, A will belong to some B. If the syllogism is negative, when the terms are universal we must take them in a similar way. Let B belong to all C, and A to no C:

[15] then *C* will belong to some *B*, and *A* to no *C*; and so *C* will be middle term. Similarly if the negative statement is universal, the affirmative particular: for *A* will belong to no *C*, and *C* to some of the *B*s. But if the negative statement is particular, no resolution will be possible, e.g. if *B* belongs to all *C*, and *A* does [20] not belong to some *C*: convert the statement *BC* and both premisses will be particular.

It is clear that in order to resolve the figures into one another the premiss which concerns the minor extreme must be converted in both the figures: for when this premiss is altered, [25] the transition to the other figure is made.

One of the syllogisms in the middle figure can, the other cannot, be resolved into the third figure. Whenever the universal statement is negative, resolution is possible. For if *A* belongs to no *B* and to some *C*, both *B* and *C* alike are convertible in relation to *A*, so that *B* [30] belongs to no *A*, and *C* to some *A*. *A* therefore is middle term. But when *A* belongs to all *B*, and not to some *C*, resolution will not be possible: for neither of the premisses is universal after conversion.

Syllogisms in the third figure can be re-[35] solved into the middle figure, whenever the negative statement is universal, e.g. if *A* belongs to no *C*, and *B* to some or all *C*. For *C* then will belong to no *A* and to some *B*. But if the negative statement is particular, no resolution will be possible: for the particular negative does not admit of conversion.

[40] It is clear then that the same syllogisms cannot be resolved in these figures which could not be resolved into the first figure, and that 51b when syllogisms are reduced to the first figure these alone are confirmed by reduction to what is impossible.

It is clear from what we have said how we ought to reduce syllogisms, and that the figures may be resolved into one another.

46

[5] In establishing or refuting, it makes some difference whether we suppose the expressions 'not to be this' and 'to be not-this' are identical or different in meaning, e.g. 'not to be white' and 'to be not-white'. For they do not mean the same thing, nor is 'to be not-white' the nega-[10] tion of 'to be white', but 'not to be white'. The reason for this is as follows. The relation of 'he can walk' to 'he can not-walk' is similar to the relation of 'it is white' to 'it is not-white'; so is that of 'he knows what is good' to 'he knows what is not-good'. For there is no difference between the expressions 'he knows what is good' and 'he is knowing what is good', or 'he [15] can walk' and 'he is able to walk': therefore there is no difference between their contraries 'he cannot walk'—'he is not able to walk'. If then 'he is not able to walk' means the same as 'he is able not to walk', capacity to walk and incapacity to walk will belong at the same time to the same person (for the same man can both walk and not-walk, and is pos-[20] sessed of knowledge of what is good and of what is not-good), but an affirmation and a denial which are opposed to one another do not belong at the same time to the same thing. As then 'not to know what is good' is not the same as 'to know what is not good', so 'to be not-good' is not the same as 'not to be good'. For when two pairs correspond, if the one pair are different from one another, the other pair [25] also must be different. Nor is 'to be not-equal' the same as 'not to be equal': for there is something underlying the one, viz. that which is not-equal, and this is the unequal, but there is nothing underlying the other. Wherefore not everything is either equal or unequal, but everything is equal or is not equal. Further the expressions 'it is a not-white log' and 'it is not a white log' do not imply one another's [30] truth. For if 'it is a not-white log', it must be a log: but that which is not a white log need not be a log at all. Therefore it is clear that 'it is not-good' is not the denial of 'it is good'. If then every single statement may truly be said to be either an affirmation or a negation, if it is not a negation clearly it must in a sense be an affirmation. But every affirmation has a corre-[35] sponding negation. The negation then of 'it is not-good' is 'it is not not-good'. The relation of these statements to one another is as follows. Let *A* stand for 'to be good', *B* for 'not to be good', let *C* stand for 'to be not-good' and be placed under *B*, and let *D* stand for 'not to be not-good' and be placed under *A*. Then either *A* or *B* will belong to everything, but they will never belong to the same thing; [40] and either *C* or *D* will belong to everything, but they will never belong to the same thing. And *B* must belong to everything to which *C* belongs. For if it is true to say 'it is 52a not-white', it is true also to say 'it is not white': for it is impossible that a thing should simultaneously be white and be not-white, or be a not-white log and be a white log; consequently if the affirmation does not belong, the denial must belong. But *C* does not always belong to *B*: for what is not a log at all, cannot

[5] be a not-white log either. On the other hand D belongs to everything to which A belongs. For either C or D belongs to everything to which A belongs. But since a thing cannot be simultaneously not-white and white, D must belong to everything to which A belongs. For of that which is white it is true to say that it is not not-white. But A is not true of all D. For of that which is not a log at all it is [10] not true to say A, viz. that it is a white log. Consequently D is true, but A is not true, i.e. that it is a white log. It is clear also that A and C cannot together belong to the same thing, and that B and D may possibly belong to the same thing.

[15] Privative terms are similarly related to positive terms in respect of this arrangement. Let A stand for 'equal', B for 'not equal', C for 'unequal', D for 'not unequal'.

In many things also, to some of which something belongs which does not belong to others, the negation may be true in a similar way, viz. [20] that all are not white or that each is not white, while that each is not-white or all are not-white is false. Similarly also 'every animal is not-white' is not the negation of 'every animal is white' (for both are false): the proper negation is 'every animal is not white'. Since it [25] is clear that 'it is not-white' and 'it is not white' mean different things, and one is an affirmation, the other a denial, it is evident that the method of proving each cannot be the same, e.g. that whatever is an animal is not white or may not be white, and that it is true to call it not-white; for this means that it is not-white. But we may prove that it is true to call [30] it white or not-white in the same way for both are proved constructively by means of the first figure. For the expression 'it is true' stands on a similar footing to 'it is'. For the negation of 'it is true to call it white' is not 'it is true to call it not-white' but 'it is not true to call it white'. If then it is to be true to say that whatever is a man is musical or is not-musical, [35] we must assume that whatever is an animal either is musical or is not-musical; and the proof has been made. That whatever is a man is not musical is proved destructively in the three ways mentioned.

In general whenever A and B are such that [40] they cannot belong at the same time to the same thing, and one of the two necessarily belongs to everything, and again C and D are **52^b** related in the same way, and A follows C but the relation cannot be reversed, then D must follow B and the relation cannot be reversed. And A and D may belong to the same thing, but B and C cannot. First it is clear [5] from the following consideration that D follows B. For since either C or D necessarily belongs to everything; and since C cannot belong to that to which B belongs, because it carries A along with it and A and B cannot belong to the same thing; it is clear that D must follow B. Again since C does not reciprocate with A, but C or D belongs to everything, [10] it is possible that A and D should belong to the same thing. But B and C cannot belong to the same thing, because A follows C; and so something impossible results. It is clear then that B does not reciprocate with D either, since it is possible that D and A should belong at the same time to the same thing.

It results sometimes even in such an arrange- [15] ment of terms that one is deceived through not apprehending the opposites rightly, one of which must belong to everything, e.g. we may reason that 'if A and B cannot belong at the same time to the same thing, but it is necessary that one of them should belong to whatever the other does not belong to: and again C and D are related in the same way, and A follows everything which C follows: it will result that B belongs necessarily to everything to which D belongs': but this is false. [20] 'Assume that F stands for the negation of A and B, and again that H stands for the negation of C and D. It is necessary then that either A or F should belong to everything: for either the affirmation or the denial must belong. And again either C or H must belong to everything: for they are related as affirmation and denial. And *ex hypothesi* A belongs to everything to which C belongs. Therefore H [25] belongs to everything to which F belongs. Again since either F or B belongs to everything, and similarly either H or D, and since H follows F, B must follow D: for we know this.[1] If then A follows C, B must follow D'. But this is false: for as we proved[2] the sequence is reversed in terms so constituted. The fallacy arises because perhaps it is not neces- [30] sary that A or F should belong to everything, or that F or B should belong to everything: for F is not the denial of A. For *not-good* is the negation of good: and not-good is not identical with 'neither good nor not-good'. Similarly also with C and D. For two negations have been assumed in respect to one term.

---
[1] From ^a 39-^b 13. [2] ^a 39-^b 13.

BOOK II

1

We have already explained the number of the figures, the character and number of the premisses, when and how a syllogism is formed;[1] further what we must look for when refuting and establishing propositions, and how we should investigate a given problem in any branch of inquiry, also by what means we shall obtain principles appropriate to each subject.[2] Since some syllogisms are universal, others particular, all the universal syllogisms give more than one result, and of particular syllogisms the affirmative yield more than one, the negative yield only the stated conclusion. For all propositions are convertible save only the particular negative: and the conclusion states one definite thing about another definite thing. Consequently all syllogisms save the particular negative yield more than one conclusion, e.g. if A has been proved to belong to all or to some B, then B must belong to some A: and if A has been proved to belong to no B, then B belongs to no A. This is a different conclusion from the former. But if A does not belong to some B, it is not necessary that B should not belong to some A: for it may possibly belong to all A.

This then is the reason common to all syllogisms whether universal or particular. But it is possible to give another reason concerning those which are universal. For all the things that are subordinate to the middle term or to the conclusion may be proved by the same syllogism, if the former are placed in the middle, the latter in the conclusion; e.g. if the conclusion AB is proved through C, whatever is subordinate to B or C must accept the predicate A: for if D is included in B as in a whole, and B is included in A, then D will be included in A. Again if E is included in C as in a whole, and C is included in A, then E will be included in A. Similarly if the syllogism is negative. In the second figure it will be possible to infer only that which is subordinate to the conclusion, e.g. if A belongs to no B and to all C; we conclude that B belongs to no C. If then D is subordinate to C, clearly B does not belong to it. But that B does not belong to what is subordinate to A, is not clear by means of the syllogism. And yet B does not belong to E, if E is subordinate to A. But while it has been proved through the syllogism that B belongs to no C, it has been assumed without proof that B does not belong to A, consequently it does not result through the syllogism that B does not belong to E.

But in particular syllogisms there will be no necessity of inferring what is subordinate to the conclusion (for a syllogism does not result when this premiss is particular), but whatever is subordinate to the middle term may be inferred, not however through the syllogism, e.g. if A belongs to all B and B to some C. Nothing can be inferred about that which is subordinate to C; something can be inferred about that which is subordinate to B, but not through the preceding syllogism. Similarly in the other figures. That which is subordinate to the conclusion cannot be proved; the other subordinate can be proved, only not through the syllogism, just as in the universal syllogisms what is subordinate to the middle term is proved (as we saw) from a premiss which is not demonstrated: consequently either a conclusion is not possible in the case of universal syllogisms or else it is possible also in the case of particular syllogisms.

2

It is possible for the premisses of the syllogism to be true, or to be false, or to be the one true, the other false. The conclusion is either true or false necessarily. From true premisses it is not possible to draw a false conclusion, but a true conclusion may be drawn from false premisses, true however only in respect to the fact, not to the reason. The reason cannot be established from false premisses: why this is so will be explained in the sequel.[3]

First then that it is not possible to draw a false conclusion from true premisses, is made clear by this consideration. If it is necessary that B should be when A is, it is necessary that A should not be when B is not. If then A is true, B must be true: otherwise it will turn out that the same thing both is and is not at the same time. But this is impossible. Let it not, because A is laid down as a single term, be supposed that it is possible, when a single fact is given, that something should necessarily result. For that is not possible. For what results necessarily is the conclusion, and the means by which this comes about are at the least three terms, and two relations of subject

---

[1] I. 1-26. [2] I. 27-31. [3] 57ª 40-ᵇ 17.

[20] and predicate or premisses. If then it is true that *A* belongs to all that to which *B* belongs, and that *B* belongs to all that to which *C* belongs, it is necessary that *A* should belong to all that to which *C* belongs, and this cannot be false: for then the same thing will belong and not belong at the same time. So *A* is posited as one thing, being two premisses taken together. The same holds good of negative [25] syllogisms: it is not possible to prove a false conclusion from true premisses.

But from what is false a true conclusion may be drawn, whether both the premisses are false or only one, provided that this is not either of the premisses indifferently, if it is taken as wholly false: but if the premiss is not taken as wholly false, it does not matter which of the [30] two is false. (1) Let *A* belong to the whole of *C*, but to none of the *B*s, neither let *B* belong to *C*. This is possible, e.g. animal belongs to no stone, nor stone to any man. If then *A* is taken to belong to all *B* and *B* to all *C*, *A* will belong to all *C*; consequently though both the premisses are false the conclusion is [35] true: for every man is an animal. Similarly with the negative. For it is possible that neither *A* nor *B* should belong to any *C*, although *A* belongs to all *B*, e.g. if the same terms are taken and man is put as middle: for neither animal nor man belongs to any stone, but animal belongs to every man. Consequently if one term is taken to belong to none [40] of that to which it does belong, and the other term is taken to belong to all of that to which it does not belong, though both the premisses are false the conclusion will be true. 54a (2) A similar proof may be given if each premiss is partially false.

(3) But if one only of the premisses is false, when the first premiss is wholly false, e.g. *AB*, the conclusion will not be true, but if the premiss *BC* is wholly false, a true conclusion will be possible. I mean by 'wholly false' the contrary [5] of the truth, e.g. if what belongs to none is assumed to belong to all, or if what belongs to all is assumed to belong to none. Let *A* belong to no *B*, and *B* to all *C*. If then the premiss *BC* which I take is true, and the premiss *AB* is wholly false, viz. that *A* belongs to all *B*, it is impossible that the conclusion should be true: for *A* belonged to none of the *C*s, since *A* belonged to nothing to which *B* belonged, [10] and *B* belonged to all *C*. Similarly there cannot be a true conclusion if *A* belongs to all *B*, and *B* to all *C*, but while the true premiss *BC* is assumed, the wholly false premiss *AB* is also assumed, viz. that *A* belongs to nothing to which *B* belongs: here the conclusion must be [15] false. For *A* will belong to all *C*, since *A* belongs to everything to which *B* belongs, and *B* to all *C*. It is clear then that when the first premiss is wholly false, whether affirmative or negative, and the other premiss is true, the conclusion cannot be true.

(4) But if the premiss is not wholly false, a true conclusion is possible. For if *A* belongs to all *C* and to some *B*, and if *B* belongs to all *C*, [20] e.g. animal to every swan and to some white thing, and white to every swan, then if we take as premisses that *A* belongs to all *B*, and *B* to all *C*, *A* will belong to all *C* truly: for every swan is an animal. Similarly if the statement *AB* is negative. For it is possible that *A* [25] should belong to some *B* and to no *C*, and that *B* should belong to all *C*, e.g. animal to some white thing, but to no snow, and white to all snow. If then one should assume that *A* belongs to no *B*, and *B* to all *C*, then *A* will belong to no *C*.

(5) But if the premiss *AB*, which is assumed, is wholly true, and the premiss *BC* is wholly false, a true syllogism will be possible: [30] for nothing prevents *A* belonging to all *B* and to all *C*, though *B* belongs to no *C*, e.g. these being species of the same genus which are not subordinate one to the other: for animal belongs both to horse and to man, but horse to no man. If then it is assumed that *A* belongs to all *B* and *B* to all *C*, the conclusion will be [35] true, although the premiss *BC* is wholly false. Similarly if the premiss *AB* is negative. For it is possible that *A* should belong neither to any *B* nor to any *C*, and that *B* should not belong to any *C*, e.g. a genus to species of another genus: for animal belongs neither to music nor to the art of healing, nor does music belong to the art of healing. If then it is assumed that *A* belongs to no *B*, and *B* to all *C*, the conclusion will be true.

(6) And if the premiss *BC* is not wholly false but in part only, even so the conclusion may be true. For nothing prevents *A* belonging [5] to the whole of *B* and of *C*, while *B* belongs to some *C*, e.g. a genus to its species and difference: for animal belongs to every man and to every footed thing, and man to some footed things though not to all. If then it is assumed that *A* belongs to all *B*, and *B* to all *C*, *A* will belong to all *C*: and this *ex hypothesi* [10] is true. Similarly if the premiss *AB* is negative. For it is possible that *A* should neither belong to any *B* nor to any *C*, though

B belongs to some C, e.g. a genus to the species of another genus and its difference: for animal neither belongs to any wisdom nor to any instance of 'speculative', but wisdom belongs to some instance of 'speculative'. If then it should [15] be assumed that A belongs to no B, and B to all C, A will belong to no C: and this *ex hypothesi* is true.

In particular syllogisms it is possible when the first premiss is wholly false, and the other true, that the conclusion should be true; also when the first premiss is false in part, and the [20] other true; and when the first is true, and the particular is false; and when both are false. (7) For nothing prevents A belonging to no B, but to some C, and B to some C, e.g. animal belongs to no snow, but to some white thing, and snow to some white thing. If then snow [25] is taken as middle, and animal as first term, and it is assumed that A belongs to the whole of B, and B to some C, then the premiss AB is wholly false, the premiss BC true, and the conclusion true. Similarly if the premiss AB is negative: for it is possible that A should belong to the whole of B, but not to some C, [30] although B belongs to some C, e.g. animal belongs to every man, but does not follow some white, but man belongs to some white; consequently if man be taken as middle term and it is assumed that A belongs to no B but B belongs to some C, the conclusion will be true although the premiss AB is wholly false. [35] (8) If the premiss AB is false in part, the conclusion may be true. For nothing prevents A belonging both to B and to some C, and B belonging to some C, e.g. animal to something beautiful and to something great, and beautiful belonging to something great. If then A is assumed to belong to all B, and B to some C, the premiss AB will be partially false, the premiss BC will be true, and the conclusion true. Similarly if the premiss AB is negative. For the same terms will serve, and in the same positions, to prove the point.

(9) Again if the premiss AB is true, and the [5] premiss BC is false, the conclusion may be true. For nothing prevents A belonging to the whole of B and to some C, while B belongs to no C, e.g. animal to every swan and to some black things, though swan belongs to no black thing. Consequently if it should be assumed that A belongs to all B, and B to some C, the [10] conclusion will be true, although the statement BC is false. Similarly if the premiss AB is negative. For it is possible that A should belong to no B, and not to some C, while B belongs to no C, e.g. a genus to the species of another genus and to the accident of its own [15] species: for animal belongs to no number and not to some white things, and number belongs to nothing white. If then number is taken as middle, and it is assumed that A belongs to no B, and B to some C, then A will not belong to some C, which *ex hypothesi* is true. And the premiss AB is true, the premiss BC false.

(10) Also if the premiss AB is partially false, [20] and the premiss BC is false too, the conclusion may be true. For nothing prevents A belonging to some B and to some C, though B belongs to no C, e.g. if B is the contrary of C, and both are accidents of the same genus: for animal belongs to some white things and to some black things, but white belongs to no [25] black thing. If then it is assumed that A belongs to all B, and B to some C, the conclusion will be true. Similarly if the premiss AB is negative: for the same terms arranged in the same way will serve for the proof.

(11) Also though both premisses are false the conclusion may be true. For it is possible that A may belong to no B and to some C, [30] while B belongs to no C, e.g. a genus in relation to the species of another genus, and to the accident of its own species: for animal belongs to no number, but to some white things, and number to nothing white. If then it is assumed that A belongs to all B and B to some [35] C, the conclusion will be true, though both premisses are false. Similarly also if the premiss AB is negative. For nothing prevents A belonging to the whole of B, and not to some C, while B belongs to no C, e.g. animal belongs to every swan, and not to some black things, and swan belongs to nothing black. [40] Consequently if it is assumed that A belongs to no B, and B to some C, then A does not belong to some C. The conclusion then is true, but the premisses are false.

3

In the middle figure it is possible in every way to reach a true conclusion through false premisses, whether the syllogisms are universal or particular, viz. when both premisses are wholly [5] false; when each is partially false; when one is true, the other wholly false (it does not matter which of the two premisses is false); if both premisses are partially false; if one is quite true, the other partially false; if one is wholly [10] false, the other partially true. For (1) if A belongs to no B and to all C, e.g. animal to no stone and to every horse, then if the premisses are stated contrariwise and it is assumed that *A* belongs to all *B* and to no *C*, though the premisses are wholly false they will yield a true [15] conclusion. Similarly if *A* belongs to all *B* and to no *C*: for we shall have the same syllogism.

(2) Again if one premiss is wholly false, the other wholly true: for nothing prevents *A* belonging to all *B* and to all *C*, though *B* belongs to no *C*, e.g. a genus to its co-ordinate species. For animal belongs to every horse and man, [20] and no man is a horse. If then it is assumed that animal belongs to all of the one, and none of the other, the one premiss will be wholly false, the other wholly true, and the conclusion will be true whichever term the negative statement concerns.

(3) Also if one premiss is partially false, the other wholly true. For it is possible that *A* should belong to some *B* and to all *C*, though [25] *B* belongs to no *C*, e.g. animal to some white things and to every raven, though white belongs to no raven. If then it is assumed that *A* belongs to no *B*, but to the whole of *C*, the premiss *AB* is partially false, the premiss *AC* wholly true, and the conclusion true. Similarly [30] if the negative statement is transposed: the proof can be made by means of the same terms. Also if the affirmative premiss is partially false, the negative wholly true, a true conclusion is possible. For nothing prevents *A* belonging to some *B*, but not to *C* as a whole, while *B* belongs to no *C*, e.g. animal belongs to some white things, but to no pitch, and [35] white belongs to no pitch. Consequently if it is assumed that *A* belongs to the whole of *B*, but to no *C*, the premiss *AB* is partially false, the premiss *AC* is wholly true, and the conclusion is true.

(4) And if both the premisses are partially false, the conclusion may be true. For it is possible that *A* should belong to some *B* and to [40] some *C*, and *B* to no *C*, e.g. animal to some white things and to some black things, 56ᵃ though white belongs to nothing black. If then it is assumed that *A* belongs to all *B* and to no *C*, both premisses are partially false, but the conclusion is true. Similarly, if the negative premiss is transposed, the proof can be made by means of the same terms.

[5] It is clear also that our thesis holds in particular syllogisms. For (5) nothing prevents *A* belonging to all *B* and to some *C*, though *B* does not belong to some *C*, e.g. animal to every man and to some white things, though man will not belong to some white things. If then it is stated that *A* belongs to no *B* and to [10] some *C*, the universal premiss is wholly false, the particular premiss is true, and the conclusion is true. Similarly if the premiss *AB* is affirmative: for it is possible that *A* should belong to no *B*, and not to some *C*, though *B* does not belong to some *C*, e.g. animal belongs to nothing lifeless, and does not belong to some [15] white things, and lifeless will not belong to some white things. If then it is stated that *A* belongs to all *B* and not to some *C*, the premiss *AB* which is universal is wholly false, the premiss *AC* is true, and the conclusion is true. Also a true conclusion is possible when the universal premiss is true, and the particular is false. For nothing prevents *A* following neither *B* [20] nor *C* at all, while *B* does not belong to some *C*, e.g. animal belongs to no number nor to anything lifeless, and number does not follow some lifeless things. If then it is stated that *A* belongs to no *B* and to some *C*, the conclusion will be true, and the universal premiss [25] true, but the particular false. Similarly if the premiss which is stated universally is affirmative. For it is possible that *A* should belong both to *B* and to *C* as wholes, though *B* does not follow some *C*, e.g. a genus in relation to its species and difference: for animal follows every man and footed things as a whole, but man does not follow every footed thing. Consequently if it is assumed that *A* belongs [30] to the whole of *B*, but does not belong to some *C*, the universal premiss is true, the particular false, and the conclusion true.

(6) It is clear too that though both premisses are false they may yield a true conclusion, since it is possible that *A* should belong both to *B* and to *C* as wholes, though *B* does not follow some *C*. For if it is assumed that *A* [35] belongs to no *B* and to some *C*, the premisses are both false, but the conclusion is true. Similarly if the universal premiss is affirmative and the particular negative. For it is possible that *A* should follow no *B* and all *C*, though *B* does [40] not belong to some *C*, e.g. animal follows no science but every man, though science does not follow every man. If then *A* is assumed to 56ᵇ belong to the whole of *B*, and not to follow some *C*, the premisses are false but the conclusion is true.

4

In the last figure a true conclusion may come through what is false, alike when both [5] premisses are wholly false, when each is partly false, when one premiss is wholly true, the other false, when one premiss is partly false, the other wholly true, and vice versa, and in every other way in which it is possible to alter the premisses. For (1) nothing prevents [10] neither A nor B from belonging to any C, while A belongs to some B, e.g. neither man nor footed follows anything lifeless, though man belongs to some footed things. If then it is assumed that A and B belong to all C, the premisses will be wholly false, but the conclusion true. Similarly if one premiss is negative, the other affirmative. For it is possible that B [15] should belong to no C, but A to all C, and that A should not belong to some B, e.g. black belongs to no swan, animal to every swan, and animal not to everything black. Consequently if it is assumed that B belongs to all C, and A to no C, A will not belong to some [20] B: and the conclusion is true, though the premisses are false.

(2) Also if each premiss is partly false, the conclusion may be true. For nothing prevents both A and B from belonging to some C while A belongs to some B, e.g. white and beautiful belong to some animals, and white to some beautiful things. If then it is stated that A and [25] B belong to all C, the premisses are partially false, but the conclusion is true. Similarly if the premiss AC is stated as negative. For nothing prevents A from not belonging, and B from belonging, to some C, while A does not belong to all B, e.g. white does not belong to some animals, beautiful belongs to some ani- [30] mals, and white does not belong to everything beautiful. Consequently if it is assumed that A belongs to no C, and B to all C, both premisses are partly false, but the conclusion is true.

(3) Similarly if one of the premisses assumed is wholly false, the other wholly true. For it is possible that both A and B should follow all C, [35] though A does not belong to some B, e.g. animal and white follow every swan, though animal does not belong to everything white. Taking these then as terms, if one assumes that B belongs to the whole of C, but A does not belong to C at all, the premiss BC will be wholly true, the premiss AC wholly false, and the conclusion true. Similarly if the statement [40] BC is false, the statement AC true, the conclusion may be true. The same terms will 57ª serve for the proof. Also if both the premisses assumed are affirmative, the conclusion may be true. For nothing prevents B from following all C, and A from not belonging to C at all, though A belongs to some B, e.g. animal belongs to every swan, black to no swan, and [5] black to some animals. Consequently if it is assumed that A and B belong to every C, the premiss BC is wholly true, the premiss AC is wholly false, and the conclusion is true. Similarly if the premiss AC which is assumed is true: the proof can be made through the same terms.

(4) Again if one premiss is wholly true, the [10] other partly false, the conclusion may be true. For it is possible that B should belong to all C, and A to some C, while A belongs to some B, e.g. biped belongs to every man, beautiful not to every man, and beautiful to some bipeds. If then it is assumed that both A and B belong to the whole of C, the premiss BC is wholly true, the premiss AC partly false, the [15] conclusion true. Similarly if of the premisses assumed AC is true and BC partly false, a true conclusion is possible: this can be proved, if the same terms as before are transposed. Also the conclusion may be true if one premiss is negative, the other affirmative. For since it is possible that B should belong to the whole of C, and A to some C, and, when they are so, [20] that A should not belong to all B, therefore it is assumed that B belongs to the whole of C, and A to no C, the negative premiss is partly false, the other premiss wholly true, and the conclusion is true. Again since it has been proved that if A belongs to no C and B to some C, it is possible that A should not belong to [25] some C, it is clear that if the premiss AC is wholly true, and the premiss BC partly false, it is possible that the conclusion should be true. For if it is assumed that A belongs to no C, and B to all C, the premiss AC is wholly true, and the premiss BC is partly false.

(5) It is clear also in the case of particular syllogisms that a true conclusion may come [30] through what is false, in every possible way. For the same terms must be taken as have been taken when the premisses are universal, positive terms in positive syllogisms, negative terms in negative. For it makes no difference to the setting out of the terms, whether one assumes that what belongs to none belongs to all [35] or that what belongs to some belongs to all. The same applies to negative statements.

It is clear then that if the conclusion is false, the premisses of the argument must be false, either all or some of them; but when the conclusion is true, it is not necessary that the premisses should be true, either one or all, yet it is possible, though no part of the syllogism is [40] true, that the conclusion may none the less be true; but it is not necessitated. The reason is that when two things are so related to one another, that if the one is, the other necessarily is, then if the latter is not, the former will not be either, but if the latter is, it is not necessary that the former should be. But it is impossible that the same thing should be necessitated by the being and by the not-being of the same thing. I mean, for example, that it is impossible that B should necessarily be great [5] since A is white and that B should necessarily be great since A is not white. For whenever since this, A, is white it is necessary that that, B, should be great, and since B is great that C should not be white, then it is necessary if A is white that C should not be white. And whenever it is necessary, since one of two [10] things is, that the other should be, it is necessary, if the latter is not, that the former (viz. A) should not be. If then B is not great A cannot be white. But if, when A is not white, it is necessary that B should be great, it necessarily results that if B is not great, B itself is great. (But this is impossible.) For if B is not great, A will necessarily not be white. If [15] then when this is not white B must be great, it results that if B is not great, it is great, just as if it were proved through three terms.

5

Circular and reciprocal proof means proof by means of the conclusion, i.e. by converting one of the premisses simply and inferring the [20] other premiss which was assumed in the original syllogism: e.g. suppose it has been necessary to prove that A belongs to all C, and it has been proved through B; suppose that A should now be proved to belong to B by assuming that A belongs to C, and C to B—so A belongs to B: but in the first syllogism the [25] converse was assumed, viz. that B belongs to C. Or suppose it is necessary to prove that B belongs to C, and A is assumed to belong to C, which was the conclusion of the first syllogism, and B to belong to A: but the converse was assumed in the earlier syllogism, viz. that A belongs to B. In no other way is reciprocal proof possible. If another term is taken as middle, the proof is not circular: for neither [30] of the propositions assumed is the same as before: if one of the accepted terms is taken as middle, only one of the premisses of the first syllogism can be assumed in the second: for if both of them are taken the same conclusion as before will result: but it must be different. If the terms are not convertible, one of the premisses from which the syllogism results must be undemonstrated: for it is not possible to demonstrate through these terms that the third belongs to the middle or the middle to the first. [35] If the terms are convertible, it is possible to demonstrate everything reciprocally, e.g. if A and B and C are convertible with one another. Suppose the proposition AC has been demonstrated through B as middle term, and again the proposition AB through the conclusion and the premiss BC converted, and similarly [40] the proposition BC through the conclusion and the premiss AB converted. But it is necessary to prove both the premiss CB, and the premiss BA: for we have used these alone without demonstrating them. If then it is assumed that B belongs to all C, and C to all A, we shall have a syllogism relating B to A. [5] Again if it is assumed that C belongs to all A, and A to all B, C must belong to all B. In both these syllogisms the premiss CA has been assumed without being demonstrated: the other premisses had *ex hypothesi* been proved. Consequently if we succeed in demonstrating this premiss, all the premisses will have been [10] proved reciprocally. If then it is assumed that C belongs to all B, and B to all A, both the premisses assumed have been proved, and C must belong to A. It is clear then that only if the terms are convertible is circular and reciprocal demonstration possible (if the terms are not convertible, the matter stands as we said [15] above). But it turns out in these also that we use for the demonstration the very thing that is being proved: for C is proved of B, and B of A, by assuming that C is said of A, and C is proved of A through these premisses, so that [20] we use the conclusion for the demonstration.

In negative syllogisms reciprocal proof is as follows. Let B belong to all C, and A to none of the Bs: we conclude that A belongs to none of the Cs. If again it is necessary to prove that A belongs to none of the Bs (which was pre- [25] viously assumed) A must belong to no C, and C to all B: thus the previous premiss is reversed. If it is necessary to prove that B belongs to C, the proposition AB must no longer be converted as before: for the premiss 'B belongs to no A' is identical with the premiss 'A belongs to no B'. But we must assume that B belongs to all of that to none of which A be- [30] longs. Let A belong to none of the Cs (which was the previous conclusion) and assume that B belongs to all of that to none of which A belongs. It is necessary then that B

should belong to all C. Consequently each of the three propositions has been made a conclusion, and this is circular demonstration, to assume the conclusion and the converse of one of [35] the premisses, and deduce the remaining premiss.

In particular syllogisms it is not possible to demonstrate the universal premiss through the other propositions, but the particular premiss can be demonstrated. Clearly it is impossible to demonstrate the universal premiss: for what is universal is proved through propositions [40] which are universal, but the conclusion is not universal, and the proof must start from the conclusion and the other premiss. Further a syllogism cannot be made at all if the other 58ᵇ premiss is converted: for the result is that both premisses are particular. But the particular premiss may be proved. Suppose that A has been proved of some C through B. If then it is assumed that B belongs to all A, and the con- [5] clusion is retained, B will belong to some C: for we obtain the first figure and A is middle. But if the syllogism is negative, it is not possible to prove the universal premiss, for the reason given above. But it is possible to prove the particular premiss, if the proposition AB is converted as in the universal syllogism, i.e. [10] 'B belongs to some of that to some of which A does not belong': otherwise no syllogism results because the particular premiss is negative.

6

In the second figure it is not possible to prove an affirmative proposition in this way, but a negative proposition may be proved. An [15] affirmative proposition is not proved because both premisses of the new syllogism are not affirmative (for the conclusion is negative) but an affirmative proposition is (as we saw) proved from premisses which are both affirmative. The negative is proved as follows. Let A belong to all B, and to no C: we conclude that [20] B belongs to no C. If then it is assumed that B belongs to all A, it is necessary that A should belong to no C: for we get the second figure, with B as middle. But if the premiss AB was negative, and the other affirmative, we shall have the first figure. For C belongs to all A, and B to no C, consequently B belongs [25] to no A: neither then does A belong to B. Through the conclusion, therefore, and one premiss, we get no syllogism, but if another premiss is assumed in addition, a syllogism will be possible. But if the syllogism is not universal, the universal premiss cannot be proved, for the same reason as we gave above,[1] but the [30] particular premiss can be proved whenever the universal statement is affirmative. Let A belong to all B, and not to all C: the conclusion is BC. If then it is assumed that B belongs to all A, but not to all C, A will not belong to some C, B being middle. But if the universal premiss is *negative*, the premiss AC will not be demonstrated by the conversion of AB: for it [35] turns out that either both or one of the premisses is negative; consequently a syllogism will not be possible. But the proof will proceed as in the universal syllogisms, if it is assumed that A belongs to some of that to some of which B does not belong.

7

In the third figure, when both premisses are [40] taken universally, it is not possible to prove them reciprocally: for that which is universal is proved through statements which are 59ᵃ universal, but the conclusion in this figure is always particular, so that it is clear that it is not possible at all to prove through this figure the universal premiss. But if one premiss is universal, the other particular, proof of the latter will sometimes be possible, sometimes not. When both the premisses assumed are affirma- [5] tive, and the universal concerns the minor extreme, proof will be possible, but when it concerns the other extreme, impossible. Let A belong to all C and B to some C: the conclusion is the statement AB. If then it is assumed that C belongs to all A, it has been proved that C belongs to some B, but that B belongs to some C has not been proved. And yet it is nec- [10] essary, if C belongs to some B, that B should belong to some C. But it is not the same that this should belong to that, and that to this: but we must assume besides that if this belongs to some of that, that belongs to some of this. But if this is assumed the syllogism no longer results from the conclusion and the oth- [15] er premiss. But if B belongs to all C, and A to some C, it will be possible to prove the proposition AC, when it is assumed that C belongs to all B, and A to some B. For if C belongs to all B and A to some B, it is necessary that A should belong to some C, B being middle. And whenever one premiss is affirmative, the other negative, and the affirmative is universal, the other premiss can be proved. Let B [20] belong to all C, and A not to some C: the conclusion is that A does not belong to some

[1] 38.

B. If then it is assumed further that C belongs to all B, it is necessary that A should not belong to some C, B being middle. But when the negative premiss is universal, the other prem- [25] iss is not proved, except as before,[1] viz. if it is assumed that *that* belongs to some of that, to some of which *this* does not belong, e.g. if A belongs to no C, and B to some C: the conclusion is that A does not belong to some B. If then it is assumed that C belongs to some of that to some of which A does not belong, it is necessary that C should belong to some of the Bs. In no other way is it possible by converting [30] the universal premiss to prove the other: for in no other way can a syllogism be formed.

It is clear then that in the first figure reciprocal proof is made both through the third and through the first figure—if the conclusion is affirmative through the first; if the conclusion [35] is negative through the last. For it is assumed that *that* belongs to all of that to none of which *this* belongs. In the middle figure, when the syllogism is universal, proof is possible through the second figure and through the first, but when particular through the second and the last. In the third figure all proofs are made through itself. It is clear also that in the [40] third figure and in the middle figure those syllogisms which are not made through those figures themselves either are not of the nature of circular proof or are imperfect.

8

59[b] To convert a syllogism means to alter the conclusion and make another syllogism to prove that either the extreme cannot belong to the middle or the middle to the last term. For it is necessary, if the conclusion has been changed into its opposite and one of the premisses stands, that the other premiss should be [5] destroyed. For if it should stand, the conclusion also must stand. It makes a difference whether the conclusion is converted into its contradictory or into its contrary. For the same syllogism does not result whichever form the conversion takes. This will be made clear by the sequel. By contradictory opposition I mean the opposition of 'to all' to 'not to all', and of 'to some' to 'to none'; by contrary opposition I [10] mean the opposition of 'to all' to 'to none', and of 'to some' to 'not to some'. Suppose that A has been proved of C, through B as middle term. If then it should be assumed that A belongs to no C, but to all B, B will belong to no C. And if A belongs to no C, and B to all C,

[1] 58[b] 9.

A will belong, not to no B at all, but not to all [15] B. For (as we saw) the universal is not proved through the last figure.[2] In a word it is not possible to refute universally by conversion the premiss which concerns the major extreme: for the refutation always proceeds through the third figure; since it is necessary to take both premisses in reference to the minor extreme. [20] Similarly if the syllogism is negative. Suppose it has been proved that A belongs to no C through B. Then if it is assumed that A belongs to all C, and to no B, B will belong to none of the Cs. And if A and B belong to all C, A will belong to some B: but in the original premiss it belonged to no B.
[25] If the conclusion is converted into its contradictory, the syllogisms will be contradictory and not universal. For one premiss is particular, so that the conclusion also will be particular. Let the syllogism be affirmative, and let it be converted as stated. Then if A belongs not to all C, but to all B, B will belong not to all [30] C. And if A belongs not to all C, but B belongs to all C, A will belong not to all B. Similarly if the syllogism is negative. For if A belongs to some C, and to no B, B will belong, not to no C at all, but—not to some C. And if A belongs to some C, and B to all C, as was [35] originally assumed, A will belong to some B.

In particular syllogisms when the conclusion is converted into its contradictory, both premisses may be refuted, but when it is converted into its contrary, neither. For the result is no [40] longer, as in the universal syllogisms,[3] a refutation in which the conclusion reached by 60[a] conversion lacks universality, but no refutation at all. Suppose that A has been proved of some C. If then it is assumed that A belongs to no C, and B to some C, A will not belong to some B: and if A belongs to no C, but to all B, B will belong to no C. Thus both premisses are refuted. But neither can be refuted if the [5] conclusion is converted into its contrary. For if A does not belong to some C, but to all B, then B will not belong to some C. But the original premiss is not yet refuted: for it is possible that B should belong to some C, and should not belong to some C. The universal premiss AB cannot be affected by a syllogism at all: for if A does not belong to some of the [10] Cs, but B belongs to some of the Cs, neither of the premisses is universal. Similarly if the syllogism is negative: for if it should be assumed that A belongs to all C, both prem-

[2] 1. 6. [3] ll. 13-20, 23-4.

isses are refuted: but if the assumption is that *A* belongs to some *C*, neither premiss is refuted. The proof is the same as before.

9

[15] In the second figure it is not possible to refute the premiss which concerns the major extreme by establishing something *contrary* to it, whichever form the conversion of the conclusion may take. For the conclusion of the refutation will always be in the third figure, and in this figure (as we saw[1]) there is no universal syllogism. The other premiss can be refuted in a manner similar to the conversion: I mean, if the conclusion of the first syllogism is con- [20] verted into its contrary, the conclusion of the refutation will be the contrary of the minor premiss of the first, if into its contradictory, the contradictory. Let *A* belong to all *B* and to no *C*: conclusion *BC*. If then it is assumed that *B* belongs to *all C*, and the proposition *AB* stands, *A* will belong to all *C*, since the first figure is produced. If *B* belongs to all *C*, and [25] *A* to no *C*, then *A* belongs not to all *B*: the figure is the last. But if the conclusion *BC* is converted into its *contradictory*, the premiss *AB* will be refuted as before, the premiss *AC* by its contradictory. For if *B* belongs to some *C*, and *A* to no *C*, then *A* will not belong to some *B*. Again if *B* belongs to some *C*, and [30] *A* to all *B*, *A* will belong to some *C*, so that the syllogism results in the contradictory of the minor premiss. A similar proof can be given if the premisses are transposed in respect of their quality.

If the syllogism is particular, when the conclusion is converted into its *contrary* neither premiss can be refuted, as also happened in the first figure,[2] but if the conclusion is converted [35] into its contradictory, both premisses can be refuted. Suppose that *A* belongs to no *B*, and to some *C*: the conclusion is *BC*. If then it is assumed that *B* belongs to some *C*, and the statement *AB* stands, the conclusion will be that *A* does not belong to some *C*. But the original statement has not been refuted: for it is possible that *A* should belong to some *C* and also not to some *C*. Again if *B* belongs to some [40] *C* and *A* to some *C*, no syllogism will be possible: for neither of the premisses taken is 60ᵇ universal. Consequently the proposition *AB* is not refuted. But if the conclusion is converted into its *contradictory*, both premisses can be refuted. For if *B* belongs to all *C*, and *A* to no *B*, *A* will belong to no *C*: but it was as- sumed to belong to some *C*. Again if *B* belongs to all *C* and *A* to some *C*, *A* will belong to some *B*. The same proof can be given if the [5] universal statement is affirmative.

10

In the third figure when the conclusion is converted into its *contrary*, neither of the premisses can be refuted in any of the syllogisms, but when the conclusion is converted into its *contradictory*, both premisses may be refuted and in all the moods. Suppose it has been proved that *A* belongs to some *B*, *C* being [10] taken as middle, and the premisses being universal. If then it is assumed that *A* does not belong to some *B*, but *B* belongs to all *C*, no syllogism is formed about *A* and *C*. Nor if *A* does not belong to some *B*, but belongs to all *C*, will a syllogism be possible about *B* and *C*. A similar proof can be given [15] if the premisses are not universal. For either both premisses arrived at by the conversion must be particular, or the universal premiss must refer to the minor extreme. But we found that no syllogism is possible thus either in the first or in the middle figure.[3] But if the conclusion is converted into its *contradictory*, [20] both the premisses can be refuted. For if *A* belongs to no *B*, and *B* to all *C*, then *A* belongs to no *C*: again if *A* belongs to no *B*, and to all *C*, *B* belongs to no *C*. And similarly if one of the premisses is not universal. For if *A* belongs to no *B*, and *B* to some *C*, *A* will not belong to some *C*: if *A* belongs to no *B*, and to [25] all *C*, *B* will belong to no *C*.

Similarly if the original syllogism is negative. Suppose it has been proved that *A* does not belong to some *B*, *BC* being affirmative, *AC* being negative: for it was thus that, as we saw,[4] a syllogism could be made. Whenever then the *contrary* of the conclusion is assumed a syllogism will not be possible. For if *A* be- [30] longs to some *B*, and *B* to all *C*, no syllogism is possible (as we saw[5]) about *A* and *C*. Nor, if *A* belongs to some *B*, and to no *C*, was a syllogism possible concerning *B* and *C*. Therefore the premisses are not refuted. But when the *contradictory* of the conclusion is assumed, they are refuted. For if *A* belongs to [35] all *B*, and *B* to *C*, *A* belongs to all *C*: but *A* was supposed originally to belong to no *C*. Again if *A* belongs to all *B*, and to no *C*, then *B* belongs to no *C*: but it was supposed to belong to all *C*. A similar proof is possible if the

[1] 1. 6.   [2] 59ᵇ 39-60ᵃ 1. 60ᵃ 5-14.
[3] 26ᵃ 17-21, 27ᵃ 4-12.   [4] 28ᵇ 1-4, 15-29ᵃ 10.
[5] 26ᵃ 30-6.

premisses are not universal. For AC becomes universal and negative, the other premiss particular and affirmative. If then A belongs to all [40] B, and B to some C, it results that A belongs to some C: but it was supposed to belong to no C. Again if A belongs to all B, and to no C, then B belongs to no C: but it was assumed to belong to some C. If A belongs to some B and B to some C, no syllogism results: nor yet if A belongs to some B, and to no C. Thus in one way the premisses are refuted, in the other way they are not.

[5] From what has been said it is clear how a syllogism results in each figure when the conclusion is converted; when a result contrary to the premiss, and when a result contradictory to the premiss, is obtained. It is clear that in the first figure the syllogisms are formed through the middle and the last figures, and the premiss which concerns the minor extreme is always [10] refuted through the middle figure, the premiss which concerns the major through the last figure. In the second figure syllogisms proceed through the first and the last figures, and the premiss which concerns the minor extreme is always refuted through the first figure, the premiss which concerns the major extreme through the last. In the third figure the refutation proceeds through the first and the middle figures; the premiss which concerns the major [15] is always refuted through the first figure, the premiss which concerns the minor through the middle figure.

11

It is clear then what conversion is, how it is effected in each figure, and what syllogism results. The syllogism *per impossibile* is proved when the contradictory of the conclusion is [20] stated and another premiss is assumed; it can be made in all the figures. For it resembles conversion, differing only in this: conversion takes place after a syllogism has been formed and both the premisses have been taken, but a reduction to the impossible takes place not because the contradictory has been [25] agreed to already, but because it is clear that it is true. The terms are alike in both, and the premisses of both are taken in the same way. For example if A belongs to all B, C being middle, then if it is supposed that A does not belong to all B or belongs to no B, but to all C (which was admitted to be true), it follows [30] that C belongs to no B or not to all B. But this is impossible: consequently the supposition is false: its contradictory then is true. Similarly in the other figures: for whatever moods admit of conversion admit also of the reduction *per impossibile*.

All the problems can be proved *per impossibile* in all the figures, excepting the universal [35] affirmative, which is proved in the middle and third figures, but not in the first. Suppose that A belongs not to all B, or to no B, and take besides another premiss concerning either of the terms, viz. that C belongs to all A, or that B belongs to all D; thus we get the [40] first figure. If then it is supposed that A does not belong to all B, no syllogism results whichever term the assumed premiss concerns; but if it is supposed that A belongs to no B, when the premiss BD is assumed as well we shall prove syllogistically what is false, but not the problem proposed. For if A belongs to no B, and B belongs to all D, A belongs to no [5] D. Let this be impossible: it is false then that A belongs to no B. But the universal affirmative is not necessarily true if the universal negative is false. But if the premiss CA is assumed as well, no syllogism results, nor does it do so when it is supposed that A does not belong to all B. Consequently it is clear that the universal affirmative cannot be proved in the first figure *per impossibile*.

[10] But the particular affirmative and the universal and particular negatives can all be proved. Suppose that A belongs to no B, and let it have been assumed that B belongs to all or to some C. Then it is necessary that A should belong to no C or not to all C. But this is impossible (for let it be true and clear that A belongs to all C): consequently if this is [15] false, it is necessary that A should belong to some B. But if the other premiss assumed relates to A, no syllogism will be possible. Nor can a conclusion be drawn when the contrary of the conclusion is supposed, e.g. that A does not belong to some B. Clearly then we must suppose the contradictory.

Again suppose that A belongs to some B, and let it have been assumed that C belongs to [20] all A. It is necessary then that C should belong to some B. But let this be impossible, so that the supposition is false: in that case it is true that A belongs to no B. We may proceed in the same way if the proposition CA has been taken as negative. But if the premiss assumed concerns B, no syllogism will be possible. If the contrary is supposed, we shall have a syllogism and an impossible conclusion, but [25] the problem in hand is not proved. Suppose that A belongs to all B, and let it have been assumed that C belongs to all A. It is necessary then that C should belong to all B. But this is impossible, so that it is false that A belongs to all B. But we have not yet shown it to be necessary that A belongs to no B, if it does not [30] belong to all B. Similarly if the other premiss taken concerns B; we shall have a syllogism and a conclusion which is impossible, but the hypothesis is not refuted. Therefore it is the *contradictory* that we must suppose.

To prove that A does not belong to all B, we must suppose that it belongs to all B: for if A belongs to all B, and C to all A, then C belongs [35] to all B; so that if this is impossible, the hypothesis is false. Similarly if the other premiss assumed concerns B. The same results if the original proposition CA was negative: for thus also we get a syllogism. But if the negative proposition concerns B, nothing is proved. If the hypothesis is that A belongs not to all [40] but to some B, it is not proved that A belongs not to all B, but that it belongs to no B. For if A belongs to some B, and C to all A, then C will belong to some B. If then this is impossible, it is false that A belongs to some 62ª B; consequently it is true that A belongs to no B. But if this is proved, the truth is refuted as well; for the original conclusion was that A belongs to some B, and does not belong to some B. Further the impossible does not result from the hypothesis: for then the hypothe-[5] sis would be false, since it is impossible to draw a false conclusion from true premisses: but in fact it is true: for A belongs to some B. Consequently we must not suppose that A belongs to some B, but that it belongs to all B. Similarly if we should be proving that A does not belong to some B: for if 'not to belong to some' and 'to belong not to all' have the same [10] meaning, the demonstration of both will be identical.

It is clear then that not the contrary but the contradictory ought to be supposed in all the syllogisms. For thus we shall have necessity of inference, and the claim we make is one that will be generally accepted. For if of everything one or other of two contradictory statements holds good, then if it is proved that the negation does not hold, the affirmation must be [15] true. Again if it is not admitted that the affirmation is true, the claim that the negation is true will be generally accepted. But in neither way does it suit to maintain the *contrary*: for it is not necessary that if the universal negative is false, the universal affirmative should be true, nor is it generally accepted that if the one is false the other is true.

12

[20] It is clear then that in the first figure all problems except the universal affirmative are proved *per impossibile*. But in the middle and the last figures this also is proved. Suppose that A does not belong to all B, and let it have been assumed that A belongs to all C. If then [25] A belongs not to all B, but to all C, C will not belong to all B. But this is impossible (for suppose it to be clear that C belongs to all B): consequently the hypothesis is false. It is true then that A belongs to all B. But if the contrary is supposed, we shall have a syllogism and a result which is impossible: but the problem in hand is not proved. For if A be-[30] longs to no B, and to all C, C will belong to no B. This is impossible; so that it is false that A belongs to no B. But though this is false, it does not follow that it is true that A belongs to all B.

When A belongs to some B, suppose that A belongs to no B, and let A belong to all C. It is necessary then that C should belong to no [35] B. Consequently, if this is impossible, A must belong to some B. But if it is supposed that A does not belong to some B, we shall have the same results as in the first figure.[1]

Again suppose that A belongs to some B, and let A belong to no C. It is necessary then that C should not belong to some B. But originally it belonged to all B, consequently the hy-[40] pothesis is false: A then will belong to no B.

When A does not belong to all B, suppose it 62ᵇ does belong to all B, and to no C. It is necessary then that C should belong to no B. But this is impossible: so that it is true that A does not belong to all B. It is clear then that all the syllogisms can be formed in the middle figure.

13

[5] Similarly they can all be formed in the last figure. Suppose that A does not belong to some B, but C belongs to all B: then A does not belong to some C. If then this is impossible, it is false that A does not belong to some B; so that it is true that A belongs to all B. But if it is supposed that A belongs to no B, we shall have a syllogism and a conclusion which is impossible: but the problem in hand is not proved: [10] for if the contrary is supposed, we shall have the same results as before.[2]

---

[1] 61ᵇ 39-62ª 8.   [2] ª 28-32.

But to prove that A belongs to some B, this hypothesis must be made. If A belongs to no B, and C to some B, A will belong not to all C. If then this is false, it is true that A belongs to some B.

[15] When A belongs to no B, suppose A belongs to some B, and let it have been assumed that C belongs to all B. Then it is necessary that A should belong to some C. But *ex hypothesi* it belongs to no C, so that it is false that A belongs to some B. But if it is supposed that A belongs to all B, the problem is not proved.

But this hypothesis must be made if we are [20] to prove that A belongs not to all B. For if A belongs to all B and C to some B, then A belongs to some C. But this we assumed not to be so, so it is false that A belongs to all B. But in that case it is true that A belongs not to all B. If however it is assumed that A belongs to some B, we shall have the same result as before.[1]

[25] It is clear then that in all the syllogisms which proceed *per impossibile* the contradictory must be assumed. And it is plain that in the middle figure an affirmative conclusion, and in the last figure a universal conclusion, are proved in a way.

14

Demonstration *per impossibile* differs from os-[30] tensive proof in that it posits what it wishes to refute by reduction to a statement admitted to be false; whereas ostensive proof starts from admitted positions. Both, indeed, take two premisses that are admitted, but the latter takes the premisses from which the syllogism starts, the former takes one of these, along with the contradictory of the original [35] conclusion. Also in the ostensive proof it is not necessary that the conclusion should be known, nor that one should suppose beforehand that it is true or not: in the other it is necessary to suppose beforehand that it is not true. It makes no difference whether the conclusion is affirmative or negative; the method is the same in both cases. Everything which is concluded ostensively can be proved *per impos-*[40] *sibile*, and that which is proved *per impossibile* can be proved ostensively, through the same terms. Whenever the syllogism is formed in the first figure, the truth will be found in the middle or the last figure, if negative in the middle, if affirmative in the last. Whenever the syllogism is formed in the middle figure, the truth will be found in the first, whatever the problem may be. Whenever the [5] syllogism is formed in the last figure, the truth will be found in the first and middle figures, if affirmative in the first, if negative in the middle. Suppose that A has been proved to belong to no B, or not to all B, through the first figure. Then the hypothesis must have been that A belongs to some B, and the original [10] premisses that C belongs to all A and to no B. For thus the syllogism was made and the impossible conclusion reached. But this is the middle figure, if C belongs to all A and to no B. And it is clear from these premisses that A belongs to no B. Similarly if A has been proved [15] not to belong to all B. For the hypothesis is that A belongs to all B; and the original premisses are that C belongs to all A but not to all B. Similarly too, if the premiss CA should be negative: for thus also we have the middle figure. Again suppose it has been proved that A belongs to some B. The hypothesis here is [20] that A belongs to no B; and the original premisses that B belongs to all C, and A either to all or to some C: for in this way we shall get what is impossible. But if A and B belong to all C, we have the last figure. And it is clear from these premisses that A must belong to some B. Similarly if B or A should be assumed to belong to some C.

[25] Again suppose it has been proved in the middle figure that A belongs to all B. Then the hypothesis must have been that A belongs not to all B, and the original premisses that A belongs to all C, and C to all B: for thus we shall get what is impossible. But if A belongs to all C, and C to all B, we have the first figure. Similarly if it has been proved that A belongs [30] to some B: for the hypothesis then must have been that A belongs to no B, and the original premisses that A belongs to all C, and C to some B. If the syllogism is negative, the hypothesis must have been that A belongs to some B, and the original premisses that A belongs to no C, and C to all B, so that the first [35] figure results. If the syllogism is not universal, but proof has been given that A does not belong to some B, we may infer in the same way. The hypothesis is that A belongs to all B, the original premisses that A belongs to no C, and C belongs to some B: for thus we get the first figure.

[40] Again suppose it has been proved in the third figure that A belongs to all B. Then the hypothesis must have been that A belongs not to all B, and the original premisses that

---

[1] 61^b 39-62^a 8.

C belongs to all B, and A belongs to all C; for thus we shall get what is impossible. And the original premisses form the first figure. Similarly if the demonstration establishes a particular proposition: the hypothesis then must have been that A belongs to no B, and the original premisses that C belongs to some B, and A to all C. If the syllogism is negative, the hypothesis must have been that A belongs to some B, and the original premisses that C belongs to no A and to all B, and this is the middle figure. Similarly if the demonstration is not universal. The hypothesis will then be that A belongs to all B, the premisses that C belongs to no A and to some B: and this is the middle figure.

It is clear then that it is possible through the same terms to prove each of the problems ostensively as well. Similarly it will be possible if the syllogisms are ostensive to reduce them *ad impossibile* in the terms which have been taken, whenever the contradictory of the conclusion of the ostensive syllogism is taken as a premiss. For the syllogisms become identical with those which are obtained by means of conversion, so that we obtain immediately the figures through which each problem will be solved. It is clear then that every thesis can be proved in both ways, i.e. *per impossibile* and ostensively, and it is not possible to separate one method from the other.

15

In what figure it is possible to draw a conclusion from premisses which are opposed, and in what figure this is not possible, will be made clear in this way. Verbally four kinds of opposition are possible, viz. universal affirmative to universal negative, universal affirmative to particular negative, particular affirmative to universal negative, and particular affirmative to particular negative: but really there are only three: for the particular affirmative is only verbally opposed to the particular negative. Of the genuine opposites I call those which are universal *contraries*, the universal affirmative and the universal negative, e.g. 'every science is good', 'no science is good'; the others I call *contradictories*.

In the first figure no syllogism whether affirmative or negative can be made out of opposed premisses: no affirmative syllogism is possible because both premisses must be affirmative, but opposites are, the one affirmative, the other negative: no negative syllogism is possible because opposites affirm and deny the same predicate of the same subject, and the middle term in the first figure is not predicated of both extremes, but one thing is denied of it, and it is affirmed of something else: but such premisses are not opposed.

In the middle figure a syllogism can be made both of contradictories and of contraries. Let A stand for good, let B and C stand for science. If then one assumes that every science is good, and no science is good, A belongs to all B and to no C, so that B belongs to no C: no science then is a science. Similarly if after taking 'every science is good' one took 'the science of medicine is not good'; for A belongs to all B but to no C, so that a particular science will not be a science. Again, a particular science will not be a science if A belongs to all C but to no B, and B is science, C medicine, and A supposition: for after taking 'no science is supposition', one has assumed that a particular science is supposition. This syllogism differs from the preceding because the relations between the terms are reversed: before, the affirmative statement concerned B, now it concerns C. Similarly if one premiss is not universal: for the middle term is always that which is stated negatively of one extreme, and affirmatively of the other. Consequently it is possible that contradictories may lead to a conclusion, though not always or in every mood, but only if the terms subordinate to the middle are such that they are either identical or related as whole to part. Otherwise it is impossible: for the premisses cannot anyhow be either contraries or contradictories.

In the third figure an affirmative syllogism can never be made out of opposite premisses, for the reason given in reference to the first figure;[1] but a negative syllogism is possible whether the terms are universal or not. Let B and C stand for science, A for medicine. If then one should assume that all medicine is science and that no medicine is science, he has asumed that B belongs to all A and C to no A, so that a particular science will not be a science. Similarly if the premiss BA is not assumed universally. For if some medicine is science and again no medicine is science, it results that some science is not science. The premisses are contrary if the terms are taken universally; if one is particular, they are contradictory.

We must recognize that it is possible to take

[1] 63^b 33.

opposites in the way we said, viz. 'all science [35] is good' and 'no science is good' or 'some science is not good'. This does not usually escape notice. But it is possible to establish one part of a contradiction through other premisses, or to assume it in the way suggested in the *Topics*.[1] Since there are three oppositions to affirmative statements, it follows that opposite statements may be assumed as premisses in six ways; we may have either universal affirmative and negative, or universal [40] affirmative and particular negative, or particular affirmative and universal negative, and the relations between the terms may be 64^b reversed; e.g. A may belong to all B and to no C, or to all C and to no B, or to all of the one, not to all of the other; here too the relation between the terms may be reversed. Similarly in the third figure. So it is clear in [5] how many ways and in what figures a syllogism can be made by means of premisses which are opposed.

It is clear too that from false premisses it is possible to draw a true conclusion, as has been said before,[2] but it is not possible if the premisses are opposed. For the syllogism is always [10] contrary to the fact, e.g. if a thing is good, it is proved that it is not good, if an animal, that it is not an animal, because the syllogism springs out of a contradiction and the terms presupposed are either identical or related as whole and part. It is evident also that in fallacious reasonings nothing prevents a contradiction to the hypothesis from resulting, e.g. if something is odd, it is not odd. For the [15] syllogism owed its contrariety to its contradictory premisses; if we assume such premisses we shall get a result that contradicts our hypothesis. But we must recognize that contraries cannot be inferred from a single syllogism in such a way that we conclude that what is not good is good, or anything of that sort, [20] unless a self-contradictory premiss is at once asumed, e.g. 'every animal is white and not white', and we proceed 'man is an animal'. Either we must introduce the contradiction by an additional assumption, assuming, e.g., that every science is supposition, and then assuming 'Medicine is a science, but none of it is supposition' (which is the mode in which refuta-[25] tions are made), or we must argue from two syllogisms. In no other way than this, as was said before, is it possible that the premisses should be really contrary.

[1] VIII. 1.   [2] Chapters 2–4.

16

To beg and assume the original question is a species of failure to demonstrate the problem [30] proposed; but this happens in many ways. A man may not reason syllogistically at all, or he may argue from premisses which are less known or equally unknown, or he may establish the antecedent by means of its consequents; for demonstration proceeds from what is more certain and is prior. Now begging the question is none of these: but since we get to know some things naturally through themselves, and other things by means of some-[35] thing else (the first principles through themselves, what is subordinate to them through something else), whenever a man tries to prove what is not self-evident by means of itself, then he begs the original question. This may be done by assuming what is in question at once; it is also possible to make a transi-[40] tion to other things which would naturally be proved through the thesis proposed, and 65^a demonstrate it through them, e.g. if A should be proved through B, and B through C, though it was natural that C should be proved through A: for it turns out that those who reason thus are proving A by means of itself. This is what those persons do who suppose that they [5] are constructing parallel straight lines: for they fail to see that they are assuming facts which it is impossible to demonstrate unless the parallels exist. So it turns out that those who reason thus merely say a particular thing is, if it is: in this way everything will be self-evident. But that is impossible.

[10] If then it is uncertain whether A belongs to C, and also whether A belongs to B, and if one should assume that A does belong to B, it is not yet clear whether he begs the original question, but it is evident that he is not demonstrating: for what is as uncertain as the question to be answered cannot be a principle of a demonstration. If however B is so related to C that they are identical, or if they are plainly [15] convertible, or the one belongs to the other, the original question is begged. For one might equally well prove that A belongs to B through those terms if they are convertible. But if they are not convertible, it is the fact that they are not that prevents such a demonstration, not the method of demonstrating. But if one were to make the conversion, then he would be doing what we have described[3]

[3] In ll. 1-4.

and effecting a reciprocal proof with three propositions.

Similarly if he should assume that B be[20]longs to C, this being as uncertain as the question whether A belongs to C, the question is not yet begged, but no demonstration is made. If however A and B are identical either because they are convertible or because A follows B, then the question is begged for the same reason as before. For we have explained the meaning of begging the question, viz. [25] proving that which is not self-evident by means of itself.

If then begging the question is proving what is not self-evident by means of itself, in other words failing to prove when the failure is due to the thesis to be proved and the premiss through which it is proved being equally uncertain, either because predicates which are identical belong to the same subject, or because the same predicate belongs to subjects which are identical, the question may be begged in [30] the middle and third figures in both ways, though, if the syllogism is affirmative, only in the third and first figures. If the syllogism is negative, the question is begged when identical predicates are denied of the same subject; and both premisses do not beg the question indifferently (in a similar way the question may be begged in the middle figure), because the terms in negative syllogisms are not converti[35]ble. In scientific demonstrations the question is begged when the terms are really related in the manner described, in dialectical arguments when they are according to common opinion so related.

17

The objection that 'this is not the reason why the result is false', which we frequently make in argument, is made primarily in the case of [40] a *reductio ad impossibile*, to rebut the proposition which was being proved by the reduction. For unless a man has contradicted this proposition he will not say, 'False cause', but urge that something false has been assumed in the earlier parts of the argument; nor will he use the formula in the case of an ostensive proof; for here what one denies is not assumed as a premiss. Further when anything is refuted ostensively by the terms ABC, it can[5] not be objected that the syllogism does not depend on the assumption laid down. For we use the expression 'false cause', when the syllogism is concluded in spite of the refutation of this position; but that is not possible in ostensive proofs: since if an assumption is refuted, a syllogism can no longer be drawn in reference to it. It is clear then that the expression 'false [10] cause' can only be used in the case of a *reductio ad impossibile*, and when the original hypothesis is so related to the impossible conclusion, that the conclusion results indifferently whether the hypothesis is made or not. The most obvious case of the irrelevance of an assumption to a conclusion which is false is when a syllogism drawn from middle terms to an [15] impossible conclusion is independent of the hypothesis, as we have explained in the *Topics*.[1] For to put that which is not the cause as the cause, is just this: e.g. if a man, wishing to prove that the diagonal of the square is incommensurate with the side, should try to prove Zeno's theorem that motion is impossible, and so establish a *reductio ad impossi*[20]*bile*: for Zeno's false theorem has no connexion at all with the original assumption. Another case is where the impossible conclusion is connected with the hypothesis, but does not result from it. This may happen whether one traces the connexion upwards or downwards, [25] e.g. if it is laid down that A belongs to B, B to C, and C to D, and it should be false that B belongs to D: for if we eliminated A and assumed all the same that B belongs to C and C to D, the false conclusion would not depend on the original hypothesis. Or again trace the connexion upwards; e.g. suppose that A [30] belongs to B, E to A, and F to E, it being false that F belongs to A. In this way too the impossible conclusion would result, though the original hypothesis were eliminated. But the impossible conclusion ought to be connected with the original terms: in this way it will depend on the hypothesis, e.g. when one traces the connexion downwards, the impossible con[35]clusion must be connected with that term which is predicate in the hypothesis: for if it is impossible that A should belong to D, the false conclusion will no longer result after A has been eliminated. If one traces the connexion upwards, the impossible conclusion must be connected with that term which is subject in the hypothesis: for if it is impossible that F should belong to B, the impossible conclusion will disappear if B is eliminated. [40] Similarly when the syllogisms are negative.

It is clear then that when the impossibility is not related to the original terms, the false conclusion does not result on account of the

[1] *On Sophistical Refutations*, 167^b 21-36.

assumption. Or perhaps even so it may sometimes be independent. For if it were laid down that A belongs not to B but to K, and that K be- [5] longs to C and C to D, the impossible conclusion would still stand. Similarly if one takes the terms in an ascending series. Consequently since the impossibility results whether the first assumption is suppressed or not, it would appear to be independent of that assumption. Or perhaps we ought not to understand the statement that the false conclusion results independently of the assumption, in the sense that if something else were supposed the impossi- [10] bility would result; but rather we mean that when the first assumption is eliminated, the same impossibility results through the remaining premises; since it is not perhaps absurd that the same false result should follow from several hypotheses, e.g. that parallels meet, both on the assumption that the interior angle is greater than the exterior and on the assumption that a triangle contains more than [15] two right angles.

18

A false argument depends on the first false statement in it. Every syllogism is made out of two or more premises. If then the false conclusion is drawn from two premises, one or both of them must be false: for (as we proved[1]) a false syllogism cannot be drawn from true [20] premises. But if the premises are more than two, e.g. if C is established through A and B, and these through D, E, F, and G, one of these higher propositions must be false, and on this the argument depends: for A and B are inferred by means of D, E, F, and G. Therefore the conclusion and the error results from one of them.

19

[25] In order to avoid having a syllogism drawn against us we must take care, whenever an opponent asks us to admit the reason without the conclusions, not to grant him the same term twice over in his premises, since we know that a syllogism cannot be drawn without a middle term, and that term which is stated more than once is the middle. How we ought to watch the middle in reference to each [30] conclusion, is evident from our knowing what kind of thesis is proved in each figure. This will not escape us since we know how we are maintaining the argument.

That which we urge men to beware of in their admissions, they ought in attack to try to conceal. This will be possible first, if, instead [35] of drawing the conclusions of preliminary syllogisms, they take the necessary premises and leave the conclusions in the dark; secondly if instead of inviting assent to propositions which are closely connected they take as far as possible those that are not connected by middle terms. For example suppose that A is to be inferred to be true of F; $B, C, D,$ and E being middle terms. One ought then to ask whether A belongs to B, and next whether D belongs to E, instead of asking whether B be- [40] longs to C; after that he may ask whether B belongs to C, and so on. If the syllogism is drawn through one middle term, he ought to begin with that: in this way he will most likely deceive his opponent.

20

Since we know when a syllogism can be [5] formed and how its terms must be related, it is clear when refutation will be possible and when impossible. A refutation is possible whether everything is conceded, or the answers alternate (one, I mean, being affirmative, the other negative). For as has been shown a syllogism is possible whether the terms are related in affirmative propositions or one proposition is affirmative, the other negative: consequently, if what is laid down is contrary to [10] the conclusion, a refutation must take place: for a refutation is a syllogism which establishes the contradictory. But if nothing is conceded, a refutation is impossible: for no syllogism is possible (as we saw[2]) when all the terms are negative: therefore no refutation is possible. For if a refutation were possible, a [15] syllogism must be possible; although if a syllogism is possible it does not follow that a refutation is possible. Similarly refutation is not possible if nothing is conceded universally: since the fields of refutation and syllogism are defined in the same way.

21

It sometimes happens that just as we are deceived in the arrangement of the terms, so error may arise in our thought about them, [20] e.g. if it is possible that the same predicate should belong to more than one subject immediately, but although knowing the one, a man may forget the other and think the opposite true. Suppose that A belongs to B and to C in virtue of their nature, and that B and C

[1] 53^b 11-25.
[2] 41^b 6.

belong to all D in the same way. If then a man thinks that A belongs to all B, and B to D, but A to no C, and C to all D, he will both know [25] and not know the same thing in respect of the same thing. Again if a man were to make a mistake about the members of a single series; e.g. suppose A belongs to B, B to C, and C to D, but some one thinks that A belongs to all B, but to no C: he will both know that A [30] belongs to D, and think that it does not. Does he then maintain after this simply that what he knows, he does not think? For he knows in a way that A belongs to C through B, since the part is included in the whole; so that what he knows in a way, this he maintains he does not think at all: but that is impossible.

[35] In the former case, where the middle term does not belong to the same series, it is not possible to think both the premisses with reference to each of the two middle terms: e.g. that A belongs to all B, but to no C, and both B and C belong to all D. For it turns out that the first premiss of the one syllogism is either wholly or partially contrary to the first premiss of the other. For if he thinks that A belongs to [40] everything to which B belongs, and he 67ᵃ knows that B belongs to D, then he knows that A belongs to D. Consequently if again he thinks that A belongs to nothing to which C belongs, he thinks that A does not belong to some of that to which B belongs; but if he thinks that A belongs to everything to which B belongs, and again thinks that A does not belong to some of that to which B belongs, these [5] beliefs are wholly or partially contrary. In this way then it is not possible to think; but nothing prevents a man thinking one premiss of each syllogism or both premisses of one of the two syllogisms: e.g. A belongs to all B, and B to D, and again A belongs to no C. An error of this kind is similar to the error into which we fall concerning particulars: e.g. if A [10] belongs to all B, and B to all C, A will belong to all C. If then a man knows that A belongs to everything to which B belongs, he knows that A belongs to C. But nothing prevents his being ignorant that C exists; e.g. let A stand for two right angles, B for triangle, C for a particular diagram of a triangle. A man might think that C did not exist, though [15] he knew that every triangle contains two right angles; consequently he will know and not know the same thing at the same time. For the expression 'to know that every triangle has its angles equal to two right angles' is ambiguous, meaning to have the knowledge either of the universal or of the particulars. Thus then he knows that C contains two right angles with a knowledge of the universal, but [20] not with a knowledge of the particulars; consequently his knowledge will not be contrary to his ignorance. The argument in the *Meno*[1] that learning is recollection may be criticized in a similar way. For it never happens that a man starts with a foreknowledge of the particular, but along with the process of being led to see the general principle he receives a knowledge of the particulars, by an act (as it were) of recognition. For we know some things directly; e.g. that the angles are equal [25] to two right angles, if we know that the figure is a triangle. Similarly in all other cases.

By a knowledge of the universal then we see the particulars, but we do not know them by the kind of knowledge which is proper to them; consequently it is possible that we may make mistakes about them, but not that we should have the knowledge and error that are contrary to one another: rather we have the knowledge of the universal but make a mis- [30] take in apprehending the particular. Similarly in the cases stated above.[2] The error in respect of the middle term is not contrary to the knowledge obtained through the syllogism, nor is the thought in respect of one middle term contrary to that in respect of the other. Nothing prevents a man who knows both that A belongs to the whole of B, and that B again belongs to C, thinking that A does not belong [35] to C, e.g. knowing that every mule is sterile and that this is a mule, and thinking that this animal is with foal: for he does not know that A belongs to C, unless he considers the two propositions together. So it is evident that if he knows the one and does not know the other, he will fall into error. And this is the relation of knowledge of the universal to 67ᵇ knowledge of the particular. For we know no sensible thing, once it has passed beyond the range of our senses, even if we happen to have perceived it, except by means of the universal *and* the possession of the knowledge which is proper to the particular, but without the actual exercise of that knowledge. For to know is used in three senses: it may mean either to have knowledge of the universal or to [5] have knowledge proper to the matter in hand or to exercise such knowledge: consequently three kinds of error also are possible. Nothing then prevents a man both knowing

---
[1] Plato, *Meno*, 81.   [2] 66ᵇ 20-6, 26-30

and being mistaken about the same thing, provided that his knowledge and his error are not contrary. And this happens also to the man whose knowledge is limited to each of the premisses and who has not previously considered the particular question. For when he thinks that the mule is with foal he has not the knowledge in the sense of its actual ex-[10]ercise, nor on the other hand has his thought caused an error contrary to his knowledge: for the error contrary to the knowledge of the universal would be a syllogism.

But he who thinks the essence of good is the essence of bad will think the same thing to be the essence of good and the essence of bad. Let A stand for the essence of good and B for the essence of bad, and again C for the essence of [15] good. Since then he thinks B and C identical, he will think that C is B, and similarly that B is A, consequently that C is A. For just as we saw that if B is *true* of all of which C is *true*, and A is true of all of which B is true, A is true of C, similarly with the word 'think'. [20] Similarly also with the word 'is'; for we saw that if C is the same as B, and B as A, C is the same as A. Similarly therefore with 'opine'. Perhaps then this is necessary if a man will grant the first point. But presumably that is false, that any one could suppose the essence of good to be the essence of bad, save [25] incidentally. For it is possible to think this in many different ways. But we must consider this matter better.

22

Whenever the extremes are convertible it is necessary that the middle should be convertible with both. For if A belongs to C through B, then if A and C are convertible and C belongs to everything to which A belongs, B is [30] convertible with A, and B belongs to everything to which A belongs, through C as middle, and C is convertible with B through A as middle. Similarly if the conclusion is negative, e.g. if B belongs to C, but A does not belong to B, neither will A belong to C. If then B is convertible with A, C will be convertible [35] with A. Suppose B does not belong to A; neither then will C: for *ex hypothesi* B belonged to all C. And if C is convertible with B, B is convertible also with A: for C is said of that of all of which B is said. And if C is convertible in relation to A and to B, B also is convertible in relation to A. For C belongs to that to which B belongs: but C does not belong to that to which A belongs. And this alone starts from the conclusion; the preceding moods do not do so as in the affirmative syllogism. Again if A and B are convertible, and [5] similarly C and D, and if A or C must belong to anything whatever, then B and D will be such that one or other belongs to anything whatever. For since B belongs to that to which A belongs, and D belongs to that to which C belongs, and since A or C belongs to everything, but not together, it is clear that B or D belongs to everything, but not together. For example if that which is uncreated is incorruptible and that which is incorruptible is uncreated, it is necessary that what is created [10] should be corruptible and what is corruptible should have been created. For two syllogisms have been put together. Again if A or B belongs to everything and if C or D belongs to everything, but they cannot belong together, then when A and C are convertible B and D are convertible. For if B does not belong to something to which D belongs, it is clear that [15] A belongs to it. But if A then C: for they are convertible. Therefore C and D belong together. But this is impossible. When A belongs to the whole of B and to C and is affirmed of nothing else, and B also belongs to all C, it is necessary that A and B should be convertible: for since A is said of B and C only, and B [20] is affirmed both of itself and of C, it is clear that B will be said of everything of which A is said, except A itself. Again when A and B belong to the whole of C, and C is convertible with B, it is necessary that A should belong to all B: for since A belongs to all C, and C to B by conversion, A will belong to all B.

[25] When, of two opposites A and B, A is preferable to B, and similarly D is preferable to C, then if A and C together are preferable to B and D together, A must be preferable to D. For A is an object of desire to the same extent as B is an object of aversion, since they are opposites: and C is similarly related to D, since they also are opposites. If then A is an [30] object of desire to the same extent as D, B is an object of aversion to the same extent as C (since each is to the same extent as each—the one an object of aversion, the other an object of desire). Therefore both A and C together, and B and D together, will be equally objects of desire or aversion. But since A and C are preferable to B and D, A cannot be equally desirable with D; for then B along with D would be equally desirable with A along with [35] C. But if D is preferable to A, then B must be less an object of aversion than C: for

the less is opposed to the less. But the greater good and lesser evil are preferable to the lesser good and greater evil: the whole BD then is preferable to the whole AC. But *ex hypothesi* this is not so. A then is preferable to D, and C consequently is less an object of aversion than B. If then every lover in virtue of his [40] love would prefer A, viz. that the beloved should be such as to grant a favour, and yet should not grant it (for which C stands), to the beloved's granting the favour (repre-**68ᵇ** sented by D) without being such as to grant it (represented by B), it is clear that A (being of such a nature) is preferable to granting the favour. To receive affection then is preferable in love to sexual intercourse. Love then is more dependent on friendship than on intercourse. And if it is most dependent on [5] receiving affection, then this is its end. Intercourse then either is not an end at all or is an end relative to the further end, the receiving of affection. And indeed the same is true of the other desires and arts.

23

It is clear then how the terms are related in conversion, and in respect of being in a higher degree objects of aversion or of desire. We [10] must now state that not only dialectical and demonstrative syllogisms are formed by means of the aforesaid figures, but also rhetorical syllogisms and in general any form of persuasion, however it may be presented. For every belief comes either through syllogism or from induction.

[15] Now induction, or rather the syllogism which springs out of induction, consists in establishing syllogistically a relation between one extreme and the middle by means of the other extreme, e.g. if B is the middle term between A and C, it consists in proving through C that A belongs to B. For this is the manner in which we make inductions. For example let A stand for long-lived, B for bileless, and C [20] for the particular long-lived animals, e.g. man, horse, mule. A then belongs to the whole of C: for whatever is bileless is long-lived. But B also ('not possessing bile') belongs to all C. If then C is convertible with B, and the middle term is not wider in extension, it is necessary that A should belong to B. For it has already [25] been proved[1] that if two things belong to the same thing, and the extreme is convertible with one of them, then the other predicate will belong to the predicate that is converted.

[1] ᵃ 21-25.

But we must apprehend C as made up of all the particulars. For induction proceeds through an enumeration of all the cases.

[30] Such is the syllogism which establishes the first and immediate premiss: for where there is a middle term the syllogism proceeds through the middle term; when there is no middle term, through induction. And in a way induction is opposed to syllogism: for the latter proves the major term to belong to the third term by means of the middle, the former proves the major to belong to the middle [35] by means of the third. In the order of nature, syllogism through the middle term is prior and better known, but syllogism through induction is clearer to *us*.

24

We have an 'example' when the major term is proved to belong to the middle by means of a term which resembles the third. It ought to be known both that the middle belongs to the [40] third term, and that the first belongs to that which resembles the third. For example let A be evil, B making war against neigh-**69ᵃ** bours, C Athenians against Thebans, D Thebans against Phocians. If then we wish to prove that to fight with the Thebans is an evil, we must assume that to fight against neighbours is an evil. Evidence of this is obtained from similar cases, e.g. that the war against [5] the Phocians was an evil to the Thebans. Since then to fight against neighbours is an evil, and to fight against the Thebans is to fight against neighbours, it is clear that to fight against the Thebans is an evil. Now it is clear that B belongs to C and to D (for both are cases of making war upon one's neighbours) and that A belongs to D (for the war against [10] the Phocians did not turn out well for the Thebans): but that A belongs to B will be proved through D. Similarly if the belief in the relation of the middle term to the extreme should be produced by several similar cases. Clearly then to argue by example is neither like reasoning from part to whole, nor like reasoning from whole to part, but rather rea-[15] soning from part to part, when both particulars are subordinate to the same term, and one of them is known. It differs from induction, because induction starting from all the particular cases proves (as we saw[2]) that the major term belongs to the middle, and does not apply the syllogistic conclusion to the minor term, whereas argument by example does

[2] Chapter 23.

25

[20] By reduction we mean an argument in which the first term clearly belongs to the middle, but the relation of the middle to the last term is uncertain though equally or more probable than the conclusion; or again an argument in which the terms intermediate between the last term and the middle are few. For in any of these cases it turns out that we approach more nearly to knowledge. For example let A [25] stand for what can be taught, B for knowledge, C for justice. Now it is clear that knowledge can be taught: but it is uncertain whether virtue is knowledge. If now the statement BC is equally or more probable than AC, we have a reduction: for we are nearer to knowledge, since we have taken a new term, being so far without knowledge that A belongs to C. Or again suppose that the terms intermediate between B and C are few: for [30] thus too we are nearer knowledge. For example let D stand for squaring, E for rectilinear figure, F for circle. If there were only one term intermediate between E and F (viz. that the circle is made equal to a rectilinear figure by the help of lunules), we should be near to knowledge. But when BC is not [35] more probable than AC, and the intermediate terms are not few, I do not call this reduction: nor again when the statement BC is immediate: for such a statement is knowledge.

26

An objection is a premiss contrary to a premiss. It differs from a premiss, because it may be particular, but a premiss either cannot be particular at all or not in universal syllogisms. An objection is brought in two ways and through two figures; in two ways because every objection is either universal or particular, by two figures because objections are brought in opposition to the premiss, and opposites can [5] be proved only in the first and third figures. If a man maintains a universal affirmative, we reply with a universal or a particular negative; the former is proved from the first figure, the latter from the third. For example let A stand for there being a single science, B for contraries. If a man premises that contraries are subjects of a single science, the ob- [10] jection may be either that opposites are never subjects of a single science, and contraries are opposites, so that we get the first figure, or that the knowable and the unknowable are not subjects of a single science: this proof is in the third figure: for it is true of C (the knowable and the unknowable) that they are contraries, and it is false that they are the subjects of a single science.

[15] Similarly if the premiss objected to is negative. For if a man maintains that contraries are not subjects of a single science, we reply either that all opposites or that certain contraries, e.g. what is healthy and what is sickly, are subjects of the same science: the former argument issues from the first, the latter from the third figure.

In general if a man urges a universal objec- [20] tion he must frame his contradiction with reference to the universal of the terms taken by his opponent, e.g. if a man maintains that *contraries* are not subjects of the same science, his opponent must reply that there is a single science of all *opposites*. Thus we must have the first figure: for the term which embraces the original subject becomes the middle term.

If the objection is particular, the objector must frame his contradiction with reference to a term relatively to which the subject of his opponent's premiss is universal, e.g. he will point [25] out that the knowable and the unknowable are not subjects of the same science: 'contraries' is universal relatively to these. And we have the third figure: for the particular term assumed is middle, e.g. the knowable and the unknowable. Premisses from which it is possible to draw the contrary conclusion are what we start from when we try to make objec- [30] tions. Consequently we bring objections in these figures only: for in them only are opposite syllogisms possible, since the second figure cannot produce an affirmative conclusion.

Besides, an objection in the middle figure would require a fuller argument, e.g. if it should not be granted that A belongs to B, because C does not follow B. This can be made [35] clear only by other premisses. But an objection ought not to turn off into other things, but have its new premiss quite clear immediately. For this reason also this is the only figure from which proof by signs cannot be obtained.

We must consider later the other kinds of objection, namely the objection from contraries, from similars, and from common opinion, and inquire whether a particular objection cannot be elicited from the first figure or a negative objection from the second.

27

A probability and a sign are not identical, but a probability is a generally approved proposition: what men know to happen or not to [5] happen, to be or not to be, for the most part thus and thus, is a probability, e.g. 'the envious hate', 'the beloved show affection'. A sign means a demonstrative proposition necessary or generally approved: for anything such that when it is another thing is, or when it has come into being the other has come into being before or after, is a sign of the other's being or having come into being. Now an enthymeme [10] is a syllogism starting from probabilities or signs, and a sign may be taken in three ways, corresponding to the position of the middle term in the figures. For it may be taken as in the first figure or the second or the third. For example the proof that a woman is with child because she has milk is in the first figure: for [15] to have milk is the middle term. Let A represent to be with child, B to have milk, C woman. The proof that wise men are good, since Pittacus is good, comes through the last figure. Let A stand for good, B for wise men, C for Pittacus. It is true then to affirm both A and B of C: only men do not say the latter, because they know it, though they state the for- [20] mer. The proof that a woman is with child because she is pale is meant to come through the middle figure: for since paleness follows women with child and is a concomitant of this woman, people suppose it has been proved that she is with child. Let A stand for paleness, B for being with child, C for woman. Now if the one proposition is stated, we have [25] only a sign, but if the other is stated as well, a syllogism, e.g. 'Pittacus is generous, since ambitious men are generous and Pittacus is ambitious.' Or again 'Wise men are good, since Pittacus is not only good but wise.' In this way then syllogisms are formed, only that which proceeds through the first figure is irrefutable if it is true (for it is universal), that which [30] proceeds through the last figure is refutable even if the conclusion is true, since the syllogism is not universal nor correlative to the matter in question: for though Pittacus is good, it is not therefore necessary that all other wise men should be good. But the syllogism which proceeds through the middle figure is always refutable in any case: for a syllogism can never [35] be formed when the terms are related in this way: for though a woman with child is pale, and this woman also is pale, it is not necessary that she should be with child. Truth then may be found in signs whatever their kind, but they have the differences we have stated.

70^b We must either divide signs in the way stated, and among them designate the middle term as the index (for people call that the index which makes us know, and the middle term above all has this character), or else we must call the arguments derived from the extremes signs, that derived from the middle term the index: for that which is proved [5] through the first figure is most generally accepted and most true.

It is possible to infer character from features, if it is granted that the body and the soul are changed together by the natural affections: I say 'natural', for though perhaps by learning music a man has made some change in his [10] soul, this is not one of those affections which are natural to us; rather I refer to passions and desires when I speak of natural emotions. If then this were granted and also that for each change there is a corresponding sign, and we could state the affection and sign proper to each kind of animal, we shall be able to infer character from features. For if there is an affection which belongs properly to an individ- [15] ual kind, e.g. courage to lions, it is necessary that there should be a sign of it: for *ex hypothesi* body and soul are affected together. Suppose this sign is the possession of large extremities: this may belong to other kinds also though not universally. For the sign is proper in the sense stated, because the affection is proper to the whole kind, though not proper to it alone, according to our usual manner of [20] speaking. The same thing then will be found in another kind, and man may be brave, and some other kinds of animal as well. They will then have the sign: for *ex hypothesi* there is one sign corresponding to each affection. If then this is so, and we can collect signs of this sort in these animals which have only one affection proper to them—but each affection has its sign, since it is necessary that it should have [25] a single sign—we shall then be able to infer character from features. But if the kind as a whole has two properties, e.g. if the lion is both brave and generous, how shall we know which of the signs which are its proper concomitants is the sign of a particular affection? Perhaps if both belong to some other kind though not to the whole of it, and if, in those kinds in which each is found though not in the whole of their members, some members possess one of the affections and not the other: e.g. if a man is brave but not generous, but [30] possesses, of the two signs, large extremities, it is clear that this is the sign of courage in the lion also. To judge character from features, then, is possible in the first figure if the middle term is convertible with the first extreme, but is wider than the third term and not convertible with it: e.g. let A stand for courage, B for large extremities, and C for lion. [35] B then belongs to everything to which C belongs, but also to others. But A belongs to everything to which B belongs, and to nothing besides, but is convertible with B: otherwise, there would not be a single sign correlative with each affection.

CONTENTS: POSTERIOR ANALYTICS

BOOK I

CHAP.		BERLIN NOS.
1.	The student's need of pre-existent knowledge; its nature	71^a 1
2.	The nature of scientific knowledge; the conditions of demonstration; the meaning of Contradiction, Enunciation, Proposition, Basic truth, Thesis, Axiom, Hypothesis, Definition	71^b 8
3.	Two erroneous views of scientific knowledge; the futility of circular demonstration	72^b 5
4.	Types of attribute: 'True in every instance', 'Essential', 'Commensurate and universal', 'Accidental'	73^a 21
5.	Causes through which we erroneously suppose a conclusion commensurate and universal when it is not; how to avoid this error	74^a 4
6.	The premisses of demonstration must be necessary and essential	74^b 5
7.	The premisses and conclusion of a demonstration must fall within a single genus; the three constituent elements of demonstration	75^a 38
8.	Only eternal connexions can be demonstrated	75^b 21
9.	Demonstration must proceed from the basic premisses peculiar to each science, except in the case of subalternate sciences	75^b 36
10.	The different sorts of basic truth	76^a 31
11.	The function of the common axioms in demonstration	77^a 5
12.	The scientific premiss in interrogative form; formal fallacy; the growth of a science	77^a 36
13.	The difference between knowledge of the fact and knowledge of the reasoned fact	78^a 22
14.	The first figure is the true type of scientific syllogism	79^a 16
15.	Immediate negative propositions	79^a 33
16.	Ignorance as erroneous inference when the premisses are immediate	79^b 23
17.	Ignorance as erroneous inference when the premisses are mediate	80^b 16
18.	Ignorance as the negation of knowledge, e.g. such as must result from the lack of a sense	81^a 37
19.	Can demonstration develop an indefinite regress of premisses, (1) supposing the primary attribute fixed? (2) supposing the ultimate subject fixed? (3) supposing both primary attribute and ultimate subject fixed?	81^b 10
20.	If (1) and (2) are answered negatively, the answer to (3) must be in the negative	82^a 21
21.	If affirmative demonstration cannot develop an indefinite regress, then negative demonstration cannot	82^a 36
22.	Dialectical and analytic proofs that the answer to both (1) and (2) is in the negative	82^b 36
23.	Corollaries	84^b 3
24.	The superiority of universal to particular demonstration	85^a 12
25.	The superiority of affirmative to negative demonstration	86^a 31
26.	The superiority of affirmative and negative demonstration to *reductio ad impossibile*	87^a 1
27.	The more abstract science is the prior and the more accurate science	87^a 31
28.	What constitutes the unity of a science	87^a 38
29.	How there may be several demonstrations of one connexion	87^b 5
30.	Chance conjunctions are not demonstrable	87^b 18
31.	There can be no demonstration through sense-perception	87^b 27
32.	Different sciences must possess different basic truths	88^a 17
33.	The relation of opinion to knowledge	88^b 30
34.	Quick wit: the faculty of instantaneously hitting upon the middle term	89^b 10

BOOK II

1.	The four possible forms of inquiry	89^b 21
2.	They all concern the middle term	89^b 36
3.	The difference between definition and demonstration	90^a 35
4.	Essential nature cannot be demonstrated	91^a 12
5.	Essential nature cannot be inferred by division	91^b 11
6.	Attempts to prove a thing's essential nature either hypothetically or through the definition of its contrary beg the question	92^a 6
7.	Definition does not touch the question of existence; demonstration proves existence; hence definition cannot demonstrate	92^a 33
8.	Yet only demonstration can reveal the	93^a 1

essential nature of things which have a cause other than themselves—i.e. attributes

9. That which is self-caused—the basic premisses—is grasped immediately $93^b\ 21$
10. Types of definition $93^b\ 28$
11. The several causes as middle terms $94^a\ 20$
12. The question of time in causal inference $95^a\ 10$
13. How to obtain the definition of a substance; the use of division for this purpose $96^a\ 20$
14. How to select a connexion for demonstration $98^a\ 1$
15. One middle will often serve to prove several connexions $98^a\ 24$
16. If the effect is present, is the cause also present? Plurality of causes is impossible where cause and effect are commensurate $98^a\ 35$
17. Different causes may produce the same effect, but not in things specifically identical $99^a\ 1$
18. The true cause of a connexion is the proximate and not the more universal cause $99^b\ 7$
19. How the individual mind comes to know the basic truths $99^b\ 15$

POSTERIOR ANALYTICS

BOOK I

1

71ª ALL instruction given or received by way of argument proceeds from pre-existent knowledge. This becomes evident upon a survey of all the species of such instruction. The mathematical sciences and all other speculative disciplines are acquired in this way, and so are the two forms of dialectical reasoning, syllogistic [5] and inductive; for each of these latter make use of old knowledge to impart new, the syllogism assuming an audience that accepts its premisses, induction exhibiting the universal as implicit in the clearly known particular. Again, the persuasion exerted by rhetorical arguments is in principle the same, since they [10] use either example, a kind of induction, or enthymeme, a form of syllogism.

The pre-existent knowledge required is of two kinds. In some cases admission of the fact must be assumed, in others comprehension of the meaning of the term used, and sometimes both assumptions are essential. Thus, we assume that every predicate can be either truly affirmed or truly denied of any subject, and that 'triangle' means so and so; as regards 'unit' we have to make the double assumption [15] of the meaning of the word and the existence of the thing. The reason is that these several objects are not equally obvious to us. Recognition of a truth may in some cases contain as factors both previous knowledge and also knowledge acquired simultaneously with that recognition—knowledge, this latter, of the particulars actually falling under the universal and therein already virtually known. For example, the student knew beforehand that the [20] angles of every triangle are equal to two right angles; but it was only at the actual moment at which he was being led on to recognize this as true in the instance before him that he came to know 'this figure inscribed in the semicircle' to be a triangle. For some things (viz. the singulars finally reached which are not predicable of anything else as subject) are only learnt in this way, i.e. there is here no recognition through a middle of a minor term as subject to a major. Before he was led on to recognition or before he actually drew a con-[25]clusion, we should perhaps say that in a manner he knew, in a manner not.

If he did not in an unqualified sense of the term *know* the existence of this triangle, how could he *know* without qualification that its angles were equal to two right angles? No: clearly he *knows* not without qualification but only in the sense that he *knows* universally. If this distinction is not drawn, we are faced with the dilemma in the *Meno*:[1] either a man will learn nothing or what he already knows; for [30] we cannot accept the solution which some people offer. A man is asked, 'Do you, or do you not, know that every pair is even?' He says he does know it. The questioner then produces a particular pair, of the existence, and so *a fortiori* of the evenness, of which he was unaware. The solution which some people offer is to assert that they do not know that every pair is even, but only that everything which they 71ᵇ know to be a pair is even: yet what they know to be even is that of which they have demonstrated evenness, i.e. what they made the subject of their premiss, viz. not merely every triangle or number which they know to be such, but any and every number or triangle without reservation. For no premiss is ever couched in the form 'every number which you know to be such', or 'every rectilinear figure which you know to be such': the predicate is always [5] construed as applicable to any and every instance of the thing. On the other hand, I imagine there is nothing to prevent a man in one sense knowing what he is learning, in another not knowing it. The strange thing would be, not if in some sense he knew what he was learning, but if he were to know it in that precise sense and manner in which he was learning it.

2

We suppose ourselves to possess unqualified scientific knowledge of a thing, as opposed to

---

NOTE: The bold face numbers and letters are approximate indications of the pages and columns of the standard Berlin Greek text; the bracketed numbers, of the lines in the Greek text; they are here assigned as they are assigned in the Oxford translation.

[1] Plato, *Meno*, 80

knowing it in the accidental way in which the sophist knows, when we think that we know the cause on which the fact depends, as the cause of that fact and of no other, and, further, that the fact could not be other than it is. Now that scientific knowing is something of this sort is evident—witness both those who falsely claim it and those who actually possess it, since the former merely imagine themselves to be, while the latter are also actually, in the condition described. Consequently the proper object of unqualified scientific knowledge is something which cannot be other than it is.

There may be another manner of knowing as well—that will be discussed later.[1] What I now assert is that at all events we do know by demonstration. By demonstration I mean a syllogism productive of scientific knowledge, a syllogism, that is, the grasp of which is *eo ipso* such knowledge. Assuming then that my thesis as to the nature of scientific knowing is correct, the premisses of demonstrated knowledge must be true, primary, immediate, better known than and prior to the conclusion, which is further related to them as effect to cause. Unless these conditions are satisfied, the basic truths will not be 'appropriate' to the conclusion. Syllogism there may indeed be without these conditions, but such syllogism, not being productive of scientific knowledge, will not be demonstration. The premisses must be true: for that which is non-existent cannot be known—we cannot know, e.g. that the diagonal of a square is commensurate with its side. The premisses must be primary and indemonstrable; otherwise they will require demonstration in order to be known, since to have knowledge, if it be not accidental knowledge, of things which are demonstrable, means precisely to have a demonstration of them. The premisses must be the causes of the conclusion, better known than it, and prior to it; its causes, since we possess scientific knowledge of a thing only when we know its cause; prior, in order to be causes; antecedently known, this antecedent knowledge being not our mere understanding of the meaning, but knowledge of the fact as well. Now 'prior' and 'better known' are ambiguous terms, for there is a difference between what is prior and better known in the order of being and what is prior and better known to man. I mean that objects nearer to sense are prior and better known to man; objects without qualification prior and better known are those further from sense. Now the most universal causes are furthest from sense and particular causes are nearest to sense, and they are thus exactly opposed to one another. In saying that the premisses of demonstrated knowledge must be primary, I mean that they must be the 'appropriate' basic truths, for I identify primary premiss and basic truth. A 'basic truth' in a demonstration is an immediate proposition. An immediate proposition is one which has no other proposition prior to it. A proposition is either part of an enunciation, i.e. it predicates a single attribute of a single subject. If a proposition is dialectical, it assumes either part indifferently; if it is demonstrative, it lays down one part to the definite exclusion of the other because that part is true. The term 'enunciation' denotes either part of a contradiction indifferently. A contradiction is an opposition which of its own nature excludes a middle. The part of a contradiction which conjoins a predicate with a subject is an affirmation; the part disjoining them is a negation. I call an immediate basic truth of syllogism a 'thesis' when, though it is not susceptible of proof by the teacher, yet ignorance of it does not constitute a total bar to progress on the part of the pupil: one which the pupil must know if he is to learn anything whatever is an axiom. I call it an axiom because there are such truths and we give them the name of axioms *par excellence*. If a thesis assumes one part or the other of an enunciation, i.e. asserts either the existence or the non-existence of a subject, it is a hypothesis; if it does not so assert, it is a definition. Definition *is* a 'thesis' or a 'laying something down', since the arithmetician lays it down that to be a unit is to be quantitatively indivisible; but it is not a hypothesis, for to define what a unit is is not the same as to affirm its existence.

Now since the required ground of our knowledge—i.e. of our conviction—of a fact is the possession of such a syllogism as we call demonstration, and the ground of the syllogism is the facts constituting its premisses, we must not only know the primary premisses—some if not all of them—beforehand, but know them better than the conclusion: for the cause of an attribute's inherence in a subject always itself inheres in the subject more firmly than that attribute; e.g. the cause of our loving anything is dearer to us than the object of our love. So since the primary premisses are the cause of our knowledge—i.e. of our conviction—it follows that we know them better—

---

[1] Cf. the following chapter and more particularly II, ch. 19.

that is, are more convinced of them—than their consequences, precisely because of our knowledge of the latter is the effect of our knowledge of the premises. Now a man cannot believe in anything more than in the things he knows, unless he has either actual knowledge of it or something better than actual knowledge. But we are faced with this [35] paradox if a student whose belief rests on demonstration has not prior knowledge; a man must believe in some, if not in all, of the basic truths more than in the conclusion. Moreover, if a man sets out to acquire the scientific knowledge that comes through demonstration, he must not only have a better knowledge of the basic truths and a firmer conviction of them than of the connexion which is being 72b demonstrated: more than this, nothing must be more certain or better known to him than these basic truths in their character as contradicting the fundamental premises which lead to the opposed and erroneous conclusion. For indeed the conviction of pure science must be unshakable.

3

[5] Some hold that, owing to the necessity of knowing the primary premises, there is no scientific knowledge. Others think there is, but that all truths are demonstrable. Neither doctrine is either true or a necessary deduction from the premises. The first school, assuming that there is no way of knowing other than by demonstration, maintain that an infinite regress is involved, on the ground that if behind the prior stands no primary, we could not [10] know the posterior through the prior (wherein they are right, for one cannot traverse an infinite series): if on the other hand—they say—the series terminates and there are primary premises, yet these are unknowable because incapable of demonstration, which according to them is the only form of knowledge. And since thus one cannot know the primary premises, knowledge of the conclusions which follow from them is not pure scientific knowledge nor properly knowing at all, but rests on the mere supposition that the premises are true. The [15] other party agree with them as regards knowing, holding that it is only possible by demonstration, but they see no difficulty in holding that all truths are demonstrated, on the ground that demonstration may be circular and reciprocal.

Our own doctrine is that not all knowledge is demonstrative: on the contrary, knowledge of the immediate premises is independent of [20] demonstration. (The necessity of this is obvious; for since we must know the prior premises from which the demonstration is drawn, and since the regress must end in immediate truths, those truths must be indemonstrable.) Such, then, is our doctrine, and in addition we maintain that besides scientific knowledge there is its originative source which enables us to recognize the definitions.

[25] Now demonstration must be based on premises prior to and better known than the conclusion; and the same things cannot simultaneously be both prior and posterior to one another: so circular demonstration is clearly not possible in the unqualified sense of 'demonstration', but only possible if 'demonstration' be extended to include that other method of argument which rests on a distinction between truths prior to us and truths without qualification prior, i.e. the method by which induction [30] produces knowledge. But if we accept this extension of its meaning, our definition of unqualified knowledge will prove faulty; for there seem to be two kinds of it. Perhaps, however, the second form of demonstration, that which proceeds from truths better known to us, is not demonstration in the unqualified sense of the term.

The advocates of circular demonstration are not only faced with the difficulty we have just stated: in addition their theory reduces to the mere statement that if a thing exists, then it does exist—an easy way of proving anything. [35] That this is so can be clearly shown by taking three terms, for to constitute the circle it makes no difference whether many terms or few or even only two are taken. Thus by direct proof, if A is, B must be; if B is, C must be; therefore if A is, C must be. Since then—by the circular proof—if A is, B must be, and if 73a B is, A must be, A may be substituted for C above. Then 'if B is, A must be' = 'if B is, C must be', which above gave the conclusion 'if A is, C must be': but C and A have been identified. Consequently the upholders of circular demonstration are in the position of say- [5] ing that if A is, A must be—a simple way of proving anything. Moreover, even such circular demonstration is impossible except in the case of attributes that imply one another, viz. 'peculiar' properties.

Now, it has been shown that the positing of one thing—be it one term or one premiss—never involves a necessary consequent:[1] two

---
[1] *Prior Analytics*, i, 25.

[10] premisses constitute the first and smallest foundation for drawing a conclusion at all and therefore *a fortiori* for the demonstrative syllogism of science. If, then, A is implied in B and C, and B and C are reciprocally implied in one another and in A, it is possible, as has been shown in my writings on the syllogism,[1] to prove all the assumptions on which the original conclusion rested, by circular demonstration in [15] the first figure. But it has also been shown that in the other figures either no conclusion is possible, or at least none which proves both the original premisses.[2] Propositions the terms of which are not convertible cannot be circularly demonstrated at all, and since convertible terms occur rarely in actual demonstrations, it is clearly frivolous and impossible to say that demonstration is reciprocal [20] and that therefore everything can be demonstrated.

4

Since the object of pure scientific knowledge cannot be other than it is, the truth obtained by demonstrative knowledge will be necessary. And since demonstrative knowledge is only present when we have a demonstration, it follows that demonstration is an inference from necessary premisses. So we must consider what are the premisses of demonstration—i.e. what [25] is their character: and as a preliminary, let us define what we mean by an attribute 'true in every instance of its subject', an 'essential' attribute, and a 'commensurate and universal' attribute. I call 'true in every instance' what is truly predicable of all instances—not of one to the exclusion of others—and at all times, not at this or that time only; e.g. if animal is [30] truly predicable of every instance of man, then if it be true to say 'this is a man', 'this is an animal' is also true, and if the one be true now the other is true now. A corresponding account holds if point is in every instance predicable as contained in line. There is evidence for this in the fact that the objection we raise against a proposition put to us as true in every instance is either an instance in which, or an occasion on which, it is not true. Essential attributes are (1) such as belong to their sub- [35] ject as elements in its essential nature (e.g. line thus belongs to triangle, point to line; for the very being or 'substance' of triangle and line is composed of these elements, which are contained in the formulae defining triangle and line): (2) such that, while they belong to cer-

[1] *Ibid.*, II, 5.   [2] *Ibid.*, II, 5 and 6.

tain subjects, the subjects to which they belong are contained in the attribute's own defining formula. Thus straight and curved belong to [40] line, odd and even, prime and compound, square and oblong, to number; and also the formula defining any one of these attributes contains its subject—e.g. line or number as the case may be.

Extending this classification to all other attributes, I distinguish those that answer the above description as belonging essentially to their respective subjects; whereas attributes related in neither of these two ways to their subjects I call accidents or 'coincidents'; e.g. musical or white is a 'coincident' of animal.

[5] Further (*a*) that is essential which is not predicated of a subject other than itself: e.g. 'the walking [thing]' walks and is white in virtue of being something else besides; whereas substance, in the sense of whatever signifies a 'this somewhat', is not what it is in virtue of being something else besides. Things, then, not predicated of a subject I call essential; things predicated of a subject I call accidental or 'coincidental'.

[10] In another sense again (*b*) a thing consequentially connected with anything is essential; one not so connected is 'coincidental'. An example of the latter is 'While he was walking it lightened': the lightning was not due to his walking; it was, we should say, a coincidence. If, on the other hand, there is a consequential connexion, the predication is essential; e.g. if a beast dies when its throat is being cut, then its death is also essentially connected with the cut- [15] ting, because the cutting was the cause of death, not death a 'coincident' of the cutting.

So far then as concerns the sphere of connexions scientifically known in the unqualified sense of that term, all attributes which (within that sphere) are essential either in the sense that their subjects are contained in them, or in the sense that they are contained in their subjects, are necessary as well as consequentially connected with their subjects. For it is impossible for them not to inhere in their subjects—either simply or in the qualified sense that one or other of a pair of opposites must inhere in [20] the subject; e.g. in line must be either straightness or curvature, in number either oddness or evenness. For within a single identical genus the contrary of a given attribute is either its privative or its contradictory; e.g. within number what is not odd is even, inasmuch as within this sphere even is a necessary consequent of not-odd. So, since any given predicate must be either affirmed or denied of any subject, essential attributes must inhere in their subjects of necessity.

[25] Thus, then, we have established the distinction between the attribute which is 'true in every instance' and the 'essential' attribute.

I term 'commensurately universal' an attribute which belongs to every instance of its subject, and to every instance essentially and as such; from which it clearly follows that all commensurate universals inhere *necessarily* in their subjects. The essential attribute, and the attribute that belongs to its subject as such, are identical. E.g. point and straight belong to line [30] essentially, for they belong to line as such; and triangle as such has two right angles, for it is *essentially* equal to two right angles.

An attribute belongs commensurately and universally to a subject when it can be shown to belong to any random instance of that subject and when the subject is the first thing to which it can be shown to belong. Thus, e.g. (1) the equality of its angles to two right angles is not a commensurately universal attribute of figure. For though it is possible to [35] show that a figure has its angles equal to two right angles, this attribute cannot be demonstrated of any figure selected at haphazard, nor in demonstrating does one take a figure at random—a square is a figure but its angles are not equal to two right angles. On the other hand, any isosceles triangle has its angles equal to two right angles, yet isosceles triangle is not the primary subject of this attribute but triangle is prior. So whatever can be shown to have [40] its angles equal to two right angles, or to possess any other attribute, in any random instance of itself and primarily—that is the first subject to which the predicate in question belongs commensurately and universally, and the demonstration, in the essential sense, of any predicate is the proof of it as belonging to this first subject commensurately and universally: while the proof of it as belonging to the other subjects to which it attaches is demonstration only in a secondary and unessential sense. Nor again (2) is equality to two right angles a commensurately universal attribute of isosceles; it is of wider application.

5

We must not fail to observe that we often fall into error because our conclusion is not in [5] fact primary and commensurately universal in the sense in which we think we prove it so. We make this mistake (1) when the subject is an individual or individuals above which there is no universal to be found: (2) when the subjects belong to different species and there is a higher universal, but it has no name: (3) when the subject which the demonstrator takes as a whole is really only a part of a larger whole; for then the demonstration will be true [10] of the individual instances within the part and will hold in every instance of it, yet the demonstration will not be true of this subject primarily and commensurately and universally. When a demonstration is true of a subject primarily and commensurately and universally, that is to be taken to mean that it is true of a given subject primarily and as such. Case (3) may be thus exemplified. If a proof were given that perpendiculars to the same line are parallel, it might be supposed that *lines thus perpendicular* were the proper subject of the demonstration because being parallel is true of every instance of them. But it is not so, [15] for the parallelism depends not on these angles being equal to one another because each is a right angle, but simply on their being equal to one another. An example of (1) would be as follows: if isosceles were the only triangle, it would be thought to have its angles equal to two right angles *qua* isosceles. An instance of (2) would be the law that proportionals alternate. Alternation used to be demonstrated separately of numbers, lines, solids, and durations, though it could have been proved of [20] them all by a single demonstration. Because there was no single name to denote that in which numbers, lengths, durations, and solids are identical, and because they differed specifically from one another, this property was proved of each of them separately. To-day, however, the proof is commensurately universal, for they do not possess this attribute *qua* lines or *qua* numbers, but *qua* manifesting this generic character which they are postulated as [25] possessing universally. Hence, even if one prove of each kind of triangle that its angles are equal to two right angles, whether by means of the same or different proofs; still, as long as one treats separately equilateral, scalene, and isosceles, one does not yet know, except sophistically, that triangle has its angles equal to two right angles, nor does one yet know that triangle has this property commensurately and universally, even if there is no other species of triangle but these. For one does [30] not know that triangle as such has this property, nor even that 'all' triangles have it —unless 'all' means 'each taken singly': if 'all' means 'as a whole class', then, though there be none in which one does not recognize this property, one does not know it of 'all triangles'.

When, then, does our knowledge fail of commensurate universality, and when it is unqualified knowledge? If triangle be identical in essence with equilateral, i.e. with each or all equilaterals, then clearly we have unqualified knowledge: if on the other hand it be not, and the attribute belongs to equilateral *qua* triangle; then our knowledge fails of commensurate [35] universality. 'But', it will be asked, 'does this attribute belong to the subject of which it has been demonstrated *qua* triangle or *qua* isosceles? What is the point at which the subject to which it belongs is primary? (i.e. to what subject can it be demonstrated as belonging commensurately and universally?)' Clearly this point is the first term in which it is found to inhere as the elimination of inferior *differentiae* proceeds. Thus the angles of a brazen isosceles triangle are equal to two right angles: but eliminate brazen and isosceles and the attribute remains. 'But'—you may say— 74ᵇ 'eliminate figure or limit, and the attribute vanishes.' True, but figure and limit are not the first *differentiae* whose elimination destroys the attribute. 'Then what is the first?' If it is triangle, it will be in virtue of triangle that the attribute belongs to all the other subjects of which it is predicable, and triangle is the subject to which it can be demonstrated as belonging commensurately and universally.

6

[5] Demonstrative knowledge must rest on necessary basic truths; for the object of scientific knowledge cannot be other than it is. Now attributes attaching essentially to their subjects attach necessarily to them: for essential attributes are either elements in the essential nature of their subjects, or contain their subjects as elements in their own essential nature. (The pairs of opposites which the latter class includes are necessary because one member or the other [10] necessarily inheres.) It follows from this that premisses of the demonstrative syllogism must be connexions essential in the sense explained: for all attributes must inhere essentially or else be accidental, and accidental attributes are not necessary to their subjects.

We must either state the case thus, or else premise that the conclusion of demonstration is necessary and that a demonstrated conclusion cannot be other than it is, and then infer that [15] the conclusion must be developed from necessary premisses. For though you may reason from true premisses without demonstrating, yet if your premisses are necessary you will assuredly demonstrate—in such necessity you have at once a distinctive character of demonstration. That demonstration proceeds from necessary premisses is also indicated by the fact that the objection we raise against a professed demonstration is that a premiss of it is [20] not a necessary truth—whether we think it altogether devoid of necessity, or at any rate so far as our opponent's previous argument goes. This shows how naïve it is to suppose one's basic truths rightly chosen if one starts with a proposition which is (1) popularly accepted and (2) true, such as the sophists' assumption that to know is the same as to possess knowledge.[1] For (1) popular acceptance or rejection is no criterion of a basic truth, which can only be the primary law of the genus constituting the subject matter of the demonstra- [25] tion; and (2) not *all* truth is 'appropriate'.

A further proof that the conclusion must be the development of necessary premisses is as follows. Where demonstration is possible, one who can give no account which includes the cause has no scientific knowledge. If, then, we suppose a syllogism in which, though *A* necessarily inheres in *C*, yet *B*, the middle term of the demonstration, is not necessarily connected with *A* and *C*, then the man who argues thus [30] has no reasoned knowledge of the conclusion, since this conclusion does not owe its necessity to the middle term; for though the conclusion is necessary, the mediating link is a contingent fact. Or again, if a man is without knowledge now, though he still retains the steps of the argument, though there is no change in himself or in the fact and no lapse of memory on his part; then neither had he knowledge previously. But the mediating link, not being necessary, may have perished in the [35] interval; and if so, though there be no change in him nor in the fact, and though he will still retain the steps of the argument, yet he has not knowledge, and therefore had not knowledge before. Even if the link has not actually perished but is liable to perish, this situation is possible and might occur. But such a condition cannot be knowledge.

75ᵃ When the conclusion is necessary, the middle through which it was proved may yet quite easily be non-necessary. You can in fact infer the necessary even from a non-necessary premiss, just as you can infer the true from the

---
[1] Plato, *Euthydemus*, 277.

not true. On the other hand, when the middle is necessary the conclusion must be necessary; [5] just as true premisses always give a true conclusion. Thus, if *A* is necessarily predicated of *B* and *B* of *C*, then *A* is necessarily predicated of *C*. But when the conclusion is non-necessary the middle cannot be necessary either. Thus: let *A* be predicated non-necessarily [10] of *C* but necessarily of *B*, and let *B* be a necessary predicate of *C*; then *A* too will be a necessary predicate of *C*, which by hypothesis it is not.

To sum up, then: demonstrative knowledge must be knowledge of a necessary nexus, and therefore must clearly be obtained through a necessary middle term; otherwise its possessor will know neither the cause nor the fact that [15] his conclusion is a necessary connexion. Either he will mistake the non-necessary for the necessary and believe the necessity of the conclusion without knowing it, or else he will not even believe it—in which case he will be equally ignorant, whether he actually infers the mere fact through middle terms or the reasoned fact and from immediate premisses.

Of accidents that are not essential according to our definition of essential there is no demonstrative knowledge; for since an accident, in [20] the sense in which I here speak of it, may also not inhere, it is impossible to prove its inherence as a necessary conclusion. A difficulty, however, might be raised as to why in dialectic, if the conclusion is not a necessary connexion, such and such determinate premisses should be proposed in order to deal with such and such determinate problems. Would not the result be the same if one asked any questions whatever and then merely stated one's conclu- [25] sion? The solution is that determinate questions have to be put, not because the replies to them affirm facts which necessitate facts affirmed by the conclusion, but because these answers are propositions which if the answerer affirm, he must affirm the conclusion—and affirm it with truth if they are true.

Since it is just those attributes within every genus which are essential and possessed by their respective subjects as such that are necessary, it is clear that both the conclusions and [30] the premisses of demonstrations which produce scientific knowledge are essential. For accidents are not necessary: and, further, since accidents are not necessary one does not necessarily have reasoned knowledge of a conclusion drawn from them (this is so even if the accidental premisses are invariable but not essential, as in proofs through signs; for though the conclusion be actually essential, one will not know it as essential nor know its reason); but [35] to have reasoned knowledge of a conclusion is to know it through its cause. We may conclude that the middle must be consequentially connected with the minor, and the major with the middle.

7

It follows that we cannot in demonstrating pass from one genus to another. We cannot, for instance, prove geometrical truths by arithmetic. For there are three elements in demon- [40] stration: (1) what is proved, the conclusion—an attribute inhering essentially in a genus; (2) the axioms, i.e. axioms which are premisses of demonstration; (3) the subject-genus whose attributes, i.e. essential properties, are revealed by the demonstration. The axioms which are premisses of demonstration may be identical in two or more sciences: but in the case of two different genera such as arithmetic and geometry you cannot apply arithmetical demonstration to the properties [5] of magnitudes unless the magnitudes in question are numbers. How in certain cases transference is possible I will explain later.[1]

Arithmetical demonstration and the other sciences likewise possess, each of them, their own genera; so that if the demonstration is to pass from one sphere to another, the genus must be either absolutely or to some extent the [10] same. If this is not so, transference is clearly impossible, because the extreme and the middle terms must be drawn from the same genus: otherwise, as predicated, they will not be essential and will thus be accidents. That is why it cannot be proved by geometry that opposites fall under one science, nor even that the product of two cubes is a cube. Nor can the theorem of any one science be demonstrated by [15] means of another science, unless these theorems are related as subordinate to superior (e.g. as optical theorems to geometry or harmonic theorems to arithmetic). Geometry again cannot prove of lines any property which they do not possess *qua* lines, i.e. in virtue of the fundamental truths of their peculiar genus: it cannot show, for example, that the straight line is the most beautiful of lines or the contrary of the circle; for these qualities do not belong to lines in virtue of their peculiar genus, but through some property which it shares [20] with other genera.

[1] Cf. 1, 9 and 13.

8

It is also clear that if the premisses from which the syllogism proceeds are commensurately universal, the conclusion of such demonstration—demonstration, i.e. in the unqualified sense—must also be eternal. Therefore no attribute can be demonstrated nor known by strictly scientific knowledge to inhere in perishable things. The proof can only be acciden- [25] tal, because the attribute's connexion with its perishable subject is not commensurately universal but temporary and special. If such a demonstration is made, one premiss must be perishable and not commensurately universal (perishable because only if it is perishable will the conclusion be perishable; not commensurately universal, because the predicate will be predicable of some instances of the subject and not of others); so that the conclusion can only be that a fact is true at the moment—not com- [30] mensurately and universally. The same is true of definitions, since a definition is either a primary premiss or a conclusion of a demonstration, or else only differs from a demonstration in the order of its terms. Demonstration and science of merely frequent occurrences— e.g. of eclipse as happening to the moon—are, as such, clearly eternal: whereas so far as they are not eternal they are not fully commensu- [35] rate. Other subjects too have properties attaching to them in the same way as eclipse attaches to the moon.

9

It is clear that if the conclusion is to show an attribute inhering as such, nothing can be demonstrated except from its 'appropriate' basic truths. Consequently a proof even from true, indemonstrable, and immediate premisses does [40] not constitute knowledge. Such proofs are like Bryson's method of squaring the circle; for they operate by taking as their middle a common character—a character, therefore, which the 76ᵃ subject may share with another—and consequently they apply equally to subjects different in kind. They therefore afford knowledge of an attribute only as inhering accidentally, not as belonging to its subject as such: otherwise they would not have been applicable to another genus.

Our knowledge of any attribute's connexion with a subject is accidental unless we know that connexion through the middle term in [5] virtue of which it inheres, and as an inference from basic premisses essential and 'appropriate' to the subject—unless we know, e.g. the property of possessing angles equal to two right angles as belonging to that subject in which it inheres essentially, and as inferred from basic premisses essential and 'appropriate' to that subject: so that if that middle term also belongs essentially to the minor, the middle must belong to the same kind as the major and minor terms. The only exceptions to this rule are such cases as theorems in harmonics which are demonstrable by arithmetic. [10] Such theorems are proved by the same middle terms as arithmetical properties, but with a qualification—the fact falls under a separate science (for the subject genus is separate), but the reasoned fact concerns the superior science, to which the attributes essentially belong. Thus, even these apparent exceptions show that no attribute is strictly demon- [15] strable except from its 'appropriate' basic truths, which, however, in the case of these sciences have the requisite identity of character.

It is no less evident that the peculiar basic truths of each inhering attribute are indemonstrable; for basic truths from which they might be deduced would be basic truths of all that is, and the science to which they belonged would possess universal sovereignty. This is so because he knows better whose knowledge is deduced from higher causes, for his knowledge [20] is from prior premisses when it derives from causes themselves uncaused: hence, if he knows better than others or best of all, his knowledge would be science in a higher or the highest degree. But, as things are, demonstration is not transferable to another genus, with such exceptions as we have mentioned of the application of geometrical demonstrations to theorems in mechanics or optics, or of arith- [25] metical demonstrations to those of harmonics.

It is hard to be sure whether one knows or not; for it is hard to be sure whether one's knowledge is based on the basic truths appropriate to each attribute—the differentia of true knowledge. We think we have scientific knowledge if we have reasoned from true and primary premisses. But that is not so: the conclusion must be homogeneous with the basic [30] facts of the science.

10

I call the basic truths of every genus those elements in it the existence of which cannot be proved. As regards both these primary truths and the attributes dependent on them the meaning of the name is assumed. The fact of their existence as regards the primary truths must be assumed; but it has to be proved of the remainder, the attributes. Thus we assume the meaning alike of unity, straight, and tri-[35] angular; but while as regards unity and magnitude we assume also the fact of their existence, in the case of the remainder proof is required.

Of the basic truths used in the demonstrative sciences some are peculiar to each science, and some are common, but common only in the sense of analogous, being of use only in so far as they fall within the genus constituting the province of the science in question. [40] Peculiar truths are, e.g. the definitions of line and straight; common truths are such as 'take equals from equals and equals remain'. Only so much of these common truths is required as falls within the genus in question: 76[b] for a truth of this kind will have the same force even if not used generally but applied by the geometer only to magnitudes, or by the arithmetician only to numbers. Also peculiar to a science are the subjects the existence as well as the meaning of which it assumes, and the essential attributes of which it investigates, e.g. [5] in arithmetic units, in geometry points and lines. Both the existence and the meaning of the subjects are assumed by these sciences; but of their essential attributes only the meaning is assumed. For example arithmetic assumes the meaning of odd and even, square and cube, geometry that of incommensurable, or of deflection or verging of lines, whereas the existence of these attributes is demonstrated by [10] means of the axioms and from previous conclusions as premisses. Astronomy too proceeds in the same way. For indeed every demonstrative science has three elements: (1) that which it posits, the subject genus whose essential attributes it examines; (2) the so-called [15] axioms, which are primary premisses of its demonstration; (3) the attributes, the meaning of which it assumes. Yet some sciences may very well pass over some of these elements; e.g. we might not expressly posit the existence of the genus if its existence were obvious (for instance, the existence of hot and cold is more evident than that of number); or we might omit to assume expressly the meaning of the attributes if it were well understood. In the [20] same way the meaning of axioms, such as 'Take equals from equals and equals remain', is well known and so not expressly assumed.

Nevertheless in the nature of the case the essential elements of demonstration are three: the subject, the attributes, and the basic premisses.

That which expresses necessary self-grounded fact, and which we must necessarily believe, is distinct both from the hypotheses of a science and from illegitimate postulate—I say 'must believe', because all syllogism, and therefore *a fortiori* demonstration, is addressed not to the [25] spoken word, but to the discourse within the soul, and though we can always raise objections to the spoken word, to the inward discourse we cannot always object. That which is capable of proof but assumed by the teacher without proof is, if the pupil believes and accepts it, hypothesis, though only in a limited sense hypothesis—that is, relatively to the pu-[30] pil; if the pupil has no opinion or a contrary opinion on the matter, the same assumption is an illegitimate postulate. Therein lies the distinction between hypothesis and illegitimate postulate: the latter is the contrary of the pupil's opinion, demonstrable, but assumed and used without demonstration.

[35] The definition—viz. those which are not expressed as statements that anything is or is not—are not hypotheses: but it is in the premisses of a science that its hypotheses are contained. Definitions require only to be understood, and this is not hypothesis—unless it be contended that the pupil's hearing is also an hypothesis required by the teacher. Hypotheses, on the contrary, postulate facts on the being of which depends the being of the fact [40] inferred. Nor are the geometer's hypotheses false, as some have held, urging that one must not employ falsehood and that the geometer is uttering falsehood in stating that the line which he draws is a foot long or straight, when it is actually neither. The truth is that 77[a] the geometer does not draw any conclusion from the being of the particular line of which he speaks, but from what his diagrams symbolize. A further distinction is that all hypotheses and illegitimate postulates are either universal or particular, whereas a definition is neither.

11

[5] So demonstration does not necessarily imply the being of Forms nor a One beside a Many, but it does necessarily imply the possibility of truly predicating one of many; since without this possibility we cannot save the universal, and if the universal goes, the middle term goes with it, and so demonstration be-

comes impossible. We conclude, then, that there must be a single identical term unequivocally predicable of a number of individuals.

[10] The law that it is impossible to affirm and deny simultaneously the same predicate of the same subject is not expressly posited by any demonstration except when the conclusion also has to be expressed in that form; in which case the proof lays down as its major premiss that the major is truly affirmed of the middle but falsely denied. It makes no difference, however, if we add to the middle, or again to the minor term, the corresponding negative. For [15] grant a minor term of which it is true to predicate man—even if it be also true to predicate not-man of it—still grant simply that man is animal and not not-animal, and the conclusion follows: for it will still be true to say that Callias—even if it be also true to say that not-Callias—is animal and not not-animal. The reason is that the major term is predicable not only of the middle, but of something other than the middle as well, being of wider appli-[20] cation; so that the conclusion is not affected even if the middle is extended to cover the original middle term and also what is not the original middle term.

The law that every predicate can be either truly affirmed or truly denied of every subject is posited by such demonstration as uses *reductio ad impossibile,* and then not always universally, but so far as it is requisite; within the limits, that is, of the genus—the genus, I mean (as I have already explained[1]), to which the [25] man of science applies his demonstrations. In virtue of the common elements of demonstration—I mean the common axioms which are used as premisses of demonstration, not the subjects nor the attributes demonstrated as belonging to them—all the sciences have communion with one another, and in communion with them all is dialectic and any science which might attempt a universal proof of axioms such as the law of excluded middle, [30] the law that the subtraction of equals from equals leaves equal remainders, or other axioms of the same kind. Dialectic has no definite sphere of this kind, not being confined to a single genus. Otherwise its method would not be interrogative; for the interrogative method is barred to the demonstrator, who cannot use the opposite facts to prove the same *nexus.* [35] This was shown in my work on the syllogism.[2]

[1] Cf. 75ª 42 ff. and 76ᵇ 13.
[2] *Prior Analytics,* I. I.

12

If a syllogistic question is equivalent to a proposition embodying one of the two sides of a contradiction, and if each science has its peculiar propositions from which its peculiar conclusion is developed, then there is such a thing as a distinctively scientific question, and it is the interrogative form of the premisses from which the 'appropriate' conclusion of each sci-[40] ence is developed. Hence it is clear that not every question will be relevant to geometry, nor to medicine, nor to any other science: only 77ᵇ those questions will be geometrical which form premisses for the proof of the theorems of geometry or of any other science, such as optics, which uses the same basic truths as geometry. Of the other sciences the like is true. Of these questions the geometer is bound to give his account, using the basic truths of geometry in conjunction with his previous con-[5] clusions; of the basic truths the geometer, as such, is not bound to give any account. The like is true of the other sciences. There is a limit, then, to the questions which we may put to each man of science; nor is each man of science bound to answer all inquiries on each several subject, but only such as fall within the defined field of his own science. If, then, in controversy with a geometer *qua* geometer the disputant confines himself to geometry and [10] proves anything from geometrical premisses, he is clearly to be applauded; if he goes outside these he will be at fault, and obviously cannot even refute the geometer except accidentally. One should therefore not discuss geometry among those who are not geometers, for in such a company an unsound argument will pass unnoticed. This is correspondingly true in [15] the other sciences.

Since there are 'geometrical' questions, does it follow that there are also distinctively 'ungeometrical' questions? Further, in each special science—geometry for instance—what kind of error is it that may vitiate questions, and yet not exclude them from that science? Again, is the erroneous conclusion one constructed from premisses opposite to the true premisses, or is [20] it formal fallacy though drawn from geometrical premisses? Or, perhaps, the erroneous conclusion is due to the drawing of premisses from another science; e.g. in a geometrical controversy a musical question is distinctively ungeometrical, whereas the notion that parallels meet is in one sense geometrical, being ungeometrical in a different fashion: the reason being that 'ungeometrical', like 'unrhythmical', is equivocal, meaning in the one case not geometry at all, in the other bad geometry? It is this error, i.e. error based on premisses of this kind—'of' the science but false—that is the contrary of science. In mathematics the formal fallacy is not so common, because it is the middle term in which the ambiguity lies, since the major is predicated of the whole of the middle and the middle of the whole of the minor (the *predicate* of course never has the prefix 'all'); and in mathematics one can, so to speak, see these middle terms with an intellectual vision, while in dialectic the ambiguity may escape detection. E.g. 'Is every circle a figure?' A diagram shows that this is so, but the minor premiss 'Are epics circles?' is shown by the diagram to be false.

If a proof has an inductive minor premiss, one should not bring an 'objection' against it. For since every premiss must be applicable to a number of cases (otherwise it will not be true in every instance, which, since the syllogism proceeds from universals, it must be), then assuredly the same is true of an 'objection'; since premisses and 'objections' are so far the same that anything which can be validly advanced as an 'objection' must be such that it could take the form of a premiss, either demonstrative or dialectical. On the other hand, arguments formally illogical do sometimes occur through taking as middles mere attributes of the major and minor terms. An instance of this is Caeneus' proof that fire increases in geometrical proportion: 'Fire', he argues, 'increases rapidly, and so does geometrical proportion'. There is no syllogism so, but there is a syllogism if the most rapidly increasing proportion is geometrical and the most rapidly increasing proportion is attributable to fire in its motion. Sometimes, no doubt, it is impossible to reason from premisses predicating mere attributes: but sometimes it is possible, though the possibility is overlooked. If false premisses could never give true conclusions 'resolution' would be easy, for premisses and conclusion would in that case inevitably reciprocate. I might then argue thus: let A be an existing fact; let the existence of A imply such and such facts actually known to me to exist, which we may call B. I can now, since they reciprocate, infer A from B.

Reciprocation of premisses and conclusion is more frequent in mathematics, because mathematics takes definitions, but never an accident, for its premisses—a second characteristic distinguishing mathematical reasoning from dialectical disputations.

A science expands not by the interposition of fresh middle terms, but by the apposition of fresh extreme terms. E.g. A is predicated of B, B of C, C of D, and so indefinitely. Or the expansion may be lateral: e.g. one major, A, may be proved of two minors, C and E. Thus let A represent number—a number or *number* taken indeterminately; B determinate odd number; C any particular odd number. We can then predicate A of C. Next let D represent determinate even number, and E even number. Then A is predicable of E.

13

Knowledge of the fact differs from knowledge of the reasoned fact. To begin with, they differ within the same science and in two ways: (1) when the premisses of the syllogism are not immediate (for then the proximate cause is not contained in them—a necessary condition of knowledge of the reasoned fact): (2) when the premisses are immediate, but instead of the cause the better known of the two reciprocals is taken as the middle; for of two reciprocally predicable terms the one which is not the cause may quite easily be the better known and so become the middle term of the demonstration. Thus (2) (a) you might prove as follows that the planets are near because they do not twinkle: let C be the planets, B not twinkling, A proximity. Then B is predicable of C; for the planets do not twinkle. But A is also predicable of B, since that which does not twinkle is near—we must take this truth as having been reached by induction or sense-perception. Therefore A is a necessary predicate of C; so that we have demonstrated that the planets are near. This syllogism, then, proves not the reasoned fact but only the fact; since they are not near because they do not twinkle, but, because they are near, do not twinkle. The major and middle of the proof, however, may be reversed, and then the demonstration will be of the reasoned fact. Thus: let C be the planets, B proximity, A not twinkling. Then B is an attribute of C, and A—not twinkling—of B. Consequently A is predicable of C, and the syllogism proves the reasoned fact, since its middle term is the proximate cause. Another example is the inference that the moon is spherical from its manner of waxing. Thus: since that which so waxes is spherical, and since the moon so waxes, clearly the moon is spherical. Put in this form, the syllogism turns out to be proof of the fact, but if the middle and major be reversed it is proof of the reasoned fact; since the moon is not spherical because it waxes in a certain manner, but waxes in such a manner because it is [10] spherical. (Let C be the moon, B spherical, and A waxing.) Again (*b*), in cases where the cause and the effect are not reciprocal and the effect is the better known, the fact is demonstrated but not the reasoned fact. This also occurs (1) when the middle falls outside the major and minor, for here too the strict cause is not given, and so the demonstration is of the [15] fact, not of the reasoned fact. For example, the question 'Why does not a wall breathe?' might be answered, 'Because it is not an animal'; but that answer would not give the strict cause, because if not being an animal causes the absence of respiration, then being an animal should be the cause of respiration, according to the rule that if the negation of x [20] causes the non-inherence of y, the affirmation of x causes the inherence of y; e.g. if the disproportion of the hot and cold elements is the cause of ill health, their proportion is the cause of health; and conversely, if the assertion of x causes the inherence of y, the negation of x must cause y's non-inherence. But in the case given this consequence does not result; for not every animal breathes. A syllogism with this kind of cause takes place in the second figure. Thus: let A be animal, B respiration, C [25] wall. Then A is predicable of all B (for all that breathes is animal), but of no C; and consequently B is predicable of no C; that is, the wall does not breathe. Such causes are like far-fetched explanations, which precisely consist in making the cause too remote, as in [30] Anacharsis' account of why the Scythians have no flute-players; namely because they have no vines.

Thus, then, do the syllogism of the fact and the syllogism of the reasoned fact differ within one science and according to the position of the middle terms. But there is another way too in which the fact and the reasoned fact differ, and that is when they are investigated respec- [35] tively by different sciences. This occurs in the case of problems related to one another as subordinate and superior, as when optical problems are subordinated to geometry, mechanical problems to stereometry, harmonic problems to arithmetic, the data of observation [40] to astronomy. (Some of these sciences bear almost the same name; e.g. mathematical and nautical astronomy, mathematical and acoustical harmonics.) Here it is the business of the empirical observers to know the fact, of the mathematicians to know the reasoned fact; for the latter are in possession of the demonstrations giving the causes, and are often ignorant of the fact: just as we have often [5] a clear insight into a universal, but through lack of observation are ignorant of some of its particular instances. These connexions have a perceptible existence though they are manifestations of forms. For the mathematical sciences concern forms: they do not demonstrate properties of a substratum, since, even though the geometrical subjects are predicable as properties of a perceptible substratum, it is not as thus predicable that the mathematician demon- [10] strates properties of them. As optics is related to geometry, so another science is related to optics, namely the theory of the rainbow. Here knowledge of the fact is within the province of the natural philosopher, knowledge of the reasoned fact within that of the optician, either *qua* optician or *qua* mathematical optician. Many sciences not standing in this mutual relation enter into it at points; e.g. medicine and geometry: it is the physician's [15] business to know that circular wounds heal more slowly, the geometer's to know the reason why.

14

Of all the figures the most scientific is the first. Thus, it is the vehicle of the demonstrations of all the mathematical sciences, such as arithmetic, geometry, and optics, and practically of [20] all sciences that investigate causes: for the syllogism of the reasoned fact is either exclusively or generally speaking and in most cases in this figure—a second proof that this figure is the most scientific; for grasp of a reasoned conclusion is the primary condition of knowledge. Thirdly, the first is the only figure [25] which enables us to pursue knowledge of the essence of a thing. In the second figure no affirmative conclusion is possible, and knowledge of a thing's essence must be affirmative; while in the third figure the conclusion can be affirmative, but cannot be universal, and essence must have a universal character: e.g. man is not two-footed animal in any qualified sense, but universally. Finally, the first figure [30] has no need of the others, while it is by means of the first that the other two figures are developed, and have their intervals close-packed until immediate premisses are reached.

Clearly, therefore, the first figure is the primary condition of knowledge.

15

Just as an attribute A may (as we saw) be atomically connected with a subject B, so its disconnexion may be atomic. I call 'atomic' connexions or disconnexions which involve no [35] intermediate term; since in that case the connexion or disconnexion will not be mediated by something other than the terms themselves. It follows that if either A or B, or both A and B, have a genus, their disconnexion cannot be primary. Thus: let C be the genus of A. Then, if C is not the genus of B—for A may well have a genus which is not the genus of [40] B—there will be a syllogism proving A's disconnexion from B thus:

all A is C,
no B is C,
∴ no B is A.

Or if it is B which has a genus D, we have

all B is D,
no D is A,
∴ no B is A, by syllogism;

[5] and the proof will be similar if both A and B have a genus. That the genus of A need not be the genus of B and vice versa, is shown by the existence of mutually exclusive coordinate series of predication. If no term in the series ACD . . . is predicable of any term in the series BEF . . ., and if G—a term in the former series—is the genus of A, clearly G will [10] not be the genus of B; since, if it were, the series would not be mutually exclusive. So also if B has a genus, it will not be the genus of A. If, on the other hand, neither A nor B has a genus and A does not inhere in B, this disconnexion must be atomic. If there be a middle term, one or other of them is bound to have a [15] genus, for the syllogism will be either in the first or the second figure. If it is in the first, B will have a genus—for the premiss containing it must be affirmative; if in the second, either A or B indifferently, since syllogism is possible if either is contained in a negative [20] premiss, but not if both premisses are negative.

Hence it is clear that one thing may be atomically disconnected from another, and we have stated when and how this is possible.

16

Ignorance—defined not as the negation of knowledge but as a positive state of mind—is error produced by inference.

[25] (1) Let us first consider propositions asserting a predicate's immediate connexion with or disconnexion from a subject. Here, it is true, positive error may befall one in alternative ways; for it may arise where one directly believes a connexion or disconnexion as well as where one's belief is acquired by inference. The error, however, that consists in a direct belief is without complication; but the error resulting from inference—which here concerns us—takes many forms. Thus, let A be atomically disconnected from all B: then the conclu- [30] sion inferred through a middle term C, that all B is A, will be a case of error produced by syllogism. Now, two cases are possible. Either (a) both premisses, or (b) one premiss only, may be false. (a) If neither A is an attribute of any C nor C of any B, whereas the contrary was posited in both cases, both prem- [35] isses will be false. (C may quite well be so related to A and B that C is neither subordinate to A nor a universal attribute of B: for B, since A was said to be primarily disconnected from B, cannot have a genus, and A need not necessarily be a universal attribute of all things. Consequently both premisses may [40] be false.) On the other hand, (b) one of the premisses may be true, though not either indifferently but only the major A–C; since, B having no genus, the premiss C–B will always be false, while A–C may be true. This is the case if, for example, A is related atomically to both C and B; because when the same term is related atomically to more terms than one, neither of those terms will belong to the other. It is, of course, equally the case if A–C [5] is not atomic.

Error of attribution, then, occurs through these causes and in this form only—for we found that no syllogism of universal attribution was possible in any figure but the first.[1] On the other hand, an error of non-attribution may occur either in the first or in the second figure. Let us therefore first explain the various forms it takes in the first figure and the char- [10] acter of the premisses in each case.

(c) It may occur when both premisses are false; e.g. supposing A atomically connected with both C and B, if it be then assumed that no C is A, and all B is C, both premisses are false.

(d) It is also possible when one is false. This [15] may be either premiss indifferently. A–C may be true, C–B false—A–C true because A is not an attribute of all things, C–B false be-

[1] *Prior Analytics*, I. 1.

cause C, which never has the attribute A, cannot be an attribute of B; for if C–B were true, the premiss A–C would no longer be true, and [20] besides if both premisses were true, the conclusion would be true. Or again, C–B may be true and A–C false; e.g. if both C and A contain B as genera, one of them must be subordinate to the other, so that if the premiss takes the form No C is A, it will be false. This makes it clear that whether either or both [25] premisses are false, the conclusion will equally be false.

In the second figure the premisses cannot both be wholly false; for if all B is A, no middle term can be with truth universally affirmed of one extreme and universally denied of the [30] other: but premisses in which the middle is affirmed of one extreme and denied of the other are the necessary condition if one is to get a valid inference at all. Therefore if, taken in this way, they are wholly false, their contraries conversely should be wholly true. But this is impossible. On the other hand, there is nothing to prevent both premisses being partially false; e.g. if actually some A is C and [35] some B is C, then if it is premised that all A is C and no B is C, both premisses are false, yet partially, not wholly, false. The same is true if the major is made negative instead of the minor. Or one premiss may be wholly false, and it may be either of them. Thus, supposing that actually an attribute of all A must also be [40] an attribute of all B, then if C is yet taken 80ᵇ to be a universal attribute of all A but universally non-attributable to B, C–A will be true but C–B false. Again, actually that which is an attribute of no B will not be an attribute of all A either; for if it be an attribute of all A, it will also be an attribute of all B, which is contrary to supposition; but if C be nevertheless assumed to be a universal attribute of A, but [5] an attribute of no B, then the premiss C–B is true but the major is false. The case is similar if the major is made the negative premiss. For in fact what is an attribute of no A will not be an attribute of any B either; and if it be yet assumed that C is universally non-attributable to A, but a universal attribute of B, the [10] premiss C–A is true but the minor wholly false. Again, in fact it is false to assume that that which is an attribute of all B is an attribute of no A, for if it be an attribute of all B, it must be an attribute of some A. If then C is nevertheless assumed to be an attribute of all B but of no A, C–B will be true but C–A false.

It is thus clear that in the case of atomic [15] propositions erroneous inference will be possible not only when both premisses are false but also when only one is false.

17

(2) In the case of attributes not atomically connected with or disconnected from their subjects, (a) (i) as long as the false conclusion is inferred through the 'appropriate' middle, only [20] the major and not both premisses can be false. By 'appropriate middle' I mean the middle term through which the contradictory—i.e. the true—conclusion is inferrible. Thus, let A be attributable to B through a middle term C: then, since to produce a conclusion the premiss C–B must be taken affirmatively, it is clear that [25] this premiss must always be true, for its quality is not changed. But the major A–C is false, for it is by a change in the quality of A–C that the conclusion becomes its contradictory —i.e. true. Similarly (ii) if the middle is taken from another series of predication; e.g. suppose D to be not only contained within A as a part within its whole but also predicable of all B. Then the premiss D–B must remain un- [30] changed, but the quality of A–D must be changed; so that D–B is always true, A–D always false. Such error is practically identical with that which is inferred through the 'appropriate' middle. On the other hand, (b) if the conclusion is not inferred through the 'appropriate' middle—(i) when the middle is subordinate to A but is predicable of no B, [35] both premisses must be false, because if there is to be a conclusion both must be posited as asserting the contrary of what is actually the fact, and so posited both become false: e.g. suppose that actually all D is A but no B is D; then if these premisses are changed in quality, a conclusion will follow and both of the new [40] premisses will be false. When, however, 81ᵃ (ii) the middle D is not subordinate to A, A–D will be true, D–B false—A–D true because A was not subordinate to D, D–B false because if it had been true, the conclusion too would have been true; but it is *ex hypothesi* false.

[5] When the erroneous inference is in the second figure, both premisses cannot be entirely false; since if B is subordinate to A, there can be no middle predicable of all of one extreme and of none of the other, as was stated before.[1] One premiss, however, may be false, and it may be either of them. Thus, if C is [10] actually an attribute of both A and B, but

[1] Cf. 80ᵃ 29.

is assumed to be an attribute of A only and not of B, $C–A$ will be true, $C–B$ false: or again if C be assumed to be attributable to B but to no A, $C–B$ will be true, $C–A$ false.

[15] We have stated when and through what kinds of premisses error will result in cases where the erroneous conclusion is negative. If the conclusion is affirmative, (a) (i) it may be inferred through the 'appropriate' middle term. In this case both premisses cannot be false since, as we said before,[1] $C–B$ must remain unchanged if there is to be a conclusion, and consequently $A–C$, the quality of which is [20] changed, will always be false. This is equally true if (ii) the middle is taken from another series of predication, as was stated to be the case also with regard to negative error;[2] for $D–B$ must remain unchanged, while the quality of $A–D$ must be converted, and the type of error is the same as before.

[25] (b) The middle may be inappropriate. Then (i) if D is subordinate to A, $A–D$ will be true, but $D–B$ false; since A may quite well be predicable of several terms no one of which can be subordinated to another. If, however, (ii) D is not subordinate to A, obviously $A–D$, since it is affirmed, will always be false, while $D–B$ may be either true or false; for A may [30] very well be an attribute of no D, whereas all B is D, e.g. no science is animal, all music is science. Equally well A may be an attribute of no D, and D of no B. It emerges, then, that if the middle term is not subordinate to the major, not only both premisses but either singly may be false.

[35] Thus we have made it clear how many varieties of erroneous inference are liable to happen and through what kinds of premisses they occur, in the case both of immediate and of demonstrable truths.

18

It is also clear that the loss of any one of the senses entails the loss of a corresponding portion of knowledge, and that, since we learn either by induction or by demonstration, this [40] knowledge cannot be acquired. Thus 81ᵇ demonstration develops from universals, induction from particulars; but since it is possible to familiarize the pupil with even the so-called mathematical abstractions only through induction—i.e. only because each subject genus possesses, in virtue of a determinate mathematical character, certain properties which can be treated as separate even though they do not

[1] Cf. 80ᵇ 17-26.   [2] Cf. 80ᵇ 26-32.

[5] exist in isolation—it is consequently impossible to come to grasp universals except through induction. But induction is impossible for those who have not sense-perception. For it is sense-perception alone which is adequate for grasping the particulars: they cannot be objects of scientific knowledge, because neither can universals give us knowledge of them without induction, nor can we get it through induction without sense-perception.

19

[10] Every syllogism is effected by means of three terms. One kind of syllogism serves to prove that A inheres in C by showing that A inheres in B and B in C; the other is negative and one of its premisses asserts one term of another, while the other denies one term of another. It is clear, then, that these are the fundamentals and so-called hypotheses of syllogism. [15] Assume them as they have been stated, and proof is bound to follow—proof that A inheres in C through B, and again that A inheres in B through some other middle term, and similarly that B inheres in C. If our reasoning aims at gaining credence and so is merely dialectical, it is obvious that we have only to see that our inference is based on prem- [20] isses as credible as possible: so that if a middle term between A and B is credible though not real, one can reason through it and complete a dialectical syllogism. If, however, one is aiming at truth, one must be guided by the real connexions of subjects and attributes. Thus: since there are attributes which are predicated of a subject essentially or naturally [25] and not coincidentally—not, that is, in the sense in which we say 'That white (thing) is a man', which is not the same mode of predication as when we say 'The man is white': the man is white not because he is something else but because he is man, but the white is man because 'being white' coincides with 'humanity' within one substratum—therefore there are terms such as are naturally subjects of predi- [30] cates. Suppose, then, C such a term not itself attributable to anything else as to a subject, but the proximate subject of the attribute B—i.e. so that $B–C$ is immediate; suppose further E related immediately to F, and F to B. The first question is, must this series terminate, or can it proceed to infinity? The second question is as follows: Suppose nothing is essentially predicated of A, but A is predicated pri- [35] marily of H and of no intermediate prior term, and suppose H similarly related to G and

G to B; then must this series also terminate, or can it too proceed to infinity? There is this much difference between the questions: the first is, is it possible to start from that which is not itself attributable to anything else but is the [40] subject of attributes, and ascend to infinity? The second is the problem whether one can start from that which is a predicate but not itself a subject of predicates, and descend to infinity? A third question is, if the extreme terms are fixed, can there be an infinity of middles? I mean this: suppose for example that A inheres in C and B is intermediate between them, but between B and A there are [5] other middles, and between these again fresh middles; can these proceed to infinity or can they not? This is the equivalent of inquiring, do demonstrations proceed to infinity, i.e. is everything demonstrable? Or do ultimate subject and primary attribute limit one another?

I hold that the same questions arise with re-[10] gard to negative conclusions and premisses: viz. if A is attributable to no B, then either this predication will be primary, or there will be an intermediate term prior to B to which A is not attributable—G, let us say, which is attributable to all B—and there may still be another term H prior to G, which is attributable to all G. The same questions arise, I say, because in these cases too either the series of prior terms to which A is not attributable is infinite or it terminates.

[15] One cannot ask the same questions in the case of reciprocating terms, since when subject and predicate are convertible there is neither primary nor ultimate subject, seeing that all the reciprocals *qua* subjects stand in the same relation to one another, whether we say that the subject has an infinity of attributes or that both subjects and attributes—and we raised the question in both cases—are infinite in number. These questions then cannot be asked—unless, indeed, the terms can reciprocate by two different modes, by accidental [20] predication in one relation and natural predication in the other.

20

Now, it is clear that if the predications terminate in both the upward and the downward direction (by 'upward' I mean the ascent to the more universal, by 'downward' the descent to the more particular), the middle terms cannot be infinite in number. For suppose that A is predicated of F, and that the in-[25] termediates—call them $BB'B''$ . . .—are infinite, then clearly you might descend from A and find one term predicated of another *ad infinitum,* since you have an infinity of terms between you and F; and equally, if you ascend from F, there are infinite terms between you and A. It follows that if these processes are impossible there cannot be an infinity of intermediates between A and F. Nor is it of any [30] effect to urge that some terms of the series $AB \ldots F$ are contiguous so as to exclude intermediates, while others cannot be taken into the argument at all: whichever terms of the series $B \ldots$ I take, the number of intermediates in the direction either of A or of F must be finite or infinite: where the infinite series starts, whether from the first term or from a later one, is of no moment, for the suc-[35] ceeding terms in any case are infinite in number.

21

Further, if in affirmative demonstration the series terminates in both directions, clearly it will terminate too in negative demonstration. Let us assume that we cannot proceed to infinity either by ascending from the ultimate term (by 'ultimate term' I mean a term such as F was, not itself attributable to a subject but itself the subject of attributes), or by descending towards an ultimate from the primary term (by 'primary term' I mean a term predicable of a subject but not itself a subject). If this assumption is justified, the series will also terminate in the case of negation. For a negative conclusion can be proved in all three fig-[5] ures. In the first figure it is proved thus: no B is A, all C is B. In packing the interval B–C we must reach immediate propositions—as is always the case with the minor premiss—since B–C is affirmative. As regards the other premiss it is plain that if the major term is denied of a term D prior to B, D will have to be [10] predicable of all B, and if the major is denied of yet another term prior to D, this term must be predicable of all D. Consequently, since the ascending series is finite, the descent will also terminate and there will be a subject of which A is primarily non-predicable. In the second figure the syllogism is, all A is B, no C is B, . . no C is A. If proof of this is [15] required, plainly it may be shown either in the first figure as above, in the second as here, or in the third. The first figure has been discussed, and we will proceed to display the second, proof by which will be as follows: all

B is D, no C is D ..., since it is required that B should be a subject of which a predicate is affirmed. Next, since D is to be proved not to belong to C, then D has a further predicate which is denied of C. Therefore, since the succession of predicates affirmed of an ever higher universal terminates, the succession of predicates denied terminates too.

The third figure shows it as follows: all B is A, some B is not C, ∴ some A is not C. This premiss, i.e. C–B, will be proved either in the same figure or in one of the two figures discussed above. In the first and second figures the series terminates. If we use the third figure, we shall take as premisses, all E is B, some E is not C, and this premiss again will be proved by a similar prosyllogism. But since it is assumed that the series of descending subjects also terminates, plainly the series of more universal non-predicables will terminate also. Even supposing that the proof is not confined to one method, but employs them all and is now in the first figure, now in the second or third—even so the regress will terminate, for the methods are finite in number, and if finite things are combined in a finite number of ways, the result must be finite.

Thus it is plain that the regress of middles terminates in the case of negative demonstration, if it does so also in the case of affirmative demonstration. That in fact the regress terminates in both these cases may be made clear by the following dialectical considerations.

22

In the case of predicates constituting the essential nature of a thing, it clearly terminates, seeing that if definition is possible, or in other words, if essential form is knowable, and an infinite series cannot be traversed, predicates constituting a thing's essential nature must be finite in number. But as regards predicates generally we have the following prefatory remarks to make. (1) We can affirm without falsehood 'the white (thing) is walking', and 'that big (thing) is a log'; or again, 'the log is big', and 'the man walks'. But the affirmation differs in the two cases. When I affirm 'the white is a log', I mean that something which happens to be white is a log—not that white is the substratum in which log inheres, for it was not *qua* white or *qua* a species of white that the white (thing) came to be a log, and the white (thing) is consequently not a log except incidentally. On the other hand, when I affirm 'the log is white', I do not mean that something else, which happens also to be a log, is white (as I should if I said 'the musician is white,' which would mean 'the man who happens also to be a musician is white'); on the contrary, log is here the substratum—the substratum which actually came to be white, and did so *qua* wood or *qua* a species of wood and *qua* nothing else.

If we must lay down a rule, let us entitle the latter kind of statement predication, and the former not predication at all, or not strict but accidental predication. 'White' and 'log' will thus serve as types respectively of predicate and subject.

We shall assume, then, that the predicate is invariably predicated strictly and not accidentally of the subject, for on such predication demonstrations depend for their force. It follows from this that when a single attribute is predicated of a single subject, the predicate must affirm of the subject either some element constituting its essential nature, or that it is in some way qualified, quantified, essentially related, active, passive, placed, or dated.

(2) Predicates which signify substance signify that the subject is identical with the predicate or with a species of the predicate. Predicates not signifying substance which are predicated of a subject not identical with themselves or with a species of themselves are accidental or coincidental; e.g. white is a coincident of man, seeing that man is not identical with white or a species of white, but rather with animal, since man *is* identical with a species of animal. These predicates which do not signify substance must be predicates of some other subject, and nothing can be white which is not also other than white. The Forms we can dispense with, for they are mere sound without sense; and even if there are such things, they are not relevant to our discussion, since demonstrations are concerned with predicates such as we have defined.

(3) If A is a quality of B, B cannot be a quality of A—a quality of a quality. Therefore A and B cannot be predicated reciprocally of one another in strict predication: they can be affirmed without falsehood of one another, but not genuinely predicated of each other. For one alternative is that they should be substantially predicated of one another, i.e. B would become the genus or differentia of A—the predicate now become subject. But it has been shown that in these substantial predications neither the ascending predicates nor the de-

scending subjects form an infinite series; e.g. neither the series, man is biped, biped is animal, &c., nor the series predicating animal of man, man of Callias, Callias of a further subject as an element of its essential nature, is in- [5] finite. For all such substance is definable, and an infinite series cannot be traversed in thought: consequently neither the ascent nor the descent is infinite, since a substance whose predicates were infinite would not be definable. Hence they will not be predicated each as the genus of the other; for this would equate a [10] genus with one of its own species. Nor (the other alternative) can a *quale* be reciprocally predicated of a *quale,* nor any term belonging to an adjectival category of another such term, except by accidental predication; for all such predicates are coincidents and are predicated of substances. On the other hand— in proof of the impossibility of an infinite ascending series—every predication displays the subject as somehow qualified or quantified or as characterized under one of the other adjectival categories, or else is an element in its sub- [15] stantial nature: these latter are limited in number, and the number of the widest kinds under which predications fall is also limited, for every predication must exhibit its subject as somehow qualified, quantified, essentially related, acting or suffering, or in some place or at some time.

I assume first that predication implies a single subject and a single attribute, and secondly that predicates which are not substantial are not predicated of one another. We assume this because such predicates are all coincidents, and though some are essential coincidents, others [20] of a different type, yet we maintain that all of them alike are predicated of some substratum and that a coincident is never a substratum—since we do not class as a coincident anything which does not owe its designation to its being something other than itself, but always hold that any coincident is predicated of some substratum other than itself, and that another group of coincidents may have a different substratum. Subject to these assumptions [25] then, neither the ascending nor the descending series of predication in which a single attribute is predicated of a single subject is infinite. For the subjects of which coincidents are predicated are as many as the constitutive elements of each individual substance, and these we have seen are not infinite in number, while in the ascending series are contained those constitutive elements with their coincidents—both of which are finite. We conclude that there is a given subject $\langle D \rangle$ of which some attribute $\langle C \rangle$ is primarily predicable; that there must be an attribute $\langle B \rangle$ primarily predicable of the first attribute, and that the series must end with a [30] term $\langle A \rangle$ not predicable of any term prior to the last subject of which it was predicated $\langle B \rangle$, and of which no term prior to it is predicable.

The argument we have given is one of the so-called proofs; an alternative proof follows. Predicates so related to their subjects that there are other predicates prior to them predicable of those subjects are demonstrable; but of demonstrable propositions one cannot have something [35] better than knowledge, nor can one know them without demonstration. Secondly, if a consequent is only known through an antecedent (viz. premisses prior to it) and we neither know this antecedent nor have something better than knowledge of it, then we shall not have scientific knowledge of the consequent. Therefore, if it is possible through demonstration to know anything without qualification and not merely as dependent on the acceptance of certain premisses—i.e. hypothetically—the series of intermediate predications must terminate. If it does not terminate, and beyond any predicate taken as higher than another there remains another still higher, then every predicate is demonstrable. Consequently, since these demonstrable predicates are infinite in number and therefore cannot be traversed, we shall *not* know them by demonstration. If, therefore, we have not something better than [5] knowledge of them, we cannot through demonstration have unqualified but only hypothetical science of anything.

As dialectical proofs of our contention these may carry conviction, but an analytic process will show more briefly that neither the ascent nor the descent of predication can be infinite in [10] the demonstrative sciences which are the object of our investigation. Demonstration proves the inherence of essential attributes in things. Now attributes may be essential for two reasons: either because they are elements in the essential nature of their subjects, or because their subjects are elements in their essential nature. An example of the latter is odd as an attribute of number—though it is number's [15] attribute, yet number itself is an element in the definition of odd; of the former, multiplicity or the indivisible, which are elements in the definition of number. In neither kind of attribution can the terms be infinite. They are not infinite where each is related to the term below it as odd is to number, for this would mean the inherence in odd of another attribute of odd in whose nature odd was an essential [20] element: but then number will be an ultimate subject of the whole infinite chain of attributes, and be an element in the definition of each of them. Hence, since an infinity of attributes such as contain their subject in their definition cannot inhere in a single thing, the ascending series is equally finite. Note, moreover, that all such attributes must so inhere in the ultimate subject—e.g. its attributes in number and number in them—as to be commensurate with the subject and not of wider extent. [25] Attributes which are essential elements in the nature of their subjects are equally finite: otherwise definition would be impossible. Hence, if all the attributes predicated are essential and these cannot be infinite, the ascending series will terminate, and consequently the descending series too.

If this is so, it follows that the intermediates between any two terms are also always limited in number. An immediately obvious con-[30] sequence of this is that demonstrations necessarily involve basic truths, and that the contention of some—referred to at the outset— that all truths are demonstrable is mistaken. For if there are basic truths, (*a*) not all truths are demonstrable, and (*b*) an infinite regress is impossible; since if either (*a*) or (*b*) were not a fact, it would mean that no interval was im-[35] mediate and indivisible, but that all intervals were divisible. This is true because a conclusion is demonstrated by the interposition, not the apposition, of a fresh term. If such interposition could continue to infinity there might be an infinite number of terms between any two terms; but this is impossible if both 84ᵇ the ascending and descending series of predication terminate; and of this fact, which before was shown dialectically, analytic proof has now been given.

23

It is an evident corollary of these conclusions that if the same attribute *A* inheres in two terms *C* and *D* predicable either not at all, or [5] not of all instances, of one another, it does not always belong to them in virtue of a common middle term. Isosceles and scalene possess the attribute of having their angles equal to two right angles in virtue of a common middle; for they possess it in so far as they are both a certain kind of figure, and not in so far as they differ from one another. But this is not always the case: for, were it so, if we take *B* as the common middle in virtue of which *A* inheres in *C* [10] and *D,* clearly *B* would inhere in *C* and *D* through a second common middle, and this in turn would inhere in *C* and *D* through a third, so that between two terms an infinity of intermediates would fall—an impossibility. Thus it need not always be in virtue of a common middle term that a single attribute inheres in several subjects, since there must be [15] immediate intervals. Yet if the attribute to be proved common to two subjects is to be one of their essential attributes, the middle terms involved must be within one subject genus and be derived from the same group of immediate premises; for we have seen that processes of proof cannot pass from one genus to another.[1]

It is also clear that when *A* inheres in *B,* this [20] can be demonstrated if there is a middle term. Further, the 'elements' of such a conclusion are the premisses containing the middle in question, and they are identical in number with the middle terms, seeing that the immediate propositions—or at least such immediate propositions as are universal—are the 'elements'. If, on the other hand, there is no middle term, demonstration ceases to be possible: we are on the way to the basic truths. Similarly if *A* does not inhere in *B,* this can be demonstrated if there is a middle term or a [25] term prior to *B* in which *A* does not inhere: otherwise there is no demonstration and a basic truth is reached. There are, moreover, as many 'elements' of the demonstrated conclusion as there are middle terms, since it is propositions containing these middle terms that are the basic premisses on which the demonstration rests; and as there are some indemonstrable basic truths asserting that 'this is that' or that 'this inheres in that', so there are [30] others denying that 'this is that' or that 'this inheres in that'—in fact some basic truths will affirm and some will deny being.

When we are to prove a conclusion, we must take a primary essential predicate—suppose it *C*—of the subject *B,* and then suppose *A* similarly predicable of *C*. If we proceed in this manner, no proposition or attribute which falls beyond *A* is admitted in the proof: the interval is constantly condensed until subject and predi-[35] cate become indivisible, i.e. one. We have our unit when the premiss becomes immediate, since the immediate premiss alone is a single

[1] I. 7.

premiss in the unqualified sense of 'single'. And as in other spheres the basic element is simple but not identical in all—in a system of weight it is the mina, in music the quartertone, and so on—so in syllogism the unit is an immediate premiss, and in the knowledge that demonstration gives it is an intuition. In syllogisms, then, which prove the inherence of an attribute, nothing falls outside the major term. In the case of negative syllogisms on the other hand, (1) in the first figure nothing falls outside the major term whose inherence is in question; e.g. to prove through a middle C that A does not inhere in B the premisses required are, all B is C, no C is A. Then if it has to be proved that no C is A, a middle must be found between A and C; and this procedure will never vary.

(2) If we have to show that E is not D by means of the premisses, all D is C; no E, or not all E, is C; then the middle will never fall beyond E, and E is the subject of which D is to be denied in the conclusion.

(3) In the third figure the middle will never fall beyond the limits of the subject and the attribute denied of it.

24

Since demonstrations may be either commensurately universal or particular, and either affirmative or negative; the question arises, which form is the better? And the same question may be put in regard to so-called 'direct' demonstration and *reductio ad impossibile*. Let us first examine the commensurately universal and the particular forms, and when we have cleared up this problem proceed to discuss 'direct' demonstration and *reductio ad impossibile*.

The following considerations might lead some minds to prefer particular demonstration.

(1) The superior demonstration is the demonstration which gives us greater knowledge (for this is the ideal of demonstration), and we have greater knowledge of a particular individual when we know it in itself than when we know it through something else; e.g. we know Coriscus the musician better when we know that Coriscus is musical than when we know only that man is musical, and a like argument holds in all other cases. But commensurately universal demonstration, instead of proving that the subject itself actually is x, proves only that something else is x—e.g. in attempting to prove that isosceles is x, it proves not that isosceles but only that triangle is x—whereas particular demonstration proves that the subject itself is x. The demonstration, then, that a subject, as such, possesses an attribute is superior. If this is so, and if the particular rather than the commensurately universal form so demonstrates, particular demonstration is superior.

(2) The universal has not a separate being over against groups of singulars. Demonstration nevertheless creates the opinion that its function is conditioned by something like this—some separate entity belonging to the real world; that, for instance, of triangle or of figure or number, over against particular triangles, figures, and numbers. But demonstration which touches the real and will not mislead is superior to that which moves among unrealities and is delusory. Now commensurately universal demonstration is of the latter kind: if we engage in it we find ourselves reasoning after a fashion well illustrated by the argument that the proportionate is what answers to the definition of some entity which is neither line, number, solid, nor plane, but a proportionate apart from all these. Since, then, such a proof is characteristically commensurate and universal, and less touches reality than does particular demonstration, and creates a false opinion, it will follow that commensurate and universal is inferior to particular demonstration.

We may retort thus. (1) The first argument applies no more to commensurate and universal than to particular demonstration. If equality to two right angles is attributable to its subject not *qua* isosceles but *qua* triangle, he who knows that isosceles possesses that attribute knows the subject as *qua* itself possessing the attribute, to a less degree than he who knows that triangle has that attribute. To sum up the whole matter: if a subject is proved to possess *qua* triangle an attribute which it does not in fact possess *qua* triangle, that is not demonstration: but if it does possess it *qua* triangle, the rule applies that the greater knowledge is his who knows the subject as possessing its attribute *qua* that in virtue of which it actually does possess it. Since, then, triangle is the wider term, and there is one identical definition of triangle—i.e. the term is not equivocal—and since equality to two right angles belongs to all triangles, it is isosceles *qua* triangle and not triangle *qua* isosceles which has its angles so related. It follows that he who knows a connexion universally has greater knowledge of it as it in fact is than he who knows the particular; and the inference is that commensurate and universal is superior to particular demonstration.

[15] (2) If there is a single identical definition—i.e. if the commensurate universal is unequivocal—then the universal will possess being not less but more than some of the particulars, inasmuch as it is universals which comprise the imperishable, particulars that tend to perish.

(3) Because the universal has a single meaning, we are not therefore compelled to suppose that in these examples it has being as a substance apart from its particulars—any more than we need make a similar supposition in the other cases of unequivocal universal predication, viz. where the predicate signifies not [20] substance but quality, essential relatedness, or action. If such a supposition is entertained, the blame rests not with the demonstration but with the hearer.

(4) Demonstration is syllogism that proves the cause, i.e. the reasoned fact, and it is rather the commensurate universal than the particular which is causative (as may be shown thus: that which possesses an attribute through its [25] own essential nature is itself the cause of the inherence, and the commensurate universal is primary; hence the commensurate universal is the cause). Consequently commensurately universal demonstration is superior as more especially proving the cause, that is the reasoned fact.

(5) Our search for the reason ceases, and we think that we know, when the coming to be or existence of the fact before us is not due to the coming to be or existence of some other fact, for the last step of a search thus conducted is [30] *eo ipso* the end and limit of the problem. Thus: 'Why did he come?' 'To get the money—wherewith to pay a debt—that he might thereby do what was right.' When in this regress we can no longer find an efficient or final cause, we regard the last step of it as the end of the coming—or being or coming to be—and we regard ourselves as then only having full knowledge of the reason why he came.

[35] If, then, all causes and reasons are alike in this respect, and if this is the means to full knowledge in the case of final causes such as we have exemplified, it follows that in the case of the other causes also full knowledge is attained when an attribute no longer inheres because of something else. Thus, when we learn that exterior angles are equal to four right angles because they are the exterior angles of an isosceles, there still remains the question 'Why 86ª has isosceles this attribute?' and its answer 'Because it is a triangle, and a triangle has it because a triangle is a rectilinear figure.' If rectilinear figure possesses the property for no further reason, at this point we have full knowledge—but at this point our knowledge has become commensurately universal, and so we conclude that commensurately universal demonstration is superior.

(6) The more demonstration becomes particular the more it sinks into an indeterminate manifold, while universal demonstration tends [5] to the simple and determinate. But objects so far as they are an indeterminate manifold are unintelligible, so far as they are determinate, intelligible: they are therefore intelligible rather in so far as they are universal than in so far as they are particular. From this it follows that universals are more demonstrable: but since relative and correlative increase concomitantly, of the more demonstrable there will be fuller demonstration. Hence the commensurate and universal form, being more truly demon-[10]stration, is the superior.

(7) Demonstration which teaches two things is preferable to demonstration which teaches only one. He who possesses commensurately universal demonstration knows the particular as well, but he who possesses particular demonstration does not know the universal. So that this is an additional reason for preferring commensurately universal demonstration. And there is yet this further argument:

(8) Proof becomes more and more proof of the commensurate universal as its middle term approaches nearer to the basic truth, and noth-[15]ing is so near as the immediate premiss which is itself the basic truth. If, then, proof from the basic truth is more accurate than proof not so derived, demonstration which depends more closely on it is more accurate than demonstration which is less closely dependent. But commensurately universal demonstration is characterized by this closer dependence, and is therefore superior. Thus, if A had to be proved to inhere in D, and the middles were B and C, B being the higher term would ren-[20]der the demonstration which it mediated the more universal.

Some of these arguments, however, are dialectical. The clearest indication of the precedence of commensurately universal demonstration is as follows: if of two propositions, a prior and a posterior, we have a grasp of the prior, we have a kind of knowledge—a potential grasp—of the posterior as well. For example, if one knows that the angles of all triangles are equal to two right angles, one knows in a sense—potentially—that the isosceles' angles also are equal to two right angles, even if one does not know that the isosceles is a triangle; but to grasp this posterior proposition is by no means to know the commensurate universal either potentially or actually. Moreover, commensurately universal demonstration is through and through intelligible; [30] particular demonstration issues in sense-perception.

25

The preceding arguments constitute our defence of the superiority of commensurately universal to particular demonstration. That affirmative demonstration excels negative may be shown as follows.

(1) We may assume the superiority *ceteris paribus* of the demonstration which derives from fewer postulates or hypotheses—in short [35] from fewer premisses; for, given that all these are equally well known, where they are fewer knowledge will be more speedily acquired, and that is a desideratum. The argument implied in our contention that demonstration from fewer assumptions is superior may be set out in universal form as follows. Assuming that in both cases alike the middle terms are known, and that middles which are prior are better known than such as are posterior, we may suppose two demonstrations of the inherence of A in E, the one proving it 86^b through the middles B, C and D, the other through F and G. Then A–D is known to the same degree as A–E (in the second proof), but A–D is better known than and prior to A–E (in the first proof); since A–E is proved through A–D, and the ground is more certain than the conclusion.

[5] Hence demonstration by fewer premisses is *ceteris paribus* superior. Now both affirmative and negative demonstration operate through three terms and two premisses, but whereas the former assumes only that something is, the latter assumes both that something is and that something else is not, and thus operating through more kinds of premiss is inferior.

[10] (2) It has been proved[1] that no conclusion follows if both premisses are negative, but that one must be negative, the other affirmative. So we are compelled to lay down the following additional rule: as the demonstration expands, the affirmative premisses must increase in number, but there cannot be more [15] than one negative premiss in each complete proof. Thus, suppose no B is A, and all C is B. Then if both the premisses are to be again expanded, a middle must be interposed. Let us interpose D between A and B, and E between B and C. Then clearly E is affirmatively re-[20] lated to B and C, while D is affirmatively related to B but negatively to A; for all B is D, but there must be no D which is A. Thus there proves to be a single negative premiss, A–D. In the further prosyllogisms too it is the same, because in the terms of an affirmative syllogism the middle is always related affirmatively to both extremes; in a negative syllogism it [25] must be negatively related only to one of them, and so this negation comes to be a single negative premiss, the other premisses being affirmative. If, then, that through which a truth is proved is a better known and more certain truth, and if the negative proposition is proved through the affirmative and not vice versa, affirmative demonstration, being prior and better known and more certain, will be superior. [30] (3) The basic truth of demonstrative syllogism is the universal immediate premiss, and the universal premiss asserts in affirmative demonstration and in negative denies: and the affirmative proposition is prior to and better known than the negative (since affirmation explains denial and is prior to denial, just as be-[35] ing is prior to not-being). It follows that the basic premiss of affirmative demonstration is superior to that of negative demonstration, and the demonstration which uses superior basic premisses is superior.

(4) Affirmative demonstration is more of the nature of a basic form of proof, because it is a *sine qua non* of negative demonstration.

26

87^a Since affirmative demonstration is superior to negative, it is clearly superior also to *reductio ad impossibile*. We must first make certain what is the difference between negative demonstration and *reductio ad impossibile*. Let us suppose that no B is A, and that all C is B: the conclusion necessarily follows that no C is A. [5] If these premisses are assumed, therefore, the negative demonstration that no C is A is direct. *Reductio ad impossibile*, on the other hand, proceeds as follows. Supposing we are to prove that A does not inhere in B, we have to assume that it does inhere, and further that

[1] *Prior Analytics*, I. 7.

B inheres in C, with the resulting inference that A inheres in C. This we have to suppose a known and admitted impossibility; and we [10] then infer that A cannot inhere in B. Thus if the inherence of B in C is not questioned, A's inherence in B is impossible.

The order of the terms is the same in both proofs: they differ according to which of the negative propositions is the better known, the one denying A of B or the one denying A of C. When the falsity of the conclusion is the better [15] known, we use *reductio ad impossibile*; when the major premiss of the syllogism is the more obvious, we use direct demonstration. All the same the proposition denying A of B is, in the order of being, prior to that denying A of C; for premisses are prior to the conclusion which follows from them, and 'no C is A' is the conclusion, 'no B is A' one of its premisses. [20] For the destructive result of *reductio ad impossibile* is not a proper conclusion, nor are its antecedents proper premisses. On the contrary: the constituents of syllogism are premisses related to one another as whole to part or part to whole, whereas the premisses $A-C$ and [25] $A-B$ are not thus related to one another. Now the superior demonstration is that which proceeds from better known and prior premisses, and while both these forms depend for credence on the not-being of something, yet the source of the one is prior to that of the other. Therefore negative demonstration will have an unqualified superiority to *reductio ad impossibile*, and affirmative demonstration, being superior to negative, will consequently [30] be superior also to *reductio ad impossibile*.

27

The science which is knowledge at once of the fact and of the reasoned fact, not of the fact by itself without the reasoned fact, is the more exact and the prior science.

A science such as arithmetic, which is not a science of properties *qua* inhering in a substratum, is more exact than and prior to a science like harmonics, which is a science of properties inhering in a substratum; and similarly a science like arithmetic, which is constituted of fewer basic elements, is more exact than and prior to geometry, which requires [35] additional elements. What I mean by 'additional elements' is this: a unit is substance without position, while a point is substance with position; the latter contains an additional element.

28

A single science is one whose domain is a single genus, viz. all the subjects constituted out of the primary entities of the genus—i.e. the parts of this total subject—and their essential properties.

One science differs from another when their basic truths have neither a common source nor are derived those of the one science from those of the other. This is verified when we reach the indemonstrable premisses of a science, for they must be within one genus with its conclusions: and this again is verified if the conclusions proved by means of them fall within one genus—i.e. are homogeneous.

29

[5] One can have several demonstrations of the same connexion not only by taking from the same series of predication middles which are other than the immediately cohering term—e.g. by taking C, D, and F severally to prove $A-B$—but also by taking a middle from another series. Thus let A be change, D alteration of a property, B feeling pleasure, and G relaxation. We can then without falsehood [10] predicate D of B and A of D, for he who is pleased suffers alteration of a property, and that which alters a property changes. Again, we can predicate A of G without falsehood, and G of B; for to feel pleasure is to relax, and to relax is to change. So the conclusion can be drawn through middles which are different, i.e. not in the same series—yet not so that neither of these middles is predicable of the [15] other, for they must both be attributable to some one subject.

A further point worth investigating is how many ways of proving the same conclusion can be obtained by varying the figure.

30

There is no knowledge by demonstration of chance conjunctions; for chance conjunctions exist neither by necessity nor as general con- [20] nexions but comprise what comes to be as something distinct from these. Now demonstration is concerned only with one or other of these two; for all reasoning proceeds from necessary or general premisses, the conclusion being necessary if the premisses are necessary and [25] general if the premisses are general. Consequently, if chance conjunctions are neither general nor necessary, they are not demonstrable.

31

Scientific knowledge is not possible through the act of perception. Even if perception as a faculty is of 'the such' and not merely of a 'this somewhat', yet one must at any rate actually perceive a 'this somewhat', and at a definite present place and time: but that which is commensurately universal and true in all cases one cannot perceive, since it is not 'this' and it is not 'now'; if it were, it would not be commensurately universal—the term we apply to what is always and everywhere. Seeing, therefore, that demonstrations are commensurately universal and universals imperceptible, we clearly cannot obtain scientific knowledge by the act of perception: nay, it is obvious that even if it were possible to perceive that a triangle has its angles equal to two right angles, we should still be looking for a demonstration—we should not (as some say) possess knowledge of it; for perception must be of a particular, whereas scientific knowledge involves the recognition of the commensurate universal. So if we were on the moon, and saw the earth shutting out the sun's light, we should not know the cause of the eclipse: we should perceive the present fact of the eclipse, but not the reasoned fact at all, since the act of perception is not of the commensurate universal. I do not, of course, deny that by watching the frequent recurrence of this event we might, after tracking the commensurate universal, possess a demonstration, for the commensurate universal is elicited from the several groups of singulars. The commensurate universal is precious because it makes clear the cause; so that in the case of facts like these which have a cause other than themselves universal knowledge is more precious than sense-perceptions and than intuition. (As regards primary truths there is of course a different account to be given.[1]) Hence it is clear that knowledge of things demonstrable cannot be acquired by perception, unless the term perception is applied to the possession of scientific knowledge through demonstration. Nevertheless certain points do arise with regard to connexions to be proved which are referred for their explanation to a failure in sense-perception: there are cases when an act of vision would terminate our inquiry, not because in seeing we should be knowing, but because we should have elicited the universal from seeing; if, for example, we saw the pores in the glass and the light passing through, the reason of the kindling would be clear to us because we should at the same time see it in each instance and intuit that it must be so in all instances.

32

All syllogisms cannot have the same basic truths. This may be shown first of all by the following dialectical considerations. (1) Some syllogisms are true and some false: for though a true inference is possible from false premisses, yet this occurs once only—I mean if *A*, for instance, is truly predicable of *C*, but *B*, the middle, is false, both *A–B* and *B–C* being false; nevertheless, if middles are taken to prove these premisses, they will be false because every conclusion which is a falsehood has false premisses, while true conclusions have true premisses, and false and true differ in kind. Then again, (2) falsehoods are not all derived from a single identical set of principles: there are falsehoods which are the contraries of one another and cannot coexist, e.g. 'justice is injustice', and 'justice is cowardice'; 'man is horse', and 'man is ox'; 'the equal is greater', and 'the equal is less.' From our established principles we may argue the case as follows, confining ourselves therefore to true conclusions. Not even all these are inferred from the same basic truths; many of them in fact have basic truths which differ generically and are not transferable; units, for instance, which are without position, cannot take the place of points, which have position. The transferred terms could only fit in as middle terms or as major or minor terms, or else have some of the other terms between them, others outside them.

Nor can any of the common axioms—such, I mean, as the law of excluded middle—serve as premisses for the proof of all conclusions. For the kinds of being are different, and some attributes attach to *quanta* and some to *qualia* only; and proof is achieved by means of the common axioms taken in conjunction with these several kinds and their attributes.

Again, it is not true that the basic truths are much fewer than the conclusions, for the basic truths are the premisses, and the premisses are formed by the apposition of a fresh extreme term or the interposition of a fresh middle. Moreover, the number of conclusions is indefinite, though the number of middle terms is finite; and lastly some of the basic truths are necessary, others variable.

---

[1] Cf., e.g., 100^b 12.

Looking at it in this way we see that, since the number of conclusions is indefinite, the basic truths cannot be identical or limited in [10] number. If, on the other hand, identity is used in another sense, and it is said, e.g. 'these and no other are the fundamental truths of geometry, these the fundamentals of calculation, these again of medicine'; would the statement mean anything except that the sciences have basic truths? To call them identical because they are self-identical is absurd, since everything can be identified with everything in that [15] sense of identity. Nor again can the contention that all conclusions have the same basic truths mean that from the mass of all possible premisses any conclusion may be drawn. That would be exceedingly naïve, for it is not the case in the clearly evident mathematical sciences, nor is it possible in analysis, since it is the immediate premisses which are the basic truths, and a fresh conclusion is only formed [20] by the addition of a new immediate premiss: but if it be admitted that it is these primary immediate premisses which are basic truths, each subject-genus will provide one basic truth. If, however, it is not argued that from the mass of all possible premisses any conclusion may be proved, nor yet admitted that basic truths differ so as to be generically different for each science, it remains to consider the possibility that, while the basic truths of all knowledge are within one genus, special premisses are re- [25] quired to prove special conclusions. But that this cannot be the case has been shown by our proof that the basic truths of things generically different themselves differ generically. For fundamental truths are of two kinds, those which are premisses of demonstration and the subject-genus; and though the former are common, the latter—number, for instance, and magnitude—are peculiar.

33

[30] Scientific knowledge and its object differ from opinion and the object of opinion in that scientific knowledge is commensurately universal and proceeds by necessary connexions, and that which is necessary cannot be otherwise. So though there are things which are true and real and yet can be otherwise, *scientific knowledge* clearly does not concern them: if it did, things which can be otherwise [35] would be incapable of being otherwise. Nor are they any concern of *rational intuition* —by rational intuition I mean an originative source of scientific knowledge—nor of indemonstrable knowledge, which is the grasping of the immediate premiss. Since then rational intuition, science, and opinion, and what is revealed by these terms, are the only things that can be 'true', it follows that it is *opinion* that is concerned with that which may be true or false, and can be otherwise: opinion in fact is the grasp of a premiss which is immediate but not necessary. This view also fits the [5] observed facts, for opinion is unstable, and so is the kind of being we have described as its object. Besides, when a man thinks a truth incapable of being otherwise he always thinks that he knows it, never that he opines it. He thinks that he opines when he thinks that a connexion, though actually so, may quite easily be otherwise; for he believes that such is the [10] proper object of opinion, while the necessary is the object of knowledge.

In what sense, then, can the same thing be the object of both opinion and knowledge? And if any one chooses to maintain that all that he knows he can also opine, why should not opinion be knowledge? For he that knows and he that opines will follow the same train of thought through the same middle terms until the immediate premisses are reached; [15] because it is possible to opine not only the fact but also the reasoned fact, and the reason is the middle term; so that, since the former knows, he that opines also has knowledge.

The truth perhaps is that if a man grasp truths that cannot be other than they are, in the way in which he grasps the definitions through which demonstrations take place, he will have not opinion but knowledge: if on the other hand he apprehends these attributes as inhering in their subjects, but not in virtue of the subjects' substance and essential nature, he [20] possesses opinion and not genuine knowledge; and his opinion, if obtained through immediate premisses, will be both of the fact and of the reasoned fact; if not so obtained, of the fact alone. The object of opinion and knowledge is not quite identical; it is only in a sense identical, just as the object of true and false [25] opinion is in a sense identical. The sense in which some maintain that true and false opinion can have the same object leads them to embrace many strange doctrines, particularly the doctrine that what a man opines falsely he does not opine at all. There are really many senses of 'identical', and in one sense the object of true and false opinion can be the same, in another it cannot. Thus, to have a true opinion that the diagonal is commensurate with [30] the side would be absurd: but because the diagonal with which they are both concerned is the same, the two opinions have objects so far the same: on the other hand, as regards their essential definable nature these objects differ. The identity of the objects of knowledge and opinion is similar. Knowledge is the apprehension of, e.g. the attribute 'animal' as incapable of being otherwise, opinion has the apprehension of 'animal' as capable of being [35] otherwise—e.g. the apprehension that animal is an element in the essential nature of man is knowledge; the apprehension of animal as predicable of man but not as an element in man's essential nature is opinion: man is the subject in both judgements, but the mode of inherence differs.

This also shows that one cannot opine and know the same thing simultaneously; for then one would apprehend the same thing as both capable and incapable of being otherwise—an **89ᵇ** impossibility. Knowledge and opinion of the same thing can co-exist in two different people in the sense we have explained, but not simultaneously in the same person. That would involve a man's simultaneously apprehending, e.g. (1) that man is essentially animal—i.e. cannot be other than animal—and (2) that [5] man is not essentially animal, that is, we may assume, may be other than animal.

Further consideration of modes of thinking and their distribution under the heads of discursive thought, intuition, science, art, practical wisdom, and metaphysical thinking, belongs rather partly to natural science, partly to moral philosophy.

34

[10] Quick wit is a faculty of hitting upon the middle term instantaneously. It would be exemplified by a man who saw that the moon has her bright side always turned towards the sun, and quickly grasped the cause of this, namely that she borrows her light from him; or observed somebody in conversation with a man of wealth and divined that he was borrowing money, or that the friendship of these people sprang from a common enmity. In all these instances he has seen the major and minor terms [15] and then grasped the causes, the middle terms.

Let A represent 'bright side turned sunward', B 'lighted from the sun', C the moon. Then B, 'lighted from the sun', is predicable of C, the moon, and A, 'having her bright side towards the source of her light', is predicable [20] of B. So A is predicable of C through B.

BOOK II

1

THE kinds of question we ask are as many as the kinds of things which we know. They are in fact four:—(1) whether the connexion of an attribute with a thing is a fact, (2) what is the reason of the connexion, (3) whether a thing [25] exists, (4) what is the nature of the thing. Thus, when our question concerns a complex of thing and attribute and we ask whether the thing is thus or otherwise qualified—whether, e.g. the sun suffers eclipse or not—then we are asking as to the fact of a connexion. That our inquiry ceases with the discovery that the sun does suffer eclipse is an indication of this; and if we know from the start that the sun suffers eclipse, we do not inquire whether it does so or not. On the other hand, when we know the fact we ask the reason; as, for example, when we know that the sun is being eclipsed [30] and that an earthquake is in progress, it is the reason of eclipse or earthquake into which we inquire.

Where a complex is concerned, then, those are the two questions we ask; but for some objects of inquiry we have a different kind of question to ask, such as whether there is or is not a centaur or a God. (By 'is or is not' I mean 'is or is not, without further qualification'; as opposed to 'is or is not (e.g.) white'.) On the other hand, when we have ascertained the thing's existence, we inquire as to its nature, asking, for instance, 'what, then, is God?' [35] or 'what is man?'.

2

These, then, are the four kinds of question we ask, and it is in the answers to these questions that our knowledge consists.

Now when we ask whether a connexion is a fact, or whether a thing without qualification *is*, we are really asking whether the connexion or the thing has a 'middle'; and when we have ascertained either that the connexion is a fact or that the thing *is*—i.e. ascertained either the partial or the unqualified being of **90ᵃ** the thing—and are proceeding to ask the reason of the connexion or the nature of the thing, then we are asking what the 'middle' is.

(By distinguishing the fact of the connexion and the existence of the thing as respectively the partial and the unqualified being of the thing, I mean that if we ask 'does the moon suffer eclipse?', or 'does the moon wax?', the question concerns a part of the thing's being; for what we are asking in such questions is whether a thing is this or that, i.e. has or has not this or that attribute: whereas, if we ask whether the moon or night exists, the question concerns the unqualified being of a thing.) [5] We conclude that in all our inquiries we are asking either whether there is a 'middle' or what the 'middle' is: for the 'middle' here is precisely the cause, and it is the cause that we seek in all our inquiries. Thus, 'Does the moon suffer eclipse?' means 'Is there or is there not a cause producing eclipse of the moon?', and when we have learnt that there is, our next question is, 'What, then, is this cause?'; for the cause through which a thing *is*—not *is this* [10] *or that,* i.e. has this or that attribute, but without qualification *is*—and the cause through which it is—not *is* without qualification, but *is this or that* as having some essential attribute or some accident—are both alike the 'middle'. By that which *is* without qualification I mean the subject, e.g. moon or earth or sun or triangle; by that which a subject *is* (in the partial sense) I mean a property, e.g. eclipse, equality or inequality, interposition or non-interposition. For in all these examples it is clear that the nature of the thing and the [15] reason of the fact are identical: the question 'What is eclipse?' and its answer 'The privation of the moon's light by the interposition of the earth' are identical with the question 'What is the reason of eclipse?' or 'Why does the moon suffer eclipse?' and the reply 'Because of the failure of light through the earth's shutting it out'. Again, for 'What is a concord? A commensurate numerical ratio of a high and a low note', we may substitute 'What reason [20] makes a high and a low note concordant? Their relation according to a commensurate numerical ratio.' 'Are the high and the low note concordant?' is equivalent to 'Is their ratio commensurate?'; and when we find that it is commensurate, we ask 'What, then, is their ratio?'.

Cases in which the 'middle' is sensible show [25] that the object of our inquiry is always the 'middle': we inquire, because we have not perceived it, whether there is or is not a 'middle' causing, e.g. an eclipse. On the other hand, if we were on the moon we should not be inquiring either as to the fact or the reason, but both fact and reason would be obvious simultaneously. For the act of perception would have enabled us to know the universal too; since, the present fact of an eclipse being evident, perception would then at the same time give us the present fact of the earth's screening the [30] sun's light, and from this would arise the universal.

Thus, as we maintain, to know a thing's nature is to know the reason why it is; and this is equally true of things in so far as they are said without qualification to *be* as opposed to being possessed of some attribute, and in so far as they are said to be possessed of some attribute such as equal to two right angles, or greater or less.

3

[35] It is clear, then, that all questions are a search for a 'middle'. Let us now state how essential nature is revealed, and in what way it can be reduced to demonstration; what definition is, and what things are definable. And let us first discuss certain difficulties which these 90ᵇ questions raise, beginning what we have to say with a point most intimately connected with our immediately preceding remarks, namely the doubt that might be felt as to whether or not it is possible to know the same thing in the same relation, both by definition and by demonstration. It might, I mean, be urged that definition is held to concern essential nature and is in every case universal and affirmative; whereas, on the other hand, some [5] conclusions are negative and some are not universal; e.g. all in the second figure are negative, none in the third are universal. And again, not even all affirmative conclusions in the first figure are definable, e.g. 'every triangle has its angles equal to two right angles'. An argument proving this difference between demonstration and definition is that to have scientific knowledge of the demonstrable is [10] identical with possessing a demonstration of it: hence if demonstration of such conclusions as these is possible, there clearly cannot also be definition of them. If there could, one might know such a conclusion also in virtue of its definition without possessing the demonstration of it; for there is nothing to stop our having the one without the other.

Induction too will sufficiently convince us of [15] this difference; for never yet by defining anything—essential attribute or accident—did we get knowledge of it. Again, if to define is to acquire knowledge of a substance, at any rate such attributes are not substances.

It is evident, then, that not everything demonstrable can be defined. What then? Can everything definable be demonstrated, or not? There is one of our previous arguments which [20] covers this too. Of a single thing *qua* single there is a single scientific knowledge. Hence, since to know the demonstrable scientifically is to possess the demonstration of it, an impossible consequence will follow:—possession of its definition without its demonstration will give knowledge of the demonstrable.

Moreover, the basic premisses of demonstrations are definitions, and it has already been shown[1] that these will be found indemonstra- [25] ble; either the basic premisses will be demonstrable and will depend on prior premisses, and the regress will be endless; or the primary truths will be indemonstrable definitions.

But if the definable and the demonstrable are not wholly the same, may they yet be partially the same? Or is that impossible, because there can be no demonstration of the defin- [30] able? There can be none, because definition is of the essential nature or being of something, and all demonstrations evidently posit and assume the essential nature—mathematical demonstrations, for example, the nature of unity and the odd, and all the other sciences likewise. Moreover, every demonstration proves a predicate of a subject as attaching or as not attaching to it, but in definition one thing is [35] not predicated of another; we do not, e.g. predicate animal of biped nor biped of animal, nor yet figure of plane—plane not being figure nor figure plane. Again, to prove essential nature is not the same as to prove the fact of a 91ᵃ connexion. Now definition reveals essential nature, demonstration reveals that a given attribute attaches or does not attach to a given subject; but different things require different demonstrations—unless the one demonstration is related to the other as part to whole. I add this because if all triangles have been proved to possess angles equal to two right angles, then this attribute has been proved to attach to isosceles; for isosceles is a part of which all tri- [5] angles constitute the whole. But in the case before us the fact and the essential nature are not so related to one another, since the one is not a part of the other.

So it emerges that not all the definable is demonstrable nor all the demonstrable defin-

[1] Cf. 72ᵇ 18-25 and 84ᵃ 30-ᵇ 2.

able; and we may draw the general conclusion that there is no identical object of which it is possible to possess both a definition and a dem- [10] onstration. It follows obviously that definition and demonstration are neither identical nor contained either within the other: if they were, their objects would be related either as identical or as whole and part.

4

So much, then, for the first stage of our problem. The next step is to raise the question whether syllogism—i.e. demonstration—of the definable nature is possible or, as our recent argument assumed, impossible.

We might argue it impossible on the following grounds:—(*a*) syllogism proves an attribute of a subject through the middle term; [15] on the other hand (*b*) its definable nature is both 'peculiar' to a subject and predicated of it as belonging to its essence. But in that case (1) the subject, its definition, and the middle term connecting them must be reciprocally predicable of one another; for if A is 'peculiar' to C, obviously A is 'peculiar' to B and B to C—in fact all three terms are 'peculiar' to one another: and further (2) if A inheres in the essence of all B and B is predicated universally of all C as belonging to C's essence, [20] A also must be predicated of C as belonging to its essence.

If one does not take this relation as thus duplicated—if, that is, A is predicated as being of the essence of B, but B is not of the essence of the subjects of which it is predicated—A will not necessarily be predicated of C as belonging to its essence. So both premisses *will* predicate essence, and consequently B also will be predicated of C as its essence. Since, there- [25] fore, both premisses do predicate essence—i.e. definable form—C's definable form will appear in the middle term before the conclusion is drawn.

We may generalize by supposing that it is possible to prove the essential nature of man. Let C be man, A man's essential nature—two-footed animal, or aught else it may be. Then, if we are to syllogize, A must be predicated of all B. But this premiss will be mediated by a [30] fresh definition, which consequently will also be the essential nature of man. Therefore the argument assumes what it has to prove, since B too is the essential nature of man. It is, however, the case in which there are only the two premisses—i.e. in which the premisses are primary and immediate—which we ought to investigate, because it best illustrates the point under discussion.

[35] Thus they who prove the essential nature of soul or man or anything else through reciprocating terms beg the question. It would be begging the question, for example, to contend that the soul is that which causes its own life, and that what causes its own life is a self-moving number; for one would have to postulate that the soul is a self-moving number in 91^b the sense of being identical with it. For if A is predicable as a mere consequent of B and B of C, A will not on that account be the definable form of C: A will merely be what it was true to say of C. Even if A is predicated of all B inasmuch as B is identical with a species of A, still it will not follow: being an animal [5] is predicated of being a man—since it is true that in all instances to be human is to be animal, just as it is also true that every man is an animal—but not as identical with being man.

We conclude, then, that unless one takes both the premisses as predicating essence, one cannot infer that A is the definable form and essence of C: but if one does so take them, in assuming B one will have assumed, before drawing the conclusion, what the definable form of [10] C is; so that there has been no inference, for one has begged the question.

5

Nor, as was said in my formal logic,[1] is the method of division a process of inference at all, since at no point does the characterization of the subject follow necessarily from the premising of certain other facts: division demon-[15] strates as little as does induction. For in a genuine demonstration the conclusion must not be put as a question nor depend on a concession, but must follow necessarily from its premisses, even if the respondent deny it. The definer asks 'Is man animal or inanimate?' and then assumes—he has not inferred—that man is animal. Next, when presented with an exhaustive division of animal into terrestrial and [20] aquatic, he assumes that man is terrestrial. Moreover, that man is the complete formula, terrestrial-animal, does not follow necessarily from the premisses: this too is an assumption, and equally an assumption whether the division comprises many differentiae or few. (Indeed as this method of division is used by those who proceed by it, even truths that can be inferred actually fail to appear as such.) For why should

[1] Cf. *Prior Analytics*, I. 31.

[25] not the whole of this formula be true of man, and yet not exhibit his essential nature or definable form? Again, what guarantee is there against an unessential addition, or against the omission of the final or of an intermediate determinant of the substantial being?

The champion of division might here urge that though these lapses do occur, yet we can solve that difficulty if all the attributes we assume are constituents of the definable form, and if, postulating the genus, we produce by division the requisite uninterrupted sequence of terms, and omit nothing; and that indeed [30] we cannot fail to fulfil these conditions if what is to be divided falls whole into the division at each stage, and none of it is omitted; and that this—the dividendum—must without further question be (ultimately) incapable of fresh specific division. Nevertheless, we reply, division does not involve inference; if it gives knowledge, it gives it in another way. Nor is there any absurdity in this: induction, perhaps, is not demonstration any more than is division, yet it does make evident some truth. Yet to [35] state a definition reached by division is not to state a conclusion: as, when conclusions are drawn without their appropriate middles, the alleged necessity by which the inference follows from the premisses is open to a question as to the reason for it, so definitions reached by division invite the same question. 92^a Thus to the question 'What is the essential nature of man?' the divider replies 'Animal, mortal, footed, biped, wingless'; and when at each step he is asked 'Why?', he will say, and, as he thinks, proves by division, that all animal is mortal or immortal: but such a formula taken in its entirety is not definition; so that even if division does demonstrate its formula, definition at any rate does not turn [5] out to be a conclusion of inference.

6

Can we nevertheless actually demonstrate what a thing essentially and substantially is, but hypothetically, i.e. by premising (1) that its definable form is constituted by the 'peculiar' attributes of its essential nature; (2) that such and such are the only attributes of its essential nature, and that the complete synthesis of them is peculiar to the thing; and thus—since in this synthesis consists the being of the thing—obtaining our conclusion? Or is the truth that, [10] since proof must be through the middle term, the definable form is once more assumed in this minor premiss too?

Further, just as in syllogizing we do not premise what syllogistic inference is (since the premisses from which we conclude must be related as whole and part), so the definable form must not fall within the syllogism but remain outside the premisses posited. It is only against [15] a doubt as to its having been a syllogistic inference at all that we have to defend our argument as conforming to the definition of syllogism. It is only when some one doubts whether the conclusion proved is the definable form that we have to defend it as conforming to the definition of definable form which we assumed. Hence syllogistic inference must be possible even without the express statement of what syllogism is or what definable form is.

[20] The following type of hypothetical proof also begs the question. If evil is definable as the divisible, and the definition of a thing's contrary—if it has one—is the contrary of the thing's definition; then, if good is the contrary of evil and the indivisible of the divisible, we conclude that to be good is essentially to be indivisible. The question is begged because definable form is assumed as a premiss, and as a premiss which is to prove definable form. 'But [25] not the same definable form', you may object. That I admit, for in demonstrations also we premise that 'this' is predicable of 'that'; but in this premiss the term we assert of the minor is neither the major itself nor a term identical in definition, or convertible, with the major.

Again, both proof by division and the syllogism just described are open to the question why man should be animal-biped-terrestrial and not merely animal *and* terrestrial, since [30] what they premise does not ensure that the predicates shall constitute a genuine unity and not merely belong to a single subject as do musical and grammatical when predicated of the same man.

7

How then by definition shall we *prove* sub-[35] stance or essential nature? We cannot show it as a fresh fact necessarily following from the assumption of premisses admitted to be facts—the method of demonstration: we may not proceed as by induction to establish a universal on the evidence of groups of particulars which offer no exception, because induction proves not what the essential nature of a thing is but that it has or has not some attribute. Therefore, since presumably one cannot prove essential nature by an appeal to sense perception or by pointing with the finger, what other method remains?

To put it another way: how shall we by definition prove *essential nature*? He who knows what human—or any other—nature is, [5] must know also that man exists; for no one knows the nature of what does not exist—one can know the meaning of the phrase or name 'goat-stag' but not what the essential nature of a goat-stag is. But further, if definition can prove what is the essential nature of a thing, can it also prove that it exists? And how will it prove them both by the same process, since definition exhibits one single thing and dem-[10]onstration another single thing, and what human nature is and the fact that man exists are not the same thing? Then too we hold that it is by *demonstration* that the being of everything must be proved—unless indeed to be were its essence; and, since being is not a genus, it is not the essence of anything. Hence the being of anything as fact is matter for dem-[15]onstration; and this is the actual procedure of the sciences, for the geometer assumes the meaning of the word triangle, but that it is possessed of some attribute he proves. What is it, then, that we shall prove in defining essential nature? Triangle? In that case a man will know by definition what a thing's nature is without knowing whether it exists. But that is impossible.

Moreover it is clear, if we consider the methods of defining actually in use, that definition does not prove that the thing defined [20] exists: since even if there does actually exist something which is equidistant from a centre, yet *why* should the thing named in the definition exist? Why, in other words, should this be the formula defining circle? One might equally well call it the definition of mountain copper. For definitions do not carry a further guarantee that the thing defined can exist or that it is what they claim to define: one can [25] always ask why.

Since, therefore, to define is to prove either a thing's essential nature or the meaning of its name, we may conclude that definition, if it in no sense proves essential nature, is a set of words signifying precisely what a name signifies. But that were a strange consequence; for (1) both what is not substance and what does not exist at all would be definable, since even non-existents can be signified by a name: (2) [30] all sets of words or sentences would be definitions, since any kind of sentence could be given a name; so that we should all be talking in definitions, and even the *Iliad* would be a definition: (3) no demonstration can prove that any particular name means any particular thing: neither, therefore, do definitions, in addition to revealing the meaning of a name, also reveal that the name has *this* meaning. It appears then from these considerations that neither definition and syllogism nor their objects are identical, and further that definition neither demonstrates nor proves anything, and that knowledge of essential nature is not to be obtained either by definition or by demonstration.

8

93ª We must now start afresh and consider which of these conclusions are sound and which are not, and what is the nature of definition, and whether essential nature is in any sense demonstrable and definable or in none.

Now to know its essential nature is, as we said,[1] the same as to know the cause of a thing's existence, and the proof of this depends on the fact that a thing must have a cause. Moreover, this cause is either identical with the essential nature of the thing or distinct from it; and if its cause is distinct from it, the essential nature of the thing is either demonstrable or indemonstrable. Consequently, if the cause is distinct from the thing's essential nature and demonstration is possible, the cause must be the middle term, and, the conclusion proved being universal and affirmative, the proof is in the first figure. So the method just examined of proving it through another essential nature would be one way of proving essential nature, because a conclusion containing essential nature must be inferred through a middle which is an essential nature just as a 'peculiar' property must be inferred through a middle which is a 'peculiar' property; so that of the two definable natures of a single thing this method will prove one and not the other.

Now it was said before[2] that this method could not amount to demonstration of essential nature—it is actually a dialectical proof of it— so let us begin again and explain by what method it can be demonstrated. When we are aware of a fact we seek its reason, and though sometimes the fact and the reason dawn on us simultaneously, yet we cannot apprehend the reason a moment sooner than the fact; and clearly in just the same way we cannot apprehend a thing's definable form without apprehending that it exists, since while we are ignorant whether it exists we cannot know its essential nature. Moreover we are aware whether a thing exists or not sometimes through apprehending an element in its character, and sometimes accidentally, as, for example, when we are aware of thunder as a noise in the clouds, of eclipse as a privation of light, or of man as some species of animal, or of the soul as a self-moving thing. As often as we have accidental knowledge that the thing exists, we must be in a wholly negative state as regards awareness of its essential nature; for we have not got genuine knowledge even of its existence, and to search for a thing's essential nature when we are unaware that it exists is to search for nothing. On the other hand, whenever we apprehend an element in the thing's character there is less difficulty. Thus it follows that the degree of our knowledge of a thing's essential nature is determined by the sense in which we are aware that it exists. Let us then take the following as our first instance of being aware of an element in the essential nature. Let A be eclipse, C the moon, B the earth's acting as a screen. Now to ask whether the moon is eclipsed or not is to ask whether or not B has occurred. But that is precisely the same as asking whether A has a defining condition; and if this condition actually exists, we assert that A also actually exists. Or again we may ask which side of a contradiction the defining condition necessitates: does it make the angles of a triangle equal or not equal to two right angles? When we have found the answer, if the premisses are immediate, we know fact and reason together; if they are not immediate, we know the fact without the reason, as in the following example: let C be the moon, A eclipse, B the fact that the moon fails to produce shadows though she is full and though no visible body intervenes between us and her. Then if B, failure to produce shadows in spite of the absence of an intervening body, is attributable to C, and A, eclipse, is attributable to B, it is clear that the moon is eclipsed, but the reason why is not yet clear, and we know that eclipse exists, but we do not know what its essential nature is. But when it is clear that A is attributable to C and we proceed to ask the reason of this fact, we are inquiring what is the nature of B: is it the earth's acting as a screen, or the moon's rotation or her extinction? But B is the definition of the other term, viz. in these examples, of the major term A; for eclipse is constituted by the earth acting as

---
[1] II. 2. [2] II. 2.

a screen. Thus, (1) 'What is thunder?' 'The quenching of fire in cloud', and (2) 'Why does it thunder?' 'Because fire is quenched in the [10] cloud', are equivalent. Let C be cloud, A thunder, B the quenching of fire. Then B is attributable to C, cloud, since fire is quenched in it; and A, noise, is attributable to B; and B is assuredly the definition of the major term A. If there be a further mediating cause of B, it will be one of the remaining partial definitions of A.

[15] We have stated then how essential nature is discovered and becomes known, and we see that, while there is no syllogism—i.e. no demonstrative syllogism—of essential nature, yet it is through syllogism, viz. demonstrative syllogism, that essential nature is exhibited. So we conclude that neither can the essential nature of anything which has a cause distinct from itself be known without demonstration, nor can it be demonstrated; and this is what we con- [20] tended in our preliminary discussions.[1]

9

Now while some things have a cause distinct from themselves, others have not. Hence it is evident that there are essential natures which are immediate, that is are basic premisses; and of these not only *that* they are but also *what* they are must be assumed or revealed in some other way. This too is the actual procedure of the arithmetician, who assumes both the na- [25] ture and the existence of unit. On the other hand, it is possible (in the manner explained) to exhibit through demonstration the essential nature of things which have a 'middle', i.e. a cause of their substantial being other than that being itself; but we do not thereby demonstrate it.

10

Since definition is said to be the statement of a thing's nature, obviously one kind of definition will be a statement of the meaning of the [30] name, or of an equivalent nominal formula. A definition in this sense tells you, e.g. the meaning of the phrase 'triangular character'. When we are aware that triangle exists, we inquire the reason why it exists. But it is difficult thus to learn the definition of things the existence of which we do not genuinely know —the cause of this difficulty being, as we said [35] before,[2] that we only know accidentally whether or not the thing exists. Moreover, a statement may be a unity in either of two ways,

[1] II. 3.　　[2] Cf. 93ª 16-27.

by conjunction, like the *Iliad,* or because it exhibits a single predicate as inhering not accidentally in a single subject.

That then is one way of defining definition. Another kind of definition is a formula exhibiting the cause of a thing's existence. Thus the former signifies without proving, but the latter will clearly be a *quasi*-demonstration of essential nature, differing from demonstration in the arrangement of its terms. For there is a difference between stating why it thunders, and stating what is the essential nature of thunder; since the first statement will be 'Because fire is quenched in the clouds', while the statement of what the nature of thunder is will be 'The noise of fire being quenched in the [5] clouds'. Thus the same statement takes a different form: in one form it is continuous demonstration, in the other definition. Again, thunder can be defined as noise in the clouds, which is the conclusion of the demonstration embodying essential nature. On the other hand the definition of immediates is an indemonstra- [10] ble positing of essential nature.

We conclude then that definition is (*a*) an indemonstrable statement of essential nature, or (*b*) a syllogism of essential nature differing from demonstration in grammatical form, or (*c*) the conclusion of a demonstration giving essential nature.

Our discussion has therefore made plain (1) in what sense and of what things the essential [15] nature is demonstrable, and in what sense and of what things it is not; (2) what are the various meanings of the term definition, and in what sense and of what things it proves the essential nature, and in what sense and of what things it does not; (3) what is the relation of definition to demonstration, and how far the same thing is both definable and demonstrable and how far it is not.

11

[20] We think we have scientific knowledge when we know the cause, and there are four causes: (1) the definable form, (2) an antecedent which necessitates a consequent, (3) the efficient cause, (4) the final cause. Hence each of these can be the middle term of a proof, for (*a*) though the inference from antecedent to necessary consequent does not hold if only [25] one premiss is assumed—two is the minimum—still when there are two it holds on condition that they have a single common middle term. So it is from the assumption of this single middle term that the conclusion follows

necessarily. The following example will also show this. Why is the angle in a semicircle a right angle?—or from what assumption does it follow that it is a right angle? Thus, let A be right angle, B the half of two right angles, [30] C the angle in a semicircle. Then B is the cause in virtue of which A, right angle, is attributable to C, the angle in a semicircle, since $B = A$ and the other, viz. $C, = B$, for C is half of two right angles. Therefore it *is* the assumption of B, the half of two right angles, from which it follows that A is attributable to C, i.e. that the angle in a semicircle is a right angle. Moreover, B is identical with (b) the de-[35] fining form of A, since it is what A's definition signifies. Moreover, the formal cause has already been shown to be the middle. (*c*) 'Why did the Athenians become involved in the Persian war?' means 'What cause originated the waging of war against the Athenians?' and the answer is, 'Because they raided Sardis with the Eretrians', since this originated the war. Let A be war, B unprovoked raiding, C the Athenians. Then B, unprovoked raiding, is true of C, the Athenians, and A is true of B, [5] since men make war on the unjust aggressor. So A, having war waged upon them, is true of B, the initial aggressors, and B is true of C, the Athenians, who were the aggressors. Hence here too the cause—in this case the efficient cause—is the middle term. (*d*) This is no less true where the cause is the final cause. E.g. why does one take a walk after supper? For the sake of one's health. Why does a house [10] exist? For the preservation of one's goods. The end in view is in the one case health, in the other preservation. To ask the reason why one must walk after supper is precisely to ask to what end one must do it. Let C be walking after supper, B the non-regurgitation of food, A health. Then let walking after supper possess the property of preventing food from ris-[15] ing to the orifice of the stomach, and let this condition be healthy; since it seems that B, the non-regurgitation of food, is attributable to C, taking a walk, and that A, health, is attributable to B. What, then, is the cause through which A, the final cause, inheres in C? It is B, the non-regurgitation of food; but B is a kind of definition of A, for A will be [20] explained by it. Why is B the cause of A's belonging to C? Because to be in a condition such as B is to be in health. The definitions must be transposed, and then the detail will become clearer. Incidentally, here the order of coming to be is the reverse of what it is in proof through the efficient cause: in the efficient order the middle term must come to be first, whereas in the teleological order the [25] minor, C, must first take place, and the end in view comes last in time.

The same thing may exist for an end and be necessitated as well. For example, light shines through a lantern (1) because that which consists of relatively small particles necessarily passes through pores larger than those [30] particles—assuming that light does issue by penetration—and (2) for an end, namely to save us from stumbling. If, then, a thing can exist through two causes, can it come to be through two causes—as for instance if thunder be a hiss and a roar necessarily produced by the quenching of fire, and also designed, as the Pythagoreans say, for a threat to terrify those that lie in Tartarus? Indeed, there are very [35] many such cases, mostly among the processes and products of the natural world; for nature, in different senses of the term 'nature', produces now for an end, now by necessity.

Necessity too is of two kinds. It may work in accordance with a thing's natural tendency, or by constraint and in opposition to it; as, for instance, by necessity a stone is borne both upwards and downwards, but not by the same necessity.

Of the products of man's intelligence some are never due to chance or necessity but always to an end, as for example a house or a [5] statue; others, such as health or safety, may result from chance as well.

It is mostly in cases where the issue is indeterminate (though only where the production does not originate in chance, and the end is consequently good), that a result is due to an end, and this is true alike in nature or in art. By chance, on the other hand, nothing comes to be for an end.

12

[10] The effect may be still coming to be, or its occurrence may be past or future, yet the cause will be the same as when it is actually existent—for it is the middle which is the cause —except that if the effect actually exists the cause is actually existent, if it is coming to be so is the cause, if its occurrence is past the cause is past, if future the cause is future. For example, the moon was eclipsed because the earth intervened, is becoming eclipsed because the [15] earth is in process of intervening, will be eclipsed because the earth will intervene, is eclipsed because the earth intervenes.

To take a second example: assuming that the definition of ice is solidified water, let C be water, A solidified, B the middle, which is the cause, namely total failure of heat. Then B is attributed to C, and A, solidification, to B: ice [20] forms when B is occurring, has formed when B has occurred, and will form when B shall occur.

This sort of cause, then, and its effect come to be simultaneously when they are in process of becoming, and exist simultaneously when they actually exist; and the same holds good when they are past and when they are future. But what of cases where they are not simultaneous? Can causes and effects different from one another form, as they seem to us to form, [25] a continuous succession, a past effect resulting from a past cause different from itself, a future effect from a future cause different from it, and an effect which is coming-to-be from a cause different from and prior to it? Now on this theory it is from the posterior event that we reason (and this though these later events actually have their source of origin in previous events—a fact which shows that also when the effect is coming-to-be we still reason from the posterior event), and from the prior event we cannot reason (we cannot argue [30] that because an event A has occurred, therefore an event B has occurred subsequently to A but still in the past—and the same holds good if the occurrence is future)—cannot reason because, be the time interval definite or indefinite, it will never be possible to infer that because it is true to say that A occurred, therefore it is true to say that B, the subsequent event, occurred; for in the interval between the events, though A has already occurred, the [35] latter statement will be false. And the same argument applies also to future events; i.e. one cannot infer from an event which occurred in the past that a future event will occur. The reason of this is that the middle must be homogeneous, past when the extremes are past, future when they are future, coming to be when they are coming-to-be, actually existent when they are actually existent; and there cannot be a middle term homogeneous with extremes respectively past and future. And it is a further difficulty in this theory that the time [40] interval can be neither indefinite nor definite, since during it the inference will be false. We have also to inquire what it is that holds events together so that the coming-to-be now occurring in actual things follows upon a past event. It is evident, we may suggest, that a past event and a present process cannot be 'contiguous', for not even two past events can be 'contiguous'. For past events are limits and [5] atomic; so just as points are not 'contiguous' neither are past events, since both are indivisible. For the same reason a past event and a present process cannot be 'contiguous', for the process is divisible, the event indivisible. Thus the relation of present process to past event is analogous to that of line to point, since [10] a process contains an infinity of past events. These questions, however, must receive a more explicit treatment in our general theory of change.[1]

The following must suffice as an account of the manner in which the middle would be identical with the cause on the supposition that coming-to-be is a series of consecutive events: for in the terms of such a series too the middle [15] and major terms must form an immediate premiss; e.g. we argue that, since C has occurred, therefore A occurred: and C's occurrence was posterior, A's prior; but C is the source of the inference because it is nearer to the present moment, and the starting-point of time is the present. We next argue that, since D has occurred, therefore C occurred. Then we conclude that, since D has occurred, therefore [20] A must have occurred; and the cause is C, for since D has occurred C must have occurred, and since C has occurred A must previously have occurred.

If we get our middle term in this way, will the series terminate in an immediate premiss, or since, as we said, no two events are 'contiguous', will a fresh middle term always intervene because there is an infinity of middles? No: though no two events are 'contiguous', yet we must start from a premiss consisting of a middle and the present event as major. The [25] like is true of future events too, since if it is true to say that D will exist, it must be a prior truth to say that A will exist, and the cause of this conclusion is C; for if D will exist, C will exist prior to D, and if C will exist, A will exist prior to it. And here too the same [30] infinite divisibility might be urged, since future events are not 'contiguous'. But here too an immediate basic premiss must be assumed. And in the world of fact this is so: if a house has been built, then blocks must have been quarried and shaped. The reason is that a house having been built necessitates a foundation having been laid, and if a foundation has [35] been laid blocks must have been shaped

[1] Cf. *Physics* vi.

beforehand. Again, if a house will be built, blocks will similarly be shaped beforehand; and proof is through the middle in the same way, for the foundation will exist before the house.

Now we observe in Nature a certain kind of circular process of coming-to-be; and this is possible only if the middle and extreme terms [40] are reciprocal, since conversion is conditioned by reciprocity in the terms of the proof. 96ᵃ This—the convertibility of conclusions and premises—has been proved in our early chapters,[1] and the circular process is an instance of this. In actual fact it is exemplified thus: when the earth had been moistened an exhalation was bound to rise, and when an exhalation had risen cloud was bound to form, and from the formation of cloud rain necessarily resulted, and by the fall of rain the earth was neces- [5] sarily moistened: but this was the starting-point, so that a circle is completed; for posit any one of the terms and another follows from it, and from that another, and from that again the first.

Some occurrences are universal (for they are, or come-to-be what they are, always and in every case); others again are not always what [10] they are but only as a general rule: for instance, not every man can grow a beard, but it is the general rule. In the case of such connexions the middle term too must be a general rule. For if A is predicated universally of B and B of C, A too must be predicated always and in every instance of C, since to hold in [15] every instance and always is of the nature of the universal. But we have assumed a connexion which is a general rule; consequently the middle term B must also be a general rule. So connexions which embody a general rule—i.e. which exist or come to be as a general rule —will also derive from immediate basic premisses.

13

[20] We have already explained how essential nature is set out in the terms of a demonstration, and the sense in which it is or is not demonstrable or definable; so let us now discuss the method to be adopted in tracing the elements predicated as constituting the definable form.

Now of the attributes which inhere always in each several thing there are some which are wider in extent than it but not wider than its [25] genus (by attributes of wider extent I mean all such as are universal attributes of each several subject, but in their application are not confined to that subject). I.e. while an attribute may inhere in every triad, yet also in a subject not a triad—as being inheres in triad but also in subjects not numbers at all—odd on the other hand is an attribute inhering in every triad and of wider application (inhering as it [30] does also in pentad), but which does not extend beyond the genus of triad; for pentad is a number, but nothing outside number is odd. It is such attributes which we have to select, up to the exact point at which they are severally of wider extent than the subject but collectively coextensive with it; for this synthesis must be the substance of the thing. For example every triad possesses the attributes number, [35] odd, and prime in both senses, i.e. not only as possessing no divisors, but also as not being a sum of numbers. This, then, is precisely what triad is, viz. a number, odd, and prime in the former and also the latter sense of the term: for these attributes taken severally 96ᵇ apply, the first two to all odd numbers, the last to the dyad also as well as to the triad, but, taken collectively, to no other subject. Now since we have shown above[2] that attributes predicated as belonging to the essential nature are necessary and that universals are necessary, and since the attributes which we select as inhering in triad, or in any other subject whose attributes we select in this way, are pred- [5] icated as belonging to its essential nature, triad will thus possess these attributes necessarily. Further, that the synthesis of them constitutes the substance of triad is shown by the following argument. If it is not identical with the being of triad, it must be related to triad as a genus named or nameless. It will then be of wider extent than triad—assuming that wider [10] potential extent is the character of a genus. If on the other hand this synthesis is applicable to no subject other than the individual triads, it will be identical with the being of triad, because we make the further assumption that the substance of each subject is the predication of elements in its essential nature down to the last differentia characterizing the individuals. It follows that any other synthesis thus exhibited will likewise be identical with the being of the subject.

[15] The author of a hand-book on a subject that is a generic whole should divide the genus into its first *infimae species*—number e.g. into triad and dyad—and then endeavour to seize

---
[1] I. 3; and *Prior Analytics*, II. 3-5, 8-10. [2] I. 4.

their definitions by the method we have described—the definition, for example, of straight line or circle or right angle. After that, having established what the category is to which the subaltern genus belongs—quantity or quality, [20] for instance—he should examine the properties 'peculiar' to the species, working through the proximate common differentiae. He should proceed thus because the attributes of the genera compounded of the *infimae species* will be clearly given by the definitions of the species; since the basic element of them all is the definition, i.e. the simple *infirma species,* and the attributes inhere essentially in the simple *infimae species,* in the genera only in virtue of these.

[25] Divisions according to differentiae are a useful accessory to this method. What force they have as proofs we did, indeed, explain above,[1] but that merely towards collecting the essential nature they may be of use we will proceed to show. They might, indeed, seem to be of no use at all, but rather to assume everything at the start and to be no better than an [30] initial assumption made without division. But, in fact, the order in which the attributes are predicated does make a difference—it matters whether we say animal—tame—biped, or biped—animal—tame. For if every definable thing consists of two elements and 'animal-tame' forms a unity, and again out of this and the further differentia man (or whatever else is the unity under construction) is constituted, then the elements we assume have necessarily been reached by division. Again, di-[35] vision is the only possible method of avoiding the omission of any element of the essential nature. Thus, if the primary genus is assumed and we then take one of the lower divisions, the dividendum will not fall whole into this division: e.g. it is not all animal which is either whole-winged or split-winged but all winged animal, for it is winged animal to which this differentiation belongs. The primary differentiation of animal is that within which all animal falls. The like is true of every other genus, whether outside animal or a subaltern genus of animal; e.g. the primary differentiation of bird is that within which falls every bird, of fish that within which falls every fish. So, if we proceed in this way, we can be sure that nothing has been omitted: by any [5] other method one is bound to omit something without knowing it.

To define and divide one need not know the

[1] II. 5; and *Prior Analytics,* I. 31.

whole of existence. Yet some hold it impossible to know the differentiae distinguishing each thing from every single other thing without knowing every single other thing; and one cannot, they say, know each thing without knowing its differentiae, since everything is [10] identical with that from which it does not differ, and other than that from which it differs. Now first of all this is a fallacy: not every differentia precludes identity, since many differentiae inhere in things specifically identical, though not in the substance of these nor essentially. Secondly, when one has taken one's differing pair of opposites and assumed that the [15] two sides exhaust the genus, and that the subject one seeks to define is present in one or other of them, and one has further verified its presence in one of them; then it does not matter whether or not one knows all the other subjects of which the differentiae are also predicated. For it is obvious that when by this process one reaches subjects incapable of further differentiation one will possess the formula defining the substance. Moreover, to postulate that the division exhausts the genus is not ille-[20] gitimate if the opposites exclude a middle; since if it is the differentia of that genus, anything contained in the genus must lie on one of the two sides.

In establishing a definition by division one should keep three objects in view: (1) the admission only of elements in the definable form, (2) the arrangement of these in the right or-[25] der, (3) the omission of no such elements. The first is feasible because one can establish genus and differentia through the topic of the genus, just as one can conclude the inherence of an accident through the topic of the accident. The right order will be achieved if the right term is assumed as primary, and this will be ensured if the term selected is predica-[30] ble of all the others but not all they of it; since there must be one such term. Having assumed this we at once proceed in the same way with the lower terms; for our second term will be the first of the remainder, our third the first of those which follow the second in a 'contiguous' series, since when the higher term is excluded, that term of the remainder which is 'contiguous' to it will be primary, and so on. Our procedure makes it clear that no elements [35] in the definable form have been omitted: we have taken the differentia that comes first in the order of division, pointing out that animal, e.g. is divisible exhaustively into *A* and *B,* and that the subject accepts one of the two as its predicate. Next we have taken the differentia of the whole thus reached, and shown that the whole we finally reach is not further divisible—i.e. that as soon as we have taken the last differentia to form the concrete totality, this totality admits of no division into species. 97ᵇ For it is clear that there is no superfluous addition, since all these terms we have selected are elements in the definable form; and nothing lacking, since any omission would have to be a genus or a differentia. Now the primary term is a genus, and this term taken in conjunction with its differentiae is a genus: moreover the differentiae are all included, because there is now no further differentia; if [5] there were, the final concrete would admit of division into species, which, we said, is not the case.

To resume our account of the right method of investigation: We must start by observing a set of similar—i.e. specifically identical—individuals, and consider what element they have in common. We must then apply the same process to another set of individuals which belong to one species and are generically but not specifically identical with the former set. When [10] we have established what the common element is in all members of this second species, and likewise in members of further species, we should again consider whether the results established possess any identity, and persevere until we reach a single formula, since this will be the definition of the thing. But if we reach not one formula but two or more, evidently the *definiendum* cannot be one thing [15] but must be more than one. I may illustrate my meaning as follows. If we were inquiring what the essential nature of pride is, we should examine instances of proud men we know of to see what, as such, they have in common; e.g. if Alcibiades was proud, or Achilles and Ajax were proud, we should find on inquiring what they all had in common, that it was intolerance of insult; it was this which drove Alcibiades to war, Achilles to [20] wrath, and Ajax to suicide. We should next examine other cases, Lysander, for example, or Socrates, and then if these have in common indifference alike to good and ill fortune, I take these two results and inquire what common element have equanimity amid the vicissitudes of life and impatience of dishonour. If [25] they have none, there will be two genera of pride. Besides, every definition is always universal and commensurate: the physician does not prescribe what is healthy for a single eye, but for all eyes or for a determinate species of eye. It is also easier by this method to define the single species than the universal, and that is why our procedure should be from the several species to the universal genera—this for [30] the further reason too that equivocation is less readily detected in genera than in *infimae species*. Indeed, perspicuity is essential in definitions, just as inferential movement is the minimum required in demonstrations; and we shall attain perspicuity if we can collect separately the definition of each species through the group of singulars which we have established—e.g. the definition of similarity not un- [35] qualified but restricted to colours and to figures; the definition of acuteness, but only of sound—and so proceed to the common universal with a careful avoidance of equivocation. We may add that if dialectical disputation must not employ metaphors, clearly metaphors and metaphorical expressions are precluded in definition: otherwise dialectic would involve metaphors.

14

98ᵃ In order to formulate the connexions we wish to prove we have to select our analyses and divisions. The method of selection consists in laying down the common genus of all our subjects of investigation—if e.g. they are animals, we lay down what the properties are which inhere in every animal. These established, we next lay down the properties essen- [5] tially connected with the first of the remaining classes—e.g. if this first subgenus is bird, the essential properties of every bird— and so on, always characterizing the proximate subgenus. This will clearly at once enable us to say in virtue of what character the subgenera —man, e.g. or horse—possess their properties. Let A be animal, B the properties of every ani- [10] mal, C D E various species of animal. Then it is clear in virtue of what character B inheres in D—namely A—and that it inheres in C and E for the same reason: and throughout the remaining subgenera always the same rule applies.

We are now taking our examples from the traditional class-names, but we must not confine ourselves to considering these. We must collect any other common character which we [15] observe, and then consider with what species it is connected and what properties belong to it. For example, as the common properties of horned animals we collect the possession of a third stomach and only one row of teeth.

Then since it is clear in virtue of what character they possess these attributes—namely their horned character—the next question is, to what species does the possession of horns attach?

[20] Yet a further method of selection is by analogy: for we cannot find a single identical name to give to a squid's pounce, a fish's spine, and an animal's bone, although these too possess common properties as if there were a single osseous nature.

15

Some connexions that require proof are identical in that they possess an identical 'middle' —e.g. a whole group might be proved through [25] 'reciprocal replacement'—and of these one class are identical in genus, namely all those whose difference consists in their concerning different subjects or in their mode of manifestation. This latter class may be exemplified by the questions as to the causes respectively of echo, of reflection, and of the rainbow: the connexions to be proved which these questions embody are identical generically, because all three are forms of repercussion; but specifically they are different.

Other connexions that require proof only differ in that the 'middle' of the one is subor- [30] dinate to the 'middle' of the other. For example: Why does the Nile rise towards the end of the month? Because towards its close the month is more stormy. Why is the month more stormy towards its close? Because the moon is waning. Here the one cause is subordinate to the other.

16

[35] The question might be raised with regard to cause and effect whether when the effect is present the cause also is present; whether, for instance, if a plant sheds its leaves or the moon is eclipsed, there is present also the cause of the eclipse or of the fall of the leaves—the possession of broad leaves, let us say, in the latter 98ᵇ case, in the former the earth's interposition. For, one might argue, if this cause is not present, these phenomena will have some other cause: if it *is* present, its effect will be at once implied by it—the eclipse by the earth's interposition, the fall of the leaves by the possession of broad leaves; but if so, they will be logically coincident and each capable of proof through [5] the other. Let me illustrate: Let A be deciduous character, B the possession of broad leaves, C vine. Now if A inheres in B (for every broad-leaved plant is deciduous), and B in C (every vine possessing broad leaves); then A inheres in C (every vine is deciduous), and the middle term B is the cause. But we can also [10] demonstrate that the vine has broad leaves because it is deciduous. Thus, let D be broad-leaved, E deciduous, F vine. Then E inheres in F (since every vine is deciduous), and D in E (for every deciduous plant has broad leaves): [15] therefore every vine has broad leaves, and the cause is its deciduous character. If, however, they cannot each be the cause of the other (for cause is prior to effect, and the earth's interposition is the cause of the moon's eclipse and not the eclipse of the interposition)—if, then, demonstration through the cause is of the [20] reasoned fact and demonstration not through the cause is of the bare fact, one who knows it through the eclipse knows the fact of the earth's interposition but not the reasoned fact. Moreover, that the eclipse is not the cause of the interposition, but the interposition of the eclipse, is obvious because the interposition is an element in the definition of eclipse, which shows that the eclipse is known through the interposition and not vice versa.

[25] On the other hand, can a single effect have more than one cause? One might argue as follows: if the same attribute is predicable of more than one thing as its primary subject, let B be a primary subject in which A inheres, and C another primary subject of A, and D and E primary subjects of B and C respectively. A will then inhere in D and E, and B will be the cause of A's inherence in D, C of A's inherence in E. The presence of the cause thus [30] necessitates that of the effect, but the presence of the effect necessitates the presence not of all that may cause it but only of *a* cause which yet need not be the whole cause. We may, however, suggest that if the connexion to be proved is always universal and commensurate, not only will the cause be a whole but also the effect will be universal and commensurate. For instance, deciduous character will belong exclusively to a subject which is a whole, and, if this whole has species, universally and commensurately to those species— i.e. either to all species of plant or to a single [35] species. So in these universal and commensurate connexions the 'middle' and its effect must reciprocate, i.e. be convertible. Supposing, for example, that the reason why trees are deciduous is the coagulation of sap, then if a tree is deciduous, coagulation must be present, and if coagulation is present—not in *any*

subject but in a tree—then that tree must be deciduous.

17

99ᵃ Can the cause of an identical effect be not identical in every instance of the effect but different? Or is that impossible? Perhaps it is impossible if the effect is demonstrated as essential and not as inhering in virtue of a symptom or an accident—because the middle is then the definition of the major term—though possible if the demonstration is not essential. Now it is [5] possible to consider the effect and its subject as an accidental conjunction, though such conjunctions would not be regarded as connexions demanding scientific proof. But if they are accepted as such, the middle will correspond to the extremes, and be equivocal if they are equivocal, generically one if they are generically one. Take the question why proportionals alternate. The cause when they are lines, and when they are numbers, is both different and identical; different in so far as lines are lines and not numbers, identical as involv- [10] ing a given determinate increment. In all proportionals this is so. Again, the cause of likeness between colour and colour is other than that between figure and figure; for likeness here is equivocal, meaning perhaps in the latter case equality of the ratios of the sides and equality of the angles, in the case of colours identity of the act of perceiving them, or some- [15] thing else of the sort. Again, connexions requiring proof which are identical by analogy have middles also analogous.

The truth is that cause, effect, and subject are reciprocally predicable in the following way. If the species are taken severally, the effect is wider than the subject (e.g. the possession of external angles equal to four right angles is an attribute wider than triangle or square), but it is coextensive with the species [20] taken collectively (in this instance with all figures whose external angles are equal to four right angles). And the middle likewise reciprocates, for the middle is a definition of the major; which is incidentally the reason why all the sciences are built up through definition.

We may illustrate as follows. Deciduous is a universal attribute of vine, and is at the same time of wider extent than vine; and of fig, and is of wider extent than fig: but it is not wider than but coextensive with the totality of the [25] species. Then if you take the middle which is proximate, it is a definition of decidu- ous. I say that, because you will first reach a middle next the subject, and a premiss asserting it of the whole subject, and after that a middle—the coagulation of sap or something of the sort—proving the connexion of the first middle with the major: but it is the coagulation of sap at the junction of leaf-stalk and stem which defines deciduous.

[30] If an explanation in formal terms of the inter-relation of cause and effect is demanded, we shall offer the following. Let A be an attribute of all B, and B of every species of D, but so that both A and B are wider than their respective subjects. Then B will be a universal attribute of each species of D (since I call such an attribute universal even if it is not commensurate, and I call an attribute primary universal if it is commensurate, not with each species severally but with their totality), and it extends beyond each of them taken separately. [35] Thus, B is the cause of A's inherence in the species of D: consequently A must be of wider extent than B; otherwise why should B be the cause of A's inherence in D any more than A the cause of B's inherence in D? Now if A is an attribute of all the species of E, all the species of E will be united by possessing some common cause other than B: otherwise how shall we be able to say that A is predicable of all of which E is predicable, while E is not 99ᵇ predicable of all of which A can be predicated? I mean how can there fail to be some special cause of A's inherence in E, as there was of A's inherence in all the species of D? Then are the species of E, too, united by possessing some common cause? This cause we must look for. Let us call it C.

We conclude, then, that the same effect may have more than one cause, but not in subjects specifically identical. For instance, the cause of [5] longevity in quadrupeds is lack of bile, in birds a dry constitution—or certainly something different.

18

If immediate premisses are not reached at once, and there is not merely one middle but several middles, i.e. several causes; is the cause of the property's inherence in the several species the middle which is proximate to the [10] primary universal, or the middle which is proximate to the species? Clearly the cause is that nearest to each species severally in which it is manifested, for that is the cause of the subject's falling under the universal. To illustrate formally: C is the cause of B's inherence in D;

hence C is the cause of A's inherence in D, B of A's inherence in C, while the cause of A's inherence in B is B itself.

19

[15] As regards syllogism and demonstration, the definition of, and the conditions required to produce each of them, are now clear, and with that also the definition of, and the conditions required to produce, demonstrative knowledge, since it is the same as demonstration. As to the basic premisses, how they become known and what is the developed state of knowledge of them is made clear by raising some preliminary problems.

[20] We have already said[1] that scientific knowledge through demonstration is impossible unless a man knows the primary immediate premisses. But there are questions which might be raised in respect of the apprehension of these immediate premisses: one might not only ask whether it is of the same kind as the apprehension of the conclusions, but also whether there is or is not scientific knowledge of both; or scientific knowledge of the latter, and of the former a different kind of knowledge; and, further, whether the developed [25] states of knowledge are not innate but come to be in us, or are innate but at first unnoticed. Now it is strange if we possess them from birth; for it means that we possess apprehensions more accurate than demonstration and fail to notice them. If on the other hand we acquire them and do not previously possess them, how could we apprehend and learn without a basis of pre-existent knowledge? For that is impossible, as we used to find[2] in the [30] case of demonstration. So it emerges that neither can we possess them from birth, nor can they come to be in us if we are without knowledge of them to the extent of having no such developed state at all. Therefore we must possess a capacity of some sort, but not such as to rank higher in accuracy than these developed states. And this at least is an obvious characteristic of all animals, for they possess a congenital [35] discriminative capacity which is called sense-perception. But though sense-perception is innate in all animals, in some the sense-impression comes to persist, in others it does not. So animals in which this persistence does not come to be have either no knowledge at all outside the act of perceiving, or no knowledge of objects of which no impression persists; animals in which it does come into being have perception and can continue to retain the sense-impression in the soul: and when such persistence is frequently repeated a further distinction at once arises between those which out of the persistence of such sense-impressions develop a power of systematizing them and those which do not. So out of sense-perception comes to be what we call memory, and out of frequently repeated memories of [5] the same thing develops experience; for a number of memories constitute a single experience. From experience again—i.e. from the universal now stabilized in its entirety within the soul, the one beside the many which is a single identity within them all—originate the skill of the craftsman and the knowledge of the man of science, skill in the sphere of coming to be and science in the sphere of being.

We conclude that these states of knowledge [10] are neither innate in a determinate form, nor developed from other higher states of knowledge, but from sense-perception. It is like a rout in battle stopped by first one man making a stand and then another, until the original formation has been restored. The soul is so constituted as to be capable of this process.

Let us now restate the account given already, [15] though with insufficient clearness. When one of a number of logically indiscriminable particulars has made a stand, the earliest universal is present in the soul: for though the act of sense-perception is of the particular, its content is universal—is man, for example, not the man Callias. A fresh stand is made among these rudimentary universals, and the process does not cease until the indivisible concepts, the true universals, are established: e.g. such and such a species of animal is a step towards the genus animal, which by the same process is a step towards a further generalization.

Thus it is clear that we must get to know the primary premisses by induction; for the method by which even sense-perception im- [5] plants the universal is inductive. Now of the thinking states by which we grasp truth, some are unfailingly true, others admit of error—opinion, for instance, and calculation, whereas scientific knowing and intuition are always true: further, no other kind of thought except intuition is more accurate than scientific knowledge, whereas primary premisses are more knowable than demonstrations, and all [10] scientific knowledge is discursive. From these considerations it follows that there will be no scientific knowledge of the primary

[1] I. 2.   [2] I. 1.

premisses, and since except intuition nothing can be truer than scientific knowledge, it will be intuition that apprehends the primary premisses—a result which also follows from the fact that demonstration cannot be the originative source of demonstration, nor, consequently, scientific knowledge of scientific knowledge. If, therefore, it is the only other kind of true thinking except scientific knowing, intuition [15] will be the originative source of scientific knowledge. And the originative source of science grasps the original basic premiss, while science as a whole is similarly related as originative source to the whole body of fact.

CONTENTS: TOPICS

BOOK I
Introductory

CHAP.		BERLIN NOS.
1.	Programme of treatise	100^a 18
2.	Uses of treatise	101^a 25
3.	Ideal aimed at	101^b 5

A. Subjects and Materials of Discussions

4.	Subjects (Problems) and materials (Propositions) classified into four groups according to nature of Predicable concerned	101^b 11
5.	The four Predicables	101^b 37
6.	How far to be treated separately	102^b 27
7.	Different kinds of sameness	103^a 6
8.	Twofold proof of division of Predicables	103^b 1
9.	The ten Categories and their relation to the Predicables	103^b 20
10.	Dialectical Propositions	104^a 3
11.	Dialectical Problems:—Theses	104^b 1
12.	Dialectical Reasoning and Induction	105^a 10

B. The Supply of Arguments

13.	Four sources of arguments:	105^a 20
14.	(1) How to secure propositions	105^a 33
15.	(2) How to distinguish ambiguous meanings	106^a 1
16.	(3) How to note differences	107^b 36
17.	(4) How to note resemblances	108^a 6
18.	The special uses of the last three processes	108^a 17

Commonplace Rules respecting Predications

(a) Of Accident: (i) Universal Predications

Part I. *Simple predications of Accidents generally*

BOOK II

1.	Proposed plan of treatment	108^b 37
2.	Various rules	109^a 34
3.	Rules for dealing with Ambiguity	110^a 23
4.	Various rules	111^a 8
5.	Rules for diverting the argument	111^b 31
6.	Various rules	112^a 24
7.	Rules drawn from contraries	112^b 26
8.	Rules drawn from different modes of opposition, or kinds of opposite	113^b 15
9.	Rules drawn from co-ordinates and inflexions, from contraries, and from processes or agents whereby things come to be or are destroyed	114^a 26
10.	Rules drawn from likeness between things or their relations, and from variations in degree	114^b 25
11.	Rules for arguing (a) from the results of adding things together to the character of the things; (b) from qualified to simple or absolute predications	115^a 25

Part II. *Comparative predications of Value-predicates of A or B*

BOOK III

1.	Various rules; including rules drawn from nature of subjects to which A or B belong (116^b 12–22); or from consideration of ends and means (116^b 22–36)	116^a 1
2.	Various rules; including rules drawn from consideration of antecedents and consequences (117^a 5–15); of numbers (117^a 16–25); of times and seasons (117^a 26–37); of self-sufficiency (117^a 37–^{b} 2); of destructions, losses, contraries, production, and acquisition (117^b 3–9); of some ideal pattern (117^b 10–27)	117^a 5
3.	Various rules; including rules drawn from comparison with some common standard (118^b 1–4); from result of adding A and B to, or subtracting them from, some other thing of known value (118^b 10–19); from comparison of grounds for desiring A or B (118^b 20–36)	118^a 26

Part III. *Simple predications of Value-predicates*

4.	How to adapt previous rules	119^a 1

Part IV. *Comparative predications of Accidents generally*

5.	Various rules	119^a 11

(ii) Particular Predications

6.	How to adapt the previous rules (119^a 32–120^a 5); proof and disproof, how affected by definiteness or indefiniteness of thesis (120^a 6–31); how to adapt the previous rules, continued (120^a 32–^{b} 7)	119^a 32

(b) Of Genus

BOOK IV

1.	Various rules	120^b 12
2.	(Continued)	121^b 24
3.	Various rules; including rules from contraries, useful for disproof (123^b 1–124^a 2), and for proof (124^a 3–10); from inflexions and co-ordinates (124^a 10–14)	123^a 20
4.	Various rules; including rules from likeness of relations (124^a 15–19); from processes or agents of generation and destruction (124^a 20–30); from capacities and uses of things (124^a 31–34); from opposition between	124^a 15

139

states and their privations (124^a 35–^{b} 6); from contradictory oppositions (124^b 7–14); from relative oppositions (124^b 15–34); from inflexions (124^b 35–125^a 4): also special rules applying where genus and species are relative terms (125^a 5–^{b} 14)

5. Various rules; including special rules applying where genus or species is a state, or a capacity or an affection. 125^b 15

6. Various rules; including rules from variations in degree, useful for disproof (127^b 18–36) and for proof (127^b 37–128^a 12); also rules for distinguishing genus from differentia (128^a 20–30) 127^a 20

(c) Of Property
BOOK V

1. Different kinds of property (128^b 16–129^a 16); suitability of each for discussion (129^a 17–31); lines of argument upon each (129^a 32–35) 128^b 14

2. *Rules for testing whether a property is rendered correctly* 129^b 1

3. (Continued) 130^b 38
Rules for testing whether a term belongs as a property at all:—

4. Various rules; including note on certain sophistical difficulties arising from ambiguity of the terms 'same' and 'different' 132^a 23

5. Various rules; including notes on difficulties arising from failure to say explicitly *how* the alleged property belongs (134^a 5–17, 18–25, 26–135^a 9); and a special rule applying to a whole consisting of like parts (135^a 20–^{b} 6) 134^a 5

6. Rules drawn from different modes of opposition—contrary opposition (135^b 7–16), relative opposition (135^b 17–26), that of a state and its privation (135^b 27–136^a 4), contradictory opposition, applied to predicates only (136^a 6–13), to both predicates and subjects (136^a 14–28), and to subjects only (136^a 29–^{b} 2); from co-ordinate members of a division (136^b 3–14) 135^b 6

7. Rules drawn from inflexions (136^b 15–32); from relations like the relation alleged to be a property (136^b 33–137^a 7); from identity of relations between the alleged property and two subjects (137^a 8–20); from processes of becoming and destruction (137^a 21–^{b} 2); from reference of the alleged property to the 'idea' of its subject (137^b 3–13) 136^b 15

8. Rules drawn from variations in degree (137^b 14–138^a 29); from comparison of an attribute-relation that is like the alleged property-relation, between a different attribute and a different subject (138^a 30–^{b} 5), between the subject of the alleged property and a different attribute (138^b 6–15), between the alleged property and a different subject (138^b 16–22); two rules (138^b 27–139^a 8, 139^a 9–20) 137^b 14

(d) Of Definition
BOOK VI

1. General division of problems relating to definition (139^a 24–35); distinction of problems treated and problems yet to be treated (139^a 36–^{b} 11) 139^a 24
Rules for testing whether definition is rendered correctly: obscurity and redundancy to be avoided (139^b 12–18)

2. Obscurity, how avoided 139^b 19

3. Redundancy, how avoided 140^a 23
Rules for testing whether the formula rendered is a definition at all:

4. Rules to secure that terms of definition shall be *prior and more intelligible;* how to detect failure in latter respect (141^b 3–142^a 21); in former (142^a 22–^{b} 19) 141^a 22

5. Rules as to *genus* 142^b 20

6. Rules as to *differentia* 143^a 29

7. Various rules, including rules for testing the definition of terms admitting variations in degree (146^a 3–20) 145^b 34

8. Rules for testing the definition of a relative term 146^a 36

9. Rules for testing the definition of a state (147^a 12–22); of a relative term (147^a 23–31); of contraries (147^a 32–^{b} 25); of a privation (147^b 26–148^a 2) or what is confused with one (148^a 3–9) 147^a 11

10. Rules drawn from like inflexions (148^a 10–13); from reference of the definition to the 'idea' of the term defined (148^a 14–22); rules for testing the definition of an ambiguous term (148^a 23–^{b} 22) 148^a 9

11. Rules for testing the definition of a complex term 148^b 22

12. Various rules, including rules for testing the definition of anything real (149^a 38–^{b} 3); of a relative term (149^b 4–23); of any term intrinsically valuable (149^b 31–39) 149^a 38

13. Definitions of the forms: 150^a 1
    (1) X is 'A and B' (150^a 1–21)
    (2) X is 'the product of A and B' (150^a 22–^{b} 26)
    (3) X is 'A+B' (150^b 27–151^a 19)

14. Various rules; including rules how to test the definition of compound whole (151^a 20–31); and how to examine an unclear definition (151^b 3–17) 151^a 20

(e) Of Sameness
BOOK VII

1. Various rules 151^b 26

2. Bearing of these rules on problem of definition 152^b 36

(f) Of Definition—*continued*

3. Rules for *establishing* a definition 153^a 6

4. Note on the comparative useful- 154^a 11

ness of the different kinds of commonplace-rules

5. Note on the comparative difficulty of proving or disproving the various kinds of Predicable — 154ᵃ 23

C. CONCERNING THE PRACTICE OF, AND PRACTICE IN, DIALECTICS

(a) *How to arrange and put questions*

BOOK VIII

1. Introductory (155ᵇ 3–17) — 155ᵇ 1
    (1) Of *necessary and other premisses*
    Premisses other than necessary premisses, and their four aims (155ᵇ 18–28)
    Use of necessary premisses (155ᵇ 29–156ᵃ 2)
    Use of premisses other than necessary:
        (1) for inductions (156ᵃ 3–7)
        (2) for concealment of intended conclusion (156ᵃ 7–157ᵃ 5)
        (3) for ornament (157ᵃ 6–13)
        (4) for clearness (157ᵃ 14–17)
2. (2) *Of inductions* (157ᵃ 18–33) — 157ᵃ 18
    (3) *Of objections* (157ᵃ 34–ᵇ 33)
    (4) Of argument *per impossibile* (157ᵇ 34–158ᵃ 2)
    (5) Miscellaneous hints (158ᵃ 3–30)
3. On the comparative difficulty or ease of certain dialectical arguments — 158ᵃ 31

(b) *How to answer*

4. Answerer's role and questioner's role — 159ᵃ 15
5. Introductory note on lack of tradition respecting discussions held for training and examination (159ᵃ 25–37) — 159ᵃ 25
    The answerer's procedure as determined by the character:
    (1) of his own thesis (159ᵃ 38–ᵇ 35)
6. (2) of the particular question put — 159ᵇ 36
    —its general acceptability and relevance
7. Its clearness — 160ᵃ 17
8. And its importance for the argument — 160ᵃ 35
9. Rules respecting the answerer's original thesis — 160ᵇ 14
10. On the solution of fallacious arguments (160ᵇ 23–39) — 160ᵇ 23
    Four types of objection distinguished (161ᵃ 1–15)

(c) *Supplementary discussions*

11. On faults of argument and faults of questioner — 161ᵃ 16
12. On clearness in argument:—its three kinds distinguished (162ᵃ 35–ᵇ 2) — 162ᵃ 35
    On fallacy in argument: its four kinds distinguished (162ᵇ 3–15); how far censurable (162ᵇ 16–24): test questions for its detection (162ᵇ 24–30)
13. On begging the question, and on the begging of contraries: five types of each distinguished — 162ᵇ 31
14. Hints upon training and practice in dialectical arguments — 163ᵃ 29

TOPICS
BOOK I

1

100ª [*18*] Our treatise proposes to find a line of inquiry whereby we shall be able to reason from opinions that are generally accepted about [*20*] every problem propounded to us, and also shall ourselves, when standing up to an argument, avoid saying anything that will obstruct us. First, then, we must say what reasoning is, and what its varieties are, in order to grasp dialectical reasoning: for this is the object of our search in the treatise before us.

[*25*] Now reasoning is an argument in which, certain things being laid down, something other than these necessarily comes about through them. (*a*) It is a 'demonstration', when the premisses from which the reasoning starts are true and primary, or are such that our knowledge of them has originally come through premisses which are primary and true: (*b*) [*30*] reasoning, on the other hand, is 'dialectical', if it reasons from opinions that are generally accepted. Things are 'true' and 'primary' **100ᵇ** [*18*] which are believed on the strength not of anything else but of themselves: for in regard to the first principles of science it is improper to ask any further for the why and [*20*] wherefore of them; each of the first principles should command belief in and by itself. On the other hand, those opinions are 'generally accepted' which are accepted by every one or by the majority or by the philosophers—i.e. by all, or by the majority, or by the most notable and illustrious of them. Again (*c*), reasoning is 'contentious' if it starts from opinions that seem to be generally accepted, but are not [*25*] really such, or again if it merely seems to reason from opinions that are or seem to be generally accepted. For not every opinion that seems to be generally accepted actually is generally accepted. For in none of the opinions which we call generally accepted is the illusion entirely on the surface, as happens in the case of the principles of contentious arguments; for the nature of the fallacy in these is obvious imme- [*30*] diately, and as a rule even to persons with little power of comprehension. So then, of **101ª** the contentious reasonings mentioned, the former really deserves to be called 'reasoning' as well, but the other should be called 'contentious reasoning', but not 'reasoning', since it appears to reason, but does not really do so.

[*5*] Further (*d*), besides all the reasonings we have mentioned there are the mis-reasonings that start from the premisses peculiar to the special sciences, as happens (for example) in the case of geometry and her sister sciences. For this form of reasoning appears to differ from the reasonings mentioned above; the man who draws a false figure reasons from things [*10*] that are neither true and primary, nor yet generally accepted. For he does not fall within the definition; he does not assume opinions that are received either by every one or by the majority or by philosophers—that is to say, by all, or by most, or by the most illustrious of them—but he conducts his reasoning upon assumptions which, though appropriate to the [*15*] science in question, are not true; for he effects his mis-reasoning either by describing the semicircles wrongly or by drawing certain lines in a way in which they could not be drawn.

The foregoing must stand for an outline survey of the species of reasoning. In general, in regard both to all that we have already dis- [*20*] cussed and to those which we shall discuss later, we may remark that that amount of distinction between them may serve, because it is not our purpose to give the exact definition of any of them; we merely want to describe them in outline; we consider it quite enough from the point of view of the line of inquiry before us to be able to recognize each of them in some sort of way.

2

[*25*] Next in order after the foregoing, we must say for how many and for what purposes the treatise is useful. They are three—intellectual training, casual encounters, and the philosophical sciences. That it is useful as a training is obvious on the face of it. The possession of a plan of inquiry will enable us more easily to

---

Note: The bold face numbers and letters are approximate indications of the pages and columns of the standard Berlin Greek text; the bracketed numbers, of the lines in the Greek text; they are here assigned as they are assigned in the Oxford translation.

[30] argue about the subject proposed. For purposes of casual encounters, it is useful because when we have counted up the opinions held by most people, we shall meet them on the ground not of other people's convictions but of their own, while we shift the ground of any argument that they appear to us to state unsoundly. For the study of the philosophical sciences it is useful, because the ability to raise [35] searching difficulties on both sides of a subject will make us detect more easily the truth and error about the several points that arise. It has a further use in relation to the ultimate bases of the principles used in the several sciences. For it is impossible to discuss them at all from the principles proper to the particular science in hand, seeing that the principles are the *prius* of everything else: it is through 101ᵇ the opinions generally held on the particular points that these have to be discussed, and this task belongs properly, or most appropriately, to dialectic: for dialectic is a process of criticism wherein lies the path to the principles of all inquiries.

3

[5] We shall be in perfect possession of the way to proceed when we are in a position like that which we occupy in regard to rhetoric and medicine and faculties of that kind: this means the doing of that which we choose with the materials that are available. For it is not every method that the rhetorician will employ to persuade, or the doctor to heal; still, if he omits none of the available means, we shall say [10] that his grasp of the science is adequate.

4

First, then, we must see of what parts our inquiry consists. Now if we were to grasp (*a*) with reference to how many, and what kind of, things arguments take place, and with what materials they start, and (*b*) how we are to become well supplied with these, we should have sufficiently won our goal. Now the materials with which arguments start are equal in number, and are identical, with the subjects on [15] which reasonings take place. For arguments start with 'propositions', while the subjects on which reasonings take place are 'problems'. Now every proposition and every problem indicates either a genus or a peculiarity or an accident—for the differentia too, applying as it does to a class (or genus), should be ranked together with the genus. Since, however, of what is peculiar to anything part signi- [20] fies its essence, while part does not, let us divide the 'peculiar' into both the aforesaid parts, and call that part which indicates the essence a 'definition', while of the remainder let us adopt the terminology which is generally current about these things, and speak of it as a 'property'. What we have said, then, makes it clear that according to our present division, the elements turn out to be four, all told, namely [25] either property or definition or genus or accident. Do not let any one suppose us to mean that each of these enunciated by itself constitutes a proposition or problem, but only that it is from these that both problems and propositions are formed. The difference between a problem and a proposition is a difference in the turn of the phrase. For if it be put [30] in this way, ' "An animal that walks on two feet" is the definition of man, is it not?' or ' "Animal" is the genus of man, is it not?' the result is a proposition: but if thus, 'Is "an animal that walks on two feet" a definition of man or no?' [or 'Is "animal" his genus or no?'] the result is a problem. Similarly too in other cases. Naturally, then, problems and proposi- [35] tions are equal in number: for out of every proposition you will make a problem if you change the turn of the phrase.

5

We must now say what are 'definition', 'property', 'genus', and 'accident'. A 'definition' is a phrase signifying a thing's essence. It is rendered in the form either of a phrase in 102ᵃ lieu of a term, or of a phrase in lieu of another phrase; for it is sometimes possible to define the meaning of a phrase as well. People whose rendering consists of a term only, try it as they may, clearly do not render the definition of the thing in question, because a definition is always a phrase of a certain kind. [5] One may, however, use the word 'definitory' also of such a remark as 'The "becoming" is "beautiful" ', and likewise also of the question, 'Are sensation and knowledge the same or different?', for argument about definitions is mostly concerned with questions of sameness and difference. In a word we may call 'definitory' everything that falls under the same branch of inquiry as definitions; and that [10] all the above-mentioned examples are of this character is clear on the face of them. For if we are able to argue that two things are the same or are different, we shall be well supplied by the same turn of argument with lines of attack upon their definitions as well: for when we have shown that they are not the same we shall have demolished the definition. Observe, please, that the converse of this last statement [15] does not hold: for to show that they are the same is not enough to establish a definition. To show, however, that they are not the same is enough of itself to overthrow it.

A 'property' is a predicate which does not indicate the essence of a thing, but yet belongs to that thing alone, and is predicated convertibly of it. Thus it is a property of man to be [20] capable of learning grammar: for if A be a man, then he is capable of learning grammar, and if he be capable of learning grammar, he is a man. For no one calls anything a 'property' which may possibly belong to something else, e.g. 'sleep' in the case of man, even though at a certain time it may happen to belong to him alone. That is to say, if any such thing were [25] actually to be called a property, it will be called not a 'property' absolutely, but a 'temporary' or a 'relative' property: for 'being on the right hand side' is a temporary property, while 'two-footed' is in point of fact ascribed as a property in certain relations; e.g. it is a property of man relatively to a horse and a dog. That nothing which may belong to anything else than A is a convertible predicate of A is clear: for it does not necessarily follow that if [30] something is asleep it is a man.

A 'genus' is what is predicated in the category of essence of a number of things exhibiting differences in kind. We should treat as predicates in the category of essence all such things as it would be appropriate to mention in reply to the question, 'What is the object before you?'; as, for example, in the case of [35] man, if asked that question, it is appropriate to say 'He is an animal'. The question, 'Is one thing in the same genus as another or in a different one?' is also a 'generic' question; for a question of that kind as well falls under the same branch of inquiry as the genus: for having argued that 'animal' is the genus of man, and likewise also of ox, we shall have argued that they are in the same genus; whereas if we 102ᵇ show that it is the genus of the one but not of the other, we shall have argued that these things are not in the same genus.

An 'accident' is (1) something which, though it is none of the foregoing—i.e. neither [5] a definition nor a property nor a genus— yet belongs to the thing: (2) something which may possibly either belong or not belong to any one and the self-same thing, as (e.g.) the 'sitting posture' may belong or not belong to some self-same thing. Likewise also 'whiteness', for there is nothing to prevent the same thing being at one time white, and at another not white. Of the definitions of accident the [10] second is the better: for if he adopts the first, any one is bound, if he is to understand it, to know already what 'definition' and 'genus' and 'property' are, whereas the second is sufficient of itself to tell us the essential meaning of the term in question. To Accident are to be [15] attached also all comparisons of things together, when expressed in language that is drawn in any kind of way from what happens (*accidit*) to be true of them; such as, for example, the question, 'Is the honourable or the expedient preferable?' and 'Is the life of virtue or the life of self-indulgence the pleasanter?', and any other problem which may happen to be phrased in terms like these. For in all such cases the question is 'to which of the two does [20] the predicate in question happen (*accidit*) to belong more closely?' It is clear on the face of it that there is nothing to prevent an accident from becoming a temporary or relative property. Thus the sitting posture is an accident, but will be a temporary property, whenever a man is the only person sitting, while if he be not the only one sitting, it is still a property relatively to those who are not sitting. So [25] then, there is nothing to prevent an accident from becoming both a relative and a temporary property; but a property absolutely it will never be.

6

We must not fail to observe that all remarks made in criticism of a 'property' and 'genus' and 'accident' will be applicable to 'definitions' as well. For when we have shown that the attribute in question fails to belong only to the [30] term defined, as we do also in the case of a property, or that the genus rendered in the definition is not the true genus, or that any of the things mentioned in the phrase used does not belong, as would be remarked also in the case of an accident, we shall have demolished the definition; so that, to use the phrase previously employed,[1] all the points we have enu- [35] merated might in a certain sense be called 'definitory'. But we must not on this account expect to find a single line of inquiry which will apply universally to them all: for this is not an easy thing to find, and, even were one found, it would be very obscure indeed, and of little service for the treatise before us. Rather,

[1] a 9.

a special plan of inquiry must be laid down for each of the classes we have distinguished, and then, starting from the rules that are appropriate in each case, it will probably be easier to 103ᵃ make our way right through the task before us. So then, as was said before,[1] we must outline a division of our subject, and other questions we must relegate each to the particular branch to which it most naturally belongs, speaking of them as 'definitory' and 'generic' questions. The questions I mean have practi-[5] cally been already assigned to their several branches.

7

First of all we must define the number of senses borne by the term 'Sameness'. Sameness would be generally regarded as falling, roughly speaking, into three divisions. We generally apply the term numerically or specifically or generically—numerically in cases where there [10] is more than one name but only one thing, e.g. 'doublet' and 'cloak'; specifically, where there is more than one thing, but they present no differences in respect of their species, as one man and another, or one horse and another: for things like this that fall under the same species are said to be 'specifically the same'. Similarly, too, those things are called generically the same which fall under the same genus, such as a horse and a man. It might appear that the sense in which water [15] from the same spring is called 'the same water' is somehow different and unlike the senses mentioned above: but really such a case as this ought to be ranked in the same class with the things that in one way or another are called 'the same' in view of unity of species. For all such things seem to be of one family and to resemble one another. For the reason [20] why all water is said to be specifically the same as all other water is because of a certain likeness it bears to it, and the only difference in the case of water drawn from the same spring is this, that the likeness is more emphatic: that is why we do not distinguish it from the things that in one way or another are called 'the same' in view of unity of species. It is generally supposed that the term 'the same' is most used in a sense agreed on by every one when applied to what is numerically [25] one. But even so, it is apt to be rendered in more than one sense; its most literal and primary use is found whenever the sameness is rendered in reference to an alternative name or definition, as when a cloak is said to be the same as a doublet, or an animal that walks on two feet is said to be the same as a man: a second sense is when it is rendered in reference to a property, as when what can acquire knowledge is called the same as a man, and what naturally travels upward the same as fire: while a third use is found when it is rendered in reference to some term drawn from Acci-[30] dent, as when the creature who is sitting, or who is musical, is called the same as Socrates. For all these uses mean to signify numerical unity. That what I have just said is true may be best seen where one form of appellation is substituted for another. For often when we give the order to call one of the people who are sitting down, indicating him by name, we change our description, whenever the person [35] to whom we give the order happens not to understand us; he will, we think, understand better from some accidental feature; so we bid him call to us 'the man who is sitting' or 'who is conversing over there'—clearly supposing ourselves to be indicating the same object by its name and by its accident.

8

103ᵇ Of 'sameness' then, as has been said,[2] three senses are to be distinguished. Now one way to confirm that the elements mentioned above are those out of which and through which and to which arguments proceed, is by induction: for if any one were to survey propositions and problems one by one, it would be [5] seen that each was formed either from the definition of something or from its property or from its genus or from its accident. Another way to confirm it is through reasoning. For every predicate of a subject must of necessity be either convertible with its subject or not: and if it is convertible, it would be its defini-[10] tion or property, for if it signifies the essence, it is the definition; if not, it is a property: for this was what a property is, viz. what is predicated convertibly, but does not signify the essence. If, on the other hand, it is not predicated convertibly of the thing, it either is or is not one of the terms contained in the definition of the subject: and if it be one of [15] those terms, then it will be the genus or the differentia, inasmuch as the definition consists of genus and differentiae; whereas, if it be not one of those terms, clearly it would be an accident, for accident was said[3] to be what belongs as an attribute to a subject without be-

---

[1] 101ᵃ 22. [2] 2ᵃ 7. [3] 102ᵇ 4.

ing either its definition or its genus or a property.

9

[20] Next, then, we must distinguish between the classes of predicates in which the four orders in question are found. These are ten in number: Essence, Quantity, Quality, Relation, Place, Time, Position, State, Activity, Passivity. For the accident and genus and property [25] and definition of anything will always be in one of these categories: for all the propositions found through these signify either something's essence or its quality or quantity or some one of the other types of predicate. It is clear, too, on the face of it that the man who signifies something's essence signifies sometimes a substance, sometimes a quality, sometimes some one of the other types of predicate. For when [30] a man is set before him and he says that what is set there is 'a man' or 'an animal', he states its essence and signifies a substance; but when a white colour is set before him and he says that what is set there is 'white' or is 'a colour', he states its essence and signifies a quality. Likewise, also, if a magnitude of a cubit be set before him and he says that what is set there is a magnitude of a cubit, he will be describing its essence and signifying a quan- [35] tity. Likewise, also, in the other cases: for each of these kinds of predicate, if either it be asserted of itself, or its genus be asserted of it, signifies an essence: if, on the other hand, one kind of predicate is asserted of another kind, it does not signify an essence, but a quantity or a quality or one of the other kinds of predicate. Such, then, and so many, are the subjects 104ᵃ on which arguments take place, and the materials with which they start. How we are to acquire them, and by what means we are to become well supplied with them, falls next to be told.

10

First, then, a definition must be given of a 'dialectical proposition' and a 'dialectical problem'. For it is not every proposition nor yet every problem that is to be set down as dialec- [5] tical: for no one in his senses would make a proposition of what no one holds, nor yet make a problem of what is obvious to everybody or to most people: for the latter admits of no doubt, while to the former no one would assent. Now a dialectical proposition consists in asking something that is held by all men or by most men or by the philosophers, i.e. either by all, or by most, or by the most notable of these, [10] provided it be not contrary to the general opinion; for a man would probably assent to the view of the philosophers, if it be not contrary to the opinions of most men. Dialectical propositions also include views which are like those generally accepted; also propositions which contradict the contraries of opinions that are taken to be generally accepted, and also all opinions that are in accordance with the recog- [15] nized arts. Thus, supposing it to be a general opinion that the knowledge of contraries is the same, it might probably pass for a general opinion also that the perception of contraries is the same: also, supposing it to be a general opinion that there is but one single science of grammar, it might pass for a general opinion that there is but one science of flute-playing as well, whereas, if it be a general opinion that there is more than one science of grammar, it might pass for a general opinion that there is more than one science of flute-playing as well: [20] for all these seem to be alike and akin. Likewise, also, propositions contradicting the contraries of general opinions will pass as general opinions: for if it be a general opinion that one ought to do good to one's friends, it will also be a general opinion that one ought not to do them harm. Here, that one ought to do harm to one's friends is contrary to the general view, and that one ought not to do them harm is the contradictory of that contrary. [25] Likewise also, if one ought to do good to one's friends, one ought not to do good to one's enemies: this too is the contradictory of the view contrary to the general view; the contrary being that one ought to do good to one's enemies. Likewise, also, in other cases. Also, on comparison, it will look like a general opinion that the contrary predicate belongs to the contrary subject: e.g. if one ought to do good to [30] one's friends, one ought also to do evil to one's enemies. it might appear also as if doing good to one's friends were a contrary to doing evil to one's enemies: but whether this is or is not so in reality as well will be stated in the course of the discussion upon contraries.[1] Clearly also, all opinions that are in accordance with the arts are dialectical propositions; for people are likely to assent to the views held by [35] those who have made a study of these things, e.g. on a question of medicine they will agree with the doctor, and on a question of geometry with the geometrician; and likewise also in other cases.

[1] II. 7.

11

104ᵇ A dialectical problem is a subject of inquiry that contributes either to choice and avoidance, or to truth and knowledge, and that either by itself, or as a help to the solution of some other such problem. It must, moreover, be something on which either people hold no opinion either way, or the masses hold a contrary opinion to the philosophers, or the phil- [5] osophers to the masses, or each of them among themselves. For some problems it is useful to know with a view to choice or avoidance, e.g. whether pleasure is to be chosen or not, while some it is useful to know merely with a view to knowledge, e.g. whether the universe is eternal or not: others, again, are not useful in and by themselves for either of these purposes, but yet help us in regard to [10] some such problems; for there are many things which we do not wish to know in and by themselves, but for the sake of other things, in order that through them we may come to know something else. Problems also include questions in regard to which reasonings conflict (the difficulty then being whether so-and-so is so or not, there being convincing argu- [15] ments for both views); others also in regard to which we have no argument because they are so vast, and we find it difficult to give our reasons, e.g. the question whether the universe is eternal or no: for into questions of that kind too it is possible to inquire.

Problems, then, and propositions are to be defined as aforesaid.[1] A 'thesis' is a supposition [20] of some eminent philosopher that conflicts with the general opinion; e.g. the view that contradiction is impossible, as Antisthenes said; or the view of Heraclitus that all things are in motion; or that Being is one, as Melissus says: for to take notice when any ordinary person expresses views contrary to men's usual opinions would be silly. Or it may be a view about which we have a reasoned theory contrary to men's usual opinions, e.g. the view [25] maintained by the sophists that what is need not in every case either have come to be or be eternal: for a musician who is a grammarian 'is' so without ever having 'come to be' so, or being so eternally. For even if a man does not accept this view, he might do so on the ground that it is reasonable.

Now a 'thesis' also is a problem, though a [30] problem is not always a thesis, inasmuch as some problems are such that we have no opinion about them either way. That a thesis, however, also forms a problem, is clear: for it follows of necessity from what has been said that either the mass of men disagree with the philosophers about the thesis, or that the one or the other class disagree among themselves, seeing that the thesis is a supposition in conflict with general opinion. Practically all dialec- [35] tical problems indeed are now called 'theses'. But it should make no difference whichever description is used; for our object in thus distinguishing them has not been to create a terminology, but to recognize what dif- **105ᵃ** ferences happen to be found between them.

Not every problem, nor every thesis, should be examined, but only one which might puzzle one of those who need argument, not punish- [5] ment or perception. For people who are puzzled to know whether one ought to honour the gods and love one's parents or not need punishment, while those who are puzzled to know whether snow is white or not need perception. The subjects should not border too closely upon the sphere of demonstration, nor yet be too far removed from it: for the former cases admit of no doubt, while the latter involve difficulties too great for the art of the trainer.

12

[10] Having drawn these definitions, we must distinguish how many species there are of dialectical arguments. There is on the one hand Induction, on the other Reasoning. Now what reasoning is has been said before:[2] induction is a passage from individuals to universals, e.g. the argument that supposing the skilled pilot is the most effective, and likewise the skilled [15] charioteer, then in general the skilled man is the best at his particular task. Induction is the more convincing and clear: it is more readily learnt by the use of the senses, and is applicable generally to the mass of men, though Reasoning is more forcible and effective against contradictious people.

13

[20] The classes, then, of things about which, and of things out of which, arguments are constructed, are to be distinguished in the way we have said before. The means whereby we are to become well supplied with reasonings are four: (1) the securing of propositions; (2) the power to distinguish in how many senses a

---
[1] b 1, a 8.
[2] 100ᵃ 25.

particular expression is used; (3) the discovery of the differences of things; (4) the investiga-[25] tion of likeness. The last three, as well, are in a certain sense propositions: for it is possible to make a proposition corresponding to each of them, e.g. (1) 'The desirable may mean either the honourable or the pleasant or the expedient'; and (2) 'Sensation differs from knowledge in that the latter may be recovered again after it has been lost, while the former [30] cannot'; and (3) 'The relation of the healthy to health is like that of the vigorous to vigour'. The first proposition depends upon the use of one term in several senses, the second upon the differences of things, the third upon their likenesses.

14

Propositions should be selected in a number of ways corresponding to the number of distinctions drawn in regard to the proposition: thus [35] one may first take in hand the opinions held by all or by most men or by the philosophers, i.e. by all, or most, or the most notable of them; or opinions contrary to those that 105b seem to be generally held; and, again, all opinions that are in accordance with the arts. We must make propositions also of the contradictories of opinions contrary to those that seem to be generally held, as was laid down before. It is useful also to make them by selecting not only those opinions that actually are [5] accepted, but also those that are like these, e.g. 'The perception of contraries is the same' —the knowledge of them being so—and 'we see by admission of something into ourselves, not by an emission'; for so it is, too, in the case of the other senses; for in hearing we admit something into ourselves; we do not emit; and we taste in the same way. Likewise also in the [10] other cases. Moreover, all statements that seem to be true in all or in most cases, should be taken as a principle or accepted position; for they are posited by those who do not also see what exception there may be. We should select also from the written handbooks of argument, and should draw up sketch-lists of them upon each several kind of subject, putting them down under separate headings, e.g. [15] 'On Good', or 'On Life'—and that 'On Good' should deal with every form of good, beginning with the category of essence. In the margin, too, one should indicate also the opinions of individual thinkers, e.g. 'Empedocles said that the elements of bodies were four': for any one might assent to the saying of some generally accepted authority.

Of propositions and problems there are—to [20] comprehend the matter in outline—three divisions: for some are ethical propositions, some are on natural philosophy, while some are logical. Propositions such as the following are ethical, e.g. 'Ought one rather to obey one's parents or the laws, if they disagree?'; such as this are logical, e.g. 'Is the knowledge of opposites the same or not?'; while such as this [25] are on natural philosophy, e.g. 'Is the universe eternal or not?' Likewise also with problems. The nature of each of the aforesaid kinds of proposition is not easily rendered in a definition, but we have to try to recognize each of them by means of the familiarity attained through induction, examining them in the light of the illustrations given above. [30] For purposes of philosophy we must treat of these things according to their truth, but for dialectic only with an eye to general opinion. All propositions should be taken in their most universal form; then, the one should be made into many. E.g. 'The knowledge of opposites is the same'; next, 'The knowledge of contraries is the same', and that 'of relative terms'. In the same way these two should again [35] be divided, as long as division is possible, e.g. the knowledge of 'good and evil', of 'white and black', or 'cold and hot'. Likewise also in other cases.

15

106a On the formation, then, of propositions, the above remarks are enough. As regards the number of senses a term bears, we must not only treat of those terms which bear different senses, but we must also try to render their definitions; e.g. we must not merely say that justice and courage are called 'good' in one [5] sense, and that what conduces to vigour and what conduces to health are called so in another, but also that the former are so called because of a certain intrinsic quality they themselves have, the latter because they are productive of a certain result and not because of any intrinsic quality in themselves. Similarly also in other cases.

Whether a term bears a number of specific [10] meanings or one only, may be considered by the following means. First, look and see if its contrary bears a number of meanings, whether the discrepancy between them be one of kind or one of names. For in some cases a difference is at once displayed even in the names; e.g. the contrary of 'sharp' in the case of a note is 'flat', while in the case of a solid edge it is 'dull'. Clearly, then, the contrary of 'sharp' bears several meanings, and if so, so [15] also does 'sharp'; for corresponding to each of the former terms the meaning of its contrary will be different. For 'sharp' will not be the same when contrary to 'dull' and to 'flat', though 'sharp' is the contrary of each. Again βαρύ ('flat', 'heavy') in the case of a note has 'sharp' as its contrary, but in the case of a solid mass 'light', so that βαρύ is used with a number of meanings, inasmuch as its con- [20] trary also is so used. Likewise, also, 'fine' as applied to a picture has 'ugly' as its contrary, but, as applied to a house, 'ramshackle'; so that 'fine' is an ambiguous term.

In some cases there is no discrepancy of any sort in the names used, but a difference of kind between the meanings is at once obvious: e.g. in the case of 'clear' and 'obscure': for sound is [25] called 'clear' and 'obscure', just as 'colour' is too. As regards the names, then, there is no discrepancy, but the difference in kind between the meanings is at once obvious: for colour is not called 'clear' in a like sense to sound. This is plain also through sensation: for of things that are the same in kind we have [30] the same sensation, whereas we do not judge clearness by the same sensation in the case of sound and of colour, but in the latter case we judge by sight, in the former by hearing. Likewise also with 'sharp' and 'dull' in regard to flavours and solid edges: here in the latter case we judge by touch, but in the former by taste. For here again there is no discrepancy in the names used, in the case either of the [35] original terms or of their contraries: for the contrary also of sharp in either sense is 'dull'.

Moreover, see if one sense of a term has a contrary, while another has absolutely none; e.g. the pleasure of drinking has a contrary in the pain of thirst, whereas the pleasure of seeing that the diagonal is incommensurate with **106^b** the side has none, so that 'pleasure' is used in more than one sense. To 'love' also, used of the frame of mind, has to 'hate' as its contrary, while as used of the physical activity (kissing) it has none: clearly, therefore, to 'love' is an ambiguous term. Further, see in regard to their intermediates, if some meanings and their contraries have an intermediate, [5] while others have none, or if both have one but not the same one, as e.g. 'clear' and 'obscure' in the case of colours have 'grey' as an intermediate, whereas in the case of sound they have none, or, if they have, it is 'harsh', as some people say that a harsh sound is intermediate. 'Clear', then, is an ambiguous term, and likewise also 'obscure'. See, moreover, if some of them have more than one intermedi- [10] ate, while others have but one, as is the case with 'clear' and 'obscure', for in the case of colours there are numbers of intermediates, whereas in regard to sound there is but one, viz. 'harsh'.

Again, in the case of the contradictory opposite, look and see if it bears more than one meaning. For if this bears more than one [15] meaning, then the opposite of it also will be used in more than one meaning; e.g. 'to fail to see' is a phrase with more than one meaning, viz. (1) to fail to possess the power of sight, (2) to fail to put that power to active use. But if this has more than one meaning, it follows necessarily that 'to see' also has more than one meaning: for there will be an opposite to each sense of 'to fail to see'; e.g. the opposite of 'not to possess the power of sight' is to possess it, [20] while of 'not to put the power of sight to active use', the opposite is to put it to active use.

Moreover, examine the case of terms that denote the privation or presence of a certain state: for if the one term bears more than one meaning, then so will the remaining term: e.g. if 'to have sense' be used with more than one meaning, as applied to the soul and to the body, then 'to be wanting in sense' too will be used with more than one meaning, as applied to the [25] soul and to the body. That the opposition between the terms now in question depends upon the privation or presence of a certain state is clear, since animals naturally possess each kind of 'sense', both as applied to the soul and as applied to the body.

Moreover, examine the inflected forms. For [30] if 'justly' has more than one meaning, then 'just', also, will be used with more than one meaning; for there will be a meaning of 'just' corresponding to each of the meanings of 'justly'; e.g. if the word 'justly' be used of judging according to one's own opinion, and also of judging as one ought, then 'just' also will be used in like manner. In the same way also, if 'healthy' has more than one meaning, then 'healthily' also will be used with more than one meaning: e.g. if 'healthy' describes [35] both what produces health and what preserves health and what betokens health, then 'healthily' also will be used to mean 'in such a way as to produce' or 'preserve' or 'betoken' health. Likewise also in other cases, whenever the original term bears more than one meaning, the inflexion also that is formed from it will be used with more than one meaning, and vice versa.

Look also at the classes of the predicates signified by the term, and see if they are the same in all cases. For if they are not the same, then [5] clearly the term is ambiguous: e.g. 'good' in the case of food means 'productive of pleasure', and in the case of medicine 'productive of health', whereas as applied to the soul it means to be of a certain quality, e.g. temperate or courageous or just: and likewise also, as applied to 'man'. Sometimes it signifies what happens at a certain time, as (e.g.) the good that happens at the right time: for what happens at the right time is called good. Often it signifies [10] what is of a certain quantity, e.g. as applied to the proper amount: for the proper amount too is called good. So then the term 'good' is ambiguous. In the same way also 'clear', as applied to a body, signifies a colour, but in regard to a note it denotes what is 'easy to hear'. 'Sharp', too, is in a closely similar case: for the same term does not bear the same meaning in all its applications: for a sharp [15] note is a swift note, as the mathematical theorists of harmony tell us, whereas a sharp (acute) angle is one that is less than a right angle, while a sharp dagger is one containing a sharp angle (point).

Look also at the genera of the objects denoted by the same term, and see if they are different without being subaltern, as (e.g.) 'donkey', which denotes both the animal and [20] the engine. For the definition of them that corresponds to the name is different: for the one will be declared to be an animal of a certain kind, and the other to be an engine of a certain kind. If, however, the genera be subaltern, there is no necessity for the definitions to be different. Thus (e.g.) 'animal' is the genus of 'raven', and so is 'bird'. Whenever therefore we say that the raven is a bird, we [25] also say that it is a certain kind of animal, so that both the genera are predicated of it. Likewise also whenever we call the raven a 'flying biped animal', we declare it to be a bird: in this way, then, as well, both the genera are predicated of raven, and also their definition. But in the case of genera that are not subaltern [30] this does not happen, for whenever we call a thing an 'engine', we do not call it an animal, nor vice versa.

Look also and see not only if the genera of the term before you are different without being subaltern, but also in the case of its contrary: for if its contrary bears several senses, [35] clearly the term before you does so as well.

It is useful also to look at the definition that arises from the use of the term in combination, e.g. of a 'clear (*lit.* white) body' and of a 'clear note'. For then if what is peculiar in each case be abstracted, the same expression ought to remain over. This does not happen in the case of ambiguous terms, e.g. in the cases just mentioned. For the former will be 'a body possessing such and such a colour', while the latter will be 'a note easy to hear'. Abstract, then, 'a body' and 'a note', and the remainder in each case is not the same. It should, however, have [5] been had the meaning of 'clear' in each case been synonymous.

Often in the actual definitions as well ambiguity creeps in unawares, and for this reason the definitions also should be examined. If (e.g.) any one describes what betokens and what produces health as 'related commensurably to health', we must not desist but go on to examine in what sense he has used the term [10] 'commensurably' in each case, e.g. if in the latter case it means that 'it is of the right amount to produce health', whereas in the former it means that 'it is such as to betoken what kind of state prevails'.

Moreover, see if the terms cannot be compared as 'more or less' or as 'in like manner', as is the case (e.g.) with a 'clear' (*lit.* white) sound and a 'clear' garment, and a 'sharp' [15] flavour and a 'sharp' note. For neither are these things said to be clear or sharp 'in a like degree', nor yet is the one said to be clearer or sharper than the other. 'Clear', then, and 'sharp' are ambiguous. For synonyms are always comparable; for they will always be used either in like manner, or else in a greater degree in one case.

Now since of genera that are different without [20] being subaltern the differentiae also are different in kind, e.g. those of 'animal' and 'knowledge' (for the differentiae of these are different), look and see if the meanings comprised under the same term are differentiae of genera that are different without being subaltern, as e.g. 'sharp' is of a 'note' and a 'solid'. For being 'sharp' differentiates note from note, and likewise also one solid from another. [25] 'Sharp', then, is an ambiguous term: for it forms differentiae of genera that are different without being subaltern.

Again, see if the actual meanings included under the same term themselves have different differentiae, e.g. 'colour' in bodies and 'colour' in tunes: for the differentiae of 'colour' in bodies are 'sight-piercing' and 'sight-[30] compressing', whereas 'colour' in melodies has not the same differentiae. Colour, then, is an ambiguous term; for things that are the same have the same differentiae.

Moreover, since the species is never the differentia of anything, look and see if one of the meanings included under the same term be a species and another a differentia, as (e.g.) [35] 'clear' (*lit.* white) as applied to a body is a species of colour, whereas in the case of a note it is a differentia; for one note is differentiated from another by being 'clear'.

16

The presence, then, of a number of meanings in a term may be investigated by these and like means. The differences which things present to each other should be examined within the same genera, e.g. 'Wherein does justice differ 108ª from courage, and wisdom from temperance?'—for all these belong to the same genus; and also from one genus to another, provided they be not very much too far apart, e.g. 'Wherein does sensation differ from knowl-[5] edge?': for in the case of genera that are very far apart, the differences are entirely obvious.

17

Likeness should be studied, first, in the case of things belonging to different genera, the formulae being 'A:B = C:D' (e.g. as knowledge stands to the object of knowledge, so is sensation related to the object of sensation), [10] and 'As A is in B, so is C in D' (e.g. as sight is in the eye, so is reason in the soul, and as is a calm in the sea, so is windlessness in the air). Practice is more especially needed in regard to terms that are far apart; for in the case of the rest, we shall be more easily able to see in one glance the points of likeness. We should [15] also look at things which belong to the same genus, to see if any identical attribute belongs to them all, e.g. to a man and a horse and a dog; for in so far as they have any identical attribute, in so far they are alike.

18

It is useful to have examined the number of meanings of a term both for clearness' sake (for a man is more likely to know what it is he asserts, if it has been made clear to him [20] how many meanings it may have), and also with a view to ensuring that our reasonings shall be in accordance with the actual facts and not addressed merely to the term used. For as long as it is not clear in how many senses a term is used, it is possible that the answerer and the questioner are not directing their minds upon the same thing: whereas when once it has been made clear how many meanings there are, and also upon which of them the former directs his mind when he [25] makes his assertion, the questioner would then look ridiculous if he failed to address his argument to this. It helps us also both to avoid being misled and to mislead by false reasoning: for if we know the number of meanings of a term, we shall certainly never be misled by false reasoning, but shall know if the questioner fails to address his argument to the same point; and when we ourselves put the [30] questions we shall be able to mislead him, if our answerer happens not to know the number of meanings of our terms. This, however, is not possible in all cases, but only when of the many senses some are true and others are false. This manner of argument, however, does not belong properly to dialectic; dialecticians [35] should therefore by all means beware of this kind of verbal discussion, unless any one is absolutely unable to discuss the subject before him in any other way.

The discovery of the differences of things helps us both in reasonings about sameness and difference, and also in recognizing what any 108ᵇ particular thing is. That it helps us in reasoning about sameness and difference is clear: for when we have discovered a difference of any kind whatever between the objects before us, we shall already have shown that they are not the same: while it helps us in recognizing what a thing is, because we usually distinguish the expression that is proper to the [5] essence of each particular thing by means of the differentiae that are proper to it.

The examination of likeness is useful with a view both to inductive arguments and to hypothetical reasonings, and also with a view to the rendering of definitions. It is useful for induc-[10] tive arguments, because it is by means of an induction of individuals in cases that are alike that we claim to bring the universal in evidence: for it is not easy to do this if we do not know the points of likeness. It is useful for hypothetical reasonings because it is a general opinion that among similars what is true of one is true also of the rest. If, then, with regard to any of them we are well supplied with [15] matter for a discussion, we shall secure a preliminary admission that however it is in these cases, so it is also in the case before us: then when we have shown the former we shall have shown, on the strength of the hypothesis, the matter before us as well: for we have first made the hypothesis that however it is in these cases, so it is also in the case before us, and have then proved the point as regards these cases. It is useful for the rendering of defini- [20] tions because, if we are able to see in one glance what is the same in each individual case of it, we shall be at no loss into what genus we ought to put the object before us when we define it: for of the common predicates that which is most definitely in the category of essence is likely to be the genus. Likewise, also, in the case of objects widely divergent, the examination of likeness is useful for purposes of definition, e.g. the sameness of a calm at sea, and [25] windlessness in the air (each being a form of rest), and of a point on a line and the unit in number—each being a starting point. If, then, we render as the genus what is common to all the cases, we shall get the credit of defining not inappropriately. Definition-mongers too nearly always render them in this way: [30] for they declare the unit to be the starting-point of number, and the point the starting-point of a line. It is clear, then, that they place them in that which is common to both as their genus.

The means, then, whereby reasonings are effected, are these: the commonplace rules, for the observance of which the aforesaid means are useful, are as follows.

BOOK II

1

[37] Of problems some are universal, others particular. Universal problems are such as 'Every pleasure is good' and 'No pleasure is good'; particular problems are such as 'Some pleasure is good' and 'Some pleasure is not good'. The methods of establishing and overthrowing a view universally are common to both kinds of problems; for when we have shown that a predicate belongs in every case, we shall also have shown that it belongs in some cases. Likewise, also, if we show that it [5] does not belong in any case, we shall also have shown that it does not belong in every case. First, then, we must speak of the methods of overthrowing a view universally, because such are common to both universal and particular problems, and because people more usually introduce theses asserting a predicate than [10] denying it, while those who argue with them overthrow it. The conversion of an appropriate name which is drawn from the element 'accident' is an extremely precarious thing; for in the case of accidents and in no other it is possible for something to be true conditionally and not universally. Names drawn from the elements 'definition' and 'property' and 'genus' are bound to be convertible; e.g. if 'to be an animal that walks on two feet is an attribute of S', then it will be true by con- [15] version to say that 'S is an animal that walks on two feet'. Likewise, also, if drawn from the genus; for if 'to be an animal is an attribute of S', then 'S is an animal'. The same is true also in the case of a property; for if 'to be capable of learning grammar is an attribute of S', then 'S will be capable of learning gram- [20] mar'. For none of these attributes can possibly belong or not belong in part; they must either belong or not belong absolutely. In the case of accidents, on the other hand, there is nothing to prevent an attribute (e.g. whiteness or justice) belonging in part, so that it is not enough to show that whiteness or justice is an attribute of a man in order to show that he is white or just; for it is open to dispute it and [25] say that he is white or just in part only. Conversion, then, is not a necessary process in the case of accidents.

We must also define the errors that occur in problems. They are of two kinds, caused either by false statement or by transgression of the established diction. For those who make false statements, and say that an attribute belongs to [30] a thing which does not belong to it, commit error; and those who call objects by the names of other objects (e.g. calling a plane-tree a 'man') transgress the established terminology.

2

Now one commonplace rule is to look and see [35] if a man has ascribed as an accident what belongs in some other way. This mistake is most commonly made in regard to the genera of things, e.g. if one were to say that white happens (*accidit*) to be a colour—for being a colour does not happen by accident to white, but colour is its genus. The assertor may of 109b course define it so in so many words, saying (e.g.) that 'Justice happens (*accidit*) to be a virtue'; but often even without such definition it is obvious that he has rendered the genus as an accident; e.g. suppose that one were to say that whiteness is coloured or that walking is in motion. For a predicate drawn from [5] the genus is never ascribed to the species in an inflected form, but always the genera are predicated of their species literally; for the species take on both the name and the definition of their genera. A man therefore who says that white is 'coloured' has not rendered 'coloured' as its genus, seeing that he has used an inflected form, nor yet as its property or as its defini- [10] tion: for the definition and property of a thing belong to it and to nothing else, whereas many things besides white are coloured, e.g. a log, a stone, a man, and a horse. Clearly then he renders it as an accident.

Another rule is to examine all cases where a predicate has been either asserted or denied universally to belong to something. Look at them species by species, and not in their infi- [15] nite multitude: for then the inquiry will proceed more directly and in fewer steps. You should look and begin with the most primary groups, and then proceed in order down to those that are not further divisible: e.g. if a man has said that the knowledge of opposites is the same, you should look and see whether it be so of relative opposites and of contraries and of terms signifying the privation or presence of certain states, and of contradictory [20] terms. Then, if no clear result be reached so far in these cases, you should again divide these until you come to those that are not further divisible, and see (e.g.) whether it be so of just deeds and unjust, or of the double and the half, or of blindness and sight, or of being and not-being: for if in any case it be shown that the knowledge of them is not the same we shall have demolished the problem. Likewise, also, if the predicate belongs in no case. [25] This rule is convertible for both destructive and constructive purposes: for, if, when we have suggested a division, the predicate appears to hold in all or in a large number of cases, we may then claim that the other should actually assert it universally, or else bring a negative instance to show in what case it is not so: for if he does neither of these things, a refusal to assert it will make him look absurd.

[30] Another rule is to make definitions both of an accident and of its subject, either of both separately or else of one of them, and then look and see if anything untrue has been assumed as true in the definitions. Thus (e.g.) to see if it is possible to wrong a god, ask what is 'to wrong'? For if it be 'to injure deliberately', clearly it is not possible for a god to be wronged: [35] for it is impossible that God should be injured. Again, to see if the good man is jealous, ask who is the 'jealous' man and what is 'jealousy'. For if 'jealousy' is pain at the apparent success of some well-behaved person, clearly the good man is not jealous: for then he would be bad. Again, to see if the indignant man is jealous, ask who each of them is: for then it will be obvious whether the statement 110a is true or false; e.g. if he is 'jealous' who grieves at the successes of the good, and he is 'indignant' who grieves at the successes of the evil, then clearly the indignant man would not be jealous. A man should substitute definitions [5] also for the terms contained in his definitions, and not stop until he comes to a familiar term: for often if the definition be rendered whole, the point at issue is not cleared up, whereas if for one of the terms used in the definition a definition be stated, it becomes obvious.

[10] Moreover, a man should make the problem into a proposition for himself, and then bring a negative instance against it: for the negative instance will be a ground of attack upon the assertion. This rule is very nearly the same as the rule to look into cases where a predicate has been attributed or denied universally: but it differs in the turn of the argument.

Moreover, you should define what kind of things should be called as most men call them, [15] and what should not. For this is useful both for establishing and for overthrowing a view: e.g. you should say that we ought to use our terms to mean the same things as most people mean by them, but when we ask what kind of things are or are not of such and such a kind, we should not here go with the multitude: e.g. it is right to call 'healthy' whatever [20] tends to produce health, as do most men: but in saying whether the object before us tends to produce health or not, we should adopt the language no longer of the multitude but of the doctor.

3

Moreover, if a term be used in several senses, and it has been laid down that it is or that it is not an attribute of S, you should show your [25] case of one of its several senses, if you cannot show it of both. This rule is to be observed in cases where the difference of meaning is undetected; for supposing this to be obvious, then the other man will object that the point which he himself questioned has not been discussed, but only the other point. This commonplace rule is convertible for purposes both of establishing and of overthrowing a view. For if we want to establish a statement, [30] we shall show that in one sense the attribute belongs, if we cannot show it of both senses: whereas if we are overthrowing a statement, we shall show that in one sense the attribute does not belong, if we cannot show it of both senses. Of course, in overthrowing a statement there is no need to start the discussion by securing any admission, either when the statement asserts or when it denies the attribute universally: for if we show that in any case [35] whatever the attribute does not belong, we shall have demolished the universal assertion of it, and likewise also if we show that it belongs in a single case, we shall demolish the universal denial of it. Whereas in establishing a statement we ought to secure a preliminary admission that if it belongs in any case whatever, it belongs universally, supposing this claim to be a plausible one. For it is not **110ᵇ** enough to discuss a single instance in order to show that an attribute belongs universally; e.g. to argue that if the soul of man be immortal, then every soul is immortal, so that a previous admission must be secured that if any soul whatever be immortal, then every soul is immortal. This is not to be done in every case, but only whenever we are not easily [5] able to quote any single argument applying to all cases in common, as (e.g.) the geometrician can argue that the triangle has its angles equal to two right angles.

If, again, the variety of meanings of a term be obvious, distinguish how many meanings it has before proceeding either to demolish or to establish it: e.g. supposing 'the right' to mean [10] 'the expedient' or 'the honourable', you should try either to establish or to demolish both descriptions of the subject in question; e.g. by showing that it is honourable and expedient, or that it is neither honourable nor expedient. Supposing, however, that it is impossible to show both, you should show the one, adding an indication that it is true in the one sense and not in the other. The same rule applies also when the number of senses into [15] which it is divided is more than two.

Again, consider those expressions whose meanings are many, but differ not by way of ambiguity of a term, but in some other way: e.g. 'The science of many things is one': here 'many things' may mean the end and the means to that end, as (e.g.) medicine is the science both of producing health and of dieting; or they may be both of them ends, as the [20] science of contraries is said to be the same (for of contraries the one is no more an end than the other); or again they may be an essential and an accidental attribute, as (e.g.) the essential fact that the triangle has its angles equal to two right angles, and the accidental fact that the equilateral figure has them so: for it is because of the accident of the equilateral triangle happening to be a triangle that we know that [25] it has its angles equal to two right angles. If, then, it is not possible in any sense of the term that the science of many things should be the same, it clearly is altogether impossible that it should be so; or, if it is possible in some sense, then clearly it is possible. Distinguish as many meanings as are required: e.g. if we want to establish a view, we should bring forward all such meanings as admit that view, [30] and should divide them only into those meanings which also are required for the establishment of our case: whereas if we want to overthrow a view, we should bring forward all that do not admit that view, and leave the rest aside. We must deal also in these cases as well with any uncertainty about the number of meanings involved. Further, that one thing is, or is not, 'of' another should be established by means of the same commonplace rules; e.g. that a particular science is of a particular thing, [35] treated either as an end or as a means to its end, or as accidentally connected with it; or again that it is not 'of' it in any of the aforesaid ways. The same rule holds true also of desire and all other terms that have more than one object. For the 'desire of X' may mean the **111ᵃ** desire of it as an end (e.g. the desire of health) or as a means to an end (e.g. the desire of being doctored), or as a thing desired accidentally, as, in the case of wine, the sweet-toothed person desires it not because it is wine but because it is sweet. For essentially he desires the sweet, and only accidentally the wine: [5] for if it be dry, he no longer desires it. His desire for it is therefore accidental. This rule is useful in dealing with relative terms: for cases of this kind are generally **cases** of relative terms.

4

Moreover, it is well to alter a term into one more familiar, e.g. to substitute 'clear' for 'exact' in describing a conception, and 'being [10] fussy' for 'being busy': for when the expression is made more familiar, the thesis becomes easier to attack. This commonplace rule also is available for both purposes alike, both for establishing and for overthrowing a view.

In order to show that contrary attributes belong [15] to the same thing, look at its genus; e.g. if we want to show that rightness and wrongness are possible in regard to perception, and to perceive is to judge, while it is possible to judge rightly or wrongly, then in regard to perception as well rightness and wrongness must be possible. In the present instance the proof proceeds from the genus and relates to the species: for 'to judge' is the genus of 'to [20] perceive'; for the man who perceives judges in a certain way. But *per contra* it may proceed from the species to the genus: for all the attributes that belong to the species belong to the genus as well; e.g. if there is a bad and a good knowledge there is also a bad and a good disposition: for 'disposition' is the genus of knowledge. Now the former commonplace argument is fallacious for purposes of establishing a view, while the second is true. For there [25] is no necessity that all the attributes that belong to the genus should belong also to the species; for 'animal' is flying and quadruped, but not so 'man'. All the attributes, on the other hand, that belong to the species must of necessity belong also to the genus; for if 'man' is good, then animal also is good. On the other hand, for purposes of overthrowing a view, the [30] former argument is true while the latter is fallacious; for all the attributes which do not belong to the genus do not belong to the species either; whereas all those that are wanting to the species are not of necessity wanting to the genus.

Since those things of which the genus is predicated must also of necessity have one of its species predicated of them, and since those things that are possessed of the genus in question, [35] or are described by terms derived from that genus, must also of necessity be possessed of one of its species or be described by terms derived from one of its species (e.g. if to anything the term 'scientific knowledge' be applied, then also there will be applied to it the term 'grammatical' or 'musical' knowledge, or knowledge of one of the other sciences; and if any one possesses scientific knowledge or is 111ᵇ described by a term derived from 'science', then he will also possess grammatical or musical knowledge or knowledge of one of the other sciences, or will be described by a term derived from one of them, e.g. as a 'grammarian' or a 'musician')—therefore if any expression be asserted that is in any way derived from the genus (e.g. that the soul is in motion), [5] look and see whether it be possible for the soul to be moved with any of the species of motion; whether (e.g.) it can grow or be destroyed or come to be, and so forth with all the other species of motion. For if it be not moved in any of these ways, clearly it does not move at all. This commonplace rule is common for both purposes, both for overthrowing and for establishing a view: for if the soul moves with [10] one of the species of motion, clearly it does move; while if it does not move with any of the species of motion, clearly it does not move.

If you are not well equipped with an argument against the assertion, look among the definitions, real or apparent, of the thing before you, and if one is not enough, draw upon [15] several. For it will be easier to attack people when committed to a definition: for an attack is always more easily made on definitions.

Moreover, look and see in regard to the thing in question, what it is whose reality conditions the reality of the thing in question, or what it is whose reality necessarily follows if the thing in question be real: if you wish to establish a view inquire what there is on whose reality the reality of the thing in question will [20] follow (for if the former be shown to be real, then the thing in question will also have been shown to be real); while if you want to overthrow a view, ask what it is that is real if the thing in question be real, for if we show that what follows from the thing in question is unreal, we shall have demolished the thing in question.

Moreover, look at the time involved, to see if there be any discrepancy anywhere: e.g. [25] suppose a man to have stated that what is being nourished of necessity grows: for animals are always of necessity being nourished, but they do not always grow. Likewise, also, if he has said that knowing is remembering: for the one is concerned with past time, whereas the other has to do also with the present and the future. For we are said to know things present and future (e.g. that there will be an

[30] eclipse), whereas it is impossible to remember anything save what is in the past.

5

Moreover, there is the sophistic turn of argument, whereby we draw our opponent into the kind of statement against which we shall be well supplied with lines of argument. This process is sometimes a real necessity, sometimes an apparent necessity, sometimes neither an apparent nor a real necessity. It is really necessary [35] whenever the answerer has denied any view that would be useful in attacking the thesis, and the questioner thereupon addresses his arguments to the support of this view, and when moreover the view in question happens to be one of a kind on which he has a good stock of lines of argument. Likewise, also, it is really necessary whenever he (the questioner) 112ᵃ first, by an induction made by means of the view laid down, arrives at a certain statement and then tries to demolish that statement: for when once this has been demolished, the view originally laid down is demolished as well. It is an apparent necessity, when the point to which the discussion comes to be directed appears to be useful, and relevant to the thesis, without being really so; whether it be [5] that the man who is standing up to the argument has refused to concede something, or whether he (the questioner) has first reached it by a plausible induction based upon the thesis and then tries to demolish it. The remaining case is when the point to which the discussion comes to be directed is neither really nor apparently necessary, and it is the answerer's luck to be confuted on a mere side issue. [10] You should beware of the last of the aforesaid methods; for it appears to be wholly disconnected from, and foreign to, the art of dialectic. For this reason, moreover, the answerer should not lose his temper, but assent to those statements that are of no use in attacking the thesis, adding an indication whenever he assents although he does not agree with the view. For, as a rule, it increases the confusion [15] of questioners if, after all propositions of this kind have been granted them, they can then draw no conclusion.

Moreover, any one who has made any statement whatever has in a certain sense made several statements, inasmuch as each statement has a number of necessary consequences: e.g. the man who said 'X is a man' has also said that it is an animal and that it is animate and a biped and capable of acquiring reason and [20] knowledge, so that by the demolition of any single one of these consequences, of whatever kind, the original statement is demolished as well. But you should beware here too of making a change to a more difficult subject: for sometimes the consequence, and sometimes the original thesis, is the easier to demolish.

6

In regard to subjects which must have one and one only of two predicates, as (e.g.) a man [25] must have either a disease or health, supposing we are well supplied as regards the one for arguing its presence or absence, we shall be well equipped as regards the remaining one as well. This rule is convertible for both purposes: for when we have shown that the one attribute belongs, we shall have shown that the remaining one does not belong; while if we show that the one does not belong, we shall have shown [30] that the remaining one does belong. Clearly then the rule is useful for both purposes.

Moreover, you may devise a line of attack by reinterpreting a term in its literal meaning, with the implication that it is most fitting so to take it rather than in its established meaning: e.g. the expression 'strong at heart' will suggest not the courageous man, according to the use now established, but the man the state [35] of whose heart is strong; just as also the expression 'of a good hope' may be taken to mean the man who hopes for good things. Likewise also 'well-starred' may be taken to mean the man whose star is good, as Xenocrates says 'well-starred is he who has a noble soul'.[1] For a man's star is his soul.
112ᵇ Some things occur of necessity, others usually, others however it may chance; if therefore a necessary event has been asserted to occur usually, or if a usual event (or, failing such an event itself, its contrary) has been stated to occur of necessity, it always gives an [5] opportunity for attack. For if a necessary event has been asserted to occur usually, clearly the speaker has denied an attribute to be universal which is universal, and so has made a mistake: and so he has if he has declared the usual attribute to be necessary: for then he declares it to belong universally when it does not so belong. Likewise also if he has declared the [10] contrary of what is usual to be necessary. For the contrary of a usual attribute is always a comparatively rare attribute: e.g. if men are usually bad, they are comparatively seldom

[1] Fr. 81, Heinze.

good, so that his mistake is even worse if he has declared them to be good of necessity. The same is true also if he has declared a mere matter of chance to happen of necessity or usually; [15] for a chance event happens neither of necessity nor usually. If the thing happens usually, then even supposing his statement does not distinguish whether he meant that it happens usually or that it happens necessarily, it is open to you to discuss it on the assumption that he meant that it happens necessarily: e.g. if he has stated without any distinction that disinherited persons are bad, you may assume in discussing [20] it that he means that they are so necessarily.

Moreover, look and see also if he has stated a thing to be an accident of itself, taking it to be a different thing because it has a different name, as Prodicus used to divide pleasures into joy and delight and good cheer: for all these are names of the same thing, to wit, Pleasure. If then any one says that joyfulness is an acci- [25] dental attribute of cheerfulness, he would be declaring it to be an accidental attribute of itself.

7

Inasmuch as contraries can be conjoined with each other in six ways, and four of these conjunctions constitute a contrariety, we must grasp the subject of contraries, in order that it may help us both in demolishing and in estab- [30] lishing a view. Well then, that the modes of conjunction are six is clear: for either (1) each of the contrary verbs will be conjoined to each of the contrary objects; and this gives two modes: e.g. to do good to friends and to do evil to enemies, or *per contra* to do evil to friends and to do good to enemies. Or else (2) both verbs may be attached to one object; and this [35] too gives two modes, e.g. to do good to friends and to do evil to friends, or to do good to enemies and to do evil to enemies. Or (3) a single verb may be attached to both objects: and this also gives two modes; e.g. to do good to friends and to do good to enemies, or to do evil to friends and evil to enemies.

113ª The first two then of the aforesaid conjunctions do not constitute any contrariety; for the doing of good to friends is not contrary to the doing of evil to enemies: for both courses are desirable and belong to the same disposition. Nor is the doing of evil to friends contrary to the doing of good to enemies: for both of [5] these are objectionable and belong to the same disposition: and one objectionable thing is not generally thought to be the contrary of another, unless the one be an expression denoting an excess, and the other an expression denoting a defect: for an excess is generally thought to belong to the class of objectionable things, and likewise also a defect. But the other four all constitute a contrariety. For to do good [10] to friends is contrary to the doing of evil to friends: for it proceeds from the contrary disposition, and the one is desirable, and the other objectionable. The case is the same also in regard to the other conjunctions: for in each combination the one course is desirable, and the other objectionable, and the one belongs to a reasonable disposition and the other to a bad. Clearly, then, from what has been said, the same course has more than one contrary. For [15] the doing of good to friends has as its contrary both the doing of good to enemies and the doing of evil to friends. Likewise, if we examine them in the same way, we shall find that the contraries of each of the others also are two in number. Select therefore whichever of the two contraries is useful in attacking the thesis.

[20] Moreover, if the accident of a thing have a contrary, see whether it belongs to the subject to which the accident in question has been declared to belong: for if the latter belongs the former could not belong; for it is impossible that contrary predicates should belong at the same time to the same thing.

Or again, look and see if anything has been said about something, of such a kind that if it be true, contrary predicates must necessarily [25] belong to the thing: e.g. if he has said that the 'Ideas' exist in us. For then the result will be that they are both in motion and at rest, and moreover that they are objects both of sensation and of thought. For according to the views of those who posit the existence of Ideas, those Ideas are at rest and are objects of thought; while if they exist in us, it is impossible that they should be unmoved: for when we move, it follows necessarily that all that is in us moves [30] with us as well. Clearly also they are objects of sensation, if they exist in us: for it is through the sensation of sight that we recognize the Form present in each individual.

Again, if there be posited an accident which has a contrary, look and see if that which admits of the accident will admit of its contrary as well: for the same thing admits of contra- [35] ries. Thus (e.g.) if he has asserted that hatred follows anger, hatred would in that case be in the 'spirited faculty': for that is where anger is. You should therefore look and see if its contrary, to wit, friendship, be also in the 'spirited faculty': for if not—if friendship is in the faculty of desire—then hatred could not follow anger. Likewise also if he has asserted that the faculty of desire is ignorant. [5] For if it were capable of ignorance, it would be capable of knowledge as well: and this is not generally held—I mean that the faculty of desire is capable of knowledge. For purposes, then, of overthrowing a view, as has been said, this rule should be observed: but for purposes of establishing one, though the rule will not help you to assert that the accident actually belongs, it will help you to assert that it may possibly belong. For having shown that the thing in question will not admit of the contrary of the accident asserted, we shall have [10] shown that the accident neither belongs nor can possibly belong; while on the other hand, if we show that the contrary belongs, or that the thing is capable of the contrary, we shall not indeed as yet have shown that the accident asserted does belong as well; our proof will merely have gone to this point, that it is possible for it to belong.

8

[15] Seeing that the modes of opposition are four in number, you should look for arguments among the contradictories of your terms, converting the order of their sequence, both when demolishing and when establishing a view, and you should secure them by means of induction—such arguments (e.g.) as that 'If man be an animal, what is not an animal is not a man': and likewise also in other instances of contradictories. For in those cases the sequence is converse: for 'animal' follows upon 'man', [20] but 'not-animal' does not follow upon 'not-man', but conversely 'not-man' upon 'not-animal'. In all cases, therefore, a postulate of this sort should be made, (e.g.) that 'If the honourable is pleasant, what is not pleasant is not honourable, while if the latter be untrue, so is the former'. Likewise, also, 'If what is not pleasant be not honourable, then what is honourable is pleasant'. Clearly, then, the conver- [25] sion of the sequence formed by contradiction of the terms of the thesis is a method convertible for both purposes.

Then look also at the case of the contraries of S and P in the thesis, and see if the contrary of the one follows upon the contrary of the other, either directly or conversely, both when you are demolishing and when you are establishing a view: secure arguments of this kind as well by means of induction, so far as may be [30] required. Now the sequence is direct in a case such as that of courage and cowardice: for upon the one of them virtue follows, and vice upon the other; and upon the one it follows that it is desirable, while upon the other it follows that it is objectionable. The sequence, therefore, in the latter case also is direct; for the desirable is the contrary of the objectionable. Likewise also in other cases. The sequence is, on the other hand, converse in such a case [35] as this: Health follows upon vigour, but disease does not follow upon debility; rather debility follows upon disease. In this case, then, clearly the sequence is converse. Converse sequence is, however, rare in the case of contraries; usually the sequence is direct. If, therefore, the contrary of the one term does not follow upon the contrary of the other either directly or conversely, clearly neither does the one term follow upon the other in the state- [5] ment made: whereas if the one followed the other in the case of the contraries, it must of necessity do so as well in the original statement.

You should look also into cases of the privation or presence of a state in like manner to the case of contraries. Only, in the case of such privations the converse sequence does not occur: the sequence is always bound to be direct: e.g. [10] as sensation follows sight, while absence of sensation follows blindness. For the opposition of sensation to absence of sensation is an opposition of the presence to the privation of a state: for the one of them is a state, and the other the privation of it.

The case of relative terms should also be studied in like manner to that of a state and its privation: for the sequence of these as well is [15] direct; e.g. if $3/1$ is a multiple, then $1/3$ is a fraction: for $3/1$ is relative to $1/3$, and so is a multiple to a fraction. Again, if knowledge be a conceiving, then also the object of knowledge is an object of conception; and if sight be a sensation, then also the object of [20] sight is an object of sensation. An objection may be made that there is no necessity for the sequence to take place, in the case of relative terms, in the way described: for the object of sensation is an object of knowledge, whereas sensation is not knowledge. The objection is, however, not generally received as really true; for many people deny that there is knowledge of objects of sensation. Moreover, the principle stated is just as useful for the contrary purpose, e.g. to show that the object of sensation [25] is not an object of knowledge, on the ground that neither is sensation knowledge.

9

Again look at the case of the co-ordinates and inflected forms of the terms in the thesis, both in demolishing and in establishing it. By 'co-ordinates' are meant terms such as the following: 'Just deeds' and the 'just man' are co-ordinates of 'justice', and 'courageous deeds' and the 'courageous man' are co-ordinates of 'courage'. Likewise also things that tend to produce and to preserve anything are called [30] co-ordinates of that which they tend to produce and to preserve, as e.g. 'healthy habits' are co-ordinates of 'health' and a 'vigorous constitutional' of a 'vigorous constitution'—and so forth also in other cases. 'Co-ordinate', then, usually describes cases such as these, whereas 'inflected forms' are such as the following: 'justly', 'courageously', 'healthily', and such as are formed in this way. It is usually [35] held that words when used in their inflected forms as well are co-ordinates, as (e.g.) 'justly' in relation to justice, and 'courageously' to courage; and then 'co-ordinate' describes all the members of the same kindred series, e.g. 'justice', 'just', of a man or an act, 'justly'. Clearly, then, when any one member, whatever its kind, of the same kindred series is 114^b shown to be good or praiseworthy, then all the rest as well come to be shown to be so: e.g. if 'justice' be something praiseworthy, then so will 'just', of a man or thing, and 'justly' connote something praiseworthy. Then 'justly' will be rendered also 'praiseworthily', derived [5] by the same inflexion from 'the praiseworthy' whereby 'justly' is derived from 'justice'.

Look not only in the case of the subject mentioned, but also in the case of its contrary, for the contrary predicate: e.g. argue that good is not necessarily pleasant; for neither is evil painful: or that, if the latter be the case, so is the former. Also, if justice be knowledge, then injustice is ignorance: and if 'justly' means [10] 'knowingly' and 'skilfully', then 'unjustly' means 'ignorantly' and 'unskilfully': whereas if the latter be not true, neither is the former, as in the instance given just now: for 'unjustly' is more likely to seem equivalent to 'skilfully' than to 'unskilfully'. This commonplace rule has been stated before in dealing with the sequence of contraries;[1] for all we are claiming

[1] 113^b 27-114^a 6.

[15] now is that the contrary of P shall follow the contrary of S.

Moreover, look at the modes of generation and destruction of a thing, and at the things which tend to produce or to destroy it, both in demolishing and in establishing a view. For those things whose modes of generation rank among good things, are themselves also good; and if they themselves be good, so also are their modes of generation. If, on the other hand, their modes of generation be evil, then they themselves also are evil. In regard to modes of destruction the converse is true: for [20] if the modes of destruction rank as good things, then they themselves rank as evil things; whereas if the modes of destruction count as evil, they themselves count as good. The same argument applies also to things tending to produce and destroy: for things whose productive causes are good, themselves also rank as good; whereas if causes destructive of them are good, they themselves rank as evil.

10

[25] Again, look at things which are like the subject in question, and see if they are in like case; e.g. if one branch of knowledge has more than one object, so also will one opinion; and if to possess sight be to see, then also to possess hearing will be to hear. Likewise also in the case of other things, both those which are and those which are generally held to be like. The rule in question is useful for both purposes; [30] for if it be as stated in the case of some one like thing, it is so with the other like things as well, whereas if it be not so in the case of some one of them, neither is it so in the case of the others. Look and see also whether the cases are alike as regards a single thing and a number of things: for sometimes there is a discrepancy. Thus, if to 'know' a thing be to 'think of' it, then also to 'know many things' is to 'be thinking of many things'; whereas this is not true; for it is possible to know many things but not to be thinking of them. If, then, the [35] latter proposition be not true, neither was the former that dealt with a single thing, viz. that to 'know' a thing is to 'think of' it.

Moreover, argue from greater and less degrees. In regard to greater degrees there are four commonplace rules. One is: See whether a greater degree of the predicate follows a greater degree of the subject: e.g. if pleasure be good, see whether also a greater pleasure be a greater good: and if to do a wrong be evil, see 115^a whether also to do a greater wrong is a greater evil. Now this rule is of use for both purposes: for if an increase of the accident follows an increase of the subject, as we have said, clearly the accident belongs; while if it [5] does not follow, the accident does not belong. You should establish this by induction. Another rule is: If one predicate be attributed to two subjects; then supposing it does not belong to the subject to which it is the more likely to belong, neither does it belong where it is less likely to belong; while if it does belong where it is less likely to belong, then it belongs as well where it is more likely. Again: If two predicates be attributed to one subject, then if the one which is more generally thought to belong does not belong, neither does the one that [10] is less generally thought to belong; or, if the one that is less generally thought to belong does belong, so also does the other. Moreover: If two predicates be attributed to two subjects, then if the one which is more usually thought to belong to the one subject does not belong, neither does the remaining predicate belong to the remaining subject; or, if the one which is less usually thought to belong to the one subject does belong, so too does the remaining predicate to the remaining subject.

[15] Moreover, you can argue from the fact that an attribute belongs, or is generally supposed to belong, in a like degree, in three ways, viz. those described in the last three rules given in regard to a greater degree.[1] For supposing that one predicate belongs, or is supposed to belong, to two subjects in a like degree, then if it does not belong to the one, neither does it belong to the other; while if it belongs to the one, it belongs to the remaining one as well. Or, supposing two predicates to belong in a [20] like degree to the same subject, then, if the one does not belong, neither does the remaining one; while if the one does belong, the remaining one belongs as well. The case is the same also if two predicates belong in a like degree to two subjects; for if the one predicate does not belong to the one subject, neither does the remaining predicate belong to the remaining subject, while if the one predicate does belong to the one subject, the remaining predicate belongs to the remaining subject as well.

11

[25] You can argue, then, from greater or less or like degrees of truth in the aforesaid number of ways. Moreover, you should argue from the addition of one thing to another. If the addition of one thing to another makes that other good or white, whereas formerly it was not white or good, then the thing added will be white or good—it will possess the character it imparts to the whole as well. Moreover, if an [30] addition of something to a given object intensifies the character which it had as given, then the thing added will itself as well be of that character. Likewise, also, in the case of other attributes. The rule is not applicable in all cases, but only in those in which the excess described as an 'increased intensity' is found to take place. The above rule is, however, not convertible for overthrowing a view. For if the thing added does not make the other good, it [35] is not thereby made clear whether in itself it may not be good: for the addition of good to evil does not necessarily make the whole good, any more than the addition of white to black makes the whole white.

Again, any predicate of which we can speak of greater or less degrees belongs also absolutely: for greater or less degrees of good or of white will not be attributed to what is not good [5] or white: for a bad thing will never be said to have a greater or less degree of goodness than another, but always of badness. This rule is not convertible, either, for the purpose of overthrowing a predication: for several predicates of which we cannot speak of a greater degree belong absolutely: for the term 'man' is not attributed in greater and less de- [10] grees, but a man is a man for all that.

You should examine in the same way predicates attributed in a given respect, and at a given time and place: for if the predicate be possible in some respect, it is possible also absolutely. Likewise, also, is what is predicated at a given time or place: for what is absolutely impossible is not possible either in any respect or at any place or time. An objection may be [15] raised that in a given respect people may be good by nature, e.g. they may be generous or temperately inclined, while absolutely they are not good by nature, because no one is prudent by nature. Likewise, also, it is possible for a destructible thing to escape destruction at a given time, whereas it is not possible for it to escape absolutely. In the same way also it is a good thing at certain places to follow such [20] and such a diet, e.g. in infected areas, though it is not a good thing absolutely. Moreover, in certain places it is possible to live singly and alone, but absolutely it is not possible to exist singly and alone. In the same way also it is in certain places honourable to sac-

[1] ll. 6-14.

rifice one's father, e.g. among the Triballi, whereas, absolutely, it is not honourable. Or possibly this may indicate a relativity not to places but to persons: for it is all the same [25] wherever they may be: for everywhere it will be held honourable among the Triballi themselves, just because they are Triballi. Again, at certain times it is a good thing to take medicines, e.g. when one is ill, but it is not so absolutely. Or possibly this again may indicate a relativity not to a certain time, but to a certain state of health: for it is all the same whenever it occurs, if only one be in that state. A thing is 'absolutely' so which without [30] any addition you are prepared to say is honourable or the contrary. Thus (e.g.) you will deny that to sacrifice one's father is honourable: it is honourable only to certain persons: it is not therefore honourable absolutely. On the other hand, to honour the gods you will declare to be honourable without adding anything, because that is honourable absolutely. So that whatever without any addition is generally accounted to be honourable or dis- [35] honourable or anything else of that kind, will be said to be so 'absolutely'.

BOOK III

I

116ᵃ The question which is the more desirable, or the better, of two or more things, should be examined upon the following lines: only first of all it must be clearly laid down that the inquiry we are making concerns not [5] things that are widely divergent and that exhibit great differences from one another (for nobody raises any doubt whether happiness or wealth is more desirable), but things that are nearly related and about which we commonly discuss for which of the two we ought rather to vote, because we do not see any advantage on either side as compared with the other. [10] Clearly, then, in such cases if we can show a single advantage, or more than one, our judgement will record our assent that whichever side happens to have the advantage is the more desirable.

First, then, that which is more lasting or secure is more desirable than that which is less so: and so is that which is more likely to be chosen by the prudent or by the good man or [15] by the right law, or by men who are good in any particular line, when they make their choice as such, or by the experts in regard to any particular class of things; i.e. either whatever most of them or what all of them would choose; e.g. in medicine or in carpentry those things are more desirable which most, or all, doctors would choose; or, in general, whatever most men or all men or all things would choose, e.g. the good: for everything aims at [20] the good. You should direct the argument you intend to employ to whatever purpose you require. Of what is 'better' or 'more desirable' the absolute standard is the verdict of the better science, though relatively to a given individual the standard may be his own particular science.

In the second place, that which is known as 'an x' is more desirable than that which does not come within the genus 'x'—e.g. justice than a just man; for the former falls within the genus 'good', whereas the other does not, and [25] the former is called 'a good', whereas the latter is not: for nothing which does not happen to belong to the genus in question is called by the generic name; e.g. a 'white man' is not 'a colour'. Likewise also in other cases.

Also, that which is desired for itself is more desirable than that which is desired for something else; e.g. health is more desirable than [30] gymnastics: for the former is desired for itself, the latter for something else. Also, that which is desirable in itself is more desirable than what is desirable *per accidens*; e.g. justice in our friends than justice in our enemies: for the former is desirable in itself, the latter *per accidens:* for we desire that our enemies should be just *per accidens,* in order that they may do us no harm. This last principle is the same as [35] the one that precedes it, with, however, a different turn of expression. For we desire justice in our friends for itself, even though it will make no difference to us, and even though they be in India; whereas in our enemies we desire it for something else, in order that they may do us no harm.

116ᵇ Also, that which is in itself the cause of good is more desirable than what is so *per accidens,* e.g. virtue than luck (for the former is in itself, and the latter *per accidens,* the cause of good things), and so in other cases of the same kind. Likewise also in the case of the [5] contrary; for what is in itself the cause of evil is more objectionable than what is so *per accidens,* e.g. vice and chance: for the one is bad in itself, whereas chance is so *per accidens.*

Also, what is good absolutely is more desirable than what is good for a particular person, e.g. recovery of health than a surgical operation; for the former is good absolutely, the lat- [10] ter only for a particular person, viz. the man who needs an operation. So too what is good by nature is more desirable than the good that is not so by nature, e.g. justice than the just man; for the one is good by nature, whereas in the other case the goodness is acquired. Also the attribute is more desirable which belongs to the better and more honourable subject, e.g. to a god rather than to a man, and to the soul rather than to the body. So too the property of the better thing is better than the property of the worse; e.g. the property of God [15] than the property of man: for whereas in respect of what is common in both of them they do not differ at all from each other, in respect of their properties the one surpasses the other. Also that is better which is inherent in things better or prior or more honourable: thus (e.g.) health is better than strength and beauty: for the former is inherent in the moist and the dry, and the hot and the cold, in fact in all the primary constituents of an animal, whereas the others are inherent in what is sec- [20] ondary, strength being a feature of the sinews and bones, while beauty is generally supposed to consist in a certain symmetry of the limbs. Also the end is generally supposed to be more desirable than the means, and of two means, that which lies nearer the end. In general, too, a means directed towards the end of life is more desirable than a means to any- [25] thing else, e.g. that which contributes to happiness than that which contributes to prudence. Also the competent is more desirable than the incompetent. Moreover, of two productive agents that one is more desirable whose end is better; while between a productive agent and an end we can decide by a proportional sum whenever the excess of the one end over the other is greater than that of the latter over its own productive means: e.g. supposing the excess of happiness over health to be greater [30] than that of health over what produces health, then what produces happiness is better than health. For what produces happiness exceeds what produces health just as much as happiness exceeds health. But health exceeds what produces health by a smaller amount; *ergo,* the excess of what produces happiness over what produces health is greater than that of health over what produces health. Clearly, [35] therefore, what produces happiness is more desirable than health: for it exceeds the same standard by a greater amount.

Moreover, what is in itself nobler and more precious and praiseworthy is more desirable than what is less so, e.g. friendship than wealth, and justice than strength. For the former belong in themselves to the class of things precious and praiseworthy, while the latter do so not in themselves but for something else: for no one prizes wealth for itself but always for something else, whereas we prize friendship for itself, even though nothing else is likely to come to us from it.

2

[5] Moreover, whenever two things are very much like one another, and we cannot see any superiority in the one over the other of them, we should look at them from the standpoint of their consequences. For the one which is followed by the greater good is the more desirable: or, if the consequences be evil, that is more desirable which is followed by the less evil. For though both may be desirable, yet [10] there may possibly be some unpleasant consequence involved to turn the scale. Our survey from the point of view of consequences lies in two directions, for there are prior consequences and later consequences: e.g. if a man learns, it follows that he was ignorant before and knows afterwards. As a rule, the later consequence is the better to consider. You should take, therefore, whichever of the consequences [15] suits your purpose.

Moreover, a greater number of good things is more desirable than a smaller, either absolutely or when the one is included in the other, viz. the smaller number in the greater. An objection may be raised suppose in some particular case the one is valued for the sake of the other; for then the two together are not more desirable than the one; e.g. recovery of [20] health and health, than health alone, inasmuch as we desire recovery of health for the sake of health. Also it is quite possible for what is not good, together with what is, to be more desirable than a greater number of good things, e.g. the combination of happiness and something else which is not good may be more desirable than the combination of justice and courage. Also, the same things are more valuable if accompanied than if unaccompanied by pleasure, and likewise when free from pain [25] than when attended with pain.

Also, everything is more desirable at the season when it is of greater consequence; e.g. freedom from pain in old age more than in youth: for it is of greater consequence in old age. On the same principle also, prudence is more desirable in old age; for no man chooses [30] the young to guide him, because he does not expect them to be prudent. With courage, the converse is the case, for it is in youth that the active exercise of courage is more imperatively required. Likewise also with temperance; for the young are more troubled by their passions than are their elders.

[35] Also, that is more desirable which is more useful at every season or at most seasons, e.g. justice and temperance rather than courage: for they are always useful, while courage is only useful at times. Also, that one of two things which if all possess, we do not need the other thing, is more desirable than that which all may possess and still we want the other one as well. Take the case of justice and courage; if everybody were just, there would be no use 117b for courage, whereas all might be courageous, and still justice would be of use.

Moreover, judge by the destructions and losses and generations and acquisitions and contraries of things: for things whose destruc- [5] tion is more objectionable are themselves more desirable. Likewise also with the losses and contraries of things; for a thing whose loss or whose contrary is more objectionable is itself more desirable. With the generations or acquisitions of things the opposite is the case: for things whose acquisition or generation is more desirable are themselves also desirable.

[10] Another commonplace rule is that what is nearer to the good is better and more desirable, i.e. what more nearly resembles the good: thus justice is better than a just man. Also, that which is more like than another thing to something better than itself, as e.g. some say that Ajax was a better man than Odysseus because he was more like Achilles. An objection may be raised to this that it is not true: for it is quite possible that Ajax did not resemble [15] Achilles more nearly than Odysseus in the points which made Achilles the best of them, and that Odysseus was a good man, though unlike Achilles. Look also to see whether the resemblance be that of a caricature, like the resemblance of a monkey to a man, whereas a horse bears none: for the monkey is not the more handsome creature, despite its nearer resemblance to a man. Again, in the case of two [20] things, if one is more like the better thing while another is more like the worse, then that is likely to be better which is more like the better. This too, however, admits of an objection: for quite possibly the one only slightly resembles the better, while the other strongly resembles the worse, e.g. supposing the resemblance of Ajax to Achilles to be slight, while that of Odysseus to Nestor is [25] strong. Also it may be that the one which is like the better type shows a degrading likeness, whereas the one which is like the worse type improves upon it: witness the likeness of a horse to a donkey, and that of a monkey to a man.

Another rule is that the more conspicuous good is more desirable than the less conspicuous, and the more difficult than the easier: for we appreciate better the possession of things [30] that cannot be easily acquired. Also the more personal possession is more desirable than the more widely shared. Also, that which is more free from connexion with evil: for what is not attended by any unpleasantness is more desirable than what is so attended.

Moreover, if A be without qualification better than B, then also the best of the members of A is better than the best of the members of B; e.g. if Man be better than Horse, then also [35] the best man is better than the best horse. Also, if the best in A be better than the best in B, then also A is better than B without qualification; e.g. if the best man be better than the best horse, then also Man is better than Horse without qualification.

118a Moreover, things which our friends can share are more desirable than those they cannot. Also, things which we like rather to do to our friend are more desirable than those we like to do to the man in the street, e.g. just dealing and the doing of good rather than the [5] semblance of them: for we would rather really do good to our friends than seem to do so, whereas towards the man in the street the converse is the case.

Also, superfluities are better than necessities, and are sometimes more desirable as well: for the good life is better than mere life, and good life is a superfluity, whereas mere life itself is a necessity. Sometimes, though, what is better is not also more desirable: for there is no neces- [10] sity that because it is better it should also be more desirable: at least to be a philosopher is better than to make money, but it is not more desirable for a man who lacks the necessities of life. The expression 'superfluity' applies whenever a man possesses the necessities of life and sets to work to secure as well other noble acquisitions. Roughly speaking, perhaps, [15] necessities are more desirable, while superfluities are better.

Also, what cannot be got from another is more desirable than what can be got from another as well, as (e.g.) is the case of justice compared with courage. Also, A is more desirable if A is desirable without B, but not B without A: power (e.g.) is not desirable without prudence, but prudence is desirable with- [20] out power. Also, if of two things we repudiate the one in order to be thought to possess the other, then that one is more desirable which we wish to be thought to possess; thus (e.g.) we repudiate the love of hard work in order that people may think us geniuses.

Moreover, that is more desirable in whose [25] absence it is less blameworthy for people to be vexed; and that is more desirable in whose absence it is more blameworthy for a man not to be vexed.

3

Moreover, of things that belong to the same species one which possesses the peculiar virtue of the species is more desirable than one which does not. If both possess it, then the one which possesses it in a greater degree is more desirable.

Moreover, if one thing makes good whatever [30] it touches, while another does not, the former is more desirable, just as also what makes things warm is warmer than what does not. If both do so, then that one is more desirable which does so in a greater degree, or if it render good the better and more important object—if (e.g.), the one makes good the soul, and the other the body.

Moreover, judge things by their inflexions [35] and uses and actions and works, and judge these by them: for they go with each other: e.g. if 'justly' means something more desirable than 'courageously', then also justice means something more desirable than courage; and if justice be more desirable than courage, then also 'justly' means something more desirable than 'courageously'. Similarly also in the other cases.

118ᵇ Moreover, if one thing exceeds while the other falls short of the same standard of good, the one which exceeds is the more desirable; or if the one exceeds an even higher standard. Nay more, if there be two things both preferable to something, the one which is more highly preferable to it is more desirable than the less highly preferable. Moreover, [5] when the excess of a thing is more desirable than the excess of something else, that thing is itself also more desirable than the other, as (e.g.) friendship than money: for an excess of friendship is more desirable than an excess of money. So also that of which a man would rather that it were his by his own doing is more desirable than what he would rather get by another's doing, e.g. friends than money. [10] Moreover, judge by means of an addition, and see if the addition of A to the same thing as B makes the whole more desirable than does the addition of B. You must, however, beware of adducing a case in which the common term uses, or in some other way helps the case of, one of the things added to it, but not the other, as (e.g.) if you took a saw and a sickle in combination with the art of carpentry: for [15] in the combination the saw is a more desirable thing, but it is not a more desirable thing without qualification. Again, a thing is more desirable if, when added to a lesser good, it makes the whole a greater good. Likewise, also, you should judge by means of subtraction: for the thing upon whose subtraction the remainder is a lesser good may be taken to be a greater good, whichever it be whose subtraction makes the remainder a lesser good.

[20] Also, if one thing be desirable for itself, and the other for the look of it, the former is more desirable, as (e.g.) health than beauty. A thing is defined as being desired for the look of it if, supposing no one knew of it, you would not care to have it. Also, it is more desirable both for itself and for the look of it, while the other thing is desirable on the one ground alone. Also, whichever is the more precious for itself, is also better and more [25] desirable. A thing may be taken to be more precious in itself which we choose rather for itself, without anything else being likely to come of it.

Moreover, you should distinguish in how many senses 'desirable' is used, and with a view to what ends, e.g. expediency or honour or pleasure. For what is useful for all or most of them may be taken to be more desirable [30] than what is not useful in like manner. If the same characters belong to both things you should look and see which possesses them more markedly, i.e. which of the two is the more pleasant or more honourable or more expedient. Again, that is more desirable which serves the better purpose, e.g. that which serves to promote virtue more than that which serves to promote pleasure. Likewise also in the case of objectionable things; for that is more objectionable which stands more in the way of [35] what is desirable, e.g. disease more than ugliness: for disease is a greater hindrance both to pleasure and to being good.

Moreover, argue by showing that the thing in question is in like measure objectionable and desirable: for a thing of such a character that a man might well desire and object to it alike is less desirable than the other which is desirable **only**.

4

119ᵃ Comparisons of things together should therefore be conducted in the manner prescribed. The same commonplace rules are useful also for showing that anything is simply desirable or objectionable: for we have only to subtract the excess of one thing over another. For if what is more precious be more desirable, then also what is precious is desirable; and if [5] what is more useful be more desirable, then also what is useful is desirable. Likewise, also, in the case of other things which admit of comparisons of that kind. For in some cases in the very course of comparing the things together we at once assert also that each of them, or the one of them, is desirable, e.g. whenever we call the one good 'by nature' and the other [10] 'not by nature': for clearly what is good by nature is desirable.

5

The commonplace rules relating to comparative degrees and amounts ought to be taken in the most general possible form: for when so taken they are likely to be useful in a larger number of instances. It is possible to render [15] some of the actual rules given above more universal by a slight alteration of the expression, e.g. that what by nature exhibits such and such a quality exhibits that quality in a greater degree than what exhibits it not by nature. Also, if one thing does, and another does not, impart such and such a quality to that which possesses it, or to which it belongs, then whichever does impart it is of that quality in greater degree than the one which does not impart it; and if both impart it, then that one exhibits it in a greater degree which imparts it in a greater degree.
[20] Moreover, if in any character one thing exceeds and another falls short of the same standard; also, if the one exceeds something which exceeds a given standard, while the other does not reach that standard, then clearly the first-named thing exhibits that character in a greater degree. Moreover, you should judge by means of addition, and see if A when added to the same thing as B imparts to the whole such and such a character in a more marked degree than B, or if, when added to a thing which exhibits that character in a less degree, it imparts that character to the whole in a [25] greater degree. Likewise, also, you may judge by means of subtraction: for a thing upon whose subtraction the remainder exhibits such and such a character in a less degree, itself exhibits that character in a greater degree. Also, things exhibit such and such a character in a greater degree if more free from admixture with their contraries; e.g. that is whiter which is more free from admixture with black. Moreover, apart from the rules given above, that has such and such a character in greater degree which admits in a greater degree of the [30] definition proper to the given character; e.g. if the definition of 'white' be 'a colour which pierces the vision', then that is whiter which is in a greater degree a colour that pierces the vision.

6

If the question be put in a particular and not in a universal form, in the first place the universal constructive or destructive commonplace rules that have been given may all be brought into use. For in demolishing or estab- [35] lishing a thing universally we also show it in particular: for if it be true of all, it is true also of some, and if untrue of all, it is untrue of some. Especially handy and of general application are the commonplace rules that are drawn from the opposites and co-ordinates and inflexions of a thing: for public opinion grants alike the claim that if all pleasure be good, then also all pain is evil, and the claim that if some 119ᵇ pleasure be good, then also some pain is evil. Moreover, if some form of sensation be not a capacity, then also some form of failure of sensation is not a failure of capacity. Also, if the object of conception is in some cases an object of knowledge, then also some form of conceiving is knowledge. Again, if what is unjust be in some cases good, then also what is [5] just is in some cases evil; and if what happens justly is in some cases evil, then also what happens unjustly is in some cases good. Also, if what is pleasant is in some cases objectionable, then pleasure is in some cases an objectionable thing. On the same principle, also, if what is pleasant is in some cases beneficial, then pleasure is in some cases a beneficial thing. The case is the same also as regards the things that destroy, and the processes of generation and destruction. For if anything that [10] destroys pleasure or knowledge be in some cases good, then we may take it that pleasure or knowledge is in some cases an evil thing. Likewise, also, if the destruction of knowledge be in some cases a good thing or its production an evil thing, then knowledge will be in some cases an evil thing; e.g. if for a man to forget his disgraceful conduct be a good thing, and to remember it be an evil thing, then the knowledge of his disgraceful [15] conduct may be taken to be an evil thing. The same holds also in other cases: in all such cases the premiss and the conclusion are equally likely to be accepted.

Moreover you should judge by means of greater or smaller or like degrees: for if some member of another genus exhibit such and such a character in a more marked degree than your object, while no member of that genus exhibits that character at all, then you may take it that neither does the object in question exhibit it; e.g. if some form of knowledge be good in a greater degree than pleasure, while [20] no form of knowledge is good, then you may take it that pleasure is not good either. Also, you should judge by a smaller or like degree in the same way: for so you will find it possible both to demolish and to establish a view, except that whereas both are possible by means of like degrees, by means of a smaller degree it is possible only to establish, not to overthrow. For if a certain form of capacity be good in a like degree to knowledge, and a cer- [25] tain form of capacity be good, then so also is knowledge; while if no form of capacity be good, then neither is knowledge. If, too, a certain form of capacity be good in a less degree than knowledge, and a certain form of capacity be good, then so also is knowledge; but if no form of capacity be good, there is no necessity that no form of knowledge either should be good. Clearly, then, it is only possible [30] to establish a view by means of a less degree.

Not only by means of another genus can you overthrow a view, but also by means of the same, if you take the most marked instance of the character in question; e.g. if it be maintained that some form of knowledge is good, then, suppose it to be shown that prudence is not good, neither will any other kind be good, seeing that not even the kind upon which there is most general agreement is so. Moreover, [35] you should go to work by means of an hypothesis; you should claim that the attribute, if it belongs or does not belong in one case, does so in a like degree in all, e.g. that if the soul of man be immortal, so are other souls as well, while if this one be not so, neither are the others. If, then, it be maintained that in some instance the attribute belongs, you must show that in some instance it does not belong: for then it will follow, by reason of the hypothesis, that it does not belong to any instance at all. If, on the other hand, it be maintained **120ᵃ** that it does not belong in some instance, you must show that it does belong in some instance, for in this way it will follow that it belongs to all instances. It is clear that the maker of the hypothesis universalizes the question, whereas it was stated in a particular form: for he claims that the maker of a particular admission should make a universal admission, [5] inasmuch as he claims that if the attribute belongs in one instance, it belongs also in all instances alike.

If the problem be indefinite, it is possible to overthrow a statement in only one way; e.g. if a man has asserted that pleasure is good or is not good, without any further definition. For if he meant that a particular pleasure is good, you must show universally that no pleasure is good, if the proposition in question is [10] to be demolished. And likewise, also, if he meant that some particular pleasure is not good you must show universally that all pleasure is good: it is impossible to demolish it in any other way. For if we show that some particular pleasure is not good or is good, the proposition in question is not yet demolished. It is clear, then, that it is possible to demolish an indefinite statement in one way only, where- [15] as it can be established in two ways: for whether we show universally that all pleasure is good, or whether we show that a particular pleasure is good, the proposition in question will have been proved. Likewise, also, supposing we are required to argue that some particular pleasure is not good, if we show that no pleasure is good or that a particular pleasure is not good, we shall have produced an argument in both ways, both universally and [20] in particular, to show that some particular pleasure is not good. If, on the other hand, the statement made be definite, it will be possible to demolish it in two ways; e.g. if it be maintained that it is an attribute of some particular pleasure to be good, while of some it is not: for whether it be shown that all pleasure, or that no pleasure, is good, the proposition in question will have been demolished. If, however, he has stated that only one single pleasure is good, it is possible to demolish it in three ways: for by showing that all pleasure, [25] or that no pleasure, or that more than one pleasure, is good, we shall have demolished the statement in question. If the statement be made still more definite, e.g. that prudence alone of the virtues is knowledge, there are four ways of demolishing it: for if it be shown that all virtue is knowledge, or that no virtue [30] is so, or that some other virtue (e.g. justice) is so, or that prudence itself is not knowledge, the proposition in question will have been demolished.

It is useful also to take a look at individual instances, in cases where some attribute has been said to belong or not to belong, as in the case of universal questions. Moreover, you should take a glance among genera, dividing [35] them by their species until you come to those that are not further divisible, as has been said before:[1] for whether the attribute is found to belong in all cases or in none, you should, after adducing several instances, claim that he should either admit your point universally, or else bring an objection showing in what case it does not hold. Moreover, in cases where it is possible to make the accident definite either specifically or numerically, you should look and see whether perhaps none of them belongs, showing e.g. that time is not moved, nor yet is a movement, by enumerating how many species there are of movement: for if none of these belong to time, clearly it does not move, nor yet is a movement. Likewise, also, you can show that the soul is not a number, by dividing all numbers into either odd or even: [5] for then, if the soul be neither odd nor even, clearly it is not a number.

In regard then to Accident, you should set to work by means like these, and in this manner.

BOOK IV

1

[12] NEXT we must go on to examine questions relating to Genus and Property. These are elements in the questions that relate to definitions, but dialecticians seldom address [15] their inquiries to these by themselves. If, then, a genus be suggested for something that is, first take a look at all objects which belong to the same genus as the thing mentioned, and see whether the genus suggested is *not* predicated of one of them, as happens in the case of an accident: e.g. if 'good' be laid down to be the genus of 'pleasure', see whether some particular pleasure be not good: for, if so, clearly 'good' is not the genus of pleasure: for the [20] genus is predicated of all the members of the same species. Secondly, see whether it be predicated not in the category of essence, but as an accident, as 'white' is predicated of 'snow', or 'self-moved' of the soul. For 'snow' is not a kind of 'white', and therefore 'white' is not the genus of snow, nor is the soul a kind of 'moving object': its motion is an accident of [25] it, as it often is of an animal to walk or to be walking. Moreover, 'moving' does not seem to indicate the essence, but rather a state of doing or of having something done to it. Likewise, also, 'white': for it indicates not the essence of snow, but a certain quality of it. So that neither of them is predicated in the category of 'essence'.

[30] Especially you should take a look at the definition of Accident, and see whether it fits the genus mentioned, as (e.g.) is also the case in the instances just given. For it is possible for a thing to be and not to be self-moved, and likewise, also, for it to be and not to be white. So that neither of these attributes is the genus but an accident, since we were saying[2] that an accident is an attribute which can belong to a [35] thing and also not belong.

Moreover, see whether the genus and the species be not found in the same division, but the one be a substance while the other is a quality, or the one be a relative while the other is a quality, as (e.g.) 'snow' and 'swan' are each a substance, while 'white' is not a substance but a quality, so that 'white' is not the genus either of 'snow' or of 'swan'. Again, 'knowledge' is a relative, while 'good' and 'noble' are each a quality, so that good, or noble, is not the genus of knowledge. For the genera of relatives ought themselves also to be relatives, as is the case with 'double': for [5] 'multiple', which is the genus of 'double', is itself also a relative. To speak generally, the genus ought to fall under the same division as the species: for if the species be a substance,

---
[1] 109^b 15.   [2] 102^b 6.

so too should be the genus, and if the species be a quality, so too the genus should be a quality; e.g. if white be a quality, so too should colour be. Likewise, also, in other cases.

[10] Again, see whether it be necessary or possible for the genus to partake of the object which has been placed in the genus. 'To partake' is defined as 'to admit the definition' of that which is partaken. Clearly, therefore, the species partake of the genera, but not the genera of the species: for the species admits the definition of the genus, whereas the genus does not admit that of the species. You must look, therefore, [15] and see whether the genus rendered partakes or can possibly partake of the species, e.g. if any one were to render anything as genus of 'being' or of 'unity': for then the result will be that the genus partakes of the species: for of everything that is, 'being' and 'unity' are predicated, and therefore their definition as well.

[20] Moreover, see if there be anything of which the species rendered is true, while the genus is not so, e.g. supposing 'being' or 'object of knowledge' were stated to be the genus of 'object of opinion'. For 'object of opinion' will be a predicate of what does not exist; for many things which do not exist are objects of opinion; whereas that 'being' or 'object of knowledge' is not predicated of what does not exist is clear. So that neither 'being' nor 'object [25] of knowledge' is the genus of 'object of opinion': for of the objects of which the species is predicated, the genus ought to be predicated as well.

Again, see whether the object placed in the genus be quite unable to partake of any of its species: for it is impossible that it should partake of the genus if it do not partake of any of its species, except it be one of the species [30] reached by the first division: these do partake of the genus alone. If, therefore, 'Motion' be stated as the genus of pleasure, you should look and see if pleasure be neither locomotion nor alteration, nor any of the rest of the given modes of motion: for clearly you may then take it that it does not partake of any of the species, and therefore not of the genus either, since what partakes of the genus must [35] necessarily partake of one of the species as well: so that pleasure could not be a species of Motion, nor yet be one of the individual phenomena comprised under the term 'motion'. For individuals as well partake in the genus and the species, as (e.g.) an individual man partakes of both 'man' and 'animal'.

121^b Moreover, see if the term placed in the genus has a wider denotation than the genus, as (e.g.) 'object of opinion' has, as compared with 'being': for both what is and what is not are objects of opinion, so that 'object of opinion' could not be a species of being: for the genus is always of wider denotation than the species. Again, see if the species and its genus [5] have an equal denotation; suppose, for instance, that of the attributes which go with everything, one were to be stated as a species and the other as its genus, as for example Being and Unity: for everything has being and unity, so that neither is the genus of the other, since their denotation is equal. Likewise, also, if the 'first' of a series and the 'beginning' were to be placed one under the other: for the be- [10] ginning is first and the first is the beginning, so that either both expressions are identical or at any rate neither is the genus of the other. The elementary principle in regard to all such cases is that the genus has a wider denotation than the species and its differentia: for the differentia as well has a narrower denotation than the genus.

[15] See also whether the genus mentioned fails, or might be generally thought to fail, to apply to some object which is not specifically different from the thing in question; or, if your argument be constructive, whether it does so apply. For all things that are not specifically different have the same genus. If, therefore, it be shown to apply to one, then clearly it applies to all, and if it fails to apply to one, clearly it fails to apply to any; e.g. if any one who assumes 'indivisible lines' were to say that the 'in- [20] divisible' is their genus. For the aforesaid term is not the genus of divisible lines, and these do not differ as regards their species from indivisible: for straight lines are never different from each other as regards their species.

2

Look and see, also, if there be any other genus [25] of the given species which neither embraces the genus rendered nor yet falls under it, e.g. suppose any one were to lay down that 'knowledge' is the genus of justice. For virtue is its genus as well, and neither of these genera embraces the remaining one, so that knowledge could not be the genus of justice: for it is generally accepted that whenever one species falls under two genera, the one is embraced by the [30] other. Yet a principle of this kind gives rise to a difficulty in some cases. For some people hold that prudence is both virtue and knowledge, and that neither of its genera is embraced by the other: although certainly not everybody admits that prudence is knowledge. If, however, any one were to admit the truth of this assertion, yet it would still be generally [35] agreed to be necessary that the genera of the same object must at any rate be subordinate either the one to the other or both to the same, as actually is the case with virtue and knowledge. For both fall under the same genus; for each of them is a state and a disposition. You should look, therefore, and see whether neither of these things is true of the genus rendered; 122a for if the genera be subordinate neither the one to the other nor both to the same, then what is rendered could not be the true genus.

Look, also, at the genus of the genus rendered, and so continually at the next higher genus, and see whether all are predicated of [5] the species, and predicated in the category of essence: for all the higher genera should be predicated of the species in the category of essence. If, then, there be anywhere a discrepancy, clearly what is rendered is not the true genus. [Again, see whether either the genus itself, or one of its higher genera, partakes of the species: for the higher genus does not partake of any of the lower.] If, then, you are [10] overthrowing a view, follow the rule as given: if establishing one, then—suppose that what has been named as genus be admitted to belong to the species, only it be disputed whether it belongs as genus—it is enough to show that one of its higher genera is predicated of the species in the category of essence. For if one of them be predicated in the category of essence, all of them, both higher and [15] lower than this one, if predicated at all of the species, will be predicated of it in the category of essence: so that what has been *rendered* as genus is also predicated in the category of essence. The premiss that when one genus is predicated in the category of essence, all the rest, if predicated at all, will be predicated in the category of essence, should be secured by induction. Supposing, however, that it be dis- [20] puted whether what has been rendered as genus belongs at all, it is not enough to show that one of the higher genera is predicated of the species in the category of essence: e.g. if any one has rendered 'locomotion' as the genus of walking, it is not enough to show that walking is 'motion' in order to show that it is 'locomotion', seeing that there are other forms of motion as well; but one must show in addition [25] that walking does not partake of any of the species of motion produced by the same division except locomotion. For of necessity what partakes of the genus partakes also of one of the species produced by the first division of the genus. If, therefore, walking does not partake either of increase or decrease or of the other kinds of motion, clearly it would partake [30] of locomotion, so that locomotion would be the genus of walking.

Again, look among the things of which the given species is predicated as genus, and see if what is rendered as its genus be also predicated in the category of essence of the very things of which the species is so predicated, and likewise if all the genera higher than this genus are so predicated as well. For if there be anywhere a discrepancy, clearly what has been [35] rendered is not the true genus: for had it been the genus, then both the genera higher than it, and it itself, would all have been predicated in the category of essence of those objects of which the species too is predicated in the category of essence. If, then, you are overthrowing a view, it is useful to see whether the genus fails to be predicated in the category of essence of those things of which the species too is predicated. If establishing a view, it is 122b useful to see whether it is predicated in the category of essence: for if so, the result will be that the genus and the species will be predicated of the same object in the category of essence, so that the same object falls under two genera: the genera must therefore of necessity be subordinate one to the other, and therefore [5] if it be shown that the one we wish to establish as genus is not subordinate to the species, clearly the species would be subordinate to it, so that you may take it as shown that it is the genus.

Look, also, at the definitions of the genera, and see whether they apply both to the given species and to the objects which partake of the species. For of necessity the definitions of its genera must be predicated of the species and [10] of the objects which partake of the species: if, then, there be anywhere a discrepancy, clearly what has been rendered is not the genus.

Again, see if he has rendered the differentia as the genus, e.g. 'immortal' as the genus of 'God'. For 'immortal' is a differentia of 'living being', seeing that of living beings some are mortal and others immortal. Clearly, then, a [15] bad mistake has been made; for the differentia of a thing is never its genus. And that this is true is clear: for a thing's differentia never signifies its essence, but rather some quality, as do 'walking' and 'biped'.

Also, see whether he has placed the differentia inside the genus, e.g. by taking 'odd' as 'a number'. For 'odd' is a differentia of num-[20] ber, not a species. Nor is the differentia generally thought to partake of the genus: for what partakes of the genus is always either a species or an individual, whereas the differentia is neither a species nor an individual. Clearly, therefore, the differentia does not partake of the genus, so that 'odd' too is no species but a differentia, seeing that it does not partake of the genus.

[25] Moreover, see whether he has placed the genus inside the species, e.g. by taking 'contact' to be a 'juncture', or 'mixture' a 'fusion', or, as in Plato's definition,[1] 'locomotion' to be the same as 'carriage'. For there is no necessity that contact should be juncture: rather, conversely, juncture must be contact: for what is in contact is not always joined, though what is joined is always in contact. Likewise, [30] also, in the remaining instances: for mixture is not always a 'fusion' (for to mix dry things does not fuse them), nor is locomotion always 'carriage'. For walking is not generally thought to be carriage: for 'carriage' is mostly used of things that change one place for another involuntarily, as happens in the case of [35] inanimate things. Clearly, also, the species, in the instances given, has a wider denotation than the genus, whereas it ought to be vice versa.

Again, see whether he has placed the differentia inside the species, by taking (e.g.) 'immortal' to be 'a god'. For the result will be that the species has an equal or wider denotation: and this cannot be, for always the differ-123ᵃ entia has an equal or a wider denotation than the species. Moreover, see whether he has placed the genus inside the differentia, by making 'colour' (e.g.) to be a thing that 'pierces', or 'number' a thing that is 'odd'. Also, see if he has mentioned the genus as differentia: for it is possible for a man to bring forward a statement of this kind as well, e.g. that 'mixture' is the differentia of 'fusion', or that [5] 'change of place' is the differentia of 'carriage'. All such cases should be examined by means of the same principles: for they depend upon common rules: for the genus should have a wider denotation that its differentia, and also should not partake of its differentia; whereas, if it be rendered in this manner, neither of the aforesaid requirements can be satisfied: for the genus will both have a narrower denotation [10] than its differentia, and will partake of it.

Again, if no differentia belonging to the genus be predicated of the given species, neither will the genus be predicated of it; e.g. of 'soul' neither 'odd' nor 'even' is predicated: neither therefore is 'number'. Moreover, see whether the species is naturally prior and abol-[15] ishes the genus along with itself: for the contrary is the general view. Moreover, if it be possible for the genus stated, or for its differentia, to be absent from the alleged species, e.g. for 'movement' to be absent from the 'soul', or 'truth and falsehood' from 'opinion', then neither of the terms stated could be its genus or its differentia: for the general view is that the genus and the differentia accompany the species, as long as it exists.

3

[20] Look and see, also, if what is placed in the genus partakes or could possibly partake of any contrary of the genus: for in that case the same thing will at the same time partake of contrary things, seeing that the genus is never absent from it, while it partakes, or can possibly partake, of the contrary genus as well. Moreover, see whether the species shares in any character which it is utterly impossible for any member of the genus to have. Thus (e.g.) [25] if the soul has a share in life, while it is impossible for any number to live, then the soul could not be a species of number.

You should look and see, also, if the species be a homonym of the genus, and employ as your elementary principles those already stated for dealing with homonymity:[2] for the genus and the species are synonymous.

[30] Seeing that of every genus there is more than one species, look and see if it be impossible that there should be another species than the given one belonging to the genus stated: for if there should be none, then clearly what has been stated could not be a genus at all.

Look and see, also, if he has rendered as genus a metaphorical expression, describing (e.g.) 'temperance' as a 'harmony': for a genus [35] is always predicated of its species in its literal sense, whereas 'harmony' is predicated of temperance not in a literal sense but metaphorically: for a harmony always consists in notes.

123ᵇ Moreover, if there be any contrary of the species, examine it. The examination may take

---
[1] *Theaetetus*, 181.

[2] 106ᵃ 9 ff.

different forms; first of all see if the contrary as well be found in the same genus as the species, supposing the genus to have no contrary; for contraries ought to be found in the same [5] genus, if there be no contrary to the genus. Supposing, on the other hand, that there is a contrary to the genus, see if the contrary of the species be found in the contrary genus: for of necessity the contrary species must be in the contrary genus, if there be any contrary to the genus. Each of these points is made plain by means of induction. Again, see whether the contrary of the species be not found in any genus at all, but be itself a genus, e.g. 'good': for if this be not found in any genus, neither will [10] its contrary be found in any genus, but will itself be a genus, as happens in the case of 'good' and 'evil': for neither of these is found in a genus, but each of them is a genus. Moreover, see if both genus and species be contrary to something, and one pair of contraries have an intermediary, but not the other. For if the genera have an intermediary, so should their [15] species as well, and if the species have, so should their genera as well, as is the case with (1) virtue and vice and (2) justice and injustice: for each pair has an intermediary. An objection to this is that there is no intermediary between health and disease, although there is one between evil and good. Or see whether, though there be indeed an intermediary between both pairs, i.e. both between the species and between the genera, yet it be not similarly related, but in one case be a mere negation of [20] the extremes, whereas in the other case it is a subject. For the general view is that the relation should be similar in both cases, as it is in the cases of virtue and vice and of justice and injustice: for the intermediaries between both are mere negations. Moreover, whenever the genus has no contrary, look and see not merely whether the contrary of the species be found in the same genus, but the intermediate as well: [25] for the genus containing the extremes contains the intermediates as well, as (e.g.) in the case of white and black: for 'colour' is the genus both of these and of all the intermediate colours as well. An objection may be raised that 'defect' and 'excess' are found in the same genus (for both are in the genus 'evil'), whereas 'moderate amount', the intermediate between them, is found not in 'evil' but in 'good'. Look [30] and see also whether, while the genus has a contrary, the species has none; for if the genus be contrary to anything, so too is the species, as virtue to vice and justice to injustice.

Likewise, also, if one were to look at other instances, one would come to see clearly a fact like this. An objection may be raised in the case of health and disease: for health in general is [35] the contrary of disease, whereas a particular disease, being a species of disease, e.g. fever and ophthalmia and any other particular disease, has no contrary.

124ᵃ If, therefore, you are demolishing a view, there are all these ways in which you should make your examination: for if the aforesaid characters do not belong to it, clearly what has been rendered is not the genus. If, on the other hand, you are establishing a view, there are three ways: in the first place, see whether the contrary of the species be found in the genus stated, suppose the genus have no contrary: for [5] if the contrary be found in it, clearly the species in question is found in it as well. Moreover, see if the intermediate species is found in the genus stated: for whatever genus contains the intermediate contains the extremes as well. Again, if the genus have a contrary, look and see whether also the contrary species is found in the contrary genus: for if so, clearly also the species in question is found in the genus in question.

[10] Again, consider in the case of the inflexions and the co-ordinates of species and genus, and see whether they follow likewise, both in demolishing and in establishing a view. For whatever attribute belongs or does not belong to one belongs or does not belong at the same time to all; e.g. if justice be a particular form of knowledge, then also 'justly' is 'knowingly' and the just man is a man of knowledge: whereas if any of these things be not so, then neither is any of the rest of them.

4

[15] Again, consider the case of things that bear a like relation to one another. Thus (e.g.) the relation of the pleasant to pleasure is like that of the useful to the good: for in each case the one produces the other. If therefore pleasure be a kind of 'good', then also the pleasant will be a kind of 'useful': for clearly it may be taken to be productive of good, seeing that pleasure is [20] good. In the same way also consider the case of processes of generation and destruction; if (e.g.) to build be to be active, then to have built is to have been active, and if to learn be to recollect, then also to have learnt is to have recollected, and if to be decomposed be to be destroyed, then to have been decomposed is to have been destroyed, and decomposition is a

kind of destruction. Consider also in the same [25] way the case of things that generate or destroy, and of the capacities and uses of things; and in general, both in demolishing and in establishing an argument, you should examine things in the light of any resemblance of whatever description, as we were saying in the case of generation and destruction. For if what tends to destroy tends to decompose, then also to be destroyed is to be decomposed: and if what tends to generate tends to produce, then [30] to be generated is to be produced, and generation is production. Likewise, also, in the case of the capacities and uses of things: for if a capacity be a disposition, then also to be capable of something is to be disposed to it, and if the use of anything be an activity, then to use it is to be active, and to have used it is to have been active.

[35] If the opposite of the species be a privation, there are two ways of demolishing an argument, first of all by looking to see if the opposite be found in the genus rendered: for either the privation is to be found absolutely nowhere in the same genus, or at least not in the same ultimate genus: e.g. if the ultimate genus containing sight be sensation, then blindness will not be a sensation. Secondly, if there be a **124ᵇ** privation opposed to both genus and species, but the opposite of the species be not found in the opposite of the genus, then neither could the species rendered be in the genus rendered. If, then, you are demolishing a view, you should follow the rule as stated; but if establishing one there is but one way: for if the opposite species be found in the opposite genus, then [5] also the species in question would be found in the genus in question: e.g. if 'blindness' be a form of 'insensibility', then 'sight' is a form of 'sensation'.

Again, look at the negations of the genus and species and convert the order of terms, according to the method described in the case of Accident:[1] e.g. if the pleasant be a kind of good, what is not good is not pleasant. For were this not [10] so, something not good as well would then be pleasant. That, however, cannot be, for it is impossible, if 'good' be the genus of pleasant, that anything not good should be pleasant: for of things of which the genus is not predicated, none of the species is predicated either. Also, in establishing a view, you should adopt the same method of examination: for if what is not good be not pleasant, then what is pleasant is good, so that 'good' is the genus of 'pleasant'.

[1] 113ᵇ 15-26.

[15] If the species be a relative term, see whether the genus be a relative term as well: for if the species be a relative term, so too is the genus, as is the case with 'double' and 'multiple': for each is a relative term. If, on the other hand, the genus be a relative term, there is no necessity that the species should be so as well: for 'knowledge' is a relative term, but not so 'grammar'. Or possibly not even the first statement [20] would be generally considered true: for virtue is a kind of 'noble' and a kind of 'good' thing, and yet, while 'virtue' is a relative term, 'good' and 'noble' are not relatives but qualities. Again, see whether the species fails to be used in the same relation when called by its own name, and when called by the name of its genus: e.g. if the term 'double' be used to [25] mean the double of a 'half', then also the term 'multiple' ought to be used to mean multiple of a 'half'. Otherwise 'multiple' could not be the genus of 'double'.

Moreover, see whether the term fail to be used in the same relation both when called by the name of its genus, and also when called by those of all the genera of its genus. For if the [30] double be a multiple of a half, then 'in excess of' will also be used in relation to a 'half': and, in general, the double will be called by the names of all the higher genera in relation to a 'half'. An objection may be raised that there is no necessity for a term to be used in the same relation when called by its own name and when called by that of its genus: for 'knowledge' is called knowledge 'of an object', whereas it is called a 'state' and 'disposition' not of an 'object' but of the 'soul'.

[35] Again, see whether the genus and the species be used in the same way in respect of the inflexions they take, e.g. datives and genitives and all the rest. For as the species is used, so should the genus be as well, as in the case of 'double' and its higher genera: for we say both 'double of' and 'multiple of' a thing. Likewise, also, in the case of 'knowledge': for both **125ᵃ** 'knowledge' itself and its genera, e.g. 'disposition' and 'state', are said to be 'of' something. An objection may be raised that in some cases it is not so: for we say 'superior *to*' and 'contrary *to*' so and so, whereas 'other', which is the genus of these terms, demands not 'to' but 'than': for the expression is 'other *than*' so and so.

[5] Again, see whether terms used in like case-relationships fail to yield a like construction when converted, as do 'double' and 'multiple'. For each of these terms takes a genitive both in

itself and in its converted form: for we say both 'a half of' and 'a fraction of' something. The case is the same also as regards both 'knowledge' and 'conception': for these take a genitive, and by conversion an 'object of knowledge' and an 'object of conception' are both alike used with a dative. If, then, in any cases the constructions after conversion be not alike, clearly the one term is not the genus of the other.

Again, see whether the species and the genus fail to be used in relation to an equal number of things: for the general view is that the uses of both are alike and equal in number, as is the case with 'present' and 'grant'. For a 'present' is of something or to some one, and also a 'grant' is of something and to some one: and 'grant' is the genus of 'present', for a 'present' is a 'grant that need not be returned'. In some cases, however, the number of relations in which the terms are used happens not to be equal, for while 'double' is double *of* something, we speak of 'in excess' or 'greater' *in* something, as well as *of* or *than* something: for what is in excess or greater is always in excess *in* something, as well as in excess *of* something. Hence the terms in question are not the genera of 'double', inasmuch as they are not used in relation to an equal number of things with the species. Or possibly it is not universally true that species and genus are used in relation to an equal number of things.

See, also, if the opposite of the species have the opposite of the genus as its genus, e.g. whether, if 'multiple' be the genus of 'double', 'fraction' be also the genus of 'half'. For the opposite of the genus should always be the genus of the opposite species. If, then, any one were to assert that knowledge is a kind of sensation, then also the object of knowledge will have to be a kind of object of sensation, whereas it is not: for an object of knowledge is not always an object of sensation: for objects of knowledge include some of the objects of intuition as well. Hence 'object of sensation' is not the genus of 'object of knowledge': and if this be so, neither is 'sensation' the genus of 'knowledge'.

Seeing that of relative terms some are of necessity found in, or used of, the things in relation to which they happen at any time to be used (e.g. 'disposition' and 'state' and 'balance'; for in nothing else can the aforesaid terms possibly be found except in the things in relation to which they are used), while others need not be found in the things in relation to which they are used at any time, though they still may be (e.g. if the term 'object of knowledge' be applied to the soul: for it is quite possible that the knowledge of itself should be possessed by the soul itself, but it is not necessary, for it is possible for this same knowledge to be found in some one else), while for others, again, it is absolutely impossible that they should be found in the things in relation to which they happen at any time to be used (as e.g. that the contrary should be found in the contrary or knowledge in the object of knowledge, unless the object of knowledge happen to be a soul or a man)—you should look, therefore, and see whether he places a term of one kind inside a genus that is not of that kind, e.g. suppose he has said that 'memory' is the 'abiding of knowledge'. For 'abiding' is always found in that which abides, and is used of that, so that the abiding of knowledge also will be found in knowledge. Memory, then, is found in knowledge, seeing that it is the abiding of knowledge. But this is impossible, for memory is always found in the soul. The aforesaid commonplace rule is common to the subject of Accident as well: for it is all the same to say that 'abiding' is the genus of memory, or to allege that it is an accident of it. For if in any way whatever memory be the abiding of knowledge, the same argument in regard to it will apply.

5

Again, see if he has placed what is a 'state' inside the genus 'activity', or an activity inside the genus 'state', e.g. by defining 'sensation' as 'movement communicated through the body': for sensation is a 'state', whereas movement is an 'activity'. Likewise, also, if he has said that memory is a 'state that is retentive of a conception', for memory is never a state, but rather an activity.

They also make a bad mistake who rank a 'state' within the 'capacity' that attends it, e.g. by defining 'good temper' as the 'control of anger', and 'courage' and 'justice' as 'control of fears' and of 'gains': for the terms 'courageous' and 'good-tempered' are applied to a man who is immune from passion, whereas 'self-controlled' describes the man who is exposed to passion and not led by it. Quite possibly, indeed, each of the former is attended by a capacity such that, if he were exposed to passion, he would control it and not be led by it: but, for all that, this is not what is meant by being 'courageous' in the one case, and 'good-tempered' in the other; what is meant is an absolute immunity from any passions of that kind at all.

Sometimes, also, people state any kind of attendant feature as the genus, e.g. 'pain' as the genus of 'anger' and 'conception' as that of [30] 'conviction'. For both of the things in question follow in a certain sense upon the given species, but neither of them is genus to it. For when the angry man feels pain, the pain has appeared in him earlier than the anger: for his anger is not the cause of his pain, but his pain of his anger, so that anger emphatically *is* not pain. By the same reasoning, neither is convic-[35] tion conception: for it is possible to have the same conception even without being convinced of it, whereas this is impossible if conviction be a species of conception: for it is impossible for a thing still to remain the same if it be entirely transferred out of its species, just as neither could the same animal at one time be, and at another not be, a man. If, on the other hand, [40] any one says that a man who has a conception must of necessity be also convinced of it, then 'conception' and 'conviction' will be 126ᵃ used with an equal denotation, so that not even so could the former be the genus of the latter: for the denotation of the genus should be wider.

See, also, whether both naturally come to be anywhere in the same thing: for what contains the species contains the genus as well: e.g. what contains 'white' contains 'colour' as well, and [5] what contains 'knowledge of grammar' contains 'knowledge' as well. If, therefore, any one says that 'shame' is 'fear', or that 'anger' is 'pain', the result will be that genus and species are not found in the same thing: for shame is found in the 'reasoning' faculty, whereas fear is in the 'spirited' faculty, and 'pain' is found in the [10] faculty of 'desires' (for in this pleasure also is found), whereas 'anger' is found in the 'spirited' faculty. Hence the terms rendered are not the genera, seeing that they do not naturally come to be in the same faculty as the species. Likewise, also, if 'friendship' be found in the faculty of desires, you may take it that it is not a form of 'wishing': for wishing is always found in the 'reasoning' faculty. This commonplace rule is useful also in dealing with Acci-[15] dent: for the accident and that of which it is an accident are both found in the same thing, so that if they do not appear in the same thing, clearly it is not an accident.

Again, see if the species partakes of the genus attributed only in some particular respect: for it is the general view that the genus is not thus imparted only in some particular respect: for a man is not an animal in a particular respect, nor is grammar knowledge in a particular respect only. Likewise also in other in-[20] stances. Look, therefore, and see if in the case of any of its species the genus be imparted only in a certain respect; e.g. if 'animal' has been described as an 'object of perception' or of 'sight'. For an animal is an object of perception or of sight in a particular respect only; for it is in respect of its body that it is perceived and seen, not in respect of its soul, so that 'object of sight' and 'object of perception' could [25] not be the genus of 'animal'.

Sometimes also people place the whole inside the part without detection, defining (e.g.) 'animal' as an 'animate body'; whereas the part is not predicated in any sense of the whole, so that 'body' could not be the genus of animal, seeing that it is a part.

[30] See also if he has put anything that is blameworthy or objectionable into the class 'capacity' or 'capable', e.g. by defining a 'sophist' or a 'slanderer', or a 'thief' as 'one who is capable of secretly thieving other people's property'. For none of the aforesaid characters is so called because he is 'capable' in one of these respects: for even God and the good man [35] are capable of doing bad things, but that is not their character: for it is always in respect of their choice that bad men are so called. Moreover, a capacity is always a desirable thing: for even the capacities for doing bad things are desirable, and therefore it is we say that even God and the good man possess them; for they are capable (we say) of doing evil. So then 'capacity' can never be the genus of any-126ᵇ thing blameworthy. Else, the result will be that what is blameworthy is sometimes desirable: for there will be a certain form of capacity that is blameworthy.

Also, see if he has put anything that is precious or desirable for its own sake into the class [5] 'capacity' or 'capable' or 'productive' of anything. For capacity, and what is capable or productive of anything, is always desirable for the sake of something else.

Or see if he has put anything that exists in two genera or more into one of them only. For some things it is impossible to place in a single genus, e.g. the 'cheat' and the 'slanderer': for neither he who has the will without the capac-[10] ity, nor he who has the capacity without the will, is a slanderer or cheat, but he who has both of them. Hence he must be put not into one genus, but into both the aforesaid genera.

Moreover, people sometimes in converse order render genus as differentia, and differentia as genus, defining (e.g.) astonishment as 'excess [15] of wonderment' and conviction as 'vehemence of conception'. For neither 'excess' nor 'vehemence' is the genus, but the differentia: for astonishment is usually taken to be an 'excessive wonderment', and conviction to be a 'vehement conception', so that 'wonderment' and 'conception' are the genus, while 'excess' and 'vehemence' are the differentia. Moreover, if any one renders 'excess' and 'vehemence' as [20] genera, then inanimate things will be convinced and astonished. For 'vehemence' and 'excess' of a thing are found in a thing which is thus vehement and in excess. If, therefore, astonishment be excess of wonderment the astonishment will be found in the wonderment, so that 'wonderment' will be astonished! Like-[25] wise, also, conviction will be found in the conception, if it be 'vehemence of conception', so that the conception will be convinced. Moreover, a man who renders an answer in this style will in consequence find himself calling vehemence vehement and excess excessive: for there is such a thing as a vehement conviction: if then conviction be 'vehemence', there would be [30] a 'vehement vehemence'. Likewise, also, there is such a thing as excessive astonishment: if then astonishment be an excess, there would be an 'excessive excess'. Whereas neither of these things is generally believed, any more than that knowledge is a knower or motion a moving thing.

Sometimes, too, people make the bad mistake of putting an affection into that which is [35] affected, as its genus, e.g. those who say that immortality is everlasting life: for immortality seems to be a certain affection or accidental feature of life. That this saying is true would appear clear if any one were to admit that a man can pass from being mortal and become immortal: for no one will assert that he takes another life, but that a certain accidental feature or affection enters into this one as it 127ᵃ is. So then 'life' is not the genus of immortality.

Again, see if to an affection he has ascribed as genus the object of which it is an affection, by defining (e.g.) wind as 'air in motion'. Rather, wind is 'a movement of air': for the [5] same air persists both when it is in motion and when it is still. Hence wind is not 'air' at all: for then there would also have been wind when the air was not in motion, seeing that the same air which formed the wind persists. Likewise, also, in other cases of the kind. Even, then, if we ought in this instance to admit the point that wind is 'air in motion', yet we should [10] accept a definition of the kind, not about all those things of which the genus is not true, but only in cases where the genus rendered is a true predicate. For in some cases, e.g. 'mud' or 'snow', it is not generally held to be true. For people tell you that snow is 'frozen water' and mud is 'earth mixed with moisture', [15] whereas snow is not water, nor mud earth, so that neither of the terms rendered could be the genus: for the genus should be true of all its species. Likewise neither is wine 'fermented water', as Empedocles speaks of 'water fermented in wood';[1] for it simply is not water at all.

6

[20] Moreover, see whether the term rendered fail to be the genus of anything at all; for then clearly it also fails to be the genus of the species mentioned. Examine the point by seeing whether the objects that partake of the genus fail to be specifically different from one another, e.g. white objects: for these do not differ specifically from one another, whereas of a genus the species are always different, so that [25] 'white' could not be the genus of anything.

Again, see whether he has named as genus or differentia some feature that goes with everything: for the number of attributes that follow everything is comparatively large: thus (e.g.) 'Being' and 'Unity' are among the number of attributes that follow everything. If, therefore, he has rendered 'Being' as a genus, clearly it would be the genus of everything, seeing that it is predicated of everything; for [30] the genus is never predicated of anything except of its species. Hence Unity, *inter alia*, will be a species of Being. The result, therefore, is that of all things of which the genus is predicated, the species is predicated as well, seeing that Being and Unity are predicates of absolutely everything, whereas the predication of the species ought to be of narrower range. [35] If, on the other hand, he has named as *differentia* some attribute that follows everything, clearly the denotation of the differentia will be equal to, or wider than, that of the genus. For if the genus, too, be some attribute that follows everything, the denotation of the differentia will be equal to its denotation, while

[1] Fr. 81.

if the genus do not follow everything, it will be still wider.

127[b] Moreover, see if the description 'inherent in S' be used of the genus rendered in relation to its species, as it is used of 'white' in the case of snow, thus showing clearly that it could not be the genus: for *true of* S' is the only description used of the genus in relation to its species. [5] Look and see also if the genus fails to be synonymous with its species. For the genus is always predicated of its species synonymously.

Moreover, beware, whenever both species and genus have a contrary, and he places the better of the contraries inside the worse genus: for the result will be that the remaining species [10] will be found in the remaining genus, seeing that contraries are found in contrary genera, so that the better species will be found in the worse genus and the worse in the better: whereas the usual view is that of the better species the genus too is better. Also see if he has placed the species inside the worse and not inside the better genus, when it is at the same time related in like manner to both, as (e.g.) [15] if he has defined the 'soul' as a 'form of motion' or 'a form of moving thing'. For the same soul is usually thought to be a principle alike of rest and of motion, so that, if rest is the better of the two, this is the genus into which the soul should have been put.

Moreover, judge by means of greater and less degrees: if overthrowing a view, see whether the genus admits of a greater degree, whereas neither the species itself does so, nor any term [20] that is called after it: e.g. if virtue admits of a greater degree, so too does justice and the just man: for one man is called 'more just than another'. If, therefore, the genus rendered admits of a greater degree, whereas neither the species does so itself nor yet any term called after it, then what has been rendered could not [25] be the genus.

Again, if what is more generally, or as generally, thought to be the genus be not so, clearly neither is the genus rendered. The commonplace rule in question is useful especially in cases where the species appears to have several predicates in the category of essence, and where no distinction has been drawn between them, and we cannot say which of them is genus; e.g. [30] both 'pain' and the 'conception of a slight' are usually thought to be predicates of 'anger' in the category of essence: for the angry man is both in pain and also conceives that he is slighted. The same mode of inquiry may be applied also to the case of the species, by comparing it with some other species: for if the one which is more generally, or as generally, thought to [35] be found in the genus rendered be not found therein, then clearly neither could the species rendered be found therein.

In demolishing a view, therefore, you should follow the rule as stated. In establishing one, on the other hand, the commonplace rule that you should see if both the genus rendered and 128[a] the species admit of a greater degree will not serve: for even though both admit it, it is still possible for one not to be the genus of the other. For both 'beautiful' and 'white' admit of a greater degree, and neither is the genus of the other. On the other hand, the comparison [5] of the genera and of the species one with another is of use: e.g. supposing A and B to have a like claim to be genus, then if one be a genus, so also is the other. Likewise, also, if what has less claim be a genus, so also is what has more claim: e.g. if 'capacity' have more claim than 'virtue' to be the genus of self-control, and virtue be the genus, so also is capacity. The same observations will apply also in the [10] case of the species. For instance, supposing A and B to have a like claim to be a species of the genus in question, then if the one be a species, so also is the other: and if that which is less generally thought to be so be a species, so also is that which is more generally thought to be so.

Moreover, to establish a view, you should look and see if the genus is predicated in the category of essence of those things of which it has been rendered as the genus, supposing the [15] species rendered to be not one single species but several different ones: for then clearly it will be the genus. If, on the other, the species rendered be single, look and see whether the genus be predicated in the category of essence of other species as well: for then, again, the result will be that it is predicated of several different species.

[20] Since some people think that the differentia, too, is a predicate of the various species in the category of essence, you should distinguish the genus from the differentia by employing the aforesaid elementary principles—(*a*) that the genus has a wider denotation than the differentia; (*b*) that in rendering the essence of a thing it is more fitting to state the genus than the differentia: for any one who says that 'man' [25] is an 'animal' shows what man is better than he who describes him as 'walking'; also (*c*) that the differentia always signifies a quality of the genus, whereas the genus does not do

this of the differentia: for he who says 'walking' describes an animal of a certain quality, whereas he who says 'animal' does not describe a walking thing of a certain quality.

[30] The differentia, then, should be distinguished from the genus in this manner. Now seeing it is generally held that if what is musical, in being musical, possesses knowledge in some respect, then also 'music' is a particular kind of 'knowledge'; and also that if what walks is moved in walking, then 'walking' is a particular kind of 'movement'; you should therefore examine in the aforesaid manner any genus in which you want to establish the existence of something; e.g. if you wish to prove [35] that 'knowledge' is a form of 'conviction', see whether the knower in knowing is convinced: for then clearly knowledge would be a particular kind of conviction. You should proceed in the same way also in regard to the other cases of this kind.

Moreover, seeing that it is difficult to distinguish whatever always follows along with a thing, and is not convertible with it, from its genus, if A follows B universally, whereas B 128[b] does not follow A universally—as e.g. 'rest' always follows a 'calm' and 'divisibility' follows 'number', but not conversely (for the divisible is not always a number, nor rest a calm)—you may yourself assume in your treatment of them that the one which always follows is the genus, whenever the other is not [5] convertible with it: if, on the other hand, some one else puts forward the proposition, do not accept it universally. An objection to it is that 'not-being' always follows what is 'coming to be' (for what is coming to be is not) and is not convertible with it (for what is not is not always coming to be), and that still 'not-being' is not the genus of 'coming to be': for 'not-being' has not any species at all.

[10] Questions, then, in regard to Genus should be investigated in the ways described.

BOOK V

1

[14] THE question whether the attribute stated is or is not a property, should be examined by the following methods:

Any 'property' rendered is always either essential and permanent or relative and temporary: e.g. it is an 'essential property' of man to be 'by nature a civilized animal': a 'relative property' is one like that of the soul in relation to the body, viz. that the one is fitted to command, and the other to obey: a 'permanent property' is one like the property which belongs [20] to God, of being an 'immortal living being': a 'temporary property' is one like the property which belongs to any particular man of walking in the gymnasium.

[The rendering of a property 'relatively' gives rise either to two problems or to four. For if he at the same time render this property of one thing and deny it of another, only two problems arise, as in the case of a statement [25] that it is a property of a man, in relation to a horse, to be a biped. For one might try both to show that a man is not a biped, and also that a horse is a biped: in both ways the property would be upset. If on the other hand he render one apiece of two attributes to each of two things, and deny it in each case of the other, there will then be four problems; as in the case of a statement that it is a property of a [30] man in relation to a horse for the former to be a biped and the latter a quadruped. For then it is possible to try to show both that a man is not naturally a biped, and that he is a quadruped, and also that the horse both is a biped, and is not a quadruped. If you show any of these at all, the intended attribute is demolished.]

An 'essential' property is one which is rendered of a thing in comparison with every-[35] thing else and distinguishes the said thing from everything else, as does 'a mortal living being capable of receiving knowledge' in the case of man. A 'relative' property is one which separates its subject off not from everything else but only from a particular definite thing, as does the property which virtue possesses, in comparison with knowledge, viz. that the former is naturally produced in more than one faculty, whereas the latter is produced in that of reason alone, and in those who have a reasoning faculty. A 'permanent' property is one 129[a] which is true at every time, and never fails, like being 'compounded of soul and body', in the case of a living creature. A 'temporary' property is one which is true at some particular time, and does not of necessity always follow; as, of some particular man, that he walks in [5] the market-place.

To render a property 'relatively' to something else means to state the difference between them as it is found either universally and always, or generally and in most cases: thus a difference that is found universally and always, is one such as man possesses in comparison with a horse, viz. being a biped: for a man is always and in every case a biped, whereas a [10] horse is never a biped at any time. On the other hand, a difference that is found generally and in most cases, is one such as the faculty of reason possesses in comparison with that of desire and spirit, in that the former commands, while the latter obeys: for the reasoning faculty does not always command, but sometimes also is under command, nor is [15] that of desire and spirit always under command, but also on occasion assumes the command, whenever the soul of a man is vicious.

Of 'properties' the most 'arguable' are the essential and permanent and the relative. For a relative property gives rise, as we said before,[1] [20] to several questions: for of necessity the questions arising are either two or four, or that arguments in regard to these are several. An essential and a permanent property you can discuss in relation to many things, or can observe in relation to many periods of time: if 'essential', discuss it in comparison with many [25] things: for the property ought to belong to its subject in comparison with every single thing that is, so that if the subject be not distinguished by it in comparison with everything else, the property could not have been rendered correctly. So a permanent property you should observe in relation to many periods of time; for if it does not or did not, or is not going to, belong, it will not be a property. On the other hand, about a temporary property we do not inquire further than in regard to the time called 'the present'; and so arguments in [30] regard to it are not many; whereas an 'arguable' question is one in regard to which it is possible for arguments both numerous and good to arise.

The so-called 'relative' property, then, should be examined by means of the commonplace arguments relating to Accident, to see whether it belongs to the one thing and not to the other: on the other hand, permanent and essential [35] properties should be considered by the following methods.

2

129ᵇ First, see whether the property has or has not been rendered correctly. Of a rendering be-

[1] 128ᵇ 22.

ing incorrect or correct, one test is to see whether the terms in which the property is stated are not or are more intelligible—for destructive purposes, whether they are not so, and for con- [5] structive purposes, whether they are so. Of the terms not being more intelligible, one test is to see whether the property which he renders is altogether more unintelligible than the subject whose property he has stated: for, if so, the property will not have been stated correctly. For the object of getting a property constituted is to be intelligible: the terms therefore in which it is rendered should be more intelligible: for in that case it will be possible to con- [10] ceive it more adequately, e.g. any one who has stated that it is a property of 'fire' to 'bear a very close resemblance to the soul', uses the term 'soul', which is less intelligible than 'fire' —for we know better what fire is than what soul is—, and therefore a 'very close resemblance to the soul' could not be correctly stated to be a property of fire. Another test is to see whether the attribution of A (property) to B (subject) fails to be more intelligible. For not only should the property be more intelligible than its sub- [15] ject, but also it should be something whose attribution to the particular subject is a more intelligible attribution. For he who does not know whether it is an attribute of the particular subject at all, will not know either whether it belongs to it alone, so that whichever of these results happens, its character as a property becomes obscure. Thus (e.g.) a man who has stated that it is a property of fire to be 'the primary element wherein the soul is naturally found', has introduced a subject which is less intelligible than 'fire', viz. whether the [20] soul is found in it, and whether it is found there primarily; and therefore to be 'the primary element in which the soul is naturally found' could not be correctly stated to be a property of 'fire'. On the other hand, for constructive purposes, see whether the terms in which the property is stated are more intelligible, and if they are more intelligible in each of the aforesaid ways. For then the property will have been correctly stated in this respect: for [25] of constructive arguments, showing the correctness of a rendering, some will show the correctness merely in this respect, while others will show it without qualification. Thus (e.g.) a man who has said that the 'possession of sensation' is a property of 'animal' has both used more intelligible terms and has rendered the property more intelligible in each of the aforesaid senses; so that to 'possess sensation' would in this respect have been correctly rendered as a property of 'animal'.

[30] Next, for destructive purposes, see whether any of the terms rendered in the property is used in more than one sense, or whether the whole expression too signifies more than one thing. For then the property will not have been correctly stated. Thus (e.g.) seeing that to 'be sentient' signifies more than one thing, viz. (1) to possess sensation, (2) to use one's sensation, [35] 'being naturally sentient' could not be a 130ᵃ correct statement of a property of 'animal'. The reason why the term you use, or the whole expression signifying the property, should not bear more than one meaning is this, that an expression bearing more than one meaning makes the object described obscure, because the man who is about to attempt an argument is in doubt which of the various senses the expression bears: and this will not do, for the object of rendering the property is [5] that he may understand. Moreover, in addition to this, it is inevitable that those who render a property after this fashion should be somehow refuted whenever any one addresses his syllogism to that one of the term's several meanings which does not agree. For constructive purposes, on the other hand, see whether both all the terms and also the expression as a [10] whole avoid bearing more than one sense: for then the property will have been correctly stated in this respect. Thus (e.g.) seeing that 'body' does not bear several meanings, nor 'quickest to move upwards in space', nor yet the whole expression made by putting them together, it would be correct in this respect to say that it is a property of fire to be the 'body quickest to move upwards in space'.

[15] Next, for destructive purposes, see if the term of which he renders the property is used in more than one sense, and no distinction has been drawn as to which of them it is whose property he is stating: for then the property will not have been correctly rendered. The reasons why this is so are quite clear from what has been said above:[1] for the same results are bound to follow. Thus (e.g.) seeing that 'the [20] knowledge of this' signifies many things —for it means (1) the possession of knowledge by it, (2) the use of its knowledge by it, (3) the existence of knowledge about it, (4) the use of knowledge about it—no property of the 'knowledge of this' could be rendered correctly unless he draw a distinction as to which of these it is whose property he is rendering. For

constructive purposes, a man should see if the term of which he is rendering the property [25] avoids bearing many senses and is one and simple: for then the property will have been correctly stated in this respect. Thus (e.g.) seeing that 'man' is used in a single sense, 'naturally civilized animal' would be correctly stated as a property of man.

Next, for destructive purposes, see whether [30] the same term has been repeated in the property. For people often do this undetected in rendering 'properties' also, just as they do in their 'definitions' as well: but a property to which this has happened will not have been correctly stated: for the repetition of it confuses the hearer; thus inevitably the meaning becomes obscure, and further, such people are thought to babble. Repetition of the same term [35] is likely to happen in two ways; one is, when a man repeatedly uses the same word, as would happen if any one were to render, as a property of fire, 'the body which is the most rarefied of bodies' (for he has repeated the word 'body'); the second is, if a man replaces words by their definitions, as would happen if 130ᵇ any one were to render, as a property of earth, 'the substance which is by its nature most easily of all bodies borne downwards in space', and were then to substitute 'substances of such and such a kind' for the word 'bodies': for 'body' and 'a substance of such and such a kind' mean one and the same thing. For he will have repeated the word 'substance', and accordingly neither of the properties would be [5] correctly stated. For constructive purposes, on the other hand, see whether he avoids ever repeating the same term; for then the property will in this respect have been correctly rendered. Thus (e.g.) seeing that he who has stated 'animal capable of acquiring knowledge' as a property of man has avoided repeating the [10] same term several times, the property would in this respect have been correctly rendered of man.

Next, for destructive purposes, see whether he has rendered in the property any such term as is a universal attribute. For one which does not distinguish its subject from other things is useless, and it is the business of the language of 'properties', as also of the language of definitions, to distinguish. In the case contemplated, therefore, the property will not have been correctly rendered. Thus (e.g.) a man who has stated that it is a property of knowledge to be a 'conception incontrovertible by argument, because of its unity', has used in the property a

---

[1] 129ᵇ 7.

term of that kind, viz. 'unity', which is a universal attribute; and therefore the property of knowledge could not have been correctly stated. For constructive purposes, on the other hand, see whether he has avoided all terms that are common to everything and used a term that distinguishes the subject from something: for then the property will in this respect have been [20] correctly stated. Thus (e.g.) inasmuch as he who has said that it is a property of a 'living creature' to 'have a soul' has used no term that is common to everything, it would in this respect have been correctly stated to be a property of a 'living creature' to 'have a soul'.

Next, for destructive purposes see whether he renders more than one property of the same thing, without a definite proviso that he is stating more than one: for then the property [25] will not have been correctly stated. For just as in the case of definitions too there should be no further addition beside the expression which shows the essence, so too in the case of properties nothing further should be rendered beside the expression that constitutes the property mentioned: for such an addition is made to no purpose. Thus (e.g.) a man who has said that it is a property of fire to be 'the most rare- [30] fied and lightest body' has rendered more than one property (for each term is a true predicate of fire alone); and so it could not be a correctly stated property of fire to be 'the most rarefied and lightest body'. On the other hand, for constructive purposes, see whether he has avoided rendering more than one property of the same thing, and has rendered one only: for then the property will in this respect have been [35] correctly stated. Thus (e.g.) a man who has said that it is a property of a liquid to be a 'body adaptable to every shape' has rendered as its property a single character and not several, and so the property of 'liquid' would in this respect have been correctly stated.

3

Next, for destructive purposes, see whether he has employed either the actual subject whose property he is rendering, or any of its species: for then the property will not have been correctly stated. For the object of rendering the property is that people may understand: now the subject itself is just as unintelligible as it was to start with, while any one of its species is posterior to it, and so is no more intelligible. Accordingly it is impossible to understand anything further by the use of these terms. Thus (e.g.) any one who has said that it is a property of 'animal' to be 'the substance to which "man" belongs as a species' has em- [5] ployed one of its species, and therefore the property could not have been correctly stated. For constructive purposes, on the other hand, see whether he avoids introducing either the subject itself or any of its species: for then the property will in this respect have been correctly stated. Thus (e.g.) a man who has stated that it is a property of a living creature to be 'compounded of soul and body' has avoided introducing among the rest either the subject it- [10] self or any of its species, and therefore in this respect the property of a 'living creature' would have been correctly rendered.

You should inquire in the same way also in the case of other terms that do or do not make the subject more intelligible: thus, for destructive purposes, see whether he has employed anything either opposite to the subject or, in [15] general, anything simultaneous by nature with it or posterior to it: for then the property will not have been correctly stated. For an opposite is simultaneous by nature with its opposite, and what is simultaneous by nature or is posterior to it does not make its subject more intelligible. Thus (e.g.) any one who has said that it is a property of good to be 'the most direct opposite of evil', has employed the opposite of good, and so the property of good could [20] not have been correctly rendered. For constructive purposes, on the other hand, see whether he has avoided employing anything either opposite to, or, in general, simultaneous by nature with the subject, or posterior to it: for then the property will in this respect have been correctly rendered. Thus (e.g.) a man who has stated that it is a property of knowledge to be 'the most convincing conception' has avoided employing anything either opposite to, or simultaneous by nature with, or pos- [25] terior to, the subject; and so the property of knowledge would in this respect have been correctly stated.

Next, for destructive purposes, see whether he has rendered as property something that does not always follow the subject but sometimes ceases to be its property: for then the property will not have been correctly described. [30] For there is no necessity either that the name of the subject must also be true of anything to which we find such an attribute belonging; nor yet that the name of the subject will be untrue of anything to which such an attribute is found not to belong. Moreover, in addition to this, even after he has rendered the property it will not be clear whether it belongs, seeing that it is the kind of attribute that may [35] fail: and so the property will not be clear. Thus (e.g.) a man who has stated that it is a property of animal 'sometimes to move and sometimes to stand still' has rendered the kind of property which sometimes is not a property, and so the property could not have been correctly stated. For constructive purposes, on the other hand, see whether he has rendered something that of necessity must always be a prop- 131^b erty: for then the property will have been in this respect correctly stated. Thus (e.g.) a man who has stated that it is a property of virtue to be 'what makes its possessor good' has rendered as property something that always follows, and so the property of virtue would in this respect have been correctly rendered.

[5] Next, for destructive purposes, see whether in rendering the property of the present time he has omitted to make a definite proviso that it is the property of the present time which he is rendering: for else the property will not have been correctly stated. For in the first place, any unusual procedure always needs a definite proviso: and it is the usual procedure for everybody to render as property some attribute that [10] always follows. In the second place, a man who omits to provide definitely whether it was the property of the present time which he intended to state, is obscure: and one should not give any occasion for adverse criticism. Thus (e.g.) a man who has stated it as the property of a particular man 'to be sitting with a particular man', states the property of the present time, and so he cannot have rendered the property correctly, seeing that he has described it without any definite proviso. For constructive purposes, on the other hand, see whether, in rendering the property of the [15] present time, he has, in stating it, made a definite proviso that it is the property of the present time that he is stating: for then the property will in this respect have been correctly stated. Thus (e.g.) a man who has said that it is the property of a particular man 'to be walking now', has made this distinction in his statement, and so the property would have been correctly stated.

Next, for destructive purposes, see whether [20] he has rendered a property of the kind whose appropriateness is not obvious except by sensation: for then the property will not have been correctly stated. For every sensible attribute, once it is taken beyond the sphere of sensation, becomes uncertain. For it is not clear whether it still belongs, because it is evidenced only by sensation. This principle will be true [25] in the case of any attributes that do not always and necessarily follow. Thus (e.g.) any one who has stated that it is a property of the sun to be 'the brightest star that moves over the earth', has used in describing the property an expression of that kind, viz. 'to move over the earth', which is evidenced by sensation; and so the sun's property could not have been correctly rendered: for it will be uncertain, whenever the sun sets, whether it continues to [30] move over the earth, because sensation then fails us. For constructive purposes, on the other hand, see whether he has rendered the property of a kind that is not obvious to sensation, or, if it be sensible, must clearly belong of necessity: for then the property will in this respect have been correctly stated. Thus (e.g.) a man who has stated that it is a property of a surface to be 'the primary thing that is coloured', has introduced amongst the rest a sensi- [35] ble quality, 'to be coloured', but still a quality such as manifestly always belongs, and so the property of 'surface' would in this respect have been correctly rendered.

Next, for destructive purposes, see whether he has rendered the definition as a property: for then the property will not have been correctly stated: for the property of a thing ought 132^a not to show its essence. Thus (e.g.) a man who has said that it is the property of man to be 'a walking, biped animal' has rendered a property of man so as to signify his essence, and so the property of man could not have been correctly rendered. For constructive purposes, on the other hand, see whether the property which he has rendered forms a predicate convertible with its subject, without, however, [5] signifying its essence: for then the property will in this respect have been correctly rendered. Thus (e.g.) he who has stated that it is a property of man to be a 'naturally civilized animal' has rendered the property so as to be convertible with its subject, without, however, showing its essence, and so the property of 'man' would in this respect have been correctly rendered.

[10] Next, for destructive purposes, see whether he has rendered the property without having placed the subject within its essence. For of properties, as also of definitions, the first term to be rendered should be the genus, and then the rest of it should be appended immediately afterwards, and should distinguish its subject from other things. Hence a property which is

not stated in this way could not have been correctly rendered. Thus (e.g.) a man who has said that it is a property of a living creature to 'have a soul' has not placed 'living creature' within its essence, and so the property of a living creature could not have been correctly stated. For constructive purposes, on the other hand, see whether a man first places within its essence the subject whose property he is rendering, and then appends the rest: for then the property will in this respect have been correctly rendered. Thus (e.g.) he who has stated that [20] it is a property of man to be an 'animal capable of receiving knowledge', has rendered the property after placing the subject within its essence, and so the property of 'man' would in this respect have been correctly rendered.

4

The inquiry, then, whether the property has been correctly rendered or no, should be made by these means. The question, on the other hand, whether what is stated is or is not a [25] property at all, you should examine from the following points of view. For the commonplace arguments which establish absolutely that the property is accurately stated will be the same as those that constitute it a property at all: accordingly they will be described in the course of them.

Firstly, then, for destructive purposes, take a look at each subject of which he has rendered the property, and see (e.g.) if it fails to belong to any of them at all, or to be true of them in that particular respect, or to be a property of [30] each of them in respect of that character of which he has rendered the property: for then what is stated to be a property will not be a property. Thus, for example, inasmuch as it is not true of the geometrician that he 'cannot be deceived by an argument' (for a geometrician is deceived when his figure is misdrawn), it could not be a property of the man of science that he is not deceived by an argument. For [35] constructive purposes, on the other hand, see whether the property rendered be true of every instance, and true in that particular respect: for then what is stated not to be a property will be a property. Thus, for example, inasmuch as the description 'an animal capable of receiving knowledge' is true of every man, and true of him *qua* man, it would be a property of man to be 'an animal capable of receiving knowledge'. [This commonplace [5] rule means—for destructive purposes, see if the description fails to be true of that of which the name is true; and if the name fails to be true of that of which the description is true: for constructive purposes, on the other hand, see if the description too is predicated of that of which the name is predicated, and if the name too is predicated of that of which the description is predicated.]

Next, for destructive purposes, see if the description fails to apply to that to which the name applies, and if the name fails to apply to [10] that to which the description applies: for then what is stated to be a property will not be a property. Thus (e.g.) inasmuch as the description 'a living being that partakes of knowledge' is true of God, while 'man' is not predicated of God, to be a living being that partakes of knowledge' could not be a property of man. For constructive purposes, on the other hand, see if the name as well be predicated of that of which the description is predicated, and if the description as well be predicated of that of [15] which the name is predicated. For then what is stated not to be a property will be a property. Thus (e.g.) the predicate 'living creature' is true of that of which 'having a soul' is true, and 'having a soul' is true of that of which the predicate 'living creature' is true; and so 'having a soul' would be a property of 'living creature'.

Next, for destructive purposes, see if he has [20] rendered a subject as a property of that which is described as 'in the subject': for then what has been stated to be a property will not be a property. Thus (e.g.) inasmuch as he who has rendered 'fire' as the property of 'the body with the most rarefied particles', has rendered the subject as the property of its predicate, 'fire' could not be a property of 'the body with the most rarefied particles'. The reason why the subject will not be a property of that which is [25] found in the subject is this, that then the same thing will be the property of a number of things that are specifically different. For the same thing has quite a number of specifically different predicates that belong to it alone, and the subject will be a property of all of these, if any one states the property in this way. For constructive purposes, on the other hand, see if he has rendered what is found in the subject as a property of the subject: for then what has [30] been stated not to be a property will be a property, if it be predicated only of the things of which it has been stated to be the property. Thus (e.g.) he who has said that it is a property of 'earth' to be 'specifically the heaviest body' has rendered of the subject as its property something that is said of the thing in question alone, and is said of it in the manner in which a property is predicated, and so the property of 'earth' would have been rightly stated.

[35] Next, for destructive purposes, see if he has rendered the property as partaken of: for then what is stated to be a property will not be a property. For an attribute of which the subject partakes is a constituent part of its essence: and an attribute of that kind would be a differentia applying to some one species. E.g. inasmuch as he who has said that 'walking on two feet' is a property of man has rendered the [5] property as partaken of, 'walking on two feet' could not be a property of 'man'. For constructive purposes, on the other hand, see if he has avoided rendering the property as partaken of, or as showing the essence, though the subject is predicated convertibly with it: for then what is stated not to be a property will be a property. Thus (e.g.) he who has stated that to be 'naturally sentient' is a property of 'animal' has rendered the property neither as partaken [10] of nor as showing the essence, though the subject is predicated convertibly with it; and so to be 'naturally sentient' would be a property of 'animal'.

Next, for destructive purposes, see if the property cannot possibly belong simultaneously, but must belong either as posterior or as prior to the attribute described in the name: for then what is stated to be a property will not [15] be a property—either never, or not always. Thus (e.g.) inasmuch as it is possible for the attribute 'walking through the market-place' to belong to an object as prior and as posterior to the attribute 'man', 'walking through the market-place' could not be a property of 'man' —either never, or not always. For constructive purposes, on the other hand, see if it always and of necessity belongs simultaneously, without being either a definition or a differentia: [20] for then what is stated not to be a property will be a property. Thus (e.g.) the attribute 'an animal capable of receiving knowledge' always and of necessity belongs simultaneously with the attribute 'man', and is neither differentia nor definition of its subject, and so 'an animal capable of receiving knowledge' would be a property of 'man'.

Next, for destructive purposes, see if the same thing fails to be a property of things that [25] are the same as the subject, so far as they are the same: for then what is stated to be a property will not be a property. Thus, for example, inasmuch as it is no property of a 'proper object of pursuit' to 'appear good to certain persons', it could not be a property of the 'desirable' either to 'appear good to certain persons': for 'proper object of pursuit' and 'desirable' mean the same. For constructive purposes, on the other hand, see if the same thing be a property of something that is the same as the subject, in so far as it is the same. For then [30] what is stated not to be a property will be a property. Thus (e.g.) inasmuch as it is called a property of a man, in so far as he is a man, 'to have a tripartite soul', it would also be a property of a mortal, in so far as he is a mortal, to have a tripartite soul. This commonplace rule is useful also in dealing with Accident: for the same attributes ought either to belong or not belong to the same things, in so far as they are the same.

[35] Next, for destructive purposes, see if the property of things that are the same in kind as the subject fails to be always the same in kind as the alleged property: for then neither will what is stated to be the property of the subject in question. Thus (e.g.) inasmuch as a man and a horse are the same in kind, and it is not always a property of a horse to stand by its own initiative, it could not be a property of a man to move by his own initiative; for to stand and to move by his own initiative are the same [5] in kind, because they belong to each of them in so far as each is an 'animal'. For constructive purposes, on the other hand, see if of things that are the same in kind as the subject the property that is the same as the alleged property is always true: for then what is stated not to be a property will be a property. Thus (e.g.) since it is a property of man to be a 'walking biped,' it would also be a property of [10] a bird to be a 'flying biped': for each of these is the same in kind, in so far as the one pair have the sameness of species that fall under the same genus, being under the genus 'animal', while the other pair have that of differentiae of the genus, viz. of 'animal'. This commonplace rule is deceptive whenever one of the properties mentioned belongs to some one species only while the other belongs to many, as does 'walking quadruped'.

[15] Inasmuch as 'same' and 'different' are terms used in several senses, it is a job to render to a sophistical questioner a property that belongs to one thing and that only. For an attribute that belongs to something qualified by an accident will also belong to the accident taken along with the subject which it qualifies; e.g. an attribute that belongs to 'man' will be-

[20] long also to 'white man', if there be a white man, and one that belongs to 'white man' will belong also to 'man'. One might, then, bring captious criticism against the majority of properties, by representing the subject as being one thing in itself, and another thing when combined with its accident, saying, for example, that 'man' is one thing, and 'white man' another, and moreover by repre-[25] senting as different a certain state and what is called after that state. For an attribute that belongs to the state will belong also to what is called after that state, and one that belongs to what is called after a state will belong also to the state: e.g. inasmuch as the condition of the scientist is called after his science, it could not be a property of 'science' that it is 'incontrovertible by argument'; for then the [30] scientist also will be incontrovertible by argument. For constructive purposes, however, you should say that the subject of an accident is not absolutely different from the accident taken along with its subject; though it is called 'another' thing because the mode of being of the two is different: for it is not the same thing for [35] a man to be a man and for a white man to be a white man. Moreover, you should take a look along at the inflections, and say that the 134a description of the man of science is wrong: one should say not 'it' but *'he* is incontrovertible by argument'; while the description of Science is wrong too: one should say not 'it' but *'she* is incontrovertible by argument'. For against an objector who sticks at nothing the defence should stick at nothing.

5

[5] Next, for destructive purposes, see if, while intending to render an attribute that naturally belongs, he states it in his language in such a way as to indicate one that invariably belongs: for then it would be generally agreed that what has been stated to be a property is upset. Thus (e.g.) the man who has said that 'biped' is a property of man intends to render the attribute [10] that naturally belongs, but his expression actually indicates one that invariably belongs: accordingly, 'biped' could not be a property of man: for not every man is possessed of two feet. For constructive purposes, on the other hand, see if he intends to render the property that naturally belongs, and indicates it in that way in his language: for then the property will not be upset in this respect. Thus (e.g.) he who renders as a property of 'man' the phrase [15] 'an animal capable of receiving knowledge' both intends, and by his language indicates, the property that belongs by nature, and so 'an animal capable of receiving knowledge' would not be upset or shown in that respect not to be a property of man.

Moreover, as regards all the things that are called as they are primarily after something else, or primarily in themselves, it is a job to render the property of such things. For if you [20] render a property as belonging to the subject that is so called after something else, then it will be true of its primary subject as well; whereas if you state it of its primary subject, then it will be predicated also of the thing that is so called after this other. Thus (e.g.) if any one renders 'coloured' as the property of 'surface', 'coloured' will be true of body as well; whereas if he render it of 'body', it will be [25] predicated also of 'surface'. Hence the name as well will not be true of that of which the description is true.

In the case of some properties it mostly happens that some error is incurred because of a failure to define how as well as to what things the property is stated to belong. For every one tries to render as the property of a thing something that belongs to it either naturally, as [30] 'biped' belongs to 'man', or actually, as 'having four fingers' belongs to a particular man, or specifically, as 'consisting of most rarefied particles' belongs to 'fire', or absolutely, as 'life' to 'living being', or one that belongs to a thing only as called after something else, as 'wisdom' to the 'soul', or on the other hand primarily, as 'wisdom' to the 'rational faculty', or because the thing is in a certain [35] state, as 'incontrovertible by argument' belongs to a 'scientist' (for simply and solely by reason of his being in a certain state will he be 'incontrovertible by argument'), or because it is the state possessed by something, as 'incontrovertible by argument' belongs to 'science', 134b or because it is partaken of, as 'sensation' belongs to 'animal' (for other things as well have sensation, e.g. man, but they have it because they already partake of 'animal'), or because it partakes of something else, as 'life' belongs to a particular kind of 'living being'. [5] Accordingly he makes a mistake if he has failed to add the word 'naturally', because what belongs naturally may fail to belong to the thing to which it naturally belongs, as (e.g.) it belongs to a man to have two feet: so too he errs if he does not make a definite proviso that he is rendering what actually belongs, because one day that attribute will not be what it now is, e.g. the man's possession of four [10] fingers. So he errs if he has not shown that he states a thing to be such and such primarily, or that he calls it so after something else, because then its name too will not be true of that of which the description is true, as is the case with 'coloured', whether rendered as a property of 'surface' or of 'body'. So he errs if he has not said beforehand that he has rendered a property to a thing either because that thing possesses a state, or because it is a state possessed by something; because then it will not be a property. For, supposing he renders the [15] property to something as being a state possessed, it will belong to what possesses that state; while supposing he renders it to what possesses the state, it will belong to the state possessed, as did 'incontrovertible by argument' when stated as a property of 'science' or of the 'scientist'. So he errs if he has not indicated beforehand that the property belongs because the thing partakes of, or is partaken of by, something; because then the property will [20] belong to certain other things as well. For if he renders it because its subject is partaken of, it will belong to the things which partake of it; whereas if he renders it because its subject partakes of something else, it will belong to the things partaken of, as (e.g.) if he were to state 'life' to be a property of a 'particular kind of living being', or just of 'living being'. So he errs if he has not expressly distinguished the property that belongs specifically, because then it will belong only to one of the things that fall under the term of which he states the property: for the superlative belongs only to one of them, [25] e.g. 'lightest' as applied to 'fire'. Sometimes, too, a man may even add the word 'specifically', and still make a mistake. For the things in question should all be of one species, whenever the word 'specifically' is added: and in some cases this does not occur, as it does not, in fact, in the case of fire. For fire is not all of one species; for live coals and flame and light are each of them 'fire', but are of different spe- [30] cies. The reason why, whenever 'specifically' is added, there should not be any species other than the one mentioned, is this, that if there be, then the property in question will belong to some of them in a greater and to others in a less degree, as happens with 'consisting of most rarefied particles' in the case of fire: for 'light' consists of more rarefied particles than live coals and flame. And this should not hap- [35] pen unless the name too be predicated in a greater degree of that of which the description is truer; otherwise the rule that where the description is truer the name too should be truer **135ᵃ** is not fulfilled. Moreover, in addition to this, the same attribute will be the property both of the term which has it absolutely and of that element therein which has it in the highest degree, as is the condition of the property 'consisting of most rarefied particles' in the case of 'fire': for this same attribute will be the prop- [5] erty of 'light' as well: for it is 'light' that 'consists of the most rarefied particles'. If, then, any one else renders a property in this way one should attack it; for oneself, one should not give occasion for this objection, but should define in what manner one states the property at the actual time of making the statement.

Next, for destructive purposes, see if he has stated a thing as a property of itself: for then [10] what has been stated to be a property will not be a property. For a thing itself always shows its own essence, and what shows the essence is not a property but a definition. Thus (e.g.) he who has said that 'becoming' is a property of 'beautiful' has rendered the term as a property of itself (for 'beautiful' and 'becoming' are the same); and so 'becoming' could not be a property of 'beautiful'. For construc- [15] tive purposes, on the other hand, see if he has avoided rendering a thing as a property of itself, but has yet stated a convertible predicate: for then what is stated not to be a property will be a property. Thus he who has stated 'animate substance' as a property of 'living-creature' has not stated 'living-creature' as a property of itself, but has rendered a convertible predicate, so that 'animate substance' would be a property of 'living-creature'.

[20] Next, in the case of things consisting of like parts, you should look and see, for destructive purposes, if the property of the whole be not true of the part, or if that of the part be not predicated of the whole: for then what has been stated to be the property will not be a property. In some cases it happens that this is so: for sometimes in rendering a property in the case [25] of things that consist of like parts a man may have his eye on the whole, while sometimes he may address himself to what is predicated of the part: and then in neither case will it have been rightly rendered. Take an instance referring to the whole: the man who has said that it is a property of the 'sea' to be 'the largest volume of salt water', has stated the property of something that consists of like parts, but has rendered an attribute of such a kind as is not [30] true of the part (for a particular sea is not

'the largest volume of salt water'); and so 'the largest volume of salt water' could not be a property of the 'sea'. Now take one referring to the part: the man who has stated that it is a property of 'air' to be 'breathable' has stated the property of something that consists of like [35] parts, but he has stated an attribute such as, though true of some air, is still not predicable of the whole (for the whole of the air is not breathable); and so 'breathable' could not be 135ᵇ a property of 'air'. For constructive purposes, on the other hand, see whether, while it is true of each of the things with similar parts, it is on the other hand a property of them taken as a collective whole: for then what has been stated not to be a property will be a property. Thus (e.g.) while it is true of earth every-[5] where that it naturally falls downwards, it is a property of the various particular pieces of earth taken as 'the Earth', so that it would be a property of 'earth' 'naturally to fall downwards'.

6

Next, look from the point of view of the respective opposites, and first (*a*) from that of the contraries, and see, for destructive purposes, if the contrary of the term rendered fails to be a property of the contrary subject. For then neither will the contrary of the first be a prop-[10] erty of the contrary of the second. Thus (e.g.) inasmuch as injustice is contrary to justice, and the lowest evil to the highest good, but 'to be the highest good' is not a property of 'justice', therefore 'to be the lowest evil' could not be a property of 'injustice'. For constructive purposes, on the other hand, see if the contrary is the property of the contrary: for then also the contrary of the first will be the property of the contrary of the second. Thus (e.g.) inas-[15] much as evil is contrary to good, and objectionable to desirable, and 'desirable' is a property of 'good', 'objectionable' would be a property of 'evil'.

Secondly (*b*) look from the point of view of relative opposites and see, for destructive purposes, if the correlative of the term rendered fails to be a property of the correlative of the subject: for then neither will the correlative of the first be a property of the correlative of the [20] second. Thus (e.g.) inasmuch as 'double' is relative to 'half', and 'in excess' to 'exceeded', while 'in excess' is not a property of 'double', 'exceeded' could not be a property of 'half'. For constructive purposes, on the other hand, see if the correlative of the alleged property is a property of the subject's correlative: for then also the correlative of the first will be a property of the correlative of the second: e.g. inasmuch as 'double' is relative to 'half', and the propor-[25] tion 1: 2 is relative to the proportion 2: 1, while it is a property of 'double' to be 'in the proportion of 2 to 1', it would be a property of 'half' to be 'in the proportion of 1 to 2'.

Thirdly (*c*) for destructive purposes, see if an attribute described in terms of a state (X) fails to be a property of the given state (Y): for then neither will the attribute described in terms of the privation (of X) be a property of the privation (of Y). Also if, on the other hand, [30] an attribute described in terms of the privation (of X) be not a property of the given privation (of Y), neither will the attribute described in terms of the state (X) be a property of the state (Y). Thus, for example, inasmuch as it is not predicated as a property of 'deafness' to be a 'lack of sensation', neither could it be a property of 'hearing' to be a 'sensation'. For constructive purposes, on the other hand, see if an attribute described in terms of a state (X) is a property of the given state (Y): for then also the attribute that is described in terms of the privation (of X) will be a property of the pri-[35] vation (of Y). Also, if an attribute described in terms of a privation (of X) be a 136ᵃ property of the privation (of Y), then also the attribute that is described in terms of the state (X) will be a property of the state (Y). Thus (e.g.) inasmuch as 'to see' is a property of 'sight', inasmuch as we have sight, 'failure to see' would be a property of 'blindness', inasmuch as we have not got the sight we should naturally have.

[5] Next, look from the point of view of positive and negative terms; and first (*a*) from the point of view of the predicates taken by themselves. This common-place rule is useful only for a destructive purpose. Thus (e.g.) see if the positive term or the attribute described in terms of it is a property of the subject: for then the negative term or the attribute described in [10] terms of it will not be a property of the subject. Also if, on the other hand, the negative term or the attribute described in terms of it is a property of the subject, then the positive term or the attribute described in terms of it will not be a property of the subject: e.g. inasmuch as 'animate' is a property of 'living creature', 'inanimate' could not be a property of 'living creature'.

Secondly (*b*) look from the point of view of [15] the predicates, positive or negative, and their respective subjects; and see, for destructive purposes, if the positive term fails to be a property of the positive subject: for then neither will the negative term be a property of the negative subject. Also, if the negative term fails to be a property of the negative subject, neither will the positive term be a property of the positive subject. Thus (e.g.) inasmuch as 'animal' is not a property of 'man', neither could 'not-animal' be a property of 'not-man'. [20] Also if 'not-animal' seems not to be a property of 'not-man', neither will 'animal' be a property of 'man'. For constructive purposes, on the other hand, see if the positive term is a property of the positive subject: for then the negative term will be a property of the negative subject as well. Also if the negative term be a property of the negative subject, the positive will be a property of the positive as well. [25] Thus (e.g.) inasmuch as it is a property of 'not-living being' 'not to live', it would be a property of 'living being' 'to live': also if it seems to be a property of 'living being' 'to live', it will also seem to be a property of 'not-living being' 'not to live'.

Thirdly (*c*) look from the point of view of the subjects taken by themselves, and see, for destructive purposes, if the property rendered [30] is a property of the positive subject: for then the same term will not be a property of the negative subject as well. Also, if the term rendered be a property of the negative subject, it will not be a property of the positive. Thus (e.g.) inasmuch as 'animate' is a property of 'living creature', 'animate' could not be a property of 'not-living creature'. For constructive purposes, on the other hand, if the term rendered fails to be a property of the affirmative [35] subject it would be a property of the negative. This commonplace rule is, however, deceptive: for a positive term is not a property of a negative, or a negative of a positive. For a positive term does not belong at all to a negative, while a negative term, though it belongs to a positive, does not belong as a property.

Next, look from the point of view of the co-ordinate members of a division, and see, for destructive purposes, if none of the co-ordinate members (parallel with the property rendered) be a property of any of the remaining set of [5] co-ordinate members (parallel with the subject): for then neither will the term stated be a property of that of which it is stated to be a property. Thus (e.g.) inasmuch as 'sensible living being' is not a property of any of the other living beings, 'intelligible living being' could not be a property of God. For constructive purposes, on the other hand, see if some one or other of the remaining co-ordinate members (parallel with the property rendered) be a property of each of these co-ordinate members (parallel with the subject): for then the re- [10] maining one too will be a property of that of which it has been stated not to be a property. Thus (e.g.) inasmuch as it is a property of 'wisdom' to be essentially 'the natural virtue of the rational faculty', then, taking each of the other virtues as well in this way, it would be a property of 'temperance' to be essentially 'the natural virtue of the faculty of desire'.

7

[15] Next, look from the point of view of the inflexions, and see, for destructive purposes, if the inflexion of the property rendered fails to be a property of the inflexion of the subject: for then neither will the other inflexion be a property of the other inflexion. Thus (e.g.) inasmuch as 'beautifully' is not a property of 'justly', neither could 'beautiful' be a property of 'just'. For constructive purposes, on the other hand, see if the inflexion of the property rendered is a property of the inflexion of the subject: for then also the other inflexion will be a property of the other inflexion. Thus (e.g.) in- [20] asmuch as 'walking biped' is a property of man, it would also be any one's property '*as* a man' to be described '*as* a walking biped'. Not only in the case of the actual term mentioned should one look at the inflexions, but also in the case of its opposites, just as has been laid down in the case of the former commonplace rules as well.[1] Thus, for destructive pur- [25] poses, see if the inflexion of the opposite of the property rendered fails to be the property of the inflexion of the opposite of the subject: for then neither will the inflexion of the other opposite be a property of the inflexion of the other opposite. Thus (e.g.) inasmuch as 'well' is not a property of 'justly', neither could 'badly' be a property of 'unjustly'. For constructive purposes, on the other hand, see if the inflexion of the opposite of the property originally suggested is a property of the inflexion of the oppo- [30] site of the original subject: for then also the inflexion of the other opposite will be a property of the inflexion of the other opposite. Thus (e.g.) inasmuch as 'best' is a property of 'the good', 'worst' also will be a property of 'the evil'.

[1] 114^b 6-15.

Next, look from the point of view of things that are in a like relation, and see, for destructive purposes, if what is in a relation like that of the property rendered fails to be a property of what is in a relation like that of the subject: for then neither will what is in a relation like [35] that of the first be a property of what is in a relation like that of the second. Thus (e.g.) inasmuch as the relation of the builder towards the production of a house is like that of the doctor towards the production of health, and it is 137ᵃ not a property of a doctor to produce health, it could not be a property of a builder to produce a house. For constructive purposes, on the other hand, see if what is in a relation like that of the property rendered is a property of what is in a relation like that of the subject: for then also what is in a relation like that of the first will be a property of what is in a relation like that of the second. Thus (e.g.) inasmuch as the relation of a doctor towards the possession of ability to produce health [5] is like that of a trainer towards the possession of ability to produce vigour, and it is a property of a trainer to possess the ability to produce vigour, it would be a property of a doctor to possess the ability to produce health.

Next look from the point of view of things that are identically related, and see, for destructive purposes, if the predicate that is identically related towards two subjects fails to be a property of the subject which is identically related to it as the subject in question; for then neither [10] will the predicate that is identically related to both subjects be a property of the subject which is identically related to it as the first. If, on the other hand, the predicate which is identically related to two subjects is the property of the subject which is identically related to it as the subject in question, then it will not be a property of that of which it has been stated to be a property. [Thus (e.g.) inasmuch as prudence is identically related to both the noble and the base, since it is knowledge of each of them, and it is not a property of prudence to be knowledge of the noble, it could not be a [15] property of prudence to be knowledge of the base. If, on the other hand, it is a property of prudence to be the knowledge of the noble, it could not be a property of it to be the knowledge of the base.] For it is impossible for the same thing to be a property of more than one subject. For constructive purposes, on the other hand, this commonplace rule is of no use: for what is 'identically related' is a single predicate [20] in process of comparison with more than one subject.

Next, for destructive purposes, see if the predicate qualified by the verb 'to be' fails to be a property of the subject qualified by the verb 'to be': for then neither will the destruction of the one be a property of the other qualified by the verb 'to be destroyed', nor will the 'becoming' the one be a property of the other qualified by the verb 'to become'. Thus (e.g.) inasmuch as it is not a property of 'man' to be an animal, neither could it be a property of becoming a [25] man to become an animal; nor could the destruction of an animal be a property of the destruction of a man. In the same way one should derive arguments also from 'becoming' to 'being' and 'being destroyed', and from 'being destroyed' to 'being' and to 'becoming', exactly [30] as they have just been given from 'being' to 'becoming' and 'being destroyed'. For constructive purposes, on the other hand, see if the subject set down as qualified by the verb 'to be' has the predicate set down as so qualified, as its property: for then also the subject qualified by the very 'to become' will have the predicate qualified by 'to become' as its property, and the subject qualified by the verb 'to be destroyed' will have as its property the predicate rendered with this qualification. Thus, for example, inasmuch as it is a property [35] of man to be a mortal, it would be a property of becoming a man to become a mortal, and the destruction of a mortal would be a property of the destruction of a man. In the same 137ᵇ way one should derive arguments also from 'becoming' and 'being destroyed' both to 'being' and to the conclusions that follow from them, exactly as was directed also for the purpose of destruction.

Next take a look at the 'idea' of the subject stated, and see, for destructive purposes, if the suggested property fails to belong to the 'idea' in question, or fails to belong to it in virtue of [5] that character which causes it to bear the description of which the property was rendered: for then what has been stated to be a property will not be a property. Thus (e.g.) inasmuch as 'being motionless' does not belong to 'man-himself' *qua* 'man', but *qua* 'idea', it could not be a property of 'man' to be motionless. For constructive purposes, on the other hand, see if the property in question belongs to the idea, and belongs to it in that respect in virtue of which there is predicated of it that [10] character of which the predicate in question has been stated not to be a property: for then what has been stated not to be a property will be a property. Thus (e.g.) inasmuch as it belongs to 'living-creature-itself' to be compounded of soul and body, and further this belongs to it *qua* 'living-creature', it would be a property of 'living-creature' to be compounded of soul and body.

8

Next look from the point of view of greater [*15*] and less degrees, and first (*a*) for destructive purposes, see if what is more-P fails to be a property of what is more-S: for then neither will what is less-P be a property of what is less-S, nor least-P of least-S, nor most-P of most-S, nor P simply of S simply. Thus (e.g.) inasmuch as being more highly coloured is not a property of what is more a body, neither could [*20*] being less highly coloured be a property of what is less a body, nor being coloured be a property of body at all. For constructive purposes, on the other hand, see if what is more-P is a property of what is more-S: for then also what is less-P will be a property of what is less-S, and least-P of least-S, and most-P of most-S, and P simply of S simply. Thus (e.g.) inasmuch as a higher degree of sensation is a property of a higher degree of life, a lower degree [*25*] of sensation also would be a property of a lower degree of life, and the highest of the highest and the lowest of the lowest degree, and sensation simply of life simply.

Also you should look at the argument from a simple predication to the same qualified types of predication, and see, for destructive purposes, if P simply fails to be a property of S [*30*] simply; for then neither will more-P be a property of more-S, nor less-P of less-S, nor most-P of most-S, nor least-P of least-S. Thus (e.g.) inasmuch as 'virtuous' is not a property of 'man', neither could 'more virtuous' be a property of what is 'more human'. For constructive purposes, on the other hand, see if P simply is a property of S simply: for then more-P also will be a property of more-S, and less-P [*35*] of less-S, and least-P of least-S, and most-P of most-S. Thus (e.g.) a tendency to move upwards by nature is a property of fire, and so 138ᵃ also a greater tendency to move upwards by nature would be a property of what is more fiery. In the same way too one should look at all these matters from the point of view of the others as well.

Secondly (*b*) for destructive purposes, see if the more likely property fails to be a property of the more likely subject: for then neither will [*5*] the less likely property be a property of the less likely subject. Thus (e.g.) inasmuch as 'perceiving' is more likely to be a property of 'animal' than 'knowing' of 'man', and 'perceiving' is not a property of 'animal', 'knowing' could not be a property of 'man'. For constructive purposes, on the other hand, see if the less likely property is a property of the less likely subject; for then too the more likely property will be a property of the more likely subject. [*10*] Thus (e.g.) inasmuch as 'to be naturally civilized' is less likely to be a property of man than 'to live' of an animal, and it is a property of man to be naturally civilized, it would be a property of animal to live.

Thirdly (*c*) for destructive purposes, see if the predicate fails to be a property of that of which it is more likely to be a property: for then neither will it be a property of that of which it is less likely to be a property: while if [*15*] it is a property of the former, it will not be a property of the latter. Thus (e.g.) inasmuch as 'to be coloured' is more likely to be a property of a 'surface' than of a 'body', and it is not a property of a surface, 'to be coloured' could not be a property of 'body'; while if it is a property of a 'surface', it could not be a property of a 'body'. For constructive purposes, on the other hand, this commonplace rule is not of [*20*] any use: for it is impossible for the same thing to be a property of more than one thing.

Fourthly (*d*) for destructive purposes, see if what is more likely to be a property of a given subject fails to be its property: for then neither will what is less likely to be a property of it be its property. Thus (e.g.) inasmuch as 'sensible' is more likely than 'divisible' to be a property of 'animal', and 'sensible' is not a property of [*25*] animal, 'divisible' could not be a property of animal. For constructive purposes, on the other hand, see if what is less likely to be a property of it is a property; for then what is more likely to be a property of it will be a property as well. Thus, for example, inasmuch as 'sensation' is less likely to be a property of 'animal' than life', and 'sensation' is a property of animal, 'life' would be a property of animal.

[*30*] Next, look from the point of view of the attributes that belong in a like manner, and first (*a*) for destructive purposes, see if what is as much a property fails to be a property of that of which it is as much a property: for then neither will that which is as much a property of it be a property of that of which it is as much a property. Thus (e.g.) inasmuch as 'desiring' is as much a property of the faculty of desire as

'reasoning' is a property of the faculty of rea-[35] son, and desiring is not a property of the faculty of desire, reasoning could not be a property of the faculty of reason. For constructive purposes, on the other hand, see if what is as much a property is a property of that of which it is as much a property: for then also what is as much a property as it will be a property of that of which it is as much a property. Thus (e.g.) inasmuch as it is as much a property of 'the faculty of reason' to be 'the primary seat of wisdom' as it is of 'the faculty of desire' to be 'the primary seat of temperance', and it is a property of the faculty of reason to be the primary seat of wisdom, it would be a property of the faculty of desire to be the [5] primary seat of temperance.

Secondly (b) for destructive purposes, see if what is as much a property of anything fails to be a property of it: for then neither will what is as much a property be a property of it. Thus (e.g.) inasmuch as 'seeing' is as much a property of man as 'hearing', and 'seeing' is not a property of man, 'hearing' could not be a property of man. For constructive purposes, on the [10] other hand, see if what is as much a property of it is its property: for then what is as much a property of it as the former will be its property as well. Thus (e.g.) it is as much a property of the soul to be the primary possessor of a part that desires as of a part that reasons, and it is a property of the soul to be the primary possessor of a part that desires, and so it [15] would be a property of the soul to be the primary possessor of a part that reasons.

Thirdly (c) for destructive purposes, see if it fails to be a property of that of which it is as much a property: for then neither will it be a property of that of which it is as much a property as of the former, while if it be a property of the former, it will not be a property of the other. Thus (e.g.) inasmuch as 'to burn' is as much a property of 'flame' as of 'live coals', and 'to burn' is not a property of flame, 'to burn' [20] could not be a property of live coals: while if it *is* a property of flame, it could not be a property of live coals. For constructive purposes, on the other hand, this commonplace rule is of no use.

The rule based on things that are in a like relation[1] differs from the rule based on attributes that belong in a like manner,[2] because the former point is secured by analogy, not [25] from reflection on the belonging of any attribute, while the latter is judged by a com-

---

[1] 136b 33–137a 7.   [2] 138a 30–b 22.

parison based on the fact that an attribute belongs.

Next, for destructive purposes, see if in rendering the property potentially, he has also through that potentiality rendered the property relatively to something that does not exist, when the potentiality in question cannot be-[30] long to what does not exist: for then what is stated to be a property will not be a property. Thus (e.g.) he who has said that 'breathable' is a property of 'air' has, on the one hand, rendered the property potentially (for that is 'breathable' which is such as can be breathed), and on the other hand has also rendered the property relatively to what does not exist:—for while air may exist, even though there exist no animal so constituted as to breathe the air, it is [35] not possible to breathe it if no animal exist: so that it will not, either, be a property of air to be such as can be breathed at a time when there exists no animal such as to breathe it—and so it follows that 'breathable' could not be a property of air.

139a For constructive purposes, see if in rendering the property potentially he renders the property either relatively to something that exists, or to something that does not exist, when the potentiality in question can belong to what does not exist: for then what has been stated not to be a property will be a property. Thus (e.g.) he who renders it as a property of 'being' [5] to be 'capable of being acted upon or of acting', in rendering the property potentially, has rendered the property relatively to something that exists: for when 'being' exists, it will also be capable of being acted upon or of acting in a certain way: so that to be 'capable of being acted upon or of acting' would be a property of 'being'.

Next, for destructive purposes, see if he has stated the property in the superlative: for then [10] what has been stated to be a property will not be a property. For people who render the property in that way find that of the object of which the description is true, the name is not true as well: for though the object perish the description will continue in being none the less; for it belongs most nearly to something that is in being. An example would be supposing any one were to render 'the lightest body' as a property of 'fire': for, though fire perish, [15] there will still be some form of body that is the lightest, so that 'the lightest body' could not be a property of fire. For constructive purposes, on the other hand, see if he has avoided rendering the property in the superlative: for then the property will in this respect have been correctly stated. Thus (e.g.) inasmuch as he who states 'a naturally civilized animal' as a property of man has not rendered the property [20] in the superlative, the property would in this respect have been correctly stated.

BOOK VI

1

The discussion of Definitions falls into five parts. For you have to show either (1) that it [25] is not true at all to apply the expression as well to that to which the term is applied (for the definition of Man ought to be true of every man); or (2) that though the object has a genus, he has failed to put the object defined into the genus, or to put it into the appropriate genus (for the framer of a definition should first place the object in its genus, and then append [30] its differences: for of all the elements of the definition the genus is usually supposed to be the principal mark of the essence of what is defined): or (3) that the expression is not peculiar to the object (for, as we said above as well,[1] a definition ought to be peculiar): or else (4) see if, though he has observed all the aforesaid cautions, he has yet failed to define the object, that is, to express its essence. (5) It remains, apart from the foregoing, to see if he [35] has defined it, but defined it incorrectly.

Whether, then, the expression be not also true of that of which the term is true you should proceed to examine according to the commonplace rules that relate to Accident. For there too the question is always 'Is so and so true or untrue?': for whenever we argue that an 139b accident belongs, we declare it to be true, while whenever we argue that it does not belong, we declare it to be untrue. If, again, he has failed to place the object in the appropriate genus, or if the expression be not peculiar to the object, we must go on to examine the case according to the commonplace rules that relate [5] to genus and property.

It remains, then, to prescribe how to investigate whether the object has been either not defined at all, or else defined incorrectly. First, then, we must proceed to examine if it has been defined incorrectly: for with anything it is easier to do it than to do it correctly. Clearly, then, more mistakes are made in the latter task on account of its greater difficulty. Accordingly [10] the attack becomes easier in the latter case than in the former.

Incorrectness falls into two branches: (1) first, the use of obscure language (for the language of a definition ought to be the very clearest possible, seeing that the whole purpose of [15] rendering it is to make something known); (2) secondly, if the expression used be longer than is necessary: for all additional matter in a definition is superfluous. Again, each of the aforesaid branches is divided into a number of others.

2

One commonplace rule, then, in regard to obscurity is, See if the meaning intended by the [20] definition involves an ambiguity with any other, e.g. 'Becoming is a passage into being', or 'Health is the balance of hot and cold elements'. Here 'passage' and 'balance' are ambiguous terms: it is accordingly not clear which of the several possible senses of the term he intends to convey. Likewise also, if the term defined be used in different senses and he has spoken without distinguishing between them: [25] for then it is not clear to which of them the definition rendered applies, and one can then bring a captious objection on the ground that the definition does not apply to all the things whose definition he has rendered: and this kind of thing is particularly easy in the case where the definer does not see the ambiguity of his terms. Or, again, the questioner may himself distinguish the various senses of the term rendered in the definition, and then [30] institute his argument against each: for if the expression used be not adequate to the subject in any of its senses, it is clear that he cannot have defined it in any sense aright.

Another rule is, See if he has used a metaphorical expression, as, for instance, if he has defined knowledge as 'unsupplantable', or the earth as a 'nurse', or temperance as a 'harmony'. For a metaphorical expression is always [35] obscure. It is possible, also, to argue sophistically against the user of a metaphorical expression as though he had used it in its literal sense: for the definition stated will not apply to the term defined, e.g. in the case of temperance: for harmony is always found between notes. Moreover, if harmony be the genus of temperance, then the same object will occur in 140a two genera of which neither contains the other: for harmony does not contain virtue, nor

[1] 101b 19.

virtue harmony. Again, see if he uses terms that are unfamiliar, as when Plato describes the eye as 'brow-shaded', or a certain spider as [5] 'poison-fanged', or the marrow as 'bone-formed'. For an unusual phrase is always obscure.

Sometimes a phrase is used neither ambiguously, nor yet metaphorically, nor yet literally, as when the law is said to be the 'measure' or 'image' of the things that are by nature just. Such phrases are worse than metaphor; for the latter does make its meaning to some extent clear because of the likeness involved; for those [10] who use metaphors do so always in view of some likeness: whereas this kind of phrase makes nothing clear; for there is no likeness to justify the description 'measure' or 'image', as applied to the law, nor is the law ordinarily so called in a literal sense. So then, if a man says that the law is literally a 'measure' or an 'image', he speaks falsely: for an image is [15] something produced by imitation, and this is not found in the case of the law. If, on the other hand, he does not mean the term literally, it is clear that he has used an unclear expression, and one that is worse than any sort of metaphorical expression.

Moreover, see if from the expression used the definition of the contrary be not clear; for definitions that have been correctly rendered also indicate their contraries as well. Or, again, [20] see if, when it is merely stated by itself, it is not evident what it defines: just as in the works of the old painters, unless there were an inscription, the figures used to be unrecognizable.

3

If, then, the definition be not clear, you should proceed to examine on lines such as these. If, on the other hand, he has phrased the definition redundantly, first of all look and see [25] whether he has used any attribute that belongs universally, either to real objects in general, or to all that fall under the same genus as the object defined: for the mention of this is sure to be redundant. For the genus ought to divide the object from things in general, and the differentia from any of the things contained in the same genus. Now any term that belongs to everything separates off the given object from absolutely nothing, while any that [30] belongs to all the things that fall under the same genus does not separate it off from the things contained in the same genus. Any addition, then, of that kind will be pointless.

Or see if, though the additional matter may be peculiar to the given term, yet even when it is struck out the rest of the expression too is peculiar and makes clear the essence of the [35] term. Thus, in the definition of man, the addition 'capable of receiving knowledge' is superfluous; for strike it out, and still the expression is peculiar and makes clear his essence. 140ᵇ Speaking generally, everything is superfluous upon whose removal the remainder still makes the term that is being defined clear. Such, for instance, would also be the definition of the soul, assuming it to be stated as a 'self-moving number';[1] for the soul is just 'the self-moving', as Plato defined it.[2] Or perhaps the expression used, though appropriate, yet does not declare the essence, if the word 'number' be [5] eliminated. Which of the two is the real state of the case it is difficult to determine clearly: the right way to treat the matter in all cases is to be guided by convenience. Thus (e.g.) it is said that the definition of phlegm is the 'undigested moisture that comes first off food'. Here the addition of the word 'undigested' is superfluous, seeing that 'the first' is one and not many, so that even when 'undi- [10] gested' is left out the definition will still be peculiar to the subject: for it is impossible that both phlegm and also something else should both be the first to arise from the food. Or perhaps the phlegm is not absolutely the first thing to come off the food, but only the first of the undigested matters, so that the addition 'undigested' is required; for stated the other way the definition would not be true unless [15] the phlegm comes first of all.

Moreover, see if anything contained in the definition fails to apply to everything that falls under the same species: for this sort of definition is worse than those which include an attribute belonging to all things universally. For in that case, if the remainder of the expression be peculiar, the whole too will be peculiar: for absolutely always, if to something peculiar any- [20] thing whatever that is true be added, the whole too becomes peculiar. Whereas if any part of the expression do not apply to everything that falls under the same species, it is impossible that the expression as a whole should be peculiar: for it will not be predicated convertibly with the object; e.g. 'a walking biped animal six feet high': for an expression of that kind is not predicated convertibly with the [25] term, because the attribute 'six feet high'

[1] Xenocrates, Fr. 60, Heinze.
[2] *Phaedrus*, 245.

does not belong to everything that falls under the same species.

Again, see if he has said the same thing more than once, saying (e.g.) 'desire' is a 'conation for the pleasant'. For 'desire' is always 'for the pleasant', so that what is the same as desire will also be 'for the pleasant'. Accordingly our defi-[30] nition of desire becomes 'conation-for-the-pleasant for the pleasant': for the word 'desire' is the exact equivalent of the words 'conation-for-the-pleasant', so that both alike will be 'for the pleasant'. Or perhaps there is no absurdity in this; for consider this instance:—'Man is a biped': therefore, what is the same as man is a biped: but 'a walking biped animal' is the same as man, and therefore 'a walking biped animal [35] is a biped'. But this involves no real absurdity. For 'biped' is not a *predicate* of 'walking animal': if it were, then we should certainly have 'biped' predicated twice of the same thing; but as a matter of fact the subject said to 141ª be a biped is 'a walking biped animal', so that the word 'biped' is only used as a predicate once. Likewise also in the case of 'desire' as well: for it is not 'conation' that is said to be 'for the pleasant', but rather the whole idea, so that there too the predication is only made [5] once. Absurdity results, not when the same word is uttered twice, but when the same thing is more than once predicated of a subject; e.g. if he says, like Xenocrates, that wisdom defines and contemplates reality:[1] for definition is a certain type of contemplation, so that by adding the words 'and contemplates' over again he says the same thing twice over. Likewise, too, those fail who say that 'cooling' is 'the privation [10] of natural heat'. For all privation is a privation of some natural attribute, so that the addition of the word 'natural' is superfluous: it would have been enough to say 'privation of heat', for the word 'privation' shows of itself that the heat meant is natural heat.

[15] Again, see if a universal have been mentioned and then a particular case of it be added as well, e.g. 'Equity is a remission of what is expedient and just'; for what is just is a branch of what is expedient and is therefore included in the latter term: its mention is therefore redundant, an addition of the particular after the universal has been already stated. So also, if he defines 'medicine' as 'knowledge of what makes for health in animals and men', or 'the [20] law' as 'the image of what is by nature noble and just'; for what is just is a branch of

[1] Fr. 7, Heinze.

what is noble, so that he says the same thing more than once.

4

Whether, then, a man defines a thing correctly or incorrectly you should proceed to examine on these and similar lines. But whether he has mentioned and defined its essence or no, [25] should be examined as follows:—

First of all, see if he has failed to make the definition through terms that are prior and more intelligible. For the reason why the definition is rendered is to make known the term stated, and we make things known by taking not any random terms, but such as are prior and more intelligible, as is done in demonstra-[30] tions (for so it is with all teaching and learning); accordingly, it is clear that a man who does not define through terms of this kind has not defined at all. Otherwise, there will be more than one definition of the same thing: for clearly he who defines through terms that are prior and more intelligible has also framed a definition, and a better one, so that both would then be definitions of the same object. This sort of view, however, does not generally find [35] acceptance: for of each real object the essence is single: if, then, there are to be a number of definitions of the same thing, the essence of the object will be the same as it is represented to be in each of the definitions, and these representations are not the same, inasmuch as 141ᵇ the definitions are different. Clearly, then, any one who has not defined a thing through terms that are prior and more intelligible has not defined it at all.

The statement that a definition has not been made through more intelligible terms may be understood in two senses, either supposing that its terms are absolutely less intelligible, or sup-[5] posing that they are less intelligible to us: for either sense is possible. Thus absolutely the prior is more intelligible than the posterior, a point, for instance, than a line, a line than a plane, and a plane than a solid; just as also a unit is more intelligible than a number; for it is the prius and starting-point of all number. Likewise, also, a letter is more intelligible than a syllable. Whereas to us it sometimes happens that the converse is the case: for the solid falls [10] under perception most of all—more than a plane—and a plane more than a line, and a line more than a point; for most people learn things like the former earlier than the latter; for any ordinary intelligence can grasp them, whereas the others require an exact and exceptional understanding.

[15] Absolutely, then, it is better to try to make what is posterior known through what is prior, inasmuch as such a way of procedure is more scientific. Of course, in dealing with persons who cannot recognize things through terms of that kind, it may perhaps be necessary to frame the expression through terms that are intelligible to them. Among definitions of this kind are those of a point, a line, and a plane, all of [20] which explain the prior by the posterior; for they say that a point is the limit of a line, a line of a plane, a plane of a solid. One must, however, not fail to observe that those who define in this way cannot show the essential nature of the term they define, unless it so hap-[25] pens that the same thing is more intelligible both to us and also absolutely, since a correct definition must define a thing through its genus and its differentiae, and these belong to the order of things which are absolutely more intelligible than, and prior to, the species. For annul the genus and differentia, and the species too is annulled, so that these are prior to the species. They are also more intelligible; for [30] if the species be known, the genus and differentia must of necessity be known as well (for any one who knows what a man is knows also what 'animal' and 'walking' are), whereas if the genus or the differentia be known it does not follow of necessity that the species is known as well: thus the species is less intelligible. Moreover, those who say that such definitions, [35] viz. those which proceed from what is intelligible to this, that, or the other man, are really and truly definitions, will have to say that there are several definitions of one and the same thing. For, as it happens, different things are more intelligible to different people, not 142ª the same things to all; and so a different definition would have to be rendered to each several person, if the definition is to be constructed from what is more intelligible to particular individuals. Moreover, to the same people different things are more intelligible at different times; first of all the objects of sense; then, as they become more sharpwitted, the converse; so that those who hold that a defini-[5] tion ought to be rendered through what is more intelligible to particular individuals would not have to render the same definition at all times even to the same person. It is clear, then, that the right way to define is not through terms of that kind, but through what is absolutely more intelligible: for only in this way could the definition come always to be one and the same. Perhaps, also, what is absolutely in-[10] telligible is what is intelligible, not to all, but to those who are in a sound state of understanding, just as what is absolutely healthy is what is healthy to those in a sound state of body. All such points as this ought to be made very precise, and made use of in the course of discussion as occasion requires. The demolition of a definition will most surely win a general [15] approval if the definer happens to have framed his expression neither from what is absolutely more intelligible nor yet from what is so to us.

One form, then, of the failure to work through more intelligible terms is the exhibition of the prior through the posterior, as we remarked before.[1] Another form occurs if we find that the definition has been rendered of [20] what is at rest and definite through what is indefinite and in motion: for what is still and definite is prior to what is indefinite and in motion.

Of the failure to use terms that are prior there are three forms:

(1) The first is when an opposite has been defined through its opposite, e.g. good through evil: for opposites are always simultaneous by nature. Some people think, also, that both are [25] objects of the same science, so that the one is not even more intelligible than the other. One must, however, observe that it is perhaps not possible to define some things in any other way, e.g. the double without the half, and all the terms that are essentially relative: for in all such cases the essential being is the same as a certain relation to something, so that it is im-[30] possible to understand the one term without the other, and accordingly in the definition of the one the other too must be embraced. One ought to learn up all such points as these, and use them as occasion may seem to require.

(2) Another is—if he has used the term defined itself. This passes unobserved when the actual name of the object is not used, e.g. sup-[35] posing any one had defined the sun as a 142ᵇ 'star that appears by day'.[2] For in bringing in 'day' he brings in the sun. To detect errors of this sort, exchange the word for its definition, e.g. the definition of 'day' as the 'passage of the sun over the earth'. Clearly, whoever has said 'the passage of the sun over the earth' has said 'the sun', so that in bringing

[1] 141ª 26. [2] Cf. Plato, *Def.* 411 A.

[5] in the 'day' he has brought in the sun.

(3) Again, see if he has defined one co-ordinate member of a division by another, e.g. 'an odd number' as 'that which is greater by one than an even number'. For the co-ordinate members of a division that are derived from the same genus are simultaneous by nature, [10] and 'odd' and 'even' are such terms: for both are differentiae of number.

Likewise also, see if he has defined a superior through a subordinate term, e.g. 'An "even number" is "a number divisible into halves"', or '"the good" is a "state of virtue"'. For 'half' is derived from 'two', and 'two' is an even number: virtue also is a kind of good, [15] so that the latter terms are subordinate to the former. Moreover, in using the subordinate term one is bound to use the other as well: for whoever employs the term 'virtue' employs the term 'good', seeing that virtue is a certain kind of good: likewise, also, whoever employs the term 'half' employs the term 'even', for to be 'divided in half' means to be divided into two, and two is even.

5

[20] Generally speaking, then, one commonplace rule relates to the failure to frame the expression by means of terms that are prior and more intelligible: and of this the subdivisions are those specified above. A second is, see whether, though the object is in a genus, it has not been placed in a genus. This sort of error is always found where the essence of the object does not stand first in the expression, e.g. the definition of 'body' as 'that which has three [25] dimensions', or the definition of 'man', supposing any one to give it, as 'that which knows how to count': for it is not stated what it is that has three dimensions, or what it is that knows how to count: whereas the genus is meant to indicate just this, and is submitted first of the terms in the definition.

[30] Moreover, see if, while the term to be defined is used in relation to many things, he has failed to render it in relation to all of them; as (e.g.) if he define 'grammar' as the 'knowledge how to write from dictation': for he ought also to say that it is a knowledge how to read as well. For in rendering it as 'knowledge of writing' he has no more defined it than by rendering it as 'knowledge of reading': neither in fact has succeeded, but only he who mentions both these things, since it is impossible that [35] there should be more than one definition of the same thing. It is only, however, in some cases that what has been said corresponds to the actual state of things: in some it does not, e.g. all those terms which are not used essentially in relation to both things: as medicine is said to deal with the production of disease and health; for it is said essentially to do the latter, but the former only by accident: for it is [5] absolutely alien to medicine to produce disease. Here, then, the man who renders medicine as relative to both of these things has not defined it any better than he who mentions the one only. In fact he has done it perhaps worse, for any one else besides the doctor is capable of producing disease.

Moreover, in a case where the term to be defined [10] is used in relation to several things, see if he has rendered it as relative to the worse rather than to the better; for every form of knowledge and potentiality is generally thought to be relative to the best.

Again, if the thing in question be not placed in its own proper genus, one must examine it according to the elementary rules in regard to genera, as has been said before.[1]

[15] Moreover, see if he uses language which transgresses the genera of the things he defines, defining, e.g. justice as a 'state that produces equality' or 'distributes what is equal': for by defining it so he passes outside the sphere of virtue, and so by leaving out the genus of justice he fails to express its essence: for the essence of a thing must in each case bring in its genus. It is the same thing if the object be not [20] put into its nearest genus; for the man who puts it into the nearest one has stated all the higher genera, seeing that all the higher genera are predicated of the lower. Either, then, it ought to be put into its nearest genus, or else to the higher genus all the differentiae ought to be appended whereby the nearest genus is defined. For then he would not have [25] left out anything: but would merely have mentioned the subordinate genus by an expression instead of by name. On the other hand, he who mentions merely the higher genus by itself, does not state the subordinate genus as well: in saying 'plant' a man does not specify 'a tree'.

6

Again, in regard to the differentiae, we must [30] examine in like manner whether the differentiae, too, that he has stated be those of the genus. For if a man has not defined the object by the differentiae peculiar to it, or has men-

[1] 139ᵇ 3.

tioned something such as is utterly incapable of being a differentia of anything, e.g. 'animal' or 'substance', clearly he has not defined it at all: for the aforesaid terms do not differentiate anything at all. Further, we must see whether the differentia stated possesses anything that is [35] co-ordinate with it in a division; for, if not, clearly the one stated could not be a differentia of the genus. For a genus is always divided by differentiae that are co-ordinate members of a division, as, for instance, 'animal' by the terms 'walking', 'flying', 'aquatic', and 'biped'. Or see if, though the contrasted differentia exists, it yet is not true of the genus, for then, clearly, neither of them could be a differentia of the genus; for differentiae that are co-ordinates in a division with the differentia of a thing are all true of the genus [5] to which the thing belongs. Likewise, also, see if, though it be true, yet the addition of it to the genus fails to make a species. For then, clearly, this could not be a specific differentia of the genus: for a specific differentia, if added to the genus, always makes a species. If, however, this be no true differentia, no more is the one [10] adduced, seeing that it is a co-ordinate member of a division with this.

Moreover, see if he divides the genus by a negation, as those do who define a line as 'length without breadth': for this means simply that it has not any breadth. The genus will then be found to partake of its own species: for, [15] since of everything either an affirmation or its negation is true, length must always either lack breadth or possess it, so that 'length' as well, i.e. the genus of 'line', will be either with or without breadth. But 'length without breadth' is the definition of a species, as also is 'length with breadth': for 'without breadth' and 'with breadth' are differentiae, and the genus and differentia constitute the definition [20] of the species. Hence the genus would admit of the definition of its species. Likewise, also, it will admit of the definition of the differentia, seeing that one or the other of the aforesaid differentiae is of necessity predicated of the genus. The usefulness of this principle is found in meeting those who assert the existence [25] of 'Ideas': for if absolute length exist, how will it be predicable of the genus that it has breadth or that it lacks it? For one assertion or the other will have to be true of 'length' universally, if it is to be true of the genus at all: and this is contrary to the fact: for there exist both lengths which have, and lengths which have not, breadth. Hence the only people against whom the rule can be employed are [30] those who assert that a genus is always numerically one; and this is what is done by those who assert the real existence of the 'Ideas'; for they allege that absolute length and absolute animal are the genus.

It may be that in some cases the definer is obliged to employ a negation as well, e.g. in defining privations. For 'blind' means a thing [35] which cannot see when its nature is to see. There is no difference between dividing the genus by a negation, and dividing it by such an affirmation as is bound to have a negation as its co-ordinate in a division, e.g. supposing he had defined something as 'length possessed of breadth'; for co-ordinate in the division with that which is possessed of breadth is that which possesses no breadth and that only, so that again the genus is divided by a negation.

[5] Again, see if he rendered the species as a differentia, as do those who define 'contumely' as 'insolence accompanied by jeering'; for jeering is a kind of insolence, i.e. it is a species and not a differentia.

Moreover, see if he has stated the genus as [10] the differentia, e.g. 'Virtue is a good or noble state: for 'good' is the genus of 'virtue'. Or possibly 'good' here is not the genus but the differentia, on the principle that the same thing cannot be in two genera of which neither contains the other: for 'good' does not include 'state', nor vice versa: for not every state is good nor every good a 'state'. Both, then, could [15] not be genera, and consequently, if 'state' is the genus of virtue, clearly 'good' cannot be its genus: it must rather be the differentia. Moreover, 'a state' indicates the essence of virtue, whereas 'good' indicates not the essence but a quality: and to indicate a quality is generally held to be the function of the differentia. [20] See, further, whether the differentia rendered indicates an individual rather than a quality: for the general view is that the differentia always expresses a quality.

Look and see, further, whether the differentia belongs only by accident to the object defined. For the differentia is never an accidental [25] attribute, any more than the genus is: for the differentia of a thing cannot both belong and not belong to it.

Moreover, if either the differentia or the species, or any of the things which are under the species, is predicable of the genus, then he could not have defined the term. For none of [30] the aforesaid can possibly be predicated of the genus, seeing that the genus is the term with the widest range of all. Again, see if the genus be predicated of the differentia; for the general view is that the genus is predicated, not of the differentia, but of the objects of which the differentia is predicated. Animal (e.g.) is [35] predicated of 'man' or 'ox' or other walking animals, not of the actual differentia itself which we predicate of the species. For if 'animal' is to be predicated of each of its differentiae, then 'animal' would be predicated of the 144b species several times over; for the differentiae are predicates of the species. Moreover, the differentiae will be all either species or individuals, if they are animals; for every animal is either a species or an individual.

Likewise you must inquire also if the species [5] or any of the objects that come under it is predicated of the differentia: for this is impossible, seeing that the differentia is a term with a wider range than the various species. Moreover, if any of the species be predicated of it, the result will be that the differentia is a species: if, for instance, 'man' be predicated, the differentia is clearly the human race. Again, see if the differentia fails to be prior to the species: [10] for the differentia ought to be posterior to the genus, but prior to the species.

Look and see also if the differentia mentioned belongs to a different genus, neither contained in nor containing the genus in question. For the general view is that the same differentia cannot be used of two non-subaltern [15] genera. Else the result will be that the same species as well will be in two non-subaltern genera: for each of the differentiae imports its own genus, e.g. 'walking' and 'biped' import with them the genus 'animal'. If, then, each of the genera as well is true of that of which the differentia is true, it clearly follows that the species must be in two non-subaltern genera. [20] Or perhaps it is not impossible for the same differentia to be used of two non-subaltern genera, and we ought to add the words 'except they both be subordinate members of the same genus'. Thus 'walking animal' and 'flying animal' are non-subaltern genera, and 'biped' is the differentia of both. The words 'ex-[25]cept they both be subordinate members of the same genus' ought therefore to be added; for both these are subordinate to 'animal'. From this possibility, that the same differentia may be used of two non-subaltern genera, it is clear also that there is no necessity for the differentia to carry with it the whole of the genus to which it belongs, but only the one or the other of its limbs together with the genera that are higher than this, as 'biped' carries with it [30] either 'flying' or 'walking animal'.

See, too, if he has rendered 'existence in' something as the differentia of a thing's essence: for the general view is that locality cannot differentiate between one essence and another. Hence, too, people condemn those who divide animals by means of the terms 'walking' and 'aquatic', on the ground that 'walking' and 'aquatic' indicate mere locality. Or possibly in this case the censure is undeserved; [35] for 'aquatic' does not mean 'in' anything; nor does it denote a locality, but a certain quality: for even if the thing be on the dry land, still it is aquatic: and likewise a land-animal, even though it be in the water, will still be a land-145a and not an aquatic-animal. But all the same, if ever the differentia does denote existence in something, clearly he will have made a bad mistake.

Again, see if he has rendered an affection as the differentia: for every affection, if intensified, subverts the essence of the thing, while the differentia is not of that kind: for the dif-[5]ferentia is generally considered rather to preserve that which it differentiates; and it is absolutely impossible for a thing to exist without its own special differentia: for if there be no 'walking', there will be no 'man'. In fact, we may lay down absolutely that a thing cannot have as its differentia anything in respect of which it is subject to alteration: for all things of that kind, if intensified, destroy its essence. [10] If, then, a man has rendered any differentia of this kind, he has made a mistake: for we undergo absolutely no alteration in respect of our differentiae.

Again, see if he has failed to render the differentia of a relative term relatively to something else; for the differentiae of relative terms are themselves relative, as in the case also of [15] knowledge. This is classed as speculative, practical and productive; and each of these denotes a relation: for it speculates upon something, and produces something and does something.

Look and see also if the definer renders each [20] relative term relatively to its natural purpose: for while in some cases the particular relative term can be used in relation to its natural purpose only and to nothing else, some can be used in relation to something else as well. Thus sight can only be used for seeing, but a strigil can also be used to dip up water. Still, if any one were to define a strigil as an instrument for dipping water, he has made a mis-

[25] take: for that is not its natural function. The definition of a thing's natural function is 'that for which it would be used by the prudent man, acting as such, and by the science that deals specially with that thing'.

Or see if, whenever a term happens to be used in a number of relations, he has failed to introduce it in its primary relation: e.g. by defining 'wisdom' as the virtue of 'man' or of the [30] 'soul', rather than of the 'reasoning faculty': for 'wisdom' is the virtue primarily of the reasoning faculty: for it is in virtue of this that both the man and his soul are said to be wise.

Moreover, if the thing of which the term defined has been stated to be an affection or disposition, or whatever it may be, be unable to admit it, the definer has made a mistake. For every disposition and every affection is formed [35] naturally in that of which it is an affection or disposition, as knowledge, too, is formed in the soul, being a disposition of soul. Sometimes, however, people make bad mistakes in matters of this sort, e.g. all those who say that 'sleep' is 145ᵇ a 'failure of sensation', or that 'perplexity' is a state of 'equality between contrary reasonings', or that 'pain' is a 'violent disruption of parts that are naturally conjoined'. For sleep is not an attribute of sensation, whereas it ought to be, if it is a failure of sensation. Like-[5] wise, perplexity is not an attribute of opposite reasonings, nor pain of parts naturally conjoined: for then inanimate things will be in pain, since pain will be present in them. Similar in character, too, is the definition of 'health', say, as a 'balance of hot and cold elements': for then health will be necessarily exhibited by the hot and cold elements: for a [10] balance of anything is an attribute inherent in those things of which it is the balance, so that health would be an attribute of them. Moreover, people who define in this way put effect for cause, or cause for effect. For the disruption of parts naturally conjoined is not pain, but only a cause of pain: nor again is a failure of sensation sleep, but the one is the [15] cause of the other: for either we go to sleep because sensation fails, or sensation fails because we go to sleep. Likewise also an equality between contrary reasonings would be generally considered to be a cause of perplexity: for it is when we reflect on both sides of a question and find everything alike to be in keeping with either course that we are per-[20] plexed which of the two we are to do.

Moreover, with regard to all periods of time look and see whether there be any discrepancy between the differentia and the thing defined: e.g. supposing the 'immortal' to be defined as a 'living thing immune at present from destruction'. For a living thing that is immune 'at present' from destruction will be immortal 'at present'. Possibly, indeed, in this case this result does not follow, owing to the ambiguity of the words 'immune at present from destruction': [25] for it may mean either that the thing has not been destroyed at present, or that it cannot be destroyed at present, or that at present it is such that it never can be destroyed. Whenever, then, we say that a living thing is at present immune from destruction, we mean that it is at present a living thing of such a kind as never to be destroyed: and this is equivalent to saying that it is immortal, so that it is not [30] meant that it is immortal only at present. Still, if ever it does happen that what has been rendered according to the definition belongs in the present only or past, whereas what is meant by the word does not so belong, then the two could not be the same. So, then, this commonplace rule ought to be followed, as we have said.

7

You should look and see also whether the term being defined is applied in consideration of something other than the definition rendered. [35] Suppose (e.g.) a definition of 'justice' as the 'ability to distribute what is equal'. This would not be right, for 'just' describes rather the man who chooses, than the man who is able to distribute what is equal: so that justice could 146ᵃ not be an ability to distribute what is equal: for then also the most just man would be the man with the most ability to distribute what is equal.

Moreover, see if the thing admits of degrees, whereas what is rendered according to the definition does not, or, vice versa, what is ren-[5] dered according to the definition admits of degrees while the thing does not. For either both must admit them or else neither, if indeed what is rendered according to the definition is the same as the thing. Moreover, see if, while both of them admit of degrees, they yet do not both become greater together: e.g. suppose sexual love to be the desire for intercourse: for [10] he who is more intensely in love has not a more intense desire for intercourse, so that both do not become intensified at once: they certainly should, however, had they been the same thing.

Moreover, suppose two things to be before

you, see if the term to be defined applies more particularly to the one to which the content of the definition is less applicable. Take, for in- [15] stance, the definition of 'fire' as the 'body that consists of the most rarefied particles'. For 'fire' denotes flame rather than light, but flame is less the body that consists of the most rarefied particles than is light: whereas both ought to be more applicable to the same thing, if they had been the same. Again, see if the one expression applies alike to both the objects before [20] you, while the other does not apply to both alike, but more particularly to one of them.

Moreover, see if he renders the definition relative to two things taken separately: thus, 'the beautiful' is 'what is pleasant to the eyes or to the ears'[1]: or 'the real' is 'what is capable of being acted upon or of acting'. For then the same thing will be both beautiful and not beautiful, and likewise will be both real and not real. For 'pleasant to the ears' will be the same [25] as 'beautiful', so that 'not pleasant to the ears' will be the same as 'not beautiful': for of identical things the opposites, too, are identical, and the opposite of 'beautiful' is 'not beautiful', while of 'pleasant to the ears' the opposite is 'not pleasant to the ears': clearly, then, 'not pleasant to the ears' is the same thing as 'not beautiful'. If, therefore, something be pleasant [30] to the eyes but not to the ears, it will be both beautiful and not beautiful. In like manner we shall show also that the same thing is both real and unreal.

Moreover, of both genera and differentiae and all the other terms rendered in definitions you should frame definitions in lieu of the [35] terms, and then see if there be any discrepancy between them.

8

If the term defined be relative, either in itself or in respect of its genus, see whether the definition fails to mention that to which the term, 146b either in itself or in respect of its genus, is relative, e.g. if he has defined 'knowledge' as an 'incontrovertible conception' or 'wishing' as 'painless conation'. For of everything relative the essence is relative to something else, seeing that the being of every relative term is identical with being in a certain relation to something. [5] He ought, therefore, to have said that knowledge is 'conception of a knowable' and that wishing is 'conation for a good'. Likewise, also, if he has defined 'grammar' as 'knowl-

[1] Cf. Plato, *Hipp. Mai.* 297 E, 299 C.

edge of letters': whereas in the definition there ought to be rendered either the thing to which the term itself is relative, or that, whatever it is, to which its genus is relative. Or see if a relative term has been described not in relation to [10] its end, the end in anything being whatever is best in it or gives its purpose to the rest. Certainly it is what is best or final that should be stated, e.g. that desire is not for the pleasant but for pleasure: for this is our purpose in choosing what is pleasant as well.

Look and see also if that in relation to which he has rendered the term be a process or an activity: for nothing of that kind is an end, [15] for the completion of the activity or process is the end rather than the process or activity itself. Or perhaps this rule is not true in all cases, for almost everybody prefers the present experience of pleasure to its cessation, so that they would count the activity as the end rather than its completion.

[20] Again see in some cases if he has failed to distinguish the quantity or quality or place or other differentiae of an object; e.g. the quality and quantity of the honour the striving for which makes a man ambitious: for all men strive for honour, so that it is not enough to define the ambitious man as him who strives for honour, but the aforesaid differentiae must be added. Likewise, also, in defining the covetous [25] man the quantity of money he aims at, or in the case of the incontinent man the quality of the pleasures, should be stated. For it is not the man who gives way to any sort of pleasure whatever who is called incontinent, but only he who gives way to a certain kind of pleasure. Or again, people sometimes define night as a 'shadow on the earth', or an earthquake as a 'movement of the earth', or a cloud as 'condensation of the air', or a wind as a 'movement of the air'; whereas they ought to specify as well [30] quantity, quality, place, and cause. Likewise, also, in other cases of the kind: for by omitting any differentiae whatever he fails to state the essence of the term. One should always attack deficiency. For a movement of the earth does not constitute an earthquake, nor a movement of the air a wind, irrespective of its [35] manner and the amount involved.

Moreover, in the case of conations, and in any other cases where it applies, see if the word 'apparent' is left out, e.g. 'wishing is a conation 147a after the good', or 'desire is a conation after the pleasant'—instead of saying 'the apparently good', or 'pleasant'. For often those who exhibit the conation do not perceive what is good or pleasant, so that their aim need not be really good or pleasant, but only apparently so. They ought, therefore, to have rendered the [5] definition also accordingly. On the other hand, any one who maintains the existence of Ideas ought to be brought face to face with his Ideas, even though he does render the word in question: for there can be no Idea of anything merely apparent: the general view is that an Idea is always spoken of in relation to an Idea: thus absolute desire is for the absolutely pleasant, and absolute wishing is for the absolutely good; they therefore cannot be for an apparently good or an apparently pleasant: for the ex- [10] istence of an absolutely-apparently-good or pleasant would be an absurdity.

9

Moreover, if the definition be of the state of anything, look at what is in the state, while if it be of what is in the state, look at the state: and likewise also in other cases of the kind. Thus if the pleasant be identical with the bene- [15] ficial, then, too, the man who is pleased is benefited. Speaking generally, in definitions of this sort it happens that what the definer defines is in a sense more than one thing: for in defining knowledge, a man in a sense defines ignorance as well, and likewise also what has knowledge and what lacks it, and what it is to know and to be ignorant. For if the first be [20] made clear, the others become in a certain sense clear as well. We have, then, to be on our guard in all such cases against discrepancy, using the elementary principles drawn from consideration of contraries and of co-ordinates.

Moreover, in the case of relative terms, see if the species is rendered as relative to a species of that to which the genus is rendered as relative, e.g. supposing belief to be relative to some ob- [25] ject of belief, see whether a particular belief is made relative to some particular object of belief: and, if a multiple be relative to a fraction, see whether a particular multiple be made relative to a particular fraction. For if it be not so rendered, clearly a mistake has been made.

See, also, if the opposite of the term has the [30] opposite definition, whether (e.g.) the definition of 'half' is the opposite of that of 'double': for if 'double' is 'that which exceeds another by an equal amount to that other', 'half' is 'that which is exceeded by an amount equal to itself'. In the same way, too, with contraries. For to the contrary term will apply the definition that is contrary in some one of the ways in which contraries are conjoined. Thus (e.g.) if 'useful' = 'productive of good', 'injurious' = 'productive of evil' or 'destructive of good', for [35] one or the other of these is bound to be contrary to the term originally used. Suppose, then, neither of these things to be the contrary of the term originally used, then clearly neither of the definitions rendered later could be the definition of the contrary of the term originally defined: and therefore the definition originally rendered of the original term has not been rightly rendered either. Seeing, moreover, that of contraries, the one is some- [5] times a word forced to denote the privation of the other, as (e.g.) inequality is generally held to be the privation of equality (for 'unequal' merely describes things that are not 'equal'), it is therefore clear that that contrary whose form denotes the privation must of necessity be defined through the other; whereas the other cannot then be defined through the one whose form denotes the privation; for else we should find that each is being interpreted by [10] the other. We must in the case of contrary terms keep an eye on this mistake, e.g. supposing any one were to define equality as the contrary of inequality: for then he is defining it through the term which denotes privation of it. Moreover, a man who so defines is bound to use in his definition the very term he is defining; and this becomes clear, if for the word we substitute its definition. For to say 'inequality' [15] is the same as to say 'privation of equality'. Therefore equality so defined will be 'the contrary of the privation of equality', so that he would have used the very word to be defined. Suppose, however, that neither of the contraries be so formed as to denote privation, but yet the definition of it be rendered in a manner like the above, e.g. suppose 'good' to be defined as 'the contrary of evil', then, since it is clear that 'evil' too will be 'the contrary of good' (for the definition of things that are contrary in this [20] way must be rendered in a like manner), the result again is that he uses the very term being defined: for 'good' is inherent in the definition of 'evil'. If, then, 'good' be the contrary of evil, and evil be nothing other than the 'contrary of good', then 'good' will be the 'contrary of the contrary of good'. Clearly, then, he has [25] used the very word to be defined.

Moreover, see if in rendering a term formed to denote privation, he has failed to render the term of which it is the privation, e.g. the state, or contrary, or whatever it may be whose privation it is: also if he has omitted to add either any term at all in which the privation is naturally formed, or else that in which it is naturally formed primarily, e.g. whether in defin- [30] ing 'ignorance' as a privation he has failed to say that it is the privation of 'knowledge'; or has failed to add in what it is naturally formed, or, though he has added this, has failed to render the thing in which it is primarily formed, placing it (e.g.) in 'man' or in 'the soul', and not in the 'reasoning faculty': for if in any of these respects he fails, he has made a mistake. Likewise, also, if he has failed to say that 'blindness' is the 'privation of sight in an eye': [35] for a proper rendering of its essence must state both of what it is the privation and what it is that is deprived.

Examine further whether he has defined by the expression 'a privation' a term that is not used to denote a privation: thus a mistake of this sort also would be generally thought to be [5] incurred in the case of 'error' by any one who is not using it as a merely negative term. For what is generally thought to be in error is not that which has no knowledge, but rather that which has been deceived, and for this reason we do not talk of inanimate things or of children as 'erring'. 'Error', then, is not used to denote a mere privation of knowledge.

10

Moreover, see whether the like inflexions in the [10] definition apply to the like inflexions of the term; e.g. if 'beneficial' means 'productive of health', does 'beneficially' mean productively of health' and a 'benefactor' a 'producer of health'?

Look too and see whether the definition given will apply to the Idea as well. For in some cases it will not do so; e.g. in the Platonic defi- [15] nition where he adds the word 'mortal' in his definitions of living creatures: for the Idea (e.g. the absolute Man) is not mortal, so that the definition will not fit the Idea. So always wherever the words 'capable of acting on' or 'capable of being acted upon' are added, the definition and the Idea are absolutely bound to [20] be discrepant: for those who assert the existence of Ideas hold that they are incapable of being acted upon, or of motion. In dealing with these people even arguments of this kind are useful.

Further, see if he has rendered a single common definition of terms that are used ambiguously. For terms whose definition corresponding to their common name is one and the same, [25] are *synonymous;* if, then, the definition applies in a like manner to the whole range of the *ambiguous* term, it is not true of any one of the objects described by the term. This is, moreover, what happens to Dionysius' definition of 'life' when stated as 'a movement of a creature sustained by nutriment, congenitally present with it': for this is found in plants as much as in animals, whereas 'life' is generally [30] understood to mean not one kind of thing only, but to be one thing in animals and another in plants. It is possible to hold the view that life is a synonymous term and is always used to describe one thing only, and therefore to render the definition in this way on purpose: or it may quite well happen that a man may see the ambiguous character of the word, and wish to render the definition of the one sense [35] only, and yet fail to see that he has rendered a definition common to both senses instead of one peculiar to the sense he intends. In either case, whichever course he pursues, he is equally at fault. Since ambiguous terms sometimes pass unobserved, it is best in questioning to treat such terms as though they were synonymous (for the definition of the one sense will not apply to the other, so that the answerer will be generally thought not to have defined it correctly, for to a synonymous term the definition should apply in its full range), whereas in answering you should yourself distinguish between the senses. Further, as some [5] answerers call 'ambiguous' what is really synonymous, whenever the definition rendered fails to apply universally, and, vice versa, call synonymous what is really ambiguous supposing their definition applies to both senses of the term, one should secure a preliminary admission on such points, or else prove beforehand that so-and-so is ambiguous or synonymous, as the case may be: for people are more ready to agree when they do not foresee what the conse- [10] quence will be. If, however, no admission has been made, and the man asserts that what is really synonymous is ambiguous because the definition he has rendered will not apply to the second sense as well, see if the definition of this second meaning applies also to the other meanings: for if so, this meaning must clearly be synonymous with those others. Otherwise, there will be more than one definition of those [15] other meanings, for there are applicable to them two distinct definitions in explanation of the term, viz. the one previously rendered and also the later one. Again, if any one were to define a term used in several senses, and, finding that his definition does not apply to them all, were to contend not that the term is ambiguous, but that even the term does not properly apply to all those senses, just because his definition will not do so either, then one may retort to such a man that though in some things [20] one must not use the language of the people, yet in a question of terminology one is bound to employ the received and traditional usage and not to upset matters of that sort.

11

Suppose now that a definition has been rendered of some complex term, take away the definition of one of the elements in the com- [25] plex, and see if also the rest of the definition defines the rest of it: if not, it is clear that neither does the whole definition define the whole complex. Suppose, e.g. that some one has defined a 'finite straight line' as 'the limit of a finite plane, such that its centre is in a line with its extremes'; if now the definition of a [30] 'finite line' be the 'limit of a finite plane', the rest (viz. 'such that its centre is in a line with its extremes') ought to be a definition of 'straight'. But an infinite straight line has neither centre nor extremes and yet is straight so that this remainder does not define the remainder of the term.

Moreover, if the term defined be a compound notion, see if the definition rendered be equimembral with the term defined. A definition is said to be equimembral with the term [35] defined when the number of the elements compounded in the latter is the same as the number of nouns and verbs in the definition. For the exchange in such cases is bound to be merely one of term for term, in the case of some if not of all, seeing that there are no more terms used now than formerly; whereas in a definition terms ought to be rendered by phrases, if possible in every case, or if not, in the majority. For at that rate, simple objects too could be defined by merely calling them by a different name, e.g. 'cloak' instead of 'doublet'.

[5] The mistake is even worse, if actually a less well known term be substituted, e.g. 'pellucid mortal' for 'white man': for it is no definition, and moreover is less intelligible when put in that form.

Look and see also whether, in the exchange of words, the sense fails still to be the same. Take, for instance, the explanation of 'speculative knowledge' as 'speculative conception': [10] for conception is not the same as knowledge—as it certainly ought to be if the whole is to be the same too: for though the word 'speculative' is common to both expressions, yet the remainder is different.

Moreover, see if in replacing one of the terms by something else he has exchanged the [15] genus and not the differentia, as in the example just given: for 'speculative' is a less familiar term than knowledge; for the one is the genus and the other the differentia, and the genus is always the most familiar term of all; so that it is not this, but the differentia, that ought to have been changed, seeing that it is the [20] less familiar. It might be held that this criticism is ridiculous: because there is no reason why the most familiar term should not describe the differentia, and not the genus; in which case, clearly, the term to be altered would also be that denoting the genus and not the differentia. If, however, a man is substituting for a term not merely another term but [25] a phrase, clearly it is of the differentia rather than of the genus that a definition should be rendered, seeing that the object of rendering the definition is to make the subject familiar; for the differentia is less familiar than the genus.

If he has rendered the definition of the dif- [30] ferentia, see whether the definition rendered is common to it and something else as well: e.g. whenever he says that an odd number is a 'number with a middle', further definition is required of how it has a middle: for the word 'number' is common to both expressions, and it is the word 'odd' for which the phrase has been substituted. Now both a line and a body have a middle, yet they are not 'odd'; so [35] that this could not be a definition of 'odd'. If, on the other hand, the phrase 'with a middle' be used in several senses, the sense here intended requires to be defined. So that this will either discredit the definition or prove that it is no definition at all.

12

Again, see if the term of which he renders the definition is a reality, whereas what is contained in the definition is not, e.g. Suppose 'white' to be defined as 'colour mingled with fire': for what is bodiless cannot be mingled with body, so that 'colour' 'mingled with fire' could not exist, whereas 'white' does exist.

Moreover, those who in the case of relative terms do not distinguish to what the object is related, but have described it only so as to in- [5] clude it among too large a number of things, are wrong either wholly or in part; e.g.

suppose some one to have defined 'medicine' as a 'science of Reality'. For if medicine be not a science of anything that is real, the definition is clearly altogether false; while if it be a science of some real thing, but not of another, it is partly false; for it ought to hold of all reality, if it is said to be of Reality essentially and not [10] accidentally: as is the case with other relative terms: for every object of knowledge is a term relative to knowledge: likewise, also, with other relative terms, inasmuch as all such are convertible. Moreover, if the right way to render account of a thing be to render it as it is not in itself but accidentally, then each and [15] every relative term would be used in relation not to one thing but to a number of things. For there is no reason why the same thing should not be both real and white and good, so that it would be a correct rendering to render the object in relation to any one whatsoever of these, if to render what it is accidentally be a correct way to render it. It is, moreover, impossible that a definition of this sort should be peculiar to the term rendered: for not only [20] medicine, but the majority of the other sciences too, have for their object some real thing, so that each will be a science of reality. Clearly, then, such a definition does not define any science at all; for a definition ought to be peculiar to its own term, not general.

Sometimes, again, people define not the [25] thing but only the thing in a good or perfect condition. Such is the definition of a rhetorician as 'one who can always see what will persuade in the given circumstances, and omit nothing'; or of a thief, as 'one who pilfers in secret': for clearly, if they each do this, then the one will be a good rhetorician, and the other a good thief: whereas it is not the actual pilfering [30] in secret, but the wish to do it, that constitutes the thief.

Again, see if he has rendered what is desirable for its own sake as desirable for what it produces or does, or as in any way desirable because of something else, e.g. by saying that justice is 'what preserves the laws' or that wisdom is 'what produces happiness'; for what produces or preserves something else is one of the things desirable for something else. It [35] might be said that it is possible for what is desirable in itself to be desirable for something else as well: but still to define what is desirable in itself in such a way is none the less wrong: for the essence contains *par excellence* what is best in anything, and it is better for a thing to be desirable in itself than to be desirable for something else, so that this is rather what the definition too ought to have indicated.

13

150ª See also whether in defining anything a man has defined it as an 'A and B', or as a 'product of A and B' or as an 'A+B'. If he defines it as 'A and B', the definition will be true of both and yet of neither of them; suppose, e.g. justice to be defined as 'temperance and [5] courage.' For if of two persons each has one of the two only, both and yet neither will be just: for both together have justice, and yet each singly fails to have it. Even if the situation here described does not so far appear very absurd because of the occurrence of this kind of thing in other cases also (for it is quite possible for two men to have a mina between them, though neither of them has it by himself), yet [10] at least that they should have contrary attributes surely seems quite absurd; and yet this will follow if the one be temperate and yet a coward, and the other, though brave, be a profligate; for then both will exhibit both justice and injustice: for if justice be temperance and bravery, then injustice will be cowardice and [15] profligacy. In general, too, all the ways of showing that the whole is not the same as the sum of its parts are useful in meeting the type just described; for a man who defines in this way seems to assert that the parts are the same as the whole. The arguments are particularly appropriate in cases where the process of putting the parts together is obvious, as in a house [20] and other things of that sort: for there, clearly, you may have the parts and yet not have the whole, so that parts and whole cannot be the same.

If, however, he has said that the term being defined is not 'A and B' but the 'product of A and B', look and see in the first place if A and B cannot in the nature of things have a single product: for some things are so related to one [25] another that nothing can come of them, e.g. a line and a number. Moreover, see if the term that has been defined is in the nature of things found primarily in some single subject, whereas the things which he has said produce it are not found primarily in any single subject, but each in a separate one. If so, clearly that term could not be the product of these things: for the whole is bound to be in the same things wherein its parts are, so that the whole will [30] then be found primarily not in one subject only, but in a number of them. If, on the other hand, both parts and whole are found primarily in some single subject, see if that medium is not the same, but one thing in the case of the whole and another in that of the parts. Again, see whether the parts perish together with the whole: for it ought to happen, vice versa, that the whole perishes when the [35] parts perish; when the whole perishes, there is no necessity that the parts should perish too. Or again, see if the whole be good or evil, and the parts neither, or, vice versa, if the parts be good or evil and the whole neither. For it is impossible either for a neutral thing to 150^b produce something good or bad, or for things good or bad to produce a neutral thing. Or again, see if the one thing is more distinctly good than the other is evil, and yet the product be no more good than evil, e.g. suppose shamelessness be defined as 'the product of courage and false opinion': here the goodness of cour[5]age exceeds the evil of false opinion; accordingly the product of these ought to have corresponded to this excess, and to be either good without qualification, or at least more good than evil. Or it may be that this does not necessarily follow, unless each be in itself good or bad; for many things that are productive are not good in themselves, but only in combination; or, *per contra*, they are good taken singly, [10] and bad or neutral in combination. What has just been said is most clearly illustrated in the case of things that make for health or sickness; for some drugs are such that each taken alone is good, but if they are both administered in a mixture, bad.

Again, see whether the whole, as produced [15] from a better and worse, fails to be worse than the better and better than the worse element. This again, however, need not necessarily be the case, unless the elements compounded be in themselves good; if they are not, the whole may very well not be good, as in the cases just instanced.

Moreover, see if the whole be synonymous with one of the elements: for it ought not to be, any more than in the case of syllables: for the [20] syllable is not synonymous with any of the letters of which it is made up.

Moreover, see if he has failed to state the manner of their composition: for the mere mention of its elements is not enough to make the thing intelligible. For the essence of any compound thing is not merely that it is a product of so-and-so, but that it is a product of them com[25]pounded in such and such a way, just as in the case of a house: for here the materials do not make a house irrespective of the way they are put together.

If a man has defined an object as 'A+B', the first thing to be said is that 'A+B' means the same either as 'A and B', or as the 'product of A and B.' for 'honey+water' means either the honey and the water, or the 'drink made of [30] honey and water'. If, then, he admits that 'A+B' is the same as either of these two things, the same criticisms will apply as have already been given for meeting each of them. Moreover, distinguish between the different senses in which one thing may be said to be '+' another, and see if there is none of them in which A could be said to exist '+ B.' Thus e.g. sup[35]posing the expression to mean that they exist either in some identical thing capable of containing them (as e.g. justice and courage are found in the soul), or else in the same place or in the same time, and if this be in no way true of the A and B in question, clearly the definition rendered could not hold of anything, as there is no possible way in which A can exist 151^a '+B'. If, however, among the various senses above distinguished, it be true that A and B are each found in the same time as the other, look and see if possibly the two are not used in the same relation. Thus e.g. suppose courage to have been defined as 'daring with right reasoning': here it is possible that the person exhibits daring in robbery, and right rea[5]soning in regard to the means of health: but he may have 'the former quality+the latter' at the same time, and not as yet be courageous! Moreover, even though both be used in the same relation as well, e.g. in relation to medical treatment (for a man may exhibit both daring and right reasoning in respect of medical treatment), still, none the less, not even this combination of 'the one+the other' makes him 'courageous'. For the two must not relate to any [10] casual object that is the same, any more than each to a different object; rather, they must relate to the function of courage, e.g. meeting the perils of war, or whatever is more properly speaking its function than this.

Some definitions rendered in this form fail to come under the aforesaid division at all, e.g. [15] a definition of anger as 'pain with a consciousness of being slighted'. For what this means to say is that it is because of a consciousness of this sort that the pain occurs; but to occur 'because of' a thing is not the same as to occur '+ a thing' in any of its aforesaid senses.

14

[20] Again, if he have described the whole compounded as the 'composition' of these things (e.g. 'a living creature' as a 'composition of soul and body'), first of all see whether he has omitted to state the kind of composition, as (e.g.) in a definition of 'flesh' or 'bone' as the 'composition of fire, earth, and air'. For it is not enough to say it is a composition, but you should also go on to define the kind of com- [25] position: for these things do not form flesh irrespective of the manner of their composition, but when compounded in one way they form flesh, when in another, bone. It appears, moreover, that neither of the aforesaid substances is the same as a 'composition' at all: for a composition always has a decomposition as its contrary, whereas neither of the aforesaid has any contrary. Moreover, if it is equally probable that every compound is a composition or [30] else that none is, and every kind of living creature, though a compound, is never a composition, then no other compound could be a composition either.

Again, if in the nature of a thing two contraries are equally liable to occur, and the thing has been defined through the one, clearly it has not been defined; else there will be more than one definition of the same thing; for how is it [35] any more a definition to define it through this one than through the other, seeing that both alike are naturally liable to occur in it? 151ᵇ Such is the definition of the soul, if defined as a substance capable of receiving knowledge: for it has a like capacity for receiving ignorance.

Also, even when one cannot attack the definition as a whole for lack of acquaintance with the whole, one should attack some part of it, if [5] one knows that part and sees it to be incorrectly rendered: for if the part be demolished, so too is the whole definition. Where, again, a definition is obscure, one should first of all correct and reshape it in order to make some part of it clear and get a handle for attack, and then proceed to examine it. For the answerer is [10] bound either to accept the sense as taken by the questioner, or else himself to explain clearly whatever it is that his definition means. Moreover, just as in the assemblies the ordinary practice is to move an emendation of the existing law and, if the emendation is better, they repeal the existing law, so one ought to do in the case of definitions as well: one ought oneself to propose a second definition: for if it [15] is seen to be better, and more indicative of the object defined, clearly the definition already laid down will have been demolished, on the principle that there cannot be more than one definition of the same thing.

In combating definitions it is always one of the chief elementary principles to take by oneself a happy shot at a definition of the object before one, or to adopt some correctly expressed [20] definition. For one is bound, with the model (as it were) before one's eyes, to discern both any shortcoming in any features that the definition ought to have, and also any superfluous addition, so that one is better supplied with lines of attack.

As to definitions, then, let so much suffice.

BOOK VII

1

WHETHER two things are 'the same' or 'different', in the most literal of the meanings ascribed to 'sameness' (and we said[1] that 'the same' applies in the most literal sense to what [30] is numerically one), may be examined in the light of their inflexions and coordinates and opposites. For if justice be the same as courage, then too the just man is the same as the brave man, and 'justly' is the same as 'bravely'. Likewise, too, in the case of their opposites: for if two things be the same, their opposites also will [35] be the same, in any of the recognized forms of opposition. For it is the same thing to take the opposite of the one or that of the other, seeing that they are the same. Again it may be examined in the light of those things which 152ᵃ tend to produce or to destroy the things in question of their formation and destruction, and in general of any thing that is related in like manner to each. For where things are absolutely the same, their formations and destructions also are the same, and so are the things that tend to produce or to destroy them. [5] Look and see also, in a case where one of two things is said to be something or other in a superlative degree, if the other of these alleged identical things can also be described by a

---
[1] 103ᵃ 23.

superlative in the same respect. Thus Xenocrates argues that the happy life and the good life are the same, seeing that of all forms of life the good life is the most desirable and so also is the happy life: for 'the most desirable' and 'the greatest' apply but to one thing.[1] Likewise [10] also in other cases of the kind. Each, however, of the two things termed 'greatest' or 'most desirable' must be numerically one: otherwise no proof will have been given that they are the same; for it does not follow because Peloponnesians and Spartans are the bravest of the Greeks, that Peloponnesians are the same as Spartans, seeing that 'Peloponnesian' is not [15] any one person nor yet 'Spartan'; it only follows that the one must be included under the other as 'Spartans' are under 'Peloponnesians': for otherwise, if the one class be not included under the other, each will be better than the other. For then the Peloponnesians are [20] bound to be better than the Spartans, seeing that the one class is not included under the other; for they are better than anybody else. Likewise also the Spartans must perforce be better than the Peloponnesians; for they too are better than anybody else; each then is better [25] than the other! Clearly therefore what is styled 'best' and 'greatest' must be a single thing, if it is to be proved to be 'the same' as another. This also is why Xenocrates fails to prove his case: for the happy life is not numerically single, nor yet the good life, so that it does not follow that, because they are both the most desirable, they are therefore the same, but only [30] that the one falls under the other.

Again, look and see if, supposing the one to be the same as something, the other also is the same as it: for if they be not both the same as the same thing, clearly neither are they the same as one another.

Moreover, examine them in the light of their accidents or of the things of which they are accidents: for any accident belonging to the [35] one must belong also to the other, and if the one belong to anything as an accident, so must the other also. If in any of these respects there is a discrepancy, clearly they are not the same.

See further whether, instead of both being found in one class of predicates, the one signifies a quality and the other a quantity or relation. Again, see if the genus of each be not the 152[b] same, the one being 'good' and the other 'evil', or the one being 'virtue' and the other

[1] Fr. 82, Heinze.

'knowledge': or see if, though the genus is the same, the differentiae predicted of either be not the same, the one (e.g.) being distinguished as a 'speculative' science, the other as a 'practical' [5] science. Likewise also in other cases.

Moreover, from the point of view of 'degrees', see if the one admits an increase of degree but not the other, or if though both admit it, they do not admit it at the same time; just as it is not the case that a man desires intercourse more intensely, the more intensely he is in love, so that love and the desire for intercourse are not the same.

[10] Moreover, examine them by means of an addition, and see whether the addition of each to the same thing fails to make the same whole; or if the subtraction of the same thing from each leaves a different remainder. Suppose (e.g.) that he has declared 'double a half' to be the same as 'a multiple of a half': then, subtracting the words 'a half' from each, the remainders ought to have signified the same [15] thing: but they do not; for 'double' and 'a multiple of' do not signify the same thing.

Inquire also not only if some impossible consequence results directly from the statement made, that A and B are the same, but also whether it is possible for a supposition to bring it about; as happens to those who assert that [20] 'empty' is the same as 'full of air': for clearly if the air be exhausted, the vessel will not be less but more empty, though it will no longer be full of air. So that by a supposition, which may be true or may be false (it makes no difference which), the one character is annulled and not the other, showing that they are not the same.

[25] Speaking generally, one ought to be on the look-out for any discrepancy anywhere in any sort of predicate of each term, and in the things of which they are predicated. For all that is predicated of the one should be predicated also of the other, and of whatever the one is a predicate, the other should be a predicate of it as well.

[30] Moreover, as 'sameness' is a term used in many senses, see whether things that are the same in one way are the same also in a different way. For there is either no necessity or even no possibility that things that are the same specifically or generically should be numerically the same, and it is with the question whether they are or are not the same in that sense that we are concerned.

Moreover, see whether the one can exist

[35] without the other; for, if so, they could not be the same.

2

Such is the number of the commonplace rules that relate to 'sameness'. It is clear from what has been said that all the destructive commonplaces relating to sameness are useful also in questions of definition, as was said before:[1] for if what is signified by the term and by the expression be not the same, clearly the 153ª expression rendered could not be a definition. None of the constructive commonplaces, on the other hand, helps in the matter of definition; for it is not enough to show the sameness of content between the expression and the term, in order to establish that the former is a definition, but a definition must have also all [5] the other characters already announced.[2]

3

This then is the way, and these the arguments, whereby the attempt to demolish a definition should always be made. If, on the other hand, we desire to establish one, the first thing to observe is that few if any who engage in discussion arrive at a definition by reasoning: they always assume something of the kind as [10] their starting point,—both in geometry and in arithmetic and the other studies of that kind. In the second place, to say accurately what a definition is, and how it should be given, belongs to another inquiry.[3] At present it concerns us only so far as is required for our present purpose, and accordingly we need only make the bare statement that to reason to a [15] thing's definition and essence is quite possible. For if a definition is an expression signifying the essence of the thing and the predicates contained therein ought also to be the only ones which are predicated of the thing in the category of essence; and genera and differentiae are so predicated in that category: it is obvious that if one were to get an admission that so and so are the only attributes predicated [20] in that category, the expression containing so and so would of necessity be a definition; for it is impossible that anything else should be a definition, seeing that there is not anything else predicated of the thing in the category of essence.

That a definition may thus be reached by a process of reasoning is obvious. The means whereby it should be established have been more precisely defined elsewhere,[4] but for the [25] purposes of the inquiry now before us the same commonplace rules serve. For we have to examine into the contraries and other opposites of the thing, surveying the expressions used both as wholes and in detail: for if the opposite definition defines that opposite term, the definition given must of necessity be that of the term before us. Seeing, however, that contra- [30] ries may be conjoined in more than one way, we have to select from those contraries the one whose contrary definition seems most obvious. The expressions, then, have to be examined each as a whole in the way we have said, and also in detail as follows. First of all, see that the genus rendered is correctly rendered; for if the contrary thing be found in the contrary genus to that stated in the definition, and the thing before you is not in that same genus, then [35] it would clearly be in the contrary genus: for contraries must of necessity be either in the same genus or in contrary genera. The differentiae, too, that are predicated of contraries we expect to be contrary, e.g. those of white and black, for the one tends to pierce the vision, 153ᵇ while the other tends to compress it. So that if contrary differentiae to those in the definition are predicated of the contrary term, then those rendered in the definition would be predicated of the term before us. Seeing, then, that both the genus and the differentiae have been rightly rendered, clearly the expression given must be the right definition. It might be replied that there is no necessity why contrary differ- [5] entiae should be predicated of contraries, unless the contraries be found within the same genus: of things whose genera are themselves contraries it may very well be that the same differentia is used of both, e.g. of justice and injustice; for the one is a virtue and the other a vice of the soul: 'of the soul', therefore, is the [10] differentia in both cases, seeing that the body as well has its virtue and vice. But this much at least is true, that the differentiae of contraries are either contrary or else the same. If, then, the contrary differentia to that given be predicated of the contrary term and not of the one in hand, clearly the differentia stated must be predicated of the latter. Speaking generally, seeing that the definition consists of ge- [15] nus and differentiae, if the definition of the contrary term be apparent, the definition of the term before you will be apparent also: for since its contrary is found either in the same genus or in the contrary genus, and like-

---

[1] 102ª 11.   [2] 139ª 27-35.
[3] *Posterior Analytics*, II. 3-13.
[4] *Ibid.*, II. 13.

wise also the differentiae predicated of opposites are either contrary to, or the same as, each other, clearly of the term before you there will be predicated either the same genus as of its [20] contrary, while, of its differentiae, either all are contrary to those of its contrary, or at least some of them are so while the rest remain the same; or, vice versa, the differentiae will be the same and the genera contrary; or both genera and differentiae will be contrary. And that is all; for that both should be the same is not possible; else contraries will have the same definition.

[25] Moreover, look at it from the point of view of its inflexions and coordinates. For genera and definitions are bound to correspond in either case. Thus if forgetfulness be the loss of knowledge, to forget is to lose knowledge, and to have forgotten is to have lost knowledge. If, then, any one whatever of these is agreed to, [30] the others must of necessity be agreed to as well. Likewise, also, if destruction is the decomposition of the thing's essence, then to be destroyed is to have its essence decomposed, and 'destructively' means 'in such a way as to decompose its essence'; if again 'destructive' means 'apt to decompose something's essence', then also 'destruction' means 'the decomposition of its essence'. Likewise also with the rest: get an admission of any one of them whatever, [35] and all the rest are admitted too.

Moreover, look at it from the point of view of things that stand in relations that are like each other. For if 'healthy' means 'productive of health', 'vigorous' too will mean 'productive of vigour', and 'useful' will mean 'productive of good.' For each of these things is related in like manner to its own peculiar end, so that if one of them is defined as 'productive of' that end, this will also be the definition of each of the rest as well.

Moreover, look at it from the point of view of greater and like degrees, in all the ways in which it is possible to establish a result by com- [5] paring two and two together. Thus if A defines α better than B defines β, and B is a definition of β, so too is A of α. Further, if A's claim to define α is like B's to define β, and B defines β, then A too defines α. This examination from the point of view of greater degrees is of no use when a single definition is com- [10] pared with two things, or two definitions with one thing; for there cannot possibly be one definition of two things or two of the same thing.

4

The most handy of all the commonplace arguments are those just mentioned and those from co-ordinates and inflexions, and these therefore are those which it is most important to master and to have ready to hand: for they are the most useful on the greatest number of occasions. Of the rest, too, the most important [15] are those of most general application: for these are the most effective, e.g. that you should examine the individual cases, and then look to see in the case of their various species whether the definition applies. For the species is synonymous with its individuals. This sort of inquiry is of service against those who assume the existence of Ideas, as has been said before.[1] [20] Moreover see if a man has used a term metaphorically, or predicated it of itself as though it were something different. So too if any other of the commonplace rules is of general application and effective, it should be employed.

5

That it is more difficult to establish than to overthrow a definition, is obvious from considerations presently to be urged. For to see for [25] oneself, and to secure from those whom one is questioning, an admission of premisses of this sort is no simple matter, e.g. that of the elements of the definition rendered the one is genus and the other differentia, and that only the genus and differentiae are predicated in the category of essence. Yet without these premisses it is impossible to reason to a definition; for if any other things as well are predicated of [30] the thing in the category of essence, there is no telling whether the formula stated or some other one is its definition, for a definition is an expression indicating the essence of a thing. The point is clear also from the following: It is easier to draw one conclusion than many. Now in demolishing a definition it is sufficient to argue against one point only (for if we have overthrown any single point whatsoever, we shall have demolished the defini- [35] tion); whereas in establishing a definition, one is bound to bring people to the view that everything contained in the definition is attributable. Moreover, in establishing a case, the reasoning brought forward must be universal: for the definition put forward must be predicated of everything of which the term is predicated, and must moreover be con-

[1] 148a 14

vertible, if the definition rendered is to be peculiar to the subject. In overthrowing a view, on the other hand, there is no longer any necessity to show one's point universally: for it is enough to show that the formula is untrue of any one of the things embraced under the term.

[5] Further, even supposing it should be necessary to overthrow something by a universal proposition, not even so is there any need to prove the converse of the proposition in the process of overthrowing the definition. For merely to show that the definition fails to be predicated of every one of the things of which the term is predicated, is enough to overthrow it universally: and there is no need to prove the converse of this in order to show that the term [10] is predicated of things of which the expression is not predicated. Moreover, even if it applies to everything embraced under the term, but not to it alone, the definition is thereby demolished.

The case stands likewise in regard to the property and genus of a term also. For in both cases it is easier to overthrow than to establish. [15] As regards the property this is clear from what has been said: for as a rule the property is rendered in a complex phrase, so that to overthrow it, it is only necessary to demolish one of the terms used, whereas to establish it it is necessary to reason to them all. Then, too, nearly all the other rules that apply to the definition will apply also to the property of a thing. For [20] in establishing a property one has to show that it is true of everything included under the term in question, whereas to overthrow one it is enough to show in a single case only that it fails to belong: further, even if it belongs to everything falling under the term, but not to that only, it is overthrown in this case as well, as was explained in the case of the definition.[1] In regard to the genus, it is clear that you are bound to establish it in one way only, viz. by [25] showing that it belongs in every case, while of overthrowing it there are two ways: for if it has been shown that it belongs either never or not in a certain case, the original statement has been demolished. Moreover, in establishing a genus it is not enough to show that it belongs, but also that it belongs as genus has to be shown; whereas in overthrowing it, it is enough to show its failure to belong either in some particular case or in every case. It appears, [30] in fact, as though, just as in other things to destroy is easier than to create, so in these

[1] l. 10.

matters too to overthrow is easier than to establish.

In the case of an accidental attribute the universal proposition is easier to overthrow than [35] to establish; for to establish it, one has to show that it belongs in every case, whereas to overthrow it, it is enough to show that it does not belong in one single case. The particular proposition is, on the contrary, easier to establish than to overthrow: for to establish it, it is enough to show that it belongs in a particular instance, whereas to overthrow it, it has to be shown that it never belongs at all.

It is clear also that the easiest thing of all is to overthrow a definition. For on account of the number of statements involved we are presented in the definition with the greatest number of points for attack, and the more plentiful [5] the material, the quicker an argument comes: for there is more likelihood of a mistake occurring in a large than in a small number of things. Moreover, the other rules too may be used as means for attacking a definition: for if either the formula be not peculiar, or the genus rendered be the wrong one, or something included in the formula fail to belong, the definition is thereby demolished. On the [10] other hand, against the others we cannot bring all of the arguments drawn from definitions, nor yet of the rest: for only those relating to accidental attributes apply generally to all the aforesaid kinds of attribute. For while each of the aforesaid kinds of attribute must belong to the thing in question, yet the genus may very well not belong as a property without as yet being thereby demolished. Likewise also the property need not belong as [15] a genus, nor the accident as a genus or property, so long as they do belong. So that it is impossible to use one set as a basis of attack upon the other except in the case of definition. Clearly, then, it is the easiest of all things to demolish a definition, while to establish one is the hardest. For there one both has to establish all those other points by reasoning (i.e. that [20] the attributes stated belong, and that the genus rendered is the true genus, and that the formula is peculiar to the term), and moreover, besides this, that the formula indicates the essence of the thing; and this has to be done correctly.

Of the rest, the property is most nearly of this kind: for it is easier to demolish, because as a rule it contains several terms; while it is the [25] hardest to establish, both because of the number of things that people must be brought to accept, and, besides this, because it belongs to its subject alone and is predicated convertibly with its subject.

The easiest thing of all to establish is an accidental predicate: for in other cases one has to show not only that the predicate belongs, but also that it belongs in such and such a par-[30] ticular way: whereas in the case of the accident it is enough to show merely that it belongs. On the other hand, an accidental predicate is the hardest thing to overthrow, because it affords the least material: for in stating an accident a man does not add how the predicate belongs; and accordingly, while in other cases it is possible to demolish what is said in two ways, by showing either that the predicate does not belong, or that it does not belong in the [35] particular way stated, in the case of an accidental predicate the only way to demolish it is to show that it does not belong at all.

The commonplace arguments through which we shall be well supplied with lines of argument with regard to our several problems have now been enumerated at about sufficient length.

BOOK VIII

I

155ᵇ NEXT there fall to be discussed the problems of arrangement and method in putting questions. Any one who intends to frame questions must, first of all, select the ground from [5] which he should make his attack; secondly, he must frame them and arrange them one by one to himself; thirdly and lastly, he must proceed actually to put them to the other party. Now so far as the selection of his ground is concerned the problem is one alike for the philosopher and the dialectician; but how to go on to arrange his points and frame his questions concerns the dialectician only: for in every problem of that kind a reference [10] to another party is involved. Not so with the philosopher, and the man who is investigating by himself: the premisses of his reasoning, although true and familiar, may be refused by the answerer because they lie too near the original statement and so he foresees what will follow if he grants them: but for this the philosopher does not care. Nay, he may possibly be even anxious to secure axioms as familiar and as near to the question in hand as pos-[15] sible: for these are the bases on which scientific reasonings are built up.

The sources from which one's commonplace arguments should be drawn have already been described:[1] we have now to discuss the arrangement and formation of questions and first to distinguish the premisses, other than the necessary premisses, which have to be adopted. [20] By necessary premisses are meant those through which the actual reasoning is constructed. Those which are secured other than these are of four kinds; they serve either inductively to secure the universal premiss being granted, or to lend weight to the argument, or to conceal the conclusion, or to render the argument more clear. Beside these there is no other [25] premiss which need be secured: these are the ones whereby you should try to multiply and formulate your questions. Those which are used to conceal the conclusion serve a controversial purpose only; but inasmuch as an undertaking of this sort is always conducted against another person, we are obliged to employ them as well.

The necessary premisses through which the [30] reasoning is effected, ought not to be propounded directly in so many words. Rather one should soar as far aloof from them as possible. Thus if one desires to secure an admission that the knowledge of contraries is one, one should ask him to admit it not of contraries, but of opposites: for, if he grants this, one will then argue that the knowledge of contraries is also the same, seeing that contraries are opposites; if he does not, one should secure the admission by induction, by formulating a proposition to that effect in the case of some particular pair [35] of contraries. For one must secure the necessary premisses either by reasoning or by induction, or else partly by one and partly by the other, although any propositions which are too obvious to be denied may be formulated in so many words. This is because the coming 156ᵃ conclusion is less easily discerned at the greater distance and in the process of induction, while at the same time, even if one cannot reach the required premisses in this way, it is still open to one to formulate them in so many words. The premisses, other than these, that were mentioned above,[2] must be secured with a view to the latter. The way to employ them respectively is as follows: Induction should [5] proceed from individual cases to the universal and from the known to the unknown;

[1] *Topics*, II-VII.　　[2] 155ᵇ 20-28.

and the objects of perception are better known, to most people if not invariably. Concealment of one's plan is obtained by securing through prosyllogisms the premisses through which the proof of the original proposition is going to be constructed—and as many of them as possible. This is likely to be effected by making syllogisms to prove not only the necessary prem- [10] isses but also some of those which are required to establish them. Moreover, do not state the conclusions of these premisses but draw them later one after another; for this is likely to keep the answerer at the greatest possible distance from the original proposition. Speaking generally, a man who desires to get information by a concealed method should so put his questions that when he has put his [15] whole argument and has stated the conclusion, people still ask 'Well, but why is that?' This result will be secured best of all by the method above described: for if one states only the final conclusion, it is unclear how it comes about; for the answerer does not foresee on what grounds it is based, because the previous syllogisms have not been made articulate to [20] him: while the final syllogism, showing the conclusion, is likely to be kept least articulate if we lay down not the secured propositions on which it is based, but only the grounds on which we reason to them.

It is a useful rule, too, not to secure the admissions claimed as the bases of the syllogisms in their proper order, but alternately those that conduce to one conclusion and those that con- [25] duce to another; for, if those which go together are set side by side, the conclusion that will result from them is more obvious in advance.

One should also, wherever possible, secure the universal premiss by a definition relating not to the precise terms themselves but to their co-ordinates; for people deceive themselves, whenever the definition is taken in regard to a [30] co-ordinate, into thinking that they are not making the admission universally. An instance would be, supposing one had to secure the admission that the angry man desires vengeance on account of an apparent slight, and were to secure this, that 'anger' is a desire for vengeance on account of an apparent slight: for, clearly, if this were secured, we should have universally what we intend. If, on the other hand, people formulate propositions relating [35] to the actual terms themselves, they often find that the answerer refuses to grant them because on the actual term itself he is readier with his objection, e.g. that the 'angry man' does not desire vengeance, because we become angry with our parents, but we do not desire vengeance on them. Very likely the objection is not valid; for upon some people it is venge- 156ᵇ ance enough to cause them pain and make them sorry; but still it gives a certain plausibility and air of reasonableness to the denial of the proposition. In the case, however, of the definition of 'anger' it is not so easy to find an objection.

Moreover, formulate your proposition as though you did so not for its own sake, but in order to get at something else: for people are [5] shy of granting what an opponent's case really requires. Speaking generally, a questioner should leave it as far as possible doubtful whether he wishes to secure an admission of his proposition or of its opposite: for if it be uncertain what their opponent's argument requires, people are more ready to say what they themselves think.

[10] Moreover, try to secure admissions by means of likeness: for such admissions are plausible, and the universal involved is less patent; e.g. make the other person admit that as knowledge and ignorance of contraries is the same, so too perception of contraries is the same; or vice versa, that since the perception is the same, so is the knowledge also. This argument resembles induction, but is not the same [15] thing; for in induction it is the universal whose admission is secured from the particulars, whereas in arguments from likeness, what is secured is not the universal under which all the like cases fall.

It is a good rule also, occasionally to bring an objection against oneself: for answerers are put off their guard against those who appear to be [20] arguing impartially. It is useful too, to add that 'So and so is generally held or commonly said'; for people are shy of upsetting the received opinion unless they have some positive objection to urge: and at the same time they are cautious about upsetting such things because they themselves too find them useful. Moreover, do not be insistent, even though you really require the point: for insistence always [25] arouses the more opposition. Further, formulate your premiss as though it were a mere illustration: for people admit the more readily a proposition made to serve some other purpose, and not required on its own account. Moreover, do not formulate the very proposition you need to secure, but rather something from which that necessarily follows: for people are more willing to admit the latter, because it is not so clear from this what the result will be, and if the one has been secured, the other has [30] been secured also. Again, one should put last the point which one most wishes to have conceded; for people are specially inclined to deny the first questions put to them, because most people in asking questions put first the points which they are most eager to secure. On the other hand, in dealing with some people propositions of this sort should be put forward first: for ill-tempered men admit most readily [35] what comes first, unless the conclusion that will result actually stares them in the face, while at the close of an argument they show their ill-temper. Likewise also with those who consider themselves smart at answering: for when they have admitted most of what you want they finally talk clap-trap to the effect that the conclusion does not follow from their admissions: yet they say 'Yes' readily, confident in their own character, and imagining that they 157ᵃ cannot suffer any reverse. Moreover, it is well to expand the argument and insert things that it does not require at all, as do those who draw false geometrical figures: for in the multitude of details the whereabouts of the fallacy is obscured. For this reason also a questioner sometimes evades observation as he adds in a [5] corner what, if he formulated it by itself, would not be granted.

For concealment, then, the rules which should be followed are the above. Ornament is attained by induction and distinction of things closely akin. What sort of process induction is is obvious: as for distinction, an instance of the kind of thing meant is the distinction of one form of knowledge as better than another by being either more accurate, or concerned with [10] better objects; or the distinction of sciences into speculative, practical, and productive. For everything of this kind lends additional ornament to the argument, though there is no necessity to say them, so far as the conclusion goes.

For clearness, examples and comparisons [15] should be adduced, and let the illustrations be relevant and drawn from things that we know, as in Homer and not as in Choerilus; for then the proposition is likely to become clearer.

2

In dialectics, syllogism should be employed in [20] reasoning against dialecticians rather than against the crowd: induction, on the other hand, is most useful against the crowd. This point has been treated previously as well.[1] In induction, it is possible in some cases to ask the question in its universal form, but in others this is not easy, because there is no established general term that covers all the resemblances: in this case, when people need to secure the universal, they use the phrase 'in all cases of this sort'. But it is one of the very hardest things [25] to distinguish which of the things adduced are 'of this sort', and which are not: and in this connexion people often throw dust in each others' eyes in their discussion, the one party asserting the likeness of things that are not alike, and the other disputing the likeness of things that are. One ought, therefore, to try [30] oneself to coin a word to cover all things of the given sort, so as to leave no opportunity either to the answerer to dispute, and say that the thing advanced does not answer to a like description, or to the questioner to suggest falsely that it does answer to a like description, for many things appear to answer to like descriptions that do not really do so.

If one has made an induction on the strength of several cases and yet the answerer refuses to grant the universal proposition, then it is fair [35] to demand his objection. But until one has oneself stated in what cases it is so, it is not fair to demand that he shall say in what cases it is not so: for one should make the induction first, and then demand the objection. One ought, moreover, to claim that the objections should not be brought in reference to the actual subject of the proposition, unless that subject happen to be the one and only thing of the kind, as for instance two is the one prime 157ᵇ number among the even numbers: for, unless he can say that this subject is unique of its kind, the objector ought to make his objection in regard to some other. People sometimes object to a universal proposition, and bring their objection not in regard to the thing itself, but in regard to some homonym of it: thus they [5] argue that a man can very well have a colour or a foot or a hand other than his own, for a painter may have a colour that is not his own, and a cook may have a foot that is not his own. To meet them, therefore, you should draw the distinction before putting your question in such cases: for so long as the ambiguity remains undetected, so long will the objection to the proposition be deemed valid. If, however, he checks the series of questions by an objection in regard not to some homonym, but to the ac-

[1] 105ᵃ 16.

tual thing asserted, the questioner should withdraw the point objected to, and form the remainder into a universal proposition, until he secures what he requires; e.g. in the case of forgetfulness and having forgotten: for people refuse to admit that the man who has lost his knowledge of a thing has forgotten it, because if the thing alters, he has lost knowledge of it, but he has not forgotten it. Accordingly the thing to do is to withdraw the part objected to, and assert the remainder, e.g. that if a person have lost knowledge of a thing while it still remains, he then has forgotten it. One should similarly treat those who object to the statement that 'the greater the good, the greater the evil that is its opposite': for they allege that health, which is a less good thing than vigour, has a greater evil as its opposite: for disease is a greater evil than debility. In this case too, therefore, we have to withdraw the point objected to; for when it has been withdrawn, the man is more likely to admit the proposition, e.g. that 'the greater good has the greater evil as its opposite, unless the one good involves the other as well', as vigour involves health. This should be done not only when he formulates an objection, but also if, without so doing, he refuses to admit the point because he foresees something of the kind: for if the point objected to be withdrawn, he will be forced to admit the proposition because he cannot foresee in the rest of it any case where it does not hold true: if he refuse to admit it, then when asked for an objection he certainly will be unable to render one. Propositions that are partly false and partly true are of this type: for in the case of these it is possible by withdrawing a part to leave the rest true. If, however, you formulate the proposition on the strength of many cases and he has no objection to bring, you may claim that he shall admit it: for a premiss is valid in dialectics which thus holds in several instances and to which no objection is forthcoming.

Whenever it is possible to reason to the same conclusion either through or without a *reductio per impossibile,* if one is demonstrating and not arguing dialectically it makes no difference which method of reasoning be adopted, but in argument with another reasoning *per impossibile* should be avoided. For where one has reasoned without the *reductio per impossibile,* no dispute can arise; if, on the other hand, one does reason to an impossible conclusion, unless its falsehood is too plainly 158ª manifest, people deny that it is impossible, so that the questioners do not get what they want.

One should put forward all propositions that hold true of several cases, and to which either no objection whatever appears or at least not any on the surface: for when people cannot see any case in which it is not so, they admit it for true.

The conclusion should not be put in the form of a question; if it be, and the man shakes his head, it looks as if the reasoning had failed. For often, even if it be not put as a question but advanced as a consequence, people deny it, and then those who do not see that it follows upon the previous admissions do not realize that those who deny it have been refuted: when, then, the one man merely asks it as a question without even saying that it so follows, and the other denies it, it looks altogether as if the reasoning had failed.

Not every universal question can form a dialectical proposition as ordinarily understood, e.g. 'What is man?' or 'How many meanings has "the good"?' For a dialectical premiss must be of a form to which it is possible to reply 'Yes' or 'No', whereas to the aforesaid it is not possible. For this reason questions of this kind are not dialectical unless the questioner himself draws distinctions or divisions before expressing them, e.g. 'Good means this, or this, does it not?' For questions of this sort are easily answered by a Yes or a No. Hence one should endeavour to formulate propositions of this kind in this form. It is at the same time also perhaps fair to ask the other man how many meanings of 'the good' there are, whenever you have yourself distinguished and formulated them, and he will not admit them at all.

Any one who keeps on asking one thing for a long time is a bad inquirer. For if he does so though the person questioned keeps on answering the questions, clearly he asks a large number of questions, or else asks the same question a large number of times: in the one case he merely babbles, in the other he fails to reason: for reasoning always consists of a small number of premisses. If, on the other hand, he does it because the person questioned does not answer the questions, he is at fault in not taking him to task or breaking off the discussion.

3

There are certain hypotheses upon which it is at once difficult to bring, and easy to stand up to, an argument. Such (e.g.) are those things which stand first and those which stand last in the order of nature. For the former require definition, while the latter have to be arrived at through many steps if one wishes to secure a [35] continuous proof from first principles, or else all discussion about them wears the air of mere sophistry: for to prove anything is impossible unless one begins with the appropriate principles, and connects inference with inference till the last are reached. Now to define first principles is just what answerers do not care to do, nor do they pay any attention if the questioner makes a definition: and yet until it is clear what it is that is proposed, it is not 158ᵇ easy to discuss it. This sort of thing happens particularly in the case of the first principles: for while the other propositions are shown through these, these cannot be shown through anything else: we are obliged to understand every item of that sort by a definition. [5] The inferences, too, that lie too close to the first principle are hard to treat in argument: for it is not possible to bring many arguments in regard to them, because of the small number of those steps, between the conclusion and the principle, whereby the succeeding propositions have to be shown. The hardest, however, of all definitions to treat in argument are those that employ terms about which, in the first place, it [10] is uncertain whether they are used in one sense or several, and, further, whether they are used literally or metaphorically by the definer. For because of their obscurity, it is impossible to argue upon such terms; and because of the impossibility of saying whether this obscurity is due to their being used metaphorically, it is [15] impossible to refute them.

In general, it is safe to suppose that, whenever any problem proves intractable, it either needs definition or else bears either several senses, or a metaphorical sense, or it is not far removed from the first principles; or else the reason is that we have yet to discover in the [20] first place just this—in which of the aforesaid directions the source of our difficulty lies: when we have made this clear, then obviously our business must be either to define or to distinguish, or to supply the intermediate premisses: for it is through these that the final conclusions are shown.

It often happens that a difficulty is found in [25] discussing or arguing a given position because the definition has not been correctly rendered: e.g. 'Has one thing one contrary or many?': here when the term 'contraries' has been properly defined, it is easy to bring people to see whether it is possible for the same thing to have several contraries or not: in the same way also with other terms requiring definition. It appears also in mathematics that [30] the difficulty in using a figure is sometimes due to a defect in definition; e.g. in proving that the line which cuts the plane parallel to one side divides similarly both the line which it cuts and the area; whereas if the definition be given, the fact asserted becomes immediately clear: for the areas have the same fraction subtracted from them as have the [35] sides: and this is the definition of 'the same ratio'. The most primary of the elementary principles are without exception very easy to show, if the definitions involved, e.g. the nature of a line or of a circle, be laid down; only the arguments that can be brought in regard to each of them are not many, because there are not many intermediate steps. If, on the other hand, the definition of the starting-points be not laid down, to show them is difficult and 159ᵃ may even prove quite impossible. The case of the significance of verbal expressions is like that of these mathematical conceptions.

One may be sure then, whenever a position is hard to discuss, that one or other of the aforesaid things has happened to it. Whenever, on the other hand, it is a harder task to argue [5] to the point claimed, i.e. the premiss, than to the resulting position, a doubt may arise whether such claims should be admitted or not: for if a man is going to refuse to admit it and claim that you shall argue to it as well, he will be giving the signal for a harder undertaking than was originally proposed: if, on the other hand, he grants it, he will be giving the original thesis credence on the strength of what is less credible than itself. If, then, it is essential not to enhance the difficulty of the [10] problem, he had better grant it; if, on the other hand, it be essential to reason through premisses that are better assured, he had better refuse. In other words, in serious inquiry he ought not to grant it, unless he be more sure about it than about the conclusion; whereas in a dialectical exercise he may do so if he is merely satisfied of its truth. Clearly, then, the circumstances under which such admissions should be claimed are different for a mere questioner and for a serious teacher.

4

[15] As to the formulation, then, and arrangement of one's questions, about enough has been said.

With regard to the giving of answers, we must first define what is the business of a good answerer, as of a good questioner. The business of the questioner is so to develop the argument as to make the answerer utter the most extrava- [20] gant paradoxes that necessarily follow because of his position: while that of the answerer is to make it appear that it is not he who is responsible for the absurdity or paradox, but only his position: for one may, perhaps, distinguish between the mistake of taking up a wrong position to start with, and that of not maintaining it properly, when once taken up.

5

[25] Inasmuch as no rules are laid down for those who argue for the sake of training and of examination:—and the aim of those engaged in teaching or learning is quite different from that of those engaged in a competition; as is the latter from that of those who discuss things together in the spirit of inquiry: for a learner should always state what he thinks: for no one is even trying to teach him [30] what is false; whereas in a competition the business of the questioner is to appear by all means to produce an effect upon the other, while that of the answerer is to appear unaffected by him; on the other hand, in an assembly of disputants discussing in the spirit not of a competition but of an examination and inquiry, there are as yet no articulate rules [35] about what the answerer should aim at, and what kind of things he should and should not grant for the correct or incorrect defence of his position:—inasmuch, then, as we have no tradition bequeathed to us by others, let us try to say something upon the matter for ourselves.

The thesis laid down by the answerer before facing the questioner's argument is bound of necessity to be one that is either generally accepted or generally rejected or else is neither: and moreover is so accepted or rejected either 159ᵇ absolutely or else with a restriction, e.g. by some given person, by the speaker or by some one else. The manner, however, of its acceptance or rejection, whatever it be, makes no difference: for the right way to answer, i.e. to admit or to refuse to admit what has been asked, will be the same in either case. If, then, the statement laid down by the answerer be generally rejected, the conclusion aimed at by [5] the questioner is bound to be one generally accepted, whereas if the former be generally accepted, the latter is generally rejected: for the conclusion which the questioner tries to draw is always the opposite of the statement laid down. If, on the other hand, what is laid down is generally neither rejected nor accepted, the conclusion will be of the same type as well. Now since a man who reasons correctly demonstrates his proposed conclusion from premises that are more generally accepted, and more familiar, it is clear that (1) where the view laid down by him is one that [10] generally is absolutely rejected, the answerer ought not to grant either what is thus absolutely not accepted at all, or what is accepted indeed, but accepted less generally than the questioner's conclusion. For if the statement laid down by the answerer be generally rejected, the conclusion aimed at by the questioner will be one that is generally accepted, so that the premises secured by the questioner should all be views generally accepted, and [15] more generally accepted than his proposed conclusion, if the less familiar is to be inferred through the more familiar. Consequently, if any of the questions put to him be not of this character, the answerer should not grant them. (2) If, on the other hand, the statement laid down by the answerer be generally accepted without qualification, clearly the conclusion sought by the questioner will be one generally rejected without qualification. Accordingly, the answerer should admit all views that are generally accepted and, of those that are not generally accepted, all that are less generally rejected than the conclusion sought by the questioner. For then he will probably be thought to have argued suffi- [20] ciently well. (3) Likewise, too, if the statement laid down by the answerer be neither rejected generally nor generally accepted; for then, too, anything that appears to be true should be granted, and, of the views not generally accepted, any that are more generally accepted than the questioner's conclusion; for in that case the result will be that the arguments will be more generally accepted. If, then, the view laid down by the answerer be one that is generally accepted or rejected without qualification, then the views that are ac- [25] cepted absolutely must be taken as the standard of comparison: whereas if the view laid down be one that is not generally accepted or rejected, but only by the answerer, then the standard whereby the latter must judge what is generally accepted or not, and must grant or refuse to grant the point asked, is himself. If, again, the answerer be defending some one else's opinion, then clearly it will be the latter's judgement to which he must have regard in granting or denying the various points. This is why those, too, who introduce other's opin-[30]ions, e.g. that 'good and evil are the same thing', as Heraclitus says,[1] refuse to admit the impossibility of contraries belonging at the same time to the same thing; not because they do not themselves believe this, but because on Heraclitus' principles one has to say so. The same thing is done also by those who take on [35] the defence of one another's positions; their aim being to speak as would the man who stated the position.

6

It is clear, then, what the aims of the answerer should be, whether the position he lays down be a view generally accepted without qualification or accepted by some definite person. Now every question asked is bound to involve some view that is either generally held or generally rejected or neither, and is also bound to be either relevant to the argument or irrelevant: if then it be a view generally accepted and ir-160ᵃ relevant, the answerer should grant it and remark that it is the accepted view: if it be a view not generally accepted and irrelevant, he should grant it but add a comment that it is not generally accepted, in order to avoid the appearance of being a simpleton. If it be relevant and also be generally accepted, he should admit that it is the view generally accepted but [5] say that it lies too close to the original proposition, and that if it be granted the problem proposed collapses. If what is claimed by the questioner be relevant but too generally rejected, the answerer, while admitting that if it be granted the conclusion sought follows, should yet protest that the proposition is too absurd to be admitted. Suppose, again, it be a view that is neither rejected generally nor generally accepted, then, if it be irrelevant to the argument, it may be granted without restric-[10]tion; if, however, it be relevant, the answerer should add the comment that, if it be granted, the original problem collapses. For then the answerer will not be held to be personally accountable for what happens to him, if he grants the several points with his eyes open, and also the questioner will be able to draw his inference, seeing that all the premisses that are more generally accepted than the conclusion are granted him. Those who try to [15] draw an inference from premisses more

[1] Frr. 58, 102, Diels.

generally rejected than the conclusion clearly do not reason correctly: hence, when men ask these things, they ought not to be granted.

7

The questioner should be met in a like manner also in the case of terms used obscurely, i.e. in several senses. For the answerer, if he does not understand, is always permitted to say 'I do not understand': he is not compelled to re-[20] ply 'Yes' or 'No' to a question which may mean different things. Clearly, then, in the first place, if what is said be not clear, he ought not to hesitate to say that he does not understand it; for often people encounter some difficulty from assenting to questions that are not clearly put. If he understands the question and yet it covers many senses, then supposing [25] what it says to be universally true or false, he should give it an unqualified assent or denial: if, on the other hand, it be partly true and partly false, he should add a comment that it bears different senses, and also that in one it is true, in the other false: for if he leave this distinction till later, it becomes uncertain whether originally as well he perceived the ambiguity or not. If he does not foresee the ambiguity, but assents to the question having in [30] view the one sense of the words, then, if the questioner takes it in the other sense, he should say, 'That was not what I had in view when I admitted it; I meant the other sense': for if a term or expression covers more than one thing, it is easy to disagree. If, however, the question is both clear and simple, he should answer either 'Yes' or 'No'.

8

[35] A premiss in reasoning always either is one of the constituent elements in the reasoning, or else goes to establish one of these: (and you can always tell when it is secured in order to establish something else by the fact of a number of similar questions being put: for as a rule people secure their universal by means either of induction or of likeness):—accordingly the particular propositions should all be 160ᵇ admitted, if they are true and generally held. On the other hand, against the universal one should try to bring some negative instance; for to bring the argument to a standstill without a negative instance, either real or apparent, shows ill-temper. If, then, a man refuses to grant the universal when supported by many

instances, although he has no negative instance to show, he obviously shows ill-temper. If, [5] moreover, he cannot even attempt a counter-proof that it is not true, far more likely is he to be thought ill-tempered—although even counter-proof is not enough: for we often hear arguments that are contrary to common opinions, whose solution is yet difficult, e.g. the argument of Zeno that it is impossible to move or to traverse the stadium;—but still, this is no reason for omitting to assert the opposites [10] of these views. If, then, a man refuses to admit the proposition without having either a negative instance or some counter-argument to bring against it, clearly he is ill-tempered: for ill-temper in argument consists in answering in ways other than the above, so as to wreck the reasoning.

9

Before maintaining either a thesis or a definition the answerer should try his hand at attack- [15] ing it by himself; for clearly his business is to oppose those positions from which questioners demolish what he has laid down.

He should beware of maintaining a hypothesis that is generally rejected: and this it may be in two ways: for it may be one which results in absurd statements, e.g. suppose any one were to say that everything is in motion or that nothing is; and also there are all those [20] which only a bad character would choose, and which are implicitly opposed to men's wishes, e.g. that pleasure is the good, and that to do injustice is better than to suffer it. For people then hate him, supposing him to maintain them not for the sake of argument but because he really thinks them.

10

Of all arguments that reason to a false conclusion the right solution is to demolish the point on which the fallacy that occurs depends: for the demolition of any random point is no solu- [25] tion, even though the point demolished be false. For the argument may contain many falsehoods, e.g. suppose some one to secure the premisses, 'He who sits, writes' and 'Socrates is sitting': for from these it follows that 'Socrates is writing'. Now we may demolish the proposition 'Socrates is sitting', and still be no nearer a solution of the argument; it may be true that [30] the point claimed is false; but it is not on that that the fallacy of the argument depends: for supposing that any one should happen to be sitting and not writing, it would be impossible in such a case to apply the same solution. Accordingly, it is not this that needs to be demolished, but rather that 'He who sits, writes': for he who sits does not always write. He, then, who has demolished the point on which the fallacy depends, has given the solution of the argument completely. Any one who knows that it is on such and such a point that [35] the argument depends, knows the solution of it, just as in the case of a figure falsely drawn. For it is not enough to object, even if the point demolished be a falsehood, but the reason of the fallacy should also be proved: for then it would be clear whether the man makes his objection with his eyes open or not.

161ª There are four possible ways of preventing a man from working his argument to a conclusion. It can be done either by demolishing the point on which the falsehood that comes about depends, or by stating an objection directed against the questioner: for often when a solution has not as a matter of fact been brought, yet the questioner is rendered thereby unable to pursue the argument any farther. [5] Thirdly, one may object to the questions asked: for it may happen that what the questioner wants does not follow from the questions he has asked because he has asked them badly, whereas if something additional be granted the conclusion comes about. If, then, the questioner be unable to pursue his argument farther, the objection would properly be directed against the questioner; if he can do so, then it would be against his questions. The fourth and worst kind of objection is that [10] which is directed to the time allowed for discussion: for some people bring objections of a kind which would take longer to answer than the length of the discussion in hand.

There are then, as we said, four ways of making objections: but of them the first alone is a solution: the others are just hindrances and [15] stumbling-blocks to prevent the conclusions.

11

Adverse criticism of an argument on its own merits, and of it when presented in the form of questions, are two different things. For often the failure to carry through the argument correctly in discussion is due to the person questioned, because he will not grant the steps of which a correct argument might have been made against his position: for it is not in the [20] power of the one side only to effect properly a result that depends on both alike. Accordingly it sometimes becomes necessary to attack the speaker and not his position, when the answerer lies in wait for the points that are contrary to the questioner and becomes abusive as well: when people lose their tempers in this way, their argument becomes a contest, not a discussion. Moreover, since argu- [25] ments of this kind are held not for the sake of instruction but for purposes of practice and examination, clearly one has to reason not only to true conclusions, but also to false ones, and not always through true premisses, but sometimes through false as well. For often, when a true proposition is put forward, the dialectician is compelled to demolish it: and then false propositions have to be formulated. [30] Sometimes also when a false proposition is put forward, it has to be demolished by means of false propositions: for it is possible for a given man to believe what is not the fact more firmly than the truth. Accordingly, if the argument be made to depend on something that he holds, it will be easier to persuade or help him. He, however, who would rightly convert any one to a different opinion should do so in a dialectical and not in a contentious [35] manner, just as a geometrician should reason geometrically, whether his conclusion be false or true: what kind of syllogisms are dialectical has already been said.[1] The principle that a man who hinders the common business is a bad partner, clearly applies to an argument as well; for in arguments as well there is a common aim in view, except with [40] mere contestants, for these cannot both reach the same goal; for more than one cannot possibly win. It makes no difference whether he effects this as answerer or as questioner: for both he who asks contentious questions is a bad dialectician, and also he who in answering fails to grant the obvious answer or [5] to understand the point of the questioner's inquiry. What has been said, then, makes it clear that adverse criticism is not to be passed in a like strain upon the argument on its own merits, and upon the questioner: for it may very well be that the argument is bad, but that the questioner has argued with the answerer in the best possible way: for when men lose their tempers, it may perhaps be impossible to make one's inferences straight-forwardly as [10] one would wish: we have to do as we can.

Inasmuch as it is indeterminate when people are claiming the admission of contrary things, and when they are claiming what originally they set out to prove—for often when they are talking by themselves they say contrary things, and admit afterwards what they have previously denied; for which reason they often assent, when questioned, to contrary things and [15] to what originally had to be proved—the argument is sure to become vitiated. The responsibility, however, for this rests with the answerer, because while refusing to grant other points, he does grant points of that kind. It is, then, clear that adverse criticism is not to be passed in a like manner upon questioners and upon their arguments.

In itself an argument is liable to five kinds of adverse criticism:
[20] (1) The first is when neither the proposed conclusion nor indeed any conclusion at all is drawn from the questions asked, and when most, if not all, of the premisses on which the conclusion rests are false or generally rejected, when, moreover, neither any withdrawals nor additions nor both together can bring the conclusions about.

[25] (2) The second is, supposing the reasoning, though constructed from the premisses, and in the manner, described above, were to be irrelevant to the original position.

(3) The third is, supposing certain additions would bring an inference about but yet these additions were to be weaker than those that were put as questions and less generally held than the conclusion.

(4) Again, supposing certain withdrawals [30] could effect the same: for sometimes people secure more premisses than are necessary, so that it is not through them that the inference comes about.

(5) Moreover, suppose the premisses be less generally held and less credible than the conclusion, or if, though true, they require more trouble to prove than the proposed view.

One must not claim that the reasoning to a [35] proposed view shall in every case equally be a view generally accepted and convincing: for it is a direct result of the nature of things that some subjects of inquiry shall be easier and some harder, so that if a man brings people to accept his point from opinions that are as generally received as the case admits, he has argued his case correctly. Clearly, then, not even the argument itself is open to the same adverse criticism when taken in relation to the proposed conclusion and when taken by itself. For there is nothing to prevent the argument [40] being open to reproach in itself, and yet commendable in relation to the proposed

---
[1] 100ᵃ 22.

conclusion, or again, vice versa, being commendable in itself, and yet open to reproach in relation to the proposed conclusion, whenever there are many propositions both generally held and also true whereby it could easily be proved. It is possible also that an argument, even though brought to a conclusion, may [5] sometimes be worse than one which is not so concluded, whenever the premisses of the former are silly, while its conclusion is not so; whereas the latter, though requiring certain additions, requires only such as are generally held and true, and moreover does not rest as an argument on these additions. With those which bring about a true conclusion by means of false premisses, it is not fair to find fault: for a false conclusion must of necessity always be [10] reached from a false premiss, but a true conclusion may sometimes be drawn even from false premisses; as is clear from the Analytics.[1]

Whenever by the argument stated something is demonstrated, but that something is other than what is wanted and has no bearing whatever on the conclusion, then no inference as to the latter can be drawn from it: and if there [15] appears to be, it will be a sophism, not a proof. A philosopheme is a demonstrative inference: an epichireme is a dialectical inference: a sophism is a contentious inference: an aporeme is an inference that reasons dialectically to a contradiction.

If something were to be shown from prem-[20]isses, both of which are views generally accepted, but not accepted with like conviction, it may very well be that the conclusion shown is something held more strongly than either. If, on the other hand, general opinion be for the one and neither for nor against the other, or if it be for the one and against the other, then, if the pro and con be alike in the case of the premisses, they will be alike for the conclusion also: if, on the other hand, the one preponderates, the conclusion too will follow suit.

It is also a fault in reasoning when a man [25] shows something through a long chain of steps, when he might employ fewer steps and those already included in his argument: suppose him to be showing (e.g.) that one opinion is more properly so called than another, and suppose him to make his postulates as follows: 'x-in-itself is more fully x than anything else': 'there genuinely exists an object of opinion in itself': therefore 'the object-of-opinion-in-itself is more fully an object of opinion than the particular objects of opinion'. Now 'a relative term is more fully itself when its correlate is more fully itself': and 'there exists a gen-[30]uine opinion-in-itself, which will be "opinion" in a more accurate sense than the particular opinions': and it has been postulated both that 'a genuine opinion-in-itself exists', and that 'x-in-itself is more fully x than anything else': therefore 'this will be opinion in a more accurate sense'. Wherein lies the viciousness of the reasoning? Simply in that it conceals the ground on which the argument depends.

12

[35] An argument is clear in one, and that the most ordinary, sense, if it be so brought to a conclusion as to make no further questions necessary: in another sense, and this is the type most usually advanced, when the propositions secured are such as compel the conclusion, and the argument is concluded through premisses that are themselves conclusions: moreover, it is so also if some step is omitted that generally is firmly accepted.

An argument is called fallacious in four senses: (1) when it appears to be brought to a conclusion, and is not really so—what is called [5] 'contentious' reasoning: (2) when it comes to a conclusion but not to the conclusion proposed—which happens principally in the case of *reductiones ad impossibile:* (3) when it comes to the proposed conclusion but not according to the mode of inquiry appropriate to the case, as happens when a non-medical argument is taken to be a medical one, or one which is not geometrical for a geometrical ar-[10]gument, or one which is not dialectical for dialectical, whether the result reached be true or false: (4) if the conclusion be reached through false premisses: of this type the conclusion is sometimes false, sometimes true: for while a false conclusion is always the result of false premisses, a true conclusion may be drawn [15] even from premisses that are not true, as was said above as well.[2]

Fallacy in argument is due to a mistake of the arguer rather than of the argument: yet it is not always the fault of the arguer either, but only when he is not aware of it: for we often accept on its merits in preference to many true ones an argument which demolishes some true [20] proposition if it does so from premisses as far as possible generally accepted. For an

---
[1] *Prior Analytics,* II. 2.

argument of that kind does demonstrate other things that are true: for one of the premisses laid down ought never to be there at all, and this will then be demonstrated. If, however, a true conclusion were to be reached through premisses that are false and utterly childish, the argument is worse than many arguments that lead to a false conclusion, though an argument which leads to a false conclusion may also be of this type. Clearly then the first thing to ask [25] in regard to the argument in itself is, 'Has it a conclusion?'; the second, 'Is the conclusion true or false?'; the third, 'Of what kind of premisses does it consist?': for if the latter, though false, be generally accepted, the argument is dialectical, whereas if, though true, they be generally rejected, it is bad: if they be both false and also entirely contrary to general opinion, clearly it is bad, either altogether or [30] else in relation to the particular matter in hand.

13

Of the ways in which a questioner may beg the original question and also beg contraries the true account has been given in the Analytics:[1] but an account on the level of general opinion must be given now.

People appear to beg their original question [35] in five ways: the first and most obvious being if any one begs the actual point requiring to be shown: this is easily detected when put in so many words; but it is more apt to escape detection in the case of different terms, 163ᵃ or a term and an expression, that mean the same thing. A second way occurs whenever any one begs universally something which he has to demonstrate in a particular case: suppose (e.g.) he were trying to prove that the knowledge of contraries is one and were to claim that the knowledge of opposites in general is one: for then he is generally thought to be begging, along with a number of other things, that which he ought to have shown by [5] itself. A third way is if any one were to beg in particular cases what he undertakes to show universally: e.g. if he undertook to show that the knowledge of contraries is always one, and begged it of certain pairs of contraries: for he also is generally considered to be begging independently and by itself what, together with a number of other things, he ought to have shown. Again, a man begs the question if he begs his conclusion piecemeal: supposing e.g. that he had to show that medicine is a sci-

[1] *Prior Analytics*, II, 16.

[10] ence of what leads to health and to disease, and were to claim first the one, then the other; or, fifthly, if he were to beg the one or the other of a pair of statements that necessarily involve one other; e.g. if he had to show that the diagonal is incommensurable with the side, and were to beg that the side is incommensurable with the diagonal.

The ways in which people assume contraries are equal in number to those in which they beg their original question. For it would happen, [15] firstly, if any one were to beg an opposite affirmation and negation; secondly, if he were to beg the contrary terms of an antithesis, e.g. that the same thing is good and evil; thirdly, suppose any one were to claim something universally and then proceed to beg its contradictory in some particular case, e.g. if having secured that the knowledge of contraries is one, he were to claim that the knowledge of what makes for health or for disease is differ- [20] ent; or, fourthly, suppose him, after postulating the latter view, to try to secure universally the contradictory statement. Again, fifthly, suppose a man begs the contrary of the conclusion which necessarily comes about through the premisses laid down; and this would happen suppose, even without begging the opposites in so many words, he were to beg two premisses such that this contradictory statement that is opposite to the first conclusion will follow from them. The securing of contraries differs from begging the original ques- [25] tion in this way: in the latter case the mistake lies in regard to the conclusion; for it is by a glance at the conclusion that we tell that the original question has been begged: whereas contrary views lie in the premisses, viz. in a certain relation which they bear to one another.

14

The best way to secure training and practice [30] in arguments of this kind is in the first place to get into the habit of converting the arguments. For in this way we shall be better equipped for dealing with the proposition stated, and after a few attempts we shall know several arguments by heart. For by 'conversion' of an argument is meant the taking the reverse of the conclusion together with the remaining propositions asked and so demolishing one of those that were conceded: for it follows neces- [35] sarily that if the conclusion be untrue, some one of the premisses is demolished, seeing that, given all the premisses, the conclusion was bound to follow. Always, in dealing with any proposition, be on the look-out for a line of 163b argument both pro and con: and on discovering it at once set about looking for the solution of it: for in this way you will soon find that you have trained yourself at the same time in both asking questions and answering them. If we cannot find any one else to argue with, we should argue with ourselves. Select, moreover, arguments relating to the same [5] thesis and range them side by side: for this produces a plentiful supply of arguments for carrying a point by sheer force, and in refutation also it is of great service, whenever one is well stocked with arguments pro and con: for then you find yourself on your guard against contrary statements to the one you wish to secure. Moreover, as contributing to knowledge and to philosophic wisdom the power of [10] discerning and holding in one view the results of either of two hypotheses is no mean instrument; for it then only remains to make a right choice of one of them. For a task of this kind a certain natural ability is required: in fact real natural ability just is the power rightly to choose the true and shun the false. Men [15] of natural ability can do this; for by a right liking or disliking for whatever is proposed to them they rightly select what is best.

It is best to know by heart arguments upon those questions which are of most frequent occurrence, and particularly in regard to those propositions which are ultimate: for in discussing these answerers frequently give up in despair. Moreover, get a good stock of defini- [20] tions: and have those of familiar and primary ideas at your fingers' ends: for it is through these that reasonings are effected. You should try, moreover, to master the heads under which other arguments mostly tend to fall. For just as in geometry it is useful to be practised in the elements, and in arithmetic to have the multiplication table up [25] to ten at one's fingers' ends—and indeed it makes a great difference in one's knowledge of the multiples of other numbers too—likewise also in arguments it is a great advantage to be well up in regard to first principles, and to have a thorough knowledge of premisses at the tip of one's tongue. For just as in a person with a trained memory, a memory of things [30] themselves is immediately caused by the mere mention of their *loci,* so these habits too will make a man readier in reasoning, because he has his premisses classified before his mind's eye, each under its number. It is better to commit to memory a premiss of general applica-

tion than an argument: for it is difficult to be even moderately ready with a first principle, or hypothesis.

Moreover, you should get into the habit of [35] turning one argument into several, and conceal your procedure as darkly as you can: this kind of effect is best produced by keeping as far as possible away from topics akin to the subject of the argument. This can be done with arguments that are entirely universal, e.g. the 164a statement that 'there cannot be one knowledge of more than one thing': for that is the case with both relative terms and contraries and co-ordinates.

Records of discussions should be made in a universal form, even though one has argued only some particular case: for this will enable [5] one to turn a single rule into several. A like rule applies in Rhetoric as well to enthymemes. For yourself, however, you should as far as possible avoid universalizing your reasonings. You should, moreover, always examine arguments to see whether they rest on principles of general application: for all particular arguments really reason universally, as well, i.e. a particular demonstration always [10] contains a universal demonstration, because it is impossible to reason at all without using universals.

You should display your training in inductive reasoning against a young man, in deductive against an expert. You should try, moreover, to secure from those skilled in deduction [15] their premisses, from inductive reasoners their parallel cases; for this is the thing in which they are respectively trained. In general, too, from your exercises in argumentation you should try to carry away either a syllogism on some subject or a refutation or a proposition or an objection, or whether some one put his question properly or improperly (whether it was yourself or some one else) and the point 164b which made it the one or the other. For this is what gives one ability, and the whole object of training is to acquire ability, especially in regard to propositions and objections. For it is the skilled propounder and objector who is, speaking generally, a dialectician. To formulate a proposition is to form a number of [5] things into one—for the conclusion to which the argument leads must be taken generally, as a single thing—whereas to formulate an objection is to make one thing into many; for the objector either distinguishes or demolishes, partly granting, partly denying the statements proposed.

Do not argue with every one, nor practise upon the man in the street: for there are some people with whom any argument is bound to [10] degenerate. For against any one who is ready to try all means in order to seem not to be beaten, it is indeed fair to try all means of bringing about one's conclusion: but it is not good form. Wherefore the best rule is, not lightly to engage with casual acquaintances, or bad argument is sure to result. For you see how in practising together people cannot re- [15] frain from contentious argument.

It is best also to have ready-made arguments relating to those questions in which a very small stock will furnish us with arguments serviceable on a very large number of occasions. These are those that are universal, and those in regard to which it is rather difficult to produce points for ourselves from matters of everyday experience.

CONTENTS: ON SOPHISTICAL REFUTATIONS

Introductory

CHAP.		BERLIN NOS.
1.	General distinction of genuine and merely apparent reasonings and refutations	164^a 20
2.	Four classes of arguments in dialogue form: Didactic arguments, Dialectical arguments, Examination arguments, and Contentious arguments (the subject of the present Book)	165^a 37

Perpetration of Fallacies

3. Aims of contentious reasoning fivefold: — 165^b 12
4. A. REFUTATION — 165^b 23
    (a) *by fallacies dependent on diction*: proof that these are six in number (165^b 24–30): due respectively to
    (1) Ambiguity (165^b 30–166^a 6)
    (2) Amphiboly (166^a 6–23)
    (3) Ambiguous combination of words (166^a 23–32)
    (4) Ambiguous division of words (166^a 33–8)
    (5) Wrong accent (166^b 1–9)
    (6) The form of expression used (166^b 10–21)
    (b) *by fallacies not dependent on diction*: seven in number (166^b 21–7): depending respectively upon
5. (1) Accident (166^b 28–36) — 166^b 28
    (2) The use of words without or with qualification (166^b 37–167^a 20)
    (3) *Ignoratio elenchi* (167^a 21–35)
    (4) *Petitio principii* (167^a 36–9)
    (5) The consequent (167^b 1–20)
    (6) False cause (167^b 21–38)
    (7) Many questions (167^b 38–168^a 16)
6. Proof that all the above can be exhibited as forms of a single fallacy, viz. *ignoratio elenchi* — 168^a 17
7. Proof that all the above arise from confusion and failure to draw proper distinctions — 169^a 22
8. (c) *by arguments (or refutations) which, though valid, are only apparently appropriate to the subject matter*) (Examination-arguments, which expose ignorance of the subject by arguments really appropriate to it (169^b 18–29) — 169^b 18
    These sophistical refutations can all be analysed by the same method as the forms of apparent proof (169^b 30–170^a 11)
    Sophistical refutation never refutes absolutely, but always relatively (to the answerer) (170^a 12–19)
9. Refutations being infinite in number, an exhaustive study of all is impossible (170^a 20–34) — 170^a 20
    Our concern is not with those that rest on principles peculiar to any particular science (170^a 34–8)
    The object of dialectic is to grasp how to construct and to solve refutations that depend on dialectic, i.e. on common principles (i.e. such refutations as are either really dialectical or apparently dialectical, or suited to an examination) (170^a 38–^{b} 11)
10. The distinction of arguments directed against the expression)(arguments directed against the thought expressed, exposed as unreal — 170^b 11
    Didactic) (dialectical argument (171^a 31–^{b}2: cf. 172^a 15–21)
11. Examination-argument and dialectical (171^b 3–6, 172^a 21–^{b} 1) — 171^b 3
    Contentious (sophistical) reasoning)(dialectical (171^b 6–7, 34–172^a 15)
    Two types of contentious reasoning (171^b 8–10, 11 ff.)
12. B. FALLACY: how to show (172^b 10–28) — 172^b 9
    C. PARADOX: how to entrap into (172^b 10–24, 29–173^a 30)
13. D. BABBLING: how to produce — 173^a 31
14. E. SOLECISM: how to produce — 173^b 16
15. How to arrange arguments most effectively — 174^a 16

Solution of Fallacies

16. General remarks: uses of studying solutions: need of practice — 175^a 1
17. Of apparent solutions — 175^a 31
18. Of genuine solutions — 176^b 29
19. A. Solution of REFUTATIONS — 177^a 9
    (a) *dependent on diction*
    (1) Ambiguity
    (2) Amphiboly
20. (3) Ambiguous division — 177^a 33
    (4) Ambiguous combination, of words
21. (5) Wrong accent — 177^b 35

225

22. (6) Like expressions for different things	178ª 4	30. (7) Many questions	181ª 36
23. General rule for solution of fallacies depending on diction	179ª 11	31. *B*. Solution of arguments tending to Babbling	181ᵇ 25
(*b*) *not dependent on diction*		32. *C*. Solution of arguments tending to Solecism	182ª 6
24. (1) Accident	179ª 26	33. Varying degrees of difficulty in respect of fallacies	182ᵇ 6
25. (2) The use of words with or without qualification	180ª 23		
26. (3) *Ignoratio elenchi*	181ª 1	Epilogue	
27. (4) *Petitio principii*	181ª 15	34. (1) Our programme and its performance (183ª 27–ᵇ 15)	183ª 27
28. (5) The consequent	181ª 21		
29. (6) Insertion of irrelevant matter (False **cause**)	181ª 31	(2) History of dialectical theory compared with that of rhetoric (183ᵇ 15–end)	

ON SOPHISTICAL REFUTATIONS

1

164[a] [20] LET us now discuss sophistic refutations, i.e. what appear to be refutations but are really fallacies instead. We will begin in the natural order with the first.

That some reasonings are genuine, while others seem to be so but are not, is evident. This happens with arguments, as also else-[25] where, through a certain likeness between the genuine and the sham. For physically some **164**[b] people are in a vigorous condition, while others merely seem to be so by blowing and [20] rigging themselves out as the tribesmen do their victims for sacrifice; and some people are beautiful thanks to their beauty, while others seem to be so, by dint of embellishing themselves. So it is, too, with inanimate things; for of these, too, some are really silver and others gold, while others are not and merely seem to be such to our sense; e.g. things made of litharge and tin seem to be of silver, while [25] those made of yellow metal look golden. In the same way both reasoning and refutation are sometimes genuine, sometimes not, though inexperience may make them appear so: for inexperienced people obtain only, as it were, a **165**[a] distant view of these things. For reasoning rests on certain statements such that they involve necessarily the assertion of something other than what has been stated, through what has been stated: refutation is reasoning involving the contradictory of the given conclusion. Now some of them do not really achieve this, though they seem to do so for a number of reasons; and of these the most prolific and usual domain is the argument that [5] turns upon names only. It is impossible in a discussion to bring in the actual things discussed: we use their names as symbols instead of them; and therefore we suppose that what follows in the names, follows in the things as well, just as people who calculate suppose in [10] regard to their counters. But the two cases (names and things) are not alike. For names are finite and so is the sum-total of formulae, while things are infinite in number. Inevitably, then, the same formulae, and a single name, have a number of meanings. Accordingly just as, in counting, those who are not clever in manipulating their counters are taken in by [15] the experts, in the same way in arguments too those who are not well acquainted with the force of names misreason both in their own discussions and when they listen to others. For this reason, then, and for others to be mentioned later, there exists both reasoning and refutation that is apparent but not real. Now for some people it is better worth while to seem [20] to be wise, than to be wise without seeming to be (for the art of the sophist is the semblance of wisdom without the reality, and the sophist is one who makes money from an apparent but unreal wisdom); for them, then, it is clearly essential also to seem to accomplish the task of a wise man rather than to accomplish it without seeming to do so. To reduce it to a single point of contrast it is the business [25] of one who knows a thing, himself to avoid fallacies in the subjects which he knows and to be able to show up the man who makes them; and of these accomplishments the one depends on the faculty to render an answer, and the other upon the securing of one. Those, then, who would be sophists are bound to study the class of arguments aforesaid: for it is [30] worth their while: for a faculty of this kind will make a man seem to be wise, and this is the purpose they happen to have in view.

Clearly, then, there exists a class of arguments of this kind, and it is at this kind of ability that those aim whom we call sophists. Let us now go on to discuss how many kinds there are of sophistical arguments, and how [35] many in number are the elements of which this faculty is composed, and how many branches there happen to be of this inquiry, and the other factors that contribute to this art.

2

Of arguments in dialogue form there are four classes:

Didactic, Dialectical, Examination-arguments, and Contentious arguments. Di-**165**[b] dactic arguments are those that reason from

NOTE: The bold face numbers and letters are approximate indications of the pages and columns of the standard Berlin Greek text; the bracketed numbers, of the lines in the Greek text; they are here assigned as they are assigned in the Oxford translation.

the principles appropriate to each subject and not from the opinions held by the answerer (for the learner should take things on trust): dialectical arguments are those that reason from premisses generally accepted, to the contradictory of a given thesis: examination-arguments are those that reason from premisses which are accepted by the answerer and which any one who pretends to possess knowledge of the subject is bound to know—in what manner, has been defined in another treatise:[1] contentious arguments are those that reason or appear to reason to a conclusion from premisses that appear to be generally accepted but are not so. The subject, then, of demonstrative arguments has been discussed in the *Analytics*, while that of dialectic arguments and examination-arguments has been discussed elsewhere:[2] let us now proceed to speak of the arguments used in competitions and contests.

3

First we must grasp the number of aims entertained by those who argue as competitors and rivals to the death. These are five in number, refutation, fallacy, paradox, solecism, and fifthly to reduce the opponent in the discussion to babbling—i.e. to constrain him to repeat himself a number of times: or it is to produce the appearance of each of these things without the reality. For they choose if possible plainly to refute the other party, or as the second best to show that he is committing some fallacy, or as a third best to lead him into paradox, or fourthly to reduce him to solecism, i.e. to make the answerer, in consequence of the argument, to use an ungrammatical expression; or, as a last resort, to make him repeat himself.

4

There are two styles of refutation: for some depend on the language used, while some are independent of language. Those ways of producing the false appearance of an argument which depend on language are six in number: they are ambiguity, amphiboly, combination, division of words, accent, form of expression. Of this we may assure ourselves both by induction, and by syllogistic proof based on this—and it may be on other assumptions as well—that this is the number of ways in which we might fail to mean the same thing by the same names or expressions. Arguments such as the following depend upon ambiguity.

[1] *Topics*, VIII. 5.   [2] *Topics*, I-VIII.

'Those learn who know: for it is those who know their letters who learn the letters dictated to them'. For to 'learn' is ambiguous; it signifies both 'to understand' by the use of knowledge, and also 'to acquire knowledge'. Again, 'Evils are good: for what needs to be is good, and evils must needs be'. For 'what needs to be' has a double meaning: it means what is inevitable, as often is the case with evils, too (for evil of some kind is inevitable), while on the other hand we say of good things as well that they 'need to be'. Moreover, 'The same man is both seated and standing and he is both sick and in health: for it is he who stood up who is standing, and he who is recovering who is in health: but it is the seated man who stood up, and the sick man who was recovering'. For 'The sick man does so and so', or 'has so and so done to him' is not single in meaning: sometimes it means 'the man who is sick or is seated now', sometimes 'the man who was sick formerly'. Of course, the man who was recovering was the sick man, who really was sick at the time: but the man who is in health is not sick at the same time: he is 'the sick man' in the sense not that he is sick now, but that he was sick formerly. Examples such as the following depend upon amphiboly: 'I wish that you the enemy may capture'. Also the thesis, 'There must be knowledge of what one knows': for it is possible by this phrase to mean that knowledge belongs to both the knower and the known. Also, 'There must be sight of what one sees: one sees the pillar: *ergo* the pillar has sight'. Also, 'What you profess to-be, that you profess-to-be: you profess a stone to-be: *ergo* you profess-to-be a stone'. Also, 'Speaking of the silent is possible': for 'speaking of the silent' also has a double meaning: it may mean that the speaker is silent or that the things of which he speaks are so. There are three varieties of these ambiguities and amphibolies: (1) When either the expression or the name has strictly more than one meaning, e.g. ἀετός and the 'dog'; (2) when by custom we use them so; (3) when words that have a simple sense taken alone have more than one meaning in combination; e.g. 'knowing letters'. For each word, both 'knowing' and 'letters', possibly has a single meaning: but both together have more than one—either that the letters themselves have knowledge or that someone else has it of them.

Amphiboly and ambiguity, then, depend on these modes of speech. Upon the combination of words there depend instances such as the following: 'A man can walk while sitting, and can write while not writing'. For the mean-[25] ing is not the same if one divides the words and if one combines them in saying that 'it is possible to walk-while-sitting' [and write while not writing]. The same applies to the latter phrase, too, if one combines the words 'to write-while-not-writing': for then it means that he has the power to write and not to write at once; whereas if one does not combine them, it means that when he is not writing he [30] has the power to write. Also, 'He knows now if he has learnt his letters'. Moreover, there is the saying that 'One single thing if you can carry a crowd you can carry too'.

Upon division depend the propositions that 5 is 2 and 3, and even and odd, and that the greater is equal: for it is that amount and more [35] besides. For the same phrase would not be thought always to have the same meaning when divided and when combined, e.g. 'I made thee a slave once a free man', and 'God-like Achilles left fifty a hundred men'.

An argument depending upon accent it is **166ᵇ** not easy to construct in unwritten discussion; in written discussions and in poetry it is easier. Thus (e.g.) some people emend Homer against those who criticize as unnatural his expression τὸ μὲν οὗ καταπύθεται ὄμβρῳ.[1] For they solve the difficulty by a change of ac- [5] cent, pronouncing the οὗ with an acuter accent. Also, in the passage about Agamemnon's dream, they say that Zeus did not himself say 'We grant him the fulfilment of his prayer',[2] but that he bade the dream grant it. Instances such as these, then, turn upon the accentuation.

[10] Others come about owing to the form of expression used, when what is really different is expressed in the same form, e.g. a masculine thing by a feminine termination, or a feminine thing by a masculine, or a neuter by either a masculine or a feminine; or, again, when a quality is expressed by a termination proper to quantity or vice versa, or what is active by a passive word, or a state by an active word, and so forth with the other divisions previously[3] [15] laid down. For it is possible to use an expression to denote what does not belong to the class of actions at all as though it did so belong. Thus (e.g.) 'flourishing' is a word which in the form of its expression is like 'cutting' or 'building': yet the one denotes a certain qual- ity—i.e. a certain condition—while the other denotes a certain action. In the same manner also in the other instances.

[20] Refutations, then, that depend upon language are drawn from these common-place rules. Of fallacies, on the other hand, that are independent of language there are seven kinds:

(1) that which depends upon Accident:

(2) the use of an expression absolutely or not absolutely but with some qualification of respect or place, or time, or relation:

(3) that which depends upon ignorance of what 'refutation' is:

[25] (4) that which depends upon the consequent:

(5) that which depends upon assuming the original conclusion:

(6) stating as cause what is not the cause:

(7) the making of more than one question into one.

5

Fallacies, then, that depend on Accident occur whenever any attribute is claimed to belong in [30] a like manner to a thing and to its accident. For since the same thing has many accidents there is no necessity that all the same attributes should belong to all of a thing's predicates and to their subject as well. Thus (e.g.), 'If Coriscus be different from "man"', he is different from himself: for he is a man': or 'If he be different from Socrates, and Socrates [35] be a man, then', they say, 'he has admitted that Coriscus is different from a man, because it so happens (*accidit*) that the person from whom he said that he (Coriscus) is different is a man'.

Those that depend on whether an expression is used absolutely or in a certain respect and not strictly, occur whenever an expression used in a particular sense is taken as though it were **167ᵃ** used absolutely, e.g. in the argument 'If what is not is the object of an opinion, then what is not is': for it is not the same thing 'to be x' and 'to be' absolutely. Or again, 'What is, is not, if it is not a particular kind of being, e.g. if it is not a man.' For it is not the same thing 'not to be x' and 'not to be' at all: it looks as if it were, because of the closeness of [5] the expression, i.e. because 'to be x' is but little different from 'to be', and 'not to be x' from 'not to be'. Likewise also with any argument that turns upon the point whether an expression is used in a certain respect or used absolutely. Thus e.g. 'Suppose an Indian to be black all over, but white in respect of his teeth;

---

[1] *Iliad*, XXIII. 328. [2] *Ibid.*, XXI. 297.
[3] *Topics*, I. 9.

then he is both white and not white.' Or if both characters belong in a particular respect, [10] then, they say, 'contrary attributes belong at the same time'. This kind of thing is in some cases easily seen by any one, e.g. suppose a man were to secure the statement that the Ethiopian is black, and were then to ask whether he is white in respect of his teeth; and then, if he be white in that respect, were to suppose at the conclusion of his questions that therefore he had proved dialectically that he was both white and not white. But in some cases it often passes undetected, viz. in all cases where, whenever a statement is made of [15] something in a certain respect, it would be generally thought that the absolute statement follows as well; and also in all cases where it is not easy to see which of the attributes ought to be rendered strictly. A situation of this kind arises, where both the opposite attributes belong alike: for then there is general support for the view that one must agree absolutely to the assertion of both, or of neither: e.g. if a thing is half white and half black, is [20] it white or black?

Other fallacies occur because the terms 'proof' or 'refutation' have not been defined, and because something is left out in their definition. For to refute is to contradict one and the same attribute—not merely the name, but the reality—and a name that is not merely synonymous but the same name—and to con- [25] fute it from the propositions granted, necessarily, without including in the reckoning the original point to be proved, in the same respect and relation and manner and time in which it was asserted. A 'false assertion' about anything has to be defined in the same way. Some people, however, omit some one of the said conditions and give a merely apparent refutation, showing (e.g.) that the same thing is both double and not double: for two is dou- [30] ble of one, but not double of three. Or, it may be, they show that it is both double and not double of the same thing, but not that it is so in the same respect: for it is double in length but not double in breadth. Or, it may be, they show it to be both double and not double of the same thing and in the same respect and manner, but not that it is so at the same time: and therefore their refutation is merely apparent. One might, with [35] some violence, bring this fallacy into the group of fallacies dependent on language as well.

Those that depend on the assumption of the original point to be proved, occur in the same way, and in as many ways, as it is possible to beg the original point; they appear to refute because men lack the power to keep their eyes at once upon what is the same and what is different.

167^b The refutation which depends upon the consequent arises because people suppose that the relation of consequence is convertible. For whenever, suppose A is, B necessarily is, they then suppose also that if B is, A necessarily is. [5] This is also the source of the deceptions that attend opinions based on sense-perception. For people often suppose bile to be honey because honey is attended by a yellow colour: also, since after rain the ground is wet in consequence, we suppose that if the ground is wet, it has been raining; whereas that does not necessarily follow. In rhetoric proofs from signs are based on consequences. For when rhetori- [10] cians wish to show that a man is an adulterer, they take hold of some consequence of an adulterous life, viz. that the man is smartly dressed, or that he is observed to wander about at night. There are, however, many people of whom these things are true, while the charge in question is untrue. It happens like this also in real reasoning; e.g. Melissus' argument, that the universe is eternal, assumes that the universe has not come to be (for from [15] what is not nothing could possibly come to be) and that what has come to be has done so from a first beginning. If, therefore, the universe has not come to be, it has no first beginning, and is therefore eternal. But this does not necessarily follow: for even if what has come to be always has a first beginning, it does not also follow that what has a first beginning has come to be; any more than it follows that if [20] a man in a fever be hot, a man who is hot must be in a fever.

The refutation which depends upon treating as cause what is not a cause, occurs whenever what is not a cause is inserted in the argument, as though the refutation depended upon it. This kind of thing happens in arguments that reason *ad impossibile:* for in these we are bound to demolish one of the premisses. If, then, the false cause be reckoned in among the ques- [25] tions that are necessary to establish the resulting impossibility, it will often be thought that the refutation depends upon it, e.g. in the proof that the 'soul' and 'life' are not the same: for if coming-to-be be contrary to perishing, then a particular form of perishing will have a particular form of coming-to-be as its contrary:

now death is a particular form of perishing and is contrary to life: life, therefore, is a coming-to-be, and to live is to come-to-be. But this is [30] impossible: accordingly, the 'soul' and 'life' are not the same. Now this is not proved: for the impossibility results all the same, even if one does not say that life is the same as the soul, but merely says that life is contrary to death, which is a form of perishing, and that perishing has 'coming-to-be' as its contrary. Arguments of that kind, then, though not inconclusive absolutely, are inconclusive in relation [35] to the proposed conclusion. Also even the questioners themselves often fail quite as much to see a point of that kind.

Such, then, are the arguments that depend upon the consequent and upon false cause. Those that depend upon the making of two questions into one occur whenever the plurality is undetected and a single answer is returned as if to a single question. Now, in some cases, it is easy to see that there is more than one, and that an answer is not to be given, e.g. 'Does the earth consist of sea, or the sky?' But in some cases it is less easy, and then people treat the question as one, and either confess their defeat by failing to answer the question, or are exposed to an apparent refutation. [5] Thus 'Is A and is B a man?' 'Yes.' 'Then if any one hits A and B, he will strike a man' (singular), 'not men' (plural). Or again, where part is good and part bad, 'is the whole good or bad?' For whichever he says, it is possible that he might be thought to expose himself to [10] an apparent refutation or to make an apparently false statement: for to say that something is good which is not good, or not good which is good, is to make a false statement. Sometimes, however, additional premisses may actually give rise to a genuine refutation; e.g. suppose a man were to grant that the descriptions 'white' and 'naked' and 'blind' apply to one thing and to a number of things in a like sense. For if 'blind' describes a thing that cannot see though nature designed it to see, it will also describe things that cannot see though nature designed them to do so. Whenever, [15] then, one thing can see while another cannot, they will either both be able to see or else both be blind; which is impossible.

6

The right way, then, is either to divide apparent proofs and refutations as above, or else to refer them all to ignorance of what 'refutation' is, and make that our starting-point: for it is possible to analyse all the aforesaid modes [20] of fallacy into breaches of the definition of a refutation. In the first place, we may see if they are inconclusive: for the conclusion ought to result from the premisses laid down, so as to compel us necessarily to state it and not merely to seem to compel us. Next we should also take the definition bit by bit, and try the fallacy thereby. For of the fallacies that consist in language, some depend upon a double meaning, e.g. ambiguity of words and of phrases, and the [25] fallacy of like verbal forms (for we habitually speak of everything as though it were a particular substance)—while fallacies of combination and division and accent arise because the phrase in question or the term as altered is not the same as was intended. Even this, however, should be the same, just as the thing signified should be as well, if a refutation or proof is to be effected; e.g. if the point concerns a [30] doublet, then you should draw the conclusion of a 'doublet', not of a 'cloak'. For the former conclusion also would be true, but it has not been proved; we need a further question to show that 'doublet' means the same thing, in order to satisfy any one who asks why you think your point proved.

Fallacies that depend on Accident are clear cases of *ignoratio elenchi* when once 'proof' has been defined. For the same definition ought [35] to hold good of 'refutation' too, except that a mention of 'the contradictory' is here added: for a refutation is a proof of the contradictory. If, then, there is no proof as regards an accident of anything, there is no refutation. For supposing, when A and B are, C must necessarily be, and C is white, there is no necessity for [40] it to be white on account of the syllogism. So, if the triangle has its angles equal to two right-angles, and it happens to be a figure, or the simplest element or starting point, it is not because it is a figure or a starting point or simplest element that it has this character. For the demonstration proves the point about it not *qua* figure or *qua* simplest element, but *qua* triangle. Likewise also in other cases. If, then, refutation is a proof, an argument which [5] argued *per accidens* could not be a refutation. It is, however, just in this that the experts and men of science generally suffer refutation at the hand of the unscientific: for the latter meet the scientists with reasonings constituted *per accidens;* and the scientists for lack of the power to draw distinctions either say 'Yes' to their questions, or else people suppose them to [10] have said 'Yes', although they have not.

Those that depend upon whether something is said in a certain respect only or said absolutely, are clear cases of *ignoratio elenchi* because the affirmation and the denial are not concerned with the same point. For of 'white in a certain respect' the negation is 'not white in a certain respect', while of 'white absolutely' it is 'not white, absolutely'. If, then, a man treats the admission that a thing is 'white in a certain respect' as though it were said to be [15] white absolutely, he does not effect a refutation, but merely appears to do so owing to ignorance of what refutation is.

The clearest cases of all, however, are those that were previously described[1] as depending upon the definition of a 'refutation': and this is also why they were called by that name. For the appearance of a refutation is produced because of the omission in the definition, and if [20] we divide fallacies in the above manner, we ought to set 'Defective definition' as a common mark upon them all.

Those that depend upon the assumption of the original point and upon stating as the cause what is not the cause, are clearly shown to be cases of *ignoratio elenchi* through the definition thereof. For the conclusion ought to come about 'because these things are so', and this does not happen where the premisses are [25] not causes of it: and again it should come about without taking into account the original point, and this is not the case with those arguments which depend upon begging the original point.

Those that depend upon the consequent are a branch of Accident: for the consequent is an accident, only it differs from the accident in this, that you may secure an admission of the accident in the case of one thing only (e.g. the [30] identity of a yellow thing and honey and of a white thing and swan), whereas the consequent always involves more than one thing: for we claim that things that are the same as one and the same thing are also the same as one another, and this is the ground of a refutation dependent on the consequent. It is, however, not always true, e.g. suppose that *A* and *B* are 'the same' as *C per accidens;* for both 'snow' and the 'swan' are the same as something [35] 'white'. Or again, as in Melissus' argument, a man assumes that to 'have been generated' and to 'have a beginning' are the same thing, or to 'become equal' and to 'assume the same magnitude'. For because what has been generated has a beginning, he claims also that what has a beginning has been generated, and argues as though both what has been generated and what is finite were the same because each has a be-[40] ginning. Likewise also in the case of things that are made equal he assumes that if 169a things that assume one and the same magnitude become equal, then also things that become equal assume one magnitude: i.e. he assumes the consequent. Inasmuch, then, as a refutation depending on accident consists in ignorance of what a refutation is, clearly so also does a refutation depending on the consequent. We shall have further to examine [5] this in another way as well.[2]

Those fallacies that depend upon the making of several questions into one consist in our failure to dissect the definition of 'proposition'. For a proposition is a single statement about a single thing. For the same definition applies to 'one single thing only' and to the 'thing', simply, e.g. to 'man' and to 'one single man only'; [10] and likewise also in other cases. If, then, a 'single proposition' be one which claims a single thing of a single thing, a 'proposition', simply, will also be the putting of a question of that kind. Now since a proof starts from propositions and refutation is a proof, refutation, too, will start from propositions. If, then, a proposition is a single statement about a single thing, it is obvious that this fallacy too consists in ignorance of what a refutation is: for in it [15] what is not a proposition appears to be one. If, then, the answerer has returned an answer as though to a single question, there will be a refutation; while if he has returned one not really but apparently, there will be an apparent refutation of his thesis. All the types of fallacy, then, fall under ignorance of what a refutation is, some of them because the contra-[20] diction, which is the distinctive mark of a refutation, is merely apparent, and the rest failing to conform to the definition of a proof.

7

The deception comes about in the case of arguments that depend on ambiguity of words and of phrases because we are unable to divide the ambiguous term (for some terms it is not easy to divide, e.g. 'unity', 'being', and 'same-[25] ness'), while in those that depend on combination and division, it is because we suppose that it makes no difference whether the phrase be combined or divided, as is indeed the case with most phrases. Likewise also with those that depend on accent: for the lowering or

---

[1] 167a 21-35.   [2] Chapters 24, 28.

raising of the voice upon a phrase is thought not to alter its meaning—with any phrase, or not with many. With those that depend on the [30] form of expression it is because of the likeness of expression. For it is hard to distinguish what kind of things are signified by the same and what by different kinds of expression: for a man who can do this is practically next door to the understanding of the truth. A special reason why a man is liable to be hurried into assent to the fallacy is that we suppose every predicate of everything to be an individual thing, and we understand it as being one with the thing: and we therefore treat it as a substance: for it is to that which is one with a [35] thing or substance, as also to substance itself, that 'individuality' and 'being' are deemed to belong in the fullest sense. For this reason, too, this type of fallacy is to be ranked among those that depend on language; in the first place, because the deception is effected the more readily when we are inquiring into a problem in company with others than when we do so by ourselves (for an inquiry with another person is carried on by means of speech, whereas an inquiry by oneself is carried on quite as much by means of the object itself); [40] secondly a man is liable to be deceived, 169ᵇ even when inquiring by himself, when he takes speech as the basis of his inquiry: moreover the deception arises out of the likeness (of two different things), and the likeness arises out of the language. With those fallacies that depend upon Accident, deception comes about because we cannot distinguish the sameness and otherness of terms, i.e. their unity [5] and multiplicity, or what kinds of predicate have all the same accidents as their subject. Likewise also with those that depend on the Consequent: for the consequent is a branch of Accident. Moreover, in many cases appearances point to this—and the claim is made—that if A is inseparable from B, so also is B from A. With those that depend upon an im- [10] perfection in the definition of a refutation, and with those that depend upon the difference between a qualified and an absolute statement, the deception consists in the smallness of the difference involved; for we treat the limitation to the particular thing or respect or manner or time as adding nothing to the meaning, and so grant the statement universally. Likewise also in the case of those that assume the original point, and those of false cause, and all that treat a number of questions [15] as one: for in all of them the deception lies in the smallness of the difference: for our failure to be quite exact in our definition of 'premiss' and of 'proof' is due to the aforesaid reason.

8

Since we know on how many points apparent syllogisms depend, we know also on how many sophistical syllogisms and refutations [20] may depend. By a sophistical refutation and syllogism I mean not only a syllogism or refutation which appears to be valid but is not, but also one which, though it is valid, only appears to be appropriate to the thing in question. These are those which fail to refute and prove people to be ignorant according to the nature of the thing in question, which was the function of the art of examination. Now the [25] art of examining is a branch of dialectic: and this may prove a false conclusion because of the ignorance of the answerer. Sophistic refutations on the other hand, even though they prove the contradictory of his thesis, do not make clear whether he is ignorant: for sophists entangle the scientist as well with these arguments.

[30] That we know them by the same line of inquiry is clear: for the same considerations which make it appear to an audience that the points required for the proof were asked in the questions and that the conclusion was proved, would make the answerer think so as well, so that false proof will occur through all or some of these means: for what a man has not been asked but thinks he has granted, he would also [35] grant if he were asked. Of course, in some cases the moment we add the missing question, we also show up its falsity, e.g. in fallacies that depend on language and on solecism. If then, fallacious proofs of the contradictory of a thesis depend on their appearing to refute, it is clear that the considerations on which both proofs of false conclusions and an apparent refutation depend must be the same in num- [40] ber. Now an apparent refutation depends upon the elements involved in a genuine one: 170ᵃ for the failure of one or other of these must make the refutation merely apparent, e.g. that which depends on the failure of the conclusion to follow from the argument (the argument *ad impossibile*) and that which treats two questions as one and so depends upon a flaw in the premiss, and that which depends on the substitution of an accident for an essential attribute, and—a branch of the last—that [5] which depends upon the consequent: more-

over, the conclusion may follow not in fact but only verbally: then, instead of proving the contradictory universally and in the same respect and relation and manner, the fallacy may be dependent on some limit of extent or on one or other of these qualifications: moreover, there is the assumption of the original point to be proved, in violation of the clause 'without reckoning in the original point'. Thus we should have the number of considerations on [10] which the fallacious proofs depend: for they could not depend on more, but all will depend on the points aforesaid.

A sophistical refutation is a refutation not absolutely but relatively to some one: and so is a proof, in the same way. For unless that which depends upon ambiguity assumes that the ambiguous term has a single meaning, and that [15] which depends on like verbal forms assumes that substance is the only category, and the rest in the same way, there will be neither refutations nor proofs, either absolutely or relatively to the answerer: whereas if they do assume these things, they will stand, relatively to the answerer; but absolutely they will not stand: for they have not secured a statement that does have a single meaning, but only one that appears to have, and that only from this particular man.

9

[20] The number of considerations on which depend the refutations of those who are refuted, we ought not to try to grasp without a knowledge of everything that is. This, however, is not the province of any special study: for possibly the sciences are infinite in number, so that obviously demonstrations may be infinite too. Now refutations may be true as well as false: for whenever it is possible to demonstrate something, it is also possible to refute the [25] man who maintains the contradictory of the truth; e.g. if a man has stated that the diagonal is commensurate with the side of the square, one might refute him by demonstrating that it is incommensurate. Accordingly, to exhaust all possible refutations we shall have to have scientific knowledge of everything: for some refutations depend upon the principles that rule in geometry and the conclusions that follow from these, others upon those that rule in medicine, and others upon those of the oth- [30] er sciences. For the matter of that, the false refutations likewise belong to the number of the infinite: for according to every art there is false proof, e.g. according to geometry there is false geometrical proof, and according to medicine there is false medical proof. By 'according to the art', I mean 'according to the principles of it'. Clearly, then, it is not of all refutations, but only of those that depend upon [35] dialectic that we need to grasp the common-place rules: for these stand in a common relation to every art and faculty. And as regards the refutation that is according to one or other of the particular sciences it is the task of that particular scientist to examine whether it is merely apparent without being real, and, if it be real, what is the reason for it: whereas it is the business of dialecticians so to examine the refutation that proceeds from the common first principles that fall under no particular special study. For if we grasp the starting-points of the accepted proofs on any subject [40] whatever we grasp those of the refutations current on that subject. For a refutation is the proof of the contradictory of a given thesis, so that either one or two proofs of the contradictory constitute a refutation. We grasp, then, the number of considerations on which all such depend: if, however, we grasp this, we also grasp their solutions as well; for the objections to these are the solutions of [5] them. We also grasp the number of considerations on which those refutations depend, that are merely apparent—apparent, I mean, not to everybody, but to people of a certain stamp; for it is an indefinite task if one is to inquire how many are the considerations that make them apparent to the man in the street. Accordingly it is clear that the dialectician's business is to be able to grasp on how many considerations depends the formation, through the common first principles, of a refutation [10] that is either real or apparent, i.e. either dialectical or apparently dialectical, or suitable for an examination.

10

It is no true distinction between arguments which some people draw when they say that some arguments are directed against the expression, and others against the thought expressed: for it is absurd to suppose that some [15] arguments are directed against the expression and others against the thought, and that they are not the same. For what is failure to direct an argument against the thought except what occurs whenever a man does not in using the expression think it to be used in his question in the same sense in which the person questioned granted it? And this is the same thing as to direct the argument against the expression. On the other hand, it is directed against the thought whenever a man uses the expression in the same sense which the answerer had in mind when he granted it. If now any [20] one (i.e. both the questioner and the person questioned), in dealing with an expression with more than one meaning, were to suppose it to have one meaning—as e.g. it may be that 'Being' and 'One' have many meanings, and yet both the answerer answers and the questioner puts his question supposing it to be one, and the argument is to the effect that 'All things are one'—will this discussion be directed any more against the expression than against [25] the thought of the person questioned? If, on the other hand, one of them supposes the expression to have many meanings, it is clear that such a discussion will not be directed against the thought. Such being the meanings of the phrases in question, they clearly cannot describe two separate classes of argument. For, in the first place, it is possible for any such argument as bears more than one meaning to be directed against the expression and against the thought, and next it is possible for any argument whatsoever; for the fact of being directed against the thought consists not in the nature of the argument, but in the special attitude of [30] the answerer towards the points he concedes. Next, all of them may be directed to the expression. For 'to be directed against the expression' means in this doctrine 'not to be directed against the thought'. For if not all are directed against either expression or thought, there will be certain other arguments directed neither against the expression nor against the thought, whereas they say that all must be one or the other, and divide them all as directed either against the expression or against the [35] thought, while others (they say) there are none. But in point of fact those that depend on mere expression are only a branch of those syllogisms that depend on a multiplicity of meanings. For the absurd statement has actually been made that the description 'dependent on mere expression' describes all the arguments that depend on language: whereas some of these are fallacies not because the answerer adopts a particular attitude towards them, but because the argument itself involves the asking [40] of a question such as bears more than one meaning.

171ᵃ It is, too, altogether absurd to discuss Refutation without first discussing Proof: for a refutation is a proof, so that one ought to discuss proof as well before describing false refutation: for a refutation of that kind is a [5] merely apparent proof of the contradictory of a thesis. Accordingly, the reason of the falsity will be either in the proof or in the contradiction (for mention of the 'contradiction' must be added), while sometimes it is in both, if the refutation be merely apparent. In the argument that speaking of the silent is possible it lies in the contradiction, not in the proof; in the argument that one can give what one [10] does not possess, it lies in both; in the proof that Homer's poem is a figure through its being a cycle it lies in the proof. An argument that does not fail in either respect is a true proof.

But, to return to the point whence our argument digressed,[1] are mathematical reasonings directed against the thought, or not? And if any one thinks 'triangle' to be a word with many meanings, and granted it in some differ- [15] ent sense from the figure which was proved to contain two right angles, has the questioner here directed his argument against the thought of the former or not?

Moreover, if the expression bears many senses, while the answerer does not understand or suppose it to have them, surely the questioner here has directed his argument against his thought! Or how else ought he to put his question except by suggesting a distinction—suppose one's question to be 'Is speaking of the silent possible or not?'—as follows, 'Is [20] the answer "No" in one sense, but "Yes" in another?' If, then, any one were to answer that it was not possible in any sense and the other were to argue that it was, has not his argument been directed against the thought of the answerer? Yet his argument is supposed to be one of those that depend on the expression. There is not, then, any definite kind of arguments that is directed against the thought. Some arguments are, indeed, directed against the expression: but these are not all even ap- [25] parent refutations, let alone all refutations. For there are also apparent refutations which do not depend upon language, e.g. those that depend upon accident, and others.

If, however, any one claims that one should actually draw the distinction, and say, 'By "speaking of the silent" I mean, in one sense this and in the other sense that', surely to [30] claim *this* is in the first place absurd (for sometimes the questioner does not see the ambiguity of his question, and he cannot possibly

---
[1] 170ᵇ 40.

draw a distinction which he does not think to be there): in the second place, what else but this will *didactic* argument be? For it will make manifest the state of the case to one who has never considered, and does not know or suppose that there is any other meaning but one. For what is there to prevent the same thing also happening to us in cases where there is no double meaning? 'Are the units in four [35] equal to the twos? Observe that the twos are contained in four in one sense in this way, in another sense in that'. Also, 'Is the knowledge of contraries one or not? Observe that some contraries are known, while others are unknown'. Thus the man who makes this claim seems to be unaware of the difference 171b between didactic and dialectical argument, and of the fact that while he who argues didactically should not ask questions but make things clear himself, the other should merely ask questions.

11

Moreover, to claim a 'Yes' or 'No' answer is the business not of a man who is showing something, but of one who is holding an examination. For the art of examining is a branch [5] of dialectic and has in view not the man who has knowledge, but the ignorant pretender. *He,* then, is a dialectician who regards the common principles with their application to the particular matter in hand, while he who only appears to do this is a sophist. Now for contentious and sophistical reasoning: (1) one such is a merely apparent reasoning, on subjects on which dialectical reasoning is the proper method of examination, even though its [10] conclusion be true: for it misleads us in regard to the cause: also (2) there are those misreasonings which do not conform to the line of inquiry proper to the particular subject, but are generally thought to conform to the art in question. For false diagrams of geometrical figures are not contentious (for the resulting fallacies conform to the subject of the art)—any more than is any false diagram that may be offered in proof of a truth—e.g. [15] Hippocrates' figure or the squaring of the circle by means of the lunules. But Bryson's method of squaring the circle, even if the circle is thereby squared, is still sophistical because it does not conform to the subject in hand. So, then, any merely apparent reasoning about these things is a contentious argument, and any reasoning that merely appears to conform [20] to the subject in hand, even though it be genuine reasoning, is a contentious argument: for it is merely apparent in its conformity to the subject-matter, so that it is deceptive and plays foul. For just as a foul in a race is a definite type of fault, and is a kind of foul fighting, so the art of contentious reasoning is foul fighting in disputation: for in the former case those who are resolved to win at all costs snatch at everything, and so in the latter case do contentious reasoners. Those, then, who do this in order to win the mere victory are generally [25] considered to be contentious and quarrelsome persons, while those who do it to win a reputation with a view to making money are sophistical. For the art of sophistry is, as we said,[1] a kind of art of money-making from a merely apparent wisdom, and this is why they aim at a merely apparent demonstration: and [30] quarrelsome persons and sophists both employ the same arguments, but not with the same motives: and the same argument will be sophistical and contentious, but not in the same respect; rather, it will be contentious in so far as its aim is an apparent victory, while in so far as its aim is an apparent wisdom, it will be sophistical: for the art of sophistry is a certain appearance of wisdom without the reality. The [35] contentious argument stands in somewhat the same relation to the dialectical as the drawer of false diagrams to the geometrician; for it beguiles by misreasoning from the same principles as dialectic uses, just as the drawer of a false diagram beguiles the geometrician. But whereas the latter is not a contentious reasoner, because he bases his false diagram on the principles and conclusions that fall under 172a the art of geometry, the argument which is subordinate to the principles of dialectic will yet clearly be contentious as regards other subjects. Thus, e.g. though the squaring of the circle by means of the lunules is not contentious, Bryson's solution is contentious: and the former argument cannot be adapted to any sub- [5] ject except geometry, because it proceeds from principles that are peculiar to geometry, whereas the latter can be adapted as an argument against all the number of people who do not know what is or is not possible in each particular context: for it will apply to them all. Or there is the method whereby Antiphon squared the circle. Or again, an argument which denied that it was better to take a walk after dinner, because of Zeno's argument, would not be a proper argument for a doctor, because Zeno's argument is of general applica-

[1] 165a 22.

tion. If, then, the relation of the contentious [10] argument to the dialectical were exactly like that of the drawer of false diagrams to the geometrician, a contentious argument upon the aforesaid subjects could not have existed. But, as it is, the dialectical argument is not concerned with any definite kind of being, nor does it show anything, nor is it even an argument such as we find in the general philosophy of being. For all beings are not contained in any one kind, nor, if they were, could they [15] possibly fall under the same principles. Accordingly, no art that is a method of showing the nature of anything proceeds by asking questions: for it does not permit a man to grant whichever he likes of the two alternatives in the question: for they will not both of them yield a proof. Dialectic, on the other hand, does proceed by questioning, whereas if it were concerned to show things, it would have refrained from putting questions, even if not about everything, at least about the first principles and the special principles that apply to the particular subject in hand. For suppose [20] the answerer not to grant these, it would then no longer have had any grounds from which to argue any longer against the objection. Dialectic is at the same time a mode of examination as well. For neither is the art of examination an accomplishment of the same kind as geometry, but one which a man may possess, even though he has not knowledge. For it is possible even for one without knowledge to hold an examination of one who is without knowledge, if also the latter grants him points taken not from thing that he knows [25] or from the special principles of the subject under discussion but from all that range of consequences attaching to the subject which a man may indeed know without knowing the theory of the subject, but which if he do not know, he is bound to be ignorant of the theory. So then clearly the art of examining does not consist in knowledge of any definite subject. For this reason, too, it deals with everything: for every 'theory' of anything employs also certain common principles. Hence everybody, [30] including even amateurs, makes use in a way of dialectic and the practice of examining: for all undertake to some extent a rough trial of those who profess to know things. What serves them here is the general principles: for they know these of themselves just as well as the scientist, even if in what they say they seem to the latter to go wildly astray from them. All, then, are engaged in refutation; for they take a hand as amateurs in the same task with [35] which dialectic is concerned professionally; and he is a dialectician who examines by the help of a theory of reasoning. Now there are many identical principles which are true of everything, though they are not such as to constitute a particular nature, i.e. a particular kind of being, but are like negative terms, while other principles are not of this kind but are special to particular subjects; accordingly it is possible from these general principles to hold an examination on everything, and that there should be a definite art of so doing, and, moreover, an art which is not of the same kind as those which demonstrate. This is why the contentious reasoner does not stand in the same condition in all respects as the drawer of a false diagram: for the contentious reasoner will not be given to misreasoning from any definite class of principles, but will deal with every class.

[5] These, then, are the types of sophistical refutations: and that it belongs to the dialectician to study these, and to be able to effect them, is not difficult to see: for the investigation of premisses comprises the whole of this study.

12

So much, then, for apparent refutations. As for showing that the answerer is committing [10] some fallacy, and drawing his argument into paradox—for this was the second item of the sophist's programme—in the first place, then, this is best brought about by a certain manner of questioning and through the question. For to put the question without framing it with reference to any definite subject is a good bait for these purposes: for people are more inclined to make mistakes when they talk at large, and they talk at large when they have [15] no definite subject before them. Also the putting of several questions, even though the position against which one is arguing be quite definite, and the claim that he shall say only what he thinks, create abundant opportunity for drawing him into paradox or fallacy, and also, whether to any of these questions he replies 'Yes' or replies 'No', of leading him on to statements against which one is well off for a line of attack. Nowadays, however, men are less [20] able to play foul by these means than they were formerly: for people rejoin with the question, 'What has that to do with the original subject?' It is, too, an elementary rule for eliciting some fallacy or paradox that one should never put a controversial question straight away, but say that one puts it from the wish for information: for the process of inquiry thus invited gives room for an attack.

[25] A rule specially appropriate for showing up a fallacy is the sophistic rule, that one should draw the answerer on to the kind of statements against which one is well supplied with arguments: this can be done both properly and improperly, as was said before.[1]

Again, to draw a paradoxical statement, look and see to what school of philosophers the person arguing with you belongs, and then question [30] him as to some point wherein their doctrine is paradoxical to most people: for with every school there is some point of that kind. It is an elementary rule in these matters to have a collection of the special 'theses' of the various schools among your propositions. The solution recommended as appropriate here, too, is to point out that the paradox does not come about because of the argument: whereas this is [35] what his opponent always really wants.

Moreover, argue from men's wishes and their professed opinions. For people do not wish the same things as they say they wish: they say what will look best, whereas they wish what appears to be to their interest: e.g. they say that a man ought to die nobly rather than to live in pleasure, and to live in honest poverty rather than in dishonourable riches; but they wish the opposite. Accordingly, a man who speaks according to his wishes must be led into stating the professed opinions of people, while he who speaks according to these must be led into admitting those that people keep [5] hidden away: for in either case they are bound to introduce a paradox; for they will speak contrary either to men's professed or to their hidden opinions.

The widest range of common-place argument for leading men into paradoxical statement is that which depends on the standards of Nature and of the Law: it is so that both Callicles is drawn as arguing in the *Gorgias*,[2] and that all the men of old supposed the result to come about: for nature (they said) and law are [10] opposites, and justice is a fine thing by a legal standard, but not by that of nature. Accordingly, they said, the man whose statement agrees with the standard of nature you should meet by the standard of the law, but the man who agrees with the law by leading him to the facts of nature: for in both ways paradoxical statements may be committed. In their view [15] the standard of nature was the truth, while that of the law was the opinion held by the majority. So that it is clear that they, too, used to try either to refute the answerer or to make him make paradoxical statements, just as the men of to-day do as well.

Some questions are such that in both forms [20] the answer is paradoxical; e.g. 'Ought one to obey the wise or one's father?' and 'Ought one to do what is expedient or what is just?' and 'Is it preferable to suffer injustice or to do an injury?' You should lead people, then, into views opposite to the majority and to the philosophers; if any one speaks as do the expert reasoners, lead him into opposition to the majority, while if he speaks as do the majority, then into opposition to the reasoners. [25] For some say that of necessity the happy man is just, whereas it is paradoxical to the many that a king should be happy. To lead a man into paradoxes of this sort is the same as to lead him into the opposition of the standards of nature and law: for the law represents the opinion of the majority, whereas philosophers [30] speak according to the standard of nature and the truth.

13

Paradoxes, then, you should seek to elicit by means of these common-place rules. Now as for making any one babble, we have already said what we mean by 'to babble'. This is the object in view in all arguments of the following kind: If it is all the same to state a term and to state its definition, the 'double' and [35] 'double of half' are the same: if then 'double' be the 'double of half', it will be the 'double of half of half'. And if, instead of 'double', 'double of half' be again put, then the same expression will be repeated three times, 'double of half of half of half'. Also 'desire is of the pleasant, isn't it?' But desire is conation for the pleasant: accordingly, 'desire' is 'conation for [40] the pleasant for the pleasant'.

All arguments of this kind occur in dealing (1) with any relative terms which not only have relative genera, but are also themselves relative, and are rendered in relation to one and the same thing, as e.g. conation is conation for something, and desire is desire of something, and double is double of something, i.e. [5] double of half: also in dealing (2) with any terms which, though they be not relative terms at all, yet have their substance, viz. the things of which they are the states or affections or what not, indicated as well in their definition,

---
[1] *Topics*, II. 5.   [2] 482.

they being predicated of these things. Thus e.g. 'odd' is a 'number containing a middle': but there is an 'odd number': therefore there is a 'number-containing-a-middle number'. Also, [10] if snub-ness be a concavity of the nose, and there be a snub nose, there is therefore a 'concave-nose nose'.

People sometimes appear to produce this result, without really producing it, because they do not add the question whether the expression 'double', just by itself, has any meaning or no, and if so, whether it has the same meaning, or a different one; but they draw their conclusion straight away. Still it seems, inasmuch as [15] the word is the same, to have the same meaning as well.

14

We have said before what kind of thing 'solecism' is.[1] It is possible both to commit it, and to seem to do so without doing so, and to do so without seeming to do so. Suppose, as Protagoras used to say that μῆνις ('wrath') [20] and πήληξ ('helmet') are masculine: according to him a man who calls wrath a 'destructress' (οὐλομένην) commits a solecism, though he does not seem to do so to other people, where he who calls it a 'destructor' (οὐλόμενον) commits no solecism though he seems to do so. It is clear, then, that any one could produce this effect by art as well: and for this reason many arguments seem to lead to solecism which do not really do so, as happens [25] in the case of refutations.

Almost all apparent solecisms depend upon the word 'this' (τόδε), and upon occasions when the inflection denotes neither a masculine nor a feminine object but a neuter. For 'he' (οὗτος) signifies a masculine, and 'she' (αὕτη) a feminine; but 'this' (τοῦτο), though meant to signify a neuter, often also signifies one or other of the former: e.g. 'What is this?' [30] 'It is Calliope'; 'it is a log'; 'it is Coriscus'. Now in the masculine and feminine the inflections are all different, whereas in the neuter some are and some are not. Often, then, when 'this' (τοῦτο) has been granted, people reason as if 'him' (τοῦτον) had been said: and likewise also they substitute one inflection for another. The fallacy comes about because 'this' [35] (τοῦτο) is a common form of several inflections: for 'this' signifies sometimes 'he' (οὗτος) and sometimes 'him' (τοῦτον). It should signify them alternately; when combined with 'is' (ἔστι) it should be 'he', while with 'being' it should be 'him': e.g. 'Coriscus (Κορίσκος) is', but 'being Coriscus' (Κορίσκον). It happens in the same way in the case of feminine nouns as well, and in the case of the [40] so-called 'chattels' that have feminine or masculine designations. For only those names which end in -ο and -ν, have the designation proper to a chattel, e.g. ξύλον ('log'), σχοινίον ('rope'); those which do not end so have that of a masculine or feminine object, though some of them we apply to chattels: e.g. ἀσκός ('wineskin') is a masculine noun, and κλίνη ('bed') a feminine. For this reason in cases of this kind as well there will be a difference of the same sort between a construction [5] with 'is' (ἔστι) or with 'being' (τὸ εἶναι). Also, Solecism resembles in a certain way those refutations which are said to depend on the like expression of unlike things. For, just as there we come upon a material solecism, so here we come upon a verbal: for 'man' is both a 'matter' for expression and also a 'word': and so is 'white'.

[10] It is clear, then, that for solecisms we must try to construct our argument out of the aforesaid inflections.

These, then, are the types of contentious arguments, and the subdivisions of those types, and the methods for conducting them aforesaid. But it makes no little difference if the materials for putting the question be arranged in a certain manner with a view to concealment, as in the case of dialectics. Following [15] then upon what we have said, this must be discussed first.

15

With a view then to refutation, one resource is length—for it is difficult to keep several things in view at once; and to secure length the elementary rules that have been stated before[2] should be employed. One resource, on the other hand, is speed; for when people are left [20] behind they look ahead less. Moreover, there is anger and contentiousness, for when agitated everybody is less able to take care of himself. Elementary rules for producing anger are to make a show of the wish to play foul, and to be altogether shameless. Moreover, there is the putting of one's questions alternately, whether one has more than one argument leading to the same conclusion, or whether one has arguments to show both that [25] something is so, and that it is not so: for the result is that he has to be on his guard at

---
[1] 165[b] 20.   [2] 155[b] 26-157[a] 5.

the same time either against more than one line, or against contrary lines, of argument. In general, all the methods described before[1] of producing concealment are useful also for purposes of contentious argument: for the object of concealment is to avoid detection, and the object of this is to deceive.

[30] To counter those who refuse to grant whatever they suppose to help one's argument, one should put the question negatively, as though desirous of the opposite answer, or at any rate as though one put the question without prejudice; for when it is obscure what answer one wants to secure, people are less refractory. Also when, in dealing with particulars, a man grants the individual case, when the induction is done you should often not put [35] the universal as a question, but take it for granted and use it: for sometimes people themselves suppose that they have granted it, and also appear to the audience to have done so, for they remember the induction and assume that the questions could not have been put for nothing. In cases where there is no term to indicate the universal, still you should avail yourself of the resemblance of the particulars to suit your purpose; for resemblance often escapes detection. Also, with a view to obtaining [40] your premiss, you ought to put it in your question side by side with its contrary. E.g. if it were necessary to secure the admission that 'A man should obey his father in everything', ask 'Should a man obey his parents in everything, or disobey them in everything?'; and to secure that 'A number multiplied by a large number is a large number', ask 'Should one agree that it is a large number or a small one?' For then, if compelled to choose, [5] one will be more inclined to think it a large one: for the placing of their contraries close beside them makes things look big to men, both relatively and absolutely, and worse and better.

A strong appearance of having been refuted is often produced by the most highly sophistical of all the unfair tricks of questioners, when without proving anything, instead of [10] putting their final proposition as a question, they state it as a conclusion, as though they had proved that 'Therefore so-and-so is not true'.

It is also a sophistical trick, when a paradox has been laid down, first to propose at the start some view that is generally accepted, and then claim that the answerer shall answer what he thinks about it, and to put one's question on matters of that kind in the form 'Do you think [15] that . . .?' For then, if the question be taken as one of the premisses of one's argument, either a refutation or a paradox is bound to result; if he grants the view, a refutation; if he refuses to grant it or even to admit it as the received opinion, a paradox; if he refuses to grant it, but admits that it is the received opinion, something very like a refutation, results.

Moreover, just as in rhetorical discourses, so [20] also in those aimed at refutation, you should examine the discrepancies of the answerer's position either with his own statements, or with those of persons whom he admits to say and do aright, moreover with those of people who are generally supposed to bear that kind of character, or who are like them, or with those of the majority or of all men. Also just as answerers, too, often, when they are in process of being confuted, draw a distinction, if their confutation is just about to [25] take place, so questioners also should resort to this from time to time to counter objectors, pointing out, supposing that against one sense of the words the objection holds, but not against the other, that they have taken it in the latter sense, as e.g. Cleophon does in the *Mandrobulus*. They should also break off their argument and cut down their other lines of attack, while in answering, if a man perceives this being done beforehand, he should [30] put in his objection and have his say first. One should also lead attacks sometimes against positions other than the one stated, on the understood condition that one cannot find lines of attack against the view laid down, as Lycophron did when ordered to deliver a eulogy upon the lyre. To counter those who demand 'Against what are you directing your effort?', since one is generally thought bound to state the charge made, while, on the other hand, [35] some ways of stating it make the defence too easy, you should state as your aim only the general result that always happens in refutations, namely the contradiction of his thesis— viz. that your effort is to deny what he has affirmed, or to affirm what he denied: don't say that you are trying to show that the knowledge of contraries is, or is not, the same. One must not ask one's conclusion in the form of a premiss, while some conclusions should not [40] even be put as questions at all; one should take and use it as granted.

---
[1] 155^b 26-157^a 5.

16

We have now therefore dealt with the sources of questions, and the methods of questioning in contentious disputations: next we have to speak of answering, and of how solutions should be made, and of what requires them, and of what use is served by arguments of this kind.

[5] The use of them, then, is, for philosophy, twofold. For in the first place, since for the most part they depend upon the expression, they put us in a better condition for seeing in how many senses any term is used, and what kind of resemblances and what kind of differences occur between things and between their names. In the second place they are useful for [10] one's own personal researches; for the man who is easily committed to a fallacy by some one else, and does not perceive it, is likely to incur this fate of himself also on many occasions. Thirdly and lastly, they further contribute to one's reputation, viz. the reputation of being well trained in everything, and not inexperienced in anything: for that a party to arguments should find fault with them, if he [15] cannot definitely point out their weakness, creates a suspicion, making it seem as though it were not the truth of the matter but merely inexperience that put him out of temper.

Answerers may clearly see how to meet arguments of this kind, if our previous account was right of the sources whence fallacies came, and also our distinctions adequate of the forms [20] of dishonesty in putting questions. But it is not the same thing to take an argument in one's hand and then to see and solve its faults, as it is to be able to meet it quickly while being subjected to questions: for what we know, we often do not know in a different context. Moreover, just as in other things speed is enhanced by training, so it is with arguments too, [25] so that supposing we are unpractised, even though a point be clear to us, we are often too late for the right moment. Sometimes too it happens as with diagrams; for there we can sometimes analyse the figure, but not construct it again: so too in refutations, though we know the thing on which the connexion of the argu- [30] ment depends, we still are at a loss to split the argument apart.

17

First then, just as we say that we ought sometimes to choose to prove something in the general estimation rather than in truth, so also we have sometimes to solve arguments rather in the general estimation than according to the truth. For it is a general rule in fighting contentious persons, to treat them not as refuting, but as merely appearing to refute: for we say [35] that they don't really prove their case, so that our object in correcting them must be to dispel the appearance of it. For if refutation be an unambiguous contradiction arrived at from certain views, there could be no need to draw distinctions against amphiboly and ambiguity: for they do not effect a proof. The only motive for drawing further distinctions is that the [40] conclusion reached looks like a refutation. What, then, we have to beware of, is not being refuted, but seeming to be, because of course the asking of amphibolies and of questions that turn upon ambiguity, and all the other tricks of that kind, conceal even a genuine refutation, and make it uncertain who is refuted and who is not. For since one has the right at the end, when the conclusion is drawn, to say that the only denial made of [5] one's statement is ambiguous, no matter how precisely he may have addressed his argument to the very same point as oneself, it is not clear whether one has been refuted: for it is not clear whether at the moment one is speaking the truth. If, on the other hand, one had drawn a distinction, and questioned him on the ambiguous term or the amphiboly, the refutation would not have been a matter of uncertainty. Also what is incidentally the object of contentious arguers, though less so nowadays than formerly, would have been fulfilled, namely that the person questioned should [10] answer either 'Yes' or 'No': whereas nowadays the improper forms in which questioners put their questions compel the party questioned to add something to his answer in correction of the faultiness of the proposition as put: for certainly, if the questioner distinguishes his meaning adequately, the answerer is bound to reply either 'Yes' or 'No'.

[15] If any one is going to suppose that an argument which turns upon ambiguity is a refutation, it will be impossible for an answerer to escape being refuted in a sense: for in the case of visible objects one is bound of necessity to deny the term one has asserted, and to assert what one has denied. For the remedy which some people have for this is quite unavailing. They say, not that Coriscus is both musical and

[20] unmusical, but that *this* Coriscus is musical and *this* Coriscus unmusical. But this will not do, for to say '*this* Coriscus is unmusical', or 'musical', and to say '*this* Coriscus' is so, is to use the same expression: and this he is both affirming and denying at once. 'But perhaps they do not mean the same.' Well, nor did the simple name in the former case: so where is the difference? If, however, he is to ascribe to [25] the one person the simple title 'Coriscus', while to the other he is to add the prefix 'one' or 'this', he commits an absurdity: for the latter is no more applicable to the one than to the other: for to whichever he adds it, it makes no difference.

All the same, since if a man does not distinguish the senses of an amphiboly, it is not clear whether he has been confuted or has not been confuted, and since in arguments the [30] right to distinguish them is granted, it is evident that to grant the question simply without drawing any distinction is a mistake, so that, even if not the man himself, at any rate his argument looks as though it had been refuted. It often happens, however, that, though they see the amphiboly, people hesitate to draw such distinctions, because of the dense crowd of persons who propose questions of the kind, [35] in order that they may not be thought to be obstructionists at every turn: then, though they would never have supposed that that was the point on which the argument turned, they often find themselves faced by a paradox. Accordingly, since the right of drawing the distinction is granted, one should not hesitate, as has been said before.[1]

If people never made two questions into one [40] question, the fallacy that turns upon ambiguity and amphiboly would not have existed either, but either genuine refutation or none. For what is the difference between asking 'Are 176ª Callias and Themistocles musical?' and what one might have asked if they, being different, had had one name? For if the term applied means more than one thing, he has asked more than one question. If then it be not right to demand simply to be given a single answer to two questions, it is evident that it is not proper to give a simple answer to any am- [5] biguous question, not even if the predicate be true of all the subjects, as some claim that one should. For this is exactly as though he had asked 'Are Coriscus and Callias at home or not at home?', supposing them to be both in or both out: for in both cases there is a number of propositions: for though the simple answer be true, that does not make the [10] question one. For it is possible for it to be true to answer even countless different questions when put to one, all together with either a 'Yes' or a 'No': but still one should not answer them with a single answer: for that is the death of discussion. Rather, the case is like as though different things has actually had the same name applied to them. If then, one should [15] not give a single answer to two questions, it is evident that we should not say simply 'Yes' or 'No' in the case of ambiguous terms either: for the remark is simply a remark, not an answer at all, although among disputants such remarks are loosely deemed to be answers, because they do not see what the consequence is.

As we said,[2] then, inasmuch as certain refutations are generally taken for such, though [20] not such really, in the same way also certain solutions will be generally taken for solutions, though not really such. Now these, we say, must sometimes be advanced rather than the true solutions in contentious reasonings and in the encounter with ambiguity. The proper answer in saying what one thinks is to say 'Granted'; for in that way the likelihood of [25] being refuted on a side issue is minimized. If, on the other hand, one is compelled to say something paradoxical, one should then be most careful to add that 'it seems' so: for in that way one avoids the impression of being either refuted or paradoxical. Since it is clear what is meant by 'begging the original question', and people think that they must at all costs overthrow the premisses that lie near the conclusion, and plead in excuse for refusing to grant him some of them that he is begging the original question, so whenever any one claims [30] from us a point such as is bound to follow as a consequence from our thesis, but is false or paradoxical, we must plead the same: for the necessary consequences are generally held to be a part of the thesis itself. Moreover, whenever the universal has been secured not under a definite name, but by a comparison of instances, one should say that the questioner assumes it not in the sense in which it was granted nor in which he proposed it in the [35] premiss: for this too is a point upon which a refutation often depends.

If one is debarred from these defences one must pass to the argument that the conclusion has not been properly shown, approaching it

---

[1] 160ª 23 ff.

[2] 164ᵇ 25.

in the light of the aforesaid distinction between the different kinds of fallacy.[1]

In the case, then, of names that are used literally one is bound to answer either simply or by drawing a distinction: the tacit understandings implied in our statements, e.g. in [40] answer to questions that are not put clearly but elliptically—it is upon this that the 176[b] consequent refutation depends. For example, 'Is what belongs to Athenians the property of Athenians?' Yes. 'And so it is likewise in other cases. But observe; man belongs to the animal kingdom, doesn't he?' Yes. 'Then man is the property of the animal kingdom.' But this is a fallacy: for we say that man 'belongs to' the animal kingdom because he is an ani- [5] mal, just as we say that Lysander 'belongs to' the Spartans, because he is a Spartan. It is evident, then, that where the premiss put forward is not clear, one must not grant it simply.

Whenever of two things it is generally thought that if the one is true the other is true of necessity, whereas, if the other is true, the first is not true of necessity, one should, if [10] asked which of them is true, grant the smaller one: for the larger the number of premisses, the harder it is to draw a conclusion from them. If, again, the sophist tries to secure that *A* has a contrary while *B* has not, suppose what he says is true, you should say that each has a contrary, only for the one there is no established name.

Since, again, in regard to some of the views [15] they express, most people would say that any one who did not admit them was telling a falsehood, while they would not say this in regard to some, e.g. to any matters whereon opinion is divided (for most people have no distinct view whether the soul of animals is destructible or immortal), accordingly (1) wherever it is uncertain in which of two senses the premiss proposed is usually meant—whether as maxims are (for people call by the name of 'maxims' both true opinions and general [20] assertions), or like the doctrine 'the diagonal of a square is incommensurate with its side': and moreover (2) whenever opinions are divided as to the truth, we then have subjects of which it is very easy to change the terminology undetected. For because of the uncertainty in which of the two senses the premiss contains the truth, one will not be thought to be playing any trick, while because of the division of opinion, one will not be thought to be telling a falsehood. Change the terminology [25] therefore, for the change will make the position irrefutable.

Moreover, whenever one foresees any question coming, one should put in one's objection and have one's say beforehand: for by doing so one is likely to embarrass the questioner most effectually.

18

Inasmuch as a proper solution is an exposure [30] of false reasoning, showing on what kind of question the falsity depends, and whereas 'false reasoning' has a double meaning—for it is used either if a false conclusion has been proved, or if there is only an apparent proof and no real one—there must be both the kind of solution just described,[2] and also the correction of a merely apparent proof, so as to show upon which of the questions the appearance [35] depends. Thus it comes about that one solves arguments that are properly reasoned by demolishing them, whereas one solves merely apparent arguments by drawing distinctions. Again, inasmuch as of arguments that are properly reasoned some have a true and others a false conclusion, those that are false in respect of their conclusion it is possible to solve in two ways; for it is possible both by demol- [40] ishing one of the premisses asked, and by showing that the conclusion is not the real 177[a] state of the case: those, on the other hand, that are false in respect of the premisses can be solved only by a demolition of one of them; for the conclusion is true. So that those who wish to solve an argument should in the first place look and see if it is properly reasoned, or is unreasoned; and next, whether the conclusion be true or false, in order that we may effect the solution either by drawing some [5] distinction or by demolishing something, and demolishing it either in this way or in that, as was laid down before. There is a very great deal of difference between solving an argument when being subjected to questions and when not: for to foresee traps is difficult, whereas to see them at one's leisure is easier.

19

Of the refutations, then, that depend upon am- [10] biguity and amphiboly some contain some question with more than one meaning, while others contain a conclusion bearing a number of senses: e.g. in the proof that 'speaking of the silent' is possible, the conclusion has a double meaning, while in the proof that 'he

---
[1] Cf. chapter 6.   [2] Chapter 17.

who knows does not understand what he knows' one of the questions contains an amphiboly. Also the double-edged saying is true [15] in one context but not in another: it means something that is and something that is not.

Whenever, then, the many senses lie in the conclusion no refutation takes place unless the sophist secures as well the contradiction of the conclusion he means to prove; e.g. in the proof that 'seeing of the blind' is possible: for without the contradiction there was no refutation. Whenever, on the other hand, the many senses lie in the questions, there is no necessity to begin by denying the double-edged premiss: for this was not the goal of the argument but only [20] its support. At the start, then, one should reply with regard to an ambiguity, whether of a term or of a phrase, in this manner, that 'in one sense it is so, and in another not so', as e.g. that 'speaking of the silent' is in one sense possible but in another not possible: also that in one sense 'one should do what must needs be done', but not in another: for 'what must needs be' bears a number of senses. If, however, the ambiguity escapes one, one [25] should correct it at the end by making an addition to the question: 'Is speaking of the silent possible?' 'No, but to speak of A while he is silent is possible.' Also, in cases which contain the ambiguity in their premisses, one should reply in like manner: 'Do people then not understand what they know?' 'Yes, but not those who know it in the manner described': for it is not the same thing to say that 'those who know cannot understand what they know', and to say that 'those who know something [30] in this particular manner cannot do so'. In general, too, even though he draws his conclusion in a quite unambiguous manner, one should contend that what he has negated is not the fact which one has asserted but only its name; and that therefore there is no refutation.

20

It is evident also how one should solve those refutations that depend upon the division and combination of words: for if the expression means something different when divided and [35] when combined, as soon as one's opponent draws his conclusion one should take the expression in the contrary way. All such expressions as the following depend upon the combination or division of the words: 'Was X being beaten with that with which you saw him being beaten?' and 'Did you see him being beaten with that with which he was being beaten?' This fallacy has also in it an element 177ᵇ of amphiboly in the questions, but it really depends upon combination. For the meaning that depends upon the division of the words is not really a double meaning (for the expression when divided is not the same), unless also the word that is pronounced, according to its breathing, as ὄρος and ὅρος is a case of double meaning. (In writing, indeed, a word is the same whenever it is written of the [5] same letters and in the same manner—and even there people nowadays put marks at the side to show the pronunciation—but the spoken words are not the same.) Accordingly an expression that depends upon division is not an ambiguous one. It is evident also that not all refutations depend upon ambiguity as some people say they do.

[10] The answerer, then, must divide the expression: for 'I-saw-a-man-being-beaten with my eyes' is not the same as to say 'I saw a man being-beaten-with-my-eyes'. Also there is the argument of Euthydemus proving 'Then you know now in Sicily that there are triremes in Piraeus': and again, 'Can a good man who is a cobbler be bad?' 'No.' 'But a good man may be a bad cobbler: therefore a good cobbler will [15] be bad.' Again, 'Things the knowledge of which is good, are good things to learn, aren't they?' 'Yes.' 'The knowledge, however, of evil is good: therefore evil is a good thing to know.' 'Yes. But, you see, evil is both evil and a thing-to-learn, so that evil is an evil-thing-to-learn, although the knowledge of [20] evils is good.' Again, 'Is it true to say in the present moment that you are born?' 'Yes.' 'Then you are born in the present moment.' 'No; the expression as divided has a different meaning: for it is true to say-in-the-present-moment that "you are born", but not "You are born-in-the-present-moment".' Again, 'Could you do what you can, and as you can?' 'Yes.' 'But when not harping, you have the power to harp: and therefore you could harp when not [25] harping.' 'No: he has not the power to harp-while-not-harping; merely, when he is not doing it, he has the power to do it.'

Some people solve this last refutation in another way as well. For, they say, if he has granted that he can do anything in the way he can, still it does not follow that he can harp when not harping: for it has not been granted that he will do anything in every way in which [30] he can; and it is not the same thing 'to do a thing in the way he can' and 'to do it in every way in which he can'. But evidently they do not solve it properly: for of arguments that depend upon the same point the solution is the same, whereas this will not fit all cases of the kind nor yet all ways of putting the questions: it is valid against the questioner, but not against his argument.

21

[35] Accentuation gives rise to no fallacious arguments, either as written or as spoken, except perhaps some few that might be made up; e.g. the following argument. 'Is οὖ καταλύεις a house?' 'Yes.' 'Is then οὐ καταλύεις the negation of καταλύεις?' 'Yes.' 'But you said that οὐ καταλύεις is a house: therefore the house is a negation.' How one should solve this, is clear: for the word does not mean the same when spoken with an acuter and when spoken with a graver accent.

22

It is clear also how one must meet those fallacies [5] that depend on the identical expressions of things that are not identical, seeing that we are in possession of the kinds of predications. For the one man, say, has granted, when asked, that a term denoting a substance does not belong as an attribute, while the other has shown that some attribute belongs which is in the Category of Relation or of Quantity, but is usually thought to denote a substance because of its expression; e.g. in the following argument: 'Is it possible to be doing and to have done the same thing at the same time?' [10] 'No.' 'But, you see, it is surely possible to be seeing and to have seen the same thing at the same time, and in the same aspect.' Again, 'Is any mode of passivity a mode of activity?' 'No.' 'Then "he is cut", "he is burnt", "he is struck by some sensible object" are alike in expression and all denote some form of passivity, while again "to say", "to run", "to see" are [15] like one another in expression: but, you see, "to see" is surely a form of being struck by a sensible object; therefore it is at the same time a form of passivity and of activity.' Suppose, however, that in that case any one, after granting that it is not possible to do and to have done the same thing in the same time, were to say that it *is* possible to see and to have seen it, still he has not yet been refuted, suppose him to say that 'to see' is not a form of 'doing' (activity) but of 'passivity': for this question is required as well, though he is supposed by [20] the listener to have already granted it, when he granted that 'to cut' is a form of present, and 'to have cut' a form of past, activity, and so on with the other things that have a like expression. For the listener adds the rest by himself, thinking the meaning to be alike: whereas really the meaning is not alike, though it appears to be so because of the expression. [25] The same thing happens here as happens in cases of ambiguity: for in dealing with ambiguous expressions the tyro in argument supposes the sophist to have negated the fact which he (the tyro) affirmed, and not merely the name: whereas there still wants the question whether in using the ambiguous term he had a single meaning in view: for if he grants that that was so, the refutation will be effected.

Like the above are also the following arguments. [30] It is asked if a man has lost what he once had and afterwards has not: for a man will no longer have ten dice even though he has only lost one die. No: rather it is that he has lost *what* he had before and has not now; but there is no necessity for him to have lost *as much* or *as many* things as he has not now. So then, he asks the questions as to *what* he has, and draws the conclusion as to the *whole number that* he has: for ten is a number. If then he had asked to begin with, whether a man no longer having the number of things [35] he once had has lost the whole number, no one would have granted it, but would have said 'Either the whole number or one of them'. Also there is the argument that 'a man may give what he has not got': for he has not got only one die. No: rather it is that he has given, not *what* he had not got, but *in a manner in which* he had not got it, viz. just the one. For the word 'only' does not signify a particular substance or quality or number, but a *manner of relation,* e.g. that it is not coupled with any other. It is therefore just as if he had asked 'Could a man give what he has not got?' and, on being given the answer 'No', were to ask if a man could give a thing quickly when he had not got it quickly, and, on this being granted, were to conclude that 'a man could give what he had not got'. It is quite evident [5] that he has not proved his point: for to 'give quickly' is not to give a thing, but to give in a certain manner; and a man could certainly give a thing in a manner in which he has not got it, e.g. he might have got it with pleasure and give it with pain.

Like these are also all arguments of the following kind: 'Could a man strike a blow with a hand which he has not got, or see with an eye which he has not got?' For he has not got [*10*] only one eye. Some people solve this case, where a man has more than one eye, or more than one of anything else, by saying also that he has only one. Others also solve it as they solve the refutation of the view that 'what a man has, he has received': for *A* gave only one vote; and certainly *B,* they say, has only one vote from *A.* Others, again, proceed by demolishing straight away the proposition asked, and admitting that it is quite possible to have what one has not received; e.g. to have received [*15*] sweet wine, but then, owing to its going bad in the course of receipt, to have it sour. But, as was said also above,[1] all these persons direct their solutions against the man, not against his argument. For if this were a genuine solution, then, suppose any one to grant the opposite, he could find no solution, just as happens in other cases; e.g. suppose the true solution to be 'So-and-so is partly true and [*20*] partly not', then, if the answerer grants the expression without any qualification, the sophist's conclusion follows. If, on the other hand, the conclusion does not follow, then that could not be the true solution: and what we say in regard to the foregoing examples is that, even if all the sophist's premises be granted, still no proof is effected.

Moreover, the following too belong to this [*25*] group of arguments. 'If something be in writing did some one write it?' 'Yes.' 'But it is now in writing that you are seated—a false statement, though it was true at the time when it was written: therefore the statement that was written is at the same time false and true.' But this is fallacious, for the falsity or truth of a statement or opinion indicates not a substance but a quality: for the same account applies to the case of an opinion as well. Again, 'Is what a learner learns what he learns?' 'Yes.' [*30*] 'But suppose some one learns "slow" quick'. Then his (the sophist's) words denote not *what* the learner learns but *how* he learns it. Also, 'Does a man tread upon what he walks through?' 'Yes.' 'But *X* walks through a whole day.' No, rather the words denote not what he walks through, but *when* he walks; just as when any one uses the words 'to drink the cup' he denotes not what he drinks, but the vessel *out of which* he drinks. Also, 'Is it either by learning or by discovery that a man knows what he knows?' 'Yes.' 'But suppose [*35*] that of a pair of things he has discovered one and learned the other, the pair is not

[1] 177ᵇ 31.

known to him by either method.' No: 'what' he knows, means 'every single thing' he knows, individually; but this does not mean 'all the things' he knows, collectively. Again, there is the proof that there is a 'third man' distinct from Man and from individual men. But that is a fallacy, for 'Man', and indeed every general predicate, denotes not an individual substance, but a particular quality, or the being related to something in a particular manner, or something of that sort. Likewise also in the case of 'Coriscus' and 'Coriscus the musician' there is the problem, 'Are they the same or different?' For the one denotes an individual substance and the other a quality, so that it cannot be isolated; though it is not the isolation which creates the 'third man', but the admission that it is an individual substance. [*5*] For 'Man' cannot be an individual substance, as Callias is. Nor is the case improved one whit even if one were to call the element he has isolated not an individual substance but a quality: for there will still be the one beside the many, just as 'Man' was. It is evident then that one must not grant that what is a common predicate applying to a class universally is an individual substance, but must say that it [*10*] denotes either a quality, or a relation, or a quantity, or something of that kind.

23

It is a general rule in dealing with arguments that depend on language that the solution always follows the opposite of the point on which the argument turns: e.g. if the argument depends upon combination, then the solution consists in division; if upon division, then in combination. Again, if it depends on an acute accent, the solution is a grave accent; if on a grave ac- [*15*] cent, it is an acute. If it depends on ambiguity, one can solve it by using the opposite term; e.g. if you find yourself calling something inanimate, despite your previous denial that it was so, show in what sense it is alive: if, on the other hand, one has declared it to be inanimate and the sophist has proved it to be animate, say how it is inanimate. Likewise also in a case [*20*] of amphiboly. If the argument depends on likeness of expression, the opposite will be the solution. 'Could a man give what he has not got?' 'No, not *what* he has not got; but he could give it *in a way in which* he has not got it, e.g. one die by itself.' Does a man know either by learning or by discovery each *thing* that he knows, singly? 'Yes, but not the *things* that he knows, collectively.' Also a man treads, perhaps, on any *thing* he walks through, but not on the *time* he walks through. Likewise [25] also in the case of the other examples.

24

In dealing with arguments that depend on Accident, one and the same solution meets all cases. For since it is indeterminate when an attribute should be ascribed to a thing, in cases where it belongs to the accident of the thing, and since in some cases it is generally agreed and people admit that it belongs, while in others they deny that it need belong, we should [30] therefore, as soon as the conclusion has been drawn, say in answer to them all alike, that there is no need for such an attribute to belong. One must, however, be prepared to adduce an example of the kind of attribute meant. All arguments such as the following depend upon Accident. 'Do you know what I am going to ask you?' 'Do you know the man who is approaching', or 'the man in the mask'? 'Is the statue your work of art?' or 'Is the dog [35] your father?' 'Is the product of a small number with a small number a small number?' For it is evident in all these cases that there is no necessity for the attribute which is true of the thing's accident to be true of the thing as well. For only to things that are indistinguishable and one in essence is it generally agreed that all the same attributes belong; whereas in the case of a good thing, to be good is not the same as to be going to be the subject of a question; nor in the case of a man approaching, or wearing a mask, is 'to be approaching' the same thing as 'to be Coriscus', so that suppose I know Coriscus, but do not know the man who is approaching, it still isn't the case that I both know and do not know the same man; nor, again, if this is mine and is [5] also a work of art, is it therefore my work of art, but my property or thing or something else. (The solution is after the same manner in the other cases as well.)

Some solve these refutations by demolishing the original proposition asked: for they say that it is possible to know and not to know the same thing, only not in the same respect: accordingly, when they don't know the man who is coming towards them, but do know Coriscus, [10] they assert that they do know and don't know the same object, but not in the same respect. Yet, as we have already remarked,[1] the correction of arguments that depend upon the same point ought to be the same, whereas this one will not stand if one adopts the same principle in regard not to knowing something, but to being, or to being in a certain state, e.g. suppose that X is a [15] father, and is also yours: for if in some cases this is true and it is possible to know and not to know the same thing, yet with that case the solution stated has nothing to do. Certainly there is nothing to prevent the same argument from having a number of flaws; but it is not the exposition of any and every fault that constitutes a solution: for it is possible for a man to show that a false conclusion has been proved, but not to show on what it depends, e.g. in the case of Zeno's argument to prove [20] that motion is impossible. So that even if any one were to try to establish that this doctrine is an impossible one, he still is mistaken, and even if he proved his case ten thousand times over, still this is no solution of Zeno's argument: for the solution was all along an exposition of false reasoning, showing on what its falsity depends. If then he has not proved his case, or is trying to establish even a true proposition, or a false one, in a false manner, [25] to point this out is a true solution. Possibly, indeed, the present suggestion may very well apply in some cases: but in these cases, at any rate, not even this would be generally agreed: for he knows both that Coriscus is Coriscus and that the approaching figure is approaching. To know and not to know the same thing is generally thought to be possible, when e.g. one knows that X is white, but does [30] not realize that he is musical: for in that way he does know and not know the same thing, though not in the same respect. But as to the approaching figure and Coriscus he knows both that it is approaching and that he is Coriscus.

A like mistake to that of those whom we have mentioned is that of those who solve the proof that every number is a small number: [35] for if, when the conclusion is not proved, they pass this over and say that a conclusion has been proved and is true, on the ground that every number is both great and small, they make a mistake.

Some people also use the principle of ambiguity to solve the aforesaid reasonings, e.g. the proof that 'X is your father', or 'son', or 'slave'. Yet it is evident that if the appearance of a proof depends upon a plurality of meanings, the term, or the expression in question, ought to bear a number of literal senses,

[1] 177^b 31.

whereas no one speaks of *A* as being '*B*'s child' in the literal sense, if *B* is the child's master, but the combination depends upon [5] Accident. 'Is *A* yours?' 'Yes.' 'And is *A* a child?' 'Yes.' 'Then the child *A* is yours,' because he happens to be both yours and a child; but he is not 'your child'.

There is also the proof that 'something "of evils" is good'; for wisdom is a 'knowledge "of evils"'. But the expression that this is 'of so-and-so' (='so-and-so's') has not a number of [10] meanings: it means that it is 'so-and-so's property'. We may suppose of course, on the other hand, that it has a number of meanings —for we also say that man is 'of the animals', though not their property; and also that any term related to 'evils' in a way expressed by a genitive case is on that account a so-and-so 'of evils', though it is not one of the evils—but in that case the apparently different meanings seem to depend on whether the term is used relatively or absolutely. 'Yet it is conceivably possible to find a real ambiguity in the phrase [15] "Something of evils is good".' Perhaps, but not with regard to the phrase in question. It would occur more nearly, suppose that 'A servant is good of the wicked'; though perhaps it is not quite found even there: for a thing may be 'good' and be '*X*'s' without being at the same time '*X*'s good'. Nor is the saying that 'Man is of the animals' a phrase with a number of meanings: for a phrase does not [20] become possessed of a number of meanings merely suppose we express it elliptically: for we express 'Give me the Iliad' by quoting half a line of it, e.g. 'Give me "Sing, goddess, of the wrath..."'

25

Those arguments which depend upon an expression that is valid of a particular thing, or in a particular respect, or place, or manner, or relation, and not valid absolutely, should be solved by considering the conclusion in rela- [25] tion to its contradictory, to see if any of these things can possibly have happened to it. For it is impossible for contraries and opposites and an affirmative and a negative to belong to the same thing absolutely; there is, however, nothing to prevent each from belonging in a particular respect or relation or manner, or to prevent one of them from belonging in a particular respect and the other absolutely. So that if this one belongs absolutely and that [30] one in a particular respect, there is as yet no refutation. This is a feature one has to find in the conclusion by examining it in comparison with its contradictory.

All arguments of the following kind have this feature: 'Is it possible for what is-not to be?' 'No.' 'But, you see, it *is* something, despite its not *being*.' Likewise also, Being will not be; for it will *not be* some particular form of being. [35] 'Is it possible for the same man at the same time to be a keeper and a breaker of his oath?' 'Can the same man at the same time both obey and disobey the same man?' Or isn't it the case that being something in particular and Being are not the same? On the other hand, Not-being, even if it be something, need not also have absolute 'being' as well. Nor if a man keeps his oath in this particular instance or in this particular respect, is he bound also to be a keeper of oaths absolutely, but he who swears that he will break his oath, and then breaks it, keeps this particular oath only; he is not a keeper of his oath: nor is the disobedient man 'obedient', though he obeys one particular command. The argument is similar, also, as regards the problem whether the same man can at the same time say what is both false and true: but it appears to be a troublesome question because it is not easy to see in which of the two connexions the word 'absolutely' is to be rendered—with 'true' or with 'false'. [5] There is, however, nothing to prevent it from being false absolutely, though true in some particular respect or relation, i.e. being true in some things, though not 'true' absolutely. Likewise also in cases of some particular relation and place and time. For all arguments of the following kind depend upon this. 'Is health, or wealth, a good thing?' 'Yes.' 'But to the fool [10] who does not use it aright it is not a good thing: therefore it is both good and not good.' 'Is health, or political power, a good thing?' 'Yes.' 'But sometimes it is not particularly good: therefore the same thing is both good and not good to the same man.' Or rather there is nothing to prevent a thing, though good absolutely, being not good to a particular man, or being good to a particular man, and yet not good [15] now or here. 'Is that which the prudent man would not wish, an evil?' 'Yes.' 'But to get rid of, he would not wish the good: therefore the good is an evil.' But that is a mistake; for it is not the same thing to say 'The good is an evil' and 'to get rid of the good is an evil'. Likewise also the argument of the thief is mistaken. For it is not the case that if the thief is an evil thing, acquiring things is also evil: what he wishes, therefore, is not what is evil

[20] but what is good; for to acquire something good is good. Also, disease is an evil thing, but not to get rid of disease. 'Is the just preferable to the unjust, and what takes place justly to what takes place unjustly?' 'Yes.' 'But to be put to death unjustly is preferable.' 'Is it just that each should have his own?' 'Yes.' 'But whatever decisions a man comes to on the [25] strength of his personal opinion, even if it be a false opinion, are valid in law: therefore the same result is both just and unjust.' Also, 'should one decide in favour of him who says what is just, or of him who says what is unjust?' 'The former.' 'But, you see, it is just for the injured party also to say fully the things he has suffered; and these were unjust.' But these are fallacies. For because to suffer a thing unjustly is preferable, unjust ways are not there- [30] fore preferable to just; but, absolutely, just ways are preferable, though in this particular case the unjust may very well be better than the just. Also, to have one's own is just, while to have what is another's is not just: all the same, the decision in question may very well be a just decision, whatever it be that the opinion of the man who gave the decision supports: for because it is just in this particular case or in this particular manner, it is not also just absolutely. Likewise also, though things are unjust, there is nothing to prevent the [35] *speaking* of them being just: for because to speak of things is just, there is no necessity that the things should be just, any more than because to speak of things be of use, the things need be of use. Likewise also in the case of what is just. So that it is not the case that because the things spoken of are unjust, the victory goes to him who speaks unjust things: for he speaks of things that are just to speak of, though absolutely, i.e. to suffer, they are unjust.

26

181ᵃ Refutations that depend on the definition of a refutation must, according to the plan sketched above,[1] be met by comparing together the conclusion with its contradictory, and seeing that it shall involve the same attribute in the same respect and relation and manner and [5] time. If this additional question be put at the start, you should not admit that it is impossible for the same thing to be both double and not double, but grant that it is possible, only not in such a way as was agreed to constitute a refutation of your case. All the following arguments depend upon a point of that kind.

[1] 167ᵃ 21.

'Does a man who knows A to be A, know the thing called A?' and in the same way, 'is one who is ignorant that A is A ignorant of the [10] thing called A?' 'Yes.' 'But one who knows that Coriscus is Coriscus might be ignorant of the fact that he is musical, so that he both knows and is ignorant of the same thing.' 'Is a thing four cubits long greater than a thing three cubits long?' 'Yes.' 'But a thing might grow from three to four cubits in length;' now what is 'greater' is greater than a 'less': accordingly the thing in question will be both greater and less than itself in the same respect.

27

[15] As to refutations that depend on begging and assuming the original point to be proved, suppose the nature of the question to be obvious, one should not grant it, even though it be a view generally held, but should tell him the truth. Suppose, however, that it escapes one, then, thanks to the badness of arguments of that kind, one should make one's error recoil upon the questioner, and say that he has brought no argument: for a refutation must be proved independently of the original point. Secondly, one should say that the point was granted under the impression that he intended [20] not to use it as a premiss, but to reason against it, in the opposite way from that adopted in refutations on side issues.

28

Also, those refutations that bring one to their conclusion through the consequent you should show up in the course of the argument itself. The mode in which consequences follow is twofold. For the argument either is that as the universal follows on its particular—as (e.g.) 'animal' follows from 'man'—so does the par- [25] ticular on its universal: for the claim is made that if A is always found with B, then B also is always found with A. Or else it proceeds by way of the opposites of the terms involved: for if A follows B, it is claimed that A's opposite will follow B's opposite. On this latter claim the argument of Melissus also depends: for he claims that because that which has come to be has a beginning, that which has not come to be has none, so that if the heaven has not come to be, it is also eternal. But that is not so; [30] for the sequence is vice versa.

29

In the case of any refutations whose reasoning depends on some addition, look and see if upon its subtraction the absurdity follows none the less: and then if so, the answerer should point this out, and say that he granted the addition not because he really thought it, but for the sake of the argument, whereas the questioner [35] has not used it for the purpose of his argument at all.

30

To meet those refutations which make several questions into one, one should draw a distinction between them straight away at the start. For a question must be single to which there is a single answer, so that one must not affirm or deny several things of one thing, nor one thing of many, but one of one. But just as in the case of ambiguous terms, an attribute belongs to a 181[b] term sometimes in both its senses, and sometimes in neither, so that a simple answer does one, as it happens, no harm despite the fact that the question is not simple, so it is in these cases of double questions too. Whenever, then, the several attributes belong to the one subject, or the one to the many, the man who [5] gives a simple answer encounters no obstacle even though he has committed this mistake: but whenever an attribute belongs to one subject but not to the other, or there is a question of a number of attributes belonging to a number of subjects and in one sense both belong to both, while in another sense, again, they do not, then there is trouble, so that one must beware of this. Thus (e.g.) in the following arguments: Supposing A to be good and B evil, you [10] will, if you give a single answer about both, be compelled to say that it is true to call these good, and that it is true to call them evil and likewise to call them neither good nor evil (for each of them has not each character), so that the same thing will be both good and evil and neither good nor evil. Also, since everything is the same as itself and different from anything else, inasmuch as the man who answers double questions simply can be made to say that several things are 'the same' not as other things but 'as themselves', and also that they are different from themselves, it follows that the same things must be both the same as and [15] different from themselves. Moreover, if what is good becomes evil while what is evil is good, then they must both become two. So of two unequal things each being equal to itself, it will follow that they are both equal and unequal to themselves.

Now these refutations fall into the province [20] of other solutions as well: for 'both' and 'all' have more than one meaning, so that the resulting affirmation and denial of the same thing does not occur, except verbally: and this is not what we meant by a refutation. But it is clear that if there be not put a single question on a number of points, but the answerer has affirmed or denied one attribute only of one subject only, the absurdity will not come to pass.

31

[25] With regard to those who draw one into repeating the same thing a number of times, it is clear that one must not grant that predications of relative terms have any meaning in abstraction by themselves, e.g. that 'double' is a significant term apart from the whole phrase 'double of half' merely on the ground that it figures in it. For ten figures in 'ten minus one' [30] and 'do' in 'not do', and generally the affirmation in the negation; but for all that, suppose any one were to say, 'This is not white', he does not say that it is white. The bare word 'double', one may perhaps say, has not even any meaning at all, any more than has 'the' in 'the half': and even if it has a meaning, yet it has not the same meaning as in the combination. Nor is 'knowledge' the same thing in a specific branch of it (suppose it, e.g. to be 'medical [35] knowledge') as it is in general: for in general it was the 'knowledge of the knowable'. In the case of terms that are predicated of the terms through which they are defined, you should say the same thing, that the term defined is not the same in abstraction as it is in the whole phrase. For 'concave' has a general meaning which is the same in the case of a snub nose, and of a bandy leg, but when added to either substantive nothing prevents it from differentiating its meaning; in fact it bears one 182[a] sense as applied to the nose, and another as applied to the leg: for in the former connexion it means 'snub' and in the latter 'bandy-shaped'; i.e. it makes no difference whether you say 'a snub nose' or 'a concave nose'. Moreover, the expression must not be granted in the nominative case: for it is a falsehood. For snubness is not a concave nose but something (e.g. an affection) belonging to a nose: hence, there [5] is no absurdity in supposing that the snub nose is a nose possessing the concavity that belongs to a nose.

32

With regard to solecisms, we have previously said[1] what it is that appears to bring them

---
[1] 165[b] 20 f.

about; the method of their solution will be clear in the course of the arguments themselves. Solecism is the result aimed at in all arguments of the following kind: 'Is a thing truly that which you truly call it?' 'Yes'. 'But, speaking of a stone, you call him real: therefore of a stone it follows that "him is real".' No: rather, talking of a stone means not saying 'which' but 'whom', and not 'that' but 'him'. If, then, any one were to ask, 'Is a stone *him whom* you truly call him?' he would be generally thought not to be speaking good Greek, any more than if he were to ask, 'Is *he* what you call *her*?' Speak in this way of a 'stick' or any neuter word, and the difference does not break out. For this reason, also, no solecism is incurred, suppose any one asks, 'Is a thing what you say it to be?' 'Yes'. 'But, speaking of a stick, you call it real: therefore, of a stick it follows that it is real.' 'Stone', however, and 'he' have masculine designations. Now suppose some one were to ask, 'Can "he" be a "she" (a female)?', and then again, 'Well, but is not he Coriscus?' and then were to say, 'Then he is a "she",' he has not proved the solecism, even if the name 'Coriscus' does signify a 'she', if, on the other hand, the answerer does not grant this: this point must be put as an additional question: while if neither is it the fact nor does he grant it, then the sophist has not proved his case either in fact or as against the person he has been questioning. In like manner, then, in the above instance as well it must be definitely put that 'he' means the stone. If, however, this neither is so nor is granted, the conclusion must not be stated: though it follows apparently, because the case (the accusative), that is really unlike, appears to be like the nominative. 'Is it true to say that this object is what you call it by name?' 'Yes'. 'But you call it by the name of a shield: this object therefore is "of a shield".' No: not necessarily, because the meaning of 'this object' is not 'of a shield' but 'a shield': 'of a shield' would be the meaning of 'this object's'. Nor again if 'He is what you call him by name', while 'the name you call him by is Cleon's', is he therefore 'Cleon's': for he is not 'Cleon's', for what was said was that '*He,* not *his,* is what I call him by name'. For the question, if put in the latter way, would not even be Greek. 'Do you know this?' 'Yes.' 'But this is he: therefore you know he'. No: rather 'this' has not the same meaning in 'Do you know this?' as in 'This is a stone'; in the first it stands for an accusative, in the second for a nominative case.

'When you have understanding of anything, do you understand it?' 'Yes.' 'But you have understanding of a stone: therefore you understand of a stone.' No: the one phrase is in the genitive, 'of a stone', while the other is in the accusative, 'a stone': and what was granted was that 'you understand *that,* not *of that,* of which you have understanding', so that you understand not 'of a stone', but 'the stone'.

Thus then that arguments of this kind do not prove solecism but merely appear to do so, and both why they so appear and how you should meet them, is clear from what has been said.

33

We must also observe that of all the arguments aforesaid it is easier with some to see why and where the reasoning leads the hearer astray, while with others it is more difficult, though often they are the same arguments as the former. For we must call an argument the same if it depends upon the same point; but the same argument is apt to be thought by some to depend on diction, by others on accident, and by others on something else, because each of them, when worked with different terms, is not so clear as it was. Accordingly, just as in fallacies that depend on ambiguity, which are generally thought to be the silliest form of fallacy, some are clear even to the man in the street (for humorous phrases nearly all depend on diction; e.g. 'The man got the cart down from the stand'; and 'Where are you bound?' 'To the yard arm'; and 'Which cow will calve afore?' 'Neither, but both behind;' and 'Is the North wind clear?' 'No, indeed; for it has murdered the beggar and the merchant.' 'Is he a Goodenough-King?' 'No, indeed; a Rob-son': and so with the great majority of the rest as well), while others appear to elude the most expert (and it is a symptom of this that they often fight about their terms, e.g. whether the meaning of 'Being' and 'One' is the same in all their applications or different; for some think that 'Being' and 'One' mean the same; while others solve the argument of Zeno and Parmenides by asserting that 'One' and 'Being' are used in a number of senses), likewise also as regards fallacies of Accident and each of the other types, some of the arguments will be easier to see while others are more difficult; also to grasp to which class a fallacy belongs, and whether it is a refutation or not a refutation, is not equally easy in all cases.

An incisive argument is one which produces

the greatest perplexity: for this is the one with the sharpest fang. Now perplexity is twofold, one which occurs in reasoned arguments, respecting which of the propositions asked one is [35] to demolish, and the other in contentious arguments, respecting the manner in which one is to assent to what is propounded. Therefore it is in syllogistic arguments that the more incisive ones produce the keenest heart-searching. Now a syllogistic argument is most incisive if from premisses that are as generally accepted as possible it demolishes a conclusion that is accepted as generally as possible. For the one argument, if the contradictory is changed about, makes all the resulting syllogisms alike in character: for always from premisses that are generally accepted it will prove a conclusion, negative or positive as the case may be, that is just as generally accepted; and therefore one is bound to feel perplexed. An argument, then, of this kind is the most incisive, viz. the one that puts its conclusion on all fours with the propositions asked; and second comes the one that argues from premisses, all of which are equally convincing: for this [5] will produce an equal perplexity as to what kind of premiss, of those asked, one should demolish. Herein is a difficulty: for one must demolish something, but what one must demolish is uncertain. Of contentious arguments, on the other hand, the most incisive is the one which, in the first place, is characterized by an initial uncertainty whether it has been properly reasoned or not; and also whether the solution depends on a false premiss or on the drawing of a distinction; while, of the rest, the second [10] place is held by that whose solution clearly depends upon a distinction or a demolition, and yet it does not reveal clearly which it is of the premisses asked, whose demolition, or the drawing of a distinction within it, will bring the solution about, but even leaves it vague whether it is on the conclusion or on one of the premisses that the deception depends.

Now sometimes an argument which has not been properly reasoned is silly, supposing the [15] assumptions required to be extremely contrary to the general view or false; but sometimes it ought not to be held in contempt. For whenever some question is left out, of the kind that concerns both the subject and the nerve of the argument, the reasoning that has both failed to secure this as well, and also failed to reason properly, is silly; but when what is omitted is some extraneous question, then it is by no means to be lightly despised, but the argu-[20]ment is quite respectable, though the questioner has not put his questions well.

Just as it is possible to bring a solution sometimes against the argument, at others against the questioner and his mode of questioning, and at others against neither of these, likewise also it is possible to marshal one's questions and reasoning both against the thesis, and against [25] the answerer and against the time, whenever the solution requires a longer time to examine than the period available.

34

As to the number, then, and kind of sources whence fallacies arise in discussion, and how we are to show that our opponent is committing a fallacy and make him utter paradoxes; moreover, by the use of what materials sole-[30]cism is brought about, and how to question and what is the way to arrange the questions; moreover, as to the question what use is served by all arguments of this kind, and concerning the answerer's part, both as a whole in general, and in particular how to solve arguments and solecisms—on all these things let the foregoing discussion suffice. It remains to [35] recall our original proposal and to bring our discussion to a close with a few words upon it.

Our programme was, then, to discover some faculty of reasoning about any theme put before us from the most generally accepted premisses that there are. For that is the essential task of the art of discussion (dialectic) and of examination (peirastic). Inasmuch, however, as it is annexed to it, on account of the near presence of the art of sophistry (sophistic), not only to be able to conduct an examination dialectically but also with a show of knowledge, we therefore proposed for our treatise not only the aforesaid aim of being able to exact an account of any view, but also the aim of [5] ensuring that in standing up to an argument we shall defend our thesis in the same manner by means of views as generally held as possible. The reason of this we have explained;[1] for this, too, was why Socrates used to ask questions and not to answer them; for he used to confess that he did not know. We have made clear, in the course of what precedes, the number both of the points with reference to which, and of the materials from which, this will be accomplished, and also from what sources we [10] can become well supplied with these: we have shown, moreover, how to question or ar-

[1] 165ª 19-27.

range the questioning as a whole, and the problems concerning the answers and solutions to be used against the reasonings of the questioner. We have also cleared up the problems concerning all other matters that belong to the same inquiry into arguments. In addition to this we have been through the subject of Fallacies, as we have already stated above.[1]

That our programme, then, has been adequately completed is clear. But we must not omit to notice what has happened in regard to this inquiry. For in the case of all discoveries the results of previous labours that have been handed down from others have been advanced bit by bit by those who have taken them on, whereas the original discoveries generally make an advance that is small at first though much more useful than the development which later springs out of them. For it may be that in everything, as the saying is, 'the first start is the main part': and for this reason also it is the most difficult; for in proportion as it is most potent in its influence, so it is smallest in its compass and therefore most difficult to see: whereas when this is once discovered, it is easier to add and develop the remainder in connexion with it. This is in fact what has happened in regard to rhetorical speeches and to practically all the other arts: for those who discovered the beginnings of them advanced them in all only a little way, whereas the celebrities of to-day are the heirs (so to speak) of a long succession of men who have advanced them bit by bit, and so have developed them to their present form, Tisias coming next after the first founders, then Thrasymachus after Tisias, and Theodorus next to him, while several people have made their several contributions to it: and therefore it is not to be wondered at that the art has attained considerable dimensions. Of this inquiry, on the other hand, it was not the case that part of the work had been thoroughly done before, while part had not. Nothing existed at all. For the training given by the paid professors of contentious arguments was like the treatment of the matter by Gorgias. For they used to hand out speeches to be learned by heart, some rhetorical, others in the form of question and answer, each side supposing that their arguments on either side generally fall among them. And therefore the teaching they gave their pupils was ready but rough. For they used to suppose that they trained people by imparting to them not the art but its products, as though any one professing that he would impart a form of knowledge to obviate any pain in the feet, were then not to teach a man the art of shoe-making or the sources whence he can acquire anything of the kind, but were to present him with several kinds of shoes of all sorts: for he has helped him to meet his need, but has not imparted an art to him. Moreover, on the subject of Rhetoric there exists much that has been said long ago, whereas on the subject of reasoning we had nothing else of an earlier date to speak of at all, but were kept at work for a long time in experimental researches. If, then, it seems to you after inspection that, such being the situation as it existed at the start, our investigation is in a satisfactory condition compared with the other inquiries that have been developed by tradition, there must remain for all of you, or for our students, the task of extending us your pardon for the shortcomings of the inquiry, and for the discoveries thereof your warm thanks.

---
[1] 183ª 27.

PHYSICAL TREATISES

CONTENTS: PHYSICS

BOOK I

CHAP.		BERLIN NOS.
1.	The scope and method of this book	184^a 10
2.	The problem: the number and character of the first principles of nature	184^b 15
	Reality is not one in the way that Parmenides and Melissus supposed (185^a 20)	
3.	Refutation of their arguments	186^a 4
4.	Statement and examination of the opinions of the natural philosophers	187^a 12
5.	The principles are contraries	188^a 18
6.	The principles are two, or three, in number	189^a 11
7.	The number and nature of the principles	189^b 30
8.	The true opinion removes the difficulty felt by the early philosophers	191^a 23
9.	Further reflections on the first principles of nature	191^b 35

BOOK II

A.

1.	Nature and the natural	192^b 8

B.

2.	Distinction of the natural philosopher from the mathematician and the metaphysician	193^b 22

C. *The conditions of change*

3.	The essential conditions	194^b 16
4.	The opinions of others about chance and spontaneity	195^b 31
5.	Do chance and spontaneity exist? What is chance and what are its characteristics?	196^b 10
6.	Distinction between chance and spontaneity, and between both and the essential conditions of change	197^a 36

D. *Proof in natural philosophy*

7.	The physicist demonstrates by means of the four conditions of change	198^a 14
8.	Does nature act for an end?	198^b 10
9.	The sense in which necessity is present in natural things	199^b 33

BOOK III

A. *Motion*

1.	The nature of motion	200^b 10
2.	The nature of motion (continued)	201^b 16
3.	The mover and the moved	202^a 12

B. *The infinite*

4.	Opinions of the early philosophers	202^b 30
	Main arguments for belief in the infinite (203^b 15)	
5.	Criticism of the Pythagorean and Platonic belief in a separately existing infinite	204^a 9
	There is no infinite sensible body (204^a 34)	
6.	That the infinite exists and how it exists	206^a 8
	What the infinite is (206^b 33)	
7.	The various kinds of infinite	207^a 33
	Which of the four conditions of change the infinite is to be referred to (207^b 34)	
8.	Refutation of the arguments for an actual infinite	208^a 5

BOOK IV

A. *Place*

1.	Does place exist?	208^a 28
	Doubts about the nature of place (209^a 2)	
2.	Is place matter or form?	209^a 31
3.	Can a thing be in itself or a place be in a place?	210^a 14
4.	What place is	210^b 33
5.	Corollaries	212^a 31

B. *The void*

6.	The views of others about the void	213^a 11
7.	What 'void' means	213^b 30
	Refutation of the arguments for belief in the void (214^a 16)	
8.	There is no void separate from bodies	214^b 11
	There is no void occupied by any body (216^a 26)	
9.	There is no void in bodies	216^b 21

C. *Time*

10.	Doubts about the existence of time	217^b 29
	Various opinions about the nature of time (218^a 31)	
11.	What time is	218^b 21
	The 'now' (219^b 9)	
12.	Various attributes of time	220^a 27
	The things that are in time (220^b 32)	
13.	Definitions of temporal terms	222^a 10
14.	Further reflections about time	222^b 30

BOOK V

1.	Classification of movements and changes	224^a 20
	Classification of changes *per se* (224^b 35)	

2. Classification of movements *per se*   225^b 10
   The unmovable (226^b 10)
3. The meaning of 'together,' 'apart,'   226^b 18
   'touch,' 'intermediate,' 'successive,' 'contiguous,' 'continuous'
4. The unity and diversity of movements   227^b 3
5. Contrariety of movement   229^a 7
6. Contrariety of movement and rest   229^b 22
   Contrariety of natural and unnatural movement or rest (230^a 18)

BOOK VI

1. Every continuum consists of continuous and divisible parts   231^a 20
2. (Continued)   232^a 23
3. A moment is indivisible and nothing is moved, or rests, in a moment   233^b 32
4. Whatever is moved is divisible   234^b 10
   Classification of movement (234^b 21)
   The time, the movement, the being-in-motion, the moving body, and the sphere of movement, are all similarly divided (235^a 13)
5. Whatever has changed is, as soon as it has changed, in that to which it has changed   235^b 6
   That in which (directly) it has changed is indivisible (235^b 32)
   In change there is a last but no first element (236^a 7)
6. In whatever time a thing changes (directly), it changes in any part of that time   236^b 20
   Whatever changes has changed before, and whatever has changed, before was changing (236^b 32)
7. The finitude or infinity of movement, of extension, and of the moved   237^b 23
8. Of coming to rest, and of rest   238^b 23
   A thing that is moved in any time directly is in no part of that time in a part of the space through which it moves (239^a 23)
9. Refutation of the arguments against the possibility of movement   239^b 5
10. That which has not parts cannot move   240^b 8
    Can change be infinite? (241^a 26)

BOOK VII

1. Whatever is moved is moved by something   241^b 24
   There is a first movent which is not moved by anything else (242^a 19)
2. The movent and the moved are together   243^a 3
3. All alteration pertains to sensible qualities   245^b 2
4. Comparison of movements   248^a 10
5. Proportion of movements   249^b 26

BOOK VIII

1. There always has been and always will be movement   250^b 10
2. Refutation of objections to the eternity of movement   252^b 7
3. There are things that are sometimes in movement, sometimes at rest   253^a 21
4. Whatever is in movement is moved by something else   254^b 7
5. The first movent is not moved by anything outside itself   256^a 3
   The first movent is immovable (257^a 31)
6. The immovable first movent is eternal and one   258^b 10
   The first movent is not moved even incidentally (259^a 20)
   The *primum mobile* is eternal (259^b 32)
7. Locomotion is the primary kind of movement   260^a 20
   No movement or change is continuous except locomotion (261^a 28)
8. Only circular movement can be continuous and infinite   261^b 26
9. Circular movement is the primary kind of locomotion   265^a 13
   Confirmation of the above doctrines (265^a 27)
10. The first movent has no parts nor magnitude, and is at the circumference of the world.   266^a 10

PHYSICS

BOOK I

1

184ª [*10*] When the objects of an inquiry, in any department, have principles, conditions, or elements, it is through acquaintance with these that knowledge, that is to say scientific knowledge, is attained. For we do not think that we know a thing until we are acquainted with its primary conditions or first principles, and have carried our analysis as far as its simplest elements. Plainly therefore in the science of Na- [*15*] ture, as in other branches of study, our first task will be to try to determine what relates to its principles.

The natural way of doing this is to start from the things which are more knowable and obvious to us and proceed towards those which are clearer and more knowable by nature; for the same things are not 'knowable relatively to us' and 'knowable' without qualification. So in the present inquiry we must follow this method and advance from what is more obscure by [*20*] nature, but clearer to us, towards what is more clear and more knowable by nature.

Now what is to us plain and obvious at first is rather confused masses, the elements and principles of which become known to us later by analysis. Thus we must advance from generalities to particulars; for it is a whole that is [*25*] best known to sense-perception, and a generality is a kind of whole, comprehending many things within it, like parts. Much the **184ᵇ** [*10*] same thing happens in the relation of the name to the formula. A name, e.g. 'round', means vaguely a sort of whole: its definition analyses this into its particular senses. Similarly a child begins by calling all men 'father', and all women 'mother', but later on distinguishes each of them.

2

[*15*] The principles in question must be either (*a*) one or (*b*) more than one.

If (*a*) one, it must be either (i) motionless, as Parmenides and Melissus assert, or (ii) in motion, as the physicists hold, some declaring air to be the first principle, others water.

If (*b*) more than one, then either (i) a finite or (ii) an infinite plurality. If (i) finite (but more than one), then either two or three or [*20*] four or some other number. If (ii) infinite, then either as Democritus believed one in kind, but differing in shape or form; or different in kind and even contrary.

A similar inquiry is made by those who inquire into the number of *existents:* for they inquire whether the ultimate constituents of existing things are one or many, and if many, whether a finite or an infinite plurality. So they too are inquiring whether the principle or element is one or many.

[*25*] Now to investigate whether Being is one and motionless is not a contribution to the sci- **185ª** ence of Nature. For just as the geometer has nothing more to say to one who denies the principles of his science—this being a question for a different science or for one common to all —so a man investigating *principles* cannot argue with one who denies their existence. For if Being is just one, and one in the way mentioned, there is a principle no longer, since a principle must be the principle of some thing or things.

[*5*] To inquire therefore whether Being is one in this sense would be like arguing against any other position maintained for the sake of argument (such as the Heraclitean thesis, or such a thesis as that Being is one man) or like refuting a merely contentious argument—a description which applies to the arguments both of Melissus and of Parmenides: their premisses [*10*] are false and their conclusions do not follow. Or rather the argument of Melissus is gross and palpable and offers no difficulty at all: accept one ridiculous proposition and the rest follows—a simple enough proceeding.

We physicists, on the other hand, must take for granted that the things that exist by nature are, either all or some of them, in motion— which is indeed made plain by induction. Moreover, no man of science is bound to solve [*15*] every kind of difficulty that may be raised, but only as many as are drawn falsely from the principles of the science: it is not our business

Note: The bold face numbers and letters are approximate indications of the pages and columns of the standard Berlin Greek text; the bracketed numbers, of the lines in the Greek text; they are here assigned as they are assigned in the Oxford translation.

to refute those that do not arise in this way: just as it is the duty of the geometer to refute the squaring of the circle by means of segments, but it is not his duty to refute Antiphon's proof. At the same time the holders of the theory of which we are speaking do incidentally raise physical questions, though Nature is not their subject: so it will perhaps be as well to spend a few words on them, especially as the inquiry is not without scientific interest.

[20] The most pertinent question with which to begin will be this: In what sense is it asserted that all things *are* one? For 'is' is used in many senses. Do they mean that all things 'are' *substance* or *quantities* or *qualities*? And, further, are all things *one* substance—one man, one horse, or one soul—or quality and that one [25] and the same—white or hot or something of the kind? These are all very different doctrines and all impossible to maintain.

For if *both* substance and quantity and quality are, then, whether these exist independently of each other or not, Being will be many.

If on the other hand it is asserted that all things are quality or quantity, then, whether substance exists or not, an absurdity results, if [30] indeed the impossible can properly be called absurd. For none of the others can exist independently: substance alone is independent: for everything is predicated of substance as subject. Now Melissus says that Being is infinite. It is then a quantity. For the infinite is in the category of quantity, whereas substance or quality or affection cannot be infinite except through a concomitant attribute, that is, if at 185ᵇ the same time they are also quantities. For to define the infinite you must use quantity in your formula, but not substance or quality. If then Being is both substance and quantity, it is two, not one: if only substance, it is not infinite and has no magnitude; for to have that it will have to be a quantity.

[5] Again, 'one' itself, no less than 'being', is used in many senses, so we must consider in what sense the word is used when it is said that the All is one.

Now we say that (*a*) the continuous is one or that (*b*) the indivisible is one, or (*c*) things are said to be 'one', when their essence is one and the same, as 'liquor' and 'drink'.

If (*a*) their One is one in the sense of continuous, it is many, for the continuous is [10] divisible *ad infinitum*.

There is, indeed, a difficulty about part and whole, perhaps not relevant to the present argument, yet deserving consideration on its own account—namely, whether the part and the whole are one or more than one, and how they can be one or many, and, if they are more than one, in what sense they are more than one. (Similarly with the parts of wholes which are [15] not continuous.) Further, if each of the two parts is indivisibly one with the whole, the difficulty arises that they will be indivisibly one with each other also.

But to proceed: If (*b*) their One is one as indivisible, nothing will have quantity or quality, and so the one will not be infinite, as Melissus says—nor, indeed, limited, as Parmenides says, for though the limit is indivisible, the limited is not.

But if (*c*) all things are one in the sense of having the same definition, like 'raiment' and [20] 'dress', then it turns out that they are maintaining the Heraclitean doctrine, for it will be the same thing 'to be good' and 'to be bad', and 'to be good' and 'to be not good', and so the same thing will be 'good' and 'not good', and man and horse; in fact, their view will be, not that all things are one, but that they are nothing; and that 'to be of such-and-such a quality' is the same as 'to be of such-and-such a size'.

[25] Even the more recent of the ancient thinkers were in a pother lest the same thing should turn out in their hands both one and many. So some, like Lycophron, were led to omit 'is', others to change the mode of expression and say 'the man has been whitened' instead of 'is white', and 'walks' instead of 'is walking', for [30] fear that if they added the word 'is' they should be making the one to *be* many—as if 'one' and 'being' were always used in one and the same sense. What 'is' may be many either in definition (for example 'to be white' is one thing, 'to be musical' another, yet the same thing may be both, so the one is many) or by division, as the whole and its parts. On this 186ᵃ point, indeed, they were already getting into difficulties and admitted that the one was many—as if there was any difficulty about the same thing being both one and many, provided that these are not opposites; for 'one' may mean either 'potentially one' or 'actually one'.

3

If, then, we approach the thesis in this way [5] it seems impossible for all things to be one. Further, the arguments they use to prove their position are not difficult to expose. For both of them reason contentiously—I mean both Me-

lissus and Parmenides. [Their premisses are false and their conclusions do not follow. Or rather the argument of Melissus is gross and palpable and offers no difficulty at all: admit one ridiculous proposition and the rest follows —a simple enough proceeding.]
[*10*] The fallacy of Melissus is obvious. For he supposes that the assumption 'what has come into being always has a beginning' justifies the assumption 'what has not come into being has no beginning'. Then this also is absurd, that in every case there should be a beginning of the *thing*—not of the time and not only in the case of coming to be in the full sense but also in the case of coming to have a quality—as if change [*15*] never took place suddenly. Again, does it follow that Being, if one, is motionless? Why should it not move, the whole of it within itself, as parts of it do which are unities, e.g. this water? Again, why is qualitative change impossible? But, further, Being cannot [*20*] be one in form, though it may be in what it is made of. (Even some of the physicists hold it to be one in the latter way, though not in the former.) Man obviously differs from horse in form, and contraries from each other.

The same kind of argument holds good against Parmenides also, besides any that may apply specially to his view: the answer to him being that '*this* is not true' and '*that* does not follow'. His assumption that one is used in a single sense only is false, because it is used in [*25*] several. His conclusion does not follow, because if we take only white things, and if 'white' has a single meaning, none the less what is white will be many and not one. For what is white will not be one either in the sense that it is continuous or in the sense that it must be defined in only one way. 'Whiteness' will be different from 'what has whiteness'. Nor does this mean that there is anything that can [*30*] exist separately, over and above what is white. For 'whiteness' and 'that which is white' differ in definition, not in the sense that they are things which can exist apart from each other. But Parmenides had not come in sight of this distinction.

It is necessary for him, then, to assume not only that 'being' has the same meaning, of whatever it is predicated, but further that it means (1) what *just is* and (2) what is *just one*.

It must be so, for (1) an attribute is predicated of some subject, so that the subject to [*35*] which 'being' is attributed will not be, as it is something different from 'being'. Some-186ᵇ thing, therefore, which is not will be. Hence 'substance' will not be a predicate of anything else. For the subject cannot be a *being*, unless 'being' means several things, in such a way that each *is* something. But *ex hypothesi* 'being' means only one thing.

If, then, 'substance' is not attributed to anything, but other things are attributed to it, how [*5*] does 'substance' mean what is rather than what is not? For suppose that 'substance' is also 'white'. Since the definition of the latter is different (for being cannot even be attributed to white, as nothing is which is not 'substance'), it follows that 'white' is not-being—and that not in the sense of a particular not-being, but in the sense that it is not at all. Hence 'sub-[*10*] stance' is not; for it is true to say that it is white, which we found to mean not-being. If to avoid this we say that even 'white' means substance, it follows that 'being' has more than one meaning.

In particular, then, Being will not have magnitude, if it is substance. For each of the two parts must *be* in a different sense.

(2) Substance is plainly divisible into other substances, if we consider the mere nature of a [*15*] definition. For instance, if 'man' is a substance, 'animal' and 'biped' must also be substances. For if not substances, they must be attributes—and if attributes, attributes either of (*a*) man or of (*b*) some other subject. But neither is possible.

(*a*) An attribute is either that which may or [*20*] may not belong to the subject or that in whose definition the subject of which it is an attribute is involved. Thus 'sitting' is an example of a separable attribute, while 'snubness' contains the definition of 'nose', to which we attribute snubness. Further, the definition of the whole is not contained in the definitions of the contents or elements of the definitory formula; that of 'man' for instance in 'biped', or [*25*] that of 'white man' in 'white'. If then this is so, and if 'biped' is supposed to be an attribute of 'man', it must be either separable, so that 'man' might possibly not be 'biped', or the definition of 'man' must come into the defini-[*30*] tion of 'biped'—which is impossible, as the converse is the case.

(*b*) If, on the other hand, we suppose that 'biped' and 'animal' are attributes not of man but of something else, and are not each of them a substance, then 'man' too will be an attribute of something else. But we must assume that substance is *not* the attribute of anything, and that the subject of which both 'biped' and 'animal' and each separately are predicated is the

subject also of the complex 'biped animal'.
[35] Are we then to say that the All is composed of indivisible substances? Some thinkers 187ᵃ did, in point of fact, give way to both arguments. To the argument that all things are one if being means one thing, they conceded that not-being is; to that from bisection, they yielded by positing atomic magnitudes. But obviously it is not true that if being means one thing, and cannot at the same time mean the [5] contradictory of this, there will be nothing which is not, for even if what is not cannot *be* without qualification, there is no reason why it should not be a particular not-being. To say that all things will be one, if there is nothing besides Being itself, is absurd. For who understands 'being itself' to be anything but a particular substance? But if this is so, there is nothing to prevent there being many beings, as has been said.
[10] It is, then, clearly impossible for Being to be one in this sense.

4

The physicists on the other hand have two modes of explanation.
The first set make the underlying body one —either one of the three or something else which is denser than fire and rarer than air— [15] then generate everything else from this, and obtain multiplicity by condensation and rarefaction. Now these are contraries, which may be generalized into 'excess and defect'. (Compare Plato's 'Great and Small'—except that he make these his matter, the one his form, while the others treat the one which underlies as matter and the contraries as differentiae, i.e. forms).
[20] The second set assert that the contrarieties are contained in the one and emerge from it by segregation, for example Anaximander and also all those who assert that 'what is' is one and many, like Empedocles and Anaxagoras; for they too produce other things from their mixture by segregation. These differ, however, from each other in that the former imagines a cycle of such changes, the latter a single series.
[25] Anaxagoras again made both his 'homœomerous' substances and his contraries infinite in multitude, whereas Empedocles posits only the so-called elements.
The theory of Anaxagoras that the principles are infinite in multitude was probably due to his acceptance of the common opinion of the physicists that nothing comes into being from not-being. For this is the reason why they use [30] the phrase 'all things were together' and the coming into being of such and such a kind of thing is reduced to change of quality, while some spoke of combination and separation. Moreover, the fact that the contraries proceed from each other led them to the conclusion. The one, they reasoned, must have already existed in the other; for since everything that comes into being must arise either from what is or from what is not, and it is impossible for it to arise from what is not (on this point all the physicists agree), they thought that the [35] truth of the alternative necessarily followed, namely that things come into being out of existent things, i.e. out of things already present, but imperceptible to our senses because 187ᵇ of the smallness of their bulk. So they assert that everything has been mixed in everything, because they saw everything arising out of everything. But things, as they say, appear different from one another and receive different names according to the nature of the particles which are numerically predominant among the innumerable constituents of the mixture. For nothing, they say, is purely and entirely [5] white or black or sweet, bone or flesh, but the nature of a thing is held to be that of which it contains the most.
Now (1) the infinite *qua* infinite is unknowable, so that what is infinite in multitude or size is unknowable in quantity, and what is infinite in variety of kind is unknowable in qual- [10] ity. But the principles in question are infinite both in multitude and in kind. Therefore it is impossible to know things which are composed of them; for it is when we know the nature and quantity of its components that we suppose we know a complex.
Further (2) if the parts of a whole may be of any size in the direction either of greatness or [15] of smallness (by 'parts' I mean components into which a whole can be divided and which are actually present in it), it is necessary that the whole thing itself may be of any size. Clearly, therefore, since it is impossible for an animal or plant to be indefinitely big or small, neither can its parts be such, or the whole will be the same. But flesh, bone, and the like are [20] the parts of animals, and the fruits are the parts of plants. Hence it is obvious that neither flesh, bone, nor any such thing can be of indefinite size in the direction either of the greater or of the less.
Again (3) according to the theory all such things are already present in one another and do not come into being but are constituents

which are separated out, and a thing receives its designation from its chief constituent. Further, anything may come out of anything—water by segregation from flesh and flesh from [25] water. Hence, since every finite body is exhausted by the repeated abstraction of a finite body, it seems obviously to follow that everything *cannot* subsist in everything else. For let flesh be extracted from water and again more flesh be produced from the remainder by repeating the process of separation: then, even though the quantity separated out will continually decrease, still it will not fall below a cer- [30] tain magnitude. If, therefore, the process comes to an end, everything will not be in everything else (for there will be no flesh in the remaining water); if on the other hand it does not, and further extraction is always possible, there will be an infinite multitude of finite equal particles in a finite quantity—which is [35] impossible. Another proof may be added: Since every body must diminish in size when something is taken from it, and flesh is quantitatively definite in respect both of greatness and smallness, it is clear that from the minimum quantity of flesh no body can be separated out; for the flesh left would be less than the minimum of flesh.

Lastly (4) in each of his infinite bodies there would be already present infinite flesh and blood and brain—having a distinct existence, however, from one another, and no less real than the infinite bodies, and each infinite: which is contrary to reason.

[5] The statement that complete separation never will take place is correct enough, though Anaxagoras is not fully aware of what it means. For affections are indeed inseparable. If then colours and states had entered into the mixture, and if separation took place, there would be a 'white' or a 'healthy' which was nothing *but* white or healthy, i.e. was not the predicate of a subject. So his 'Mind' is an absurd person aiming at the impossible, if he is supposed to [10] wish to separate them, and it is impossible to do so, both in respect of quantity and of quality—of quantity, because there is no minimum magnitude, and of quality, because affections are inseparable.

Nor is Anaxagoras right about the coming to be of homogeneous bodies. It is true there is a sense in which clay is divided into pieces of clay, but there is another in which it is not. [15] Water and air are, and are generated 'from' each other, but not in the way in which bricks come 'from' a house and again a house 'from' bricks; and it is better to assume a smaller and finite number of principles, as Empedocles does.

5

All thinkers then agree in making the contraries principles, both those who describe the All as one and unmoved (for even Parmeni- [20] des treats hot and cold as principles under the names of fire and earth) and those too who use the rare and the dense. The same is true of Democritus also, with his plenum and void, both of which exist, he says, the one as being, the other as not-being. Again he speaks of differences in position, shape, and order, and these are genera of which the species are contraries, namely, of position, above and below, before and behind; of shape, angular and [25] angle-less, straight and round.

It is plain then that they all in one way or another identify the contraries with the principles. And with good reason. For first principles must not be derived from one another nor from anything else, while everything has to be derived from them. But these conditions are fulfilled by the primary contraries, which are not derived from anything else because they are primary, nor from each other because they are contraries.

[30] But we must see how this can be arrived at as a reasoned result, as well as in the way just indicated.

Our first presupposition must be that in nature nothing acts on, or is acted on by, any other thing at random, nor may anything come from anything else, unless we mean that it does so in virtue of a concomitant attribute. For [35] how could 'white' come from 'musical', unless 'musical' happened to be an attribute of the not-white or of the black? No, 'white' comes from 'not-white'—and not from *any* 'not-white', but from black or some intermediate colour. Similarly, 'musical' comes to be from 'not-musical', but not from *any* thing other than musical, but from 'unmusical' or any intermediate state there may be.

Nor again do things pass into the first chance thing; 'white' does not pass into 'musical' (except, it may be, in virtue of a concomitant attribute), but into 'not-white'—and not into any chance thing which is not white, but into black or an intermediate colour; 'musical' passes into [5] 'not-musical'—and not into any chance thing other than musical, but into 'unmusical' or any intermediate state there may be.

The same holds of other things also: even

things which are not simple but complex fol-[10]low the same principle, but the opposite state has not received a name, so we fail to notice the fact. What is in tune must come from what is not in tune, and *vice versa;* the tuned passes into untunedness—and not into *any* untunedness, but into the corresponding oppo-[15]site. It does not matter whether we take attunement, order, or composition for our illustration; the principle is obviously the same in all, and in fact applies equally to the production of a house, a statue, or any other complex. A house comes from certain things in a certain state of separation instead of conjunction, a statue (or any other thing that has been [20] shaped) from shapelessness—each of these objects being partly order and partly composition.

If then this is true, everything that comes to be or passes away from, or passes into, its contrary or an intermediate state. But the intermediates are derived from the contraries—colours, for instance, from black and white. Ev-[25]erything, therefore, that comes to be by a natural process is either a contrary or a product of contraries.

Up to this point we have practically had most of the other writers on the subject with us, as I have said already[1]: for all of them identify their elements, and what they call their principles, with the contraries, giving no reason indeed for the theory, but contrained as it were by the truth itself. They differ, however, [30] from one another in that some assume contraries which are more primary, others contraries which are less so: some those more knowable in the order of explanation, others those more familiar to sense. For some make hot and cold, or again moist and dry, the conditions of becoming; while others make odd [35] and even, or again Love and Strife; and these differ from each other in the way mentioned.

Hence their principles are in one sense the same, in another different; different certainly, as indeed most people think, but the same in-189ª asmuch as they are analogous; for all are taken from the same table of columns,[2] some of the pairs being wider, others narrower in extent. In this way then their theories are both the same and different, some better, some worse; some, as I have said, take as their contraries what is more knowable in the order of explanation, others what is more familiar to [5] sense. (The universal is more knowable in the order of explanation, the particular in the order of sense: for explanation has to do with the universal, sense with the particular.) 'The great and the small', for example, belong to the former class, 'the dense and the rare' to the latter.

[10] It is clear then that our principles must be contraries.

6

The next question is whether the principles are two or three or more in number.

One they cannot be, for there cannot be one contrary. Nor can they be innumerable, because, if so, Being will not be knowable: and in any one genus there is only one contrariety, and substance is one genus: also a finite num-[15]ber is sufficient, and a finite number, such as the principles of Empedocles, is better than an infinite multitude; for Empedocles professes to obtain from his principles all that Anaxagoras obtains from his innumerable principles. Lastly, some contraries are more primary than others, and some arise from others—for example sweet and bitter, white and black—whereas the principles must always remain principles.

[20] This will suffice to show that the principles are neither one nor innumerable.

Granted, then, that they are a limited number, it is plausible to suppose them more than two. For it is difficult to see how either density should be of such a nature as to act in any way on rarity or rarity on density. The same is true of any other pair of contraries; for Love does [25] not gather Strife together and make things out of it, nor does Strife make anything out of Love, but both act on a third thing different from both. Some indeed assume more than one such thing from which they construct the world of nature.

Other objections to the view that it is not necessary to assume a third principle as a substratum may be added. (1) We do not find that the contraries constitute the *substance* of [30] any thing. But what is a first principle ought not to be the *predicate* of any subject. If it were, there would be a principle of the supposed principle: for the subject is a principle, and prior presumably to what is predicated of it. Again (2) we hold that a substance is not contrary to another substance. How then can substance be derived from what are not substances? Or how can non-substances be prior to substance?

If then we accept both the former argument

---

[1] a19-30. [2] *Metaphysics,* I. 986ª 23.

[35] and this one, we must, to preserve both, assume a third somewhat as the substratum of the contraries, such as is spoken of by those who describe the All as one nature—water or fire or what is intermediate between them. What is intermediate seems preferable; for fire, earth, air, and water are already in- [5] volved with pairs of contraries. There is, therefore, much to be said for those who make the underlying substance different from these four; of the rest, the next best choice is air, as presenting sensible differences in a less degree than the others; and after air, water. All, however, agree in this, that they differentiate their One by means of the contraries, such as density [10] and rarity and more and less, which may of course be generalized, as has already been said,[1] into excess and defect. Indeed this doctrine too (that the One and excess and defect are the principles of things) would appear to be of old standing, though in different forms; for the early thinkers made the two the active and the one the passive principle, whereas [15] some of the more recent maintain the reverse.

To suppose then that the elements are three in number would seem, from these and similar considerations, a plausible view, as I said before.[2] On the other hand, the view that they are more than three in number would seem to be untenable.

For the one substratum is sufficient to be [20] acted on; but if we have four contraries, there will be two contrarieties, and we shall have to suppose an intermediate nature for each pair separately. If, on the other hand, the contrarieties, being two, can generate from each other, the second contrariety will be superfluous. Moreover, it is impossible that there should be more than one *primary* contrariety. For substance is a single genus of being, so that the principles can differ only as prior and [25] posterior, *not* in genus; in a single genus there is always a single contrariety, all the other contrarieties in it being held to be reducible to one.

It is clear then that the number of elements is neither one nor more than two or three; but whether two or three is, as I said, a question of considerable difficulty.

7

[30] We will now give our own account, approaching the question first with reference to becoming in its widest sense: for we shall be

[1] 187ª 16.   [2] ª 21.

following the natural order of inquiry if we speak first of common characteristics, and then investigate the characteristics of special cases.

We say that one thing comes to be from another thing, and one sort of thing from another sort of thing, both in the case of simple and of complex things. I mean the following. We can say (1) the 'man becomes musical', (2) what [35] is 'not-musical becomes musical', or (3) the 'not-musical man becomes a musical man'. Now what becomes in (1) and (2)— 'man' and 'not musical'—I call *simple*, and what each becomes—'musical'—simple also. But when (3) we say the 'not-musical man becomes a musical man', both what becomes and what it becomes are *complex*.

[5] As regards one of these simple 'things that become' we say not only 'this becomes so-and-so', but also 'from being this, comes to be so-and-so', as 'from being not-musical comes to be musical'; as regards the other we do not say this in all cases, as we do not say (1) 'from being a man he came to be musical' but only 'the man became musical'.

When a 'simple' thing is said to become something, in one case (1) it survives through the process, in the other (2) it does not. For [10] the man remains a man and is such even when he becomes musical, whereas what is not musical or is unmusical does not continue to exist, either simply or combined with the subject.

These distinctions drawn, one can gather from surveying the various cases of becoming in the way we are describing that, as we say, there must always be an underlying something, [15] namely that which becomes, and that this, though always one numerically, in form at least is not one. (By that I mean that it can be described in different ways.) For 'to be man' is not the same as 'to be unmusical'. One part survives, the other does not: what is not an opposite survives (for 'man' survives), but 'not-musical' or 'unmusical' does not survive, [20] nor does the compound of the two, namely 'unmusical man'.

We speak of 'becoming that from this' instead of 'this becoming that' more in the case of what does not survive the change—'becoming musical from unmusical', not 'from man' —but there are exceptions, as we sometimes [25] use the latter form of expression even of what survives; we speak of 'a statue coming to be from bronze', not of the 'bronze becoming a statue'. The change, however, from an opposite which does not survive is described indifferently in both ways, 'becoming that from this' or 'this becoming that'. We say both that [30] 'the unmusical becomes musical', and that 'from unmusical he becomes musical'. And so both forms are used of the complex, 'becoming a musical man from an unmusical man', and 'an unmusical man becoming a musical man'.

But there are different senses of 'coming to be'. In some cases we do not use the expression 'come to be', but 'come to be so-and-so'. Only substances are said to 'come to be' in the unqualified sense.

Now in all cases other than substance it is plain that there must be some subject, namely, that which becomes. For we know that when a thing comes to be of such a quantity or quality [35] or in such a relation, time, or place, a subject is always presupposed, since substance alone is not predicated of another subject, but everything else of substance.

190[b] But that substances too, and anything else that can be said 'to be' without qualification, come to be from some substratum, will appear on examination. For we find in every case something that underlies from which proceeds that which comes to be; for instance, animals and plants from seed.

[5] Generally things which come to be, come to be in different ways: (1) by change of shape, as a statue; (2) by addition, as things which grow; (3) by taking away, as the Hermes from the stone; (4) by putting together, as a house; (5) by alteration, as things which 'turn' in respect of their material substance.

It is plain that these are all cases of coming to be from a substratum.

[10] Thus, clearly, from what has been said, whatever comes to be is always complex. There is, on the one hand, (a) something which comes into existence, and again (b) something which becomes that—the latter (b) in two senses, either the subject or the opposite. By the 'opposite' I mean the 'unmusical', by the 'subject' 'man', and similarly I call the absence [15] of shape or form or order the 'opposite', and the bronze or stone or gold the 'subject'.

Plainly then, if there are conditions and principles which constitute natural objects and from which they primarily are or have come to be—have come to be, I mean, what each is said to be in its essential nature, not what each is in respect of a concomitant attribute—plain- [20] ly, I say, everything comes to be from both subject and form. For 'musical man' is composed (in a way) of 'man' and 'musical': you can analyse it into the definitions of its elements. It is clear then that what comes to be will come to be from these elements.

Now the subject is one numerically, though it is two in form. (For it is the man, the gold —the 'matter' generally—that is counted, for [25] it is more of the nature of a 'this', and what comes to be does not come from it in virtue of a concomitant attribute; the privation, on the other hand, and the contrary *are* incidental in the process.) And the positive form is one—the order, the acquired art of music, or any similar predicate.

There is a sense, therefore, in which we must declare the principles to be two, and a sense in [30] which they are three; a sense in which the contraries are the principles—say for example the musical and the unmusical, the hot and the cold, the tuned and the untuned—and a sense in which they are not, since it is impossible for the contraries to be acted on by each other. But this difficulty also is solved by the fact that the substratum is different from the contraries, [35] for it is itself not a contrary. The principles therefore are, in a way, not more in number than the contraries, but as it were two, nor yet precisely two, since there is a difference 191[a] of essential nature, but three. For 'to be man' is different from 'to be unmusical', and 'to be unformed' from 'to be bronze'.

We have now stated the number of the principles of natural objects which are subject to generation, and how the number is reached: and it is clear that there must be a substratum for the contraries, and that the contraries must [5] be two. (Yet in another way of putting it this is not necessary, as one of the contraries will serve to effect the change by its successive absence and presence.)

The underlying nature is an object of scientific knowledge, by an analogy. For as the bronze is to the statue, the wood to the bed, [10] or the matter and the formless before receiving form to any thing which has form, so is the underlying nature to substance, i.e. the 'this' or existent.

This then is one principle (though not one or existent in the same sense as the 'this'), and the definition was one as we agreed; then further there is its contrary, the privation. In what sense these are two, and in what sense more, [15] has been stated above. Briefly, we explained first[1] that only the contraries were principles, and later[2] that a substratum was in-

[1] Chapter 5. [2] Chapter 6.

dispensable, and that the principles were three; our last statement[1] has elucidated the difference between the contraries, the mutual relation of the principles, and the nature of the substratum. Whether the form or the substratum is the essential nature of a physical ob-[20] ject is not yet clear. But that the principles are three, and in what sense, and the way in which each is a principle, is clear.

So much then for the question of the number and the nature of the principles.

8

We will now proceed to show that the difficulty of the early thinkers, as well as our own, is solved in this way alone.

The first of those who studied science were [25] misled in their search for truth and the nature of things by their inexperience, which as it were thrust them into another path. So they say that none of the things that are either comes to be or passes out of existence, because what comes to be must do so either from what is or from what is not, both of which are im-[30] possible. For what is cannot come to be (because it *is* already), and from what is not nothing could have come to be (because something must be present as a substratum). So too they exaggerated the consequence of this, and went so far as to deny even the *existence* of a plurality of things, maintaining that only Being itself is. Such then was their opinion, and such the reason for its adoption.

Our explanation on the other hand is that the phrases 'something comes to be from what is or from what is not', 'what is not or what is [35] does something or has something done to it or becomes some particular thing', are to be taken (in the first way of putting our explana-191ᵇ tion) in the same sense as 'a doctor does something or has something done to him', 'is or becomes something from being a doctor'. These expressions may be taken in two senses, and so too, clearly, may 'from being', and 'being acts or is acted on'. A doctor builds a house, not *qua* doctor, but *qua* housebuilder, [5] and turns gray, not *qua* doctor, but *qua* darkhaired. On the other hand he doctors or fails to doctor *qua* doctor. But we are using words most appropriately when we say that a doctor does something or undergoes something, or becomes something from being a doctor, if he does, undergoes, or becomes *qua* doctor. Clearly then also 'to come to be so-and-so from not-being' means '*qua* not-being'.

[10] It was through failure to make this distinction that those thinkers gave the matter up, and through this error that they went so much farther astray as to suppose that nothing else comes to be or exists apart from Being itself, thus doing away with all becoming.

We ourselves are in agreement with them in holding that nothing can be said without qualification to come from what is not. But nevertheless we maintain that a thing may 'come to be from what is not'—that is, in a qualified [15] sense. For a thing comes to be from the privation, which in its own nature is not-being, —this not surviving as a constituent of the result. Yet this causes surprise, and it is thought impossible that something should come to be in the way described from what is not.

In the same way we maintain that nothing comes to be from being, and that being does not come to be except in a qualified sense. In that way, however, it does, just as animal might come to be from animal, and an animal [20] of a certain kind from an animal of a certain kind. Thus, suppose a dog to come to be from a horse. The dog would then, it is true, come to be from animal (as well as from an animal of a certain kind) but not as *animal*, for that is already there. But if anything is to become an animal, *not* in a qualified sense, it will not be from animal: and if being, not [25] from being—nor from not-being either, for it has been explained[2] that by 'from not-being' we mean from not-being *qua* not-being.

Note further that we do not subvert the principle that everything either is or is not.

This then is one way of solving the difficulty. Another consists in pointing out that the same things can be explained in terms of potentiality and actuality. But this has been done with greater precision elsewhere.[3]

[30] So, as we said, the difficulties which constrain people to deny the existence of some of the things we mentioned are now solved. For it was this reason which also caused some of the earlier thinkers to turn so far aside from the road which leads to coming to be and passing away and change generally. If they had come in sight of this nature, all their ignorance would have been dispelled.

9

[35] Others, indeed, have apprehended the nature in question, but not adequately.

In the first place they allow that a thing may come to be without qualification from not-

---

[1] Chapter 7.   [2] l. 9.   [3] *Metaphysics*, IX, and V (1017ᵃ 35–ᵇ 9).

being, accepting on this point the statement of Parmenides. Secondly, they think that if the substratum is one numerically, it must have also only a single potentiality—which is a very different thing.

Now we distinguish matter and privation, and hold that one of these, namely the matter, is not-being only in virtue of an attribute which it has, while the privation in its own [5] nature is not-being; and that the matter is nearly, in a sense *is*, substance, while the privation in no sense is. They, on the other hand, identify their Great and Small alike with not-being, and that whether they are taken together as one or separately. Their triad is therefore of quite a different kind from ours. For they got so far as to see that there must [10] be some underlying nature, but they make it one—for even if one philosopher[1] makes a dyad of it, which he calls Great and Small, the effect is the same, for he overlooked the other nature. For the one which persists is a joint cause, with the form, of what comes to be—a mother, as it were. But the negative part [15] of the contrariety may often seem, if you concentrate your attention on it as an evil agent, not to exist at all.

For admitting with them that there is something divine, good, and desirable, we hold that there are two other principles, the one contrary to it, the other such as of its own nature to desire and yearn for it. But the consequence of their view is that the contrary desires its own [20] extinction. Yet the form cannot desire itself, for it is not defective; nor can the contrary desire it, for contraries are mutually destructive. The truth is that what desires the form is matter, as the female desires the male and the ugly the beautiful—only the ugly or the female not *per se* but *per accidens*.

[25] The matter comes to be and ceases to be in one sense, while in another it does not. As that which contains the privation, it ceases to be in its own nature, for what ceases to be—the privation—is contained within it. But as potentiality it does not cease to be in its own nature, but is necessarily outside the sphere of becoming and ceasing to be. For if it came to be, something must have existed as a primary substratum from which it should come and [30] which should persist in it; but this is its own special nature, so that it will be before coming to be. (For my definition of matter is just this—the primary substratum of each thing, from which it comes to be without qualification, and which persists in the result.) And if it ceases to be it will pass into that at the last, so it will have ceased to be before ceasing to be.

The accurate determination of the first principle in respect of form, whether it is one or many and what it is or what they are, is the [35] province of the primary type of science; so these questions may stand over till then.[2] But of the natural, i.e. perishable, forms we shall speak in the expositions which follow.[3]

The above, then, may be taken as sufficient to establish that there are principles and what they are and how many there are. Now let us make a fresh start and proceed.

BOOK II

1

Of things that exist, some exist by nature, some from other causes.

'By nature' the animals and their parts exist, [10] and the plants and the simple bodies (earth, fire, air, water)—for we say that these and the like exist 'by nature'.

All the things mentioned present a feature in which they differ from things which are *not* constituted by nature. Each of them has *within itself* a principle of motion and of stationari- [15] ness (in respect of place, or of growth and decrease, or by way of alteration). On the other hand, a bed and a coat and anything else of that sort, *qua* receiving these designations— i.e. in so far as they are products of art—have no innate impulse to change. But in so far as they happen to be composed of stone or of [20] earth or of a mixture of the two, they *do* have such an impulse, and just to that extent— which seems to indicate that *nature is a source or cause of being moved and of being at rest in that to which it belongs primarily,* in virtue of itself and not in virtue of a concomitant attribute.

I say 'not in virtue of a concomitant attribute', because (for instance) a man who is a doctor might cure himself. Nevertheless it is

---

[1] Plato.
[2] *Metaphysics*, xii. 7–9.
[3] I.e. the rest of the *Physics*, the *On the Heavens, On Generation and Corruption*, etc. (especially *On Generation and Corruption*, ii).

not in so far as he is a patient that he possesses the art of medicine: it merely has happened that the same man is doctor and patient—and that is why these attributes are not always found together. So it is with all other artificial products. None of them has in itself the source of its own production. But while in some cases (for instance houses and the other products of manual labour) that principle is in something else external to the thing, in others [30]—those which may cause a change in themselves in virtue of a concomitant attribute—it lies in the things themselves (but not in virtue of what they are).

'Nature' then is what has been stated. Things 'have a nature' which have a principle of this kind. Each of them is a substance; for it is a subject, and nature always implies a subject in which it inheres.

[35] The term 'according to nature' is applied to all these things and also to the attributes which belong to them in virtue of what they are, for instance the property of fire to be carried upwards—which is not a 'nature' nor 'has a nature' but is 'by nature' or 'according to nature'.

193ª *What* nature is, then, and the meaning of the terms 'by nature' and 'according to nature', has been stated. *That* nature exists, it would be absurd to try to prove; for it is obvious that there are many things of this kind, [5] and to prove what is obvious by what is not is the mark of a man who is unable to distinguish what is self-evident from what is not. (This state of mind is clearly possible. A man blind from birth might reason about colours. Presumably therefore such persons must be talking about words without any thought to correspond.)

Some identify the nature or substance of a [10] natural object with that immediate constituent of it which taken by itself is without arrangement, e.g. the wood is the 'nature' of the bed, and the bronze the 'nature' of the statue.

As an indication of this Antiphon points out that if you planted a bed and the rotting wood acquired the power of sending up a shoot, it would not be a bed that would come up, but *wood*—which shows that the arrangement in [15] accordance with the rules of the art is merely an incidental attribute, whereas the real nature is the other, which, further, persists continuously through the process of making.

But if the material of each of these objects has itself the same relation to something else, [20] say bronze (or gold) to water, bones (or wood) to earth and so on, *that* (they say) would be their nature and essence. Consequently some assert earth, others fire or air or water or some or all of these, to be the nature of the things that are. For whatever any one of them supposed to have this character—whether one thing or more than one thing—[25] this or these he declared to be the whole of substance, all else being its affections, states, or dispositions. Every such thing they held to be eternal (for it could not pass into anything else), but other things to come into being and cease to be times without number.

This then is one account of 'nature', namely that it is the immediate material substratum of things which have in themselves a principle of motion or change.

[30] Another account is that 'nature' is the shape or form which is specified in the definition of the thing.

For the word 'nature' is applied to what is according to nature and the natural in the same way as 'art' is applied to what is artistic or a work of art. We should not say in the latter case that there is anything artistic about a thing, if it is a bed only potentially, not yet having the form of a bed; nor should we call [35] it a work of art. The same is true of natural compounds. What is potentially flesh or bone has not yet its own 'nature', and does not exist 'by nature', until it receives the form specified in the definition, which we name 193ᵇ in defining what flesh or bone is. Thus in the second sense of 'nature' it would be the shape or form (not separable except in statement) of [5] things which have in themselves a source of motion. (The combination of the two, e.g. man, is not 'nature' but 'by nature' or 'natural'.)

The form indeed is 'nature' rather than the matter; for a thing is more properly said to be what it is when it has attained to fulfilment than when it exists potentially. Again man is born from man, but not bed from bed. That is why people say that the figure is not the nature [10] of a bed, but the wood is—if the bed sprouted not a bed but wood would come up. But even if the figure *is* art, then on the same principle the shape of man is his nature. For man is born from man.

We also speak of a thing's nature as being exhibited in the process of growth by which its nature is attained. The 'nature' in this sense is not like 'doctoring', which leads not to the [15] art of doctoring but to health. Doctoring must start from the art, not lead to it. But it is not in this way that nature (in the one sense) is related to nature (in the other). What grows *qua* growing grows from something into something. Into what then does it grow? Not into that from which it arose but into that to which it tends. The shape then is nature.

'Shape' and 'nature', it should be added, are [20] used in two senses. For the privation too is in a way form. But whether in unqualified coming to be there is privation, i.e. a contrary to what comes to be, we must consider later.[1]

2

We have distinguished, then, the different ways in which the term 'nature' is used.

The next point to consider is how the mathematician differs from the physicist. Obviously physical bodies contain surfaces and volumes, lines and points, and these are the subject-matter of mathematics.

[25] Further, is astronomy different from physics or a department of it? It seems absurd that the physicist should be supposed to know the nature of sun or moon, but not to know any of their essential attributes, particularly as the writers on physics obviously do discuss [30] their shape also and whether the earth and the world are spherical or not.

Now the mathematician, though he too treats of these things, nevertheless does not treat of them as the limits of a physical body; nor does he consider the attributes indicated as the attributes of such bodies. That is why he separates them; for in thought they are separable from motion, and it makes no difference, nor does any falsity result, if they are [35] separated. The holders of the theory of Forms do the same, though they are not aware of it; for they separate the objects of physics, which are less separable than those of mathematics. This becomes plain if one tries to state in each of the two cases the definitions of the things and of their attributes. 'Odd' and 'even', 'straight' and 'curved', and likewise 'number', 'line', and 'figure', do not involve [5] motion; not so 'flesh' and 'bone' and 'man' —*these* are defined like 'snub nose', not like 'curved'.

Similar evidence is supplied by the more physical of the branches of mathematics, such as optics, harmonics, and astronomy. These are in a way the converse of geometry. While geometry investigates physical lines but not [10] *qua* physical, optics investigates mathematical lines, but *qua* physical, not *qua* mathematical.

Since 'nature' has two senses, the form and the matter, we must investigate its objects as we would the essence of snubness. That is, such things are neither independent of matter nor can be defined in terms of matter only. Here [15] too indeed one might raise a difficulty. Since there are two natures, with which is the physicist concerned? Or should he investigate the combination of the two? But if the combination of the two, then also each severally. Does it belong then to the same or to different sciences to know each severally?

If we look at the ancients, physics would [20] seem to be concerned with the *matter*. (It was only very slightly that Empedocles and Democritus touched on the forms and the essence.)

But if on the other hand art imitates nature, and it is the part of the same discipline to know the form and the matter up to a point (e.g. the doctor has a knowledge of health and also of bile and phlegm, in which health is realized, and the builder both of the form of the house [25] and of the matter, namely that it is bricks and beams, and so forth): if this is so, it would be the part of physics also to know nature in both its senses.

Again, 'that for the sake of which', or the end, belongs to the same department of knowledge as the means. But the nature is the end or 'that for the sake of which'. For if a thing undergoes a continuous change and there is a stage which is last, this stage is the end or [30] 'that for the sake of which'. (That is why the poet was carried away into making an absurd statement when he said 'he has the end for the sake of which he was born'.[2] For not every stage that is last claims to be an end, but only that which is best.)

For the arts make their material (some simply 'make' it, others make it serviceable), and we use everything as if it was there for our [35] sake. (We also are in a sense an end. 'That for the sake of which' has two senses: the distinction is made in our work *On Philosophy*.[3]) The arts, therefore, which govern the matter and have knowledge are two, namely the art which uses the product and the art which directs the production of it. That is why the using art also is in a sense directive; but it differs in that it knows the form, whereas the art which is directive as being concerned

---

[1] *On Generation and Corruption*, I. 3.
[2] Kock, *Com. Att. Fr.* III, p. 493.
[3] I.e. in the dialogue *De Philosophia*.

with production knows the matter. For the [5] helmsman knows and prescribes what sort of form a helm should have, the other from what wood it should be made and by means of what operations. In the products of art, however, we make the material with a view to the function, whereas in the products of nature the matter is there all along.

Again, matter is a relative term: to each form there corresponds a special matter. How far then must the physicist know the form or [10] essence? Up to a point, perhaps, as the doctor must know sinew or the smith bronze (i.e. until he understands the purpose of each): and the physicist is concerned only with things whose forms are separable indeed, but do not exist apart from matter. Man is begotten by man and by the sun as well. The mode of existence and essence of the separable it is [15] the business of the primary type of philosophy to define.

3

Now that we have established these distinctions, we must proceed to consider causes, their character and number. Knowledge is the object of our inquiry, and men do not think they know a thing till they have grasped the 'why' of it [20] (which is to grasp its primary cause). So clearly we too must do this as regards both coming to be and passing away and every kind of physical change, in order that, knowing their principles, we may try to refer to these principles each of our problems.

In one sense, then, (1) that out of which a thing comes to be and which persists, is called 'cause', e.g. the bronze of the statue, the silver [25] of the bowl, and the genera of which the bronze and the silver are species.

In another sense (2) the form or the archetype, i.e. the statement of the essence, and its genera, are called 'causes' (e.g. of the octave the relation of 2 : 1, and generally number), and the parts in the definition.

Again (3) the primary source of the change [30] or coming to rest; e.g. the man who gave advice is a cause, the father is cause of the child, and generally what makes of what is made and what causes change of what is changed.

Again (4) in the sense of end or 'that for the sake of which' a thing is done, e.g. health is the cause of walking about. ('Why is he walking about?' we say. 'To be healthy', and, having said that, we think we have assigned [35] the cause.) The same is true also of all the intermediate steps which are brought about through the action of something else as means towards the end, e.g. reduction of flesh, purging, drugs, or surgical instruments are means 195ª towards health. All these things are 'for the sake of' the end, though they differ from one another in that some are activities, others instruments.

This then perhaps exhausts the number of ways in which the term 'cause' is used.

As the word has several senses, it follows that there are several causes of the same thing (not merely in virtue of a concomitant attri- [5] bute), e.g. both the art of the sculptor and the bronze are causes of the statue. These are causes of the statue *qua* statue, not in virtue of anything else that it may be—only not in the same way, the one being the material cause, the other the cause whence the motion comes. Some things cause each other recipro- [10] cally, e.g. hard work causes fitness and *vice versa*, but again not in the same way, but the one as end, the other as the origin of change. Further the same thing is the cause of contrary results. For that which by its presence brings about one result is sometimes blamed for bringing about the contrary by its absence. Thus we ascribe the wreck of a ship to the absence of the pilot whose presence was the cause of its safety.

[15] All the causes now mentioned fall into four familiar divisions. The letters are the causes of syllables, the material of artificial products, fire, &c., of bodies, the parts of the whole, and the premisses of the conclusion, in the sense of 'that from which'. Of these pairs [20] the one set are causes in the sense of substratum, e.g. the parts, the other set in the sense of essence—the whole and the combination and the form. But the seed and the doctor and the adviser, and generally the maker, are all sources whence the change or stationariness originates, while the others are causes in the sense of the end or the good of the rest; for 'that for the sake of which' means what is best [25] and the end of the things that lead up to it. (Whether we say the 'good itself' or the 'apparent good' makes no difference.)

Such then is the number and nature of the kinds of cause.

Now the modes of causation are many, though when brought under heads they too can be reduced in number. For 'cause' is used in many senses and even within the same kind [30] one may be prior to another (e.g. the doctor and the expert are causes of health, the relation 2 : 1 and number of the octave), and always what is inclusive to what is particular. Another mode of causation is the incidental and its genera, e.g. in one way 'Polyclitus', in another 'sculptor' is the cause of a statue, be-[35] cause 'being Polyclitus' and 'sculptor' are incidentally conjoined. Also the classes in which the incidental attribute is included; thus 'a man' could be said to be the cause of a 195[b] statue or, generally, 'a living creature'. An incidental attribute too may be more or less remote, e.g. suppose that 'a pale man' or 'a musical man' were said to be the cause of the statue.

All causes, both proper and incidental, may [5] be spoken of either as potential or as actual; e.g. the cause of a house being built is either 'house-builder' or 'house-builder building'.

Similar distinctions can be made in the things of which the causes are causes, e.g. of 'this statue' or of 'statue' or of 'image' generally, of 'this bronze' or of 'bronze' or of 'material' generally. So too with the incidental at-[10] tributes. Again we may use a complex expression for either and say, e.g. neither 'Polyclitus' nor 'sculptor' but 'Polyclitus, sculptor'.

All these various uses, however, come to six in number, under each of which again the usage is twofold. Cause means either what is particular or a genus, or an incidental attri-[15] bute or a genus of that, and these either as a complex or each by itself; and all six either as actual or as potential. The difference is this much, that causes which are actually at work and particular exist and cease to exist simultaneously with their effect, e.g. this healing person with this being-healed person and that housebuilding man with that being-built house; but this is not always true of potential [20] causes—the house and the housebuilder do not pass away simultaneously.

In investigating the cause of each thing it is always necessary to seek what is most precise (as also in other things): thus man builds because he is a builder, and a builder builds in virtue of his art of building. This last cause then is prior: and so generally.
[25] Further, generic effects should be assigned to generic causes, particular effects to particular causes, e.g. statue to sculptor, this statue to this sculptor; and powers are relative to possible effects, actually operating causes to things which are actually being effected.

This must suffice for our account of the [30] number of causes and the modes of causation.

4

But chance also and spontaneity are reckoned among causes: many things are said both to be and to come to be as a result of chance and spontaneity. We must inquire therefore in what manner chance and spontaneity are present among the causes enumerated, and [35] whether they are the same or different, and generally what chance and spontaneity are.

Some people even question whether they are 196[a] real or not. They say that nothing happens by chance, but that everything which we ascribe to chance or spontaneity has some definite cause, e.g. coming 'by chance' into the market and finding there a man whom one wanted but did not expect to meet is due to one's wish to go and buy in the market. Sim-[5] ilarly in other cases of chance it is always possible, they maintain, to find something which is the cause; but not chance, for if chance were real, it would seem strange indeed, and the question might be raised, why on earth none of the wise men of old in speaking of the causes of generation and decay took ac-[10] count of chance; whence it would seem that they too did not believe that anything is by chance. But there is a further circumstance that is surprising. Many things both come to be and are by chance and spontaneity, and although all know that each of them can be ascribed to some cause (as the old argument said which [15] denied chance), nevertheless they speak of some of these things as happening by chance and others not. For this reason also they ought to have at least referred to the matter in some way or other.

Certainly the early physicists found no place for chance among the causes which they recognized—love, strife, mind, fire, or the like. This is strange, whether they supposed that there is no such thing as chance or whether they [20] thought there is but omitted to mention it—and that too when they sometimes used it, as Empedocles does when he says that the air is not always separated into the highest region, but 'as it may chance'. At any rate he says in his cosmogony that 'it happened to run that way at that time, but it often ran otherwise.'[1] He tells us also that most of the parts of animals came to be by chance.
[25] There are some too who ascribe this heavenly sphere and all the worlds to spon-

---
[1] Fr. 53.

taneity. They say that the vortex arose spontaneously, i.e. the motion that separated and arranged in its present order all that exists. This statement might well cause surprise. For they are asserting that chance is not responsible for the existence or generation of animals and [30] plants, nature or mind or something of the kind being the cause of them (for it is not any chance thing that comes from a given seed but an olive from one kind and a man from another); and yet at the same time they assert that the heavenly sphere and the divinest of visible things arose spontaneously, having no [35] such cause as is assigned to animals and plants. Yet if this is so, it is a fact which deserves to be dwelt upon, and something might **196ᵇ** well have been said about it. For besides the other absurdities of the statement, it is the more absurd that people should make it when they see nothing coming to be spontaneously in the heavens, but much happening by chance among the things which as they say are not due to chance; whereas we should have expected exactly the opposite.

[5] Others there are who, indeed, believe that chance is a cause, but that it is inscrutable to human intelligence, as being a divine thing and full of mystery.

Thus we must inquire what chance and spontaneity are, whether they are the same or different, and how they fit into our division of causes.

5

[10] First then we observe that some things always come to pass in the same way, and others for the most part. It is clearly of neither of these that chance is said to be the cause, nor can the 'effect of chance' be identified with any of the things that come to pass by necessity and always, or for the most part. But as there is a third class of events besides these two—events which all say are 'by chance'—it is plain that there is such a thing as chance and spontaneity; [15] for we know that things of this kind are due to chance and that things due to chance are of this kind.

But, secondly, some events are for the sake of something, others not. Again, some of the former class are in accordance with deliberate intention, others not, but both are in the class of things which are for the sake of something. [20] Hence it is clear that even among the things which are outside the necessary and the normal, there are some in connexion with which the phrase 'for the sake of something' is applicable. (Events that are for the sake of something include whatever may be done as a result of thought or of nature.) Things of this kind, then, when they come to pass incidentally are said to be 'by chance'. For just as a thing [25] is something either in virtue of itself or incidentally, so may it be a cause. For instance, the housebuilding faculty is in virtue of itself the cause of a house, whereas the pale or the musical is the incidental cause. That which is *per se* cause of the effect is determinate, but the incidental cause is indeterminable, for the possible attributes of an individual are innumerable. To resume then; when a thing of this [30] kind comes to pass among events which are for the sake of something, it is said to be spontaneous or by chance. (The distinction between the two must be made later[1]—for the present it is sufficient if it is plain that both are in the sphere of things done for the sake of something.)

Example: A man is engaged in collecting subscriptions for a feast. He would have gone to such and such a place for the purpose of getting the money, if he had known. He [35] actually went there for another purpose, and it was only incidentally that he got his money by going there; and this was not due to the fact that he went there as a rule or necessarily, nor is the end effected (getting the money) a cause present in himself—it belongs to the class of things that are intentional and the result of intelligent deliberation. It is when these conditions are satisfied that the man is said to have gone 'by chance'. If he had gone of deliberate purpose and for the sake of this—if he always or normally went there when he was collecting payments—he would not be said to have gone 'by chance'.

[5] It is clear then that chance is an incidental cause in the sphere of those actions for the sake of something which involve purpose. Intelligent reflection, then, and chance are in the same sphere, for purpose implies intelligent reflection.

It is necessary, no doubt, that the causes of what comes to pass by chance be indefinite; and that is why chance is supposed to belong to the class of the indefinite and to be inscrutable to man, and why it might be [10] thought that, in a way, nothing occurs by chance. For all these statements are correct, because they are well grounded. Things *do*, in a way, occur by chance, for they occur incidentally and chance is an *incidental cause*. But

[1] In chapter 6.

strictly it is not the *cause*—without qualification—of anything; for instance, a housebuilder is the cause of a house; incidentally, a flute-player may be so.

[15] And the causes of the man's coming and getting the money (when he did not come for the sake of that) are innumerable. He may have wished to see somebody or been following somebody or avoiding somebody, or may have gone to see a spectacle. Thus to say that chance is a thing contrary to rule is correct. For 'rule' applies to what is always true or true for the most part, whereas chance be- [20] longs to a third type of event. Hence, to conclude, since causes of this kind are indefinite, chance too is indefinite. (Yet in some cases one might raise the question whether *any* incidental fact might be the cause of the chance occurrence, e.g. of health the fresh air or the sun's heat may be the cause, but having had one's hair cut *cannot;* for some incidental causes are more relevant to the effect than others.)

[25] Chance or fortune is called 'good' when the result is good, 'evil' when it is evil. The terms 'good fortune' and 'ill fortune' are used when either result is of considerable magnitude. Thus one who comes within an ace of some great evil or great good is said to be fortunate or unfortunate. The mind affirms the presence of the attribute, ignoring the hair's [30] breadth of difference. Further, it is with reason that good fortune is regarded as unstable; for chance is unstable, as none of the things which result from it can be invariable or normal.

Both are then, as I have said, incidental causes—both chance and spontaneity—in the sphere of things which are capable of coming to pass not necessarily, nor normally, and with [35] reference to such of these as might come to pass for the sake of something.

6

They differ in that 'spontaneity' is the wider term. Every result of chance is from what is spontaneous, but not everything that is from what is spontaneous is from chance.
197b Chance and what results from chance are appropriate to agents that are capable of good fortune and of moral action generally. Therefore necessarily chance is in the sphere of moral actions. This is indicated by the fact that good fortune is thought to be the same, or nearly the same, as happiness, and happiness to be a kind of moral action, since it is [5] well-doing. Hence what is not capable of moral action cannot do anything by chance. Thus an inanimate thing or a lower animal or a child cannot do anything by chance, because it is incapable of deliberate intention; nor can 'good fortune' or 'ill fortune' be ascribed to them, except metaphorically, as Protarchus,[1] for example, said that the stones of which altars are made are fortunate because they are [10] held in honour, while their fellows are trodden under foot. Even these things, however, can in a way be affected by chance, when one who is dealing with them does something to them by chance, but not otherwise.

The spontaneous on the other hand is found [15] both in the lower animals and in many inanimate objects. We say, for example, that the horse came 'spontaneously', because, though his coming saved him, he did not come for the sake of safety. Again, the tripod fell 'of itself', because, though when it fell it stood on its feet so as to serve for a seat, it did not fall for the sake of that.

Hence it is clear that events which (1) belong to the general class of things that may come to pass for the sake of something, (2) do not come to pass for the sake of what actually results, and (3) have an external cause, may be [20] described by the phrase 'from spontaneity'. These 'spontaneous' events are said to be 'from chance' if they have the further characteristics of being the objects of deliberate intention and due to agents capable of that mode of action. This is indicated by the phrase 'in vain', which is used when *A,* which is for the sake of *B,* does not result in *B.* For instance, taking a walk is for the sake of evacuation of the bowels; if this does not follow after walking, we say that we have walked 'in vain' and that the walking was 'vain'. This implies that [25] what is naturally the means to an end is 'in vain', when it does not effect the end towards which it was the natural means—for it would be absurd for a man to say that he had bathed in vain because the sun was not eclipsed, since the one was not done with a view to the other. Thus the spontaneous is even according to its derivation the case in which the thing itself happens in vain. The stone that [30] struck the man did not fall for the purpose of striking him; therefore it fell spontaneously, because it might have fallen by the action of an agent and for the purpose of striking. The difference between spontaneity

---
[1] Probably the reference is to the Protarchus described as a pupil of Gorgias in Plato, *Philebus,* 58.

and what results by chance is greatest in things that come to be by nature; for when anything comes to be contrary to nature, we do not say [35] that it came to be by chance, but by spontaneity. Yet strictly this too is different from the spontaneous proper; for the cause of the latter is external, that of the former internal.

198ª We have now explained what chance is and what spontaneity is, and in what they differ from each other. Both belong to the mode of causation 'source of change', for either some natural or some intelligent agent is always the cause; but in this sort of causation the number of possible causes is infinite.
[5] Spontaneity and chance are causes of effects which though they might result from intelligence or nature, have in fact been caused by something *incidentally*. Now since nothing which is incidental is prior to what is *per se*, it is clear that no incidental cause can be prior to a cause *per se*. Spontaneity and chance, therefore, are posterior to intelligence and na- [10] ture. Hence, however true it may be that the heavens are due to spontaneity, it will still be true that intelligence and nature will be prior causes of this All and of many things in it besides.

7

It is clear then that there are causes, and that [15] the number of them is what we have stated. The number is the same as that of the things comprehended under the question 'why'. The 'why' is referred ultimately either (1), in things which do not involve motion, e.g. in mathematics, to the 'what' (to the definition of 'straight line' or 'commensurable', &c.), or (2) to what initiated a motion, e.g. 'why did they go to war?—because there had been a raid'; [20] or (3) we are inquiring 'for the sake of what?'—'that they may rule'; or (4), in the case of things that come into being, we are looking for the matter. The causes, therefore, are these and so many in number.

Now, the causes being four, it is the business of the physicist to know about them all, and if he refers his problems back to all of them, he will assign the 'why' in the way proper to his science—the matter, the form, the [25] mover, 'that for the sake of which'. The last three often coincide; for the 'what' and 'that for the sake of which' are one, while the primary source of motion is the same in species as these (for man generates man), and so too, in general, are all things which cause movement by being themselves moved; and such as are not of this kind are no longer inside the province of physics, for they cause motion not by possessing motion or a source of motion in themselves, but being themselves incapable of motion. Hence there are three [30] branches of study, one of things which are incapable of motion, the second of things in motion, but indestructible, the third of destructible things.

The question 'why', then, is answered by reference to the matter, to the form, and to the primary moving cause. For in respect of coming to be it is mostly in this last way that causes are investigated—'what comes to be after what? what was the primary agent or patient?' and so at each step of the series.
[35] Now the principles which cause motion in a physical way are two, of which one is not physical, as it has no principle of motion in 198ᵇ itself. Of this kind is whatever causes movement, not being itself moved, such as (1) that which is completely unchangeable, the primary reality, and (2) the essence of that which is coming to be, i.e. the form; for this is the end or 'that for the sake of which'. Hence since nature is for the sake of something, we must know this cause also. We must [5] explain the 'why' in all the senses of the term, namely, (1) that from this that will necessarily result ('from this' either without qualification or in most cases); (2) that 'this must be so if that is to be so' (as the conclusion presupposes the premisses); (3) that this was the essence of the thing; and (4) because it is better thus (not without qualification, but with reference to the essential nature in each case).

8

[10] We must explain then (1) that Nature belongs to the class of causes which act for the sake of something; (2) about the necessary and its place in physical problems, for all writers ascribe things to this cause, arguing that since the hot and the cold, &c., are of such and such a kind, therefore certain things *necessarily* are and come to be—and if they mention any other [15] cause (one his 'friendship and strife', another his 'mind'), it is only to touch on it, and then good-bye to it.

A difficulty presents itself: why should not nature work, not for the sake of something, nor because it is better so, but just as the sky rains, not in order to make the corn grow, but of necessity? What is drawn up must cool, and [20] what has been cooled must become water and descend, the result of this being that the corn grows. Similarly if a man's crop is spoiled on the threshing-floor, the rain did not fall for the sake of this—in order that the crop might be spoiled—but that result just followed. Why then should it not be the same with the parts in nature, e.g. that our teeth should come up *of necessity*—the front teeth sharp, fitted for [25] tearing, the molars broad and useful for grinding down the food—since they did not arise for this end, but it was merely a coincident result; and so with all other parts in which we suppose that there is purpose? Wherever then all the parts came about just what they would have been if they had come [30] to be for an end, such things survived, being organized spontaneously in a fitting way; whereas those which grew otherwise perished and continue to perish, as Empedocles says his 'man-faced ox-progeny' did.[1]

Such are the arguments (and others of the kind) which may cause difficulty on this point. Yet it is impossible that this should be the true view. For teeth and all other natural [35] things either invariably or normally come about in a given way; but of not one of the results of chance or spontaneity is this true. We do not ascribe to chance or mere coincidence the frequency of rain in winter, but frequent rain in summer we do; nor heat in the dog-days, but only if we have it in winter. If then, it is agreed that things are either the result of coincidence or for an end, and these cannot be the result of coincidence or [5] spontaneity, it follows that they must be for an end; and that such things are all due to nature even the champions of the theory which is before us would agree. Therefore action for an end is present in things which come to be and are by nature.

Further, where a series has a completion, all the preceding steps are for the sake of that. Now surely as in intelligent action, so in nature; [10] and as in nature, so it is in each action, if nothing interferes. Now intelligent action is for the sake of an end; therefore the nature of things also is so. Thus if a house, e.g. had been a thing made by nature, it would have been made in the same way as it is now by art; and if things made by nature were made also by art, they would come to be in the same way as by nature. Each step then [15] in the series is for the sake of the next; and generally art partly completes what nature cannot bring to a finish, and partly imitates her. If, therefore, artificial products are for the sake of an end, so clearly also are natural products. The relation of the later to the earlier terms of the series is the same in both. [20] This is most obvious in the animals other than man: they make things neither by art nor after inquiry or deliberation. Wherefore people discuss whether it is by intelligence or by some other faculty that these creatures work,—spiders, ants, and the like. By gradual advance in this direction we come to see clearly that in [25] plants too that is produced which is conducive to the end—leaves, e.g. grow to provide shade for the fruit. If then it is both by nature and for an end that the swallow makes its nest and the spider its web, and plants grow leaves for the sake of the fruit and send their roots down (not up) for the sake of nourishment, it is plain that this kind of cause is [30] operative in things which come to be and are by nature. And since 'nature' means two things, the matter and the form, of which the latter is the end, and since all the rest is for the sake of the end, the form must be the cause in the sense of 'that for the sake of which'.

Now mistakes come to pass even in the operations of art: the grammarian makes a mistake in writing and the doctor pours out [35] the wrong dose. Hence clearly mistakes are possible in the operations of nature also. If then in art there are cases in which what is rightly produced serves a purpose, and if where mistakes occur there was a purpose in what was attempted, only it was not attained, so must it be also in natural products, and [5] monstrosities will be failures in the purposive effort. Thus in the original combinations the 'ox-progeny' if they failed to reach a determinate end must have arisen through the corruption of some principle corresponding to what is now the seed.

Further, seed must have come into being first, and not straightway the animals: the words 'whole-natured first . . .'[2] must have meant seed.

Again, in plants too we find the relation of [10] means to end, though the degree of organization is less. Were there then in plants also 'olive-headed vine-progeny', like the 'man-headed ox-progeny', or not? An absurd suggestion; yet there must have been, if there were such things among animals.

Moreover, among the seeds anything must have come to be at random. But the person who asserts this entirely does away with 'na-

[1] Fr. 61. 2.

[2] Empedocles, Fr. 62. 4.

[*15*] ture' and what exists 'by nature'. For those things are natural which, by a continuous movement originated from an internal principle, arrive at some completion: the same completion is not reached from every principle; nor any chance completion, but always the tendency in each is towards the same end, if there is no impediment.

The end and the means towards it may come [*20*] about by chance. We say, for instance, that a stranger has come by chance, paid the ransom, and gone away, when he does so as if he had come for that purpose, though it was not for that that he came. This is incidental, for chance is an incidental cause, as I remarked before.[1] But when an event takes place always or for the most part, it is not [*25*] incidental or by chance. In natural products the sequence is invariable, if there is no impediment.

It is absurd to suppose that purpose is not present because we do not observe the agent deliberating. Art does not deliberate. If the ship-building art were in the wood, it would produce the same results *by nature*. If, therefore, purpose is present in art, it is present [*30*] also in nature. The best illustration is a doctor doctoring himself: nature is like that.

It is plain then that nature is a cause, a cause that operates for a purpose.

9

As regards what is 'of necessity', we must ask [*35*] whether the necessity is 'hypothetical', or 'simple' as well. The current view places what is of necessity in the process of production, just **200a** as if one were to suppose that the wall of a house necessarily comes to be because what is heavy is naturally carried downwards and what is light to the top, wherefore the stones and foundations take the lowest place, with earth above because it is lighter, and wood at [*5*] the top of all as being the lightest. Whereas, though the wall does not come to be *without* these, it is not *due* to these, except as its material cause: it comes to be for the sake of sheltering and guarding certain things. Similarly in all other things which involve production for an end; the product cannot come to be without things which have a necessary nature, but it is not due to these (except as its ma- [*10*] terial); it comes to be for an end. For instance, why is a saw such as it is? To effect so-and-so and for the sake of so-and-so. This

[1] 106b 23-7.

end, however, cannot be realized unless the saw is made of iron. It is, therefore, necessary for it to be of iron, *if* we are to have a saw and perform the operation of sawing. What is necessary then, is necessary *on a hypothesis;* it is not a result necessarily determined by antecedents. Necessity is in the matter, while 'that for the sake of which' is in the definition.

[*15*] Necessity in mathematics is in a way similar to necessity in things which come to be through the operation of nature. Since a straight line is what it is, it is necessary that the angles of a triangle should equal two right angles. But not conversely; though if the angles are *not* equal to two right angles, then the straight line is not what it is either. But in things which come to be for an end, the reverse is true. If the end is to exist or does exist, [*20*] that also which precedes it will exist or does exist; otherwise just as there, if the conclusion is not true, the premiss will not be true, so here the end or 'that for the sake of which' will not exist. For this too is itself a starting-point, but of the reasoning, not of the action; while in mathematics the starting-point is the starting-point of the reasoning only, as there is no action. If then there is to be [*25*] a house, such-and-such things must be made or be there already or exist, or generally the matter relative to the end, bricks and stones if it is a house. But the end is not due to these except as the matter, nor will it come to exist because of them. Yet if they do not exist at all, neither will the house, or the saw —the former in the absence of stones, the latter in the absence of iron—just as in the other case the premisses will not be true, if the angles of the triangle are not equal to two right angles.

[*30*] The necessary in nature, then, is plainly what we call by the name of matter, and the changes in it. Both causes must be stated by the physicist, but especially the end; for that is the cause of the matter, not *vice versa;* and the end is 'that for the sake of which', and the beginning starts from the definition or es- [*35*] sence; as in artificial products, since a **200b** house is of such-and-such a kind, certain things must *necessarily* come to be or be there already, or since health is this, these things must necessarily come to be or be there already. Similarly if man is this, then these; if these, then those. Perhaps the necessary is present also in the definition. For if one defines the [*5*] operation of sawing as being a certain kind of dividing, then this cannot come about un-

less the saw has teeth of a certain kind; and these cannot be unless it is of iron. For in the definition too there are some parts that are, as it were, its matter.

BOOK III

1

NATURE has been defined as a 'principle of motion and change', and it is the subject of our inquiry. We must therefore see that we understand the meaning of 'motion'; for if it were unknown, the meaning of 'nature' too would be unknown.
[15] When we have determined the nature of motion, our next task will be to attack in the same way the terms which are involved in it. Now motion is supposed to belong to the class of things which are *continuous;* and the *infinite* presents itself first in the continuous— that is how it comes about that 'infinite' is often used in definitions of the continuous ('what is infinitely divisible is continuous').
[20] Besides these, *place, void,* and *time* are thought to be necessary conditions of motion.

Clearly, then, for these reasons and also because the attributes mentioned are common to, and coextensive with, all the objects of our science, we must first take each of them in hand and discuss it. For the investigation of special attributes comes after that of the common attributes.
[25] To begin then, as we said, with motion.

We may start by distinguishing (1) what exists in a state of fulfilment only, (2) what exists as potential, (3) what exists as potential and also in fulfilment—one being a 'this', another 'so much', a third 'such', and similarly in each of the other modes of the predication of being.

Further, the word 'relative' is used with [30] reference to (1) excess and defect, (2) agent and patient and generally what can move and what can be moved. For 'what can cause movement' is relative to 'what can be moved', and *vice versa.*

Again, there is no such thing as motion *over and above* the things. It is always with respect to substance or to quantity or to quality or to place that what changes changes. But it is impossible, as we assert, to find anything com- [35] mon to these which is neither 'this' nor 201ª *quantum* nor *quale* nor any of the other predicates. Hence neither will motion and change have reference to something over and above the things mentioned, for there *is* nothing over and above them.

Now each of these belongs to all its subjects in either of two ways: namely (1) substance— the one is positive form, the other privation; [5] (2) in quality, white and black; (3) in quantity, complete and incomplete; (4) in respect of locomotion, upwards and downwards or light and heavy. Hence there are as many types of motion or change as there are meanings of the word 'is'.

We have now before us the distinctions in the various classes of being between what is fully real and what is potential.
[10] Def. *The fulfilment of what exists potentially, in so far as it exists potentially, is motion*—namely, of what is alterable *qua* alterable, *alteration:* of what can be increased and its opposite what can be decreased (there is no common name), *increase* and *decrease:* of what can come to be and can pass away, *coming to be* and *passing away:* of what can be carried along, *locomotion.*
[15] Examples will elucidate this definition of motion. When the buildable, in so far as it is just *that,* is fully real, it is *being built,* and this is build*ing.* Similarly, learning, doctoring, rolling, leaping, ripening, ageing.

The same thing, if it is of a certain kind, can [20] be both potential and fully real, not indeed at the same time or not in the same respect, but e.g. potentially hot and actually cold. Hence at once such things will act and be acted on by one another in many ways: each of them will be capable at the same time of causing alteration and of being altered. Hence, too, what effects motion as a physical agent can be moved: when a thing of this kind causes motion, it is [25] itself also moved. This, indeed, has led some people to suppose that every mover is moved. But this question depends on another set of arguments, and the truth will be made clear later.[1] It *is* possible for a thing to cause motion, though it is itself incapable of being moved.

It is the fulfilment of what is potential when it is already fully real and operates not as *itself* but as *movable,* that is motion. What I mean by 'as' is this: Bronze is potentially a statue. [30] But it is not the fulfilment of bronze as *bronze* which is motion. For 'to be bronze' and 'to be a certain potentiality' are not the same.

[1] VIII. 5.

If they were identical without qualification, i.e. in *definition,* the fulfilment of bronze as bronze *would* have been motion. But they are not the same, as has been said. (This is obvious in con-[35] traries. 'To be capable of health' and 'to be capable of illness' are not the same, for if they were there would be no difference between being ill and being well. Yet the *subject* both of health and of sickness—whether it is humour or blood—is one and the same.)

We can distinguish, then, between the two —just as, to give another example, 'colour' and 'visible' are different—and clearly it is the fulfilment of what is potential *as* potential that is [5] motion. So this, precisely, is motion.

Further it is evident that motion is an attribute of a thing just *when* it is fully real in this way, and neither before nor after. For each thing of this kind is capable of being at one time actual, at another not. Take for instance the buildable as buildable. The actuality of the [10] buildable as buildable is the process of building. For the actuality of the buildable must be either this or the house. But when there is a house, the buildable is no longer buildable. On the other hand, it *is* the buildable which is *being* built. The process then of being built must be the kind of actuality required. But building is a kind of motion, and the same account will apply to the other kinds [15] also.

2

The soundness of this definition is evident both when we consider the accounts of motion that the others have given, and also from the difficulty of defining it otherwise.

One could not easily put motion and change in another genus—this is plain if we consider where some people put it; they identify motion [20] with 'difference' or 'inequality' or 'not being'; but such things are not necessarily moved, whether they are 'different' or 'unequal' or 'non-existent'; Nor is change either *to* or from *these* rather than to or from their opposites.

The reason why they put motion into these [25] genera is that it is thought to be something indefinite, and the principles in the second column are indefinite because they are privative: none of them is either 'this' or 'such' or comes under any of the other modes of predication. The reason in turn why motion is thought to be indefinite is that it cannot be classed simply as a potentiality or as an actuality—a thing that is merely *capable* of having a [30] certain size is not undergoing change, nor yet a thing that is *actually* of a certain size, and motion is thought to be a sort of *actuality,* but incomplete, the reason for this view being that the potential whose actuality it is is incomplete. This is why it is hard to grasp what motion is. It is necessary to class it with privation or with potentiality or with sheer actuality, yet none of these seems possible. There remains then the [35] suggested mode of definition, namely that it is a sort of actuality, or actuality of the kind described, hard to grasp, but not incapable of existing.

The mover too is moved, as has been said—every mover, that is, which is capable of motion, and whose immobility is rest—when a thing is subject to motion its immobility is rest. [5] For to act on the movable as such is just to *move* it. But this it does by *contact,* so that at the same time it is also acted on. Hence we can define motion as *the fulfilment of the movable qua movable, the cause of the attribute being contact with what can move,* so that the mover is also acted on. The mover or agent will always be the vehicle of a form, either a 'this' or [10] a 'such', which, when it acts, will be the source and cause of the change, e.g. the full-formed man begets man from what is potentially man.

3

The solution of the difficulty that is raised about the motion—whether it is in the *movable*—is plain. It is the fulfilment of this potentiality, and by the action of that which has the power of causing motion; and the actuality of that which has the power of causing motion is [15] not other than the actuality of the movable, for it must be the fulfilment of *both*. A thing is capable of causing motion because it *can* do this, it is a mover because it actually *does* it. But it is on the movable that it is capable of acting. Hence there is a single actuality of both alike, just as one to two and two to one are the same interval, and the steep ascent and [20] the steep descent are one—for these are one and the same, although they can be described in different ways. So it is with the mover and the moved.

This view has a dialectical difficulty. Perhaps it is necessary that the actuality of the agent and that of the patient should not be the same. The one is 'agency' and the other 'patiency'; and the outcome and completion of the one is an 'action', that of the other a 'passion'. [25] Since then they are both motions, we may ask: *in* what are they, if they are different?

Either (*a*) both are in what is acted on and moved, or (*b*) the agency is in the agent and the patiency in the patient. (If we ought to call the latter also 'agency', the word would be used in two senses.)

Now, in alternative (*b*), the motion will be in the mover, for the same statement will hold of 'mover' and 'moved'. Hence either *every* [30] mover will be moved, or, though having motion, it will not be moved.

If on the other hand (*a*) both are in what is moved and acted on—both the agency and the patiency (e.g. both teaching and learning, though they are *two,* in the *learner*), then, first, the actuality of each will not be present *in* each, and, a second absurdity, a thing will have two motions at the same time. How will there [35] be two alterations of quality in *one* subject towards *one* definite quality? The thing is impossible: the actualization will be one.

202[b] But (some one will say) it is contrary to reason to suppose that there should be one identical actualization of two things which are different in kind. Yet there will be, if teaching and learning are the same, and agency and patiency. To teach will be the same as to learn, and to act the same as to be acted on—the teacher will necessarily be learning everything that he teaches, and the agent will be acted on. [5] One may reply:

(1) It is *not* absurd that the actualization of one thing should be in another. Teaching is the activity of a person who can teach, yet the operation is performed *on* some patient—it is not cut adrift from a subject, but is of *A* on *B*.

(2) There is nothing to prevent two things having one and the same actualization, provided the actualizations are not *described* in the same way, but are related as what can act to what is acting.
[10] (3) Nor is it necessary that the teacher should learn, even if to act and to be acted on are one and the same, provided they are not the same in *definition* (as 'raiment' and 'dress'), but are the same merely in the sense in which the road from Thebes to Athens and the road from Athens to Thebes are the same, as has been explained above.[1] For it is not things which are in a way the same that have all their [15] attributes the same, but only such as have the same definition. But indeed it by no means follows from the fact that teaching is the same as learning, that to learn is the same as to teach, any more than it follows from the fact that there is one *distance* between two things which

[1] Cf. [a]18–20.

are at a distance from each other, that the two *vectors AB* and *BA* are one and the same. To generalize, teaching is not the same as learning, or agency as patiency, in the full sense, [20] though they belong to the same *subject,* the motion; for the 'actualization of *X* in *Y*' and the 'actualization of *Y* through the action of *X*' differ in *definition.*

What then Motion is, has been stated both generally and particularly. It is not difficult to see how each of its types will be defined—al- [25] teration is the fulfillment of the alterable *qua* alterable (or, more scientifically, the fulfilment of what can act and what can be acted on, as such)—generally and again in each particular case, building, healing, &c. A similar definition will apply to each of the other kinds of motion.

4

[30] The science of nature is concerned with spatial magnitudes and motion and time, and each of these at least is necessarily infinite or finite, even if some things dealt with by the science are not, e.g. a quality or a point—it is not necessary perhaps that such things should be put under either head. Hence it is incumbent on the person who specializes in physics [35] to discuss the infinite and to inquire whether there *is* such a thing or not, and, if there is, *what* it is.

The appropriateness to the science of this problem is clearly indicated. All who have touched on this kind of science in a way worth considering have formulated views about the infinite, and indeed, to a man, make it a principle of things.

(1) Some, as the Pythagoreans and Plato, [5] make the infinite a principle in the sense of a self-subsistent substance, and not as a mere attribute of some other thing. Only the Pythagoreans place the infinite among the objects of sense (they do not regard number as separable from these), and assert that what is outside the heaven is infinite. Plato, on the other hand, holds that there is no body outside (the Forms are not outside, because they are nowhere), yet that the infinite is present not only in the objects of sense but in the Forms also.

[10] Further, the Pythagoreans identify the infinite with the even. For this, they say, when it is cut off and shut in by the odd, provides things with the element of infinity. An indication of this is what happens with numbers. If the gnomons are placed round the one, and without the one, in the one construction the

figure that results is always different, in the [15] other it is always the same. But Plato has two infinites, the Great and the Small.

The physicists, on the other hand, all of them, always regard the infinite as an attribute of a substance which is different from it and belongs to the class of the so-called elements— water or air or what is intermediate between them. Those who make them limited in number never make them infinite in amount. But those who make the elements infinite in num- [20] ber, as Anaxagoras and Democritus do, say that the infinite is continuous by contact— compounded of the homogeneous parts according to the one, of the seed-mass of the atomic shapes according to the other.

Further, Anaxagoras held that any part is a mixture in the same way as the All, on the ground of the observed fact that anything comes out of anything. For it is probably for this reason that he maintains that once upon a [25] time all things were together. (*This* flesh and *this* bone were together, and so of *any* thing: therefore *all* things: and at the same time too.) For there is a beginning of separation, not only for each thing, but for all. Each thing that comes to be comes from a similar body, and there is a coming to be of all things, though not, it is true, at the same time. Hence [30] there must also be an origin of coming to be. One such source there is which he calls Mind, and Mind begins its work of thinking from some starting-point. So necessarily all things must have been together at a certain time, and must have begun to be moved at a certain time.

Democritus, for his part, asserts the contrary, namely that no element arises from another element. Nevertheless for him the com- 203ᵇ mon body is a source of all things, differing from part to part in size and in shape.

It is clear then from these considerations that the inquiry concerns the physicist. Nor is it without reason that they all make it a principle or source. We cannot say that the infinite [5] has no effect, and the only effectiveness which we can ascribe to it is that of a principle. Everything is either a source or derived from a source. But there cannot be a source of the infinite or limitless, for that would be a limit of it. Further, as it is a beginning, it is both uncreatable and indestructible. For there must be a point at which what has come to be reaches completion, and also a termination of all pass- [10] ing away. That is why, as we say, there is no principle of *this,* but it is this which is held to be the principle of other things, and to encompass all and to steer all, as those assert who do not recognize, alongside the infinite, other causes, such as Mind or Friendship. Further they identify it with the Divine, for it is 'deathless and imperishable' as Anaximander says, with the majority of the physicists.

[15] Belief in the existence of the infinite comes mainly from five considerations:

(1) From the nature of time—for it is infinite.

(2) From the division of magnitudes—for the mathematicians also use the notion of the infinite.

(3) If coming to be and passing away do not give out, it is only because that from which things come to be is infinite.

[20] (4) Because the limited always finds its limit in something, so that there must be *no* limit, if everything is *always* limited by something different from itself.

(5) Most of all, a reason which is peculiarly appropriate and presents the difficulty that is felt by everybody—not only number but also mathematical magnitudes and what is outside the heaven are supposed to be infinite because they never give out in our *thought*.

[25] The last fact (that what is outside is infinite) leads people to suppose that body also is infinite, and that there is an infinite number of worlds. Why should there be body in one part of the void rather than in another? Grant only that mass is anywhere and it follows that it must be everywhere. Also, if void and place are infinite, there must be infinite body too, for in the case of eternal things what may be must be.

[30] But the problem of the infinite is difficult: many contradictions result whether we suppose it to exist or not to exist. If it exists, we have still to ask *how* it exists; as a substance or as the essential attribute of some entity? Or in neither way, yet none the less is there something which is infinite or some things which are infinitely many?

204ᵃ The problem, however, which specially belongs to the physicist is to investigate whether there is a sensible magnitude which is infinite.

We must begin by distinguishing the various senses in which the term 'infinite' is used.

(1) What is incapable of being gone through, because it is not in its nature to be gone through (the sense in which the voice is 'invisible').

(2) What admits of being gone through, the process however having no termination, or

(3) what scarcely admits of being gone through.

(4) What naturally admits of being gone through, but is not actually gone through or does not actually reach an end.

Further, everything that is infinite may be so in respect of addition or division or both.

5

Now it is impossible that the infinite should be a thing which is itself infinite, separable from sensible objects. If the infinite is neither a magnitude nor an aggregate, but is itself a substance and not an attribute, it will be indivisible; for the divisible must be either a magnitude or an aggregate. But if indivisible, then not infinite, except in the sense (1) in which the voice is 'invisible'. But this is not the sense in which it is used by those who say that the infinite exsts, nor that in which we are investigating it, namely as (2), 'that which cannot be gone through'. But if the infinite exists as an attribute, it would not be, *qua* infinite, an element in substances, any more than the invisible would be an element of speech, though the voice is invisible.

Further, how can the infinite be itself any thing, unless both number and magnitude, of which it is an essential attribute, exist in that way? If *they* are not substances, *a fortiori* the infinite is not.

It is plain, too, that the infinite cannot be an actual thing and a substance and principle. For any part of it that is taken will be infinite, if it has parts: for 'to be infinite' and 'the infinite' are the same, if it is a substance and not predicated of a subject. Hence it will be either indivisible or divisible into infinites. But the same thing cannot be many infinites. (Yet just as part of air is air, so a part of the infinite would be infinite, if it is supposed to be a substance and principle.) Therefore the infinite must be without parts and indivisible. But this cannot be true of what is infinite in full completion: for it must be a definite quantity.

Suppose then that infinity belongs to substance as an attribute. But, if so, it cannot, as we have said, be described as a principle, but rather that of which it is an attribute—the air or the even number.

Thus the view of those who speak after the manner of the Pythagoreans is absurd. With the same breath they treat the infinite as substance, and divide it into parts.

This discussion, however, involves the more general question whether the infinite can be present in mathematical objects and things which are intelligible and do not have extension, as well as among sensible objects. Our inquiry (as physicists) is limited to its special subject-matter, the objects of sense, and we have to ask whether there is or is not among *them* a body which is infinite in the direction of increase.

We may begin with a dialectical argument and show as follows that there is no such thing. If 'bounded by a surface' is the definition of body there cannot be an infinite body either intelligible or sensible. Nor can number taken in abstraction be infinite, for number or that which has number is numerable. If then the numerable can be numbered, it would also be possible to go through the infinite.

If, on the other hand, we investigate the question more in accordance with principles appropriate to physics, we are led as follows to the same result.

The infinite body must be either (1) compound, or (2) simple; yet neither alternative is possible.

(1) Compound the infinite body will not be, if the elements are finite in number. For they must be more than one, and the contraries must always balance, and no *one* of them can be infinite. If one of the bodies falls in any degree short of the other in potency—suppose fire is finite in amount while air is infinite and a given quantity of fire exceeds in power the same amount of air in any ratio provided it is numerically definite—the infinite body will obviously prevail over and annihilate the finite body. On the other hand, it is impossible that *each* should be infinite. 'Body' is what has extension in all directions and the infinite is what is boundlessly extended, so that the infinite body would be extended in all directions *ad infinitum*.

Nor (2) can the infinite body be one and simple, whether it is, as some hold, a thing over and above the elements (from which they generate the elements) or is not thus qualified.

(*a*) We must consider the former alternative; for there *are* some people who make this the infinite, and not air or water, in order that the other elements may not be annihilated by the element which is infinite. They have contrariety with each other—air is cold, water moist, fire hot; if one were infinite, the others by now would have ceased to be. As it is, they say, the infinite is different from them and is their source.

It is impossible, however, that there should

[30] be such a body; not because it is infinite—on that point a general proof can be given which applies equally to all, air, water, or anything else—but simply because there is, as a matter of fact, no such *sensible* body, alongside the so-called elements. Everything can be resolved into the elements of which it is composed. Hence the body in question would have been present in our world here, alongside air and fire and earth and water: but nothing of the kind is observed.

[35] (*b*) Nor can fire or any other of the elements be infinite. For generally, and apart from 205ᵃ the question of how any of them could be infinite, the All, even if it were limited, cannot either be or become one of them, as Heraclitus says that at some time all things become fire. (The same argument applies also to the [5] one which the physicists suppose to exist alongside the elements: for everything changes from contrary to contrary, e.g. from hot to cold).

The preceding consideration of the various cases serves to show us whether it is or is not possible that there should be an infinite sensible body. The following arguments give a general demonstration that it is not possible.

[10] It is the nature of every kind of sensible body to be somewhere, and there is a place appropriate to each, the same for the part and for the whole, e.g. for the whole earth and for a single clod, and for fire and for a spark.

Suppose (*a*) that the infinite sensible body is homogeneous. Then each part will be either immovable or always being carried along. Yet neither is possible. For why downwards rather than upwards or in any other direction? I mean, e.g. if you take a clod, where will it be [15] moved or where will it be at rest? For *ex hypothesi* the place of the body akin to it is infinite. Will it occupy the whole place, then? And how? What then will be the nature of its rest and of its movement, or where will they be? It will either be at home everywhere—then it will not be moved; or it will be moved everywhere—then it will not come to rest.

But if (*b*) the All has dissimilar parts, the proper places of the parts will be dissimilar [20] also, and the body of the All will have no unity except that of contact. Then, further, the parts will be either finite or infinite in variety of kind. (i) *Finite* they cannot be, for if the All is to be infinite, some of them would have to be infinite, while the others were not, e.g. fire or water will be infinite. But, as we have seen before, such an element would destroy [25] what is contrary to it. (This indeed is the reason why none of the physicists made fire or earth the one infinite body, but either water or air or what is intermediate between them, because the abode of each of the two was plainly determinate, while the others have an ambiguous place between up and down.)

But (ii) if the parts are *infinite* in number and simple, their proper places too will be infinite in number, and the same will be true of [30] the elements themselves. If that is impossible, and the places are finite, the whole too must be finite; for the place and the body cannot but fit each other. Neither is the whole place larger than what can be filled by the body (and then the body would no longer be [35] infinite), nor is the body larger than the place; for either there would be an empty space or a body whose nature it is to be nowhere.

205ᵇ Anaxagoras gives an absurd account of why the infinite is at rest. He says that the infinite itself is the cause of its being fixed. This because it is *in* itself, since nothing else contains it—on the assumption that wherever any[5]thing is, it is there by its own nature. But this is not true: a thing could be somewhere by compulsion, and not where it is its nature to be.

Even if it is true as true can be that the whole is not moved (for what is fixed by itself and is in itself must be immovable), yet we must explain *why* it is not its nature to be moved. It is not enough just to make this statement and then decamp. Anything else might [10] be in a state of rest, but there is no reason why it should not be its nature to be moved. The earth is not carried along, and would not be carried along if it were infinite, provided it is held together by the centre. But it would not be because there was no other region in which it could be carried along that it would remain at the centre, but because this is its nature. Yet in this case also we may say that it fixes itself. If then in the case of the earth, supposed to be [15] infinite, it is at rest, not because it is infinite, but because it has weight and what is heavy rests at the centre and the earth is at the centre, similarly the infinite also would rest in itself, not because it is infinite and fixes itself, but owing to some other cause.

Another difficulty emerges at the same time. Any part of the infinite body ought to remain at rest. Just as the infinite remains at rest in itself because it fixes itself, so too any part of it [20] you may take will remain in itself. The appropriate places of the whole and of the part are alike, e.g. of the whole earth and of a clod the appropriate place is the lower region; of fire as a whole and of a spark, the upper region. If, therefore, to be in itself is the place of the infinite, that also will be appropriate to the part. Therefore it will remain in itself.

In general, the view that there is an infinite [25] body is plainly incompatible with the doctrine that there is necessarily a proper place for each kind of body, if every sensible body has either weight or lightness, and if a body has a natural locomotion towards the centre if it is heavy, and upwards if it is light. This would need to be true of the infinite also. But neither character can belong to it: it cannot be either as a whole, nor can it be half the one and half [30] the other. For how should you divide it? or how can the infinite have the one part up and the other down, or an extremity and a centre?

Further, every sensible body is in place, and the kinds or differences of place are up-down, before-behind, right-left; and these distinctions hold not only in relation to us and by arbitrary [35] agreement, but also in the whole itself. But in the infinite body they cannot exist. In general, if it is impossible that there should be an infinite place, and if every body is in place, 206ᵃ there cannot be an infinite body.

Surely what is in a special place is in place, and what is in place is in a special place. Just, then, as the infinite cannot be quantity—that would imply that it has a particular quantity, e.g. two or three cubits; quantity just means [5] these—so a thing's being in place means that it is *some*where, and that is either up or down or in some other of the six differences of position: but each of these is a limit.

It is plain from these arguments that there is no body which is *actually* infinite.

6

But on the other hand to suppose that the infinite does not exist in any way leads obviously to many impossible consequences: there will be [10] a beginning and an end of time, a magnitude will not be divisible into magnitudes, number will not be infinite. If, then, in view of the above considerations, neither alternative seems possible, an arbiter must be called in; and clearly there is a sense in which the infinite exists and another in which it does not.

We must keep in mind that the word 'is' means either what *potentially* is or what *fully* is. [15] Further, a thing is infinite either by addition or by division.

Now, as we have seen, magnitude is not actually infinite. But by division it is infinite. (There is no difficulty in refuting the theory of indivisible lines.) The alternative then remains that the infinite has a potential existence.

But the phrase 'potential existence' is ambiguous. When we speak of the potential existence of a statue we mean that there will be an [20] actual statue. It is not so with the infinite. There will not be an actual infinite. The word 'is' has many senses, and we say that the infinite 'is' in the sense in which we say 'it is day' or 'it is the games', because one thing after another is always coming into existence. For of these things too the distinction between potential and actual existence holds. We say that there are Olympic games, both in the sense that they may occur and that they are actually occurring.

[25] The infinite exhibits itself in different ways—in time, in the generations of man, and in the division of magnitudes. For generally the infinite has this mode of existence: one thing is always being taken after another, and each thing that is taken is always finite, but always different. Again, 'being' has more than one [30] sense, so that we must not regard the infinite as a 'this', such as a man or a horse, but must suppose it to exist in the sense in which we speak of the day or the games as existing—things whose being has not come to them like that of a substance, but consists in a process of coming to be or passing away; definite if you like at each stage, yet always different.

206ᵇ But when this takes place in spatial magnitudes, what is taken perists, while in the succession of time and of men it takes place by the passing away of these in such a way that the source of supply never gives out.

In a way the infinite by addition is the same thing as the infinite by division. In a finite magnitude, the infinite by addition comes about in a way inverse to that of the other. For [5] in proportion as we see division going on, in the same proportion we see addition being made to what is already marked off. For if we take a determinate part of a finite magnitude and add another part *determined by the same ratio* (not taking in the same amount of the original whole), and so on, we shall not trav- [10] erse the given magnitude. But if we increase the ratio of the part, so as always to take in the same amount, we shall traverse the magnitude, for every finite magnitude is exhausted by means of any determinate quantity however small.

The infinite, then, exists in no other way, but in this way it does exist, potentially and by reduction. It exists fully in the sense in which we say 'it is day' or 'it is the games'; and po- [15] tentially as matter exists, not independently as what is finite does.

By addition then, also, there is potentially an infinite, namely, what we have described as being in a sense the same as the infinite in respect of division. For it will always be possible to take something *ab extra*. Yet the sum of the parts taken will not exceed every determinate magnitude, just as in the direction of division every determinate magnitude is surpassed in smallness and there will be a smaller part.

[20] But in respect of addition there cannot be an infinite which even potentially exceeds every assignable magnitude, unless it has the attribute of being actually infinite, as the physicists hold to be true of the body which is outside the world, whose essential nature is air or something of the kind. But if there cannot be in this way a sensible body which is infinite in [25] the full sense, evidently there can no more be a body which is potentially infinite in respect of addition, except as the inverse of the infinite by division, as we have said. It is for this reason that Plato also made the infinites two in number, because it is supposed to be possible to exceed all limits and to proceed *ad infinitum* in the direction both of increase and of reduction. Yet though he makes the infinites two, he does not use them. For in the [30] numbers the infinite in the direction of reduction is not present, as the monad is the smallest; nor is the infinite in the direction of increase, for the parts number only up to the decad.

The infinite turns out to be the contrary of what it is said to be. It is not what has nothing 207ᵃ outside it that is infinite, but what always has something outside it. This is indicated by the fact that rings also that have no bezel are described as 'endless', because it is always possible to take a part which is outside a given part. The description depends on a certain similarity, but it is not true in the full sense of the [5] word. This condition alone is not sufficient: it is necessary also that the next part which is taken should never be the same. In the circle, the latter condition is not satisfied: it is only the adjacent part from which the new part is different.

Our definition then is as follows:

A quantity is infinite if it is such that we can always take a part outside what has been already taken. On the other hand, what has nothing outside it is complete and whole. For thus we define the whole—that from which noth- [10] ing is wanting, as a whole man or a whole box. What is true of each particular is true of the whole as such—the whole is that of which nothing is outside. On the other hand that from which something is absent and outside, however small that may be, is not 'all'. 'Whole' and 'complete' are either quite identical or closely akin. Nothing is complete (τέλειον) which has no end (τέλος); and the end is a limit.

[15] Hence Parmenides must be thought to have spoken better than Melissus. The latter says that the whole is infinite, but the former describes it as limited, 'equally balanced from the middle'.[1] For to connect the infinite with the all and the whole is not like joining two pieces of string; for it is from this they get the dignity they ascribe to the infinite—its contain- [20] ing all things and holding the all in itself—from its having a certain similarity to the whole. It is in fact the matter of the completeness which belongs to size, and what is potentially a whole, though not in the full sense. It is divisible both in the direction of reduction and of the inverse addition. It is a whole and limited; not, however, in virtue of its own nature, but in virtue of what is other than it. It does not contain, but, in so far as it is infinite, [25] is contained. Consequently, also, it is unknowable, *qua* infinite; for the matter has no form. (Hence it is plain that the infinite stands in the relation of part rather than of whole. For the matter is part of the whole, as the bronze is of the bronze statue.) If it contains in the case of sensible things, in the case of intelligible things the great and the small ought to [30] contain them. But it is absurd and impossible to suppose that the unknowable and indeterminate should contain and determine.

7

It is reasonable that there should not be held to be an infinite in respect of addition such as to surpass every magnitude, but that there should be thought to be such an infinite in the direction of division. For the matter and the [35] infinite are contained inside what contains them, while it is the form which con- 207ᵇ tains. It is natural too to suppose that in number there is a limit in the direction of the minimum, and that in the other direction every assigned number is surpassed. In magnitude,

[1] Fr. 8. 44.

on the contrary, every assigned magnitude is surpassed in the direction of smallness, while [5] in the other direction there is no infinite magnitude. The reason is that what is one is indivisible whatever it may be, e.g. a man is one man, not many. Number on the other hand is a plurality of 'ones' and a certain quantity of them. Hence number must stop at the indivisible: for 'two' and 'three' are merely derivative terms, and so with each of the other [10] numbers. But in the direction of largeness it is always possible to think of a larger number: for the number of times a magnitude can be bisected is infinite. Hence this infinite is potential, never actual: the number of parts that can be taken always surpasses any assigned number. But this number is not separable from the process of bisection, and its infinity is not a permanent actuality but consists in a process of coming to be, like time and the number of time.

[15] With magnitudes the contrary holds. What is continuous is divided *ad infinitum,* but there is no infinite in the direction of increase. For the size which it can potentially be, it can also actually be. Hence since no sensible magnitude is infinite, it is impossible to exceed every assigned magnitude; for if it were possi- [20] ble there would be something bigger than the heavens.

The infinite is not the same in magnitude and movement and time, in the sense of a single nature, but its secondary sense depends on its primary sense, i.e. movement is called infinite in virtue of the magnitude covered by the movement (or alteration or growth), and time because of the movement. (I use these terms [25] for the moment. Later I shall explain what each of them means, and also why every magnitude is divisible into magnitudes.)

Our account does not rob the mathematicians of their science, by disproving the actual existence of the infinite in the direction of increase, in the sense of the untraversable. In point of fact they do not need the infinite and [30] do not use it. They postulate only that the finite straight line may be produced as far as they wish. It is possible to have divided in the same ratio as the largest quantity another magnitude of any size you like. Hence, for the purposes of proof, it will make no difference to them to have such an infinite instead, while its existence will be in the sphere of real magnitudes.

[35] In the fourfold scheme of causes, it is plain that the infinite is a cause in the sense of matter, and that its essence is privation, the 208^a subject as such being what is continuous and sensible. All the other thinkers, too, evidently treat the infinite as matter—that is why it is inconsistent in them to make it what contains, and not what is contained.

8

[5] It remains to dispose of the arguments which are supposed to support the view that the infinite exists not only potentially but as a separate thing. Some have no cogency; others can be met by fresh objections that are valid.

(1) In order that coming to be should not fail, it is not necessary that there should be a sensible body which is actually infinite. The passing away of one thing may be the coming [10] to be of another, the All being limited.

(2) There is a difference between touching and being limited. The former is relative to something and is the touching of something (for everything that touches touches something), and further is an attribute of some one of the things which are limited. On the other hand, what is limited is not limited in relation to anything. Again, contact is not necessarily possible between any two things taken at random.

[15] (3) To rely on mere thinking is absurd, for then the excess or defect is not in the thing but in the thought. One might think that one of us is bigger than he is and magnify him *ad infinitum*. But it does not follow that he is bigger than the size we are, just because some one thinks he is, but only because he *is* the size he is. The thought is an accident.

[20] (*a*) Time indeed and movement are infinite, and also thinking, in the sense that each part that is taken passes in succession out of existence.

(*b*) Magnitude is not infinite either in the way of reduction or of magnification in thought.

This concludes my account of the way in which the infinite exists, and of the way in which it does not exist, and of what it is.

BOOK IV

1

THE physicist must have a knowledge of Place, too, as well as of the infinite—namely, whether there is such a thing or not, and the manner of its existence and what it is—both [30] because all suppose that things which exist are *somewhere* (the non-existent is nowhere—where is the goat-stag or the sphinx?), and because 'motion' in its most general and primary sense is change of place, which we call 'locomotion'.

The question, what is place? presents many difficulties. An examination of all the relevant facts seems to lead to divergent conclusions. [35] Moreover, we have inherited nothing from previous thinkers, whether in the way of a statement of difficulties or of a solution.

208ᵇ The existence of place is held to be obvious from the fact of mutual replacement. Where water now is, there in turn, when the water has gone out as from a vessel, air is pres- [5] ent. When therefore another body occupies this same place, the place is thought to be different from all the bodies which come to be in it and replace one another. What now contains air formerly contained water, so that clearly the place or space into which and out of which they passed was something different from both.

Further, the typical locomotions of the elementary natural bodies—namely, fire, earth, and the like—show not only that place is some- [10] thing, but also that it exerts a certain influence. Each is carried to its own place, if it is not hindered, the one up, the other down. Now these are regions or kinds of place—up and down and the rest of the six directions. Nor do such distinctions (up and down and right and [15] left, &c.) hold only in relation to us. To *us* they are not always the same but change with the direction in which we are turned: that is why the same thing may be both right *and* left, up *and* down, before *and* behind. But in *nature* each is distinct, taken apart by itself. It is not every chance direction which is 'up', but where fire and what is light are carried; [20] similarly, too, 'down' is not any chance direction but where what has weight and what is made of earth are carried—the implication being that these places do not differ merely in relative position, but also as possessing distinct potencies. This is made plain also by the objects studied by mathematics. Though they have no real place, they nevertheless, in respect of their position relatively to us, have a right and left as attributes ascribed to them only in consequence of their relative position, not having by nature these various characteristics. [25] Again, the theory that the void exists involves the existence of place: for one would define void as place bereft of body.

These considerations then would lead us to suppose that place is something distinct from bodies, and that every sensible body is in place. Hesiod too might be held to have given a correct account of it when he made chaos first. [30] At least he says:

First of all things came chaos to being, then broad-breasted earth,[1]

implying that things need to have space first, because he thought, with most people, that everything is somewhere and in place. If this is its nature, the potency of place must be a marvellous thing, and take precedence of all other [35] things. For that without which nothing else can exist, while it can exist without the others, must needs be first; for place does not 209ᵃ pass out of existence when the things in it are annihilated.

True, but even if we suppose its existence settled, the question of its *nature* presents difficulty—whether it is some sort of 'bulk' of body or some entity other than that, for we must first determine its genus.

[5] (1) Now it has three dimensions, length, breadth, depth, the dimensions by which all body also is bounded. But the place cannot *be* body; for if it were there would be two bodies in the same place.

(2) Further, if body has a place and space, clearly so too have surface and the other limits of body; for the same statement will apply to them: where the bounding planes of the [10] water were, there in turn will be those of the air. But when we come to a point we cannot make a distinction between it and its place. Hence if the place of a point is not different from the point, no more will that of any of the others be different, and place will not be something different from each of them.

(3) What in the world then are we to suppose place to be? If it has the sort of nature described, it cannot be an element or composed [15] of elements, whether these be corporeal or incorporeal: for while it has size, it has not

[1] *Theogony*, 116 f.

body. But the elements of sensible bodies are bodies, while nothing that has size results from a combination of intelligible elements.

(4) Also we may ask: of what in things is space the cause? None of the four modes of causation can be ascribed to it. It is neither [20] cause in the sense of the matter of existents (for nothing is composed of it), nor as the form and definition of things, nor as end, nor does it move existents.

(5) Further, too, if it is itself an existent, *where* will it be? Zeno's difficulty demands an explanation: for if everything that exists has a [25] place, place too will have a place, and so on *ad infinitum*.

(6) Again, just as every body is in place, so, too, every place has a body in it. What then shall we say about *growing* things? It follows from these premisses that their place must grow with them, if their place is neither less nor greater than they are.

By asking these questions, then, we must raise the whole problem about place—not only [30] as to what it is, but even whether there is such a thing.

2

We may distinguish generally between predicating B of A because it (A) is itself, and because it is something else; and particularly between place which is common and in which all bodies are, and the special place occupied primarily by each. I mean, for instance, that you are now in the heavens because you are in the air and it is in the heavens; and you are in the air because you are on the earth; and simi-[35] larly on the earth because you are in this place which contains no more than you.

209b Now if place is what *primarily* contains each body, it would be a limit, so that the place would be the form or shape of each body by which the magnitude or the matter of the magnitude is defined: for this is the limit of each body.

[5] If, then, we look at the question in this way the place of a thing is its form. But, if we regard the place as the *extension* of the magnitude, it is the matter. For this is different from the magnitude: it is what is contained and defined by the form, as by a bounding plane. Matter or the indeterminate is of this nature; when the boundary and attributes of a sphere [10] are taken away, nothing but the matter is left.

This is why Plato in the *Timaeus*[1] says that

[1] 52.

matter and space are the same; for the 'participant' and space are identical. (It is true, indeed, that the account he gives there of the 'participant' is different from what he says in [15] his so-called 'unwritten teaching'. Nevertheless, he did identify place and space.) I mention Plato because, while all hold place to be something, he alone tried to say *what* it is.

In view of these facts we should naturally expect to find difficulty in determining what place is, if indeed it *is* one of these two things, [20] matter or form. They demand a very close scrutiny, especially as it is not easy to recognize them apart.

But it is at any rate not difficult to see that place cannot be either of them. The form and the matter are not separate from the thing, whereas the place can be separated. As we pointed out,[2] where air was, water in turn comes to be, the one replacing the other; and [25] similarly with other bodies. Hence the place of a thing is neither a part nor a state of it, but is separable from it. For place is supposed to be something like a vessel—the vessel being a transportable place. But the vessel is no part of the thing.

[30] In so far then as it is separable from the thing, it is not the form: *qua* containing, it is different from the matter.

Also it is held that what is anywhere is both itself something and that there is a different thing outside it. (Plato of course, if we may digress, ought to tell us why the form and the [35] numbers are not in place, if 'what participates' is place—whether what participates is the Great and the Small or the matter, as he 210a called it in writing in the *Timaeus*.)[3]

Further, how could a body be carried to its own place, if place was the matter or the form? It is impossible that what has no reference to motion or the distinction of up and down can be place. So place must be looked for among things which have these characteristics.

[5] If the place is in the thing (it must be if it is either shape or matter) place will have a place: for both the form and the indeterminate undergo change and motion along with the thing, and are not always in the same place, but are where the thing is. Hence the place will have a place.

Further, when water is produced from air, [10] the place has been destroyed, for the resulting body is not in the same place. What sort of destruction then is that?

This concludes my statement of the rea-

[2] 208b 2.   [3] 52.

sons why space must be something, and again of the difficulties that may be raised about its essential nature.

3

The next step we must take is to see in how many senses one thing is said to be 'in' another.

[15] (1) As the finger is 'in' the hand and generally the part 'in' the whole.

(2) As the whole is 'in' the parts: for there is no whole over and above the parts.

(3) As man is 'in' animal and generally species 'in' genus.

(4) As the genus is 'in' the species and generally the part of the specific form 'in' the definition of the specific form.

[20] (5) As health is 'in' the hot and the cold and generally the form 'in' the matter.

(6) As the affairs of Greece centre 'in' the king, and generally events centre 'in' their primary motive agent.

(7) As the existence of a thing centres 'in' its good and generally 'in' its end, i.e. in 'that for the sake of which' it exists.

(8) In the strictest sense of all, as a thing is 'in' a vessel, and generally 'in' place.

[25] One might raise the question whether a thing can be in itself, or whether nothing can be in itself—everything being either *nowhere* or in something *else*.

The question is ambiguous; we may mean the thing *qua* itself or *qua* something else.

When there are parts of a whole—the one that in which a thing is, the other the thing which is in it—the whole will be described as being in itself. For a thing is described in terms of its parts, as well as in terms of the thing as a whole, e.g. a man is said to be white because the visible surface of him is white, or to be scientific because his thinking faculty [30] has been trained. The jar then will not be in itself and the wine will not be in itself. But the jar of wine will: for the contents and the container are both parts of the same whole.

In this sense then, but not primarily, a thing can be in itself, namely, as 'white' is in body (for the visible surface is in body), and science is in the mind.

210ᵇ It is from these, which are 'parts' (in the sense at least of being 'in' the man), that the man is called white, &c. But the jar and the wine in separation are not parts of a whole, though together they are. So when there are parts, a thing will be in itself, as 'white' is in man because it is in body, and in body because it resides in the visible surface. We cannot go [5] further and say that it is in surface in virtue of something other than itself. (Yet it is not in itself: though these are in a way the same thing,) they differ in essence, each having a special nature and capacity, 'surface' and 'white'.

Thus if we look at the matter inductively we do not find anything to be 'in' itself in any of the senses that have been distinguished; and it can be seen by argument that it is impossible. [10] For each of two things will have to be both, e.g. the jar will have to be both vessel and wine, and the wine both wine and jar, if it is possible for a thing to be in itself; so that, however true it might be that they were in each other, the jar will receive the wine in virtue [15] not of *its* being wine but of the wine's being wine, and the wine will be in the jar in virtue not of *its* being a jar but of the jar's being a jar. Now that they are different in respect of their essence is evident; for 'that in which something is' and 'that which is in it' would be differently defined.

Nor is it possible for a thing to be in itself even incidentally: for two things would be at [20] the same time in the same thing. The jar would be in itself—if a thing whose nature it is to receive can be in itself; and that which it receives, namely (if wine) wine, will be in it.

Obviously then a thing cannot be in itself *primarily*.

Zeno's problem—that if Place is something it must be in something—is not difficult to solve. There is nothing to prevent the first place from being 'in' something else—not in- [25] deed in that as 'in' place, but as health is 'in' the hot as a positive determination of it or as the hot is 'in' body as an affection. So we escape the infinite regress.

Another thing is plain: since the vessel is no part of what is in it (what contains in the *strict* sense is different from what is contained), place could not be either the matter or the form of the thing contained, but must [30] be different—for the latter, both the matter and the shape, are parts of what is contained.

This then may serve as a critical statement of the difficulties involved.

4

What then after all is place? The answer to this question may be elucidated as follows.

Let us take for granted about it the various characteristics which are supposed correctly to belong to it essentially. We assume then—

(1) Place is what contains that of which it is the place.

211ᵃ (2) Place is no part of the thing.

(3) The immediate place of a thing is neither less nor greater than the thing.

(4) Place can be left behind by the thing and is separable. In addition:

(5) All place admits of the distinction of up and down, and each of the bodies is naturally [5] carried to its appropriate place and rests there, and this makes the place either up or down.

Having laid these foundations, we must complete the theory. We ought to try to make our investigation such as will render an account of place, and will not only solve the difficulties connected with it, but will also show that the attributes supposed to belong to it do really belong to it, and further will make clear [10] the cause of the trouble and of the difficulties about it. Such is the most satisfactory kind of exposition.

First then we must understand that place would not have been thought of, if there had not been a special kind of motion, namely that with respect to place. It is chiefly for this reason that we suppose the heaven also to be in place, because it is in constant movement. Of this kind of change there are two species—locomotion on the one hand and, on the other, [15] increase and diminution. For these too involve variation of place: what was then in this place has now in turn changed to what is larger or smaller.

Again, when we say a thing is 'moved', the predicate either (1) belongs to it actually, in virtue of its own nature, or (2) in virtue of something conjoined with it. In the latter case it may be either (*a*) something which by its own [20] nature is capable of being moved, e.g. the parts of the body or the nail in the ship, or (*b*) something which is not in itself capable of being moved, but is *always* moved through its conjunction with something else, as 'whiteness' or 'science'. These have changed their place only because the subjects to which they belong do so.

We say that a thing is in the world, in the [25] sense of in place, because it is in the air, and the air is in the world; and when we say it is in the air, we do not mean it is in every part of the air, but that it is in the air because of the outer surface of the air which surrounds it; for if all the air were its place, the place of a thing would not be equal to the thing—which it is supposed to be, and which the primary place in which a thing is actually is.

When what surrounds, then, is not separate [30] from the thing, but is in continuity with it, the thing is said to be in what surrounds it, not in the sense of in place, but as a part in a whole. But when the thing is separate and in contact, it is immediately 'in' the inner surface of the surrounding body, and this surface is neither a part of what is in it nor yet greater than its extension, but equal to it; for the extremities of things which touch are coincident.

Further, if one body is in continuity with an- [35] other, it is not moved *in* that but *with* that. On the other hand it is moved *in* that if it is separate. It makes no difference whether what contains is moved or not.

211ᵇ Again, when it is not separate it is described as a part in a whole, as the pupil in the eye or the hand in the body: when it is separate, as the water in the cask or the wine in the jar. For the hand is moved *with* the body and the water *in* the cask.

[5] It will now be plain from these considerations what place is. There are just four things of which place must be one—the shape, or the matter, or some sort of extension between the bounding surfaces of the containing body, or this boundary itself if it contains no extension over and above the bulk of the body which comes to be in it.

Three of these it obviously cannot be:

[10] (1) The shape is supposed to be place because it surrounds, for the extremities of what contains and of what is contained are coincident. Both the shape and the place, it is true, are boundaries. But not of the same thing: the form is the boundary of the thing, the place is the boundary of the body which contains it.

(2) The extension between the extremities is thought to be something, because what is contained and separate may often be changed [15] while the container remains the same (as water may be poured from a vessel)—the assumption being that the extension is something over and above the body displaced. But there is no such extension. One of the bodies which change places and are naturally capable of being in contact with the container falls in—whichever it may chance to be.

If there were an extension which were such [20] as to exist independently and be permanent, there would be an infinity of places in the same thing. For when the water and the air change places, all the portions of the two together will play the same part in the whole which was previously played by all the water in the vessel; at the same time the place too will be undergoing change; so that there will be another place which is the place of the [25] place, and many places will be coincident. There is not a different place of the part, in which it is moved, when the whole vessel changes its place: it is always the same: for it is in the (proximate) place where they are that the air and the water (or the parts of the water) succeed each other, not in that place in which they come to be, which is part of the place which is the place of the whole world.

[30] (3) The matter, too, might seem to be place, at least if we consider it in what is at rest and is thus separate but in continuity. For just as in change of quality there is something which was formerly black and is now white, or formerly soft and now hard—this is just why we say that the matter exists—so place, because it presents a similar phenomenon, is [35] thought to exist—only in the one case we say so because *what* was air is now water, in the other because *where* air formerly was there 212ª is now water. But the matter, as we said before,[1] is neither separable from the thing nor contains it, whereas place has both characteristics.

Well, then, if place is none of the three—neither the form nor the matter nor an extension which is always there, different from, and over and above, the extension of the thing [5] which is displaced—place necessarily is the one of the four which is left, namely, the boundary of the containing body at which it is in contact with the contained body. (By the contained body is meant what can be moved by way of locomotion.)

Place is thought to be something important and hard to grasp, both because the matter and the shape present themselves along with it, and because the displacement of the body that is moved takes place in a stationary con- [10] tainer, for it seems possible that there should be an interval which is other than the bodies which are moved. The air, too, which is thought to be incorporeal, contributes something to the belief: it is not only the boundaries of the vessel which seem to be place, but also what is between them, regarded as empty. Just, in fact, as the vessel is transportable [15] place, so place is a non-portable vessel. So when what is within a thing which is moved, is moved and changes its place, as a boat on a river, what contains plays the part of a vessel rather than that of place. Place on the other hand is rather what is motionless: so it is rather the whole river that is place, because as a whole it is motionless.

[20] Hence we conclude that *the innermost motionless boundary of what contains is place*.

This explains why the middle of the heaven and the surface which faces us of the rotating system are held to be 'up' and 'down' in the strict and fullest sense for all men: for the one is always at rest, while the inner side of the rotating body remains always coincident with [25] itself. Hence since the light is what is naturally carried up, and the heavy what is carried down, the boundary which contains in the direction of the middle of the universe, and the middle itself, are down, and that which contains in the direction of the outermost part of the universe, and the outermost part itself, are up.

For this reason, too, place is thought to be a kind of surface, and as it were a vessel, i.e. a container of the thing.

[30] Further, place is coincident with the thing, for boundaries are coincident with the bounded.

5

If then a body has another body outside it and containing it, it is in place, and if not, not. That is why, even if there were to be water which had not a container, the parts of it, on the one hand, will be moved (for one part is contained in another), while, on the other hand, the whole will be moved in one sense, [35] but not in another. For as a whole it does not simultaneously change its place, though it 212ᵇ will be moved in a circle: for this place is the place of its parts. (Some things are moved, not up and down, but in a circle; others up and down, such things namely as admit of condensation and rarefaction.)

As was explained,[2] some things are potentially in place, others actually. So, when you have a homogeneous substance which is con- [5] tinuous, the parts are potentially in place: when the parts are separated, but in contact, like a heap, they are actually in place.

Again, (1) some things are *per se* in place, namely every body which is movable either by way of locomotion or by way of increase is *per se* somewhere, but the heaven, as has been said,[3] is not anywhere as a whole, nor in any [10] place, if at least, as we must suppose, no

[1] 209ᵇ 22–32.   [2] 211ª 17–ᵇ5.   [3] ª32.

body contains it. On the line on which it is moved, its parts have place: for each is contiguous to the next.

But (2) other things are in place indirectly, through something conjoined with them, as the soul and the heaven. The latter is, in a way, in place, for all its parts are: for on the orb one part contains another. That is why the upper part is moved in a circle, while the All [15] is not anywhere. For what is somewhere is itself something, and there must be alongside it some other thing wherein it is and which contains it. But alongside the All or the Whole there is nothing outside the All, and for this reason all things are in the heaven; for the heaven, we may say, is the All. Yet their place is not the same as the heaven. It is part of it, the innermost part of it, which is in [20] contact with the movable body; and for this reason the earth is in water, and this in the air, and the air in the aether, and the aether in heaven, but we cannot go on and say that the heaven is in anything else.

It is clear, too, from these considerations that all the problems which were raised about place will be solved when it is explained in this way:

(1) There is no necessity that the place should grow with the body in it,

(2) Nor that a point should have a place,

[25] (3) Nor that two bodies should be in the same place,

(4) Nor that place should be a corporeal interval: for what is between the boundaries of the place is any body which may chance to be there, not an interval in body.

Further, (5) place is also somewhere, not in the sense of being in a place, but as the limit is in the limited; for not everything that is is in place, but only movable body.

Also (6) it is reasonable that each kind of [30] body should be carried to its own place. For a body which is next in the series and in contact (not by compulsion) is akin, and bodies which are united do not affect each other, while those which are in contact interact on each other.

Nor (7) is it without reason that each should remain naturally in its proper place. For this part has the same relation to its place, as a [35] separable part to its whole, as when one 213ª moves a part of water or air: so, too, air is related to water, for the one is like matter, the other form—water is the matter of air, air as it were the actuality of water, for water is potentially air, while air is potentially water, though in another way.

These distinctions will be drawn more carefully later.[1] On the present occasion it was necessary to refer to them: what has now been stated obscurely will then be made more clear. If the matter and the fulfilment are the same thing (for water is both, the one potentially, the other completely), water will be related to air in a way as part to whole. That is why these have *contact*: it is *organic union* when both become actually one.

[10] This concludes my account of place—both of its existence and of its nature.

6

The investigation of similar questions about the void, also, must be held to belong to the physicist—namely whether it exists or not, and how it exists or what it is—just as about place. The views taken of it involve arguments both for and against, in much the same sort [15] of way. For those who hold that the void exists regard it as a sort of place or vessel which is supposed to be 'full' when it holds the bulk which it is capable of containing, 'void' when it is deprived of that—as if 'void' and 'full' and 'place' denoted the same thing, though the essence of the three is different.

[20] We must begin the inquiry by putting down the account given by those who say that it exists, then the account of those who say that it does not exist, and third the current view on these questions.

Those who try to show that the void does not exist do not disprove what people really mean by it, but only their erroneous way of speaking; this is true of Anaxagoras and of those who refute the existence of the void in this [25] way. They merely give an ingenious demonstration that air is something—by straining wine-skins and showing the resistance of the air, and by cutting it off in clepsydras. But people really mean that there is an empty interval in which there is *no* sensible body. They hold that everything which is is [30] body and say that what has nothing in it at all is void (so what is full of air is void). It is not then the existence of air that needs to be proved, but the non-existence of an interval, different from the bodies, either separable or actual—an interval which divides the whole body so as to break its continuity, as Democritus and Leucippus hold, and many other 213ᵇ physicists—or even perhaps as something which is outside the whole body, which remains continuous.

[1] *On Generation and Corruption*, I. 3.

These people, then, have not reached even the threshold of the problem, but rather those who say that the void exists.

(1) They argue, for one thing, that change [5] in place (i.e. locomotion and increase) would not be. For it is maintained that motion would seem not to exist, if there were no void, since what is full cannot contain anything more. If it could, and there were two bodies in the same place, it would also be true that any number of bodies could be together; for it is impossible to draw a line of division beyond which the statement would become untrue. If this were possible, it would follow also that [10] the smallest body would contain the greatest; for 'many a little makes a mickle': thus if many equal bodies can be together, so also can many unequal bodies.

Melissus, indeed, infers from these considerations that the All is immovable; for if it were moved there must, he says, be void, but void is not among the things that exist.

This argument, then, is one way in which they show that there is a void.

[15] (2) They reason from the fact that some things are observed to contract and be compressed, as people say that a cask will hold the wine which formerly filled it, along with the skins into which the wine has been decanted, which implies that the compressed body contracts into the voids present in it.

Again (3) increase, too, is thought to take [20] place always by means of void, for nutriment is body, and it is impossible for two bodies to be together. A proof of this they find also in what happens to ashes, which absorb as much water as the empty vessel.

The Pythagoreans, too, (4) held that void exists and that it enters the heaven itself, which as it were inhales it, from the infinite air. Further it is the void which distinguishes the na-[25] tures of things, as if it were like what separates and distinguishes the terms of a series. This holds primarily in the numbers, for the void distinguishes their nature.

These, then, and so many, are the main grounds on which people have argued for and against the existence of the void.

7

[30] As a step towards settling which view is true, we must determine the meaning of the name.

The void is thought to be place with nothing in it. The reason for this is that people take what exists to be body, and hold that while every body is in place, void is place in which there is no body, so that where there is no body, there must be void.

214ª Every body, again, they suppose to be tangible; and of this nature is whatever has weight or lightness.

Hence, by a syllogism, what has nothing heavy or light in it, is void.

This result, then, as I have said, is reached [5] by syllogism. It would be absurd to suppose that the point is void; for the void must be *place* which has in it an interval in tangible body.

But at all events we observe then that in one way the void is described as what is not full of body perceptible to touch; and what has heaviness and lightness is perceptible to touch. So we would raise the question: what would they say of an interval that has colour or sound—is [10] it void or not? Clearly they would reply that if it *could* receive what is tangible it was void, and if not, not.

In another way void is that in which there is no 'this' or corporeal substance. So some say that the void is the matter of the body (they identify the place, too, with this), and in this they speak incorrectly; for the matter is not [15] separable from the things, but they are inquiring about the void as about something separable.

Since we have determined the nature of place, and void must, if it exists, be place deprived of body, and we have stated both in what sense place exists and in what sense it does not, it is plain that on this showing void does not exist, either unseparated or separated; [20] for the void is meant to be, not body but rather an interval in body. This is why the void is thought to be something, viz. because place is, and for the same reasons. For the fact of motion in respect of place comes to the aid both of those who maintain that place is something over and above the bodies that come to occupy it, and of those who maintain that the void is something. They state that the void is the condition of movement in the sense of that in which movement takes place; [25] and this would be the kind of thing that some say place is.

But there is no necessity for there being a void if there is movement. It is not in the least needed as a condition of movement in general, for a reason which, incidentally, escaped Melissus; viz. that the full can suffer *qualitative* change.

But not even movement in respect of place

involves a void; for bodies may simultaneously make room for one another, though there is no [30] interval separate and apart from the bodies that are in movement. And this is plain even in the rotaion of continuous things, as in that of liquids.

And things can also be compressed not into a void but because they squeeze out what is contained in them (as, for instance, when water is compressed the air within it is squeezed 214[b] out); and things can increase in size not only by the entrance of something but also by qualitative change; e.g. if water were to be transformed into air.

In general, both the argument about increase of size and that about water poured on to the [5] ashes get in their own way. For either not any and every part of the body is increased, or bodies may be increased otherwise than by the addition of body, or there may be two bodies in the same place (in which case they are claiming to solve a quite general difficulty, but are not proving the existence of void), or the *whole* body must be void, if it is increased in every part and is increased by means of void. The same argument applies to the ashes.
[10] It is evident, then, that it is easy to refute the arguments by which they prove the existence of the void.

8

Let us explain again that there is no void existing separately, as some maintain. If each of the simple bodies has a natural locomotion, e.g. fire upward and earth downward and [15] towards the middle of the universe, it is clear that it cannot be the void that is the condition of locomotion. What, then, *will* the void be the condition of? It is thought to be the condition of movement in respect of place, and it is not the condition of this.

Again, if void is a sort of place deprived of body, when there is a void where will a body placed in it move to? It certainly cannot move into the whole of the void. The same argu- [20] ment applies as against those who think that place is something separate, into which things are carried; viz. how will what is placed in it move, or rest? Much the same argument will apply to the void as to the 'up' and 'down' in place, as is natural enough since those who maintain the existence of the void make it a place.

And in what way will things be present [25] either in place or in the void? For the expected result does not take place when a body is placed as a whole in a place conceived of as separate and permanent; for a part of it, unless it be placed apart, will not be in a place but in the whole. Further, if separate place does not exist, neither will void.

If people say that the void must exist, as being necessary if there is to be movement, what rather turns out to be the case, if one [30] studies the matter, is the opposite, that not a single thing can be moved if there *is* a void; for as with those who for a like reason say the earth is at rest, so, too, in the void things must be at rest; for there is no place to which things can move more or less than to another; since the void in so far as it is void admits no difference.

215[a] The second reason is this: all movement is either compulsory or according to nature, and if there is compulsory movement there must also be natural (for compulsory movement is contrary to nature, and movement contrary to nature is posterior to that according to nature, so that if each of the natural bodies has not a natural movement, none of the [5] other movements can exist); but how can there be natural movement if there is no difference throughout the void or the infinite? For in so far as it is infinite, there will be no up or down or middle, and in so far as it is a void, up differs no whit from down; for as [10] there is no difference in what is nothing, there is none in the void (for the void seems to be a non-existent and a privation of being), but natural locomotion seems to be differentiated, so that the things that exist by nature must be differentiated. Either, then, nothing has a natural locomotion, or else there is no void.

Further, in point of fact things that are thrown move though that which gave them their impulse is not touching them, either by [15] reason of mutual replacement, as some maintain, or because the air that has been pushed pushes them with a movement quicker than the natural locomotion of the projectile wherewith it moves to its proper place. But in a void none of these things can take place, nor can anything be moved save as that which is carried is moved.

Further, no one could say why a thing once [20] set in motion should stop anywhere; for why should it stop *here* rather than *here*? So that a thing will either be at rest or must be moved *ad infinitum,* unless something more powerful get in its way.

Further, things are now thought to move

into the void because it yields; but in a void this quality is present equally everywhere, so that things should move in all directions.

Further, the truth of what we assert is plain [25] from the following considerations. We see the same weight or body moving faster than another for two reasons, either because there is a difference in what it moves through, as between water, air, and earth, or because, other things being equal, the moving body differs from the other owing to excess of weight or of lightness.

Now the medium causes a difference because it impedes the moving thing, most of all if it is moving in the opposite direction, but in [30] a secondary degree even if it is at rest; and especially a medium that is not easily divided, i.e. a medium that is somewhat dense. 215^b A, then, will move through B in time Γ, and through Δ, which is thinner, in time E (if the length of B is equal to Δ), in proportion to the density of the hindering body. For let B be water and Δ air; then by so much as [5] air is thinner and more incorporeal than water, A will move through Δ faster than through B. Let the speed have the same ratio to the speed, then, that air has to water. Then if air is twice as thin, the body will traverse B in twice the time that it does Δ, and the time Γ will be twice the time E. And always, by so [10] much as the medium is more incorporeal and less resistant and more easily divided, the faster will be the movement.

Now there is no ratio in which the void is exceeded by body, as there is no ratio of 0 to a number. For if 4 exceeds 3 by 1, and 2 by more than 1, and 1 by still more than it exceeds 2, [15] still there is no ratio by which it exceeds 0; for that which exceeds must be divisible into the excess + that which is exceeded, so that 4 will be what it exceeds 0 by + 0. For this reason, too, a line does not exceed a point—unless it is composed of points! Similarly the [20] void can bear no ratio to the full, and therefore neither can movement through the one to movement through the other, but if a thing moves through the thickest medium such and such a distance in such and such a time, it moves through the void with a speed beyond any ratio. For let Z be void, equal in magnitude to B and to Δ. Then if A is to traverse and move through it in a certain time, H, a [25] time less than E, however, the void will bear this ratio to the full. But in a time equal to H, A will traverse the part Θ of Δ. And it will surely also traverse in that time any substance Z which exceeds air in thickness in the [30] ratio which the time E bears to the time H. For if the body Z be as much thinner than Δ as E exceeds H, A, if it moves through Z, will traverse it in a time inverse to the speed of 216^a the movement, i.e. in a time equal to H. If, then, there is *no* body in Z, A will traverse Z still more quickly. But we supposed that its traverse of Z when Z was void occupied the time H. So that it will traverse Z in an equal time whether Z be full or void. But this is impossible. It is plain, then, that if there is a time in which it will move through any part of the void, this impossible result will follow: it will [5] be found to traverse a certain distance, whether this be full or void, in an equal time; for there will be some *body* which is in the same ratio to the other body as the time is to the time.

To sum the matter up, the cause of this result is obvious, viz. that between any two movements there is a ratio (for they occupy [10] time, and there is a ratio between any two times, so long as both are finite), but there is no ratio of void to full.

These are the consequences that result from a difference in the media; the following depend upon an excess of one moving body over another. We see that bodies which have a greater impulse either of weight or of light- [15] ness, if they are alike in other respects, move faster over an equal space, and in the ratio which their magnitudes bear to each other. Therefore they will also move through the void with this ratio of speed. But that is impossible; for why should one move faster? (In moving through *plena* it must be so; for the greater divides them faster by its force. For a moving thing cleaves the medium either by its shape, or by the impulse which the body [20] that is carried along or is projected possesses.) Therefore all will possess equal velocity. But this is impossible.

It is evident from what has been said, then, that, if there is a void, a result follows which is the very opposite of the reason for which those who believe in a void set it up. They think that if movement in respect of place is to exist, the void cannot exist, separated all by itself; but this is the same as to say that place [25] is a separate cavity; and this has already been stated to be impossible.

But even if we consider it on its own merits the so-called vacuum will be found to be really vacuous. For as, if one puts a cube in water, an amount of water equal to the cube will be displaced; so too in air; but the effect is imperceptible to sense. And indeed always, in the [30] case of any body that can be displaced, it must, if it is not compressed, be displaced in the direction in which it is its nature to be displaced—always either down, if its locomotion is downwards as in the case of earth, or up, if it is fire, or in both directions—whatever be the nature of the inserted body. Now in the void this is impossible; for it is not body; the void must have penetrated the cube to a dis- [35] tance equal to that which this portion of void formerly occupied in the void, just as if 216^b the water or air had not been displaced by the wooden cube, but had penetrated right through it.

But the cube also has a magnitude equal to that occupied by the void; a magnitude which, if it is also hot or cold, or heavy or light, is [5] none the less different in essence from all its attributes, even if it is not separable from them; I mean the *volume* of the wooden cube. So that even if it were separated from everything else and were neither heavy nor light, it will occupy an equal amount of void, and fill the same place, as the part of place or of the void equal to itself. How then will the body of [10] the cube differ from the void or place that is equal to it? And if there can be two such things, why cannot there be any number coinciding?

This, then, is one absurd and impossible implication of the theory. It is also evident that the cube will have this same volume even if it is displaced, which is an attribute possessed by all other bodies also. Therefore if this differs in no respect from its place, why need we assume a place for bodies over and above the volume of each, if their volume be conceived [15] of as free from attributes? It contributes nothing to the situation if there is an equal interval attached to it as well. [Further, it ought to be clear by the study of moving things what sort of thing void is. But in fact it is found nowhere in the world. For air is something, though it does not *seem* to be so—nor, for that matter, would water, if fishes were made of iron; for the discrimination of the tangible is by touch.]
[20] It is clear, then, from these considerations that there is no separate void.

9

There are some who think that the existence of rarity and density shows that there is a void. If rarity and density do not exist, they say, neither can things contract and be compressed. But if this were not to take place, [25] either there would be no movement at all, or the universe would bulge, as Xuthus said, or air and water must always change into equal amounts (e.g. if air has been made out of a cupful of water, at the same time out of an equal amount of air a cupful of water must have been made), or void must necessarily exist; for compression and expansion cannot take place otherwise.
[30] Now, if they mean by the rare that which has many voids existing separately, it is plain that if void cannot exist separate any more than a place can exist with an extension all to itself, neither can the rare exist in this sense. But if they mean that there is void, not separately existent, but still present in the rare, this is less impossible, yet, first, the void turns out not to be a condition of *all* movement, but [35] only of movement upwards (for the rare 217^a is light, which is the reason why they say fire is rare); second, the void turns out to be a condition of movement not as that in which it takes place, but in that the void carries things up as skins by being carried up themselves carry up what is continuous with them. Yet how can void have a local movement or a place? For thus that into which void moves is till then void of a void.

[5] Again, how will they explain, in the case of what is heavy, its movement downwards? And it is plain that if the rarer and more void a thing is the quicker it will move upwards, if it were completely void it would move with a maximum speed! But perhaps even this is impossible, that it should move at all; the same reason which showed that in the void all things are incapable of moving shows that the void cannot move, viz. the fact that the speeds are incomparable.

[10] Since we deny that a void exists, but for the rest the problem has been truly stated, that *either* there will be no movement, if there is not to be condensation and rarefaction, *or* the universe will bulge, *or* a transformation of water into air will always be balanced by an equal transformation of air into water (for it is clear that the air produced from water is bulkier [15] than the water): it is necessary therefore, if compression does not exist, *either* that the next portion will be pushed outwards and make the outermost part bulge, *or* that somewhere else there must be an equal amount of water produced out of air, so that the entire bulk of the whole may be equal, *or* that noth-

ing moves. For when anything is displaced this will always happen, unless it comes round in a circle; but locomotion is not always circular, but sometimes in a straight line.

[20] These then are the reasons for which they might say that there is a void; *our* statement is based on the assumption that there is a single matter for contraries, hot and cold and the other natural contrarieties, and that what exists actually is produced from a potential existent, and that matter is not separable from the con-[25] traries but its being is different, and that a single matter may serve for colour and heat and cold.

The same matter also serves for both a large and a small body. This is evident; for when air is produced from water, the same matter has become something different, not by acquiring an addition to it, but has become actually what it was potentially, and, again, water is produced from air in the same way, the [30] change being sometimes from smallness to greatness, and sometimes from greatness to smallness. Similarly, therefore, if air which is large in extent comes to have a smaller volume, or becomes greater from being smaller, it is the matter which is potentially both that comes to be each of the two.

For as the same matter becomes hot from being cold, and cold from being hot, because it was potentially both, so too from hot it can 217ᵇ become more hot, though nothing in the matter has become hot that was not hot when the thing was less hot; just as, if the arc or curve of a greater circle becomes that of a smaller, whether it remains the same or becomes a different curve, convexity has not come [5] to exist in anything that was not convex but straight (for differences of degree do not depend on an intermission of the quality); nor can we get any portion of a flame, in which both heat and whiteness are not present. So too, then, is the earlier heat related to the later. So that the greatness and smallness, also, of the sensible volume are extended, not by the matter's acquiring anything new, but because the matter is potentially matter for both states; so [10] that the same thing is dense and rare, and the two qualities have one matter.

The dense is heavy, and the rare is light. [Again, as the arc of a circle when contracted into a smaller space does not acquire a new part which is convex, but what was there has been contracted; and as any part of fire that [15] one takes will be hot; so, too, it is all a question of contraction and expansion of the same matter.] There are two types in each case, both in the dense and in the rare; for both the heavy and the hard are thought to be dense, and contrariwise both the light and the soft are rare; and weight and hardness fail to coincide in the case of lead and iron.

[20] From what has been said it is evident, then, that void does not exist either separate (either absolutely separate or as a separate element in the rare) or potentially, unless one is willing to call the condition of movement void, whatever it may be. At that rate the matter of the heavy and the light, *qua* matter of them, would be the void; for the dense and the rare are productive of locomotion in virtue of *this* [25] contrariety, and in virtue of their hardness and softness productive of passivity and impassivity, i.e. not of locomotion but rather of qualitative change.

So much, then, for the discussion of the void, and of the sense in which it exists and the sense in which it does not exist.

10

Next for discussion after the subjects men-[30] tioned is Time. The best plan will be to begin by working out the difficulties connected with it, making use of the current arguments. First, does it belong to the class of things that exist or to that of things that do not exist? Then secondly, what is its nature? To start, then: the following considerations would make one suspect that it either does not exist at all or barely, and in an obscure way. One part of it has been and is not, while the other 218ᵃ is going to be and is not yet. Yet time—both infinite time and any time you like to take—is made up of these. One would naturally suppose that what is made up of things which do not exist could have no share in reality.

Further, if a divisible thing is to exist, it is necessary that, when it exists, all or some of its [5] parts must exist. But of time some parts have been, while others have to be, and no part of it *is*, though it is divisible. For what is 'now' is not a part: a part is a measure of the whole, which must be made up of parts. Time, on the other hand, is not held to be made up of 'nows'.

Again, the 'now' which seems to bound the past and the future—does it always remain one [10] and the same or is it always other and other? It is hard to say.

(1) If it is always different and different, and if none of the *parts* in time which are other and other are simultaneous (unless the

one contains and the other is contained, as the shorter time is by the longer), and if the 'now' which is not, but formerly was, must have [15] ceased-to-be at some time, the *'nows'* too cannot be simultaneous with one another, but the prior 'now' must always have ceased-to-be. But the prior 'now' cannot have ceased-to-be in itself (since it then existed); yet it cannot have ceased-to-be in another 'now'. For we may lay it down that one 'now' cannot be next to another, any more than point to point. If then it did not cease-to-be in the next 'now' [20] but in another, it would exist simultaneously with the innumerable 'nows' between the two—which is impossible.

Yes, but (2) neither is it possible for the 'now' to remain always the same. No determinate divisible thing has a single termination, whether it is continuously extended in one or in more than one dimension: but the 'now' is a termination, and it is possible to cut off a [25] determinate time. Further, if coincidence in time (i.e. being neither prior nor posterior) means to be 'in one and the same "now"', then, if both what is before and what is after are in this same 'now', things which happened ten thousand years ago would be simultaneous with what has happened to-day, and nothing would be before or after anything else.
[30] This may serve as a statement of the difficulties about the attributes of time.

As to what time is or what is its nature, the traditional accounts give us as little light as the preliminary problems which we have worked through.

Some assert that it is (1) the movement of 218ᵇ the whole, others that it is (2) the sphere itself.

(1) Yet part, too, of the revolution is a time, but it certainly is not a revolution: for what is taken is part of a revolution, not a revolution. Besides, if there were more heavens than one, the movement of any of them equally would be time, so that there would be many times at the same time.
[5] (2) Those who said that time is the sphere of the whole thought so, no doubt, on the ground that all things are in time and all things are in the sphere of the whole. The view is too naive for it to be worth while to consider the impossibilities implied in it.

But as time is most usually supposed to be (3) motion and a kind of change, we must consider this view.
[10] Now (*a*) the change or movement of each thing is only *in* the thing which changes or *where* the thing itself which moves or changes may chance to be. But time is present equally everywhere and with all things.

Again, (*b*) change is always faster or slower, [15] whereas time is not: for 'fast' and 'slow' are defined by time—'fast' is what moves much in a short time, 'slow' what moves little in a long time; but time is not defined by time, by being either a certain amount or a certain kind of it.

Clearly then it is not movement. (We need [20] not distinguish at present between 'movement' and 'change'.)

11

But neither does time exist without change; for when the state of our own minds does not change at all, or we have not noticed its changing, we do not realize that time has elapsed, any more than those who are fabled to [25] sleep among the heroes in Sardinia do when they are awakened; for they connect the earlier 'now' with the later and make them one, cutting out the interval because of their failure to notice it. So, just as, if the 'now' were not different but one and the same, there would not have been time, so too when its difference escapes our notice the interval does not seem to be time. If, then, the non-realiza- [30] tion of the existence of time happens to us when we do not distinguish any change, but the soul seems to stay in one indivisible state, and when we perceive and distinguish we say time has elapsed, evidently time is not independent of movement and change. It is evi- 219ᵃ dent, then, that time is neither movement nor independent of movement.

We must take this as our starting-point and try to discover—since we wish to know what time is—what exactly it has to do with movement.

Now we perceive movement and time together: for even when it is dark and we are not [5] being affected through the body, if any movement takes place in the mind we at once suppose that some time also has elapsed; and not only that but also, when some time is thought to have passed, some movement also along with it seems to have taken place. Hence time is either movement or something that belongs to movement. Since then it is not movement, it must be the other.
[10] But what is moved is moved from something to something, and all magnitude is continuous. Therefore the movement goes with the magnitude. Because the magnitude is con-

tinuous, the movement too must be continuous, and if the movement, then the time; for the time that has passed is always thought to be in proportion to the movement.

The distinction of 'before' and 'after' holds primarily, then, in place; and there in virtue [15] of relative position. Since then 'before' and 'after' hold in magnitude, they must hold also in movement, these corresponding to those. But also in time the distinction of 'before' and 'after' must hold, for time and movement always correspond with each other. The 'before' and 'after' in motion is identical in sub- [20] stratum with motion yet differs from it in definition, and is not identical with motion.

But we apprehend time only when we have marked motion, marking it by 'before' and 'after'; and it is only when we have perceived 'before' and 'after' in motion that we say that [25] time has elapsed. Now we mark them by judging that A and B are different, and that some third thing is intermediate to them. When we think of the extremes as different from the middle and the mind pronounces that the 'nows' are two, one before and one after, it is then that we say that there is time, and this that we say is time. For what is bounded by the 'now' is thought to be time— we may assume this.

[30] When, therefore, we perceive the 'now' as one, and neither as before and after in a motion nor as an identity but in relation to a 'before' and an 'after', no time is thought to have elapsed, because there has been no motion either. On the other hand, when we do perceive a 'before' and an 'after', then we say that there is time. For time is just this—number of motion in respect of 'before' and 'after'.

Hence time is not movement, but only movement in so far as it admits of enumeration. A proof of this: we discriminate the more or the less by number, but more or less movement by time. Time then is a kind of number. (Num- [5] ber, we must note, is used in two senses— both of what is counted or the countable and also of that with which we count. Time obviously is what is counted, not that with which we count: there are different kinds of thing.)

Just as motion is a perpetual succession, so [10] also is time. But every simultaneous time is self-identical; for the 'now' as a subject is an identity, but it accepts different attributes. The 'now' measures time, in so far as time involves the 'before and after'.

The 'now' in one sense is the same, in another it is not the same. In so far as it is in succession, it is different (which is just what its being now was supposed to mean), but its [15] substratum is an identity: for motion, as was said,[1] goes with magnitude, and time, as we maintain, with motion. Similarly, then, there corresponds to the point the body which is carried along, and by which we are aware of the motion and of the 'before and after' involved in it. This is an identical *substratum* (whether a point or a stone or something else of the kind), but it has different *attributes*— [20] as the sophists assume that Coriscus' being in the Lyceum is a different thing from Coriscus' being in the market-place. And the body which is carried along is different, in so far as it is at one time here and at another there. But the 'now' corresponds to the body that is carried along, as time corresponds to the motion. For it is by means of the body that is carried along that we become aware of the 'be- [25] fore and after' in the motion, and if we regard these as countable we get the 'now'. Hence in these also the 'now' as substratum remains the same (for it is what is before and after in movement), but what is predicated of it is different; for it is in so far as the 'before and after' is numerable that we get the 'now'. This is what is most knowable: for, similarly, motion is known because of that which is moved, locomotion because of that which is carried. [30] For what is carried is a real thing, the movement is not. Thus what is called 'now' in one sense is always the same; in another it is not the same: for this is true also of what is carried.

Clearly, too, if there were no time, there would be no 'now', and vice versa. Just as the moving body and its locomotion involve each other mutually, so too do the number of the moving body and the number of its locomotion. For the number of the locomotion is time, while the 'now' corresponds to the moving body, and is like the unit of number.

Time, then, also is both made continuous by [5] the 'now' and divided at it. For here too there is a correspondence with the locomotion and the moving body. For the motion or locomotion is made one by the thing which is moved, because *it* is one—not because it is one in its own nature (for there might be pauses in the movement of such a thing)—but because it is one in definition: for this determines the movement as 'before' and 'after'. Here, too, [10] there is a correspondence with the point; for the point also both connects and terminates

[1] 11.

the length—it is the beginning of one and the end of another. But when you take it in this way, using the one point as two, a pause is necessary, if the same point is to be the beginning and the end. The 'now' on the other hand, since the body carried is moving, is always different.

Hence time is not number in the sense in which there is 'number' of the same point because it is beginning and end, but rather as [15] the extremities of a line form a number, and not as the parts of the line do so, both for the reason given (for we can use the middle point as two, so that on that analogy time might stand still), and further because obviously the 'now' is no *part* of time nor the section any part of the movement, any more than the points are parts of the line—for it is two [20] *lines* that are *parts* of one line.

In so far then as the 'now' is a boundary, it is not time, but an attribute of it; in so far as it numbers, it is number; for boundaries belong only to that which they bound, but number (e.g. ten) is the number of these horses, and belongs also elsewhere.

It is clear, then, that time is 'number of [25] movement in respect of the before and after', and is continuous since it is an attribute of what is continuous.

12

The smallest number, in the strict sense of the word 'number', is two. But of number as concrete, sometimes there is a minimum, sometimes not: e.g. of a 'line', the smallest in respect of *multiplicity* is two (or, if you like, one), [30] but in respect of *size* there is no minimum; for every line is divided *ad infinitum*. Hence it is so with time. In respect of number the minimum is one (or two); in point of extent there is no minimum.

It is clear, too, that time is not described as 220[b] fast or slow, but as many or few and as long or short. For as continuous it is long or short and as a number many or few, but it is not fast or slow—any more than any number with which we number is fast or slow.
[5] Further, there is the same time everywhere at once, but not the same time before and after, for while the present change is one, the change which has happened and that which will happen are different. Time is not number with which we count, but the number of things which are counted, and this according as it occurs before or after is always different, [10] for the 'nows' are different. And the number of a hundred horses and a hundred men is the same, but the things numbered are different—the horses from the men. Further, as a movement can be one and the same again and again, so too can time, e.g. a year or a spring or an autumn.

[15] Not only do we measure the movement by the time, but also the time by the movement, because they define each other. The time marks the movement, since it is its number, and the movement the time. We describe the time as much or little, measuring it by the movement, just as we know the number by what is numbered, e.g. the number of the [20] horses by one horse as the unit. For we know how many horses there are by the use of the number; and again by using the one horse as unit we know the number of the horses itself. So it is with the time and the movement; for we measure the movement by the time and vice versa. It is natural that this should happen; [25] for the movement goes with the distance and the time with the movement, because they are quanta and continuous and divisible. The movement has these attributes because the distance is of this nature, and the time has them because of the movement. And we measure both the distance by the movement and the movement by the distance; for we say that the road is long, if the journey is long, and that [30] this is long, if the road is long—the time, too, if the movement, and the movement, if the time.

221[a] Time is a measure of motion and of being moved, and it measures the motion by determining a motion which will measure exactly the whole motion, as the cubit does the length by determining an amount which will measure out the whole. Further 'to be in time' means, for movement, that both it and its essence are measured by time (for simultaneously it meas-[5] ures both the movement and its essence, and this is what being in time means for it, that its essence should be measured).

Clearly then 'to be in time' has the same meaning for other things also, namely, that their being should be measured by time. 'To be in time' is one of two things: (1) to exist [10] when time exists, (2) as we say of some things that they are 'in number'. The latter means either what is a part or mode of number—in general, something which belongs to number—or that things have a number.

Now, since time is number, the 'now' and [15] the 'before' and the like are in time, just as 'unit' and 'odd' and 'even' are in number, i.e. in the sense that the one set belongs to number, the other to time. But things are in time as they are in number. If this is so, they are contained by time as things in place are contained by place.

Plainly, too, to be in time does not mean to [20] co-exist with time, any more than to be in motion or in place means to co-exist with motion or place. For if 'to be in something' is to mean this, then all things will be in anything, and the heaven will be in a grain; for when the grain is, then also is the heaven. But this is a merely incidental conjunction, whereas the other is necessarily involved: that which is in [25] time necessarily involves that there is time when *it* is, and that which is in motion that there is motion when *it* is.

Since what is 'in time' is so in the same sense as what is in number is so, a time greater than everything in time can be found. So it is necessary that all the things in time should be contained by time, just like other things also which are 'in anything', e.g. the things 'in place' by place.

[30] A thing, then, will be affected by time, just as we are accustomed to say that time wastes things away, and that all things grow old through time, and that there is oblivion owing to the lapse of time, but we do not 221[b] say the same of getting to know or of becoming young or fair. For time is by its nature the cause rather of decay, since it is the number of change, and change removes what is.

Hence, plainly, things which are always are not, as such, in time, for they are not contained by time, nor is their being measured by time. [5] A proof of this is that none of them is *affected* by time, which indicates that they are not in time.

Since time is the measure of motion, it will be the measure of rest too—indirectly. For all rest is in time. For it does not follow that what is in time is moved, though what is in motion [10] is necessarily moved. For time is not motion, but 'number of motion': and what is at rest, also, can be in the number of motion. Not everything that is not in motion can be said to be 'at rest'—but only that which can be moved, though it actually is not moved, as was said above.[1]

'To be in number' means that there is a [15] number of the thing, and that its being is measured by the number in which it is. Hence if a thing is 'in time' it will be measured by time. But time will measure what is moved and what is at rest, the one *qua* moved, the other *qua* at rest; for it will measure their motion and rest respectively.

Hence what is moved will not be measurable by the time simply in so far as it has quantity, [20] but in so far as its *motion* has quantity. Thus none of the things which are neither moved nor at rest are in time: for 'to be in time' is 'to be measured by time', while time is the measure of motion and rest.

Plainly, then, neither will everything that does not exist be in time, i.e. those non-existent things that cannot exist, as the diagonal cannot be commensurate with the side.

[25] Generally, if time is directly the measure of motion and indirectly of other things, it is clear that a thing whose existence is measured by it will have its existence in rest or motion. Those things therefore which are subject to perishing and becoming — generally, those which at one time exist, at another do not— [30] are necessarily in time: for there is a greater time which will extend both beyond their existence and beyond the time which measures their existence. Of things which do not exist but are contained by time some were, 222[a] e.g. Homer once was, some will be, e.g. a future event; this depends on the direction in which time contains them; if on both, they have both modes of existence. As to such things as it does not contain in any way, they neither were nor are nor will be. These are those nonexistents whose opposites always are, as the [5] incommensurability of the diagonal always is—and this will not be in time. Nor will the commensurability, therefore; hence this eternally is not, because it is contrary to what eternally is. A thing whose contrary is not eternal can be and not be, and it is of such things that there is coming to be and passing away.

13

[10] The 'now' is the link of time, as has been said[2] (for it connects past and future time), and it is a limit of time (for it is the beginning of the one and the end of the other). But this is not obvious as it is with the point, which is fixed. It divides potentially, and in so far as it [15] is dividing the 'now' is always different, but in so far as it connects it is always the same, as it is with mathematical lines. For the intellect it is not always one and the same point, since it is other and other when one divides

---

[1] 202[a] 4.

[2] 220[a] 5.

the line; but in so far as it is one, it is the same in every respect.

So the 'now' also is in one way a potential dividing of time, in another the termination of both parts, and their unity. And the dividing and the uniting are the same thing and in the same reference, but in essence they are not the same.

[20] So one kind of 'now' is described in this way: another is when the time is *near* this kind of 'now'. 'He will come now' because he will come to-day; 'he has come now' because he came to-day. But the things in the *Iliad* have not happened 'now', nor is the flood 'now'— not that the time from now to them is not continuous, but because they are not near.

'At some time' means a time determined in [25] relation to the first of the two types of 'now', e.g. 'at some time' Troy was taken, and 'at some time' there will be a flood; for it must be determined with reference to the 'now'. There *will* thus be a determinate time from this 'now' to that, and there *was* such in reference to the past event. But if there be no time which is not 'sometime', every time will be determined.

Will time then fail? Surely not, if motion al-[30]ways exists. Is time then always different or does the same time recur? Clearly time is, in the same way as motion is. For if one and the same motion sometimes recurs, it will be one and the same time, and if not, not.

222[b] Since the 'now' is an end and a beginning of time, not of the same time however, but the end of that which is past and the beginning of that which is to come, it follows that, as the circle has its convexity and its concavity, in a sense, in the same thing, so time is always at a beginning and at an end. And for this reason it seems to be always different; for [5] the 'now' is not the beginning and the end of the same thing; if it were, it would be at the same time and in the same respect two opposites. And time will not fail; for it is always at a beginning.

'Presently' or 'just' refers to the part of fu-[10]ture time which is near the indivisible present 'now' ('When do you walk?' 'Presently', because the time in which he is going to do so is near), and to the part of past time which is not far from the 'now' ('When do you walk?' 'I have just been walking'). But to say that Troy has just been taken—we do not say that, because it is too far from the 'now'. 'Lately', too, refers to the part of past time which is near the present 'now'. 'When did you go?' 'Lately', if the time is near the existing now. 'Long ago' refers to the distant past.

[15] 'Suddenly' refers to what has departed from its former condition in a time imperceptible because of its smallness; but it is the nature of *all* change to alter things from their former condition. In time all things come into being and pass away; for which reason some called it the wisest of all things, but the Pythagorean Paron called it the most stupid, because in it we also forget; and his was the truer view. It is clear then that it must be in itself, as we said [20] before,[1] the condition of destruction rather than of coming into being (for change, in itself, makes things depart from their former condition), and only incidentally of coming into being, and of being. A sufficient evidence of this is that nothing comes into being without itself moving somehow and acting, but a thing can be destroyed even if it does not move at all. And this is what, as a rule, we [25] chiefly mean by a thing's being destroyed by time. Still, time does not work even this change; even this sort of change takes place *incidentally* in time.

We have stated, then, that time exists and what it is, and in how many senses we speak of the 'now', and what 'at some time', 'lately', 'presently' or 'just', 'long ago', and 'suddenly' mean.

14

[30] These distinctions having been drawn, it is evident that every change and everything that moves is in time; for the distinction of faster and slower exists in reference to all change, since it is found in every instance. In the phrase 'moving faster' I refer to that which 223[a] changes before another into the condition in question, when it moves over the same interval and with a regular movement; e.g. in the case of locomotion, if both things move along the circumference of a circle, or both along a straight line; and similarly in all other cases. But what is *before* is in time; for we say 'be-[5]fore' and 'after' with reference to the distance from the 'now', and the 'now' is the boundary of the past and the future; so that since 'nows' are in time, the before and the after will be in time too; for in that in which the 'now' is, the distance from the 'now' will also be. But 'before' is used contrariwise with refer-[10]ence to past and to future time; for in the past we call 'before' what is farther from the 'now', and 'after' what is nearer, but in the

[1] 221[b] 1.

future we call the nearer 'before' and the farther 'after'. So that since the 'before' is in time, [15] and every movement involves a 'before', evidently every change and every movement is in time.

It is also worth considering how time can be related to the soul; and why time is thought to be in everything, both in earth and in sea and in heaven. Is it because it is an attribute, or state, or movement (since it is the number of movement) and all these things are movable (for they are all in place), and time and [20] movement are together, both in respect of potentiality and in respect of actuality?

Whether if soul did not exist time would exist or not, is a question that may fairly be asked; for if there cannot be some one to count there cannot be anything that can be counted, so that evidently there cannot be number; for number is either what has been, or what can [25] be, counted. But if nothing but soul, or in soul reason, is qualified to count, there would not be time unless there were soul, but only that of which time is an attribute, i.e. if *movement* can exist without soul, and the before and after are attributes of movement, and time is these *qua* numerable.

One might also raise the question what sort [30] of movement time is the number of. Must we not say 'of *any* kind'? For things both come into being in time and pass away, and grow, and are altered in time, and are moved locally; thus it is of each movement *qua* movement that time is the number. And so it is simply the number of continuous movement, not of any particular kind of it.

223ᵇ But other things as well may have been moved now, and there would be a number of each of the two movements. Is there another time, then, and will there be two equal times at once? Surely not. For a time that is both equal and simultaneous is one and the same time, and even those that are not simultaneous are one in kind; for if there were dogs, and [5] horses, and seven of each, it would be the same number. So, too, movements that have simultaneous limits have the same time, yet the one may in fact be fast and the other not, and one may be locomotion and the other alteration; still the time of the two changes is the same if their number also is equal and simul-[10]taneous; and for this reason, while the movements are different and separate, the time is everywhere the same, because the number of equal and simultaneous movements is everywhere one and the same.

Now there is such a thing as locomotion, and in locomotion there is included circular movement, and everything is measured by some one thing homogeneous with it, units by a unit, horses by a horse, and similarly times [15] by some definite time, and, as we said,[1] time is measured by motion as well as motion by time (this being so because by a motion definite in time the quantity both of the motion and of the time is measured): if, then, what is first is the measure of everything homogeneous with it, regular circular motion is above all else the measure, because the num-[20]ber of this is the best known. Now neither alteration nor increase nor coming into being can be regular, but locomotion can be. This also is why time is thought to be the movement of the sphere, viz. because the other movements are measured by this, and time by this movement.

This also explains the common saying that [25] human affairs form a circle, and that there is a circle in all other things that have a natural movement and coming into being and passing away. This is because all other things are discriminated by time, and end and begin as though conforming to a cycle; for even time itself is thought to be a circle. And this opin-[30]ion again is held because time is the measure of this kind of locomotion and is itself measured by such. So that to say that the things that come into being form a circle is to say that there is a circle of time; and this is to say that it is measured by the circular movement; for apart from the meas-224ᵃ ure nothing else to be measured is observed; the whole is just a plurality of measures.

It is said rightly, too, that the number of the sheep and of the dogs is the same *number* if the two numbers are equal, but not the same *decad* or the same *ten;* just as the equilateral [5] and the scalene are not the same *triangle,* yet they are the same *figure,* because they are both triangles. For things are called the same so-and-so if they do not differ by a differentia of that thing, but not if they do; e.g. triangle differs from triangle by a differentia of triangle, therefore they are different triangles; but they do not differ by a differentia of figure, but are in one and the same division of it. For a figure of the one kind is a circle and a figure [10] of another kind of triangle, and a triangle of one kind is equilateral and a triangle of another kind scalene. They are the same figure,

---
[1] 220ᵇ 28.

then, and that, triangle, but not the same triangle. Therefore the number of two groups also is the same number (for their number does not differ by a differentia of number), but it is not the same decad; for the things of which it is asserted differ; one group are dogs, and the other horses.

[15] We have now discussed time—both time itself and the matters appropriate to the consideration of it.

BOOK V

1

EVERYTHING which changes does so in one of three senses. It may change (1) *accidentally*, as for instance when we say that something musical walks, that which walks being something in which aptitude for music is an *accident*. Again (2) a thing is said without qualification to change because *something belonging to it* changes, i.e. in statements which refer [25] to part of the thing in question: thus the body is restored to health because the eye or the chest, that is to say *a part* of the whole body, is restored to health. And above all there is (3) the case of a thing which is in motion neither accidentally nor in respect of something else belonging to it, but in virtue of being *itself* directly in motion. Here we have a thing which is *essentially* movable: and that which is so is a different thing according to the particular variety of motion: for instance it may be a thing capable of alteration: and within the sphere of alteration it is again a different thing according [30] as it is capable of being restored to health or capable of being heated. And there are the same distinctions in the case of the mover: (1) one thing causes motion accidentally, (2) another partially (because something belonging to it causes motion), (3) another of itself directly, as, for instance, the physician heals, the hand strikes. We have, then, the following factors: (*a*) on the one hand that which directly causes motion, and (*b*) on the other hand that which is in motion: further, we have (*c*) that [35] in which motion takes place, namely time, and (distinct from these three) (*d*) that 224ᵇ from which and (*e*) that to which it proceeds: for every motion proceeds from something and to something, that which is directly in motion being distinct from that to which it is in motion and that from which it is in motion: for instance, we may take the three things 'wood', 'hot', and 'cold', of which the first is that which is in motion, the second is that to which the motion proceeds, and the third is that from which it proceeds. This being so, it is clear that the motion is in the wood, not in [5] its form: for the motion is neither caused nor experienced by the form or the place or the quantity. So we are left with a mover, a moved, and a goal of motion. I do not include the starting-point of motion: for it is the goal rather than the starting-point of motion that gives its name to a particular process of change. Thus 'perishing' is change *to not-being*, though it is also true that that which perishes changes *from being*: and 'becoming' is change *to being*, though it is also change *from not-being*.

[10] Now a definition of motion has been given above,[1] from which it will be seen that every goal of motion, whether it be a form, an affection, or a place, is immovable, as, for instance, knowledge and heat. Here, however, a difficulty may be raised. Affections, it may be said, are motions, and whiteness is an affection: thus there may be change *to* a motion. To this [15] we may reply that it is not whiteness but whitening that is a motion. Here also the same distinctions are to be observed: a goal of motion may be so accidentally, or partially or with reference to something other than itself, or directly and with no reference to anything else: for instance, a thing which is becoming white changes accidentally to an object of thought, the *colour* being only accidentally the [20] object of thought; it changes to colour, because white is a part of colour, or to Europe, because Athens is a part of Europe; but it changes essentially to white colour. It is now clear in what sense a thing is in motion essentially, accidentally, or in respect of something other than itself, and in what sense the phrase 'itself directly' is used in the case both of the [25] mover and of the moved: and it is also clear that the motion is not in the form but in that which is in motion, that is to say 'the movable in activity'. Now accidental change we may leave out of account: for it is to be found in everything, at any time, and in any respect. Change which is not accidental on the other hand is not to be found in everything, but only in contraries, in things intermediate between [30] contraries, and in contradictories, as may be proved by induction. An intermediate may be a starting-point of change, since for the

[1] 201ᵃ 10.

purposes of the change it serves as contrary to either of two contraries: for the intermediate is in a sense the extremes. Hence we speak of the intermediate as in a sense a contrary relatively to the extremes and of either extreme as a contrary relatively to the intermediate: for instance, the central note is low relatively to the highest and high relatively to the lowest, and grey is light relatively to black and dark relatively to white.

[35] And since every change is *from* something 225ᵃ *to* something—as the word itself (μεταβολή) indicates, implying something 'after' (μετά) something else, that is to say something earlier and something later—that which changes must change in one of four ways: from subject to subject, from subject to non-[5] subject, from non-subject to subject, or from non-subject to non-subject, where by 'subject' I mean what is affirmatively expressed. So it follows necessarily from what has been said above[1] that there are only three kinds of change, that from subject to subject, that from subject to non-subject, and that from non-[10] subject to subject: for the fourth conceivable kind, that from non-subject to non-subject, is not change, as in that case there is no opposition either of contraries or of contradictories.

Now change from non-subject to subject, the relation being that of contradiction, is 'coming to be'—'unqualified coming to be' when the change takes place in an unqualified way, 'particular coming to be' when the change is change in a particular character: for instance, a change from not-white to white is a coming to be of the particular thing, white, while [15] change from unqualified not-being to being is coming to be in an unqualified way, in respect of which we say that a thing 'comes to be' without qualification, not that it 'comes to be' some particular thing. Change from subject to non-subject is 'perishing'—'unqualified perishing' when the change is from being to not-being, 'particular perishing' when the change is to the opposite negation, the distinction being the same as that made in the case of coming to be.

[20] Now the expression 'not-being' is used in several senses: and there can be motion neither of that which 'is not' in respect of the affirmation or negation of a predicate, nor of that which 'is not' in the sense that it only *potentially* 'is', that is to say the opposite of that which *actually* 'is' in an unqualified sense:

[1] 224ᵇ 28, 29.

for although that which is 'not-white' or 'not-good' may nevertheless be in motion *accidentally* (for example that which is 'not-white' might be a man), yet that which is without qualification 'not-so-and-so' cannot in [25] any sense be in motion: therefore it is impossible for that which *is not* to be in motion. This being so, it follows that 'becoming' cannot be a motion: for it is that which 'is not' that 'becomes'. For however true it may be that it *accidentally* 'becomes', it is nevertheless correct to say that it is that which 'is not' that in an unqualified sense 'becomes'. And similarly it is impossible for that which 'is not' to be at rest.

[30] There are these difficulties, then, in the way of the assumption that that which 'is not' can be in motion: and it may be further objected that, whereas everything which is in motion is in space, that which 'is not' is not in space: for then it would be *somewhere*.

So, too, 'perishing' is not a motion: for a motion has for its contrary either another motion or rest, whereas 'perishing' is the contrary of 'becoming'.

Since, then, every motion is a kind of change, and there are only the three kinds of [35] change mentioned above,[2] and since of these three those which take the form of 'be- 225ᵇ coming' and 'perishing', that is to say those which imply a relation of contradiction, are not motions: it necessarily follows that only change from subject to subject is motion. And every such subject is either a contrary or an intermediate (for a privation may be allowed to rank as a contrary) and can be affirmatively expressed, as naked, toothless, or black. If, then, [5] the categories are severally distinguished as Being, Quality, Place, Time, Relation, Quantity, and Activity or Passivity, it necessarily follows that there are three kinds of motion— qualitative, quantitative, and local.

2

[10] In respect of Substance there is no motion, because Substance has no contrary among things that are. Nor is there motion in respect of Relation: for it may happen that when one correlative changes, the other, although this does not itself change, is no longer applicable, so that in these cases the motion is accidental. Nor is there motion in respect of Agent and Patient—in fact there can never be motion of mover and moved, because there cannot be

[2] l. 7.

[15] motion of motion or becoming of becoming or in general change of change.

For in the first place there are two senses in which motion of motion is conceivable. (1) The motion of which there is motion might be conceived as subject; e.g. a man is in motion because he changes from fair to dark. Can it be that in this sense motion grows hot or cold, or [20] changes place, or increases or decreases? Impossible: for change is not a subject. Or (2) can there be motion of motion in the sense that some other subject changes from a change to another mode of being, as e.g. a man changes from falling ill to getting well? Even this is possible only in an accidental sense. For, whatever the subject may be, movement is change from one form to another. (And the same [25] holds good of becoming and perishing, except that in these processes we have a change to a particular kind of opposite, while the other, motion, is a change to a different kind.) So, if there is to be motion of motion, that which is changing from health to sickness must simultaneously be changing from this very change to another. It is clear, then, that by the time that it has become sick, it must also have changed to whatever may be the other change concerned (for that it should be at rest, though logically possible, is excluded by the theory). Moreover this other can never be any casual change, but must be a change from [30] something definite to some other definite thing. So in this case it must be the opposite change, viz. convalescence. It is only accidentally that there can be change of change, e.g. there is a change from remembering to forgetting only because the subject of this change changes at one time to knowledge, at another to ignorance.

In the second place, if there is to be change of change and becoming of becoming, we shall have an infinite regress. Thus if one of a series [35] of changes is to be a change of change, 226ᵃ the preceding change must also be so: e.g. if simple becoming was ever in process of becoming, then that which was becoming simple becoming was also in process of becoming, so that we should not yet have arrived at what was in process of simple becoming but only at what was already in process of becoming in process of becoming. And this again was sometime in process of becoming, so that even then we should not have arrived at what was in process of simple becoming. And since in an infinite series there is no first term, here there will be no first stage and therefore no follow-[5]ing stage either. On this hypothesis, then, nothing can become or be moved or change.

Thirdly, if a thing is capable of any particular motion, it is also capable of the corresponding contrary motion or the corresponding coming to rest, and a thing that is capable of becoming is also capable of perishing: consequently, if there be becoming of becoming, that which is in process of becoming is in process of perishing at the very moment when it has reached the stage of becoming: since it cannot be in process of perishing when it is just beginning to become or after it has ceased to become: for that which is in process of perishing must be in existence.

[10] Fourthly, there must be a substrate underlying all processes of becoming and changing. What can this be in the present case? It is either the body or the soul that undergoes alteration: what is it that correspondingly becomes motion or becoming? And again what is the goal of their motion? It must be the motion or becoming of something from something to something else. But in what sense [15] can this be so? For the becoming of learning cannot be learning: so neither can the becoming of becoming be becoming, nor can the becoming of any process be that process.

Finally, since there are three kinds of motion, the substratum and the goal of motion must be one or other of these, e.g. locomotion will have to be altered or to be locally moved.

To sum up, then, since everything that is moved is moved in one of three ways, either accidentally, or partially, or essentially, change [20] can change only accidentally, as e.g. when a man who is being restored to health runs or learns: and accidental change we have long ago[1] decided to leave out of account.

Since, then, motion can belong neither to Being nor to Relation nor to Agent and Patient, it remains that there can be motion only in respect of Quality, Quantity, and Place: for [25] with each of these we have a pair of contraries. Motion in respect of Quality let us call alteration, a general designation that is used to include both contraries: and by Quality I do not here mean a property of substance (in that sense that which constitutes a specific distinction is a quality) but a passive quality in virtue of which a thing is said to be acted on or to be incapable of being acted on. Motion in [30] respect of Quantity has no name that includes both contraries, but it is called increase or decrease according as one or the other is

[1] 224ᵇ 26.

designated: that is to say motion in the direction of complete magnitude is increase, motion in the contrary direction is decrease. Motion in respect of Place has no name either general or particular: but we may designate it by the general name of locomotion, though strictly the term 'locomotion' is applicable to things that change their place only when they have not [35] the power to come to a stand, and to things that do not move *themselves* locally.

226^b Change within the same kind from a lesser to a greater or from a greater to a lesser degree is alteration: for it is motion either from a contrary or to a contrary, whether in an unqualified or in a qualified sense: for change to a lesser degree of a quality will be called change to the contrary of that quality, [5] and change to a greater degree of a quality will be regarded as change from the contrary of that quality to the quality itself. It makes no difference whether the change be qualified or unqualified, except that in the former case the contraries will have to be contrary to one another only in a qualified sense: and a thing's possessing a quality in a greater or in a lesser degree means the presence or absence in it of more or less of the opposite quality. It is now clear, then, that there are only these three kinds of motion.

[10] The term 'immovable' we apply in the first place to that which is absolutely incapable of being moved (just as we correspondingly apply the term invisible to sound); in the second place to that which is moved with difficulty after a long time or whose movement is slow at the start—in fact, what we describe as hard to move; and in the third place to that which is naturally designed for and capable of motion, but is not in motion when, where, and as it naturally would be so. This last is the only kind of immovable thing of which I use the term 'being at rest': for rest is con-[15]trary to motion, so that rest will be negation of motion in that which is capable of admitting motion.

The foregoing remarks are sufficient to explain the essential nature of motion and rest, the number of kinds of change, and the different varieties of motion.

3

Let us now proceed to define the terms 'together' and 'apart', 'in contact', 'between', 'in [20] succession', 'contiguous', and 'continuous', and to show in what circumstances each of these terms is naturally applicable.

Things are said to be together in place when they are in one place (in the strictest sense of the word 'place') and to be apart when they are in different places.

Things are said to be in contact when their extremities are together.

That which a changing thing, if it changes [25] continuously in a natural manner, naturally reaches before it reaches that to which it changes last, is between. Thus 'between' implies the presence of at least three things: for in a process of change it is the contrary that is 'last': and a thing is moved continuously if it leaves no gap or only the smallest possible gap in the material—not in the time (for a gap in the time does not prevent things having a 'between', while, on the other hand, there is nothing to prevent the highest note sounding [30] immediately after the lowest) but in the material in which the motion takes place. This is manifestly true not only in local changes but in every other kind as well. ⟨Now every 227^a [7] change implies a pair of opposites, and opposites may be either contraries or contradictories; since then contradiction admits of no mean term, it is obvious that 'between' must imply a pair of contraries.⟩ That is locally con-226^b [32]trary which is most distant in a straight line: for the shortest line is definitely limited, and that which is definitely limited constitutes a measure.

A thing is 'in succession' when it is after [35] the beginning in position or in form or in some other respect in which it is definitely 227^a so regarded, and when further there is nothing of the *same* kind as itself between it and that to which it is in succession, e.g. a line or lines if it is a line, a unit or units if it is a unit, a house if it is a house (there is nothing to prevent something of a *different* kind being between). For that which is in succession is in succession to a particular thing, and is something posterior: for one is not 'in succession' to [5] two, nor is the first day of the month to be second: in each case the latter is 'in succession' to the former.

A thing that is in succession and touches is [10] 'contiguous'. The 'continuous' is a subdivision of the contiguous: things are called continuous when the touching limits of each become one and the same and are, as the word implies, contained in each other: continuity is impossible if these extremities are two. This definition makes it plain that continuity belongs to things that naturally in virtue of their [15] mutual contact form a unity. And in whatever way that which holds them together is one, so too will the whole be one, e.g. by a rivet or glue or contact or organic union.

It is obvious that of these terms 'in succession' is first in order of analysis: for that which touches is necessarily in succession, but not everything that is in succession touches: and so succession is a property of things prior in [20] definition, e.g. numbers, while contact is not. And if there is continuity there is necessarily contact, but if there is contact, that alone does not imply continuity: for the extremities of things may be *'together'* without necessarily being *one:* but they cannot be one without being necessarily together. So natural junction is last in coming to be: for the extremities must necessarily come into contact if they are to be [25] naturally joined: but things that are in contact are not all naturally joined, while there is no contact clearly there is no natural junction either. Hence, if as some say 'point' and 'unit' have an independent existence of their own, it is impossible for the two to be identical: for points can touch while units can [30] only be in succession. Moreover, there can always be something between points (for all lines are intermediate between points), whereas it is not necessary that there should possibly be anything between units: for there can be nothing between the numbers one and two.

We have now defined what is meant by 'to-227[b] gether' and 'apart', 'contact', 'between' and 'in succession', 'contiguous' and 'continuous': and we have shown in what circumstances each of these terms is applicable.

4

There are many senses in which motion is said to be 'one': for we use the term 'one' in many senses.

Motion is one *generically* according to the [5] different categories to which it may be assigned: thus any locomotion is one generically with any other locomotion, whereas alteration is different generically from locomotion.

Motion is one specifically when besides being one generically it also takes place in a species incapable of subdivision: e.g. colour has specific differences: therefore blackening and whitening differ specifically; but at all events every whitening will be specifically the same with every other whitening and every blackening with every other blackening. But white-[10] ness is not further subdivided by specific differences: hence any whitening is specifically one with any other whitening. Where it happens that the genus is at the same time a species, it is clear that the motion will then in a sense be one specifically though not in an unqualified sense: learning is an example of this, knowledge being on the one hand a species of apprehension and on the other hand a genus including the various knowledges. A difficulty, however, may be raised as to whether a mo-[15] tion is specifically one when the same thing changes from the same to the same, e.g. when one point changes again and again from a particular place to a particular place: if this motion is specifically one, circular motion will be the same as rectilinear motion, and rolling the same as walking. But is not this difficulty removed by the principle already laid down that if that in which the motion takes place is specifically different (as in the present instance the circular path is specifically different from [20] the straight) the motion itself is also different? We have explained, then, what is meant by saying that motion is one generically or one specifically.

Motion is one in an unqualified sense when it is one essentially or numerically: and the following distinctions will make clear what this kind of motion is. There are three classes of things in connexion with which we speak of motion, the 'that which', the 'that in which', and the 'that during which'. I mean that there [25] must *be* something that is in motion, e.g. a man or gold, and it must be in motion *in* something, e.g. a place or an affection, and *during* something, for all motion takes place during a time. Of these three it is the thing in which the motion takes place that makes it one generically or specifically, it is the thing moved that makes the motion one in subject, and it is the time that makes it consecutive: but it is the three together that make it one without qualification: to effect this, that in [30] which the motion takes place (the species) must be one and incapable of subdivision, that during which it takes place (the time) must be one and unintermittent, and that which is in motion must be one—not in an accidental sense (i.e. it must be one as the white that blackens is one or Coriscus who walks is one, not in the accidental sense in 228[a] which Coriscus and white may be one), nor merely in virtue of community of nature (for there might be a case of two men being restored to health at the same time in the same way, e.g. from inflammation of the eye, yet this motion is not really one, but only specifically one).

Suppose, however, that Socrates undergoes an alteration specifically the same but at one time and again at another: in this case if it is possible for that which ceased to be again to come into being and remain numerically the [5] same, then this motion too will be one: otherwise it will be the same but not one. And akin to this difficulty there is another; viz. is health one? and generally are the states and affections in bodies severally one in essence although (as is clear) the things that contain them are obviously in motion and in flux? Thus if a person's health at daybreak and at [10] the present moment is one and the same, why should not this health be numerically one with that which he recovers after an interval? The same argument applies in each case. There is, however, we may answer, this difference: that if the states are two then it follows simply from this fact that the activities must also in point of number be two (for only that which is numerically one can give rise to an activity [15] that is numerically one), but if the state is one, this is not in itself enough to make us regard the activity also as one: for when a man ceases walking, the walking no longer is, but it will again be if he begins to walk again. But, be this as it may, if in the above instance the health is one and the same, then it must be possible for that which is one and the same to come to be and to cease to be many times. However, these difficulties lie outside our present inquiry.

[20] Since every motion is continuous, a motion that is one in an unqualified sense must (since every motion is divisible) be continuous, and a continuous motion must be one. There will not be continuity between any motion and any other indiscriminately any more than there is between any two things chosen at random in any other sphere: there can be continuity only when the extremities of the two things are one. Now some things have no extremities at all: and the extremities of others differ specifically although we give them the same [25] name of 'end': how should e.g. the 'end' of a line and the 'end' of walking touch or come to be one? Motions that are not the same either specifically or generically may, it is true, be *consecutive* (e.g. a man may run and then at once fall ill of a fever), and again, in the torch-race we have consecutive but not continuous locomotion: for according to our definition there can be continuity only when the ends of the two things are one. Hence motions [30] may be consecutive or successive in virtue of the time being continuous, but there can be continuity only in virtue of the motions themselves being continuous, that is when the end of each is one with the end of the other. Motion, therefore, that is in an unqualified sense continuous and one must be specifically the same, of one thing, and in one time. Unity is required in respect of time in order that there may be no interval of immobility, for where there is intermission of motion there must be rest, and a motion that includes intervals of rest will be not one but many, so that [5] a motion that is interrupted by stationariness is not one or continuous, and it is so interrupted if there is an interval of time. And though of a motion that is not specifically one (even if the time is unintermittent) the time is one, the motion is specifically different, and so cannot really be one, for motion that is one [10] must be specifically one, though motion that is specifically one is not necessarily one in an unqualified sense. We have now explained what we mean when we call a motion one without qualification.

Further, a motion is also said to be one generically, specifically, or essentially when it is complete, just as in other cases completeness and wholeness are characteristics of what is one: and sometimes a motion even if incomplete is said to be one, provided only that it is continuous.

[15] And besides the cases already mentioned there is another in which a motion is said to be one, viz. when it is regular: for in a sense a motion that is irregular is not regarded as one, that title belonging rather to that which is regular, as a straight line is regular, the irregular being as such divisible. But the difference would seem to be one of degree. In every kind of motion we may have regularity or irregu-[20]larity: thus there may be regular alteration, and locomotion in a regular path, e.g. in a circle or on a straight line, and it is the same with regard to increase and decrease. The difference that makes a motion irregular is sometimes to be found in its path: thus a motion cannot be regular if its path is an irregular magnitude, e.g. a broken line, a spiral, or any other magnitude that is not such that any part of it taken at random fits on to any other that [25] may be chosen. Sometimes it is found neither in the place nor in the time nor in the goal but in the manner of the motion: for in some cases the motion is differentiated by

quickness and slowness: thus if its velocity is uniform a motion is regular, if not it is irregular. So quickness and slowness are not species of motion nor do they constitute specific differences of motion, because this distinction occurs in connexion with all the distinct species [30] of motion. The same is true of heaviness and lightness when they refer to the same thing: e.g. they do not specifically distinguish earth from itself or fire from itself. Irregular 229ᵃ motion, therefore, while in virtue of being continuous it is one, is so in a lesser degree, as is the case with locomotion in a broken line: and a lesser degree of something always means an admixture of its contrary. And since every motion that is one can be both regular and irregular, motions that are consecutive [5] but not specifically the same cannot be one and continuous: for how should a motion composed of alteration and locomotion be regular? If a motion is to be regular its parts ought to fit one another.

5

We have further to determine what motions are contrary to each other, and to determine similarly how it is with rest. And we have first to decide whether contrary motions are motions respectively from and to the same thing, e.g. [10] a motion from health and a motion to health (where the opposition, it would seem, is of the same kind as that between coming to be and ceasing to be); or motions respectively from contraries, e.g. a motion from health and a motion from disease; or motions respectively to contraries, e.g. a motion to health and a motion to disease; or motions respectively from a contrary and to the opposite contrary, e.g. a motion from health and a motion to disease; or motions respectively from a contrary to the opposite contrary and from the latter to the former, e.g. a motion from health to disease and a motion from disease to health: for motions [15] must be contrary to one another in one or more of these ways, as there is no other way in which they can be opposed.

Now motions respectively from a contrary and to the opposite contrary, e.g. a motion from health and a motion to disease, are not contrary motions: for they are one and the same. (Yet their essence is not the same, just as changing from health is different from changing to disease.) Nor are motions re-[20]spectively from a contrary and from the opposite contrary contrary motions, for a motion from a contrary is at the same time a motion to a contrary or to an intermediate (of this, however, we shall speak later),[1] but changing to a contrary rather than changing from a contrary would seem to be the cause of the contrariety of motions, the latter being the loss, the former the gain, of con-[25]trariness. Moreover, each several motion takes its name rather from the goal than from the starting-point of change, e.g. motion to health we call convalescence, motion to disease sickening. Thus we are left with motions respectively to contraries, and motions respectively to contraries from the opposite contraries. Now it would seem that motions to contraries are at the same time motions from contraries (though their essence may not be the same; 'to health' is distinct, I mean, from 'from disease', and 'from health' from 'to disease').

[30] Since then change differs from motion (motion being change from a particular subject to a particular subject), it follows that contrary motions are motions respectively from a contrary to the opposite contrary and from the 229ᵇ latter to the former, e.g. a motion from health to disease and a motion from disease to health. Moreover, the consideration of particular examples will also show what kinds of processes are generally recognized as contrary: thus falling ill is regarded as contrary to recov-[5]ering one's health, these processes having contrary goals, and being taught as contrary to being led into error by another, it being possible to acquire error, like knowledge, either by one's own agency or by that of another. Similarly we have upward locomotion and downward locomotion, which are contrary lengthwise, locomotion to the right and locomotion to the left, which are contrary breadthwise, and forward locomotion and backward locomotion, which too are contraries. On the other [10] hand, a process simply to a contrary, e.g. that denoted by the expression 'becoming white', where no starting-point is specified, is a change but not a motion. And in all cases of a thing that has no contrary we have as contraries change from and change to the same thing. Thus coming to be is contrary to ceasing to be, and losing to gaining. But these are changes and not motions. And wher-[15]ever a pair of contraries admit of an intermediate, motions to that intermediate must be held to be in a sense motions to one or other of the contraries: for the intermediate serves as a contrary for the purposes of the motion, in

[1] l. 28 sqq.

whichever direction the change may be, e.g. grey in a motion from grey to white takes the place of black as starting-point, in a motion from white to grey it takes the place of black as goal, and in a motion from black to grey it takes the place of white as goal: for the middle [20] is opposed in a sense to either of the extremes, as has been said above.[1] Thus we see that two motions are contrary to each other only when one is a motion from a contrary to the opposite contrary and the other is a motion from the latter to the former.

6

But since a motion appears to have contrary to it not only another motion but also a state of rest, we must determine how this is so. A motion has for its contrary in the strict sense of the term another motion, but it also has for an opposite a state of rest (for rest is the priva-[25] tion of motion and the privation of anything may be called its contrary), and motion of one kind has for its opposite rest of that kind, e.g. local motion has local rest. This statement, however, needs further qualification: there remains the question, is the opposite of remaining at a particular place motion from or motion to that place? It is surely clear that since there are two subjects between which [30] motion takes place, motion from one of these (*A*) to its contrary (*B*) has for its opposite remaining in *A*, while the reverse motion has for its opposite remaining in *B*. At the same time these two are also contrary to each other: for it would be absurd to suppose that there are contrary motions and not opposite states of 230ᵃ rest. States of rest in contraries *are* opposed. To take an example, a state of rest in health is (1) contrary to a state of rest in disease, and (2) the motion to which it is contrary is that from health to disease. For (2) it would be absurd that its contrary motion should be that from disease to health, since motion to that in which a thing is at rest is [5] rather a coming to rest, the coming to rest being found to come into being simultaneously with the motion; and one of these two motions it must be. And (1) rest in *whiteness* is of course not contrary to rest in health.

Of all things that have no contraries there are opposite *changes* (viz. change from the thing and change to the thing, e.g. change from being and change to being), but no *motion*. So, too, of such things there is no remaining though there is absence of change. Should

[1] 224ᵇ 32 sqq.

[10] there be a particular subject, absence of change in its being will be contrary to absence of change in its not-being. And here a difficulty may be raised: if not-being is not a particular something, what is it, it may be asked, that is contrary to absence of change in a thing's being? and is this absence of change a state of rest? If it is, then either it is not true that every state of rest is contrary to a motion or else coming to be and ceasing to be are motion. [15] It is clear then that, since we exclude these from among motions, we must not say that this absence of change is a state of rest: we must say that it is similar to a state of rest and call it absence of change. And it will have for its contrary either nothing or absence of change in the thing's not-being, or the ceasing to be of the thing: for such ceasing to be is change from it and the thing's coming to be is change to it.

Again, a further difficulty may be raised. How is it, it may be asked, that whereas in local change both remaining and moving may [20] be natural or unnatural, in the other changes this is not so? e.g. alteration is not now natural and now unnatural, for convalescence is no more natural or unnatural than falling ill, whitening no more natural or unnatural than blackening; so, too, with increase and decrease: these are not contrary to each other in the sense [25] that either of them is natural while the other is unnatural, nor is one increase contrary to another in this sense; and the same account may be given of becoming and perishing: it is not true that becoming is natural and perishing unnatural (for growing old is natural), nor do we observe one becoming to be natural and another unnatural. We answer that if [30] what happens under violence is unnatural, then violent perishing is unnatural and as such contrary to natural perishing. Are there then also some becomings that are violent and not the result of natural necessity, and are therefore contrary to natural becomings, and 230ᵇ violent increases and decreases, e.g. the rapid growth to maturity of profligates and the rapid ripening of seeds even when not packed close in the earth? And how is it with alterations? Surely just the same: we may say that some alterations are violent while others are natural, e.g. patients alter naturally or unnat-[5] urally according as they throw off fevers on the critical days or not. But, it may be objected, then we shall have perishings contrary to one another, not to becoming. Certainly: and why should not this in a sense be so? Thus it is so if one perishing is pleasant and another painful: and so one perishing will be contrary to another not in an unqualified sense, but in so far as one has this quality and the other that.

[10] Now motions and states of rest universally exhibit contrariety in the manner described above,[1] e.g. upward motion and rest above are respectively contrary to downward motion and rest below, these being instances of local contrariety; and upward locomotion belongs naturally to fire and downward to earth, i.e. the locomotions of the two are contrary to each other. And again, fire moves up naturally and down unnaturally: and its natural motion is [15] certainly contrary to its unnatural motion. Similarly with remaining: remaining above is contrary to motion from above downwards, and to earth this remaining comes unnaturally, this motion naturally. So the unnatural remaining of a thing is contrary to its natural motion, just as we find a similar contrariety in the motion of the same thing: [20] one of its motions, the upward or the downward, will be natural, the other unnatural.

Here, however, the question arises, has every state of rest that is not permanent a becoming, and is this becoming a coming to a standstill? If so, there must be a becoming of that which is at rest unnaturally, e.g. of earth at rest above: and therefore this earth during the time that it was being carried violently upward was coming to a standstill. But whereas the velocity of that which comes to a standstill seems always to increase, the velocity of that which is [25] carried violently seems always to decrease: so it will *be* in a state of rest without having *become* so. Moreover 'coming to a standstill' is generally recognized to be identical or at least concomitant with the locomotion of a thing to its proper place.

There is also another difficulty involved in the view that remaining in a particular place is contrary to motion from that place. For when a thing is moving from or discarding something, it still appears to have that which is [30] being discarded, so that if a state of rest is itself contrary to the motion from the state of rest to its contrary, the contraries rest and motion will be simultaneously predicable of the same thing. May we not say, however, that in so far as the thing is still stationary it is in a state of rest in a qualified sense? For, in fact, whenever a thing is in motion, part of it is at the starting-point while part is at the goal to 231[a] which it is changing: and consequently a motion finds its true contrary rather in another motion than in a state of rest.

With regard to motion and rest, then, we have now explained in what sense each of them is one and under what conditions they exhibit contrariety.

[5] [With regard to coming to a standstill the question may be raised whether there is an opposite state of rest to unnatural as well as to natural motions. It would be absurd if this were not the case: for a thing may remain still merely under violence: thus we shall have a thing being in a non-permanent state of rest without having become so. But it is clear that it must be the case: for just as there is unnatural motion, so, too, a thing may be in an un- [10] natural state of rest. Further, some things have a natural and an unnatural motion, e.g. fire has a natural upward motion and an unnatural downward motion: is it, then, this unnatural downward motion or is it the natural downward motion of earth that is contrary to the natural upward motion? Surely it is clear that both are contrary to it though not in the same sense: the natural motion of earth is contrary inasmuch as the motion of fire is [15] also natural, whereas the upward motion of fire as being natural is contrary to the downward motion of fire as being unnatural. The same is true of the corresponding cases of remaining. But there would seem to be a sense in which a state of rest and a motion are opposites.]

BOOK VI

1

Now if the terms 'continuous', 'in contact', and 'in succession' are understood as defined above[2] —things being 'continuous' if their extremities are one, 'in contact' if their extremities are together, and 'in succession' if there is nothing of their own kind intermediate between them —nothing that is continuous can be composed [25] of indivisibles: e.g. a line cannot be composed of points, the line being continuous and the point indivisible. For the extremities of two points can neither be *one* (since of an indivisible there can be no extremity as distinct from some other part) nor *together* (since that which has no parts can have no extremity, the

[1] In chapter 5. [2] v. 3.

extremity and the thing of which it is the extremity being distinct).

Moreover, if that which is continuous is [30] composed of points, these points must be either *continuous* or *in contact* with one another: and the same reasoning applies in the case of all indivisibles. Now for the reason given above they cannot be continuous: and one thing can be in contact with another only if whole is in contact with whole or part with part or part with whole. But since indivisibles have no parts, they must be in contact with one another as whole with whole. And if they are in contact with one another as whole with whole, they will not be continuous: [5] for that which is continuous has distinct parts: and these parts into which it is divisible are different in this way, i.e. spatially separate.

Nor, again, can a point be *in succession* to a point or a moment to a moment in such a way that length can be composed of points or time of moments: for things are in succession if there is nothing of their own kind intermediate between them, whereas that which is intermediate between points is always a line and that which is intermediate between moments is always a period of time.

[10] Again, if length and time could thus be composed of indivisibles, they could be divided into indivisibles, since each is divisible into the parts of which it is composed. But, as we saw, no continuous thing is divisible into things without parts. Nor can there be anything of any other kind intermediate between the parts or between the moments: for if there could be any such thing it is clear that it must be either indivisible or divisible, and if it is divisible, it must be divisible either into indivisibles or into divisibles that are infinitely divisible, in which case it is continuous.

[15] Moreover, it is plain that everything continuous is divisible into divisibles that are infinitely divisible: for if it were divisible into indivisibles, we should have an indivisible in contact with an indivisible, since the extremities of things that are continuous with one another are one and are in contact.

The same reasoning applies equally to magnitude, to time, and to motion: either all of these are composed of indivisibles and are divisible into indivisibles, or none. This may be [20] made clear as follows. If a magnitude is composed of indivisibles, the motion over that magnitude must be composed of corresponding indivisible motions: e.g. if the magnitude $AB\Gamma$ is composed of the indivisibles A, B, Γ, each corresponding part of the motion ΔEZ [25] of Ω over $AB\Gamma$ is indivisible. Therefore, since where there is motion there must be something that is in motion, and where there is something in motion there must be motion, therefore the being-moved will also be composed of indivisibles. So Ω traversed A when its motion was Δ, B when its motion was E, and Γ similarly when its motion was Z. Now a thing that is in motion from one place to another cannot at the moment when it was in motion both be in motion and at the same time have completed its motion at the place to which it was in motion: e.g. if a man is walking to Thebes, he cannot be walking to Thebes [30] and at the same time have completed his walk to Thebes: and, as we saw, Ω traverses the partless section A in virtue of the presence of the motion Δ. Consequently, if Ω actually passed through A *after* being in process of passing through, the motion must be divisible: for at the time when Ω was passing through, it neither was at rest nor had completed its passage but was in an intermediate state: while if it is passing through and has completed its passage *at the same moment,* [5] then that which is walking will at the moment when it is walking have completed its walk and will be in the place to which it is walking; that is to say, it will have completed its motion at the place to which it is in motion. And if a thing is in motion over the whole $\Lambda B \Gamma$ and its motion is the three Δ, E, and Z, and if it is not in motion at all over the partless section A but has completed its motion over it, then the motion will consist not of motions but of starts, and will take place by a thing's having completed a motion without being in motion: for on this assumption it has completed its passage through A without pass- [10] ing through it. So it will be possible for a thing to have completed a walk without ever walking: for on this assumption it has completed a walk over a particular distance without walking over that distance. Since, then, everything must be either at rest or in motion, and Ω is therefore at rest in each of the sections A, B, and Γ, it follows that a thing can be continuously at rest and at the same time in motion: for, as we saw, Ω is in motion over the whole $AB\Gamma$ and at rest in any part (and conse- [15] quently in the whole) of it. Moreover, if the indivisibles composing ΔEZ are motions, it would be possible for a thing in spite of the presence in it of motion to be not in motion but at rest, while if they are not motions, it would be possible for motion to be composed of something other than motions.

And if length and motion are thus indivisible, it is neither more nor less necessary that time also be similarly indivisible, that is to say be composed of indivisible moments: for if [20] the whole distance is divisible and an equal velocity will cause a thing to pass through less of it in less time, the time must also be divisible, and conversely, if the time in which a thing is carried over the section A is divisible, this section A must also be divisible.

2

And since every magnitude is divisible into magnitudes—for we have shown that it is impossible for anything continuous to be composed of indivisible parts, and every magni- [25] tude is continuous—it necessarily follows that the quicker of two things traverses a greater magnitude in an equal time, an equal magnitude in less time, and a greater magnitude in less time, in conformity with the definition sometimes given of 'the quicker'. Suppose that A is quicker than B. Now since of two things that which changes sooner is quicker, in the time ZH, in which A has [30] changed from Γ to Δ, B will not yet have arrived at Δ but will be short of it: so that in an equal time the quicker will pass over a greater magnitude. More than this, it will pass over a greater magnitude in less time: for in the time in which A has arrived at Δ, B being the slower has arrived, let us say, at E. Then since A has occupied the whole time ZH in 232ᵇ arriving at Δ, it will have arrived at Θ in less time than this, say ZK. Now the magnitude ΓΘ that A has passed over is greater than the magnitude ΓE, and the time ZK is less than the whole time ZH: so that the quicker will pass over a greater magnitude in less time. [5] And from this it is also clear that the quicker will pass over an equal magnitude in less time than the slower. For since it passes over the greater magnitude in less time than the slower, and (regarded by itself) passes over ΛM the greater in more time than ΛΞ the lesser, the time ΠP in which it passes over ΛM will be more than the time ΠΣ in which [10] it passes over ΛΞ: so that, the time ΠP being less than the time ΠX in which the slower passes over ΛΞ, the time ΠΣ will also be less than the time ΠX: for it is less than the time ΠP, and that which is less than something else that is less than a thing is also itself less than that thing. Hence it follows that the quicker will traverse an equal magnitude in less time than the slower. Again, since the mo- [15] tion of anything must always occupy either an equal time or less or more time in comparison with that of another thing, and since, whereas a thing is slower if its motion occupies more time and of equal velocity if its motion occupies an equal time, the quicker is neither of equal velocity nor slower, it follows that the motion of the quicker can occupy neither an equal time nor more time. It can only be, then, that it occupies less time, and thus we get the necessary consequence that the quicker will pass over an equal magnitude [20] (as well as a greater) in less time than the slower.

And since every motion is in time and a motion may occupy any time, and the motion of everything that is in motion may be either quicker or slower, both quicker motion and slower motion may occupy any time: and this being so, it necessarily follows that time also is continuous. By continuous I mean that which is divisible into divisibles that are infinitely [25] divisible: and if we take this as the definition of continuous, it follows necessarily that time is continuous. For since it has been shown that the quicker will pass over an equal magnitude in less time than the slower, suppose that A is quicker and B slower, and that the [30] slower has traversed the magnitude ΓΔ in the time ZH. Now it is clear that the quicker will traverse the same magnitude in less time than this: let us say in the time ZΘ. Again, since the quicker has passed over the whole ΓΔ in the time ZΘ, the slower will in the same time pass over ΓK, say, which is less 233ᵃ than ΓΔ. And since B, the slower, has passed over ΓK in the time ZΘ, the quicker will pass over it in less time: so that the time ZΘ will again be divided. And if this is divided the magnitude ΓK will also be divided just as ΓΔ was: and again, if the magnitude is divided, the time will also be divided. And [5] we can carry on this process for ever, taking the slower after the quicker and the quicker after the slower alternately, and using what has been demonstrated at each stage as a new point of departure: for the quicker will divide the time and the slower will divide the length. If, then, this alternation always holds good, and at every turn involves a division, it [10] is evident that all time must be continuous. And at the same time it is clear that all magnitude is also continuous; for the divisions of which time and magnitude respectively are susceptible are the same and equal.

Moreover, the current popular arguments make it plain that, if time is continuous, magnitude is continuous also, inasmuch as a thing passes over half a given magnitude in half the [15] time taken to cover the whole: in fact without qualification it passes over a less magnitude in less time; for the divisions of time and of magnitude will be the same. And if either is infinite, so is the other, and the one is so in the same way as the other; i.e. if time is infinite in respect of its extremities, length is also infinite in respect of its extremities: if time is infinite in respect of divisibility, [20] length is also infinite in respect of divisibility: and if time is infinite in both respects, magnitude is also infinite in both respects.

Hence Zeno's argument makes a false assumption in asserting that it is impossible for a thing to pass over or severally to come in contact with infinite things in a finite time. For there are two senses in which length and time and generally anything continuous are called [25] 'infinite': they are called so either in respect of divisibility or in respect of their extremities. So while a thing in a finite time cannot come in contact with things quantitatively infinite, it can come in contact with things infinite in respect of divisibility: for in this sense the time itself is also infinite: and so we find that the time occupied by the passage over the [30] infinite is not a finite but an infinite time, and the contact with the infinites is made by means of moments not finite but infinite in number.

The passage over the infinite, then, cannot occupy a finite time, and the passage over the finite cannot occupy an infinite time: if the time is infinite the magnitude must be infinite also, and if the magnitude is infinite, so also is the time. This may be shown as follows. Let AB be a finite magnitude, and let us suppose that it is traversed in infinite time Γ, and let [35] a finite period ΓΔ of the time be taken. 233^b Now in this period the thing in motion will pass over a certain segment of the magnitude: let BE be the segment that it has thus passed over. (This will be either an exact measure of AB or less or greater than an exact measure: it makes no difference which it is.) Then, since a magnitude equal to BE will always be passed over in an equal time, and BE [5] measures the whole magnitude, the whole time occupied in passing over AB will be finite: for it will be divisible into periods equal in number to the segments into which the magnitude is divisible. Moreover, if it is the case that infinite time is not occupied in passing over every magnitude, but it is possible to pass over some magnitude, say BE, in a finite [10] time, and if this BE measures the whole of which it is a part, and if an equal magnitude is passed over in an equal time, then it follows that the time like the magnitude is finite. That infinite time will not be occupied in passing over BE is evident if the time be taken as limited in one direction: for as the part will be passed over in less time than the whole, the time occupied in traversing this part must be finite, the limit in one direction being given. The same reasoning will also show the falsity of the assumption that infinite length can be [15] traversed in a finite time. It is evident, then, from what has been said that neither a line nor a surface nor in fact anything continuous can be indivisible.

This conclusion follows not only from the present argument but from the consideration that the opposite assumption implies the divisibility of the indivisible. For since the distinction of quicker and slower may apply to [20] motions occupying any period of time and in an equal time the quicker passes over a greater length, it may happen that it will pass over a length twice, or one and a half times, as great as that passed over by the slower: for their respective velocities may stand to one another in this proportion. Suppose, then, that the quicker has in the same time been carried over a length one and a half times as great as that traversed by the slower, and that the respective magnitudes are divided, that of the quicker, the magnitude ABΓΔ, into three indivisibles, and that of the slower into the two [25] indivisibles EZ, ZH. Then the time may also be divided into three indivisibles, for an equal magnitude will be passed over in an equal time. Suppose then that it is thus divided into KΛ, ΛM, MN. Again, since in the same time the slower has been carried over EZ, ZH, the time may also be similarly divided into two. Thus the indivisible will be divisible, and that [30] which has no parts will be passed over not in an indivisible but in a greater time. It is evident, therefore, that nothing continuous is without parts.

3

The present also is necessarily indivisible—the present, that is, not in the sense in which the word is applied to one thing in virtue of another, but in its proper and primary sense; in

[35] which sense it is inherent in all time. For 234ᵃ the present is something that is an extremity of the past (no part of the future being on this side of it) and also of the future (no part of the past being on the other side of it): it is, as we have said,[1] a limit of both. And if it is once shown that it is essentially of this character and one and the same, it will at once be evident also that it is indivisible.

[5] Now the present that is the extremity of both times must be one and the same: for if each extremity were different, the one could not be in succession to the other, because nothing continuous can be composed of things having no parts: and if the one is apart from the other, there will be time intermediate between them, because everything continuous is such that there is something intermediate between its limits and described by the same name as itself. But if the intermediate thing is time, it will be [10] divisible: for all time has been shown[2] to be divisible. Thus on this assumption the present is divisible. But if the present is divisible, there will be part of the past in the future and part of the future in the past: for past time will be marked off from future time at the actual point of division. Also the present will [15] be a present not in the proper sense but in virtue of something else: for the division which yields it will not be a division proper. Furthermore, there will be a part of the present that is past and a part that is future, and it will not always be the same part that is past or future: in fact one and the same present will not be simultaneous: for the time may be divided at many points. If, therefore, the present cannot possibly have these characteristics, it follows that it must be the same present that belongs [20] to each of the two times. But if this is so it is evident that the present is also indivisible: for if it is divisible it will be involved in the same implications as before. It is clear, then, from what has been said that time contains something indivisible, and this is what we call a present.

We will now show that nothing can be in [25] motion in a present. For if this is possible, there can be both quicker and slower motion in the present. Suppose then that in the present N the quicker has traversed the distance AB. That being so, the slower will in the same present traverse a distance less than AB, say AΓ. But since the slower will have occupied the whole present in traversing AΓ, the [30] quicker will occupy less than this in trav-ersing it. Thus we shall have a division of the present, whereas we found it to be indivisible. It is impossible, therefore, for anything to be in motion in a present.

Nor can anything be at rest in a present: for, as we were saying,[3] that only can be at rest which is naturally designed to be in motion but is not in motion when, where, or as it would naturally be so: since, therefore, nothing is naturally designed to be in motion in a present, it is clear that nothing can be at rest in a present either.

Moreover, inasmuch as it is the same present [35] that belongs to both the times, and it is possible for a thing to be in motion throughout one time and to be at rest throughout the 234ᵇ other, and that which is in motion or at rest for the whole of a time will be in motion or at rest as the case may be in any part of it in which it is naturally designed to be in motion or at rest: this being so, the assumption that there can be motion or rest in a present will carry with it the implication that the same thing can at the same time be at rest and in motion: for both the times have the same extremity, viz. the present.

[5] Again, when we say that a thing is at rest, we imply that its condition in whole and in part is at the time of speaking uniform with what it was previously: but the present contains no 'previously': consequently, there can be no rest in it.

It follows then that the motion of that which is in motion and the rest of that which is at rest must occupy time.

4

[10] Further, everything that changes must be divisible. For since every change is from something to something, and when a thing is at the goal of its change it is no longer changing, and when both it itself and all its parts are at the starting-point of its change it is not changing (for that which is in whole and in part in an unvarying condition is not in a state of [15] change); it follows, therefore, that part of that which is changing must be at the starting-point and part at the goal: for as a whole it cannot be in both or in neither. (Here by 'goal of change' I mean that which comes first in the process of change: e.g. in a process of change from white the goal in question will be grey, not black: for it is not necessary that that which [20] is changing should be at either of the extremes.) It is evident, therefore, that

---

[1] 222ᵃ 12. [2] Chapter 2. [3] 226ᵇ 12 sqq.

everything that changes must be divisible.

Now motion is divisible in two senses. In the first place it is divisible in virtue of the time that it occupies. In the second place it is divisible according to the motions of the several parts of that which is in motion: e.g. if the whole AΓ is in motion, there will be a motion of AB and a motion of BΓ. That being so, let ΔE be the motion of the part AB and EZ the [25] motion of the part BΓ. Then the whole ΔZ must be the motion of AΓ: for ΔZ must constitute the motion of AΓ inasmuch as ΔE and EZ severally constitute the motions of each of its parts. But the motion of a thing can never be constituted by the motion of something else: consequently the whole motion is the motion of the whole magnitude.

Again, since every motion is a motion of something, and the whole motion ΔZ is not the motion of either of the parts (for each of the parts ΔE, EZ is the motion of one of the [30] parts AB, BΓ) or of anything else (for, the whole motion being the motion of a whole, the parts of the motion are the motions of the parts of that whole: and the parts of ΔZ are the motions of AB, BΓ and of nothing else: for, as we saw,[1] a motion that is one cannot be the motion of more things than one): since this is so, the whole motion will be the motion of the magnitude ABΓ.

Again, if there is a motion of the whole other than ΔZ, say ΘI, the motion of each of the parts may be subtracted from it: and these [35] motions will be equal to ΔE, EZ respectively: for the motion of that which is one must be one. So if the whole motion ΘI may be divided into the motions of the parts, ΘI will be equal to ΔZ: if on the other hand there is any remainder, say KI, this will be a [5] motion of nothing: for it can be the motion neither of the whole nor of the parts (as the motion of that which is one must be one) nor of anything else: for a motion that is continuous must be the motion of things that are continuous. And the same result follows if the division of ΘI reveals a surplus on the side of the motions of the parts. Consequently, if this is impossible, the whole motion must be the same as and equal to ΔZ.

This then is what is meant by the division of motion according to the motions of the parts: and it must be applicable to everything that is divisible into parts.

[10] Motion is also susceptible of another kind of division, that according to time. For since all motion is in time and all time is divisible, and in less time the motion is less, it follows that every motion must be divisible according to time. And since everything that is in motion is in motion in a certain sphere and for a certain time and has a motion belonging to it, it [15] follows that the time, the motion, the being-in-motion, the thing that is in motion, and the sphere of the motion must all be susceptible of the same divisions (though spheres of motion are not all divisible in a like manner: thus quantity is essentially, quality accidentally divisible). For suppose that A is the time occupied by the motion B. Then if all the [20] time has been occupied by the whole motion, it will take less of the motion to occupy half the time, less again to occupy a further subdivision of the time, and so on to infinity. Again, the time will be divisible similarly to the motion: for if the whole motion occupies all the time half the motion will occupy half the time, and less of the motion again will occupy less of the time.

[25] In the same way the being-in-motion will also be divisible. For let Γ be the whole being-in-motion. Then the being-in-motion that corresponds to half the motion will be less than the whole being-in-motion, that which corresponds to a quarter of the motion will be less again, and so on to infinity. Moreover by setting out successively the being-in-motion corresponding to each of the two motions ΔΓ (say) and ΓE, we may argue that the whole [30] being-in-motion will correspond to the whole motion (for if it were some other being-in-motion that corresponded to the whole motion, there would be more than one being-in-motion corresponding to the same motion), the argument being the same as that whereby we showed[2] that the motion of a thing is divisible into the motions of the parts of the thing: for if we take separately the being-in-motion corresponding to each of the two motions, we shall see that the whole being-in-motion is continuous.

The same reasoning will show the divisibility of the length, and in fact of everything that forms a sphere of change (though some [35] of these are only accidentally divisible because that which changes is so): for the division of one term will involve the division of all. So, too, in the matter of their being finite or infinite, they will all alike be either the one or the other. And we now see that in most cases the fact that all the terms are divisi-

---

[1] 223[b] 1 sqq.   [2] 234[b] 24 sqq., especially 234[b] 34 sqq.

ble or infinite is a direct consequence of the fact that the thing that changes is divisible or infinite: for the attributes 'divisible' and 'infinite' belong in the first instance to the thing [5] that changes. That divisibility does so we have already[1] shown: that infinity does so will be made clear in what follows.[2]

5

Since everything that changes changes from something to something, that which has changed must at the moment when it has first changed be in that to which it has changed. For that which changes retires from or leaves that from which it changes: and leaving, if not identical with changing, is at any rate a con- [10] sequence of it. And if leaving is a consequence of changing, having left is a consequence of having changed: for there is a like relation between the two in each case.

One kind of change, then, being change in a relation of contradiction, where a thing has changed from not-being to being it has left [15] not-being. Therefore it will be in being: for everything must either be or not be. It is evident, then, that in contradictory change that which has changed must be in that to which it has changed. And if this is true in this kind of change, it will be true in all other kinds as well: for in this matter what holds good in the case of one will hold good likewise in the case of the rest.

Moreover, if we take each kind of change separately, the truth of our conclusion will be equally evident, on the ground that that which has changed must be somewhere or in some- [20] thing. For, since it has left that from which it has changed and must be somewhere, it must be either in that to which it has changed or in something else. If, then, that which has changed to B is in something other than B, say Γ, it must again be changing from Γ to B: for it cannot be assumed that there is no interval be- [25] tween Γ and B, since change is continuous. Thus we have the result that the thing that has changed, at the moment when it has changed, is changing to that to which it has changed, which is impossible: that which has changed, therefore, must be in that to which it has changed. So it is evident likewise that that which has come to be, at the moment when it has come to be, will *be,* and that which has ceased to be will *not-be:* for what we have said applies universally to every kind of change, and its truth is most obvious in the case of

[1] 234^b 10-20. [2] Chapter 7.

[30] contradictory change. It is clear, then, that that which has changed, at the moment when it has first changed, is in that to which it has changed.

We will now show that the 'primary when' in which that which has changed effected the completion of its change must be indivisible, where by 'primary' I mean possessing the characteristics in question of itself and not in virtue of the possession of them by something else belonging to it. For let AΓ be divisible, and [35] let it be divided at B. If then the completion of change has been effected in AB or again in BΓ, AΓ cannot be the primary thing in which the completion of change has been effected. If, on the other hand, it has been changing in both AB and BΓ (for it must either have changed or be changing in each of them), it must have been changing in the whole AΓ: but our assumption was that AΓ contains only the *completion* of the change. It is equally impossible to suppose that one part of AΓ contains the process and the other the completion of the change: for then we shall have something prior to what is primary. So that in which the completion of change has been effected must be indivisible. [5] It is also evident, therefore, that that in which that which has ceased to be has ceased to be and that in which that which has come to be has come to be are indivisible.

But there are two senses of the expression 'the primary when in which something has changed'. On the one hand it may mean the primary when containing the *completion* of the process of change—the moment when it is correct to say 'it has changed': on the other hand it may mean the primary when containing the *beginning* of the process of change. Now the [10] primary when that has reference to the *end* of the change is something really existent: for a change may really be completed, and there is such a thing as an end of change, which we have in fact shown to be indivisible because it is a limit. But that which has reference to the beginning is not existent at all: for there is no such thing as a beginning of a process of change, and the time occupied by the change does not contain any primary when [15] in which the change began. For suppose that AΔ is such a primary when. Then it cannot be indivisible: for, if it were, the moment immediately preceding the change and the moment in which the change begins would be consecutive (and moments cannot be consecutive). Again, if the changing thing is at rest in the whole preceding time ΓA (for we may suppose that it is at rest), it is at rest in A also: so if AΔ is without parts, it will simultaneously be at rest and have changed: for it is [20] at rest in A and has changed in Δ. Since then AΔ is not without parts, it must be divisible, and the changing thing must have changed in every part of it (for if it has changed in neither of the two parts into which AΔ is divided, it has not changed in the whole either: if, on the other hand, it is in process of change in both parts, it is likewise in process of change in the whole: and if, again, it has changed in one of the two parts, the whole is not the primary when in which it has changed: [25] it must therefore have changed in every part). It is evident, then, that with reference to the beginning of change there is no primary when in which change has been effected: for the divisions are infinite.

So, too, of that which has changed there is no primary part that has changed. For suppose that of ΔE the primary part that has changed is ΔZ (everything that changes having been [30] shown[1] to be divisible): and let ΘI be the time in which ΔZ has changed. If, then, in the whole time ΔZ has changed, in half the time there will be a part that has changed, less than and therefore prior to ΔZ: and again there will be another part prior to this, and yet another, and so on to infinity. Thus of that which changes there cannot be any primary part that [35] has changed. It is evident, then, from what has been said, that neither of that which changes nor of the time in which it changes is there any primary part.

236[b] With regard, however, to the actual subject of change—that is to say that in respect of which a thing changes—there is a difference to be observed. For in a process of change we may distinguish three terms—that which changes, that in which it changes, and the actual subject of change, e.g. the man, the time, and the fair complexion. Of these the man and the time [5] are divisible: but with the fair complexion it is otherwise (though they are all divisible accidentally, for that in which the fair complexion or any other quality is an accident is divisible). For of actual subjects of change it will be seen that those which are classed as essentially, not accidentally, divisible have no [10] primary part. Take the case of magnitudes: let AB be a magnitude, and suppose that it has moved from B to a primary 'where' Γ. Then if BΓ is taken to be indivisible, two things without parts will have to be contiguous (which is impossible): if on the other hand it is taken to be divisible, there will be something prior to Γ to which the magnitude has changed, and something else again prior to that, and so on to infinity, because the process [15] of division may be continued without end. Thus there can be no primary 'where' to which a thing has changed. And if we take the case of quantitative change, we shall get a like result, for here too the change is in something continuous. It is evident, then, that only in qualitative motion can there be anything essentially indivisible.

6

[20] Now everything that changes changes in time, and that in two senses: for the time in which a thing is said to change may be the primary time, or on the other hand it may have an extended reference, as e.g. when we say that a thing changes in a particular year because it changes in a particular day. That being so, that which changes must be changing in any part of the primary time in which it changes. This is clear from our definition of 'primary',[2] in which the word is said to express just this: it may also, however, be made evident by the following argument. Let XP be the pri-[25] mary time in which that which is in motion is in motion: and (as all time is divisible) let it be divided at K. Now in the time XK it either is in motion or is not in motion, and the same is likewise true of the time KP. Then if it is in motion in neither of the two parts, it will be at rest in the whole: for it is impossible that it should be in motion in a time in no [30] part of which it is in motion. If on the other hand it is in motion in only one of the two parts of the time, XP cannot be the primary time in which it is in motion: for its motion will have reference to a time other than XP. It must, then, have been in motion in any part of XP.

And now that this has been proved, it is evident that everything that is in motion must have been in motion before. For if that which is in motion has traversed the distance KΛ in [35] the primary time XP, in half the time a thing that is in motion with equal velocity and began its motion at the same time will have traversed half the distance. But if this second thing whose velocity is equal has traversed a 237[a] certain distance in a certain time, the original thing that is in motion must have

---
[1] 234[b] 10 sqq.   [2] 235[b] 33.

traversed the same distance in the same time. Hence that which is in motion must have been in motion before.

Again, if by taking the extreme moment of [5] the time—for it is the moment that defines the time, and time is that which is intermediate between moments—we are enabled to say that motion has taken place in the whole time XP or in fact in any period of it, motion may likewise be said to have taken place in every other such period. But half the time finds an extreme in the point of division. Therefore motion will have taken place in half the time and in fact in any part of it: for as soon as any division is made there is always a time defined by moments. If, then, all time is divisible, and [10] that which is intermediate between moments is time, everything that is changing must have completed an infinite number of changes.

Again, since a thing that changes continuously and has not perished or ceased from its change must either be changing or have changed in any part of the time of its change, and since it cannot be changing in a moment, it follows that it must have changed at every [15] moment in the time: consequently, since the moments are infinite in number, everything that is changing must have completed an infinite number of changes.

And not only must that which is changing have changed, but that which has changed must also previously have been changing, since everything that has changed from something [20] to something has changed in a period of time. For suppose that a thing has changed from A to B in a moment. Now the moment in which it has changed cannot be the same as that in which it is at A (since in that case it would be in A and B at once): for we have shown above[1] that that which has changed, when it has changed, is not in that from which it has changed. If, on the other hand, it is a different moment, there will be a period of time intermediate between the two: for, as we saw,[2] moments are not consecutive. Since, then, [25] it has changed in a period of time, and all time is divisible, in half the time it will have completed another change, in a quarter another, and so on to infinity: consequently when it has changed, it must have previously been changing.

Moreover, the truth of what has been said is more evident in the case of magnitude, because [30] the magnitude over which what is changing changes is continuous. For suppose that a

[1] 235^b 6 sqq.   [2] 231^b 6 sqq.

thing has changed from Γ to Δ. Then if ΓΔ is indivisible, two things without parts will be consecutive. But since this is impossible, that which is intermediate between them must be a magnitude and divisible into an infinite number of segments: consequently, before the change is completed, the thing changes to those segments. Everything that has changed, therefore, must previously have been changing: for [35] the same proof also holds good of change 237^b with respect to what is not continuous, changes, that is to say, between contraries and between contradictories. In such cases we have only to take the time in which a thing has changed and again apply the same reasoning. So that which has changed must have been changing and that which is changing must have changed, and a process of change is preceded by a completion of change and a completion by a process: and we can never take [5] any stage and say that it is absolutely the first. The reason of this is that no two things without parts can be contiguous, and therefore in change the process of division is infinite, just as lines may be infinitely divided so that one part is continually increasing and the other continually decreasing.

[10] So it is evident also that that which has become must previously have been in process of becoming, and that which is in process of becoming must previously have become, everything (that is) that is divisible and continuous: though it is not always the actual thing that is in process of becoming of which this is true: sometimes it is something else, that is to say, some part of the thing in question, e.g. the foundation-stone of a house. So, too, in the case of that which is perishing and that which has perished: for that which becomes and that which perishes must contain an element of infiniteness as an immediate consequence of [15] the fact that they are continuous things: and so a thing cannot be in process of becoming without having become or have become without having been in process of becoming. So, too, in the case of perishing and having perished: perishing must be preceded by having perished, and having perished must be preceded by perishing. It is evident, then, that that which has become must previously have been in process of becoming, and that which is in [20] process of becoming must previously have become: for all magnitudes and all periods of time are infinitely divisible.

Consequently no absolutely first stage of change can be represented by any particular part of space or time which the changing thing may occupy.

7

Now since the motion of everything that is in motion occupies a period of time, and a greater magnitude is traversed in a longer time, it is impossible that a thing should undergo a finite [25] motion in an infinite time, if this is understood to mean not that the same motion or a part of it is continually repeated, but that the whole infinite time is occupied by the whole finite motion. In all cases where a thing is in motion with uniform velocity it is clear that the finite magnitude is traversed in a finite time. For if we take a part of the motion which shall be a measure of the whole, the whole motion is completed in as many equal periods of [30] the time as there are parts of the motion. Consequently, since these parts are finite, both in size individually and in number collectively, the whole time must also be finite: for it will be a multiple of the portion, equal to the time occupied in completing the aforesaid part multiplied by the number of the parts.

But it makes no difference even if the velocity is not uniform. For let us suppose that the [35] line AB represents a finite stretch over which a thing has been moved in the given time, and let ΓΔ be the infinite time. Now if one part of the stretch must have been traversed before another part (this is clear, that in the earlier and in the later part of the time a different part of the stretch has been traversed: for as the time lengthens a different part of the motion will always be completed in it, [5] whether the thing in motion changes with uniform velocity or not: and whether the rate of motion increases or diminishes or remains stationary this is none the less so), let us then take AE a part of the whole stretch of motion AB which shall be a measure of AB. Now this part of the motion occupies a certain period of the infinite time: it cannot itself occupy an infinite time, for we are assuming that that is occupied by the whole AB. And if again I take [10] another part equal to AE, that also must occupy a finite time in consequence of the same assumption. And if I go on taking parts in this way, on the one hand there is no part which will be a measure of the infinite time (for the infinite cannot be composed of finite parts whether equal or unequal, because there must be some unity which will be a measure [15] of things finite in multitude or in magnitude, which, whether they are equal or unequal, are none the less limited in magnitude); while on the other hand the finite stretch of motion AB is a certain multiple of AE: consequently the motion AB must be accomplished in a finite time. Moreover it is the same with coming to rest as with motion. And so it is impossible for one and the same thing to be infinitely in process of becoming or of perishing. [20] The same reasoning will prove that in a finite time there cannot be an infinite extent of motion or of coming to rest, whether the motion is regular or irregular. For if we take a part which shall be a measure of the whole time, in this part a certain fraction, not the whole, of the magnitude will be traversed, because we assume that the traversing of the whole occupies all the time. Again, in another equal part of the time another part of the mag- [25] nitude will be traversed: and similarly in each part of the time that we take, whether equal or unequal to the part originally taken. It makes no difference whether the parts are equal or not, if only each is finite: for it is clear that while the time is exhausted by the subtraction of its parts, the infinite magnitude will not be thus exhausted, since the process of subtraction is finite both in respect of the quantity subtracted and of the number of times a subtraction is made. Consequently the infinite magnitude will not be traversed in a [30] finite time: and it makes no difference whether the magnitude is infinite in only one direction or in both: for the same reasoning will hold good.

This having been proved, it is evident that neither can a finite magnitude traverse an infinite magnitude in a finite time, the reason being the same as that given above: in part of [35] the time it will traverse a finite magnitude and in each several part likewise, so that in the whole time it will traverse a finite magnitude.

And since a finite magnitude will not traverse an infinite in a finite time, it is clear that neither will an infinite traverse a finite in a finite time. For if the infinite could traverse the finite, the finite could traverse the infinite; for it makes no difference which of the two is the thing in motion; either case involves the traversing of the infinite by the finite. For [5] when the infinite magnitude A is in motion a part of it, say ΓΔ, will occupy the finite B, and then another, and then another, and so on to infinity. Thus the two results will coincide: the infinite will have completed a motion over the finite and the finite will have traversed the infinite: for it would seem to be [10] impossible for the motion of the infinite over the finite to occur in any way other than by the finite traversing the infinite either by locomotion over it or by measuring it. Therefore, since this is impossible, the infinite cannot traverse the finite.

Nor again will the infinite traverse the infinite in a finite time. Otherwise it would also [15] traverse the finite, for the infinite includes the finite. We can further prove this in the same way by taking the time as our starting-point.

Since, then, it is established that in a finite time neither will the finite traverse the infinite, nor the infinite the finite, nor the infinite the [20] infinite, it is evident also that in a finite time there cannot be infinite motion: for what difference does it make whether we take the motion or the magnitude to be infinite? If either of the two is infinite, the other must be so likewise: for all locomotion is in space.

8

Since everything to which motion or rest is natural is in motion or at rest in the natural time, place, and manner, that which is coming to a stand, when it is coming to a stand, must [25] be in motion: for if it is not in motion it must be at rest: but that which is at rest cannot be coming to rest. From this it evidently follows that coming to a stand must occupy a period of time: for the motion of that which is in motion occupies a period of time, and that which is coming to a stand has been shown to be in motion: consequently coming to a stand must occupy a period of time.

Again, since the terms 'quicker' and 'slower' [30] are used only of that which occupies a period of time, and the process of coming to a stand may be quicker or slower, the same conclusion follows.

And that which is coming to a stand must be coming to a stand in any part of the primary time in which it is coming to a stand. For if it is coming to a stand in neither of two parts into which the time may be divided, it cannot be coming to a stand in the whole time, with the result that that which is coming to a stand will not be coming to a stand. If on the other hand it is coming to a stand in only one of the two parts of the time, the whole cannot be the pri- [35] mary time in which it is coming to a stand: for it is coming to a stand in the whole time not primarily but in virtue of something distinct from itself, the argument being the same as that which we used above about things in motion.[1]

And just as there is no primary time in which that which is in motion is in motion, so too there is no primary time in which that which is coming to a stand is coming to a stand, there being no primary stage either of being in motion or of coming to a stand. For let AB be the primary time in which a thing is coming to a stand. Now AB cannot be without parts: for there cannot be motion in that which is without parts, because the moving thing would necessarily have been already moved for part of the time of its movement: [5] and that which is coming to a stand has been shown to be in motion. But since AB is therefore divisible, the thing is coming to a stand in every one of the parts of AB: for we have shown above[2] that it is coming to a stand in every one of the parts in which it is primarily coming to a stand. Since then, that in which primarily a thing is coming to a stand must be a period of time and not something indivisible, and since all time is infinitely divisible, there cannot be anything in which primarily it is coming to a stand.

[10] Nor again can there be a primary time at which the being at rest of that which is at rest occurred: for it cannot have occurred in that which has no parts, because there cannot be motion in that which is indivisible, and that in which rest takes place is the same as that in which motion takes place: for we defined[3] a state of rest to be the state of a thing to which motion is natural but which is not in motion when (that is to say in that in which) motion would be natural to it. Again, our use of the [15] phrase 'being at rest' also implies that the previous state of a thing is still unaltered, not one point only but two at least being thus needed to determine its presence: consequently that in which a thing is at rest cannot be without parts. Since, then it is divisible, it must be a period of time, and the thing must be at rest in every one of its parts, as may be shown by the same method as that used above in similar demonstrations.

[20] So there can be no primary part of the time: and the reason is that rest and motion are always in a period of time, and a period of time has no primary part any more than a magnitude or in fact anything continuous: for everything continuous is divisible into an infinite number of parts.

And since everything that is in motion is in

[1] Chapter 6.   [2] 238^b 31 sqq.   [3] 226^b 12 sqq.

motion in a period of time and changes from something to something, when its motion is comprised within a particular period of time essentially—that is to say when it fills the whole [25] and not merely a part of the time in question—it is impossible that in that time that which is in motion should be over against some particular thing primarily. For if a thing— itself and each of its parts—occupies the same space for a definite period of time, it is at rest: for it is in just these circumstances that we use the term 'being at rest'—when at one moment after another it can be said with truth that a thing, itself and its parts, occupies the same [30] space. So if this is being at rest it is impossible for that which is changing to be as a whole, at the time when it is primarily changing, over against any particular thing (for the whole period of time is divisible), so that in one part of it after another it will be true to say that the thing, itself and its parts, occupies the same space. If this is not so and the aforesaid proposition is true only at a single moment, then the thing will be over against a particular thing not for any period of time but only at a moment that limits the time. It is true that at [35] any moment it is always over against 239[b] something stationary: but it is not at rest: for at a moment it is not possible for anything to be either in motion or at rest. So while it is true to say that that which is in motion is at a moment not in motion and is opposite some particular thing, it cannot in a period of time be over against that which is at rest: for that would involve the conclusion that that which is in locomotion is at rest.

9

[5] Zeno's reasoning, however, is fallacious, when he says that if everything when it occupies an equal space is at rest, and if that which is in locomotion is always occupying such a space at any moment, the flying arrow is therefore motionless. This is false, for time is not composed of indivisible moments any more than any other magnitude is composed of indivisibles.
[10] Zeno's arguments about motion, which cause so much disquietude to those who try to solve the problems that they present, are four in number. The first asserts the non-existence of motion on the ground that that which is in locomotion must arrive at the half-way stage before it arrives at the goal. This we have discussed above.[1]

[1] 233[a] 13 sqq.

The second is the so-called 'Achilles', and it [15] amounts to this, that in a race the quickest runner can never overtake the slowest, since the pursuer must first reach the point whence the pursued started, so that the slower must always hold a lead. This argument is the same in principle as that which depends on bisection, though it differs from it in that the spaces with which we successively have to deal are not [20] divided into halves. The result of the argument is that the slower is not overtaken: but it proceeds along the same lines as the bisection-argument (for in both a division of the space in a certain way leads to the result that the goal is not reached, though the 'Achilles' goes further in that it affirms that even the quickest runner in legendary tradition must [25] fail in his pursuit of the slowest), so that the solution must be the same. And the axiom that that which holds a lead is never overtaken is false: it is not overtaken, it is true, while it holds a lead: but it is overtaken nevertheless if it is granted that it traverses the finite distance prescribed. These then are two of his arguments.
[30] The third is that already given above, to the effect that the flying arrow is at rest, which result follows from the assumption that time is composed of moments: if this assumption is not granted, the conclusion will not follow.

The fourth argument is that concerning the two rows of bodies, each row being composed of an equal number of bodies of equal size, passing each other on a race-course as they proceed with equal velocity in opposite directions, the one row originally occupying the space between the goal and the middle point of the course and the other that between the middle [35] point and the starting-post. This, he thinks, involves the conclusion that half a given time is equal to double that time. The fallacy 240[a] of the reasoning lies in the assumption that a body occupies an equal time in passing with equal velocity a body that is in motion and a body of equal size that is at rest; which is false. For instance (so runs the argument), let A, A ... be the stationary bodies of equal size, [5] B, B ... the bodies, equal in number and in size to A, A ..., originally occupying the half of the course from the starting-post to the middle of the A's, and Γ, Γ ... those originally occupying the other half from the goal to the middle of the A's, equal in number, size, and velocity to B, B .... Then three consequences follow:

First, as the B's and the Γ's pass one another,

the first B reaches the last Γ at the same moment as the first Γ reaches the last B. Secondly, [10] at this moment the first Γ has passed all the A's, whereas the first B has passed only half the A's, and has consequently occupied only half the time occupied by the first Γ, since each of the two occupies an equal time in passing each A. Thirdly, at the same moment all the B's have passed all the Γ's: for the first Γ and the first B will simultaneously reach the oppo-[15] site ends of the course, since (so says Zeno) the time occupied by the first Γ in passing each of the B's is equal to that occupied by it in passing each of the A's, because an equal time is occupied by both the first B and the first Γ in passing all the A's. This is the argument, but it presupposed the aforesaid fallacious assumption.

Nor in reference to contradictory change shall we find anything unanswerable in the ar-[20] gument that if a thing is changing from not-white, say, to white, and is in neither condition, then it will be neither white nor not-white: for the fact that it is not *wholly* in either condition will not preclude us from calling it white or not-white. We call a thing white or not-white not necessarily because it is wholly either one or the other, but because most of its parts or the most essential parts of it are so: not [25] being in a certain condition is different from not being wholly in that condition. So, too, in the case of being and not-being and all other conditions which stand in a contradictory relation: while the changing thing must of necessity be in one of the two opposites, it is never wholly in either.

Again, in the case of circles and spheres and everything whose motion is confined within the space that it occupies, it is not true to say [30] that the motion can be nothing but rest, on the ground that such things in motion, themselves and their parts, will occupy the same position for a period of time, and that therefore they will be at once at rest and in motion. For in the first place the parts do not occupy the same position for any period of time: and in the second place the whole also is always changing to a different position: for if we 240ᵇ take the orbit as described from a point A on a circumference, it will not be the same as the orbit as described from B or Γ or any other point on the same circumference except in an accidental sense, the sense that is to say in which a musical man is the same as a man. [5] Thus one orbit is always changing into another, and the thing will never be at rest. And it is the same with the sphere and everything else whose motion is confined within the space that it occupies.

10

Our next point is that that which is without parts cannot be in motion except accidentally: i.e. it can be in motion only in so far as the body or the magnitude is in motion and the [10] partless is in motion by inclusion therein, just as that which is in a boat may be in motion in consequence of the locomotion of the boat, or a part may be in motion in virtue of the motion of the whole. (It must be remembered, however, that by 'that which is without parts' I mean that which is quantitatively indivisible ⟨and that the case of the motion of a part is not exactly parallel⟩: for parts have motions belonging essentially and severally to [15] themselves distinct from the motion of the whole. The distinction may be seen most clearly in the case of a revolving sphere, in which the velocities of the parts near the centre and of those on the surface are different from one another and from that of the whole; this implies that there is not one motion but many). As we have said, then, that which is without parts can be in motion in the sense in which a man sitting in a boat is in motion when the boat is travelling, but it cannot be in motion of [20] itself. For suppose that it is changing from AB to BΓ—either from one magnitude to another, or from one form to another, or from some state to its contradictory—and let Δ be the primary time in which it undergoes the change. Then in the time in which it is changing it must be either in AB or in BΓ or partly [25] in one and partly in the other: for this, as we saw,[1] is true of everything that is changing. Now it cannot be partly in each of the two: for then it would be divisible into parts. Nor again can it be in BΓ: for then it will have completed the change, whereas the assumption is that the change is in process. It remains, then, that in the time in which it is changing, it is in AB. That being so, it will be at rest: for, as we saw,[2] to be in the same condition for a period of time [30] is to be at rest. So it is not possible for that which has no parts to be in motion or to change in any way: for only one condition could have made it possible for it to have motion, viz. that time should be composed of moments, in which case at any moment it would have completed a 241ᵃ motion or a change, so that it would never be in motion, but would always have been in

---
[1] 234ᵇ 10 sqq.   [2] 239ᵃ 27.

motion. But this we have already shown above[1] to be impossible: time is not composed of moments, just as a line is not composed of points, and motion is not composed of starts: for this [5] theory simply makes motion consist of indivisibles in exactly the same way as time is made to consist of moments or a length of points.

Again, it may be shown in the following way that there can be no motion of a point or of any other indivisible. That which is in motion can never traverse a space greater than itself without first traversing a space equal to or less than itself. That being so, it is evident that the point [10] also must first traverse a space equal to or less than itself. But since it is indivisible, there can be no space less than itself for it to traverse first: so it will have to traverse a distance equal to itself. Thus the line will be composed of points, for the point, as it continually traverses a distance equal to itself, will be a measure of the whole line. But since this is impossible, it is likewise impossible for the indivisible to be in motion.

[15] Again, since motion is always in a period of time and never in a moment, and all time is divisible, for everything that is in motion there must be a time less than that in which it traverses a distance as great as itself. For that in which it is in motion will be a time, because all motion is in a period of time; and all time has been shown above[2] to be divisible. Therefore, if a point is in motion, there must be a time less than that in which it has itself traversed [20] any distance. But this is impossible, for in less time it must traverse less distance, and thus the indivisible will be divisible into something less than itself, just as the time is so divisible: the fact being that the only condition under which that which is without parts and indivisible could be in motion would have been the possibility of the infinitely small being in mo- [25] tion in a moment: for in the two questions—that of motion in a moment and that of motion of something indivisible—the same principle is involved.

Our next point is that no process of change is infinite: for every change, whether between contradictories or between contraries, is a change from something to something. Thus in contradictory changes the positive or the nega-

[1] 231[b] 18 sqq.   [2] 232[b] 23 sqq.

tive, as the case may be, is the limit, e.g. being is the limit of coming to be and not-being is the limit of ceasing to be: and in contrary changes the particular contraries are the limits, [30] since these are the extreme points of any such process of change, and consequently of every process of alteration: for alteration is always dependent upon some contraries. Similarly contraries are the extreme points of processes of increase and decrease: the limit of increase is to be found in the complete magnitude proper to the peculiar nature of the thing that is increasing, while the limit of decrease is the complete loss of such magnitude. Locomotion, it is true, we cannot show to be finite in this way, since it is not always between contraries. But since that which cannot be cut (in the sense that it is inconceivable that it should be cut, the term 'cannot' being used in several [5] senses)—since it is inconceivable that that which in this sense cannot be cut should be in process of being cut, and generally that that which cannot come to be should be in process of coming to be, it follows that it is inconceivable that that which cannot complete a change should be in process of changing to that to which it cannot complete a change. If, then, it is to be assumed that that which is in locomotion is in process of changing, it must be capable of completing the change. Consequently its motion is not infinite, and [10] it will not be in locomotion over an infinite distance, for it cannot traverse such a distance.

It is evident, then, that a process of change cannot be infinite in the sense that it is not defined by limits. But it remains to be considered whether it is possible in the sense that one and the same process of change may be infinite in respect of the time which it occupies. If it is not one process, it would seem that there is nothing [15] to prevent its being infinite in this sense; e.g. if a process of locomotion be succeeded by a process of alteration and that by a process of increase and that again by a process of coming to be: in this way there may be motion for ever so far as the time is concerned, but it will not be one motion, because all these motions do not compose one. If it is to be one process, no motion can be infinite in respect of the time that it occupies, with the single exception of rota- [20] tory locomotion.

BOOK VII

1

EVERYTHING that is in motion must be moved [25] by something. For if it has not the source of its motion in itself it is evident that it is moved by something other than itself, for there must be something else that moves it. If on the other hand it has the source of its motion in itself, let AB be taken to represent that which is in motion essentially of itself and not in virtue of the fact that something belonging to it is in motion. Now in the first place to assume that [30] AB, because it is in motion as a whole and is not moved by anything external to itself, is therefore moved by itself—this is just as if, supposing that KΛ is moving ΛM and is also itself in motion, we were to deny that KM is moved by anything on the ground that it is not evident which is the part that is moving it and which the part that is moved. In the second place that which is in motion without being moved by anything does not necessarily cease from its motion because something else is at rest, but a thing must be moved by something if the fact of something else having ceased from its motion causes it to be at rest. Thus, if this is accepted, everything that is in motion must be [5] moved by something. For AB, which has been taken to represent that which is in motion, must be divisible, since everything that is in motion is divisible. Let it be divided, then, at Γ. Now if ΓB is not in motion, then AB will not be in motion: for if it is, it is clear that AΓ would be in motion while BΓ is at rest, and [10] thus AB cannot be in motion essentially and primarily. But *ex hypothesi* AB is in motion essentially and primarily. Therefore if ΓB is not in motion AB will be at rest. But we have agreed that that which is at rest if something else is not in motion must be moved by something. Consequently, everything that is in motion must be moved by something: for that [15] which is in motion will always be divisible, and if a part of it is not in motion the whole must be at rest.

Since everything that is in motion must be moved by something, let us take the case in which a thing is in locomotion and is moved by something that is itself in motion, and that again is moved by something else that is in motion, and that by something else, and so on continually: then the series cannot go on to [20] infinity, but there must be some first movent. For let us suppose that this is not so and take the series to be infinite. Let A then be moved by B, B by Γ, Γ by Δ, and so on, each member of the series being moved by that which comes next to it. Then since *ex hypothesi* the movent while causing motion is also itself in motion, and the motion of the moved and the motion of the movent must proceed simultaneously (for the movent is causing motion and the [25] moved is being moved simultaneously) it is evident that the respective motions of A, B, Γ, and each of the other moved movents are simultaneous. Let us take the motion of each separately and let E be the motion of A, Z of B, and H and Θ respectively the motions of Γ and Δ : for though they are all moved severally one by another, yet we may still take the motion of each as numerically one, since every mo- [30] tion is from something to something and is not infinite in respect of its extreme points. By a motion that is numerically one I mean a motion that proceeds from something numerically one and the same to something numerically one and the same in a period of time numerically one and the same: for a motion may [35] be the same generically, specifically, or numerically: it is generically the same if it belongs to the same category, e.g. substance or quality: it is specifically the same if it proceeds from something specifically the same to something specifically the same, e.g. from white to black or from good to bad, which is not of a kind specifically distinct: it is numerically the same if it proceeds from something numerically one to something numerically one in the same period of time, e.g. from a particular white to a particular black, or from a particular place to a particular place, in a particular period of time: for if the period of time were not one and the same, the motion would no longer be numerically one though it would still be specifically one. [4, 8] We have dealt with this question above.[1] Now let us further take the time in which A has completed its motion, and let it be represented by K. Then since the motion of A is finite the time will also be finite. But since the movents and the things moved are infinite, the motion EZHΘ, i.e. the motion that is composed of all [15] the individual motions, must be infinite. For the motions of A, B, and the others may be equal, or the motions of the others may be greater: but assuming what is conceivable, we

[1] v. 4 (227^b 3 sqq.).

find that whether they are equal or some are greater, in both cases the whole motion is infinite. And since the motion of A and that of each of the others are simultaneous, the whole motion must occupy the same time as the motion of A: but the time occupied by the motion of A is finite: consequently the motion will be infinite in a finite time, which is impossible.

It might be thought that what we set out to [20] prove has thus been shown, but our argument so far does not prove it, because it does not yet prove that anything impossible results from the contrary supposition: for in a finite time there may be an infinite motion, though not of one thing, but of many: and in the case that we are considering this is so: for each thing accomplishes its own motion, and there is no impossibility in many things being in motion simultaneously. But if (as we see to be universally the case) that which primarily is moved locally and corporeally must be either [25] in contact with or continuous with that which moves it, the things moved and the movents must be continuous or in contact with one another, so that together they all form a single unity: whether this unity is finite or infinite makes no difference to our present argument; for in any case since the things in motion are infinite in number the whole motion will be infinite, if, as is theoretically possible, each motion is either equal to or greater than that which follows it in the series: for we shall take as actual that which is theoretically possible. [30] If, then, A, B, Γ, Δ form an infinite magnitude that passes through the motion EZHΘ in the finite time K, this involves the conclusion that an infinite motion is passed through in a finite time: and whether the magnitude in question is finite or infinite this is in either case impossible. Therefore the series must come to an end, and there must be a first movent and a first moved: for the fact that this impossibil-
243ᵃ ity results only from the assumption of a particular case is immaterial, since the case assumed is theoretically possible, and the assumption of a theoretically possible case ought not to give rise to any impossible result.

2

That which is the first movement of a thing—in the sense that it supplies not 'that for the sake of which' but the source of the motion—is always together with that which is moved by it (by 'together' I mean that there is nothing [5] intermediate between them). This is universally true wherever one thing is moved by another. And since there are three kinds of motion, local, qualitative, and quantitative, there [10] must also be three kinds of movent, that which causes locomotion, that which causes alteration, and that which causes increase or decrease.

Let us begin with locomotion, for this is the primary motion. Everything that is in locomotion is moved either by itself or by something else. In the case of things that are moved by themselves it is evident that the moved and the movent are together: for they contain within themselves their first movent, so that there is [15] nothing in between. The motion of things that are moved by something else must proceed in one of four ways: for there are four kinds of locomotion caused by something other than that which is in motion, viz. pulling, pushing, carrying, and twirling. All forms of locomotion are reducible to these. Thus pushing on is a form of pushing in which that which is causing motion away from itself follows up that which it pushes and continues to push it: pushing off occurs when the movent does not follow up the thing that it has moved: throw-[20]ing when the movent causes a motion
243ᵇ away from itself more violent than the natural locomotion of the thing moved, which continues its course so long as it is controlled by the motion imparted to it. Again, pushing apart and pushing together are forms respectively of pushing off and pulling: pushing apart is pushing off, which may be a motion either away from the pusher or away from something [5] else, while pushing together is pulling, which may be a motion towards something else as well as towards the puller. We may similarly classify all the varieties of these last two, e.g. packing and combing: the former is a form of pushing together, the latter a form of pushing apart. The same is true of the other processes of combination and separation (they will all be found to be forms of pushing apart or of pushing together), except such as are involved in the processes of becoming and perishing. (At [10] the same time it is evident that there is no other kind of motion but combination and separation: for they may all be apportioned to one or other of those already mentioned.) Again, inhaling is a form of pulling, exhaling a form of pushing: and the same is true of spitting and of all other motions that proceed through the body, whether secretive or assimilative, the assimilative being forms of pulling, the secretive [15] of pushing off. All other kinds of locomotion must be similarly reduced, for they all fall

under one or other of our four heads. And again, of these four, carrying and twirling are reducible to pulling and pushing. For carrying always follows one of the other three methods, for that which is carried is in motion accidentally, because it is in or upon something that is [20] in motion, and that which carries it is in doing so being either pulled or pushed or 244ᵃ twirled; thus carrying belongs to all the other three kinds of motion in common. And twirling is a compound of pulling and pushing, for that which is twirling a thing must be pulling one part of the thing and pushing another part, since it impels one part away from itself and another part towards itself. If, therefore, it can be shown that that which is pushing and that which is pulling are adjacent respectively to that which is being pushed and that which [5] is being pulled, it will be evident that in all locomotion there is nothing intermediate between moved and movent. But the former fact is clear even from the definitions of pushing and pulling, for pushing is motion to something else from oneself or from something else, and pulling is motion from something else to oneself or to something else, when the motion of that which is pulling is quicker than the motion [10] that would separate from one another the two things that are continuous: for it is this that causes one thing to be pulled on along with the other. (It might indeed be thought that there is a form of pulling that arises in another way: that wood, e.g. pulls fire in a manner different from that described above. But it makes no difference whether that which pulls is in motion or is stationary when it is pulling: in the latter case it pulls to the place where it is, while in the former it pulls to the place where it was.) Now it is impossible to move anything [15] either from oneself to something else or from something else to oneself without being 244ᵇ in contact with it: it is evident, therefore, that in all locomotion there is nothing intermediate between moved and movent.

Nor again is there anything intermediate between that which undergoes and that which causes alteration: this can be proved by induction: for in every case we find that the respective extremities of that which causes and that which undergoes alteration are adjacent. For our assumption is that things that are undergoing alteration are altered in virtue of their being affected in respect of their so-called affective qualities, since that which is of a certain quality is altered in so far as it is sensible, and the characteristics in which bodies differ from one another are sensible characteristics: for every body differs from another in possessing a greater or lesser number of sensible characteristics or in possessing the same sensible characteristics in a greater or lesser degree. But the alteration of that which undergoes alteration is also caused by the above-mentioned character- [5] istics, which are affections of some particular underlying quality. Thus we say that a thing is altered by becoming hot or sweet or thick or dry or white: and we make these assertions alike of what is inanimate and of what is animate, and further, where animate things are in question, we make them both of the parts that have no power of sense-perception and of [10] the senses themselves. For in a way even the senses undergo alteration, since the active sense is a motion through the body in the course of which the sense is affected in a certain way. We see, then, that the animate is capable of every kind of alteration of which the inanimate is capable: but the inanimate is not capable of every kind of alteration of which the animate is capable, since it is not capable of alteration in respect of the senses: moreover [15] the inanimate is unconscious of being af- 245ᵃ fected by alteration, whereas the animate is conscious of it, though there is nothing to prevent the animate also being unconscious of it when the process of the alteration does not concern the senses. Since, then, the alteration of that which undergoes alteration is caused by sensible things, in every case of such alteration it is evident that the respective extremities of that which causes and that which undergoes [5] alteration are adjacent. Thus the air is continuous with that which causes the alteration, and the body that undergoes alteration is continuous with the air. Again, the colour is continuous with the light and the light with the sight. And the same is true of hearing and smelling: for the primary movent in respect to the moved is the air. Similarly, in the case of tasting, the flavour is adjacent to the sense of [10] taste. And it is just the same in the case of things that are inanimate and incapable of sense-perception. Thus there can be nothing intermediate between that which undergoes and that which causes alteration.

Nor, again, can there be anything intermediate between that which suffers and that which causes increase: for the part of the latter that starts the increase does so by becoming attached in such a way to the former that the whole becomes one. Again, the decrease of that which suffers decrease is caused by a part of the thing becoming detached. So that which [15] causes increase and that which causes decrease must be continuous with that which suffers increase and that which suffers decrease respectively: and if two things are continuous with one another there can be nothing intermediate between them.

It is evident, therefore, that between the extremities of the moved and the movent that are respectively first and last in reference to the moved there is nothing intermediate.

3

Everything, we say, that undergoes alteration is altered by sensible causes, and there is alteration only in things that are said to be essentially affected by sensible things. The truth [5] of this is to be seen from the following considerations. Of all other things it would be most natural to suppose that there is alteration in figures and shapes, and in acquired states and in the processes of acquiring and losing these: but as a matter of fact in neither of these two classes of things is there alteration.

In the first place, when a particular forma- [10] tion of a thing is completed, we do not call it by the name of its material: e.g. we do not call the statue 'bronze' or the pyramid 'wax' or the bed 'wood', but we use a derived expression and call them 'of bronze', 'waxen', and 'wooden' respectively. But when a thing has been affected and altered in any way we still call it by the original name: thus we speak of the bronze or the wax being dry or fluid or hard or hot.

[15] And not only so: we also speak of the particular fluid or hot substance as being bronze, giving the material the same name as that which we use to describe the affection.

246ª Since, therefore, having regard to the figure or shape of a thing we no longer call that which has become of a certain figure by the name of the material that exhibits the figure, whereas having regard to a thing's affections or alterations we still call it by the name of its material, it is evident that becomings of the former kind cannot be alterations.

Moreover it would seem absurd even to speak in *this* way, to speak, that is to say, of a [5] man or house or anything else that has come into existence as having been altered. Though it may be true that every such becoming is necessarily the result of something's being altered, the result, e.g. of the material's being condensed or rarefied or heated or cooled, nevertheless it is not the things that are coming into existence that are altered, and their becoming is not an alteration.

[10] Again, acquired states, whether of the body or of the soul, are not alterations. For some are excellences and others are defects, and neither excellence nor defect is an alteration: excellence is a perfection (for when anything acquires its proper excellence we call it perfect, since it is then if ever that we have a [15] thing in its natural state: e.g. we have a perfect circle when we have one as good as possible), while defect is a perishing of or departure from this condition. So just as when speaking of a house we do not call its arrival at perfection an alteration (for it would be absurd to suppose that the coping or the tiling is an alter- [20] ation or that in receiving its coping or its tiling a house is altered and not perfected), the same also holds good in the case of excellences and defects and of the persons or things that 246ᵇ possess or acquire them: for excellences are perfections of a thing's nature and defects are departures from it: consequently they are not alterations.

Further, we say that all excellences depend upon particular relations. Thus bodily excellences such as health and a good state of body [5] we regard as consisting in a blending of hot and cold elements within the body in due proportion, in relation either to one another or to the surrounding atmosphere: and in like manner we regard beauty, strength, and all the other bodily excellences and defects. Each of them exists in virtue of a particular relation and puts that which possesses it in a good or bad condition with regard to its proper affections, where by 'proper' affections I mean those influences that from the natural constitution of a thing tend to promote or destroy its existence. Since, [10] then, relatives are neither themselves alterations nor the subjects of alteration or of becoming or in fact of any change whatever, it is evident that neither states nor the processes of losing and acquiring states are alterations, though it may be true that their becoming or perishing [15] is necessarily, like the becoming or perishing of a specific character or form, the result of the alteration of certain other things, e.g. hot and cold or dry and wet elements or the elements, whatever they may be, on which the states primarily depend. For each several bodily defect or excellence involves a relation with those things from which the possessor of the defect or excellence is naturally subject to alteration: thus excellence disposes its possessor to be unaffected by these influences or to be affected by those of them that ought to be admitted, while defect disposes its possessor to be affected by them or to be unaffected by those of them that ought to be admitted.

[20] And the case is similar in regard to the 247a states of the soul, all of which (like those of body) exist in virtue of particular relations, the excellences being perfections of nature and the defects departures from it: moreover, excellence puts its possessor in good condition, while defect puts its possessor in a bad condition, to meet his proper affections. Consequently these cannot any more than the bodily states be alter-[5] ations, nor can the processes of losing and acquiring them be so, though their becoming is necessarily the result of an alteration of the sensitive part of the soul, and this is altered by sensible objects: for all moral excellence is concerned with bodily pleasures and pains, which again depend either upon acting or upon remembering or upon anticipating. Now those that depend upon action are determined by [10] sense-perception, i.e. they are stimulated by something sensible: and those that depend upon memory or anticipation are likewise to be traced to sense-perception, for in these cases pleasure is felt either in remembering what one has experienced or in anticipating what one is going to experience. Thus all pleasure of this kind must be produced by sensible things: and since the presence in any one of moral defect or excellence involves the presence in him of [15] pleasure or pain (with which moral excellence and defect are always concerned), and these pleasures and pains are alterations of the sensitive part, it is evident that the loss and acquisition of these states no less than the loss and acquisition of the states of the body must be the result of the alteration of something else. Consequently, though their becoming is accompanied by an alteration, they are not themselves alterations.

247b Again, the states of the intellectual part of the soul are not alterations, nor is there any becoming of them. In the first place it is much more true of the possession of knowledge that it depends upon a particular relation. And further, it is evident that there is no becoming of these states. For that which is potentially possessed of knowledge becomes actually possessed of it not by being set in motion at all itself [5] but by reason of the presence of something else: i.e. it is when it meets with the particular object that it knows in a manner the particular through its knowledge of the universal. (Again, there is no becoming of the actual use and activity of these states, unless it is thought that there is a becoming of vision and touching and that the activity in question is similar to these.) And the original acquisition of knowledge is not a becoming or an alteration: for the terms [10] 'knowing' and 'understanding' imply that the intellect has reached a state of rest and come to a standstill, and there is no becoming that leads to a state of rest, since, as we have said above,[1] no change at all can have a becoming. Moreover, just as to say, when any one has passed from a state of intoxication or sleep or disease to the contrary state, that he has become [15] possessed of knowledge again is incorrect in spite of the fact that he was previously incapable of using his knowledge, so, too, when any one originally acquires the state, it is incorrect to say that he becomes possessed of knowledge: for the possession of understanding and knowledge is produced by the soul's settling down out of the restlessness natural to it. Hence, too, in learning and in forming judgements on matters relating to their sense-percep- 248a tions children are inferior to adults owing to the great amount of restlessness and motion in their souls. Nature itself causes the soul to settle down and come to a state of rest for the performance of some of its functions, while for the performance of others other things do so: but in either case the result is brought about through the alteration of something in the body, as we see in the case of the use and activ-[5] ity of the intellect arising from a man's becoming sober or being awakened. It is evident, then, from the preceding argument that alteration and being altered occur in sensible things and in the sensitive part of the soul, and, except accidentally, in nothing else.

4

[10] A difficulty may be raised as to whether every motion is commensurable with every other or not. Now if they are all commensurable and if two things to have the same velocity must accomplish an equal motion in an equal time, then we may have a circumference equal to a straight line, or, of course, the one may be greater or less than the other. Further, if one thing alters and another accomplishes a locomotion in an equal time, we may have an alter-[15] ation and a locomotion equal to one another: thus an affection will be equal to a length, which is impossible. But is it not only when an equal motion is accomplished by two things in an equal time that the velocities of

[1] v. 2 (225b 15 sqq.).

the two are equal? Now an affection cannot be equal to a length. Therefore there cannot be an alteration equal to or less than a locomotion: and consequently it is not the case that every motion is commensurable with every other.

But how will our conclusion work out in the case of the circle and the straight line? It would be absurd to suppose that the motion of one [20] thing in a circle and of another in a straight line cannot be similar, but that the one must inevitably move more quickly or more slowly than the other, just as if the course of one were downhill and of the other uphill. Moreover it does not as a matter of fact make any difference to the argument to say that the one motion must inevitably be quicker or slower than the other: for then the circumference can be greater or less than the straight line; and if so it is possible for the two to be equal. [25] For if in the time A the quicker (B) passes over the distance B′ and the slower (Γ) 248^b passes over the distance Γ′, B′ will be greater than Γ′: for this is what we[1] took 'quicker' to mean: and so quicker motion also implies that one thing traverses an equal distance in less time than another: consequently there will be a part of A in which B will pass over a part of the circle equal to Γ′, while Γ will occupy the whole of A in passing over Γ′. None the less, if the two motions are commen- [5] surable, we are confronted with the consequence stated above, viz. that there may be a straight line equal to a circle. But these are not commensurable: and so the corresponding motions are not commensurable either.

But may we say that things are always commensurable if the same terms are applied to them without equivocation? e.g. a pen, a wine, and the highest note in a scale are not commensurable: we cannot say whether any one of them is sharper than any other: and why is this? they are incommensurable because it is only equivocally that the same term 'sharp' is applied to them: whereas the highest note in a scale is commensurable with the leading-note, because the term 'sharp' has the same meaning [10] as applied to both. Can it be, then, that the term 'quick' has not the same meaning as applied to straight motion and to circular motion respectively? If so, far less will it have the same meaning as applied to alteration and to locomotion.

Or shall we in the first place deny that things are always commensurable if the same terms are applied to them without equivocation? For the term 'much' has the same meaning whether applied to water or to air, yet water and air are not commensurable in respect of it: or, if this illustration is not considered satisfactory, 'double' at any rate would seem to have the same meaning as applied to each (denoting in each case the proportion of two to one), yet water and air are not commensurable in re- [15] spect of it. But here again may we not take up the same position and say that the term 'much' is equivocal? In fact there are some terms of which even the definitions are equivocal; e.g. if 'much' were defined as 'so much and more', 'so much' would mean something different in different cases: 'equal' is similarly equivocal; and 'one' again is perhaps in- [20] evitably an equivocal term; and if 'one' is equivocal, so is 'two'. Otherwise why is it that some things are commensurable while others are not, if the nature of the attribute in the two cases is really one and the same?

Can it be that the incommensurability of two things in respect of any attribute is due to a difference in that which is primarily capable of carrying the attribute? Thus horse and dog are so commensurable that we may say which is the whiter, since that which primarily contains the whiteness is the same in both, viz. the surface: and similarly they are commensurable in respect of size. But water and speech are not commensurable in respect of clearness, since that which primarily contains the attribute is [25] different in the two cases. It would seem, however, that we must reject this solution, since clearly we could thus make all equivocal attributes univocal and say merely that that which contains each of them is different in different cases: thus 'equality', 'sweetness', and 'whiteness' will severally always be the same, though that which contains them is different in different cases. Moreover, it is not any casual thing that is capable of carrying any attribute: each single attribute can be carried primarily only by one single thing.

Must we then say that, if two things are to be commensurable in respect of any attribute, not only must the attribute in question be applicable to both without equivocation, but there must also be no specific differences either in the attribute itself or in that which contains the [5] attribute—that these, I mean, must not be divisible in the way in which colour is divided into kinds? Thus in this respect one thing will not be commensurable with another, i.e. we cannot say that one is more coloured than the other where only colour in general and not any

---

[1] vi. 2(232^a 25 sqq.).

particular colour is meant; but they are commensurable in respect of whiteness.

Similarly in the case of motion: two things are of the same velocity if they occupy an equal time in accomplishing a certain equal amount of motion. Suppose, then, that in a certain time an alteration is undergone by one half of a body's length and a locomotion is accomplished by [10] the other half: can be say that in this case the alteration is equal to the locomotion and of the same velocity? That would be absurd, and the reason is that there are different species of motion. And if in consequence of this we must say that two things are of equal velocity if they accomplish locomotion over an equal distance in an equal tme, we have to admit the equality of a straight line and a circumference. What, then, is the reason of this? Is it that locomo- [15] tion is a genus or that line is a genus? (We may leave the time out of account, since that is one and the same.) If the lines are specifically different, the locomotions also differ specifically from one another: for locomotion is specifically differentiated according to the specific differentiation of that over which it takes place. (It is also similarly differentiated, it would seem, accordingly as the instrument of the locomotion is different: thus if feet are the instrument, it is walking, if wings it is flying; but perhaps we should rather say that this is not so, and that in this case the differences in the locomotion are merely differences of posture in that which is in motion.) We may say, therefore, that things are of equal velocity [20] if in an equal time they traverse the same magnitude: and when I call it 'the same' I mean that it contains no specific difference and therefore no difference in the motion that takes place over it. So we have now to consider how motion is differentiated: and this discussion serves to show that the genus is not a unity but contains a plurality latent in it and distinct from it, and that in the case of equivocal terms sometimes the different senses in which they are used are far removed from one another, while sometimes there is a certain likeness between them, and sometimes again they are nearly related either generically or analogically, with the result that they seem not to be equivocal though they really are.
[25] When, then, is there a difference of species? Is an attribute specifically different if the subject is different while the attribute is the same, or must the attribute itself be different as well? And how are we to define the limits of a species? What will enable us to decide that particular instances of whiteness or sweetness are the same or different? Is it enough that it appears different in one subject from what it appears in another? Or must there be no sameness at all? And further, where alteration is in question, how is one alteration to be of equal velocity with another? One person may be cured quickly and another slowly, and cures [30] may also be simultaneous: so that, recovery of health being an alteration, we have here alterations of equal velocity, since each altera- 249^b tion occupies an equal time. But what alteration? We cannot here speak of an 'equal' alteration: what corresponds in the category of quality to equality in the category of quantity is 'likeness'. However, let us say that there is equal velocity where *the same* change is accom- [5] plished in an equal time. Are we, then, to find the commensurability in the subject of the affection or in the affection itself? In the case that we have just been considering it is the fact that health is one and the same that enables us to arrive at the conclusion that the one alteration is neither more nor less than the other, but that both are alike. If on the other hand the affection is different in the two cases, e.g. when the alterations take the form of becoming white and becoming healthy respectively, here there is no sameness or equality or likeness inasmuch as the difference in the affections at [10] once makes the alterations specifically different, and there is no unity of alteration any more than there would be unity of locomotion under like conditions. So we must find out how many species there are of alteration and of locomotion respectively. Now if the things that are in motion—that is to say, the things to which the motions belong essentially and not accidentally—differ specifically, then their respective motions will also differ specifically: if on the other hand they differ generically or numerically, the motions also will differ generically or numerically as the case may be. But [15] there still remains the question whether, supposing that two alterations are of equal velocity, we ought to look for this equality in the sameness (or likeness) of the affections, or in the things altered, to see e.g. whether a certain quantity of each has become white. Or ought we not rather to look for it in both? That is to say, the alterations are the same or different according as the affections are the same or different, while they are equal or unequal according as the things altered are equal or unequal.

And now we must consider the same ques-

[20] tion in the case of becoming and perishing: how is one becoming of equal velocity with another? They are of equal velocity if in an equal time there are produced two things that are the same and specifically inseparable, e.g. two men (not merely generically inseparable as e.g. two animals). Similarly one is quicker than the other if in an equal time the product is different in the two cases. I state it thus because we have no pair of terms that will convey this 'difference' in the way in which unlikeness is conveyed. If we adopt the theory that it is number that constitutes being, we may indeed speak of a 'greater number' and a 'lesser number' within the same species, but there is no common term that will include both relations, nor are there terms to express each of [25] them separately in the same way as we indicate a higher degree or preponderance of an affection by 'more', of a quantity by 'greater.'

5

Now since wherever there is a movent, its motion always acts upon something, is always in something, and always extends to something (by 'is always in something' I mean that it occupies a time: and by 'extends to something' I mean that it involves the traversing of a certain amount of distance: for at any moment when a thing is causing motion, it also has caused motion, so that there must always be a certain amount of distance that has been traversed and a certain amount of time that has been occu- [30] pied). If, then, A the movent have moved B a distance Γ in a time Δ, then in the same time the same force A will move $\frac{1}{2}$B twice the distance Γ, and in $\frac{1}{2}\Delta$ it will move $\frac{1}{2}$B the whole distance Γ: for thus the rules of proportion will be observed. Again if a given [5] force move a given weight a certain distance in a certain time and half the distance in half the time, half the motive power will move half the weight the same distance in the same time. Let E represent half the motive power A and Z half the weight B: then the ratio between the motive power and the weight in the one case is similar and proportionate to the ratio in the other, so that each force will cause the same distance to be traversed in the same time. [10] But if E move Z a distance Γ in a time Δ, it does not necessarily follow that E can move twice Z half the distance Γ in the same time. If, then, A move B a distance Γ in a time Δ, it does not follow that E, being half of A, will in the time Δ or in any fraction of it cause B to traverse a part of Γ the ratio between which and the whole of Γ is proportionate to that between A and E (whatever fraction of A E may [15] be): in fact it might well be that it will cause no motion at all; for it does not follow that, if a given motive power causes a certain amount of motion, half that power will cause motion either of any particular amount or in any length of time: otherwise one man might move a ship, since both the motive power of the ship-haulers and the distance that they all cause the ship to traverse are divisible into as many parts as there are men. Hence Zeno's rea- [20] soning is false when he argues that there is no part of the millet that does not make a sound: for there is no reason why any such part should not in any length of time fail to move the air that the whole bushel moves in falling. In fact it does not of itself move even such a quantity of the air as it would move if this part were by itself: for no part even exists otherwise than potentially.

[25] If on the other hand we have two forces each of which separately moves one of two weights a given distance in a given time, then the forces in combination will move the combined weights an equal distance in an equal time: for in this case the rules of proportion apply.

Then does this hold good of alteration and of increase also? Surely it does, for in any given case we have a definite thing that causes in- [30] crease and a definite thing that suffers increase, and the one causes and the other suffers a certain amount of increase in a certain amount of time. Similarly we have a definite thing that causes alteration and a definite thing that undergoes alteration, and a certain amount, or rather degree, of alteration is completed in a certain amount of time: thus in twice as much time twice as much alteration will be completed and conversely twice as much alteration will occupy twice as much time: and the alteration of half of its object will occupy half as much time and in half as much time half of the object will be altered: or again, in the same amount of time it will be altered twice as much.

On the other hand if that which causes alteration or increase causes a certain amount of increase or alteration respectively in a certain [5] amount of time, it does not necessarily follow that half the force will occupy twice the time in altering or increasing the object, or that in twice the time the alteration or increase will be completed by it: it may happen that there will be no alteration or increase at all, the case being the same as with the weight.

BOOK VIII

1

It remains to consider the following question. Was there ever a becoming of motion before which it had no being, and is it perishing again so as to leave nothing in motion? Or are we to say that it never had any becoming and is not perishing, but always was and always will be? Is it in fact an immortal never-failing property of things that are, a sort of life as it were to all naturally constituted things?

[15] Now the *existence* of motion is asserted by all who have anything to say about nature, because they all concern themselves with the construction of the world and study the question of becoming and perishing, which processes could not come about without the existence of motion. But those who say that there is an infinite number of worlds, some of which are in process of becoming while others are in [20] process of perishing, assert that there is always motion (for these processes of becoming and perishing of the worlds necessarily involve motion), whereas those who hold that there is only one world, whether everlasting or not, make corresponding assumptions in regard to motion. If then it is possible that at any time nothing should be in motion, this must come about in one of two ways: either in the manner described by Anaxagoras, who says that all [25] things were together and at rest for an infinite period of time, and that then Mind introduced motion and separated them; or in the manner described by Empedocles, according to whom the universe is alternately in motion and at rest—in motion, when Love is making the one out of many, or Strife is making many out of one, and at rest in the intermediate periods of time—his account being as follows:

[30] '*Since One hath learned to spring from Manifold,*

And One disjoined makes Manifold arise,

251ᵃ *Thus they Become, nor stable is their life:*

But since their motion must alternate be,

Thus have they ever Rest upon their round':

for we must suppose that he means by this that [5] they alternate from the one motion to the other. We must consider, then, how this matter stands, for the discovery of the truth about it is of importance, not only for the study of nature, but also for the investigation of the First Principle.

Let us take our start from what we have already[1] laid down in our course on Physics. Motion, we say, is the fulfilment of the movable in [10] so far as it is movable. Each kind of motion, therefore, necessarily involves the presence of the things that are capable of that motion. In fact, even apart from the definition of motion, every one would admit that in each kind of motion it is that which is capable of that motion that is in motion: thus it is that which is capable of alteration that is altered, and that which is capable of local change that [15] is in locomotion: and so there must be something capable of being burned before there can be a process of being burned, and something capable of burning before there can be a process of burning. Moreover, these things also must either have a beginning before which they had no being, or they must be eternal. Now if there was a becoming of every movable thing, it follows that before the motion in question another change or motion must have taken place in which that which was capable of being moved or of causing motion had its becoming. [20] To suppose, on the other hand, that these things were in being throughout all previous time without there being any motion appears unreasonable on a moment's thought, and still more unreasonable, we shall find, on further consideration. For if we are to say that, while there are on the one hand things that are movable, and on the other hand things that are motive, there is a time when there is a first movent and a first moved, and another time when there is no such thing but only something that is at [25] rest, then this thing that is at rest must previously have been in process of change: for there must have been some cause of its rest, rest being the privation of motion. Therefore, before this first change there will be a previous change. For some things cause motion in only one way, while others can produce either of two contrary motions: thus fire causes heating [30] but not cooling, whereas it would seem that knowledge may be directed to two contrary ends while remaining one and the same. Even in the former class, however, there seems to be something similar, for a cold thing in a sense causes heating by turning away and retiring, just as one possessed of knowledge vol-

[1] III. 1.

untarily makes an error when he uses his 251ᵇ knowledge in the reverse way. But at any rate all things that are capable respectively of affecting and being affected, or of causing motion and being moved, are capable of it not under all conditions, but only when they are in a particular condition and approach one another: so it is on the approach of one thing to another that the one causes motion and the other is moved, and when they are present under such conditions as rendered the one motive and [5] the other movable. So if the motion was not always in process, it is clear that they must have been in a condition not such as to render them capable respectively of being moved and of causing motion, and one or other of them must have been in process of change: for in what is relative this is a necessary consequence: e.g. if one thing is double another when before it was not so, one or other of them, if not both, must have been in process of change. It follows, then, that there will be a process of change previous to the first.

[10] (Further, how can there be any 'before' and 'after' without the existence of time? Or how can there be any time without the existence of motion? If, then, time is the number of motion or itself a kind of motion, it follows that, if there is always time, motion must also be eternal. But so far as time is concerned we see that all with one exception are in agreement in saying that it is uncreated: in fact, it is just [15] this that enables Democritus to show that all things cannot have had a becoming: for time, he says, is uncreated. Plato alone asserts the creation of time, saying¹ that it had a becoming together with the universe, the universe according to him having had a becoming. Now since time cannot exist and is unthinkable apart from the moment, and the moment [20] is a kind of middle-point, uniting as it does in itself both a beginning and an end, a beginning of future time and an end of past time, it follows that there must always be time: for the extremity of the last period of time that we take must be found in some moment, since time contains no point of contact for us except [25] the moment. Therefore, since the moment is both a beginning and an end, there must always be time on both sides of it. But if this is true of time, it is evident that it must also be true of motion, time being a kind of affection of motion.)

The same reasoning will also serve to show the imperishability of motion: just as a becoming of motion would involve, as we saw, the [30] existence of a process of change previous to the first, in the same way a perishing of motion would involve the existence of a process of change subsequent to the last: for when a thing ceases to be moved, it does not therefore at the same time cease to be movable—e.g. the cessation of the process of being burned does not involve the cessation of the capacity of being burned, since a thing may be capable of being burned without being in process of being burned—nor, when a thing ceases to be movent, does it therefore at the same time cease to 252ᵃ be motive. Again, the destructive agent will have to be destroyed, after what it destroys has been destroyed, and then that which has the capacity of destroying *it* will have to be destroyed afterwards, ⟨so that there will be a process of change subsequent to the last,⟩ for being destroyed also is a kind of change. If, then, the view which we are criticizing involves these impossible consequences, it is clear that motion is eternal and cannot have existed at one time and not at another: in fact, such a view can hardly be described as anything else than fantastic.

[5] And much the same may be said of the view that such is the ordinance of nature and that this must be regarded as a principle, as would seem to be the view of Empedocles when he says that the constitution of the world is of necessity such that Love and Strife alternately predominate and cause motion, while in the intermediate period of time there is a state of rest. [10] Probably also those who, like Anaxagoras, assert a single principle ⟨of motion⟩ would hold this view. But that which is produced or directed by nature can never be anything disorderly: for nature is everywhere the cause of order. Moreover, there is no ratio in the relation of the infinite to the infinite, whereas order always means ratio. But if we say that there is first a state of rest for an infinite time, and [15] then motion is started at some moment, and that the fact that it is this rather than a previous moment is of no importance, and involves no order, then we can no longer say that it is nature's work: for if anything is of a certain character *naturally,* it either is so invariably and is not sometimes of this and sometimes of another character (e.g. fire, which travels upwards naturally, does not sometimes do so and sometimes not) or there is a ratio in the variation. It would be better, therefore, to [20] say with Empedocles and any one else who may have maintained such a theory as

---
¹Aristotle is thinking of a passage in the *Timaeus* (38).

his that the universe is alternately at rest and in motion: for in a system of this kind we have at once a certain order. But even here the holder of the theory ought not only to assert the fact: he ought to explain the cause of it: i.e. he should not make any mere assumption or lay down any gratuitous axiom, but should em-[25] ploy either inductive or demonstrative reasoning. The Love and Strife postulated by Empedocles are not in themselves causes of the fact in question, nor is it of the essence of either that it should be so, the essential function of the former being to unite, of the latter to separate. If he is to go on to explain this alternate predominance, he should adduce cases where such a state of things exists, as he points to the fact that among mankind we have something that unites men, namely Love, while on the [30] other hand enemies avoid one another: thus from the observed fact that this occurs in certain cases comes the assumption that it occurs also in the universe. Then, again, some argument is needed to explain why the predominance of each of the two forces lasts for an equal period of time. But it is a wrong assumption to suppose universally that we have an adequate first principle in virtue of the fact that something always is so or always happens so. Thus Democritus reduces the causes that explain nature to the fact that things happened in the past in the same way as they happen [35] now: but he does not think fit to seek for 252^b a first principle to explain this 'always': so, while his theory is right in so far as it is applied to certain individual cases, he is wrong in making it of universal application. Thus, a triangle always has its angles equal to two right angles, but there is nevertheless an ulterior cause of the eternity of this truth, whereas first principles are eternal and have no ulterior [5] cause. Let this conclude what we have to say in support of our contention that there never was a time when there was not motion, and never will be a time when there will not be motion.

2

The arguments that may be advanced against this position are not difficult to dispose of. The chief considerations that might be thought to indicate that motion may exist though at one time it had not existed at all are the following:

First, it may be said that no process of change is eternal: for the nature of all change [10] is such that it proceeds *from* something *to* something, so that every process of change must be bounded by the contraries that mark its course, and no motion can go on to infinity.

Secondly, we see that a thing that neither is in motion nor contains any motion within itself can be set in motion; e.g. inanimate things that are (whether the whole or some part is in question) not in motion but at rest, are at [15] some moment set in motion: whereas, if motion cannot have a becoming before which it had no being, these things ought to be either always or never in motion.

Thirdly, the fact is evident above all in the case of animate beings: for it sometimes happens that there is no motion in us and we are quite still, and that nevertheless we are then at some moment set in motion, that is to say it sometimes happens that we produce a begin-[20] ning of motion in ourselves spontaneously without anything having set us in motion from without. We see nothing like this in the case of inanimate things, which are always set in motion by something else from without: the animal, on the other hand, we say, moves itself: therefore, if an animal is ever in a state of absolute rest, we have a motionless thing in which motion can be produced from the thing itself, and not from without. Now if this [25] can occur in an animal, why should not the same be true also of the universe as a whole? If it can occur in a small world it could also occur in a great one: and if it can occur in the world, it could also occur in the infinite; that is, if the infinite could as a whole possibly be in motion or at rest.

Of these objections, then, the first-mentioned [30]—that motion to opposites is not always the same and numerically one—is a correct statement; in fact, this may be said to be a necessary conclusion, provided that it is possible for the motion of that which is one and the same to be not always one and the same. (I mean that e.g. we may question whether the note given by a single string is one and the same, or is different each time the string is struck, although the string is in the same condition and is moved in the same way.) But [35] still, however this may be, there is nothing to prevent there being a motion that is the 253^a same in virtue of being continuous and eternal: we shall have something to say later[1] that will make this point clearer.

As regards the second objection, no absurdity is involved in the fact that something not in motion may be set in motion, that which caused the motion from without being at one

---
[1] Chapter 8.

time present, and at another absent. Nevertheless, how this can be so remains matter for inquiry; how it comes about, I mean, that the same motive force at one time causes a thing to be in motion, and at another does not do so: [5] for the difficulty raised by our objector really amounts to this—why is it that some things are not always at rest, and the rest always in motion?

The third objection may be thought to present more difficulty than the others, namely, that which alleges that motion arises in things in which it did not exist before, and adduces in proof the case of animate things: thus an [10] animal is first at rest and afterwards walks, not having been set in motion apparently by anything from without. This, however, is false: for we observe that there is always some part of the animal's organism in motion, and the cause of the motion of this part is not the animal itself, but, it may be, its environment. Moreover, we say that the animal itself originates not all of its motions but its locomotion. [15] So it may well be the case—or rather we may perhaps say that it must necessarily be the case—that many motions are produced in the body by its environment, and some of these set in motion the intellect or the appetite, and this again then sets the whole animal in motion: this is what happens when animals are asleep: though there is then no perceptive motion in them, there is some motion that causes [20] them to wake up again. But we will leave this point also to be elucidated at a later[1] stage in our discussion.

3

Our enquiry will resolve itself at the outset into a consideration of the above-mentioned problem—what can be the reason why some things in the world at one time are in motion and at another are at rest again? Now one of three things must be true: either all things are al- [25] ways at rest, or all things are always in motion, or some things are in motion and others at rest: and in this last case again either the things that are in motion are always in motion and the things that are at rest are always at rest, or they are all constituted so as to be capable alike of motion and of rest; or there is yet a third possibility remaining—it may be that some things in the world are always motionless, others always in motion, while others again admit of both conditions. This last is [30] the account of the matter that we must

[1] Chapter 6.

give: for herein lies the solution of all the difficulties raised and the conclusion of the investigation upon which we are engaged.

To maintain that all things are at rest, and to disregard sense-perception in an attempt to show the theory to be reasonable, would be an instance of intellectual weakness: it would call in question a whole system, not a particular [35] detail: moreover, it would be an attack not only on the physicist but on almost all sciences and all received opinions, since motion plays a part in all of them. Further, just as in arguments about mathematics objections that involve first principles do not affect the mathematician—and the other sciences are in similar case—so, too, objections involving the point that we have just raised do not affect the [5] physicist: for it is a fundamental assumption with him that motion is ultimately referable to nature herself.

The assertion that all things are in motion we may fairly regard as equally false, though it is less subversive of physical science: for though in our course on physics it was laid down that rest no less than motion is ultimately referable to nature herself, nevertheless motion is the characteristic fact of nature: moreover, the view is actually held by some that not [10] merely some things but all things in the world are in motion and always in motion, though we cannot apprehend the fact by sense-perception. Although the supporters of this theory do not state clearly what kind of motion they mean, or whether they mean all kinds, it is no hard matter to reply to them: thus we may point out that there cannot be a continuous process either of increase or of decrease: that which comes between the two has [15] to be included. The theory resembles that about the stone being worn away by the drop of water or split by plants growing out of it: if so much has been extruded or removed by the drop, it does not follow that half the amount has previously been extruded or removed in half the time: the case of the hauled ship is exactly comparable: here we have so many drops setting so much in motion, but a part of them will not set as much in motion in any period of time. The amount removed is, it is true, di- [20] visible into a number of parts, but no one of these was set in motion separately: they were all set in motion together. It is evident, then, that from the fact that the decrease is divisible into an infinite number of parts it does not follow that some part must always be passing away: it all passes away at a particular moment. Similarly, too, in the case of any alteration whatever if that which suffers alteration is infinitely divisible it does not follow from [25] this that the same is true of the alteration itself, which often occurs all at once, as in freezing. Again, when any one has fallen ill, there must follow a period of time in which his restoration to health is in the future: the process of change cannot take place in an instant: yet the change cannot be a change to anything else but health. The assertion, therefore, that alteration is continuous is an extravagant call- [30] ing into question of the obvious: for alteration is a change from one contrary to another. Moreover, we notice that a stone becomes neither harder nor softer. Again, in the matter of locomotion, it would be a strange thing if a stone could be falling or resting on the ground without our being able to perceive the fact. Further, it is a law of nature that earth and all other bodies should remain in [35] their proper places and be moved from them only by violence: from the fact then that some of them are in their proper places it follows that in respect of place also all things can- 254ᵃ not be in motion. These and other similar arguments, then, should convince us that it is impossible either that all things are always in motion or that all things are always at rest.

Nor again can it be that some things are always at rest, others always in motion, and nothing sometimes at rest and sometimes in [5] motion. This theory must be pronounced impossible on the same grounds as those previously mentioned: viz. that we see the above-mentioned changes occurring in the case of the same things. We may further point out that the defender of this position is fighting against the obvious, for on this theory there can be no such thing as increase: nor can there be any such thing as compulsory motion, if it is impossible that a thing can be at rest before being [10] set in motion unnaturally. This theory, then, does away with becoming and perishing. Moreover, motion, it would seem, is generally thought to be a sort of becoming and perishing, for that to which a thing changes comes to be, or occupancy of it comes to be, and that from which a thing changes ceases to be, or there ceases to be occupancy of it. It is clear, therefore, that there are cases of occasional motion and occasional rest.

[15] We have now to take the assertion that all things are sometimes at rest and sometimes in motion and to confront it with the arguments previously advanced. We must take our start as before from the possibilities that we distinguished just above. Either all things are at rest, or all things are in motion, or some things are at rest and others in motion. And if some things are at rest and others in motion, [20] then it must be that either all things are sometimes at rest and sometimes in motion, or some things are always at rest and the remainder always in motion, or some of the things are always at rest and others always in motion while others again are sometimes at rest and sometimes in motion. Now we have said before that it is impossible that all things should be at rest: nevertheless we may now repeat that assertion. We may point out that, [25] even if it is really the case, as certain persons assert, that the existent is infinite and motionless, it certainly does not appear to be so if we follow sense-perception: many things that exist appear to be in motion. Now if there is such a thing as false opinion or opinion at all, there is also motion; and similarly if there is such a thing as imagination, or if it is the case that anything seems to be different at different times: for imagination and opinion are [30] thought to be motions of a kind. But to investigate this question at all—to seek a reasoned justification of a belief with regard to which we are too well off to require reasoned justification—implies bad judgement of what is better and what is worse, what commends itself to belief and what does not, what is ultimate and what is not. It is likewise impossible that all things should be in motion or that some things should be always in motion and [35] the remainder always at rest. We have sufficient ground for rejecting all these theories in the single fact that we *see* some things that 254ᵇ are sometimes in motion and sometimes at rest. It is evident, therefore, that it is no less impossible that some things should be always in motion and the remainder always at rest than that all things should be at rest or that all things should be in motion continuously. It remains, then, to consider whether all things are so constituted as to be capable both of being in motion and of being at rest, or whether, [5] while some things are so constituted, some are always at rest and some are always in motion: for it is this last view that we have to show to be true.

4

Now of things that cause motion or suffer motion, to some the motion is accidental, to others essential: thus it is accidental to what merely belongs to or contains as a part a thing that causes motion or suffers motion, essential to a [10] thing that causes motion or suffers motion not merely by belonging to such a thing or containing it as a part.

Of things to which the motion is essential some derive their motion from themselves, others from something else: and in some cases their motion is natural, in others violent and unnatural. Thus in things that derive their [15] motion from themselves, e.g. all animals, the motion is natural (for when an animal is in motion its motion is derived from itself): and whenever the source of the motion of a thing is in the thing itself we say that the motion of that thing is natural. Therefore the animal as a whole moves itself naturally: but the body of the animal may be in motion unnaturally as well as naturally: it depends upon the kind of motion that it may chance to be suffering and [20] the kind of element of which it is composed. And the motion of things that derive their motion from something else is in some cases natural, in other unnatural: e.g. upward motion of earthy things and downward motion of fire are unnatural. Moreover the parts of animals are often in motion in an unnatural way, their positions and the character of the motion being abnormal. The fact that a thing [25] that is in motion derives its motion from something is most evident in things that are in motion unnaturally, because in such cases it is clear that the motion is derived from something other than the thing itself. Next to things that are in motion unnaturally those whose motion while natural is derived from themselves—e.g. animals—make this fact clear: for here the uncertainty is not as to whether the motion is derived from something but as to how we ought to distinguish in the thing between the movent and the moved. It would [30] seem that in animals, just as in ships and things not naturally organized, that which causes motion is separate from that which suffers motion, and that it is only in this sense that the animal as a whole causes its own motion.

The greatest difficulty, however, is presented by the remaining case of those that we last distinguished. Where things derive their motion from something else we distinguished [35] the cases in which the motion is unnatural: we are left with those that are to be contrasted with the others by reason of the fact 255ᵃ that the motion is natural. It is in these cases that difficulty would be experienced in deciding whence the motion is derived, e.g. in the case of light and heavy things. When these things are in motion to positions the reverse of those they would properly occupy, their motion is violent: when they are in motion to their proper positions—the light thing up and the heavy thing down—their motion is natural; but in this latter case it is no longer evident, as it is when the motion is unnatural, [5] whence their motion is derived. It is impossible to say that their motion is derived from themselves: this is a characteristic of life and peculiar to living things. Further, if it were, it would have been in their power to stop themselves (I mean that if e.g. a thing can cause itself to walk it can also cause itself not to walk), and so, since on this supposition fire itself possesses the power of upward locomotion, it is clear that it should also possess the [10] power of downward locomotion. Moreover if things move themselves, it would be unreasonable to suppose that in only one kind of motion is their motion derived from themselves. Again, how can anything of continuous and naturally connected substance move itself? In so far as a thing is one and continuous not merely in virtue of contact, it is impassive: it is only in so far as a thing is divided that one part of it is by nature active and another [15] passive. Therefore none of the things that we are now considering move themselves (for they are of naturally connected substance), nor does anything else that is continuous: in each case the movent must be separate from the moved, as we see to be the case with inanimate things when an animate thing moves them. It is the fact that these things also always derive their motion from something: what it is would become evident if we were to distinguish the different kinds of cause.

[20] The above-mentioned distinctions can also be made in the case of things that cause motion: some of them are capable of causing motion unnaturally (e.g. the lever is not naturally capable of moving the weight), others naturally (e.g. what is actually hot is naturally capable of moving what is potentially hot): and similarly in the case of all other things of this kind.

In the same way, too, what is potentially of a certain quality or of a certain quantity or in a [25] certain place is naturally movable when it contains the corresponding principle in itself and not accidentally (for the same thing may be both of a certain quality and of a certain quantity, but the one is an accidental, not an essential property of the other). So when fire or earth is moved by something the motion is violent when it is unnatural, and natural when it brings to actuality the proper activities that [30] they potentially possess. But the fact that the term 'potentially' is used in more than one sense is the reason why it is not evident whence such motions as the upward motion of fire and the downward motion of earth are derived. One who is learning a science potentially knows it in a different sense from one who while already possessing the knowledge is not actually exercising it. Wherever we have something capable of acting and something capable of being correspondingly acted on, in the event [35] of any such pair being in contact what is 255[b] potential becomes at times actual: e.g. the learner becomes from one potential something another potential something: for one who possesses knowledge of a science but is not actually exercising it knows the science potentially in a sense, though not in the same sense as he knew it potentially before he learnt it. And when he is in this condition, if something does not prevent him, he actively exercises his knowledge: otherwise he would be in the contradictory state of not knowing. In re- [5] gard to natural bodies also the case is similar. Thus what is cold is potentially hot: then a change takes place and it is fire, and it burns, unless something prevents and hinders it. So, too, with heavy and light: light is generated from heavy, e.g. air from water (for water is [10] the first thing that is potentially light), and air is actually light, and will at once realize its proper activity as such unless something prevents it. The activity of lightness consists in the light thing being in a certain situation, namely high up: when it is in the contrary situation, it is being prevented from rising. The case is similar also in regard to quantity and quality. But, be it noted, this is the question we are trying to answer—how can we account for the motion of light things and heavy things to their proper situations? The reason for it is [15] that they have a natural tendency respectively towards a certain position: and this constitutes the essence of lightness and heaviness, the former being determined by an upward, the latter by a downward, tendency. As we have said, a thing may be potentially light or heavy in more senses than one. Thus not only when a thing is water is it in a sense potentially light, but when it has become air it may be still potentially light: for it may be that through some hindrance it does not occupy an upper [20] position, whereas, if what hinders it is removed, it realizes its activity and continues to rise higher. The process whereby what is of a certain quality changes to a condition of active existence is similar: thus the exercise of knowledge follows at once upon the possession of it unless something prevents it. So, too, what is of a certain quantity extends itself over a certain space unless something prevents it. The thing in a sense is and in a sense is not moved by one who moves what is obstructing and [25] preventing its motion (e.g. one who pulls away a pillar from under a roof or one who removes a stone from a wineskin in the water is the accidental cause of motion): and in the same way the real cause of the motion of a ball rebounding from a wall is not the wall but the thrower. So it is clear that in all these cases the [30] thing does not move itself, but it contains within itself the source of motion—not of moving something or of causing motion, but of suffering it.

If then the motion of all things that are in motion is either natural or unnatural and violent, and all things whose motion is violent and unnatural are moved by something, and something other than themselves, and again all things whose motion is natural are moved by something—both those that are moved by themselves and those that are not moved by them- [35] selves (e.g. light things and heavy things, 256[a] which are moved either by that which brought the thing into existence as such and made it light and heavy, or by that which released what was hindering and preventing it); then all things that are in motion must be moved by something.

5

Now this may come about in either of two ways. Either the movent is not itself responsible for the motion, which is to be referred to something else which moves the movent, [5] or the movent is itself responsible for the motion. Further, in the latter case, either the movent immediately precedes the last thing in the series, or there may be one or more intermediate links: e.g. the stick moves the stone and is moved by the hand, which again is moved by the man: in the man, however, we have reached a movent that is not so in virtue of being moved by something else. Now we say that the thing is moved both by the last and by the first movent in the series, but more

[10] strictly by the first, since the first movent moves the last, whereas the last does not move the first, and the first will move the thing without the last, but the last will not move it without the first: e.g. the stick will not move anything unless it is itself moved by the man. If then everything that is in motion must be moved by something, and the movent must either itself be moved by something else or not, [15] and in the former case there must be some first movent that is not itself moved by anything else, while in the case of the immediate movent being of this kind there is no need of an intermediate movent that is also moved (for it is impossible that there should be an infinite series of movents, each of which is itself moved by something else, since in an infinite series there is no first term)—if then everything that is in motion is moved by some-[20] thing, and the first movent is moved but not by anything else, it much be moved by itself.

This same argument may also be stated in another way as follows. Every movent moves something and moves it with something, either with itself or with something else: e.g. a man moves a thing either himself or with a stick, and a thing is knocked down either by the [25] wind itself or by a stone propelled by the wind. But it is impossible for that with which a thing is moved to move it without being moved by that which imparts motion by its own agency: on the other hand, if a thing imparts motion by its own agency, it is not necessary that there should be anything else with which it imparts motion, whereas if there is a different thing with which it imparts motion, there must be something that imparts motion not with something else but with itself, or else there will be an infinite series. If, then, anything is a movent while being itself moved, [30] the series must stop somewhere and not be infinite. Thus, if the stick moves something in virtue of being moved by the hand, the hand moves the stick: and if something else moves with the *hand*, the hand also is moved by something different from itself. So when motion by means of an instrument is at each stage caused by something different from the instrument, this must always be preceded by something else which imparts motion with itself. Therefore, if this last movent is in motion and there **256ᵇ** is nothing else that moves it, it must move itself. So this reasoning also shows that, when a thing is moved, if it is not moved immediately by something that moves itself, the series brings us at some time or other to a movent of this kind.

And if we consider the matter in yet a third way we shall get this same result as follows. [5] If everything that is in motion is moved by something that is in motion, ether this being in motion is an accidental attribute of the movents in question, so that each of them moves something while being itself in motion, but not always because it is itself in motion, or it is not accidental but an essential attribute. Let us consider the former alternative. If then it is an accidental attribute, it is not necessary that that which is in motion should be in motion: and if this is so it is clear that there may be a time when nothing that exists is in motion, since the accidental is not [10] necessary but contingent. Now if we assume the existence of a possibility, any conclusion that we thereby reach will not be an impossibility, though it may be contrary to fact. But the non-existence of motion is an impossibility: for we have shown above[1] that there must always be motion.

Moreover, the conclusion to which we have been led is a reasonable one. For there must be three things—the moved, the movent, and the [15] instrument of motion. Now the moved must be in motion, but it need not move anything else: the instrument of motion must both move something else and be itself in motion (for it changes together with the moved, with which it is in contact and continuous, as is clear in the case of things that move other things locally, in which case the two things must up to a certain point be in contact): and the movent—that is to say, that which causes motion in such a manner that it is not merely the instrument of motion—must be unmoved. [20] Now we have visual experience of the last term in this series, namely that which has the capacity of being in motion, but does not contain a motive principle, and also of that which is in motion but is moved by itself and not by anything else: it is reasonable, therefore, not to say necessary, to suppose the existence of the third term also, that which causes motion but is itself unmoved. So, too, Anaxagoras [25] is right when he says that Mind is impassive and unmixed, since he makes it the principle of motion: for it could cause motion in this sense only by being itself unmoved, and have supreme control only by being unmixed.

We will now take the second alternative. If the movent is not accidentally but necessarily

[1] Chapter 1.

in motion—so that, if it were not in motion, it would not move anything—then the movent, in so far as it is in motion, must be in motion [30] in one of two ways: it is moved either as that is which is moved with the same kind of motion, or with a different kind—either that which is heating, I mean, is itself in process of becoming hot, that which is making healthy in process of becoming healthy, and that which is causing locomotion in process of locomotion, or else that which is making healthy is, let us say, in process of locomotion, and that which is causing locomotion in process of, say, increase. But it is evident that this is impossible. For if we adopt the first assumption we have to make it apply within each of the very lowest species 257a into which motion can be divided: e.g. we must say that if some one is teaching some lesson in geometry, he is also in process of being taught that same lesson in geometry, and that if he is throwing he is in process of being thrown in just the same manner. Or if we reject this assumption we must say that one kind of motion is derived from another; e.g. that that which is causing locomotion is in process [5] of increase, that which is causing this increase is in process of being altered by something else, and that which is causing this alteration is in process of suffering some different kind of motion. But the series must stop somewhere, since the kinds of motion are limited; and if we say that the process is reversible, and that that which is causing alteration is in process of locomotion, we do no more than if we had said at the outset that that which is causing locomotion is in process of locomotion, and [10] that one who is teaching is in process of being taught: for it is clear that everything that is moved is moved by the movent that is further back in the series as well as by that which immediately moves it: in fact the earlier movent is that which more strictly moves it. But this is of course impossible: for it involves the consequence that one who is teaching is in process of learning what he is teaching, whereas teaching necessarily implies possessing knowledge, and learning not possessing it. Still more unreasonable is the consequence involved [15] that, since everything that is moved is moved by something that is itself moved by something else, everything that has a capacity for causing motion has as such a corresponding capacity for being moved: i.e. it will have a capacity for being moved in the sense in which one might say that everything that has a capacity for making healthy, and exercises that capacity, has as such a capacity for being made healthy, and that which has a capacity for building has as such a capacity for being built. It will have the capacity for being thus moved either immediately or through one or more links (as it will if, while everything that has a capacity for causing motion has as such a capacity for being moved by something [20] else, the motion that it has the capacity for suffering is not that with which it affects what is next to it, but a motion of a different kind; e.g. that which has a capacity for making healthy might as such have a capacity for learning: the series, however, could be traced back, as we said before, until at some time or other we arrived at the same kind of motion). Now the first alternative is impossible, and the second is fantastic: it is absurd that that which has a capacity for causing alteration should as [25] such necessarily have a capacity, let us say, for increase. It is not necessary, therefore, that that which is moved should always be moved by something else that is itself moved by something else: so there will be an end to the series. Consequently the first thing that is in motion will derive its motion either from something that is at rest or from itself. But if there *were* any need to consider which of the two, that which moves itself or that which is moved by something else, is the cause and principle of motion, every one would decide [30] for the former: for that which is itself independently a cause is always prior as a cause to that which is so only in virtue of being itself dependent upon something else that makes it so.

We must therefore make a fresh start and consider the question; if a thing moves itself, in what sense and in what manner does it do so? Now everything that is in motion must be infinitely divisible, for it has been shown already[1] in our general course on Physics, 257b that everything that is essentially in motion is continuous. Now it is impossible that that which moves itself should in its entirety move itself: for then, while being specifically one and indivisible, it would as a whole both undergo and cause the same locomotion or alteration: thus it would at the same time be both [5] teaching and being taught ⟨the same thing⟩, or both restoring to and being restored to the same health. Moreover, we have established the fact that it is the movable that is moved; and this is potentially, not actually, in motion, but the potential is in process to actu-

[1] The reference is apparently to vi. 4 (234b 10 sqq.).

ality, and motion is an incomplete actuality of the movable. The movent on the other hand is already in activity: e.g. it is that which is hot that produces heat: in fact, that which produces the form is always something that pos-[10] sesses it. Consequently (if a thing can move itself as a whole), the same thing in respect of the same thing may be at the same time both hot and not hot. So, too, in every other case where the movent must be described by the same name in the same sense as the moved. Therefore when a thing moves itself it is one part of it that is the movent and another part that is moved. But it is not self-moving in the sense that each of the two parts is moved by the other part: the following considerations [15] make this evident. In the first place, if each of the two parts is to move the other, there will be no first movent. If a thing is moved by a series of movents, that which is earlier in the series is more the cause of its being moved than that which comes next, and will be more truly the movent: for we found that there are two kinds of movent, that which is itself moved by something else and that which derives its motion from itself: and that which is further from the thing that is moved is nearer to the principle of motion than that [20] which is intermediate. In the second place, there is no necessity for the movent part to be moved by anything but itself: so it can only be accidentally that the other part moves it in return. I take then the possible case of its not moving it: then there will be a part that is moved and a part that is an unmoved movent. In the third place, there is no necessity for the movent to be moved in return: on the contrary the necessity that there should always be motion makes it necessary that there should be some movent that is either unmoved or moved [25] by itself. In the fourth place we should then have a thing undergoing the same motion that it is causing—that which is producing heat, therefore, being heated. But as a matter of fact that which primarily moves itself cannot contain either a single part that moves itself or a number of parts each of which moves itself. For, if the whole is moved by itself, it must be moved either by some part of itself or [30] as a whole by itself as a whole. If, then, it is moved in virtue of some part of it being moved by that part itself, it is this part that will be the primary self-movent, since, if this part is separated from the whole, the part will still move itself, but the whole will do so no longer. If on the other hand the whole is moved by itself as a whole, it must be accidentally that the parts move themselves: and therefore, their self-motion not being necessary, we may 258ᵃ take the case of their not being moved by themselves. Therefore in the whole of the thing we may distinguish that which imparts motion without itself being moved and that which is moved: for only in this way is it possible for a thing to be self-moved. Further, if the whole moves itself we may distinguish in it that which imparts the motion and that which is moved: so while we say that AB is moved by [5] itself, we may also say that it is moved by A. And since that which imparts motion may be either a thing that is moved by something else or a thing that is unmoved, and that which is moved may be either a thing that imparts motion to something else or a thing that does not, that which moves itself must be composed of something that is unmoved but imparts motion and also of something that is moved but does not necessarily impart motion but may or may not do so. Thus let A be something that imparts motion but is unmoved, B something that is moved by A and moves Γ, Γ some-[10] thing that is moved by B but moves nothing (granted that we eventually arrive at Γ we may take it that there is only one intermediate term, though there may be more). Then the whole ABΓ moves itself. But if I take away Γ, AB will move itself, A imparting motion and B being moved, whereas Γ will not move itself or in fact be moved at all. Nor [15] again will BΓ move itself apart from A: for B imparts motion only through being moved by something else, not through being moved by any part of itself. So only AB moves itself. That which moves itself, therefore, must comprise something that imparts motion but is unmoved and something that is moved but [20] does not necessarily move anything else: and each of these two things, or at any rate one of them, must be in contact with the other. If, then, that which imparts motion is a continuous substance—that which is moved must of course be so—it is clear that it is not through some part of the whole being of such a nature as to be capable of moving itself that the whole moves itself: it moves itself as a whole, both being moved and imparting motion through [25] containing a part that imparts motion and a part that is moved. It does not impart motion as a whole nor is it moved as a whole: it is A alone that imparts motion and B alone that is moved. It is not true, further, that Γ is moved by A, which is impossible.

Here a difficulty arises: if something is taken away from A (supposing that that which imparts motion but is unmoved is a continuous substance), or from B the part that is moved, will the remainder of A continue to impart mo-[30] tion or the remainder of B continue to be moved? If so, it will not be AB primarily that is moved by itself, since, when something is taken away from AB, the remainder of AB will still continue to move itself. Perhaps we 258b may state the case thus: there is nothing to prevent each of the two parts, or at any rate one of them, that which is moved, being divisible though actually undivided, so that if it is divided it will not continue in the possession of the same capacity: and so there is nothing to prevent self-motion residing primarily in things that are potentially divisible.

From what has been said, then, it is evident [5] that that which primarily imparts motion is unmoved: for, whether the series is closed at once by that which is in motion but moved by something else deriving its motion directly from the first unmoved, or whether the motion is derived from what is in motion but moves itself and stops its own motion, on both suppositions we have the result that in all cases of things being in motion that which primarily imparts motion is unmoved.

6

[10] Since there must always be motion without intermission, there must necessarily be something, one thing or it may be a plurality, that first imparts motion, and this first movent must be unmoved. Now the question whether each of the things that are unmoved but impart motion is eternal is irrelevant to our present argument: but the following considerations will make it clear that there must necessarily be some such thing, which, while it has the capacity of moving something else, is itself unmoved and exempt from all change, which [15] can affect it neither in an unqualified nor in an accidental sense. Let us suppose, if any one likes, that in the case of certain things it is possible for them at different times to be and not to be, without any process of becoming and perishing (in fact it would seem to be necessary, if a thing that has not parts at one time is and at another time is not, that any such thing should without undergoing any process of change at one time be and at another time [20] not be). And let us further suppose it possible that some principles that are unmoved but capable of imparting motion at one time are and at another time are not. Even so, this cannot be true of *all* such principles, since there must clearly be something that *causes* things that move themselves at one time to be and at another not to be. For, since nothing that has not parts can be in motion, that which [25] moves itself must as a whole have magnitude, though nothing that we have said makes this necessarily true of every movent. So the fact that some things become and others perish, and that this is so continuously, cannot be caused by any one of those things that, though they are unmoved, do not always exist: nor again can it be caused by any of those which move certain particular things, while others move other things. The eternity and continuity of the process cannot be caused either by any one of them singly or by the sum of them, [30] because this causal relation must be eternal and necessary, whereas the sum of these movents is infinite and they do not all exist together. It is clear, then, that though there may be countless instances of the perishing of 259a some principles that are unmoved but impart motion, and though many things that move themselves perish and are succeeded by others that come into being, and though one thing that is unmoved moves one thing while another moves another, nevertheless there is something that comprehends them all, and that as something apart from each one of them, and this it is that is the cause of the fact that some things are and others are not and of the con-[5] tinuous process of change: and this causes the motion of the other movents, while they are the causes of the motion of other things. Motion, then, being eternal, the first movent, if there is but one, will be eternal also: if there are more than one, there will be a plurality of such eternal movents. We ought, however, to suppose that there is one rather than many, and a finite rather than an infinite number. When the consequences of either assumption are the same, we should always assume that things are finite rather than infinite in number, since [10] in things constituted by nature that which is finite and that which is better ought, if possible, to be present rather than the reverse: and here it is sufficient to assume only one movent, the first of unmoved things, which being eternal will be the principle of motion to everything else.

The following argument also makes it evident that the first movent must be something that is one and eternal. We have shown[1] that

[1] Chapter 1.

[15] there must always be motion. That being so, motion must also be continuous, because what is always is continuous, whereas what is merely in succession is not continuous. But further, if motion is continuous, it is one: and it is one only if the movent and the moved that constitute it are each of them one, since in the event of a thing's being moved now by one thing and now by another the whole motion will not be continuous but successive.

[20] Moreover a conviction that there is a first unmoved something may be reached not only from the foregoing arguments, but also by considering again the principles operative in movents. Now it is evident that among existing things there are some that are sometimes in motion and sometimes at rest. This fact has served above[1] to make it clear that it is not true either that all things are in motion or that all things are at rest or that some things are al- [25] ways at rest and the remainder always in motion: on this matter proof is supplied by things that fluctuate between the two and have the capacity of being sometimes in motion and sometimes at rest. The existence of things of this kind is clear to all: but we wish to explain also the nature of each of the other two kinds and show that there are some things that are always unmoved and some things that are always in motion. In the course of our argument [30] directed to this end we established the fact that everything that is in motion is moved by something, and that the movent is either unmoved or in motion, and that, if it is in motion, it is moved either by itself or by something else and so on throughout the series: and so we proceeded to the position that the first principle that directly causes things that are in motion to be moved is that which moves itself, and the first principle of the whole series is **259ᵇ** the unmoved. Further it is evident from actual observation that there are things that have the characteristic of moving themselves, e.g. the animal kingdom and the whole class of living things. This being so, then, the view was suggested that perhaps it may be possible for motion to come to be in a thing without having been in existence at all before, because we [5] see this actually occurring in animals: they are unmoved at one time and then again they are in motion, as it seems. We must grasp the fact, therefore, that animals move themselves only with one kind of motion, and that this is not strictly originated by them. The cause of it is not derived from the animal itself: it is

[1] Chapter 3.

connected with other natural motions in animals, which they do not experience through their own instrumentality, e.g. increase, de- [10] crease, and respiration: these are experienced by every animal while it is at rest and not in motion in respect of the motion set up by its own agency: here the motion is caused by the atmosphere and by many things that enter into the animal: thus in some cases the cause is nourishment: when it is being digested animals sleep, and when it is being distributed through the system they awake and move themselves, the first principle of this motion being thus originally derived from outside. Therefore animals are not always in continuous motion by their own agency: it is some- [15] thing else that moves them, itself being in motion and changing as it comes into relation with each several thing that moves itself. (Moreover in all these self-moving things the first movent and cause of their self-motion is itself moved by itself, though in an accidental sense: that is to say, the body changes its place, so that that which is in the body changes its place also and is a self-movent through its [20] exercise of leverage.) Hence we may confidently conclude that if a thing belongs to the class of unmoved movents that are also themselves moved accidentally, it is impossible that it should cause continuous motion. So the necessity that there should be motion continuously requires that there should be a first movent that is unmoved even accidentally, if, as we [25] have said,[2] there is to be in the world of things an unceasing and undying motion, and the world is to remain permanently self-contained and within the same limits: for if the first principle is permanent, the universe must also be permanent, since it is continuous with the first principle. (We must distinguish, however, between accidental motion of a thing by itself and such motion by something else, the former being confined to perishable things, whereas the latter belongs also to certain first principles of heavenly bodies, of all those, that [30] is to say, that experience more than one locomotion.)

And further, if there is always something of **260ᵃ** this nature, a movent that is itself unmoved and eternal, then that which is first moved by it must be eternal. Indeed this is clear also from the consideration that there would otherwise be no becoming and perishing and no change of any kind in other things, which require something that is in motion to

[2] Chapter 1.

move them: for the motion imparted by the unmoved will always be imparted in the same way and be one and the same, since the unmoved does not itself change in relation to [5] that which is moved by it. But that which is moved by something that, though it is in motion, is moved directly by the unmoved stands in varying relations to the things that it moves, so that the motion that it causes will not be always the same: by reason of the fact that it occupies contrary positions or assumes contrary forms at different times it will pro-[10] duce contrary motions in each several thing that it moves and will cause it to be at one time at rest and at another time in motion.

The foregoing argument, then, has served to clear up the point about which we raised a difficulty at the outset[1]—why is it that instead of all things being either in motion or at rest, or some things being always in motion and the remainder always at rest, there are things that are sometimes in motion and sometimes not? The cause of this is now plain: it is because, while some things are moved by an eternal unmoved movent and are therefore always in [15] motion, other things are moved by a movent that is in motion and changing, so that they too must change. But the unmoved movent, as has been said, since it remains permanently simple and unvarying and in the same state, will cause motion that is one and simple.

7

[20] This matter will be made clearer, however, if we start afresh from another point. We must consider whether it is or is not possible that there should be a continuous motion, and, if it is possible, which this motion is, and which is the primary motion: for it is plain that if there must always be motion, and a particular motion is primary and continuous, then it is [25] this motion that is imparted by the first movent, and so it is necessarily one and the same and continuous and primary.

Now of the three kinds of motion that there are—motion in respect of magnitude, motion in respect of affection, and motion in respect of place—it is this last, which we call locomotion, that must be primary. This may be shown as follows. It is impossible that there should be [30] increase without the previous occurrence of alteration: for that which is increased, although in a sense it is increased by what is like itself, is in a sense increased by what is unlike

[1] Chapter 3.

itself: thus it is said that contrary is nourishment to contrary: but growth is effected only by things becoming like to like. There must be alteration, then, in that there is this change 260ᵇ from contrary to contrary. But the fact that a thing is altered requires that there should be something that alters it, something e.g. that makes the potentially hot into the actually hot: so it is plain that the movent does not maintain a uniform relation to it but is at one time nearer to and at another farther from that [5] which is altered: and we cannot have this without locomotion. If, therefore, there must always be motion, there must also always be locomotion as the primary motion, and, if there is a primary as distinguished from a secondary form of locomotion, it must be the primary form. Again, all affections have their origin in condensation and rarefaction: thus [10] heavy and light, soft and hard, hot and cold, are considered to be forms of density and rarity. But condensation and rarefaction are nothing more than combination and separation, processes in accordance with which substances are said to become and perish: and in being combined and separated things must change in respect of place. And further, when a thing is increased or decreased its magnitude changes in respect of place.

[15] Again, there is another point of view from which it will be clearly seen that locomotion is primary. As in the case of other things so too in the case of motion the word 'primary' may be used in several senses. A thing is said to be prior to other things when, if it does not exist, the others will not exist, whereas it can exist without the others: and there is also priority in time and priority in perfection of existence. Let us begin, then, with the first sense. [20] Now there must be motion continuously, and there may be continuously either continuous motion or successive motion, the former, however, in a higher degree than the latter: moreover it is better that it should be continuous rather than successive motion, and we always assume the presence in nature of the better, if it be possible: since, then, continuous motion is possible (this will be proved later:[2] for the present let us take it for granted), and [25] no other motion can be continuous except locomotion, locomotion must be primary. For there is no necessity for the subject of locomotion to be the subject either of increase or of alteration, nor need it become or perish: on the other hand there cannot be any one of these

[2] Chapter 8.

processes without the existence of the continuous motion imparted by the first movent.

Secondly, locomotion must be primary in time: for this is the only motion possible for [30] eternal things. It is true indeed that, in the case of any individual thing that has a becoming, locomotion must be the last of its motions: for after its becoming it first experiences alteration and increase, and locomotion is a motion that belongs to such things only when they 261ᵃ are perfected. But there must previously be something else that is in process of locomotion to be the cause even of the becoming of things that become, without itself being in process of becoming, as e.g. the begotten is preceded by what begot it: otherwise becoming might be thought to be the primary motion on the ground that the thing must first become. [5] But though this is so in the case of any individual thing that becomes, nevertheless before anything becomes, something else must be in motion, not itself becoming but being, and before this there must again be something else. And since becoming cannot be primary—for, if it were, everything that is in motion would be perishable—it is plain that no one of the motions next in order can be prior to locomotion. [10] By the motions next in order I mean increase and then alteration, decrease, and perishing. All these are posterior to becoming: consequently, if not even becoming is prior to locomotion, then no one of the other processes of change is so either.

Thirdly, that which is in process of becoming appears universally as something imperfect and proceeding to a first principle: and so what is posterior in the order of becoming is prior in the order of nature. Now all things that go through the process of becoming acquire locomotion last. It is this that accounts for the fact [15] that some living things, e.g. plants and many kinds of animals, owing to lack of the requisite organ, are entirely without motion, whereas others acquire it in the course of their being perfected. Therefore, if the degree in which things possess locomotion corresponds to the degree in which they have realized their natural development, then this motion must be prior to all others in respect of perfection of ex- [20] istence: and not only for this reason but also because a thing that is in motion loses its essential character less in the process of locomotion than in any other kind of motion: it is the only motion that does not involve a change of being in the sense in which there is a change in quality when a thing is altered and a change in quantity when a thing is increased or decreased. Above all it is plain that this motion, motion in respect of place, is what is in the strictest sense produced by that which moves [25] itself; but it is the self-movent that we declare to be the first principle of things that are moved and impart motion and the primary source to which things that are in motion are to be referred.

It is clear, then, from the foregoing arguments that locomotion is the primary motion. We have now to show which kind of locomotion is primary. The same process of reasoning will also make clear at the same time the truth of the assumption we have made both now and [30] at a previous stage[1] that it is possible that there should be a motion that is continuous and eternal. Now it is clear from the following considerations that no other than locomotion can be continuous. Every other motion and change is from an opposite to an opposite: thus for the processes of becoming and perishing the limits are the existent and the non-existent, for alteration the various pairs of contrary affections, [35] and for increase and decrease either greatness and smallness or perfection and imperfection of magnitude: and changes to the respective contraries are contrary changes. Now a 261ᵇ thing that is undergoing any particular kind of motion, but though previously existent has not always undergone it, must previously have been at rest so far as that motion is concerned. It is clear, then, that for the changing thing the contraries will be states of rest. And we have a similar result in the case of changes that are not motions: for becoming and perishing, whether regarded simply as such without qualification or as affecting something in par- [5] ticular, are opposites: therefore provided it is impossible for a thing to undergo opposite changes at the same time, the change will not be continuous, but a period of time will intervene between the opposite processes. The question whether these contradictory changes are contraries or not makes no difference, provided only it is impossible for them both to be present to the same thing at the same time: the point is of no importance to the argument. Nor [10] does it matter if the thing need not *rest* in the contradictory state, or if there is no state of rest as a contrary to the process of change: it may be true that the non-existent is not at rest, and that perishing is a process to the non-existent. All that matters is the intervention of a time: it is this that prevents the change from

[1] 253ᵃ 29.

being continuous: so, too, in our previous instances the important thing was not the relation of contrariety but the impossibility of the two processes being present to a thing at the [15] same time. And there is no need to be disturbed by the fact that on this showing there may be more than one contrary to the same thing, that a particular motion will be contrary both to rest and to motion in the contrary direction. We have only to grasp the fact that a particular motion is in a sense the opposite both of a state of rest and of the contrary motion, in the same way as that which is of equal or standard measure is the opposite both of that which surpasses it and of that which it surpasses, and [20] that it is impossible for the opposite motions or changes to be present to a thing at the same time. Furthermore, in the case of becoming and perishing it would seem to be an utterly absurd thing if as soon as anything has become it must necessarily perish and cannot continue to exist for any time: and, if this is true of becoming and perishing, we have fair grounds [25] for inferring the same to be true of the other kinds of change, since it would be in the natural order of things that they should be uniform in this respect.

8

Let us now proceed to maintain that it is possible that there should be an infinite motion that is single and continuous, and that this motion is rotatory motion. The motion of everything that is in process of locomotion is either rotatory or rectilinear or a compound of the two: consequently, if one of the former two is not continuous, that which is composed of [30] them both cannot be continuous either. Now it is plain that if the locomotion of a thing is rectilinear and finite it is not continuous locomotion: for the thing must turn back, and that which turns back in a straight line undergoes two contrary locomotions, since, so far as motion in respect of place is concerned, upward motion is the contrary of downward motion, forward motion of backward motion, and mo- [35] tion to the left of motion to the right, these being the pairs of contraries in the sphere 262ª of place. But we have already[1] defined single and continuous motion to be motion of a single thing in a single period of time and operating within a sphere admitting of no further specific differentiation (for we have three things to consider, first that which is in motion, e.g. a man or a god, secondly the 'when' of the

[1] v. 4.

motion, that is to say, the time, and thirdly the sphere within which it operates, which may be either place or affection or essential form or [5] magnitude): and contraries are specifically not one and the same but distinct: and within the sphere of place we have the above-mentioned distinctions. Moreover we have an indication that motion from A to B is the contrary of motion from B to A in the fact that, if they occur at the same time, they arrest and stop each other. And the same is true in the case of a circle: the motion from A towards B is the contrary of the motion from A towards Γ: for [10] even if they are continuous and there is no turning back they arrest each other, because contraries annihilate or obstruct one another. On the other hand lateral motion is not the contrary of upward motion. But what shows most clearly that rectilinear motion cannot be continuous is the fact that turning back necessarily implies coming to a stand, not only when it is a straight line that is traversed, but also in [15] the case of locomotion in a circle (which is not the same thing as rotatory locomotion: for, when a thing merely traverses a circle, it may either proceed on its course without a break or turn back again when it has reached the same point from which it started). We may assure ourselves of the necessity of this coming to a stand not only on the strength of observation, but also on theoretical grounds. We may start as follows: we have three points, starting-point, middle-point, and finishing-point, of [20] which the middle-point in virtue of the relations in which it stands severally to the other two is both a starting-point and a finishing-point, and though numerically one is theoretically two. We have further the distinction between the potential and the actual. So in the straight line in question any one of the points lying between the two extremes is potentially a middle-point: but it is not actually so unless that which is in motion divides the line by coming to a stand at that point and beginning its motion again: thus [25] the middle-point becomes both a starting-point and a goal, the starting-point of the latter part and the finishing-point of the first part of the motion. This is the case e.g. when A in the course of its locomotion comes to a stand at B and starts again towards Γ: but when its motion is continuous A cannot either have come to be or have ceased to be at the point B: it can [30] only have been there at the moment of passing, its passage not being contained within any period of time except the whole of which the particular moment is a dividing-point. To maintain that it has come to be and ceased to be there will involve the consequence that A in the course of its locomotion will always be coming to a stand: for it is impossible that A should simultaneously have come to be at B and ceased to be there, so that the two things must have happened at different points of time, and therefore there will be the intervening period of time: consequently A will be in a state of rest at B, and similarly at all other points, since the same reasoning holds good in every [5] case. When to A, that which is in process of locomotion, B, the middle-point, serves both as a finishing-point and as a starting-point for its motion, A must come to a stand at B, because it makes it two just as one might do in thought. However, the point A is the real starting-point at which the moving body has ceased to be, and it is at Γ that it has really come to be when its course is finished and it comes to a stand. So this is how we must meet the difficulty that [10] then arises, which is as follows. Suppose the line E is equal to the line Z, that A proceeds in continuous locomotion from the extreme point of E to Γ, and that, at the moment when A is at the point B, Δ is proceeding in uniform locomotion and with the same velocity as A from the extremity of Z to H: then, says the argument, Δ will have reached H before A has reached Γ: for that which makes an earlier start and departure must make an earlier ar- [15] rival: the reason, then, for the late arrival of A is that it has not simultaneously come to be and ceased to be at B: otherwise it will not arrive later: for this to happen it will be necessary that it should come to a stand there. Therefore we must not hold that there was a moment when A came to be at B and that at the same moment Δ was in motion from the extremity of Z: for the fact of A's having come to [20] be at B will involve the fact of its also ceasing to be there, and the two events will not be simultaneous, whereas the truth is that A is at B at a sectional point of time and does not occupy time there. In this case, therefore, where the motion of a thing is continuous, it is impossible to use this form of expression. On the other hand in the case of a thing that turns back in its course we must do so. For suppose H in the course of its locomotion proceeds to Δ and then turns back and proceeds downwards again: then the extreme point Δ has served as finishing-point and as starting-point for it, one point thus serving as two: therefore H must [25] have come to a stand there: it cannot have come to be at Δ and departed from Δ simul-taneously, for in that case it would simultaneously be there and not be there at the same moment. And here we cannot apply the argument used to solve the difficulty stated above: we cannot argue that H is at Δ at a sectional point of time and has not come to be or ceased to be there. For here the goal that is reached is [30] necessarily one that is actually, not potentially, existent. Now the point in the middle is potential: but this one is actual, and regarded from below it is a finishing-point, while regarded from above it is a starting-point, so that it stands in these same two respective relations to the two motions. Therefore that which turns back in traversing a rectilinear course must in so doing come to a stand. Consequently there cannot be a continuous rectilinear motion that is eternal.

The same method should also be adopted in replying to those who ask, in the terms of [5] Zeno's argument, whether we admit that before any distance can be traversed half the distance must be traversed, that these half-distances are infinite in number, and that it is impossible to traverse distances infinite in number—or some on the lines of this same argument put the questions in another form, and would have us grant that in the time during which a motion is in progress it should be possible to reckon a half-motion before the whole for every half-distance that we get, so that we have the result that when the whole distance is trav- [10] ersed we have reckoned an infinite number, which is admittedly impossible. Now when we first discussed the question of motion we put forward a solution[1] of this difficulty turning on the fact that the period of time occupied in traversing the distance contains within itself an infinite number of units: there is no absurdity, we said, in supposing the traversing of infinite distances in infinite time, and the element of infinity is present in the time no less [15] than in the distance. But, although this solution is adequate as a reply to the questioner (the question asked being whether it is possible in a finite time to traverse or reckon an infinite number of units), nevertheless as an account of the fact and explanation of its true nature it is inadequate. For suppose the distance to be left out of account and the question asked to be no longer whether it is possible in a finite [20] time to traverse an infinite number of distances, and suppose that the inquiry is made to refer to the time taken by itself (for the time contains an infinite number of divisions): then

---

[1] VI. 2 (233ᵃ 21 sqq.), and VI. 9.

this solution will no longer be adequate, and we must apply the truth that we enunciated in our recent discussion, stating it in the following way. In the act of dividing the continuous distance into two halves one point is treated as two, since we make it a starting-point and a finishing-point: and this same result is also produced by the act of reckoning halves as well as by the act of dividing into halves. But if divisions are made in this way, neither the distance nor the motion will be continuous: for motion if it is to be continuous must relate to what is continuous: and though what is continuous contains an infinite number of halves, they are not actual but potential halves. If the halves are made actual, we shall get not a continuous but an intermittent motion. In the case of reckoning the halves, it is clear that this result follows: for then one point must be reckoned as two: it will be the finishing-point of the one half and the starting-point of the other, if we reckon not the one continuous whole but the two halves. Therefore to the question whether it is possible to pass through an infinite number of units either of time or of distance we must reply that in a sense it is and in a sense it is not. If the units are actual, it is not possible: if they are potential, it is possible. For in the course of a continuous motion the traveller has traversed an infinite number of units in an accidental sense but not in an unqualified sense: for though it is an accidental characteristic of the distance to be an infinite number of half-distances, this is not its real and essential character. It is also plain that unless we hold that the point of time that divides earlier from later always belongs only to the later so far as the thing is concerned, we shall be involved in the consequence that the same thing is at the same moment existent and not existent, and that a thing is not existent at the moment when it has become. It is true that the point is common to both times, the earlier as well as the later, and that, while numerically one and the same, it is theoretically not so, being the finishing-point of the one and the starting-point of the other: but so far as the thing is concerned it belongs to the later stage of what happens to it. Let us suppose a time $AB\Gamma$ and a thing Δ, Δ being white in the time A and not-white in the time B. Then Δ is at the moment Γ white and not-white: for if we were right in saying that it is white during the whole time A, it is true to call it white at any moment of A, and not-white in B, and Γ is in both A and B. We must not allow, therefore, that it is white in the whole of A, but must say that it is so in all of it except the last moment Γ. Γ belongs already to the later period, and if in the whole of A not-white was in process of becoming and white of perishing, at Γ the process is complete. And so Γ is the first moment at which it is true to call the thing white or not-white respectively. Otherwise a thing may be non-existent at the moment when it has become and existent at the moment when it has perished: or else it must be possible for a thing at the same time to be white and not white and in fact to be existent and non-existent. Further, if anything that exists after having been previously non-existent must become existent and does not exist when it is becoming, time cannot be divisible into time-atoms. For suppose that Δ was becoming white in the time A and that at another time B, a time-atom consecutive with the last atom of A, Δ has already become white and so is white at that moment: then, inasmuch as in the time A it was becoming white and so was not white and at the moment B it is white, there must have been a becoming between A and B and therefore also a time in which the becoming took place. On the other hand, those who deny atoms of time ⟨as we do⟩ are not affected by this argument: according to them Δ has become and so is white at the last point of the actual time in which it was becoming white: and this point has no other point consecutive with or in succession to it, whereas time-atoms are conceived as successive. Moreover it is clear that if Δ was becoming white in the whole time A, the time occupied by it in having become white in addition to having been in process of becoming white is no more than all that it occupied in the mere process of becoming white.

These and such-like, then, are the arguments for our conclusion that derive cogency from the fact that they have a special bearing on the point at issue. If we look at the question from the point of view of general theory, the same result would also appear to be indicated by the following arguments. Everything whose motion is continuous must, on arriving at any point in the course of its locomotion, have been previously also in process of locomotion to that point, if it is not forced out of its path by anything: e.g. on arriving at B a thing must also have been in process of locomotion to B, and that not merely when it was near to B, but from the moment of its starting on its course, since there can be no reason for its being so at any particular stage rather than at an earlier one. So, too, in the case of the other kinds of motion. Now we are to suppose that a thing proceeds in locomotion from A to Γ and that at [15] the moment of its arrival at Γ the continuity of its motion is unbroken and will remain so until it has arrived back at A. Then when it is undergoing locomotion from A to Γ it is at the same time undergoing also its locomotion to A from Γ: consequently it is simultaneously undergoing two contrary motions, since the two motions that follow the same straight line are contrary to each other. With this consequence there also follows another: we have a thing that is in process of change from a position in which it has not yet been: so, inasmuch as this is impossible, the thing must come to a [20] stand at Γ. Therefore the motion is not a single motion, since motion that is interrupted by stationariness is not single.

Further, the following argument will serve better to make this point clear universally in respect of every kind of motion. If the motion undergone by that which is in motion is always one of those already enumerated, and the state of rest that it undergoes is one of those that are the opposites of the motions (for we found[1] that there could be no other besides these), and moreover that which is undergoing but does not always undergo a particular motion (by [25] this I mean one of the various specifically distinct motions, not some particular part of the whole motion) must have been previously undergoing the state of rest that is the opposite of the motion, the state of rest being privation of motion; then, inasmuch as the two motions that follow the same straight line are contrary motions, and it is impossible for a thing to undergo simultaneously two contrary motions, that which is undergoing locomotion from A [30] to Γ cannot also simultaneously be undergoing locomotion from Γ to A: and since the latter locomotion is not simultaneous with the former but is still to be undergone, before it is undergone there must occur a state of rest at Γ: for this, as we found,[2] is the state of rest that is the opposite of the motion from Γ. The foregoing argument, then, makes it plain that the motion in question is not continuous.

264^b Our next argument has a more special bearing than the foregoing on the point at issue. We will suppose that there has occurred in something simultaneously a perishing of not-white and a becoming of white. Then if the alteration to white and from white is a continuous process and the white does not remain any [5] time, there must have occurred simultaneously a perishing of not-white, a becoming of white, and a becoming of not-white: for the time of the three will be the same.

Again, from the continuity of the time in which the motion takes place we cannot infer continuity in the motion, but only successiveness: in fact, how could contraries, e.g. whiteness and blackness, meet in the same extreme point?

On the other hand, in motion on a circular line we shall find singleness and continuity: for here we are met by no impossible consequence: [10] that which is in motion from A will in virtue of the same direction of energy be simultaneously in motion to A (since it is in motion to the point at which it will finally arrive), and yet will not be undergoing two contrary or opposite motions: for a motion to a point and a motion from that point are not always contraries or opposites: they are contraries only if they are on the same straight line (for then [15] they are contrary to one another in respect of place, as e.g. the two motions along the diameter of the circle, since the ends of this are at the greatest possible distance from one another), and they are opposites only if they are along the same line. Therefore in the case we are now considering there is nothing to prevent the motion being continuous and free from all intermission: for rotatory motion is motion of a thing from its place to its place, whereas [20] rectilinear motion is motion from its place to another place.

Moreover the progress of rotatory motion is never localized within certain fixed limits, whereas that of rectilinear motion repeatedly is so. Now a motion that is always shifting its ground from moment to moment can be continuous: but a motion that is repeatedly localized within certain fixed limits cannot be so, since then the same thing would have to undergo simultaneously two opposite motions. So, too, there cannot be continuous motion in a [25] semicircle or in any other arc of a circle, since here also the same ground must be traversed repeatedly and two contrary processes of change must occur. The reason is that in these motions the starting-point and the termination do not coincide, whereas in motion over a circle they do coincide, and so this is the only perfect motion.

This differentiation also provides another means of showing that the other kinds of motion cannot be continuous either: for in all of

---
[1] v. 2. [2] v. 6 (229^b 28 sqq.).

[30] them we find that there is the same ground to be traversed repeatedly; thus in alteration there are the intermediate stages of the process, and in quantitative change there are the intervening degrees of magnitude: and in becoming and perishing the same thing is true. It makes no difference whether we take the intermediate stages of the process to be few or many, or whether we add or subtract one: for 265ᵃ in either case we find that there is still the same ground to be traversed repeatedly. Moreover it is plain from what has been said that those physicists who assert that all sensible things are always in motion are wrong: for their motion must be one or other of the mo- [5] tions just mentioned: in fact they mostly conceive it as alteration (things are always in flux and decay, they say), and they go so far as to speak even of becoming and perishing as a process of alteration. On the other hand, our argument has enabled us to assert the fact, applying universally to all motions, that no motion admits of continuity except rotatory motion: consequently neither alteration nor in- [10] crease admits of continuity. We need now say no more in support of the position that there is no process of change that admits of infinity or continuity except rotatory locomotion.

9

It can now be shown plainly that rotation is the primary locomotion. Every locomotion, as we said before,[1] is either rotatory or rectilinear [15] or a compound of the two: and the two former must be prior to the last, since they are the elements of which the latter consists. Moreover rotatory locomotion is prior to rectilinear locomotion, because it is more simple and complete, which may be shown as follows. The straight line traversed in rectilinear motion cannot be infinite: for there is no such thing as an infinite straight line; and even if there were, it would not be traversed by anything in motion: for the impossible does not happen and it is im- [20] possible to traverse an infinite distance. On the other hand rectilinear motion on a finite straight line is if it turns back a composite motion, in fact two motions, while if it does not turn back it is incomplete and perishable: and in the order of nature, of definition, and of time alike the complete is prior to the incomplete and the imperishable to the perishable. Again, a motion that admits of being eternal is [25] prior to one that does not. Now rotatory motion can be eternal: but no other motion,

[1]Chapter 8 (261ᵇ 28).

whether locomotion or motion of any other kind, can be so, since in all of them rest must occur and with the occurrence of rest the motion has perished. Moreover the result at which we have arrived, that rotatory motion is single and continuous, and rectilinear motion is not, is a reasonable one. In rectilinear motion we have a definite starting-point, finishing-point, [30] and middle-point, which all have their place in it in such a way that there is a point from which that which is in motion can be said to start and a point at which it can be said to finish its course (for when anything is at the limits of its course, whether at the starting-point or at the finishing-point, it must be in a state of rest). On the other hand in circular motion there are no such definite points: for why should any one point on the line be a limit rather than any other? Any one point as much as any other is alike starting-point, middle-point, and finishing-point, so that we can say of certain things both that they are always and that they never are at a starting-point and at a 265ᵇ finishing-point (so that a revolving sphere, while it is in motion, is also in a sense at rest, for it continues to occupy the same place). The reason of this is that in this case all these characteristics belong to the centre: that is to say, the centre is alike starting-point, middle-point, and finishing-point of the space traversed; consequently since this point is not a [5] point on the circular line, there is no point at which that which is in process of locomotion can be in a state of rest as having traversed its course, because in its locomotion it is proceeding always about a central point and not to an extreme point: therefore it remains still, and the whole is in a sense always at rest as well as continuously in motion. Our next point gives a convertible result: on the one hand, because rotation is the measure of motions it must be the primary motion (for all things are meas- [10] ured by what is primary): on the other hand, because rotation is the primary motion it is the measure of all other motions. Again, rotatory motion is also the only motion that admits of being regular. In rectilinear locomotion the motion of things in leaving the starting-point is not uniform with their motion in approaching the finishing-point, since the velocity of a thing always increases proportionately as it removes itself farther from its position of rest: on the other hand rotatory motion is the only motion whose course is naturally such that [15] it has no starting-point or finishing-point in itself but is determined from elsewhere.

As to locomotion being the primary motion, this is a truth that is attested by all who have ever made mention of motion in their theories: they all assign their first principles of motion to things that impart motion of this kind. Thus 'separation' and 'combination' are motions in [20] respect of place, and the motion imparted by 'Love' and 'Strife' takes these forms, the latter 'separating' and the former 'combining'. Anaxagoras, too, says that 'Mind', his first movent, 'separates'. Similarly those who assert no cause of this kind but say that 'void' accounts [25] for motion—they also hold that the motion of natural substance is motion in respect of place: for their motion that is accounted for by 'void' is locomotion, and its sphere of operation may be said to be place. Moreover they are of opinion that the primary substances are not subject to any of the other motions, though the things that are compounds of these substances are so subject: the processes of increase and decrease and alteration, they say, are effects [30] of the 'combination' and 'separation' of 'atoms'. It is the same, too, with those who make out that the becoming or perishing of a thing is accounted for by 'density' or 'rarity': for it is by 'combination' and 'separation' that the place of these things in their systems is determined. Moreover to these we may add those who make Soul the cause of motion: for they say that things that undergo motion have as their first principle 'that which moves itself': and when animals and all living things move themselves, the motion is motion in respect of place. Finally it is to be noted that we say that a thing 'is in motion' in the strict sense of the term only when its motion is motion in respect of place: if a thing is in process of increase or decrease or is undergoing some alteration while remaining at rest in the same place, we say that it is in motion in some particular respect: we do not say that it 'is in motion' [5] without qualification.

Our present position, then, is this: We have argued that there always was motion and always will be motion throughout all time, and we have explained what is the first principle of this eternal motion: we have explained further which is the primary motion and which is the only motion that can be eternal: and we have pronounced the first movent to be unmoved.

10

[10] We have now to assert that the first movent must be without parts and without magnitude, beginning with the establishment of the premisses on which this conclusion depends.

One of these premisses is that nothing finite can cause motion during an infinite time. We have three things, the movent, the moved, and thirdly that in which the motion takes place, namely the time: and these are either all infinite or all finite or partly—that is to say two of them [15] or one of them—finite and partly infinite. Let A be the movent, B the moved, and Γ the infinite time. Now let us suppose that Δ moves E, a part of B. Then the time occupied by this motion cannot be equal to Γ: for the greater the amount moved, the longer the time occupied. It follows that the time Z is not infinite. Now we see that by continuing to add to Δ I shall use up A and by continuing to add to E I shall [20] use up B: but I shall not use up the time by continually subtracting a corresponding amount from it, because it is infinite. Consequently the duration of the part of Γ which is occupied by all A in moving the whole of B, will be finite. Therefore a finite thing cannot impart to anything an infinite motion. It is clear, then, that it is impossible for the finite to cause motion during an infinite time.

[25] It has now to be shown that in no case is it possible for an infinite force to reside in a finite magnitude. This can be shown as follows: we take it for granted that the greater force is always that which in less time than another does an equal amount of work when engaged in any activity—in heating, for example, or sweetening or throwing; in fact, in causing any kind of motion. Then that on which the forces act must be affected to some extent by our supposed finite magnitude possessing an infinite force as well as by anything else, in fact to a greater extent than by anything else, since the [30] infinite force is greater than any other. But then there cannot be any time in which its action could take place. Suppose that A is the time occupied by the infinite power in the performance of an act of heating or pushing, and that AB is the time occupied by a finite power in the performance of the same act: then by adding to the latter another finite power and continually increasing the magnitude of the power so added I shall at some time or other reach a point at which the finite power has completed the motive act in the time A: for by continual addition to a finite magnitude I must arrive at a magnitude that exceeds any assigned limit, and in the same way by continual subtraction I must arrive at one that falls short of any assigned limit. So we get the result that the finite force will occupy the same amount of

time in performing the motive act as the infi-[5]nite force. But this is impossible. Therefore nothing finite can possess an infinite force. So it is also impossible for a finite force to reside in an infinite magnitude. It is true that a greater force can reside in a lesser magnitude: but the superiority of any such greater force can be still greater if the magnitude in which it resides is greater. Now let AB be an infinite magnitude. Then BΓ possesses a certain force that occupies a certain time, let us say the time EZ, [10] in moving Δ. Now if I take a magnitude twice as great at BΓ, the time occupied by this magnitude in moving Δ will be half of EZ (assuming this to be the proportion): so we may call this time ZH. That being so, by continually taking a greater magnitude in this way I shall never arrive at the full AB, whereas I shall always be getting a lesser fraction of the time originally given. Therefore the force must [15] be infinite, since it exceeds any finite force. Moreover the time occupied by the action of any finite force must also be finite: for if a given force moves something in a certain time, a greater force will do so in a lesser time, but still a definite time, in inverse proportion. But a force must always be infinite—just as a number or a magnitude is—if it exceeds all definite [20] limits. This point may also be proved in another way—by taking a finite magnitude in which there resides a force the same in kind as that which resides in the infinite magnitude, so that this force will be a measure of the finite force residing in the infinite magnitude.

[25] It is plain, then, from the foregoing arguments that it is impossible for an infinite force to reside in a finite magnitude or for a finite force to reside in an infinite magnitude. But before proceeding to our conclusion it will be well to discuss a difficulty that arises in connexion with locomotion. If everything that is in motion with the exception of things that move themselves is moved by something else, how is it that some things, e.g. things thrown, continue to be in motion when their movent is no longer in contact with them? If we say [30] that the movent in such cases moves something else at the same time, that the thrower e.g. also moves the air, and that this in being moved is also a movent, then it would be no more possible for this second thing than for the original thing to be in motion when the original movent is not in contact with it or moving it: all the things moved would have to be in motion simultaneously and also to have ceased simultaneously to be in motion when the orig-267ª inal movent ceases to move them, even if, like the magnet, it makes that which it has moved capable of being a movent. Therefore, while we must accept this explanation to the extent of saying that the original movent gives the power of being a movent either to air or to water or to something else of the kind, nat-[5] urally adapted for imparting and undergoing motion, we must say further that this thing does not cease simultaneously to impart motion and to undergo motion: it ceases to be in motion at the moment when its movent ceases to move it, but it still remains a movent, and so it causes something else consecutive with it to be in motion, and of this again the same may be said. The motion begins to cease when the motive force produced in one member of the consecutive series is at each stage less than that possessed by the preceding member, and it finally ceases when one member no longer causes the next member to be a movent but [10] only causes it to be in motion. The motion of these last two—of the one as movent and of the other as moved—must cease simultaneously, and with this the whole motion ceases. Now the things in which this motion is produced are things that admit of being sometimes in motion and sometimes at rest, and the motion is not continuous but only appears so: for it is motion of things that are either successive or in contact, there being not [15] one movent but a number of movents consecutive with one another: and so motion of this kind takes place in air and water. Some say that it is 'mutual replacement': but we must recognize that the difficulty raised cannot be solved otherwise than in the way we have described. So far as they are affected by 'mutual replacement', all the members of the series are moved and impart motion simultaneously, so that their motions also cease simultaneously: but our present problem concerns the appearance of continuous motion in a sin-[20] gle thing, and therefore, since it cannot be moved throughout its motion by the same movent, the question is, what moves it?

Resuming our main argument, we proceed from the positions that there must be continuous motion in the world of things, that this is a single motion, that a single motion must be a motion of a magnitude (for that which is without magnitude cannot be in motion), and that the magnitude must be a single magnitude moved by a single movent (for otherwise there will not be continuous motion but a consecutive series of separate motions), and that if the movent is a single thing, it is either itself in [25] motion or itself unmoved: if, then, it is in motion, it will have to be subject to the same conditions as that which it moves, that is to say it will itself be in process of change and in being so will also have to be moved by something: so we have a series that must come to an end, and a point will be reached at which motion is imparted by something that is unmoved. Thus we have a movent that has no need to change along with that which it moves but will be able to cause motion always (for the causing of motion under these conditions involves no effort): and this motion alone is regular, or at least it is so in a higher degree than any other, since the movent is never subject to any change. So, too, in order that [5] the motion may continue to be of the same character, the moved must not be subject to change in respect of its relation to the movent. Moreover the movent must occupy either the centre or the circumference, since these are the first principles from which a sphere is derived. But the things nearest the movent are those whose motion is quickest, and in this case it is the motion of the circumference that is the quickest: therefore the movent occupies the circumference.

There is a further difficulty in supposing it to be possible for anything that is in motion to cause motion continuously and not merely in [10] the way in which it is caused by something repeatedly pushing (in which case the continuity amounts to no more than successiveness). Such a movent must either itself continue to push or pull or perform both these actions, or else the action must be taken up by something else and be passed on from one movent to another (the process that we described before as occurring in the case of things thrown, since the air or the water, being divisible, is a movent only in virtue of the fact that different parts of the air are moved one after [15] another): and in either case the motion cannot be a single motion, but only a consecutive series of motions. The only continuous motion, then, is that which is caused by the unmoved movent: and this motion is continuous because the movent remains always invariable, so that its relation to that which it moves remains also invariable and continuous.

Now that these points are settled, it is clear that the first unmoved movent cannot have any magnitude. For if it has magnitude, this must be either a finite or an infinite magnitude. Now [20] we have already[1] proved in our course on Physics that there cannot be an infinite magnitude: and we have now proved that it is impossible for a finite magnitude to have an infinite force, and also that it is impossible for a thing to be moved by a finite magnitude during an infinite time. But the first movent causes a motion that is eternal and does [25] cause it during an infinite time. It is clear, therefore, that the first movent is indivisible and is without parts and without magnitude.

[1] III. 5.

CONTENTS: ON THE HEAVENS

Of the Heavenly Bodies
BOOK I

CHAP.		BERLIN NOS.
1.	The subject of inquiry	268^a 1
2.	That in addition to the four elements, earth, water, air, and fire, there is a fifth element, the movement of which is circular	268^b 11
3.	That this body is exempt from alteration and decay	269^b 18
4.	That the circular movement has no contrary	270^b 31
5.	That no body is infinite: (i) Not the primary body, or fifth element	271^b 1
6.	(ii) None of the other elements	273^a 6
7.	(iii) In general, an infinite body is impossible	274^a 30
8.	That there cannot be more than one Heaven: (i) Proved from a consideration of the natural movements and places of the elements	276^a 18
9.	(ii) Proved by the principles of form and matter, the three different senses of the term 'heaven' being explained. Corollary: There is no place or void or time outside the Heaven	277^b 26
10.	That the Heaven is ungenerated and indestructible: (i) Review of previous theories	279^b 4
11.	(ii) Definition of the terms 'ungenerated' and 'indestructible', and of their opposites	280^b 1
12.	(iii) Proof of the thesis	281^a 28

BOOK II

1.	Corroboration of this result	283^b 26
2.	Of the sense in which the spatial oppositions, up and down, right and left, can be attributed to the Heaven	284^b 6
3.	Why there is a plurality of movements and of bodies within the Heaven	286^a 3
4.	That the Heaven is perfectly spherical	286^b 10
5.	Why the first Heaven revolves in one direction rather than the other	287^b 22
6.	That the movement of the first Heaven is regular	288^a 13
7.	Of the stars: (i) That they are not composed of fire	289^a 11
8.	(ii) That their movement is due to the movement of circles to which they are attached	289^b 1
9.	(iii) That no 'harmony of the spheres' results from their movement	290^b 12
10.	(iv) Of their order	291^a 30
11.	(v) Of their spherical shape	291^b 11
12.	(vi) Solution of two problems concerning their order and movements	291^b 24
13.	Of the Earth: (i) Review of previous theories	293^a 15
14.	(ii) That it is at rest at the centre, and spherical in shape	296^a 24

Of the Sublunary Bodies
BOOK III

1.	Previous theories concerning generation stated; the analysis of bodies into planes refuted	298^a 24
2.	That every simple body possesses a natural movement; that this movement is either upward or downward; how unnatural movement occurs. General results concerning generation	300^a 20
3.	Of bodies subject to generation: (i) What the elements are	302^a 10
4.	(ii) That the elements are limited in number; the view of Leucippus and Democritus refuted	302^b 10
5.	(iii) That the elements cannot be reduced to one	303^b 9
6.	(iv) That the elements are not eternal, but are generated out of one another	304^b 24
7.	(v) Of the manner of their generation: the view of Empedocles and the explanation by planes refuted	305^a 34
8.	(vi) Refutation of the attempt to differentiate the elements by their shapes	306^b 3

BOOK IV

1.	Of the meaning of the terms 'heavy' and 'light'	307^b 29
2.	Review of previous theories concerning these	308^a 34
3.	Explanation of the variety of motions exhibited by the elements	310^a 14
4.	Of the distinctive constitution and properties of the four elements	311^a 15
5.	In what sense the matter of which the elements are composed may be regarded as one	312^a 22
6.	That the shape of a body cannot account for the direction, but only for the pace, of its movement	313^a 14

ON THE HEAVENS

BOOK I

1

268ª THE science which has to do with nature clearly concerns itself for the most part with bodies and magnitudes and their properties and movements, but also with the principles of this sort of substance, as many as they may be. [5] For of things constituted by nature some are bodies and magnitudes, some possess body and magnitude, and some are principles of things which possess these. Now a continuum is that which is divisible into parts always capable of subdivision, and a body is that which is every way divisible. A magnitude if divisible one way is a line, if two ways a surface, and if three a body. Beyond these there is no other [10] magnitude, because the three dimensions are all that there are, and that which is divisible in three directions is divisible in all. For, as the Pythagoreans say, the world and all that is in it is determined by the number three, since beginning and middle and end give the number of an 'all', and the number they give is the triad. And so, having taken these three from nature as (so to speak) laws of it, we make [15] further use of the number three in the worship of the Gods. Further, we use the terms in practice in this way. Of two things, or men, we say 'both', but not 'all': three is the first number to which the term 'all' has been appropriated. And in this, as we have said, we do [20] but follow the lead which nature gives. Therefore, since 'every' and 'all' and 'complete' do not differ from one another in respect of form, but only, if at all, in their matter and in that to which they are applied, body alone among magnitudes can be complete. For it alone is determined by the three dimensions, that is, is an 'all'. But if it is divisible in three dimensions it is every way divisible, while the [25] other magnitudes are divisible in one dimension or in two alone: for the divisibility and continuity of magnitudes depend upon the number of the dimensions, one sort being continuous in one direction, another in two, another in all. All magnitudes, then, which are divisible are also continuous. Whether we can also say that whatever is continuous is divisible [30] does not yet, on our present grounds, appear. One thing, however, is clear. We cannot **268ᵇ** pass beyond body to a further kind, as we passed from length to surface, and from surface to body. For if we could, it would cease to be true that body is complete magnitude. We could pass beyond it only in virtue of a defect in it; and that which is complete cannot be de-[5]fective, since it has being in every respect. Now bodies which are classed as parts of the whole are each complete according to our formula, since each possesses every dimension. But each is determined relatively to that part which is next to it by contact, for which reason each of them is in a sense many bodies. But the whole of which they are parts must necessarily be complete, and thus, in accordance with the [10] meaning of the word, have being, not in some respect only, but in every respect.

2

The question as to the nature of the whole, whether it is infinite in size or limited in its total mass, is a matter for subsequent inquiry.[1] We will now speak of those parts of the whole which are specifically distinct. Let us take this [15] as our starting-point. All natural bodies and magnitudes we hold to be, as such, capable of locomotion; for nature, we say, is their principle of movement.[2] But all movement that is in place, all locomotion, as we term it, is either straight or circular or a combination of these two, which are the only simple movements. And the reason of this is that these two, the [20] straight and the circular line, are the only simple magnitudes. Now revolution about the centre is circular motion, while the upward and downward movements are in a straight line, 'upward' meaning motion away from the centre, and 'downward' motion towards it. All simple motion, then, must be motion either away from or towards or about the centre. This [25] seems to be in exact accord with what we said above: as body found its completion in

---

[1] See chapter 7. [2] Cf. *Physics*, 192ᵇ 20.

NOTE: The bold face numbers and letters are approximate indications of the pages and columns of the standard Berlin Greek text; the bracketed numbers, of the lines in the Greek text; they are here assigned as they are assigned in the Oxford translation.

three dimensions, so its movement completes itself in three forms.

Bodies are either simple or compounded of such; and by simple bodies I mean those which possess a principle of movement in their own nature, such as fire and earth with their kinds, and whatever is akin to them. Necessarily, then, [30] movements also will be either simple or in some sort compound—simple in the case of the simple bodies, compound in that of the composite—and in the latter case the motion will be that of the simple body which prevails in the composition. Supposing, then, that there is such a thing as simple movement, and that circular movement is an instance of it, and that both movement of a simple body is simple and simple movement is of a simple body (for if it is movement of a compound it will be in [5] virtue of a prevailing simple element), then there must necessarily be some simple body which revolves naturally and in virtue of its own nature with a circular movement. By constraint, of course, it may be brought to move with the motion of something else different from itself, but it cannot so move naturally, since there is one sort of movement natural to each of the simple bodies. Again, if the unnatural movement is the contrary of the natural and [10] a thing can have no more than one contrary, it will follow that circular movement, being a simple motion, must be unnatural, if it is not natural, to the body moved. If then (1) the body, whose movement is circular, is fire or some other element, its natural motion must be the contrary of the circular motion. But a single thing has a single contrary; and upward and downward motion are the contraries of one [15] another. If, on the other hand, (2) the body moving with this circular motion which is unnatural to it is something different from the elements, there will be some other motion which is natural to it. But this cannot be. For if the natural motion is upward, it will be fire or air, and if downward, water or earth. Further, this circular motion is necessarily primary. For [20] the perfect is naturally prior to the imperfect, and the circle is a perfect thing. This cannot be said of any straight line:—not of an infinite line; for, if it were perfect, it would have a limit and an end: nor of any finite line; for in every case there is something beyond it, since any finite line can be extended. And so, since the prior movement belongs to the body which [25] is naturally prior, and circular movement is prior to straight, and movement in a straight line belongs to simple bodies—fire moving straight upward and earthy bodies straight downward towards the centre—since this is so, it follows that circular movement also must be the movement of some simple body. For the movement of composite bodies is, as we said, determined by that simple body which preponderates [30] in the composition. These premises clearly give the conclusion that there is in nature some bodily substance other than the formations we know, prior to them all and more divine than they. But it may also be proved as follows. We may take it that all movement is either natural or unnatural, and that the movement which is unnatural to one body is natural to another—as, for instance, is the case with the upward and downward movements, [35] which are natural and unnatural to fire and earth respectively. It necessarily follows that circular movement, being unnatural to these bodies, is the natural movement of some other. Further, if, on the one hand, circular movement is *natural* to something, it must surely be some simple and primary body which is ordained to move with a natural circular [5] motion, as fire is ordained to fly up and earth down. If, on the other hand, the movement of the rotating bodies about the centre is *unnatural,* it would be remarkable and indeed quite inconceivable that this movement alone should be continuous and eternal, being nevertheless contrary to nature. At any rate the evidence of all other cases goes to show that it [10] is the unnatural which quickest passes away. And so, if, as some say, the body so moved is fire, this movement is just as unnatural to it as downward movement; for any one can see that fire moves in a straight line away from the centre. On all these grounds, therefore, we may infer with confidence that there [15] is something beyond the bodies that are about us on this earth, different and separate from them; and that the superior glory of its nature is proportionate to its distance from this world of ours.

3

In consequence of what has been said, in part by way of assumption and in part by way of proof, it is clear that not every body either possesses [20] lightness or heaviness. As a preliminary we must explain in what sense we are using the words 'heavy' and 'light', sufficiently, at least, for our present purpose: we can examine the terms more closely later, when we come to consider their essential nature. Let us then apply the term 'heavy' to that which naturally moves towards the centre, and 'light' to that which moves naturally away from the centre. The heaviest thing will be that which sinks to [25] the bottom of all things that move downward, and the lightest that which rises to the surface of everything that moves upward. Now, necessarily, everything which moves either up or down possesses lightness or heaviness or both —but not both relatively to the same thing: for things are heavy and light relatively to one another; air, for instance, is light relatively to wa- [30] ter, and water light relatively to earth. The body, then, which moves in a circle cannot possibly possess either heaviness or lightness. For neither naturally nor unnaturally can it move either towards or away from the centre. Movement in a straight line certainly does not belong to it *naturally,* since one sort of movement is, as we saw, appropriate to each simple body, and so we should be compelled to iden- [35] tify it with one of the bodies which move in this way. Suppose, then, that the movement is *unnatural.* In that case, if it is the downward 270ᵃ movement which is unnatural, the upward movement will be natural; and if it is the upward which is unnatural, the downward will be natural. For we decided that of contrary movements, if the one is unnatural to anything, the other will be natural to it. But since the natural movement of the whole and of its part— of earth, for instance, as a whole and of a small [5] clod—have one and the same direction, it results, in the first place, that this body can possess no lightness or heaviness at all (for that would mean that it could move by its own nature either from or towards the centre, which, as we know, is impossible); and, secondly, that it cannot possibly move in the way of locomotion by being forced violently aside in an up- [10] ward or downward direction. For neither naturally nor unnaturally can it move with any other motion but its own, either itself or any part of it, since the reasoning which applies to the whole applies also to the part.

It is equally reasonable to assume that this body will be ungenerated and indestructible and exempt from increase and alteration, since everything that comes to be comes into being [15] from its contrary and in some substrate, and passes away likewise in a substrate by the action of the contrary into the contrary, as we explained in our opening discussions.[1] Now the motions of contraries are contrary. If then this body can have no contrary, because there can be no contrary motion to the circular, na-

[1]*Physics,* i. 7-9.

[20] ture seems justly to have exempted from contraries the body which was to be ungenerated and indestructible. For it is in contraries that generation and decay subsist. Again, that which is subject to increase increases upon contact with a kindred body, which is resolved [25] into its matter. But there is nothing out of which this body can have been generated. And if it is exempt from increase and diminution, the same reasoning leads us to suppose that it is also unalterable. For alteration is movement in respect of quality; and qualitative states and dispositions, such as health and disease, do not come into being without changes of properties. But all natural bodies which [30] change their properties we see to be subject without exception to increase and diminution. This is the case, for instance, with the bodies of animals and their parts and with vegetable bodies, and similarly also with those of the elements. And so, if the body which moves with a circular motion cannot admit of in- [35] crease or diminution, it is reasonable to suppose that it is also unalterable.

270ᵇ The reasons why the primary body is eternal and not subject to increase or diminution, but unaging and unalterable and unmodified, will be clear from what has been said to any one who believes in our assumptions. Our theory seems to confirm experience and to be [5] confirmed by it. For all men have some conception of the nature of the gods, and all who believe in the existence of gods at all, whether barbarian or Greek, agree in allotting the highest place to the deity, surely because they suppose that immortal is linked with immortal and regard any other supposition as in- [10] conceivable. If then there is, as there certainly is, anything divine, what we have just said about the primary bodily substance was well said. The mere evidence of the senses is enough to convince us of this, at least with human certainty. For in the whole range of time past, so far as our inherited records reach, no [15] change appears to have taken place either in the whole scheme of the outermost heaven or in any of its proper parts. The common name, too, which has been handed down from our distant ancestors even to our own day, seems to show that they conceived of it in the fashion which we have been expressing. The same ideas, one must believe, recur in men's [20] minds not once or twice but again and again. And so, implying that the primary body is something else beyond earth, fire, air, and water, they gave the highest place a name of its own, *aither,* derived from the fact that it 'runs always' for an eternity of time. Anaxagoras, [25] however, scandalously misuses this name, taking *aither* as equivalent to fire.

It is also clear from what has been said why the number of what we call simple bodies cannot be greater than it is. The motion of a simple body must iself be simple, and we assert that there are only these two simple motions, [30] the circular and the straight, the latter being subdivided into motion away from and motion towards the centre.

4

That there is no other form of motion opposed as contrary to the circular may be proved in various ways. In the first place, there is an obvious tendency to oppose the straight line to [35] the circular. For concave and convex are 271ᵃ not only regarded as opposed to one another, but they are also coupled together and treated as a unity in opposition to the straight. And so, if there is a contrary to circular motion, motion in a straight line must be recognized as having the best claim to that name. But the two forms of rectilinear motion are opposed to one [5] another by reason of their places; for up and down is a difference and a contrary opposition in place. Secondly, it may be thought that the same reasoning which holds good of the rectilinear path applies also the circular, movement from A to B being opposed as contrary to movement from B to A. But what is meant is still rectilinear motion. For that is limited to a [10] single path, while the circular paths which pass through the same two points are infinite in number. Even if we are confined to the single semicircle and the opposition is between movement from C to D and from D to C along that semicircle, the case is no better. For the motion is the same as that along the diameter, since we invariably regard the distance between two points as the length of the straight line which joins them. It is no more satisfactory to construct a circle and treat motion [15] along one semicircle as contrary to motion along the other. For example, taking a complete circle, motion from E to F on the semicircle G may be opposed to motion from F to E on the semicircle H. But even supposing these are contraries, it in no way follows that the reverse motions on the complete circumference [20] are contraries. Nor again can motion along the circle from A to B be regarded as the contrary of motion from A to C: for the motion goes from the same point towards the same point, and contrary motion was distinguished as motion from a contrary to its contrary. And even if the motion round a circle is the contrary of the reverse motion, one of the two would be ineffective: for both move to the same point, because that which moves in a circle, at what- [25] ever point it begins, must necessarily pass through all the contrary places alike. (By contrarieties of place I mean up and down, back and front, and right and left; and the contrary oppositions of movements are determined by those of places.) One of the motions, then, would be ineffective, for if the two motions were of equal strength, there would be no movement either way, and if one of the two [30] were preponderant, the other would be inoperative. So that if both bodies were there, one of them, inasmuch as it would not be moving with its own movement, would be useless, in the sense in which a shoe is useless when it is not worn. But God and nature create nothing that has not its use.

5

271ᵇ This being clear, we must go on to consider the questions which remain. First, is there an infinite body, as the majority of the ancient philosophers thought, or is this an impossibility? The decision of this question, either way, [5] is not unimportant, but rather all-important, to our search for the truth. It is this problem which has practically always been the source of the differences of those who have written about nature as a whole. So it has been and so it must be; since the least initial deviation from the truth is multiplied later a thou- [10] sandfold. Admit, for instance, the existence of a minimum magnitude, and you will find that the minimum which you have introduced, small as it is, causes the greatest truths of mathematics to totter. The reason is that a principle is great rather in power than in extent; hence that which was small at the start turns out a giant at the end. Now the conception of the infinite possesses this power of principles, and indeed in the sphere of quantity [15] possesses it in a higher degree than any other conception; so that it is in no way absurd or unreasonable that the assumption that an infinite body exists should be of peculiar moment to our inquiry. The infinite, then, we must now discuss, opening the whole matter from the beginning.

Every body is necessarily to be classed either as simple or as composite; the infinite body, therefore, will be either simple or composite.

[20] But it is clear, further, that if the simple bodies are finite, the composite must also be finite, since that which is composed of bodies finite both in number and in magnitude is itself finite in respect of number and magnitude: its quantity is in fact the same as that of the bodies which compose it. What remains for us to consider, then, is whether any of the simple bodies can be infinite in magnitude, or wheth- [25] er this is impossible. Let us try the primary body first, and then go on to consider the others.

The body which moves in a circle must necessarily be finite in every respect, for the following reasons. (1) If the body so moving is infinite, the radii drawn from the centre will be [30] infinite. But the space between infinite radii is infinite: and by the space between the radii I mean the area outside which no magnitude which is in contact with the two lines can be conceived as falling. This, I say, will be infinite: first, because in the case of finite radii it 272ᵃ is always finite; and secondly, because in it one can always go on to a width greater than any given width; thus the reasoning which forces us to believe in infinite number, because there is no maximum, applies also to the space between the radii. Now the infinite cannot be traversed, and if the body is infinite the interval between the radii is necessarily infinite: circu- [5] lar motion therefore is an impossibility. Yet our eyes tell us that the heavens revolve in a circle, and by argument also we have determined that there is something to which circular movement belongs.

(2) Again, if from a finite time a finite time be subtracted, what remains must be finite and have a beginning. And if the time of a journey [10] has a beginning, there must be a beginning also of the movement, and consequently also of the distance traversed. This applies universally. Take a line, ACE, infinite in one direction, E, and another line, BB, infinite in both directions. Let ACE describe a circle, re- [15] volving upon C as centre. In its movement it will cut BB continuously for a certain time. This will be a finite time, since the total time is finite in which the heavens complete their circular orbit, and consequently the time subtracted from it, during which the one line in its motion cuts the other, is also finite. Therefore there will be a point at which ACE began for the first time to cut BB. This, however, is impossible. The infinite, then, cannot revolve in [20] a circle; nor could the world, if it were infinite.

(3) That the infinite cannot move may also be shown as follows. Let A be a finite line moving past the finite line, B. Of necessity A will pass clear of B and B of A at the same mo- [25] ment; for each overlaps the other to precisely the same extent. Now if the two were both moving, and moving in contrary directions, they would pass clear of one another more rapidly; if one were still and the other moving past it, less rapidly; provided that the speed of the latter were the same in both cases. This, however, is clear: that it is impossible to traverse an infinite line in a finite time. Infinite time, then, [30] would be required. (This we demonstrated above in the discussion of movement.[1]) And it makes no difference whether a finite is pass- 272ᵇ ing by an infinite or an infinite by a finite. For when A is passing B, then B overlaps A, and it makes no difference whether B is moved or unmoved, except that, if both move, they pass clear of one another more quickly. It is, however, quite possible that a moving line should in certain cases pass one which is stationary quicker than it passes one moving in an [5] opposite direction. One has only to imagine the movement to be slow where both move and much faster where one is stationary. To suppose one line stationary, then, makes no difficulty for our argument, since it is quite possible for A to pass B at a slower rate when both are moving than when only one is. If, [10] therefore, the time which the finite moving line takes to pass the other is infinite, then necessarily the time occupied by the motion of the infinite past the finite is also infinite. For the infinite to move at all is thus absolutely impossible; since the very smallest movement conceivable must take an infinity of time. Moreover the heavens certainly revolve, and they complete their circular orbit in a finite time; so [15] that they pass round the whole extent of any line within their orbit, such as the finite line AB. The revolving body, therefore, cannot be infinite.

(4) Again, as a line which has a limit cannot be infinite, or, if it is infinite, is so only in length, so a surface cannot be infinite in that respect in which it has a limit; or, indeed, if it is completely determinate, in any respect what- [20] ever. Whether it be a square or a circle or a sphere, it cannot be infinite, any more than a foot-rule can. There is then no such thing as an infinite sphere or square or circle, and where there is no circle there can be no circular movement, and similarly where there is no infinite

[1] *Physics*, VI. 7.

at all there can be no infinite movement; and from this it follows that, an infinite circle being itself an impossibility, there can be no circular motion of an infinite body.

[25] (5) Again, take a centre C, an infinite line, AB, another infinite line at right angles to it, E, and a moving radius, CD. CD will never cease contact with E, but the position will always be something like CE, CD cutting E at F. The infinite line, therefore, refuses to complete the circle.

[30] (6) Again, if the heaven is infinite and moves in a circle, we shall have to admit that in a finite time it has traversed the infinite. For suppose the fixed heaven infinite, and that which moves within it equal to it. It results that when the infinite body has completed its revolution, it has traversed an infinite equal to itself in a finite time. But that we know to be impossible.

(7) It can also be shown, conversely, that if the time of revolution is finite, the area traversed must also be finite; but the area traversed was equal to itself; therefore, it is itself finite.

[5] We have now shown that the body which moves in a circle is not endless or infinite, but has its limit.

6

Further, neither that which moves towards nor that which moves away from the centre can be infinite. For the upward and downward motions are contraries and are therefore motions towards contrary places. But if one of a [10] pair of contraries is determinate, the other must be determinate also. Now the centre is determined; for, from whatever point the body which sinks to the bottom starts its downward motion, it cannot go farther than the centre. The centre, therefore, being determinate, the upper place must also be determinate. But if these two places are determined and finite, the [15] corresponding bodies must also be finite. Further, if up and down are determinate, the intermediate place is also necessarily determinate. For, if it is indeterminate, the movement within it will be infinite; and that we have already shown to be an impossibility.[1] The middle region then is determinate, and consequently any body which either is in it, or might be in it, is determinate. But the bodies which move [20] up and down may be in it, since the one moves naturally away from the centre and the other towards it.

[1] *Physics*, VIII. 8.

From this alone it is clear that an infinite body is an impossibility; but there is a further point. If there is no such thing as infinite weight, then it follows that none of these bodies can be infinite. For the supposed infinite [25] body would have to be infinite in weight. (The same argument applies to lightness: for as the one supposition involves infinite weight, so the infinity of the body which rises to the surface involves infinite lightness.) This is proved as follows. Assume the weight to be finite, and take an infinite body, AB, of the weight C. Subtract from the infinite body a fi- [30] nite mass, BD, the weight of which shall be E. E then is less than C, since it is the weight of a lesser mass. Suppose then that the smaller goes into the greater a certain number of times, and take BF bearing the same proportion to BD which the greater weight bears to the smaller. For you may subtract as much as you please from an infinite. If now the masses are proportionate to the weights, and the lesser weight is that of the lesser mass, the greater [5] must be that of the greater. The weights, therefore, of the finite and of the infinite body are equal. Again, if the weight of a greater body is greater than that of a less, the weight of GB will be greater than that of FB; and thus the weight of the finite body is greater than that of the infinite. And, further, the weight of unequal masses will be the same, since the infinite and the finite cannot be equal. It does [10] not matter whether the weights are commensurable or not. If (a) they are *incommensurable* the same reasoning holds. For instance, suppose E multiplied by three is rather more than C: the weight of three masses of the full size of BD will be greater than C. We thus ar- [15] rive at the same impossibility as before. Again (b) we may assume weights which are *commensurate*; for it makes no difference whether we begin with the weight or with the mass. For example, assume the weight E to be commensurate with C, and take from the infinite mass a part BD of weight E. Then let a [20] mass BF be taken having the same proportion to BD which the two weights have to one another. (For the mass being infinite you may subtract from it as much as you please.) These assumed bodies will be commensurate in mass and in weight alike. Nor again does it make any difference to our demonstration whether the total mass has its weight equally or unequally distributed. For it must always be [25] possible to take from the infinite mass a body of equal weight to BD by diminishing or increasing the size of the section to the necessary extent.

From what we have said, then, it is clear that the weight of the infinite body cannot be finite. It must then be infinite. We have therefore only to show this to be impossible in order to prove an infinite body impossible. But the impossibility of infinite weight can be shown [30] in the following way. A given weight moves a given distance in a given time; a weight which is as great and more moves the same distance in a less time, the times being in inverse proportion to the weights. For instance, if one weight is twice another, it will take half as long over a given movement. Further, a finite weight traverses any finite distance in a finite time. It necessarily follows from this that infinite weight, if there is such a thing, being, on [5] the one hand, as great and more than as great as the finite, will move accordingly, but being, on the other hand, compelled to move in a time inversely proportionate to its greatness, cannot move at all. The time should be less in proportion as the weight is greater. But there is no proportion between the infinite and the finite: proportion can only hold between a less and a greater *finite* time. And though you may say that the time of the movement can be continually diminished, yet there is no minimum. [10] Nor, if there were, would it help us. For some finite body could have been found greater than the given finite in the same proportion which is supposed to hold between the infinite and the given finite; so that an infinite and a finite weight must have traversed an equal distance in equal time. But that is impossible. Again, whatever the time, so long as it is finite, [15] in which the infinite performs the motion, a finite weight must necessarily move a certain finite distance in that same time. Infinite weight is therefore impossible, and the same reasoning applies also to infinite lightness. Bodies then of infinite weight and of infinite lightness are equally impossible.

That there is no infinite body may be shown, as we have shown it, by a detailed consideration [20] of the various cases. But it may also be shown universally, not only by such reasoning as we advanced in our discussion of principles[1] (though in that passage we have already determined universally the sense in which the existence of an infinite is to be asserted or denied), but also suitably to our present purpose in the following way. That will lead us to a further [25] question. Even if the total mass is not infinite, it may yet be great enough to admit a plurality of universes. The question might possibly be raised whether there is any obstacle to our believing that there are other universes composed on the pattern of our own, more than one, though stopping short of infinity. First, however, let us treat of the infinite universally.

7

[30] Every body must necessarily be either finite or infinite, and if infinite, either of similar or of dissimilar parts. If its parts are *dissimilar*, they must represent either a finite or an infinite number of kinds. That the kinds cannot be *infinite* is evident, if our original presuppositions remain unchallenged. For the primary movements being finite in number, the kinds of simple body are necessarily also finite, since the movement of a simple body is simple, and the simple movements are finite, and every natural body must always have its proper motion. [5] Now if the infinite body is to be composed of a *finite* number of kinds, then each of its parts must necessarily be infinite in quantity, that is to say, the water, fire, &c., which compose it. But this is impossible, because, as we have already shown, infinite weight and lightness do not exist. Moreover it would be necessary also that their places should be infinite in [10] extent, so that the movements too of all these bodies would be infinite. But this is not possible, if we are to hold to the truth of our original presuppositions and to the view that neither that which moves downward, nor, by the same reasoning, that which moves upward, can prolong its movement to infinity. For it is true in regard to quality, quantity, and place alike that any process of change is impossible [15] which can have no end. I mean that if it is impossible for a thing to have come to be white, or a cubit long, or in Egypt, it is also impossible for it to be in process of coming to be any of these. It is thus impossible for a thing to be moving to a place at which in its motion it can never by any possibility arrive. Again, suppose the body to exist in dispersion, it may be maintained none the less that the total of all these scattered particles, say, of fire, is infinite. [20] But body we saw to be that which has extension every way. How can there be several dissimilar elements, each infinite? Each would have to be infinitely extended every way.

It is no more conceivable, again, that the infinite should exist as a whole of *similar* parts. For, in the first place, there is no other

---
[1] *Physics*, III. 4-8.

⟨straight⟩ movement beyond those mentioned: we must therefore give it one of them. And if [25] so, we shall have to admit either infinite weight or infinite lightness. Nor, secondly, could the body whose movement is circular be infinite, since it is impossible for the infinite to move in a circle. This, indeed, would be as good as saying that the heavens are infinite, which we have shown to be impossible.

[30] Moreover, in general, it is impossible that the infinite should move at all. If it did, it would move either naturally or by constraint: and if by constraint, it possesses also a natural motion, that is to say, there is another place, infinite like itself, to which it will move. But that is impossible.

That in general it is impossible for the infinite to be acted upon by the finite or to act upon it may be shown as follows.

275ª ⟨1. *The infinite cannot be acted upon by the finite.*⟩ Let A be an infinite, B a finite, C the time of a given movement produced by one in the other. Suppose, then, that A was heated, or impelled, or modified in any way, or caused to undergo any sort of movement whatever, by B in the time C. Let D be less than B; and, assuming that a lesser agent moves a lesser pa- [5] tient in an equal time, call the quantity thus modified by D, E. Then, as D is to B, so is E to some finite quantum. We assume that the alteration of equal by equal takes equal time, and the alteration of less by less or of greater by greater takes the same time, if the quantity of the patient is such as to keep the proportion [10] which obtains between the agents, greater and less. If so, no movement can be caused in the infinite by any finite agent in any time whatever. For a less agent will produce that movement in a less patient in an equal time, and the proportionate equivalent of that patient will be a finite quantity, since no proportion holds between finite and infinite.

⟨2. *The infinite cannot act upon the finite.*⟩ Nor, again, can the infinite produce a move- [15] ment in the finite in any time whatever. Let A be an infinite, B a finite, C the time of action. In the time C, D will produce that motion in a patient less than B, say F. Then take E, bearing the same proportion to D as the whole BF bears to F. E will produce the motion in BF in the time C. Thus the finite and [20] the infinite effect the same alteration in equal times. But this is impossible; for the assumption is that the greater effects it in a shorter time. It will be the same with any time that can be taken, so that there will no time in which the infinite can effect this movement. And, as to infinite time, in that nothing can move another or be moved by it. For such time has no limit, while the action and reaction have.

⟨3. *There is no interaction between infinites.*⟩ Nor can infinite be acted upon in any [25] way by infinite. Let A and B be infinites, CD being the time of the action of A upon B. Now the whole B was modified in a certain time, and the part of this infinite, E, cannot be so modified in the same time, since we assume that a less quantity makes the movement in a less time. Let E then, when acted upon by A, [30] complete the movement in the time D. Then, as D is to CD, so is E to some finite part of B. This part will necessarily be moved by A in the time CD. For we suppose that the same agent produces a given effect on a greater and 275ᵇ a smaller mass in longer and shorter times, the times and masses varying proportionately. There is thus no finite time in which infinites can move one another. Is their time then infinite? No, for infinite time has no end, but the movement communicated has.

[5] If therefore every perceptible body possesses the power of acting or of being acted upon, or both of these, it is impossible that an infinite body should be perceptible. All bodies, however, that occupy place are perceptible. There is therefore no infinite body beyond the heaven. Nor again is there anything of limited extent beyond it. And so beyond the heaven there is no body at all. For if you suppose it an [10] object of intelligence, it will be in a place —since place is what 'within' and 'beyond' denote—and therefore an object of perception. But nothing that is not in a place is perceptible.

The question may also be examined in the light of more general considerations as follows. The infinite, considered as a whole of similar parts, cannot, on the one hand, move in a circle. For there is no centre of the infinite, and [15] that which moves in a circle moves about the centre. Nor again can the infinite move in a straight line. For there would have to be another place infinite like itself to be the goal of its natural movement and another, equally great, for the goal of its unnatural movement. Moreover, whether its rectilinear movement is natural or constrained, in either case the force [20] which causes its motion will have to be infinite. For infinite force is force of an infinite body, and of an infinite body the force is infinite. So the motive body also will be infinite. (The proof of this is given in our discussion of movement,[1] where it is shown that no finite thing possesses infinite power, and no infinite thing finite power.) If then that which moves naturally can also move unnaturally, there will [25] be two infinites, one which causes, and another which exhibits the latter motion. Again, what is it that moves the infinite? If it moves itself, it must be animate. But how can it possibly be conceived as an infinite animal? And if there is something else that moves it, there will be two infinites, that which moves and that which is moved, differing in their form and power.

[30] If the whole is not continuous, but exists, as Democritus and Leucippus think, in the form of parts separated by void, there must necessarily be one movement of all the multitude. They are distinguished, we are told, from 276a one another by their figures; but their nature is one, like many pieces of gold separated from one another. But each piece must, as we assert, have the same motion. For a single clod moves to the same place as the whole mass of earth, and a spark to the same place as the whole mass of fire. So that if it be weight that all possess, no body is, strictly speaking, light: and if [5] lightness be universal, none is heavy. Moreover, whatever possesses weight or lightness will have its place either at one of the extremes or in the middle region. But this is impossible while the world is conceived as infinite. And, generally, that which has no centre or extreme limit, no up or down, gives the bod-[10] ies no place for their motion; and without that movement is impossible. A thing must move either naturally or unnaturally, and the two movements are determined by the proper and alien places. Again, a place in which a thing rests or to which it moves unnaturally, [15] must be the natural place for some other body, as experience shows. Necessarily, therefore, not everything possesses weight or lightness, but some things do and some do not. From these arguments then it is clear that the body of the universe is not infinite.

8

We must now proceed to explain why there cannot be more than one heaven—the further question mentioned above. For it may be thought that we have not proved universally [20] of bodies that none whatever can exist outside our universe, and that our argument applied only to those of indeterminate extent.

Now all things rest and move naturally and

[1] *Physics*, VIII. 10.

by constraint. A thing moves naturally to a place in which it rests without constraint, and rests naturally in a place to which it moves [25] without constraint. On the other hand, a thing moves by constraint to a place in which it rests by constraint, and rests by constraint in a place to which it moves by constraint. Further, if a given movement is due to constraint, its contrary is natural. If, then, it is by constraint that earth moves from a certain place to the centre here, its movement from here to there will be natural, and if earth from there rests here without constraint, its movement hith-[30] er will be natural. And the natural movement in each case is one. Further, these worlds, being similar in nature to ours, must all be composed of the same bodies as it. Moreover each of the bodies, fire, I mean, and earth and 276b their intermediates, must have the same power as in our world. For if these names are used equivocally, if the identity of name does not rest upon an identity of form in these elements and ours, then the whole to which they belong can only be called a world by equivoca-[5] tion. Clearly, then, one of the bodies will move naturally away from the centre and another towards the centre, since fire must be identical with fire, earth with earth, and so on, as the fragments of each are identical in this world. That this must be the case is evident from the principles laid down in our discussion of the movements,[2] for these are limited in number, and the distinction of the elements [10] depends upon the distinction of the movements. Therefore, since the movements are the same, the elements must also be the same everywhere. The particles of earth, then, in another world move naturally also to our centre and its fire to our circumference. This, [15] however, is impossible, since, if it were true, earth must, in its own world, move upwards, and fire to the centre; in the same way the earth of our world must move naturally away from the centre when it moves towards the centre of another universe. This follows from the supposed juxtaposition of the worlds. For either we must refuse to admit the iden-[20] tical nature of the simple bodies in the various universes, or, admitting this, we must make the centre and the extremity one as suggested. This being so, it follows that there cannot be more worlds than one.

To postulate a difference of nature in the simple bodies according as they are more or less distant from their proper places is unrea-

[2] Above, Chapters 2-4.

sonable. For what difference can it make whether we say that a thing is this distance [25] away or that? One would have to suppose a difference proportionate to the distance and increasing with it, but the form is in fact the same. Moreover, the bodies must have some movement, since the fact that they move is quite evident. Are we to say then that all their movements, even those which are mutually contrary, are due to constraint? No, for a body which has no natural movement at all cannot be moved by constraint. If then the [30] bodies have a natural movement, the movement of the particular instances of each form must necessarily have for goal a place numerically one, i.e. a particular centre or a particular extremity. If it be suggested that the goal in each case is one in form but numer-277ª ically more than one, on the analogy of particulars which are many though each undifferentiated in form, we reply that the variety of goal cannot be limited to this portion or that but must extend to all alike. For all are equally undifferentiated in form, but any one [5] is different numerically from any other. What I mean is this: if the portions in this world behave similarly both to one another and to those in another world, then the portion which is taken hence will not behave differently either from the portions in another world or from those in the same world, but similarly to them, since in form no portion differs from another. The result is that we must either abandon our present assumptions [10] or assert that the centre and the extremity are each numerically one. But this being so, the heaven, by the same evidence and the same necessary inferences, must be one only and no more.

A consideration of the other kinds of movement also makes it plain that there is some point to which earth and fire move naturally. For in general that which is moved changes [15] from something into something, the starting-point and the goal being different in form, and always it is a finite change. For instance, to recover health is to change from disease to health, to increase is to change from smallness to greatness. Locomotion must be similar: for it also has its goal and starting-point—and therefore the starting-point and the goal of the natural movement must differ in form—just as the movement of coming to [20] health does not take any direction which chance or the wishes of the mover may select. Thus, too, fire and earth move not to infinity but to opposite points; and since the opposition in place is between above and below, these will be the limits of their movement. (Even in circular movement there is a sort of opposition between the ends of the diameter, though the movement as a whole has no contrary: so that [25] here too the movement has in a sense an opposed and finite goal.) There must therefore be some end to locomotion: it cannot continue to infinity.

This conclusion that local movement is not continued to infinity is corroborated by the fact that earth moves more quickly the nearer it is to the centre, and fire the nearer it is to [30] the upper place. But if movement were infinite speed would be infinite also; and if speed then weight and lightness. For as superior speed in downward movement implies superior weight, so infinite increase of weight necessitates infinite increase of speed.

277ᵇ Further, it is not the action of another body that makes one of these bodies move up and the other down; nor is it constraint, like the 'extrusion' of some writers. For in that case the larger the mass of fire or earth the slower would be the upward or downward movement; but the fact is the reverse: the greater the mass of fire or earth the quicker [5] always is its movement towards its own place. Again, the speed of the movement would not increase towards the end if it were due to constraint or extrusion; for a constrained movement always diminishes in speed as the source of constraint becomes more distant, and a body moves without constraint to the place whence it was moved by constraint.

A consideration of these points, then, gives adequate assurance of the truth of our contentions. The same could also be shown with the [10] aid of the discussions which fall under First Philosophy, as well as from the nature of the circular movement, which must be eternal both here and in the other worlds. It is plain, too, from the following considerations that the universe must be one.

The bodily elements are three, and there-[15] fore the places of the elements will be three also; the place, first, of the body which sinks to the bottom, namely the region about the centre; the place, secondly, of the revolving body, namely the outermost place, and thirdly, the intermediate place, belonging to the intermediate body. Here in this third place will be the body which rises to the surface; since, if not here, it will be elsewhere, and it cannot be elsewhere: for we have two bodies, one weightless, one endowed with weight, and below is [20] the place of the body endowed with weight, since the region about the centre has been given to the heavy body. And its position cannot be unnatural to it, for it would have to be natural to something else, and there is nothing else. It must then occupy the intermediate place. What distinctions there are within the intermediate itself we will explain later on.

We have now said enough to make plain the character and number of the bodily elements, the place of each, and further, in gen- [25] eral, how many in number the various places are.

9

We must show not only that the heaven is one, but also that more than one heaven is impossible, and, further, that, as exempt from decay and generation, the heaven is eternal. We may begin by raising a difficulty. From one point of [30] view it might seem impossible that the heaven should be one and unique, since in all formations and products whether of nature or of art we can distinguish the shape in itself and the shape in combination with matter. For 278ª instance the form of the sphere is one thing and the gold or bronze sphere another; the shape of the circle again is one thing, the bronze or wooden circle another. For when we state the essential nature of the sphere or circle we do not include in the formula gold or [5] bronze, because they do not belong to the essence, but if we are speaking of the copper or gold sphere we do include them. We still make the distinction even if we cannot conceive or apprehend any other example beside the particular thing. This may, of course, sometimes be the case: it might be, for instance, that only one circle could be found; yet none the less the difference will remain between the being of circle and of this particular circle, the one being form, the other form in matter, i.e. a par- [10] ticular thing. Now since the universe is perceptible it must be regarded as a particular; for everything that is perceptible subsists, as we know, in matter. But if it is a particular, there will be a distinction between the being of 'this universe' and of 'universe' unqualified. There is a difference, then, between 'this universe' and simple 'universe'; the second is form and [15] shape, the first form in combination with matter; and any shape or form has, or may have, more than one particular instance.

On the supposition of Forms such as some assert, this must be the case, and equally on the view that no such entity has a separate existence. For in every case in which the essence is in matter it is a fact of observation that the particulars of like form are several or infinite [20] in number. Hence there either are, or may be, more heavens than one. On these grounds, then, it might be inferred either that there are or that there might be several heavens. We must, however, return and ask how much of this argument is correct and how much not.

Now it is quite right to say that the formula of the shape apart from the matter must be different [25] from that of the shape in the matter, and we may allow this to be true. We are not, however, therefore compelled to assert a plurality of worlds. Such a plurality is in fact impossible if this world contains the entirety of matter, as in fact it does. But perhaps our contention can be made clearer in this way. Suppose 'aquilinity' to be curvature in the nose [30] or flesh, and flesh to be the matter of aquilinity. Suppose further, that all flesh came together into a single whole of flesh endowed with this aquiline quality. Then neither would there be, nor could there arise, any other thing that was aquiline. Similarly, suppose flesh and bones to be the matter of man, and suppose a [35] man to be created of all flesh and all bones in indissoluble union. The possibility of another man would be removed. Whatever case you took it would be the same. The general rule is this: a thing whose essence resides in a substratum of matter can never come into being in the absence of all matter. Now the universe is certainly a particular and a material thing: if however, it is composed not of a part [5] but of the whole of matter, then though the being of 'universe' and of 'this universe' are still distinct, yet there is no other universe, and no possibility of others being made, because all the matter is already included in this. It remains, then, only to prove that it is composed of all natural perceptible body.

[10] First, however, we must explain what we mean by 'heaven' and in how many senses we use the word, in order to make clearer the object of our inquiry. (*a*) In one sense, then, we call 'heaven' the substance of the extreme circumference of the whole, or that natural body whose place is at the extreme circumference. We recognize habitually a special right to the [15] name 'heaven' in the extremity or upper region, which we take to be the seat of all that is divine. (*b*) In another sense, we use this

name for the body continuous with the extreme circumference which contains the moon, the sun, and some of the stars; these we say are 'in the heaven'. (c) In yet another sense we give the name to all body included within [20] the extreme circumference, since we habitually call the whole or totality 'the heaven'. The word, then, is used in three senses.

Now the whole included within the extreme circumference must be composed of *all* physical and sensible body, because there neither is, nor can come into being, any body outside the [25] heaven. For if there is a natural body outside the extreme circumference it must be either a simple or a composite body, and its position must be either natural or unnatural. But it cannot be any of the simple bodies. For, first, it has been shown[1] that that which moves [30] in a circle cannot change its place. And, secondly, it cannot be that which moves from the centre or that which lies lowest. *Naturally* they could not be there, since their proper places are elsewhere; and if these are there *unnaturally,* the exterior place will be natural to some other body, since a place which is unnatural to one body must be natural to another: but we saw that there is no other body besides [35] these.[2] Then it is not possible that any simple body should be outside the heaven. But, if no simple body, neither can any mixed body be there: for the presence of the simple body is involved in the presence of the mixture. Further neither can any body come into that place: for it will do so either naturally or unnaturally, and will be either simple [5] or composite; so that the same argument will apply, since it makes no difference whether the question is 'does *A* exist?' or 'could *A* come to exist?' From our arguments then it is evident not only that there is not, but also that there could never come to be, any bodily mass whatever outside the circumference. The world as a whole, therefore, includes *all* its appropriate matter, which is, as we saw, natural perceptible body. So that neither are there now, nor have there ever been, nor can [10] there ever be formed more heavens than one, but this heaven of ours is one and unique and complete.

It is therefore evident that there is also no place or void or time outside the heaven. For in every place body can be present; and void is said to be that in which the presence of [15] body, though not actual, is possible; and

[1] Chapters 2 and 3 above.
[2] Chapter 2 above.

time is the number of movement. But in the absence of natural body there is no movement, and outside the heaven, as we have shown, body neither exists nor can come to exist. It is clear then that there is neither place, nor void, nor time, outside the heaven. Hence whatever is there, is of such a nature as not to occupy any place, nor does time age it; nor is there any [20] change in any of the things which lie beyond the outermost motion; they continue through their entire duration unalterable and unmodified, living the best and most self-sufficient of lives. As a matter of fact, this word 'duration' possessed a divine significance for the ancients, for the fulfilment which includes the period of life of any creature, outside of which no natural development can fall, has [25] been called its duration. On the same principle the fulfilment of the whole heaven, the fulfilment which includes all time and infinity, is 'duration'—a name based upon the fact that it *is always*—duration immortal and divine. From it derive the being and life which [30] other things, some more or less articulately but others feebly, enjoy. So, too, in its discussions concerning the divine, popular philosophy often propounds the view that whatever is divine, whatever is primary and supreme, is necessarily unchangeable. This fact confirms what we have said. For there is nothing else stronger than it to move it—since that [35] would mean more divine—and it has no defect and lacks none of its proper excellences. Its unceasing movement, then, is also reasonable, since everything ceases to move when it comes to its proper place, but the body whose path is the circle has one and the same place for starting-point and goal.

10

Having established these distinctions, we may [5] now proceed to the question whether the heaven is ungenerated or generated, indestructible or destructible. Let us start with a review of the theories of other thinkers; for the proofs of a theory are difficulties for the contrary theory. Besides, those who have first heard the pleas of our adversaries will be more likely to credit the [10] assertions which we are going to make. We shall be less open to the charge of procuring judgement by default. To give a satisfactory decision as to the truth it is necessary to be rather an arbitrator than a party to the dispute.

That the world was generated all are agreed, but, generation over, some say that it is eternal, others say that it is destructible like any other natural formation. Others again, with Empedocles of Acragas and Heraclitus of Ephesus, believe that there is alternation in the destructive process, which takes now this direction, now that, and continues without end.

Now to assert that it was generated and yet is eternal is to assert the impossible; for we cannot reasonably attribute to anything any characteristics but those which observation detects in many or all instances. But in this case the facts point the other way: generated things are seen always to be destroyed. Further, a thing whose present state had no beginning and which could not have been other than it was at any previous moment throughout its entire duration, cannot possibly be changed. For there will have to be some cause of change, and if this had been present earlier it would have made possible another condition of that to which any other condition was impossible. Suppose that the world was formed out of elements which were formerly otherwise conditioned than as they are now. Then (1) if their condition was always so and could not have been otherwise, the world could never have come into being. And (2) if the world did come into being, then, clearly, their condition must have been capable of change and not eternal: after combination therefore they will be dispersed, just as in the past after dispersion they came into combination, and this process either has been, or could have been, indefinitely repeated. But if this is so, the world cannot be indestructible, and it does not matter whether the change of condition has actually occurred or remains a possibility.

Some of those who hold that the world, though indestructible, was yet generated, try to support their case by a parallel which is illusory. They say that in their statements about its generation they are doing what geometricians do when they construct their figures, not implying that the universe really had a beginning, but for didactic reasons facilitating understanding by exhibiting the object, like the figure, as in course of formation. The two cases, as we said, are not parallel; for, in the construction of the figure, when the various steps are completed the required figure forthwith results; but in these other demonstrations what results is not that which was required. Indeed it cannot be so; for antecedent and consequent, as assumed, are in contradiction. The ordered, it is said,[1] arose out of the unordered; and the same thing cannot be at the same time both ordered and unordered; there must be a process and a lapse of time separating the two states. In the figure, on the other hand, there is no temporal separation. It is clear then that the universe cannot be at once eternal and generated.

To say that the universe alternately combines and dissolves is no more paradoxical than to make it eternal but varying in shape. It is as if one were to think that there was now destruction and now existence when from a child a man is generated, and from a man a child. For it is clear that when the elements come together the result is not a chance system and combination, but the very same as before —especially on the view of those who hold this theory, since they say that the contrary is the cause of each state. So that if the totality of body, which is a continuum, is now in this order or disposition and now in that, and if the combination of the whole is a world or heaven, then it will not be the world that comes into being and is destroyed, but only its dispositions.

If the world is believed to be one, it is impossible to suppose that it should be, as a whole, first generated and then destroyed, never to reappear; since before it came into being there was always present the combination prior to it, and that, we hold, could never change if it was never generated. If, on the other hand, the worlds are infinite in number the view is more plausible. But whether this is, or is not, impossible will be clear from what follows. For there are some who think it possible both for the ungenerated to be destroyed and for the generated to persist undestroyed. (This is held in the *Timaeus,* where Plato says that the heaven, though it was generated, will none the less exist to eternity.) So far as the heaven is concerned we have answered this view with arguments appropriate to the nature of the heaven: on the general question we shall attain clearness when we examine the matter universally.

11

We must first distinguish the senses in which we use the words 'ungenerated' and 'generated', 'destructible' and 'indestructible'. These have many meanings, and though it may make no difference to the argument, yet some confusion of mind must result from treating

[1] Cp. Plato, *Timaeus,* 30.

[5] as uniform in its use a word which has several distinct applications. The character which is the ground of the predication will always remain obscure.

The word 'ungenerated' then is used (*a*) in one sense whenever something now is which formerly was not, no process of becoming or change being involved. Such is the case, according to some, with contact and motion, since there is no process of coming to be in contact or in motion. (*b*) It is used in another sense, when something which is capable of coming [10] to be, with or without process, does not exist; such a thing is ungenerated in the sense that its generation is not a fact but a possibility. (*c*) It is also applied where there is general impossibility of any generation such that the thing now is which then was not. And 'impossibility' has two uses: first, where it is untrue to say that the thing can ever come into being, and secondly, where it cannot do so easily, quickly, or well. In the same way the [15] word 'generated' is used, (*a*) first, where what formerly was not afterwards is, whether a process of becoming was or was not involved, so long as that which then was not, now is; (*b*) secondly, of anything capable of existing, 'capable' being defined with reference either to truth or to facility; (*c*) thirdly, of anything to which the passage from not being to being belongs, whether already actual, if its existence is due to a past process of becoming, or not [20] yet actual but only possible. The uses of the words 'destructible' and 'indestructible' are similar. 'Destructible' is applied (*a*) to that which formerly was and afterwards either is not or might not be, whether a period of being destroyed and changed intervenes or not; and (*b*) sometimes we apply the word to that which a process of destruction may cause not to be; and also (*c*) in a third sense, to that [25] which is easily destructible, to the 'easily-destroyed', so to speak. Of the indestructible the same account holds good. It is either (*a*) that which now is and now is not, without any process of destruction, like contact, which without being destroyed afterwards is not, though formerly it was; or (*b*) that which is but might not be, or which will at some time not be, though it now is. For you exist now and [30] so does the contact; yet both are destructible, because a time will come when it will not be true of you that you exist, nor of these things that they are in contact. Thirdly (*c*) in its most proper use, it is that which is, but is incapable of any destruction such that the thing which now is later ceases to be or might cease to be; or again, that which has not yet been destroyed, but in the future may cease to be. 281ª For indestructible is also used of that which is destroyed with difficulty.

This being so, we must ask what we mean by 'possible' and 'impossible'. For in its most proper use the predicate 'indestructible' is given because it is impossible that the thing should be destroyed, i.e. exist at one time and [5] not at another. And 'ungenerated' also involves impossibility when used for that which cannot be generated, in such fashion that, while formerly it was not, later it is. An instance is a commensurable diagonal. Now when we speak of a power to move or to lift weights, we refer always to the maximum. We speak, for instance, of a power to lift a hundred talents or walk a hundred stades—though a power to effect the maximum is also a power [10] to effect any part of the maximum—since we feel obliged in defining the power to give the limit or maximum. A thing, then, which is capable of a certain amount as maximum must also be capable of that which lies within it. If, for example, a man can lift a hundred talents, he can also lift two, and if he can walk a hundred stades, he can also walk two. But the power [15] is of the maximum, and a thing said, with reference to its maximum, to be incapable of so much is also incapable of any greater amount. It is, for instance, clear that a person who cannot walk a thousand stades will also be unable to walk a thousand and one. This point need not trouble us, for we may take it as settled that what is, in the strict sense, possible is determined by a limiting maximum. Now [20] perhaps the objection might be raised [25] that there is no necessity in this, since he who sees a stade need not see the smaller measures contained in it, while, on the contrary, he who can see a dot or hear a small sound will perceive what is greater. This, however, does not touch our argument. The maximum may be determined either in the power or in its object. The application of this is plain. Superior sight is sight of the smaller body, but superior speed is that of the greater body.

12

Having established these distinctions we can now proceed to the sequel. If there are things capable both of being and of not being, there must be some definite maximum time of their [30] being and not being; a time, I mean, during which continued existence is possible to them and a time during which continued non-existence is possible. And this is true in every category, whether the thing is, for example, 'man', or 'white', or 'three cubits long', or whatever it may be. For if the time is not definite in quantity, but longer than any that can be suggested and shorter than none, then it will be possible for one and the same thing to exist for infinite time and not to exist for another infinity. This, however, is impossible.

Let us take our start from this point. The impossible and the false have not the same significance. One use of 'impossible' and 'possible', and 'false' and 'true', is hypothetical. It is impossible, for instance, on a certain hypothesis that the triangle should have its angles equal to two right angles, and on another the diagonal is commensurable. But there are also things possible and impossible, false and true, absolutely. Now it is one thing to be absolutely false, and another thing to be absolutely impossible. To say that you are standing when you are not standing is to assert a falsehood, [10] but not an impossibility. Similarly to say that a man who is playing the harp, but not singing, is singing, is to say what is false but not impossible. To say, however, that you are at once standing and sitting, or that the diagonal is commensurable, is to say what is not only false but also impossible. Thus it is not the same thing to make a false and to make an impossible hypothesis, and from the impossible [15] hypothesis impossible results follow. A man has, it is true, the capacity at once of sitting and of standing, because when he possesses the one he also possesses the other; but it does not follow that he can at once sit and stand, only that at another time he can do the other also. But if a thing has for infinite time more than one capacity, another time is impossible and the times must coincide. Thus if any- [20] thing which exists for infinite time is destructible, it will have the capacity of not being. Now if it exists for infinite time let this capacity be actualized; and it will be in actuality at once existent and non-existent. Thus a false conclusion would follow because a false assumption was made, but if what was assumed had not been impossible its consequence [25] would not have been impossible.

Anything then which always exists is absolutely imperishable. It is also ungenerated, since if it was generated it will have the power for some time of not being. For as that which formerly was, but now is not, or is capable at some future time of not being, is destructible, so that which is capable of formerly not having been is generated. But in the case of that which always is, there is no time for such a capacity of [30] not being, whether the supposed time is finite or infinite; for its capacity of being must include the finite time since it covers infinite time.

It is therefore impossible that one and the same thing should be capable of always existing and of always not-existing. And 'not always existing', the contradictory, is also excluded. Thus it is impossible for a thing always 282ª to exist and yet to be destructible. Nor, similarly, can it be generated. For of two attributes if B cannot be present without A, the impossibility of A proves the impossibility of B. What always is, then, since it is incapable of ever not being, cannot possibly be generated. [5] But since the contradictory of 'that which is always capable of being' is 'that which is not always capable of being'; while 'that which is always capable of not being' is the contrary, whose contradictory in turn is 'that which is not always capable of not being', it is necessary that the contradictories of both terms should be predicable of one and the same thing, and thus that, intermediate between what always is and what always is not, there should be that [10] to which being and not-being are both possible; for the contradictory of each will at times be true of it unless it always exists. Hence that which not always is not will sometimes be and sometimes not be; and it is clear that this is true also of that which cannot always be but sometimes is and therefore sometimes is not. One thing, then, will have the power of being, and will thus be intermediate between the other two.

Expressed universally our argument is as fol- [15] lows. Let there be two attributes, A and B, not capable of being present in any one thing together, while either A or C and either B or D are capable of being present in everything. Then C and D must be predicated of everything of which neither A nor B is predicated. Let E lie between A and B; for that which is neither of two contraries is a mean between them. In E both C and D must be present, for [20] either A or C is present everywhere and therefore in E. Since then A is impossible, C must be present, and the same argument holds of D.

Neither that which always is, therefore, nor that which always is not is either generated or destructible. And clearly whatever is generated or destructible is not eternal. If it were, it would be at once capable of always being and [25] capable of not always being, but it has already been shown[1] that this is impossible. Surely then whatever is ungenerated and in being must be eternal, and whatever is indestructible and in being must equally be so. (I use the words 'ungenerated' and 'indestructible' in their proper sense, 'ungenerated' for that which now is and could not at any previous time have been truly said not to be; 'indestructible' for that which now is and cannot [30] at any future time be truly said not to be.) If, again, the two terms are coincident, if the ungenerated is indestructible, and the indestructible ungenearted, then each of them is 282b coincident with 'eternal'; anything ungenerated is eternal and anything indestructible is eternal. This is clear too from the definition of the terms, Whatever is destructible must be generated; for it is either ungenerated, or generated, but, if ungenerated, it is by hypothesis indestructible. Whatever, further, is generated must be destructible. For it is either [5]destructible or indestructible, but, if indestructible, it is by hypothesis ungenerated.

If, however, 'indestructible' and 'ungenerated' are not coincident, there is no necessity that either the ungenerated or the indestructible should be eternal. But they must be coincident, for the following reasons. The terms 'generated' and 'destructible' are coincident; [10] this is obvious from our former remarks, since between what always is and what always is not there is an intermediate which is neither, and that intermediate is the generated and destructible. For whatever is either of these is capable both of being and of not being for a definite time: in either case, I mean, there is a certain period of time during which the thing is and another during which it is not. Anything [15] therefore which is generated or destructible must be intermediate. Now let A be that which always is and B that which always is not, C the generated, and D the destructible. Then C must be intermediate between A and B. For in their case there is no time in the direction of either limit, in which either A is not or B is. But for the generated there must be such a [20] time either actually or potentially, though not for A and B in either way. C then will be, and also not be, for a limited length of time, and this is true also of D, the destructible. Therefore each is both generated and destructible. Therefore 'generated' and 'destructible' are coincident. Now let E stand for the ungen- [25] erated, F for the generated, G for the indestructible, and H for the destructible. As for F and H, it has been shown that they are coincident. But when terms stand to one another as these do, F and H coincident, E and F never predicated of the same thing but one or other of everything, and G and H likewise, then E [30] and G must needs be coincident. For suppose that E is not coincident with G, then F will be, since either E or F is predictable of everything. But of that of which F is predicated H will be predicable also. H will then be 283a coincident with G, but this we saw to be impossible. And the same argument shows that G is coincident with E.

Now the relation of the ungenerated (E) to the generated (F) is the same as that of the indestructible (G) to the destructible (H). To say then that there is no reason why anything should not be generated and yet indestructible [5] or ungenerated and yet destroyed, to imagine that in the one case generation and in the other case destruction occurs once for all, is to destroy part of the data. For (1) everything is capable of acting or being acted upon, of being or not being, either for an infinite, or for a definitely limited space of time; and the infinite time is only a possible alternative because it is after a fashion defined, as a length of time [10] which cannot be exceeded. But infinity in one direction is neither infinite or finite. (2) Further, why, after always existing, was the thing destroyed, why, after an infinity of not being, was it generated, at one moment rather than another? If every moment is alike and the moments are infinite in number, it is clear that a generated or destructible thing existed for an infinite time. It has therefore for an infinite time the capacity of not being (since the capacity [15] of being and the capacity of not being will be present together), if destructible, in the time before destruction, if generated, in the time after generation. If then we assume the two capacities to be actualized, opposites will be present together. (3) Further, this second capacity will be present like the first at every moment, so that the thing will have for an infinite time the capacity both of being and of not being; but this has been shown to be im- [20] possible. (4) Again, if the capacity is present prior to the activity, it will be present for all time, even while the thing was as yet ungenerated and non-existent, throughout the infinite time in which it was capable of being

---
[1] 281b 18 ff.

generated. At the time, then, when it was not, at that same time it had the capacity of being, both of being then and of being thereafter, and therefore for an infinity of time.

[25] It is clear also on other grounds that it is impossible that the destructible should not at some time be destroyed. For otherwise it will always be at once destructible and in actuality indestructible, so that it will be at the same time capable of always existing and of not always existing. Thus the destructible is at some time actually destroyed. The generable, similarly, has been generated, for it is capable of having been generated and thus also of not always existing.

[30] We may also see in the following way how impossible it is either for a thing which is generated to be thenceforward indestructible, or for a thing which is ungenerated and has always hitherto existed to be destroyed. Nothing that is by chance can be indestructible or ungenerated, since the products of chance and 283b fortune are opposed to what is, or comes to be, always or usually, while anything which exists for a time infinite either absolutely or in one direction, is in existence either always or usually. That which is by chance, then, is by nature such as to exist at one time and not at another. But in things of that character the [5] contradictory states proceed from one and the same capacity, the matter of the thing being the cause equally of its existence and of its non-existence. Hence contradictories would be present together in actuality.

Further, it cannot truly be said of a thing now that it exists last year, nor could it be said last year that it exists now. It is therefore impossible for what once did not exist later to be eternal. For in its later state it will possess the capacity of not existing, only not of not [10] existing at a time when it exists—since then it exists in actuality—but of not existing last year or in the past. Now suppose it to be in actuality what it is capable of being. It will then be true to say now that it does not exist last year. But this is impossible. No capacity relates to being in the past, but always to being in the present or future. It is the same with the notion of an eternity of existence followed later [15] by non-existence. In the later state the capacity will be present for that which is not there in actuality. Actualize, then, the capacity. It will be true to say now that this exists last year or in the past generally.

Considerations also not general like these but proper to the subject show it to be impossible that what was formerly eternal should later be destroyed or that what formerly was not should [20] later be eternal. Whatever is destructible or generated is always alterable. Now alteration is due to contraries, and the things which compose the natural body are the very same that destroy it.

· · ·

BOOK II

1

THAT the heaven as a whole neither came into being nor admits of destruction, as some assert, but is one and eternal, with no end or beginning of its total duration, containing and em-[30] bracing in itself the infinity of time, we may convince ourselves not only by the arguments already set forth but also by a consideration of the views of those who differ from us in providing for its generation. If our view is a possible one, and the manner of generation 284a which they assert is impossible, this fact will have great weight in convincing us of the immortality and eternity of the world. Hence it is well to persuade oneself of the truth of the ancient and truly traditional theories, that there is some immortal and divine thing which possesses movement, but movement such as [5] has no limit and is rather itself the limit of all other movement. A limit is a thing which contains; and this motion, being perfect, contains those imperfect motions which have a limit and a goal, having itself no beginning or end, but unceasing through the infinity of [10] time, and of other movements, to some the cause of their beginning, to others offering the goal. The ancients gave to the Gods the heaven or upper place, as being alone immortal; and our present argument testifies that it is indestructible and ungenerated. Further, it is unaffected by any mortal discomfort, and, [15] in addition, effortless; for it needs no constraining necessity to keep it to its path, and prevent it from moving with some other movement more natural to itself. Such a constrained movement would necessarily involve effort—the more so, the more eternal it were—and would be inconsistent with perfection. Hence we must not believe the old tale which says [20] that the world needs some Atlas to keep it safe—a tale composed, it would seem, by men who, like later thinkers, conceived of all the upper bodies as earthy and endowed with weight, and therefore supported it in their fabulous way upon animate necessity. We must no more believe that than follow Empedocles when he says that the world, by being whirled [25] round, received a movement quick enough to overpower its own downward tendency, and thus has been kept from destruction all this time. Nor, again, is it conceivable that it should persist eternally by the necessitation of a soul. For a soul could not live in such conditions painlessly or happily, since the movement [30] involves constraint, being imposed on the first body, whose natural motion is different, and imposed continuously. It must therefore be uneasy and devoid of all rational satisfaction; for it could not even, like the soul of mortal animals, take recreation in the bodily relaxation of [35] sleep. An Ixion's lot must needs possess it, 284b without end or respite. If then, as we said, the view already stated of the first motion is a possible one, it is not only more appropriate so to conceive of its eternity, but also on this hypothesis alone are we able to advance a [5] theory consistent with popular divinations of the divine nature. But of this enough for the present.

2

Since there are some who say that there is a right and a left in the heaven, with those who are known as Pythagoreans—to whom indeed the view really belongs—we must consider whether, if we are to apply these principles to [10] the body of the universe, we should follow their statement of the matter or find a better way. At the start we may say that, if right and left are applicable, there are prior principles which must first be applied. These principles have been analysed in the discussion of the movements of animals,[1] for the reason that they are proper to animal nature. For in some [15] animals we find all such distinctions of parts as this of right and left clearly present, and in others some; but in plants we find only above and below. Now if we are to apply to the heaven such a distinction of parts, we must expect, as we have said, to find in it also that [20] distinction which in animals is found first of them all. The distinctions are three, namely, above and below, front and its opposite, right and left—all these three oppositions we expect to find in the perfect body—and each may be called a principle. Above is the principle of

[1] *On the Gait of Animals*, chapters 4, 5.

[25] length, right of breadth, front of depth. Or again we may connect them with the various movements, taking principle to mean that part, in a thing capable of movement, from which movement first begins. Growth starts from above, locomotion from the right, sense-movement from in front (for front is simply [30] the part to which the senses are directed). Hence we must not look for above and below, right and left, front and back, in every kind of body, but only in those which, being animate, have a principle of movement within themselves. For in no inanimate thing do we observe a part from which movement originates. Some do not move at all, some move, but not [35] indifferently in any direction; fire, for ex-285a ample, only upward, and earth only to the centre. It is true that we speak of above and below, right and left, in these bodies relatively to ourselves. The reference may be to our own right hands, as with the diviner, or to some similarity to our own members, such as the [5] parts of a statue possess; or we may take the contrary spatial order, calling right that which is to our left, and left that which is to our right. We observe, however, in the things themselves none of these distinctions; indeed if they are turned round we proceed to speak of the opposite parts as right and left, above [10] and below, front and back. Hence it is remarkable that the Pythagoreans should have spoken of these two principles, right and left, only, to the exclusion of the other four, which have as good a title as they. There is no less difference between above and below or front [15] and back in animals generally than between right and left. The difference is sometimes only one of function, sometimes also one of shape; and while the distinction of above and below is characteristic of all animate things, whether plants or animals, that of right and left is not found in plants. Further, inasmuch as length is prior to breadth, if above is the [20] principle of length, right of breadth, and if the principle of that which is prior is itself prior, then above will be prior to right, or let us say, since 'prior' is ambiguous, prior in order of generation. If, in addition, above is the region from which movement originates, right the region in which it starts, front the region [25] to which it is directed, then on this ground too above has a certain original character as compared with the other forms of position. On these two grounds, then, they may fairly be criticized, first, for omitting the more fundamental principles, and secondly, for thinking

that the two they mentioned were attributable equally to everything.

Since we have already determined that functions of this kind belong to things which possess a principle of movement, and that the [30] heaven is animate and possesses a principle of movement, clearly the heaven must also exhibit above and below, right and left. We need not be troubled by the question, arising from the spherical shape of the world, how there can be a distinction of right and left 285ᵇ within it, all parts being alike and all for ever in motion. We must think of the world as of something in which right differs from left in shape as well as in other respects, which subsequently is included in a sphere. The difference of function will persist, but will appear [5] not to by reason of the regularity of shape. In the same fashion must we conceive of the beginning of its movement. For even if it never began to move, yet it must possess a principle from which it would have begun to move if it had begun, and from which it would begin again if it came to a stand. Now by its length I mean the interval between its poles, one pole [10] being above and the other below; for two hemispheres are specially distinguished from all others by the immobility of the poles. Further, by 'transverse' in the universe we commonly mean, not above and below, but a direction crossing the line of the poles, which, by implication, is length: for transverse motion is [15] motion crossing motion up and down. Of the poles, that which we see above us is the lower region, and that which we do not see is the upper. For right in anything is, as we say, the region in which locomotion originates, and the rotation of the heaven originates in the region from which the stars rise. So this will be the right, and the region where they set the [20] left. If then they begin from the right and move round to the right, the upper must be the unseen pole. For if it is the pole we see, the movement will be leftward, which we deny to be the fact. Clearly then the invisible pole is above. And those who live in the other [25] hemisphere are above and to the right, while we are below and to the left. This is just the opposite of the view of the Pythagoreans, who make us above and on the right side and those in the other hemisphere below and on the left side; the fact being the exact opposite. Relatively, however, to the secondary revolution, I mean that of the planets, we are above and on [30] the right and they are below and on the left. For the principle of their movement has the reverse position, since the movement itself is the contrary of the other: hence it follows that we are at its beginning and they at its 286ᵃ end. Here we may end our discussion of the distinctions of parts created by the three dimensions and of the consequent differences of position.

3

Since circular motion is not the contrary of the reverse circular motion, we must consider why [5] there is more than one motion, though we have to pursue our inquiries at a distance—a distance created not so much by our spatial position as by the fact that our senses enable us to perceive very few of the attributes of the heavenly bodies. But let not that deter us. The reason must be sought in the following facts. Everything which has a function exists for its function. The activity of God is immortality, [10] i.e. eternal life. Therefore the movement of that which is divine must be eternal. But such is the heaven, viz. a divine body, and for that reason to it is given the circular body whose nature it is to move always in a circle. Why, then, is not the whole body of the heaven of the same character as that part? Because there must be something at rest at the centre of the revolving body; and of that body no part [15] can be at rest, either elsewhere or at the centre. It could do so only if the body's natural movement were towards the centre. But the circular movement is natural, since otherwise it could not be eternal: for nothing unnatural is eternal. The unnatural is subsequent to the natural, being a derangement of the natural [20] which occurs in the course of its generation. Earth then has to exist; for it is earth which is at rest at the centre. (At present we may take this for granted: it shall be explained later.[1]) But if earth must exist, so must fire. For, if one of a pair of contraries naturally exists, the other, if it is really contrary, exists also naturally. In some form it must be present, [25] since the matter of contraries is the same. Also, the positive is prior to its privation (warm, for instance, to cold), and rest and heaviness stand for the privation of lightness and movement. But further, if fire and earth exist, the intermediate bodies must exist also: [30] for each element stands in a contrary relation to every other. (This, again, we will here take for granted and try later to explain.[2]) With these four elements generation clearly is

[1] See chapter 14.
[2] See *On Generation and Corruption*, II. 3, 4.

involved, since none of them can be eternal: for contraries interact with one another and destroy one another. Further, it is inconceivable that a movable body should be eternal, if [35] its movement cannot be regarded as naturally eternal: and these bodies we know to possess movement. Thus we see that generation is necessarily involved. But if so, there must be at least one other circular motion: for a single movement of the whole heaven would necessitate an identical relation of the elements [5] of bodies to one another. This matter also shall be cleared up in what follows: but for the present so much is clear, that the reason why there is more than one circular body is the necessity of generation, which follows on the presence of fire, which, with that of the other bodies, follows on that of earth; and earth is required because eternal movement in one body necessitates eternal rest in another.

4

[10] The shape of the heaven is of necessity spherical; for that is the shape most appropriate to its substance and also by nature primary.

First, let us consider generally which shape is primary among planes and solids alike. Every plane figure must be either rectilinear [15] or curvilinear. Now the rectilinear is bounded by more than one line, the curvilinear by one only. But since in any kind the one is naturally prior to the many and the simple to the complex, the circle will be the first of plane figures. Again, if by complete, as previously [20] defined,[1] we mean a thing outside which no part of itself can be found, and if addition is always possible to the straight line but never to the circular, clearly the line which embraces the circle is complete. If then the complete is prior to the incomplete, it follows on this ground also that the circle is primary among figures. And the sphere holds the same position among solids. For it alone is embraced by [25] a single surface, while rectilinear solids have several. The sphere is among solids what the circle is among plane figures. Further, those who divide bodies into planes and generate them out of planes seem to bear witness to the truth of this. Alone among solids they leave the sphere undivided, as not possessing [30] more than one surface: for the division into surfaces is not just dividing a whole by cutting it into its parts, but division of another fashion into parts different in form. It is

[1]*Physics*, III. 207ª 8.

clear, then, that the sphere is first of solid figures.

If, again, one orders figures according to [35] their numbers, it is most natural to arrange them in this way. The circle corresponds to the number one, the triangle, being the sum of two right angles, to the number two. But if one is assigned to the triangle, the circle will not be a figure at all.

Now the first figure belongs to the first body, and the first body is that at the farthest circumference. It follows that the body which revolves with a circular movement must be [5] spherical. The same then will be true of the body continuous with it: for that which is continuous with the spherical is spherical. The same again holds of the bodies between these and the centre. Bodies which are bounded by the spherical and in contact with it must be, as wholes, spherical; and the bodies below the sphere of the planets are contiguous with the sphere above them. The sphere then will be [10] spherical throughout; for every body within it is contiguous and continuous with spheres.

Again, since the whole revolves, palpably and by assumption, in a circle, and since it has been shown that outside the farthest circumference there is neither void nor place, from these grounds also it will follow necessarily that the heaven is spherical. For if it is to be rectilinear in shape, it will follow that there is [15] place and body and void without it. For a rectilinear figure as it revolves never continues in the same room, but where formerly was body, is now none, and where now is none, body will be in a moment because of the projection at the corners. Similarly, if the world [20] had some other figure with unequal radii, if, for instance, it were lentiform, or oviform, in every case we should have to admit space and void outside the moving body, because the whole body would not always occupy the same room.

Again, if the motion of the heaven is the measure of all movements whatever in virtue of being alone continuous and regular and eternal, [25] and if, in each kind, the measure is the minimum, and the minimum movement is the swiftest, then, clearly, the movement of the heaven must be the swiftest of all movements. Now of lines which return upon themselves the line which bounds the circle is the shortest; and that movement is the swiftest which follows the shortest line. Therefore, if the heaven moves in a circle and moves more swiftly than

[30] anything else, it must necessarily be spherical.

Corroborative evidence may be drawn from the bodies whose position is about the centre. If earth is enclosed by water, water by air, air by fire, and these similarly by the upper bodies —which while not continuous are yet contiguous with them—and if the surface of water is spherical, and that which is continuous with or embraces the spherical must itself be spherical, then on these grounds also it is clear that the heavens are spherical. But the surface [5] of water is seen to be spherical if we take as our starting-point the fact that water naturally tends to collect in a hollow place—'hollow' meaning 'nearer the centre'. Draw from the centre the lines AB, AC, and let their extremities be joined by the straight line BC. The line AD, drawn to the base of the triangle, will be shorter than either of the radii. Therefore the [10] place in which it terminates will be a hollow place. The water then will collect there until equality is established, that is until the line AE is equal to the two radii. Thus water forces its way to the ends of the radii, and there only will it rest: but the line which connects the extremities of the radii is circular: therefore the surface of the water BEC is spherical.

[15] It is plain from the foregoing that the universe is spherical. It is plain, further, that it is turned (so to speak) with a finish which no manufactured thing nor anything else within the range of our observation can even approach. For the matter of which these are composed does not admit of anything like the same regularity and finish as the substance of the enveloping body; since with each step away [20] from earth the matter manifestly becomes finer in the same proportion as water is finer than earth.

5

Now there are two ways of moving along a circle, from A to B or from A to C, and we have already explained[1] that these movements are not contrary to one another. But nothing [25] which concerns the eternal can be a matter of chance or spontaneity, and the heaven and its circular motion are eternal. We must therefore ask why this motion takes one direction and not the other. Either this is itself an ultimate fact or there is an ultimate fact behind it. It may seem evidence of excessive folly or excessive zeal to try to provide an explanation [30] of some things, or of everything, admit-

[1] I. 4.

ting no exception. The criticism, however, is not always just: one should first consider what reason there is for speaking, and also what kind of certainty is looked for, whether human merely or of a more cogent kind. When any 288ᵃ one shall succeed in finding proofs of greater precision, gratitude will be due to him for the discovery, but at present we must be content with a probable solution. If nature always follows the best course possible, and, just as upward movement is the superior form of rectilinear movement, since the upper region [5] is more divine than the lower, so forward movement is superior to backward, then front and back exhibits, like right and left, as we said before and as the difficulty just stated itself suggests, the distinction of prior and posterior, which provides a reason and so solves our difficulty. Supposing that nature is ordered in the [10] best way possible, this may stand as the reason of the fact mentioned. For it is best to move with a movement simple and unceasing, and, further, in the superior of two possible directions.

6

We have next to show that the movement of the heaven is regular and not irregular. This [15] applies only to the first heaven and the first movement; for the lower spheres exhibit a composition of several movements into one. If the movement is uneven, clearly there will be acceleration, maximum speed, and retardation, since these appear in all irregular mo- [20] tions. The maximum may occur either at the starting-point or at the goal or between the two; and we expect natural motion to reach its maximum at the goal, unnatural motion at the starting-point, and missiles midway between the two. But circular movement, having no beginning or limit or middle in the direct sense of the words, has neither whence nor whither nor middle: for in time it is eternal, and in [25] length it returns upon itself without a break. If then its movement has no maximum, it can have no irregularity, since irregularity is produced by retardation and acceleration. Further, since everything that is moved is moved by something, the cause of the irregularity of movement must lie either in the mover or in the [30] moved or both. For if the mover moved not always with the same force, or if the moved were altered and did not remain the same, or if both were to change, the result might well be an irregular movement in the moved. But none of these possibilities can be conceived as actual in the case of the heavens. As to that which is moved, we have shown that it is primary and **288ᵇ** simple and ungenerated and indestructible and generally unchanging; and the mover has an even better right to these attributes. It is the primary that moves the primary, the simple the simple, the indestructible and ungenerated that which is indestructible and ungener- [5] ated. Since then that which is moved, being a body, is nevertheless unchanging, how should the mover, which is incorporeal, be changed?

It follows then, further, that the motion cannot be irregular. For if irregularity occurs, there must be change either in the movement as a whole, from fast to slow and slow to fast, or in its parts. That there is no irregularity in [10] the parts is obvious, since, if there were, some divergence of the stars would have taken place before now in the infinity of time, as one moved slower and another faster: but no alteration of their intervals is ever observed. Nor again is a change in the movement as a whole admissible. Retardation is always due to incapacity, and incapacity is unnatural. The inca- [15] pacities of animals, age, decay, and the like, are all unnatural, due, it seems, to the fact that the whole animal complex is made up of materials which differ in respect of their proper places, and no single part occupies its own place. If therefore that which is primary con- [20] tains nothing unnatural, being simple and unmixed and in its proper place and having no contrary, then it has no place for incapacity, nor, consequently, for retardation or (since acceleration involves retardation) for acceleration. Again, it is inconceivable that the mover should first show incapacity for an infinite time, and capacity afterwards for another infinity. For clearly nothing which, like incapacity, [25] is unnatural ever continues for an infinity of time; nor does the unnatural endure as long as the natural, or any form of incapacity as long as the capacity. But if the movement is retarded it must necessarily be retarded for an infinite time. Equally impossible is perpetual acceleration or perpetual retardation. For such movement would be infinite and indefinite, but every movement, in our view, proceeds from [30] one point to another and is definite in character. Again, suppose one assumes a minimum time in less than which the heaven could not complete its movement. For, as a given walk or a given exercise on the harp cannot take any and every time, but every performance has its definite minimum time which is unsurpassable, so, one might suppose, the movement of the heaven could not be complet- **289ᵃ** ed in any and every time. But in that case perpetual acceleration is impossible (and, equally, perpetual retardation: for the argument holds of both and each), if we may take acceleration to proceed by identical or increasing additions of speed and for an infinite time. The [5] remaining alternative is to say that the movement exhibits an alternation of slower and faster: but this is a mere fiction and quite inconceivable. Further, irregularity of this kind would be particularly unlikely to pass unobserved, since contrast makes observation easy.

That there is one heaven, then, only, and that it is ungenerated and eternal, and further that its movement is regular, has now been [10] sufficiently explained.

7

We have next to speak of the stars, as they are called, of their composition, shape, and movements. It would be most natural and consequent upon what has been said that each of [15] the stars should be composed of that substance in which their path lies, since, as we said, there is an element whose natural movement is circular. In so saying we are only following the same line of thought as those who say that the stars are fiery because they believe the upper body to be fire, the presumption being that a thing is composed of the same stuff as that in which it is situated. The warmth and light [20] which proceed from them are caused by the friction set up in the air by their motion. Movement tends to create fire in wood, stone, and iron; and with even more reason should it have that effect on air, a substance which is closer to fire than these. An example is that of missiles, which as they move are themselves fired so strongly that leaden balls are melted; [25] and if they are fired the surrounding air must be similarly affected. Now while the missiles are heated by reason of their motion in air, which is turned into fire by the agitation produced by their movement, the upper bodies are carried on a moving sphere, so that, though [30] they are not themselves fired, yet the air underneath the sphere of the revolving body is necessarily heated by its motion, and particularly in that part where the sun is attached to it. Hence warmth increases as the sun gets nearer or higher or overhead. Of the fact, then, [35] that the stars are neither fiery nor move in fire, enough has been said.

8

289ᵇ Since changes evidently occur not only in the position of the stars but also in that of the whole heaven, there are three possibilities. Either (1) both are at rest, or (2) both are in motion, or (3) the one is at rest and the other in motion.

(1) That both should be at rest is impossible; for, if the earth is at rest, the hypothesis [5] does not account for the observations; and we take it as granted that the earth is at rest. It remains either that both are moved, or that the one is moved and the other at rest.

(2) On the view, first, that both are in motion, we have the absurdity that the stars and the circles move with the same speed, i.e. that the pace of every star is that of the circle in [10] which it moves. For star and circle are seen to come back to the same place at the same moment; from which it follows that the star has traversed the circle and the circle has completed its own movement, i.e. traversed its own circumference, at one and the same moment. But it is difficult to conceive that the pace of [15] each star should be exactly proportioned to the size of its circle. That the pace of each circle should be proportionate to its size is not absurd but inevitable: but that the same should be true of the movement of the stars contained in the circles is quite incredible. For if, on the one hand, we suppose that the star which moves on the greater circle is necessarily swifter, clearly we also admit that if stars shifted their position [20] so as to exchange circles, the slower would become swifter and the swifter slower. But this would show that their movement was not their own, but due to the circles. If, on the other hand, the arrangement was a chance combination, the coincidence in every case of a greater circle with a swifter movement of the star contained in it is too much to believe. In one or [25] two cases it might not inconceivably fall out so, but to imagine it in every case alike is a mere fiction. Besides, chance has no place in that which is natural, and what happens everywhere and in every case is no matter of chance.

(3) The same absurdity is equally plain if it is supposed that the circles stand still and that it is the stars themselves which move. For it will follow that the outer stars are the swifter, [30] and that the pace of the stars corresponds to the size of their circles.

Since, then, we cannot reasonably suppose either that both are in motion or that the star alone moves, the remaining alternative is that the circles should move, while the stars are at rest and move with the circles to which they are attached. Only on this supposition are we involved in no absurd consequence. For, in the first place, the quicker movement of the larger [35] circle is natural when all the circles are **290ᵃ** attached to the same centre. Whenever bodies are moving with their proper motion, the larger moves quicker. It is the same here with the revolving bodies: for the arc intercepted by two radii will be larger in the larger circle, and hence it is not surprising that the [5] revolution of the larger circle should take the same time as that of the smaller. And secondly, the fact that the heavens do not break in pieces follows not only from this but also from the proof already given[1] of the continuity of the whole.

Again, since the stars are spherical, as our opponents assert and we may consistently admit, inasmuch as we construct them out of the spherical body, and since the spherical body has [10] two movements proper to itself, namely rolling and spinning, it follows that if the stars have a movement of their own, it will be one of these. But neither is observed. (1) Suppose them to *spin*. They would then stay where they were, and not change their place, as, by observation and general consent, they do. Further, one would expect them all to exhibit the same movement: but the only star which appears [15] to possess this movement is the sun, at sunrise or sunset, and this appearance is due not to the sun itself but to the distance from which we observe it. The visual ray being excessively prolonged becomes weak and wavering. The same reason probably accounts for the apparent twinkling of the fixed stars and the [20] absence of twinkling in the planets. The planets are near, so that the visual ray reaches them in its full vigour, but when it comes to the fixed stars it is quivering because of the distance and its excessive extension; and its tremor produces an appearance of movement in the star: for it makes no difference whether movement is set up in the ray or in the object of vision.

[25] (2) On the other hand, it is also clear that the stars do not *roll*. For rolling involves rotation: but the 'face', as it is called, of the moon is always seen. Therefore, since any movement of their own which the stars possessed would presumably be one proper to themselves, and no such movement is observed in them, clearly they have no movement of their own.

[1] Cf. chapter 4.

[30] There is, further, the absurdity that nature has bestowed upon them no organ appropriate to such movement. For nature leaves nothing to chance, and would not, while caring for animals, overlook things so precious. Indeed, nature seems deliberately to have stripped them of everything which makes self-originated progression possible, and to have removed them as far as possible from things [35] which have organs of movement. This is just why it seems proper that the whole heaven 290[b] and every star should be spherical. For while of all shapes the sphere is the most convenient for movement in one place, making possible, as it does, the swiftest and most self-contained motion, for forward movement it is [5] the most unsuitable, least of all resembling shapes which are self-moved, in that it has no dependent or projecting part, as a rectilinear figure has, and is in fact as far as possible removed in shape from ambulatory bodies. Since, therefore, the heavens have to move in one place, and the stars are not required to move [10] themselves forward, it is natural that both should be spherical—a shape which best suits the movement of the one and the immobility of the other.

9

From all this it is clear that the theory that the movement of the stars produces a harmony, i.e. that the sounds they make are concordant, in spite of the grace and originality with which [15] it has been stated, is nevertheless untrue. Some thinkers suppose that the motion of bodies of that size must produce a noise, since on our earth the motion of bodies far inferior in size and in speed of movement has that effect. Also, when the sun and the moon, they say, and all the stars, so great in number and in size, are [20] moving with so rapid a motion, how should they not produce a sound immensely great? Starting from this argument and from the observation that their speeds, as measured by their distances, are in the same ratios as musical concordances, they assert that the sound given forth by the circular movement of the stars is a harmony. Since, however, it appears unaccountable that we should not hear this [25] music, they explain this by saying that the sound is in our ears from the very moment of birth and is thus indistinguishable from its contrary silence, since sound and silence are discriminated by mutual contrast. What happens to men, then, is just what happens to coppersmiths, who are so accustomed to the noise of the smithy that it makes no difference to [30] them. But, as we said before, melodious and poetical as the theory is, it cannot be a true account of the facts. There is not only the absurdity of our hearing nothing, the ground of which they try to remove, but also the fact that no effect other than sensitive is produced upon us. Excessive noises, we know, shatter the solid [35] bodies even of inanimate things: the noise 291[a] of thunder, for instance, splits rocks and the strongest of bodies. But if the moving bodies are so great, and the sound which penetrates to us is proportionate to their size, that sound must needs reach us in an intensity many times that of thunder, and the force of its action must be immense. Indeed the reason [5] why we do not hear, and show in our bodies none of the effects of violent force, is easily given: it is that there is no noise. But not only is the explanation evident; it is also a corroboration of the truth of the views we have advanced. For the very difficulty which made the Pythagoreans say that the motion of the stars produces a concord corroborates our view. [10] Bodies which are themselves in motion, produce noise and friction: but those which are attached or fixed to a moving body, as the parts to a ship, can no more create noise, than a ship on a river moving with the stream. Yet by the same argument one might say it was absurd that on a large vessel the motion of mast and [15] poop should not make a great noise, and the like might be said of the movement of the vessel itself. But sound is caused when a moving body is enclosed in an unmoved body, and cannot be caused by one enclosed in, and continuous with, a moving body which creates no friction. We may say, then, in this matter that if the heavenly bodies moved in a generally [20] diffused mass of air or fire, as every one supposes, their motion would necessarily cause a noise of tremendous strength and such a noise would necessarily reach and shatter us. Since, therefore, this effect is evidently not produced, it follows that none of them can move with the motion either of animate nature or of constraint. It is as though nature had foreseen [25] the result, that if their movement were other than it is, nothing on this earth could maintain its character.

That the stars are spherical and are not self-moved, has now been explained.

10

[30] With their order—I mean the position of each, as involving the priority of some and the

posteriority of others, and their respective distances from the extremity—with this astronomy may be left to deal, since the astronomical discussion is adequate. This discussion shows that the movements of the several stars depend, as regards the varieties of speed which they exhibit, on the distance of each from the extrem-[35] ity. It is established that the outermost revolution of the heavens is a simple movement and the swiftest of all, and that the movement of all other bodies is composite and relatively slow, for the reason that each is moving on its own circle with the reverse motion to that of the heavens. This at once leads us to expect that the body which is nearest to that first simple revolution should take the longest [5] time to complete its circle, and that which is farthest from it the shortest, the others taking a longer time the nearer they are and a shorter time the farther away they are. For it is the nearest body which is most strongly influenced, and the most remote, by reason of its distance, which is least affected, the influence on the intermediate bodies varying, as the mathemati-[10] cians show, with their distance.

11

With regard to the shape of each star, the most reasonable view is that they are spherical. It has been shown[1] that it is not in their nature to move themselves, and, since nature is no wanton or random creator, clearly she will [15] have given things which possess no movement a shape particularly unadapted to movement. Such a shape is the sphere, since it possesses no instrument of movement. Clearly then their mass will have the form of a sphere. Again, what holds of one holds of all, and the evidence of our eyes shows us that the moon is spherical. For how else should the moon as it [20] waxes and wanes show for the most part a crescent-shaped or gibbous figure, and only at one moment a half-moon? And astronomical arguments give further confirmation; for no other hypothesis accounts for the crescent shape of the sun's eclipses. One, then, of the heavenly bodies being spherical, clearly the rest will be spherical also.

12

There are two difficulties, which may very reasonably here be raised, of which we must [25] now attempt to state the probable solution: for we regard the zeal of one whose thirst after philosophy leads him to accept even slight

[1]Chapter 8.

indications where it is very difficult to see one's way, as a proof rather of modesty than of overconfidence.

Of many such problems one of the strangest [30] is the problem why we find the greatest number of movements in the intermediate bodies, and not, rather, in each successive body a variety of movement proportionate to its distance from the primary motion. For we should expect, since the primary body shows one motion only, that the body which is nearest to it should move with the fewest movements, say two, and the one next after that with three, or [35] some similar arrangement. But the opposite is the case. The movements of the sun and moon are fewer than those of some of the planets. Yet these planets are farther from the centre and thus nearer to the primary body than they, as observation has itself revealed. For we have seen the moon, half-full, pass be-[5] neath the planet Mars, which vanished on its shadow side and came forth by the bright and shining part. Similar accounts of other stars are given by the Egyptians and Babylonians, whose observations have been kept for very many years past, and from whom much of our evidence about particular stars is derived. [10] A second difficulty which may with equal justice be raised is this. Why is it that the primary motion includes such a multitude of stars that their whole array seems to defy counting, while of the other stars each one is separated off, and in no case do we find two or more attached to the same motion?

On these questions, I say, it is well that we should seek to increase our understanding, [15] though we have but little to go upon, and are placed at so great a distance from the facts in question. Nevertheless there are certain principles on which if we base our consideration we shall not find this difficulty by any means insoluble. We may object that we have been thinking of the stars as mere bodies, and as [20] units with a serial order indeed but entirely inanimate; but should rather conceive them as enjoying life and action. On this view the facts cease to appear surprising. For it is natural that the best-conditioned of all things should have its good without action, that that which is nearest to it should achieve it by little and simple action, and that which is farther removed by a complexity of actions, just as with [25] men's bodies one is in good condition without exercise at all, another after a short walk, while another requires running and wrestling and hard training, and there are yet others who however hard they worked themselves could never secure this good, but only some substitute for it. To succeed often or in many things is difficult. For instance, to throw [30] ten thousand Coan throws with the dice would be impossible, but to throw one or two is comparatively easy. In action, again, when *A* has to be done to get *B*, *B* to get *C*, and *C* to get *D*, one step or two present little difficulty, but 292ᵇ as the series extends the difficulty grows. We must, then, think of the action of the lower stars as similar to that of animals and plants. For on our earth it is man that has the greatest variety of actions—for there are many goods that man can secure; hence his actions are various and directed to ends beyond them—while [5] the perfectly conditioned has no need of action, since it is itself the end, and action always requires two terms, end and means. The lower animals have less variety of action than man; and plants perhaps have little action and of one kind only. For either they have but one attainable good (as indeed man has), or, if several, [10] each contributes directly to their ultimate good. One thing then has and enjoys the ultimate good, other things attain to it, one immediately by few steps, another by many, while yet another does not even attempt to secure it but is satisfied to reach a point not far removed from that consummation. Thus, taking health as the end, there will be one thing that always possesses health, others that attain it, one by reducing flesh, another by running and thus reducing flesh, another by taking steps to enable [15] himself to run, thus further increasing the number of movements, while another cannot attain health itself, but only running or reduction of flesh, so that one or other of these is for such a being the end. For while it is clearly best for any being to attain the real end, yet, if that cannot be, the nearer it is to the best the better [20] will be its state. It is for this reason that the earth moves not at all and the bodies near to it with few movements. For they do not attain the final end, but only come as near to it as their share in the divine principle permits. But the first heaven finds it immediately with a single [25] movement, and the bodies intermediate between the first and last heavens attain it indeed, but at the cost of a multiplicity of movement.

As to the difficulty that into the one primary motion is crowded a vast multitude of stars, while of the other stars each has been separately given special movements of its own, there is in the first place this reason for regarding the arrangement as a natural one. In thinking of the life and moving principle of the several heavens one must regard the first as far superior [30] to the others. Such a superiority would be reasonable. For this single first motion has to move many of the divine bodies, 293ᵃ while the numerous other motions move only one each, since each single planet moves with a variety of motions. Thus, then, nature makes matters equal and establishes a certain order, giving to the single motion many bodies and to the single body many motions. And there is a second reason why the other motions [5] have each only one body, in that each of them except the last, i.e. that which contains the one star, is really moving many bodies. For this last sphere moves with many others, to which it is fixed, each sphere being actually a body; so that its movement will be a joint product. Each sphere, in fact, has its particular natural [10] motion, to which the general movement is, as it were, added. But the force of any limited body is only adequate to moving a limited body.

The characteristics of the stars which move with a circular motion, in respect of substance and shape, movement and order, have now been sufficiently explained.

13

[15] It remains to speak of the earth, of its position, of the question whether it is at rest or in motion, and of its shape.

1. As to its *position* there is some difference of opinion. Most people—all, in fact, who regard the whole heaven as finite—say it lies at [20] the centre. But the Italian philosophers known as Pythagoreans take the contrary view. At the centre, they say, is fire, and the earth is one of the stars, creating night and day by its circular motion about the centre. They further construct another earth in opposition to ours [25] to which they give the name counter-earth. In all this they are not seeking for theories and causes to account for observed facts, but rather forcing their observations and trying to accommodate them to certain theories and opinions of their own. But there are many others who would agree that it is wrong to give the earth the central position, looking for confirmation [30] rather to theory than to the facts of observation. Their view is that the most precious place befits the most precious thing: but fire, they say, is more precious than earth, and the limit than the intermediate, and the circumference and the centre are limits. Reason-

ing on this basis they take the view that it is not earth that lies at the centre of the sphere, but rather fire. The Pythagoreans have a further reason. They hold that the most important part of the world, which is the centre, should be most strictly guarded, and name it, or rather the fire which occupies that place, the 'Guardhouse of Zeus', as if the word 'centre' were quite unequivocal, and the centre of the mathe- [5] matical figure were always the same with that of the thing or the natural centre. But it is better to conceive of the case of the whole heaven as analogous to that of animals, in which the centre of the animal and that of the body are different. For this reason they have no need to be so disturbed about the world, or to call in [10] a guard for its centre: rather let them look for the centre in the other sense and tell us what it is like and where nature has set it. That centre will be something primary and precious; but to the mere position we should give the last place rather than the first. For the middle is what is defined, and what defines it is the limit, and that which contains or limits is more precious than that which is limited, see- [15] ing that the latter is the matter and the former the essence of the system.

11. As to the position of the earth, then, this is the view which some advance, and the views advanced concerning its *rest or motion* are similar. For here too there is no general agreement. All who deny that the earth lies at the centre think that it revolves about the centre, [20] and not the earth only but, as we said before, the counter-earth as well. Some of them even consider it possible that there are several bodies so moving, which are invisible to us owing to the interposition of the earth. This, they say, accounts for the fact that eclipses of the moon are more frequent than eclipses of the sun: for in addition to the earth each of these [25] moving bodies can obstruct it. Indeed, as in any case the surface of the earth is not actually a centre but distant from it a full hemisphere, there is no more difficulty, they think, in accounting for the observed facts on their view that we do not dwell at the centre, than on the common view that the earth is in the middle. Even as it is, there is nothing in the observations to suggest that we are removed [30] from the centre by half the diameter of the earth. Others, again, say that the earth, which lies at the centre, is 'rolled', and thus in motion, about the axis of the whole heaven, So it stands written in the *Timaeus*.[1]

[1]40.

111. There are similar disputes about the *shape* of the earth. Some think it is spherical, others that it is flat and drum-shaped. For evidence they bring the fact that, as the sun rises and sets, the part concealed by the earth shows a straight and not a curved edge, whereas if the earth were spherical the line of section would have to be circular. In this they leave out [5] of account the great distance of the sun from the earth and the great size of the circumference, which, seen from a distance on these apparently small circles appears straight. Such an appearance ought not to make them doubt the circular shape of the earth. But they have another argument. They say that because it is [10] at rest, the earth must necessarily have this shape. For there are many different ways in which the movement or rest of the earth has been conceived.

The difficulty must have occurred to every one. It would indeed be a complacent mind that felt no surprise that, while a little bit of earth, let loose in mid-air, moves and will not [15] stay still, and the more there is of it the faster it moves, the whole earth, free in midair, should show no movement at all. Yet here is this great weight of earth, and it is at rest. And again, from beneath one of these moving fragments of earth, before it falls, take away the earth, and it will continue its downward movement with nothing to stop it. The difficulty then, has naturally passed into a com- [20] monplace of philosophy; and one may well wonder that the solutions offered are not seen to involve greater absurdities than the problem itself.

By these considerations some have been led to assert that the earth below us is infinite, saying, with Xenophanes of Colophon, that it has 'pushed its roots to infinity',[2]—in order to save the trouble of seeking for the cause. Hence the [25] sharp rebuke of Empedocles, in the words 'if the deeps of the earth are endless and endless the ample ether—such is the vain tale told by many a tongue, poured from the mouths of those who have seen but little of the whole'.[3] Others say the earth rests upon water. This, indeed, is the oldest theory that has been preserved, and is attributed to Thales of Miletus. [30] It was supposed to stay still because it floated like wood and other similar substances, which are so constituted as to rest upon water

[2]Diels, *Vorsokratiker*[3], 11 A 47 (53, 38 ff.), B 28 (63, 8). Ritter and Preller, 103 b. Cf. Burnet, E.G.P.[3] § 60.

[3]Diels, *Vors.*[3] 21 B 39 (241, 16). Ritter and Preller, 103 b. Burnet, E.G.P.[3] p. 212.

but not upon air. As if the same account had not to be given of the water which carries the earth as of the earth itself! It is not the nature of water, any more than of earth, to stay in mid-air: it must have something to rest upon. Again, as air is lighter than water, so is water than earth: how then can they think that the naturally lighter substance lies below the heavier? Again, if the earth as a whole is capable of floating upon water, that must obviously be the case with any part of it. But observation [5] shows that this is not the case. Any piece of earth goes to the bottom, the quicker the larger it is. These thinkers seem to push their inquiries some way into the problem, but not so far as they might. It is what we are all inclined to do, to direct our inquiry not by the matter itself, but by the views of our opponents: and even when interrogating oneself one [10] pushes the inquiry only to the point at which one can no longer offer any opposition. Hence a good inquirer will be one who is ready in bringing forward the objections proper to the genus, and that he will be when he has gained an understanding of all the differences.

Anaximenes and Anaxagoras and Democritus give the flatness of the earth as the cause of [15] its staying still. Thus, they say, it does not cut, but covers like a lid, the air beneath it. This seems to be the way of flat-shaped bodies: for even the wind can scarcely move them because of their power of resistance. The same immobility, they say, is produced by the flatness of the surface which the earth presents to the air which underlies it; while the air, not [20] having room enough to change its place because it is underneath the earth, stays there in a mass, like the water in the case of the water-clock. And they adduce an amount of evidence to prove that air, when cut off and at rest, can bear a considerable weight.

Now, first, if the shape of the earth is not flat, its flatness cannot be the cause of its immobility. But in their own account it is rather [25] the size of the earth than its flatness that causes it to remain at rest. For the reason why the air is so closely confined that it cannot find a passage, and therefore stays where it is, is its great amount: and this amount is great because the body which isolates it, the earth, is very large. This result, then, will follow, even if the [30] earth is spherical, so long as it retains its size. So far as their arguments go, the earth will still be at rest.

In general, our quarrel with those who speak of movement in this way cannot be confined to the parts; it concerns the whole universe. One must decide at the outset whether bodies have a natural movement or not, whether there is no natural but only constrained movement. Seeing, however, that we have already decided this matter to the best of our ability, we are entitled to treat our results as representing fact. Bodies, we say, which have no natural movement, have no constrained movement; and where there is no natural and no constrained movement there will be no movement [5] at all. This is a conclusion, the necessity of which we have already decided,[1] and we have seen further that rest also will be inconceivable, since rest, like movement, is either natural or constrained. But if there is any natural movement, constraint will not be the sole principle of motion or of rest. If, then, it is by constraint that the earth now keeps its place, the so-called [10] 'whirling' movement by which its parts came together at the centre was also constrained. (The form of causation supposed they all borrow from observations of liquids and of air, in which the larger and heavier bodies always move to the centre of the whirl. This is thought by all those who try to generate the heavens to explain why the earth came together [15] at the centre. They then seek a reason for its staying there; and some say, in the manner explained, that the reason is its size and flatness, others, with Empedocles, that the motion of the heavens, moving about it at a higher speed, prevents movement of the earth, as the [20] water in a cup, when the cup is given a circular motion, though it is often underneath the bronze, is for this same reason prevented from moving with the downward movement which is natural to it.) But suppose both the 'whirl' and its flatness (the air beneath being withdrawn) cease to prevent the earth's motion, where will the earth move to then? Its movement to the centre was constrained, and its rest at the centre is due to constraint; but there must be some motion which is natural to [25] it. Will this be upward motion or downward or what? It must have some motion; and if upward and downward motion are alike to it, and the air above the earth does not prevent upward movement, then no more could air below it prevent downward movement. For the same cause must necessarily have the same effect on the same thing.

[30] Further, against Empedocles there is another point which might be made. When the elements were separated off by Hate, what

[1] I. 2-4.

caused the earth to keep its place? Surely the 'whirl' cannot have been then also the cause. It is absurd too not to perceive that, while the whirling movement may have been responsible for the original coming together of the parts of earth at the centre, the question re-[35] mains, why *now* do all heavy bodies move to the earth. For the whirl surely does not come 295ᵇ near us. Why, again, does fire move upward? Not, surely, because of the whirl. But if fire is naturally such as to move in a certain direction, clearly the same may be supposed to hold of earth. Again, it cannot be the whirl which determines the heavy and the light. [5] Rather that movement caused the pre-existent heavy and light things to go to the middle and stay on the surface respectively. Thus, before ever the whirl began, heavy and light existed; and what can have been the ground of their distinction, or the manner and direction of their natural movements? In the infinite chaos there can have been neither above nor below, and it is by these that heavy and light are determined.

[10] It is to these causes that most writers pay attention: but there are some, Anaximander, for instance, among the ancients, who say that the earth keeps its place because of its indifference. Motion upward and downward and sideways were all, they thought, equally inappropriate to that which is set at the centre and indifferently related to every extreme point; and [15] to move in contrary directions at the same time was impossible: so it must needs remain still. This view is ingenious but not true. The argument would prove that everything, whatever it be, which is put at the centre, must stay there. Fire, then, will rest at the centre: for the proof turns on no peculiar property of earth. But this [20] does not follow. The observed facts about earth are not only that it remains at the centre, but also that it moves to the centre. The place to which any fragment of earth moves must necessarily be the place to which the whole moves; and in the place to which a thing naturally moves, it will naturally rest. The reason then is not in the fact that the earth is indifferently related to every extreme point: for this [25] would apply to any body, whereas movement to the centre is peculiar to earth. Again it is absurd to look for a reason why the earth remains at the centre and not for a reason why fire remains at the extremity. If the extremity is the natural place of fire, clearly earth must also have a natural place. But suppose that the [30] centre is not its place, and that the reason of its remaining there is this necessity of indifference—on the analogy of the hair which, it is said, however great the tension, will not break under it, if it be evenly distributed, or of the men who, though exceedingly hungry and thirsty, and both equally, yet being equidistant from food and drink, is therefore bound to stay [35] where he is—even so, it still remains to 296ᵃ explain why fire stays at the extremities. It is strange, too, to ask about things staying still but not about their motion,—why, I mean, one thing, if nothing stops it, moves up, and another thing to the centre. Again, their statements are not true. It happens, indeed, to be the [5] case that a thing to which movement this way and that is equally inappropriate is obliged to remain at the centre. But so far as their argument goes, instead of remaining there, it will move, only not as a mass but in fragments. For the argument applies equally to fire. Fire, if set at the centre, should stay there, like earth, since [10] it will be indifferently related to every point on the extremity. Nevertheless it will move, as in fact it always does move when nothing stops it, away from the centre to the extremity. It will not, however, move in a mass to a single point on the circumference—the only possible result on the lines of the indifference theory—but rather each corresponding [15] portion of fire to the corresponding part of the extremity, each fourth part, for instance, to a fourth part of the circumference. For since no body is a point, it will have parts. The expansion, when the body increased the place occupied, would be on the same principle as the contraction, in which the place was diminished. Thus, for all the indifference theory shows to the contrary, earth also would have moved in [20] this manner away from the centre, unless the centre had been its natural place.

We have now outlined the views held as to the shape, position, and rest or movement of the earth.

14

Let us first decide the question whether the earth moves or is at rest. For, as we said, there [25] are some who make it one of the stars, and others who, setting it at the centre, suppose it to be 'rolled' and in motion about the pole as axis. That both views are untenable will be clear if we take as our starting-point the fact that the earth's motion, whether the earth be at the centre or away from it, must needs be a con-[30] strained motion. It cannot be the movement of the earth itself. If it were, any portion of it would have this movement; but in fact every part moves in a straight line to the centre. Being, then, constrained and unnatural, the movement could not be eternal. But the order of the universe is eternal. Again, everything that moves with the circular movement, except [35] the first sphere, is observed to be passed, 296ᵇ and to move with more than one motion. The earth, then, also, whether it move about the centre or as stationary at it, must necessarily move with two motions. But if this were so, there would have to be passings and [5] turnings of the fixed stars. Yet no such thing is observed. The same stars always rise and set in the same parts of the earth.

Further, the natural movement of the earth, part and whole alike, is the centre of the whole —whence the fact that it is now actually situated at the centre—but it might be questioned, [10] since both centres are the same, which centre it is that portions of earth and other heavy things move to. Is this their goal because it is the centre of the earth or because it is the centre of the whole? The goal, surely, must be the centre of the whole. For fire and other light things move to the extremity of the area which [15] contains the centre. It happens, however, that the centre of the earth and of the whole is the same. Thus they do move to the centre of the earth, but accidentally, in virtue of the fact that the earth's centre lies at the centre of the whole. That the centre of the earth is the goal of their movement is indicated by the fact that heavy bodies moving towards the earth do not [20] move parallel but so as to make equal angles, and thus to a single centre, that of the earth. It is clear, then, that the earth must be at the centre and immovable, not only for the reasons already given, but also because heavy bodies forcibly thrown quite straight upward return to the point from which they started, even [25] if they are thrown to an infinite distance. From these considerations then it is clear that the earth does not move and does not lie elsewhere than at the centre.

From what we have said the explanation of the earth's immobility is also apparent. If it is the nature of earth, as observation shows, to move from any point to the centre, as of fire contrariwise to move from the centre to the ex- [30] tremity, it is impossible that any portion of earth should move away from the centre except by constraint. For a single thing has a single movement, and a simple thing a simple: contrary movements cannot belong to the same thing, and movement away from the centre is the contrary of movement to it. If then no portion of earth can move away from the centre, obviously still less can the earth as a whole so [35] move. For it is the nature of the whole to move to the point to which the part naturally 297ᵃ moves. Since, then, it would require a force greater than itself to move it, it must needs stay at the centre. This view is further supported by the contributions of mathematicians to astronomy, since the observations made [5] as the shapes change by which the order of the stars is determined, are fully accounted for on the hypothesis that the earth lies at the centre. Of the position of the earth and of the manner of its rest or movement, our discussion may here end.

Its shape must necessarily be spherical. For [10] every portion of earth has weight until it reaches the centre, and the jostling of parts greater and smaller would bring about not a waved surface, but rather compression and convergence of part and part until the centre is reached. The process should be conceived by supposing the earth to come into being in the way that some of the natural philosophers de- [15] scribe. Only they attribute the downward movement to constraint, and it is better to keep to the truth and say that the reason of this motion is that a thing which possesses weight is naturally endowed with a centripetal movement. When the mixture, then, was merely potential, the things that were separated off moved similarly from every side towards the centre. Whether the parts which came together [20] at the centre were distributed at the extremities evenly, or in some other way, makes no difference. If, on the one hand, there were a similar movement from each quarter of the extremity to the single centre, it is obvious that the resulting mass would be similar on every side. For if an equal amount is added on every side the extremity of the mass will be every- [25] where equidistant from its centre, i.e. the figure will be spherical. But neither will it in any way affect the argument if there is not a similar accession of concurrent fragments from every side. For the greater quantity, finding a lesser in front of it, must necessarily drive it on, both having an impulse whose goal is the centre, [30] and the greater weight driving the lesser forward till this goal is reached. In this we have also the solution of a possible difficulty. The earth, it might be argued, is at the centre and spherical in shape: if, then, a weight many times that of the earth were added to one hemisphere, the centre of the earth and of the whole will no longer be coincident. So that either the earth will not stay still at the centre, or if it 297^b does, it will be at rest without having its centre at the place to which it is still its nature to move. Such is the difficulty. A short consideration will give us an easy answer, if we first give precision to our postulate that any body endowed with weight, of whatever size, moves [5] towards the centre. Clearly it will not stop when its edge touches the centre. The greater quantity must prevail until the body's centre occupies the centre. For that is the goal of its impulse. Now it makes no difference whether we apply this to a clod or common fragment of earth or to the earth as a whole. The fact indicated does not depend upon degrees of size but [10] applies universally to everything that has the centripetal impulse. Therefore earth in motion, whether in a mass or in fragments, necessarily continues to move until it occupies the centre equally every way, the less being forced to equalize itself by the greater owing to the forward drive of the impulse.

If the earth was generated, then, it must have [15] been formed in this way, and so clearly its generation was spherical; and if it is ungenerated and has remained so always, its character must be that which the initial generation, if it had occurred, would have given it. But the spherical shape, necessitated by this argument, follows also from the fact that the motions of heavy bodies always make equal angles, and [20] are not parallel. This would be the natural form of movement towards what is naturally spherical. Either then the earth is spherical or it is at least naturally spherical. And it is right to call anything that which nature intends it to be, and which belongs to it, rather than that which it is by constraint and contrary to nature. The evidence of the senses further corrob- [25] orates this. How else would eclipses of the moon show segments shaped as we see them? As it is, the shapes which the moon itself each month shows are of every kind— straight, gibbous, and concave—but in eclipses the outline is always curved: and, since it is the interposition of the earth that makes the eclipse, [30] the form of this line will be caused by the form of the earth's surface, which is therefore spherical. Again, our observations of the stars make it evident, not only that the earth is circular, but also that it is a circle of no great size. For quite a small change of position to south or north causes a manifest alteration of the hori- 298^a zon. There is much change, I mean, in the stars which are overhead, and the stars seen are different, as one moves northward or southward. Indeed there are some stars seen in Egypt and in the neighbourhood of Cyprus which are not seen in the northerly regions; [5] and stars, which in the north are never beyond the range of observation, in those regions rise and set. All of which goes to show not only that the earth is circular in shape, but also that it is a sphere of no great size: for otherwise the effect of so slight a change of place would not be so quickly apparent. Hence one should not [10] be too sure of the incredibility of the view of those who conceive that there is continuity between the parts about the pillars of Hercules and the parts about India, and that in this way the ocean is one. As further evidence in favour of this they quote the case of elephants, a species occurring in each of these extreme regions, suggesting that the common characteristic of [15] these extremes is explained by their continuity. Also, those mathematicians who try to calculate the size of the earth's circumference arrive at the figure 400,000 stades. This indicates not only that the earth's mass is spherical in shape, but also that as compared with the [20] stars it is not of great size.

BOOK III

1

We have already discussed the first heaven and its parts, the moving stars within it, the [25] matter of which these are composed and their bodily constitution, and we have also shown that they are ungenerated and indestructible. Now things that we call natural are either substances or functions and attributes of substances. As substances I class the simple [30] bodies—fire, earth, and the other terms of the series—and all things composed of them; for example, the heaven as a whole and its parts, animals, again, and plants and their parts. By attributes and functions I mean the movements of these and of all other things in which they have power in themselves to cause movement, and also their alterations and re- 298^b ciprocal transformations. It is obvious, then, that the greater part of the inquiry into nature concerns bodies: for a natural substance is either a body or a thing which cannot come into existence without body and magnitude. [5] This appears plainly from an analysis of the character of natural things, and equally from an inspection of the instances of inquiry into nature. Since, then, we have spoken of the primary element, of its bodily constitution, and of its freedom from destruction and generation, it remains to speak of the other two. In speaking of them we shall be obliged also to in- [10] quire into generation and destruction. For if there is generation anywhere, it must be in these elements and things composed of them.

This is indeed the first question we have to ask: is generation a fact or not? Earlier speculation was at variance both with itself and with the views here put forward as to the true an- [15] swer to this question. Some removed generation and destruction from the world altogether. Nothing that is, they said, is generated or destroyed, and our conviction to the contrary is an illusion. So maintained the school of Melissus and Parmenides. But however excellent their theories may otherwise be, anyhow they cannot be held to speak as students of nature. There may be things not subject to generation or any kind of movement, but if so they [20] belong to another and a higher inquiry than the study of nature. They, however, had no idea of any form of being other than the substance of things perceived; and when they saw, what no one previously had seen, that there could be no knowledge or wisdom without some such unchanging entities, they naturally transferred what was true of them to things perceived. Others, perhaps intentionally, [25] maintain precisely the contrary opinion to this. It has been asserted that everything in the world was subject to generation and nothing was ungenerated, but that after being generated some things remained indestructible while the rest were again destroyed. This had been asserted in the first instance by Hesiod and his followers, but afterwards outside his circle by the earliest natural philosophers. But what these thinkers maintained was that all [30] else has been generated and, as they said, 'is flowing away', nothing having any solidity, except one single thing which persists as the basis of all these transformations. So we may interpret the statements of Heraclitus of Ephesus and many others. And some subject all bodies whatever to generation, by means of 299ᵃ the composition and separation of planes.

Discussion of the other views may be postponed. But this last theory which composes every body of planes is, as the most superficial observation shows, in many respects in plain contradiction with mathematics. It is, however, [5] wrong to remove the foundations of a science unless you can replace them with others more convincing. And, secondly, the same theory which composes solids of planes clearly composes planes of lines and lines of points, so that a part of a line need not be a line. This matter has been already considered in our dis- [10] cussion of movement, where we have shown that an indivisible length is impossible.[1] But with respect to natural bodies there are impossibilities involved in the view which asserts indivisible lines, which we may briefly consider at this point. For the impossible consequences which result from this view in the mathematical sphere will reproduce themselves when it is applied to physical bodies, but there will be [15] difficulties in physics which are not present in mathematics; for mathematics deals with an abstract and physics with a more concrete object. There are many attributes necessarily present in physical bodies which are necessarily excluded by indivisibility; all attributes, in fact, which are divisible. There can be nothing divisible in an indivisible thing, but the attributes of bodies are all divisible in one of [20] two ways. They are divisible into kinds, as colour is divided into white and black, and they are divisible *per accidens* when that which has them is divisible. In this latter sense attributes which are simple are nevertheless divisible. Attributes of this kind will serve, therefore, to illustrate the impossibility of the view. [25] It is impossible, if two parts of a thing have no weight, that the two together should have weight. But either all perceptible bodies or some, such as earth and water, have weight, as these thinkers would themselves admit. Now if the point has no weight, clearly the lines have not either, and, if they have not, neither have the planes. Therefore no body has [30] weight. It is, further, manifest that their point cannot have weight. For while a heavy thing may always be heavier than something and a light thing lighter than something, a thing which is heavier or lighter than something need not be itself heavy or light, just as a large thing is larger than others, but what is larger is not always large. A thing which, judged absolutely, is small may none the less [5] be larger than other things. Whatever, then, is heavy and also heavier than something else, must exceed this by something which is heavy. A heavy thing therefore is always divisible. But it is common ground that a point is indivisible. Again, suppose that what is heavy

[1] *Physics*, VI. 1.

is a dense body, and what is light rare. Dense differs from rare in containing more matter in the same cubic area. A point, then, if it may be [10] heavy or light, may be dense or rare. But the dense is divisible while a point is indivisible. And if what is heavy must be either hard or soft, an impossible consequence is easy to draw. For a thing is soft if its surface can be pressed in, hard if it cannot; and if it can be pressed in it is divisible.

[15] Moreover, no weight can consist of parts not possessing weight. For how, except by the merest fiction, can they specify the number and character of the parts which will produce weight? And, further, when one weight is greater than another, the difference is a third weight; from which it will follow that every indivisible part possesses weight. For suppose that a body of four points possesses weight. A body composed of more than four points will [20] be superior in weight to it, a thing which has weight. But the difference between weight and weight must be a weight, as the difference between white and whiter is white. Here the difference which makes the superior weight heavier is the single point which remains when the common number, four, is subtracted. A single point, therefore, has weight.

Further, to assume, on the one hand, that the [25] planes can only be put in linear contact would be ridiculous. For just as there are two ways of putting lines together, namely, end to end and side by side, so there must be two ways of putting planes together. Lines can be put together so that contact is linear by laying one along the other, though not by putting them end to end. But if, similarly, in putting the planes together, superficial contact is al-[30] lowed as an alternative to linear, that method will give them bodies which are not any element nor composed of elements. Again, if it is the number of planes in a body that makes 300ª one heavier than another, as the *Timaeus*[1] explains, clearly the line and the point will have weight. For the three cases are, as we said before, analogous. But if the reason of differences of weight is not this, but rather the [5] heaviness of earth and the lightness of fire, then some of the planes will be light and others heavy (which involves a similar distinction in the lines and the points); the earthplane, I mean, will be heavier than the fire-plane. In general, the result is either that there is no magnitude at all, or that all magnitude could be done away with. For a point is to a line as

[1] Plato, *Timaeus*, 56.

[10] a line is to a plane and as a plane is to a body. Now the various forms in passing into one another will each be resolved into its ultimate constituents. It might happen therefore that nothing existed except points, and that there was no body at all. A further consideration is that if time is similarly constituted, there would be, or might be, a time at which it was done away with. For the indivisible now [15] is like a point in a line. The same consequences follow from composing the heaven of numbers, as some of the Pythagoreans do who make all nature out of numbers. For natural bodies are manifestly endowed with weight and lightness, but an assemblage of units can neither be composed to form a body nor possess weight.

2

[20] The necessity that each of the simple bodies should have a natural movement may be shown as follows. They manifestly move, and if they have no proper movement they must move by constraint: and the constrained is the same as the unnatural. Now an unnatural movement presupposes a natural move-[25] ment which it contravenes, and which, however many the unnatural movements, is always one. For naturally a thing moves in one way, while its unnatural movements are manifold. The same may be shown from the fact of rest. Rest, also, must either be constrained or natural, constrained in a place to which movement was constrained, natural in a place movement to which was natural. Now manifestly [30] there is a body which is at rest at the centre. If then this rest is natural to it, clearly motion to this place is natural to it. If, on the other hand, its rest is constrained, what is hindering its motion? Something, perhaps, which is at rest: but if so, we shall simply repeat the same argument; and either we shall come to an ulti-300ᵇ mate something to which rest where it is is natural, or we shall have an infinite process, which is impossible. The hindrance to its movement, then, we will suppose, is a moving thing—as Empedocles says that it is the vortex which keeps the earth still—: but in that case we ask, where would it have moved to but for the vortex? It could not move infinitely; for to [5] traverse an infinite is impossible, and impossibilities do not happen. So the moving thing must stop somewhere, and there rest not by constraint but naturally. But a natural rest proves a natural movement to the place of rest. Hence Leucippus and Democritus, who say

that the primary bodies are in perpetual move-
[10] ment in the void or infinite, may be
asked to explain the manner of their motion
and the kind of movement which is natural to
them. For if the various elements are constrained by one another to move as they do,
each must still have a natural movement which
the constrained contravenes, and the prime
mover must cause motion not by constraint but
[15] naturally. If there is no ultimate natural
cause of movement and each preceding term in
the series is always moved by constraint, we
shall have an infinite process. The same difficulty is involved even if it is supposed, as we
read in the *Timaeus*,[1] that before the ordered
world was made the elements moved without
order. Their movement must have been due
either to constraint or to their nature. And if
[20] their movement was natural, a moment's
consideration shows that there was already an
ordered world. For the prime mover must
cause motion in virtue of its own natural movement, and the other bodies, moving without
constraint, as they came to rest in their proper
places, would fall into the order in which they
now stand, the heavy bodies moving towards
[25] the centre and the light bodies away from
it. But that is the order of their distribution in
our world. There is a further question, too,
which might be asked. Is it possible or impossible that bodies in unordered movement
should combine in some cases into combinations like those of which bodies of nature's
composing are composed, such, I mean, as
bones and flesh? Yet this is what Empedocles
[30] asserts to have occurred under Love.
'Many a head', says he, 'came to birth without
a neck.'[2] The answer to the view that there are
infinite bodies moving in an infinite is that,
if the cause of movement is single, they must
move with a single motion, and therefore not
without order; and if, on the other hand, the
301ᵃ causes are of infinite variety, their motions too must be infinitely varied. For a finite
number of causes would produce a kind of
order, since absence of order is not proved by
diversity of direction in motions: indeed, in the
world we know, not all bodies, but only bodies
of the same kind, have a common goal of
[5] movement. Again, disorderly movement
means in reality unnatural movement, since
the order proper to perceptible things is their
nature. And there is also absurdity and impossibility in the notion that the disorderly move-

[1] Plato, *Timaeus*, 30.
[2] Fr. 57, l. 1, Diels, *Vors.*³ 245, 20.

ment is infinitely continued. For the nature of
things is the nature which most of them possess
for most of the time. Thus their view brings
[10] them into the contrary position that disorder is natural, and order or system unnatural.
But no natural fact can originate in chance.
This is a point which Anaxagoras seems to
have thoroughly grasped; for he starts his cosmogony from unmoved things. The others, it
is true, make things collect together somehow before they try to produce motion and separation. But there is no sense in starting gen-
[15] eration from an original state in which
bodies are separated and in movement. Hence
Empedocles begins after the process ruled by
Love: for he could not have constructed the
heaven by building it up out of bodies in separation, making them to combine by the power
of Love, since our world has its constituent
elements in separation, and therefore presup-
[20] poses a previous state of unity and combination.

These arguments make it plain that every
body has its natural movement, which is not
constrained or contrary to its nature. We go
on to show that there are certain bodies whose
necessary impetus is that of weight and lightness. Of necessity, we assert, they must move,
[25] and a moved thing which has no natural
impetus cannot move either towards or away
from the centre. Suppose a body A without
weight, and a body B endowed with weight.
Suppose the weightless body to move the distance CD, while B in the same time moves the
distance CE, which will be greater since the
heavy thing must move further. Let the heavy
[30] body then be divided in the proportion
$CE : CD$ (for there is no reason why a part of
B should not stand in this relation to the
whole). Now if the whole moves the whole
distance CE, the part must in the same time
move the distance CD. A weightless body,
therefore, and one which has weight will move
301ᵇ the same distance, which is impossible.
And the same argument would fit the case of
lightness. Again, a body which is in motion but
has neither weight nor lightness, must be
moved by constraint, and must continue its
constrained movement infinitely. For there will
[5] be a force which moves it, and the smaller
and lighter a body is the further will a given
force move it. Now let A, the weightless body,
be moved the distance CE, and B, which has
weight, be moved in the same time the distance CD. Dividing the heavy body in the proportion $CE:CD$, we subtract from the heavy

[10] body a part which will in the same time move the distance CE, since the whole moved CD: for the relative speeds of the two bodies will be in inverse ratio to their respective sizes. Thus the weightless body will move the same distance as the heavy in the same time. But [15] this is impossible. Hence, since the motion of the weightless body will cover a greater distance than any that is suggested, it will continue infinitely. It is therefore obvious that every body must have a definite weight or lightness. But since 'nature' means a source of movement within the thing itself, while a force is a source of movement in something other than it or in itself *qua* other, and since [20] movement is always due either to nature or to constraint, movement which is natural, as downward movement is to a stone, will be merely accelerated by an external force, while an unnatural movement will be due to the force alone. In either case the air is as it were instrumental to the force. For air is both light and heavy, and thus *qua* light produces upward motion, being propelled and set in mo- [25] tion by the force, and *qua* heavy produces a downward motion. In either case the force transmits the movement to the body by first, as it were, impregnating the air. That is why a body moved by constraint continues to move when that which gave the impulse ceases to accompany it. Otherwise, i.e. if the air were not endowed with this function, constrained movement would be impossible. And the natural [30] movement of a body may be helped on in the same way. This discussion suffices to show (1) that all bodies are either light or heavy, and (2) how unnatural movement takes place.

From what has been said earlier[1] it is plain that there cannot be generation either of everything or in an absolute sense of anything. It is impossible that everything should be generated, unless an extra-corporeal void is possible. For, assuming generation, the place which is to be occupied by that which is coming to be, must have been previously occupied by void in which no body was. Now it is quite possible for one body to be generated out of [5] another, air for instance out of fire, but in the absence of any pre-existing mass generation is impossible. That which is potentially a certain kind of body may, it is true, become such in actuality. But if the potential body was not already in actuality some other kind of body, the existence of an extra-corporeal void must be admitted.

[1] *Physics,* IV. 6–9.

3

[10] It remains to say what bodies are subject to generation, and why. Since in every case knowledge depends on what is primary, and the elements are the primary constituents of bodies, we must ask which of such bodies are elements, and why; and after that what is their [15] number and character. The answer will be plain if we first explain what kind of substance an element is. An element, we take it, is a body into which other bodies may be analysed, present in them potentially or in actuality (which of these, is still disputable), and not itself divisible into bodies different in form. That, or something like it, is what all men in every case mean by element. Now if what we [20] have described is an element, clearly there must be such bodies. For flesh and wood and all other similar bodies contain potentially fire and earth, since one sees these elements exuded from them; and, on the other hand, neither in potentiality nor in actuality does fire contain [25] flesh or wood, or it would exude them. Similarly, even if there were only one elementary body, it would not contain them. For though it will be either flesh or bone or something else, that does not at once show that it contained these in potentiality: the further question remains, in what manner it becomes them. Now Anaxagoras opposes Empedocles' view of the elements. Empedocles says that fire [30] and earth and the related bodies are elementary bodies of which all things are composed; but this Anaxagoras denies. His elements are the homoeomerous things, viz. flesh, bone, and the like. Earth and fire are mixtures, composed of them and all the other seeds, each consisting of a collection of all the homoeomerous bodies, separately invisible; and that explains why from these two bodies all others are generated. (To him fire and [5] *aither* are the same thing.) But since every natural body has it proper movement, and movements are either simple or mixed, mixed in mixed bodies and simple in simple, there must obviously be simple bodies; for there are simple movements. It is plain, then, that there are elements, and why.

4

[10] The next question to consider is whether the elements are finite or infinite in number, and, if finite, what their number is. Let us first show reason or denying that their number is infinite, as some suppose. We begin with the

view of Anaxagoras that all the homoeomerous [15] bodies are elements. Any one who adopts this view misapprehends the meaning of element. Observation shows that even mixed bodies are often divisible into homoeomerous parts; examples are flesh, bone, wood, and stone. Since then the composite cannot be an element, not every homoeomerous body can be an element; only, as we said before,[1] that [20] which is not divisible into bodies different in form. But even taking 'element' as they do, they need not assert an infinity of elements, since the hypothesis of a finite number will give identical results. Indeed even two or three such bodies serve the purpose as well, as Empedocles' attempt shows. Again, even on their view it turns out that all things are not com- [25] posed of homoeomerous bodies. They do not pretend that a face is composed of faces, or that any other natural conformation is composed of parts like itself. Obviously then it would be better to assume a finite number of principles. They should, in fact, be as few as possible, consistently with proving what has to [30] be proved. This is the common demand of mathematicians, who always assume as principles things finite either in kind or in number. Again, if body is distinguished from body by the appropriate qualitative difference, and there is a limit to the number of differ- 303ᵃ ences (for the difference lies in qualities apprehended by sense, which are in fact finite in number, though this requires proof), then manifestly there is necessarily a limit to the number of elements.

There is, further, another view—that of Leucippus and Democritus of Abdera—the implications of which are also unacceptable. [5] The primary masses, according to them, are infinite in number and indivisible in mass: one cannot turn into many nor many into one; and all things are generated by their combination and involution. Now this view in a sense makes things out to be numbers or composed [10] of numbers. The exposition is not clear, but this is its real meaning. And further, they say that since the atomic bodies differ in shape, and there is an infinity of shapes, there is an infinity of simple bodies. But they have never explained in detail the shapes of the various [15] elements, except so far to allot the sphere to fire. Air, water, and the rest they distinguished by the relative size of the atom, assuming that the atomic substance was a sort of master-seed for each and every element. Now,

in the first place, they make the mistake already noticed. The principles which they assume are not limited in number, though such limitation would necessitate no other alteration in their theory. Further, if the differences of [20] bodies are not infinite, plainly the elements will not be an infinity. Besides, a view which asserts atomic bodies must needs come into conflict with the mathematical sciences, in addition to invalidating many common opinions and apparent data of sense perception. But of these things we have already spoken in our discussion of time and movement.[2] They are [25] also bound to contradict themselves. For if the elements are atomic, air, earth, and water cannot be differentiated by the relative sizes of their atoms, since then they could not be generated out of one another. The extrusion of the largest atoms is a process that will in time exhaust the supply; and it is by such a process that they account for the generation of water, air, and earth from one another. Again, even [30] on their own presuppositions it does not seem as if the elements would be infinite in number. The atoms differ in figure, and all figures are composed of pyramids, rectilinear 303ᵇ in the case of rectilinear figures, while the sphere has eight pyramidal parts. The figures must have their principles, and, whether these are one or two or more, the simple bodies must be the same in number as they. Again, if every element has its proper movement, and a [5] simple body has a simple movement, and the number of simple movements is not infinite, because the simple motions are only two and the number of places is not infinite, on these grounds also we should have to deny that the number of elements is infinite.

5

Since the number of the elements must be lim- [10] ited, it remains to inquire whether there is more than one element. Some assume one only, which is according to some water, to others air, to others fire, to others again something finer than water and denser than air, an infinite body—so they say—embracing all the heavens.

Now those who decide for a single element, which is either water or air or a body finer than water and denser than air, and proceed to [15] generate other things out of it by use of the attributes density and rarity, all alike fail to observe the fact that they are depriving the

---

[1] Above, 302ᵃ 18.   [2] Especially *Physics*, vi. 1–2 (231ᵃ 18 ff.).

element of its priority. Generation out of the elements is, as they say, synthesis, and generation into the elements is analysis, so that the body with the finer parts must have priority [20] in the order of nature. But they say that fire is of all bodies the finest. Hence fire will be first in the natural order. And whether the finest body is fire or not makes no difference; anyhow it must be one of the other bodies that is primary and not that which is intermediate. Again, density and rarity, as instruments of generation, are equivalent to fineness and coarseness, since the fine is rare, and coarse in [25] their use means dense. But fineness and coarseness, again, are equivalent to greatness and smallness, since a thing with small parts is fine and a thing with large parts coarse. For that which spreads itself out widely is fine, and a thing composed of small parts is so spread out. In the end, then, they distinguish the various other substances from the element [30] by the greatness and smallness of their parts. This method of distinction makes all judgement relative. There will be no absolute distinction between fire, water, and air, but one and the same body will be relatively to this 304ᵃ fire, relatively to something else air. The same difficulty is involved equally in the view which recognizes several elements and distinguishes them by their greatness and smallness. The principle of distinction between bodies being quantity, the various sizes will be in a [5] definite ratio, and whatever bodies are in this ratio to one another must be air, fire, earth, and water respectively. For the ratios of smaller bodies may be repeated among greater bodies.

Those who start from fire as the single element, while avoiding this difficulty, involve themselves in many others. Some of them give [10] fire a particular shape, like those who make it a pyramid, and this on one of two grounds. The reason given may be—more crudely—that the pyramid is the most piercing of figures as fire is of bodies, or—more ingeniously—the position may be supported by the following argument. As all bodies are composed of that which has the finest parts, [15] posed of that which has the finest parts, so all solid figures are composed of pyramids: but the finest body is fire, while among figures the pyramid is primary and has the smallest parts; and the primary body must have the primary figure: therefore fire will be a pyramid. Others, again, express no opinion on the subject of its figure, but simply regard it as the [20] body of the finest parts, which in combination will form other bodies, as the fusing of gold-dust produces solid gold. Both of these views involve the same difficulties. For (1) if, on the one hand, they make the primary body an atom, the view will be open to the objections already advanced against the atomic theory. And further the theory is inconsistent [25] with a regard for the facts of nature. For if all bodies are quantitatively commensurable, and the relative size of the various homoeomerous masses and of their several elements are in the same ratio, so that the total mass of water, for instance, is related to the total mass of air as the elements of each are to one another, and [30] so on, and if there is more air than water and, generally, more of the finer body than of the coarser, obviously the element of water will be smaller than that of air. But the lesser quantity is contained in the greater. Therefore 304ᵇ the air element is divisible. And the same could be shown of fire and of all bodies whose parts are relatively fine. (2) If, on the other hand, the primary body is divisible, then (a) those who give fire a special shape will have to say that a part of fire is not fire, because [5] a pyramid is not composed of pyramids, and also that not every body is either an element or composed of elements, since a part of fire will be neither fire nor any other element. And (b) those whose ground of distinction is size will have to recognize an element prior to the element, a regress which continues infinitely, since every body is divisible and that which has the smallest parts is the element. Further, they too will have to say that the same [10] body is relatively to this fire and relatively to that air, to others again water and earth.

The common error of all views which assume a single element is that they allow only one natural movement, which is the same for every body. For it is a matter of observation that a natural body possesses a principle of [15] movement. If then all bodies are one, all will have one movement. With this motion the greater their quantity the more they will move, just as fire, in proportion as its quantity is greater, moves faster with the upward motion which belongs to it. But the fact is that increase of quantity makes many things move the faster downward. For these reasons, then, [20] as well as from the distinction already established[1] of a plurality of natural movements, it is impossible that there should be only one element. But if the elements are not an

---
[1] Book I, chapter 2.

6

First we must inquire whether the elements are eternal or subject to generation and destruction; for when this question has been answered their number and character will be manifest. In the first place, they cannot be eternal. It is a matter of observation that fire, water, and every simple body undergo a process of analysis, which must either continue infinitely or stop somewhere. (1) Suppose it infinite. Then the time occupied by the process will be infinite, and also that occupied by the reverse process of synthesis. For the processes of analysis and synthesis succeed one another in the various parts. It will follow that there are two infinite times which are mutually exclusive, the time occupied by the synthesis, which is infinite, being preceded by the period of analysis. There are thus two mutually exclusive infinites, which is impossible. (2) Suppose, on the other hand, that the analysis stops somewhere. Then the body at which it stops will be either atomic or, as Empedocles seems to have intended, a divisible body which will yet never be divided. The foregoing arguments[1] show that it cannot be an atom; but neither can it be a divisible body which analysis will never reach. For a smaller body is more easily destroyed than a larger; and a destructive process which succeeds in destroying, that is, in resolving into smaller bodies, a body of some size, cannot reasonably be expected to fail with the smaller body. Now in fire we observe a destruction of two kinds: it is destroyed by its contrary when it is quenched, and by itself when it dies out. But the effect is produced by a greater quantity upon a lesser, and the more quickly the smaller it is. The elements of bodies must therefore be subject to destruction and generation.

Since they are generated, they must be generated either from something incorporeal or from a body, and if from a body, either from one another or from something else. The theory which generates them from something incorporeal requires an extra-corporeal void. For everything that comes to be comes to be in something, and that in which the generation takes place must either be incorporeal or possess body; and if it has body, there will be two bodies in the same place at the same time, viz. that which is coming to be and that which was previously there, while if it is incorporeal, there must be an extra-corporeal void. But we have already shown[2] that this is impossible. But, on the other hand, it is equally impossible that the elements should be generated from some kind of body. That would involve a body distinct from the elements and prior to them. But if this body possesses weight or lightness, it will be one of the elements; and if it has no tendency to movement, it will be an immovable or mathematical entity, and therefore not in a place at all. A place in which a thing is at rest is a place in which it might move, either by constraint, i.e. unnaturally, or in the absence of constraint, i.e. naturally. If, then, it is in a place and somewhere, it will be one of the elements; and if it is not in a place, nothing can come from it, since that which comes into being and that out of which it comes must needs be together. The elements therefore cannot be generated from something incorporeal nor from a body which is not an element, and the only remaining alternative is that they are generated from one another.

7

We must, therefore, turn to the question, what is the manner of their generation from one another? Is it as Empedocles and Democritus say, or as those who resolve bodies into planes say, or is there yet another possibility? (1) What the followers of Empedocles do, though without observing it themselves, is to reduce the generation of elements out of one another to an illusion. They make it a process of excretion from a body of what was in it all the time—as though generation required a vessel rather than a material—so that it involves no change of anything. And even if this were accepted, there are other implications equally unsatisfactory. We do not expect a mass of matter to be made heavier by compression. But they will be bound to maintain this, if they say that water is a body present in air and excreted from air, since air becomes heavier when it turns into water. Again, when the mixed body is divided, they can show no reason why one of the constituents must by itself take up more room than the body did: but when water turns into air, the room occupied is increased. The fact is that the finer body takes up more room, as is obvious in any case of transformation. As the liquid is converted into vapour or air the vessel which contains it is often burst because it does not

---
[1] Chapter 4.
[2] *Physics*, IV. 8.

contain room enough. Now, if there is no void at all, and if, as those who take this view say, there is no expansion of bodies, the impossibility of this is manifest: and if there is void and expansion, there is no accounting for the fact that the body which results from division occu- [20] pies of necessity a greater space. It is inevitable, too, that generation of one out of another should come to a stop, since a finite quantum cannot contain an infinity of finite quanta. When earth produces water something is taken away from the earth, for the process is one of excretion. The same thing happens again when the residue produces water. But [25] this can only go on for ever, if the finite body contains an infinity, which is impossible. Therefore the generation of elements out of one another will not always continue.

(2) We have now explained that the mutual transformations of the elements cannot take place by means of excretion. The remaining alternative is that they should be generated by changing into one another. And this in one of [30] two ways, either by change of shape, as the same wax takes the shape both of a sphere and of a cube, or, as some assert, by resolution into planes. (*a*) Generation by change of shape would necessarily involve the assertion of atomic bodies. For if the particles were divisible there would be a part of fire which was not fire and a part of earth which was not earth, [35] for the reason that not every part of a pyramid is a pyramid nor of a cube a cube. But if (*b*) the process is resolution into planes, the first difficulty is that the elements cannot all be generated out of one another. This they are obliged to assert, and do assert. It is absurd, because it is unreasonable that one element alone should have no part in the transformations, and also contrary to the observed [5] data of sense, according to which all alike change into one another. In fact their explanation of the observations is not consistent with the observations. And the reason is that their ultimate principles are wrongly assumed: they had certain predetermined views, and were resolved to bring everything into line with them. [10] It seems that perceptible things require perceptible principles, eternal things eternal principles, corruptible things corruptible principles; and, in general, every subject matter principles homogeneous with itself. But they, owing to their love for their principles, fall into the attitude of men who undertake the defence of a position in argument. In the confidence that the principles are true they are ready to accept any consequence of their ap- [15] plication. As though some principles did not require to be judged from their results, and particularly from their final issue! And that issue, which in the case of productive knowledge is the product, in the knowledge of nature is the unimpeachable evidence of the senses as to each fact.

The result of their view is that earth has the best right to the name element, and is alone indestructible; for that which is indissoluble is [20] indestructible and elementary, and earth alone cannot be dissolved into any body but itself. Again, in the case of those elements which do suffer dissolution, the 'suspension' of the triangles is unsatisfactory. But this takes place whenever one is dissolved into another, because of the numerical inequality of the triangles which compose them. Further, those who hold these views must needs suppose that [25] generation does not start from a body. For what is generated out of planes cannot be said to have been generated from a body. And they must also assert that not all bodies are divisible, coming thus into conflict with our most accurate sciences, namely the mathematical, which assume that even the intelligible is divisible, while they, in their anxiety to save their hy- [30] pothesis, cannot even admit this of every perceptible thing. For any one who gives each element a shape of its own, and makes this the ground of distinction between the substances, has to attribute to them indivisibility; since division of a pyramid or a sphere must leave somewhere at least a residue which is not a sphere or a pyramid. Either, then, a part of fire is not fire, so that there is a body prior to the element—for every body is either an element or composed of elements—or not every body is divisible.

8

In general, the attempt to give a shape to each of the simple bodies is unsound, for the reason, [5] first, that they will not succeed in filling the whole. It is agreed that there are only three plane figures which can fill a space, the triangle, the square, and the hexagon, and only two solids, the pyramid and the cube. But the theory needs more than these because the elements which it recognizes are more in number. Secondly, it is manifest that the simple bodies [10] are often given a shape by the place in which they are included, particularly water and air. In such a case the shape of the element cannot persist; for, if it did, the contained mass would not be in continuous contact with the containing body; while, if its shape is changed, it will cease to be water, since the distinctive [15] quality is shape. Clearly, then, their shapes are not fixed. Indeed, nature itself seems to offer corroboration of this theoretical conclusion. Just as in other cases the substratum must be formless and unshapen—for thus the 'all-receptive', as we read in the *Timaeus*,[1] will be best for modelling—so the elements should [20] be conceived as a material for composite things; and that is why they can put off their qualitative distinctions and pass into one another. Further, how can they account for the generation of flesh and bone or any other continuous body? The elements alone can-[25] not produce them because their collocation cannot produce a continuum. Nor can the composition of planes; for this produces the elements themselves, not bodies made up of them. Any one then who insists upon an exact statement of this kind of theory, instead of assenting after a passing glance at it, will see that it removes generation from the world.

[30] Further, the very properties, powers, and motions, to which they paid particular attention in allotting shapes, show the shapes not to be in accord with the bodies. Because fire is mobile and productive of heat and combustion, some made it a sphere, others a pyramid. These shapes, they thought, were the most mobile because they offer the fewest points of con- 307ᵃ tact and are the least stable of any; they were also the most apt to produce warmth and combustion, because the one is angular throughout while the other has the most acute angles, and the angles, they say, produce warmth and combustion. Now, in the first place, with regard to movement both are in [5] error. These may be the figures best adapted to movement; they are not, however, well adapted to the movement of fire, which is an upward and rectilinear movement, but rather to that form of circular movement which we call rolling. Earth, again, they call a cube because it is stable and at rest. But it rests only in its own place, not anywhere; from any other [10] it moves if nothing hinders, and fire and the other bodies do the same. The obvious inference, therefore, is that fire and each several element is in a foreign place a sphere or a pyramid, but in its own a cube. Again, if the possession of angles makes a body produce heat [15] and combustion, every element produces

[1] Plato, *Timaeus*, 51.

heat, though one may do so more than another. For they all possess angles, the octahedron and dodecahedron as well as the pyramid; and Democritus makes even the sphere a kind of angle, which cuts things because of its mobility. The difference, then, will be one of degree: and this is plainly false. They must also accept the inference that the mathematical [20] solids produce heat and combustion, since they too possess angles and contain atomic spheres and pyramids, especially if there are, as they allege, atomic figures. Anyhow if these functions belong to some of these things and not to others, they should explain the difference, instead of speaking in quite general terms as they do. Again, combustion of a body [25] produces fire, and fire is a sphere or a pyramid. The body, then, is turned into spheres or pyramids. Let us grant that these figures may reasonably be supposed to cut and break up bodies as fire does; still it remains quite inexplicable that a pyramid must needs produce pyramids or a sphere spheres. One might as well postulate that a knife or a saw [30] divides things into knives or saws. It is also ridiculous to think only of division when allotting fire its shape. Fire is generally thought of as combining and connecting rather than as 307ᵇ separating. For though it separates bodies different in kind, it combines those which are the same; and the combining is essential to it, the functions of connecting and uniting being a mark of fire, while the separating is incidental. For the expulsion of the foreign body is an incident in the compacting of the homogeneous. In choosing the shape, then, they [5] should have thought either of both functions or preferably of the combining function. In addition, since hot and cold are contrary powers, it is impossible to allot any shape to the cold. For the shape given must be the contrary of that given to the hot, but there is no contrariety between figures. That is why they have all left the cold out, though properly either all [10] or none should have their distinguishing figures. Some of them, however, do attempt to explain this power, and they contradict themselves. A body of large particles, they say, is cold because instead of penetrating through the passages it crushes. Clearly, then, that which is hot is that which penetrates these passages, or in other words that which has fine [15] particles. It results that hot and cold are distinguished not by the figure but by the size of the particles. Again, if the pyramids are unequal in size, the large ones will not be fire and that figure will produce not combustion but its contrary.

From what has been said it is clear that the difference of the elements does not depend upon their shape. Now their most important [20] differences are those of property, function, and power; for every natural body has, we maintain, its own functions, properties, and powers. Our first business, then, will be to speak of these, and that inquiry will enable us to explain the differences of each from each.

BOOK IV

1

We have now to consider the terms 'heavy' and 'light'. We must ask what the bodies so called are, how they are constituted, and what [30] is the reason of their possessing these powers. The consideration of these questions is a proper part of the theory of movement, since we call things heavy and light because they have the power of being moved naturally in a certain way. The activities corresponding to these powers have not been given any name, 308a unless it is thought that 'impetus' is such a name. But because the inquiry into nature is concerned with movement, and these things have in themselves some spark (as it were) of movement, all inquirers avail themselves of these powers, though in all but a few cases without exact discrimination. We must then [5] first look at whatever others have said, and formulate the questions which require settlement in the interests of this inquiry, before we go on to state our own view of the matter.

Language recognizes (*a*) an absolute, (*b*) a relative heavy and light. Of two heavy things, such as wood and bronze, we say that the one is relatively light, the other relatively heavy. [10] Our predecessors have not dealt at all with the absolute use of the terms, but only with the relative. I mean, they do not explain what the heavy is or what the light is, but only the relative heaviness and lightness of things possessing weight. This can be made clearer as follows. There are things whose constant nature it is to move away from the centre, while others [15] move constantly towards the centre; and of these movements that which is away from the centre I call upward movement and that which is towards it I call downward movement. (The view, urged by some,[1] that there is no up and no down in the heaven, is absurd. There can be, they say, no up and no down, [20] since the universe is similar every way, and from any point on the earth's surface a man by advancing far enough will come to stand foot to foot with himself. But the extremity of the whole, which we call 'above', is in position above and in nature primary. And since the universe has an extremity and a centre, it must clearly have an up and down. Common usage is thus correct, though inadequate. And the reason of its inadequacy is that men think that the universe is not similar every way. They recognize only the hemisphere which is over us. But if they went on to think of the world as formed on this pattern all round, with a centre identically related to each point on the extremity, they would have to admit that the extremity was above and the centre below.) By absolutely light, then, we [30] mean that which moves upward or to the extremity, and by absolutely heavy that which moves downward or to the centre. By lighter or relatively light we mean that one, of two bodies endowed with weight and equal in bulk, which is exceeded by the other in the speed of its natural downward movement.

2

Those of our predecessors who have entered [35] upon this inquiry have for the most part spoken of light and heavy things only in the 308b sense in which one of two things both endowed with weight is said to be the lighter. And this treatment they consider a sufficient analysis also of the notions of absolute heaviness, to which their account does not apply. This, however, will become clearer as we advance. One use of the terms 'lighter' and [5] 'heavier' is that which is set forth in writing in the *Timaeus*,[2] that the body which is composed of the greater number of identical parts is relatively heavy, while that which is composed of a smaller number is relatively light. As a larger quantity of lead or of bronze is heavier than a smaller—and this holds good of all homogeneous masses, the superior weight always depending upon a numerical superi- [10] ority of equal parts—in precisely the same way, they assert, lead is heavier than wood. For all bodies, in spite of the general opinion to the contrary, are composed of identical parts

[1] Plato, *Timaeus*, 62.
[2] 63.

and of a single material. But this analysis says nothing of the absolutely heavy and light. The facts are that fire is always light and moves upward, while earth and all earthy things move downwards or towards the centre. It [15] cannot then be the fewness of the triangles (of which, in their view, all these bodies are composed) which disposes fire to move upward. If it were, the greater the quantity of fire the slower it would move, owing to the increase of weight due to the increased number of triangles. But the palpable fact, on the contrary, is that the greater the quantity, the lighter the mass is and the quicker its upward [20] movement: and, similarly, in the reverse movement from above downward, the small mass will move quicker and the large slower. Further, since to be lighter is to have fewer of these homogeneous parts and to be heavier is to have more, and air, water, and fire are composed of the same triangles, the only difference [25] being in the number of such parts, which must therefore explain any distinction of relatively light and heavy between these bodies, it follows that there must be a certain quantum of air which is heavier than water. But the facts are directly opposed to this. The larger the quantity of air the more readily it moves upward, and any portion of air without exception will rise up out of the water.

So much for one view of the distinction be-[30] tween light and heavy. To others the analysis seems insufficient; and their views on the subject, though they belong to an older generation than ours, have an air of novelty. It is apparent that there are bodies which, when smaller in bulk than others, yet exceed them in weight. It is therefore obviously insufficient to say that bodies of equal weight are [35] composed of an equal number of primary parts: for that would give equality of bulk. Those who maintain that the primary or atomic parts, of which bodies endowed with 309ᵃ weight are composed, are planes, cannot so speak without absurdity; but those who regard them as solids are in a better position to assert that of such bodies the larger is the heavier. But since in composite bodies the weight obviously does not correspond in this way to the [5] bulk, the lesser bulk being often superior in weight (as, for instance, if one be wool and the other bronze), there are some who think and say that the cause is to be found elsewhere. The void, they say, which is imprisoned in bodies, lightens them and sometimes makes the larger body the lighter. The reason is that there is more void. And this would also account for the fact that a body composed of a number of solid parts equal to, or even smaller than, that of another is sometimes larger in bulk than it. [10] In short, generally and in every case a body is relatively light when it contains a relatively large amount of void. This is the way they put it themselves, but their account requires an addition. Relative lightness must depend not only on an excess of void, but also an a defect of solid: for if the ratio of solid to void [15] exceeds a certain proportion, the relative lightness will disappear. Thus fire, they say, is the lightest of things just for this reason that it has the most void. But it would follow that a large mass of gold, as containing more void than a small mass of fire, is lighter than it, unless it also contains many times as much solid. The addition is therefore necessary.

Of those who deny the existence of a void some, like Anaxagoras and Empedocles, have not tried to analyse the notions of light and [20] heavy at all; and those who, while still denying the existence of a void, have attempted this,[1] have failed to explain why there are bodies which are absolutely heavy and light, or in other words why some move upward and others downward. The fact, again, [25] that the body of greater bulk is sometimes lighter than smaller bodies is one which they have passed over in silence, and what they have said gives no obvious suggestion for reconciling their views with the observed facts.

But those who attribute the lightness of fire to its containing so much void are necessarily involved in practically the same difficulties. For though fire be supposed to contain less [30] solid than any other body, as well as more void, yet there will be a certain quantum of fire in which the amount of solid or plenum is in excess of the solids contained in some small quantity of earth. They may reply that there is an excess of void also. But the question is, how will they discriminate the absolutely heavy? Presumably, either by its excess of solid or by its defect of void. On the former 309ᵇ view there could be an amount of earth so small as to contain less solid than a large mass of fire. And similarly, if the distinction rests on the amount of void, there will be a body, lighter than the absolutely light, which nevertheless moves downward as constantly as [5] the other moves upward. But that cannot be so, since the absolutely light is always lighter than bodies which have weight and move

[1] Plato, in the *Timaeus*.

downward, while, on the other hand, that which is lighter need not be light, because in common speech we distinguish a lighter and a heavier (viz. water and earth) among bodies endowed with weight. Again, the suggestion of a certain ratio between the void and the solid in a body is no more equal to solving the prob-[10] lem before us. The manner of speaking will issue in a similar impossibility. For any two portions of fire, small or great, will exhibit the same ratio of solid to void; but the upward movement of the greater is quicker than that of the less, just as the downward movement of a mass of gold or lead, or of any other body en-[15] dowed with weight, is quicker in proportion to its size. This, however, should not be the case if the ratio is the ground of distinction between heavy things and light. There is also an absurdity in attributing the upward movement of bodies to a void which does not itself move. If, however, it is the nature of a void to move upward and of a plenum to move downward, and therefore each causes a like move-[20] ment in other things, there was no need to raise the question why composite bodies are some light and some heavy; they had only to explain why these two things are themselves light and heavy respectively, and to give, further, the reason why the plenum and the void are not eternally separated. It is also unreason-[25] able to imagine a place for the void, as if the void were not itself a kind of place. But if the void is to move, it must have a place out of which and into which the change carries it. Also what is the cause of its movement? Not, surely, its voidness: for it is not the void only which is moved, but also the solid.

Similar difficulties are involved in all other methods of distinction, whether they account [30] for the relative lightness and heaviness of bodies by distinctions of size, or proceed on any other principle, so long as they attribute to each the same matter, or even if they recognize more than one matter, so long as that means only a pair of contraries. If there is a single matter, as with those who compose things of triangles, nothing can be absolutely heavy or 310ª light: and if there is one matter and its contrary—the void, for instance, and the plenum—no reason can be given for the relative lightness and heaviness of the bodies intermediate between the absolutely light and heavy when compared either with one another or with these themselves. The view which bases the distinction upon differences of size is more [5] like a mere fiction than those previously mentioned, but, in that it is able to make distinctions between the four elements, it is in a stronger position for meeting the foregoing difficulties. Since, however, it imagines that these bodies which differ in size are all made of one substance, it implies, equally with the view that there is but one matter, that there is nothing absolutely light and nothing which moves up-[10] ward (except as being passed by other things or forced up by them); and since a multitude of small atoms are heavier than a few large ones, it will follow that much air or fire is heavier than a little water or earth, which is impossible.

3

These, then, are the views which have been advanced by others and the terms in which [15] they state them. We may begin our own statement by settling a question which to some has been the main difficulty—the question why some bodies move always and naturally upward and others downward, while others again move both upward and downward. After that we will inquire into light and heavy and the [20] explanation of the various phenomena connected with them. The local movement of each body into its own place must be regarded as similar to what happens in connexion with other forms of generation and change. There are, in fact, three kinds of movement, affecting respectively the size, the form, and the place of a thing, and in each it is observable that change [25] proceeds from a contrary to a contrary or to something intermediate: it is never the change of any chance subject in any chance direction, nor, similarly, is the relation of the mover to its object fortuitous: the thing altered is different from the thing increased, and precisely the same difference holds between that which produces alteration and that which pro-[30] duces increase. In the same manner it must be thought that that which produces local motion and that which is so moved are not fortuitously related. Now, that which produces upward and downward movement is that which produces weight and lightness, and that which is moved is that which is potentially heavy or light, and the movement of each body to its own place is motion towards its own 310ᵇ form. (It is best to interpret in this sense the common statement of the older writers that 'like moves to like'. For the words are not in every sense true to fact. If one were to remove the earth to where the moon now is, the various fragments of earth would each move not

[5] towards it but to the place in which it now is. In general, when a number of similar and undifferentiated bodies are moved with the same motion this result is necessarily produced, viz. that the place which is the natural goal of the movement of each single part is also that of the whole. But since the place of a thing is the boundary of that which contains it, and the continent of all things that move upward or downward is the extremity and the centre, and [10] this boundary comes to be, in a sense, the form of that which is contained, it is to its like that a body moves when it moves to its own place. For the successive members of the series are like one another: water, I mean, is like air and air like fire, and between intermediates the relation may be converted, though not between them and the extremes; thus air is like water, but water is like earth: for the relation of each [15] outer body to that which is next within it is of form to matter.) Thus to ask why fire moves upward and earth downward is the same as to ask why the healable, when moved and changed *qua* healable, attains health and not whiteness; and similar questions might be asked concerning any other subject of altera- [20] tion. Of course the subject of increase, when changed *qua* increasable, attains not health but a superior size. The same applies in the other cases. One thing changes in quality, another in quantity: and so in place, a light thing goes upward, a heavy thing downward. The only difference is that in the last case, viz. that of the heavy and the light, the bodies are [25] thought to have a spring of change within themselves, while the subjects of healing and increase are thought to be moved purely from without. Sometimes, however, even they change of themselves, i.e. in response to a slight external movement reach health or increase, as the case may be. And since the same thing which is [30] healable is also receptive of disease, it depends on whether it is moved *qua* healable or *qua* liable to disease whether the motion is towards health or towards disease. But the reason why the heavy and the light appear more than these things to contain within themselves the source of their movements is that their matter is nearest to being. This is indicated by the fact that locomotion belongs to bodies only when isolated from other bodies, and is generated last of the several kinds of movement; in order of being then it will be first. Now when311ª ever air comes into being out of water, light out of heavy, it goes to the upper place. It is forthwith light: becoming is at an end, and in that place it has being. Obviously, then, it is a potentiality, which, in its passage to actuality, [5] comes into that place and quantity and quality which belong to its actuality. And the same fact explains why what is already actually fire or earth moves, when nothing obstructs it, towards its own place. For motion is equally immediate in the case of nutriment, when nothing hinders, and in the case of the thing healed, when nothing stays the healing. But the movement is also due to the origi[10] nal creative force and to that which removes the hindrance or off which the moving thing rebounded, as was explained in our opening discussions, where we tried to show how none of these things moves itself.[1] The reason of the various motions of the various bodies, and the meaning of the motion of a body to its own place, have now been explained.

4

[15] We have now to speak of the distinctive properties of these bodies and of the various phenomena connected with them. In accordance with general conviction we may distinguish the absolutely heavy, as that which sinks to the bottom of all things, from the absolutely light, which is that which rises to the surface of all things. I use the term 'absolutely', in view of the generic character of 'light' and 'heavy', in order to confine the application to bodies which do not combine lightness and heaviness. [20] It is apparent, I mean, that fire, in whatever quantity, so long as there is no external obstacle moves upward, and earth downward; and, if the quantity is increased, the movement is the same, though swifter. But the heaviness and lightness of bodies which combine these qualities is different from this, since while they rise to the surface of some bodies they sink to the bottom of others. Such are air and water. Neither of them is absolutely either light or heavy. [25] Both are lighter than earth—for any portion of either rises to the surface of it—but heavier than fire, since a portion of either, whatever its quantity, sinks to the bottom of fire; compared together, however, the one has absolute weight, the other absolute lightness, since air in any quantity rises to the surface of water, while water in any quantity sinks to the bottom of air. [30] Now other bodies are severally light and heavy, and evidently in them the attributes are due to the difference of their uncompounded parts: that is to say, according as the one or the other happens to preponderate the bodies will

[1] *Physics*, VII. 1(241ᵇ 24); VIII. 4(254ᵇ 7).

be heavy and light respectively. Therefore we need only speak of these parts, since they are [35] primary and all else consequential: and in so doing we shall be following the advice which we gave[1] to those whose attribute heaviness to the presence of plenum and lightness to that of void. It is due to the properties of the elementary bodies that a body which is regarded as light in one place is regarded as heavy in another, and vice versa. In air, for instance, a talent's weight of wood is heavier than a mina of lead, but in water the wood is the lighter. The reason is that all the elements [5] except fire have weight and all but earth lightness. Earth, then, and bodies in which earth preponderates, must needs have weight everywhere, while water is heavy anywhere but in earth, and air is heavy when not in water or earth. In its own place each of these bodies has weight except fire, even air. Of this we [10] have evidence in the fact that a bladder when inflated weighs more than when empty. A body, then, in which air preponderates over earth and water, may well be lighter than something in water and yet heavier than it in air, since such a body does not rise in air but rises to the surface in water.

[15] The following account will make it plain that there is an absolutely light and an absolutely heavy body. And by absolutely light I mean one which of its own nature always moves upward, by absolutely heavy one which of its own nature always moves downward, if no obstacle is in the way. There are, I say, these two kinds of body, and it is not the case, as some maintain, that all bodies have weight. Different views are in fact agreed that there is a heavy body, which moves uniformly towards the centre. But [20] there is also similarly a light body. For we see with our eyes, as we said before,[2] that earthy things sink to the bottom of all things and move towards the centre. But the centre is a fixed point. If therefore there is some body which rises to the surface of all things—and we observe fire to move upward even in air itself, while the air remains at rest—clearly this body is moving towards the extremity. It cannot then have any weight. If it had, there would be [25] another body in which it sank: and if that had weight, there would be yet another which moved to the extremity and thus rose to the surface of all moving things. In fact, however, we have no evidence of such a body. Fire, then, has no weight. Neither has earth any lightness, since it sinks to the bottom of all things, and

[1] Above, 309ᵇ 20.   [2] Above, 311ᵃ 20.

that which sinks moves to the centre. That there is a centre towards which the motion of [30] heavy things, and away from which that of light things is directed, is manifest in many ways. First, because no movement can continue to infinity. For what cannot be can no more come-to-be than be, and movement is a coming-to-be in one place from another. Secondly, like the upward movement of fire, the downward [35] movement of earth and all heavy things makes equal angles on every side with the earth's surface: it must therefore be directed towards the centre. Whether it is really the centre of the earth and not rather that of the whole to which it moves, may be left to another inquiry, since these are coincident. But since that which sinks to the bottom of all things moves to the centre, necessarily that which rises to the surface moves to the extremity of the re- [5] gion in which the movement of these bodies takes place. For the centre is opposed as contrary to the extremity, as that which sinks is opposed to that which rises to the surface. This also gives a reasonable ground for the duality of heavy and light in the spatial duality centre and extremity. Now there is also the intermediate region to which each name is given in op- [10] position to the other extreme. For that which is intermediate between the two is in a sense both extremity and centre. For this reason there is another heavy and light; namely, water and air. But in our view the continent pertains to form and the contained to matter: and this distinction is present in every genus. Alike in the sphere of quality and in that of [15] quantity there is that which corresponds rather to form and that which corresponds to matter. In the same way, among spatial distinctions, the above belongs to the determinate, the below to matter. The same holds, consequently, also of the matter itself of that which is heavy and light: as potentially possessing the one character, it is matter for the heavy, and as potentially possessing the other, for the light. It is the same matter, but its being is different, as [20] that which is receptive of disease is the same as that which is receptive of health, though in being different from it, and therefore diseasedness is different from healthiness.

5

A thing then which has the one kind of matter is light and always moves upward, while a thing which has the opposite matter is heavy and always moves downward. Bodies composed of kinds of matter different from these but having relatively to each other the charac-[25] ter which these have absolutely, possess both the upward and the downward motion. Hence air and water each have both lightness and weight, and water sinks to the bottom of all things except earth, while air rises to the surface of all things except fire. But since there is one body only which rises to the surface of all things and one only which sinks to the bottom of all things, there must needs be two [30] other bodies which sink in some bodies and rise to the surface of others. The kinds of matter, then, must be as numerous as these bodies, i.e. four, but though they are four there must be a common matter of all—particularly if they pass into one another—which in each is in being different. There is no reason why 312[b] there should not be one or more intermediates between the contraries, as in the case of colour; for 'intermediate' and 'mean' are capable of more than one application.

Now in its own place every body endowed with both weight and lightness has weight—whereas earth has weight everywhere—but [5] they only have lightness among bodies to whose surface they rise. Hence when a support is withdrawn such a body moves downward until it reaches the body next below it, air to the place of water and water to that of earth. But if the fire above air is removed, it will not move upward to the place of fire, except by constraint; and in that way water also may be drawn up, when the upward movement of air [10] which has had a common surface with it is swift enough to overpower the downward impulse of the water. Nor does water move upward to the place of air, except in the manner just described. Earth is not so affected at all, because a common surface is not possible to it. Hence water is drawn up into the vessel to which fire is applied, but not earth. As earth [15] fails to move upward, so fire fails to move downward when air is withdrawn from beneath it: for fire has no weight even in its own place, as earth has no lightness. The other two move downward when the body beneath is withdrawn because, while the absolutely heavy is that which sinks to the bottom of all things, the relatively heavy sinks to its own place or to the surface of the body in which it rises, since it is similar in matter to it.

[20] It is plain that one must suppose as many distinct species of matter as there are bodies. For if, *first*, there is a single matter of all things, as, for instance, the void or the plenum or extension or the triangles, either all things will move upward or all things will move downward, and the second motion will be abolished. And so, either there will be no absolutely light body, if superiority of weight is [25] due to superior size or number of the constituent bodies or to the fullness of the body: but the contrary is a matter of observation, and it has been shown that the downward and upward movements are equally constant and universal: or, if the matter in question is the void or something similar, which moves uniformly upward, there will be nothing to move uniformly downward. Further, it will follow that the intermediate bodies move downward in some cases quicker than earth: for air in sufficiently large quantity will con-[30] tain a larger number of triangles or solids or particles. It is, however, manifest that no portion of air whatever moves downward. And the same reasoning applies to lightness, if that is supposed to depend on superiority of quantity of matter. But if, *secondly,* the kinds of matter are two, it will be difficult to make the intermediate bodies behave as air and water 313[a] behave. Suppose, for example, that the two asserted are void and plenum. Fire, then, as moving upward, will be void, earth, as moving downward, plenum; and in air, it will be said, fire preponderates, in water, earth. There will then be a quantity of water containing more fire than a little air, and a large amount of air will contain more earth than a little water: [5] consequently we shall have to say that air in a certain quantity moves downward more quickly than a little water. But such a thing has never been observed anywhere. Necessarily, then, as fire goes up because it has something, e.g. void, which other things do not have, and earth goes downward because it has plenum, so air goes to its own place above [10] water because it has something else, and water goes downward because of some special kind of body. But if the two bodies are one matter, or two matters both present in each, there will be a certain quantity of each at which water will excel a little air in the upward movement and air excel water in the downward movement, as we have already often said.

6

The shape of bodies will not account for their [15] moving upward or downward in general, though it will account for their moving faster or slower. The reasons for this are not difficult to see. For the problem thus raised is why a flat piece of iron or lead floats upon water, while smaller and less heavy things, so long as they are round or long—a needle, for instance—sink down; and sometimes a thing floats be-[20] cause it is small, as with gold dust and the various earthy and dusty materials which throng the air. With regard to these questions, it is wrong to accept the explanation offered by Democritus. He says that the warm bodies moving up out of the water hold up heavy bodies which are broad, while the narrow ones fall through, because the bodies which offer this resistance are not numerous. But this would be even more likely to happen in air—an objection which he himself raises. His reply to the objection is feeble. In the air, he [5] says, the 'drive' (meaning by drive the movement of the upward moving bodies) is not uniform in direction. But since some continua are easily divided and others less easily, and things which produce division differ similarly in the ease with which they produce it, the explanation must be found in this fact. It is the easily bounded, in proportion as it is easily bounded, which is easily divided; and air is [10] more so than water, water than earth. Further, the smaller the quantity in each kind, the more easily it is divided and disrupted. Thus the reason why broad things keep their place is because they cover so wide a surface and the greater quantity is less easily disrupted. Bodies of the opposite shape sink down be-[15] cause they occupy so little of the surface, which is therefore easily parted. And these considerations apply with far greater force to air, since it is so much more easily divided than water. But since there are two factors, the force responsible for the downward motion of the heavy body and the disruption-resisting force of the continuous surface, there must be some ratio between the two. For in proportion as the force applied by the heavy thing towards [20] disruption and division exceeds that which resides in the continuum, the quicker will it force its way down; only if the force of the heavy thing is the weaker, will it ride upon the surface.

We have now finished our examination of the heavy and the light and of the phenomena connected with them.

CONTENTS:

ON GENERATION AND CORRUPTION

BOOK I

Coming-to-be and passing-away are distinguished from 'alteration' and from growth and diminution

CHAP.   BERLIN NOS.

1. Are coming-to-be and passing-away distinct from 'alteration'? It is clear that, amongst the ancient philosophers, the monists are logically bound to identify, and the pluralists to distinguish, these changes. Hence both Anaxagoras and Empedocles (who are pluralists) are inconsistent in their statements on this subject. Empedocles, it must be added, is inconsistent and obscure in many other respects as well 314^a 1

2. There are no indivisible magnitudes. Nevertheless, coming-to-be and passing-away may well occur and be distinct from 'alteration'. For coming-to-be is not effected by the 'association' of discrete constituents, nor passing-away by their 'dissociation'; and 'change in what is continuous' is not always 'alteration' 315^a 26

3. Coming-to-be and passing-away (in the strict or 'unqualified' sense of the terms) are in fact always occurring in Nature. Their ceaseless occurrence is made possible by the character of Matter (*materia prima*) 317^a 32

4. 'Alteration' is change of quality. It is thus essentially distinct from coming-to-be and passing-away, which are changes of substance 319^b 5

5. Definition and explanation of growth and diminution 320^a 8

What comes-to-be is formed out of certain material constituents, by their 'combination'. Combination implies 'action and passion', which in turn imply 'contact'

6. Definition and explanation of 'contact' 322^b 1

7. Agent and patient are neither absolutely identical with, nor sheerly other than, one another. They must be contrasted species of the same genus, opposed formations of the same matter 323^b 1

8. Bodies do not consist of indivisible solids with void interspaces, as the Atomists maintain: nor are there 'pores' or empty channels running through them, as Empedocles supposes. Neither of these theories could account for 'action-passion' 324^b 26

9. The true explanation of 'action-passion' depends (*a*) upon the distinction between a body's *actual* and *potential* possession of a quality, and (*b*) upon the fact that *potential* possession (i.e. 'susceptibility') may vary in intensity or degree in different parts of the body 326^b 29

10. What 'combination' is, and how it can take place 327^a 30

BOOK II

The material constituents of all that comes-to-be and passes-away are the so-called 'elements', i.e. the 'simple' bodies. What these are, how they are transformed into one another, and how they 'combine'

1. Earth, Air, Fire, and Water are not really 'elements' of body, but 'simple' bodies. The 'elements' of body are 'primary matter' and certain 'contrarieties' 328^b 25

2. The 'contrarieties' in question are 'the hot and the cold' and 'the dry and the moist' 329^b 6

3. These four 'elementary qualities' (hot, cold, dry, moist) are diversely coupled so as to constitute four 'simple' bodies analogous to, but purer than, Earth, Air, Fire, and Water 330^a 30

4. The four 'simple' bodies undergo reciprocal transformation in various manners 331^a 6

5. Restatement and confirmation of the preceding doctrine 332^a 5

6. Empedocles maintains that his four 'elements' cannot be transformed into one another. How then can they be 'equal' (i.e. comparable) as he asserts? His whole theory, indeed, is thoroughly unsatisfactory. In particular, he entirely fails to explain how compounds (e.g. bone or flesh) come-to-be out of his 'elements' 333^a 16

7. How the 'simple' bodies combine to form compounds 334^a 16

8. Every compound body requires all four 'simple' bodies as its constituents   334^b 31

The causes of coming-to-be and passing-away

9. Material, formal, and final causes of coming-to-be and passing-away. The failure of earlier theories—e.g. of the 'materialist' theory and of the theory advanced by Socrates in the *Phaedo*—must be ascribed to inadequate recognition of the efficient cause   335^a 24

10. The sun's annual movement in the ecliptic or zodiac circle is the efficient cause of coming-to-be and passing-away. It explains the occurrence of these changes and their ceaseless alternation   336^a 13

Appendix

11. In what sense, and under what conditions, the things which come-to-be are 'necessary'. Absolute necessity characterizes every sequence of transformations which is cyclical   337^a 34

ON GENERATION AND CORRUPTION
BOOK I

1

314ᵃ Our next task is to study coming-to-be and passing-away. We are to distinguish the causes, and to state the definitions, of these processes considered in general—as changes predicable uniformly of all the things that come-to-be and pass-away by nature. Further, we are to study growth and 'alteration'. We must inquire what each of them is; and [5] whether 'alteration' is to be identified with coming-to-be, or whether to these different names there correspond two separate processes with distinct natures.

On this question, indeed, the early philosophers are divided. Some of them assert that the so-called 'unqualified coming-to-be' is 'alteration', while others maintain that 'alteration' and coming-to-be are distinct. For those who say that the universe is one something (i.e. those who generate all things out of one thing) are bound to assert that coming-to-be [10] is 'alteration', and that whatever 'comes-to-be' in the proper sense of the term is 'being altered': but those who make the matter of things more than one must distinguish coming-to-be from 'alteration'. To this latter class belong Empedocles, Anaxagoras, and Leucippus. And yet Anaxagoras himself failed to understand his own utterance. He *says,* at all events, that coming-to-be and passing-away [15] are the same as 'being altered':[1] yet, in common with other thinkers, he affirms that the elements are many. Thus Empedocles holds that the corporeal elements are four, while all the elements—including those which initiate movement—are six in number; whereas Anaxagoras agrees with Leucippus and Democritus that the elements are infinite.

(Anaxagoras posits as elements the 'homoe- [20] omeries', viz. bone, flesh, marrow, and everything else which is such that part and whole are the same in name and nature; while

[1] Cf. fr. 17, Diels, pp. 320–1.

Note: The bold face numbers and letters are approximate indications of the pages and columns of the standard Berlin Greek text; the bracketed numbers, of the lines in the Greek text; they are here assigned as they are assigned in the Oxford translation.

Democritus and Leucippus say that there are indivisible bodies, infinite both in number and in the varieties of their shapes, of which everything else is composed—the compounds differing one from another according to the shapes, 'positions', and 'groupings' of their constituents.)

[25] For the views of the school of Anaxagoras seem diametrically opposed to those of the followers of Empedocles. Empedocles says that Fire, Water, Air, and Earth are four elements, and are thus 'simple' rather than flesh, bone, and bodies which, like these, are 'homoeomeries'. But the followers of Anaxagoras regard the 'homoeomeries' as 'simple' and elements, whilst they affirm that Earth, Fire, Water, and Air are composite; for each of 314ᵇ these is (according to them) a 'common seminary' of all the 'homoeomeries'.

Those, then, who construct all things out of a single element, must maintain that coming-to-be and passing-away are 'alteration'. For they must affirm that the underlying something always remains identical and one; and change of such a *substratum* is what we call 'altering'. Those, on the other hand, who make the ulti- [5] mate kinds of things more than one, must maintain that 'alteration' is distinct from coming-to-be: for coming-to-be and passing-away result from the consilience and the dissolution of the many kinds. That is why Empedocles too uses language to this effect, when he says 'There is no coming-to-be of anything, but only a mingling and a divorce of what has been mingled'.[2] Thus it is clear (i) that to describe coming-to-be and passing-away in these terms [10] is in accordance with their fundamental assumption, and (ii) that they do in fact so describe them: nevertheless, they too must recognize 'alteration' as a fact distinct from coming-to-be, though it is impossible for them to do so consistently with what they say.

That we are right in this criticism is easy to perceive. For 'alteration' is a fact of observation. While the substance of the thing remains unchanged, we *see* it 'altering' just as we *see* in [15] it the changes of magnitude called

[2] Cf. fr. 8, Diels, p. 175, and the paraphrase in MXG, 975ᵃ 36–ᵇ16.

'growth' and 'diminution'. Nevertheless, the statements of those who posit more 'original reals' than one make 'alteration' impossible. For 'alteration', as we assert, takes place in respect to certain qualities: and these qualities (I mean, e.g. hot-cold, white-black, dry-moist, [20] soft-hard, and so forth) are, all of them, differences characterizing the 'elements'. The actual words of Empedocles may be quoted in illustration—

The sun everywhere bright to see, and hot;
The rain everywhere dark and cold;[1]

and he distinctively characterizes his remaining elements in a similar manner. Since, therefore, it is not possible for Fire to become Water, or Water to become Earth, neither will it be possible for anything white to become black, or [25] anything soft to become hard; and the same argument applies to all the other qualities. Yet this is what 'alteration' essentially is.

It follows, as an obvious corollary, that a single matter must always be assumed as underlying the contrary 'poles' of any change—whether change of place, or growth and diminution, or 'alteration'; further, that the being of this matter and the being of 'alteration' stand and fall together. For if the change is 315ᵃ 'alteration', then the *substratum* is a single element; i.e. all things which admit of change into one another have a single matter. And, conversely, if the *substratum* of the changing things is one, there is 'alteration'.

Empedocles, indeed, seems to contradict his [5] own statements as well as the observed facts. For he denies that any one of his elements comes-to-be out of any other, insisting on the contrary that they are the things out of which everything else comes-to-be; and yet (having brought the entirety of existing things, except Strife, together into one) he maintains, simultaneously with this denial, that each thing once more comes-to-be out of the One. Hence it was clearly out of a One that *this* came-to-be Water, and *that* Fire, various por- [10] tions of it being separated off by certain characteristic differences or qualities—as indeed he calls the sun 'white and hot', and the earth 'heavy and hard'. If, therefore, these characteristic differences be taken away (for they can be taken away, since they came-to-be), it will clearly be inevitable for Earth to come-to-be out of Water and Water out of Earth, and for each of the other elements to undergo a similar transformation—not only *then,* but

[1] Cf. fr. 21, ll. 3 and 5, Diels, p. 180.

[15] also *now*—if, and because, they change their qualities. And, to judge by what he says, the qualities are such that they *can* be 'attached' to things and *can* again be 'separated' from them, especially since Strife and Love are still fighting with one another for the mastery. It was owing to this same conflict that the elements were generated from a One at the former period. I say 'generated', for presumably Fire, Earth, and Water had no distinctive existence at all while merged in one.

There is another obscurity in the theory of [20] Empedocles. Are we to regard the One as his 'original real'? Or is it the Many—i.e. Fire and Earth, and the bodies co-ordinate with these? For the One is an 'element' in so far as it underlies the process as matter—as that out of which Earth and Fire come-to-be through a change of qualities due to 'the motion'. On the other hand, in so far as the One results from *composition* (by a consilience of the Many), whereas they result from *disintegration,* the Many are more 'elementary' [25] than the One, and prior to it in their nature.

2

We have therefore to discuss the whole subject of 'unqualified' coming-to-be and passing-away; we have to inquire whether these changes do or do not occur and, if they occur, to explain the precise conditions of their occurrence. We must also discuss the remaining forms of change, viz. growth and 'alteration'. For though, no doubt, Plato investigated the conditions under which things come-to-be and [30] pass-away, he confined his inquiry to these changes; and he discussed not *all* coming-to-be, but only that of the elements. He asked no questions as to how flesh or bones, or any of the other similar compound things, come-to-be; nor again did he examine the conditions under which 'alteration' or growth are attributable to things.

A similar criticism applies to all our prede- [35] cessors with the single exception of Democritus. Not one of them penetrated below the surface or made a thorough examination of a single one of the problems. Democritus, however, does seem not only to have thought carefully about all the problems, but also to be 315ᵇ distinguished from the outset by his method. For, as we are saying, none of the other philosophers made any definite statement about growth, except such as any amateur might have made. They said that things grow 'by the accession of like to like', but they did not proceed to explain the manner of this accession. Nor did they give any account of 'combination': and they neglected almost every single one of the remaining problems, offering [5] no explanation, e.g. of 'action' or 'passion' —how in physical actions one thing acts and the other undergoes action. Democritus and Leucippus, however, postulate the 'figures', and make 'alteration' and coming-to-be result from them. They explain coming-to-be and passing-away by their 'dissociation' and 'association', but 'alteration' by their 'grouping' and 'position'. And since they thought that the [10] truth lay in the appearance, and the appearances are conflicting and infinitely many, they made the 'figures' infinite in number. Hence—owing to the changes of the compound—*the same* thing seems different and conflicting to different people: it is 'transposed' by a small additional ingredient, and appears utterly other by the 'transposition' of [15] a single constituent. For Tragedy and Comedy are both composed of *the same* letters.

Since almost all our predecessors think (i) that coming-to-be is distinct from 'alteration', and (ii) that, whereas things 'alter' by change of their qualities, it is by 'association' and 'dissociation' that they come-to-be and pass-away, we must concentrate our attention on these theses. For they lead to many perplexing and [20] well-grounded dilemmas. If, on the one hand, coming-to-be *is* 'association', many impossible consequences result: and yet there are other arguments, not easy to unravel, which force the conclusion upon us that coming-to-be cannot possibly be anything else. If, on the other hand, coming-to-be *is not* 'association', either there is no such thing as coming-to-be at all or it is 'alteration': or else we must endeavour to unravel this dilemma too—and a stubborn one we shall find it.

[25] The fundamental question, in dealing with all these difficulties, is this: 'Do things come-to-be and "alter" and grow, and undergo the contrary changes, because the primary "reals" are indivisible magnitudes? Or is no magnitude indivisible?' For the answer we give to this question makes the greatest difference. And again, if the primary 'reals' are [30] indivisible magnitudes, are these *bodies*, as Democritus and Leucippus maintain? Or are they *planes*, as is asserted in the *Timaeus*?

To resolve bodies into planes and no further —this, as we have also remarked elsewhere,[1] is

[1] Cf., e.g. *On The Heavens*, 299^a 6–11.

in itself a paradox. Hence there is more to be said for the view that there are indivisible bodies. Yet even these involve much of paradox. Still, as we have said, it is possible to con- [35] struct 'alteration' and coming-to-be with them, if one 'transposes' *the same* by 'turning' and 'intercontact', and by 'the varieties of the figures', as Democritus does. (His denial of the reality of colour is a corollary from this position: for, according to him, things get coloured by 'turning' of the 'figures'.) But the possibility of such a construction no longer exists for those who divide bodies into planes. For nothing except solids results from putting planes together: they do not even attempt to generate any quality from them.

[5] Lack of experience diminishes our power of taking a comprehensive view of the admitted facts. Hence those who dwell in intimate association with nature and its phenomena grow more and more able to formulate, as the foundations of their theories, principles such as to admit of a wide and coherent development: while those whom devotion to abstract discussions has rendered unobservant of [10] the facts are too ready to dogmatize on the basis of a few observations. The rival treatments of the subject now before us will serve to illustrate how great is the difference between a 'scientific' and a 'dialectical' method of inquiry. For, whereas the Platonists argue that there must be atomic magnitudes 'because otherwise "The Triangle" will be more than one', Democritus would appear to have been convinced by arguments appropriate to the subject, i.e. drawn from the science of nature. Our meaning will become clear as we proceed. [15] For to suppose that a body (i.e. a magnitude) is divisible through and through, and that this division is possible, involves a difficulty. What will there be in the body which escapes the division?

If it is divisible through and through, and if this division is possible, then it might *be,* at one and the same moment, *divided* through and through, even though the dividings had not been effected simultaneously: and the actual occurrence of this result would involve no impossibility. Hence the same principle will [20] apply whenever a body is by nature divisible through and through, whether by bisection, or generally by any method whatever: nothing impossible will have resulted if it has actually been divided—not even if it has been divided into innumerable parts, themselves divided innumerable times. Nothing impossible will have resulted, though perhaps nobody in fact could so divide it.

Since, therefore, the body is divisible through and through, let it have been divided. What, then, will remain? A magnitude? No: that is impossible, since then there will be something [25] not divided, whereas *ex hypothesi* the body was divisible *through and through*. But if it be admitted that neither a body nor a magnitude will remain, and yet division is to take place, the constituents of the body will *either* be points (i.e. without magnitude) *or* absolutely nothing. If its constituents are nothings, then it might both come-to-be out of nothings and exist as a composite of nothings: and thus presumably the whole body will be nothing but an appearance. But if it consists [30] of points, a similar absurdity will result: it will not possess any magnitude. For when the points were in contact and coincided to form a single magnitude, they did not make the whole any bigger (since, when the body was divided into two or more parts, the whole was not a bit smaller or bigger than it was before the division): hence, even if all the points be put together, they will not make any magnitude.

But suppose that, as the body is being divided, a minute section—a piece of sawdust, 316b as it were—is extracted, and that in this sense a body 'comes away' from the magnitude, evading the division. Even then the same argument applies. For in what sense is that section divisible? But if what 'came away' was not a body but a separable form or quality, and if the magnitude *is* 'points or contacts thus quali- [5] fied': it is paradoxical that a magnitude should consist of elements which are not magnitudes. Moreover, *where* will the points be? And are they motionless or moving? And every contact is always a contact of two somethings, i.e. there is always something besides the contact or the division or the point.

These, then, are the difficulties resulting from the supposition that any and every body, whatever its size, is divisible through and through. There is, besides, this further con- [10] sideration. If, having divided a piece of wood or anything else, I put it together, it is again equal to what it was, and is one. Clearly this is so, whatever the point at which I cut the wood. The wood, therefore, has been divided *potentially* through and through. What, then, is there in the wood besides the division? For even if we suppose there is some quality, yet how is the wood dissolved into such constituents and how does it come-to-be out of them? Or how are such constituents separated so as to exist apart from one another?

[15] Since, therefore, it is impossible for magnitudes to consist of contacts or points, there must be indivisible bodies and magnitudes. Yet, if we *do* postulate the latter, we are confronted with equally impossible consequences, which we have examined in other works.[1] But we must try to disentangle these perplexities, and must therefore formulate the whole problem over again.

[20] On the one hand, then, it is in no way paradoxical that every perceptible body should be indivisible as well as divisible at any and every point. For the second predicate will attach to it *potentially*, but the first *actually*. On the other hand, it would seem to be impossible for a body to be, even potentially, divisible at all points simultaneously. For if it were possible, then it might actually occur, with the result, not that the body would simultaneously be actually *both* (indivisible and divided), but [25] that it would be simultaneously divided at any and every point. Consequently, nothing will remain and the body will have passed-away into what is incorporeal: and so it might come-to-be again either out of points or absolutely out of nothing. And how is that possible?

But now it is obvious that a body is in fact divided into separable magnitudes which are smaller at each division—into magnitudes which fall apart from one another and are actually separated. Hence (it is urged) the [30] process of dividing a body part by part is not a 'breaking up' which could continue *ad infinitum;* nor can a body be simultaneously divided at every point, for that is not possible; but there is a limit, beyond which the 'breaking up' cannot proceed. The necessary consequence—especially if coming-to-be and passing-away are to take place by 'association' and 'dissociation' respectively—is that a body must contain atomic magnitudes which are invisible. 317a Such is the argument which is believed to establish the necessity of atomic magnitudes: we must now show that it conceals a faulty inference, and exactly where it conceals it.

For, since point is not 'immediately-next' to point, magnitudes are 'divisible through and through' in one sense, and yet not in another. When, however, it is admitted that a magni- [5] tude is 'divisible through and through', it is thought there is a point not only anywhere,

[1] Cf. *Physics*, 231a 21 ff.; *On the Heavens*, 303a 3 ff.

but also everywhere, in it: hence it is supposed to follow, from the admission, that the magnitude must be divided away into nothing. For—it is supposed—there is a point everywhere within it, so that it consists either of contacts or of points. But it is only *in one sense* that the magnitude is 'divisible through and through', viz. in so far as there is one point *anywhere* within it and all its points are *everywhere* within it if you take them singly one by one. But there are not more points than one *anywhere* within it, for the points are not 'consecutive': hence it is not simultaneously 'divis-[*10*] ible through and through'. For if it were, then, if it be divisible at its centre, it will be divisible also at a point 'immediately-next' to its centre. But it is not so divisible: for position is not 'immediately-next' to position, nor point to point—in other words, division is not 'immediately-next' to division, nor composition to composition.

Hence there are both 'association' and 'dissociation', though neither (*a*) into, and out of, atomic magnitudes (for that involves many [*15*] impossibilities), nor (*b*) so that division takes place through and through—for this would have resulted only if point had been 'immediately-next' to point: but 'dissociation' takes place into small (i.e. relatively small) parts, and 'association' takes place out of relatively small parts.

It is wrong, however, to suppose, as some assert, that coming-to-be and passing-away in the unqualified and complete sense are distinctively defined by 'association' and 'dissociation', while the change that takes place in what is continuous is 'alteration'. On the contrary, [*20*] this is where the whole error lies. For unqualified coming-to-be and passing-away are not effected by 'association' and 'dissociation'. They take place when a thing changes, from *this* to *that*, as a whole. But the philosophers we are criticizing suppose that all such change is 'alteration': whereas in fact there is a difference. For in that which underlies the change there is a factor corresponding to the defini-[*25*] tion and there is a material factor. When, then, the change is in these constitutive factors, there will be coming-to-be or passing-away: but when it is in the thing's qualities, i.e. a change of the thing *per accidens,* there will be 'alteration'.

'Dissociation' and 'association' affect the thing's susceptibility to passing-away. For if water has first been 'dissociated' into smallish drops, air comes-to-be out of it more quickly: while, if drops of water have first been 'associated', air comes-to-be more slowly. Our doc-[*30*] trine will become clearer in the sequel.[1] Meantime, so much may be taken as established —viz. that coming-to-be cannot be 'association', at least not the kind of 'association' some philosophers assert it to be.

3

Now that we have established the preceding distinctions, we must first consider whether there is anything which comes-to-be and passes-away in the unqualified sense: or whether nothing comes-to-be in this strict sense, but everything always comes-to-be *something* and [*35*] *out of something*—I mean, e.g. comes-to-be-healthy out of being-ill and ill out of being-healthy, comes-to-be-small out of being-big and big out of being-small, and so on in every other instance. For if there is to be coming-to-be without qualification, 'something' must—without qualification—'come-to-be out of not-being', so that it would be true to say that 'not-being is an attribute of some things'. For *qualified* coming-to-be is a process out of *qualified* not-being (e.g. out of not-[*5*] white or not-beautiful), but *unqualified* coming-to-be is a process out of *unqualified* not-being.

Now 'unqualified' means either (i) the primary predication within each Category, or (ii) the universal, i.e. the all-comprehensive, predication. Hence, if 'unqualified not-being' means the negation of 'being' in the sense of the primary term of the Category in question, we shall have, in 'unqualified coming-to-be', a coming-to-be of a substance out of not-substance. But that which is not a substance or a 'this' clearly cannot possess predicates drawn [*10*] from any of the other Categories either —e.g. we cannot attribute to it any quality, quantity, or position. Otherwise, properties would admit of existence in separation from substances. If, on the other hand, 'unqualified not-being' means 'what is not in any sense at all', it will be a universal negation of all forms of being, so that what comes-to-be will have to come-to-be out of nothing.

Although we have dealt with these problems at greater length in another work,[2] where we have set forth the difficulties and established the distinguishing definitions, the fol-[*15*] lowing concise restatement of our results must here be offered:—

In one sense things come-to-be out of that

[1] Cf. 328ª 23 ff. [2] *Physics*, I. 6–9.

which has no 'being' without qualification: yet in another sense they come-to-be always out of 'what is'. For coming-to-be necessarily implies the pre-existence of something which *potentially* 'is', but *actually* 'is not'; and this something is spoken of both as 'being' and as 'not-being'.

These distinctions may be taken as established: but even then it is extraordinarily difficult to see how there can be 'unqualified coming-to-be' (whether we suppose it to occur out [20] of what potentially 'is', or in some other way), and we must recall this problem for further examination. For the question might be raised whether substance (i.e. the 'this') comes-to-be at all. Is it not rather the 'such', the 'so great', or the 'somewhere', which comes-to-be? And the same question might be raised about 'passing-away' also. For if a substantial thing comes-to-be, it is clear that there will 'be' (not actually, but potentially) a substance, out of which its coming-to-be will proceed and into [25] which the thing that is passing-away will necessarily change. Then will any predicate belonging to the remaining Categories attach *actually* to this presupposed substance? In other words, will that which is only potentially a 'this' (which only potentially *is*), while without the qualification 'potentially' it is not a 'this' (i.e. *is not*), possess, e.g. any determinate size or quality or position? For (i) if it possesses none of these determinations actually, but all of them only potentially, the result is *first* that a being, which is not a determinate being, is capable of separate existence; and *in addition* that coming-to-be proceeds out of nothing pre-existing—a thesis [30] which, more than any other, preoccupied and alarmed the earliest philosophers. On the other hand (ii) if, although it is not a 'this somewhat' or a substance, it is to possess some of the remaining determinations quoted above, then (as we said)[1] properties will be separable from substances.

We must therefore concentrate all our powers on the discussion of these difficulties and on [35] the solution of a further question—viz. What is the cause of the perpetuity of coming-to-be? Why is there always unqualified, as well as *partial*, coming-to-be?

318ª 'Cause' in this connexion has two senses. It means (i) the source from which, as we say, the process 'originates', and (ii) the matter. It is the material cause that we have here to state. For, as to the other cause, we have already explained (in our treatise on Motion[2]) that it involves (*a*) something immovable through all time and (*b*) something always [5] being moved. And the accurate treatment of the first of these—of the immovable 'originative source'—belongs to the province of the other, or 'prior', philosophy: while as regards 'that which sets everything else in motion by being itself continuously moved', we shall have to explain later[3] which amongst the so-called 'specific' causes exhibits this character. But at present we are to state the material cause—the cause classed under the head of matter—to [10] which it is due that passing-away and coming-to-be never fail to occur in Nature. For perhaps, if we succeed in clearing up this question, it will simultaneously become clear what account we ought to give of that which perplexed us just now, i.e. of *unqualified* passing-away and coming-to-be.

Our new question too—viz. 'what is the cause of the unbroken continuity of coming-to-be?'—is sufficiently perplexing, if in fact what passes-away vanishes into 'what is not' [15] and 'what is not' is nothing (since 'what is not' is neither a thing, nor possessed of a quality or quantity, nor in any place). If, then, some one of the things 'which are' is constantly disappearing, why has not the whole of 'what is' been used up long ago and vanished away—assuming of course that the material of all the several comings-to-be was finite? For, presumably, the unfailing continuity of coming-to-be cannot be attributed to the infinity of the [20] material. That is impossible, for nothing is actually infinite. A thing is infinite only potentially, i.e. the dividing of it can continue indefinitely: so that we should have to suppose there is only one kind of coming-to-be in the world—viz. one which never fails, because it is such that what comes-to-be is on each successive occasion smaller than before. But in fact this is not what we see occurring.

[25] Why, then, is this form of change necessarily ceaseless? Is it because the passing-away of *this* is a coming-to-be of *something else*, and the coming-to-be of *this* a passing-away of *something else?*

The cause implied in this solution must no doubt be considered adequate to account for coming-to-be and passing-away in their general character as they occur in all existing things [30] alike. Yet, if the same process is a coming-to-be of *this* but a passing-away of *that,* and a

---

[1] Cf. above, 317ᵇ 10-11.
[2] *Physics*, VIII. 3 ff., especially 258ᵇ 10 ff.
[3] Cf. below, II. 10.

passing-away of *this* but a coming-to-be of *that*, why are some things said to come-to-be and pass-away without qualification, but others only with a qualification?

The distinction must be investigated once more, for it demands some explanation. ⟨It is applied in a twofold manner.⟩ For (i) we say 'it is now passing-away' without qualification, and not merely '*this* is passing-away': and we call *this* change 'coming-to-be', and *that* 'passing-away', without qualification. And (ii) so-and-so 'comes-to-be-something', but does not 'come-to-be' without qualification; for we say [35] that the student 'comes-to-be-learned', not 'comes-to-be' without qualification.

318^b (i) Now we often divide terms into those which signify a 'this somewhat' and those which do not. And ⟨the first form of⟩ the distinction, which we are investigating, results from a similar division of terms: for it makes a difference *into what* the changing thing changes. Perhaps, e.g. the passage into Fire is 'coming-to-be' *unqualified*, but 'passing-away-of-something' (e.g. of Earth): whilst the [5] coming-to-be of Earth is *qualified* (not *unqualified*) 'coming-to-be', though *unqualified* 'passing-away' (e.g. of Fire). This would be the case on the theory set forth in Parmenides: for he says that the things into which change takes place are two, and he asserts that these two, viz. *what is* and *what is not,* are Fire and Earth. Whether we postulate these, or other things of a similar kind, makes no difference. For we are trying to discover not what undergoes these changes, but what is their characteristic manner. The passage, then, [10] into what 'is' not except with a qualification is unqualified passing-away, while the passage into what 'is' without qualification is unqualified coming-to-be. Hence whatever the contrasted 'poles' of the changes may be—whether Fire and Earth, or some other couple—the one of them will be 'a being' and the other 'a not-being'.

We have thus stated one characteristic manner in which *unqualified* will be distinguished from *qualified* coming-to-be and passing-away: but they are also distinguished according to the special nature of the material of the chang- [15] ing thing. For a material, whose constitutive differences signify more a 'this somewhat', is itself more 'substantial' or 'real': while a material, whose constitutive differences signify privation, is 'not real'. (Suppose, e.g. that 'the hot' is a positive predication, i.e. a 'form', whereas 'cold' is a privation, and that Earth and Fire differ from one another by these constitutive differences.)

The opinion, however, which most people are inclined to prefer, is that the distinction depends upon the difference between 'the perceptible' and 'the imperceptible'. Thus, when [20] there is a change into perceptible material, people say there is 'coming-to-be'; but when there is a change into invisible material, they call it 'passing-away'. For they distinguish 'what is' and 'what is not' by their perceiving and not-perceiving, just as what is knowable 'is' and what is unknowable 'is not'—perception on their view having the force of knowledge. [25] Hence, just as they deem themselves to live and to 'be' in virtue of their perceiving or their capacity to perceive, so too they deem the things to 'be' *qua* perceived or perceptible —and in this they are in a sense on the track of the truth, though what they actually say is not true.

Thus unqualified coming-to-be and passing-away turn out to be different according to common opinion from what they are in truth. For Wind and Air are in truth more real— more a 'this somewhat' or a 'form'—than Earth. But they are less real to perception— which explains why things are commonly said [30] to 'pass-away' without qualification when they change into Wind and Air, and to 'come-to-be' when they change into what is tangible, i.e. into Earth.

We have now explained why there is 'unqualified coming-to-be' (though it is a passing-away-of-something) and 'unqualified passing-away' (though it is a coming-to-be-of-some- [35] thing). For this distinction of appellation depends upon a difference in the material out of which, and into which, the changes are effected. It depends *either* upon whether the 319^a material is or is not 'substantial', *or* upon whether it is more or less 'substantial', *or* upon whether it is more or less perceptible.

(ii) But why are some things said to 'come-to-be' without qualification, and others only to 'come-to-be-so-and-so', in cases different from the one we have been considering where two things come-to-be reciprocally out of one [5] another? For at present we have explained no more than this:—why, when two things change reciprocally into one another, we do not attribute coming-to-be and passing-away *uniformly* to them both, although every coming-to-be is a passing-away of something else and every passing-away some other thing's coming-to-be. But the question subsequently formulated involves a different problem—viz. why, although the learning thing is said to [10] 'come-to-be-learned' but not to 'come-to-be' without qualification, yet the growing thing *is* said to 'come-to-be'.

The distinction here turns upon the difference of the Categories. For some things signify a *this somewhat,* others a *such,* and others a *so-much.* Those things, then, which do not signify substance, are not said to 'come-to-be' without qualification, but only to 'come-to-be-so-and-so'. Nevertheless, in all changing things alike, we speak of 'coming-to-be' when the [15] thing comes-to-be something in *one* of the two Columns—e.g. in Substance, if it comes-to-be Fire but not if it comes-to-be Earth; and in Quality, if it comes-to-be learned but not when it comes-to-be ignorant.

We have explained why some things come-to-be without qualification, but not others—both in general, and also when the changing things are substances and nothing else; and we have stated that the *substratum* is the material cause of the continuous occurrence of coming-to-be, because it is such as to change from contrary [20] to contrary and because, in substances, the coming-to-be of one thing is always a passing-away of another, and the passing-away of one thing is always another's coming-to-be. But there is no need even to discuss the other question we raised—viz. why coming-to-be continues though things are constantly being destroyed. For just as people speak of 'a passing-away' without qualification when a thing has passed into what is imperceptible and what in that sense 'is not', so [25] also they speak of 'a coming-to-be out of a not-being' when a thing emerges from an imperceptible. Whether, therefore, the *substratum* is or is not something, what comes-to-be emerges out of a 'not-being': so that a thing 'comes-to-be out of a not-being' just as much as it 'passes-away into what is not'. Hence it is reasonable enough that coming-to-be should never fail. For coming-to-be is a passing-away of 'what is not' and passing-away is a coming-to-be of 'what is not'.

But what about that which 'is' not except [30] with a qualification? Is it one of the two contrary poles of the change—e.g. is Earth (i.e. the heavy) a 'not-being', but Fire (i.e. the light) a 'being'? Or, on the contrary, does 'what is' include Earth as well as Fire, whereas 'what is not' is matter—the matter of Earth and Fire alike? And again, is the matter of each different? Or is it the same, since otherwise they would not come-to-be reciprocally out of one another, i.e. contraries out of contraries? For these things—Fire, Earth, Water, Air—are characterized by 'the contraries'.

Perhaps the solution is that their matter is in one sense the same, but in another sense different. For that which underlies them, whatever its nature may be *qua* underlying them, is the same: but its actual being is not the same. So much, then, on these topics.

4

[5] Next we must state what the difference is between coming-to-be and 'alteration'—for we maintain that these changes are distinct from one another.

Since, then, we must distinguish (*a*) the *substratum,* and (*b*) the property whose nature it is to be predicated of the *substratum;* [10] and since change of each of these occurs; there is 'alteration' when the *substratum* is perceptible and persists, but changes in its own properties, the properties in question being opposed to one another either as contraries or as intermediates. The body, e.g. although persisting as the same body, is now healthy and now ill; and the bronze is now spherical and at another time angular, and yet remains the same [15] bronze. But when nothing perceptible persists in its identity as a *substratum,* and the thing changes as a whole (when e.g. the seed as a whole is converted into blood, or water into air, or air as a whole into water), such an occurrence is no longer 'alteration'. It is a coming-to-be of one substance and a passing-away of the other—especially if the change proceeds from an imperceptible something to something perceptible (either to touch or to all the senses), [20] as when water comes-to-be out of, or passes-away into, air: for air is pretty well imperceptible. If, however, in such cases, any property (being one of a pair of contraries) persists, in the thing that has come-to-be, the same as it was in the thing which has passed-away—if, e.g. when water comes-to-be out of air, both are transparent or cold—the *second* thing, into which the *first* changes, must not be a property of this persistent identical something. Otherwise the change will be 'alteration.' [25] Suppose, e.g. that *the musical man* passed-away and *an unmusical man* came-to-be, and that *the man* persists as something identical. Now, if 'musicalness and unmusicalness' had not been a property essentially inhering in man, these changes would have been a coming-to-be of unmusicalness and a passing-away of musicalness: but in fact 'musicalness and unmusicalness' are a property of the persistent identity, viz. man. (Hence, as regards *man*, these changes are 'modifications'; though, [*30*] as regards *musical man* and *unmusical man*, they are a passing-away and a coming-to-be.) Consequently such changes are 'alteration.'

When the change from contrary to contrary is *in quantity*, it is 'growth and diminution'; when it is *in place*, it is 'motion'; when it is in property, i.e. *in quality*, it is 'alteration': but 320ᵃ when nothing persists, of which the resultant is a property (or an 'accident' in any sense of the term), it is 'coming-to-be', and the converse change is 'passing-away'.

'Matter', in the most proper sense of the term, is to be identified with the *substratum* which is receptive of coming-to-be and passing-away: but the *substratum* of the remaining kinds of change is also, in a certain sense, 'mat-[*5*] ter', because all these *substrata* are receptive of 'contrarieties' of some kind. So much, then, as an answer to the questions (i) whether coming-to-be 'is' or 'is not'—i.e. what are the precise conditions of its occurrence and (ii) what 'alteration' is: but we have still to treat of growth.

5

We must explain (i) wherein growth differs from coming-to-be and from 'alteration', and (ii) what is the process of growing and the [*10*] process of diminishing in each and all of the things that grow and diminish.

Hence our first question is this: Do these changes differ from one another solely because of a difference in their respective 'spheres'? In other words, do they differ because, while a change from *this* to *that* (viz. from potential to actual *substance*) is coming-to-be, a change in the sphere of *magnitude* is growth and one in [*15*] the sphere of *quality* is 'alteration'—both growth and 'alteration' being changes from what is-potentially to what is-actually magnitude and quality respectively? Or is there also a difference in the manner of the change, since it is evident that, whereas neither what is 'altering' nor what is coming-to-be necessarily changes its place, what is growing or diminishing changes its spatial position of necessity, though in a different manner from that in which the moving thing does so? For that [*20*] which is being moved changes its place as a whole: but the growing thing changes its place like a metal that is being beaten, retaining its position as a whole while its parts change their places. They change their places, but not in the same way as the parts of a revolving globe. For the parts of the globe change their places while the whole continues to occupy an equal place: but the parts of the growing thing expand over an ever-increas-[*25*] ing place and the parts of the diminishing thing contract within an ever-diminishing area.

It is clear, then, that these changes—the changes of that which is coming-to-be, of that which is 'altering', and of that which is growing—differ *in manner* as well as *in sphere*. But how are we to conceive the 'sphere' of the change which is growth and diminution? The 'sphere' of growing and diminishing is believed to be magnitude. Are we to suppose that body and magnitude come-to-be out of some-[*30*] thing which, though potentially magnitude and body, is actually incorporeal and devoid of magnitude? And since this description may be understood in two different ways, in which of these two ways are we to apply it to the process of growth? Is the matter, out of which growth takes place, (i) 'separate' and existing alone by itself, or (ii) 'separate' but contained in another body?

Perhaps it is impossible for growth to take place in either of these ways. For since the mat-320ᵇ ter is 'separate', either (*a*) it will occupy no place (as if it were a point), or (*b*) it will be a 'void', i.e. a non-perceptible body. But the first of these alternatives is impossible. For since what comes-to-be out of this incorporeal and sizeless something will always be 'somewhere', it too must be 'somewhere'—either in-[*5*] trinsically or indirectly. And the second alternative necessarily implies that the matter is contained in some other body. But if it is to be 'in' another body and yet remains 'separate' in such a way that it is in no sense a part of that body (neither a part of its substantial being nor an 'accident' of it), many impossibilities will result. It is as if we were to suppose that when, e.g. air comes-to-be out of water the process were due not to a change of the [*10*] water, but to the matter of the air being 'contained in' the water as in a vessel. This is impossible. For (i) there is nothing to prevent an indeterminate number of matters being thus 'contained in' the water, so that they might come-to-be actually an indeterminate quantity of air; and (ii) we do not in fact see air coming-to-be out of water in this fashion, viz. withdrawing out of it and leaving it unchanged.

It is therefore better to suppose that in all instances of coming-to-be the matter is inseparable, being numerically identical and one with the 'containing' body, though isolable from it by definition. But the same reasons also forbid [15] us to regard the matter, out of which the body comes-to-be, as points or lines. The matter is that of which points and lines are limits, and it is something that can never exist without quality and without form.

Now it is no doubt true, as we have also established elsewhere,[1] that one thing 'comes-to-be' (in the unqualified sense) out of another thing: and further it is true that the efficient cause of its coming-to-be is either (i) an actual thing (which is the same as the effect either *generically*—for the efficient cause of the coming-to-be of a hard thing is not a hard thing— [20] or *specifically,* as e.g. fire is the efficient cause of the coming-to-be of fire or one man of the birth of another), or (ii) an actuality. Nevertheless, since there is also a matter out of which corporeal substance itself comes-to-be (corporeal substance, however, already characterized as such-and-such a determinate body, for there is no such thing as body in general), this same matter is also the matter of magnitude and quality—being separable from these matters by definition, but not separable in place [25] unless Qualities are, in their turn, separable.

It is evident, from the preceding[2] development and discussion of difficulties, that growth is not a change out of something which, though potentially a magnitude, actually possesses no magnitude. For, if it were, the 'void' would exist in separation; but we have explained in a former work[3] that this is impossible. Moreover, a change of that kind is not peculiarly distinctive of growth, but characterizes [30] coming-to-be as such or in general. For growth is an increase, and diminution is a lessening, of the magnitude which is there already —that, indeed, is why the growing thing must possess some magnitude. Hence growth must not be regarded as a process from a matter without magnitude to an actuality of magnitude: for this would be a body's coming-to-be rather than its growth.

We must therefore come to closer quarters 321ᵃ with the subject of our inquiry. We must 'grapple' with it (as it were) from its beginning, and determine the precise character of the growing and diminishing whose causes we are investigating.

[1] Cf. *Physics,* I. 7; *Metaphysics,* 1032ᵃ 12 ff.
[2] Cf. above, 320ᵃ 27-ᵇ 12.
[3] Cf. *Physics,* IV. 6-9.

It is evident (i) that any and every part of the growing thing has increased, and that similarly in diminution every part has become smaller: also (ii) that a thing grows by the [5] accession, and diminishes by the departure, of something. Hence it must grow by the accession either (*a*) of something incorporeal or (*b*) of a body. Now, if (*a*) it grows by the accession of something incorporeal, there will exist *separate* a void: but (as we have stated before)[4] it is impossible for *a matter of magnitude* to exist 'separate'. If, on the other hand (*b*) it grows by the accession of a body, there will be two bodies—that which grows and that which increases it—in the same place: and this too is impossible.

[10] But neither is it open to us to say that growth or diminution occurs in the way in which e.g. air is generated from water. For, although the volume has then become greater, the change will not be growth, but a coming-to-be of the one—viz. of that into which the change is taking place—and a passing-away of the contrasted body. It is not a *growth* of either. Nothing grows in the process; unless indeed there be something common to both [15] things (to that which is coming-to-be and to that which passed-away), e.g. 'body', and this grows. The water has not grown, nor has the air: but the former has passed-away and the latter has come-to-be, and—if anything has grown—there has been a growth of 'body.' Yet this too is impossible. For our account of growth must preserve the characteristics of that which is growing and diminishing. And these characteristics are three: (i) any and every part [20] of the growing magnitude is made bigger (e.g. if flesh grows, every particle of the flesh gets bigger), (ii) by the accession of something, and (iii) in such a way that the growing thing is preserved and persists. For whereas a thing does not persist in the processes of unqualified coming-to-be or passing-away, that which grows or 'alters' persists in its identity through the 'altering' and through the growing or di- [25] minishing, though the quality (in 'alteration') and the size (in growth) do not remain the same. Now if the generation of air from water is to be regarded as growth, a thing might grow without the accession (and without the persistence) of anything, and diminish without the departure of anything—and that which grows need not persist. But this characteristic must be preserved: for the growth we

[4] Cf. above, 320ᵃ 27-ᵇ 25.

are discussing has been assumed to be thus characterized.

[30] One might raise a further difficulty. What is 'that which grows'? Is it that to which something is added? If, e.g. a man grows in his shin, is it the shin which is greater—but not that 'whereby' he grows, viz. not the food? Then why have not both 'grown'? For when A is added to B, both A and B are greater, as when you mix wine with water; for each ingredient is alike increased in volume. Perhaps the explanation is that the substance of the one [35] remains unchanged, but the substance of the other (viz. of the food) does not. For indeed, even in the mixture of wine and water, it 321^b is the prevailing ingredient which is said to have increased in volume. We say, e.g. that the wine has increased, because the whole mixture acts as wine but not as water. A similar principle applies also to 'alteration'. Flesh is said to have been 'altered' if, while its character and substance remain, some one of its essential properties, which was not there before, [5] now qualifies it: on the other hand, that 'whereby' it has been 'altered' may have undergone no change, though sometimes it too has been affected. The altering agent, however, and the originative source of the process are in the growing thing and in that which is being 'altered': for the efficient cause is in these. No doubt the food, which has come in, may sometimes expand as well as the body that has consumed it (that is so, e.g. if, after having come in, a food is converted into wind), but when [10] it has undergone this change it has passed-away: and the efficient cause is not in the food.

We have now developed the difficulties sufficiently and must therefore try to find a solution of the problem. Our solution must preserve intact the three characteristics of growth—that the growing thing persists, that it grows by the accession (and diminishes by the departure) of something, and further that every perceptible particle of it has become either larger or smaller. [15] We must recognize also (a) that the growing body is not 'void' and that yet there are not two magnitudes in the same place, and (b) that it does not grow by the accession of something incorporeal.

Two preliminary distinctions will prepare us to grasp the cause of growth. We must note (i) that the organic parts grow by the growth of the tissues (for every organ is composed of these as its constituents); and (ii) that flesh, [20] bone, and every such part—like every other thing which has its form immersed in matter—has a twofold nature: for the form as well as the matter is called 'flesh' or 'bone'.

Now, that any and every part of the tissue *qua* form should grow—and grow by the accession of something—is possible, but not that any and every part of the tissue *qua* matter should do so. For we must think of the tissue [25] after the image of flowing water that is measured by one and the same measure: particle after particle comes-to-be, and each successive particle is different. And it is in this sense that the matter of the flesh grows, some flowing out and some flowing in fresh; not in the sense that fresh matter accedes to every particle of it. There is, however, an accession to every part of its figure or 'form'.

That growth has taken place proportionally, is more manifest in the organic parts—e.g. in the hand. For *there* the fact that the matter is [30] distinct from the form is more manifest than in flesh, i.e. than in the tissues. That is why there is a greater tendency to suppose that a corpse still possesses flesh and bone than that it still has a hand or an arm.

Hence in one sense it is true that any and every part of the flesh has grown; but in another sense it is false. For there has been an accession to every part of the flesh in respect to its form, but not in respect to its matter. The [35] whole, however, has become larger. And this increase is due (a) on the one hand to the accession of something, which is called 'food' 322^a and is said to be 'contrary' to flesh, but (b) on the other hand to the transformation of this food into the same form as that of flesh—as if, e.g. 'moist' were to accede to 'dry' and, having acceded, were to be transformed and to become 'dry'. For in one sense 'Like grows by Like', but in another sense 'Unlike grows by Unlike'.

One might discuss what must be the charac-[5]ter of that 'whereby' a thing grows. Clearly it must be potentially that which is growing—potentially flesh, e.g. if it is flesh that is growing. Actually, therefore, it must be 'other' than the growing thing. This 'actual other', then, has passed-away and come-to-be flesh. But it has not been transformed into flesh alone by itself (for that would have been a coming-to-be, not a growth): on the contrary, it is the growing thing which has come-to-be flesh ⟨and grown⟩ *by* the food. In what way, then, has the food been modified by the growing thing? Perhaps we should say that it has been 'mixed' with it, as if one were to pour water into wine and the [10] wine were able to convert the new ingredient into wine. And as fire lays hold of the inflammable, so the active principle of growth, dwelling in the growing thing (i.e. in that which is actually flesh), lays hold of an acceding food which is potentially flesh and converts it into actual flesh. The acceding food, therefore, must be *together with* the growing thing: for if it were apart from it, the change would be a com-[15]ing-to-be. For it is possible to produce fire by piling logs on to the already burning fire. That is 'growth'. But when the logs themselves are set on fire, that is 'coming-to-be'.

'Quantum-in-general' does not come-to-be any more than 'animal' which is neither man nor any other of the specific forms of animal: what 'animal-in-general' is in coming-to-be, that 'quantum-in-general' is in growth. But what does come-to-be in growth is flesh or bone —or a hand or arm (i.e. the tissues of these or-[20]ganic parts). Such things come-to-be, then, by the accession not of quantified-flesh but of a quantified-something. In so far as this acceding food is potentially the double result— e.g. is potentially so-much-flesh—it produces growth: for it is bound to become actually both *so-much* and *flesh*. But in so far as it is potentially flesh only, it nourishes: for it is thus that 'nutrition' and 'growth' differ by their definition. That is why a body's 'nutrition' continues so long as it is kept alive (even when it is diminishing), though not its 'growth'; and why nu-[25]trition, though 'the same' as growth, is yet different from it in its actual being. For in so far as that which accedes is potentially 'so-much-flesh' it tends to increase flesh: whereas, in so far as it is potentially 'flesh' only, it is nourishment.

The form of which we have spoken is a kind of power immersed in matter—a duct, as it were. If, then, a matter accedes—a mat-[30]ter, which is potentially a duct and also potentially possesses determinate quantity— the ducts to which it accedes will become bigger. But if it is no longer able to act—if it has been weakened by the continued influx of matter, just as water, continually mixed in greater and greater quantity with wine, in the end makes the wine watery and converts it into water—then it wil cause a diminution of the *quantum;* though still the form persists.

6

322ᵇ ⟨In discussing the causes of coming-to-be⟩ we must first investigate the *matter,* i.e. the so-called 'elements'. We must ask whether they really are elements or not, i.e. whether each of them is eternal or whether there is a sense in which they come-to-be: and, if they do come-to-be, whether all of them come-to-be in the same manner reciprocally out of one another, or whether one amongst them is something [5] primary. Hence we must begin by explaining certain preliminary matters, about which the statements now current are vague.

For all ⟨the pluralist philosophers⟩—those who generate the 'elements' as well as those who generate the bodies that are compounded of the elements—make use of 'dissociation' and 'association', and of 'action' and 'passion'. Now 'association' is 'combination'; but the precise meaning of the process we call 'combining' has not been explained. Again, ⟨all the monists make use of 'alteration': but⟩ without an agent [10] and a patient there cannot be 'altering' any more than there can be 'dissociating' and 'associating'. For not only those who postulate a plurality of elements employ their reciprocal action and passion to generate the compounds: those who derive things from a single element are equally compelled to introduce 'acting'. And in this respect Diogenes is right when he argues that 'unless all things were derived from [15] one, reciprocal action and passion could not have occurred'.[1] The hot thing, e.g. would not be cooled and the cold thing in turn be warmed: for heat and cold do not change reciprocally into one another, but what changes (it is clear) is the *substratum*. Hence, whenever there is action and passion between two things, that which underlies them must be a single something. No doubt, it is not true to say that *all* things are of this character: but it [20] is true of all things between which there is reciprocal action and passion.

But if we must investigate 'action-passion' and 'combination', we must also investigate 'contact'. For action and passion (in the proper sense of the terms) can only occur between things which are such as to touch one another; [25] nor can things enter into combination at all unless they have come into a certain kind of contact. Hence we must give a definite account of these three things—of 'contact', 'combination', and 'acting'.

Let us start as follows. All things which admit of 'combination' must be capable of reciprocal contact: and the same is true of any two things, of which one 'acts' and the other 'suffers action' in the proper sense of the terms. For this reason we must treat of 'contact' first. [30] Now every term which possesses a variety

[1] Cf. Diogenes, fr. 2, Diels, p. 334.

of meanings includes those various meanings *either* owing to a mere coincidence of language, *or* owing to a real order of derivation in the different things to which it is applied: but, though this may be taken to hold of 'contact' as of all such terms, it is nevertheless true that 'contact' *in the proper sense* applies only to things which have 'position'. And 'position' belongs only to those things which also have a 'place': for in so far as we attribute 'contact' to the mathematical things, we must also attribute 'place' to them, whether they exist in separation or in some other fashion. Assuming, therefore, that 'to touch' is—as we have defined it in a previous work[1]—'to have the extremes together', only those things will touch [5] one another which, being separate magnitudes and possessing position, have their extremes 'together'. And since position belongs only to those things which also have a 'place', while the primary differentiation of 'place' is 'the above' and 'the below' (and the similar pairs of opposites), all things which touch one another will have 'weight' or 'lightness'—*either* both these qualities *or* one or the other of them. But bodies which are heavy or light are [10] such as to 'act' and 'suffer action'. Hence it is clear that those things which are by nature such as to touch one another, which (being separate magnitudes) have their extremes 'together' and are able to move, and be moved by, one another.

The manner in which the 'mover' moves the 'moved' is not always the same: on the contrary, whereas one kind of 'mover' can only impart motion by being itself moved, another kind can do so though remaining itself unmoved. Clear-[15]ly therefore we must recognize a corresponding variety in speaking of the 'acting' thing too: for the 'mover' is said to 'act' (in a sense) and the 'acting' thing to 'impart motion'. Nevertheless there is a difference and we must draw a distinction. For not every 'mover' can 'act', if (*a*) the term 'agent' is to be used in contrast to 'patient' and (*b*) 'patient' is to be applied only to those things whose motion is a [20] 'qualitative affection'—i.e. a quality, like 'white' or 'hot', in respect to which they are 'moved' only in the sense that they are 'altered': on the contrary, to 'impart motion' is a wider term than to 'act'. Still, so much, at any rate, is clear: the things which are 'such as to impart motion', if that description be interpreted in one sense, will touch the things which are 'such as to be moved by them'—while they will not touch them, if the description be interpreted in a different sense. But the disjunctive definition of 'touching' must include and distinguish (*a*) 'contact in general' as the relation between two things which, having position, are such that one is able to impart motion and the other to be moved, and (*b*) 'reciprocal contact' as the relation between two things, one able to impart motion and the other able to be moved in such a way that 'action and passion' [25] are predicable of them.

As a rule, no doubt, if A touches B, B touches A. For indeed practically all the 'movers' within our ordinary experience impart motion by being moved: in their case, what touches inevitably must, and also evidently does, touch something which reciprocally touches it. Yet, if A moves B, it is possible—as we sometimes express it—for A 'merely to touch' B, and that which touches need not touch a something [30] which touches it. Nevertheless it is commonly supposed that 'touching' must be reciprocal. The reason of this belief is that 'movers' which belong to the same kind as the 'moved' impart motion by being moved. Hence if anything imparts motion without itself being moved, it may touch the 'moved' and yet itself be touched by nothing—for we say sometimes that the man who grieves us 'touches' us, but not that we 'touch' him.

The account just given may serve to distinguish and define the 'contact' which occurs in the things of Nature.

7

323[b] Next in order we must discuss 'action' and 'passion'. The traditional theories on the subject are conflicting. For (i) most thinkers are unanimous in maintaining (*a*) that 'like' is always unaffected by 'like', because (as they [5] argue) neither of two 'likes' is more apt than the other either to act or to suffer action, since all the properties which belong to the one belong identically and in the same degree to the other; and (*b*) that 'unlikes', i.e. 'differents', are by nature such as to act and suffer action reciprocally. For even when the smaller fire is destroyed by the greater, it suffers this effect (they say) owing to its 'contrariety'—[10] since the great is contrary to the small. But (ii) Democritus dissented from all the other thinkers and maintained a theory peculiar to himself. He asserts that agent and patient are identical, i.e. 'like'. It is not possible (he says) that 'others', i.e. 'differents', should suffer action from one another: on the contrary, even if two things, being 'others', do act in

---

[1] Cf. *Physics*, 226[b] 21-23.

[15] some way on one another, this happens to them not *qua* 'others' but *qua* possessing an identical property.

Such, then, are the traditional theories, and it looks as if the statements of their advocates were in manifest conflict. But the reason of this conflict is that each group is in fact stating *a part*, whereas they ought to have taken a comprehensive view of the subject *as a whole*. For (i) if A and B are 'like'—absolutely and in all respects without difference from one another [20]—it is reasonable to infer that neither is in any way affected by the other. Why, indeed, should either of them tend to act any more than the other? Moreover, if 'like' can be affected by 'like', a thing can also be affected by itself: and yet if that were so—if 'like' tended in fact to act *qua* 'like'—there would be nothing indestructible or immovable, for everything would move itself. And (ii) the same [25] consequence follows if A and B are absolutely 'other', i.e. in no respect identical. *Whiteness* could not be affected in any way by *line* nor *line* by *whiteness*—except perhaps 'coincidentally', viz. if the line happened to be white or black: for unless two things either are, or are composed of, 'contraries', neither drives the other out of its natural condition. But (iii) [30] since only those things which either involve a 'contrariety' or are 'contraries'—and not any things selected at random—are such as to suffer action and to act, agent and patient must be 'like' (i.e. identical) in kind and yet 'unlike' (i.e. contrary) in species. (For it is a law of nature that body is affected by body, flavour by flavour, colour by colour, and so in general what belongs to any kind by a member of the same kind—the reason being that 'contraries' are in every case within a single identical kind, and it is 'contraries' which reciprocally act and suffer action.) Hence agent and patient must be in one sense identical, but in another sense other than (i.e. 'unlike') one [5] another. And since (*a*) patient and agent are generically identical (i.e. 'like') but specifically 'unlike', while (*b*) it is 'contraries' that exhibit this character: it is clear that 'contraries' and their 'intermediates' are such as to suffer action and to act reciprocally—for indeed it is these that constitute the entire sphere of passing-away and coming-to-be.

[10] We can now understand why fire heats and the cold thing cools, and in general why the active thing assimilates to itself the patient. For agent and patient are contrary to one another, and coming-to-be is a process into the contrary: hence the patient *must* change into the agent, since it is only thus that coming-to-be will be a process into the contrary. And, again, it is intelligible that the advocates of both views, although their theories are not the [15] same, are yet in contact with the nature of the facts. For sometimes we speak of the *substratum* as suffering action (e.g. of 'the man' as being healed, being warmed and chilled, and similarly in all the other cases), but at other times we say 'what is cold is being warmed', 'what is sick is being healed': and in both these ways of speaking we express the truth, since in one sense it is the 'matter', while in another sense it is the 'contrary', which suffers action. (We make the same distinction in speaking of [20] the agent: for sometimes we say that 'the man', but at other times that 'what is hot', produces heat.) Now the one group of thinkers supposed that agent and patient must possess something identical, because they fastened their attention on the *substratum*: while the other group maintained the opposite because their attention was concentrated on the 'contraries'.

[25] We must conceive the same account to hold of action and passion as that which is true of 'being moved' and 'imparting motion'. For the 'mover', like the 'agent', has two meanings. Both (*a*) that which contains the originative source of the motion is thought to 'impart motion' (for the originative source is first amongst the causes), and also (*b*) that which is last, i.e. immediately next to the moved thing and to the coming-to-be. A similar distinction holds [30] also of the agent: for we speak not only (*a*) of the doctor, but also (*b*) of the wine, as healing. Now, in motion, there is nothing to prevent *the first mover* being unmoved (indeed, as regards some 'first movers' this is actually necessary) although *the last mover* always imparts motion by being itself moved: and, in action, there is nothing to prevent *the first agent* being unaffected, while *the last agent* only acts by suffering action itself. For (*a*) if agent and patient have not the same [35] matter, agent acts without being affected: thus the art of healing produces health without itself being acted upon in any way by that which is being healed. But (*b*) the food, in acting, is itself in some way acted upon: for, in acting, it is simultaneously heated or cooled or otherwise affected. Now the art of healing corresponds to an 'originative source', while the food corresponds to 'the last' (i.e. 'contiguous') mover.

[5] Those active powers, then, whose forms

are not embodied in matter, are unaffected: but those whose forms are in matter are such as to be affected in acting. For we maintain that one and the same 'matter' is *equally,* so to say, the basis of either of the two opposed things—being as it were a 'kind'; and that *that which can be hot* must be made hot, provided the heating agent is there, i.e. comes near. Hence (as we [10] have said) some of the active powers are unaffected while others are such as to be affected; and what holds of motion is true also of the active powers. For as in motion 'the first mover' is unmoved, so among the active powers 'the first agent' is unaffected.

The active power is a 'cause' in the sense of that from which the process originates: but the end, for the sake of which it takes place, is not [15] 'active'. (That is why *health* is not 'active', except metaphorically.) For when the agent is there, the patient *becomes* something: but when 'states' are there, the patient no longer *becomes* but already *is*—and 'forms' (i.e. 'ends') are a kind of 'state'. As to the 'matter', it (*qua* matter) is passive. Now fire contains 'the hot' embodied in matter: but a 'hot' sepa-[20] rate from matter (if such a thing existed) could not suffer any action. Perhaps, indeed, it is impossible that 'the hot' should exist in separation from matter: but if there are any entities thus separable, what we are saying would be true of them.

We have thus explained what action and passion are, what things exhibit them, why they do so, and in what manner. We must go [25] on to discuss how it is possible for action and passion to take place.

8

Some philosophers think that the 'last' agent—the 'agent' in the strictest sense—enters in through certain pores, and so the patient suffers action. It is in this way, they assert, that we see and hear and exercise all our other senses. Moreover, according to them, things are seen through air and water and other trans-[30] parent bodies, because such bodies possess pores, invisible indeed owing to their minuteness, but close-set and arranged in rows: and the more transparent the body, the more frequent and serial they suppose its pores to be.

Such was the theory which some philosophers (including Empedocles) advanced in regard to the structure of certain bodies. They do not restrict it to the bodies which act and suffer action: but 'combination' too, they say, [35] takes place 'only between bodies whose pores are in reciprocal symmetry'. The most systematic and consistent theory, however, and one that applied to all bodies, was advanced by Leucippus and Democritus: and, in maintaining it, they took as their starting-point what naturally comes first.

For some of the older philosophers thought that 'what is' must of necessity be 'one' and immovable. The void, they argue, 'is not': but [5] unless there is a void with a separate being of its own, 'what is' cannot be moved—nor again can it be 'many', since there is nothing to keep things apart. And in *this* respect, they insist, the view that the universe is not 'continuous' but 'discretes-in-contact' is no better than the view that there are 'many' (and not 'one') and a void. For ⟨suppose that the universe is discretes-in-contact. Then⟩, if it is divisible through and through, there is no 'one', and therefore no 'many' either, but the Whole is void; while to maintain that it is divisible at [10] some points, but not at others, looks like an arbitrary fiction. For up to what limit is it divisible? And for what reason is part of the Whole indivisible, i.e. a *plenum,* and part divided? Further, they maintain, it is equally necessary to deny the existence of motion.

Reasoning in this way, therefore, they were led to transcend sense-perception, and to disregard it on the ground that 'one ought to follow the argument': and so they assert that the uni-[15] verse is 'one' and immovable. Some of them add that it is 'infinite', since the limit (if it had one) would be a limit against the void.

There were, then, certain thinkers who, for the reasons we have stated, enunciated views of this kind as their theory of 'The Truth'.... Moreover, although these opinions appear to follow logically in a dialectical discussion, yet to believe them seems next door to madness [20] when one considers the facts. For indeed no lunatic seems to be so far out of his senses as to suppose that fire and ice are 'one': it is only between what *is* right and what *seems* right from habit, that some people are mad enough to see no difference.

Leucippus, however, thought he had a theory which harmonized with sense-perception and would not abolish either coming-to-be or [25] passing-away or motion and the multiplicity of things. He made these concessions to the facts of perception: on the other hand, he conceded to the Monists that there could be no motion without a void. The result is a theory which he states as follows: 'The void is a "not-being", and no part of "what is" is a "not-being"; for what "is" in the strict sense of the term is an absolute *plenum*. This *plenum*, however, is not "one": on the contrary, it is a [30] "many" infinite in number and invisible owing to the minuteness of their bulk. The "many" move in the void (for there is a void): and by coming together they produce "coming-to-be", while by separating they produce "passing-away". Moreover, they act and suffer action wherever they chance to be in contact (for *there* they are not "one"), and they generate by being put together and becoming intertwined. From the genuinely-one, on the other [35] hand, there never could have come-to-be a multiplicity, nor from the genuinely-many a 325ᵇ "one": that is impossible. But' (just as Empedocles and some of the other philosophers say that things suffer action through their pores, so) 'all "alteration" and all "passion" take place in the way that has been explained: breaking-up (i.e. passing-away) is effected by means of the void, and so too is growth—solids [5] creeping in to fill the void places.'

Empedocles too is practically bound to adopt the same theory as Leucippus. For he must say that there are certain solids which, however, are indivisible—unless there are continuous pores all through the body. But this last alternative is impossible: for *then* there will be nothing solid in the body (nothing beside the pores) but all of it will be void. It is necessary, therefore, for his 'contiguous discretes' to be [10] indivisible, while the intervals between them—which he calls 'pores'—must be void. But this is precisely Leucippus' theory of action and passion.

Such, approximately, are the current explanations of the manner in which some things 'act' while others 'suffer action'. And as regards the Atomists, it is not only clear what their explanation is: it is also obvious that it follows [15] with tolerable consistency from the assumptions they employ. But there is less obvious consistency in the explanation offered by the other thinkers. It is not clear, for instance, how, on the theory of Empedocles, there is to be 'passing-away' as well as 'alteration'. For the primary bodies of the Atomists—the primary constituents of which bodies are composed, and the ultimate elements into which they are dissolved—are indivisible, differing from one another only in figure. In the philosophy of Empedocles, on the other hand, it is evident that all [20] the other bodies down to the 'elements' have their coming-to-be and their passing-away: but it is not clear how the 'elements'

themselves, severally in their aggregated masses, come-to-be and pass-away. Nor is it possible for Empedocles to explain how they do so, since he does not assert that Fire too (and similarly every one of his other 'elements') possesses 'elementary constituents' of itself.

Such an assertion would commit him to doctrines like those which Plato has set forth in [25] the *Timaeus*. For although both Plato and Leucippus postulate elementary constituents that are indivisible and distinctively characterized by figures, there is this great difference between the two theories: the 'indivisibles' of Leucippus (i) are solids, while those of Plato are planes, and (ii) are characterized by an infinite variety of figures, while the characterizing figures employed by Plato are limited in num- [30] ber. Thus the 'comings-to-be' and the 'dissociations' result from the 'indivisibles' (*a*) *according to Leucippus* through the void and through contact (for it is at the point of contact that each of the composite bodies is divisible), but (*b*) *according to Plato* in virtue of contact alone, since he denies there is a void.

Now we have discussed 'indivisible planes' in the preceding treatise.[1] But with regard to the [35] assumption of 'indivisible solids', although we must not now enter upon a detailed study of its consequences, the following criticisms fall within the compass of a short digression:— 326ᵃ 1. The Atomists are committed to the view that every 'indivisible' is incapable alike of receiving a sensible property (for nothing can 'suffer action' except through the void) and of producing one—no 'indivisible' can be, e.g. either hard or cold. Yet it is surely a paradox that an exception is made of 'the hot'—'the hot' [5] being assigned as peculiar to the spherical figure: for, that being so, its 'contrary' also ('the cold') is bound to belong to another of the figures. If, however, these properties (heat and cold) do belong to the 'indivisibles', it is a further paradox that they should not possess heaviness and lightness, and hardness and soft- [10] ness. And yet Democritus says 'the more any indivisible exceeds, the heavier it is'—to which we must clearly add 'and the hotter it is'. But if *that* is their character, it is impossible they should not be affected by one another: the 'slightly-hot indivisible', e.g. will inevitably suffer action from one which far exceeds it in heat. Again, if any 'indivisible' is 'hard', there must also be one which is 'soft': but 'the soft' derives its very name from the fact that it suf-

[1] Cf. *On the Heavens*, III. 1, especially 298ᵇ 33 ff., III. 7 and IV. 2.

fers a certain action—for 'soft' is that which yields to pressure.

II. But further, not only is it paradoxical (i) [*15*] that no property except figure should belong to the 'indivisibles': it is also paradoxical (ii) that, if other properties do belong to them, one only of these additional properties should attach to each—e.g. that *this* 'indivisible' should be cold and *that* 'indivisible' hot. For, on that supposition, their substance would not even be uniform. And it is equally impossible (iii) that more than one of these additional properties should belong to the single 'indivisible'. For, being *indivisible,* it will possess these properties in the same point—so that, if it 'suffers ac-[*20*] tion' by being chilled, it will also, *qua* chilled, 'act' or 'suffer action' in some other way. And the same line of argument applies to all the other properties too: for the difficulty we have just raised confronts, as a necessary consequence, all who advocate 'indivisibles' (whether solids or planes), since their 'indivisibles' cannot become either 'rarer' or 'denser' inasmuch as there is no void in them.

[*25*] III. It is a further paradox that there should be small 'indivisibles', but not large ones. For it is natural enough, from the ordinary point of view, that the larger bodies should be more liable to fracture than the small ones, since they (viz. the large bodies) are easily broken up because they collide with many other bodies. But why should indivisibility *as such* be the property of small, rather than of large, [*30*] bodies?

IV. Again, is the substance of all those solids uniform, or do they fall into sets which differ from one another—as if, e.g. some of them, in their aggregated bulk, were 'fiery', others 'earthy'? For (i) if all of them are uniform in substance, what is it that separated one from another? Or why, when they come into contact, do they not coalesce into one, as drops of water run together when drop touches drop (for the two cases are precisely parallel)? On the other hand (ii) if they fall into differing sets, how [*35*] are these characterized? It is clear, too, that *these,* rather than the 'figures', ought to be 326ᵇ postulated as 'original reals', i.e. causes from which the phenomena result. Moreover, if they differed in substance, they would both act and suffer action on coming into reciprocal contact.

V. Again, what is it which sets them moving? For if their 'mover' is other than themselves, they are such as to 'suffer action'. If, on the other hand, each of them sets itself in motion, either (*a*) it will be divisible ('imparting motion' *qua this,* 'being moved' *qua that*), or [*5*] (*b*) contrary properties will attach to it in the same respect—i.e. 'matter' will be identical-in-potentiality as well as numerically-identical.

As to the thinkers who explain modification of property through the movement facilitated by the pores, if this is supposed to occur notwithstanding the fact that the pores are filled, their postulate of pores is superfluous. For if the whole body suffers action under these conditions, it would suffer action in the same way [*10*] even if it had no pores but were just its own continuous self. Moreover, how can their account of 'vision through a *medium*' be correct? It is impossible for ⟨the visual ray⟩ to penetrate the transparent bodies at their 'contacts'; and impossible for it to pass through their pores if every pore be full. For how will that differ from having no pores at all? The body will be uniformly 'full' throughout. But, [*15*] further, even if these passages, though they must *contain* bodies, are 'void', the same consequence will follow once more. And if they are 'too minute to admit any body', it is absurd to suppose there is a 'minute' void and yet to deny the existence of a 'big' one (no matter how small the 'big' may be), or to imagine 'the void' means anything else than a body's [*20*] place—whence it clearly follows that to every body there will correspond a void of equal cubic capacity.

As a general criticism we must urge that to postulate pores is superfluous. For if the agent produces no effect by touching the patient, neither will it produce any by passing through its pores. On the other hand, if it acts by contact, then—even without pores—some things will 'suffer action' and others will 'act', provided they are by nature adapted for reciprocal action and passion. Our arguments have shown [*25*] that it is either false or futile to advocate pores in the sense in which some thinkers conceive them. But since bodies are divisible through and through, the postulate of pores is ridiculous: for, *qua* divisible, a body can fall into separate parts.

9

Let us explain the way in which things in [*30*] fact possess the power of generating, and of acting and suffering action: and let us start from the principle we have often enunciated. For, assuming the distinction between (*a*) that which is *potentially* and (*b*) that which is *actually* such-and-such, it is the nature of the first, precisely in so far as it is what it is, to suffer action *through and through,* not merely to be susceptible in some parts while insusceptible in others. But its susceptibility varies in degree, according as it is more or less such-and-such, and one would be more justified in speaking of 'pores' in this connexion: for instance, in the metals there are veins of 'the sus-[35] ceptible' stretching continuously through 327ª the substance.

So long, indeed, as any body is naturally coherent and one, it is insusceptible. So, too, bodies are insusceptible so long as they are not in contact either with one another or with other bodies which are by nature such as to act and suffer action. (To illustrate my meaning: Fire heats not only when in contact, but also from a distance. For the fire heats the air, and the [5] air—being by nature such as both to act and suffer action—heats the body.) But the supposition that a body is 'susceptible in some parts, but insusceptible in others' (is only possible for those who hold an erroneous view concerning the divisibility of magnitudes. For us) the following account results from the distinctions we established at the beginning.[1] For (i) if magnitudes are not divisible through and through—if, on the contrary, there are indivisible solids or planes—then indeed no body would be susceptible through and through: [10] but neither would any be continuous. Since, however, (ii) this is false, i.e. since every body is divisible, there is no difference between 'having been divided into parts which remain in contact' and 'being divisible'. For if a body '*can* be separated at the contacts' (as some thinkers express it), then, even though it has not yet been divided, it will be in a state of dividedness—since, as it *can* be divided, nothing inconceivable results. And (iii) the supposition is open to this general objection—it is [15] a paradox that 'passion' should occur in this manner *only,* viz. by the bodies being split. For this theory abolishes 'alteration': but we see the same body *liquid* at one time and *solid* at another, without losing its continuity. It has suffered this change not by 'division' and 'composition', nor yet by 'turning' and 'inter-[20] contact' as Democritus asserts; for it has passed from the liquid to the solid state without any change of 'grouping' or 'position' in the constituents of its substance. Nor are there contained within it those 'hard' (i.e. congealed) particles 'indivisible in their bulk': on the contrary, it is liquid—and again, solid and

[1] Cf. above, 316ª 14-317ª 17.

congealed—uniformly all through. This theory, it must be added, makes growth and diminution impossible also. For if there is to be *opposition* (instead of the growing thing having [25] changed as a whole, either by the admixture of something or by its own transformation), increase of size will not have resulted in any and every part.

So much, then, to establish that things generate and are generated, act and suffer action, reciprocally; and to distinguish the way in which these processes *can* occur from the (impossible) way in which some thinkers say they occur.

10

[30] But we have still to explain 'combination', for that was the third of the subjects we originally proposed to discuss. Our explanation will proceed on the same method as before. We must inquire: What is 'combination', and what is that which can 'combine'? Of what things, and under what conditions, is 'combination' a property? And, further, does 'combination' exist in fact, or is it false to assert its existence?

[35] For, according to some thinkers, it is impossible for one thing to be combined with another. They argue that (i) if *both* the 'com-327ᵇ bined' constituents persist unaltered, they are no more 'combined' now than they were before, but are in the same condition: while (ii) if *one* has been destroyed, the constituents have not been 'combined'—on the contrary, one constituent *is* and the other *is not,* whereas 'combination' demands uniformity of condition in them both: and on the same principle [5] (iii) even if *both* the combining constituents have been destroyed as the result of their coalescence, *they* cannot 'have been combined' since *they* have no being at all.

What we have in this argument is, it would seem, a demand for the precise distinction of 'combination' from coming-to-be and passing-away (for it is obvious that 'combination', if it exists, must differ from these processes) and for the precise distinction of the 'combinable' from that which is such as to come-to-be and pass-away. As soon, therefore, as these distinc-[10] tions are clear, the difficulties raised by the argument would be solved.

Now (i) we do not speak of the wood as 'combined' with the fire, nor of its burning as a 'combining' either of its particles with one another or of itself with the fire: what we say is that 'the fire is coming-to-be, but the wood is passing-away'. Similarly, we speak neither (ii) [*15*] of the food as 'combining' with the body, nor (iii) of the shape as 'combining' with the wax and thus fashioning the lump. Nor can body 'combine' with white, nor (to generalize) 'properties' and 'states' with 'things': for we *see* them persisting unaltered. But again (iv) white and knowledge cannot be 'combined' either, nor any other of the 'adjectivals'. (Indeed, this is a blemish in the theory of [*20*] those who assert that 'once upon a time all things were together and combined'. For not everything can 'combine' with everything. On the contrary, both of the constituents that are combined in the compound must originally have existed in separation: but no property can have separate existence.)

Since, however, some things *are-potentially* while others *are-actually*, the constituents combined in a compound can 'be' in a sense and yet 'not-be'. The compound may *be-actually* [*25*] other than the constituents from which it has resulted; nevertheless each of them may still *be-potentially* what it was before they were combined, and both of them may survive undestroyed. (For this was the difficulty that emerged in the previous argument: and it is evident that the combining constituents not only coalesce, having formerly existed in separation, but also can again be separated out from the compound.) The constituents, there- [*30*] fore, neither (*a*) *persist actually*, as 'body' and 'white' persist: nor (*b*) are they *destroyed* (either one of them or both), for their 'power of action' is preserved. Hence these difficulties may be dismissed: but the problem immediately connected with them—'whether combination is something relative to perception'—must be set out and discussed.

When the combining constituents have been divided into parts so small, and have been juxtaposed in such a manner, that perception [*35*] fails to discriminate them one from another, have they then 'been combined'? Or ought we to say 'No, not until any and every part of one constituent is juxtaposed to a part of the other'? The term, no doubt, is applied in the former sense: we speak, e.g. of wheat having been 'combined' with barley when each *grain* of the one is juxtaposed to a *grain* of the other. But every body is divisible and therefore, since body 'combined' with body is uniform in texture throughout, *any and* [*5*] *every part* of each constituent ought to be juxtaposed to a part of the other.

No body, however, can be divided into its 'least' parts: and 'composition' is not identical with 'combination', but other than it. From these premises it clearly follows (i) that so long as the constituents are preserved in small particles, we must not speak of them as 'combined'. (For this will be a 'composition' instead of a 'blending' or 'combination': nor will every portion of the resultant exhibit the same [*10*] ratio between its constituents as the whole. But we maintain that, if 'combination' has taken place, the compound *must* be uniform in texture throughout—any part of such a compound being the same as the whole, just as any part of water is water: whereas, if 'combination' is 'composition of the small particles', nothing of the kind will happen. On the contrary, the constituents will only be 'combined' relatively to perception: and the same thing will be 'combined' to one percipient, if his [*15*] sight is not sharp, ⟨but not to another,⟩ while to the eye of Lynceus nothing will be 'combined'.) It clearly follows (ii) that we must not speak of the constituents as 'combined in virtue of a division such that *any and every part* of each is juxtaposed to a part of the other: for it is impossible for them to be thus divided. Either, then, there is no 'combination', or we have still to explain the manner in which it can take place.

Now, as we maintain, some things are such as to act and others such as to suffer action from them. Moreover, some things—viz. those [*20*] which have the same matter—'reciprocate', i.e. are such as to act upon one another and to suffer action from one another; while other things, viz. agents which have not the same matter as their patients, act without themselves suffering action. Such agents cannot 'combine'—that is why neither the art of healing nor health produces health by 'combining' with the bodies of the patients. Amongst those things, however, which are reciprocally active and passive, some are easily-divisible. Now (i) if a great quantity (or a large bulk) of one of these easily-divisible 'reciprocating' [*25*] materials be brought together with a little (or with a small piece) of another, the effect produced is not 'combination', but increase of the dominant: for the other material is transformed into the dominant. (That is why a drop of wine does not 'combine' with ten thousand gallons of water: for its form is dissolved, and it is changed so as to merge in the total volume of water.) On the other hand (ii) when there is a certain equilibrium between [*30*] their 'powers of action', then each of them changes out of its own nature towards the dominant: yet neither becomes the other, but both become an intermediate with properties common to both.

Thus it is clear that only those agents are 'combinable' which involve a contrariety—for these are such as to suffer action reciprocally. And, further, they combine more freely if small pieces of each of them are juxtaposed. For in that condition they change one another more [35] easily and more quickly; whereas this effect takes a long time when agent and patient are present in bulk.

328[b] Hence, amongst the divisible susceptible materials, those whose shape is readily adaptable have a tendency to combine: for they are easily divided into small particles, since that is precisely what 'being readily adaptable in shape' implies. For instance, liquids are the most 'combinable' of all bodies—because, of all divisible materials, the liquid is most readily adaptable in shape, unless it be viscous. Vis- [5] cous liquids, it is true, produce no effect except to increase the volume and bulk. But when one of the constituents is alone susceptible—or superlatively susceptible, the other being susceptible in a very slight degree—the compound resulting from their combination is either no greater in volume or only a little greater. This is what happens when tin is combined with bronze. For some things display a hesitating and ambiguous attitude towards one [10] another—showing a slight tendency to combine and also an inclination to behave as 'receptive matter' and 'form' respectively. The behaviour of these metals is a case in point. For the tin almost vanishes, behaving as if it were an immaterial property of the bronze: having been combined, it disappears, leaving no trace except the colour it has imparted to the bronze. The same phenomenon occurs in other instances too.

[15] It is clear, then, from the foregoing account, that 'combination' occurs, what it is, to what it is due, and what kind of thing is 'combinable'. The phenomenon depends upon the fact that some things are such as to be (a) reciprocally susceptible and (b) readily adaptable in shape, i.e. easily divisible. For such things can be 'combined' without its being necessary *either* that they should have been destroyed *or* that they should survive absolutely unaltered: and their 'combination' need not be [20] a 'composition', nor merely 'relative to perception'. On the contrary: anything is 'combinable' which, being readily adaptable in shape, is such as to suffer action and to act; and it is 'combinable with' another thing similarly characterized (for the 'combinable' is relative to the 'combinable'); and 'combination' is unification of the 'combinables', resulting from their 'alteration'.

BOOK II

1

WE have explained under what conditions 'combination', 'contact', and 'action-passion' are attributable to the things which undergo natural change. Further, we have discussed 'unqualified' coming-to-be and passing-away, and explained under what conditions they are predicable, of what subject, and owing to what [30] cause. Similarly, we have also discussed 'alteration', and explained what 'altering' is and how it differs from coming-to-be and passing-away. But we have still to investigate the so-called 'elements' of bodies.

For the complex substances whose formation and maintenance are due to natural processes all presuppose the perceptible bodies as the condition of their coming-to-be and passing-away: but philosophers disagree in regard to the matter which underlies these perceptible bodies. Some maintain it is single, supposing it to be, e.g. Air or Fire, or an 'intermediate' [35] between these two (but still a body with 329[a] a separate existence). Others, on the contrary, postulate two or more materials—ascribing to their 'association' and 'dissociation', or to their 'alteration', the coming-to-be and passing-away of things. (Some, for instance, postulate Fire and Earth: some add Air, making three: and some, like Empedocles, reckon Water as well, thus postulating four.)

[5] Now we may agree that the primary materials, whose change (whether it be 'association and dissociation' or a process of another kind) results in coming-to-be and passing-away, are rightly described as 'originative sources', i.e. elements'. But (i) those thinkers are in error who postulate, beside the bodies we have mentioned, a single matter—and that [10] a corporeal and separable matter. For this 'body' of theirs cannot possibly exist without a 'perceptible contrariety': this 'Boundless', which some thinkers identify with the 'original real', must be either light or heavy, either

cold or hot. And (ii) what Plato has written in the *Timaeus* is not based on any precisely-articulated conception. For he has not stated [*15*] clearly whether his 'Omnirecipient'[1] exists in separation from the 'elements'; nor does he make any use of it. He says, indeed, that it is a *substratum* prior to the so-called 'elements' —underlying them, as gold underlies the things that are fashioned of gold. (And yet this comparison, if thus expressed, is itself open [*20*] to criticism. Things which come-to-be and pass-away cannot be called by the name of the material out of which they have come-to-be: it is only the results of 'alteration' which retain the name of the *substratum* whose 'alterations' they are. However, he actually says[2] that 'far the truest account is to affirm that each of them is "gold" '.) Nevertheless he carries his analysis of the 'elements'—solids though they are—back to 'planes',[3] and it is impossible for 'the Nurse'[4] (i.e. the primary matter) to be identical with 'the planes'.

Our own doctrine is that although there is [*25*] a matter of the perceptible bodies (a matter out of which the so-called 'elements' come-to-be), it has no separate existence, but is always bound up with a contrariety. A more precise account of these presuppositions has been given in another work[5]: we must, however, give a detailed explanation of the primary bodies as well, since they too are simi-[*30*]larly derived from the matter. We must reckon as an 'originative source' and as 'primary' the matter which underlies, though it is inseparable from, the contrary qualities: for 'the hot' is not matter for 'the cold' nor 'the cold' for 'the hot', but the *substratum* is matter for them both. We therefore have to recognize three 'originative sources': *firstly* that which is potentially perceptible body, *secondly* [*35*] the contrarieties (I mean, e.g. heat and cold), and *thirdly* Fire, Water, and the like. *Only* 'thirdly', however: for these bodies change 329[b] into one another (they are not immutable as Empedocles and other thinkers assert, since 'alteration' would then have been impossible), whereas the contrarieties do not change.

Nevertheless, even so the question remains: What sorts of contrarieties, and how many of them, are to be accounted 'originative sources'

---
[1] Cf. *Timaeus*, 51.
[2] Cf. *Timaeus*, 49-50.
[3] Cf. *Timaeus*, 53 ff.
[4] Cf. *Timaeus*, e.g. 49, 52.
[5] Cf. *Physics*, I, 6-9.

of body? For all the other thinkers assume [*5*] and use them without explaining why they are *these* or why they are just *so many*.

2

Since, then, we are looking for 'originative sources' of perceptible body; and since 'perceptible' is equivalent to 'tangible', and 'tangible' is that of which the perception is touch; it is clear that not all the contrarieties constitute [*10*] 'forms' and 'originative sources' of body, but only those which correspond to touch. For it is in accordance with a contrariety—a contrariety, moreover, of *tangible* qualities—that the primary bodies are differentiated. That is why neither whiteness (and blackness), nor sweetness (and bitterness), nor (similarly) any quality belonging to the other perceptible contrarieties either, constitutes an 'element'. And yet vision is prior to touch, so that its [*15*] object also is prior to the object of touch. The object of vision, however, is a quality of tangible body not *qua* tangible, but *qua* something else—*qua* something which may well be naturally prior to the object of touch.

Accordingly, we must segregate the tangible differences and contrarieties, and distinguish which amongst them are primary. Contrarieties correlative to touch are the following: hot-[*20*] cold, dry-moist, heavy-light, hard-soft, viscous-brittle, rough-smooth, coarse-fine. Of these (i) heavy and light are neither active nor susceptible. Things are not called 'heavy' and 'light' because they act upon, or suffer action from, other things. But the 'elements' must be reciprocally active and susceptible, since they 'combine' and are transformed into one another. On the other hand (ii) hot and cold, [*25*] and dry and moist, are terms, of which the first pair implies *power to act* and the second pair *susceptibility*. 'Hot' is that which 'associates' things of the same kind (for 'dissociating', which people attribute to Fire as its function, *is* 'associating' things of the same class, since its effect is to eliminate what is foreign), while 'cold' is that which brings to-[*30*]gether, i.e. 'associates', homogeneous and heterogeneous things alike. And 'moist' is that which, being readily adaptable in shape, is not determinable by any limit of its own: while 'dry' is that which is readily determinable by its own limit, but not readily adaptable in shape.

From moist and dry are derived (iii) the fine and coarse, viscous and brittle, hard and soft, and the remaining tangible differences. For

[35] (*a*) since the moist has no determinate shape, but is readily adaptable and follows the outline of that which is in contact with it, it is characteristic of it to be 'such as to fill up'. Now 'the fine' is 'such as to fill up'. For 'the fine' consists of subtle particles; but that which consists of small particles is 'such as to fill up', inasmuch as it is in contact whole with whole—and 'the fine' exhibits this character in a superlative degree. Hence it is evident that the fine derives from the moist, while the [5] coarse derives from the dry. Again (*b*) 'the viscous' derives from the moist: for 'the viscous' (e.g. oil) is a 'moist' modified in a certain way. 'The brittle', on the other hand, derives from the dry: for 'brittle' is that which is *completely* dry—so completely, that its solidification has actually been due to failure of moisture. Further (*c*) 'the soft' derives from the moist. For 'soft' is that which yields to pressure by retiring into itself, though it does not yield by total displacement as the moist [10] does—which explains why the moist is not 'soft', although 'the soft' derives from the moist. 'The hard', on the other hand, derives from the dry: for 'hard' is that which is solidified, and the solidified is dry.

The terms 'dry' and 'moist' have more senses than one. For 'the damp', as well as the moist, is opposed to the dry: and again 'the solidified', as well as the dry, is opposed to the moist. But [15] all these qualities derive from the dry and moist we mentioned first.[1] For (i) the dry is opposed to the damp: i.e. 'damp' is that which has foreign moisture on its surface ('sodden' being that which is penetrated to its core), while 'dry' is that which has lost foreign moisture. Hence it is evident that the damp will derive from the moist, and 'the dry' which is opposed to it will derive from the primary [20] dry. Again (ii) the 'moist' and the solidified derive in the same way from the primary pair. For 'moist' is that which contains moisture *of its own* deep within it ('sodden' being that which is deeply penetrated by *foreign* mosture), whereas 'solidified' is that which has lost this inner moisture. Hence these too derive from the primary pair, the 'solidified' from the dry and the 'liquefiable' from the moist.

[25] It is clear, then, that all the other differences reduce to the first four, but that these admit of no further reduction. For the hot is not *essentially* moist or dry, nor the moist *essentially* hot or cold: nor are the cold and the dry derivative forms, either of one another or of the hot and the moist. Hence these must be four.

3

[30] The elementary qualities are four, and any four terms can be combined in six couples. Contraries, however, refuse to be coupled: for it is impossible for the same thing to be hot and cold, or moist and dry. Hence it is evident that the 'couplings' of the elementary qualities will be four: hot with dry and moist with hot, and again cold with dry and cold with moist. And these four couples have attached themselves to the *apparently* 'simple' bodies (Fire, Air, Water, and Earth) in a manner consonant with theory. For Fire is hot and dry, whereas Air is hot and moist (Air being [5] a sort of aqueous vapour); and Water is cold and moist, while Earth is cold and dry. Thus the differences are reasonably distributed among the primary bodies, and the number of the latter is consonant with theory. For all who make the simple bodies 'elements' postulate either one, or two, or three, or four. Now (i) [10] those who assert there is *one* only, and then generate everything else by condensation and rarefaction, are in effect making their 'originative sources' two, viz. the rare and the dense, or rather the hot and the cold: for it is these which are the moulding forces, while the 'one' underlies them as a 'matter'. But (ii) those who postulate *two* from the start—as Parmenides postulated Fire and Earth—make [15] the intermediates (e.g. Air and Water) blends of these. The same course is followed (iii) by those who advocate *three*. (We may compare what Plato does in 'The Divisions': for he makes 'the middle' a blend.) Indeed, there is practically no difference between those who postulate *two* and those who postulate *three,* except that the former split the middle 'element' into two, while the latter treat it [20] as only one. But (iv) some advocate *four* from the start, e.g. Empedocles: yet he too draws them together so as to reduce them to *the two,* for he opposes all the others to Fire.

In fact, however, fire and air, and each of the bodies we have mentioned, are not simple, but blended. The 'simple' bodies are indeed similar in nature to them, but not identical with them. Thus the 'simple' body corresponding to fire is 'such-as-fire', not fire: that which corresponds to air is 'such-as-air': and [25] so on with the rest of them. But fire is an excess of heat, just as ice is an excess of cold. For freezing and boiling are excesses of heat

[1] Cf. above, 329ᵇ 30-2.

and cold respectively. Assuming, therefore, that ice is a freezing of moist and cold, fire analogously will be a boiling of dry and hot: a fact, by the way, which explains why nothing [30] comes-to-be either out of ice or out of fire.

The 'simple' bodies, since they are four, fall into two pairs which belong to the two regions, each to each: for Fire and Air are forms of the body moving towards the 'limit', while Earth and Water are forms of the body which moves towards the 'centre'. Fire and Earth, moreover, are extremes and purest: Water and Air, on the contrary are intermediates and more like blends. And, further, the members of either pair are contrary to those of the other, Water being contrary to Fire and Earth to Air; for the qualities constituting Water and Earth are contrary to those that constitute Fire and Air. Nevertheless, since they are four, each of them is characterized *par excellence* by a single quality: Earth by dry rather than [5] by cold, Water by cold rather than by moist, Air by moist rather than by hot, and Fire by hot rather than by dry.

4

It has been established before[1] that the coming-to-be of the 'simple' bodies is reciprocal. At the same time, it is manifest, even on the evidence of perception, that they *do* come-to-be: for otherwise there would not have been 'al- [10] teration', since 'alteration' is change in respect to the qualities of the objects of touch. Consequently, we must explain (i) what is the manner of their reciprocal transformation, and (ii) whether every one of them can come-to-be out of every one—or whether some can do so, but not others.

Now it is evident that all of them are by nature such as to change into one another: for coming-to-be is a change into contraries and [15] out of contraries, and the 'elements' all involve a contrariety in their mutual relations because their distinctive qualities are contrary. For in some of them *both* qualities are contrary—e.g. in Fire and Water, the first of these being dry and hot, and the second moist and cold: while in others *one* of the qualities (though only one) is contrary—e.g. in Air and Water, the first being moist and hot, and the [20] second moist and cold. It is evident, therefore, if we consider them in general, that every one is by nature such as to come-to-be out of every one: and when we come to con-

[1] The reference is probably to *On the Heavens*, 304ᵇ 23 ff

sider them severally, it is not difficult to see the manner in which their transformation is effected. For, though all will result from all, both the speed and the facility of their conversion will differ in degree.

[25] Thus (i) the process of conversion will be quick between those which have interchangeable 'complementary factors', but slow between those which have none. The reason is that it is easier for a single thing to change than for many. Air, e.g. will result from Fire if a single quality changes: for Fire, as we saw, is hot and dry while Air is hot and moist, so that there will be Air if the dry be overcome by the [30] moist. Again, Water will result from Air if the hot be overcome by the cold: for Air, as we saw, is hot and moist while Water is cold and moist, so that, if the hot changes, there will be Water. So too, in the same manner, Earth will result from Water and Fire from Earth, since the two 'elements' in both these couples have interchangeable 'complementary factors'. For Water is moist and cold while [35] Earth is cold and dry—so that, if the moist be overcome, there will be Earth: and again, since Fire is dry and hot while Earth is cold and dry, Fire will result from Earth if the cold pass-away.

It is evident, therefore, that the coming-to-be of the 'simple' bodies will be cyclical; and that this cyclical method of transformation is the easiest, because the *consecutive* 'elements' contain interchangeable 'complementary factors'. On the other hand (ii) the transformation of [5] Fire into Water and of Air into Earth, and again of Water and Earth into Fire and Air respectively, though possible, is more difficult because it involves the change of more qualities. For if Fire is to result from Water, both the cold and the moist must pass-away: and again, both the cold and the dry must pass-away if Air is to result from Earth. So, [10] too, if Water and Earth are to result from Fire and Air respectively—both qualities must change.

This second method of coming-to-be, then, takes a longer time. But (iii) if one quality in each of two 'elements' pass-away, the transformation, though easier, is not reciprocal. Still, from Fire *plus* Water there will result Earth and Air, and from Air *plus* Earth Fire and [15] Water. For there will be Air, when the cold of the Water and the dry of the Fire have passed-away (since the hot of the latter and the moist of the former are left): whereas, when the hot of the Fire and the moist of the

Water have passed-away, there will be Earth, owing to the survival of the dry of the Fire and the cold of the Water. So, too, in the same way, Fire and Water will result from Air *plus* [20] Earth. For there will be Water, when the hot of the Air and the dry of the Earth have passed-away (since the moist of the former and the cold of the latter are left): whereas, when the moist of the Air and the cold of the Earth have passed-away, there will be Fire, owing to the survival of the hot of the Air and the dry of the Earth—qualities essentially constitutive of Fire. Moreover, this mode of Fire's [25] coming-to-be is confirmed by perception. For flame is *par excellence* Fire: but flame is burning smoke, and smoke consists of Air and Earth.

No transformation, however, into any of the 'simple' bodies can result from the passing-away of one elementary quality in each of two 'elements' when they are taken in their consecutive order, because either *identical* or *contrary* [30] qualities are left in the pair: but no 'simple' body can be formed either out of identical, or out of contrary, qualities. Thus no 'simple' body would result, if the dry of Fire and the moist of Air were to pass-away: for the hot is left in both. On the other hand, if the hot pass-away out of both, the contraries—dry and moist—are left. A similar result will occur in all the others too: for all the *consecutive* 'elements' contain one identical, and one contrary, [35] quality. Hence, too, it clearly follows that, when one of the *consecutive* 'elements' is transformed into one, the coming-to-be is effected by the passing-away of a single quality: whereas, when two of them are transformed into a third, more than one quality must have passed-away.

332ª We have stated that all the 'elements' come-to-be out of any one of them; and we have explained the manner in which their mutual conversion takes place. Let us nevertheless supplement our theory by the following speculations concerning them.

5

[5] If Water, Air, and the like are a 'matter' of which the natural bodies consist, as some thinkers in fact believe, these 'elements' must be either one, or two, or more. Now they cannot all of them be *one*—they cannot, e.g. all be Air or Water or Fire or Earth—because 'Change is into contraries'. For if they all were Air, then (assuming Air to persist) there will be 'alteration' instead of coming-to-be. Besides, nobody supposes a single 'element' to [10] persist, as the basis of all, in such a way that it is Water as well as Air (or any other 'element') *at the same time*. So there will be a certain contrariety, i.e. a differentiating quality: and the other member of this contrariety, e.g. heat, will belong to some other 'element', e.g. to Fire. But Fire will certainly not be 'hot Air'. For a change of that kind (*a*) is 'alteration', and (*b*) is not what is observed. Moreover (*c*) if Air is again to result out of the Fire, [15] it will do so by the conversion of the hot into its contrary: this contrary, therefore, will belong to Air, and Air will be a cold something: hence it is impossible for Fire to be 'hot Air', since in that case the same thing will be simultaneously hot and cold. Both Fire and Air, therefore, will be something else which is the same; i.e. there will be some 'matter', other than either, common to both.

The same argument applies to all the 'ele-[20] ments', proving that there is no single one of them out of which they all originate. But neither is there, beside these four, some other body from which they originate—a something intermediate, e.g. between Air and Water (coarser than Air, but finer than Water), or between Air and Fire (coarser than Fire, but finer than Air). For the supposed 'intermediate' will be Air and Fire when a pair of contrasted qualities is added to it: but, since one of every two contrary qualities is a 'privation', the 'intermediate' never can exist—as some [25] thinkers assert the 'Boundless' or the 'Environing' exists—in isolation. It is, therefore, equally and indifferently any one of the 'elements', or else it is nothing.

Since, then, there is nothing—at least, nothing *perceptible*—prior to these, they must be all. That being so, either they must always persist and not be transformable into one another: or they must undergo transformation—either [30] all of them, or some only (as Plato wrote in the *Timaeus*).[1] Now it has been proved before that they must undergo reciprocal transformation. It has also been proved that the speed with which they come-to-be, one out of another, is not uniform—since the process of reciprocal transformation is relatively *quick* between the 'elements' with a 'complementary factor', but relatively *slow* between those which possess no such factor. Assuming, then, that the contrariety, in respect to which they are transformed, is *one,* the 'elements' will [35] inevitably be two: for it is 'matter' that is

[1] Cf. *Timaeus*, 54.

the 'mean' between the two contraries, and matter is imperceptible and inseparable from them. Since, however, the 'elements' are seen to be more than two, the contrarieties must at the least be two. But the contrarieties being two, the 'elements' must be four (as they evidently are) and cannot be three: for the 'couplings' are four, since, though six are possible, the two in which the qualities are contrary to one another cannot occur.

These subjects have been discussed before:[1] but the following arguments will make it clear that, since the 'elements' are transformed into one another, it is impossible for any one of them—whether it be at the end or in the middle—to be an 'originative source' of the rest. There can be no such 'originative element' at the ends: for all of them would then be Fire or Earth, and this theory amounts to the assertion that all things are made of Fire or Earth. Nor can a 'middle-element' be such an 'originative source'—as some thinkers suppose that Air is transformed both into Fire and into Water, and Water both into Air and into Earth, while the 'end-elements' are not further transformed into one another. For the process must come to a stop, and cannot continue *ad infinitum* in a straight line in either direction, since otherwise an infinite number of contrarieties would attach to the single 'element'. Let E stand for Earth, W for Water, A for Air, and F for Fire. Then (i) since A is transformed into F and W, there will be a contrariety belonging to A F. Let these contraries be whiteness and blackness. Again (ii) since A is transformed into W, there will be another contrariety: for W is not the same as F. Let this second contrariety be dryness and moistness, D being dryness and M moistness. Now if, when A is transformed into W, the 'white' persists, Water will be moist and white: but if it does not persist, Water will be black since change is into contraries. Water, therefore, must be either white or black. Let it then be the first. On similar grounds, therefore, D (dryness) will also belong to F. Consequently F (Fire) as well as Air will be able to be transformed into Water: for it has qualities contrary to those of Water, since Fire was *first* taken to be black and *then* to be dry, while Water was moist and *then* showed itself white. Thus it is evident that all the 'elements' will be able to be transformed out of one another; and that, in the instances we have taken, E (Earth) also will contain the remaining two 'complementary factors', viz. the black and the moist (for these have not yet been coupled).

We have dealt with this last topic before the thesis we set out to prove.[2] That thesis—viz. that the process cannot continue *ad infinitum* —will be clear from the following considerations. If Fire (which is represented by F) is not to revert, but is to be transformed in turn into some other 'element' (e.g. into Q), a new contrariety, other than those mentioned, will belong to Fire and Q: for it has been assumed that Q is not the same as any of the four, E W A and F. Let K, then, belong to F and Y to Q. Then K will belong to all four, E W A and F: for they are transformed into one another. This last point, however, we may admit, has not yet been proved: but at any rate it is clear that if Q is to be transformed in turn into yet another 'element', yet another contrariety will belong not only to Q but also to F (Fire). And, similarly, every addition of a new 'element' will carry with it the attachment of a new contrariety to the preceding 'elements'. Consequently, if the 'elements' are infinitely many, there will also belong *to the single 'element'* an infinite number of contrarieties. But if that be so, it will be impossible to define any 'element': impossible also for any to come-to-be. For if one is to result from another, it will have to pass through such a vast number of contrarieties—and indeed even more than any determinate number. Consequently (i) into some 'elements' transformation will never be effected—viz. if the intermediates are infinite in number, as they must be if the 'elements' are infinitely many: further (ii) there will not even be a transformation of Air into Fire, if the contrarieties are infinitely many: moreover (iii) all the 'elements' become one. For all the contrarieties of the 'elements' above F must belong to those below F, and *vice versa*: hence they will all be one.

6

As for those who agree with Empedocles that the 'elements' of body are more than one, so that they are not transformed into one another—one may well wonder in what sense it is open to them to maintain that the 'elements' are comparable. Yet Empedocles says 'For these are all not only equal . . .'[3]

If (i) it is meant that they are comparable in their amount, all the 'comparables' must pos-

[1] Cf. above, II. 2 and 3.
[2] Cf. above, 332[b] 12-13.
[3] Empedocles, fr. 17. l, 27, Diels, p. 179.

sess an identical something whereby they are measured. If, e.g. one pint of Water yields ten of Air, both are measured by the same unit; and therefore both were from the first an identical something. On the other hand, suppose (ii) they are not 'comparable in their amount' in the sense that so-much of the one yields so-much of the other, but comparable in 'power [25] of action (a pint of Water, e.g. having a power of cooling equal to that of ten pints of Air); even so, they *are* 'comparable in their amount', though not *qua* 'amount' but *qua* 'so-much power'. There is also (iii) a third possibility. Instead of comparing their powers by the measure of their amount, they might be compared as terms in a 'correspondence': e.g. 'as *x* is hot, so correspondingly *y* is white'. But [30] 'correspondence', though it means equality in the *quantum,* means similarity in a *quale*. Thus it is manifestly absurd that the 'simple' bodies, though they are not transformable, are comparable not merely as 'corresponding', but by a measure of their powers; i.e. that so-much Fire is comparable with many-times-that-amount of Air, as being 'equally' or 'similarly' hot. For the same thing, if it be greater in amount, will, since it belongs to the same kind, have its *ratio* correspondingly increased.

[35] A further objection to the theory of Empedocles is that it makes even *growth* impossible, unless it be increase by addition. For his 333[b] Fire increases by Fire: 'And Earth increases its own frame and Ether increases Ether.'[1] These, however, are cases of addition: but it is not by addition that growing things are believed to increase. And it is far more difficult for him to account for the *coming-to-* [5] *be* which occurs in nature. For the things which come-to-be by natural process all exhibit, in their coming-to-be, a uniformity either absolute or highly regular: while any exceptions—any results which are in accordance neither with the invariable nor with the general rule—are products of chance and luck. Then what is the cause determining that man comes-to-be from man, that wheat (instead of an olive) comes-to-be from wheat, either invariably or generally? Are we to say 'Bone comes-to-be if the "elements" be put together in such-and-such a manner'? For, according to his own [10] statements, nothing comes-to-be from their 'fortuitous consilience', but only from their 'consilience' in a certain proportion. What, then, is the cause of this proportional con-

silience? Presumably not Fire or Earth. But neither is it Love and Strife: for the former is a cause of 'association' only, and the latter only of 'dissociation'. No: the cause in question is the essential nature of each thing—not merely (to quote his words) 'a mingling and a divorce [15] of what has been mingled'.[2] And *chance*, not *proportion*, 'is the name given to these occurrences': for things can be 'mingled' fortuitously.

The cause, therefore, of the coming-to-be of the things which owe their existence to nature is that they are in such-and-such a determinate condition: and it is *this* which constitutes the 'nature' of each thing—a 'nature' about which he says nothing. What he says, therefore, is no explanation of 'nature'. Moreover, it is *this* which is both 'the excellence' of each thing and its 'good': whereas he assigns the whole credit [20] to the 'mingling'. (And yet *the 'elements'* at all events are 'dissociated' not by Strife, but by Love: since the 'elements' are by nature prior to the Deity, and they too are Deities.)

Again, his account of motion is vague. For it is not an adequate explanation to say that 'Love and Strife set things moving', unless the very nature of Love is a movement of *this* kind and the very nature of Strife a movement of [25] *that* kind. He ought, then, either to have defined or to have postulated these characteristic movements, or to have demonstrated them—whether strictly or laxly or in some other fashion. Moreover, since (*a*) the 'simple' bodies *appear* to move 'naturally' as well as by compulsion, i.e. in a manner contrary to nature (fire, e.g. appears to move upwards without compulsion, though it appears to move by compulsion downwards); and since (*b*) what is 'natural' is contrary to that which is due to compulsion, and movement by compulsion actually occurs; it follows that 'natural movement' [30] can also occur in fact. Is *this,* then, the movement that Love sets going? No: for, on the contrary, the 'natural movement' moves Earth downwards and resembles 'dissociation', and Strife rather than Love is its cause—so that in general, too, Love rather than Strife would seem to be contrary to nature. And unless Love or Strife is actually setting them in motion, the 'simple' bodies themselves have [35] absolutely no movement or rest. But this is paradoxical: and what is more, they do in 334[a] fact obviously move. For though Strife 'dissociated', it was not by Strife that the 'Ether' was borne upwards. On the contrary,

---

[1] Cf. Empedocles, fr. 37, Diels, p. 186.

[2] Cf. Empedocles, fr. 8, Diels, p. 175.

sometimes he attributes its movement to something like *chance* ('For *thus,* as it ran, it *happened* to meet them then, though often otherwise'[1]), while at other times he says it is the *nature* of Fire to be borne upwards, but 'the [5] Ether' (to quote his words) 'sank down upon the Earth with long roots'.[2] With such statements, too, he combines the assertion that the Order of the World is the same *now,* in the reign of Strife, as it was *formerly* in the reign of Love. What, then, is the 'first mover' of the 'elements'? What causes their motion? Presumably not Love and Strife: on the contrary, these are causes of a *particular* motion, if at least we assume that 'first mover' to be an 'originative source'.

[10] An additional paradox is that the soul should consist of the 'elements', or that it should be one of them. How are the soul's 'alterations' to take place? How, e.g. is the change from being musical to being unmusical, or how is memory or forgetting, to occur? For clearly, if the soul be Fire, only such modifications will happen to it as characterize Fire *qua* Fire: while if it be compounded out of the 'elements', only the corporeal modifications will occur in it. But the changes we have mentioned [15] are none of them corporeal.

7

The discussion of these difficulties, however, is a task appropriate to a different investigation:[3] let us return to the 'elements' of which bodies are composed. The theories that 'there is something common to all the "elements"', and that 'they are reciprocally transformed', are so related that those who accept *either* are bound to accept *the other* as well. Those, on the other hand, who do not make their coming-to-be reciprocal—who refuse to suppose that any one of the 'elements' comes-to-be out of any other [20] *taken singly,* except in the sense in which bricks come-to-be out of a wall—are faced with a paradox. How, on their theory, are flesh and bones or any of the other compounds to result from the 'elements' *taken together?*

Indeed, the point we have raised constitutes a problem even for those who generate the 'elements' out of one another. In what manner does anything other than, and beside, the 'elements' come-to-be out of them? Let me illustrate my meaning. Water can come-to-be out of Fire and Fire out of Water; for their *substratum* is [25] something common to them both. But flesh too, presumably, and marrow come-to-be out of them. How, then, do such things come-to-be? For (*a*) how is the manner of their coming-to-be to be conceived by those who maintain a theory like that of Empedocles? They must conceive it as *composition*—just as a wall comes-to-be out of bricks and stones: and the 'Mixture', of which they speak, will be composed of the 'elements', these being preserved [30] in it unaltered but with their small particles juxtaposed each to each. That will be the manner, presumably, in which flesh and every other compound results from the 'elements'. Consequently, it follows that Fire and Water do not come-to-be 'out of any and every part of flesh'. For instance, although a sphere might come-to-be out of *this* part of a lump of wax and a pyramid out of *some other* part, it was nevertheless possible for either figure to have [35] come-to-be out of either part indifferently: *that* is the manner of coming-to-be when 'both Fire and Water come-to-be out of any and every part of flesh'. Those, however, who maintain 334ᵇ the theory in question, are not at liberty to conceive that 'both come-to-be out of flesh' in that manner, but only as a stone and a brick 'both come-to-be out of a wall'—viz. each out of a different place or part. Similarly (*b*) even for those who postulate a single matter of their 'elements' there is a certain difficulty in explaining how anything is to result from two of them taken together—e.g. from 'cold' and [5] 'hot', or from Fire and Earth. For if flesh consists of both and is neither of them, nor again is a 'composition' of them in which they are preserved unaltered, what alternative is left except to identify the resultant of the two 'elements' with their matter? For the passing-away of either 'element' produces *either* the other *or* the matter.

Perhaps we may suggest the following solution. (i) There are differences of degree in hot and cold. Although, therefore, when either is fully real without qualification, the other will [10] exist potentially; yet, when neither exists in the full completeness of its being, but both by combining destroy one another's excesses so that there exist instead a hot which (for a 'hot') is cold and a cold which (for a 'cold') is hot; then what results from these two contraries will be neither their matter, nor either of them existing in its full reality without qualification. There will result instead an 'intermediate': and this 'intermediate', according

---

[1] Cf. Empedocles, fr. 53, Diels, p. 189.
[2] Cf. fr. 54, *ibid.*
[3] Cf. *On the Soul,* I. 4 and 5, especially 408ᵃ 18-23 and 409ᵇ 23 ff.

[15] as it is potentially more hot than cold or *vice versa*, will possess a power-of-heating that is double or triple its power-of-cooling, or otherwise related thereto in some similar ratio. Thus all the other bodies will result from the contraries, or rather from the 'elements', in so far as these have been 'combined': while the 'elements' will result from the contraries, in so far as these 'exist potentially' in a special sense—not as matter 'exists potentially', but in the sense explained above. And when a thing comes-to-be in *this* manner, the process is 'com-[20] bination'; whereas what comes-to-be in the other manner is matter. Moreover (ii) contraries also 'suffer action', in accordance with the disjunctively-articulated definition established in the early part of this work.[1] For the actually-hot is potentially-cold and the actually-cold potentially-hot; so that hot and cold, unless they are equally balanced, are transformed into one another (and all the other contraries [25] behave in a similar way). It is thus, then, that *in the first place* the 'elements' are transformed; and that (*in the second place*) out of the 'elements' there come-to-be flesh and bones and the like—the hot becoming cold and the cold becoming hot when they have been brought to the 'mean'. For at the 'mean' is neither hot nor cold. The 'mean', however, is of considerable extent and not indivisible. Similarly, it is *qua* reduced to a 'mean' condition that the dry and the moist, as well as the contraries we have used as examples, produce flesh and bone and [30] the remaining compounds.

8

All the compound bodies—all of which exist in the region belonging to the central body—are composed of all the 'simple' bodies. For they all contain Earth because every 'simple' body is to be found specially and most abundantly in its own place. And they all contain Water be-[35] cause (*a*) the compound must possess a definite outline and Water, alone of the 'simple' bodies, is readily adaptable in shape: moreover (*b*) Earth has no power of cohesion without the moist. On the contrary, the moist is what holds it together; for it would fall to pieces if the moist were eliminated from it completely.

They contain Earth and Water, then, for the reasons we have given: and they contain Air and Fire, because these are contrary to Earth [5] and Water (Earth being contrary to Air and Water to Fire, in so far as one Substance

[1] Cf. above, I. 7.

can be 'contrary' to another). Now all compounds presuppose in their coming-to-be constituents which are contrary to one another: and in all compounds there is contained one set of the contrasted extremes. Hence the other set must be contained in them also, so that every compound will include all the 'simple' bodies.

[10] Additional evidence seems to be furnished by the food each compound takes. For all of them are fed by substances which are the same as their constituents, and all of them are fed by more substances than one. Indeed, even the plants, though it might be thought they are fed by one substance only, viz. by Water, are fed by more than one: for Earth has been mixed with the Water. That is why farmers too endeavour to mix before watering.

[15] Although food is akin to the matter, that which is fed is the 'figure'—i.e. the 'form'—taken along with the matter. This fact enables us to understand why, whereas all the 'simple' bodies come-to-be out of one another, Fire is the only one of them which (as our predecessors also assert) 'is fed'. For Fire alone—or more than all the rest—is akin to the 'form' because it tends by nature to be borne towards [20] the limit. Now each of them naturally tends to be borne towards its own place; but the 'figure'—i.e. the 'form'—of them all is at the limits.

Thus we have explained that all the compound bodies are composed of all the 'simple' bodies.

9

Since some things are such as to come-to-be [25] and pass-away, and since coming-to-be in fact occurs in the region about the centre, we must explain the *number* and the *nature* of the 'originative sources' of all coming-to-be alike: for a grasp of the true theory of any universal facilitates the understanding of its specific forms.

The 'originative sources', then, of the things which come-to-be are equal in number to, and identical in kind with, those in the sphere of the eternal and primary things. For there is *one* [30] in the sense of 'matter', and a *second* in the sense of 'form': and, in addition, the *third* 'originative source' must be present as well. For the two first are not sufficient to bring things into being, any more than they are adequate to account for the primary things.

Now cause, in the sense of material origin, for the things which are such as to come-to-be is 'that which can be-and-not-be': and this is identical with 'that which can come-to-be-and-pass-away', since the latter, while it *is* at one time, at another time *is* not. (For whereas some things *are* of necessity, viz. the eternal things, others of necessity *are not*. And of these [35] two sets of things, since they cannot 335ᵇ diverge from the necessity of their nature, it is impossible for the first *not to be* and impossible for the second *to be*. Other things, however, can both *be* and *not be*.) Hence coming-to-be and passing-away must occur [5] within the field of 'that which can be-and-not-be'. This, therefore, is cause in the sense of material origin for the things which are such as to come-to-be; while cause, in the sense of their 'end', is their 'figure' or 'form'—and that is the formula expressing the essential nature of each of them.

But the third 'originative source' must be present as well—the cause vaguely dreamed of by all our predecessors, definitely stated by none of them. On the contrary (*a*) some [10] amongst them thought the nature of 'the Forms' was adequate to account for coming-to-be. Thus Socrates in the *Phaedo* first blames everybody else for having given no explanation;¹ and then lays it down that 'some things are Forms, others Participants in the Forms', and that 'while a thing is said to "be" in virtue of the Form, it is said to "come-to-be" *qua* "sharing in," to "pass-away" *qua* "losing," the [15] Form'. Hence he thinks that 'assuming the truth of these theses, the Forms *must* be causes both of coming-to-be and of passing-away'.² On the other hand (*b*) there were others who thought 'the matter' was adequate by itself to account for coming-to-be, since 'the movement originates from the matter'.

Neither of these theories, however, is sound. For (*a*) if the Forms are causes, why is their generating activity intermittent instead of perpetual and continuous—since there always *are* [20] Participants as well as Forms? Besides, in some instances we *see* that the cause is other than the Form. For it is the doctor who implants health and the man of science who implants science, although 'Health itself' and 'Science itself' *are* as well as the Participants: and the same principle applies to everything else that is produced in accordance with an art. On the other hand (*b*) to say that 'matter [25] generates owing to its movement' would be, no doubt, more scientific than to make such statements as are made by the thinkers we have been criticizing. For what 'alters' and transfigures plays a greater part in bringing things into being; and we are everywhere accustomed, in the products of nature and of art alike, to look upon that which can initiate movement as the producing cause. Nevertheless this second theory is not right either.

[30] For, to begin with, it is characteristic of matter to suffer action, i.e. to be moved: but to move, i.e. to act, belongs to a different 'power'. This is obvious both in the things that come-to-be by art and in those that come-to-be by nature. Water does not of itself produce out of itself an animal: and it is the art, not the wood, that makes a bed. Nor is this their only error. They make a second mistake [35] in omitting the more controlling cause: 336ᵃ for they eliminate the essential nature, i.e. the 'form'. And what is more, since they remove the formal cause, they invest the forces they assign to the 'simple' bodies—the forces which enable these bodies to bring things into being—with too instrumental a character. For 'since' (as they say) 'it is the nature of the hot to dissociate, of the cold to bring together, and [5] of each remaining contrary either to act or to suffer action', it is out of such materials and by their agency (so they maintain) that everything else comes-to-be and passes-away. Yet (*a*) it is evident that even Fire is itself moved, i.e. suffers action. Moreover (*b*) their procedure is virtually the same as if one were to treat the saw (and the various instruments of carpentry) as 'the cause' of the things that [10] come-to-be: for the wood *must* be divided if a man saws, *must* become smooth if he planes, and so on with the remaining tools. Hence, however true it may be that Fire is active, i.e. sets things moving, there is a further point they fail to observe—viz. that Fire is inferior to the tools or instruments in the manner in which it sets things moving.

10

As to our own theory—we have given a general account of the causes in an earlier work,³ and we have now explained and distinguished the 'matter' and the 'form'.⁴ Further, since the [15] change which is motion has been proved⁵ to be eternal, the continuity of the occurrence of coming-to-be follows necessarily from what we have established: for the eternal motion, by causing 'the generator' to approach and

---

¹ Cf. Plato, *Phaedo*, 96-99.
² Cf. Plato, *Phaedo*, 100-101.
³ Cf. *Physics*, II. 3-9. ⁴ Cf. above, 335ᵃ 32-ᵇ 7.
⁵ Cf. *Physics*, VIII. 7-9.

retire, will produce coming-to-be uninterruptedly. At the same time it is clear that we were [20] also right when, in an earlier work,[1] we called motion (not coming-to-be) 'the primary form of change'. For it is far more reasonable that *what is* should cause the coming-to-be of *what is not,* than that *what is not* should cause the being of *what is.* Now that which is being moved *is,* but that which is coming-to-be *is not:* hence, also, motion is prior to coming-to-be.

We have assumed, and have proved, that [25] coming-to-be and passing-away happen to things continuously; and we assert that motion causes coming-to-be. That being so, it is evident that, if the motion be single, *both* processes cannot occur since they are contrary to one another: for it is a law of nature that the same cause, provided it remain in the same condition, always produces the same effect, so that, from a single motion, either coming-to-be or passing-away will always result. The movements must, on the contrary, be more [30] than one, and they must be contrasted with one another either by the sense of their motion or by its irregularity: for contrary effects demand contraries as their causes.

This explains why it is not the primary motion that causes coming-to-be and passing-away, but the motion along the inclined circle: for this motion not only possesses the necessary continuity, but includes a duality of movements as well. For if coming-to-be and passing-away are always to be continuous, there must be some body always being moved (in order that these changes may not fail) and moved with a duality of movements (in order that both changes, not one only, may result). Now the continuity of this movement is caused by the motion of the whole: but the approaching and retreating of the moving body are caused by the inclination. For the consequence [5] of the inclination is that the body becomes alternately remote and near; and since its distance is thus unequal, its movement will be irregular. Therefore, if it generates by approaching and by its proximity, it—this very same body—destroys by retreating and becoming remote: and if it generates by many successive approaches, it also destroys by many successive retirements. For contrary effects demand contraries as their causes; and the natural [10] processes of passing-away and coming-to-be occupy equal periods of time. Hence, too, the times—i.e. the lives—of the several kinds of living things have a number by which they are distinguished: for there is an Order controlling all things, and every time (i.e. every life) is measured by a period. Not all of them, however, are measured by the same period, but some by a smaller and others by a greater one: for to some of them the period, which is their [15] measure, is a year, while to some it is longer and to others shorter.

And there are facts of observation in manifest agreement with our theories. Thus we see that coming-to-be occurs as the sun approaches and decay as it retreats; and we see that the two processes occupy equal times. For the durations of the natural processes of passing-away and coming-to-be are equal. Nevertheless it [20] often happens that things pass-away in too short a time. This is due to the 'intermingling' by which the things that come-to-be and pass-away are implicated with one another. For their matter is 'irregular', i.e. is not everywhere the same: hence the processes by which they come-to-be must be 'irregular' too, i.e. some too quick and others too slow. Consequently the phenomenon in question occurs, because the 'irregular' coming-to-be of these things is the passing-away of other things.

[25] Coming-to-be and passing-away will, as we have said, always be continuous, and will never fail owing to the cause we stated.[2] And this continuity has a sufficient reason on our theory. For in all things, as we affirm, Nature always strives after 'the better'. Now 'being' (we have explained elsewhere[3] the exact variety of meanings we recognize in this term) is [30] better than 'not-being': but not all things can possess 'being', since they are too far removed from the 'originative source.' God therefore adopted the remaining alternative, and fulfilled the perfection of the universe by making coming-to-be uninterrupted: for the greatest possible coherence would thus be secured to existence, because that 'coming-to-be should itself come-to-be perpetually' is the closest approximation to eternal being.

The cause of this perpetuity of coming-to-be, as we have often said, is circular motion: for that is the only motion which is continuous. That, too, is why all the other things—the things, I mean, which are reciprocally transformed in virtue of their 'passions' and their 'powers of action', e.g. the 'simple' bodies— imitate circular motion. For when Water is [5] transformed into Air, Air into Fire, and the Fire back into Water, we say the coming-

---

[1] Cf. *Physics*, 260^{a}26-261^{a}26.

[2] Cf. above, 318^a 9 ff.

[3] Cf., e.g. *Metaphysics*, 1017^a 7 ff.

to-be 'has completed the circle', because it reverts again to the beginning. Hence it is by imitating circular motion that rectilinear motion too is continuous.

These considerations serve at the same time to explain what is to some people a baffling problem—viz. why the 'simple' bodies, since each them is travelling towards its own place, [10] have not become dissevered from one another in the infinite lapse of time. The reason is their reciprocal transformation. For, had each of them persisted in its own place instead of being transformed by its neighbour, they would have got dissevered long ago. They are transformed, however, owing to the motion with its dual character: and because they are transformed, none of them is able to persist in [15] any place allotted to it by the Order.

It is clear from what has been said (i) that coming-to-be and passing-away actually occur, (ii) what causes them, and (iii) what subject undergoes them. But (*a*) if there is to be movement (as we have explained elsewhere, in an earlier work[1]) there must be something which initiates it; if there is to be movement always, there must always be something which initiates it; if the movement is to be continuous, what [20] initiates it must be single, unmoved, ungenerated, and incapable of 'alteration'; and if the circular movements are more than one, their initiating causes must all of them, in spite of their plurality, be in some way subordinated to a single 'originative source'. Further (*b*) since time is continuous, movement must be continuous, inasmuch as there can be no time without movement. Time, therefore, is a 'number' of some continuous movement—a 'num-[25]ber', therefore, of the circular movement, as was established in the discussions at the beginning.[2] But (*c*) is movement continuous because of the continuity of that which is moved, or because that in which the movement occurs (I mean, e.g. the place or the quality) is continuous? The answer must clearly be 'because that which is moved is continuous'. (For how can the quality be continuous except in virtue of the continuity of the thing to which it belongs? But if the continuity of 'that in which' contributes to make the movement continuous, [30] this is true only of 'the place in which'; for that has 'magnitude' in a sense.) But (*d*) amongst continuous bodies which are moved, only that which is moved in a circle is 'continuous' in such a way that it preserves its continu-

[1] *Physics*, 255^b 31-260^a 10.
[2] *Physics*, 217^b 29-224^a 17.

ity with itself throughout the movement. The conclusion therefore is that *this* is what produces continuous movement, viz. the body which is being moved in a circle; and its movement makes time continuous.

11

Wherever there is continuity in any process [35] (coming-to-be or 'alteration' or any kind of change whatever) we observe 'consecutive-ness', i.e. *this* coming-to-be after *that* without any interval. Hence we must investigate whether, amongst the consecutive members, there is any whose future being is necessary; or whether, on the contrary, every one of them may fail to come-to-be. For that some of them may fail to occur, is clear. (*a*) We need only appeal to the distinction between the statements '*x* will be' and '*x* is about to . . .', which depends upon this fact. For if it be true [5] to say of *x* that it 'will be', it must at some time be true to say of it that 'it is': whereas, though it be true to say of *x now* that 'it is about to occur', it is quite possible for it not to come-to-be—thus a man might not walk, though he is now 'about to' walk. And (*b*) since (to appeal to a general principle) amongst the things which 'are' some are capable also of 'not-being', it is clear that the same ambiguous character will attach to them no less when they are coming-to-be: in other words, their coming-to-be will not be necessary.

[10] Then are all the things that come-to-be of this contingent character? Or, on the contrary, is it absolutely necessary for some of them to come-to-be? Is there, in fact, a distinction in the field of 'coming-to-be' corresponding to the distinction, within the field of 'being', between things that cannot possibly 'not-be' and things that can 'not-be'? For instance, is it necessary that solstices shall come-to-be, i.e. impossible that they should fail to be able to occur?

Assuming that the antecedent must have come-to-be if the consequent is to be (e.g. that [15] foundations must have come-to-be if there is to be a house: clay, if there are to be foundations), is the converse also true? If foundations have come-to-be, must a house come-to-be? The answer seems to be that the necessary *nexus* no longer holds, unless it is 'necessary' for the consequent (as well as for the antecedent) to come-to-be—'necessary' *absolutely*. If that be the case, however, 'a house must come-to-be if foundations have come-to-be', as well as *vice versa*. For the antecedent was assumed to be so related to the consequent that, if the latter is to be, the antecedent must have come-to-[20] be before it. If, therefore, it is necessary that the consequent should come-to-be, the antecedent also must have come-to-be: and if the antecedent has come-to-be, then the consequent also must come-to-be—not, however, because of the antecedent, but because the future being of the consequent was assumed as necessary. Hence, in any sequence, when the being of the consequent is necessary, the *nexus* is reciprocal —in other words, when the antecedent has [25] come-to-be the consequent must always come-to-be too.

Now (i) if the sequence of occurrences is to proceed *ad infinitum* 'downwards', the coming-to-be of any determinate 'this' amongst the later members of the sequence will not be *absolutely*, but only *conditionally*, necessary. For it will always be necessary that some other member shall have come-to-be before 'this' as the presupposed condition of the necessity that 'this' should come-to-be: consequently, since what is 'infinite' has no 'originative source', neither will there be in the infinite sequence any 'primary' member which will make it 'necessary' for the remaining members to come-to-be.

[30] Nor again (ii) will it be possible to say with truth, even in regard to the members of a limited sequence, that it is 'absolutely necessary' for any one of them to come-to-be. We cannot truly say, e.g. that 'it is absolutely necessary for a house to come-to-be when foundations have been laid': for (unless it is *always* necessary for a house to be coming-to-be) we should be faced with the consequence that, when foundations have been laid, a thing, which need not always be, must always be. No: if its coming-to-be is to be 'necessary', it must [35] be 'always' in its coming-to-be. For what is 'of necessity' coincides with what is 'always', 338ª since that which 'must be' cannot possibly 'not-be'. Hence a thing is eternal if its 'being' is necessary: and if it is eternal, its 'being' is necessary. And if, therefore, the 'coming-to-be' of a thing is necessary, its 'coming-to-be' is eternal; and if eternal, necessary.

It follows that the coming-to-be of anything, [5] if it is absolutely necessary, must be cyclical—i.e. must return upon itself. For coming-to-be must either be limited or not limited: and if not limited, it must be either rectilinear or cyclical. But the first of these last two alternatives is impossible if coming-to-be is to be eternal, because there could not be any 'originative source' whatever in an infinite rectilinear sequence, whether its members be taken 'downwards' (as future events) or 'upwards' (as past events). Yet coming-to-be must have an 'originative source' ⟨if it is to be necessary and therefore eternal⟩, nor can it be eternal if it is [10] limited. Consequently it must be cyclical. Hence the *nexus* must be reciprocal. By this I mean that the necessary occurrence of 'this' involves the necessary occurrence of its antecedent: and conversely that, given the antecedent, it is also necessary for the consequent to come-to-be. And this reciprocal *nexus* will hold continuously throughout the sequence: for it makes no difference whether the reciprocal *nexus*, of which we are speaking, is mediated by two, or by many, members.

[15] It is in circular movement, therefore, and in cyclical coming-to-be that the 'absolutely necessary' is to be found. In other words, if the coming-to-be of any things is cyclical, it is 'necessary' that each of them is coming-to-be and has come-to-be: and if the coming-to-be of any things is 'necessary', their coming-to-be is cyclical.

The result we have reached is logically concordant with the eternity of circular motion, i.e. the eternity of the revolution of the heavens (a fact which approved itself on other and independent evidence),[1] since precisely those 338ᵇ movements which belong to, and depend upon, this eternal revolution 'come-to-be' of necessity, and of necessity 'will be'. For since the revolving body is always setting something else in motion, the movement of the things it moves must also be circular. Thus, from the being of the 'upper revolution' it follows that the sun revolves in this determinate manner; and since the sun revolves *thus*, the seasons in consequence come-to-be in a cycle, i.e. return upon [5] themselves; and since they come-to-be cyclically, so in their turn do the things whose coming-to-be the seasons initiate.

Then why do some things manifestly come-to-be in this cyclical fashion (as, e.g. showers and air, so that it must rain if there is to be a cloud and, conversely, there must be a cloud if it is to rain), while men and animals do not 'return upon themselves' so that the same indi-[10] vidual comes-to-be a second time (for though your coming-to-be presupposes your father's, his coming-to-be does not presuppose yours)? Why, on the contrary, does this coming-to-be seem to constitute a rectilinear sequence?

In discussing this new problem, we must begin by inquiring whether all things 'return

[1] Cf. *Physics*, VIII. 7-9.

upon themselves' in a uniform manner; or whether, on the contrary, though in some sequences what recurs is *numerically* the same, in other sequences it is the same *only in species*. In consequence of this distinction, it is evident that those things, whose 'substance'—that which is undergoing the process—is imperish-[15] able, will be numerically, as well as specifically, the same in their recurrence: for the character of the process is determined by the character of that which undergoes it. Those things, on the other hand, whose 'substance' is perishable (not imperishable) must 'return upon themselves' in the sense that what recurs, though specifically the same, is not the same numerically. That is why, when Water comes-to-be from Air and Air from Water, the Air is the same 'specifically', not 'numerically': and if these too recur numerically the same, at any rate this does not happen with things whose 'substance' comes-to-be—whose 'substance' is such that it is essentially capable of not-being.

CONTENTS: METEOROLOGY

BOOK I

CHAP.		BERLIN NOS.
1.	Summary of subject-matter of meteorology	338^a 20
2.	The material and the efficient cause of the phenomena to be studied	339^a 11
3.	The position of air and fire relatively to the celestial sphere. Why clouds and water do not form in ether	339^a 32
4.	The cause of shooting-stars and the like	341^b 1
5.	The cause of the appearance of 'chasms', &c., in the sky	342^a 35
6.	Refutation of earlier theories of comets	342^b 25
7.	The cause of comets	344^a 5
8.	The milky way	345^a 11
9.	The causes of rain, and the difference between cloud and mist	346^b 16
10.	The causes of dew and hoar-frost	347^a 13
11.	The causes and concomitants of snow	347^b 13
12.	Hail—where and when it is produced	347^b 34
13.	Winds, rivers, and springs	349^a 11
14.	Why the same parts of the earth are not always watered by rivers, or always dry. Floods	351^a 19

BOOK II

1.	Three theories of the origin of the sea. It cannot have springs. Why it flows as it does	353^a 30
2.	Its place. It is the end rather than the beginning of water. Why it is not increased by the influx of rivers	354^b 1
3.	Why is it salt? Is it eternal? The cause of different tastes and colours in water	356^b 2
4.	The causes of winds	359^b 26
5.	Why winds blow at some times and not at others. From where, and when, each wind blows	361^b 14
6.	The direction of the winds; which are contrary; and which can blow together. Their number, concomitants, and natures	363^a 21
7.	Three theories of earthquakes	365^a 13
8.	The causes of earthquakes. Indications that they are due to exhalation	365^b 21
9.	Early theories of thunder and lightning	369^a 10

BOOK III

CHAP.		BERLIN NOS.
1.	The causes of, and difference between, ecnephias, typhon, and prester. The kinds of thunderbolt	370^b 1
2.	The causes and concomitants of halos	371^b 18
3.	Why halos are circular, and what they indicate	372^b 11
4.	The rainbow—how it is produced by reflection, and the causes of its properties (e.g its colours). How it differs from the halo	373^a 32
5.	Some properties of the rainbow	375^b 16
6.	The causes of 'rods' and mock suns	377^a 28

BOOK IV

1.	Hot and cold are active, dry and moist passive principles. True or natural generation is due to these. The contrary of true generation is putrefaction. Putrefaction further considered	378^b 10
2.	Concoction and inconcoction	379^b 10
3.	Three kinds of concoction—ripening, boiling, broiling; and their contraries	380^a 11
4.	Dry and moist, and the properties consequent on them in composite bodies—hard and soft	381^b 23
5.	Every well-defined body must be hard or soft, and solid. Solidification and its causes	382^a 22
6.	Things that can be solidified are made either of water, or of earth and water. Various modes of solidification and solution	382^b 28
7.	Things are thickened by fire or by cold according as they have more water or earth in them	383^b 17
8.	The properties of composite bodies —nineteen positive and nineteen negative. What can and what cannot be solidified; what can and what cannot be melted	384^b 24
9.	The remaining seventeen properties	385^b 7
10.	Homoeomerous bodies	388^a 10
11.	Which mixtures are warm and which are cold	389^a 23
12.	Homoeomerous bodies are composed of the elements. End and function more evident in non-homoeomerous bodies than in the homoeomerous bodies which compose them, and in these than in the elements	389^b 22

METEOROLOGY
BOOK I

1

338ª [20] We have already discussed the first causes of nature, and all natural motion,[1] also the stars ordered in the motion of the heavens,[2] and the physical elements—enumerating and specifying them and showing how they change into one another—and becoming and perishing in general.[3] There remains for consideration a part of this inquiry which all our predecessors called meteorology. It is concerned with **338ᵇ** events that are natural, though their or-[21] der is less perfect than that of the first of the elements of bodies. They take place in the region nearest to the motion of the stars. Such are the milky way, and comets, and the movements of meteors. It studies also all the affections we may call common to air and water, and the kinds and parts of the earth and the affections of its parts. These throw light on the **339ª** causes of winds and earthquakes and all the consequences the motions of these kinds and parts involve. Of these things some puzzle us, while others admit of explanation in some degree. Further, the inquiry is concerned with the falling of thunderbolts and with whirlwinds and fire-winds, and further, the recur-[5] rent affections produced in these same bodies by concretion. When the inquiry into these matters is concluded let us consider what account we can give, in accordance with the method we have followed, of animals and plants, both generally and in detail. When that has been done we may say that the whole of our original undertaking will have been carried out.

[10] After this introduction let us begin by discussing our immediate subject.

2

We have already laid down that there is one physical element which makes up the system

[1] *Physics.*   [2] *On the Heavens,* especially I and II.
[3] *On Generation and Corruption,* and perhaps *On the Heavens,* III and IV.

NOTE: The bold face numbers and letters are approximate indications of the pages and columns of the standard Berlin Greek text; the bracketed numbers, of the lines in the Greek text; they are here assigned as they are assigned in the Oxford translation.

of the bodies that move in a circle, and besides this four bodies owing their existence to the four principles, the motion of these latter bod-[15] ies being of two kinds: either from the centre or to the centre. These four bodies are fire, air, water, earth. Fire occupies the highest place among them all, earth the lowest, and two elements correspond to these in their relation to one another, air being nearest to fire, water to earth. The whole world surrounding [20] the earth, then, the affections of which are our subject, is made up of these bodies. This world necessarily has a certain continuity with the upper motions: consequently all its power and order is derived from them. (For the originating principle of all motion is the [25] first cause. Besides, that element is eternal and its motion has no limit in space, but is always complete; whereas all these other bodies have separate regions which limit one another.) So we must treat fire and earth and the elements like them as the material causes of the [30] events in this world (meaning by material what is subject and is affected), but must assign causality in the sense of the originating principle of motion to the influence of the eternally moving bodies.

3

Let us first recall our original principles and the distinctions already drawn and then explain [35] the 'milky way' and comets and the other phenomena akin to these.

Fire, air, water, earth, we assert, originate **339ᵇ** from one another, and each of them exists potentially in each, as all things do that can be resolved into a common and ultimate substrate.

The first difficulty is raised by what is called the air. What are we to take its nature to be in [5] the world surrounding the earth? And what is its position relatively to the other physical elements. (For there is no question as to the relation of the bulk of the earth to the size of the bodies which exist around it, since astronomical demonstrations have by this time proved to us that it is actually far smaller than some individual stars. As for the water, it is [10] not observed to exist collectively and separately, nor can it do so apart from that volume of it which has its seat about the earth: the sea, that is, and rivers, which we can see, and any subterranean water that may be hidden from our observation.) The question is really about that which lies between the earth and the nearest stars. Are we to consider it to be one kind [15] of body or more than one? And if more than one, how many are there and what are the bounds of their regions?

We have already described and characterized the first element, and explained that the whole world of the upper motions is full of that body.[1]

[20] This is an opinion we are not alone in holding: it appears to be an old assumption and one which men have held in the past, for the word ether has long been used to denote that element. Anaxagoras, it is true, seems to me to think that the word means the same as fire. For he thought that the upper regions were full of fire, and that men referred to those regions when they spoke of ether. In the latter [25] point he was right, for men seem to have assumed that a body that was eternally in motion was also divine in nature; and, as such a body was different from any of the terrestrial elements, they determined to call it 'ether'.

For the same opinions appear in cycles among men not once nor twice, but infinitely often.

[30] Now there are some who maintain that not only the bodies in motion but that which contains them is pure fire, and the interval between the earth and the stars air: but if they had considered what is now satisfactorily established by mathematics, they might have given up this puerile opinion. For it is altogether childish to suppose that the moving [35] bodies are all of them of a small size, because they seem so to us, looking at them from the earth.

This a matter which we have already discussed in our treatment of the upper region, but we may return to the point now.

340ᵃ If the intervals were full of fire and the bodies consisted of fire every one of the other elements would long ago have vanished.

However, they cannot simply be said to be full of air either; for even if there were two elements to fill the space between the earth and the heavens, the air would far exceed the quantity required to maintain its proper proportion [5] to the other elements. For the bulk of the

[1] *On the Heavens,* 1. 3.

earth (which includes the whole volume of water) is infinitesimal in comparison with the whole world that surrounds it. Now we find that the excess in volume is not proportionate- [10] ly great where water dissolves into air or air into fire. Whereas the *proportion* between any given small quantity of water and the air that is generated from it ought to hold good between the total amount of air and the total amount of water. Nor does it make any difference if any one denies that the elements *originate from one another,* but asserts that they [15] are equal in power. For on this view it is certain amounts of each that are equal in power, just as would be the case if they actually *originated from one another.*

So it is clear that neither air nor fire alone fills the intermediate space.

It remains to explain, after a preliminary discussion of difficulties, the relation of the two elements air and fire to the position of the first [20] element, and the reason why the stars in the upper region impart heat to the earth and its neighbourhood. Let us first treat of the air, as we proposed, and then go on to these questions.

Since water is generated from air, and air from water, why are clouds not formed in the [25] upper air? They ought to form there the more, the further from the earth and the colder that region is. For it is neither appreciably near to the heat of the stars, nor to the rays reflected [30] from the earth. It is these that dissolve any formation by their heat and so prevent clouds from forming near the earth. For clouds gather at the point where the reflected rays disperse in the infinity of space and are lost. To explain this we must suppose either that it is not all air from which water is generated, or, if it is produced from all air alike, that what immediately surrounds the earth is not mere air, but a sort of vapour, and that its vaporous nature is [35] the reason why it condenses back to water again. But if the whole of that vast region is vapour, the amount of air and of water will be disproportionately great. For the spaces left by the heavenly bodies must be filled by some element. This cannot be fire, for then all the rest would have been dried up. Consequently, what fills it must be air and the water that surrounds the whole earth—vapour being water dissolved.

After this exposition of the difficulties involved, let us go on to lay down the truth, with [5] a view at once to what follows and to what has already been said. The upper region as far as the moon we affirm to consist of a body distinct both from fire and from air, but varying [10] in degree of purity and in kind, especially towards its limit on the side of the air, and of the world surrounding the earth. Now the circular motion of the first element and of the bodies it contains dissolves, and inflames by its motion, whatever part of the lower world is nearest to it, and so generates heat. From another point of view we may look at the motion [15] as follows. The body that lies below the circular motion of the heavens is, in a sort, matter, and is potentially hot, cold, dry, moist, and possessed of whatever other qualities are derived from these. But it actually acquires or retains one of these in virtue of motion or rest, the cause and principle of which has already been explained.[1] So at the centre and round it [20] we get earth and water, the heaviest and coldest elements, by themselves; round them and contiguous with them, air and what we commonly call fire. It is not really fire, for fire is an excess of heat and a sort of ebullition; but in reality, of what we call air, the part sur- [25] rounding the earth is moist and warm, because it contains both vapour and a dry exhalation from the earth. But the next part, above that, is warm and dry. For vapour is naturally moist and cold, but the exhalation warm and dry; and vapour is potentially like water, the exhalation potentially like fire. So we must take the reason why clouds are not [30] formed in the upper region to be this: that it is filled not with mere air but rather with a sort of fire.

However, it may well be that the formation of clouds in that upper region is also prevented by the circular motion. For the air round the earth is necessarily all of it in motion, except [35] that which is cut off inside the circumference which makes the earth a complete sphere. In the case of winds it is actually observable that they originate in marshy districts of the earth; and they do not seem to blow above the level of the highest mountains. It is the revolution of the heaven which carries the air with it and causes its circular motion, fire being continuous with the upper element and air with fire. Thus its motion is a second reason why that air is not condensed into water.

[5] But whenever a particle of air grows heavy, the warmth in it is squeezed out into the upper region and it sinks, and other particles in turn are carried up together with the fiery exhalation. Thus the one region is always full of air and the other of fire, and each of them is perpetually in a state of change.

[10] So much to explain why clouds are not formed and why the air is not condensed into water, and what account must be given of the space between the stars and the earth, and what is the body that fills it.

As for the heat derived from the sun, the right place for a special and scientific account of it is in the treatise about sense, since heat is [15] an affection of sense, but we may now explain how it can be produced by the heavenly bodies which are not themselves hot.

We see that motion is able to dissolve and inflame the air; indeed, moving bodies are often actually found to melt. Now the sun's motion alone is sufficient to account for the origin of [20] terrestrial warmth and heat. For a motion that is to have this effect must be rapid and near, and that of the stars is rapid but distant, while that of the moon is near but slow, whereas the sun's motion combines both conditions in a sufficient degree. That most heat should be [25] generated where the sun is present is easy to understand if we consider the analogy of terrestrial phenomena, for here, too, it is the air that is nearest to a thing in rapid motion which is heated most. This is just what we should expect, as it is the nearest air that is most dissolved by the motion of a solid body.

[30] This then is one reason why heat reaches our world. Another is that the fire surrounding the air is often scattered by the motion of the heavens and driven downwards in spite of itself.

Shooting-stars further suffice to prove that the celestial sphere is not hot or fiery: for they do not occur in that upper region but below: yet the more and the faster a thing moves, [35] the more apt it is to take fire. Besides, the sun, which most of all the stars is considered to be hot, is really white and not fiery in colour.

4

Having determined these principles let us explain the cause of the appearance in the sky of burning flames and of shooting-stars, and of 'torches', and 'goats', as some people call them. All these phenomena are one and the [5] same thing, and are due to the same cause, the difference between them being one of degree.

The explanation of these and many other phenomena is this. When the sun warms the

---
[1] *On Generation and Corruption*, II. 10.

earth the evaporation which takes place is necessarily of two kinds, not of one only as some think. One kind is rather of the nature of vapour, the other of the nature of a windy exhalation. That which rises from the moisture contained in the earth and on its surface is vapour, [10] while that rising from the earth itself, which is dry, is like smoke. Of these the windy exhalation, being warm, rises above the moister vapour, which is heavy and sinks below the other. Hence the world surrounding the earth is ordered as follows. First below the circular motion comes the warm and dry element, which we call fire, for there is no word fully [15] adequate to every state of the fumid evaporation: but we must use this terminology since this element is the most inflammable of all bodies. Below this comes air. We must think of what we just called fire as being spread [20] round the terrestrial sphere on the outside like a kind of fuel, so that a little motion often makes it burst into flame just as smoke does: for flame is the ebullition of a dry exhalation. So whenever the circular motion stirs this stuff up in any way, it catches fire at the point at which it is most inflammable. The result differs according to the disposition and quantity [25] of the combustible material. If this is broad and long, we often see a flame burning as in a field of stubble: if it burns lengthwise only, we see what are called 'torches' and 'goats' and shooting-stars. Now when the inflammable material is longer than it is broad [30] sometimes it seems to throw off sparks as it burns. (This happens because matter catches fire at the sides in small portions but continuously with the main body.) Then it is called a 'goat'. When this does not happen it is a 'torch'. But if the whole length of the exhalation is scattered in small parts and in many directions and in breadth and depth alike, we [35] get what are called shooting-stars.

The cause of these shooting-stars is sometimes the motion which ignites the exhalation. 342ª At other times the air is condensed by cold and squeezes out and ejects the hot element; making their motion look more like that of a thing thrown than like a running fire. For the question might be raised whether the 'shooting' of a 'star' is the same thing as when [5] you put an exhalation below a lamp and it lights the lower lamp from the flame above. For here too the flame passes wonderfully quickly and looks like a thing thrown, and not as if one thing after another caught fire. Or is a 'star' when it 'shoots' a single body that is thrown? Apparently both cases occur: sometimes it is like the flame from the lamp and sometimes bodies are projected by being [10] squeezed out (like fruit stones from one's fingers) and so are seen to fall into the sea and on the dry land, both by night and by day when the sky is clear. They are thrown downwards because the condensation which propels them inclines downwards. Thunderbolts fall downwards for the same reason: their origin [15] is never combustion but ejection under pressure, since naturally all heat tends upwards.

When the phenomenon is formed in the upper region it is due to the combustion of the exhalation. When it takes place at a lower level it is due to the ejection of the exhalation by the condensing and cooling of the moister evapo- [20] ration: for this latter as it condenses and inclines downward contracts, and thrusts out the hot element and causes it to be thrown downwards. The motion is upwards or downwards or sideways according to the way in which the evaporation lies, and its disposition in respect of breadth and depth. In most cases the direction is sideways because two motions [25] are involved, a compulsory motion downwards and a natural motion upwards, and under these circumstances an object always moves obliquely. Hence the motion of 'shooting-stars' is generally oblique.

So the material cause of all these phenomena is the exhalation, the efficient cause sometimes the [30] upper motion, sometimes the contraction and condensation of the air. Further, all these things happen below the moon. This is shown by their apparent speed, which is equal to that of things thrown by us; for it is because they are close to us, that these latter seem far to exceed in speed the stars, the sun, and the moon.

5

[35] Sometimes on a fine night we see a variety of appearances that form in the sky: 'chasms' for instance and 'trenches' and blood-red colours. These, too, have the same cause. For we 342ᵇ have seen that the upper air condenses into an inflammable condition and that the combustion sometimes takes on the appearance of a burning flame, sometimes that of moving [5] torches and stars. So it is not surprising that this same air when condensing should assume a variety of colours. For a weak light shining through a dense air, and the air when it acts as a mirror, will cause all kinds of colours to appear, but especially crimson and pur-

ple. For these colours generally appear when fire-colour and white are combined by superposition. Thus on a hot day, or through a smoky [10] medium, the stars when they rise and set look crimson. The light will also create colours by reflection when the mirror is such as to reflect colour only and not shape.

These appearances do not persist long, because the condensation of the air is transient. [15] 'Chasms' get their appearance of depth from light breaking out of a dark blue or black mass of air. When the process of condensation goes further in such a case we often find 'torches' ejected. When the 'chasm' contracts it presents the appearance of a 'trench'.

In general, white in contrast with black creates a variety of colours; like flame, for instance, through a medium of smoke. But by [20] day the sun obscures them, and, with the exception of crimson, the colours are not seen at night because they are dark.

These then must be taken to be the causes of 'shooting-stars' and the phenomena of combustion and also of the other transient appearances of this kind.

6

[25] Let us go on to explain the nature of comets and the 'milky way', after a preliminary discussion of the views of others.

Anaxagoras and Democritus declare that comets are a conjunction of the planets approaching one another and so appearing to touch one another.

[30] Some of the Italians called Pythagoreans say that the comet is one of the planets, but that it appears at great intervals of time and only rises a little above the horizon. This is the case with Mercury too; because it only rises a little above the horizon it often fails to be seen [35] and consequently appears at great intervals of time.

A view like theirs was also expressed by Hippocrates of Chios and his pupil Aeschylus. 343ª Only they say that the tail does not belong to the comet iself, but is occasionally assumed by it on its course in certain situations, when our sight is reflected to the sun from the moisture attracted by the comet. It appears at greater intervals than the other stars because it [5] is slowest to get clear of the sun and has been left behind by the sun to the extent of the whole of its circle before it reappears at the same point. It gets clear of the sun both towards the north and towards the south. In the space between the tropics it does not draw water to itself because that region is dried up by [10] the sun on its course. When it moves towards the south it has no lack of the necessary moisture, but because the segment of its circle which is above the horizon is small, and that below it many times as large, it is impossible for the sun to be reflected to our sight, either [15] when it approaches the southern tropic, or at the summer solstice. Hence in these regions it does not develop a tail at all. But when it is visible in the north it assumes a tail because the arc above the horizon is large and that below it small. For under these circumstances there is nothing to prevent our vision [20] from being reflected to the sun.

These views involve impossibilities, some of which are common to all of them, while others are peculiar to some only.

This is the case, first, with those who say that the comet is one of the planets. For all the planets appear in the circle of the zodiac, [25] whereas many comets have been seen outside that circle. Again more comets than one have often appeared simultaneously. Besides, if their tail is due to reflection, as Aeschylus and Hippocrates say, this planet ought sometimes to be visible without a tail since, as they [30] say, it does not possess a tail in every place in which it appears. But, as a matter of fact, no planet has been observed besides the five. And all of them are often visible above the horizon together at the same time. Further, comets are often found to appear, as well when all the planets are visible as when some are not, but are obscured by the neighbourhood of the sun. [35] Moreover the statement that a comet only appears in the north, with the sun at the summer solstice, is not true either. The great comet which appeared at the time of the earthquake in Achaea and the tidal wave rose due west; and many have been known to appear in the south. Again in the archonship of Euclees, [5] son of Molon, at Athens there appeared a comet in the north in the month Gamelion, the sun being about the winter solstice. Yet they themselves admit that reflection over so great a space is an impossibility.

An objection that tells equally against those who hold this theory and those who say that comets are a coalescence of the planets is, first, the fact that some of the fixed stars too get a [10] tail. For this we must not only accept the authority of the Egyptians who assert it, but we have ourselves observed the fact. For a star in the thigh of the Dog had a tail, though a faint one. If you fixed your sight on it its light was dim, but if you just glanced at it, it appeared [15] brighter. Besides, all the comets that have been seen in our day have vanished without setting, gradually fading away above the horizon; and they have not left behind them either one or more stars. For instance the great comet we mentioned before[1] appeared to the west in winter in frosty weather when the sky was clear, in the archonship of Asteius. On the first [20] day it set before the sun and was then not seen. On the next day it was seen, being ever so little behind the sun and immediately setting. But its light extended over a third part of the sky like a leap, so that people called it a 'path'. [25] This comet receded as far as Orion's belt and there dissolved. Democritus however, insists upon the truth of his view and affirms that certain stars have been seen when comets dissolve. But on his theory this ought not to occur occasionally but always. Besides, the Egyptians affirm that conjunctions of the planets with one another, and with the fixed stars, take place, [30] and we have ourselves observed Jupiter coinciding with one of the stars in the Twins and hiding it, and yet no comet was formed. Further, we can also give a rational proof of our point. It is true that some stars seem to be bigger than others, yet each one by itself looks indivisible. Consequently, just as, if they really [35] had been indivisible, their conjunction could not have created any greater magnitude, so now that they are not in fact indivisible but look as if they were, their conjunction will not make them look any bigger.

Enough has been said, without further argument, to show that the causes brought forward to explain comets are false.

7

[5] We consider a satisfactory explanation of phenomena inaccessible to observation to have been given when our account of them is free from impossibilities. The observations before us suggest the following account of the phenomena we are now considering. We know [10] that the dry and warm exhalation is the outermost part of the terrestrial world which falls below the circular motion. It, and a great part of the air that is continuous with it below, is carried round the earth by the motion of the circular revolution. In the course of this motion it often ignites wherever it may happen to be of the right consistency, and this we maintain [15] to be the cause of the 'shooting' of scattered 'stars'. We may say, then, that a comet is formed when the upper motion introduces into a gathering of this kind a fiery principle not of such excessive strength as to burn up much of the material quickly, nor so weak as soon to be extinguished, but stronger and capable of burn- [20] ing up much material, and when exhalation of the right consistency rises from below and meets it. The kind of comet varies according to the shape which the exhalation happens to take. If it is diffused equally on every side the star is said to be fringed, if it stretches out in one direction it is called bearded. We have seen that when a fiery principle of this kind [25] moves we seem to have a shooting-star: similarly when it stands still we seem to have a star standing still. We may compare these phenomena to a heap or mass of chaff into which a torch is thrust, or a spark thrown. That is what a shooting-star is like. The fuel is so inflammable that the fire runs through it [30] quickly in a line. Now if this fire were to persist instead of running through the fuel and perishing away, its course through the fuel would stop at the point where the latter was densest, and then the whole might begin to move. Such is a comet—like a shooting-star that contains its beginning and end in itself.

When the matter begins to gather in the lower region independently the comet appears by [35] itself. But when the exhalation is constituted by one of the fixed stars or the planets, owing to their motion, one of them becomes a comet. The fringe is not close to the stars themselves. Just as haloes appear to follow the sun and the moon as they move, and encircle [5] them, when the air is dense enough for them to form along under the sun's course, so too the fringe. It stands in the relation of a halo to the stars, except that the colour of the halo is due to reflection, whereas in the case of comets the colour is something that appears actually on them.

Now when this matter gathers in relation to [10] a star the comet necessarily appears to follow the same course as the star. But when the comet is formed independently it falls behind the motion of the universe, like the rest of the terrestrial world. It is this fact, that a comet often forms independently, indeed oftener than round one of the regular stars, that makes it impossible to maintain that a comet is a sort of [15] reflection, not indeed, as Hippocrates and his school say, to the sun, but to the very star it is alleged to accompany—in fact, a kind of halo in the pure fuel of fire.

As for the halo we shall explain its cause later.[1]

The fact that comets when frequent fore-[20] shadow wind and drought must be taken as an indication of their fiery constitution. For their origin is plainly due to the plentiful supply of that secretion. Hence the air is necessarily drier and the moist evaporation is so dissolved and dissipated by the quantity of the hot exhalation as not readily to condense into water. [25]—But this phenomenon too shall be explained more clearly later when the time comes to speak of the winds.—So when there are many comets and they are dense, it is as we say, and the years are clearly dry and windy. When they are fewer and fainter this effect does not appear in the same degree, though as a rule the [30] wind is found to be excessive either in duration or strength. For instance when the stone at Aegospotami fell out of the air—it had been carried up by a wind and fell down in the daytime—then too a comet happened to have appeared in the west. And at the time of the great [35] comet the winter was dry and north winds prevailed, and the wave was due to an opposition of winds. For in the gulf a north wind blew and outside it a violent south wind. Again in the archonship of Nicomachus a comet appeared for a few days about the equinoctial circle (this one had not risen in the west), and simultaneously with it there happened [5] the storm at Corinth.

That there are few comets and that they appear rarely and outside the tropic circles more than within them is due to the motion of the sun and the stars. For this motion does not only cause the hot principle to be secreted but also dissolves it when it is gathering. But the chief reason is that most of this stuff collects in [10] the region of the milky way.

8

Let us now explain the origin, cause, and nature of the milky way. And here too let us begin by discussing the statements of others on the subject.

(1) Of the so-called Pythagoreans some say that this is the path of one of the stars that fell [15] from heaven at the time of Phaethon's downfall. Others say that the sun used once to move in this circle and that this region was scorched or met with some other affection of this kind, because of the sun and its motion.

But it is absurd not to see that if this were the reason the circle of the Zodiac ought to be affected in the same way, and indeed more so [20] than that of the milky way, since not the sun only but all the planets move in it. We can see the whole of this circle (half of it being visible at any time of the night), but it shows no signs of any such affection except where a part of it touches the circle of the milky way.

[25] (2) Anaxagoras, Democritus, and their schools say that the milky way is the light of certain stars. For, they say, when the sun passes below the earth some of the stars are hidden from it. Now the light of those on which the sun shines is invisible, being obscured by the rays of the sun. But the milky way is the pecu-[30] liar light of those stars which are shaded by the earth from the sun's rays.

This, too, is obviously impossible. The milky way is always unchanged and among the same constellations (for it is clearly a greatest circle), whereas, since the sun does not remain in the same place, what is hidden from it differs at [35] different times. Consequently with the change of the sun's position the milky way ought to change its position too: but we find that this does not happen. Besides, if astronomical demonstrations are correct and the size of the sun is greater than that of the earth and the distance of the stars from the earth many times greater than that of the sun (just as the sun is further from the earth than the moon), then [5] the cone made by the rays of the sun would terminate at no great distance from the earth, and the shadow of the earth (what we call night) would not reach the stars. On the contrary, the sun shines on all the stars and the earth screens none of them.

[10] (3) There is a third theory about the milky way. Some say that it is a reflection of our sight to the sun, just as they say that the comet is.

But this too is impossible. For if the eye and the mirror and the whole of the object were severally at rest, then the same part of the image would appear at the same point in the mir-[15] ror. But if the mirror and the object move, keeping the same distance from the eye which is at rest, but at different rates of speed and so not always at the same interval from one another, then it is impossible for the same image always to appear in the same part of the mirror. Now the constellations included in the circle of the milky way move; and so does the sun, the object to which our sight is reflected; but we [20] stand still. And the distance of those two from us is constant and uniform, but their distance from one another varies. For the Dolphin

[1] III. 2.

sometimes rises at midnight, sometimes in the morning. But in each case the same parts of the milky way are found near it. But if it were a reflection and not a genuine affection of these regions, this ought not to be the case.

[25] Again, we can see the milky way reflected at night in water and similar mirrors. But under these circumstances it is impossible for our sight to be reflected to the sun.

These considerations show that the milky way is not the path of one of the planets, nor the light of imperceptible stars, nor a reflection. [30] And those are the chief theories handed down by others hitherto.

Let us recall our fundamental principle and then explain our views. We have already laid down[1] that the outermost part of what is called the air is potentially fire and that therefore when the air is dissolved by motion, there is separated off a kind of matter—and of this matter we assert that comets consist. We must [35] suppose that what happens is the same as in the case of the comets when the matter does 346ᵃ not form independently but is formed by one of the fixed stars or the planets. Then these stars appear to be fringed, because matter of this kind follows their course. In the same way, a certain kind of matter follows the sun, and [5] we explain the halo as a reflection from it when the air is of the right constitution. Now we must assume that what happens in the case of the stars severally happens in the case of the whole of the heavens and all the upper motion. For it is natural to suppose that, if the motion of a single star excites a flame, that of all the stars should have a similar result, and espe- [10] cially in that region in which the stars are biggest and most numerous and nearest to one another. Now the circle of the zodiac dissolves this kind of matter because of the motion of the sun and the planets, and for this reason most comets are found outside the tropic circles. Again, no fringe appears round the sun or [15] moon: for they dissolve such matter too quickly to admit of its formation. But this circle in which the milky way appears to our sight is the greatest circle, and its position is such that it extends far outside the tropic circles. Besides the region is full of the biggest and brightest constellations and also of what [20] are called 'scattered' stars (you have only to look to see this clearly). So for these reasons all this matter is continually and ceaselessly collecting there. A proof of the theory is this: In the circle itself the light is stronger in that half where the milky way is divided, and in it the constellations are more numerous and closer to [25] one another than in the other half; which shows that the cause of the light is the motion of the constellations and nothing else. For if it is found in the circle in which there are most constellations and at that point in the circle at which they are densest and contain the biggest and the most stars, it is natural to suppose that [30] they are the true cause of the affection in question. The circle and the constellations in it may be seen in the diagram.[2] The so-called 'scattered' stars it is not possible to set down in the same way on the sphere because none of them have an evident permanent position; but if you look up to the sky the point is clear. For [35] in this circle alone are the intervals full of these stars: in the other circles there are ob- 346ᵇ vious gaps. Hence if we accept the cause assigned for the appearance of comets as plausible we must assume that the same kind of thing holds good of the milky way. For the fringe which in the former case is an affection of a single star here forms in the same way in [5] relation to a whole circle. So if we are to define the milky way we may call it 'a fringe attaching to the greatest circle, and due to the matter secreted'. This, as we said before,[3] explains why there are few comets and why they appear rarely; it is because at each revolution of the heavens this matter has always been and is always being separated off and gathered into this region.

[10] We have now explained the phenomena that occur in that part of the terrestrial world which is continuous with the motions of the heavens, namely, shooting-stars and the burning flame, comets and the milky way, these be- [15] ing the chief affections that appear in that region.

9

Let us go on to treat of the region which follows next in order after this and which immediately surrounds the earth. It is the region common to water and air, and the processes attending the formation of water above take place in it. We must consider the principles and causes of all these phenomena too as before. [20] The efficient and chief and first cause is the circle in which the sun moves. For the sun

---

[1] 340ᵇ 4-32.

[2] Aristotle must be supposed to have illustrated his theory here by a diagram of the milky way, but the Greek commentators have not preserved any tradition of the particular diagram used.

[3] 345ᵃ 7.

as it approaches or recedes, obviously causes dissipation and condensation and so gives rise to generation and destruction. Now the earth remains but the moisture surrounding it is made to evaporate by the sun's rays and the [25] other heat from above, and rises. But when the heat which was raising it leaves it, in part dispersing to the higher region, in part quenched through rising so far into the upper air, then the vapour cools because its heat is gone and because the place is cold, and condenses again and turns from air into water. And after the water has formed it falls down again to the earth.

The exhalation of water is vapour: air condensing into water is cloud. Mist is what is left over when a cloud condenses into water, and is therefore rather a sign of fine weather than of rain; for mist might be called a barren cloud. [35] So we get a circular process that follows the course of the sun. For according as the sun moves to this side or that, the moisture in this process rises or falls. We must think of it as a river flowing up and down in a circle and made up partly of air, partly of water. When the sun is near, the stream of vapour flows upwards; when it recedes, the stream of [5] water flows down: and the order of sequence, at all events, in this process always remains the same. So if 'Oceanus' had some secret meaning in early writers, perhaps they may have meant this river that flows in a circle about the earth.

So the moisture is always raised by the heat and descends to the earth again when it gets [10] cold. These processes and, in some cases, their varieties are distinguished by special names. When the water falls in small drops it is called a drizzle; when the drops are larger it is rain.

10

Some of the vapour that is formed by day does not rise high because the ratio of the fire that is raising it to the water that is being [15] raised is small. When this cools and descends at night it is called dew and hoar-frost. When the vapour is frozen before it has condensed to water again it is hoar-frost; and this appears in winter and is commoner in cold places. It is dew when the vapour has condensed into water and the heat is not so great as to dry up the moisture that has been raised, [20] nor the cold sufficient (owing to the warmth of the climate or season) for the vapour itself to freeze. For dew is more commonly found when the season or the place is warm, whereas the opposite, as has been said, is the case with hoar-frost. For obviously vapour is warmer than water, having still the fire that [25] raised it: consequently more cold is needed to freeze it.

Both dew and hoar-frost are found when the sky is clear and there is no wind. For the vapour could not be raised unless the sky were clear, and if a wind were blowing it could not condense.

The fact that hoar-frost is not found on mountains contributes to prove that these phenomena occur because the vapour does not rise [30] high. One reason for this is that it rises from hollow and watery places, so that the heat that is raising it, bearing as it were too heavy a burden cannot lift it to a great height but soon lets it fall again. A second reason is that the motion of the air is more pronounced at a height, and this dissolves a gathering of this kind.

[35] Everywhere, except in Pontus, dew is found with south winds and not with north winds. There the opposite is the case and it is found with north winds and not with south. The reason is the same as that which explains why dew is found in warm weather and not in cold. For the south wind brings warm, and the north, wintry weather. For the north wind is cold and so quenches the heat of the evaporation. But in Pontus the south wind does not bring warmth enough to cause evapora- [5] tion, whereas the coldness of the north wind concentrates the heat by a sort of recoil, so that there is more evaporation and not less. This is a thing which we can often observe in other places too. Wells, for instance, give off more vapour in a north than in a south wind. Only the north winds quench the heat before [10] any considerable quantity of vapour has gathered, while in a south wind the evaporation is allowed to accumulate.

Water, once formed, does not freeze on the surface of the earth, in the way that it does in the region of the clouds.

11

From the latter there fall three bodies condensed by cold, namely rain, snow, hail. Two of these correspond to the phenomena on the lower level and are due to the same causes, [15] differing from them only in degree and quantity.

Snow and hoar-frost are one and the same thing, and so are rain and dew: only there is a great deal of the former and little of the latter. For rain is due to the cooling of a great amount of vapour, for the region from which and the time during which the vapour is collected are [20] considerable. But of dew there is little: for the vapour collects for it in a single day and from a small area, as its quick formation and scanty quantity show.

The relation of hoar-frost and snow is the same: when cloud freezes there is snow, when vapour freezes there is hoar-frost. Hence snow is a sign of a cold season or country. For a great [25] deal of heat is still present and unless the cold were overpowering it the cloud would not freeze. For there still survives in it a great deal of the heat which caused the moisture to rise as vapour from the earth.

Hail on the other hand is found in the upper region, but the corresponding phenomenon in the vaporous region near the earth is lack- [30] ing. For, as we said, to snow in the upper region corresponds hoar-frost in the lower, and to rain in the upper region, dew in the lower. But there is nothing here to correspond to hail in the upper region. Why this is so will be clear when we have explained the nature of hail.

12

But we must go on to collect the facts bear- [35] ing on the origin of it, both those which raise no difficulties and those which seem paradoxical.

348ª Hail is ice, and water freezes in winter; yet hailstorms occur chiefly in spring and autumn and less often in the late summer, but rarely in winter and then only when the cold is less intense. And in general hailstorms occur in warmer, and snow in colder places. Again, [5] there is a difficulty about water freezing in the upper region. It cannot have frozen before becoming water: and water cannot remain suspended in the air for any space of time. Nor can we say that the case is like that of particles of moisture which are carried up owing to their small size and rest on the air [10] (the water swimming on the air just as small particles of earth and gold often swim on water). In that case large drops are formed by the union of many small, and so fall down. This cannot take place in the case of hail, since solid bodies cannot coalesce like liquid ones. Clearly then drops of that size were suspended in the air or else they could not have been so large when frozen.

Some think that the cause and origin of hail [15] is this. The cloud is thrust up into the upper atmosphere, which is colder because the reflection of the sun's rays from the earth ceases there, and upon its arrival there the water freezes. They think that this explains why hailstorms are commoner in summer and in warm countries; the heat is greater and it thrusts the clouds further up from the earth. [20] But the fact is that hail does not occur at all at a great height: yet it ought to do so, on their theory, just as we see that snow falls most on high mountains. Again clouds have often been observed moving with a great noise close [25] to the earth, terrifying those who heard and saw them as portents of some catastrophe. Sometimes, too, when such clouds have been seen, without any noise, there follows a violent hailstorm, and the stones are of incredible size, and angular in shape. This shows that they have not been falling for long and that they were frozen near to the earth, and not as [30] that theory would have it. Moreover, where the hailstones are large, the cause of their freezing must be present in the highest degree: for hail is ice as every one can see. Now those hailstones are large which are angular in shape. And this shows that they froze close to [35] the earth, for those that fall far are worn away by the length of their fall and become round and smaller in size.

348ᵇ It clearly follows that the congelation does not take place because the cloud is thrust up into the cold upper region.

Now we see that warm and cold react upon one another by recoil. Hence in warm weather the lower parts of the earth are cold and in a [5] frost they are warm. The same thing, we must suppose, happens in the air, so that in the warmer seasons the cold is concentrated by the surrounding heat and causes the cloud to go over into water suddenly. (For this reason rain-drops are much larger on warm days than in winter, and showers more violent. A shower [10] is said to be more violent in proportion as the water comes down in a body, and this happens when the condensation takes place quickly,—though this is just the opposite of what Anaxagoras says. He says that this happens when the cloud has risen into the cold air; whereas we say that it happens when the cloud has descended into the warm air, and that the more the further the cloud has de- [15] scended). But when the cold has been concentrated within still more by the outer heat, it freezes the water it has formed and there is hail. We get hail when the process of freezing is quicker than the descent of the water. For if the water falls in a certain time and the cold is sufficient to freeze it in less, [20] there is no difficulty about its having frozen in the air, provided that the freezing takes place in a shorter time than its fall. The nearer to the earth, and the more suddenly, this process takes place, the more violent is the rain that results and the larger the raindrops [25] and the hailstones because of the shortness of their fall. For the same reason large raindrops do not fall thickly. Hail is rarer in summer than in spring and autumn, though commoner than in winter, because the air is drier in summer, whereas in spring it is still moist, and in autumn it is beginning to grow moist. It is for the same reason that hailstorms sometimes occur in the late summer as we have said.[1]

[30] The fact that the water has previously been warmed contributes to its freezing quickly: for so it cools sooner. Hence many people, when they want to cool hot water quickly, begin by putting it in the sun. So the inhabitants [35] of Pontus when they encamp on the ice to fish (they cut a hole in the ice and then fish) pour warm water round their reeds that it may 349ª freeze the quicker, for they use the ice like lead to fix the reeds. Now it is in hot countries and seasons that the water which forms soon grows warm.

It is for the same reason that rain falls in [5] summer and not in winter in Arabia and Ethiopia too, and that in torrents and repeatedly on the same day. For the concentration or recoil due to the extreme heat of the country cools the clouds quickly.

[10] So much for an account of the nature and causes of rain, dew, snow, hoar-frost, and hail.

13

Let us explain the nature of winds, and all windy vapours, also of rivers and of the sea. But here, too, we must first discuss the difficulties involved: for, as in other matters, so in [15] this no theory has been handed down to us that the most ordinary man could not have thought of.

Some say that what is called air, when it is in motion and flows, is wind, and that this same air when it condenses again becomes cloud and water, implying that the nature of wind and water is the same. So they define wind as [20] a motion of the air. Hence some, wishing to say a clever thing, assert that all the winds

[1]ª 1.

are one wind, because the air that moves is in fact all of it one and the same; they maintain that the winds appear to differ owing to the region from which the air may happen to flow [25] on each occasion, but really do not differ at all. This is just like thinking that all rivers are one and the same river, and the ordinary unscientific view is better than a scientific theory like this. If all rivers flow from one source, and the same is true in the case of the [30] winds, there might be some truth in this theory; but if it is no more true in the one case than in the other, this ingenious idea is plainly false. What requires investigation is this: the nature of wind and how it originates, its efficient cause and whence they derive their source; whether one ought to think of the wind as issuing from a sort of vessel and flowing [35] until the vessel is empty, as if let out of a wineskin, or, as painters represent the winds, as drawing their source from themselves.

We find analogous views about the origin of rivers. It is thought that the water is raised by the sun and descends in rain and gathers below the earth and so flows from a great reservoir, all the rivers from one, or each from [5] a different one. No water at all is generated, but the volume of the rivers consists of the water that is gathered into such reservoirs in winter. Hence rivers are always fuller in winter than in summer, and some are perennial, others not. Rivers are perennial where the [10] reservoir is large and so enough water has collected in it to last out and not be used up before the winter rain returns. Where the reservoirs are smaller there is less water in the rivers, and they are dried up and their vessel empty before the fresh rain comes on.

[15] But if any one will picture to himself a reservoir adequate to the water that is continuously flowing day by day, and consider the amount of the water, it is obvious that a receptacle that is to contain all the water that flows in the year would be larger than the earth, or, at any rate, not much smaller.

[20] Though it is evident that many reservoirs of this kind do exist in many parts of the earth, yet it is unreasonable for any one to refuse to admit that air becomes water in the earth for the same reason as it does above it. If the cold causes the vaporous air to condense into water above the earth we must suppose the cold in the earth to produce this same ef- [25] fect, and recognize that there not only exists in it and flows out of it actually formed

water, but that water is continually forming in it too.

Again, even in the case of the water that is not being formed from day to day but exists as such, we must not suppose as some do that [30] rivers have their source in definite subterranean lakes. On the contrary, just as above the earth small drops form and these join others, till finally the water descends in a body as rain, so too we must suppose that in the earth the water at first trickles together little by little, and that the sources of the rivers drip, [35] as it were, out of the earth and then unite. This is proved by facts. When men construct an aqueduct they collect the water in pipes and trenches, as if the earth in the higher ground were sweating the water out. Hence, too, the head-waters of rivers are found to flow from mountains, and from the greatest mountains there flow the most numerous and [5] greatest rivers. Again, most springs are in the neighbourhood of mountains and of high ground, whereas if we except rivers, water rarely appears in the plains. For mountains and high ground, suspended over the country like a saturated sponge, make the water ooze out and trickle together in minute quantities but in many places. They receive a great deal of [10] water falling as rain (for it makes no difference whether a spongy receptacle is concave and turned up or convex and turned down: in either case it will contain the same volume of matter) and they also cool the vapour that rises and condense it back into water.

Hence, as we said, we find that the greatest [15] rivers flow from the greatest mountains. This can be seen by looking at itineraries: what is recorded in them consists either of things which the writer has seen himself or of such as he has compiled after inquiry from those who have seen them.

In Asia we find that the most numerous and [20] greatest rivers flow from the mountain called Parnassus, admittedly the greatest of all mountains towards the south-east. When you have crossed it you see the outer ocean, the further limit of which is unknown to the dwellers in our world. Besides other rivers there flow from it the Bactrus, the Choaspes, the Araxes: from the last a branch separates off and flows [25] into lake Maeotis as the Tanais. From it, too, flows the Indus, the volume of whose stream is greatest of all rivers. From the Caucasus flows the Phasis, and very many other great rivers besides. Now the Caucasus is the greatest of the mountains that lie to the north-[30] east, both as regards its extent and its height. A proof of its height is the fact that it can be seen from the so-called 'deeps' and from the entrance to the lake. Again, the sun shines on its peaks for a third part of the night before sunrise and again after sunset. Its extent is proved by the fact that though it contains many inhabitable regions which are occupied by many nations and in which there are said [35] to be great lakes, yet they say that all these regions are visible up to the last peak. From Pyrene (this is a mountain towards the west in Celtice) there flow the Istrus and the Tartessus. The latter flows outside the pillars, while the Istrus flows through all Europe into the Euxine. Most of the remaining rivers flow [5] northwards from the Hercynian mountains, which are the greatest in height and extent about that region. In the extreme north, beyond furthest Scythia, are the mountains called Rhipae. The stories about their size are altogether too fabulous: however, they say that the most and (after the Istrus) the greatest [10] rivers flow from them. So, too, in Libya there flow from the Aethiopian mountains the Aegon and the Nyses; and from the so-called Silver Mountain the two greatest of named rivers, the river called Chremetes that flows [15] into the outer ocean, and the main source of the Nile. Of the rivers in the Greek world, the Achelous flows from Pindus, the Inachus from the same mountain; the Strymon, the Nestus, and the Hebrus all three from Scombrus; many rivers, too, flow from Rhodope.

All other rivers would be found to flow in [20] the same way, but we have mentioned these as examples. Even where rivers flow from marshes, the marshes in almost every case are found to lie below mountains or gradually rising ground.

It is clear then that we must not suppose rivers to originate from definite reservoirs: for the whole earth, we might almost say, would [25] not be sufficient (any more than the region of the clouds would be) if we were to suppose that they were fed by actually existing water only and it were not the case that as some water passed out of existence some more came into existence, but rivers always drew their stream from an existing store. Secondly, the fact that rivers rise at the foot of mountains proves that a place transmits the water it contains by gradual percolation of many drops, little by little, and that this is how the sources [30] of rivers originate. However, there is nothing impossible about the existence of such places containing a quantity of water like lakes: only they cannot be big enough to produce the supposed effect. To think that they are is just as absurd as if one were to suppose that rivers drew all their water from the sources we see (for most rivers do flow from springs). So it is no more reasonable to suppose those lakes to contain the whole volume of water than these springs.

351ᵃ That there exist such chasms and cavities in the earth we are taught by the rivers that are swallowed up. They are found in many parts of the earth: in the Peloponnesus, for instance, there are many such rivers in Arcadia. The reason is that Arcadia is mountainous and [5] there are no channels from its valleys to the sea. So these places get full of water, and this, having no outlet, under the pressure of the water that is added above, finds a way out for itself underground. In Greece this kind of thing happens on quite a small scale, but the lake at the foot of the Caucasus, which the inhabitants of these parts call a sea, is consider-[10] able. Many great rivers fall into it and it has no visible outlet but issues below the earth off the land of the Coraxi about the so-called 'deeps of Pontus'. This is a place of unfathomable depth in the sea: at any rate no one has yet been able to find bottom there by sounding. At this spot, about three hundred stadia from [15] land, there comes up sweet water over a large area, not all of it together but in three places. And in Liguria a river equal in size to the Rhodanus is swallowed up and appears again elsewhere: the Rhodanus being a navigable river.

14

The same parts of the earth are not always [20] moist or dry, but they change according as rivers come into existence and dry up. And so the relation of land to sea changes too and a place does not always remain land or sea throughout all time, but where there was dry land there comes to be sea, and where there is now sea, there one day comes to be dry land. [25] But we must suppose these changes to follow some order and cycle. The principle and cause of these changes is that the interior of the earth grows and decays, like the bodies of plants and animals. Only in the case of these latter the process does not go on by parts, but [30] each of them necessarily grows or decays as a whole, whereas it does go on by parts in the case of the earth. Here the causes are cold and heat, which increase and diminish on account of the sun and its course. It is owing to them that the parts of the earth come to have a different character, that some parts remain moist for a certain time, and then dry up and [35] grow old, while other parts in their turn are filled with life and moisture. Now when places become drier the springs necessarily 351ᵇ give out, and when this happens the rivers first decrease in size and then finally become dry; and when rivers change and disappear in one part and come into existence correspondingly in another, the sea must needs be affected.

[5] If the sea was once pushed out by rivers and encroached upon the land anywhere, it necessarily leaves that place dry when it recedes; again, if the dry land has encroached on the sea at all by a process of silting set up by the rivers when at their full, the time must come when this place will be flooded again.

But the whole vital process of the earth takes place so gradually and in periods of time which [10] are so immense compared with the length of our life, that these changes are not observed, and before their course can be recorded from beginning to end whole nations perish and are destroyed. Of such destructions the most utter and sudden are due to wars; but pestilence or famine cause them too. Famines, again, are [15] either sudden and severe or else gradual. In the latter case the disappearance of a nation is not noticed because some leave the country while others remain; and this goes on until the land is unable to maintain any inhabitants at all. So a long period of time is likely to [20] elapse from the first departure to the last, and no one remembers and the lapse of time destroys all record even before the last inhabitants have disappeared. In the same way a nation must be supposed to lose account of the time when it first settled in a land that was changing from a marshy and watery state and [25] becoming dry. Here, too, the change is gradual and lasts a long time and men do not remember who came first, or when, or what the land was like when they came. This has been the case with Egypt. Here it is obvious that the land is continually getting drier and that the whole country is a deposit of the river [30] Nile. But because the neighbouring peoples settled in the land gradually as the marshes dried, the lapse of time has hidden the beginning of the process. However, all the mouths of the Nile, with the single exception of that at Canopus, are obviously artificial and not natural. And Egypt was nothing more than [35] what is called Thebes, as Homer, too, shows, modern though he is in relation to such changes. For Thebes is the place that he mentions; which implies that Memphis did not yet exist, or at any rate was not as important as it is now. That this should be so is natural, since the lower land came to be inhabited later than that which lay higher. For the parts that lie nearer to the place where the river is depositing the silt are necessarily marshy for a longer time since the water always lies most [5] in the newly formed land. But in time this land changes its character, and in its turn enjoys a period of prosperity. For these places dry up and come to be in good condition while the places that were formerly well-tempered some day grow excessively dry and deteriorate. This happened to the land of Argos and Mycenae in Greece. In the time of the Trojan wars the [10] Argive land was marshy and could only support a small population, whereas the land of Mycenae was in good condition (and for this reason Mycenae was the superior). But now the opposite is the case, for the reason we have mentioned: the land of Mycenae has become completely dry and barren, while the Argive land that was formerly barren owing to the water has now become fruitful. Now the same process that has taken place in this [15] small district must be supposed to be going on over whole countries and on a large scale.

Men whose outlook is narrow suppose the cause of such events to be change in the universe, in the sense of a coming to be of the world as a whole. Hence they say that the sea [20] is being dried up and is growing less, because this is observed to have happened in more places now than formerly. But this is only partially true. It is true that many places are now dry, that formerly were covered with water. But the opposite is true too: for if they look they will find that there are many places where the sea has invaded the land. But we [25] must not suppose that the cause of this is that the world is in process of becoming. For it is absurd to make the universe to be in process because of small and trifling changes, when the bulk and size of the earth are surely as nothing in comparison with the whole world. Rather we must take the cause of all these changes to be that, just as winter occurs in the seasons of the year, so in determined [30] periods there comes a great winter of a great year and with it excess of rain. But this excess does not always occur in the same place. The deluge in the time of Deucalion, for instance, [35] took place chiefly in the Greek world and in it especially about ancient Hellas, the country about Dodona and the Achelous, a river which has often changed its course. Here the Selli dwelt and those who were formerly called Graeci and now Hellenes. When, therefore, such an excess of rain occurs we must suppose that it suffices for a long time. We have [5] seen that some[1] say that the size of the subterranean cavities is what makes some rivers perennial and others not, whereas we maintain that the size of the mountains is the cause, and their density and coldness; for great, dense, and cold mountains catch and keep and create most water: whereas if the mountains that overhang [10] the sources of rivers are small or porous and stony and clayey, these rivers run dry earlier. We must recognize the same kind of thing in this case too. Where such abundance of rain falls in the great winter it tends to make the moisture of those places almost everlasting. But as time goes on places of the latter type dry up more, while those of the former, moist [15] type, do so less: until at last the beginning of the same cycle returns.

Since there is necessarily some change in the whole world, but not in the way of coming into existence or perishing (for the universe is permanent), it must be, as we say, that the same places are not for ever moist through the presence of sea and rivers, nor for ever dry. And the facts prove this. The whole land of [20] the Egyptians, whom we take to be the most ancient of men, has evidently gradually come into existence and been produced by the river. This is clear from an observation of the country, and the facts about the Red Sea suffice to prove it too. One of their kings tried [25] to make a canal to it (for it would have been of no little advantage to them for the whole region to have become navigable; Sesostris is said to have been the first of the ancient kings to try), but he found that the sea was higher than the land. So he first, and Darius afterwards, stopped making the canal, lest the sea should mix with the river water and spoil [30] it. So it is clear that all this part was once unbroken sea. For the same reason Libya—the country of Ammon—is, strangely enough, lower and hollower than the land to the seaward of it. For it is clear that a barrier of silt [35] was formed and after it lakes and dry land, but in course of time the water that was

[1] 349^b 3.

left behind in the lakes dried up and is now all gone. Again the silting up of the lake Maeotis by the rivers has advanced so much that the limit to the size of the ships which can now sail into it to trade is much lower than it was sixty years ago. Hence it is easy to infer [5] that it, too, like most lakes, was originally produced by the rivers and that it must end by drying up entirely.

Again, this process of silting up causes a continuous current through the Bosporus; and in this case we can directly observe the nature of the process. Whenever the current from the Asiatic shore threw up a sandbank, there first [10] formed a small lake behind it. Later it dried up and a second sandbank formed in front of the first and a second lake. This process went on uniformly and without interruption. Now when this has been repeated often enough, in the course of time the strait must become like a river, and in the end the river itself must dry up.

[15] So it is clear, since there will be no end to time and the world is eternal, that neither the Tanais nor the Nile has always been flowing, but that the region whence they flow was once dry: for their effect may be fulfilled, but time cannot. And this will be equally true of [20] all other rivers. But if rivers come into existence and perish and the same parts of the earth were not always moist, the sea must needs change correspondingly. And if the sea is always advancing in one place and receding in another it is clear that the same parts of the whole earth are not always either sea or land, but that all this changes in course of time.

[25] So we have explained that the same parts of the earth are not always land or sea and why that is so: and also why some rivers are perennial and others not.

BOOK II

1

Let us explain the nature of the sea and the reason why such a large mass of water is salt and the way in which it originally came to be.

The old writers who invented theogonies say [35] that the sea has springs, for they want earth and sea to have foundations and roots of their own. Presumably they thought that this view was grander and more impressive as implying that our earth was an important part of the universe. For they believed that the whole world had been built up round our earth and for its sake, and that the earth was the most important and primary part of it. [5] Others, wiser in human knowledge, give an account of its origin. At first, they say, the earth was surrounded by moisture. Then the sun began to dry it up, part of it evaporated and is the cause of winds and the turnings back of the sun and the moon, while the remainder [10] forms the sea. So the sea is being dried up and is growing less, and will end by being some day entirely dried up. Others say that the sea is a kind of sweat exuded by the earth when the sun heats it, and that this explains its saltness: for all sweat is salt. Others say that the saltness is due to the earth. Just as water strained through ashes becomes salt, so the sea [15] owes its saltness to the admixture of earth with similar properties.

We must now consider the facts which prove that the sea cannot possibly have springs. The waters we find on the earth either flow or are stationary. All flowing water has springs. (By [20] a spring, as we have explained above,[1] we must not understand a source from which waters are ladled as it were from a vessel, but a first point at which the water which is continually forming and percolating gathers.) Stationary water is either that which has collected and has been left standing, marshy pools, for instance, and lakes, which differ merely in size, or else it comes from springs. In this case [25] it is always artificial, I mean as in the case of wells, otherwise the spring would have to be above the outlet. Hence the water from fountains and rivers flows of itself, whereas wells need to be worked artificially. All the waters that exist belong to one or other of these classes.

[30] On the basis of this division we can see that the sea cannot have springs. For it falls under neither of the two classes; it does not flow and it is not artificial; whereas all water from springs must belong to one or other of them. Natural standing water from springs is never found on such a large scale.

[35] Again, there are several seas that have no communication with one another at all. The Red Sea, for instance, communicates but slightly with the ocean outside the straits, and the Hyrcanian and Caspian seas are distinct from this ocean and people dwell all round them. Hence, if these seas had had any springs

---

[1] 349b 27.

anywhere they must have been discovered.

[5] It is true that in straits, where the land on either side contracts an open sea into a small space, the sea appears to flow. But this is because it is swinging to and fro. In the open sea this motion is not observed, but where the [10] land narrows and contracts the sea the motion that was imperceptible in the open necessarily strikes the attention.

The whole of the Mediterranean does actually flow. The direction of this flow is determined by the depth of the basins and by the number of rivers. Maeotis flows into Pontus and Pontus into the Aegean. After that the [15] flow of the remaining seas is not so easy to observe. The current of Maeotis and Pontus is due to the number of rivers (more rivers flow into the Euxine and Maeotis than into the whole Mediterranean with its much larger basin), and to their own shallowness. For we [20] find the sea getting deeper and deeper. Pontus is deeper than Maeotis, the Aegean than Pontus, the Sicilian sea than the Aegean; the Sardinian and Tyrrhenic being the deepest of all. (Outside the pillars of Heracles the sea is shallow owing to the mud, but calm, for it lies in a hollow.) We see, then, that just as single rivers flow from mountains, so it is with [25] the earth as a whole: the greatest volume of water flows from the higher regions in the north. Their alluvium makes the northern seas shallow, while the outer seas are deeper. Some further evidence of the height of the northern regions of the earth is afforded by the view of many of the ancient meteorologists. They believed that the sun did not pass below [30] the earth, but round its northern part, and that it was the height of this which obscured the sun and caused night.

So much to prove that there cannot be sources of the sea and to explain its observed flow.

2

354ᵇ We must now discuss the origin of the sea, if it has an origin, and the cause of its salt and bitter taste.

What made earlier writers consider the sea to be the original and main body of water is this. It seems reasonable to suppose that to be [5] the case on the analogy of the other elements. Each of them has a main bulk which by reason of its mass is the origin of that element, and any parts which change and mix with the other elements come from it. Thus the main body of fire is in the upper region; that of air occupies the place next inside the region of fire; while the mass of the earth is that [10] round which the rest of the elements are seen to lie. So we must clearly look for something analogous in the case of water. But here we can find no such single mass, as in the case of the other elements, except the sea. River water is not a unity, nor is it stable, but is seen to be in a continuous process of becoming [15] from day to day. It was this difficulty which made people regard the sea as the origin and source of moisture and of all water. And so we find it maintained that rivers not only flow into the sea but originate from it, the salt water becoming sweet by filtration.

But this view involves another difficulty. If [20] this body of water is the origin and source of all water, why is it salt and not sweet? The reason for this, besides answering this question, will ensure our having a right first conception of the nature of the sea.

The earth is surrounded by water, just as that is by the sphere of air, and that again by the sphere called that of fire (which is the [25] outermost both on the common view and on ours). Now the sun, moving as it does, sets up processes of change and becoming and decay, and by its agency the finest and sweetest water is every day carried up and is dissolved into vapour and rises to the upper re- [30] gion, where it is condensed again by the cold and so returns to the earth. This, as we have said before,[1] is the regular course of nature.

Hence all my predecessors who supposed that the sun was nourished by moisture are absurdly mistaken. Some go on to say that the 355ᵃ solstices are due to this, the reason being that the same places cannot always supply the sun with nourishment and that without it he [5] must perish. For the fire we are familiar with lives as long as it is fed, and the only food for fire is moisture. As if the moisture that is raised could reach the sun! or this ascent were really like that performed by flame as it comes into being, and to which they supposed the case of the sun to be analogous! Really there is no similarity. A flame is a process of becoming, involving a constant interchange of [10] moist and dry. It cannot be said to be nourished since it scarcely persists as one and the same for a moment. This cannot be true of the sun; for if it were nourished like that, as they say it is, we should obviously not only have a new sun every day, as Heraclitus says,

[1] I. 9.

[15] but a new sun every moment. Again, when the sun causes the moisture to rise, this is like fire heating water. So, as the fire is not fed by the water above it, it is absurd to suppose that the sun feeds on that moisture, even if its heat made all the water in the world evaporate. Again, it is absurd, considering the number and size of the stars, that these think- [20] ers should consider the sun only and overlook the question how the rest of the heavenly bodies subsist. Again, they are met by the same difficulty as those who say that at first the earth itself was moist and the world round the earth was warmed by the sun, and so air was generated and the whole firmament grew, and the air caused winds and solstices. The [25] objection is that we always plainly see the water that has been carried up coming down again. Even if the same amount does not come back in a year or in a given country, yet in a certain period all that has been carried up is returned. This implies that the celestial bodies do not feed on it, and that we cannot distinguish between some air which preserves its character once it is generated and some other [30] which is generated but becomes water again and so perishes; on the contrary, all the moisture alike is dissolved and all of it condensed back into water.

The drinkable, sweet water, then, is light and is all of it drawn up: the salt water is heavy and remains behind, but not in its natural place. For this is a question which has been [35] sufficiently discussed (I mean about the natural place that water, like the other elements, must in reason have), and the answer 355ᵇ is this. The place which we see the sea filling is not its natural place but that of water. [5] It seems to belong to the sea because the weight of the salt water makes it remain there, while the sweet, drinkable water which is light is carried up. The same thing happens in animal bodies. Here, too, the food when it enters the body is sweet, yet the residuum and dregs of liquid food are found to be bitter and salt. This is because the sweet and drinkable [10] part of it has been drawn away by the natural animal heat and has passed into the flesh and the other parts of the body according to their several natures. Now just as here it would be wrong for any one to refuse to call the belly the place of liquid food because that disappears from it soon, and to call it the place of the residuum because this is seen to remain, so in the case of our present subject. This [15] place, we say, is the place of water. Hence all rivers and all the water that is generated flow into it: for water flows into the deepest place, and the deepest part of the earth is filled by the sea. Only all the light and sweet part of it is quickly carried off by the sun, while the [20] rest remains for the reason we have explained. It is quite natural that some people should have been puzzled by the old question why such a mass of water leaves no trace anywhere (for the sea does not increase though innumerable and vast rivers are flowing into it every day). But if one considers the matter [25] the solution is easy. The same amount of water does not take as long to dry up when it is spread out as when it is gathered in a body, and indeed the difference is so great that in the one case it might persist the whole day long while in the other it might all disappear in a moment—as for instance if one [30] were to spread out a cup of water over a large table. This is the case with the rivers: all the time they are flowing their water forms a compact mass, but when it arrives at a vast wide place it quickly and imperceptibly evaporates.

But the theory of the *Phaedo*[1] about rivers and the sea is impossible. There it is said that the earth is pierced by intercommunicating [35] channels and that the original head and 356ᵃ source of all waters is what is called Tartarus—a mass of water about the centre, from which all waters, flowing and standing, are derived. This primary and original water is always surging to and fro, and so it causes the rivers to flow on this side of the earth's centre and on that; for it has no fixed seat but is always oscillating about the centre. Its motion [5] up and down is what fills rivers. Many of these form lakes in various places (our sea is an instance of one of these), but all of them come round again in a circle to the original source of their flow, many at the same point, but some at a point opposite to that from which [10] they issued; for instance, if they started from the other side of the earth's centre, they might return from this side of it. They descend only as far as the centre, for after that all motion is upwards. Water gets its tastes and colours from the kind of earth the rivers happened to flow through.

But on this theory rivers do not always flow [15] in the same sense. For since they flow to the centre from which they issue forth they will not be flowing down any more than up, but in whatever direction the surging of Tar-

---
[1] *Phaedo*, 111 sq.

tarus inclines to. But at this rate we shall get the proverbial rivers flowing upwards, which is impossible. Again, where is the water that is generated and what goes up again as vapour to come from? For this must all of it [20] simply be ignored, since the quantity of water is always the same and all the water that flows out from the original source flows back to it again. This itself is not true, since all rivers are seen to end in the sea except where one flows into another. Not one of them ends in the earth, but even when one is swal- [25] lowed up it comes to the surface again. And those rivers are large which flow for a long distance through a low-lying country, for by their situation and length they cut off the course of many others and swallow them up. This is why the Istrus and the Nile are the greatest of the rivers which flow into our sea. Indeed, so many rivers fall into them that there [30] is disagreement as to the sources of them both. All of which is plainly impossible on the theory, and the more so as it derives the sea from Tartarus.

Enough has been said to prove that this is the natural place of water and not of the sea, and to explain why sweet water is only found [35] in rivers, while salt water is stationary, 356ᵇ and to show that the sea is the end rather than the source of water, analogous to the residual matter of all food, and especially liquid food, in animal bodies.

3

We must now explain why the sea is salt, and ask whether it eternally exists as identically the same body, or whether it did not exist at all once and some day will exist no longer, but [5] will dry up as some people think.

Every one admits this, that if the whole world originated the sea did too; for they make them come into being at the same time. It follows that if the universe is eternal the same must be true of the sea. Any one who thinks [10] like Democritus that the sea is diminishing and will disappear in the end reminds us of Aesop's tales. His story was that Charybdis had twice sucked in the sea: the first time she made the mountains visible; the second time the islands; and when she sucks it in for the [15] last time she will dry it up entirely. Such a tale is appropriate enough to Aesop in a rage with the ferryman, but not to serious inquirers. Whatever made the sea remain at first, whether it was its weight, as some even of those who hold these views say (for it is easy to see the cause here), or some other reason—clearly the [20] same thing must make it persist for ever. They must either deny that the water raised by the sun will return at all, or, if it does, they must admit that the sea persists for ever or as long as this process goes on, and again, that for the same period of time that sweet water must have been carried up beforehand. So the [25] sea will never dry up: for before that can happen the water that has gone up beforehand will return to it: for if you say that this happens once you must admit its recurrence. If you stop the sun's course there is no drying agency. If you let it go on it will draw up the sweet water as we have said whenever it ap- [30] proaches, and let it descend again when it recedes. This notion about the sea is derived from the fact that many places are found to be drier now than they once were. Why this is so we have explained.[1] The phenomenon is due to temporary excess of rain and not to any process of becoming in which the universe or [35] its parts are involved. Some day the oppo- 357ᵃ site will take place and after that the earth will grow dry once again. We must recognize that this process always goes on thus in a cycle, for that is more satisfactory than to suppose a change in the whole world in order to explain these facts. But we have dwelt longer on this point than it deserves.

[5] To return to the saltness of the sea: those who create the sea once for all, or indeed generate it at all, cannot account for its saltness. It makes no difference whether the sea is the residue of all the moisture that is about the earth and has been drawn up by the sun, or whether all the flavour existing in the whole mass of sweet water is due to the admixture of a certain kind of earth. Since the total volume [10] of the sea is the same once the water that evaporated has returned, it follows that it must either have been salt at first too, or, if not at first, then not now either. If it was salt from the very beginning, then we want to know why that was so; and why, if salt water was drawn up then, that is not the case now.

Again, if it is maintained that an admixture [15] of earth makes the sea salt (for they say that earth has many flavours and is washed down by the rivers and so makes the sea salt by its admixture), it is strange that rivers should not be salt too. How can the admixture [20] of this earth have such a striking effect in a great quantity of water and not in each

[1] I. 14.

river singly? For the sea, differing in nothing from rivers but in being salt, is evidently simply the totality of river water, and the rivers are the vehicle in which that earth is carried to their common destination.

It is equally absurd to suppose that anything [25] has been explained by calling the sea 'the sweat of the earth', like Empedocles.[1] Metaphors are poetical and so that expression of his may satisfy the requirements of a poem, but as a scientific theory it is unsatisfactory. Even in the case of the body it is a question how the sweet liquid drunk becomes salt sweat— whether it is merely by the departure of some [30] element in it which is sweetest, or by the admixture of something, as when water is strained through ashes. Actually the saltness seems to be due to the same cause as in the case of the residual liquid that gathers in the bladder. That, too, becomes bitter and salt though the liquid we drink and that contained 357^b in our food is sweet. If then the bitterness is due in these cases (as with the water strained through lye) to the presence of a certain sort of stuff that is carried along by the urine (as indeed we actually find a salt deposit settling in chamber-pots) and is secreted [5] from the flesh in sweat (as if the departing moisture were washing the stuff out of the body), then no doubt the admixture of something earthy with the water is what makes the sea salt.

Now in the body stuff of this kind, viz. the sediment of food, is due to failure to digest: but how there came to be any such thing in the [10] earth requires explanation. Besides, how can the drying and warming of the earth cause the secretion of such a great quantity of water; especially as that must be a mere fragment of what is left in the earth? Again, waiving the question of quantity, why does not the earth sweat now when it happens to be in process of [15] drying? If it did so then, it ought to do so now. But it does not: on the contrary, when it is dry it grows moist, but when it is moist it does not secrete anything at all. How then was it possible for the earth at the beginning when it was moist to sweat as it grew dry? Indeed, the theory that maintains that most of the moisture departed and was drawn up by [20] the sun and that what was left over is the sea is more reasonable; but for the earth to sweat when it is moist is impossible.

Since all the attempts to account for the saltness of the sea seem unsuccessful let us explain it by the help of the principle we have used already.[2]

[25] Since we recognize two kinds of evaporation, one moist, the other dry, it is clear that the latter must be recognized as the source of phenomena like those we are concerned with.

But there is a question which we must discuss first. Does the sea always remain numerically one and consisting of the same parts, or is it, too, one in form and volume while its parts are in continual change, like air and sweet [30] water and fire? All of these are in a constant state of change, but the form and the quantity of each of them are fixed, just as they are in the case of a flowing river or a burning flame. The answer is clear, and there is no doubt that the same account holds good of all these things alike. They differ in that some of 358^a them change more rapidly or more slowly than others; and they all are involved in a process of perishing and becoming which yet affects them all in a regular course.

This being so we must go on to try to explain why the sea is salt. There are many facts which make it clear that this taste is due to the [5] admixture of something. First, in animal bodies what is least digested, the residue of liquid food, is salt and bitter, as we said before. All animal excreta are undigested, but especially that which gathers in the bladder (its extreme lightness proves this; for every- [10] thing that is digested is condensed), and also sweat; in these then is excreted (along with other matter) an identical substance to which this flavour is due. The case of things burnt is analogous. What heat fails to assimilate becomes the excrementary residue in animal bodies, and, in things burnt, ashes. That is why some people say that it was burnt earth that made the sea salt. To say that it was burnt [15] earth is absurd; but to say that it was something like burnt earth is true. We must suppose that just as in the cases we have described, so in the world as a whole, everything that grows and is naturally generated always leaves an undigested residue, like that of things burnt, consisting of this sort of earth. All [20] the earthy stuff in the dry exhalation is of this nature, and it is the dry exhalation which accounts for its great quantity. Now since, as we have said, the moist and the dry evaporations are mixed, some quantity of this stuff must always be included in the clouds and the water that are formed by condensation, and [25] must redescend to the earth in rain. This

---
[1] Diels, 21A. 66; B. 55.
[2] 341^b 6 ff.

process must always go on with such regularity as the sublunary world admits of, and it is the answer to the question how the sea comes to be salt.

It also explains why rain that comes from the south, and the first rains of autumn, are brackish. The south is the warmest of winds [30] and it blows from dry and hot regions. Hence it carries little moist vapour and that is why it is hot. (It makes no difference even if this is not its true character and it is originally a cold wind, for it becomes warm on its way by incorporating with itself a great quantity of dry evaporation from the places it passes over.) [35] The north wind, on the other hand, com-358b ing from moist regions, is full of vapour and therefore cold. It is dry in our part of the world because it drives the clouds away before it, but in the south it is rainy; just as the south is a dry wind in Libya. So the south wind charges the rain that falls with a great quantity of this stuff. Autumn rain is brackish be- [5] cause the heaviest water must fall first; so that that which contains the greatest quantity of this kind of earth descends quickest.

This, too, is why the sea is warm. Everything that has been exposed to fire contains heat potentially, as we see in the case of lye and ashes and the dry and liquid excreta of [10] animals. Indeed those animals which are hottest in the belly have the hottest excreta.

The action of this cause is continually making the sea more salt, but some part of its saltness is always being drawn up with the sweet water. This is less than the sweet water in the same ratio in which the salt and brackish [15] element in rain is less than the sweet, and so the saltness of the sea remains constant on the whole. Salt water when it turns into vapour becomes sweet, and the vapour does not form salt water when it condenses again. This I know by experiment. The same thing is true in every case of the kind: wine and all fluids that evaporate and condense back into a liquid [20] state become water. They all are water modified by a certain admixture, the nature of which determines their flavour. But this subject must be considered on another more suitable occasion.

For the present let us say this. The sea is [25] there and some of it is continually being drawn up and becoming sweet; this returns from above with the rain. But it is now different from what it was when it was drawn up, and its weight makes it sink below the sweet water. This process prevents the sea, as it does rivers, from drying up except from local causes (this must happen to sea and rivers alike). [30] On the other hand the parts neither of the earth nor of the sea remain constant but only their whole bulk. For the same thing is true of the earth as of the sea: some of it is carried up and some comes down with the rain, and both that which remains on the surface and that which comes down again change their situations.

There is more evidence to prove that saltness is due to the admixture of some substance, [35] besides that which we have adduced. 359a Make a vessel of wax and put it in the sea, fastening its mouth in such a way as to prevent any water getting in. Then the water that percolates through the wax sides of the vessel is sweet, the earthy stuff, the admixture of which makes the water salt, being separated off as it were by a filter. It is this stuff [5] which make salt water heavy (it weighs more than fresh water) and thick. The difference in consistency is such that ships with the same cargo very nearly sink in a river when they are quite fit to navigate in the sea. [10] This circumstance has before now caused loss to shippers freighting their ships in a river. That the thicker consistency is due to an admixture of something is proved by the fact that if you make strong brine by the admixture of salt, eggs, even when they are full, float in it. It almost becomes like mud; such a [15] quantity of earthy matter is there in the sea. The same thing is done in salting fish.

Again if, as is fabled, there is a lake in Palestine, such that if you bind a man or beast and throw it in it floats and does not sink, this [20] would bear out what we have said. They say that this lake is so bitter and salt that no fish live in it and that if you soak clothes in it and shake them it cleans them. The following facts all of them support our theory that it is some earthy stuff in the water which [25] makes it salt. In Chaonia there is a spring of brackish water that flows into a neighbouring river which is sweet but contains no fish. The local story is that when Heracles came from Erytheia driving the oxen and gave the inhabitants the choice, they chose salt in pref- [30] erence to fish. They get the salt from the spring. They boil off some of the water and let the rest stand; when it has cooled and the heat and moisture have evaporated together it gives them salt, not in lumps but loose and light like snow. It is weaker than ordinary salt and [35] added freely gives a sweet taste, and it is not as white as salt generally is. Another instance of this is found in Umbria. There is a place there where reeds and rushes grow. They burn some of these, put the ashes into water and boil it off. When a little water is left and has cooled it gives a quantity of salt.

[5] Most salt rivers and springs must once have been hot. Then the original fire in them was extinguished but the earth through which they percolate preserves the character of lye or ashes. Springs and rivers with all kinds of flavours are found in many places. These flavours must in every case be due to the fire [10] that is or was in them, for if you expose earth to different degrees of heat it assumes various kinds and shades of flavour. It becomes full of alum and lye and other things of the kind, and the fresh water percolates through these and changes its character. Sometimes it [15] becomes acid as in Sicania, a part of Sicily. There they get a salt and acid water which they use as vinegar to season some of their dishes. In the neighbourhood of Lyncus, too, there is a spring of acid water, and in Scythia a bitter spring. The water from this makes the whole of the river into which it flows bitter. These differences are explained [20] by a knowledge of the particular mixtures that determine different savours. But these have been explained in another treatise.[1]

We have now given an account of waters and the sea, why they persist, how they change, what their nature is, and have ex- [25] plained most of their natural operations and affections.

4

Let us proceed to the theory of winds. Its basis is a distinction we have already made.[2] We recognize two kinds of evaporation, one moist, the other dry. The former is called [30] vapour: for the other there is no general name but we must call it a sort of smoke, applying to the whole of it a word that is proper to one of its forms. The moist cannot exist without the dry nor the dry without the moist: whenever we speak of either we mean that it predominates. Now when the sun in its circular course approaches, it draws up by [35] its heat the moist evaporation: when it recedes the cold makes the vapour that had been raised condense back into water which falls and is distributed through the earth. (This explains why there is more rain in winter and more by night than by day: though the fact is not recognized because rain by night is more apt to escape observation than [5] by day.) But there is a great quantity of fire and heat in the earth, and the sun not only draws up the moisture that lies on the surface of it, but warms and dries the earth itself. Consequently, since there are two kinds of evaporation, as we have said, one like vapour, [10] the other like smoke, both of them are necessarily generated. That in which moisture predominates is the source of rain, as we explained before,[3] while the dry evaporation is the source and substance of all winds. That things must necessarily take this course is clear from the resulting phenomena themselves, [15] for the evaporation that is to produce them must necessarily differ; and the sun and the warmth in the earth not only can but must produce these evaporations.

Since the two evaporations are specifically distinct, wind and rain obviously differ and their substance is not the same, as those say [20] who maintain that one and the same air when in motion is wind, but when it condenses again is water. Air, as we have explained in an earlier book,[4] is made up of these as constituents. Vapour is moist and cold (for its fluidity is due to its moistness, and because it derives from water it is naturally cold, like water that has not been warmed): whereas [25] the smoky evaporation is hot and dry. Hence each contributes a part, and air is moist and hot. It is absurd that this air that surrounds us should become wind when in motion, whatever be the source of its motion—on the contrary the case of winds is like that [30] of rivers. We do not call water that flows anyhow a river, even if there is a great quantity of it, but only if the flow comes from a spring. So too with the winds; a great quantity of air might be moved by the fall of some large object without flowing from any source or spring.

The facts bear out our theory. It is because [35] the evaporation takes place uninterruptedly but differs in degree and quantity that clouds and winds appear in their natural proportion according to the season; and it is because there is now a great excess of the vaporous, now of the dry and smoky exhalation, that some years are rainy and wet, others [5] windy and dry. Sometimes there is much drought or rain, and it prevails over a great

---

[1] Perhaps *On Sense and Sensibility*, chapter 4.
[2] 341[b] 6 ff.
[3] I. 9.
[4] *On Generation and Corruption*, II. 4.

and continuous stretch of country. At other times it is local; the surrounding country often getting seasonable or even excessive rains while [10] there is drought in a certain part; or, contrariwise, all the surrounding country gets little or even no rain while a certain part gets rain in abundance. The reason for all this is that while the same affection is generally apt to prevail over a considerable district because adjacent places (unless there is something special to differentiate them) stand in the same [15] relation to the sun, yet on occasion the dry evaporation will prevail in one part and the moist in another, or conversely. Again the reason for this latter is that each evaporation goes over to that of the neighbouring district: for instance, the dry evaporation circulates in its [20] own place while the moist migrates to the next district or is even driven by winds to some distant place: or else the moist evaporation remains and the dry moves away. Just as in the case of the body when the stomach is dry the lower belly is often in the contrary state, and when it is dry the stomach is moist [25] and cold, so it often happens that the evaporations reciprocally take one another's place and interchange.

Further, after rain wind generally rises in those places where the rain fell, and when rain has come on the wind ceases. These are necessary effects of the principles we have ex-[30] plained. After rain the earth is being dried by its own heat and that from above and gives off the evaporation which we saw to be the material cause of wind. Again, suppose this secretion is present and wind prevails; the heat is continually being thrown off, rising to [35] the upper region, and so the wind ceases; then the fall in temperature makes vapour 361ᵃ form and condense into water. Water also forms and cools the dry evaporation when the clouds are driven together and the cold concentrated in them. These are the causes that make wind cease on the advent of rain, and rain fall on the cessation of wind.

[5] The cause of the predominance of winds from the north and from the south is the same. (Most winds, as a matter of fact, are north winds or south winds.) These are the only regions which the sun does not visit: it approaches them and recedes from them, but its course is always over the west and the east. Hence [10] clouds collect on either side, and when the sun approaches it provokes the moist evaporation, and when it recedes to the opposite side there are storms and rain. So summer and winter are due to the sun's motion to and from the solstices, and water ascends and falls again for the same reason. Now since most rain falls [15] in those regions towards which and from which the sun turns and these are the north and the south, and since most evaporation must take place where there is the greatest rainfall, just as green wood gives most smoke, [20] and since this evaporation is wind, it is natural that the most and most important winds should come from these quarters. (The winds from the north are called Boreae, those from the south Noti.)

The course of winds is oblique: for though the evaporation rises straight up from the earth, they blow round it because all the surrounding air follows the motion of the heav-[25] ens. Hence the question might be asked whether winds originate from above or from below. The motion comes from above: before we feel the wind blowing the air betrays its presence if there are clouds or a mist, for their motion shows that the wind has begun to blow before it has actually reached us; and this implies that the source of winds is above. But [30] since wind is defined as 'a quantity of dry evaporation from the earth moving round the earth', it is clear that while the origin of the motion is from above, the matter and the generation of wind come from below. The oblique movement of the rising evaporation is caused from above: for the motion of the heavens determines the processes that are at a distance from the earth, and the motion from [35] below is vertical and every cause is more active where it is nearest to the effect; but in its generation and origin wind plainly derives from the earth.

361ᵇ The facts bear out the view that winds are formed by the gradual union of many evaporations just as rivers derive their sources from the water that oozes from the earth. Every wind is weakest in the spot from which it blows; as they proceed and leave their source at a distance they gather strength. Thus the [5] winter in the north is windless and calm: that is, in the north itself; but the breeze that blows from there so gently as to escape observation becomes a great wind as it passes on.

We have explained the nature and origin of [10] wind, the occurrence of drought and rains, the reason why rain stops wind and wind rises after rain, the prevalence of north and south winds and also why wind moves in the way it does.

5

The sun both checks the formation of winds [15] and stimulates it. When the evaporation is small in amount and faint the sun wastes it and dissipates by its greater heat the lesser heat contained in the evaporation. It also dries up the earth, the source of the evaporation, before the latter has appeared in bulk: just as, when you throw a little fuel into a great fire, it is often burnt up before giving off any smoke. [20] In these ways the sun checks winds and prevents them from rising at all: it checks them by wasting the evaporation, and prevents their rising by drying up the earth quickly. Hence calm is very apt to prevail about the rising of Orion and lasts until the coming of the Etesiae and their 'forerunners'.

[25] Calm is due to two causes. Either cold quenches the evaporation, for instance a sharp frost: or excessive heat wastes it. In the intermediate periods, too, the causes are generally either that the evaporation has not had time to develop or that it has passed away and there is [30] none as yet to replace it.

Both the setting and the rising of Orion are considered to be treacherous and stormy, because they take place at a change of season (namely of summer or winter; and because the size of the constellation makes its rise last over many days) and a state of change is always indefinite and therefore liable to disturbance.

[35] The Etesiae blow after the summer solstice and the rising of the dog-star: not at the time when the sun is closest nor when it is distant; and they blow by day and cease at night. The reason is that when the sun is near it dries up the earth before evaporation has taken place, but when it has receded a little its heat and the evaporation are present in the [5] right proportion; so the ice melts and the earth, dried by its own heat and that of the sun, smokes and vapours. They abate at night because the cold of the nights checks the melting of the ice. What is frozen gives off no evapora- [10] tion, nor does that which contains no dryness at all: it is only where something dry contains moisture that it gives off evaporation under the influence of heat.

The question is sometimes asked: why do the north winds which we call the Etesiae blow continuously after the summer solstice, when there are no corresponding south winds after the winter solstice? The facts are reasonable enough: for the so-called 'white south winds' do blow at the corresponding season, though they are not equally continuous and so escape [15] observation and give rise to this inquiry. The reason for this is that the north wind blows from the arctic regions which are full of water and snow. The sun thaws them and so the Etesiae blow: after rather than at the summer [20] solstice. (For the greatest heat is developed not when the sun is nearest to the north, but when its heat has been felt for a considerable period and it has not yet receded far. The 'bird winds' blow in the same way after the winter solstice. They, too, are weak Etesiae, but they blow less and later than the Etesiae. [25] They begin to blow only on the seventieth day because the sun is distant and therefore weaker. They do not blow so continuously because only things on the surface of the earth and offering little resistance evaporate then, the thoroughly frozen parts requiring greater heat to melt them. So they blow intermittently till the true Etesiae come on again at the summer [30] solstice: for from that time onwards the wind tends to blow continuously.) But the south wind blows from the tropic of Cancer and not from the antarctic region.

There are two inhabitable sections of the earth: one near our upper, or nothern pole, the other near the other or southern pole; and their [35] shape is like that of a tambourine. If you draw lines from the centre of the earth they cut out a drum-shaped figure. The lines form two cones; the base of the one is the tropic, of the other the ever visible circle, their vertex is at the centre of the earth. Two other cones towards the south pole give corresponding segments of the earth. These sections alone [5] are habitable. Beyond the tropics no one can live: for there the shade would not fall to the north, whereas the earth is known to be uninhabitable before the sun is in the zenith or the shade is thrown to the south: and the regions below the Bear are uninhabitable because of the cold.

[10] [The Crown, too, moves over this region: for it is in the zenith when it is on our meridian].

So we see that the way in which they now describe the geography of the earth is ridiculous. They depict the inhabited earth as round, but both ascertained facts and general considerations show this to be impossible. If we reflect we see that the inhabited region is limited [15] in breadth, while the climate admits of its extending all round the earth. For we meet with no excessive heat or cold in the direction of its length but only in that of its breadth; so that there is nothing to prevent our travelling round the earth unless the extent of the sea presents an obstacle anywhere. The records of journeys by sea and land bear this out. They [20] make the length far greater than the breadth. If we compute these voyages and journeys the distance from the Pillars of Heracles to India exceeds that from Aethiopia to Maeotis and the northernmost Scythians by a ratio of more than 5 to 3, as far as such matters ad- [25] mit of accurate statement. Yet we know the whole breadth of the region we dwell in up to the uninhabited parts: in one direction no one lives because of the cold, in the other because of the heat.

But it is the sea which divides as it seems the parts beyond India from those beyond the Pillars of Heracles and prevents the earth from being inhabited all round. [30] Now since there must be a region bearing the same relation to the southern pole as the place we live in bears to our pole, it will clearly correspond in the ordering of its winds as well as in other things. So just as we have a north wind here, they must have a corre- [35] sponding wind from the antarctic. This wind cannot reach us since our own north wind is like 363ª a land breeze and does not even reach the limits of the region we live in. The prevalence of north winds here is due to [5] our lying near the north. Yet even here they give out and fail to penetrate far: in the southern sea beyond Libya east and west winds are always blowing alternately, like north and south winds with us. So it is clear that the south wind is not the wind that blows from the south pole. It is neither that nor the wind from [10] the winter tropic. For symmetry would require another wind blowing from the summer tropic, which there is not, since we know that only one wind blows from that quarter. So the south wind clearly blows from the torrid region. Now the sun is so near to that region [15] that it has no water, or snow which might melt and cause Etesiae. But because that place is far more extensive and open the south wind is greater and stronger and warmer than the north and penetrates farther to the north than the north wind does to the south.

The origin of these winds and their relation [20] to one another has now been explained.

6

Let us now explain the position of the winds, their oppositions, which can blow simultaneously with which, and which cannot, their names and number, and any other of their af- [25] fections that have not been treated in the 'particular questions'. What we say about their position must be followed with the help of the figure. For clearness' sake we have drawn the circle of the horizon, which is round, but it represents the zone in which we [30] live; for that can be divided in the same

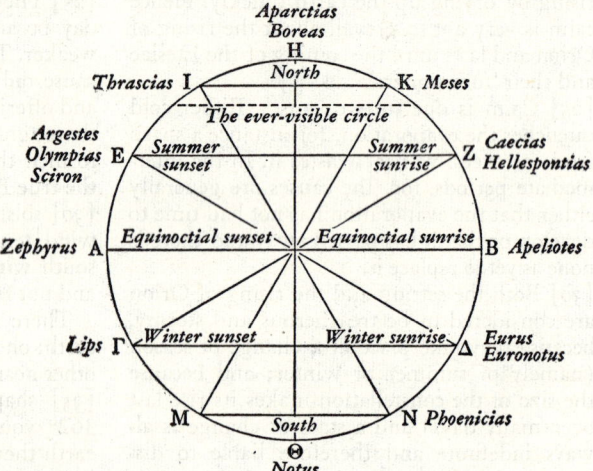

way. Let us also begin by laying down that those things are locally contrary which are locally most distant from one another, just as things specifically most remote from one another are specific contraries. Now things that face one another from opposite ends of a diameter are locally most distant from one another.

Let A be the point where the sun sets at the equinox and B, the point opposite, the place where it rises at the equinox. Let there be another diameter cutting this at right angles, and let the point H on it be the north and its diametrical opposite Θ the south. Let Z be the rising of the sun at the summer solstice and E its setting at the summer solstice; Δ its rising [5] at the winter solstice, and Γ its setting at the winter solstice. Draw a diameter from Z to Γ and from Δ to E. Then since those things are locally contrary which are most distant from one another in space, and points diametrically opposite are most distant from one another, those winds must necessarily be contrary to one

[10] another that blow from opposite ends of a diameter.

The names of the winds according to their position are these. Zephyrus is the wind that blows from A, this being the point where the sun sets at the equinox. Its contrary is Apeliotes blowing from B the point where the sun rises at the equinox. The wind blowing from H, the north, is the true north wind, called [15] Aparctias: while Notus blowing from Θ is its contrary; for this point is the south and Θ is contrary to H, being diametrically opposite to it. Caecias blows from Z, where the sun rises at the summer solstice. Its contrary is not the wind blowing from E but Lips blowing from Γ. For Lips blows from the point where the sun sets at the winter solstice and is dia- [20] metrically opposite to Caecias: so it is its contrary. Eurus blows from Δ, coming from the point where the sun rises at the winter solstice. It borders on Notus, and so we often find that people speak of 'Euro-Noti'. Its contrary is not Lips blowing from Γ but the wind that blows from E which some call Argestes, some [25] Olympias, and some Sciron. This blows from the point where the sun sets at the summer solstice, and is the only wind that is diametrically opposite to Eurus. These are the winds that are diametrically opposite to one another and their contraries.

There are other winds which have no contraries. The wind they call Thrascias, which lies between Argestes and Aparctias, blows [30] from I; and the wind called Meses, which lies between Caecias and Aparctias, from K. (The line IK nearly coincides with the ever visible circle, but not quite.) These winds have no contraries. Meses has not, or else there would be a wind blowing from the point M 364ᵃ which is diametrically opposite. Thrascias corresponding to the point I has not, for then there would be a wind blowing from N, the point which is diametrically opposite. (But perhaps a local wind which the inhabitants of those parts call Phoenicias blows from that point.)

These are the most important and definite winds and these their places.

[5] There are more winds from the north than from the south. The reason for this is that the region in which we live lies nearer to the north. Also, much more water and snow is pushed aside into this quarter because the oth- [10] er lies under the sun and its course. When this thaws and soaks into the earth and is exposed to the heat of the sun and the earth it necessarily causes evaporation to rise in greater quantities and over a greater space.

Of the winds we have described Aparctias is the north wind in the strict sense. Thrascias and Meses are north winds too. (Caecias is [15] half north and half east.) South are that which blows from due south and Lips. East, the wind from the rising of the sun at the equinox and Eurus. Phoenicias is half south and half east. West, the wind from the true west and that called Argestes. More generally these winds are classified as northerly or southerly. [20] The west winds are counted as northerly, for they blow from the place of sunset and are therefore colder; the east winds as southerly, for they are warmer because they blow from the place of sunrise. So the distinction of cold and hot or warm is the basis for the division of the winds into northerly and southerly. East winds are warmer than west winds be- [25] cause the sun shines on the east longer, whereas it leaves the west sooner and reaches it later.

Since this is the distribution of the winds it is clear that contrary winds cannot blow simultaneously. They are diametrically opposite to one another and one of the two must be overpowered and cease. Winds that are not diametrically opposite to one another may blow simul- [30] taneously: for instance the winds from Z and from Δ. Hence it sometimes happens that both of them, though different winds and blowing from different quarters, are favourable to sailors making for the same point.

Contrary winds commonly blow at opposite seasons. Thus Caecias and in general the winds north of the summer solstice blow about the time of the spring equinox, but about the autumn equinox Lips; and Zephyrus about the summer solstice, but about the winter solstice Eurus.

Aparctias, Thrascias, and Argestes are the [5] winds that fall on others most and stop them. Their source is so close to us that they are greater and stronger than other winds. They bring fair weather most of all winds for the same reason, for, blowing as they do, from close at hand, they overpower the other winds and stop them; they also blow away the clouds that are forming and leave a clear sky—unless [10] they happen to be very cold. Then they do not bring fair weather, but being colder than they are strong they condense the clouds before driving them away.

Caecias does not bring fair weather because

it returns upon itself. Hence the saying: 'Bringing it on himself as Caecias does clouds.'

When they cease, winds are succeeded by [15] their neighbours in the direction of the movement of the sun. For an effect is most apt to be produced in the neighbourhood of its cause, and the cause of winds moves with the sun.

Contrary winds have either the same or contrary effects. Thus Lips and Caecias, sometimes called Hellespontias, are both rainy. Ar- [20] gestes and Eurus are dry: the latter being dry at first and rainy afterwards. Meses and Aparctias are coldest and bring most snow. Aparctias, Thrascias, and Argestes bring hail. Notus, Zephyrus, and Eurus are hot. Caecias covers the sky with heavy clouds, Lips with [25] lighter ones. Caecias does this because it returns upon itself and combines the qualities of Boreas and Eurus. By being cold it condenses and gathers the vaporous air, and because it is easterly it carries with it and drives before it a great quantity of such matter. Aparctias, Thrascias, and Argestes bring fair weather for the reason we have explained be- [30] fore.[1] These winds and Meses are most commonly accompanied by lightning. They are cold because they blow from the north, and lightning is due to cold, being ejected when the clouds contract. Some of these same winds 365ª bring hail with them for the same reason; namely, that they cause a sudden condensation.

Hurricanes are commonest in autumn, and next in spring: Aparctias, Thrascias, and Argestes give rise to them most. This is because hurricanes are generally formed when some winds are blowing and others fall on them; and these are the winds which are most apt to fall on others that are blowing; the reason for [5] which, too, we have explained before.[2]

The Etesiae veer round: they begin from the north, and become for dwellers in the west Thrasciae, Argestae, and Zephyrus (for Zephyrus belongs to the north). For dwellers in the east they veer round as far as Apeliotes.

[10] So much for the winds, their origin and nature and the properties common to them all or peculiar to each.

7

We must go on to discuss earthquakes next, for their cause is akin to our last subject.

[15] The theories that have been put forward up to the present date are three, and their authors three men, Anaxagoras of Clazomenae, and before him Anaximenes of Miletus, and later Democritus of Abdera.

Anaxagoras says that the ether, which naturally moves upwards, is caught in hollows be- [20] low the earth and so shakes it, for though the earth is really all of it equally porous, its surface is clogged up by rain. This implies that part of the whole sphere is 'above' and part 'below': 'above' being the part on which we live, 'below' the other.

[25] This theory is perhaps too primitive to require refutation. It is absurd to think of up and down otherwise than as meaning that heavy bodies move to the earth from every quarter, and light ones, such as fire, away from [30] it; especially as we see that, as far as our knowledge of the earth goes, the horizon always changes with a change in our position, which proves that the earth is convex and spherical. It is absurd, too, to maintain that the earth rests on the air because of its size, and then to say that impact upwards from below shakes it right through. Besides he gives no account of the circumstances attendant on earth- [35] quakes: for not every country or every season is subject to them.

365ᵇ Democritus says that the earth is full of water and that when a quantity of rain-water is added to this an earthquake is the result. The hollows in the earth being unable to admit the excess of water it forces its way in and so causes an earthquake. Or again, the earth as it dries draws the water from the fuller to the [5] emptier parts, and the inrush of the water as it changes its place causes the earthquake.

Anaximenes says that the earth breaks up when it grows wet or dry, and earthquakes are due to the fall of these masses as they break away. Hence earthquakes take place in times [10] of drought and again of heavy rain, since, as we have explained, the earth grows dry in time of drought and breaks up, whereas the rain makes it sodden and destroys its cohesion.

But if this were the case the earth ought to be found to be sinking in many places. Again, why do earthquakes frequently occur in places which are not excessively subject to drought or [15] rain, as they ought to be on the theory? Besides, on this view, earthquakes ought always to be getting fewer, and should come to an end entirely some day: the notion of contraction by packing together implies this. So [20] if this is impossible the theory must be impossible too.

---
[1] b 6. [2] 364ᵇ 3.

8

We have already shown[1] that wet and dry must both give rise to an evaporation: earthquakes are a necessary consequence of this fact. The earth is essentially dry, but rain fills it [25] with moisture. Then the sun and its own fire warm it and give rise to a quantity of wind both outside and inside it. This wind sometimes flows outwards in a single body, sometimes inwards, and sometimes it is divided. All these are necessary laws. Next we must find [30] out what body has the greatest motive force. This will certainly be the body that naturally moves farthest and is most violent. Now that which has the most rapid motion is necessarily the most violent; for its swiftness gives its impact the greatest force. Again, the rarest body, that which can most readily pass through every other body, is that which naturally moves [35] farthest. Wind satisfies these conditions in the highest degree (fire only becomes flame and moves rapidly when wind accompanies it): so that not water nor earth is the cause of earthquakes but wind—that is, the inrush of the external evaporation into the earth.

[5] Hence, since the evaporation generally follows in a continuous body in the direction in which it first started, and either all of it flows inwards or all outwards, most earthquakes and the greatest are accompanied by calm. It is true that some take place when a wind is blowing, but this presents no difficulty. We sometimes find several winds blowing simultaneously. If [10] one of these enters the earth we get an earthquake attended by wind. Only these earthquakes are less severe because their source and cause is divided.

Again, most earthquakes and the severest occur at night or, if by day, about noon, that being generally the calmest part of the day. For [15] when the sun exerts its full power (as it does about noon) it shuts the evaporation into the earth. Night, too, is calmer than day. The absence of the sun makes the evaporation return into the earth like a sort of ebb tide, corresponding to the outward flow; especially to- [20] wards dawn, for the winds, as a rule, begin to blow then, and if their source changes about like the Euripus and flows inwards the quantity of wind in the earth is greater and a more violent earthquake results.

[25] The severest earthquakes take place where the sea is full of currents or the earth spongy and cavernous: so they occur near the Hellespont and in Achaea and Sicily, and those parts of Euboea which correspond to our description—where the sea is supposed to flow in channels below the earth. The hot springs, too, near Aedepsus are due to a cause of this kind. It is the confined character of these places that [30] makes them so liable to earthquakes. A great and therefore violent wind is developed, which would naturally blow away from the earth: but the onrush of the sea in a great mass thrusts it back into the earth. The countries that are spongy below the surface are exposed to earthquakes because they have room for so much wind.

For the same reason earthquakes usually take place in spring and autumn and in times of wet and of drought—because these are the windiest seasons. Summer with its heat and [5] winter with its frost cause calm: winter is too cold, summer too dry for winds to form. In time of drought the air is full of wind; drought is just the predominance of the dry over the moist evaporation. Again, excessive [10] rain causes more of the evaporation to form in the earth. Then this secretion is shut up in a narrow compass and forced into a smaller space by the water that fills the cavities. Thus a great wind is compressed into a smaller space and so gets the upper hand, and then breaks out and beats against the earth and shakes it violently.

[15] We must suppose the action of the wind in the earth to be analogous to the tremors and throbbings caused in us by the force of the wind contained in our bodies. Thus some earthquakes are a sort of tremor, others a sort of throbbing. Again, we must think of an earthquake as something like the tremor that often runs through the body after passing wa- [20] ter as the wind returns inwards from without in one volume.

The force wind can have may be gathered not only from what happens in the air (where one might suppose that it owed its power to produce such effects to its volume), but also [25] from what is observed in animal bodies. Tetanus and spasms are motions of wind, and their force is such that the united efforts of many men do not succeed in overcoming the movements of the patients. We must suppose, then (to compare great things with small), that what happens in the earth is just like that. [30] Our theory has been verified by actual observation in many places. It has been known to happen that an earthquake has continued until the wind that caused it burst through the earth

---
[1] 341^b 6.

into the air and appeared visibly like a hurricane. This happened lately near Heracleia in Pontus and some time past at the island Hiera, one of the group called the Aeolian islands. Here a portion of the earth swelled up and a lump like a mound rose with a noise: [5] finally it burst, and a great wind came out of it and threw up live cinders and ashes which buried the neighbouring town of Lipara and reached some of the towns in Italy. The spot where this eruption occurred is still to be seen.

Indeed, this must be recognized as the cause [10] of the fire that is generated in the earth: the air is first broken up in small particles and then the wind is beaten about and so catches fire.

A phenomenon in these islands affords further evidence of the fact that winds move below the surface of the earth. When a south wind is going to blow there is a premonitory indication: a sound is heard in the places from [15] which the eruptions issue. This is because the sea is being pushed on from a distance and its advance thrusts back into the earth the wind that was issuing from it. The reason why there is a noise and no earthquake is that the underground spaces are so extensive in proportion to the quantity of the air that is being driven on that the wind slips away into the void beyond.

[20] Again, our theory is supported by the facts that the sun appears hazy and is darkened in the absence of clouds, and that there is sometimes calm and sharp frost before earthquakes at sunrise. The sun is necessarily obscured and darkened when the evaporation which dissolves and rarefies the air begins to withdraw into the earth. The calm, too, and the cold to- [25] wards sunrise and dawn follow from the theory. The calm we have already explained. There must as a rule be calm because the wind flows back into the earth: again, it must be most marked before the more violent earthquakes, for when the wind is not part outside [30] the earth, part inside, but moves in a single body, its strength must be greater. The cold comes because the evaporation which is naturally and essentially hot enters the earth. (Wind is not recognized to be hot, because it sets the air in motion, and that is full of a quantity of cold vapour. It is the same with the breath we blow from our mouth: close by it is warm, as it is when we breathe out through the mouth, but there is so little of it that it is scarcely noticed, whereas at a distance it is cold for the same reason as wind.) Well, when this evaporation disappears into the earth the vaporous [5] exhalation concentrates and causes cold in any place in which this disappearance occurs.

A sign which sometimes precedes earthquakes can be explained in the same way. Either by day or a little after sunset, in fine weather, a little, light, long-drawn cloud is [10] seen, like a long very straight line. This is because the wind is leaving the air and dying down. Something analogous to this happens on the sea-shore. When the sea breaks in great waves the marks left on the sand are very thick [15] and crooked, but when the sea is calm they are slight and straight (because the secretion is small). As the sea is to the shore so the wind is to the cloudy air; so, when the wind drops, this very straight and thin cloud is left, a sort of wave-mark in the air.

[20] An earthquake sometimes coincides with an eclipse of the moon for the same reason. When the earth is on the point of being interposed, but the light and heat of the sun has not quite vanished from the air but is dying away, the wind which causes the earthquake before the eclipse, turns off into the earth, and calm [25] ensues. For there often are winds before eclipses: at nightfall if the eclipse is at midnight, and at midnight if the eclipse is at dawn. They are caused by the lessening of the warmth from the moon when its sphere approaches the point at which the eclipse is going to take [30] place. So the influence which restrained and quieted the air weakens and the air moves again and a wind rises, and does so later, the later the eclipse.

A severe earthquake does not stop at once or after a single shock, but first the shocks go on, often for about forty days; after that, for one or even two years it gives premonitory indications in the same place. The severity of the earthquake is determined by the quantity of wind and the shape of the passages through which it flows. Where it is beaten back and cannot easily find its way out the shocks are most violent, and there it must remain in a [5] cramped space like water that cannot escape. Any throbbing in the body does not cease suddenly or quickly, but by degrees according as the affection passes off. So here the agency which created the evaporation and gave it an impulse to motion clearly does not at once ex- [10] haust the whole of the material from which it forms the wind which we call an earthquake. So until the rest of this is exhausted the shocks must continue, though more gently, and they must go on until there is too little of the evaporation left to have any perceptible effect on the earth at all.

Subterranean noises, too, are due to the wind; sometimes they portend earthquakes but [15] sometimes they have been heard without any earthquake following. Just as the air gives off various sounds when it is struck, so it does when it strikes other things; for striking involves being struck and so the two cases are the same. The sound precedes the shock because [20] sound is thinner and passes through things more readily than wind. But when the wind is too weak by reason of thinness to cause an earthquake the absence of a shock is due to its filtering through readily, though by striking hard and hollow masses of different shapes it makes various noises, so that the earth some-[25] times seems to 'bellow' as the portent-mongers say.

Water has been known to burst out during an earthquake. But that does not make water the cause of the earthquake. The wind is the efficient cause whether it drives the water along the surface or up from below: just as winds are [30] the causes of waves and not waves of winds. Else we might as well say that earth was the cause; for it is upset in an earthquake, just like water (for effusion is a form of upsetting). No, earth and water are material causes (being patients, not agents): the true cause is the wind.

The combination of a tidal wave with an [35] earthquake is due to the presence of contrary winds. It occurs when the wind which is 368^b shaking the earth does not entirely succeed in driving off the sea which another wind is bringing on, but pushes it back and heaps it up in a great mass in one place. Given this situation it follows that when this wind gives [5] way the whole body of the sea, driven on by the other wind, will burst out and overwhelm the land. This is what happened in Achaea. There a south wind was blowing, but outside a north wind; then there was a calm and the wind entered the earth, and then the tidal wave came on and simultaneously there was an earthquake. This was the more violent as the sea allowed no exit to the wind that had entered the earth, but shut it in. So in their [10] struggle with one another the wind caused the earthquake, and the wave by its settling down the inundation.

Earthquakes are local and often affect a small district only; whereas winds are not local. Such phenomena are local when the evaporations at [15] a given place are joined by those from the next and unite; this, as we explained, is what happens when there is drought or excessive rain locally. Now earthquakes do come about in this way but winds do not. For earthquakes, rains, and droughts have their source and origin inside the earth, so that the sun is not [20] equally able to direct all the evaporations in one direction. But on the evaporations in the air the sun has more influence so that, when once they have been given an impulse by its motion, which is determined by its various positions, they flow in one direction.

When the wind is present in sufficient quantity there is an earthquake. The shocks are horizontal like a tremor; except occasionally, in a few places, where they act vertically, up-[25] wards from below, like a throbbing. It is the vertical direction which makes this kind of earthquake so rare. The motive force does not easily accumulate in great quantity in the position required, since the surface of the earth secretes far more of the evaporation than its depths. Wherever an earthquake of this kind does occur a quantity of stones comes to the surface of the earth (as when you throw up [30] things in a winnowing fan), as we see from Sipylus and the Phlegraean plain and the district in Liguria, which were devastated by this kind of earthquake.

Islands in the middle of the sea are less exposed to earthquakes than those near land. First, the volume of the sea cools the evapora-[35] tions and overpowers them by its weight 369^a and so crushes them. Then, currents and not shocks are produced in the sea by the action of the winds. Again, it is so extensive that evaporations do not collect in it but issue from it, and these draw the evaporations from the earth after them. Islands near the continent really form part of it: the intervening sea is not enough to make any difference; but those in [5] the open sea can only be shaken if the whole of the sea that surrounds them is shaken too.

We have now explained earthquakes, their nature and cause, and the most important of the circumstances attendant on their appearance.

9

[10] Let us go on to explain lightning and thunder, and further whirlwind, fire-wind, and thunderbolts: for the cause of them all is the same.

As we have said,[1] there are two kinds of exhalation, moist and dry, and the atmosphere contains them both potentially. It, as we have

---
[1] E. g. 341^b 6.

[15] said before,[1] condenses into cloud, and the density of the clouds is highest at their upper limit. (For they must be denser and colder on the side where the heat escapes to the upper region and leaves them. This explains why hurricanes and thunderbolts and all analogous phe- [20] nomena move downwards in spite of the fact that everything hot has a natural tendency upwards. Just as the pips that we squeeze between our fingers are heavy but often jump upwards: so these things are necessarily squeezed out away from the densest part of the cloud.) Now the heat that escapes disperses to the upper region. But if any of the dry exhalation is [25] caught in the process as the air cools, it is squeezed out as the clouds contract, and collides in its rapid course with the neighbouring clouds, and the sound of this collision is what we call thunder. This collision is analogous, to [30] compare small with great, to the sound we hear in a flame which men call the laughter or the threat of Hephaestus or of Hestia. This occurs when the wood dries and cracks and the exhalation rushes on the flame in a body. So in [35] the clouds, the exhalation is projected and 369[b] its impact on dense clouds causes thunder: the variety of the sound is due to the irregularity of the clouds and the hollows that intervene where their density is interrupted. This, then, is thunder, and this its cause.

[5] It usually happens that the exhalation that is ejected is inflamed and burns with a thin and faint fire: this is what we call lightning, where we see as it were the exhalation coloured in the act of its ejection. It comes into existence after the collision and the thunder, though we see it earlier because sight is quicker than hearing. The rowing of triremes illustrates this: the oars [10] are going back again before the sound of their striking the water reaches us.

However, there are some who maintain that there is actually fire in the clouds. Empedocles says that it consists of some of the sun's rays which are intercepted: Anaxagoras that it is part of the upper ether (which he calls fire) [15] which has descended from above. Lightning, then, is the gleam of this fire, and thunder the hissing noise of its extinction in the cloud.

But this involves the view that lightning actually is prior to thunder and does not merely appear to be so. Again, this intercepting of the fire is impossible on either theory, but especially [20] when it is said to be drawn down from the upper ether. Some reason ought to be given

[1] E. g. 341[b] 36 sqq., 346[b] 23 sqq.

why that which naturally ascends should descend, and why it should not always do so, but only when it is cloudy. When the sky is clear there is no lightning: to say that there is, is altogether wanton.

[25] The view that the heat of the sun's rays intercepted in the clouds is the cause of these phenomena is equally unattractive: this, too, is a most careless explanation. Thunder, lightning, and the rest must have a separate and de- [30] terminate cause assigned to them on which they ensue. But this theory does nothing of the sort. It is like supposing that water, snow, and hail existed all along and were produced when the time came and not generated at all, as if the atmosphere brought each to hand out of its stock from time to time. They are concretions in the same way as thunder and [35] lightning are discretions, so that if it is true of either that they are not generated but pre-exist, the same must be true of the other. 370[a] Again, how can any distinction be made about the intercepting between this case and that of interception in denser substances such as water? Water, too, is heated by the sun and by fire: yet when it contracts again and grows cold and freezes no such ejection as they de- [5] scribe occurs, though it ought on their theory to take place on a proportionate scale. Boiling is due to the exhalation generated by fire: but it is impossible for it to exist in the water beforehand; and besides they call the noise 'hissing', not 'boiling'. But hissing is really boiling on a small scale: for when that which is brought into contact with moisture and is in process of being extinguished gets the better of it, then it boils and makes the noise in question.

[10] Some—Cleidemus is one of them—say that lightning is nothing objective but merely an appearance. They compare it to what happens when you strike the sea with a rod by night and the water is seen to shine. They say that the moisture in the cloud is beaten about in the same way, and that lightning is the ap- [15] pearance of brightness that ensues.

This theory is due to ignorance of the theory of reflection, which is the real cause of that phenomenon. The water appears to shine when struck because our sight is reflected from it to some bright object: hence the phenomenon oc- [20] curs mainly by night: the appearance is not seen by day because the daylight is too intense and obscures it.

These are the theories of others about thunder and lightning: some maintaining that lightning is a reflection, the others that lightning is fire shining through the cloud and thunder its extinction, the fire not being generated in each [25] case but existing beforehand. We say that the same stuff is wind on the earth, and earthquake under it, and in the clouds thunder. The essential constituent of all these phenomena is the same: namely, the dry exhalation. If it flows in one direction it is wind, in another it causes earthquakes; in the clouds, when they are in a process of change and contract and [30] condense into water, it is ejected and causes thunder and lightning and the other phenomena of the same nature.

So much for thunder and lightning.

BOOK III

1

370[b] Let us explain the remaining operations of this secretion in the same way as we have treated the rest. When this exhalation is secret- [5] ed in small and scattered quantities and frequently, and is transitory, and its constitution rare, it gives rise to thunder and lightning. But if it is secreted in a body and is denser, that is, less rare, we get a hurricane. The fact that it issues in a body explains its violence: it is due [10] to the rapidity of the secretion. Now when this secretion issues in a great and continuous current the result corresponds to what we get when the opposite development takes place and rain and a quantity of water are produced. As far as the matter from which they are developed goes both sets of phenomena are the same. As soon as a stimulus to the development of either potentiality appears, that of [15] which there is the greater quantity present in the cloud is at once secreted from it, and there results either rain, or, if the other exhalation prevails, a hurricane.

Sometimes the exhalation in the cloud, when it is being secreted, collides with another under circumstances like those found when a wind is forced from an open into a narrow space in a gateway or a road. It often happens [20] in such cases that the first part of the moving body is deflected because of the resistance due either to the narrowness or to a contrary current, and so the wind forms a circle and eddy. It is prevented from advancing in a straight line: at the same time it is pushed on from behind; so it is compelled to move sideways in the direction of least resistance. The [25] same thing happens to the next part, and the next, and so on, till the series becomes one, that is, till a circle is formed: for if a figure is described by a single motion that figure must itself be one. This is how eddies are generated on the earth, and the case is the same in the clouds as far as the beginning of them goes. Only here (as in the case of the hurricane which shakes off the cloud without cessation [30] and becomes a continuous wind) the cloud follows the exhalation unbroken, and the exhalation, failing to break away from the cloud because of its density, first moves in a circle for the reason given and then descends, because clouds are always densest on the side where the 371[a] heat escapes. This phenomenon is called a whirlwind when it is colourless; and it is a sort of undigested hurricane. There is never a whirlwind when the weather is northerly, nor a hurricane when there is snow. The reason is that all these phenomena are 'wind', and wind [5] is a dry and warm evaporation. Now frost and cold prevail over this principle and quench it at its birth: that they do prevail is clear or there could be no snow or northerly rain, since these occur when the cold does prevail.

[10] So the whirlwind originates in the failure of an incipient hurricane to escape from its cloud: it is due to the resistance which generates the eddy, and it consists in the spiral which descends to the earth and drags with it the cloud which it cannot shake off. It moves things by its wind in the direction in which it is blowing in a straight line, and whirls round by its circular motion and forcibly snatches up whatever it meets.

[15] When the cloud burns as it is drawn downwards, that is, when the exhalation becomes rarer, it is called a fire-wind, for its fire colours the neighbouring air and inflames it.

When there is a great quantity of exhalation and it is rare and is squeezed out in the cloud itself we get a thunderbolt. If the exhalation is [20] exceedingly rare this rareness prevents the thunderbolt from scorching and the poets call it 'bright': if the rareness is less it does scorch and they call it 'smoky'. The former moves rapidly because of its rareness, and because of its rapidity passes through an object before setting fire to it or dwelling on it so as to blacken it: the slower one does blacken the object, but passes through it before it can actually burn it. [25] Further, resisting substances are affected, unresisting ones are not. For instance, it has happened that the bronze of a shield has been melted while the woodwork remained intact because its texture was so loose that the exhalation filtered through without affecting it. So it has passed through clothes, too, without burning them, and has merely reduced them to shreds.

Such evidence is enough by itself to show [30] that the exhalation is at work in all these cases, but we sometimes get direct evidence as well, as in the case of the conflagration of the temple at Ephesus which we lately witnessed. There independent sheets of flame left the main fire and were carried bodily in many directions. Now that smoke is exhalation and that smoke burns is certain, and has been stated 371^b in another place before[1]; but when the flame moves bodily, then we have ocular proof that smoke is exhalation. On this occasion what is seen in small fires appeared on a much larger scale because of the quantity of matter that was burning. The beams which were the source of [5] the exhalation split, and a quantity of it rushed in a body from the place from which it issued forth and went up in a blaze: so that the flame was actually seen moving through the air away and falling on the houses. For we must recognize that exhalation accompanies and precedes thunderbolts though it is colourless and so invisible. Hence, where the thunderbolt is [10] going to strike, the object moves before it is struck, showing that the exhalation leads the way and falls on the object first. Thunder, too, splits things not by its noise but because the exhalation that strikes the object and that which makes the noise are ejected simultaneously. This exhalation splits the thing it strikes but does not scorch it at all.

We have now explained thunder and lightning [15] and hurricane, and further firewinds, whirlwinds, and thunderbolts, and shown that they are all of them forms of the same thing and wherein they all differ.

2

Let us now explain the nature and cause of halo, rainbow, mock suns, and rods, since the [20] same account applies to them all.

We must first describe the phenomena and the circumstances in which each of them occurs. The halo often appears as a complete circle: it is seen round the sun and the moon and bright stars, by night as well as by day, and at [25] midday or in the afternoon, more rarely about sunrise or sunset.

[1] Cf. 341^b 21, 388^a 2, and *On Generation and Corruption*, 331^b 25.

The rainbow never forms a full circle, nor any segment greater than a semicircle. At sunset and sunrise the circle is smallest and the segment largest: as the sun rises higher the circle [30] is larger and the segment smaller. After the autumn equinox in the shorter days it is seen at every hour of the day, in the summer not about midday. There are never more than two rainbows at one time. Each of them is three-coloured; the colours are the same in both and their number is the same, but in the outer rainbow they are fainter and their position is reversed. In the inner rainbow the first and largest band is red; in the outer rainbow the band that is nearest to this one and smallest is of the same colour: the other bands correspond on the same principle. These are al- [5] most the only colours which painters cannot manufacture: for there are colours which they create by mixing, but no mixing will give red, green, or purple. These are the colours of the rainbow, though between the red and the green an orange colour is often seen.

[10] Mock suns and rods are always seen by the side of the sun, not above or below it nor in the opposite quarter of the sky. They are not seen at night but always in the neighbourhood of the sun, either as it is rising or setting but more commonly towards sunset. They have scarcely ever appeared when the sun was on the meridian, though this once happened in [15] Bosporus where two mock suns rose with the sun and followed it all through the day till sunset.

These are the facts about each of these phenomena: the cause of them all is the same, for they are all reflections. But they are different varieties, and are distinguished by the surface [20] from which and the way in which the reflection to the sun or some other bright object takes place.

The rainbow is seen by day, and it was formerly thought that it never appeared by night as a moon rainbow. This opinion was due to the rarity of the occurrence: it was not observed, for though it does happen it does so rarely. The reason is that the colours are not so easy to see in the dark and that many other [25] conditions must coincide, and all that in a single day in the month. For if there is to be one it must be at full moon, and then as the moon is either rising or setting. So we have only met with two instances of a moon rainbow in more than fifty years.

We must accept from the theory of optics the [30] fact that sight is reflected from air and any object with a smooth surface just as it is from water; also that in some mirrors the forms of things are reflected, in others only their colours. Of the latter kind are those mirrors which are so small as to be indivisible for sense. It is impossible that the figure of a thing should be reflected in them, for if it is the mirror will be sensibly divisible since divisibility is involved in the notion of figure. But since something must be reflected in them and [5] figure cannot be, it remains that colour alone should be reflected. The colour of a bright object sometimes appears bright in the reflection, but it sometimes, either owing to the admixture of the colour of the mirror or to weakness of sight, gives rise to the appearance of another colour.

However, we must accept the account we have given of these things in the theory of sen- [10] sation, and take some things for granted while we explain others.

3

Let us begin by explaining the shape of the halo; why it is a circle and why it appears round the sun or the moon or one of the other stars: the explanation being in all these cases the same.

[15] Sight is reflected in this way when air and vapour are condensed into a cloud and the condensed matter is uniform and consists of small parts. Hence in itself it is a sign of rain, but if it fades away, of fine weather, if it is broken up, [20] of wind. For if it does not fade away and is not broken up but is allowed to attain its normal state, it is naturally a sign of rain since it shows that a process of condensation is proceeding which must, when it is carried to an end, result in rain. For the same reason these haloes are the darkest. It is a sign of wind when [25] it is broken up because its breaking up is due to a wind which exists there but has not reached us. This view finds support in the fact that the wind blows from the quarter in which the main division appears in the halo. Its fading away is a sign of fine weather because if the [30] air is not yet in a state to get the better of the heat it contains and proceed to condense into water, this shows that the moist vapour has not yet separated from the dry and firelike exhalation: and this is the cause of fine weather.

So much for the atmospheric conditions under which the reflection takes place. The reflection is from the mist that forms round the sun or the moon, and that is why the halo is not seen opposite the sun like the rainbow.

Since the reflection takes place in the same way from every point the result is necessarily a circle or a segment of a circle: for if the lines start from the same point and end at the same point and are equal, the points where they form an [5] angle will always lie on a circle.

Let AΓB and AZB and AΔB be lines each of which goes from the point A to the point B and forms an angle. Let the lines AΓ, AZ, AΔ be equal and those at B, ΓB, ZB, ΔB equal too.

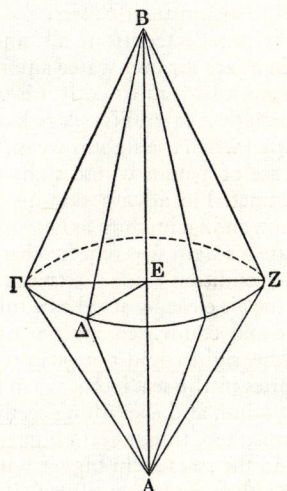

Draw the line AEB. Then the triangles are [10] equal; for their base AEB is equal. Draw perpendiculars to AEB from the angles; ΓE from Γ, ZE from Z, ΔE from Δ. Then these perpendiculars are equal, being in equal triangles. And they are all in one plane, being all at [15] right angles to AEB and meeting at a single point E. So if you draw the line it will be a circle and E its centre. Now B is the sun, A the eye, and the circumference passing through the points ΓZΔ the cloud from which the line of sight is reflected to the sun.

The mirrors must be thought of as contiguous: [20] each of them is too small to be visible, but their contiguity makes the whole made up of them all to seem one. The bright band is the sun, which is seen as a circle, appearing successively in each of the mirrors as a point indivisible to sense. The band of cloud next to it [25] is black, its colour being intensified by contrast with the brightness of the halo. The halo is formed rather near the earth because that is calmer: for where there is wind it is clear that no halo can maintain its position.

Haloes are commoner round the moon because the greater heat of the sun dissolves the condensations of the air more rapidly.

[30] Haloes are formed round stars for the same reasons, but they are not prognostic in the same way because the condensation they imply is so insignificant as to be barren.

4

We have already stated that the rainbow is a reflection: we have now to explain what sort of reflection it is, to describe its various concomitants, and to assign their causes.

[35] Sight is reflected from all smooth surfaces, such as are air and water among others. 373[b] Air must be condensed if it is to act as a mirror, though it often gives a reflection even uncondensed when the sight is weak. Such was [5] the case of a man whose sight was faint and indistinct. He always saw an image in front of him and facing him as he walked. This was because his sight was reflected back to him. Its morbid condition made it so weak and delicate that the air close by acted as a mirror, just as distant and condensed air normally does, [10] and his sight could not push it back. So promontories in the sea 'loom' when there is a south-east wind, and everything seems bigger, and in a mist, too, things seem bigger: so, too, the sun and the stars seem bigger when rising and setting than on the meridian. But things are best reflected from water, and even in proc- [15] ess of formation it is a better mirror than air, for each of the particles, the union of which constitutes a raindrop, is necessarily a better mirror than mist. Now it is obvious and has already been stated[1] that a mirror of this kind renders the colour of an object only, but not its [20] shape. Hence it follows that when it is on the point of raining and the air in the clouds is in process of forming into raindrops but the rain is not yet actually there, if the sun is opposite, or any other object bright enough to make the cloud a mirror and cause the sight to be reflected to the object then the reflection must render the colour of the object without its shape. Since each of the mirrors is so small as [25] to be invisible and what we see is the continuous magnitude made up of them all, the reflection necessarily gives us a continuous magnitude made up of one colour; each of the mirrors contributing the same colour to the whole. We may deduce that since these conditions are realizable there will be an appearance [30] due to reflection whenever the sun and the cloud are related in the way described and

[1] 372[a] 34.

we are between them. But these are just the conditions under which the rainbow appears. So it is clear that the rainbow is a reflection of sight to the sun.

So the rainbow always appears opposite the [35] sun whereas the halo is round it. They are both reflections, but the rainbow is distin- 374[a] guished by the variety of its colours. The reflection in the one case is from water which is dark and from a distance; in the other from air which is nearer and lighter in colour. White light through a dark medium or on a dark surface (it makes no difference) looks red. We [5] know how red the flame of green wood is: this is because so much smoke is mixed with the bright white firelight: so, too, the sun appears red through smoke and mist. That is why in the rainbow reflection the outer circumference is red (the reflection being from small particles of water), but not in the case of the halo. [10] The other colours shall be explained later. Again, a condensation of this kind cannot persist in the neighbourhood of the sun: it must either turn to rain or be dissolved, but opposite to the sun there is an interval during which the water is formed. If there were not this distinc- [15] tion haloes would be coloured like the rainbow. Actually no complete or circular halo presents this colour, only small and fragmentary appearances called 'rods'. But if a haze due to water or any other dark substance formed there we should have had, as we maintain, a complete rainbow like that which we do find [20] round lamps. A rainbow appears round these in winter, generally with southerly winds. Persons whose eyes are moist see it most clearly because their sight is weak and easily reflected. It is due to the moistness of the air and the soot which the flame gives off and which mixes [25] with the air and makes it a mirror, and to the blackness which that mirror derives from the smoky nature of the soot. The light of the lamp appears as a circle which is not white but purple. It shows the colours of the rainbow; but because the sight that is reflected is too weak and the mirror too dark, red is absent. [30] The rainbow that is seen when oars are raised out of the sea involves the same relative positions as that in the sky, but its colour is more like that round the lamps, being purple rather than red. The reflection is from very small particles continuous with one another, and in this case the particles are fully formed [35] water. We get a rainbow, too, if a man 374[b] sprinkles fine drops in a room turned to the sun so that the sun is shining in part of the room and throwing a shadow in the rest. Then if one man sprinkles in the room, another, standing outside, sees a rainbow where the [5] sun's rays cease and make the shadow. Its nature and colour is like that from the oars and its cause is the same, for the sprinkling hand corresponds to the oar.

That the colours of the rainbow are those we described[1] and how the other colours come to appear in it will be clear from the following considerations. We must recognize, as we have [10] said,[2] and lay down: first, that white colour on a black surface or seen through a black medium gives red; second, that sight when strained to a distance becomes weaker and less; third, that black is in a sort the negation of sight: an object is black because sight fails; so everything at a distance looks blacker, because sight does not reach it. The theory of these [15] matters belongs to the account of the senses, which are the proper subjects of such an inquiry; we need only state about them what is necessary for us. At all events, that is the reason why distant objects and objects seen in a mirror look darker and smaller and smoother, [20] and why the reflection of clouds in water is darker than the clouds themselves. This latter is clearly the case: the reflection diminishes the sight that reaches them. It makes no difference whether the change is in the object seen or in the sight, the result being in either case the same. The following fact further is worth [25] noticing. When there is a cloud near the sun and we look at it it does not look coloured at all but white, but when we look at the same cloud in water it shows a trace of rainbow colouring. Clearly, then, when sight is reflected it is weakened and, as it makes dark look darker, so it makes white look less white, changing it [30] and bringing it nearer to black. When the sight is relatively strong the change is to red; the next stage is green, and a further degree of weakness gives violet. No further change is visible, but three completes the series of colours (as we find three does in most other things), and the change into the rest is imperceptible to sense. Hence also the rainbow appears with 375ᵃ three colours; this is true of each of the two, but in a contrary way. The outer band of the primary rainbow is red: for the largest band reflects most sight to the sun, and the outer band is largest. The middle band and the third go on the same principle. So if the principles we laid down[3] about the appearance of

[5] colours are true the rainbow necessarily has three colours, and these three and no others. The appearance of yellow is due to contrast, for the red is whitened by its juxtaposition with green. We can see this from the fact that the [10] rainbow is purest when the cloud is blackest; and then the red shows most yellow. (Yellow in the rainbow comes between red and green.) So the whole of the red shows white by contrast with the blackness of the cloud around: for it is white compared to the cloud and the green. Again, when the rainbow is fading away [15] and the red is dissolving, the white cloud is brought into contact with the green and becomes yellow. But the moon rainbow affords the best instance of this colour contrast. It looks quite white: this is because it appears on the dark cloud and at night. So, just as fire is in-[20] tensified by added fire, black beside black makes that which is in some degree white look quite white. Bright dyes too show the effect of contrast. In woven and embroidered stuffs the appearance of colours is profoundly affected by their juxtaposition with one another (purple, [25] for instance, appears different on white and on black wool), and also by differences of illumination. Thus embroiderers say that they often make mistakes in their colours when they work by lamplight, and use the wrong ones.

We have now shown why the rainbow has three colours and that these are its only colours. [30] The same cause explains the double rainbow and the faintness of the colours in the outer one and their inverted order. When sight is strained to a great distance the appearance of the distant object is affected in a certain way: and the same thing holds good here. So the re-375ᵇ flection from the outer rainbow is weaker because it takes place from a greater distance

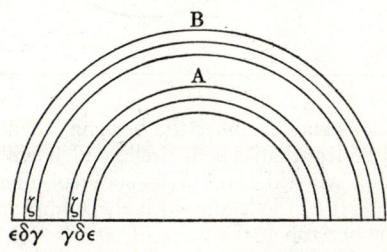

γ = Red; δ = Green; ϵ = Violet; ζ = Yellow

and less of it reaches the sun, and so the colours seen are fainter. Their order is reversed because more reflection reaches the sun from the small-[5] er, inner band. For that reflection is nearer

---

[1] 372ᵃ 7, cf. 375ᵃ 28 below.   [2] 374ᵃ 3.
[3] 374ᵇ 9 above.

to our sight which is reflected from the band which is nearest to the primary rainbow. Now the smallest band in the outer rainbow is that which is nearest, and so it will be red; and the second and the third will follow the same principle. Let B be the outer rainbow, A the inner [10] one; let γ stand for the red colour, Δ for green, E for violet; yellow appears at the point ζ. Three rainbows or more are not found because even the second is fainter, so that the third reflection can have no strength whatever [15] and cannot reach the sun at all.

5

The rainbow can never be a circle nor a segment of a circle greater than a semicircle. The consideration of the diagram will prove this and the other properties of the rainbow.

Let A be a hemisphere resting on the circle [20] of the horizon, let its centre be K and let H be another point appearing on the horizon. Then, if the lines that fall in a cone from K have HK as their axis, and, K and M being joined, the lines KM are reflected from the hemisphere to H over the greater angle, the lines from K will fall on the circumference of [25] a circle. If the reflection takes place when the luminous body is rising or setting the segment of the circle above the earth which is cut off by the horizon will be a semi-circle; if the

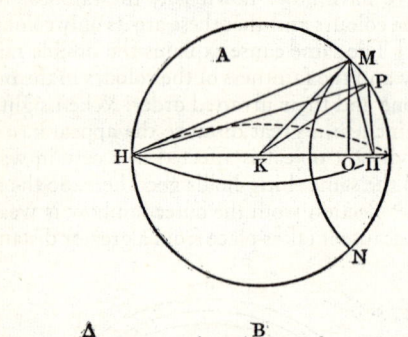

luminous body is above the horizon it will always be less than a semicircle, and it will be smallest when the luminous body culminates. [30] First let the luminous body be appearing on the horizon at the point H, and let KM be reflected to H, and let the plane in which A is, determined by the triangle HKM, be produced. Then the section of the sphere will be a great circle. Let it be A (for it makes no difference which of the planes passing through the line HK and determined by the triangle KMH

376ᵃ is produced). Now the lines drawn from H and K to a point on the semicircle A are in a certain ratio to one another, and no lines drawn from the same points to another point on that semicircle can have the same ratio. For since both the points H and K and the line KH are given, the line MH will be given too; consequently the ratio of the line MH to the line [5] MK will be given too. So M will touch a given circumference. Let this be NM. Then the intersection of the circumferences is given, and the same ratio cannot hold between lines in the same plane drawn from the same points to any other circumference but MN.

[10] Draw a line ΔB outside of the figure and divide it so that Δ:B = MH:MK. But MH is greater than MK since the reflection of the cone is over the greater angle (for it subtends the greater angle of the triangle KMH). Therefore [15] Δ is greater than B. Then add to B a line Z such that B+Z:Δ = Δ:B. Then make another line KΠ having the same ratio to B as KH has to Z, and join MΠ.

Then Π is the pole of the circle on which the [20] lines from K fall. For the ratio of Δ to ΠM is the same as that of Z to KH and of B to KΠ. If not, let Δ be in the same ratio to a line indifferently lesser or greater than ΠM, and let this line be ΠP. Then HK and KΠ and ΠP will have the same ratios to one another as Z, B, and Δ. But the ratios between Z, B, and Δ were such that Z+B:Δ = Δ:B. [25] Therefore ΠH:ΠP = ΠP:ΠK. Now, if the points K, H be joined with the point P by the lines HP, KP, these lines will be to one another as ΠH is to ΠP, for the sides of the triangles HΠP, KPΠ about the angle Π are [30] homologous. Therefore, HP too will be to KP as HΠ is to ΠP. But this is also the ratio of MH to MK, for the ratio both of HΠ to ΠP and of MH to MK is the same as that of Δ to B. Therefore, from the points H, K there will have been drawn lines with the same ratio to one another, not only to the circumference MN but to another point as well, which is impossible. Since then Δ cannot bear that ratio to any line either lesser or greater [5] than ΠM (the proof being in either case the same), it follows that it must stand in that ratio to MΠ itself. Therefore as MΠ is to ΠK so ΠH will be to MΠ and finally MH to MK.

If, then, a circle be described with Π as pole at the distance MΠ it will touch all the angles which the lines from H and K make by their

[10] reflection. If not, it can be shown, as before, that lines drawn to different points in the semicircle will have the same ratio to one another, which was impossible. If, then, the semicircle A be revolved about the diameter HKΠ, the lines reflected from the points H, K at the [15] point M will have the same ratio, and will make the angle KMH equal, in every plane. Further, the angle which HM and MΠ make with HΠ will always be the same. So there are a number of triangles on HΠ and KΠ equal to the triangles HMΠ and KMΠ. Their perpendiculars will fall on HΠ at the same point [20] and will be equal. Let O be the point on which they fall. Then O is the centre of the circle, half of which, MN, is cut off by the horizon.

Next let the horizon be ABΓ but let H have [30] risen above the horizon. Let the axis now be HΠ. The proof will be the same for the rest as before, but the pole Π of the circle will be below the horizon AΓ since the point H has risen above the horizon. But the pole, and the centre of the circle, and the centre of that circle (namely HΠ) which now determines the position of the sun are on the same line. But since KH lies above the diameter AΓ, the cen- [5] tre will be at O on the line KΠ below the plane of the circle AΓ which determined the position of the sun before. So the segment ΨΥ which is above the horizon will be less than a semicircle. For ΨΥΩ was a semicircle and it has now been cut off by the horizon AΓ. So part of it, ΥΩ, will be invisible when the sun has risen above the horizon, and the segment

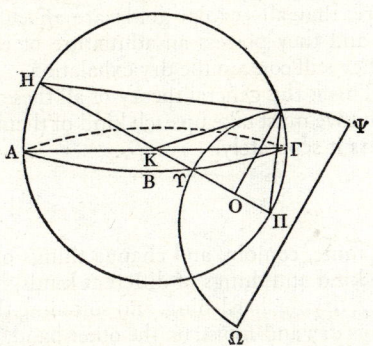

visible will be smallest when the sun is on the [10] meridian; for the higher H is the lower the pole and the centre of the circle will be.

In the shorter days after the autumn equinox there may be a rainbow at any time of the day, but in the longer days from the spring to the autumn equinox there cannot be a rainbow [15] about midday. The reason for this is that when the sun is north of the equator the visible arcs of its course are all greater than a semicircle, and go on increasing, while the invisible arc is small, but when the sun is south of the equator the visible arc is small and the invisible arc great, and the farther the sun moves south of the equator the greater is the invisible [20] arc. Consequently, in the days near the summer solstice, the size of the visible arc is such that before the point H reaches the middle of that arc, that is its point of culmination, the point Π is well below the horizon; the reason for this being the great size of the visible arc, and the consequent distance of the point of culmination from the earth. But in the days [25] near the winter solstice the visible arcs are small, and the contrary is necessarily the case: for the sun is on the meridian before the point H has risen far.

6

Mock suns, and rods too, are due to the [30] causes we have described. A mock sun is caused by the reflection of sight to the sun. Rods are seen when sight reaches the sun under circumstances like those which we described,[1] when there are clouds near the sun and sight is reflected from some liquid surface to the cloud. Here the clouds themselves are colourless when you look at them directly, but in the water they are full of rods. The only difference is that in this latter case the colour of the cloud seems to reside in the water, but in the case of rods on the cloud itself. Rods [5] appear when the composition of the cloud is uneven, dense in part and in part rare, and more and less watery in different parts. Then the sight is reflected to the sun: the mirrors are too small for the shape of the sun to appear, but, the bright white light of the sun, to which the sight is reflected, being seen on the uneven mirror, its colour appears partly red, partly [10] green or yellow. It makes no difference whether sight passes through or is reflected from a medium of that kind; the colour is the same in both cases; if it is red in the first case it must be the same in the other.

Rods then are occasioned by the unevenness [15] of the mirror—as regards colour, not form. The mock sun, on the contrary, appears when the air is very uniform, and of the same density throughout. This is why it is white: the uniform character of the mirror gives the

[1] 374^b 24.

reflection in it a single colour, while the fact that the sight is reflected in a body and is thrown on the sun all together by the mist, [20] which is dense and watery though not yet quite water, causes the sun's true colour to appear just as it does when the reflection is from the dense, smooth surface of copper. So the sun's colour being white, the mock sun is white too. This, too, is the reason why the mock sun is a surer sign of rain than the rods; it indi-[25] cates, more than they do, that the air is ripe for the production of water. Further a mock sun to the south is a surer sign of rain than one to the north, for the air in the south is readier to turn into water than that in the north.

Mock suns and rods are found, as we stated,[1] about sunset and sunrise, not above the sun nor [30] below it, but beside it. They are not found very close to the sun, nor very far from it, for the sun dissolves the cloud if it is near, but if it is far off the reflection cannot take place, since sight weakens when it is reflected from a small mirror to a very distant object. (This is why a halo is never found opposite to the sun.) If the 378ª cloud is above the sun and close to it the sun will dissolve it; if it is above the sun but at a distance the sight is too weak for the reflection to take place, and so it will not reach the sun. But at the side of the sun, it is possible for the mirror to be at such an interval that the sun does not dissolve the cloud, and yet sight reaches [5] it undiminished because it moves close to the earth and is not dissipated in the immensity of space. It cannot subsist below the sun because close to the earth the sun's rays would dissolve it, but if it were high up and the sun in the middle of the heavens, sight would be dissipated. Indeed, even by the side of the sun, it is not found when the sun is in the middle of the sky, for then the line of vision is not close [10] to the earth, and so but little sight reaches

the mirror and the reflection from it is altogether feeble.

Some account has now been given of the ef-[15] fects of the secretion above the surface of the earth; we must go on to describe its operations below, when it is shut up in the parts of the earth.

Just as its twofold nature gives rise to various effects in the upper region, so here it causes two varieties of bodies. We maintain that there are two exhalations, one vaporous the other smoky, and there correspond two kinds of [20] bodies that originate in the earth, 'fossils' and metals. The heat of the dry exhalation is the cause of all 'fossils'. Such are the kinds of stones that cannot be melted, and realgar, and ochre, and ruddle, and sulphur, and the other [25] things of that kind, most 'fossils' being either coloured lye or, like cinnabar, a stone compounded of it. The vaporous exhalation is the cause of all metals, those bodies which are either fusible or malleable such as iron, copper, gold. All these originate from the imprisonment of the vaporous exhalation in the earth, [30] and especially in stones. Their dryness compresses it, and it congeals just as dew or hoar-frost does when it has been separated off, though in the present case the metals are generated before that segregation occurs. Hence, they are water in a sense, and in a sense not. Their matter was that which might have become water, but it can no longer do so: nor are 378ᵇ they, like savours, due to a qualitative change in actual water. Copper and gold are not formed like that, but in every case the evaporation congealed before water was formed. Hence, they all (except gold) are affected by fire, and they possess an admixture of earth; for they still contain the dry exhalation. [5] This is the general theory of all these bodies, but we must take up each kind of them and discuss it separately.

BOOK IV

I

[10] WE have explained that the qualities that constitute the elements are four, and that their combinations determine the number of the elements to be four.

Two of the qualities, the hot and the cold, are active; two, the dry and the moist, passive. We can satisfy ourselves of this by looking at instances. In every case heat and cold deter-

[1] 372ª 10.

[15] mine, conjoin, and change things of the same kind and things of different kinds, moistening, drying, hardening, and softening them. Things dry and moist, on the other hand, both in isolation and when present together in the same body are the subjects of that determina-[20] tion and of the other affections enumerated. The account we give of the qualities when we define their character shows this too. Hot and cold we describe as active, for 'congregating' is essentially a species of 'being active':

moist and dry are passive, for it is in virtue of its being acted upon in a certain way that a thing is said to be 'easy to determine' or 'diffi- [25] cult to determine'. So it is clear that some of the qualities are active and some passive.

Next we must describe the operations of the active qualities and the forms taken by the passive. First of all, true becoming, that is, natural change, is always the work of these powers and so is the corresponding natural destruction; [30] and this becoming and this destruction are found in plants and animals and their parts. True natural becoming is a change introduced by these powers into the matter underlying a given thing when they are in a certain ratio to that matter, which is the passive qualities we 379a have mentioned. When the hot and the cold are masters of the matter they generate a thing: if they are not, and the failure is partial, the object is imperfectly boiled or otherwise unconcocted. But the strictest general opposite of true becoming is putrefaction. All natural destruction is on the way to it, as are, for instance, growing old or growing dry. Putrescence is the [5] end of all these things, that is of all natural objects, except such as are destroyed by violence: you can burn, for instance, flesh, bone, or anything else, but the natural course of their destruction ends in putrefaction. Hence things that putrefy begin by being moist and end by being dry. For the moist and the dry were their [10] matter, and the operation of the active qualities caused the dry to be determined by the moist.

Destruction supervenes when the determined gets the better of the determining by the help of the environment (though in a special sense the word putrefaction is applied to partial destruction, when a thing's nature is perverted). [15] Hence everything, except fire, is liable to putrefy; for earth, water, and air putrefy, being all of them matter relatively to fire. The definition of putrefaction is: the destruction of the peculiar and natural heat in any moist subject by external heat, that is, by the heat of the environment. So since lack of heat is the ground of this affection and everything in as far as it [20] lacks heat is cold, both heat and cold will be the causes of putrefaction, which will be due indifferently to cold in the putrefying subject or to heat in the environment.

This explains why everything that putrefies grows drier and ends by becoming earth or dung. The subject's own heat departs and causes the natural moisture to evaporate with it, and then there is nothing left to draw in [25] moisture, for it is a thing's peculiar heat that attracts moisture and draws it in. Again, putrefaction takes place less in cold that in hot seasons, for in winter the surrounding air and water contain but little heat and it has no power, but in summer there is more. Again, what is frozen does not putrefy, for its cold is greater [30] that the heat of the air and so is not mastered, whereas what affects a thing does master it. Nor does that which is boiling or hot putrefy, for the heat in the air being less than that in the object does not prevail over it or set up any change. So too anything that is flowing or in motion is less apt to putrefy than a thing at [35] rest, for the motion set up by the heat in 379b the air is weaker than that pre-existing in the object, and so it causes no change. For the same reason a great quantity of a thing putrefies less readily than a little, for the greater quantity contains too much proper fire and cold for the corresponding qualities in the environment to get the better of. Hence, the sea [5] putrefies quickly when broken up into parts, but not as a whole; and all other waters likewise. Animals too are generated in putrefying bodies, because the heat that has been secreted, being natural, organizes the particles secreted with it.

So much for the nature of becoming and of destruction.

2

[10] We must now describe the next kinds of processes which the qualities already mentioned set up in actually existing natural objects as matter.

Of these concoction is due to heat; its species are ripening, boiling, broiling. Inconcoction is due to cold and its species are rawness, imperfect boiling, imperfect broiling. (We must recognize that the things are not prop- [15] erly denoted by these words: the various classes of similar objects have no names universally applicable to them; consequently we must think of the species enumerated as being not what those words denote but something like it.) Let us say what each of them is. Concoction is a process in which the natural and proper heat of an object perfects the corresponding passive qualities, which are the proper matter [20] of any given object. For when concoction has taken place we say that a thing has been perfected and has come to be itself. It is the proper heat of a thing that sets up this perfecting, though external influences may contribute in some degrees to its fulfilment. Baths, for instance, and other things of the kind contribute to the digestion of food, but the primary cause [25] is the proper heat of the body. In some cases of concoction the end of the process is the nature of the thing—nature, that is, in the sense of the formal cause and essence. In other cases it leads to some *presupposed state* which is attained when the moisture has acquired certain properties or a certain magnitude in the process of being broiled or boiled or of putrefying, or however else it is being heated. This state is the end, for when it has been reached the thing has some use and we say that concoction has taken place. Must is an instance of this, [30] and the matter in boils when it becomes purulent, and tears when they become rheum, and so with the rest.

Concoction ensues whenever the matter, the moisture, is mastered. For the matter is what is determined by the heat connatural to the [35] object, and as long as the ratio between them exists in it a thing maintains its nature. 380ᵃ Hence things like the liquid and solid excreta and ejecta in general are signs of health, and concoction is said to have taken place in them, for they show that the proper heat has got the better of the indeterminate matter.

Things that undergo a process of concoction necessarily become thicker and hotter, for the action of heat is to make things more compact, [5] thicker, and drier.

This then is the nature of concoction: but inconcoction is an imperfect state due to lack of proper heat, that is, to cold. That *of* which the imperfect state is, is the corresponding passive qualities which are the natural matter of anything.

[10] So much for the definition of concoction and inconcoction.

3

Ripening is a sort of concoction; for we call it ripening when there is a concoction of the nutriment in fruit. And since concoction is a sort of perfecting, the process of ripening is perfect when the seeds in fruit are able to re- [15] produce the fruit in which they are found; for in all other cases as well this is what we mean by 'perfect'. This is what 'ripening' means when the word is applied to fruit. However, many other things that have undergone concoction are said to be 'ripe', the general character of the process being the same, though the word is applied by an extension of meaning. The reason for this extension is, as we explained before,[1] that the various modes in which natural heat and cold perfect the matter they determine have not special names appropriated to them. In the case of boils and [20] phlegm, and the like, the process of ripening is the concoction of the moisture in them by their natural heat, for only that which gets the better of matter can determine it. So everything that ripens is condensed from a spirituous into a watery state, and from a watery into an earthy state, and in general from being rare becomes [25] dense. In this process the nature of the thing that is ripening incorporates some of the matter in itself, and some it rejects. So much for the definition of ripening.

Rawness is its opposite and is therefore an imperfect concoction of the nutriment in the fruit, namely, of the undetermined moisture. Consequently a raw thing is either spirituous or watery or contains both spirit and water. [30] Ripening being a kind of perfecting, rawness will be an imperfect state, and this state is due to a lack of natural heat and its disproportion to the moisture that is undergoing the process of ripening. (Nothing moist ripens without the admixture of some dry matter: water alone of liquids does not thicken.) This dis- 380ᵇ proportion may be due either to defect of heat or to excess of the matter to be determined: hence the juice of raw things is thin, cold rather than hot, and unfit for food or drink. Rawness, like ripening, is used to denote a variety [5] of states. Thus the liquid and solid excreta and catarrhs are called raw for the same reason, for in every case the word is applied to things because their heat has not got the mastery in them and compacted them. If we go further, brick is called raw and so is milk and many other things too when they are such as to admit of being changed and compacted by heat but have remained unaffected. Hence, while [10] we speak of 'boiled' water, we cannot speak of raw water, since it does not thicken. We have now defined ripening and rawness and assigned their causes.

Boiling is, in general, a concoction by moist heat of the indeterminate matter contained in the moisture of the thing boiled, and the word is strictly applicable only to things boiled in the [15] way of cooking. The indeterminate matter, as we said,[2] will be either spirituous or watery. The cause of the concoction is the fire contained in the moisture; for what is cooked in a frying-pan is broiled: it is the heat outside that affects it and, as for the moisture in which

---

[1] 379ᵇ 14. [2] ᵃ 29.

it is contained, it dries this up and draws it into itself. But a thing that is being boiled behaves in the opposite way: the moisture contained in [20] it is drawn out of it by the heat in the liquid outside. Hence boiled meats are drier than broiled; for, in boiling, things do not draw the moisture into themselves, since the external heat gets the better of the internal: if the internal heat had got the better it would have drawn the moisture to itself. Not every body admits of [25] the process of boiling: if there is no moisture in it, it does not (for instance, stones), nor does it if there is moisture in it but the density of the body is too great for it to be mastered, as in the case of wood. But only those bodies can be boiled that contain moisture which can be acted on by the heat contained in the liquid outside. It is true that gold and wood and many other things are said to be 'boiled': but this is a stretch of the meaning of the word, though the [30] kind of thing intended is the same, the reason for the usage being that the various cases have no names appropriated to them. Liquids too, like milk and must, are said to undergo a process of 'boiling' when the external fire that surrounds and heats them changes the savour in the liquid into a given form, the process being thus in a way like what we have called boiling.

381ᵃ The end of the things that undergo boiling, or indeed any form of concoction, is not always the same: some are meant to be eaten, some drunk, and some are intended for other uses; for instance dyes, too, are said to be 'boiled'.

All those things then admit of 'boiling' which [5] can grow denser, smaller, or heavier; also those which do that with a part of themselves and with a part do the opposite, dividing in such a way that one portion thickens while the other grows thinner, like milk when it divides into whey and curd. Oil by itself is affected in none of these ways, and therefore cannot be said to admit of 'boiling'. Such then is the spe- [10] cies of concoction known as 'boiling', and the process is the same in an artificial and in a natural instrument, for the cause will be the same in every case.

Imperfect boiling is the form of inconcoction opposed to boiling. Now the opposite of boiling properly so called is an inconcoction of the undetermined matter in a body due to lack of heat in the surrounding liquid. (Lack of heat [15] implies, as we have pointed out, the presence of cold.) The motion which causes imperfect boiling is different from that which causes boiling, for the heat which operates the concoction is driven out. The lack of heat is due either to the amount of cold in the liquid or to the quantity of moisture in the object undergoing the process of boiling. Where either of these conditions is realized the heat in the surrounding liquid is too great to have no effect at all, but too small to carry out the process of concoction uniformly and thoroughly. Hence [20] things are harder when they are imperfectly boiled than when they are boiled, and the moisture in them more distinct from the solid parts. So much for the definition and causes of boiling and imperfect boiling.

Broiling is concoction by dry foreign heat. Hence if a man were to boil a thing but the change and concoction in it were due, not to [25] the heat of the liquid but to that of the fire, the thing will have been broiled and not boiled when the process has been carried to completion: if the process has gone too far we use the word 'scorched' to describe it. If the process leaves the thing drier at the end the agent has been dry heat. Hence the outside is drier than the inside, the opposite being true [30] of things boiled. Where the process is artificial, broiling is more difficult than boiling, for it is difficult to heat the inside and the outside uniformly, since the parts nearer to the fire are the first to get dry and consequently 381ᵇ get more intensely dry. In this way the outer pores contract and the moisture in the thing cannot be secreted but is shut in by the closing of the pores. Now broiling and boiling are artificial processes, but the same general kind of thing, as we said,[1] is found in nature [5] too. The affections produced are similar though they lack a name; for art imitates nature. For instance, the concoction of food in the body is like boiling, for it takes place in a hot and moist medium and the agent is the heat of the body. So, too, certain forms of indigestion are like imperfect boiling. And it is not true that animals are generated in the concoction of [10] food, as some say. Really they are generated in the excretion which putrefies in the lower belly, and they ascend afterwards. For concoction goes on in the upper belly but the excretion putrefies in the lower: the reason for this has been explained elsewhere.

We have seen that the opposite of boiling is imperfect boiling: now there is something correspondingly opposed to the species of concoc- [15] tion called broiling, but it is more difficult to find a name for it. It would be the kind of

[1] 379ᵇ 14, 380ᵃ 16.

thing that would happen if there were imperfect broiling instead of broiling proper through lack of heat due to deficiency in the external fire or to the quantity of water in the thing undergoing the process. For then we should get too much heat for no effect to be produced, but too little for concoction to take place.

[20] We have now explained concoction and inconcoction, ripening and rawness, boiling and broiling, and their opposites.

4

We must now describe the forms taken by the passive qualities the moist and the dry. The elements of bodies, that is, the passive ones, are [25] the moist and the dry; the bodies themselves are compounded of them and whichever predominates determines the nature of the body; thus some bodies partake more of the dry, others of the moist. All the forms to be described will exist either actually, or potentially and in their opposite: for instance, there is actual melting and on the other hand that which admits of being melted.

Since the moist is easily determined and the [30] dry determined with difficulty, their relation to one another is like that of a dish and its condiments. The moist is what makes the dry determinable, and each serves as a sort of glue 382ᵃ to the other—as Empedocles said in his poem on Nature,[1] 'glueing meal together by means of water.' Thus the determined body involves them both. Of the elements earth is especially representative of the dry, water of the moist, and therefore all determinate bodies in our world involve earth and water. Every body [5] shows the quality of that element which predominates in it. It is because earth and water are the material elements of all bodies that animals live in them alone and not in air or fire.

Of the qualities of bodies hardness and softness are those which must primarily belong to [10] a determined thing, for anything made up of the dry and the moist is necessarily either hard or soft. Hard is that the surface of which does not yield into itself; soft that which does yield but not by interchange of place: water, for instance, is not soft, for its surface does not yield to pressure or sink in but there is an interchange of place. Those things are absolutely [15] hard and soft which satisfy the definition absolutely, and those things relatively so which do so compared with another thing. Now relatively to one another hard and soft are indefinable, because it is a matter of degree, but since all the objects of sense are determined by reference to the faculty of sense it is clearly the relation to touch which determines that which is hard and soft absolutely, and touch is that which we use as a standard or mean. So we call [20] that which exceeds it hard and that which falls short of it soft.

5

A body determined by its own boundary must be either hard or soft; for it either yields or does not.

It must also be concrete: or it could not be so determined. So since everything that is determined and solid is either hard or soft and [25] these qualities are due to concretion, all composite and determined bodies must involve concretion. Concretion therefore must be discussed.

Now there are two causes besides matter, the agent and the quality brought about, the agent being the efficient cause, the quality the formal cause. Hence concretion and disaggregation, [30] drying and moistening, must have these two causes.

382ᵇ But since concretion is a form of drying let us speak of the latter first.

382ᵃ As we have explained, the agent operates by means of two qualities and the patient is acted on in virtue of two qualities: action takes place by means of heat or cold, and the quality is produced either by the presence or by the absence 382ᵇ of heat or cold; but that which is acted upon is moist or dry or a compound of both. Water is the element characterized by the moist, earth that characterized by the dry, for these among the elements that admit the qualities moist and dry are passive. Therefore cold, too, being found in water and earth (both of [5] which we recognize to be cold), must be reckoned rather as a passive quality. It is active only as contributing to destruction or incidentally in the manner described before[2]; for cold is sometimes actually said to burn and to warm, but not in the same way as heat does, but by collecting and concentrating heat.

[10] The subjects of drying are water and the various watery fluids and those bodies which contain water either foreign or connatural. By foreign I mean like the water in wool, by connatural, like that in milk. The watery fluids are wine, urine, whey, and in general those fluids which have no sediment or only a little, except where this absence of sediment is due to [15] viscosity. For in some cases, in oil and

---
[1] Diels, 21 B. 34.
[2] 347ᵇ 4-9.

pitch for instance, it is the viscosity which prevents any sediment from appearing.

It is always a process of heating or cooling that dries things, but the agent in both cases is heat, either internal or external. For even when things are dried by cooling, like a garment, [20] where the moisture exists separately it is the internal heat that dries them. It carries off the moisture in the shape of vapour (if there is not too much of it), being itself driven out by the surrounding cold. So everything is dried, as we have said, by a process either of heating or cooling, but the agent is always heat, either [25] internal or external, carrying off the moisture in vapour. By external heat I mean as where things are boiled: by internal where the heat breathes out and takes away and uses up its moisture. So much for drying.

6

Liquefaction is, first, condensation into water; second, the melting of a solidified body. The first, condensation, is due to the cooling of [30] vapour: what melting is will appear from the account of solidification.

Whatever solidifies is either water or a mixture of earth and water, and the agent is either dry heat or cold. Hence those of the bodies solidified by heat or cold which are soluble at all 383ª are dissolved by their opposites. Bodies solidified by the dry-hot are dissolved by water, which is the moist-cold, while bodies solidified by cold are dissolved by fire, which is hot. Some things seem to be solidified by water, e.g. [5] boiled honey, but really it is not the water but the cold in the water which effects the solidification. Aqueous bodies are not solidified by fire: for it is fire that dissolves them, and the same cause in the same relation cannot have opposite effects upon the same thing. Again, water solidifies owing to the departure of heat; so it will clearly be dissolved by the entry into it of heat: cold, therefore, must be the agent in solidifying it.

[10] Hence aqueous bodies do not thicken when they solidify; for thickening occurs when the moisture goes off and the dry matter comes together, but water is the only liquid that does not thicken. Those bodies that are made up of both earth and water are solidified both by fire and by cold and in either case are thickened. The operation of the two is in a way the same [15] and in a way different. Heat acts by drawing off the moisture, and as the moisture goes off in vapour the dry matter thickens and collects. Cold acts by driving out the heat, which is accompanied by the moisture as this goes off in vapour with it. Bodies that are soft but not [20] liquid do not thicken but solidify when the moisture leaves them, e.g. potter's clay in process of baking: but those mixed bodies that are liquid thicken besides solidifying, like milk. Those bodies which have first been thickened or hardened by cold often begin by becoming moist: thus potter's clay at first in the process of baking steams and grows softer, and is liable [25] to distortion in the ovens for that reason.

Now of the bodies solidified by cold which are made up both of earth and water but in which the earth preponderates, those which solidify by the departure of heat melt by heat when it enters into them again; this is the case [30] with frozen mud. But those which solidify by refrigeration, where all the moisture has gone off in vapour with the heat, like iron and horn, cannot be dissolved except by excessive heat, but they can be softened—though manufactured iron does melt, to the point of becoming fluid and then solidifying again. This is how steel is made. The dross sinks to the bottom 383ᵇ and is purged away: when this has been done often and the metal is pure we have steel. The process is not repeated often because the purification of the metal involves great waste and loss of weight. But the iron that has [5] less dross is the better iron. The stone *pyrimachus*, too, melts and forms into drops and becomes fluid; after having been in a fluid state it solidifies and becomes hard again. Millstones, too, melt and become fluid: when the fluid mass begins to solidify it is black but its consistency comes to be like that of lime. [Mud and earth, too, melt].

[10] Of the bodies which are solidified by dry heat some are insoluble, others are dissolved by liquid. Pottery and some kinds of stone that are formed out of earth burnt up by fire, such as millstones, cannot be dissolved. Natron and salt are soluble by liquid, but not all liquid but only such as is cold. Hence water and any of its varieties melt them, but oil does not. For the [15] opposite of the dry-hot is the cold-moist and what the one solidified the other will dissolve, and so opposites will have opposite effects.

7

If a body contains more water than earth fire only thickens it: if it contains more earth fire solidifies it. Hence natron and salt and stone and potter's clay must contain more earth.

[20] The nature of oil presents the greatest

problem. If water preponderated in it, cold ought to solidify it; if earth preponderated, then fire ought to do so. Actually neither solidifies, but both thicken it. The reason is that it [25] is full of air (hence it floats on the top of water, since air tends to rise). Cold thickens it by turning the air in it into water, for any mixture of oil and water is thicker than either. Fire and the lapse of time thicken and whiten it. The whitening follows on the evaporation of any water that may have been in it; the [30] thickening is due to the change of the air into water as the heat in the oil is dissipated. The effect in both cases is the same and the cause is the same, but the manner of its operation is different. Both heat and cold thicken it, but neither dries it (neither the sun nor cold 384a dries oil), not only because it is glutinous but because it contains air. Its glutinous nature prevents it from giving off vapour and so fire does not dry it or boil it off.

Those bodies which are made up of earth and water may be classified according to the preponderance of either. There is a kind of wine, for instance, which both solidifies and [5] thickens by boiling—I mean, must. All bodies of this kind lose their water as they dry. That it is their water may be seen from the fact that the vapour from them condenses into water when collected. So wherever some sediment is left this is of the nature of earth. Some of these bodies, as we have said,[1] are also thickened and dried by cold. For cold not only solid- [10] ifies but also dries water, and thickens things by turning air into water. (Solidifying, as we have said,[2] is a form of drying.) Now those things that are not thickened by cold, but solidified, belong rather to water, e.g. wine, urine, vinegar, lye, whey. But those things that are thickened (not by evaporation due to [15] fire) are made up either of earth or of water and air: honey of earth, while oil contains air. Milk and blood, too, are made up of both water and earth, though earth generally predominates in them. So, too, are the liquids out of which natron and salt are formed; and stones are also formed from some mixtures of this kind. Hence, if the whey has not been separated, it burns away if you boil it over a [20] fire. But the earthy element in milk can also be coagulated by the help of fig-juice, if you boil it in a certain way as doctors do when they treat it with fig-juice, and this is how the whey and the cheese are commonly separated. Whey, once separated, does not thicken, as the milk did, but boils away like water. Sometimes, however, there is little or no cheese in milk, and such milk is not nutritive and is [25] more like water. The case of blood is similar: cold dries and so solidifies it. Those kinds of blood that do not solidify, like that of the stag, belong rather to water and are very cold. Hence they contain no fibres: for the fibres are of earth and solid, and blood from which they have been removed does not solidify. This is because it cannot dry; for what remains is wa- [30] ter, just as what remains of milk when cheese has been removed is water. The fact that diseased blood will not solidify is evidence of the same thing, for such blood is of the nature of serum and that is phlegm and water, the nature of the animal having failed to get the better of it and digest it.

Some of these bodies are soluble, e.g. natron, 384b some insoluble, e.g. pottery: of the latter, some, like horn, can be softened by heat, others, like pottery and stone, cannot. The reason is that opposite causes have opposite effects: consequently, if solidification is due to two causes, the cold and the dry, solution must be due to the hot and the moist, that is, to fire [5] and to water (these being opposites): water dissolving what was solidified by fire alone, fire what was solidified by cold alone. Consequently, if any things happen to be solidified by the action of both, these are least apt to be soluble. Such a case we find where things have been heated and are then solidified by cold. When the heat in leaving them has caused most of the moisture to evaporate, the cold so compacts these bodies together again [10] as to leave no entrance even for moisture. Therefore heat does not dissolve them (for it only dissolves those bodies that are solidified by cold alone), nor does water (for it does not dissolve what cold solidifies, but only what is solidified by dry heat). But iron is melted by [15] heat and solidified by cold. Wood consists of earth and air and is therefore combustible but cannot be melted or softened by heat. (For the same reason it floats in water—all except ebony. This does not, for other kinds of wood contain a preponderance of air, but in black ebony the air has escaped and so earth preponderates in it.) Pottery consists of earth [20] alone because it solidified gradually in the process of drying. Water cannot get into it, for the pores were only large enough to admit of vapour escaping: and seeing that fire solidified it, that cannot dissolve it either.

So solidification and melting, their causes,

---

[1] 383a 13.   [2] 382b 1.

and the kinds of subjects in which they occur have been described.

8

All this makes it clear that bodies are formed [25] by heat and cold and that these agents operate by thickening and solidifying. It is because these qualities fashion bodies that we find heat in all of them, and in some cold in so far as heat is absent. These qualities, then, are present as active, and the moist and the dry as passive, and consequently all four are found in [30] mixed bodies. So water and earth are the constituents of homogeneous bodies both in plants and in animals and of metals such as gold, silver, and the rest—water and earth and their respective exhalations shut up in the compound bodies, as we have explained elsewhere.[1]

385ᵃ All these mixed bodies are distinguished from one another, firstly by the qualities special to the various senses, that is, by their capacities of action. (For a thing is white, fragrant, sonant, sweet, hot, cold in virtue of a power of acting on sense). Secondly by other more characteristic affections which express [5] their aptitude to be affected: I mean, for instance, the aptitude to melt or solidify or bend and so forth, all these qualities, like moist and dry, being passive. These are the qualities that differentiate bone, flesh, sinew, wood, bark, stone and all other homogeneous natural [10] bodies. Let us begin by enumerating these qualities expressing the aptitude or inaptitude of a thing to be affected in a certain way. They are as follows: to be apt or inapt to solidify, melt, be softened by heat, be softened [15] by water, bend, break, be comminuted, impressed, moulded, squeezed; to be tractile or non-tractile, malleable or non-malleable, to be fissile or non-fissile, apt or inapt to be cut; to be viscous or friable, compressible or incompressible, combustible or incombustible; to be apt or inapt to give off fumes. These affections differentiate most bodies from one another. Let us go on to explain the nature of each of them. [20] We have already given a general account of that which is apt or inapt to solidify or to melt, but let us return to them again now. Of all the bodies that admit of solidification and hardening, some are brought into this state by heat, others by cold. Heat does this by drying [25] up their moisture, cold by driving out their heat. Consequently some bodies are affected in this way by defect of moisture, some by defect

[1] E. g. 378ᵃ 15-ᵇ 6, in relation to metals.

of heat: watery bodies by defect of heat, earthy bodies of moisture. Now those bodies that are so affected by defect of moisture are dissolved by water, unless like pottery they have so contracted that their pores are too small for the [30] particles of water to enter. All those bodies in which this is not the case are dissolved by water, e.g. natron, salt, dry mud. Those bodies that solidified through defect of heat are melted by heat, e.g. ice, lead, copper. So much for the bodies that admit of solidification and of melting, and those that do not admit of melting.

385ᵇ The bodies which do not admit of solidification are those which contain no aqueous moisture and are not watery, but in which heat and earth preponderate, like honey and must (for these are in a sort of state of effervescence), and those which do possess some water but have a preponderance of air, like oil [5] and quicksilver, and all viscous substances such as pitch and birdlime.

9

Those bodies admit of softening which are not (like ice) made up of water, but in which earth predominates. All their moisture must not have left them (as in the case of natron and salt), nor must the relation of dry to moist [10] in them be incongruous (as in the case of pottery). They must be tractile (without admitting water) or malleable (without consisting of water), and the agent in softening them is fire. Such are iron and horn.

Both of bodies that can melt and of bodies that cannot, some do and some do not admit of softening in water. Copper, for instance, which can be melted, cannot be softened in water, whereas wool and earth can be softened in water, for they can be soaked. (It is true that [15] though copper can be melted the agent in its case is not water, but some of the bodies that can be melted by water too such as natron and salt cannot be softened in water: for nothing is said to be so affected unless the water soaks into it and makes it softer.) Some things, on the other hand, such as wool and grain, can be softened by water though they cannot be melted. Any body that is to be softened by water must be of earth and must have its pores larger than the particles of water, and the pores [20] themselves must be able to resist the action of water, whereas bodies that can be 'melted' by water must have pores throughout.

[Why is it that earth is both 'melted' and softened by moisture, while natron is 'melted' but not softened? Because natron is pervaded throughout by pores so that the parts are im- [25] mediately divided by the water, but earth has also pores which do not connect and is therefore differently affected according as the water enters by one or the other set of pores.]

Some bodies can be bent or straightened, like the reed or the withy, some cannot, like pottery and stone. Those bodies are apt to be bent and straightened which can change from being [30] curved to being straight and from being straight to being curved, and bending and straightening consist in the change or motion to the straight or to a curve, for a thing is said to be in process of being bent whether it is be- 386ᵃ ing made to assume a convex or a concave shape. So bending is defined as motion to the convex or the concave without a change of length. For if we added 'or to the straight', we should have a thing bent and straight at once, and it is impossible for that which is straight to be bent. And if all bending is a bending back or a bending down, the former being a [5] change to the convex, the latter to the concave, a motion that leads to the straight cannot be called bending, but bending and straightening are two different things. These, then, are the things that can, and those that cannot be bent, and be straightened.

Some things can be both broken and comminuted, others admit only one or the other. Wood, for instance, can be broken but not [10] comminuted, ice and stone can be comminuted but not broken, while pottery may either be comminuted or broken. The distinction is this: breaking is a division and separation into large parts, comminution into parts of any size, but there must be more of them than two. Now those solids that have many pores not communicating with one another are [15] comminuible (for the limit to their subdivision is set by the pores), but those whose pores stretch continuously for a long way are breakable, while those which have pores of both kinds are both comminuible and breakable.

Some things, e.g. copper and wax, are impressible, others, e.g. pottery and water, are not. The process of being impressed is the sinking of a part of the surface of a thing in response to pressure or a blow, in general to [20] contact. Such bodies are either soft, like wax, where part of the surface is depressed while the rest remains, or hard, like copper. Non-impressible bodies are either hard, like pottery (its surface does not give way and sink in), or liquid, like water (for though water does give way it is not in a part of it, for there is a reciprocal change of place of all its parts). [25] Those impressibles that retain the shape impressed on them and are easily moulded by the hand are called 'plastic'; those that are not easily moulded, such as stone or wood, or are easily moulded but do not retain the shape impressed, like wool or a sponge, are not plastic. The last group are said to be 'squeezable'. Things are 'squeezable' when they can contract into themselves under pressure, their sur- [30] face sinking in without being broken and without the parts interchanging position as happens in the case of water. (We speak of pressure when there is movement and the 386ᵇ motor remains in contact with the thing moved, of impact when the movement is due to the local movement of the motor.) Those bodies are subject to squeezing which have empty pores—empty, that is, of the stuff of which the body itself consists—and that can sink upon the void spaces within them, or rather upon their pores. For sometimes the pores upon which a body sinks in are not [5] empty (a wet sponge, for instance, has its pores full). But the pores, if full, must be full of something softer than the body itself which is to contract. Examples of things squeezable are the sponge, wax, flesh. Those things are not squeezable which cannot be made to contract upon their own pores by pressure, either because they have no pores or because their [10] pores are full of something too hard. Thus iron, stone, water and all liquids are incapable of being squeezed.

Things are tractile when their surface can be made to elongate, for being drawn out is a movement of the surface, remaining unbroken, in the direction of the mover. Some things are tractile, e.g. hair, thongs, sinew, dough, bird- [15] lime, and some are not, e.g. water, stone. Some things are both tractile and squeezable, e.g. wool; in other cases the two qualities do not coincide; phlegm, for instance, is tractile but not squeezable, and a sponge squeezable but not tractile.

Some things are malleable, like copper. Some are not, like stone and wood. Things are malleable when their surface can be made to move [20] (but only in part) both downwards and sideways with one and the same blow: when this is not possible a body is not malleable. All malleable bodies are impressible, but not all impressible bodies are malleable, e.g. wood, though on the whole the two go together. Of squeezable things some are malleable and some not: wax and mud are malleable, wool is not. [25] Some things are fissile, e.g. wood, some are not, e.g. potter's clay. A thing is fissile when it is apt to divide in advance of the instrument dividing it, for a body is said to split when it divides to a further point than that to which the dividing instrument divides it and the act of division advances: which is not the case with [30] cutting. Those bodies which cannot behave like this are non-fissile. Nothing soft is fissile (by soft I mean absolutely soft and not relatively: for iron itself may be relatively 387ª soft); nor are all hard things fissile, but only such as are neither liquid nor impressible nor comminuible. Such are the bodies that have the pores along which they cohere lengthwise and not crosswise.

Those hard or soft solids are apt to be cut [5] which do not necessarily either split in advance of the instrument or break into minute fragments when they are being divided. Those that necessarily do so and liquids cannot be cut. Some things can be both split and cut, like wood, though generally it is lengthwise that a thing can be split and crosswise that it can be cut. For, a body being divided into many parts, [10] in so far as its unity is made up of many lengths it is apt to be split, in so far as it is made up of many breadths it is apt to be cut.

A thing is viscous when, being moist or soft, it is tractile. Bodies owe this property to the interlocking of their parts when they are composed like chains, for then they can be drawn out to a great length and contracted again. Bodies that are not like this are friable. [15] Bodies are compressible when they are squeezable and retain the shape they have been squeezed into; incompressible when they are either inapt to be squeezed at all or do not retain the shape they have been squeezed into.

Some bodies are combustible and some are not. Wood, wool, bone are combustible; stone, ice are not. Bodies are combustible when their [20] pores are such as to admit fire and their longitudinal pores contain moisture weaker than fire. If they have no moisture, or if, as in ice or very green wood, the moisture is stronger than fire, they are not combustible.

Those bodies give off fumes which **contain** moisture, but in such a form that it does not go off separately in vapour when they are exposed to fire. For vapour is a moist secretion [25] tending to the nature of air produced from a liquid by the agency of burning heat. Bodies that give off fumes give off secretions of the nature of air by the lapse of time: as they perish away they dry up or become earth. But the kind of secretion we are concerned with now differs from others in that it is not moist nor does it become wind (which is a continuous flow of air in a given direction). Fumes are [30] a common secretion of dry and moist together caused by the agency of burning heat. Hence they do not moisten things but rather colour them.

387ᵇ The fumes of a woody body are called smoke. (I mean to include bones and hair and everything of this kind in the same class. For there is no name common to all the objects that I mean, but, for all that, these things are all in the same class by analogy. Compare what Empedocles says: They are one and the same, hair [5] and leaves and the thick wings of birds and scales that grow on stout limbs.[1]) The fumes of fat are a sooty smoke and those of oily substances a greasy steam. Oil does not boil away or thicken by evaporation because it does not give off vapour but fumes. Water on the other hand does not give off fumes, but vapour. Sweet wine does give off fumes, for it contains [10] fat and behaves like oil. It does not solidify under the influence of cold and it is apt to burn. Really it is not wine at all in spite of its name: for it does not taste like wine and consequently does not inebriate as ordinary wine does. It contains but little fumigable stuff and consequently is inflammable.

All bodies are combustible that dissolve into [15] ashes, and all bodies do this that solidify under the influence either of heat or of both heat and cold; for we find that all these bodies are mastered by fire. Of stones the precious stone called carbuncle is least amenable to fire.

Of combustible bodies some are inflammable and some are not, and some of the former are reduced to coals. Those are called 'inflamma- [20] ble' which produce flame and those which do not are called 'non-inflammable'. Those fumigable bodies that are not liquid are inflammable, but pitch, oil, wax are inflammable in conjunction with other bodies rather than by themselves. Most inflammable are those bodies that give off smoke. Of bodies of this kind those that contain more earth than smoke are apt to be reduced to coals. Some bodies that can be melted are not inflammable, e.g. cop- [25] per; and some bodies that cannot be melted are inflammable, e.g. wood; and some bodies can be melted and are also inflammable, e.g. frankincense. The reason is that wood has

[1] Diels, 21 B. 82.

its moisture all together and this is continuous throughout and so it burns up: whereas copper has it in each part but not continuous, and in-[30] sufficient in quantity to give rise to flame. In frankincense it is disposed in both of these ways. Fumigable bodies are inflammable when earth predominates in them and they are consequently such as to be unable to melt. These 388a are inflammable because they are dry like fire. When this dry comes to be hot there is fire. This is why flame is burning smoke or dry exhalation. The fumes of wood are smoke, those of wax and frankincense and such-like, and pitch and whatever contains pitch or such-like are sooty smoke, while the fumes of oil and [5] oily substances are a greasy steam; so are those of all substances which are not at all combustible by themselves because there is too little of the dry in them (the dry being the means by which the transition to fire is effected), but burn very readily in conjunction with something else. (For the fat is just the conjunction of the oily with the dry.) So those bodies that give off fumes, like oil and pitch, belong rather to the moist, but those that burn to the dry.

10

[10] Homogeneous bodies differ to touch by these affections and differences, as we have said.[1] They also differ in respect of their smell, taste, and colour.

By homogeneous bodies I mean, for instance, 'metals', gold, copper, silver, tin, iron, stone, [15] and everything else of this kind and the bodies that are extracted from them; also the substances found in animals and plants, for instance, flesh, bones, sinew, skin, viscera, hair, fibres, veins (these are the elements of which the non-homogeneous bodies like the face, a hand, a foot, and everything of that kind are made up), and in plants, wood, bark, leaves, roots, and the rest like them.

[20] The homogeneous bodies, it is true, are constituted by a different cause, but the matter of which they are composed is the dry and the moist, that is, water and earth (for these bodies exhibit those qualities most clearly). The agents are the hot and the cold, for they constitute and make concrete the homogeneous bodies out of earth and water as matter. Let [25] us consider, then, which of the homogeneous bodies are made of earth and which of water, and which of both.

Of organized bodies some are liquid, some

[1] 385a 8.

soft, some hard. The soft and the hard are constituted by a process of solidification, as we have already explained.

Those liquids that go off in vapour are made [30] of water, those that do not are either of the nature of earth, or a mixture either of earth and water, like milk, or of earth and air, like wood, or of water and air, like oil. Those liquids which are thickened by heat are a mix-388b ture. (Wine is a liquid which raises a difficulty: for it is both liable to evaporation and it also thickens; for instance new wine does. The reason is that the word 'wine' is ambiguous and different 'wines' behave in different ways. New wine is more earthy than old, and for this reason it is more apt to be thickened by heat and less apt to be congealed [5] by cold. For it contains much heat and a great proportion of earth, as in Arcadia, where it is so dried up in its skins by the smoke that you scrape it to drink. If all wine has some sediment in it then it will belong to earth or to water according to the quantity of the sediment it possesses.) The liquids that are thickened by cold are of the nature of earth; those that are thickened either by heat or by cold consist of more than one element, like oil and honey and 'sweet wine'.

[10] Of solid bodies those that have been solidified by cold are of water, e.g. ice, snow, hail, hoar-frost. Those solidified by heat are of earth, e.g. pottery, cheese, natron, salt. Some bodies are solidified by both heat and cold. Of this kind are those solidified by refrigeration, that is by the privation both of heat and of the moisture which departs with the heat. For salt [15] and the bodies that are purely of earth solidify by the privation of moisture only, ice by that of heat only, these bodies by that of both. So both the active qualities and both kinds of matter were involved in the process. Of these bodies those from which all the moisture has gone are all of them of earth, like pottery or amber. (For amber, also, and the bodies called 'tears' are formed by refrigera-[20] tion, like myrrh, frankincense, gum. Amber, too, appears to belong to this class of things: the animals enclosed in it show that it is formed by solidification. The heat is driven out of it by the cold of the river and causes the moisture to evaporate with it, as in the case of honey when it has been heated and is immersed in water.) Some of these bodies cannot [25] be melted or softened; for instance, amber and certain stones, e.g. the stalactites in caves. (For these stalactites, too, are formed in

the same way: the agent is not fire, but cold which drives out the heat, which, as it leaves the body, draws out the moisture with it: in the other class of bodies the agent is external [30] fire.) In those from which the moisture has not wholly gone earth still preponderates, but they admit of softening by heat, e.g. iron and horn.

Now since we must include among 'meltables' those bodies which are melted by fire, these contain some water: indeed some of them, like wax, are common to earth and water alike. 389ᵃ But those that are melted by water are of earth. Those that are not melted either by fire or water are of earth, or of earth and water.

Since, then, all bodies are either liquid or solid, and since the things that display the affections we have enumerated belong to these two classes and there is nothing intermediate, it follows that we have given a complete ac- [5] count of the criteria for distinguishing whether a body consists of earth or of water or of more elements than one, and whether fire was the agent in its formation, or cold, or both.

Gold, then, and silver and copper and tin and lead and glass and many nameless stones [10] are of water: for they are all melted by heat. Of water, too, are some wines and urine and vinegar and lye and whey and serum: for they are all congealed by cold. In iron, horn, nails, bones, sinews, wood, hair, leaves, bark, earth preponderates. So, too, in amber, myrrh, frankincense, and all the substances called [15] 'tears', and stalactites, and fruits, such as leguminous plants and corn. For things of this kind are, to a greater or less degree, of earth. For of all these bodies some admit of softening by heat, the rest give off fumes and are formed by refrigeration. So again in natron, salt, and those kinds of stones that are not formed by refrigeration and cannot be melted. Blood, on the other hand, and semen, are made up of [20] earth and water and air. If the blood contains fibres, earth preponderates in it: consequently its solidifies by refrigeration and is melted by liquids; if not, it is of water and therefore does not solidify. Semen solidifies by refrigeration, its moisture leaving it together with its heat.

11

We must investigate in the light of the results we have arrived at what solid or liquid bodies are hot and what cold.

[25] Bodies consisting of water are commonly cold, unless (like lye, urine, wine) they contain foreign heat. Bodies consisting of earth, on the other hand, are commonly hot because heat was active in forming them: for instance lime and ashes.

We must recognize that cold is in a sense the matter of bodies. For the dry and the moist are matter (being passive) and earth and water are [30] the elements that primarily embody them, and they are characterized by cold. Consequently cold must predominate in every body that consists of one or other of the elements simply, unless such a body contains foreign heat as water does when it boils or when it has been strained through ashes. This latter, too, has acquired heat from the ashes, for everything that has been burnt contains more or [5] less heat. This explains the generation of animals in putrefying bodies: the putrefying body contains the heat which destroyed its proper heat.

Bodies made up of earth and water are hot, for most of them derive their existence from concoction and heat, though some, like the waste products of the body, are products of putrefaction. Thus blood, semen, marrow, fig-juice, and all things of the kinds are hot as long [10] as they are in their natural state, but when they perish and fall away from that state they are so no longer. For what is left of them is their matter and that is earth and water. Hence both views are held about them, some people maintaining them to be cold and others to be warm; for they are observed to be hot when they are in their natural state, but to solidify [15] when they have fallen away from it. That, then, is the case of mixed bodies. However, the distinction we laid down holds good: if its matter is predominantly water a body is cold (water being the complete opposite of fire), but if earth or air it tends to be warm.

It sometimes happens that the coldest bodies can be raised to the highest temperature by foreign heat; for the most solid and the hardest [20] bodies are coldest when deprived of heat and most burning after exposure to fire: thus water is more burning than smoke and stone than water.

12

Having explained all this we must describe the nature of flesh, bone, and the other homogeneous bodies severally.

Our account of the formation of the homogeneous bodies has given us the elements out of which they are compounded and the classes [25] into which they fall, and has made it clear to which class each of those bodies belongs. The homogeneous bodies are made up of the elements, and all the works of nature in turn of the homogeneous bodies as matter. All the homogeneous bodies consist of the elements described, as matter, but their essential nature is determined by their definition. This fact is always clearer in the case of the later products, [30] of those, in fact, that are intruments, as it were, and have an end: it is clearer, for instance, that a dead man is a man only in name. And so the hand of a dead man, too, will in the same way be a hand in name only, just as stone 390ª flutes might still be called flutes: for these members, too, are instruments of a kind. But in the case of flesh and bone the fact is not so clear to see, and in that of fire and water even less. For the end is least obvious there where matter predominates most. If you take the extremes, [5] matter is pure matter and the essence is pure definition; but the bodies intermediate between the two are matter or definition in proportion as they are near to either. For each of those elements has an end and is not water or fire in any and every condition of itself, just as flesh is not flesh nor viscera viscera, and the same is true in a higher degree with [10] face and hand. What a thing is is always determined by its function: a thing really is itself when it can perform its function; an eye, for instance, when it can see. When a thing cannot do so it is that thing only in name, like a dead eye or one made of stone, just as a wooden saw is no more a saw than one in a picture. The same, then, is true of flesh, except that its [15] function is less clear than that of the tongue. So, too, with fire; but its function is perhaps even harder to specify by physical inquiry than that of flesh. The parts of plants, and inanimate bodies like copper and silver, are in the same case. They all are what they are in virtue of a certain power of action or passion —just like flesh and sinew. But we cannot state [20] their form accurately, and so it is not easy to tell when they are really there and when they are not unless the body is thoroughly corrupted and its shape only remains. So ancient corpses suddenly become ashes in the grave and very old fruit preserves its shape only but not its taste: so, too, with the solids that form from milk.

Now heat and cold and the motions they set up as the bodies are solidified by the hot and the cold are sufficient to form all such parts as [5] are the homogeneous bodies, flesh, bone, hair, sinew, and the rest. For they are all of them differentiated by the various qualities enumerated above, tension, tractility, comminuibility, hardness, softness, and the rest of them: all of which are derived from the hot and the cold and the mixture of their motions. But no one would go as far as to consider them sufficient in the case of the non-homogeneous [10] parts (like the head, the hand, or the foot) which these homogeneous parts go to make up. Cold and heat and their motion would be admitted to account for the formation of copper or silver, but not for that of a saw, a bowl, or a box. So here, save that in the examples given the cause is art, but in the non-homogeneous bodies nature or some other cause.

Since, then, we know to what element each [15] of the homogeneous bodies belongs, we must now find the definition of each of them, the answer, that is, to the question, 'what is' flesh, semen, and the rest? For we know the cause of a thing and its definition when we know the material or the formal or, better, both the material and the formal conditions of its generation and destruction, and the efficient cause of it.

After the homogeneous bodies have been explained [20] we must consider the non-homogeneous too, and lastly the bodies made up of these, such as man, plants, and the rest.

CONTENTS: METAPHYSICS

BOOK I

CHAP.		BERLIN NOS.
1.	The advance from sensation through memory, experience, and art, to theoretical knowledge	980^a 22
2.	Characteristics of 'wisdom' (philosophy)	982^a 5
3.	The successive recognition by earlier philosophers of the material, efficient, and final causes	983^a 24
4.	Inadequacy of the treatment of these causes	984^b 23
5.	The Pythagorean and Eleatic schools; the former recognizes vaguely the formal cause	985^b 23
6.	The Platonic philosophy; it uses only the material and formal causes	987^a 29
7.	The relation of the various systems to the four causes	988^a 18
8.	Criticism of the pre-Platonic philosophers	988^b 22
9.	Criticism of the doctrine of Ideas	990^a 33
10.	The history of philosophy reveals no causes other than the four	993^a 11

BOOK II

1.	General considerations about the study of philosophy	993^a 30
2.	There cannot be an infinite series, nor an infinite variety of kinds, of causes	994^a 1
3.	Different methods are appropriate to different studies	994^b 32

BOOK III

1. Sketch of the main problems of philosophy — 995^a 24
2. Fuller statement of the problems: — 996^a 18
    (i) Can one science treat of all the four causes?
    (ii) Are the primary axioms treated of by the science of substance, and if not, by what science? — 996^b 26
    (iii) Can one science treat of all substances? — 997^a 15
    (iv) Does the science of substance treat also of its attributes? — 997^a 25
    (v) Are there any non-sensible substances, and if so, of how many kinds? — 997^a 34
3. (vi) Are the genera, or the constituent parts, of things their first principles? — 998^a 20
    (vii) If the genera, is it the highest genera or the lowest? — 998^b 14
4. (viii) Is there anything apart from individual things? — 999^a 24
    (ix) Is each of the first principles one in kind, or in number? — 999^b 24
    (x) Are the principles of perishable and of imperishable things the same? — 1000^a 5
    (xi) Are being and unity substances or attributes? — 1001^a 4
5. (xii) Are the objects of mathematics substances? — 1001^b 26
6. (xiii) Do Ideas exist, as well as sensible things and the objects of mathematics? — 1002^b 12
    (xiv) Do the first principles exist potentially or actually? — 1002^b 32
    (xv) Are the first principles universal or individual? — 1003^a 5

BOOK IV

1. Our object is the study of being as such — 1003^a 21
2. We must therefore study primary being (viz. substance), unity and plurality, and the derivative contraries, and the attributes of being and of substance — 1003^a 33
3. We must study also the primary axioms, and especially the law of contradiction — 1005^a 19
4. Fatal difficulties involved in the denial of this law — 1005^b 35
5. The connexion of such denial with Protagoras' doctrine of relativity; the doctrine refuted — 1009^a 6
6. Further refutation of Protagoras — 1011^a 3
7. The law of excluded middle defended — 1011^b 23
8. All judgements are not true, nor are all false; all things are not at rest, nor are all in motion — 1012^a 29

BOOK V

Philosophical Lexicon

1. 'Beginning' — 1012^b 34
2. 'Cause' — 1013^a 24
3. 'Element' — 1014^a 26
4. 'Nature' — 1014^b 16
5. 'Necessary' — 1015^a 20
6. 'One,' 'Many' — 1015^b 16
7. 'Being' — 1017^a 7
8. 'Substance' — 1017^b 10
9. 'The Same,' 'Other,' 'Different,' 'Like,' 'Unlike' — 1017^b 27
10. 'Opposite,' 'Contrary,' 'Other in species,' 'The same in species' — 1018^a 20
11. 'Prior,' 'Posterior' — 1018^b 9

12. 'Potency,' 'Capable,' 'Incapacity,' 1019^a 15
'Possible,' 'Impossible'
13. 'Quantum' 1020^a 7
14. 'Quality' 1020^a 33
15. 'Relative' 1020^b 26
16. 'Complete' 1021^b 12
17. 'Limit' 1022^a 4
18. 'That in virtue of which,' 'In 1022^a 14
virtue of itself'
19. 'Disposition' 1022^b 1
20. 'Having' or 'habit' (ἕξις) 1022^b 4
21. 'Affection' 1022^b 15
22. 'Privation' 1022^b 22
23. 'Have' or 'hold' (ἔχειν), 'Be in' 1023^a 8
24. 'From' 1023^a 26
25. 'Part' 1023^b 12
26. 'Whole,' 'Total,' 'All' 1023^b 26
27. 'Mutilated' 1024^a 11
28. 'Race' or 'genus' (γένος), 'Other in 1024^a 29
genus'
29. 'False' 1024^b 17
30. 'Accident' 1025^a 14

BOOK VI

1. Distinction of 'theology,' the science of being as such, from the other theoretical sciences, mathematics and physics 1025^b 3
2. Four senses of 'being'; of these (i) accidental being is the object of no science 1026^a 33
3. The nature and origin of accident 1027^a 29
4. (ii) Being as truth is not primary being 1027^b 17

BOOK VII

1. The study of being is primarily the study of substance 1028^a 10
2. Various opinions on the question, what things are substances? 1028^b 8
3. Four things are commonly held to be substantial—the essence, the universal, the genus, the substratum. The last may be conceived as matter, form, or the concrete individual. Reasons why *matter* and the *concrete individual* cannot be primary substance. *Form* to be studied first in sensible things 1028^b 33
4. What is essence and to what does it belong, i.e. what things can be defined? Primarily substance 1029^b 1
5. Combinations of a subject with one of its proper attributes have no definition nor essence 1030^b 14
6. Is a thing the same as its essence? Yes, if it is a substance 1031^a 15
(7. Analysis of generation, whether by nature, art, or spontaneity 1032^a 12
8. Form is not generated, but put into matter; yet it did not previously exist apart—the agent in generation is form embodied in another individual of the same species 1033^a 24
9. Why spontaneous generation sometimes takes place. The conditions of generation in the categories other than substance) 1034^a 9
10. When are definitions of the parts included in the definition of the whole? When the parts are parts of the form 1034^b 20
11. Which parts are parts of the form, which of the concrete individual? 1036^a 26
12. Wherein consists the unity of an object of definition? In the appropriateness of the differentia to the genus 1037^b 8
13. A universal cannot be either the substance or an element in the substance of anything (yet how else can a thing be defined?) 1038^b 1
14. Hence it is fatal to make Ideas substances and yet hold that they are composed of other Ideas 1039^a 24
15. No individual can be defined, whether sensible or, like the Ideas, intelligible 1039^b 20
16. The parts of sensible things are only potencies. Unity and being are not the substance of things 1040^b 5
17. Substance is the cause or form which puts matter into a determinate state; it is that in a thing which is distinct from its material elements 1041^a 6

BOOK VIII

1. The discussion of sensible substances continued. Their matter is itself substance 1042^a 3
2. The main types of form or actuality. Definitions of matter, of form, and of the concrete individual distinguished 1042^b 9
3. Form distinguished from the material elements; Antisthenes' attack on definition; definition analogous to number 1043^a 29
4. Remote and proximate matter; the substratum of *attributes* not matter but the concrete individual 1044^a 15
5. The relation of matter to its contrary states 1044^b 21
6. What gives unity to a definition? The fact that the genus is simply the potency of the differentia, the differentia the actuality of the genus 1045^a 7

BOOK IX

1. Being as potency and actuality. Potency in the strict sense, as potency of motion, active or passive 1045^b 27
2. Non-rational potencies are single, rational potencies twofold 1046^a 36
3. Potency defended against the attack of the Megaric school 1046^b 29
4. Potency as possibility 1047^b 3
5. How potency is acquired, and the conditions of its actualization 1047^b 31
6. Actuality distinguished from potency; a special type of potency described; actuality distinguished from movement 1048^a 25
7. When one thing may be called the potency or matter of another; how things 1048^b 35

CONTENTS

are described by names derived from their matter or their accidents

8. Actuality prior to potency in definition, time, and substantiality; nothing eternal or necessary is a mere potency   1049^b 4
9. Good actuality better than potency, and bad actuality worse; therefore no separate evil principle in the universe. Geometrical truths found by actualization of potencies   1051^a 4
10. Being as truth, with regard to both composite and simple objects   1051^a 34

BOOK X

1. Four kinds of unit; the essence of a unit is to be a measure of quantity or of quality; various types of measure   1052^a 15
2. Unity not a substance but a universal predicate; its denotation the same as that of being   1053^b 9
3. Unity and plurality; identity; likeness; otherness; difference   1054^a 20
4. Contrariety is complete difference; how related to privation and contradiction   1055^a 3
5. The opposition of the equal to the great and the small   1055^b 30
6. The opposition of the one to the many   1056^b 3
7. Intermediates are homogeneous with each other and with the extremes, stand between contraries, and are compounded out of these contraries   1057^a 18
8. Otherness *in* species is otherness *of* the genus and is contrariety; its nature further described   1057^b 35
9. What contrarieties constitute otherness in species   1058^a 29
10. The perishable and the imperishable differ in kind   1058^b 26

BOOK XI

1. Shorter form of III. 2, 3   1059^a 18
2. Shorter form of III. 4–6   1060^a 3
3. Shorter form of IV. 1, 2   1060^b 31
4. Shorter form of IV. 3, 4   1061^b 17
5. Shorter form of IV. 3, 4   1061^b 34
6. Shorter form of IV. 5–8   1062^b 12
7. Shorter form of VI. 1   1063^b 36
8. Shorter form of VI. 2–4   1064^b 15
   Extracts from *Physics*:
   II. 5, 6, on luck   1064^b 30
9. III. 1–3, on potency, actuality, and movement   1065^b 5
10. III. 4, 5, 7, on the infinite; there is no actual infinite, and especially no infinite body   1066^a 35
11. V. 1, on change and movement   1067^b 1
12. V. 2, on the three kinds of movement   1068^a 8
    V. 3, definitions of 'together in place,' 'apart,' 'touch,' 'between,' 'contrary in place,' 'successive,' 'contiguous,' 'continuous'   1068^b 26

BOOK XII

1. Substance the primary subject of inquiry. Three kinds of substance—perishable sensible, eternal sensible, and unmovable (non-sensible)   1069^a 18
2. Change implies not only form and privation but matter   1069^b 3
3. Neither matter nor form comes into being. Whatever comes into being comes from a substance of the same kind. If form ever exists apart from the concrete individual, it is in the case of natural objects   1069^b 35
4. Different things have elements numerically different but the same in kind; they all have form, privation, and matter. They also have a proximate and an ultimate moving cause   1070^a 31
5. Again actuality and potency are principles common to all things, though they apply differently in different cases. The principles of all things are only analogous, not identical   1070^b 36
6. Since movement must be eternal, there must be an eternal mover, and one whose essence is actuality (actuality being prior to potency). To account for the uniform change in the universe, there must be one principle which acts always alike, and one whose action varies   1071^b 3
7. The eternal mover originates motion by being the primary object of desire (as it is of thought); being thoroughly actual, it cannot change or move; it is a living being, perfect, separate from sensible things, and without parts   1072^a 19
8. Besides the first mover there must be as many unmoved movers as there are simple motions involved in the motions of the planets. The number is probably either 55 or 47. As there is but one prime mover, there must be but one heaven   1073^a 13
9. The divine thought must be concerned with the most divine object, which is itself. Thought and the object of thought are never different when the object is immaterial   1074^b 15
10. How the good is present in the universe both as the order of the parts and (more primarily) as their ruler. Difficulties which attend the views of other philosophers   1075^a 11

BOOK XIII

1. We pass to immaterial substance. Two kinds of immaterial substances have been believed in, mathematical objects and Ideas. We shall discuss first the former, then the latter, then the view that numbers and Ideas are the substance of sensible things   1076^a 8
2. (i) Mathematical objects cannot exist as distinct substances either in or apart from sensible things   1076^a 38
3. They can be separated only in   1077^b 17

thought. Mathematics is not entirely divorced from consideration of the beautiful, as is sometimes alleged

4. (ii) Arguments which led to the belief in Ideas. Some prove too little, others too much 1078^b 7

5. Even if there were Ideas, they would not explain the changes in the sensible world 1079^b 12

6. (iii) Various ways in which numbers may be conceived as the substance of things 1080^a 12

7. (a) If all units are associable, this gives only mathematical, not ideal number. (b) If all units are inassociable, this gives neither mathematical nor ideal number. (c) If only the units in the same number are associable, this leads to equal difficulties; units must have no difference of kind 1080^b 37

8. The views of Platonists who disagree with Plato, and those of the Pythagoreans, lead to equal difficulties. Further objections to ideal numbers: (a) How are the units derived from the indefinite dyad? (b) Is the series of numbers infinite or finite; and if finite, what is its limit? (c) What sort of principle is the One? 1083^a 1

9. Discussion of the principles of geometrical objects. Criticism of the generation of numbers from unity and plurality, and of spatial magnitudes from similar principles. The criticism of ideal numbers summed up. The upholders of Ideas make them at once universal and individual 1085^a 3

10. Are the first principles of substances individual or universal? 1086^b 14

BOOK XIV

1. The principles cannot be contraries. The Platonists in making them contraries treated one of the contraries as matter. Various forms of this theory. The nature of unity and plurality expounded 1087^a 29

2. Eternal substances cannot be compounded out of elements. The object of the Platonists is to explain the presence of plurality in the world, but in this they do not succeed. What justifies the belief in the separate existence of numbers? 1088^b 14

3. Difficulties in the various theories of number. The Pythagoreans ascribe generation to numbers, which are eternal 1090^a 16

4. The relation between the first principles and the good 1091^a 23

5. How is number supposed to be derived from its elements? How is it the cause of substances? 1092^a 9

6. The causal agency ascribed to numbers is purely fanciful 1092^b 26

METAPHYSICS
BOOK I

1

980ᵃ ALL men by nature desire to know. An indication of this is the delight we take in our senses; for even apart from their usefulness they are loved for themselves; and above all others the sense of sight. For not only with a [25] view to action, but even when we are not going to do anything, we prefer seeing (one might say) to everything else. The reason is that this, most of all the senses, makes us know and brings to light many differences between things.

By nature animals are born with the faculty of sensation, and from sensation memory is produced in some of them, though not in oth-**980ᵇ** ers. And therefore the former are more intelligent and apt at learning than those which cannot remember; those which are incapable of hearing sounds are intelligent though they cannot be taught, e.g. the bee, and any other race of animals that may be like it; and those which besides memory have this sense of hearing can be taught.

[25] The animals other than man live by appearances and memories, and have but little of connected experience; but the human race lives also by art and reasonings. Now from memory experience is produced in men; for the several memories of the same thing produce finally the **981ᵃ** capacity for a single experience. And experience seems pretty much like science and art, but really science and art come to men *through* experience; for 'experience made art', [5] as Polus says,[1] 'but inexperience luck'. Now art arises when from many notions gained by experience one universal judgement about a class of objects is produced. For to have a judgement that when Callias was ill of this disease this did him good, and similarly in the case of Socrates and in many individual cases, is a mat-[10] ter of experience; but to judge that it has done good to all persons of a certain constitution, marked off in one class, when they were ill of this disease, e.g. to phlegmatic or bilious people when burning with fever,—this is a matter of art.

With a view to action experience seems in no respect inferior to art, and men of experience succeed even better than those who have theory [15] without experience. (The reason is that experience is knowledge of individuals, art of universals, and actions and productions are all concerned with the individual; for the physician does not cure *man,* except in an incidental way, but Callias or Socrates or some other called by some such individual name, who hap-[20] pens to be a man. If, then, a man has the theory without the experience, and recognizes the universal but does not know the individual included in this, he will often fail to cure; for it is the individual that is to be cured.) But yet we think that *knowledge* and *understanding* [25] belong to art rather than to experience, and we suppose artists to be wiser than men of experience (which implies that Wisdom depends in all cases rather on knowledge); and this because the former know the cause, but the latter do not. For men of experience know that the thing is so, but do not know why, [30] while the others know the 'why' and the cause. Hence we think also that the masterworkers in each craft are more honourable and know in a truer sense and are wiser than the **981ᵇ** manual workers, because they know the causes of the things that are done (we think the manual workers are like certain lifeless things which act indeed, but act without knowing what they do, as fire burns,—but while the lifeless things perform each of their functions by a natural tendency, the labourers perform [5] them through habit); thus we view them as being wiser not in virtue of being able to act, but of having the theory for themselves and knowing the causes. And in general it is a sign of the man who knows and of the man who does not know, that the former can teach, and therefore we think art more truly knowledge than experience is; for artists can teach, and men of mere experience cannot.

[10] Again, we do not regard any of the senses as Wisdom; yet surely these give the most authoritative knowledge of particulars. But they

---
[1] Cf. Plato, *Gorgias*, 448, 462.

NOTE: The bold face numbers and letters are approximate indications of the pages and columns of the standard Berlin Greek text; the bracketed numbers, of the lines in the Greek text; they are here assigned as they are assigned in the Oxford translation.

do not tell us the 'why' of anything—e.g. why fire is hot; they only say *that* it is hot.

At first he who invented any art whatever that went beyond the common perceptions of man was naturally admired by men, not only [15] because there was something useful in the inventions, but because he was thought wise and superior to the rest. But as more arts were invented, and some were directed to the necessities of life, others to recreation, the inventors of the latter were naturally always regarded as wiser than the inventors of the former, because their branches of knowledge did not aim at [20] utility. Hence when all such inventions were already established, the sciences which do not aim at giving pleasure or at the necessities of life were discovered, and first in the places where men first began to have leisure. This is why the mathematical arts were founded in Egypt; for there the priestly caste was allowed to be at leisure.

[25] We have said in the *Ethics*[1] what the difference is between art and science and the other kindred faculties; but the point of our present discussion is this, that all men suppose what is called Wisdom to deal with the first causes and the principles of things; so that, as [30] has been said before, the man of experience is thought to be wiser than the possessors of any sense-perception whatever, the artist wiser than the men of experience, the master-worker than the mechanic, and the theoretical kinds of knowledge to be more of the nature of Wisdom than the productive. Clearly then 982ª Wisdom is knowledge about certain principles and causes.

2

[5] Since we are seeking this knowledge, we must inquire of what kind are the causes and the principles, the knowledge of which is Wisdom. If one were to take the notions we have about the wise man, this might perhaps make the answer more evident. We suppose first, then, that the wise man knows all things, as far as possible, although he has not knowledge [10] of each of them in detail; secondly, that he who can learn things that are difficult, and not easy for man to know, is wise (sense-perception is common to all, and therefore easy and no mark of Wisdom); again, that he who is more exact and more capable of teaching the causes is wiser, in every branch of knowledge; and that of the sciences, also, that which is de- [15] sirable on its own account and for the sake of knowing it is more of the nature of Wisdom than that which is desirable on account of its results, and the superior science is more of the nature of Wisdom than the ancillary; for the wise man must not be ordered but must order, and he must not obey another, but the less wise must obey *him*.

[20] Such and so many are the notions, then, which we have about Wisdom and the wise. Now of these characteristics that of knowing all things must belong to him who has in the highest degree universal knowledge; for he knows in a sense all the instances that fall under the universal. And these things, the most universal, are on the whole the hardest for men to know; for they are farthest from the senses. [25] And the most exact of the sciences are those which deal most with first principles; for those which involve fewer principles are more exact than those which involve additional principles, e.g. arithmetic than geometry. But the science which investigates causes is also *instructive,* in a higher degree, for the people who instruct us are those who tell the causes of each [30] thing. And understanding and knowledge pursued for their own sake are found most in the knowledge of that which is most knowable (for he who chooses to know for the sake of knowing will choose most readily that 982ᵇ which is most truly knowledge, and such is the knowledge of that which is most knowable); and the first principles and the causes are most knowable; for by reason of these, and from these, all other things come to be known, and not these by means of the things subordinate to them. And the science which knows to what end each thing must be done is [5] the most authoritative of the sciences, and more authoritative than any ancillary science; and this end is the good of that thing, and in general the supreme good in the whole of nature. Judged by all the tests we have mentioned, then, the name in question falls to the same science; this must be a science that investigates [10] the first principles and causes; for the good, i.e. the end, is one of the causes.

That it is not a science of production is clear even from the history of the earliest philosophers. For it is owing to their wonder that men both now begin and at first began to philosophize; they wondered originally at the obvious difficulties, then advanced little by little and [15] stated difficulties about the greater matters, e.g. about the phenomena of the moon and those of the sun and of the stars, and about the genesis of the universe. And a man who is puz-

[1] 1139ᵇ 14-1141ᵇ 8.

zled and wonders thinks himself ignorant (whence even the lover of myth is in a sense a lover of Wisdom, for the myth is composed of wonders); therefore since they philosophized [20] in order to escape from ignorance, evidently they were pursuing science in order to know, and not for any utilitarian end. And this is confirmed by the facts; for it was when almost all the necessities of life and the things that make for comfort and recreation had been secured, that such knowledge began to be sought. Evidently then we do not seek it for [25] the sake of any other advantage; but as the man is free, we say, who exists for his own sake and not for another's, so we pursue this as the only free science, for it alone exists for its own sake.

Hence also the possession of it might be justly regarded as beyond human power; for in many ways human nature is in bondage, so [30] that according to Simonides[1] 'God alone can have this privilege', and it is unfitting that man should not be content to seek the knowledge that is suited to him. If, then, there is something in what the poets say, and jealousy 983ª is natural to the divine power, it would probably occur in this case above all, and all who excelled in this knowledge would be unfortunate. But the divine power cannot be jealous (nay, according to the proverb, 'bards tell many a lie'), nor should any other science be [5] thought more honourable than one of this sort. For the most divine science is also most honourable; and this science alone must be, in two ways, most divine. For the science which it would be most meet for God to have is a divine science, and so is any science that deals with divine objects; and this science alone has both these qualities; for (1) God is thought to be among the causes of all things and to be a first principle, and (2) such a science either God alone can have, or God above all oth-[10]ers. All the sciences, indeed, are more necessary than this, but none is better.

Yet the acquisition of it must in a sense end in something which is the opposite of our original inquiries. For all men begin, as we said, by wondering that things are as they are, as [15] they do about self-moving marionettes, or about the solstices or the incommensurability of the diagonal of a square with the side; for it seems wonderful to all who have not yet seen the reason, that there is a thing which cannot be measured even by the smallest unit. But we must end in the contrary and, according to the proverb, the better state, as is the case in these instances too when men learn the cause; for there is nothing which would surprise a geome-[20]ter so much as if the diagonal turned out to be commensurable.

We have stated, then, what is the nature of the science we are searching for, and what is the mark which our search and our whole investigation must reach.

3

Evidently we have to acquire knowledge of [25] the original causes (for we say we know each thing only when we think we recognize its first cause), and causes are spoken of in four senses. In one of these we mean the substance, i.e. the essence (for the 'why' is reducible finally to the definition, and the ultimate 'why' is a cause and principle); in another the matter [30] or substratum, in a third the source of the change, and in a fourth the cause opposed to this, the purpose and the good (for this is the end of all generation and change). We have studied these causes sufficiently in our work on 983ᵇ nature,[2] but yet let us call to our aid those who have attacked the investigation of being and philosophized about reality before us. For obviously they too speak of certain principles and causes; to go over their views, then, will [5] be of profit to the present inquiry, for we shall either find another kind of cause, or be more convinced of the correctness of those which we now maintain.

Of the first philosophers, then, most thought the principles which were of the nature of matter were the only principles of all things. That of which all things that are consist, the first from which they come to be, the last into which they are resolved (the substance remaining, but [10] changing in its modifications), this they say is the element and this the principle of things, and therefore they think nothing is either generated or destroyed, since this sort of entity is always conserved, as we say Socrates neither comes to be absolutely when he comes to be beautiful or musical, nor ceases to be [15] when he loses these characteristics, because the substratum, Socrates himself remains. Just so they say nothing else comes to be or ceases to be; for there must be some entity—either one or more than one—from which all other things come to be, it being conserved.

Yet they do not all agree as to the number [20] and the nature of these principles. Thales, the founder of this type of philosophy, says the

---

[1] Fr. 3, Hiller.　　　　　[2] *Physics*, II. 3, 7.

principle is water (for which reason he declared that the earth rests on water), getting the notion perhaps from seeing that the nutriment of all things is moist, and that heat itself is generated from the moist and kept alive by it (and that from which they come to be is a [25] principle of all things). He got his notion from this fact, and from the fact that the seeds of all things have a moist nature, and that water is the origin of the nature of moist things.

Some think that even the ancients who lived long before the present generation, and first framed accounts of the gods, had a similar [30] view of nature; for they made Ocean and Tethys the parents of creation, and described the oath of the gods as being by water, to which they give the name of Styx; for what is oldest is most honourable, and the most honourable thing is that by which one swears. It may perhaps be uncertain whether this opinion about nature is primitive and ancient, but Thales at any rate is said to have declared himself thus about the first cause. Hippo no one would think fit to include among these thinkers, because of the paltriness of his thought.

[5] Anaximenes and Diogenes make air prior to water, and the most primary of the simple bodies, while Hippasus of Metapontium and Heraclitus of Ephesus say this of fire, and Empedocles says it of the four elements (adding a fourth—earth—to those which have been named); for these, he says, always remain and do not come to be, except that they come to be [10] more or fewer, being aggregated into one and segregated out of one.

Anaxagoras of Clazomenae, who, though older than Empedocles, was later in his philosophical activity, says the principles are infinite in number; for he says almost all the things that are made of parts like themselves, in the manner of water or fire, are generated and destroyed in this way, only by aggregation and [15] segregation, and are not in any other sense generated or destroyed, but remain eternally.

From these facts one might think that the only cause is the so-called material cause; but as men thus advanced, the very facts opened the way for them and joined in forcing them to investigate the subject. However true it may [20] be that all generation and destruction proceed from some one or (for that matter) from more elements, why does this happen and what is the cause? For at least the substratum itself does not make itself change; e.g. neither the wood nor the bronze causes the change of either of them, nor does the wood manufacture a bed and the bronze a statue, but something [25] else is the cause of the change. And to seek this is to seek the second cause, as *we* should say,—that from which comes the beginning of the movement. Now those who at the very beginning set themselves to this kind of inquiry, and said the substratum was one, were not at all dissatisfied with themselves; but some at least of those who maintain it to be one—as [30] though defeated by this search for the second cause—say the one and nature as a whole is unchangeable not only in respect of generation and destruction (for this is a primitive belief, and all agreed in it), but also of all other change; and this view is peculiar to them.

984^b Of those who said the universe was one, then none succeeded in discovering a cause of this sort, except perhaps Parmenides, and he only inasmuch as he supposes that there is not only one but also in some sense two causes. But [5] for those who make more elements it is more possible to state the second cause, e.g. for those who make hot and cold, or fire and earth, the elements; for they treat fire as having a nature which fits it to move things, and water and earth and such things they treat in the contrary way.

When these men and the principles of this kind had had their day, as the latter were found inadequate to generate the nature of things [10] men were again forced by the truth itself, as we said,[1] to inquire into the next kind of cause. For it is not likely either that fire or earth or any such element should be the reason why things manifest goodness and beauty both in their being and in their coming to be, or that those thinkers should have supposed it was; nor again could it be right to entrust so great a [15] matter to spontaneity and chance. When one man said, then, that reason was present—as in animals, so throughout nature—as the cause of order and of all arrangement, he seemed like a sober man in contrast with the random talk of his predecessors. We know that Anaxagoras certainly adopted these views, but Hermotimus of Clazomenae is credited with [20] expressing them earlier. Those who thought thus stated that there is a principle of things which is at the same time the cause of beauty, and that sort of cause from which things acquire movement.

4

One might suspect that Hesiod was the first to look for such a thing—or some one else who
[1] 984^{a}18.

put love or desire among existing things as a principle, as Parmenides, too, does; for he, in [25] constructing the genesis of the universe, says[1]:—
Love first of all the Gods she planned.
And Hesiod says[2]:—
First of all things was chaos made, and then Broad-breasted earth, . . .
And love, 'mid all the gods pre-eminent,
[30] which implies that among existing things there must be from the first a cause which will move things and bring them together. How these thinkers should be arranged with regard to priority of discovery let us be allowed to decide later; but since the contraries of the various forms of good were also perceived to be present in nature—not only order and the beautiful, but also disorder and the ugly, and 985a bad things in greater number than good, and ignoble things than beautiful—therefore another thinker introduced friendship and strife, each of the two the cause of one of these two sets of qualities. For if we were to follow out the view of Empedocles, and interpret it according to its meaning and not to its lisping [5] expression, we should find that friendship is the cause of good things, and strife of bad. Therefore, if we said that Empedocles in a sense both mentions, and is the first to mention, the bad and the good as principles, we should perhaps be right, since the cause of all goods is the good itself.

[10] These thinkers, as we say, evidently grasped, and to this extent, two of the causes which we distinguished in our work on nature[3]—the matter and the source of the movement—vaguely, however, and with no clearness, but as untrained men behave in fights; for they go round their opponents and often [15] strike fine blows, but they do not fight on scientific principles, and so too these thinkers do not seem to know what they say; for it is evident that, as a rule, they make no use of their causes except to a small extent. For Anaxagoras uses reason as a *deus ex machina* for the making of the world, and when he is at a loss [20] to tell from what cause something necessarily is, then he drags reason in, but in all other cases ascribes events to anything rather than to reason. And Empedocles, though he uses the causes to a greater extent than this, neither does so sufficiently nor attains consistency in their use. At least, in many cases he makes love segregate things, and strife ag-

[1] Fr. 13.   [2] *Theogony*, 116-120.
[3] *Physics*, II. 3, 7.

[25] gregate them. For whenever the universe is dissolved into its elements by strife, fire is aggregated into one, and so is each of the other elements; but whenever again under the influence of love they come together into one, the parts must again be segregated out of each element.

Empedocles, then, in contrast with his pred- [30] ecessors, was the first to introduce the dividing of this cause, not positing one source of movement, but different and contrary sources. Again, he was the first to speak of four material elements; yet he does not *use* 985b four, but treats them as two only; he treats fire by itself, and its opposites—earth, air, and water—as one kind of thing. We may learn this by study of his verses.

This philosopher then, as we say, has spoken of the principles in this way, and made them [5] of this number. Leucippus and his associate Democritus say that the full and the empty are the elements, calling the one being and the other non-being—the full and solid being being, the empty non-being (whence they say being no more is than non-being, because the solid no more is than the empty); and they [10] make these the material causes of things. And as those who make the underlying substance one generate all other things by its modifications, supposing the rare and the dense to be the sources of the modifications, in the same way these philosophers say the differences in the elements are the causes of all other qualities. These differences, they say, are three— [15] shape and order and position. For they say the real is differentiated only by 'rhythm' and 'inter-contact' and 'turning'; and of these rhythm is shape, inter-contact is order, and turning is position; for A differs from N in shape, AN from NA in order, ⊒ from H in position. The question of movement—whence or how it is to belong to things—these thinkers, like the others, lazily neglected.

[20] Regarding the two causes, then, as we say, the inquiry seems to have been pushed thus far by the early philosophers.

5

Contemporaneously with these philosophers and before them, the so-called Pythagoreans, who were the first to take up mathematics, not only advanced this study, but also having been [25] brought up in it they thought its principles were the principles of all things. Since of these principles numbers are by nature the first, and in numbers they seemed to see many resemblances to the things that exist and come into being—more than in fire and earth and water (such and such a modification of num-[30] bers being justice, another being soul and reason, another being opportunity—and similarly almost all other things being numerically expressible); since, again, they saw that the modifications and the ratios of the musical scales were expressible in numbers;—since, then, all other things seemed in their whole nature to be modelled on numbers, and numbers seemed to be the first things in the whole 986ª of nature, they supposed the elements of numbers to be the elements of all things, and the whole heaven to be a musical scale and a number. And all the properties of numbers and scales which they could show to agree with [5] the attributes and parts and the whole arrangement of the heavens, they collected and fitted into their scheme; and if there was a gap anywhere, they readily made additions so as to make their whole theory coherent. E.g. as the number 10 is thought to be perfect and to comprise the whole nature of numbers, they [10] say that the bodies which move through the heavens are ten, but as the visible bodies are only nine, to meet this they invent a tenth —the 'counter-earth'. We have discussed these matters more exactly elsewhere.[1]

But the object of our review is that we may learn from these philosophers also what they suppose to be the principles and how these fall [15] under the causes we have named. Evidently, then, these thinkers also consider that number is the principle both as matter for things and as forming both their modifications and their permanent states, and hold that the elements of number are the even and the odd, and that of these the latter is limited, and the former unlimited; and that the One proceeds from both of these (for it is both even and [20] odd), and number from the One; and that the whole heaven, as has been said, is numbers.

Other members of this same school say there are ten principles, which they arrange in two columns of cognates—limit and unlimited, odd and even, one and plurality, right and left, [25] male and female, resting and moving, straight and curved, light and darkness, good and bad, square and oblong. In this way Alcmaeon of Croton seems also to have conceived the matter, and either he got this view from [30] them or they got it from him; for he expressed himself similarly to them. For he says most human affairs go in pairs, meaning not definite contrarieties such as the Pythagoreans speak of, but any chance contrarieties, e.g. white and black, sweet and bitter, good and bad, great and small. He threw out indefinite suggestions about the other contrarieties, but 986ᵇ the Pythagoreans declared both how many and which their contrarieties are.

From both these schools, then, we can learn this much, that the contraries are the principles of things; and how many these principles are and which they are, we can learn from one of the two schools. But how these principles can [5] be brought together under the causes we have named has not been clearly and articulately stated by them; they seem, however, to range the elements under the head of matter; for out of these as immanent parts they say substance is composed and moulded.

From these facts we may sufficiently perceive the meaning of the ancients who said the elements of nature were more than one; but [10] there are some who spoke of the universe as if it were one entity, though they were not all alike either in the excellence of their statement or in its conformity to the facts of nature. The discussion of them is in no way appropriate to our present investigation of causes, for they do not, like some of the natural philosophers, assume being to be one and yet gen-[15] erate it out of the one as out of matter, but they speak in another way; those others add change, since they generate the universe, but these thinkers say the universe is unchangeable. Yet *this* much is germane to the present inquiry: Parmenides seems to fasten on that which is one in definition, Melissus on [20] that which is one in matter, for which reason the former says that it is limited, the latter that it is unlimited; while Xenophanes, the first of these partisans of the One (for Parmenides is said to have been his pupil), gave no clear statement, nor does he seem to have grasped the nature of either of these causes, but with reference to the whole ma-[25] terial universe he says the One is God. Now these thinkers, as we said, must be neglected for the purposes of the present inquiry —two of them entirely, as being a little too naïve, viz. Xenophanes and Melissus; but Parmenides seems in places to speak with more insight. For, claiming that, besides the existent, nothing non-existent exists, he thinks that of necessity one thing exists, viz. the ex-[30] istent and nothing else (on this we have

---
[1] *On the Heavens*, II. 13.

spoken more clearly in our work on nature),[1] but being forced to follow the observed facts, and supposing the existence of that which is one in definition, but more than one according to our sensations, he now posits two causes and two principles, calling them hot and cold, i.e. fire and earth; and of these he ranges the hot 987ª with the existent, and the other with the non-existent.

From what has been said, then, and from the wise men who have now sat in council with us, we have got thus much—on the one hand from the earliest philosophers, who regard the first principle as corporeal (for water and fire [5] and such things are bodies), and of whom some suppose that there is one corporeal principle, others that there are more than one, but both put these under the head of matter; and on the other hand from some who posit both this cause and besides this the source of movement, which we have got from some as single and from others as twofold.

Down to the Italian school, then, and apart [10] from it, philosophers have treated these subjects rather obscurely, except that, as we said, they have in fact used two kinds of cause, and one of these—the source of movement—some treat as one and others as two. But the Pythagoreans have said in the same way that there are two principles, but added this much, [15] which is peculiar to them, that they thought that finitude and infinity were not attributes of certain other things, e.g. of fire or earth or anything else of this kind, but that infinity itself and unity itself were the substance of the things of which they are predicated. This is why number was the substance of all things. On this subject, then, they expressed [20] themselves thus; and regarding the question of essence they began to make statements and definitions, but treated the matter too simply. For they both defined superficially and thought that the first subject of which a given definition was predicable was the substance of the thing defined, as if one supposed that 'double' and '2' were the same, because 2 is the [25] first thing of which 'double' is predicable. But surely to be double and to be 2 are not the same; if they are, one thing will be many—a consequence which they actually drew. From the earlier philosophers, then, and from their successors we can learn thus much.

6

After the systems we have named came the

[1] *Physics*, I. 3.

[30] philosophy of Plato, which in most respects followed these thinkers, but had peculiarities that distinguished it from the philosophy of the Italians. For, having in his youth first become familiar with Cratylus and with the Heraclitean doctrines (that all sensible things are ever in a state of flux and there is no knowledge about them), these views he held even in later years. Socrates, however, 987ᵇ was busying himself about ethical matters and neglecting the world of nature as a whole but seeking the universal in these ethical matters, and fixed thought for the first time on definitions; Plato accepted his teaching, but [5] held that the problem applied not to sensible things but to entities of another kind—for this reason, that the common definition could not be a definition of any sensible thing, as they were always changing. Things of this other sort, then, he called Ideas, and sensible things, he said, were all named after these, and in virtue of a relation to these; for the many existed by participation in the Ideas that have [10] the same name as they. Only the name 'participation' was new; for the Pythagoreans say that things exist by 'imitation' of numbers, and Plato says they exist by participation, changing the name. But what the participation or the imitation of the Forms could be they left an open question.

Further, besides sensible things and Forms [15] he says there are the objects of mathematics, which occupy an intermediate position, differing from sensible things in being eternal and unchangeable, from Forms in that there are many alike, while the Form itself is in each case unique.

Since the Forms were the causes of all other [20] things, he thought their elements were the elements of all things. As matter, the great and the small were principles; as essential reality, the One; for from the great and the small, by participation in the One, come the Numbers.

But he agreed with the Pythagoreans in saying that the One is substance and not a predicate of something else; and in saying that the Numbers are the causes of the reality of other [25] things he agreed with them; but positing a dyad and constructing the infinite out of great and small, instead of treating the infinite as one, is peculiar to him; and so is his view that the Numbers exist apart from sensible things, while *they* say that the things themselves are Numbers, and do not place the objects of mathematics between Forms and sensi-

[30] ble things. His divergence from the Pythagoreans in making the One and the Numbers separate from things, and his introduction of the Forms, were due to his inquiries in the region of definitions (for the earlier thinkers had no tincture of dialectic), and his making the other entity besides the One a dyad was due to the belief that the numbers, except those which were prime, could be neatly produced out of the dyad as out of some plastic material. 988ᵃ Yet what *happens* is the contrary; the theory is not a reasonable one. For they make many things out of the matter, and the form generates only once, but what we observe is that one table is made from one matter, while the man who applies the form, though he is [5] one, makes many tables. And the relation of the male to the female is similar; for the latter is impregnated by one copulation, but the male impregnates many females; yet these are analogues of those first principles.

Plato, then, declared himself thus on the points in question; it is evident from what has been said that he has used only two causes, that of the essence and the material cause (for the [10] Forms are the causes of the essence of all other things, and the One is the cause of the essence of the Forms); and it is evident what the underlying matter is, of which the Forms are predicated in the case of sensible things, and the One in the case of Forms, viz. that this is a dyad, the great and the small. Further, he has assigned the cause of good and that of evil to the elements, one to each of the two, as we [15] say some of his predecessors sought to do, e.g. Empedocles and Anaxagoras.

7

Our review of those who have spoken about first principles and reality and of the way in which they have spoken, has been concise and [20] summary; but yet we have learnt *this* much from them, that of those who speak about 'principle' and 'cause' no one has mentioned any principle except those which have been distinguished in our work on nature,[1] but all evidently have some inkling of *them,* though only vaguely. For some speak of the first principle as matter, whether they suppose [25] one or more first principles, and whether they suppose this to be a body or to be incorporeal; e.g. Plato spoke of the great and the small, the Italians of the infinite, Empedocles of fire, earth, water, and air, Anaxagoras of the infinity of things composed of similar parts.

[1] *Physics*, II. 3, 7.

These, then, have all had a notion of this kind of cause, and so have all who speak of air or [30] fire or water, or something denser than fire and rarer than air; for some have said the prime element is of this kind.

These thinkers grasped this cause only; but certain others have mentioned the source of movement, e.g. those who make friendship and strife, or reason, or love, a principle.

The essence, i.e. the substantial reality, no [35] one has expressed distinctly. It is hinted at chiefly by those who believe in the Forms; 988ᵇ for they do not suppose either that the Forms are the matter of sensible things, and the One the matter of the Forms, or that they are the source of movement (for they say these are causes rather of immobility and of being at rest), but they furnish the Forms as the es- [5] sence of every other thing, and the One as the essence of the Forms.

That for whose sake actions and changes and movements take place, they assert to be a cause in a way, but not in this way, i.e. not in the way in which it is its *nature* to be a cause. For those who speak of reason or friendship class these causes as goods; they do not speak, however, as if anything that exists either existed or came into being for the sake of these, [10] but as if movements started from these. In the same way those who say the One or the existent is the good, say that it is the cause of substance, but not that substance either is or comes to be for the sake of this. Therefore it turns out that in a sense they both say and do [15] not say the good is a cause; for they do not call it a cause *qua* good but only incidentally.

All these thinkers, then, as they cannot pitch on another cause, seem to testify that we have determined rightly both how many and of what sort the causes are. Besides this it is plain that when the causes are being looked for, either all four must be sought thus or they must be sought in one of these four ways. Let [20] us next discuss the possible difficulties with regard to the way in which each of these thinkers has spoken, and with regard to his situation relatively to the first principles.

8

Those, then, who say the universe is one and posit one kind of thing as matter, and as corporeal matter which has spatial magnitude, evidently go astray in many ways. For they [25] posit the elements of bodies only, not of incorporeal things, though there are also incorporeal things. And in trying to state the causes of generation and destruction, and in giving a physical account of all things, they do away with the cause of movement. Further, they err in not positing the substance, i.e. the essence, as the cause of anything, and besides this in lightly calling any of the simple bodies [30] except earth the first principle, without inquiring how they are produced out of one another,—I mean fire, water, earth, and air. For some things are produced out of each other by combination, others by separation, and this makes the greatest difference to their priority [35] and posteriority. For (1) in a way the property of being most elementary of all would seem to belong to the first thing from which they are 989ª produced by combination, and *this* property would belong to the most fine-grained and subtle of bodies. For this reason those who make fire the principle would be most in agreement with this argument. But each of the other thinkers agrees that the element of cor- [5] poreal things is of this sort. At least none of those who named one element claimed that earth was the element, evidently because of the coarseness of its grain. (Of the other three elements each has found some judge on its side; for some maintain that fire, others that water, others that air is the element. Yet why, after all, do they not name earth also, as most men do? For people say all things are earth. [10] And Hesiod says earth was produced first of corporeal things; so primitive and popular has the opinion been.) According to this argument, then, no one would be right who either says the first principle is any of the elements other than fire, or supposes it to be denser than [15] air but rarer than water. But (2) if that which is later in generation is prior in nature, and that which is concocted and compounded is later in generation, the contrary of what we have been saying must be true,—water must be prior to air, and earth to water.

So much, then, for those who posit one cause such as we mentioned; but the same is true if one supposes more of these, as Empedocles says [20] the matter of things is four bodies. For he too is confronted by consequences some of which are the same as have been mentioned, while others are peculiar to him. For we see these bodies produced from one another, which implies that the same body does not always remain fire or earth (we have spoken about this [25] in our works on nature[1]); and regarding the cause of movement and the question whether we must posit one or two, he must be

[1] *On the Heavens*, III. 7.

thought to have spoken neither correctly nor altogether plausibly. And in general, change of quality is necessarily done away with for those who speak thus, for on their view cold will not come from hot nor hot from cold. For if it did there would be something that accepted the contraries themselves, and there would be some one entity that became fire and water, which Empedocles denies.

[30] As regards Anaxagoras, if one were to suppose that he said there were two elements, the supposition would accord thoroughly with an argument which Anaxagoras himself did not state articulately, but which he must have accepted if any one had led him on to it. True, to say that in the beginning all things were mixed is absurd both on other grounds and because it follows that they must have existed 989ᵇ before in an unmixed form, and because nature does not allow any chance thing to be mixed with any chance thing, and also because on this view modifications and accidents could be separated from substances (for the same things which are mixed can be separated); yet if one were to follow him up, piecing together [5] what he means, he would perhaps be seen to be somewhat modern in his views. For when nothing was separated out, evidently nothing could be truly asserted of the substance that then existed. I mean, e.g. that it was neither white nor black, nor grey nor any other colour, but of necessity colourless; for if it had been coloured, it would have had one of these col- [10] ours. And similarly, by this same argument, it was flavourless, nor had it any similar attribute; for it could not be either of any quality or of any size, nor could it be any definite kind of thing. For if it were, one of the particular forms would have belonged to it, and this is impossible, since all were mixed together; for the particular form would necessarily have been already separated out, but he [15] says all were mixed except reason, and this alone was unmixed and pure. From this it follows, then, that he must say the principles are the One (for this is simple and unmixed) and the Other, which is of such a nature as we suppose the indefinite to be before it is defined and partakes of some form. Therefore, while expressing himself neither rightly nor clearly, he means something like what the later [20] thinkers say and what is now more clearly seen to be the case.

But these thinkers are, after all, at home only in arguments about generation and destruction and movement; for it is practically only of this sort of substance that they seek the principles and the causes. But those who ex-[25] tend their vision to all things that exist, and of existing things suppose some to be perceptible and others not perceptible, evidently study both classes, which is all the more reason why one should devote some time to seeing what is good in their views and what bad from the standpoint of the inquiry we have now before us.

The 'Pythagoreans' treat of principles and [30] elements stranger than those of the physical philosophers (the reason is that they got the principles from non-sensible things, for the objects of mathematics, except those of astronomy, are of the class of things without movement); yet their discussions and investigations are all about nature; for they generate 990ª the heavens, and with regard to their parts and attributes and functions they observe the phenomena, and use up the principles and the causes in explaining these, which implies that they agree with the others, the physical philosophers, that the *real* is just all that which [5] is perceptible and contained by the so-called 'heavens'. But the causes and the principles which they mention are, as we said,[1] sufficient to act as steps even up to the higher realms of reality, and are more suited to these than to theories about nature. They do not tell us at all, however, how there can be movement if limit and unlimited and odd and even are [10] the only things assumed, or how without movement and change there can be generation and destruction, or the bodies that move through the heavens can do what they do.

Further, if one either granted them that spatial magnitude consists of these elements, or this were proved, still how would some bodies be light and others have weight? To judge [15] from what they assume and maintain they are speaking no more of mathematical bodies than of perceptible; hence they have said nothing whatever about fire or earth or the other bodies of this sort, I suppose because they have nothing to say which applies *peculiarly* to perceptible things.

Further, how are we to combine the beliefs [20] that the attributes of number, and number itself, are causes of what exists and happens in the heavens both from the beginning and now, and that there is no other number than this number out of which the world is composed? When in one particular region they place opinion and opportunity, and, a little

[1] 989b 31-3.

above or below, injustice and decision or mixture, and allege, as proof, that each of these is [25] a number, and that there happens to be already in this place a plurality of the extended bodies composed of numbers, because these attributes of number attach to the various places,—this being so, is this number, which we must suppose each of these abstractions to be, the same number which is exhibited in the material universe, or is it another than this? Plato says [30] it is different; yet even he thinks that both these bodies and their causes are numbers, but that the *intelligible* numbers are causes, while the others are *sensible*.

9

Let us leave the Pythagoreans for the present; for it is enough to have touched on them as much as we have done. But as for those who 990b posit the Ideas as causes, firstly, in seeking to grasp the causes of the things around us, they introduced others equal in number to these, as if a man who wanted to count things thought he would not be able to do it while they were few, but tried to count them when he had added to their number. For the Forms [5] are practically equal to—or not fewer than—the things, in trying to explain which these thinkers proceeded from them to the Forms. For to each thing there answers an entity which has the same name and exists apart from the substances, and so also in the case of all other groups there is a one over many, whether the many are in this world or are eternal.

Further, of the ways in which we prove that [10] the Forms exist, none is convincing; for from some no inference necessarily follows, and from some arise Forms even of things of which we think there are no Forms. For according to the arguments from the existence of the sciences there will be Forms of all things of which there are sciences and according to the 'one over many' argument there will be Forms even of negations, and according to the argument that there is an object for thought even when the thing has perished, there will be Forms of perishable things; for we have [15] an image of these. Further, of the more accurate arguments, some lead to Ideas of relations, of which we say there is no independent class, and others introduce the 'third man'.

And in general the arguments for the Forms destroy the things for whose existence we are more zealous than for the existence of the Ideas; for it follows that not the dyad but

[20] number is first, i.e. that the relative is prior to the absolute,—besides all the other points on which certain people by following out the opinions held about the Ideas have come into conflict with the principles of the theory.

Further, according to the assumption on which our belief in the Ideas rests, there will be Forms not only of substances but also of many other things (for the concept is single not only [25] in the case of substances but also in the other cases, and there are sciences not only of substance but also of other things, and a thousand other such difficulties confront them). But according to the necessities of the case and the opinions held about the Forms, if Forms can be shared in there must be Ideas of sub-[30] stances only. For they are not shared in incidentally, but a thing must share in its Form as in something not predicated of a subject (by 'being shared in incidentally' I mean that e.g. if a thing shares in 'double itself', it shares also in 'eternal', but incidentally; for 'eternal' happens to be predicable of the 'double'). Therefore the Forms will be substance; but the same terms indicate substance in this and in the ideal 991ᵃ world (or what will be the meaning of saying that there is something apart from the particulars—the one over many?). And if the Ideas and the particulars that share in them have the same form, there will be something common to these; for why should '2' be one and the same in the perishable 2's or in those which are many but eternal, and not the same [5] in the '2 itself' as in the particular 2? But if they have not the same form, they must have only the name in common, and it is as if one were to call both Callias and a wooden image a 'man', without observing any community between them.

Above all one might discuss the question what on earth the Forms contribute to sensible things, either to those that are eternal or to [10] those that come into being and cease to be. For they cause neither movement nor any change in them. But again they help in no wise either towards the knowledge of the other things (for they are not even the substance of these, else they would have been in them), or towards their being, if they are not *in* the particulars which share in them; though if they were, they might be thought to be causes, as [15] white causes whiteness in a white object by entering into its composition. But this argument, which first Anaxagoras and later Eudoxus and certain others used, is very easily upset; for it is not difficult to collect many insuperable objections to such a view.

But, further, all other things cannot come [20] from the Forms in any of the usual senses of 'from'. And to say that they are patterns and the other things share in them is to use empty words and poetical metaphors. For what is it that works, looking to the Ideas? And anything can either be, or become, like another without being copied from it, so that whether [25] Socrates exists or not a man like Socrates might come to be; and evidently this might be so even if Socrates were eternal. And there will be several patterns of the same thing, and therefore several Forms; e.g. 'animal' and 'two-footed' and also 'man himself' will be Forms of man. Again, the Forms are patterns not only [30] of sensible things, but of Forms themselves also; i.e. the genus, as genus of various species, will be so; therefore the same thing will be pattern and copy.

991ᵇ Again, it would seem impossible that the substance and that of which it is the substance should exist apart; how, therefore, could the Ideas, being the substances of things, exist apart? In the *Phaedo*[1] the case is stated in this way—that the Forms are causes both of being and of becoming; yet when the Forms exist, still the things that share in them do not come [5] into being, unless there is something to originate movement; and many other things come into being (e.g. a house or a ring) of which we say there are no Forms. Clearly, therefore, even the other things can both be and come into being owing to such causes as produce the things just mentioned.

Again, if the Forms are numbers, how can [10] they be causes? Is it because existing things are other numbers, e.g. one number is man, another is Socrates, another Callias? Why then are the one set of numbers causes of the other set? It will not make any difference even if the former are eternal and the latter are not. But if it is because things in this sensible world (e.g. harmony) are ratios of numbers, evidently the things between which they are ratios are some one class of things. If, then, this—the [15] matter—is some definite thing, evidently the numbers themselves too will be ratios of something to something else. E.g. if Callias is a numerical ratio between fire and earth and water and air, his Idea also will be a number of certain other underlying things; and man-himself, whether it is a number in a sense or not, will still be a numerical ratio of certain things

[1] 100.

and not a number proper, nor will it be a kind [20] of number merely because it is a numerical ratio.

Again, from many numbers one number is produced, but how can one Form come from many Forms? And if the number comes not from the many numbers themselves but from the units in them, e.g. in 10,000, how is it with the units? If they are specifically alike, numer-[25] ous absurdities will follow, and also if they are not alike (neither the units in one number being themselves like one another nor those in other numbers being all like to all); for in what will they differ, as they are without quality? This is not a plausible view, nor is it consistent with our thought on the matter.

Further, they must set up a second kind of number (with which arithmetic deals), and all the objects which are called 'intermediate' by some thinkers; and how do these exist or from what principles do they proceed? Or why must [30] they be intermediate between the things in this sensible world and the things-themselves?

Further, the units in 2 must each come from a prior 2; but this is impossible.

992ª Further, why is a number, when taken all together, one?

Again, besides what has been said, if the units are *diverse* the Platonists should have spoken like those who say there are four, or two, elements; for each of these thinkers gives the name of element not to that which is com-[5] mon, e.g. to body, but to fire and earth, whether there is something common to them, viz. body, or not. But in fact the Platonists speak as if the One were *homogeneous* like fire or water; and if this is so, the numbers will not be substances. Evidently, if there is a One-itself and this is a first principle, 'one' is being used in more than one sense; for otherwise the theory is impossible.

[10] When we wish to reduce substances to their principles, we state that lines come from the short and long (i.e. from a kind of small and great), and the plane from the broad and narrow, and body from the deep and shallow. Yet how then can either the plane contain a line, or the solid a line or a plane? For the broad and narrow is a different class from the [15] deep and shallow. Therefore, just as number is not present in these, because the many and few are different from these, evidently no other of the higher classes will be present in the lower. But again the broad is not a genus which includes the deep, for then the solid would have been a species of plane. Further, from what principle will the presence of the *points* in the line be derived? Plato even used [20] to object to this class of things as being a geometrical fiction. He gave the name of principle of the line—and this he often posited —to the indivisible lines. Yet these must have a limit; therefore the argument from which the existence of the line follows proves also the existence of the point.

In general, though philosophy seeks the [25] cause of perceptible things, we have given this up (for we say nothing of the cause from which change takes its start), but while we fancy we are stating the substance of perceptible things, we assert the existence of a second class of substances, while our account of the way in which they are the substances of perceptible things is empty talk; for 'sharing', as we said before,[1] means nothing.

Nor have the Forms any connexion with [30] what we see to be the cause in the case of the arts, that for whose sake both all mind and the whole of nature are operative,—with this cause which we assert to be one of the first principles; but mathematics has come to be identical with philosophy for modern thinkers, though they say that it should be studied for the sake of other things.[2]

992ᵇ Further, one might suppose that the substance which according to them underlies as matter is too mathematical, and is a predicate and differentia of the substance, i.e. of the matter, rather than matter itself; i.e. the great and the small are like the rare and the dense which the physical philosophers speak of, call-[5] ing these the primary differentiae of the substratum; for these are a kind of excess and defect. And regarding movement, if the great and the small are to *be* movement, evidently the Forms will be moved; but if they are not to be movement, whence did movement come? The whole study of nature has been annihilated.

And what is thought to be easy—to show [10] that all things are one—is not done; for what is proved by the method of setting out instances is not that all things are one but that there is a One itself,—if we grant all the assumptions. And not even this follows, if we do not grant that the universal is a genus; and this in some cases it cannot be.

Nor can it be explained either how the lines and planes and solids that come after the num-

---

[1] 991ª 20-22.
[2] Cf. Plato, *Republic*, VII. 531, 533.

[15] bers exist or can exist, or what significance they have; for these can neither be Forms (for they are not numbers), nor the intermediates (for those are the objects of mathematics), nor the perishable things. This is evidently a distinct fourth class.

In general, if we search for the elements of existing things without distinguishing the many senses in which things are said to exist, we cannot find them, especially if the search [20] for the elements of which things are made is conducted in this manner. For it is surely impossible to discover what 'acting' or 'being acted on', or 'the straight', is made of, but if elements can be discovered at all, it is only the elements of substances; therefore either to seek the elements of all existing things or to think one has them is incorrect.

And how could we *learn* the elements of all [25] things? Evidently we cannot start by knowing anything before. For as he who is learning geometry, though he may know other things before, knows none of the things with which the science deals and about which he is to learn, so is it in all other cases. Therefore if there is a science of all things, such as some assert to exist, he who is learning this will [30] know nothing before. Yet all learning is by means of premisses which are (either all or some of them) known before,—whether the learning be by demonstration or by definitions; for the elements of the definition must be known before and be familiar; and learning by induction proceeds similarly. But again, if 993ª the science were actually innate, it were strange that we are unaware of our possession of the greatest of sciences.

Again, how is one to *come to know* what all things are made of, and how is this to be made *evident*? This also affords a difficulty; for there might be a conflict of opinion, as there is about [5] certain syllables; some say *za* is made out of *s* and *d* and *a,* while others say it is a distinct sound and none of those that are familiar.

Further, how could we know the objects of sense without having the sense in question? Yet we ought to, if the elements of which all things consist, as complex sounds consist of [10] the elements proper to sound, are the same.

10

It is evident, then, even from what we have said before, that all men seem to seek the causes named in the *Physics*,[1] and that we cannot name any beyond these; but they seek these vaguely; and though in a sense they have all been described before, in a sense they have not been described at all. For the earliest philos- [15] ophy is, on all subjects, like one who lisps, since it is young and in its beginnings. For even Empedocles says bone exists by virtue of the ratio in it. Now this is the essence and the substance of the thing. But it is similarly necessary that flesh and each of the other tissues should be the ratio of its elements, or that not [20] one of them should; for it is on account of this that both flesh and bone and everything else will exist, and not on account of the matter, which he names,—fire and earth and water and air. But while he would necessarily have agreed if another had said this, he has not said it clearly.

On these questions our views have been ex- [25] pressed before; but let us return to enumerate the difficulties that might be raised on these same points;[2] for perhaps we may get from them some help towards our later difficulties.

BOOK II

I

[30] THE investigation of the truth is in one way hard, in another easy. An indication of this is found in the fact that no one is able to attain the truth adequately, while, on the other 993ᵇ hand, we do not collectively fail, but every one says something true about the nature of things, and while individually we contribute little or nothing to the truth, by the union of all a considerable amount is amassed. Therefore, since the truth seems to be like the pro- [5] verbial door, which no one can fail to hit, in this respect it must be easy, but the fact that we can have a whole truth and not the particular part we aim at shows the difficulty of it.

Perhaps, too, as difficulties are of two kinds, the cause of the present difficulty is not in the facts but in us. For as the eyes of bats are to [10] the blaze of day, so is the reason in our soul to the things which are by nature most evident of all.

It is just that we should be grateful, not only to those with whose views we may agree, but

---

[1] II. 3, 7.
[2] The reference is to Book III.

also to those who have expressed more superficial views; for these also contributed something, by developing before us the powers of [15] thought. It is true that if there had been no Timotheus we should have been without much of our lyric poetry; but if there had been no Phrynis there would have been no Timotheus. The same holds good of those who have expressed views about the truth; for from some thinkers we have inherited certain opinions, while the others have been responsible for the appearance of the former.

It is right also that philosophy should be [20] called knowledge of the truth. For the end of theoretical knowledge is truth, while that of practical knowledge is action (for even if they consider how things are, practical men do not study the eternal, but what is relative and in the present). Now we do not know a truth without its cause; and a thing has a quality in a higher degree than other things if in virtue of it the similar quality belongs to the other things as well (e.g. fire is the hottest [25] of things; for it is the cause of the heat of all other things); so that that which causes derivative truths to be true is most true. Hence the principles of eternal things must be always most true (for they are not merely sometimes true, nor is there any cause of their being, but they themselves are the cause of the being of [30] other things), so that as each thing is in respect of being, so is it in respect of truth.

2

994ᵃ But evidently there *is* a first principle, and the causes of things are neither an infinite series nor infinitely various in kind. For (1) neither can one thing proceed from another, as from matter, *ad infinitum* (e.g. flesh from [5] earth, earth from air, air from fire, and so on without stopping), nor can the sources of movement form an endless series (man for instance being acted on by air, air by the sun, the sun by Strife, and so on without limit). Similarly the final causes cannot go on *ad infinitum*,—walking being for the sake of health, this for the sake of happiness, happiness for the sake of something else, and so one thing always for the sake of another. And the case of [10] the essence is similar. For in the case of intermediates, which have a last term and a term prior to them, the prior must be the cause of the later terms. For if we had to say which of the three is the cause, we should say the first; surely not the last, for the final term is the [15] cause of none; nor even the intermediate, for it is the cause only of one. (It makes no difference whether there is one intermediate or more, nor whether they are infinite or finite in number.) But of series which are infinite in this way, and of the infinite in general, all the parts down to that now present are alike intermediates; so that if there is no first there is no cause at all.

Nor can there be an infinite process downwards, [20] with a beginning in the upward direction, so that water should proceed from fire, earth from water, and so always some other kind should be produced. For one thing comes *from* another in two ways—not in the sense in which 'from' means 'after' (as we say 'from the Isthmian games come the Olympian'), but either (i) as the man comes from the boy, by the boy's changing, or (ii) as air [25] comes from water. By 'as the man comes from the boy' we mean 'as that which has come to be from that which is coming to be, or as that which is finished from that which is being achieved' (for as becoming is between being and not being, so that which is becoming is always between that which is and that which is not; for the learner is a man of science in the making, and this is what is meant when we say [30] that *from* a learner a man of science is being made); on the other hand, coming from another thing as water comes from air implies the destruction of the other thing. This is why changes of the former kind are not reversible, and the boy does not come from the man (for it is not that which comes to be something that comes to be as a result of coming to be, but that 994ᵇ which exists after the coming to be; for it is thus that the day, too, comes from the morning—in the sense that it comes after the morning; which is the reason why the morning cannot come from the day); but changes of the other kind are reversible. But in both cases it is impossible that the number of terms should be infinite. For terms of the former kind, being intermediates, must have an end, and terms of [5] the latter kind change back into *one another*; for the destruction of either is the generation of the other.

At the same time it is impossible that the first cause, being eternal, should be destroyed; for since the process of becoming is not infinite in the upward direction, that which is the first thing by whose destruction something came to be must be non-eternal.

Further, the *final cause* is an end, and that sort of end which is not for the sake of something else, but for whose sake everything else

[10] is; so that if there is to be a last term of this sort, the process will not be infinite; but if there is no such term, there will be no final cause, but those who maintain the infinite series eliminate the Good without knowing it (yet no one would try to do anything if he were not going to come to a limit); nor would there be reason in the world; the reasonable man, [15] at least, always acts for a purpose, and this is a limit; for the end is a limit.

But the *essence,* also, cannot be reduced to another definition which is fuller in expression. For the original definition is always more of a definition, and not the later one; and in a series in which the first term has not the required [20] character, the next has not it either.— Further, those who speak thus destroy science; for it is not possible to have this till one comes to the unanalysable terms. And knowledge becomes impossible; for how can one apprehend things that are infinite in this way? For this is not like the case of the line, to whose divisibility there is no stop, but which we cannot think if we do not make a stop (for which reason one who is tracing the infinitely divisible line cannot be counting the possibilities of section), but [25] the whole line also must be apprehended by something in us that does not move from part to part.—Again, nothing infinite can exist; and if it could, at least the notion of infinity is not infinite.

But (2) if the *kinds* of causes had been infinite in number, then also knowledge would have been impossible; for we think we know, only when we have ascertained the causes, but [30] that which is infinite by addition cannot be gone through in a finite time.

3

The effect which lectures produce on a hearer depends on his habits; for we demand the language we are accustomed to, and that which is different from this seems not in keeping but somewhat unintelligible and foreign because of its unwontedness. For it is the customary that is intelligible. The force of habit is shown by the laws, in which the legendary and [5] childish elements prevail over our knowledge about them, owing to habit. Thus some people do not listen to a speaker unless he speaks mathematically, others unless he gives instances, while others expect him to cite a poet as witness. And some want to have everything done accurately, while others are annoyed by accuracy, either because they cannot follow the connexion of thought or because they regard it [10] as pettifoggery. For accuracy has something of this character, so that as in trade so in argument some people think it mean. Hence one must be already trained to know how to take each sort of argument, since it is absurd to seek at the same time knowledge and the way of attaining knowledge; and it is not easy to get even one of the two.

[15] The minute accuracy of mathematics is not to be demanded in all cases, but only in the case of things which have no matter. Hence its method is not that of natural science; for presumably the whole of nature has matter. Hence we must inquire first what nature is: for thus we shall also see what natural science treats of [and whether it belongs to one science or to more to investigate the causes and the [20] principles of things].

BOOK III

1

We must, with a view to the science which we are seeking, first recount the subjects that should be first discussed. These include both [25] the other opinions that some have held on the first principles, and any point besides these that happens to have been overlooked. For those who wish to get clear of difficulties it is advantageous to discuss the difficulties well; for the subsequent free play of thought implies the solution of the previous difficulties, and it is [30] not possible to untie a knot of which one does not know. But the difficulty of our thinking points to a 'knot' in the object; for in so far as our thought is in difficulties, it is in like case with those who are bound; for in either case it is impossible to go forward. Hence one should have surveyed all the difficulties beforehand, both for the purposes we have stated and because people who inquire without first stat-[35] ing the difficulties are like those who do not know where they have to go; besides, a man does not otherwise know even whether he has at any given time found what he is looking for or not; for the end is not clear to such a man, while to him who has first discussed the difficulties it is clear. Further, he who has heard all the contending arguments, as if they were the parties to a case, must be in a better position for judging.

The first problem concerns the subject which

[5] we discussed in our prefatory remarks. It is this—(1) whether the investigation of the causes belongs to one or to more sciences, and (2) whether such a science should survey only the first principles of substance, or also the principles on which all men base their proofs, e.g. whether it is possible at the same time to assert and deny one and the same thing or not, [10] and all other such questions; and (3) if the science in question deals with substance, whether *one* science deals with all substances, or more than one, and if more, whether all are akin, or some of them must be called forms of Wisdom and the others something else. And (4) this itself is also one of the things that must be discussed—whether sensible substances alone should be said to exist or others [15] also besides them, and whether these others are of one kind or there are several classes of substances, as is supposed by those who believe both in Forms and in mathematical objects intermediate between these and sensible things. Into these questions, then, as we say, we must inquire, and also (5) whether our investigation is concerned only with substances or also with the essential attributes of sub- [20] stances. Further, with regard to the same and other and like and unlike and contrariety, and with regard to prior and posterior and all other such terms about which the dialecticians try to inquire, starting their investigation from probable premises only,—whose business is it to inquire into all these? Further, we must dis- [25] cuss the essential attributes of these themselves; and we must ask not only what each of these is, but also whether one thing always has one contrary. Again (6), are the principles and elements of things the *genera,* or the parts *present* in each thing, into which it is divided; and (7) if they are the genera, are they the genera that are predicated proximately of the individuals, or the highest genera, e.g. is animal or [30] man the first principle and the more independent of the individual instance? And (8) we must inquire and discuss especially whether there is, besides the matter, any thing that is a cause in itself or not, and whether this can exist apart or not, and whether it is one or more in number, and whether there is something [35] apart from the concrete thing (by the concrete thing I mean the matter with something already predicated of it), or there is nothing apart, or there is something in some cases though not in others, and what sort of cases these are. Again (9) we ask whether the principles are limited in number or in kind, both those in the definitions and those in the substratum; and (10) whether the principles of perishable and of imperishable things are the same or different; and whether they are all imperishable or those of perishable things are perishable. Further (11) there is the question [5] which is hardest of all and most perplexing, whether unity and being, as the Pythagoreans and Plato said, are not attributes of something else but the substance of existing things, or this is not the case, but the substratum is something else,—as Empedocles says, love; as some one else says, fire; while another says water or air. Again (12) we ask whether the principles are universal or like individual [10] things, and (13) whether they exist potentially or actually, and further, whether they are potential or actual in any other sense than in reference to movement; for these questions also would present much difficulty. Further (14), are numbers and lines and figures and points a kind of substance or not, and if they are substances are they separate from sensible [15] things or present in them? With regard to all these matters not only is it hard to get possession of the truth, but it is not easy even to think out the difficulties well.

2

(1) First then with regard to what we mentioned first, does it belong to one or to more sciences to investigate all the kinds of causes? [20] How could it belong to one science to recognize the principles if these are not contrary?

Further, there are many things to which not all the principles pertain. For how can a principle of change or the nature of the good exist for unchangeable things, since everything that in itself and by its own nature is good is an [25] end, and a cause in the sense that for its sake the other things both come to be and are, and since an end or purpose is the end of some action, and all actions imply change? So in the case of unchangeable things this principle could not exist, nor could there be a good-itself. This is why in mathematics nothing is proved by means of this kind of cause, nor is there any [30] demonstration of this kind—'because it is better, or worse'; indeed no one even mentions anything of the kind. And so for this reason some of the Sophists, e.g. Aristippus, used to ridicule mathematics; for in the arts (he maintained), even in the industrial arts, e.g. in carpentry and cobbling, the reason always given [35] is 'because it is better, or worse,' but the mathematical sciences take no account of goods and evils.

996ᵇ But if there are *several* sciences of the causes, and a different science for each different principle, which of these sciences should be said to be that which we seek, or which of the people who possess them has the most scientific [5] knowledge of the object in question? The same thing may have all the kinds of causes, e.g. the moving cause of a house is the art or the builder, the final cause is the function it fulfils, the matter is earth and stones, and the form is the definition. To judge from our previous discussion[1] of the question which of the sciences should be called Wisdom, there is reason for applying the name to each of them. For [10] inasmuch as it is most architectonic and authoritative and the other sciences, like slave-women, may not even contradict it, the science of the *end* and of the *good* is of the nature of Wisdom (for the other things are for the sake of the end). But inasmuch as it was described[2] as dealing with the first causes and that which is in the highest sense object of knowledge, the science of *substance* must be of the nature of Wisdom. For since men may know the same [15] thing in many ways, we say that he who recognizes what a thing is by its being so and so knows more fully than he who recognizes it by its not being so and so, and in the former class itself one knows more fully than another, and he knows most fully who knows what a thing is, not he who knows its quantity or quality or what it can by nature do or have done to it. And further in all cases also we think that the knowledge of each even of the things of which demonstration is possible is present only when [20] we know what the thing is, e.g. what squaring a rectangle is, viz. that it is the finding of a mean; and similarly in all other cases. And we know about becomings and actions and about every change when we know the *source of the movement;* and this is other than and opposed to the end. Therefore it would [25] seem to belong to different sciences to investigate these causes severally.

But (2), taking the starting-points of demonstration as well as the causes, it is a disputable question whether they are the object of one science or of more (by the starting-points of demonstration I mean the common beliefs, on which all men base their proofs); e.g. that everything must be either affirmed or denied, and that a thing cannot at the same time be and not [30] be, and all other such premises:—the question is whether the same science deals with them as with substance, or a different science, and if it is not one science, which of the two must be identified with that which we now seek.—It is not reasonable that these topics should be the object of one science; for why should it be peculiarly appropriate to geometry or to any other science to understand these mat- [35] ters? If then it belongs to every science 997ᵃ alike, and cannot belong to all, it is not peculiar to the science which investigates substances, any more than to any other science, to know about these topics.—And, at the same time, in what way can there be a *science* of the first principles? For we are aware even now what each of them in fact is (at least even other [5] sciences use them as familiar); but if there is a demonstrative science which deals with them, there will have to be an underlying kind, and some of them must be demonstrable attributes and others must be axioms (for it is impossible that there should be demonstration about all of them); for the demonstration must start from certain premises and be about a certain subject and prove certain attributes. Therefore it follows that all attributes that are proved must [10] belong to a single class; for all demonstrative sciences use the axioms.

But if the science of substance and the science which deals with the axioms are different, which of them is by nature more authoritative and prior? The *axioms* are most universal and are principles of all things. And if it is not the business of the philosopher, to whom else will it belong to inquire what is true and what is untrue about them?

[15] (3) In general, do all substances fall under one science or under more than one? If the latter, to what sort of substance is the present science to be assigned?—On the other hand, it is not reasonable that one science should deal with all. For then there would be one demonstrative science dealing with all attributes. For every demonstrative science investigates with [20] regard to some subject its essential attributes, starting from the common beliefs. Therefore to investigate the essential attributes of one class of things, starting from one set of beliefs, is the business of one science. For the subject belongs to one science, and the premises belong to one, whether to the same or to another; so that the attributes do so too, whether they are investigated by these sciences or by one compounded out of them.

[25] (5)[3] Further, does our investigation deal with substances alone or also with their attri

---

[1] Cf. 1. 982ᵃ 8-19. [2] *Ibid.* 30-ᵇ 2. [3] Problem nos. as in ch. 1.

butes? I mean for instance, if the solid is a substance and so are lines and planes, is it the business of the same science to know these and to know the attributes of each of these classes (the attributes about which the mathematical sciences offer proofs), or of a different science? [30] If of the *same,* the science of substance also must be a demonstrative science, but it is thought that there is *no* demonstration of the essence of things. And if of *another,* what will be the science that investigates the attributes of substance? This is a very difficult question.

(4) Further, must we say that sensible substances alone exist, or that there are others be-[35] sides these? And are substances of one kind or are there in fact several kinds of sub-998[b] stances, as those say who assert the existence both of the Forms and of the intermediates, with which they say the mathematical sciences deal?—The sense in which we say the Forms are both causes and self-dependent substances has been explained in our first remarks [5] about them;[1] while the theory presents difficulties in many ways, the most paradoxical thing of all is the statement that there are certain things besides those in the material universe, and that these are the same as sensible things except that they are eternal while the latter are perishable. For they say there is a man-himself and a horse-itself and health-itself, with no further qualification,—a procedure like that of the people who said there are gods, [10] but in human form. For they were positing nothing but eternal men, nor are the Platonists making the Forms anything other than eternal sensible things.

Further, if we are to posit besides the Forms and the sensibles the intermediates between them, we shall have many difficulties. For clearly on the same principle there will be lines besides the lines-themselves and the sensible lines, [15] and so with each of the other classes of things; so that since astronomy is one of these mathematical sciences there will also be a heaven besides the sensible heaven, and a sun and a moon (and so with the other heavenly bodies) besides the sensible. Yet how are we to believe in these things? It is not reasonable even to suppose such a body immovable, but to suppose it *moving* is quite impossible.—And similarly [20] with the things of which optics and mathematical harmonics treat; for these also cannot exist apart from the sensible things, for the same reasons. For if there are sensible things

[1] Cf. 1. 6 and 9.

and sensations intermediate between Form and individual, evidently there will also be animals intermediate between animals-themselves and [25] the perishable animals.—We might also raise the question, with reference to *which kind* of existing things we must look for these sciences of intermediates. If geometry is to differ from mensuration only in this, that the latter deals with things that we perceive, and the former with things that are not perceptible, evidently there will also be a science other than medicine, intermediate between medical-science-itself and this individual medical science, and so with each of the other sciences. Yet how [30] is this possible? There would have to be also healthy things besides the perceptible healthy things and the healthy-itself.—And at the same time not even this is true, that mensuration deals with perceptible and perishable magnitudes; for then it would have perished when they perished.

But on the other hand astronomy cannot be dealing with perceptible magnitudes nor with this heaven above us. For neither are percepti-[35] ble lines such lines as the geometer speaks 998[a] of (for no perceptible thing is straight or round in the way in which he defines 'straight' and 'round'; for a hoop touches a straight edge not at a point, but as Protagoras used to say it did, in his refutation of the geometers), nor are the movements and spiral orbits in the [5] heavens like those of which astronomy treats, nor have geometrical points the same nature as the actual stars.—Now there are some who say that these so-called intermediates between the Forms and the perceptible things exist, not apart from the perceptible things, however, but in these; the impossible results of this [10] view would take too long to enumerate, but it is enough to consider even such points as the following:—It is not reasonable that this should be so only in the case of these *intermediates,* but clearly the *Forms* also might be in the perceptible things; for both statements are parts of the same theory. Further, it follows from this theory that there are two solids in the same place, and that the intermediates are not immovable, since they are in the moving percep-[15] tible things. And in general to what purpose would one suppose them to *exist* indeed, but to exist *in* perceptible things? For the same paradoxical results will follow which we have already mentioned; there will be a heaven besides *the* heaven, only it will be not apart but in the same place; which is still more impossible.

3

[20] (6) Apart from the great difficulty of stating the case truly with regard to these matters, it is very hard to say, with regard to the first principles, whether it is the genera that should be taken as elements and principles, or rather the primary constituents of a thing; e.g. it is the primary parts of which articulate sounds consist that are thought to be elements and principles of articulate sound, not the [25] common genus—articulate sound; and we give the name of 'elements' to those geometrical propositions, the proofs of which are implied in the proofs of the others, either of all or of most. Further, both those who say there are several elements of corporeal things and those who say there is one, say the parts of which bodies are compounded and consist are princi- [30] ples; e.g. Empedocles says fire and water and the rest are the constituent elements of things, but does not describe these as genera of existing things. Besides this, if we want to examine the nature of anything else, we examine **998ᵇ** the parts of which, e.g. a bed consists and how they are put together, and then we know its nature.

To judge from these arguments, then, the principles of things would not be the genera; but if we know each thing by its definition, and [5] the genera are the principles or starting-points of definitions, the genera must also be the principles of definable things. And if to get the knowledge of the species according to which things are named is to get the knowledge of things, the genera are at least starting-points of the *species*. And some also of those who say unity or being, or the great and the [10] small, are elements of things, seem to treat them as genera.

But, again, it is not possible to describe the principles in *both* ways. For the formula of the essence is one; but definition by genera will be different from that which states the constituent parts of a thing.

(7) Besides this, even if the genera are in the [15] highest degree principles, should one regard the first of the genera as principles, or those which are predicated directly of the individuals? This also admits of dispute. For if the universals are always more of the nature of principles, evidently the uppermost of the genera are the principles; for these are predicated of all things. There will, then, be as many principles of things as there are primary [20] genera, so that both being and unity will be principles and substances; for these are most of all predicated of all existing things. But it is not possible that either unity or being should be a single genus of things; for the differentiae of any genus must each of them both have being and be one, but it is not possible for the genus taken apart from its species (any [25] more than for the species of the genus) to be predicated of its proper differentiae; so that if unity or being is a genus, no differentia will either have being or be one. But if unity and being are not genera, neither will they be principles, if the genera are the principles.— Again, the intermediate kinds, in whose nature the differentiae are included, will on this theory be genera, down to the indivisible species; but as it is, some are thought to be genera [30] and others are not thought to be so. Besides this, the differentiae are principles even more than the genera; and if these also are principles, there comes to be practically an infinite number of principles, especially if we **999ᵃ** suppose the highest genus to be a principle.—But again, if unity *is* more of the nature of a principle, and the indivisible is one, and everything indivisible is so either in quantity or in species, and that which is so in species is the prior, and genera are divisible into species (for man is not the *genus* of individual men), [5] that which is predicated directly of the individuals will have more unity.—Further, in the case of things in which the distinction of prior and posterior is present, that which is predicable of these things cannot be something apart from them (e.g. if two is the first of numbers, there will not be a Number apart from the kinds of numbers; and similarly there will not be a Figure apart from the kinds of [10] figures; and if the genera of these things do not exist apart from the species, the genera of *other* things will scarcely do so; for genera of these things are thought to exist if any do). But among the individuals one is not prior and another posterior. Further, where one thing is better and another worse, the better is always prior; so that of these also no genus can exist. [15] From these considerations, then, the species predicated of individuals seem to be principles rather than the genera. But again, it is not easy to say in what sense these are to be taken as principles. For the principle or cause must exist alongside of the things of which it is the principle, and must be capable of existing in separation from them; but for what reason should we suppose any such thing to exist [20] alongside of the individual, except that it

is predicated universally and of all? But if this is the reason, the things that are more universal must be supposed to be more of the nature of principles; so that the highest genera would be the principles.

4

(8) There is a difficulty connected with these, [25] the hardest of all and the most necessary to examine, and of this the discussion now awaits us. If, on the one hand, there is nothing apart from individual things, and the individuals are infinite in number, how then is it possible to get knowledge of the infinite individuals? For all things that we come to know, we come to know in so far as they have some unity and identity, and in so far as some attribute belongs to them universally.

But if this is necessary, and there must be [30] something apart from the individuals, it will be necessary that the genera exist apart from the individuals,—either the lowest or the highest genera; but we found by discussion just now that this is impossible.[1]

Further, if we admit in the fullest sense that something exists apart from the concrete thing, whenever something is predicated of the matter, must there, if there is something apart, be something apart from each set of individuals, **999ᵇ** or from some and not from others, or from none? (A) If there is nothing apart from individuals, there will be no object of thought, but all things will be objects of sense, and there will not be knowledge of anything, unless we say that sensation is knowledge. Further, nothing will be eternal or unmovable; for all perceptible things perish and are in movement. [5] But if there is nothing eternal, neither can there be a process of coming to be; for there must be something that comes to be, i.e. from which something comes to be, and the ultimate term in this series cannot have come to be, since the series has a limit and since nothing can come to be out of that which is not. Further, if generation and movement exist there must [10] also be a limit; for no movement is infinite, but every movement has an end, and that which is incapable of completing its coming to be cannot be in process of coming to be; and that which has completed its coming to be must *be* as soon as it has come to be. Further, since the matter exists, because it is ungenerated, it is *a fortiori* reasonable that the substance or essence, that which the matter is at any time coming to be, should exist; for if

[1] Chapter 3.

neither essence nor matter is to be, nothing [15] will be at all, and since this is impossible there must be something besides the concrete thing, viz. the shape or form.

But again (B) if we are to suppose this, it is hard to say in which cases we are to suppose it and in which not. For evidently it is not possible to suppose it in all cases; we could not suppose that there is a house besides the par- [20] ticular houses.—Besides this, will the substance of all the individuals, e.g. of all men, be one? This is paradoxical, for all the things whose substance is one are one. But are the substances many and different? This also is unreasonable.—At the same time, how does the matter become each of the individuals, and how *is* the concrete thing these two elements?

(9) Again, one might ask the following [25] question also about the first principles. If they are one *in kind* only, nothing will be numerically one, not even unity-itself and being-itself; and how will knowing exist, if there is not to be something common to a whole set of individuals?

But if there is a common element which is *numerically* one, and each of the principles is one, and the principles are not as in the case of perceptible things different for different things (e.g. since this particular syllable is the same in kind whenever it occurs, the elements [30] of it are also the same in kind; only in kind, for these also, like the syllable, are numerically different in different contexts),—if it is not like this but the principles of things are numerically one, there will be nothing else besides the elements (for there is no difference of meaning between 'numerically one' and 'individual'; for this is just what we mean by the individual—the numerically one, and by the **1000ᵃ** universal we mean that which is predicable of the individuals). Therefore it will be just as if the elements of articulate sound were limited in number; all the language in the world would be confined to the ABC, since there could not be two or more letters of the same kind.

[5] (10) One difficulty which is as great as any has been neglected both by modern philosophers and by their predecessors—whether the principles of perishable and those of imperishable things are the same or different. If they are the same, how are some things perishable and others imperishable, and for what reason? The school of Hesiod and all the theologians thought only of what was plausible to them- [10] selves, and had no regard to us. For,

asserting the first principles to be gods and born of gods, they say that the beings which did not taste of nectar and ambrosia became mortal; and clearly they are using words which are familiar to themselves, yet what they have said about the very application of these causes is above our comprehension. For if the gods [15] taste of nectar and ambrosia for their pleasure, these are in no wise the causes of their existence; and if they taste them to maintain their existence, how can gods who need food be eternal?—But into the subtleties of the mythologists it is not worth our while to inquire seriously; those, however, who use the language of proof we must cross-examine and [20] ask why, after all, things which consist of the same elements are, some of them, eternal in nature, while others perish. Since these philosophers mention no cause, and it is unreasonable that things should be as they say, evidently the principles or causes of things cannot be the same. Even the man whom one might sup- [25] pose to speak most consistently—Empedocles,—even he has made the same mistake; for he maintains that strife is a principle that causes *destruction,* but even strife would seem no less to *produce* everything, except the One; for all things excepting God proceed from strife. At least he says:—

> From which all that was and is and will be hereafter—
> [30] Trees, and men and women, took their growth,
> And beasts and birds and water-nourished fish,
> And long-aged gods.[1]

The implication is evident even apart from 1000[b] these words; for if strife had not been present in things, all things would have been one, according to him; for when they have come together, 'then strife stood outermost.'[2] Hence it also follows on his theory that God most blessed is less wise than all others; for he [5] does not know all the elements; for he has in him no strife, and knowledge is of the like by the like. 'For by earth,' he says,

> we see earth, by water water,
> By ether godlike ether, by fire wasting fire,
> Love by love, and strife by gloomy strife.[3]

But—and this is the point we started from— [10] this at least is evident, that on his theory it follows that strife is as much the cause of existence as of destruction. And similarly love is not specially the cause of existence; for in collecting things into the One it destroys all other things. And at the same time Empedocles mentions no cause of the change itself, except that things are so by nature.

> But when strife at last waxed great in the limbs of the Sphere,
> And sprang to assert its rights as the time was fulfilled
> [15] Which is fixed for them in turn by a mighty oath.[4]

This implies that change was necessary; but he shows no cause of the necessity. But yet so far at least he alone speaks consistently; for he does not make some things perishable and others imperishable, but makes all perishable [20] except the elements. The difficulty we are speaking of now is, why some things are perishable and others are not, if they consist of the same principles.

Let this suffice as proof of the fact that the principles cannot be the same. But if there are different principles, one difficulty is whether these also will be imperishable or perishable. For if they are *perishable,* evidently these also [25] must consist of certain elements (for all things that perish, perish by being resolved into the elements of which they consist); so that it follows that prior to the principles there are other principles. But this is impossible, whether the process has a limit or proceeds to infinity. Further, how will perishable things exist, if their principles are to be annulled? But if the principles are *imperishable,* why will things composed of *some* imperishable principles be [30] perishable, while those composed of the others are imperishable? This is not probable, but is either impossible or needs much proof. Further, no one has even tried to maintain different principles; they maintain the same principles for all things. But they swallow the difficulty we stated first[5] as if they took it to be something trifling.

(11) The inquiry that is both the hardest of [5] all and the most necessary for knowledge of the truth is whether being and unity are the substances of things, and whether each of them, without being anything else, is being or unity respectively, *or* we must inquire what being and unity are, with the implication that they have some other underlying nature. For some people think they are of the former, others think they are of the latter character. Plato and the Pythagoreans thought being and [10] unity were nothing else, but this was their nature, their essence being just unity and being. But the natural philosophers take a dif-

---
[1] Fr. 21.   [2] Fr. 36.   [3] Fr. 109.   [4] Fr. 30.   [5] 1000[a] 5-[b] 21.

ferent line; e.g. Empedocles—as though reducing it to something more intelligible—says what unity is; for he would seem to say it is love: at least, this is for all things the cause of [15] their being one. Others say this unity and being, of which things consist and have been made, is fire, and others say it is air. A similar view is expressed by those who make the elements more than one; for these also must say that unity and being are precisely all the things which they say are principles.

(A) If we do not suppose unity and being to [20] be substances, it follows that none of the other universals is a substance; for these are most universal of all, and if there is no unity-itself or being-itself, there will scarcely be in any *other* case anything apart from what are [25] called the individuals. Further, if unity is not a substance, evidently number also will not exist as an entity separate from the individual things; for number is units, and the unit is precisely a certain kind of one.

But (B) if there is a unity-itself and a being-itself, unity and being must be their substance; for it is not something else that is predicated universally of the things that are and are one, but just unity and being. But if there *is* to be [30] a being-itself and a unity-itself, there is much difficulty in seeing how there will be anything else besides these,—I mean, how things will be more than one in number. For what is different from being does not exist, so that it necessarily follows, according to the argument of Parmenides, that all things that are are one and this is being.

1001[b] There are objections to both views. For whether unity is not a substance or there *is* a unity-itself, number cannot be a substance. We have already[1] said why this result follows if unity is not a substance; and if it is, the same difficulty arises as arose with regard to being. [5] For whence is there to be another one besides unity-itself? It must be not-one; but all things are either one or many, and of the many each is one.

Further, if unity-itself is indivisible, according to Zeno's postulate it will be nothing. For that which neither when added makes a thing greater nor when subtracted makes it less, he asserts to have no being, evidently assuming [10] that whatever has being is a spatial magnitude. And if it is a magnitude, it is corporeal; for the corporeal has being in every dimension, while the other objects of mathematics, e.g. a plane or a line, added in one way will increase

[1] a 24-27.

what they are added to, but in another way will not do so, and a point or a unit does so in no way. But, since his theory is of a low order, and an indivisible thing *can* exist in such a way [15] as to have a defence even against him (for the indivisible when added will make the number, though not the size, greater),—yet how can a *magnitude* proceed from one such indivisible or from many? It is like saying that the line is made out of points.

[20] But even if one supposes the case to be such that, as some say, number proceeds from unity-itself and something else which is not one, none the less we must inquire why and how the product will be sometimes a number and sometimes a magnitude, if the not-one was inequality and was the same principle in either case. For it is not evident how magnitudes could proceed either from the one and [25] this principle, or from some number and this principle.

5

(14) A question connected with these is whether numbers and bodies and planes and points are substances of a kind, or not. If they are not, it baffles us to say what being is and what the substances of things are. For modifica- [30] tions and movements and relations and dispositions and ratios do not seem to indicate the substance of anything; for all are predicated of a subject, and none is a 'this'. And as to the things which might seem most of all to indicate substance, water and earth and fire and air, of which composite bodies consist, heat and **1002**[a] cold and the like are modifications of these, not substances, and the body which is thus modified alone persists as something real and as a substance. But, on the other hand, the body is surely less of a substance than the surface, [5] and the surface than the line, and the line than the unit and the point. For the body is bounded by these; and they are thought to be capable of existing without body, but body incapable of existing without these. This is why, while most of the philosophers and the earlier among them thought that substance and being were identical with *body,* and that all other [10] things were modifications of this, so that the first principles of the bodies were the first principles of being, the more recent and those who were held to be wiser thought *numbers* were the first principles. As we said, then, if these are not substance, there is no substance and no being at all; for the *accidents* of these it cannot be right to call beings.

[15] But if this is admitted, that lines and points are substance more than bodies, but we do not see to what sort of bodies these could belong (for they cannot be in perceptible bodies), there can be no substance.—Further, these are all evidently divisions of body,—one in breadth, another in depth, another in length. [20] —Besides this, no sort of shape is present in the solid more than any other; so that if the Hermes is not in the stone, neither is the half of the cube in the cube as something determinate; therefore the surface is not in it either; for if any sort of surface were in it, the surface which marks off the half of the cube would [25] be in it too. And the same account applies to the line and to the point and the unit. Therefore, if on the one hand body is in the highest degree substance, and on the other hand these things are so more than body, but these are not even instances of substance, it baffles us to say what being is and what the substance of things is.—For besides what has been said, the questions of generation and de-[30] struction confront us with further paradoxes. For if substance, not having existed before, now exists, or having existed before, afterwards does not exist, this change is thought to be accompanied by a process of becoming or perishing; but points and lines and surfaces cannot be in process either of becoming or of perishing, when they at one time exist and at another do not. For when bodies come into **1002ᵇ** contact or are divided, their boundaries simultaneously become one in the one case—when they touch, and two in the other—when they are divided; so that when they have been put together one boundary does not exist but has perished, and when they have been divided the boundaries exist which before did not exist (for it cannot be said that the point, which is indivisible, was divided into two). And if the boundaries come into being and cease to be, from what do they come into being? A sim-[5] ilar account may also be given of the 'now' in time; for this also cannot be in process of coming into being or of ceasing to be, but yet seems to be always different, which shows that it is not a substance. And evidently the same is true of points and lines and planes; for the [10] same argument applies, since they are all alike either limits or divisions.

6

In general one might raise the question why after all, besides perceptible things and the intermediates, we have to look for another class of things, i.e. the Forms which we posit. If it is for this reason, because the objects of mathematics, while they differ from the things [15] in this world in some other respect, differ not at all in that there are many of the same kind, so that their first principles cannot be limited in number (just as the elements of all the language in this sensible world are not limited in number, but in kind, unless one takes the elements of this individual syllable or of [20] this individual articulate sound—whose elements will be limited even in number; so is it also in the case of the intermediates; for there also the members of the same kind are infinite in number), so that if there are not—besides perceptible and mathematical objects—others such as some maintain the Forms to be, there will be no substance which is one in number, but only in kind, nor will the first principles of things be determinate in number, [25] but only in kind:—if then this must be so, the Forms also must therefore be held to exist. Even if those who support this view do not express it articulately, still this is what they mean, and they must be maintaining the Forms just because each of the Forms is a substance and none is by accident.

[30] But if we *are* to suppose both that the Forms exist and that the principles are one in number, not in kind, we have mentioned[1] the impossible results that necessarily follow.

(13) Closely connected with this is the question whether the elements exist potentially or in some other manner. If in some other way, there will be something else prior to the first **1003ᵃ** principles; for the potency is prior to the actual cause, and it is not necessary for everything potential to be actual.—But if the elements exist potentially, it is possible that everything that is should not be. For even that which is not yet is capable of being; for that which is not comes to be, but nothing that is incapable of being comes to be.

[5] (12) We must not only raise these questions about the first principles, but also ask whether they are universal or what we call individuals. If they are universal, they will not be substances; for everything that is common indicates not a 'this' but a 'such', but substance is a 'this'. And if we are to be allowed to lay it down that a common predicate is a 'this' and [10] a single thing, Socrates will be several animals—himself and 'man' and 'animal', if each of these indicates a 'this' and a single thing.

[1] 999ᵇ 27–1000ᵃ 4.

If, then, the principles are universals, these results follow; if they are not universals but of the nature of individuals, they will not be knowable; for the knowledge of anything is [*15*] universal. Therefore if there is to be knowledge of the principles there must be other principles prior to them, namely those that are universally predicated of them.

BOOK IV

1

THERE is a science which investigates being as being and the attributes which belong to this in virtue of its own nature. Now this is not the same as any of the so-called special sciences; for none of these others treats universally of being as being. They cut off a part of being and [*25*] investigate the attribute of this part; this is what the mathematical sciences for instance do. Now since we are seeking the first principles and the highest causes, clearly there must be some thing to which these belong in virtue of its own nature. If then those who sought the elements of existing things were seeking these same principles, it is necessary [*30*] that the elements must be elements of being not by accident but just because it *is* being. Therefore it is of being as being that we also must grasp the first causes.

2

There are many senses in which a thing may be said to 'be', but all that 'is' is related to one central point, one definite kind of thing, and is not said to 'be' by a mere ambiguity. Everything which is healthy is related to health, one [*35*] thing in the sense that it preserves health, another in the sense that it produces it, another in the sense that it is a symptom of health, another because it is capable of it. And that 1003ᵇ which is medical is relative to the medical art, one thing being called medical because it possesses it, another because it is naturally adapted to it, another because it is a function of the medical art. And we shall find other [*5*] words used similarly to these. So, too, there are many senses in which a thing is said to be, but all refer to one starting-point; some things are said to be because they are substances, others because they are affections of substance, others because they are a process towards substance, or destructions or privations or qualities of substance, or productive or generative of substance, or of things which are relative to substance, or negations of one of these things [*10*] or of substance itself. It is for this reason that we say even of non-being that it *is* non-being. As, then, there is one science which deals with all healthy things, the same applies in the other cases also. For not only in the case of things which have one common notion does the investigation belong to one science, but also in the case of things which are related to one common nature; for even these in [*15*] a sense have one common notion. It is clear then that it is the work of one science also to study the things that are, *qua* being.—But everywhere science deals chiefly with that which is primary, and on which the other things depend, and in virtue of which they get their names. If, then, this is substance, it will be of substances that the philosopher must grasp the principles and the causes.

Now for each one class of things, as there is [*20*] one perception, so there is one science, as for instance grammar, being one science, investigates all articulate sounds. Hence to investigate all the species of being *qua* being is the work of a science which is generically one, and to investigate the several species is the work of the specific parts of the science.

If, now, being and unity are the same and are one thing in the sense that they are implied in one another as principle and cause are, not in the sense that they are explained by the same [*25*] definition (though it makes no difference even if we suppose them to be like that—in fact this would even strengthen our case); for 'one man' and 'man' are the same thing, and so are 'existent man' and 'man', and the doubling of the words in 'one man and one *existent* man' does not express anything different (it is clear that the two things are not separated either in coming to be or in ceasing [*30*] to be); and similarly '*one* existent man' adds nothing to 'existent man', and that it is obvious that the addition in these cases means the same thing, and unity is nothing apart from being; and if, further, the substance of each thing is one in no merely accidental way, and similarly is from its very nature something that *is*:—all this being so, there must be exactly as many species of being as of unity. And to investigate the essence of these is the work of a [*35*] science which is generically one—I mean, for instance, the discussion of the same and the similar and the other concepts of this sort; and nearly all contraries may be referred to this origin; let us take them as having been investigated in the 'Selection of Contraries'.

And there are as many parts of philosophy as there are kinds of substance, so that there must necessarily be among them a first philosophy and one which follows this. For being [5] falls immediately into genera; for which reason the sciences too will correspond to these genera. For the philosopher is like the mathematician, as that word is used; for mathematics also has parts, and there is a first and a second science and other successive ones within the sphere of mathematics.

Now since it is the work of one science to [10] investigate opposites, and plurality is opposed to unity—and it belongs to one science to investigate the negation and the privation because in both cases we are really investigating the one thing of which the negation or the privation is a negation or privation (for we either say simply that that thing is not present, or that it is not present in some particular class; in the latter case difference is present over and above what is implied in negation; for negation means just the absence of the thing in [15] question, while in privation there is also employed an underlying nature of which the privation is asserted):—in view of all these facts, the contraries of the concepts we named above, the other and the dissimilar and the unequal, and everything else which is derived either from these or from plurality and unity, must fall within the province of the science [20] above named. And contrariety is one of these concepts; for contrariety is a kind of difference, and difference is a kind of otherness. Therefore, since there are many senses in which a thing is said to be one, these terms also will have many senses, but yet it belongs to one science to know them all; for a term belongs to different sciences not if it has different senses, but if it has not one meaning [25] and its definitions cannot be referred to one central meaning. And since all things are referred to that which is primary, as for instance all things which are called one are referred to the primary one, we must say that this holds good also of the same and the other and of contraries in general; so that after distinguishing the various senses of each, we must then explain by reference to what is primary in the case of each of the predicates in question, saying how they are related to it; for [30] some will be called what they are called because they possess it, others because they produce it, and others in other such ways.

It is evident, then, that it belongs to one science to be able to give an account of these concepts as well as of substance (this was one of the questions in our book of problems), and that it is the function of the philosopher to be able to investigate all things. For if it is not the function of the philosopher, who is it who will inquire whether Socrates and Socrates seated are the same thing, or whether one thing has one contrary, or what contrariety is, or how many meanings it has? And similarly with all other such questions. Since, then, these [5] are essential modifications of unity *qua* unity and of being *qua* being, not *qua* numbers or lines or fire, it is clear that it belongs to this science to investigate both the essence of these concepts and their properties. And those who study these properties err not by leaving the sphere of philosophy, but by forgetting that substance, of which they have no correct idea, is prior to these other things. For [10] number *qua* number has peculiar attributes, such as oddness and evenness, commensurability and equality, excess and defect, and these belong to numbers either in themselves or in relation to one another. And similarly the solid and the motionless and that which is in motion and the weightless and that which has weight have other peculiar properties. So [15] too there are certain properties peculiar to being as such, and it is about these that the philosopher has to investigate the truth.—An indication of this may be mentioned:—dialecticians and sophists assume the same guise as the philosopher, for sophistic is Wisdom which exists only in semblance, and dialecticians embrace all things in their dialectic, and being is common to all things; but evidently their dialectic embraces these subjects because these are proper to philosophy.—For sophistic and dialectic turn on the same class of things as philosophy, but this differs from dialectic in the nature of the faculty required and from sophistic in respect of the purpose of the philosophic life. Dialectic is merely critical where philosophy claims to know, and sophistic is what appears to be philosophy but is not.

Again, in the list of contraries one of the two columns is privative, and all contraries are reducible to being and non-being, and to unity and plurality, as for instance rest belongs to unity and movement to plurality. And nearly [30] all thinkers agree that being and substance are composed of contraries; at least all name contraries as their first principles—some name odd and even, some hot and cold, some limit and the unlimited, some love and strife. And all the others as well are evidently reducible to unity and plurality (this reduction we 1005ª must take for granted), and the principles stated by other thinkers fall entirely under these as their genera. It is obvious then from these considerations too that it belongs to one science to examine being *qua* being. For all things are either contraries or composed of contraries, and unity and plurality are the starting-points of all contraries. And [5] these belong to one science, whether they have or have not one single meaning. Probably the truth is that they have not; yet even if 'one' has several meanings, the other meanings will be related to the primary meaning (and similarly in the case of the contraries), even if being or unity is not a universal and the same in every instance or is not separable [10] from the particular instances (as in fact it probably is not; the unity is in some cases that of common reference, in some cases that of serial succession). And for this reason it does not belong to the geometer to inquire what is contrariety or completeness or unity or being or the same or the other, but only to presuppose these concepts and reason from this starting-point.—Obviously then it is the work of one science to examine being *qua* being, and the attributes which belong to it *qua* being, and the same science will examine not only substances [15] but also their attributes, both those above named and the concepts 'prior' and 'posterior', 'genus' and 'species', 'whole' and 'part', and the others of this sort.

3

We must state whether it belongs to one or to different sciences to inquire into the truths which are in mathematics called axioms, and [20] into substance. Evidently, the inquiry into these also belongs to one science, and that the science of the philosopher; for these truths hold good for everything that is, and not for some special genus apart from others. And all men use them, because they are true of being *qua* [25] being and each genus has being. But men use them just so far as to satisfy their purposes; that is, as far as the genus to which their demonstrations refer extends. Therefore since these truths clearly hold good for all things *qua* being (for this is what is common to them), to him who studies being *qua* being belongs the inquiry into these as well. And for this reason no one who is conducting a special inquiry [30] tries to say anything about their truth or falsity,—neither the geometer nor the arithmetician. Some natural philosophers indeed have done so, and their procedure was intelligible enough; for they thought that they alone were inquiring about the whole of nature and about being. But since there is one kind of thinker who is above even the natural philosopher (for nature is only one particular [35] genus of being), the discussion of these truths also will belong to him whose inquiry is universal and deals with primary substance. 1005ᵇ Physics also is a kind of Wisdom, but it is not the first kind.—And the attempts of some of those who discuss the terms on which truth should be accepted, are due to a want of training in logic; for they should know these things already when they come to a special study, and not be inquiring into them while they are listening to lectures on it.

[5] Evidently then it belongs to the philosopher, i.e. to him who is studying the nature of all substance, to inquire also into the principles of syllogism. But he who knows best about each genus must be able to state the most [10] certain principles of his subject, so that he whose subject is existing things *qua* existing must be able to state the most certain principles of all things. This is the philosopher, and the most certain principle of all is that regarding which it is impossible to be mistaken; for such a principle must be both the best known (for all men may be mistaken about things which they do not know), and non-hypothet- [15] ical. For a principle which every one must have who understands anything that is, is not a hypothesis; and that which every one must know who knows anything, he must already have when he comes to a special study. Evidently then such a principle is the most certain of all; which principle this is, let us proceed to say. It is, that the same attribute cannot at the same time belong and not belong to the same [20] subject and in the same respect; we must presuppose, to guard against dialectical objections, any further qualifications which might be added. This, then, is the most certain of all principles, since it answers to the definition given above. For it is impossible for any one to believe the same thing to be and not to be, as [25] some think Heraclitus says. For what a man says, he does not necessarily believe; and if it is impossible that contrary attributes should belong at the same time to the same subject (the usual qualifications must be presupposed in this premiss too), and if an opinion which

contradicts another is contrary to it, obviously it is impossible for the same man at the same time to believe the same thing to be and not to [30] be; for if a man were mistaken on this point he would have contrary opinions at the same time. It is for this reason that all who are carrying out a demonstration reduce it to this as an ultimate belief; for this is naturally the starting-point even for all the other axioms.

4

[35] There are some who, as we said,[1] both themselves assert that it is possible for the same thing to be and not to be, and say that people can judge this to be the case. And among others many writers about nature use this language. But we have now posited that it is impossible for anything at the same time to be and not to be, and by this means have shown that this is the most indisputable [5] of all principles.—Some indeed demand that even this shall be demonstrated, but this they do through want of education, for not to know of what things one should demand demonstration, and of what one should not, argues want of education. For it is impossible that there should be demonstration of absolutely everything (there would be an infinite regress, [10] so that there would still be no demonstration); but if there are things of which one should not demand demonstration, these persons could not say what principle they maintain to be more self-evident than the present one.

We can, however, demonstrate negatively even that this view is impossible, if our opponent will only say something; and if he says nothing, it is absurd to seek to give an account of our views to one who cannot give an account of anything, in so far as he cannot do so. [15] For such a man, as such, is from the start no better than a vegetable. Now negative demonstration I distinguish from demonstration proper, because in a demonstration one might be thought to be begging the question, but if another person is responsible for the assumption we shall have negative proof, not demonstration. The starting-point for all such arguments is not the demand that our opponent [20] shall say that something either is or is not (for this one might perhaps take to be a begging of the question), but that he shall say something which is *significant* both for himself and for another; for this is necessary, if he really is to say anything. For, if he means nothing, such a man will not be capable of reasoning, either with himself or with another. But if any one grants this, demonstration will be [25] possible; for we shall already have something definite. The person responsible for the proof, however, is not he who demonstrates but he who listens; for while disowning reason he listens to reason. And again he who admits this has admitted that something is true apart from demonstration [so that not everything will be 'so and not so'].

First then this at least is obviously true, that [30] the word 'be' or 'not be' has a definite meaning, so that not everything will be 'so and not so'.[2]—Again, if 'man' has one meaning, let this be 'two-footed animal'; by having one meaning I understand this:—if 'man' means '*X*', then if *A* is a man '*X*' will be what 'being a man' means for him. (It makes no difference even if one were to say a word has several meanings, if only they are limited in number; for to each definition there might be assigned a different word. For instance, we might say that 'man' has not one meaning but several, one of which would have one definition, viz. 'two-footed animal', while there might be also several other definitions if only they were limited in number; for a peculiar name might be assigned to each of the definitions. If, however, [5] they were not limited but one were to say that the word has an infinite number of meanings, obviously reasoning would be impossible; for not to have one meaning is to have no meaning, and if words have no meaning our reasoning with one another, and indeed with [10] ourselves, has been annihilated; for it is impossible to think of anything if we do not think of one thing; but if this *is* possible, one name might be assigned to this thing.)

Let it be assumed then, as was said at the beginning,[3] that the name has a meaning and has one meaning; it is impossible, then, that 'being a man' should mean precisely 'not being a man', if 'man' not only signifies something about one subject but also has one [15] significance (for we do not identify 'having one significance' with 'signifying something about one subject', since on *that* assumption even 'musical' and 'white' and 'man' would have had one significance, so that all things would have been one; for they would all have had the same significance).

And it will not be possible to be and not to be the same thing, except in virtue of an ambiguity, just as if one whom we call 'man',

---

[1] Apparently a loose reference to 1005[b] 23-5.   [2] Cf. Plato, *Theaetetus*, 183.   [3] [a]21, 31.

[20] others were to call 'not-man'; but the point in question is not this, whether the same thing can at the same time be and not be a man in name, but whether it can in fact.—Now if 'man' and 'not-man' mean nothing different, obviously 'not being a man' will mean nothing different from 'being a man'; so that 'being a man' will be 'not being a man'; for [25] they will be one. For being one means this—being related as 'raiment' and 'dress' are, if their definition is one. And if 'being a man' and 'being a not-man' are to be one, they must mean one thing. But it was shown earlier[1] that they mean different things.—Therefore, if it is true to say of anything that it is a man, it must be a two-footed animal (for this was what [30] 'man' meant); and if this is necessary, it is impossible that the same thing should not at that time be a two-footed animal; for this is what 'being necessary' means—that it is impossible for the thing not to be. It is, then, impossible that it should be at the same time true to say the same thing is a man and is not a man.

The same account holds good with regard 1007ª to 'not being a man', for 'being a man' and 'being a not-man' mean different things, since even 'being white' and 'being a man' are different; for the former terms are much more opposed, so that they must *a fortiori* mean different things. And if any one says that 'white' means one and the same thing as 'man', [5] again we shall say the same as what was said before,[2] that it would follow that *all* things are one, and not only opposites. But if this is impossible, then what we have maintained will follow, if our opponent will only answer our question.

And if, when one asks the question simply, [10] he adds the contradictories, he is not answering the question. For there is nothing to prevent the same thing from being both a man and white and countless other things: but still, if one asks whether it is or is not true to say that this is a man, our opponent must give an answer which means one thing, and not add that 'it is also white and large'. For, besides other reasons, it is impossible to enumerate its [15] accidental attributes, which are infinite in number; let him, then, enumerate either all or none. Similarly, therefore, even if the same thing is a thousand times a man and a not-man, he must not, in answering the question whether this is a man, add that it is also at the same time a not-man, unless he is bound to add

[1] ll. 11-15. [2] 1006ᵇ 17.

also all the other accidents, all that the subject is or is not; and if he does this, he is not observing the rules of argument.

[20] And in general those who say this do away with substance and essence. For they must say that all attributes are accidents, and that there is no such thing as 'being essentially a man' or 'an animal'. For if there is to be any such thing as 'being essentially a man' this will not be 'being a not-man' or 'not being a man' [25] (yet these are negations of it); for there was one thing which it meant, and this was the substance of something. And denoting the substance of a thing means that the essence of the thing is nothing else. But if its being essentially a man is to be the same as either being essentially a not-man or essentially not being a man, then its essence *will* be something else. Therefore our opponents must say that there [30] cannot be such a definition of anything, but that all attributes are accidental; for this is the distinction between substance and accident —'white' is accidental to man, because though he is white, whiteness is not his essence. But if *all* statements are accidental, there will be nothing primary about which they are made, if the [35] accidental always implies predication 1007ᵇ about a subject. The predication, then, must go on *ad infinitum*. But this is impossible; for not even more than two terms can be combined in accidental predication. For (1) an accident is not an accident of an accident, unless it be because both are accidents of the same subject. I mean, for instance, that the white is musical and the latter is white, only because [5] both are accidental to man. But (2) Socrates is musical, not in this sense, that both terms are accidental to something else. Since then some predicates are accidental in this and some in that sense, (*a*) those which are accidental in the latter sense, in which white is accidental to Socrates, cannot form an infinite series in the upward direction; e.g. Socrates the white has not yet another accident; for no [10] unity can be got out of such a sum. Nor again (*b*) will 'white' have another term accidental to it, e.g. 'musical'. For this is no more accidental to that than that is to this; and at the same time we have drawn the distinction, that while some predicates are accidental in this sense, others are so in the sense in which 'musical' is accidental to Socrates; and the accident is an accident of an accident not in cases of [15] the latter kind, but only in cases of the other kind, so that not *all* terms will be accidental. There must, then, even so be some-

thing which denotes substance. And if this is so, it has been shown that contradictories cannot be predicated at the same time.

Again, if all contradictory statements are true of the same subject at the same time, evidently all things will be one. For the same [20] thing will be a trireme, a wall, and a man, if of everything it is possible either to affirm or to deny anything (and this premiss must be accepted by those who share the views of Protagoras). For if any one thinks that the man is not a trireme, evidently he is not a trireme; so that he also *is* a trireme, if, as they say, con- [25] tradictory statements are both true. And we thus get the doctrine of Anaxagoras, that all things are mixed together; so that nothing really exists. They seem, then, to be speaking of the indeterminate, and, while fancying themselves to be speaking of being, they are speaking about non-being; for it is that which exists potentially and not in complete reality that is indeterminate. But they *must* predicate of every subject the affirmation or the negation [30] of every attribute. For it is absurd if of each subject its own negation is to be predicable, while the negation of something else which cannot be predicated of it is not to be predicable of it; for instance, if it is true to say of a man that he is not a man, evidently it is also true to say that he is either a trireme or not a trireme. If, then, the affirmative can be predi- [35] cated, the negative must be predicable too; and if the affirmative is not predicable, the negative, at least, will be more predicable than **1008ª** the negative of the subject itself. If, then, even the latter negative is predicable, the negative of 'trireme' will be also predicable; and, if this is predicable, the affirmative will be so too.

Those, then, who maintain this view are driven to this conclusion, and to the further conclusion that it is not necessary either to assert or to deny. For if it is true that a thing is a [5] man and a not-man, evidently also it will be neither a man nor a not-man. For to the two assertions there answer two negations, and if the former is treated as a single proposition compounded out of two, the latter also is a single proposition opposite to the former.

Again, either the theory is true in all cases, and a thing is both white and not-white, and existent and non-existent, and all other assertions and negations are similarly compatible, [10] or the theory is true of some statements and not of others. And if not of all, the exceptions will be contradictories of which admittedly only one is true; but if of all, again either the negation will be true wherever the assertion is, and the assertion true wherever the negation is, or the negation will be true where the assertion is, but the assertion not always [15] true where the negation is. And (*a*) in the latter case there will be something which fixedly *is not,* and this will be an indisputable belief; and if non-being is something indisputable and knowable, the opposite assertion will be more knowable. But (*b*) if it is equally possible also to assert all that it is possible to deny, one must either be saying what is true when one separates the predicates (and says, for instance, that a thing is white, and again [20] that it is not-white), or not. And if (i) it is not true to apply the predicates separately, our opponent is not saying what he professes to say, and also nothing at all exists; but how could non-existent things speak or walk, as he does? Also all things would on this view be one, as has been already said,[1] and man and God and trireme and their contradictories will [25] be the same. For if contradictories can be predicated alike of each subject, one thing will in no wise differ from another; for if it differ, this difference will be something true and peculiar to it. And (ii) if one may with truth apply the predicates separately, the above-mentioned result follows none the less, and, further, it follows that all would then be right and all would be in error, and our opponent himself confesses himself to be in error.—And [30] at the same time our discussion with him is evidently about nothing at all; for he says nothing. For he says neither 'yes' nor 'no', but 'yes and no'; and again he denies both of these and says 'neither yes nor no'; for otherwise there would already be something definite.

Again, if when the assertion is true, the nega- [35] tion is false, and when this is true, the affirmation is false, it will not be possible to assert and deny the same thing truly at the **1008ᵇ** same time. But perhaps they might say this was the very question at issue.

Again, is he in error who judges either that the thing is so or that it is not so, and is he right who judges both? If he is right, what can they mean by saying that the nature of [5] existing things is of this kind? And if he is not right, but more right than he who judges in the other way, being will already be of a definite nature, and this will be true, and not at the same time also not true. But if all are

---
[1] 1006ᵇ 17, 1007ª 6.

alike both wrong and right, one who is in this condition will not be able either to speak or to say anything intelligible; for he says at the [10] same time both 'yes' and 'no.' And if he makes no judgement but 'thinks' and 'does not think', indifferently, what difference will there be between him and a vegetable?—Thus, then, it is in the highest degree evident that neither any one of those who maintain this view nor any one else is really in this position. For why does a man walk to Megara and not stay at home, when he thinks he ought to be [15] walking there? Why does he not walk early some morning into a well or over a precipice, if one happens to be in his way? Why do we observe him guarding against this, evidently because he does not think that falling in is alike good and not good? Evidently, then, he judges one thing to be better and another worse. And if this is so, he must also judge one thing to be a man and another to be not-[20] a-man, one thing to be sweet and another to be not-sweet. For he does not aim at and judge all things alike, when, thinking it desirable to drink water or to see a man, he proceeds to aim at these things; yet he *ought,* if the same thing were alike a man and not-a-man. But, as was said, there is no one who does [25] not obviously avoid some things and not others. Therefore, as it seems, all men make unqualified judgements, if not about all things, still about what is better and worse. And if this is not knowledge but opinion, they should be all the more anxious about the truth, as a sick man should be more anxious about his [30] health than one who is healthy; for he who has opinions is, in comparison with the man who knows, not in a healthy state as far as the truth is concerned.

Again, however much all things may be 'so and not so', still there is a more and a less in the nature of things; for we should not say that two and three are equally even, nor is he who thinks four things are five equally wrong [35] with him who thinks they are a thousand. If then they are not equally wrong, obviously one is less wrong and therefore more right. If then that which has more of any **1009**ᵃ quality is nearer the norm, there must be some truth to which the more true is nearer. And even if there is not, still there is already something better founded and liker the truth, and we shall have got rid of the [5] unqualified doctrine which would prevent us from determining anything in our thought.

5

From the same opinion proceeds the doctrine of Protagoras, and both doctrines must be alike true or alike untrue. For on the one hand, if all opinions and appearances are true, all statements must be at the same time true and false. For many men hold beliefs in which they con-[10] flict with one another, and think those mistaken who have not the same opinions as themselves; so that the same thing must both be and not be. And on the other hand, if this is so, all opinions must be true; for those who are mistaken and those who are right are opposed to one another in their opinions; if, then, reality is such as the view in question supposes, all will be right in their beliefs.

[15] Evidently, then, both doctrines proceed from the same way of thinking. But the same method of discussion must not be used with all opponents; for some need persuasion, and others compulsion. Those who have been driven to this position by difficulties in their thinking can easily be cured of their ignorance; for it is not their expressed argument but their [20] thought that one has to meet. But those who argue for the sake of argument can be cured only by refuting the argument as expressed in speech and in words.

Those who really feel the difficulties have been led to this opinion by observation of the sensible world. (1) They think that contradictories or contraries are true at the same time, because they see contraries coming into existence out [25] of the same thing. If, then, that which is not cannot come to be, the thing must have existed before as both contraries alike, as Anaxagoras says all is mixed in all, and Democritus too; for *he* says the void and the full exist alike in every part, and yet one of these is being, and the other non-being. To those, then, [30] whose belief rests on these grounds, we shall say that in a sense they speak rightly and in a sense they err. For 'that which is' has two meanings, so that in some sense a thing can come to be out of that which is not, while in some sense it cannot, and the same thing can at the same time be in being and not in being—but not in the same respect. For the same thing [35] can be potentially at the same time two contraries, but it cannot actually. And again we shall ask them to believe that among existing things there is also another kind of substance to which neither movement nor destruction nor generation at all belongs.

1009ᵇ And (2) similarly some have inferred

from observation of the sensible world the truth of appearances. For they think that the truth should not be determined by the large or small number of those who hold a belief, and that the same thing is thought sweet by some when they taste it, and bitter by others, so that [5] if all were ill or all were mad, and only two or three were well or sane, these would be thought ill and mad, and not the others.

And again, they say that many of the other animals receive impressions contrary to ours; and that even to the senses of each individual, things do not always seem the same. Which, then, of these impressions are true and which [10] are false is not obvious; for the one set is no more true than the other, but both are alike. And this is why Democritus, at any rate, says that either there is no truth or to us at least it is not evident.

And in general it is because these thinkers suppose knowledge to be sensation, and this to be a physical alteration, that they say that what appears to our senses must be true; for it is for [15] these reasons that both Empedocles and Democritus and, one may almost say, all the others have fallen victims to opinions of this sort. For Empedocles says that when men change their condition they change their knowledge;

For wisdom increases in men according to what is before them.[1]

And elsewhere he says that

[20] *So far as their nature changed, so far to them always*
Came changed thoughts into mind.[2]

And Parmenides also expresses himself in the same way:

For as at each time the much-bent limbs are composed,
So is the mind of men; for in each and all men
'Tis one thing thinks—the substance of their limbs:
For that of which there is more is thought.[3]

[25] A saying of Anaxagoras to some of his friends is also related,—that things would be for them such as they supposed them to be. And they say that Homer also evidently had this opinion, because he made Hector, when he was unconscious from the blow, lie 'thinking other [30] thoughts',[4]—which implies that even those who are bereft of thought have thoughts, though not the same thoughts. Evidently, then,

if both are forms of knowledge, the real things also are at the same time 'both so and not so'. And it is in this direction that the consequences are most difficult. For if those who have seen most of such truth as is possible for us (and [35] these are those who seek and love it most) —if these have such opinions and express these views about the truth, is it not natural that beginners in philosophy should lose heart? For to seek the truth would be to follow flying game.

1010ᵃ But the reason why these thinkers held this opinion is that while they were inquiring into the truth of that which is, they thought, 'that which is' was identical with the sensible world; in this, however, there is largely present the nature of the indeterminate—of that which exists in the peculiar sense which we have explained;[5] and therefore, while they speak plausibly, they do not say what is true (for it is fit-[5] ting to put the matter so rather than as Epicharmus put it against Xenophanes). And again, because they saw that all this world of nature is in movement, and that about that which changes no true statement can be made, they said that of course, regarding that which everywhere in every respect is changing, nothing could truly be affirmed. It was this belief [10] that blossomed into the most extreme of the views above mentioned, that of the professed Heracliteans, such as was held by Cratylus, who finally did not think it right to say anything but only moved his finger, and criticized Heraclitus for saying that it is impossible to step twice into the same river; for *he* thought one could not do it even once.

[15] But we shall say in answer to this argument also, that while there is some justification for their thinking that the changing, when it is changing, does not exist, yet it is after all disputable; for that which is losing a quality has something of that which is being lost, and of that which is coming to be, something must already be. And in general if a thing is perishing, there will be present something that exists; [20] and if a thing is coming to be, there must be something from which it comes to be and something by which it is generated, and this process cannot go on *ad infinitum.*—But, leaving these arguments, let us insist on this, that it is not the same thing to change in quantity and in quality. Grant that in quantity a thing is not constant; still it is in respect of its form that we [25] know each thing.—And again, it would be fair to criticize those who hold this view for

---
[1] Fr. 106. [2] Fr. 108. [3] Fr. 16.
[4] Cf. *Iliad*, xxiii. 698, which does not, however, refer to Hector.
[5] Cf. 1009ᵃ 32.

asserting about the whole material universe what they saw only in a minority even of sensible things. For only that region of the sensible world which immediately surrounds us is al- [30] ways in process of destruction and generation; but this is—so to speak—not even a fraction of the whole, so that it would have been juster to acquit this part of the world because of the other part, than to condemn the other because of this.—And again, obviously we shall make to them also the same reply that we made long ago;[1] we must show them and persuade them that there is something whose [35] nature is changeless. Indeed, those who say that things at the same time are and are not, should in consequence say that all things are at rest rather than that they are in movement; for there is nothing into which they can change, since all attributes belong already to all subjects.

1010[b] Regarding the nature of truth, we must maintain that not everything which appears is true; firstly, because even if sensation—at least of the object peculiar to the sense in question —is not false, still appearance is not the same as sensation.—Again, it is fair to express surprise at our opponents' raising the question whether magnitudes are as great, and colours are of [5] such a nature, as they appear to people at a distance, or as they appear to those close at hand, and whether they are such as they appear to the healthy or to the sick, and whether those things are heavy which appear so to the weak or those which appear so to the strong, and those things true which appear to the sleeping or to the waking. For obviously they [10] do not think these to be open questions; no one, at least, if when he is in Libya he has fancied one night that he is in Athens, starts for the concert hall.—And again with regard to the future, as Plato says,[2] surely the opinion of the physician and that of the ignorant man are not equally weighty, for instance, on the question whether a man will get well or not.— [15] And again, among sensations themselves the sensation of a foreign object and that of the appropriate object, or that of a kindred object and that of the object of the sense in question, are not equally authoritative, but in the case of colour sight, not taste, has the authority, and in the case of flavour taste, not sight; each of which senses never says at the same time of the same object that it simultaneously is 'so and not so'.—But not even at different times does one [20] sense disagree about the quality, but only

[1] Cf. 1009[a] 36-8.   [2] Cf. *Theaetetus*, 178-179.

about that to which the quality belongs. I mean, for instance, that the same wine might seem, if either it or one's body changed, at one time sweet and at another time not sweet; but at least the sweet, such as it is when it exists, has [25] never yet changed, but one is always right about it, and that which is to be sweet is of necessity of such and such a nature. Yet all these views destroy this necessity, leaving nothing to be of necessity, as they leave no essence of anything; for the necessary cannot be in this way and also in that, so that if anything is of necessity, it will not be 'both so and not so'.
[30] And, in general, if only the sensible exists, there would be nothing if animate things were not; for there would be no faculty of sense. Now the view that neither the sensible qualities nor the sensations would exist is doubtless true (for they are affections of the perceiver), but that the substrata which cause the sensation should not exist even apart from sensation [35] is impossible. For sensation is surely not the sensation of itself, but there is something beyond the sensation, which must be prior to the sensation; for that which moves is prior in 1011[a] nature to that which is moved, and if they are correlative terms, this is no less the case.

6

There are, both among those who have these convictions and among those who merely profess these views, some who raise a difficulty by [5] asking, who is to be the judge of the healthy man, and in general who is likely to judge rightly on each class of questions. But such inquiries are like puzzling over the question whether we are now asleep or awake. And all such questions have the same meaning. These people demand that a reason shall be given for everything; for they seek a starting-point, and they seek to get this by demonstration, while it [10] is obvious from their actions that they have no conviction. But their mistake is what we have stated it to be; they seek a reason for things for which no reason can be given; for the starting-point of demonstration is not demonstration.

These, then, might be easily persuaded of this truth, for it is not difficult to grasp; but [15] those who seek merely compulsion in argument seek what is impossible; for they demand to be allowed to contradict themselves— a claim which contradicts itself from the very first.—But if not all things are relative, but some are self-existent, not everything that appears will be true; for that which appears is apparent to some one; so that he who says all [20] things that appear are true, makes all things relative. And, therefore, those who ask for an irresistible argument, and at the same time demand to be called to account for their views, must guard themselves by saying that the truth is not that what appears exists, but that what appears exists *for him to whom* it appears, and *when,* and *to the sense to which,* and *under the conditions under which* it appears. And if they give an account of their view, but do not give it in this way, they will soon find themselves contradicting themselves. For it is [25] possible that the same thing may appear to be honey to the sight, but not to the taste, and that, since we have two eyes, things may not appear the same to each, if their sight is unlike. For to those who for the reasons named [30] some time ago[1] say that what appears is true, and therefore that all things are alike false and true, for things do not appear either the same to all men or always the same to the same man, but often have contrary appearances at the same time (for touch says there are two objects when we cross our fingers, while sight says there is one),—to these we shall say 'yes, but not to the same sense and in the same part [35] of it and under the same conditions and at the same time', so that what appears will be 1011[b] with these qualifications true. But perhaps for this reason those who argue thus not because they feel a difficulty but for the sake of argument, should say that this is not true, but true for this man. And as has been said[2] before, they must make everything relative—relative [5] to opinion and perception, so that nothing either has come to be or will be without some one's first thinking so. But if things *have* come to be or will be, evidently not all things will be relative to opinion.—Again, if a thing is one, it is in relation to one thing or to a definite number of things; and if the same thing is both half and equal, it is not to the double that the equal is correlative. If, then, in relation to that which thinks, man and that which is thought are the [10] same, man will not be that which thinks, but only that which is thought. And if each thing is to be relative to that which thinks, that which thinks will be relative to an infinity of specifically different things.

Let this, then, suffice to show (1) that the most indisputable of all beliefs is that contradictory statements are not at the same time true, and (2) what consequences follow from

[1] Cf. 1009[a] 38–1010[a] 15.   [2] [a] 19 f.

the assertion that they are, and (3) why people [15] do assert this. Now since it is impossible that contradictories should be at the same time true of the same thing, obviously contraries also cannot belong at the same time to the same thing. For of contraries, one is a privation no less than it is a contrary—and a privation of the essential nature; and privation is the denial of a predicate to a determinate genus. If, then, [20] it is impossible to affirm and deny truly at the same time, it is also impossible that contraries should belong to a subject at the same time, unless both belong to it in particular relations, or one in a particular relation and one without qualification.

7

But on the other hand there cannot be an intermediate between contradictories, but of one subject we must either affirm or deny any one [25] predicate. This is clear, in the first place, if we define what the true and the false are. To say of what is that it is not, or of what is not that it is, is false, while to say of what is that it is, and of what is not that it is not, is true; so that he who says of anything that it is, or that it is not, will say either what is true or what is false; but neither what is nor what is not is said to be or not to be.—Again, the intermediate between the contradictories will be so either in [30] the way in which grey is between black and white, or as that which is neither man nor horse is between man and horse. (*a*) If it were of the latter kind, it could not change into the extremes (for change is from not-good to good, or from good to not-good), but as a matter of fact when there is an intermediate it is always observed to change into the extremes. For there is no change except to opposites and to their [35] intermediates. (*b*) But if it is really intermediate, in this way too there would have to be a change to white, which was not from not-white; but as it is, this is never seen.—Again, 1012[a] every object of understanding or reason the understanding either affirms or denies— this is obvious from the definition—whenever it says what is true or false. When it connects in one way by assertion or negation, it says what is true, and when it does so in another [5] way, what is false.—Again, there must be an intermediate between *all* contradictories, if one is not arguing merely for the sake of argument; so that it will be possible for a man to say what is neither true nor untrue, and there will be a middle between that which is and that which is not, so that there will also be a kind of change intermediate between generation and destruction.—Again, in all classes in which the negation of an attribute involves the assertion [10] of its contrary, even in these there will be an intermediate; for instance, in the sphere of numbers there will be number which is neither odd nor not-odd. But this is impossible, as is obvious from the definition.—Again, the process will go on *ad infinitum,* and the number of realities will be not only half as great again, but even greater. For again it will be possible to deny this intermediate with reference both to its assertion and to its negation, and this new term will be some definite thing; for its essence [15] is something different.—Again, when a man, on being asked whether a thing is white, says 'no', he has denied nothing except that it is; and its not being is a negation.

Some people have acquired this opinion as other paradoxical opinions have been acquired; when men cannot refute eristical arguments, they give in to the argument and agree that the [20] conclusion is true. This, then, is why some express this view; others do so because they demand a reason for everything. And the starting-point in dealing with all such people is definition. Now the definition rests on the necessity of their meaning something; for the form of words of which the word is a sign will be its definition.—While the doctrine of Heraclitus, that all things are and are not, seems to make [25] everything true, that of Anaxagoras, that there is an intermediate between the terms of a contradiction, seems to make everything false; for when things are mixed, the mixture is neither good nor not-good, so that one cannot say anything that is true.

8

In view of these distinctions it is obvious that [30] the one-sided theories which some people express about all things cannot be valid—on the one hand the theory that nothing is true (for, say they, there is nothing to prevent every statement from being like the statement 'the diagonal of a square is commensurate with the side'), on the other hand the theory that everything is true. These views are practically the same as that of Heraclitus; for he who says that [35] 'all things are true and all are false' also makes each of these statements separately, so 1012^b that since they are impossible, the double statement must be impossible too.—Again, there are obviously contradictories which cannot be at the same time true—nor on the other hand can all statements be false; yet this would *seem* more possible in the light of what has [5] been said.—But against all such views we must postulate, as we said above,[1] not that something is or is not, but that something has a meaning, so that we must argue from a definition, viz. by assuming what falsity or truth means. If that which it is true to affirm is nothing other than that which it is false to deny, it [10] is impossible that all statements should be false; for one side of the contradiction must be true. Again, if it is necessary with regard to everything either to assert or to deny it, it is impossible that both should be false; for it is *one* side of the contradiction that is false.—Therefore all such views are also exposed to the often expressed objection, that they destroy them- [15] selves. For he who says that everything is true makes even the statement contrary to his own true, and therefore his own not true (for the contrary statement denies that it is true), while he who says everything is false makes himself also false.—And if the former person excepts the contrary statement, saying it alone is not true, while the latter excepts his own as [20] being not false, none the less they are driven to postulate the truth or falsity of an infinite number of statements; for that which says the true statement is true is true, and this process will go on to infinity.

Evidently, again, those who say all things are at rest are not right, nor are those who say all things are in movement. For if all things are at rest, the same statements will always be true and the same always false,—but this obviously [25] changes; for he who makes a statement, himself at one time was not and again will not be. And if all things are in motion, nothing will be true; everything therefore will be false. But it has been shown that this is impossible. Again, it must be that which is that changes; for change is from something to something. But again it is not the case that all things are at rest or in motion *sometimes,* and nothing *for* [30] *ever;* for there is something which always moves the things that are in motion, and the first mover is itself unmoved.

[1] Cf. 1006^a 18-22.

BOOK V

1

'Beginning' means (1) that part of a thing from which one would start first, e.g. a line or a road has a beginning in either of the contrary directions. (2) That from which each thing would best be originated, e.g. even in learning we must sometimes begin not from the first point and the beginning of the subject, but from the point from which we should learn most easily. (3) That from which, as an immanent part, a thing first comes to be, e.g. as the keel of a ship and the foundation of a house, while in animals some suppose the heart, others the brain, others some other part, to be of this nature. (4) That from which, *not* as an immanent part, a thing first comes to be, and from which the movement or the change naturally first begins, as a child comes from its father and its mother, and a fight from abusive language. (5) That at whose will that which is moved is moved and that which changes changes, e.g. the magistracies in cities, and oligarchies and monarchies and tyrannies, are called ἀρχαί, and so are the arts, and of these especially the architectonic arts. (6) That from which a thing can first be known,—this also is called the beginning of the thing, e.g. the hypotheses are the beginnings of demonstrations. (Causes are spoken of in an equal number of senses; for all causes are beginnings.) It is common, then, to all beginnings to be the first point from which a thing either is or comes to be or is known; but of these some are immanent in the thing and others are outside. Hence the nature of a thing is a beginning, and so is the element of a thing, and thought and will, and essence, and the final cause—for the good and the beautiful are the beginning both of the knowledge and of the movement of many things.

2

'Cause' means (1) that from which, as immanent material, a thing comes into being, e.g. the bronze is the cause of the statue and the silver of the saucer, and so are the classes which include these. (2) The form or pattern, i.e. the definition of the essence, and the classes which include this (e.g. the ratio 2:1 and number in general are causes of the octave), and the parts included in the definition. (3) That from which the change or the resting from change first begins; e.g. the adviser is a cause of the action, and the father a cause of the child, and in general the maker a cause of the thing made and the change-producing of the changing. (4) The end, i.e. that for the sake of which a thing is; e.g. health is the cause of walking. For 'Why does one walk?' we say; 'that one may be healthy'; and in speaking thus we think we have given the cause. The same is true of all the means that intervene before the end, when something else has put the process in motion, as e.g. thinning or purging or drugs or instruments intervene before health is reached; for all these are for the sake of the end, though they differ from one another in that some are instruments and others are actions.

These, then, are practically all the senses in which causes are spoken of, and as they are spoken of in several senses it follows both that there are several causes of the same thing, and in no accidental sense (e.g. both the art of sculpture and the bronze are causes of the statue not in respect of anything else but *qua* statue; not, however, in the same way, but the one as matter and the other as source of the movement), and that things can be causes of one another (e.g. exercise of good condition, and the latter of exercise; not, however, in the same way, but the one as end and the other as source of movement).—Again, the same thing is the cause of contraries; for that which when present causes a particular thing, we sometimes charge, when absent, with the contrary, e.g. we impute the shipwreck to the absence of the steersman, whose presence was the cause of safety; and both—the presence and the privation—are causes as sources of movement.

All the causes now mentioned fall under four senses which are the most obvious. For the letters are the cause of syllables, and the material is the cause of manufactured things, and fire and earth and all such things are the causes of bodies, and the parts are causes of the whole, and the hypotheses are causes of the conclusion, in the sense that they are that out of which these respectively are made; but of these some are cause as the *substratum* (e.g. the parts), others as the *essence* (the whole, the synthesis, and the form). The semen, the physician, the adviser, and in general the agent, are all *sources of change* or of rest. The remainder are causes as the *end* and the good of the other things; for that for the sake of which other things are tends to be the best and the end of the other things; let us take it as making no difference whether we call it good or apparent good.

These, then, are the causes, and this is the number of their kinds, but the *varieties* of causes are many in number, though when summarized these also are comparatively few. [30] Causes are spoken of in many senses, and even of those which are of the same kind some are causes in a prior and others in a posterior sense, e.g. both 'the physician' and 'the professional man' are causes of health, and both 'the ratio 2:1' and 'number' are causes of the octave, and the classes that include any particular cause are always causes of the particular effect. Again, there are accidental causes and the [35] classes which include these; e.g. while in one sense 'the sculptor' causes the statue, in another sense 'Polyclitus' causes it, because the sculptor happens to be Polyclitus; and the 1014ᵃ classes that include the accidental cause are also causes, e.g. 'man'—or in general 'animal'—is the cause of the statue, because Polyclitus is a man, and man is an animal. Of accidental causes also some are more remote or [5] nearer than others, as, for instance, if 'the white' and 'the musical' were called causes of the statue, and not only 'Polyclitus' or 'man'. But besides all these varieties of causes, whether proper or accidental, some are called causes as being able to act, others as acting; e.g. the cause of the house's being built is a builder, or a builder who is building.—The same variety [10] of language will be found with regard to the effects of causes; e.g. a thing may be called the cause of this statue or of a statue or in general of an image, and of this bronze or of bronze or of matter in general; and similarly in the case of accidental effects. Again, both accidental and proper causes may be spoken of in combination; e.g. we may say not 'Polyclitus' nor 'the sculptor', but 'Polyclitus the sculptor'. [15] Yet all these are but six in number, while each is spoken of in two ways; for (A) they are causes either as the individual, or as the genus, or as the accidental, or as the genus that includes the accidental, and these either as combined, or as taken simply; and (B) all may be taken as acting or as having a capacity. But [20] they differ inasmuch as the acting causes, i.e. the individuals, exist, or do not exist, simultaneously with the things of which they are causes, e.g. this particular man who is healing, with this particular man who is recovering health, and this particular builder with this particular thing that is being built; but the potential causes are not always in this case; for the house does not perish at the same time as [25] the builder.

3

'Element' means (1) the primary component immanent in a thing, and indivisible in kind into other kinds; e.g. the elements of speech are the parts of which speech consists and into which it is ultimately divided, while *they* are no longer divided into other forms of speech [30] different in kind from them. If they *are* divided, their parts are of the same kind, as a part of water is water (while a part of the syllable is not a syllable). Similarly those who speak of the elements of bodies mean the things into which bodies are ultimately divided, while *they* are no longer divided into other things differing in kind; and whether the things of [35] this sort are one or more, they call these elements. The so-called elements of geometrical proofs, and in general the elements of demonstrations, have a similar character; for the primary demonstrations, each of which is 1014ᵇ implied in many demonstrations, are called elements of demonstrations; and the primary syllogisms, which have three terms and proceed by means of one middle, are of this nature.

(2) People also transfer the word 'element' from this meaning and apply it to that which, being one and small, is useful for many pur- [5] poses; for which reason what is small and simple and indivisible is called an element. Hence come the facts that the most universal things are elements (because each of them being one and simple is present in a plurality of things, either in all or in as many as possible), and that unity and the point are thought by some to be first principles. Now, since the so-called genera are universal and indivisible (for there is no definition of them), some say the [10] genera are elements, and more so than the differentia, because the genus is more universal; for where the differentia is present, the genus accompanies it, but where the genus is present, the differentia is not always so. It is common to all the meanings that the element [15] of each thing is the first component immanent in each.

4

'Nature' means (1) the genesis of growing things—the meaning which would be suggested if one were to pronounce the υ in φύσις long. (2) That immanent part of a growing thing, from which its growth first proceeds. (3) The source from which the primary movement in each natural object is present in it in [20] virtue of its own essence. Those things are said to grow which derive increase from something else by contact and either by organic unity, or by organic adhesion as in the case of embryos. Organic unity differs from contact; for in the latter case there need not be anything besides the contact, but in organic unities there is something identical in both parts, [25] which makes them grow together instead of merely touching, and be one in respect of continuity and quantity, though not of quality. —(4) 'Nature' means the primary material of which any natural object consists or out of which it is made, which is relatively unshaped and cannot be changed from its own potency, as e.g. bronze is said to be the nature of a statue and of bronze utensils, and wood the nature of wooden things; and so in all other [30] cases; for when a product is made out of these materials, the first matter is preserved throughout. For it is in this way that people call the elements of natural objects also their nature, some naming fire, others earth, others air, others water, others something else of the sort, and some naming more than one of these, and others all of them.—(5) 'Nature' means [35] the *essence* of natural objects, as with those who say the nature is the primary mode 1015ᵃ of composition, or as Empedocles[1] says:—

> Nothing that is has a nature,
> But only mixing and parting of the mixed,
> And nature is but a name given them by men.

Hence as regards the things that are or come to be by nature, though that *from which* they naturally come to be or are is already present, we say they have not their nature yet, unless [5] they have their form or shape. That which comprises both of these exists *by* nature, e.g. the animals and their parts; and not only is the first matter nature (and this in two senses, either the first, counting from the thing, or the first in general; e.g. in the case of works in bronze, bronze is first with reference to them, but in general perhaps water is first, if all things that can be melted are water), but also [10] the form or essence, which is the end of the process of becoming.—(6) By an extension of meaning from this sense of 'nature' every essence in general has come to be called a 'nature', because the nature of a thing is one kind of essence.

From what has been said, then, it is plain that nature in the primary and strict sense is the essence of things which have in themselves, [15] as such, a source of movement; for the matter is called the nature because it is qualified to receive this, and processes of becoming and growing are called nature because they are movements proceeding from this. And nature in this sense is the source of the movement of natural objects, being present in them somehow, either potentially or in complete reality.

5

[20] We call 'necessary' (1) (*a*) that without which, as a condition, a thing cannot live; e.g. breathing and food are necessary for an animal; for it is incapable of existing without these; (*b*) the conditions without which good cannot be or come to be, or without which we cannot get rid or be freed of evil; e.g. drinking the medicine is necessary in order that we may [25] be cured of disease, and a man's sailing to Aegina is necessary in order that he may get his money.—(2) The compulsory and compulsion, i.e. that which impedes and tends to hinder, contrary to impulse and purpose. For the compulsory is called necessary (whence the necessary is painful, as Evenus[2] says: 'For every [30] necessary thing is ever irksome'), and compulsion is a form of necessity, as Sophocles[3] says: 'But force necessitates me to this act'. And necessity is held to be something that cannot be persuaded—and rightly, for it is contrary to the movement which accords with purpose and with reasoning.—(3) We say that that which cannot be otherwise is necessarily [35] as it is. And from this sense of 'necessary' all the others are somehow derived; for a thing is said to do or suffer what is necessary in the 1015ᵇ sense of compulsory, only when it cannot act according to its impulse because of the compelling force,—which implies that necessity is that because of which a thing cannot be otherwise; and similarly as regards the conditions of life and of good; for when in the one case [5] good, in the other life and being, are not possible without certain conditions, these are necessary, and this kind of cause is a sort of necessity. Again, demonstration is a necessary thing because the conclusion cannot be otherwise, if there has been demonstration in the unqualified sense; and the causes of this necessity are the first premisses, i.e. the fact that the

---
[1] Fr. 8.   [2] Fr. 8, Hiller.   [3] *Electra*, 256.

propositions from which the syllogism proceeds cannot be otherwise.

Now some things owe their necessity to something other than themselves; others do [10] not, but are themselves the source of necessity in other things. Therefore the necessary in the primary and strict sense is the simple; for this does not admit of more states than one, so that it cannot even be in one state and also in another; for if it did it would already be in more than one. If, then, there are any things [15] that are eternal and unmovable, nothing compulsory or against their nature attaches to them.

6

'One' means (1) that which is one by accident, (2) that which is one by its own nature. (1) Instances of the accidentally one are 'Coriscus and what is musical', and 'musical Coriscus' (for it is the same thing to say 'Coriscus and what is musical', and 'musical Coriscus'), and 'what is musical and what is just', and 'musical Coriscus and just Coriscus'. For all of these are called [20] one by virtue of an accident, 'what is just and what is musical' because they are accidents of one substance, 'what is musical and Coriscus' because the one is an accident of the other; and similarly in a sense 'musical Coriscus' is one with 'Coriscus' because one of the parts of [25] the phrase is an accident of the other, i.e. 'musical' is an accident of Coriscus; and 'musical Coriscus' is one with 'just Coriscus' because one part of each is an accident of one and the same subject. The case is similar if the accident is predicated of a genus or of any universal [30] name, e.g. if one says that man is the same as 'musical man'; for this is either because 'musical' is an accident of man, which is one substance, or because both are accidents of some individual, e.g. Coriscus. Both, however, do not belong to him in the same way, but one presumably as genus and included in his substance, the other as a state or affection of the substance.

[35] The things, then, that are called one in virtue of an accident, are called so in this way. (2) Of things that are called one in virtue of their own nature some (*a*) are so called because 1016ᵃ they are continuous, e.g. a bundle is made one by a band, and pieces of wood are made one by glue; and a line, even if it is bent, is called one if it is continuous, as each part of the body is, e.g. the leg or the arm. Of these themselves, the continuous by nature are more one than the continuous by art. A thing is [5] called continuous which has by its own nature one movement and cannot have any other; and the movement is one when it is indivisible, and it is indivisible in respect of time. Those things are continuous by their own nature which are one not merely by contact; for if you put pieces of wood touching one another, you will not say these are one piece of wood or one body or one *continuum* of any other sort. Things, then, that are continuous in any way [10] are called one, even if they admit of being bent, and still more those which cannot be bent; e.g. the shin or the thigh is more one than the leg, because the movement of the leg need not be one. And the straight line is more one than the bent; but that which is bent and has an angle we call both one and not one, because its movement may be either simultaneous or [15] not simultaneous; but that of the straight line is always simultaneous, and no part of it which has magnitude rests while another moves, as in the bent line.

(*b*) (i) Things are called one in another sense because their substratum does not differ in kind; it does not differ in the case of things whose kind is indivisible to sense. The substratum meant is either the nearest to, or the far- [20] thest from, the final state. For, one the one hand, wine is said to be one and water is said to be one, *qua* indivisible in kind; and, on the other hand, *all* juices, e.g. oil and wine, are said to be one, and so are all things that can be melted, because the ultimate substratum of all is the same; for all of these are water or air.

(ii) Those things also are called one whose [25] genus is one though distinguished by opposite differentiae—these too are all called one because the genus which underlies the differentiae is one (e.g. horse, man, and dog form a unity, because all are animals), and indeed in a way similar to that in which the matter is one. These are sometimes called one in this way, but sometimes it is the higher genus that is said to be the same (if they are *infimae spe-* [30] *cies* of their genus)—the genus above the proximate genera; e.g. the isosceles and the equilateral are one and the same *figure* because both are triangles; but they are not the same triangles.

(*c*) Two things are called one, when the definition which states the essence of one is indivisible from another definition which shows us the other (though *in itself* every [35] definition is divisible). Thus even that which has increased or is diminishing is one, because its definition is one, as, in the case of plane figures, is the definition of their form. In general those things the thought of whose essence is indivisible, and cannot separate them either in time or in place or in definition, are most of all one, and of these especially those which are substances. For in general those things that do not admit of division are called one in so far as they do not admit of [5] it; e.g. if two things are indistinguishable *qua* man, they are one kind of man; if *qua* animal, one kind of animal; if *qua* magnitude, one kind of magnitude.—Now most things are called one because they either do or have or suffer or are related to something else that is one, but the things that are primarily called one are those whose substance is one,—and one either in continuity or in form or in definition; for we count as more than one either [10] things that are not continuous, or those whose form is not one, or those whose definition is not one.

While in a sense we call anything one if it is a quantity and continuous, in a sense we do not unless it is a whole, i.e. unless it has unity of form; e.g. if we saw the parts of a shoe put together anyhow we should not call them one [15] all the same (unless because of their continuity); we do this only if they are put together so as to be a shoe and to have already a certain single form. This is why the circle is of all lines most truly one, because it is whole and complete.

(3) The *essence* of what is one is to be some kind of beginning of number; for the first measure is the beginning, since that by which we first know each class is the first measure [20] of the class; the one, then, is the beginning of the knowable regarding each class. But the one is not the same in all classes. For here it is a quarter-tone, and there it is the vowel or the consonant; and there is another unit of weight and another of movement. But everywhere the one is indivisible either in quantity or in kind. [25] Now that which is indivisible in quantity is called a unit if it is not divisible in any dimension and is without position, a point if it is not divisible in any dimension and has position, a line if it is divisible in one dimension, a plane if in two, a body if divisible in quantity in all—i.e. in three—dimensions. And, reversing the order, that which is divisible in two dimensions is a plane, that which is divisible in one a line, that which is in no way di- [30] visible in quantity is a point or a unit,— that which has not position a unit, that which has position a point.

Again, some things are one in number, others in species, others in genus, others by analogy; in number those whose matter is one, in species those whose definition is one, in genus those to which the same figure of predication applies, by analogy those which are related as a third thing is to a fourth. The latter [35] kinds of unity are always found when the former are; e.g. things that are one in number are also one in species, while things that are one in species are not all one in number; but things that are one in species are all one in genus, while things that are so in genus are not all one in species but are all one by analogy; while things that are one by analogy are not all one in genus.

Evidently 'many' will have meanings opposite to those of 'one'; some things are many because they are not continuous, others because [5] their matter—either the proximate matter or the ultimate—is divisible in kind, others because the definitions which state their essence are more than one.

7

Things are said to 'be' (1) in an accidental sense, (2) by their own nature.

(1) In an accidental sense, e.g. we say 'the righteous doer is musical', and 'the man is musical', and 'the musician is a man', just as we [10] say 'the musician builds', because the builder happens to be musical or the musician to be a builder; for here 'one thing is another' means 'one is an accident of another'. So in the cases we have mentioned; for when we say 'the man is musical' and 'the musician is a man', [15] or 'he who is pale is musical' or 'the musician is pale', the last two mean that both attributes are accidents of the same thing; the first that the attribute is an accident of that which *is;* while 'the musical is a man' means that 'musical' is an accident of a man. (In this sense, too, the not-pale is said to *be,* because that of which it is an accident *is.*) Thus when one thing is said in an accidental sense to be [20] another, this is either because both belong to the same thing, and this *is,* or because that to which the attribute belongs *is,* or because the subject which has as an attribute that of which it is itself predicated, itself *is.*

(2) The kinds of essential being are precisely those that are indicated by the figures of predication; for the senses of 'being' are just as many as these figures. Since, then, some pred- [25] icates indicate what the subject is, others its quality, others quantity, others relation,

others activity or passivity, others its 'where', others its 'when', 'being' has a meaning answering to each of these. For there is no difference between 'the man is recovering' and 'the man recovers', nor between 'the man is walking' or [30] 'cutting' and 'the man walks' or 'cuts'; and similarly in all other cases.

(3) Again, 'being' and 'is' mean that a statement is true, 'not being' that it is not true but false,—and this alike in the case of affirmation and of negation; e.g. 'Socrates *is* musical' means that this is true, or 'Socrates *is* not-pale' means that this is true; but 'the diagonal of the square *is not* commensurate with the side' means that it is false to say it is.

[35] (4) Again, 'being' and 'that which is' mean that some of the things we have mentioned 'are' potentially, others in complete reality. For we say both of that which sees potentially and of that which sees actually, that it is 'seeing', and both of that which can actualize its knowledge and of that which is [5] actualizing it, that it knows, and both of that to which rest is already present and of that which can rest, that it rests. And similarly in the case of substances; we say the Hermes is in the stone, and the half of the line is in the line, and we say of that which is not yet ripe that it is corn. *When* a thing is potential and when it is not yet potential must be explained elsewhere.[1]

8

[10] We call 'substance' (1) the simple bodies, i.e. earth and fire and water and everything of the sort, and in general bodies and the things composed of them, both animals and divine beings, and the parts of these. All these are called substance because they are not predicated of a subject but everything else is predicated of them.—(2) That which, being pres-[15]ent in such things as are not predicated of a subject, is the cause of their being, as the soul is of the being of an animal.—(3) The parts which are present in such things, limiting them and marking them as individuals, and by whose destruction the whole is destroyed, as the body is by the destruction of the plane, as some say, and the plane by the destruction of [20] the line; and in general number is thought by some to be of this nature; for if it is destroyed, they say, nothing exists, and it limits all things.—(4) The essence, the formula of which is a definition, is also called the substance of each thing.

[1] IX. 7.

It follows, then, that 'substance' has two senses, (*A*) the ultimate substratum, which is no longer predicated of anything else, and (*B*) that which, being a 'this', is also separable—[25] and of this nature is the shape or form of each thing.

9

'The same' means (1) that which is the same in an accidental sense, e.g. 'the pale' and 'the musical' are the same because they are accidents of the same thing, and 'a man' and 'musical' because the one is an accident of the other; and 'the musical' is 'a man' because it is an accident of the man. (The complex entity [30] is the same as either of the simple ones and each of these is the same as it; for both 'the man' and 'the musical' are said to be the same as 'the musical man', and this the same as they.) This is why all of these statements are made not universally; for it is not true to [35] say that *every* man is the same as 'the musical' (for universal attributes belong to things in virtue of their own nature, but accidents do not belong to them in virtue of their own nature); but of the individuals the statements are made without qualification. For 'Socrates' and 'musical Socrates' are thought to be the same; but 'Socrates' is not predicable of more than one subject, and therefore we do not say 'every Socrates' as we say 'every man'.

Some things are said to be the same in this sense, others (2) are the same by their own nature, in as many senses as that which is one [5] by its own nature is so; for both the things whose matter is one either in kind or in number, and those whose essence is one, are said to be the same. Clearly, therefore, sameness is a unity of the being either of more than one thing or of one thing when it is treated as more than one, i.e. when we say a thing is the same as itself; for we treat it as two.

[10] Things are called 'other' if either their kinds or their matters or the definitions of their essence are more than one; and in general 'other' has meanings opposite to those of 'the same'.

'Different' is applied (1) to those things which though other are the same in some respect, only not in number but either in species or in genus or by analogy; (2) to those whose genus is other, and to contraries, and to all things that have their otherness in their essence.

[15] Those things are called 'like' which have the same attributes in every respect, and those

which have more attributes the same than different, and those whose quality is one; and that which shares with another thing the greater number or the more important of the attributes (each of them one of two contraries) in respect of which things are capable of altering, is like that other thing. The senses of 'unlike' are opposite to those of 'like'.

10

[20] The term 'opposite' is applied to contradictories, and to contraries, and to relative terms, and to privation and possession, and to the extremes from which and into which generation and dissolution take place; and the attributes that cannot be present at the same time in that which is receptive of both, are said to be opposed,—either themselves of their constituents. Grey and white colour do not belong at the same time to the same thing; hence their constituents are opposed.

[25] The term 'contrary' is applied (1) to those attributes differing in genus which cannot belong at the same time to the same subject, (2) to the most different of the things in the same genus, (3) to the most different of the attributes in the same recipient subject, (4) to the most different of the things that fall [30] under the same faculty, (5) to the things whose difference is greatest either absolutely or in genus or in species. The other things that are called contrary are so called, some because they possess contraries of the above kind, some because they are receptive of such, some because they are productive of or susceptible to such, or are producing or suffering them, or are losses or acquisitions, or possessions or [35] privations, of such. Since 'one' and 'being' have many senses, the other terms which are derived from these, and therefore 'same', 'other', and 'contrary', must correspond, so that they must be different for each category.

The term 'other in species' is applied to things which being of the same genus are not subordinate the one to the other, or which 1018ᵇ being in the same genus have a difference, or which have a contrariety in their substance; and contraries are other than one another in species (either all contraries or those which are so called in the primary sense), and so are those things whose definitions differ in [5] the *infima species* of the genus (e.g. man and horse are indivisible in genus, but their definitions are different), and those which being in the same substance have a difference. 'The same in species' has the various meanings opposite to these.

11

The words 'prior' and 'posterior' are applied (1) to some things (on the assumption that there is a first, i.e. a beginning, in each class) [10] because they are nearer some beginning determined either absolutely and by nature, or by reference to something or in some place or by certain people; e.g. things are prior in place because they are nearer either to some place determined by nature (e.g. the middle or the last place), or to some chance object; and that which is farther is posterior.—Other things are [15] prior in time; some by being farther from the present, i.e. in the case of past events (for the Trojan war is prior to the Persian, because it is farther from the present), others by being nearer the present, i.e. in the case of future events (for the Nemean games are prior to the Pythian, if we treat the present as beginning and first point, because they are nearer the present).—Other things are prior in move- [20] ment; for that which is nearer the first mover is prior (e.g. the boy is prior to the man); and the prime mover also is a beginning absolutely.—Others are prior in power; for that which exceeds in power, i.e. the more powerful, is prior; and such is that according to whose will the other—i.e. the posterior— must follow, so that if the prior does not set it in motion the other does not move, and if it sets [25] it in motion it does move; and here will is a beginning.—Others are prior in arrangement; these are the things that are placed at intervals in reference to some one definite thing according to some rule, e.g. in the chorus the second man is prior to the third, and in the lyre the second lowest string is prior to the lowest; for in the one case the leader and in the other the middle string is the beginning.

[30] These, then, are called prior in this sense, but (2) in another sense that which is prior for knowledge is treated as also absolutely prior; of these, the things that are prior in definition do not coincide with those that are prior in relation to perception. For in definition universals are prior, in relation to perception individuals. And in definition also the accident is prior to the whole, e.g. 'musical' to [35] 'musical man', for the definition cannot exist as a whole without the part; yet musicalness cannot exist unless there is some one who is musical.

(3) The attributes of prior things are called

prior, e.g. straightness is prior to smoothness; for one is an attribute of a line as such, and the other of a surface.

1019ª Some things then are called prior and posterior in this sense, others (4) in respect of nature and substance, i.e. those which can be without other things, while the others cannot be without *them*,—a distinction which Plato used. (If we consider the various senses of 'be-[5] ing', firstly the subject is prior, so that substance is prior; secondly, according as potency or complete reality is taken into account, different things are prior, for some things are prior in respect of potency, others in respect of complete reality, e.g. in potency the half line is prior to the whole line, and the part to the whole, and the matter to the concrete substance, but in complete reality these are pos-[10] terior; for it is only when the whole has been dissolved that they will exist in complete reality.) In a sense, therefore, all things that are called prior and posterior are so called with reference to this fourth sense; for some things can exist without others in respect of generation, e.g. the whole without the parts, and others in respect of dissolution, e.g. the part without the whole. And the same is true in all other cases.

12

[*15*] 'Potency' means (1) a source of movement or change, which is in another thing than the thing moved or in the same thing *qua* other; e.g. the art of building is a potency which is not in the thing built, while the art of healing, which is a potency, may be in the man healed, but not in him *qua* healed. 'Potency' then means the source, in general, of change or movement in another thing or in the [*20*] same thing *qua* other, and also (2) the source of a thing's being moved by another thing or by itself *qua* other. For in virtue of that principle, in virtue of which a patient suffers anything, we call it 'capable' of suffering; and this we do sometimes if it suffers anything at all, sometimes not in respect of everything it suffers, but only if it suffers a change for the better.—(3) The capacity of performing this well or according to intention; for sometimes we say of those who merely can walk or speak but not well or not as they in-[*25*] tend, that they cannot speak or walk. So too (4) in the case of passivity.—(5) The states in virtue of which things are absolutely impassive or unchangeable, or not easily changed for the worse, are called potencies; for things are broken and crushed and bent and in gen-[*30*] eral destroyed not by having a potency but by not having one and by lacking something, and things are impassive with respect to such processes if they are scarcely and slightly affected by them, because of a 'potency' and because they 'can' do something and are in some positive state.

'Potency' having this variety of meanings, so too the 'potent' or 'capable' in one sense will mean that which can begin a movement (or a change in general, for even that which can bring things to rest is a 'potent' thing) in an-[*35*] other thing or in itself *qua* other; and in **1019ᵇ** one sense that over which something else has such a potency; and in one sense that which has a potency of changing into something, whether for the worse or for the better (for even that which perishes is thought to be 'capable' of perishing, for it would not have perished if it had not been capable of it; but, as a matter of fact, it has a certain disposition [5] and cause and principle which fits it to suffer this; sometimes it is thought to be of this sort because it has something, sometimes because it is deprived of something; but if privation is in a sense 'having' or 'habit', everything will be capable by having something, so that things are capable both by having a positive habit and principle, and by having the privation of this, if it is possible to *have* a privation; and if privation is *not* in a sense 'habit', [*10*] 'capable' is used in two distinct senses); and a thing is capable in another sense because neither any other thing, nor itself *qua* other, has a potency or principle which can destroy it. Again, all of these are capable either merely because the thing might chance to happen or not to happen, or because it might do so *well*. This sort of potency is found even in lifeless things, e.g. in instruments; for we say one lyre can speak, and another cannot speak at all, if it has not a good tone.

[*15*] Incapacity is privation of capacity—i.e. of such a principle as has been described—either in general or in the case of something that would naturally have the capacity, or even at the time when it would naturally already have it; for the senses in which we should call a boy and a man and a eunuch 'incapable of begetting' are distinct.—Again, to either kind of capacity there is an opposite incapacity—both [*20*] to that which only *can* produce movement and to that which can produce it well.

Some things, then, are called ἀδύνατα in virtue of this kind of incapacity, while others are so in another sense; i.e. both δυνατόν and ἀδύνατον are used as follows. The impossible is that of which the contrary is of necessity true, e.g. that the diagonal of a square is commensurate with the side is impossible, because [25] such a statement is a falsity of which the contrary is not only true but also necessary; that it is commensurate, then, is not only false but also of necessity false. The contrary of this, the possible, is found when it is not necessary that the contrary is false, e.g. that a man should be seated is possible; for that he is not seated [30] is not of necessity false. The possible, then, in one sense, as has been said, means that which is not of necessity false; in one, that which is true; in one, that which may be true.—A 'potency' or 'power' in geometry is so called by a change of meaning.—These senses of 'capable' [35] or 'possible' involve no reference to potency. But the senses which involve a reference to potency all refer to the primary kind of 1020ᵃ potency; and this is a source of change in another thing or in the same thing *qua* other. For other things are called 'capable', some because something else has such a potency over them, some because it has not, some because it has it in a particular way. The same is true of the things that are incapable. Therefore the proper definition of the primary kind [5] of potency will be 'a source of change in another thing or in the same thing *qua* other'.

13

'Quantum' means that which is divisible into two or more constituent parts of which each is by nature a 'one' and a 'this'. A quantum is a plurality if it is numerable, a magnitude if it is [10] measurable. 'Plurality' means that which is divisible potentially into non-continuous parts, 'magnitude' that which is divisible into continuous parts; of magnitude, that which is continuous in one dimension is length; in two breadth, in three depth. Of these, limited plurality is number, limited length is a line, breadth a surface, depth a solid.

Again, some things are called quanta in vir-[15]tue of their own nature, others incidentally; e.g. the line is a quantum by its own nature, the musical is one incidentally. Of the things that are quanta by their own nature some are so as substances, e.g. the line is a quantum (for 'a certain kind of quantum' is present in the definition which states what it is), and others are modifications and states of this kind of substance, e.g. much and little, [20] long and short, broad and narrow, deep and shallow, heavy and light, and all other such attributes. And also great and small, and greater and smaller, both in themselves and when taken relatively to each other, are by their own nature attributes of what is quantita-[25]tive; but these names are transferred to other things also. Of things that are quanta incidentally, some are so called in the sense in which it was said that the musical and the white were quanta, viz. because that to which musicalness and whiteness belong is a quantum, and some are quanta in the way in which movement and time are so; for these also are [30] called quanta of a sort and continuous because the things of which these are attributes are divisible. I mean not that which is moved, but the space through which it is moved; for because that is a quantum movement also is a quantum, and because this is a quantum time is one.

14

'Quality' means (1) the differentia of the essence, e.g. man is an animal of a certain quality because he is two-footed, and the horse is so [35] because it is four-footed; and a circle is a figure of particular quality because it is with-1020ᵇ out angles,—which shows that the essential differentia is a quality.—This, then, is one meaning of quality—the differentia of the essence, but (2) there is another sense in which it applies to the unmovable objects of mathematics, the sense in which the numbers have a certain quality, e.g. the composite numbers which are not in one dimension only, but of [5] which the plane and the solid are copies (these are those which have two or three factors); and in general that which exists in the essence of numbers besides quantity is quality; for the essence of each is what it is once, e.g. that of 6 is not what it is twice or thrice, but what it is once; for 6 is once 6.

(3) All the modifications of substances that [10] move (e.g. heat and cold, whiteness and blackness, heaviness and lightness, and the others of the sort) in virtue of which, when they change, bodies are said to alter. (4) Quality in respect of virtue and vice, and in general, of evil and good.

Quality, then, seems to have practically two meanings, and one of these is the more proper. The primary quality is the differentia of the [15] essence, and of this the quality in numbers is a part; for it is a differentia of essences, but either not of things that move or not of them *qua* moving. Secondly, there are the modifications of things that move, *qua* moving, and the differentiae of movements. Virtue and vice fall among these modifications; for they indicate differentiae of the movement or [20] activity, according to which the things in motion act or are acted on well or badly; for that which can be moved or act in one way is good, and that which can do so in another—the contrary—way is vicious. Good and evil indicate quality especially in living things, and [25] among these especially in those which have purpose.

15

Things are 'relative' (1) as double to half, and treble to a third, and in general that which contains something else many times to that which is contained many times in something else, and that which exceeds to that which is exceeded; (2) as that which can heat to that which can be heated, and that which can cut to that which can be cut, and in general the [30] active to the passive; (3) as the measurable to the measure, and the knowable to knowledge, and the perceptible to perception.

(1) Relative terms of the first kind are numerically related either indefinitely or definitely, to numbers themselves or to 1. E.g. the double is in a definite numerical relation to 1, and that which is 'many times as great' is in [35] a numerical, but not a definite, relation to 1, i.e. not in this or in that numerical relation to it; the relation of that which is half as big again as something else to that something is a definite numerical relation to a number; that which is $\frac{n+1}{n}$ times something else is in an indefinite relation to that something, as that which is 'many times as great' is in an indefinite relation to 1; the relation of that which exceeds to that which is exceeded is nu-[5] merically quite indefinite; for number is always commensurate, and 'number' is not predicated of that which is not commensurate, but that which exceeds is, in relation to that which is exceeded, so much and something more; and this something is indefinite; for it can, indifferently, be either equal or not equal to that which is exceeded.—All these relations, then, are numerically expressed and are determinations of number, and so in another way are the equal and the like and the same. For [10] all refer to unity. Those things are the same whose substance is one; those are like whose quality is one; those are equal whose quantity is one; and 1 is the beginning and measure of number, so that all these relations imply number, though not in the same way.

[15] (2) Things that are active or passive imply an active or a passive potency and the actualizations of the potencies; e.g. that which is capable of heating is related to that which is capable of being heated, because it *can* heat it, and, again, that which heats is related to that which is heated and that which cuts to that which is cut, in the sense that they actually do these things. But *numerical* relations are not actualized except in the sense which has been [20] elsewhere stated; actualizations in the sense of movement they have not. Of relations which imply potency some further imply particular periods of time, e.g. that which has made is relative to that which has been made, and that which will make to that which will be made. For it is in this way that a father is called the father of his son; for the one has acted and the other has been acted on [25] in a certain way. Further, some relative terms imply *privation* of potency, i.e. 'incapable' and terms of this sort, e.g. 'invisible'.

Relative terms which imply number or potency, therefore, are all relative because their very essence includes in its nature a reference to something else, not because something else involves a reference to *it;* but (3) that which is [30] measurable or knowable or thinkable is called relative because something else involves a reference to it. For 'that which is thinkable' implies that the thought of it is possible, but the thought is not relative to 'that of which it is the thought'; for we should then have said the same thing twice. Similarly sight is the sight of something, not 'of that of which it is the sight' (though of course it is true to say this); in fact it is relative to colour or to something else of the sort. But according to the other way of speaking the same thing would be said twice,—'the sight is of that of which it is.'

Things that are by their own nature called relative are called so sometimes in these senses, sometimes if the classes that include them are [5] of this sort; e.g. medicine is a relative term because its genus, science, is thought to be a relative term. Further, there are the properties in virtue of which the things that have them are called relative, e.g. equality is relative because the equal is, and likeness because the like is. Other things are relative by accident; e.g. a man is relative because he happens to be double [10] of something and double is a relative term; or the white is relative, if the same thing happens to be double and white.

16

What is called 'complete' is (1) that outside which it is not possible to find any, even one, of its parts; e.g. the complete time of each thing is that outside which it is not possible to find any time which is a part proper to it.—[15] (2) That which in respect of excellence and goodness cannot be excelled in its kind; e.g. we have a complete doctor or a complete flute-player, when they lack nothing in respect of the form of their proper excellence. And thus, transferring the word to bad things, we speak of a complete scandal-monger and a complete thief; indeed we even call them *good,* i.e. [20] a good thief and a good scandal-monger. And excellence is a completion; for each thing is complete and every substance is complete, when in respect of the form of its proper excellence it lacks no part of its natural magnitude.—(3) The things which have attained their end, this being good, are called complete; for things are complete in virtue of having attained their end. Therefore, since the end [25] is something ultimate, we transfer the word to bad things and say a thing has been completely spoilt, and completely destroyed, when it in no wise falls short of destruction and badness, but is at its last point. This is why death, too, is by a figure of speech called the end, because both are last things. But the ultimate purpose is also [30] an end.—Things, then, that are called complete in virtue of their *own* nature are so called in all these senses, some because in respect of goodness they lack nothing and cannot be excelled and no part proper to them can be found outside them, others in general because they cannot be exceeded in their several classes and no part proper to them is outside them; the *others* presuppose these first two kinds, and are called complete because they either make or have something of the sort or are adapted to it or in some way or other involve a reference to the things that are called complete in the primary sense.

17

'Limit' means (1) the last point of each thing, i.e. the first point beyond which it is not possible to find any part, and the first point within [5] which every part is; (2) the form, whatever it may be, of a spatial magnitude or of a thing that has magnitude; (3) the end of each thing (and of this nature is that towards which the movement and the action are, not that from which they are,—though sometimes it is both, that from which and that to which the movement is, i.e. the final cause); (4) the substance of each thing, and the essence of each; for this is the limit of knowledge; and if of knowledge, [10] of the object also. Evidently, therefore, 'limit' has as many senses as 'beginning', and yet more; for the beginning is a limit, but not every limit is a beginning.

18

'That in virtue of which' has several meanings:—[15] (1) the form or substance of each thing, e.g. that in virtue of which a man is good is the good itself, (2) the proximate subject in which it is the nature of an attribute to be found, e.g. colour in a surface. 'That in virtue of which', then, in the primary sense is the form, and in a secondary sense the matter of each thing and the proximate substratum of each.—In general 'that in virtue of which' will [20] be found in the same number of senses as 'cause'; for we say indifferently (3) 'in virtue of what has he come?' or 'for what end has he come?'; and (4) 'in virtue of what has he inferred wrongly, or inferred?' or 'what is the cause of the inference, or of the wrong inference?'—Further (5) καθ' ὅ is used in reference to position, e.g. 'at which he stands' or 'along which he walks'; for all such phrases indicate place and position.

Therefore 'in virtue of itself' must likewise [25] have several meanings. The following belong to a thing in virtue of itself:—(1) the essence of each thing, e.g. Callias is in virtue of himself Callias and what it was to be Callias; (2) whatever is present in the 'what', e.g. Callias is in virtue of himself an animal. For 'animal' is present in his definition; Callias is a particular animal.—(3) Whatever attribute a thing receives in itself directly or in one of its [30] parts; e.g. a surface is white in virtue of itself, and a man is alive in virtue of himself; for the soul, in which life directly resides, is a part of the man.—(4) That which has no cause other than itself; man has more than one cause—animal, two-footed—but yet man is man in virtue of himself.—(5) Whatever attri- [35] butes belong to a thing alone, and in so far as they belong to it merely by virtue of itself considered apart by itself.

19

'Disposition' means the arrangement of that which has parts, in respect either of place or of potency or of kind; for there must be a certain position, as even the *word* 'disposition' shows.

20

'Having' means (1) a kind of activity of the haver and of what he has—something like an action or movement. For when one thing makes [5] and one is made, between them there is a making; so too between him who has a garment and the garment which he has there is a having. This sort of having, then, evidently we cannot *have;* for the process will go on to infinity, if it is to be possible to have the having [10] of what we have.—(2) 'Having' or 'habit' means a disposition according to which that which is disposed is either well or ill disposed, and either in itself or with reference to something else; e.g. health is a 'habit'; for it is such a disposition.—(3) We speak of a 'habit' if there is a portion of such a disposition; and so even the excellence of the parts is a 'habit' of the whole thing.

21

[15] 'Affection' means (1) a quality in respect of which a thing can be altered, e.g. white and black, sweet and bitter, heaviness and lightness, and all others of the kind.—(2) The actualization of these—the already accomplished alterations.—(3) Especially, injurious alterations and movements, and, above all, [20] painful injuries.—(4) Misfortunes and painful experiences when on a large scale are called affections.

22

We speak of 'privation' (1) if something has not one of the attributes which a thing might naturally have, even if this thing itself would not naturally have it; e.g. a plant is said to be 'deprived' of eyes.—(2) If, though either the thing itself or its genus would naturally have [25] an attribute, it has it not; e.g. a blind man and a mole are in different senses 'deprived' of sight; the latter in contrast with its genus, the former in contrast with his own normal nature.—(3) If, though it would naturally have the attribute, and when it would naturally have it, it has it not; for blindness is a privation, but one is not 'blind' at any and every age, but only if one has not sight at the [30] age at which one would naturally have it. Similarly a thing is called blind if it has not sight in the medium in which, and in respect of the organ in respect of which, and with reference to the object with reference to which, and in the circumstances in which, it would naturally have it.—(4) The violent taking away of anything is called privation.

Indeed there are just as many kinds of privations as there are of words with negative prefixes; for a thing is called unequal because it has not equality though it would naturally have it, and invisible either because it has no [35] colour at all or because it has a poor colour, and apodous either because it has no feet at all or because it has imperfect feet. Again, a privative term may be used because the thing 1023ᵃ has little of the attribute (and this means having it in a sense imperfectly), e.g. 'kernel-less'; or because it has it not easily or not well (e.g. we call a thing uncuttable not only if it cannot be cut but also if it cannot be cut easily or well); or because it has not the attribute at all; for it is not the one-eyed man but he who is sightless in both eyes that is [5] called blind. This is why not every man is 'good' or 'bad', 'just' or 'unjust', but there is also an intermediate state.

23

To 'have' or 'hold' means many things:—(1) to treat a thing according to one's own nature or according to one's own impulse; so that [10] fever is said to have a man, and tyrants to have their cities, and people to have the clothes they wear.—(2) That in which a thing is present as in something receptive of it is said to have the thing; e.g. the bronze has the form of the statue, and the body has the disease.—(3) As that which contains holds the things contained; for a thing is said to be held by that in which it is as in a container; e.g. [15] we say that the vessel holds the liquid and the city holds men and the ship sailors; and so too that the whole holds the parts.—(4) That which hinders a thing from moving or acting according to its own impulse is said to hold it, as pillars hold the incumbent weights, and as [20] the poets make Atlas hold the heavens, implying that otherwise they would collapse on the earth, as some of the natural philosophers also say. In this way also that which holds things together is said to hold the things it holds together, since they would otherwise separate, each according to its own impulse.

'Being in something' has similar and cor- [25] responding meanings to 'holding' or 'having'.

24

'To come *from* something' means (1) to come from something as from matter, and this in two senses, either in respect of the highest genus or in respect of the lowest species; e.g. in a sense all things that can be melted come from water, but in a sense the statue comes [30] from bronze.—(2) As from the first moving principle; e.g. 'what did the fight come from?' From abusive language, because this was the origin of the fight.—(3) From the compound of matter and shape, as the parts come from the whole, and the verse from the *Iliad,* and the stones from the house; ⟨in every such case the whole is a compound of matter and shape,⟩ for the shape is the end, and only that which attains an end is complete.—(4) [35] As the form from its part, e.g. man from 'two-footed' and syllable from 'letter'; for this is a different sense from that in which the 1023[b] statue comes from bronze; for the composite substance comes from the sensible matter, but the form also comes from the matter of the form.—Some things, then, are said to come from something else in these senses; but (5) others are so described if one of these senses is applicable to a part of that other thing; e.g. the child comes from its father and mother, and plants come from the earth, because they come [5] from a part of those things.—(6) It means coming after a thing in time, e.g. night comes from day and storm from fine weather, because the one comes after the other. Of these things some are so described because they admit of change into one another, as in the cases now mentioned; some merely because they are successive in time, e.g. the voyage took place 'from' the equinox, because it took place after the [10] equinox, and the festival of the Thargelia comes 'from' the Dionysia, because after the Dionysia.

25

'Part' means (1) (*a*) that into which a quantum can in any way be divided; for that which is taken from a quantum *qua* quantum is always called a part of it, e.g. two is called in a sense a [15] part of three. It means (*b*), of the parts in the first sense, only those which measure the whole; this is why two, though in one sense it is, in another is not, called a part of three.—(2) The elements into which a kind might be divided apart from the quantity are also called parts of it; for which reason we say the species are parts of the genus.—(3) The elements into which a whole is divided, or of which it consists—the 'whole' meaning either the form or [20] that which has the form; e.g. of the bronze sphere or of the bronze cube both the bronze—i.e. the matter in which the form is—and the characteristic angle are parts.—(4) The elements in the definition which explains a thing are also parts of the whole; this is why the genus is called a part of the species, though in another [25] sense the species is part of the genus.

26

'A whole' means (1) that from which is absent none of the parts of which it is said to be naturally a whole, and (2) that which so contains the things it contains that they form a unity; and this in two senses—either as being each severally one single thing, or as making up the unity between them. For (*a*) that which is true of a whole class and is said to hold good as a whole (which implies that it is a kind of [30] whole) is true of a whole in the sense that it contains many things by being predicated of each, and by all of them, e.g. man, horse, god, being severally one single thing, because all are living things. But (*b*) the continuous and limited is a whole, when it is a unity consisting of several parts, especially if they are present only potentially, but, failing this, even if they are present actually. Of these things themselves, those which are so by nature are wholes in a [35] higher degree than those which are so by art, as we said[1] in the case of unity also, wholeness being in fact a sort of oneness.

Again (3), of quanta that have a beginning and a middle and an end, those to which the position does not make a difference are called totals, and those to which it does, wholes. Those which admit of both descriptions are both wholes and totals. These are the things whose nature remains the same after transposition, but whose form does not, e.g. wax or a [5] coat; they are called both wholes and totals; for they have both characteristics. Water and all liquids and number are called totals, but 'the whole number' or 'the whole water' one does not speak of, except by an extension of meaning. To things, to which *qua* one the term 'total' is applied, the term 'all' is applied when [10] they are treated as separate; 'this total number,' 'all these units.'

27

It is not any chance quantitative thing that can be said to be 'mutilated'; it must be a whole as

---
[1] Cf. 1016[a] 4.

well as divisible. For not only is two not 'mutilated' if one of the two ones is taken away (for the part removed by mutilation is never equal to the remainder), but in general no number is thus mutilated; for it is also necessary that the essence remain; if a cup is mutilated, it must [15] still be a cup; but the number is no longer the same. Further, even if things consist of unlike parts, not even these things can all be said to be mutilated, for in a sense a number has unlike parts (e.g. two and three) as well as like; but in general of the things to which their position makes no difference, e.g. water or fire, none can be mutilated; to be mutilated, things must be such as in virtue of their essence have a certain position. Again, they must be continu- [20] ous; for a musical scale consists of unlike parts and has position, but cannot become mutilated. Besides, not even the things that are wholes are mutilated by the privation of *any* part. For the parts removed must be neither those which determine the essence nor any chance parts, irrespective of their position; e.g. a cup is not mutilated if it is bored through, but [25] only if the handle or a projecting part is removed, and a man is mutilated not if the flesh or the spleen is removed, but if an extremity is, and that not every extremity but one which when completely removed cannot grow again. Therefore baldness is not a mutilation.

28

The term 'race' or 'genus' is used (1) if genera- [30] tion of things which have the same form is continuous, e.g. 'while the race of men lasts' means 'while the generation of them goes on continuously'.—(2) It is used with reference to that which first brought things into existence; for it is thus that some are called Hellenes by race and others Ionians, because the former proceed from Hellen and the latter from Ion as their first begetter. And the word is used in [35] reference to the begetter more than to the matter, though people also get a race-name from the female, e.g. 'the descendants of Pyrrha'.—(3) There is genus in the sense in which 1024^b 'plane' is the genus of plane figures and 'solid' of solids; for each of the figures is in the one case a plane of such and such a kind, and in the other a solid of such and such a kind; and this is what underlies the differentiae. Again (4), in definitions the first constituent element, which is included in the 'what', is the [5] genus, whose differentiae the qualities are said to be.—'Genus' then is used in all these ways, (1) in reference to continuous genera-tion of the same kind, (2) in reference to the first mover which is of the same kind as the things it moves, (3) as matter; for that to which the differentia or quality belongs is the substratum, which we call matter.

[10] Those things are said to be 'other in genus' whose proximate substratum is different, and which are not analysed the one into the other nor both into the same thing (e.g. form and matter are different in genus); and things which belong to different categories of being (for some of the things that are said to 'be' signify essence, others a quality, others the other categories we have before distinguished[1]); [15] these also are not analysed either into one another or into some one thing.

29

'The false' means (1) that which is false as a *thing,* and that (*a*) because it is not put together or cannot be put together, e.g. 'that the diagonal of a square is commensurate with the side' [20] or 'that you are sitting'; for one of these is false always, and the other sometimes; it is in these two senses that they are non-existent. (*b*) There are things which exist, but whose nature it is to appear either not to be such as they are or to be things that do not exist, e.g. a sketch or a dream; for these are something, but are not the things the appearance of which they produce in us. We call things false in this way, [25] then,—either because they themselves do not exist, or because the appearance which results from them is that of something that does not exist.

(2) A false *account* is the account of non-existent objects, in so far as it is false. Hence every account is false when applied to something other than that of which it is true; e.g. the account of a circle is false when applied to a triangle. In a sense there is one account of each thing, i.e. the account of its essence, but in a sense there are many, since the thing itself and the [30] thing itself with an attribute are in a sense the same, e.g. Socrates and musical Socrates (a false account is not the account of anything, except in a qualified sense). Hence Antisthenes was too simple-minded when he claimed that nothing could be described except by the account proper to it,—one predicate to one subject; from which the conclusion used to be drawn that there could be no contradiction, and almost that there could be no error. But it is possible to describe each thing not only by the ac- [35] count of itself, but also by that of some-

[1] 1017^a 24-27.

thing else. This may be done altogether falsely indeed, but there is also a way in which it may be done truly; e.g. eight may be described as a double number by the use of the definition of two.

1025ᵃ These things, then, are called false in these senses, but (3) a false *man* is one who is ready at and fond of such accounts, not for any other reason but for their own sake, and one who is good at impressing such accounts on other [5] people, just as we say *things* are false, which produce a false appearance. This is why the proof in the *Hippias* that the same man is false and true is misleading. For it assumes that he is false who can deceive (i.e. the man who knows and is wise); and further that he who is *willingly* bad is better. This is a false result of [10] induction—for a man who limps willingly is better than one who does so unwillingly—by 'limping' Plato means 'mimicking a limp', for if the man *were* lame willingly, he would presumably be worse in this case as in the corresponding case of moral character.

30

'Accident' means (1) that which attaches to something and can be truly asserted, but neither of necessity nor usually, e.g. if some one in [15] digging a hole for a plant has found treasure. This—the finding of treasure—is for the man who dug the hole an accident; for neither does the one come of necessity from the other or after the other, nor, if a man plants, does he usually find treasure. And a musical man [20] *might* be pale; but since this does not happen of necessity nor usually, we call it an accident. Therefore since there are attributes and they attach to subjects, and some of them attach to these only in a particular place and at a particular time, whatever attaches to a subject, but not because it was this subject, or the time this time, or the place this place, will be an accident. Therefore, too, there is no definite cause for an accident, but a chance cause, i.e. an in- [25] definite one. Going to Aegina was an accident for a man, if he went not in order to get there, but because he was carried out of his way by a storm or captured by pirates. The accident has happened or exists,—not in virtue of the subject's nature, however, but of something else; for the *storm* was the cause of his coming to a place for which he was not sailing, and this was Aegina.

[30] 'Accident' has also (2) another meaning, i.e. all that attaches to each thing in virtue of itself but is not in its essence, as having its angles equal to two right angles attaches to the triangle. And accidents of this sort may be eternal, but no accident of the other sort is. This is explained elsewhere.[1]

BOOK VI

1

1025ᵇ We are seeking the principles and the causes of the things that are, and obviously of them *qua* being. For, while there is a cause of health and of good condition, and the objects of mathematics have first principles and ele- [5] ments and causes, and in general every science which is ratiocinative or at all involves reasoning deals with causes and principles, more or less precise, all these sciences mark off some particular being—some genus, and inquire into [10] this, but not into being simply nor *qua* being, nor do they offer any discussion of the essence of the things of which they treat; but starting from the essence—some making it plain to the senses, others assuming it as a hypothesis—they then demonstrate, more or less cogently, the essential attributes of the genus with which they deal. It is obvious, therefore, that such an induction yields no demonstra- [15] tion of substance or of the essence, but some other way of exhibiting it. And similarly the sciences omit the question whether the genus with which they deal exists or does not exist, because it belongs to the same kind of thinking to show what it is and that it is.

And since natural science, like other sciences, is in fact about one class of being, i.e. to that sort of substance which has the principle of its [20] movement and rest present in itself, evidently it is neither practical nor productive. For in the case of things made the principle is in the maker—it is either reason or art or some faculty, while in the case of things done it is in the doer—viz. will, for that which is done and [25] that which is willed are the same. Therefore, if all thought is either practical or productive or theoretical, physics must be a theoretical science, but it will theorize about such being as admits of being moved, and about substance-as-defined for the most part only as not separable from matter. Now, we must not fail to notice the mode of being of the essence and of its definition, for, without this, inquiry is but

[1] *Posterior Analytics*, i. 75ᵃ 18-22, 39-41, 76ᵇ 11-16.

[30] idle. Of things defined, i.e. of 'whats', some are like 'snub', and some like 'concave'. And these differ because 'snub' is bound up with matter (for what is snub is a concave *nose*), while concavity is independent of perceptible matter. If then all natural things are 1026ᵃ analogous to the snub in their nature— e.g. nose, eye, face, flesh, bone, and, in general, animal; leaf, root, bark, and, in general, plant (for none of these can be defined without reference to movement—they always have matter), it is clear how we must seek and define the 'what' in the case of natural objects, and [5] also that it belongs to the student of nature to study even soul in a certain sense, i.e. so much of it as is not independent of matter.

That physics, then, is a theoretical science, is plain from these considerations. Mathematics also, however, is theoretical; but whether its objects are immovable and separable from matter, is not at present clear; still, it is clear that *some* mathematical theorems *consider* them [10] *qua* immovable and *qua* separable from matter. But if there is something which is eternal and immovable and separable, clearly the knowledge of it belongs to a theoretical science, —not, however, to physics (for physics deals with certain movable things) nor to mathematics, but to a science prior to both. For physics deals with things which exist separately but are not immovable, and some parts of mathematics deal with things which are immovable but pre- [15] sumably do not exist separately, but as embodied in matter; while the first science deals with things which both exist separately and are immovable. Now all causes must be eternal, but especially these; for they are the causes that operate on so much of the divine as appears to us. There must, then, be three theoretical philosophies, mathematics, physics, and what we may call theology, since it is obvious [20] that if the divine is present anywhere, it is present in things of this sort. And the highest science must deal with the highest genus. Thus, while the theoretical sciences are more to be desired than the other sciences, this is more to be desired than the other theoretical sciences. For one might raise the question whether first philosophy is universal, or deals with one genus, i.e. some one kind of being; for not even the [25] mathematical sciences are all alike in this respect,—geometry and astronomy deal with a certain particular kind of thing, while universal mathematics applies alike to all. We answer that if there is no substance other than those which are formed by nature, natural science will be the first science; but if there is an immovable substance, the science of this must be [30] prior and must be first philosophy, and universal in this way, because it is first. And it will belong to this to consider being *qua* being —both what it is and the attributes which belong to it *qua* being.

2

But since the unqualified term 'being' has several meanings, of which one was seen[1] to be the accidental, and another the true ('non-being' [35] being the false), while besides these there are the figures of predication (e.g. the 'what', quality, quantity, place, time, and any similar meanings which 'being' may have), and again 1026ᵇ besides all these there is that which 'is' potentially or actually:—since 'being' has many meanings, we must say regarding the *accidental,* that there can be no scientific treatment of it. This is confirmed by the fact that no science [5] —practical, productive, or theoretical— troubles itself about it. For on the one hand he who produces a house does not produce all the attributes that come into being along with the house; for these are innumerable; the house that has been made may quite well be pleasant for some people, hurtful for some, and useful to others, and different—to put it shortly— from all things that are; and the science of building does not aim at producing any of these [10] attributes. And in the same way the geometer does not consider the attributes which attach thus to figures, nor whether 'triangle' is different from 'triangle whose angles are equal to two right angles'.—And this happens naturally enough; for the accidental is practically a mere name. And so Plato was in a sense not wrong in ranking sophistic as dealing with that [15] which is not. For the arguments of the sophists deal, we may say, above all with the accidental; e.g. the question whether 'musical' and 'lettered' are different or the same, and whether 'musical Coriscus' and 'Coriscus' are the same, and whether 'everything which is, but is not eternal, has come to be', with the paradoxical conclusion that if one who was musical has come to be lettered, he must also have been lettered and have come to be musical,— [20] and all the other arguments of this sort; the accidental is obviously akin to non-being. And this is clear also from arguments such as the following: things which are in another sense come into being and pass out of being by a process, but things which are accidentally do

[1] Cf. v. 7.

not. But still we must, as far as we can, say further, regarding the accidental, what its nature is and from what cause it proceeds; for it will perhaps at the same time become clear why there is no science of it.

Since, among things which are, some are always in the same state and are of necessity (not necessity in the sense of compulsion but that which we assert of things because they cannot be otherwise), and some are not of necessity nor always, but for the most part, this is the principle and this the cause of the existence of the accidental; for that which is neither always nor for the most part, we call accidental. For instance, if in the dog-days there is wintry and cold weather, we say this is an accident, but not if there is sultry heat, because the latter is always or for the most part so, but not the former. And it is an accident that a man is pale (for this is neither always nor for the most part so), but it is not by accident that he is an animal. And that the builder produces health is an accident, because it is the nature not of the builder but of the doctor to do this,—but the builder happened to be a doctor. Again, a confectioner, aiming at giving pleasure, may make something wholesome, but not in virtue of the confectioner's art; and therefore we say 'it was an accident', and while there is a sense in which he makes it, in the unqualified sense he does not. For to other things answer faculties productive of them, but to accidental results there corresponds no determinate art nor faculty; for of things which are or come to be by accident, the cause also is accidental. Therefore, since not all things either are or come to be of necessity and always, but the majority of things are *for the most part,* the accidental must exist; for instance a pale man is not always nor for the most part musical, but since this sometimes happens, it must be accidental (if not, everything will be of necessity). The matter, therefore, which is capable of being otherwise than as it usually is, must be the cause of the accidental. And we must take as our starting-point the question whether there is nothing that is neither always nor for the most part. Surely this is impossible. There is, then, besides these something which is fortuitous and accidental. But while the usual exists, can nothing be said to be always, or are there eternal things? This must be considered later,[1] but that there is no science of the accidental is obvious; for all science is either of that which is always or of that which is for the most part. (For how else is one to learn or to teach another? The thing must be determined as occurring either always or for the most part, e.g. that honey-water is useful for a patient in a fever is true for the most part.) But that which is contrary to the usual law science will be unable to state, i.e. when the thing does *not* happen, e.g. 'on the day of new moon'; for even that which happens on the day of new moon happens then either always or for the most part; but the accidental is contrary to such laws. We have stated, then, what the accidental is, and from what cause it arises, and that there is no science which deals with it.

3

That there are principles and causes which are generable and destructible without ever being in course of being generated or destroyed, is obvious. For otherwise all things will be of necessity, since that which is being generated or destroyed must have a cause which is not accidentally its cause. Will A exist or not? It will *if B* happens; and if not, not. And B will exist if C happens. And thus if time is constantly subtracted from a limited extent of time, one will obviously come to the present. This man, then, will die by violence, *if* he goes out; and he will do this if he gets thirsty; and he will get thirsty if something else happens; and thus we shall come to that which is now present, or to some past event. For instance, he will go out if he gets thirsty; and he will get thirsty if he is eating pungent food; and this is either the case or not; so that he will of necessity die, or of necessity not die. And similarly if one jumps over to past events, the same account will hold good; for this—I mean the past condition—is already present in something. Everything, therefore, that will be, will be of necessity; e.g. it is necessary that he who lives shall one day die; for already some condition has come into existence, e.g. the presence of contraries in the same body. But whether he is to die by disease or by violence is not yet determined, but depends on the happening of something else. Clearly then the process goes back to a certain starting-point, but this no longer points to something further. This then will be the starting-point for the fortuitous, and will have nothing else as cause of its coming to be. But to what sort of starting-point and what sort of cause we thus refer the fortuitous—whether to matter or to the purpose or to the motive power, must be carefully considered.

[1] Cf. xii. 6-8.

4

Let us dismiss accidental being; for we have sufficiently determined its nature. But since that which *is* in the sense of being true, or *is not* in the sense of being false, depends on combination and separation, and truth and falsity together depend on the allocation of a pair of [20] contradictory judgements (for the true judgement affirms where the subject and predicate really are combined, and denies where they are separated, while the false judgement has the opposite of this allocation; it is another question, how it happens that we think things together or apart; by 'together' and 'apart' I mean thinking them so that there is no succes-[25] sion in the thoughts but they become a unity); for falsity and truth are not in things—it is not as if the good were true, and the bad were in itself false—but in thought; while with regard to simple concepts and 'whats' falsity and truth do not exist even in thought:—this being so, we must consider later[2] what has to be discussed with regard to that which is or is not in this sense. But since the combination and the [30] separation are in thought and not in the things, and that which is in this sense is a different sort of 'being' from the things that are in the full sense (for the thought attaches or removes either the subject's 'what' or its having a certain quality or quantity or something else), that which *is* accidentally and that which *is* in the sense of being true must be dismissed. For the cause of the former is indeterminate, and that of the latter is some affection of the 1028ª thought, and both are related to the remaining genus of being, and do not indicate the existence of any separate class of being. Therefore let these be dismissed, and let us consider the causes and the principles of being itself, *qua* being. [It was clear in our discussion of the various meanings of terms, that 'being' [5] has several meanings.]

BOOK VII

1

[10] There are several senses in which a thing may be said to 'be', as we pointed out previously in our book on the various senses of words;[1] for in one sense the 'being' meant is 'what a thing is' or a 'this', and in another sense it means a quality or quantity or one of the other things that are predicated as these are. While 'being' has all these senses, obviously that which 'is' primarily is the 'what', which indi-[15] cates the substance of the thing. For when we say of what quality a thing is, we say that it is good or bad, not that it is three cubits long or that it is a man; but when we say *what* it is, we do not say 'white' or 'hot' or 'three cubits long', but 'a man' or 'a god'. And all other things are said to be because they are, some of them, quantities of that which *is* in this primary sense, others qualities of it, others affections of it, and others some other determination of it. And [20] so one might even raise the question whether the words 'to walk', 'to be healthy', 'to sit' imply that each of these things is existent, and similarly in any other case of this sort; for none of them is either self-subsistent or capable of being separated from substance, but rather, if anything, it is that which walks or sits or is healthy that is an exist-[25] ent thing. Now these are seen to be more real because there is something definite which underlies them (i.e. the substance or individual), which is implied in such a predicate; for we never use the word 'good' or 'sitting' without implying this. Clearly then it is in virtue of this category that each of the others also *is*. Therefore that which is primarily, i.e. not in [30] a qualified sense but without qualification, must be substance.

Now there are several senses in which a thing is said to be first; yet substance is first in every sense—(1) in definition, (2) in order of knowledge, (3) in time. For (3) of the other categories none can exist independently, but only sub-[35] stance. And (1) in definition also this is first; for in the definition of each term the definition of its substance must be present. And (2) we think we know each thing most fully, when we know what it is, e.g. what man is or what fire is, rather than when we know its 1028ᵇ quality, its quantity, or its place; since we know each of these predicates also, only when we know *what* the quantity or the quality *is*.

And indeed the question which was raised of old and is raised now and always, and is always the subject of doubt, viz. what being is, is just the question, what is substance? For it is this that some assert to be one, others more [5] than one, and that some assert to be limit-

---
[1] Cf. v. 7.   [2] Cf. ix. 10.

ed in number, others unlimited. And so we also must consider chiefly and primarily and almost exclusively what that is which *is* in *this* sense.

2

Substance is thought to belong most obviously to bodies; and so we say that not only animals and plants and their parts are substances, but [*10*] also natural bodies such as fire and water and earth and everything of the sort, and all things that are either parts of these or composed of these (either of parts or of the whole bodies), e.g. the physical universe and its parts, stars and moon and sun. But whether these alone are substances, or there are also others, or only some of these, or others as well, or none [*15*] of these but only some other things, are substances, must be considered. Some think the limits of body, i.e. surface, line, point, and unit, are substances, and more so than body or the solid.

Further, some do not think there is anything substantial besides sensible things, but others think there are eternal substances which are more in number and more real; e.g. Plato posited two kinds of substance—the Forms and the [*20*] objects of mathematics—as well as a third kind, viz. the substance of sensible bodies. And Speusippus made still more kinds of substance, beginning with the One, and assuming principles for each kind of substance, one for numbers, another for spatial magnitudes, and then another for the soul; and by going on in this way he multiplies the kinds of substance. And [*25*] some say Forms and numbers have the same nature, and the other things come after them—lines and planes—until we come to the substance of the material universe and to sensible bodies.

Regarding these matters, then, we must inquire which of the common statements are right and which are not right, and what substances there are, and whether there are or are not any besides sensible substances, and how [*30*] sensible substances exist, and whether there is a substance capable of separate existence (and if so why and how) or no such substance, apart from sensible substances; and we must first sketch the nature of substance.

3

The word 'substance' is applied, if not in more senses, still at least to four main objects; for both the essence and the universal and the genus are thought to be the substance of each [*35*] thing, and fourthly the substratum. Now the substratum is that of which everything else is predicated, while it is itself not predicated of anything else. And so we must first determine 1029ª the nature of this; for that which underlies a thing primarily is thought to be in the truest sense its substance. And in one sense matter is said to be of the nature of substratum, in another, shape, and in a third, the compound of these. (By the matter I mean, for instance, the bronze, by the shape the pattern of its form, and by the compound of these the [*5*] statue, the concrete whole.) Therefore if the form is prior to the matter and more real, it will be prior also to the compound of both, for the same reason.

We have now outlined the nature of substance, showing that it is that which is not predicated of a stratum, but of which all else is predicated. But we must not merely state the matter thus; for this is not enough. The statement itself is obscure, and further, on this view, *matter* becomes substance. For if this is [*10*] not substance, it baffles us to say what else is. When all else is stripped off evidently nothing but matter remains. For while the rest are affections, products, and potencies of bodies, length, breadth, and depth are quantities and not substances (for a quantity is not a sub- [*15*] stance), but the substance is rather that to which these belong primarily. But when length and breadth and depth are taken away we see nothing left unless there is something that is bounded by these; so that to those who consider the question thus matter alone must seem to be substance. By matter I mean that [*20*] which in itself is neither a particular thing nor of a certain quantity nor assigned to any other of the categories by which being is determined. For there is something of which each of these is predicated, whose being is different from that of each of the predicates (for the predicates other than substance are predicated of substance, while substance is predicated of matter). Therefore the ultimate substratum is of itself neither a particular thing nor of a particular quantity nor otherwise posi- [*25*] tively characterized; nor yet is it the negations of these, for negations also will belong to it only by accident.

If we adopt this point of view, then, it follows that matter is substance. But this is impossible; for both separability and 'thisness' are thought to belong chiefly to substance. And so form and the compound of form and matter [*30*] would be thought to be substance, rather than matter. The substance compounded of both, i.e. of matter and shape, may be dismissed; for it is posterior and its nature is obvious. And matter also is in a sense manifest. But we must inquire into the third kind of substance; for this is the most perplexing.

Some of the sensible substances are generally admitted to be substances, so that we must look first among these. For it is an advantage 1029ᵇ [3] to advance to that which is more knowable. For learning proceeds for all in this way—through that which is less knowable by [5] nature to that which is more knowable; and just as in conduct our task is to start from what is good for each and make what is without qualification good good for each, so it is our task to start from what is more knowable to oneself and make what is knowable by nature knowable to oneself. Now what is knowable and primary for particular sets of people is often knowable to a very small extent, and has [10] little or nothing of reality. But yet one must start from that which is barely knowable but knowable to oneself, and try to know what is knowable without qualification, passing, as has been said, by way of those very things which one does know.

4

[1] Since at the start[1] we distinguished the various marks by which we determine substance, and one of these was thought to be the essence, [13] we must investigate this. And first let us make some linguistic remarks about it. The essence of each thing is what it is said to be *propter se*. For being you is not being musical, since [15] you are not by your very nature musical. What, then, you are by your very nature is your essence.

Nor yet is the whole of this the essence of a thing; not that which is *propter se* as white is to a surface, because being a surface is not *identical* with being white. But again the combination of both—'being a white surface'—is not the essence of surface, because 'surface' itself is added. The formula, therefore, in which the term itself is not present but its meaning is [20] expressed, this is the formula of the essence of each thing. Therefore if to be a white surface is to be a smooth surface, to be white and to be smooth are one and the same.

But since there are also compounds answering to the other categories (for there is a substratum for each category, e.g. for quality,

[1] 1028ᵇ 33-6.

[25] quantity, time, place, and motion), we must inquire whether there is a formula of the essence of each of them, i.e. whether to these compounds also there belongs an essence, e.g. to 'white man'. Let the compound be denoted by 'cloak'. What is the essence of cloak? But, it may be said, this also is not a *propter se* expression. We reply that there are just two ways in which a predicate may fail to be true [30] of a subject *propter se,* and one of these results from the addition, and the other from the omission, of a determinant. One kind of predicate is not *propter se* because the term that is being defined is combined with another determinant, e.g. if in defining the essence of white one were to state the formula of white *man;* the *other* because in the subject another determinant is combined with that which is expressed in the formula, e.g. if 'cloak' meant 'white man', and one were to define cloak as 1030ᵃ white; white man is white indeed, but its essence is not to be white.

But is being-a-cloak an essence at all? Probably not. For the essence is precisely what something *is;* but when an attribute is asserted of a subject other than itself, the complex is not precisely what some 'this' *is*, e.g. white man is [5] not precisely what some 'this' *is*, since thisness belongs only to substances. Therefore there is an essence only of those things whose formula is a definition. But we have a definition not where we have a word and a formula identical in meaning (for in that case all formulae or sets of words would be definitions; for there will be some name for any set of words whatever, so that even the *Iliad* will be a definition), but where there is a formula of [10] something primary; and primary things are those which do not imply the predication of one element in them of another element. Nothing, then, which is not a species of a genus will have an *essence*—only species will have it, for these are thought to imply not merely that the subject participates in the attribute and has it as an affection, or has it by accident; but for everything else as well, if it has a name, there [15] will be a *formula of its meaning*—viz. that this attribute belongs to this subject; or instead of a simple formula we shall be able to give a more accurate one; but there will be no definition nor essence.

Or has 'definition', like 'what a thing is', several meanings? 'What a thing is' in one sense means substance and the 'this', in another [20] one or other of the predicates, quantity, quality, and the like. For as 'is' belongs to all things, not however in the same sense, but to one sort of thing primarily and to others in a secondary way, so too 'what a thing is' belongs in the simple sense to substance, but in a limited sense to the other categories. For even of a quality we might ask what it is, so that qual- [25] ity also is a 'what a thing is',—not in the simple sense, however, but just as, in the case of that which is not, some say,[1] emphasizing the linguistic form, that that which is not *is*—not *is* simply, but *is* non-existent; so too with quality.

We must no doubt inquire how we should express ourselves on each point, but certainly not more than how the facts actually stand. And so now also, since it is evident what language we use, essence will belong, just as 'what a thing is' does, primarily and in the simple sense to substance, and in a secondary way to [30] the other categories also,—not essence in the simple sense, but the essence of a quality or of a quantity. For it must be either by an equivocation that we say these *are,* or by adding to and taking from the meaning of 'are' (in the way in which that which is not known may be said to be known),—the truth being that we use the word neither ambiguously nor in the [35] same sense, but just as we apply the word 'medical' by virtue of a *reference* to one and the same thing, not *meaning* one and the same **1030**[b] thing, nor yet speaking ambiguously; for a patient and an operation and an instrument are called medical neither by an ambiguity nor with a single meaning, but with reference to a common end. But it does not matter at all in which of the two ways one [5] likes to describe the facts; this is evident, that definition and essence in the primary and simple sense belong to substances. Still they belong to other things as well, only not in the primary sense. For if we suppose this it does not follow that there is a definition of every word which means the same as any formula; it must mean the same as a particular kind of formula; and this condition is satisfied if it is a formula of something which is one, not by continuity like the *Iliad* or the things that are [10] one by being bound together, but in one of the main senses of 'one', which answer to the senses of 'is'; now 'that which is' in one sense denotes a 'this', in another a quantity, in another a quality. And so there can be a formula or definition even of white man, but not in the sense in which there is a definition either of white or of a substance.

[1] Cf. Plato, *Sophist,* 237, 256 ff.

5

It is a difficult question, if one denies that a formula with an added determinant is a defi- [15] nition, whether any of the terms that are not simple but coupled will be definable. For we *must* explain them by adding a determinant. E.g. there is the nose, and concavity, and snubness, which is compounded out of the two by the presence of the one in the other, and it is not by *accident* that the nose has the attribute either of concavity or of snubness, but in virtue [20] of its nature; nor do they attach to it as whiteness does to Callias, or to man (because Callias, who happens to be a man, is white), but as 'male' attaches to animal and 'equal' to quantity, and as all so-called 'attributes *propter se*' attach to their subjects. And such attributes are those in which is involved either the *formula* or the *name* of the subject of the particular attribute, and which cannot be ex- [25] plained without this; e.g. white can be explained apart from man, but not female apart from animal. Therefore there is either no essence and definition of any of these things, or if there is, it is in another sense, as we have said.[2]

But there is also a second difficulty about them. For if snub nose and concave nose are the same thing, snub and concave will be the [30] same thing; but if snub and concave are not the same (because it is impossible to speak of snubness apart from the thing of which it is an attribute *propter se,* for snubness is concavity-*in-a-nose*), either it is impossible to say 'snub nose' or the same thing will have been said twice, concave-nose nose; for snub nose will be concave-nose nose. And so it is absurd that such things should have an essence; if they [35] have, there will be an infinite regress; for in snub-nose nose yet another 'nose' will be involved.

1031[a] Clearly, then, only substance is definable. For if the other categories also are definable, it must be by addition of a determinant, e.g. the qualitative is defined thus, and so is the odd, for it cannot be defined apart from number; nor can female be defined apart from animal. (When I say 'by addition' I mean the expressions in which it turns out that we are saying the same thing twice, as in these in- [5] stances.) And if this is true, coupled terms also, like 'odd number', will not be definable (but this escapes our notice because our formulae are not accurate.). But if these also are

[2] a 17-b 13.

definable, either it is in some other way or, as we said,[1] definition and essence must be said to have more than one sense. Therefore in one [10] sense nothing will have a definition and nothing will have an essence, except substances, but in another sense other things will have them. Clearly, then, definition is the formula of the essence, and essence belongs to substances either alone or chiefly and primarily and in the unqualified sense.

6

[15] We must inquire whether each thing and its essence are the same or different. This is of some use for the inquiry concerning substance; for each thing is thought to be not different from its substance, and the essence is said to be the substance of each thing.

Now in the case of accidental unities the two [20] would be generally thought to be different, e.g. white man would be thought to be different from the essence of white man. For if they are the same, the essence of man and that of white man are also the same; for a man and a white man are the same thing, as people say, so that the essence of white man and that of man would be also the same. But perhaps it does not follow that the essence of accidental unities should be the same as that of the simple terms. For the extreme terms are not in the same way identical with the middle term. But [25] perhaps *this* might be thought to follow, that the extreme terms, the accidents, should turn out to be the same, e.g. the essence of white and that of musical; but this is not actually thought to be the case.

But in the case of so-called self-subsistent things, is a thing necessarily the same as its essence? E.g. if there are some substances which have no other substances nor entities [30] prior to them—substances such as some assert the Ideas to be?—If the essence of good is to be different from good-itself, and the essence of animal from animal-itself, and the essence of being from being-itself, there will, firstly, be other substances and entities and Ideas besides those which are asserted, and, secondly, these others will be prior substances, if essence is substance. And if the posterior substances and the prior are severed from each other, (α) there will be no knowledge of the [5] former, and (β) the latter will have no being. (By 'severed' I mean, if the good-itself has not the essence of good, and the latter has not the property of being good.) For (α) there

[1] 1030ᵃ17-ᵇ13.

is knowledge of each thing only when we know its essence. And (β) the case is the same for other things as for the good; so that if the essence of good is not good, neither is the essence of reality real, nor the essence of unity [10] one. And all essences alike exist or none of them does; so that if the essence of reality is not real, neither is any of the others. Again, that to which the essence of good does not belong is not good.—The good, then, must be one with the essence of good, and the beautiful with the essence of beauty, and so with all things which do not depend on something else but are self-subsistent and primary. For it is enough if they are this, even if they are not Forms; or rather, perhaps, even if they *are* [15] Forms. (At the same time it is clear that if there are Ideas such as some people say there are, it will not be substratum that is substance; for these must be substances, but not predicable of a substratum; for if they were they would exist only by being participated in.)

Each thing itself, then, and its essence are one and the same in no merely accidental way, [20] as is evident both from the preceding arguments and because to *know* each thing, at least, is just to know its essence, so that even by the exhibition of instances it becomes clear that both must be one.

(But of an accidental term, e.g. 'the musical' or 'the white', since it has two meanings, it is not true to say that it itself is identical with its essence; for both that to which the accidental quality belongs, and the accidental quality, are [25] white, so that in a sense the accident and its essence are the same, and in a sense they are not; for the essence of white is not the same as the man or the white man, but it is the same as the attribute white.)

The absurdity of the separation would appear also if one were to assign a name to each of the essences; for there would be yet another [30] essence besides the original one, e.g. to the essence of horse there will belong a second essence. Yet why should not some things be their essences from the start, since essence is substance? But indeed not only are a thing and its essence one, but the formula of them is also the same, as is clear even from what has been said; for it is not by accident that the essence of one, and the one, are one. Further, if they are to be different, the process will go on to infinity; for we shall have (1) the essence of one, and (2) the one, so that to terms of the former kind the same argument will be applicable.

[5] Clearly, then, each primary and self-subsistent thing is one and the same as its essence. The sophistical objections to this position, and the question whether Socrates and to be Socrates are the same thing, are obviously answered by the same solution; for there is no difference either in the standpoint from which the question would be asked, or in that from [10] which one could answer it successfully. We have explained, then, in what sense each thing is the same as its essence and in what sense it is not.

7

Of things that come to be, some come to be by nature, some by art, some spontaneously. Now everything that comes to be comes to be by the agency of something and from something and comes to be something. And the something which I say it comes to be may be found in any category; it may come to be either a 'this' or of some size or of some quality or somewhere. [15] Now natural comings to be are the comings to be of those things which come to be by nature; and that out of which they come to be is what we call matter; and that by which they come to be is something which exists naturally; and the something which they come to be is a man or a plant or one of the things of this kind, which we say are substances if anything [20] is—all things produced either by nature or by art have matter; for each of them is capable both of being and of not being, and this capacity is the matter in each—and, in general, both that from which they are produced is nature, and the type according to which they are produced is nature (for that which is produced, e.g. a plant or an animal, has a nature), and so is that by which they are produced—the so-called 'formal' nature, which is specifically the same (though this is in another individual); for man begets man.
[25] Thus, then, are natural products produced; all other productions are called 'makings'. And all makings proceed either from art or from a faculty or from thought. Some of them happen also spontaneously or by luck [30] just as natural products sometimes do; for there also the same things sometimes are produced without seed as well as from seed. Concerning these cases, then, we must inquire later,[1] but from art proceed the things of which the form is in the soul of the artist. (By form 1032[b] I mean the essence of each thing and its primary substance.) For even contraries

[1] Cf. [b]23-30, 1034[a] 9-21, [b] 4-7.

have in a sense the same form; for the substance of a privation is the opposite substance, e.g. health is the substance of disease (for dis- [5] ease is the absence of health); and health is the formula in the soul or the knowledge of it. The healthy subject is produced as the result of the following train of thought:—since *this* is health, if the subject is to be healthy *this* must first be present, e.g. a uniform state of body, and if this is to be present, there must be heat; and the physician goes on thinking thus until he reduces the matter to a final something which he himself can produce. Then the proc- [10] ess from this point onward, i.e. the process towards health, is called a 'making'. Therefore it follows that in a sense health comes from health and house from house, that with matter from that without matter; for the medical art and the building art are the form of health and of the house, and when I speak of substance without matter I mean the essence.
[15] Of the productions or processes one part is called thinking and the other making,—that which proceeds from the starting-point and the form is thinking, and that which proceeds from the final step of the thinking is making. And each of the other, intermediate, things is produced in the same way. I mean, for instance, if the subject is to be healthy his bodily state must be made uniform. What then does being made uniform imply? This or that. And this de- [20] pends on his being made warm. What does this imply? Something else. And this something is present potentially; and what is present potentially is already in the physician's power.

The active principle then and the starting point for the process of becoming healthy is, if it happens by art, the form in the soul, and if spontaneously, it is that, whatever it is, which starts the making, for the man who makes by [25] art, as in healing the starting-point is perhaps the production of warmth (and this the physician produces by rubbing). Warmth in the body, then, is either a part of health or is followed (either directly or through several intermediate steps) by something similar which is a part of health; and this, viz. that which produces the part of health, is the limiting-point,—and so too with a house (the stones are the limiting-point here) and in all other cases. [30] Therefore, as the saying goes, it is impossible that anything should be produced if there were nothing existing before. Obviously then some part of the result will pre-exist of necessity; for the matter is a part; for this is present in the process and it is this that becomes something. But is the matter an element even in the *formula*? We certainly describe in both ways what brazen circles are; we describe both the matter by saying it is brass, and the form by saying that it is such and such a figure; and figure is the proximate genus in which it is placed. The brazen circle, then, has its matter *in its formula.*

[5] As for that out of which as matter they are produced, some things are said, when they have been produced, to be not that but 'thaten'; e.g. the statue is not gold but golden. And a healthy man is not said to be that from which he has come. The reason is that though a thing comes both from its privation and from its substratum, which we call its matter (e.g. what [10] becomes healthy is both a man and an invalid), it is said to come rather from its privation (e.g. it is from an invalid rather than from a man that a healthy subject is produced). And so the healthy subject is not said to *be* an invalid, but to be a man, and the man is said to be healthy. But as for the things whose privation is obscure and nameless, e.g. in brass the privation of a particular shape or in bricks and timber the privation of arrangement as a [15] house, the thing is thought to be produced *from* these materials, as in the former case the healthy man is produced *from* an invalid. And so, as there also a thing is not said to be that from which it comes, here the statue is not said to be wood but is said by a verbal change to be wooden, not brass but brazen, not gold but golden, and the house is said to be not bricks [20] but bricken (though we should not say without qualification, if we looked at the matter carefully, even that a statue is produced from wood or a house from bricks, because coming to be implies change in that from which a thing comes to be, and not permanence). It is for this reason, then, that we use this way of speaking.

8

Since anything which is produced is produced by something (and this I call the starting-point of the production), and from something (and [25] let this be taken to be not the privation but the matter; for the meaning we attach to this has already[1] been explained), and since something is produced (and this is either a sphere or a circle or whatever else it may chance to be), just as we do not make the substratum (the brass), so we do not make the sphere, except incidentally, because the brazen sphere is a sphere and we make the former. [30] For to make a 'this' is to make a 'this' out of the substratum in the full sense of the word. (I mean that to make the brass round is not to make the round or the sphere, but something else, i.e. to produce this form in something different from itself. For if we make the form, we must make it out of something else; for this was assumed.[2] E.g. we make a brazen sphere; and that in the sense that out of this, which is brass, we make this other, which is a sphere.) If, then, we also make the substratum itself, clearly we shall make it in the same way, and the processes of making will [5] regress to infinity. Obviously then the form also, or whatever we ought to call the shape present in the sensible thing, is not produced, nor is there any production of it, nor is the essence produced; for this is that which is made to be in something else either by art or by nature or by some faculty. But that there is a *brazen sphere,* this we make. For we make it out of brass and the sphere; we bring the form [10] into this particular matter, and the result is a brazen sphere. But if the essence of sphere in general is to be produced, something must be produced out of something. For the product will always have to be divisible, and one part must be this and another that; I mean the one must be matter and the other form. If, then, a sphere is 'the figure whose circumference is at all points equidistant from the centre', part of [15] this will be the medium in which the thing made will be, and part will be in that medium, and the whole will be the thing produced, which corresponds to the brazen sphere. It is obvious, then, from what has been said, that that which is spoken of as form or substance is not produced, but the concrete thing which gets its name from this is produced, and that in everything which is generated matter is present, and one part of the thing is matter and the other form.

Is there, then, a sphere apart from the individual [20] spheres or a house apart from the bricks? Rather we may say that no 'this' would ever have been coming to be, if this had been so, but that the 'form' means the 'such', and is not a 'this'—a definite thing; but the artist makes, or the father begets, a 'such' out of a 'this'; and when it has been begotten, it is a 'this such'. And the whole 'this', Callias or Socrates, is analogous to 'this brazen sphere', but [25] man and animal to 'brazen sphere' in gen-

---
[1] Cf. 1032ª 17.   [2] a 25.

eral. Obviously, then, the cause which consists of the Forms (taken in the sense in which some maintain the existence of the Forms, i.e. if they are something apart from the individuals) is useless, at least with regard to comings-to-be and to substances; and the Forms need not, for this reason at least, be self-subsistent substances. In some cases indeed it is even obvious [30] that the begetter is of the same kind as the begotten (not, however, the *same* nor one in number, but in form), i.e. in the case of natural products (for man begets man), unless something happens contrary to nature, e.g. the production of a mule by a horse. (And even these cases are similar; for that which would be found to be common to horse and ass, the genus next above them, has not received a name, but it would doubtless be both in fact something like a mule.) Obviously, therefore, it is quite unnecessary to set up a Form as a pattern (for we should have looked for Forms in these cases if in any; for these are substances if anything is so); the begetter is adequate to the making of the product and [5] to the causing of the form in the matter. And when we have the whole, such and such a form in this flesh and in these bones, this is Callias or Socrates; and they are different in virtue of their matter (for that is different), but the same in form; for their form is indivisible.

9

The question might be raised, why some things are produced spontaneously as well as by art, [10] e.g. health, while others are not, e.g. a house. The reason is that in some cases the matter which governs the production in the making and producing of any work of art, and in which a part of the product is present,—some matter is such as to be set in motion by itself and some is not of this nature, and of the former kind some can move itself in the particular way required, while other matter is incapable of this; for many things can be set in motion by themselves but not in some par- [15] ticular way, e.g. that of dancing. The things, then, whose matter is of this sort, e.g. stones, cannot be moved in the particular way required, except by something else, but in another way they can move themselves—and so it is with fire. Therefore some things will not exist apart from some one who has the art of making them, while others will; for motion will be started by these things which have not [20] the art but can themselves be moved by other things which have not the art or with a motion starting from a part of the product.

And it is clear also from what has been said that in a sense every product of art is produced from a thing which shares its name (as natural products are produced), or from a part of itself which shares its name (e.g. the house is produced from a house, *qua* produced by reason; for the art of building is the form of the house), or from something which contains a part of it,—if we exclude things produced by [25] accident; for the cause of the thing's producing the product directly *per se* is a part of the product. The heat in the movement caused heat in the body, and this is either health, or a part of health, or is followed by a part of health or by health itself. And so it is said to cause health, because it causes that to which health attaches as a consequence.

[30] Therefore, as in syllogisms, substance is the starting-point of everything. It is from 'what a thing is' that syllogisms start; and from it also we now find processes of production to start.

Things which are formed by nature are in the same case as these products of art. For the seed is productive in the same way as the things that work by art; for it has the form potentially, and that from which the seed comes has in a sense the same name as the offspring—only in a sense, for we must not expect parent and offspring always to have exactly the same name, as in the production of 'human being' from 'human being'; for a 'woman' also can be produced by a 'man'—unless the offspring be an imperfect form; which is the reason why the parent of a mule is not a mule. The natural things which (like the artificial objects previ- [5] ously considered[1]) can be produced spontaneously are those whose matter can be moved even by itself in the way in which the seed usually moves it; those things which have not such matter cannot be produced except from the parent animals themselves.

But not only regarding substance does our argument prove that its form does not come to be, but the argument applies to all the primary classes alike, i.e. quantity, quality, and the [10] other categories. For as the brazen sphere comes to be, but not the sphere nor the brass, and so too in the case of brass itself, if it comes to be, it is its concrete unity that comes to be (for the matter and the form must always exist before), so is it both in the case of substance and in that of quality and quantity and

[1] Cf. ᵃ9-32.

the other categories likewise; for the quality does not come to be, but the wood of that qual-[15] ity, and the quantity does not come to be, but the wood or the animal of that size. But we may learn from these instances a peculiarity of substance, that there must exist beforehand in complete reality another substance which produces it, e.g. an animal if an animal is produced; but it is not necessary that a quality or quantity should pre-exist otherwise than potentially.

10

[20] Since a definition is a formula, and every formula has parts, and as the formula is to the thing, so is the part of the formula to the part of the thing, the question is already being asked whether the formula of the parts must be present in the formula of the whole or not. For in some cases the formulae of the parts are seen to be present, and in some not. The formula of the circle does not include that of [25] the segments, but that of the syllable includes that of the letters; yet the circle is divided into segments as the syllable is into letters.—And further if the parts are prior to the whole, and the acute angle is a part of the right angle and the finger a part of the animal, the acute angle will be prior to the right angle and [30] the finger to the man. But the latter are thought to be prior; for in formula the parts are explained by reference to them, and in respect also of the power of existing apart from each other the wholes are prior to the parts.

Perhaps we should rather say that 'part' is used in several senses. One of these is 'that which measures another thing in respect of quantity'. But let this sense be set aside; let us inquire about the parts of which *substance* 1035^a consists. If then matter is one thing, form another, the compound of these a third, and both the matter and the form and the compound are substance, even the matter is in a sense called part of a thing, while in a sense *it* is not, but only the elements of which the formula of the form consists. E.g. of concavity flesh (for this is the matter in which it is pro-[5] duced) is not a part, but of snubness it is a part; and the bronze is a part of the concrete statue, but not of the statue when this is spoken of in the sense of the form. (For the form, or the thing as having form, should be said to be the thing, but the material element by itself must never be said to be so.) And so the formula of the circle does not include that of the [10] segments, but the formula of the syllable includes that of the letters; for the letters are parts of the formula of the form, and not matter, but the segments are parts in the sense of matter on which the form supervenes; yet they are nearer the form than the bronze is when roundness is produced in bronze. But in a sense not even every kind of letter will be present in the formula of the syllable, e.g. particular waxen letters or the letters as movements in the air; for in these also we have already something that is part of the syllable only in the sense that it is its perceptible matter. For even if the line when divided passes away into its halves, or the man into bones and muscles and flesh, it does not follow that they are composed of these as parts of their essence, [20] but rather as matter; and these are parts of the concrete thing, but not also of the form, i.e. of that to which the formula refers; wherefore also they are not present in the formulae. In one kind of formula, then, the formula of such parts will be present, but in another it must not be present, where the formula does not refer to the concrete object. For it is for this reason that some things have as their constituent principles parts into which they pass away, while some have not. Those things [25] which are the form and the matter taken together, e.g. the snub, or the bronze circle, pass away into these materials, and the matter is a part of them; but those things which do not involve matter but are without matter, and whose formulae are formulae of the form only, do not pass away,—either not at all or at any [30] rate not in this way. Therefore these materials are principles and parts of the concrete things, while of the form they are neither parts nor principles. And therefore the clay statue is resolved into clay and the ball into bronze and Callias into flesh and bones, and again the circle into its segments; for there is a sense of 'circle' in which it involves matter. For 'circle' 1035^b is used ambiguously, meaning both the circle, unqualified, and the individual circle, because there is no name peculiar to the individuals.

The truth has indeed now been stated, but still let us state it yet more clearly, taking up the question again. The parts of the formula, [5] into which the formula is divided, are prior to it, either all or some of them. The formula of the right angle, however, does not include the formula of the acute, but the formula of the acute includes that of the right angle; for he who defines the acute uses the right angle; for the acute is 'less than a right angle'.

The circle and the semicircle also are in a like relation; for the semicircle is defined by the [10] circle; and so is the finger by the whole body, for a finger is 'such and such a part of a man'. Therefore the parts which are of the nature of matter, and into which as its matter a thing is divided, are posterior; but those which are of the nature of parts of the formula, and of the substance according to its formula, are prior, either all or some of them. And since the soul of animals (for this is the substance [15] of a living being) is their substance according to the formula, i.e. the form and the essence of a body of a certain kind (at least we shall define each part, if we define it well, not without reference to its function, and this cannot belong to it without perception), so that the parts of soul are prior, either all or some of them, to the concrete 'animal', and so too with each individual animal; and the body and [20] its parts are posterior to this, the essential substance, and it is not the substance but the concrete thing that is divided into these parts as its matter:—this being so, to the concrete thing these are in a sense prior, but in a sense they are not. For they cannot even exist if severed from the whole; for it is not a finger in any and every state that is the finger of a liv-[25] ing thing, but a dead finger is a finger only in name. Some parts are neither prior nor posterior to the whole, i.e. those which are dominant and in which the formula, i.e. the essential substance, is immediately present, e.g. perhaps the heart or the brain; for it does not matter in the least which of the two has this quality. But man and horse and terms which are thus applied to individuals, but universally, are not substance but something composed of this particular formula and this particular mat-[30] ter treated as universal; and as regards the individual, Socrates already includes in him ultimate individual matter; and similarly in all other cases. 'A part' may be a part either of the form (i.e. of the essence), or of the compound of the form and the matter, or of the matter itself. But only the parts of the form are parts of the formula, and the formula is of the 1036ᵃ universal; for 'being a circle' is the same as the circle, and 'being a soul' the same as the soul. But when we come to the concrete thing, e.g. *this* circle, i.e. one of the individual circles, whether perceptible or intelligible (I mean by intelligible circles the mathematical, and by [5] perceptible circles those of bronze and of wood),—of these there is no definition, but they are known by the aid of intuitive thinking or of perception; and when they pass out of this complete realization it is not clear whether they exist or not; but they are always stated and recognized by means of the universal formula. But matter is unknowable in itself. And [10] some matter is perceptible and some intelligible, perceptible matter being for instance bronze and wood and all matter that is changeable, and intelligible matter being that which is present in perceptible things not *qua* perceptible, i.e. the objects of mathematics.

We have stated, then, how matters stand with regard to whole and part, and their priority and posteriority. But when any one asks whether the right angle and the circle and the [15] animal are prior, or the things into which they are divided and of which they consist, i.e. the parts, we must meet the inquiry by saying that the question cannot be answered simply. For if even bare soul is the animal or the living thing, or the soul of each individual is the individual itself, and 'being a circle' is the circle, and 'being a right angle' and the essence of the right angle is the right angle, then the whole in one sense must be called posterior to the part in one sense, i.e. to the parts included in the [20] formula and to the parts of the individual right angle (for both the material right angle which is made of bronze, and that which is formed by individual lines, are posterior to their parts); while the immaterial right angle is posterior to the parts included in the formula, but prior to those included in the particular instance, and the question must not be answered simply. If, however, the soul is something different and is not identical with the animal, even so some parts must, as we have main-[25] tained, be called prior and others must not.

11

Another question is naturally raised, viz. what sort of parts belong to the form and what sort not to the form, but to the concrete thing. Yet if this is not plain it is not possible to define any thing; for definition is of the universal and of the form. If then it is not evident what sort [30] of parts are of the nature of matter and what sort are not, neither will the formula of the thing be evident. In the case of things which are found to occur in specifically different materials, as a circle may exist in bronze or stone or wood, it seems plain that these, the bronze or the stone, are no part of the essence of the circle, since it is found apart from them. [35] Of things which are *not* seen to exist

1036ᵇ apart, there is no reason why the same may not be true, just as if all circles that had ever been seen were of bronze; for none the less the bronze would be no part of the form; but it is hard to eliminate it in thought. E.g. the form of man is always found in flesh and bones and parts of this kind; are these then [5] also parts of the form and the formula? No, they are matter; but because man is not found also in other matters we are unable to perform the abstraction.

Since this is thought to be possible, but it is not clear *when* it is the case, some people already raise the question even in the case of the circle and the triangle, thinking that it is not right to define these by reference to lines and to [10] the continuous, but that all these are to the circle or the triangle as flesh and bones are to man, and bronze or stone to the statue; and they reduce all things to numbers, and they say the formula of 'line' is that of 'two'. And of those who assert the Ideas some make 'two' the [15] line-itself, and others make it the Form of the line; for in some cases they say the Form and that of which it is the Form are the same, e.g. 'two' and the Form of two; but in the case of 'line' they say this is no longer so.

It follows then that there is one Form for many things whose form is evidently different (a conclusion which confronted the Pythagoreans also); and it is possible to make one thing the Form-itself of all, and to hold that the oth- [20] ers are not Forms; but thus all things will be one.

We have pointed out, then, that the question of definitions contains some difficulty, and why this is so. And so to reduce all things thus to Forms and to eliminate the matter is useless labour; for some things surely are a particular form in a particular matter, or particular things in a particular state. And the comparison which Socrates the younger used to make [25] in the case of 'animal' is not sound; for it leads away from the truth, and makes one suppose that man can possibly exist without his parts, as the circle can without the bronze. But the case is not similar; for an animal is something perceptible, and it is not possible to define it without reference to movement—nor, therefore, without reference to the parts' being [30] in a certain state. For it is not a hand in any and every state that is a part of man, but only when it can fulfil its work, and therefore only when it is alive; if it is not alive it is not a part.

Regarding the objects of mathematics, why are the formulae of the parts not parts of the formulae of the wholes; e.g. why are not the semicircles included in the formula of the circle? It cannot be said, 'because these parts are perceptible things'; for they are not. But per- [35] haps this makes no difference; for even 1037ᵃ some things which are not perceptible must have matter; indeed there is some matter in everything which is not an essence and a bare form but a 'this'. The semicircles, then, will not be parts of the universal circle, but will be parts of the individual circles, as has been said before[1]; for while one kind of matter is perceptible, there is another which is intelligible.

[5] It is clear also that the soul is the primary substance and the body is matter, and man or animal is the compound of both taken universally; and 'Socrates' or 'Coriscus', if even the soul of Socrates may be called Socrates, has two meanings (for some mean by such a term the soul, and others mean the concrete thing), but if 'Socrates' or 'Coriscus' means simply this particular soul and this particular body, the individual is analogous to the universal in its composition.

[10] Whether there is, apart from the matter of such substances, another kind of matter, and one should look for some substance other than these, e.g. numbers or something of the sort, must be considered later.[2] For it is for the sake of this that we are trying to determine the nature of perceptible substances as well, since in a sense the inquiry about perceptible substances [15] is the work of physics, i.e. of second philosophy; for the physicist must come to know not only about the matter, but also about the substance expressed in the formula, and even more than about the other. And in the case of definitions, how the elements in the formula are parts of the definition, and why the definition is one formula (for clearly the thing is one, but in virtue of *what* is the thing one, although [20] it has parts?),—this must be considered later.[3]

What the essence is and in what sense it is independent, has been stated universally in a way which is true of every case, and also why the formula of the essence of some things contains the parts of the thing defined, while that of others does not. And we have stated that in [25] the formula of the substance the material parts will not be present (for they are not even parts of the substance in that sense, but of the

---
[1] 1035ᵃ 30-ᵇ 3. [2] Cf. XIII, XIV.
[3] Cf. VII. 12, VIII. 6.

concrete substance; but of *this* there is in a sense a formula, and in a sense there is not; for there is no formula of it with its matter, for this is indefinite, but there is a formula of it with reference to its primary substance—e.g. in the case of man the formula of the soul—, for the substance is the indwelling form, from which and the matter the so-called concrete substance is derived; e.g. concavity is a form of [30] this sort, for from this and the nose arise 'snub nose' and 'snubness'); but in the concrete substance, e.g. a snub nose or Callias, the matter also will be present. And we have stated that the essence and the thing itself are in some 1037ᵇ cases the same; i.e. in the case of primary substances, e.g. curvature and the essence of curvature, if this is primary. (By a 'primary' substance I mean one which does not imply the presence of something in something else, i.e. in something that underlies it which acts as matter.) But things which are of the nature of matter, or of wholes that include matter, are not the same as their essences, nor are acciden-[5] tal unities like that of 'Socrates' and 'musical'; for these are the same only by accident.

12

Now let us treat first of definition, in so far as we have not treated of it in the *Analytics*[1]; for the problem stated in them is useful for our inquiries concerning substance. I mean this prob-[10] lem:—wherein can consist the unity of that, the formula of which we call a definition, as for instance, in the case of man, 'two-footed animal'; for let this be the formula of man. Why, then, is this one, and not many, viz. 'animal' *and* 'two-footed'? For in the case of [15] 'man' and 'pale' there is a plurality when one term does not belong to the other, but a unity when it does belong and the subject, man, has a certain attribute; for then a unity is produced and we have 'the pale man'. In the present case, on the other hand, one does not share in the other; the genus is not thought to share in its differentiae (for then the same thing would share in contraries; for the differentiae [20] by which the genus is divided are contrary). And even if the genus does share in them, the same argument applies, since the differentiae present in man are many, e.g. endowed with feet, two-footed, featherless. Why are these one and not many? Not because they are present in one thing; for on this principle a unity can be made out of *all* the attributes of a thing. But surely all the attributes in the defi-[25] nition *must* be one; for the definition is a single formula and a formula of substance, so that it must be a formula of some one thing; for substance means a 'one' and a 'this', as we maintain.

We must first inquire about definitions reached by the method of divisions. There is nothing in the definition except the first-named [30] genus and the differentiae. The other genera are the first genus and along with this the differentiae that are taken with it, e.g. the first may be 'animal', the next 'animal which is two-footed', and again 'animal which is two-footed and featherless', and similarly if the definition 1038ᵃ includes more terms. And in general it makes no difference whether it includes many or few terms,—nor, therefore, whether it includes few or simply two; and of the two the one is differentia and the other genus; e.g. in 'two-footed animal' 'animal' is genus, and the other is differentia.

[5] If then the genus absolutely does not exist apart from the species-of-a-genus, or if it exists but exists as matter (for the voice is genus and matter, but its differentiae make the species, i.e. the letters, out of it), clearly the definition is the formula which comprises the differentiae.

But it is also necessary that the division be by the differentia *of the differentia;* e.g. 'endowed with feet' is a differentia of 'animal'; [10] again the differentia of 'animal endowed with feet' must be of it *qua* endowed with feet. Therefore we must not say, if we are to speak rightly, that of that which is endowed with feet one part has feathers and one is featherless (if we do this we do it through incapacity); we must divide it only into cloven-footed and not-cloven; for these are differentiae in the foot; cloven-footedness is a form of footedness. And [15] the process wants always to go on so till it reaches the species that contain no differences. And then there will be as many kinds of foot as there are differentiae, and the kinds of animals endowed with feet will be equal in number to the differentiae. If then this is so, clearly the *last* differentia will be the substance [20] of the thing and its definition, since it is not right to state the same things more than once in our definitions; for it is superfluous. And this does happen; for when we say 'animal endowed with feet and two-footed' we have said nothing other than 'animal having feet, having two feet'; and if we divide this by the proper division, we shall be saying the same thing more than once—as many times as there are differentiae.

---
[1] Cf. *Posterior Analytics*, II. 3-10, 13.

[25] If then a differentia of a differentia be taken at each step, one differentia—the last—will be the form and the substance; but if we divide according to accidental qualities, e.g. if we were to divide that which is endowed with feet into the white and the black, there will be as many differentiae as there are cuts. Therefore it is plain that the definition is the formula which contains the differentiae, or, according to [30] the right method, the last of these. This would be evident, if we were to change the order of such definitions, e.g. of that of man, saying 'animal which is two-footed and endowed with feet'; for 'endowed with feet' is superfluous when 'two-footed' has been said. But there is no order in the substance; for how are we to think the one element posterior and the other prior? Regarding the definitions, then, which are reached by the method of divisions, let this [35] suffice as our first attempt at stating their nature.

13

1038[b] Let us return to the subject of our inquiry, which is substance. As the substratum and the essence and the compound of these are called substance, so also is the universal. About two of these we have spoken; both about the essence[1] and about the substratum,[2] of which [5] we have said[3] that it underlies in two senses, either being a 'this'—which is the way in which an animal underlies its attributes—or as the matter underlies the complete reality. The universal also is thought by some to be in the fullest sense a cause, and a principle; therefore let us attack the discussion of this point also. For it seems impossible that any universal term should be the name of a substance. For firstly the substance of each thing is that which [10] is peculiar to it, which does not belong to anything else; but the universal is common, since that is called universal which is such as to belong to more than one thing. Of which individual then will this be the substance? Either of all or of none; but it cannot be the substance of all. And if it is to be the substance of one, this one will be the others also; for things whose substance is one and whose essence is one are themselves also one.

[15] Further, substance means that which is not predicable of a subject, but the universal is predicable of some subject always.

But perhaps the universal, while it cannot be substance in the way in which the essence is

---
[1] Chapters 4-6, 10-12.   [2] Chapter 3.
[3] 1029[a] 2-3, 23-4.

so, can be present in this; e.g. 'animal' can be present in 'man' and 'horse'. Then clearly it is a formula of the essence. And it makes no difference even if it is not a formula of everything that is in the substance; for none the less [20] the universal will be the substance of something, as 'man' is the substance of the individual man in whom it is present, so that the same result will follow once more; for the universal, e.g. 'animal', will be the substance of that in which it is present as something peculiar to it. And further it is impossible and absurd that the 'this', i.e. the substance, if it con-[25] sists of parts, should not consist of substances nor of what is a 'this', but of quality; for that which is not substance, i.e. the quality, will then be prior to substance and to the 'this'. Which is impossible; for neither in formula nor in time nor in coming to be can the modifications be prior to the substance; for then they will also be separable from it. Further, Socrates will contain a substance present in a substance, so that this will be the substance of two [30] things. And in general it follows, if man and such things are substance, that none of the elements in their formulae is the substance of anything, nor does it exist apart from the species or in anything else; I mean, for instance, that no 'animal' exists apart from the particular kinds of animal, nor does any other of the elements present in formulae exist apart.

If, then, we view the matter from these standpoints, it is plain that no universal attri-[35] bute is a substance, and this is plain also from the fact that no common predicate indi-1039[a] cates a 'this', but rather a 'such'. If not, many difficulties follow and especially the 'third man'.

The conclusion is evident also from the following consideration. A substance cannot consist of substances present in it in complete reality; for things that are thus in complete reality [5] two are never in complete reality one, though if they are *potentially* two, they can be one (e.g. the double line consists of two halves —potentially; for the complete realization of the halves divides them from one another); therefore if the substance is one, it will not consist of substances present in it and present in this way, which Democritus describes rightly; he says one thing cannot be made out of two [10] nor two out of one; for he identifies substances with his indivisible magnitudes. It is clear therefore that the same will hold good of number, if number is a synthesis of units, as is said by some; for two is either not one, or there is no unit present in it in complete reality. [*15*] But our result involves a difficulty. If no substance can consist of universals because a universal indicates a 'such', not a 'this', and if no substance can be composed of substances existing in complete reality, every substance would be incomposite, so that there would not even be a formula of any substance. But it is *thought* by all and was stated long ago[1] that it is either only, or primarily, substance that can [*20*] be defined; yet now it seems that not even substance can. There cannot, then, be a definition of anything; or in a sense there can be, and in a sense there cannot. And what we are saying will be plainer from what follows.[2]

14

It is clear also from these very facts what consequence confronts those who say the Ideas are substances capable of separate existence, and at [*25*] the same time make the Form consist of the genus and the differentiae. For if the Forms exist and 'animal' is present in 'man' and 'horse', it is either one and the same in number, or different. (In formula it is clearly one; for he who states the formula will go through the [*30*] same formula in either case.) If then there is a 'man-in-himself' who is a 'this' and exists apart, the parts also of which he consists, e.g. 'animal' and 'two-footed', must indicate 'thises', and be capable of separate existence, and substances; therefore 'animal', as well as 'man', must be of this sort.

Now (1) if the 'animal' in 'the horse' and in 'man' is one and the same, as you are with yourself, (*a*) how will the one in things that 1039[b] exist apart be one, and how will this 'animal' escape being divided even from itself?

Further, (*b*) if it is to share in 'two-footed' and 'many-footed', an impossible conclusion follows; for contrary attributes will belong at the same time to it although it is one and a 'this'. If it is not to share in them, what is the relation implied when one says the animal is two-footed or possessed of feet? But perhaps [*5*] the two things are 'put together' and are 'in contact', or are 'mixed'. Yet all these expressions are absurd.

But (2) suppose the Form to be different in each species. Then there will be practically an infinite number of things whose *substance* is 'animal'; for it is not by accident that 'man' has 'animal' for one of its elements. Further, many things will be 'animal-itself'. For (i) the 'animal' in each species will be the substance of [*10*] the species; for it is after nothing else that the species is called; if it were, that other would be an element in 'man', i.e. would be the genus of man. And further, (ii) all the elements of which 'man' is composed will be Ideas. None of them, then, will be the Idea of one thing and the substance of another; this is impossible. The 'animal', then, present in each species of animals will be animal-itself. Further, from what is this 'animal' in each species derived, and how will it be derived from animal-itself? [*15*] Or how can this 'animal', whose essence is simply animality, exist apart from animal-itself?

Further, (3) in the case of sensible things both these consequences and others still more absurd follow. If, then, these consequences are impossible, clearly there are not Forms of sensible things in the sense in which some maintain their existence.

15

[*20*] Since substance is of two kinds, the concrete thing and the formula (I mean that one kind of substance is the formula taken with the matter, while another kind is the formula in its generality), substances in the former sense are capable of destruction (for they are capable also of generation), but there is no destruction of the formula in the sense that it is ever in course of being destroyed (for there is no generation of it either; the being of house is not generated, [*25*] but only the being of *this* house), but without generation and destruction formulae are and are not; for it has been shown[3] that no one begets nor makes these. For this reason, also, there is neither definition of nor demonstration about sensible individual substances, because they have matter whose nature is such [*30*] that they are capable both of being and of not being; for which reason all the individual instances of them are destructible. If then demonstration is of necessary truths and definition is a scientific process, and if, just as knowledge cannot be sometimes knowledge and sometimes ignorance, but the state which varies thus is opinion, so too demonstration and definition cannot vary thus, but it is opinion that deals with that which can be otherwise than as it is, clearly there can neither be definition of nor demonstration about sensible individuals. For perishing things are obscure to those who have the relevant knowledge, when they have passed from our perception; and though the formulae remain

---

[1] Cf. 1031[a] 11-14. [2] Cf. VII. 15, VIII. 6. [3] Chapter 8.

in the soul unchanged, there will no longer be [5] either definition or demonstration. And so when one of the definition-mongers defines any individual, he must recognize that his definition may always be overthrown; for it is not possible to define such things.

Nor is it possible to define any Idea. For the Idea is, as its supporters say, an individual, and can exist apart; and the formula must con-[10]sist of words; and he who defines must not invent a word (for it would be unknown), but the established words are common to all the members of a class; these then must apply to something besides the thing defined; e.g. if one were defining you, he would say 'an animal which is lean' or 'pale', or something else which will apply also to some one other than you. If any one were to say that perhaps all the attributes taken apart may belong to many subjects, but together they belong only to this one, [15] we must reply first that they belong also to both the elements; e.g. 'two-footed animal' belongs to animal and to the two-footed. (And in the case of eternal entities this is even necessary, since the elements are prior to and parts of the compound; nay more, they can also exist apart, if 'man' can exist apart. For either [20] neither or both can. If, then, neither can, the genus will not exist apart from the various species; but if it does, the differentia will also.) Secondly, we must reply that 'animal' and 'two-footed' are prior in being to 'two-footed animal'; and things which are prior to others are not destroyed when the others are.

Again, if the Ideas consist of Ideas (as they must, since elements are simpler than the compound), it will be further necessary that the elements also of which the Idea consists, e.g. 'animal' and 'two-footed', should be predicated [25] of many subjects. If not, how will they come to be known? For there will then be an Idea which cannot be predicated of more subjects than one. But this is not thought possible —every Idea is thought to be capable of being shared.

As has been said,[1] then, the impossibility of defining individuals escapes notice in the case of eternal things, especially those which are unique, like the sun or the moon. For people [30] err not only by adding attributes whose removal the sun would survive, e.g. 'going round the earth' or 'night-hidden' (for from their view it follows that if it stands still or is visible, it will no longer be the sun; but it is strange if this is so; for 'the sun' means a cer-

[1] Cf. l. 17.

tain *substance*); but also by the mention of attributes which can belong to another subject; e.g. if another thing with the stated attributes comes into existence, clearly it will be a sun; 1040^b the formula therefore is general. But the sun was supposed to be an individual, like Cleon or Socrates. After all, why does not one of the supporters of the Ideas produce a definition of an Idea? It would become clear, if they tried, that what has now been said is true.

16

[5] Evidently even of the things that are thought to be substances, most are only potencies,—both the parts of animals (for none of them exists separately; and when they *are* separated, then too they exist, all of them, merely as matter) and earth and fire and air; for none of them is a unity, but as it were a mere heap, till they are worked up and some [10] unity is made out of them. One might most readily suppose the parts of living things and the parts of the soul nearly related to them to turn out to be both, i.e. existent in complete reality as well as in potency, because they have sources of movement in something in their joints; for which reason some animals live when divided. Yet all the parts must exist only potentially, when they are one and con-[15]tinuous by nature,—not by force or by growing into one, for such a phenomenon is an abnormality.

Since the term 'unity' is used like the term 'being', and the substance of that which is one is one, and things whose substance is numerically one are numerically one, evidently neither unity nor being can be the substance of things, just as being an element or a principle cannot [20] be the substance, but we ask what, then, the principle is, that we may reduce the thing to something more knowable. Now of these concepts 'being' and 'unity' are more substantial than 'principle' or 'element' or 'cause', but not even the former are substance, since in general nothing that is common is substance; for substance does not belong to anything but to itself and to that which has it, of which it is the [25] substance. Further, that which is one cannot be in many places at the same time, but that which is common is present in many places at the same time; so that clearly no universal exists apart from its individuals.

But those who say the Forms exist, in one respect are right, in giving the Forms separate existence, *if* they are substances; but in another respect they are not right, because they say the

[30] one over many is a Form. The reason for their doing this is that they cannot declare what are the substances of this sort, the imperishable substances which exist apart from the individual and sensible substances. They make them, then, the same in kind as the perishable things (for this kind of substance we know)—'man-himself' and 'horse-itself', adding to the sensible things the word 'itself'. 1041ª Yet even if we had not seen the stars, none the less, I suppose, would they have been eternal substances apart from those which we knew; so that now also if we do not know what non-sensible substances there are, yet it is doubtless necessary that there should *be* some.—Clearly, then, no universal term is the name of a substance, and no substance is com-[5] posed of substances.

17

Let us state what, i.e. what kind of thing, substance should be said to be, taking once more another starting-point; for perhaps from this we shall get a clear view also of that substance which exists apart from sensible substances. Since, then, substance is a principle and a cause, let us pursue it from this starting-point. [10] The 'why' is always sought in this form—'why does one thing attach to some other?' For to inquire why the musical man is a musical man, is either to inquire—as we have said—why the man is musical, or it is something else. Now 'why a thing is itself' is a meaningless in-[15] quiry (for ⟨to give meaning to the question 'why'⟩ the fact or the existence of the thing must already be evident—e.g. that the moon is eclipsed—but the fact that a thing is itself is the single reason and the single cause to be given in answer to all such questions as 'why the man is man, or the musician musical', unless one were to answer 'because each thing is inseparable from itself, and its being one just meant this'; this, however, is common to all things and is a short and easy way with the [20] question). But we *can* inquire why man is an animal of such and such a nature. This, then, is plain, that we are not inquiring why he who is a man is a man. We are inquiring, then, why something is predicable of something (that it is predicable must be clear; for if not, the inquiry is an inquiry into nothing). E.g. why does it thunder? This is the same as 'why is sound produced in the clouds?' Thus [25] the inquiry is about the predication of one thing of another. And why are these things, i.e. bricks and stones, a house? Plainly we are seeking the cause. And this is the essence (to speak abstractly), which in some cases is the end, e.g. perhaps in the case of a house or a [30] bed, and in some cases is the first mover; for this also is a cause. But while the efficient cause is sought in the case of genesis and destruction, the final cause is sought in the case of being also.

The object of the inquiry is most easily overlooked where one term is not expressly predicated of another (e.g. when we inquire 'what 1041ᵇ man is'), because we do not distinguish and do not say definitely that certain elements make up a certain whole. But we must articulate our meaning before we begin to inquire; if not, the inquiry is on the border-line between being a search for something and a search for nothing. Since we must have the existence of the thing as something given, clearly the question is *why* the matter is some definite thing; e.g. why are these materials a [5] house? Because that which was the essence of a house is present. And why is this individual thing, or this body having this form, a man? Therefore what we seek is the cause, i.e. the form, by reason of which the matter is some definite thing; and this is the substance of the thing. Evidently, then, in the case of [10] *simple* terms no inquiry nor teaching is possible; our attitude towards such things is other than that of inquiry.

Since that which is compounded out of something so that the whole is one, not like a heap but like a syllable,—now the syllable is not its elements, *ba* is not the same as *b* and *a*, nor is flesh fire and earth (for when these are separated the wholes, i.e. the flesh and the syllable, no longer exist, but the elements of the [15] syllable exist, and so do fire and earth); the syllable, then, is something—not only its elements (the vowel and the consonant) but also something else, and the flesh is not only fire and earth or the hot and the cold, but also something else:—if, then, that something must itself be either an element or composed of ele-[20] ments, (1) if it is an element the same argument will again apply; for flesh will consist of this and fire and earth and something still further, so that the process will go on to infinity. But (2) if it is a compound, clearly it will be a compound not of one but of more than one (or else that one will be the thing itself), so that again in this case we can use the same argument as in the case of flesh or of the [25] syllable. But it would seem that this 'other' is something, and not an element, and that it is the *cause* which makes *this* thing flesh and *that* a syllable. And similarly in all other cases. And this is the *substance* of each thing (for this is the primary cause of its being); and since, while some things are not substances, as many as are substances are formed in accordance with a nature of their own and by a proc- [30] ess of nature, their substance would seem to be this kind of 'nature', which is not an element but a principle. An *element,* on the other hand, is that into which a thing is divided and which is present in it as matter; e.g. *a* and *b* are the elements of the syllable.

BOOK VIII

1

1042ª WE must reckon up the results arising from what has been said, and compute the sum of them, and put the finishing touch to our [5] inquiry. We have said that the causes, principles, and elements of substances are the object of our search. And some substances are recognized by every one, but some have been advocated by particular schools. Those generally recognized are the natural substances, i.e. fire, earth, water, air, &c., the simple bodies; secondly, plants and their parts, and animals [10] and the parts of animals; and finally the physical universe and its parts; while some particular schools say that Forms and the objects of mathematics are substances. But there are arguments which lead to the conclusion that there are other substances, the essence and the substratum. Again, in another way the genus seems more substantial than the various spe- [15] cies, and the universal than the particulars. And with the universal and the genus the Ideas are connected; it is in virtue of the same argument that they are thought to be substances. And since the essence is substance, and the definition is a formula of the essence, for this reason we have discussed definition and essential predication. Since the definition is a formula, and a formula has parts, we had to [20] consider also with respect to the notion of 'part', what are parts of the substance and what are not, and whether the parts of the substance are also parts of the definition. Further, too, neither the universal nor the genus is a substance; we must inquire later into the Ideas and the objects of mathematics; for some say these are substances as well as the sensible substances.

But now let us resume the discussion of the [25] generally recognized substances. These are the sensible substances, and sensible substances all have matter. The substratum is substance, and this is in one sense the matter (and by matter I mean that which, not being a 'this' actually, is potentially a 'this'), and in another sense the formula or shape (that which being a 'this' can be separately formulated), and third- [30] ly the complex of these two, which alone is generated and destroyed, and is, without qualification, capable of separate existence; for of substances completely expressible in a formula some are separable and some are not.

But clearly matter also is substance; for in all the opposite changes that occur there is something which underlies the changes, e.g. in respect of place that which is now here and again [35] elsewhere, and in respect of increase that which is now of one size and again less or greater, and in respect of alteration that which is now healthy and again diseased; and sim- 1042ᵇ ilarly in respect of substance there is something that is now being generated and again being destroyed, and now underlies the process as a 'this' and again underlies it in respect of a privation of positive character. And in *this* change the others are involved. But in either one or two of the others this is not in- [5] volved; for it is not necessary if a thing has matter for change of place that it should also have matter for generation and destruction.

The difference between becoming in the full sense and becoming in a qualified sense has been stated in our physical works.[1]

2

Since the substance which exists as underlying and as matter is generally recognized, and this [10] is that which exists potentially, it remains for us to say what is the substance, in the sense of *actuality,* of sensible things. Democritus seems to think there are three kinds of difference between things; the underlying body, the matter, is one and the same, but they differ either in rhythm, i.e. shape, or in turning, i.e. position, or in inter-contact, i.e. order. But [15] evidently there are many differences; for instance, some things are characterized by the mode of composition of their matter, e.g. the things formed by blending, such as honey-

[1] Cf. *Physics,* 225ª 12-20; *On Generation and Corruption,* 317ª 17-31.

water; and others by being bound together, e.g. a bundle; and others by being glued together, e.g. a book; and others by being nailed together, e.g. a casket; and others in more than one of these ways; and others by position, e.g. threshold and lintel (for these differ by being [20] placed in a certain way); and others by time, e.g. dinner and breakfast; and others by place, e.g. the winds; and others by the affections proper to sensible things, e.g. hardness and softness, density and rarity, dryness and wetness; and some things by some of these qualities, others by them all, and in general some by excess and some by defect. Clearly, [25] then, the word 'is' has just as many meanings; a thing *is* a threshold because it lies in such and such a position, and its being means its lying in that position, while being ice means having been solidified in such and such a way. And the being of some things will be defined by *all* these qualities, because some parts of them are mixed, others are blended, others are [30] bound together, others are solidified, and others use the other differentiae; e.g. the hand or the foot requires such complex definition. We must grasp, then, the kinds of differentiae (for these will be the principles of the being of things), e.g. the things characterized by the more and the less, or by the dense and the rare, and by other such qualities; for all these are [35] forms of excess and defect. And anything that is characterized by shape or by smoothness and roughness is characterized by the straight and the curved. And for other things 1043ª their being will mean their being mixed, and their not being will mean the opposite.

It is clear, then, from these facts that, since its substance is the cause of each thing's being, we must seek in these differentiae what is the cause of the being of each of these things. Now none of these differentiae is substance, even when coupled with matter, yet it is what is [5] analogous to substance in each case; and as in substances that which is predicated of the matter is the actuality itself, in all other definitions also it is what most resembles full actuality. E.g. if we had to define a threshold, we should say 'wood or stone in such and such a position', and a house we should define as 'bricks and timbers in such and such a position' (or a purpose may exist as well in some cases), and if we had to define ice we should say 'water frozen or solidified in such and such [10] a way', and harmony is 'such and such a blending of high and low'; and similarly in all other cases.

Obviously, then, the actuality or the formula is different when the matter is different; for in some cases it is the composition, in others the mixing, and in others some other of the attributes we have named. And so, of the people who go in for defining, those who define a house as stones, bricks, and timbers are speak-[15] ing of the potential house, for these are the matter; but those who propose 'a receptacle to shelter chattels and living beings', or something of the sort, speak of the actuality. Those who combine both of these speak of the third kind of substance, which is composed of matter and form (for the formula that gives the differentiae seems to be an account of the form [20] or actuality, while that which gives the components is rather an account of the matter); and the same is true of the kind of definitions which Archytas used to accept; they are accounts of the combined form and matter. E.g. what is still weather? Absence of motion in a large expanse of air; air is the matter, and absence of motion is the actuality and sub-[25] stance. What is a calm? Smoothness of sea; the material substratum is the sea, and the actuality or shape is smoothness. It is obvious then, from what has been said, what sensible substance is and how it exists—one kind of it as matter, another as form or actuality, while the third kind is that which is composed of these two.

3

We must not fail to notice that sometimes it is [30] not clear whether a name means the composite substance, or the actuality or form, e.g. whether 'house' is a sign for the composite thing, 'a covering consisting of bricks and stones laid thus and thus', or for the actuality or form, 'a covering', and whether a line is 'twoness in length' or 'twoness', and whether [35] an animal is 'a soul in a body' or 'a soul'; for soul is the substance or actuality of some body. 'Animal' might even be applied to both, not as something definable by one formula, but as related to a single thing. But this question, while important for another purpose, is of no importance for the inquiry into sensible substance; for the essence certainly attaches to the form and the actuality. For 'soul' and 'to be soul' are the same, but 'to be man' and 'man' are not the same, unless even the bare soul is to be called man; and thus on one interpretation the thing is the same as its essence, and on another it is not.

[5] If we examine we find that the syllable

does not consist of the letters + juxtaposition, nor is the house bricks + juxtaposition. And this is right; for the juxtaposition or mixing does not consist of those things of which it is the juxtaposition or mixing. And the same is true in all other cases; e.g. if the threshold is characterized by its position, the position is not constituted by the threshold, but rather the [10] latter is constituted by the former. Nor is man animal + biped, but there must be something besides these, if these are matter,—something which is neither an element in the whole nor a compound, but is the substance; but this people eliminate, and state only the matter. If, then, this is the cause of the thing's being, and if the cause of its being is its substance, they will not be stating the substance itself.

[15] (This, then, must either be eternal or it must be destructible without being ever in course of being destroyed, and must have come to be without ever being in course of coming to be. But it has been proved and explained elsewhere[1] that no one makes or begets the form, but it is the individual that is made, i.e. the complex of form and matter that is generated. Whether the substances of destructible things can exist apart, is not yet at all clear; [20] except that obviously this is impossible in *some* cases—in the case of things which cannot exist apart from the individual instances, e.g. house or utensil. Perhaps, indeed, neither these things themselves, nor any of the other things which are not formed by nature, are substances at all; for one might say that the nature in natural objects is the only substance to be found in destructible things.)

Therefore the difficulty which used to be raised by the school of Antisthenes and other such uneducated people has a certain timeli-[25] ness. They said that the 'what' cannot be defined (for the definition so called is a 'long rigmarole') but of what *sort* a thing, e.g. silver, is, they thought it possible actually to explain, not saying what it is, but that it is like tin. Therefore one kind of substance can be defined and formulated, i.e. the composite kind, wheth-[30] er it be perceptible or intelligible; but the primary parts of which this consists cannot be defined, since a definitory formula predicates something of something, and one part of the definition must play the part of matter and the other that of form.

It is also obvious that, if substances are in a sense numbers, they are so in this sense and not, as some say, as numbers of units. For a

[1] Cf. VII. 8.

definition is a sort of number; for (1) it is [35] divisible, and into indivisible parts (for definitory formulae are not infinite), and number also is of this nature. And (2) as, when one of the parts of which a number consists has been taken from or added to the number, it is no longer the same number, but a different one, even if it is the very smallest part that has been **1044ª** taken away or added, so the definition and the essence will no longer remain when anything has been taken away or added. And (3) the number must be something in virtue of which it is one, and this these thinkers cannot state, what makes it one, if it is one (for either it is not one but a sort of heap, or if it is, we ought to say what it is that makes one out of [5] many); and the definition is one, but similarly they cannot say what makes *it* one. And this is a natural result; for the same reason is applicable, and substance is one in the sense which we have explained, and not, as some say, by being a sort of unit or point; each is a complete reality and a definite nature. And [10] (4) as number does not admit of the more and the less, neither does substance, in the sense of form, but if any substance does, it is only the substance which involves matter. Let this, then, suffice for an account of the generation and destruction of so-called substances—in what sense it is possible and in what sense impossible—and of the reduction of things to number.

4

[15] Regarding material substance we must not forget that even if all things come from the same first cause or have the same things for their first causes, and if the same matter serves as starting-point for their generation, yet there is a matter proper to each, e.g. for phlegm the sweet or the fat, and for bile the bitter, or something else; though perhaps these [20] come from the same original matter. And there come to be several matters for the same thing, when the one matter is matter for the other; e.g. phlegm comes from the fat and from the sweet, if the fat comes from the sweet; and it comes from bile by analysis of the bile into its ultimate matter. For one thing comes from another in two senses, either because it will be found at a later stage, or because it is produced if the other is analysed into its orig-[25] inal constituents. When the matter is one, different things may be produced owing to difference in the moving cause; e.g. from wood may be made both a chest and a bed. But *some*

different things must have their matter different; e.g. a saw could not be made of wood, nor is this in the power of the moving cause; for it could not make a saw of wool or of wood. But if, as a matter of fact, the same thing can be [30] made of different material, clearly the art, i.e. the moving principle, is the same; for if both the matter and the moving cause were different, the product would be so too.

When one inquires into the cause of something, one should, since 'causes' are spoken of in several senses, state all the possible causes. E.g. what is the material cause of man? Shall [35] we say 'the menstrual fluid'? What is the moving cause? Shall we say 'the seed'? The formal cause? His essence. The final cause? His end. But perhaps the latter two are the **1044ᵇ** same.—It is the proximate causes we must state. What is the material cause? We must name not fire or earth, but the matter peculiar to the thing.

Regarding the substances that are natural and generable, *if* the causes are really these and of this number and we have to learn the causes, [5] we must inquire thus, if we are to inquire rightly. But in the case of natural but *eternal* substances another account must be given. For perhaps some have no matter, or not matter of this sort but only such as can be moved in respect of place. Nor does matter belong to those things which exist by nature but are not substances; their substratum is the *substance*. E.g. [10] what is the cause of eclipse? What is its matter? There is none; the *moon* is that which suffers eclipse. What is the moving cause which extinguished the light? The earth. The final cause perhaps does not exist. The formal principle is the definitory formula, but this is obscure if it does not include the cause. E.g. what is eclipse? Deprivation of light. But if we add 'by the earth's coming in between', this is [15] the formula which includes the cause. In the case of sleep it is not clear what it is that proximately has this affection. Shall we say that it is the animal? Yes, but the animal in virtue of what, i.e. what is the proximate subject? The heart or some other part. Next, by what is it produced? Next, what is the affection —that of the proximate subject, not of the whole animal? Shall we say that it is immobility of such and such a kind? Yes, but to what [20] process in the proximate subject is this due?

5

Since some things are and are not, without coming to be and ceasing to be, e.g. points, if they can be said to *be,* and in general forms (for it is not 'white' that comes to be, but the wood comes to be white, if everything that comes to be comes from something and comes to be something), not all contraries can come [25] from one another, but it is in different senses that a pale man comes from a dark man, and pale comes from dark. Nor has everything matter, but only those things which come to be and change into one another. Those things which, without ever being in course of changing, are or are not, have no matter.

There is difficulty in the question how the [30] matter of each thing is related to its contrary states. E.g. if the body is potentially healthy, and disease is contrary to health, is it potentially both healthy and diseased? And is water potentially wine and vinegar? We answer that it is the matter of one in virtue of its positive state and its form, and of the other in virtue of the privation of its positive state and the corruption of it contrary to its nature. It is also hard to say why wine is not said to be the matter of vinegar nor potentially vinegar [35] (though vinegar is produced from it), and why a living man is not said to be potentially dead. In fact they are not, but the corruptions in question are accidental, and it is **1045ᵃ** the *matter* of the animal that is itself in virtue of its corruption the potency and matter of a corpse, and it is water that is the matter of vinegar. For the corpse comes from the animal, and vinegar from wine, as night from day. And *all* the things which change thus into one another must go back to their matter; e.g. if from a corpse is produced an animal, the corpse first goes back to its matter, and only [5] then becomes an animal; and vinegar first goes back to water, and only then becomes wine.

6

To return to the difficulty which has been stated[1] with respect both to definitions and to numbers, what is the cause of their unity? In the case of all things which have several parts and in which the totality is not, as it were, a mere heap, but the whole is something besides [10] the parts, there is a cause; for even in bodies contact is the cause of unity in some cases, and in others viscosity or some other such quality. And a definition is a set of words which is one not by being connected together, like the *Iliad,* but by dealing with one object. —What then, is it that makes man one; why is

[1] Cf. vii. 12, viii. 1044ᵃ 2-6.

he one and not many, e.g. animal + biped, es-
[15] pecially if there are, as some say, an animal-itself and a biped-itself? Why are not those Forms themselves the man, so that men would exist by participation not in man, nor in one Form, but in two, animal and biped, and in general man would be not one but more than one thing, animal and biped?
[20] Clearly, then, if people proceed thus in their usual manner of definition and speech, they cannot explain and solve the difficulty. But if, as we say, one element is matter and another is form, and one is potentially and the [25] other actually, the question will no longer be thought a difficulty. For this difficulty is the same as would arise if 'round bronze' were the definition of 'cloak'; for this word would be a sign of the definitory formula, so that the question is, what is the cause of the unity of 'round' and 'bronze'? The difficulty disappears, because the one is matter, the other form. [30] What, then, causes this—that which was potentially to be actually—except, in the case of things which are generated, the agent? For there is no other cause of the potential sphere's becoming actually a sphere, but this was the essence of either. Of matter some is intelligible, some perceptible, and in a formula there is al-[35] ways an element of matter as well as one of actuality; e.g. the circle is 'a plane figure'. But of the things which have no matter, either intelligible or perceptible, each is by its nature **1045ᵇ** essentially a kind of unity, as it is essentially a kind of being—individual substance, quality, or quantity (and so neither 'existent' nor 'one' is present in their definitions), and the essence of each of them is by its very nature a kind of unity as it is a kind of being—and so none of these has any reason outside itself, [5] for being one, nor for being a kind of being; for each is by its nature a kind of being and a kind of unity, not as being in the genus 'being' or 'one' nor in the sense that being and unity can exist apart from particulars.

Owing to the difficulty about unity some speak of 'participation', and raise the question, what is the cause of participation and what is it to participate; and others speak of 'com-[10] munion', as Lycophron says knowledge is a communion of knowing with the soul; and others say life is a 'composition' or 'connexion' of soul with body. Yet the same account applies to all cases; for being healthy, too, will on this showing be either a 'communion' or a 'connexion' or a 'composition' of soul and health, and the fact that the bronze is a triangle will be a 'composition' of bronze and triangle, [15] and the fact that a thing is white will be a 'composition' of surface and whiteness. The reason is that people look for a unifying formula, and a difference, between potency and complete reality. But, as has been said,[2] the proximate matter and the form are one and the same thing, the one potentially, and the other actually. Therefore it is like asking what in general is the cause of unity and of a thing's [20] being one; for each thing is a unity, and the potential and the actual are somehow one. Therefore there is no other cause here unless there is something which caused the movement from potency into actuality. And all things which have *no* matter are *without qualification* essentially unities.

BOOK IX

I

WE have treated of that which *is* primarily and to which all the other categories of being are referred—i.e. of substance. For it is in virtue of the concept of substance that the others [30] also are said to be—quantity and quality and the like; for all will be found to involve the concept of substance, as we said in the first part of our work.[1] And since 'being' is in one way divided into individual thing, quality, and quantity, and is in another way distinguished in respect of potency and complete reality, and of function, let us now add a discussion of po-[35] tency and complete reality. And first let us explain potency in the strictest sense, which **1046ᵃ** is, however, not the most *useful* for our present purpose. For potency and actuality extend beyond the cases that involve a reference to motion. But when we have spoken of this first kind, we shall in our discussions of actuality[3] explain the other kinds of potency as well.

We have pointed out elsewhere[4] that 'potency' and the word 'can' have several senses. [5] Of these we may neglect all the potencies that are so called by an equivocation. For some are called so by analogy, as in geometry we say one thing is or is not a 'power' of another by virtue of the presence or absence of some rela-

---

[1] Cf. VII. 1.
[2] Cf. ᵃ 23-33.
[3] Cf. IX, 1048ᵃ 27-ᵇ 6.
[4] Cf. V. 12.

tion between them. But all potencies that conform to the same type are originative sources [10] of some kind, and are called potencies in reference to one primary kind of potency, which is an originative source of change in another thing or in the thing itself *qua* other. For one kind is a potency of being acted on, i.e. the originative source, in the very thing acted on, of its being passively changed by another thing or by itself *qua* other; and another kind is a state of insusceptibility to change for the worse and to destruction by another thing or by the thing itself *qua* other by virtue [15] of an originative source of change. In all these definitions is implied the formula of potency in the primary sense.—And again these so-called potencies are potencies either of merely acting or being acted on, or of acting or being acted on *well,* so that even in the formulae of the latter the formulae of the prior kinds of potency are somehow implied.

Obviously, then, in a sense the potency of [20] acting and of being acted on is one (for a thing may be 'capable' either because it can itself be acted on or because something else can be acted on by it), but in a sense the potencies are different. For the one is in the thing acted on; it is because it contains a certain originative source, and because even the matter is an originative source, that the thing acted on is acted on, and one thing by one, another by another; for that which is oily can be burnt, and that which yields in a particular way can [25] be crushed; and similarly in all other cases. But the other potency is in the agent, e.g. heat and the art of building are present, one in that which can produce heat and the other in the man who can build. And so, in so far as a thing is an organic unity, it cannot be acted on by itself; for it is one and not two different things. And 'impotence' and 'impotent' stand for the privation which is contrary to [30] potency of this sort, so that every potency belongs to the same subject and refers to the same process as a corresponding impotence. Privation has several senses; for it means (1) that which has not a certain quality and (2) that which might naturally have it but has not it, either (*a*) in general or (*b*) when it might naturally have it, and either (*a*) in some particular way, e.g. when it has not it completely, or (*β*) when it has not it at all. And in certain [35] cases if things which naturally have a quality lose it by violence, we say they have suffered privation.

2

Since some such originative sources are present in soulless things, and others in things possessed of soul, and in soul, and in the rational part of the soul, clearly some potencies will be non-rational and some will be accompanied by a rational formula. This is why all arts, i.e. all productive forms of knowledge, are potencies; they are originative sources of change in another thing or in the artist himself considered as other.

And each of those which are accompanied by [5] a rational formula is alike capable of contrary effects, but one non-rational power produces one effect; e.g. the hot is capable only of heating, but the medical art can produce both disease and health. The reason is that science is a rational formula, and the same rational formula explains a thing and its privation, only not in the same way; and in a sense it applies to both, but in a sense it applies rather to the [10] positive fact. Therefore such sciences must deal with contraries, but with one in virtue of their own nature and with the other not in virtue of their nature; for the rational formula applies to one object in virtue of that object's nature, and to the other, in a sense, accidentally. For it is by denial and removal that it exhibits the contrary; for the contrary is the primary privation, and this is the removal of [15] the positive term. Now since contraries do not occur in the same thing, but science is a potency which depends on the possession of a rational formula, and the soul possesses an originative source of movement; therefore, while the wholesome produces only health and the calorific only heat and the frigorific only cold, the scientific man produces both the contrary [20] effects. For the rational formula is one which applies to both, though not in the same way, and it is in a soul which possesses an originative source of movement; so that the soul will start both processes from the same originative source, having linked them up with the same thing. And so the things whose potency is according to a rational formula act contrariwise to the things whose potency is non-rational; for the products of the former are included under one originative source, the rational formula.

[25] It is obvious also that the potency of merely doing a thing or having it done to one is implied in that of doing it or having it done *well,* but the latter is not always implied in the former: for he who does a thing well must

also do it, but he who does it merely need not also do it well.

3

There are some who say, as the Megaric school does, that a thing 'can' act only when it is acting, and when it is not acting it 'cannot' act, [30] e.g. that he who is not building cannot build, but only he who is building, when he is building; and so in all other cases. It is not hard to see the absurdities that attend this view.

For it is clear that on this view a man will not be a builder unless he is building (for to be a builder is to be able to build), and so with [35] the other arts. If, then, it is impossible to have such arts if one has not at some time learnt and acquired them, and it is then impossible not to have them if one has not some-1047ª time lost them (either by forgetfulness or by some accident or by time; for it cannot be by the destruction of the *object,* for that lasts for ever), a man will not have the art when he has ceased to use it, and yet he may immediately build again; how then will he have got the art? And similarly with regard to [5] lifeless things; nothing will be either cold or hot or sweet or perceptible at all if people are not perceiving it; so that the upholders of this view will have to maintain the doctrine of Protagoras. But, indeed, nothing will even have perception if it is not perceiving, i.e. exercising its perception. If, then, that is blind which has not sight though it would naturally have it, when it would naturally have it and when it still exists, the same people will be blind many times in the day—and deaf too. [10] Again, if that which is deprived of potency is incapable, that which is not happening will be incapable of happening; but he who says of that which is incapable of happening either that it is or that it will be will say what is untrue; for this is what incapacity meant. Therefore these views do away with both move-[15] ment and becoming. For that which stands will always stand, and that which sits will always sit, since if it is sitting it will not get up; for that which, as we are told, cannot get up will be incapable of getting up. But we cannot say this, so that evidently potency and actuality are different (but these views make potency and actuality the same, and so it is no [20] small thing they are seeking to annihilate), so that it is possible that a thing may be capable of being and not *be,* and capable of not being and yet *be,* and similarly with the other kinds of predicate; it may be capable of walking and yet not walk, or capable of not walking and yet walk. And a thing is capable of doing something if there will be nothing im-[25] possible in its having the actuality of that of which it is said to have the capacity. I mean, for instance, if a thing is capable of sitting and it is open to it to sit, there will be nothing impossible in its actually sitting; and similarly if it is capable of being moved or moving, or of standing or making to stand, or of being or coming to be, or of not being or not coming to be.

[30] The word 'actuality', which we connect with 'complete reality', has, in the main, been extended from movements to other things; for actuality in the strict sense is thought to be identical with movement. And so people do not assign movement to non-existent things, though they do assign some other predicates. E.g. they say that non-existent things are objects of [35] thought and desire, but not that they are moved; and this because, while *ex hypothesi* they do not actually exist, they would have to exist actually if they were moved. For 1047ᵇ of non-existent things some exist potentially; but they do not *exist,* because they do not exist in complete reality.

4

If what we have described[1] is identical with the capable or convertible with it, evidently it cannot be true to say 'this is capable of being [5] but will not be', which would imply that the things *in*capable of being would on this showing vanish. Suppose, for instance, that a man—one who did not take account of that which is incapable of being—were to say that the diagonal of the square is capable of being measured but will not be measured, because a thing may well be capable of being or coming to be, and yet not be or be about to be. But from the premisses this necessarily follows, that if [10] we actually supposed that which is not, but is capable of being, to be or to have come to be, there will be nothing impossible in this; but the result *will* be impossible, for the measuring of the diagonal is impossible. For the false and the impossible are *not* the same; that you are standing now is false, but that you should be standing is not impossible.

At the same time it is clear that if, when *A* [15] is real, *B* must be real, then, when *A* is possible, *B* also must be possible. For if *B* need not be possible, there is nothing to prevent its not being possible. Now let *A* be supposed pos-

---
[1] Cf. 1047ª 24-26.

sible. Then, when A was possible, we agreed that nothing impossible followed if A were supposed to be real; and then B must of course [20] be real. But we supposed B to be impossible. Let it be impossible then. If, then, B is impossible, A also must be so. But the first *was* supposed impossible; therefore the second also is impossible. If, then, A is possible, B also will be possible, if they were so related that if A is real, B must be real. If, then, A and B [25] being thus related, B is not possible on this condition, A and B will not be related as was supposed. And if when A is possible, B must be possible, then if A is real, B also must be real. For to say that B must be possible, if A is possible, means this, that if A is real both at the time when and in the way in which it was supposed capable of being real, B also must [30] then and in that way be real.

5

As all potencies are either innate, like the senses, or come by practice, like the power of playing the flute, or by learning, like artistic power, those which come by practice or by rational formula we must acquire by previous exercise but this is not necessary with those which are not of this nature and which imply passivity.
[35] Since that which is 'capable' is capable of something and at some time in some way (with 1048ᵃ all the other qualifications which must be present in the definition), and since some things can produce change according to a rational formula and their potencies involve such a formula, while other things are nonrational and their potencies are non-rational, and the former potencies must be in a living [5] thing, while the latter can be both in the living and in the lifeless; as regards potencies of the latter kind, when the agent and the patient meet in the way appropriate to the potency in question, the one must act and the other be acted on, but with the former kind of potency this is not necessary. For the nonrational potencies are all productive of one effect each, but the rational produce contrary effects, so that if they produced their effects necessarily they would produce contrary effects [10] at the same time; but this is impossible. There must, then, be something else that decides; I mean by this, desire or will. For whichever of two things the animal desires decisively, it will do, when it is present, and meets the passive object, in the way appropriate to the potency in question. Therefore everything which has a rational potency, when it desires that for which it has a potency and in the circumstances in which it has the potency, [15] must do this. And it has the potency in question when the passive object is present and is in a certain state; if not it will not be able to act. (To add the qualification 'if nothing external prevents it' is not further necessary; for it has the potency on the terms on which this is a potency of acting, and it is this not in all circumstances but on certain conditions, among which will be the exclusion of external [20] hindrances; for these are barred by some of the positive qualifications.) And so even if one has a rational wish, or an appetite, to do two things or contrary things at the same time, one will not do them; for it is not on these terms that one has the potency for them, nor is it a potency of doing both at the same time, since one will do the things which it is a potency of doing, on the terms on which one has the potency.

6

[25] Since we have treated[1] of the kind of potency which is related to movement, let us discuss actuality—what, and what kind of thing, actuality is. For in the course of our analysis it will also become clear, with regard to the potential, that we not only ascribe potency to that whose nature it is to move something else, or to be moved by something else, either without qualification or in some particular way, but also use the word in another sense, which is the reason of the inquiry [30] in the course of which we have discussed these previous senses also. Actuality, then, is the existence of a thing not in the way which we express by 'potentially'; we say that potentially, for instance, a statue of Hermes is in the block of wood and the half-line is in the whole, because it might be separated out, and we call even the man who is not studying a man of science, if he is capable of studying; [35] the thing that stands in contrast to each of these exists actually. Our meaning can be seen in the particular cases by induction, and we must not seek a definition of everything but be content to grasp the analogy, that it is as that which is building is to that which is cap-1048ᵇ able of building, and the waking to the sleeping, and that which is seeing to that which has its eyes shut but has sight, and that which has been shaped out of the matter to the matter, and that which has been wrought up to the

[1] Cf. IX. 1-5.

unwrought. Let actuality be defined by one [5] member of this antithesis, and the potential by the other. But all things are not said in the *same sense* to exist actually, but only by analogy —as *A* is in *B* or to *B*, *C* is in *D* or to *D*; for some are as movement to potency, and the others as substance to some sort of matter.

But also the infinite and the void and all [10] similar things are said to exist potentially and actually in a different sense from that which applies to many other things, e.g. to that which sees or walks or is seen. For of the latter class these predicates can at some time be also truly asserted without qualification; for the seen is so called sometimes because it is being seen, sometimes because it is capable of being seen. But the infinite does not exist potentially in the sense that it will ever actually have separate existence; it exists po- [15] tentially only for knowledge. For the fact that the process of dividing never comes to an end ensures that this activity exists potentially, but not that the infinite exists separately.

Since of the actions which have a limit none is an end but all are relative to the end, e.g. the removing of fat, or fat-removal, and the [20] bodily parts themselves when one is making them thin are in movement in this way (i.e. without being already that at which the movement aims), this is not an action or at least not a complete one (for it is not an end); but that movement in which the end is present is an action. E.g. at the same time we are seeing and have seen, are understanding and have understood, are thinking and have thought (while it is not true that at the same time we are learning and have learnt, or are being cured [25] and have been cured). At the same time we are living well and have lived well, and are happy and have been happy. If not, the process would have had sometime to cease, as the process of making thin ceases: but, as things are, it does not cease; we are living and have lived. Of these processes, then, we must call the one set movements, and the other actualities. For every movement is incomplete—making thin, learning, walking, building; [30] these are movements, and incomplete at that. For it is not true that at the same time a thing is walking and has walked, or is building and has built, or is coming to be and has come to be, or is being moved and has been moved, but what is being moved is different from what has been moved, and what is moving from what has moved. But it is the same thing that at the same time has seen and is seeing, or is thinking and has thought. The latter sort of process, then, I call an actuality, and the former a movement.

7

[35] What, and what kind of thing, the actual is, may be taken as explained by these and similar considerations. But we must distinguish when a thing exists potentially and when it does not; for it is not at any and every time. 1049ª E.g. is earth potentially a man? No— but rather when it has already become seed, and perhaps not even then. It is just as it is with being healed; not everything can be healed by the medical art or by luck, but there is a certain kind of thing which is capable of it, and only this is potentially healthy. And (1) [5] the delimiting mark of that which as a result of *thought* comes to exist in complete reality from having existed potentially is that if the agent has willed it it comes to pass if nothing external hinders, while the condition on the other side—viz. in that which is healed —is that nothing in it hinders the result. It is on similar terms that we have what is potentially a house; if nothing in the thing acted on [10] —i.e. in the matter—prevents it from becoming a house, and if there is nothing which must be added or taken away or changed, this is potentially a house; and the same is true of all other things the source of whose becoming is external. And (2) in the cases in which the source of the becoming is in the very thing which comes to be, a thing is potentially all those things which it will be of itself if nothing external hinders it. E.g. the seed is not yet potentially a man; for it must be deposited in some- [15] thing other than itself and undergo a change. But when through its own motive principle it has already got such and such attributes, in this state it is already potentially a man; while in the former state it needs another motive principle, just as earth is not yet potentially a statue (for it must first change in order to become brass.)

It seems that when we call a thing not something else but 'thaten'—e.g. a casket is not [20] 'wood' but 'wooden', and wood is not 'earth' but 'earthen', and again earth will illustrate our point if it is similarly not something else but 'thaten'—that other thing is always potentially (in the full sense of that word) the thing which comes after it in this series. E.g. a casket is not 'earthen' nor 'earth', but 'wooden'; for this is potentially a casket and this is the matter of a casket, wood in general of a casket in general, and this particular wood of this particular casket. And if there is a first thing, which is no longer, in reference to something [25] else, called 'thaten', this is prime matter; e.g. if earth is 'airy' and air is not 'fire' but 'fiery', fire is prime matter, which is not a 'this'. For the subject or substratum is differentiated by being a 'this' or not being one; i.e. the substratum of *modifications* is, e.g. a man, i.e. a body and a soul, while the modification is [30] 'musical' or 'pale'. (The subject is called, when music comes to be present in it, not 'music' but 'musical', and the man is not 'paleness' but 'pale', and not 'ambulation' or 'movement' but 'walking' or 'moving',—which is akin to the 'thaten'.) Wherever this is so, then, the ultimate subject is a substance; but when this is not so but the predicate is a *form* [35] and a 'this', the ultimate subject is matter and material substance. And it is only right that 'thaten' should be used with reference **1049ᵇ** both to the matter and to the accidents; for both are indeterminates.

We have stated, then, when a thing is to be said to exist potentially and when it is not.

8

From our discussion of the various senses of [5] 'prior',[1] it is clear that actuality is prior to potency. And I mean by potency not only that definite kind which is said to be a principle of change in another thing or in the thing itself regarded as other, but in general every principle of movement or of rest. For nature also is in the same genus as potency; for it is a [10] principle of movement—not, however, in something else but in the thing itself *qua* itself. To all such potency, then, actuality is prior both in formula and in substantiality; and in time it is prior in one sense, and in another not.

(1) Clearly it is prior in formula; for that which is in the primary sense potential is potential because it is possible for it to become active; e.g. I mean by 'capable of building' that [15] which can build, and by 'capable of seeing' that which can see, and by 'visible' that which can be seen. And the same account applies to all other cases, so that the formula and the knowledge of the one must precede the knowledge of the other.

(2) In time it is prior in this sense: the actual which is identical in species though not in number with a potentially existing thing is prior to it. I mean that to this particular man [20] who now exists actually and to the corn

[1] Cf. v. 11.

and to the seeing subject the matter and the seed and that which is capable of seeing, which are potentially a man and corn and seeing, but not yet actually so, are prior in time; but prior in time to these are other actually existing things, from which they were produced. For from the potentially existing the actually existing is always produced by an actually existing [25] thing, e.g. man from man, musician by musician; there is always a first mover, and the mover already exists actually. We have said in our account of substance[2] that everything that is produced is something produced from something and by something, and that the same in species as it.

This is why it is thought impossible to be a [30] builder if one has built nothing or a harper if one has never played the harp; for he who learns to play the harp learns to play it by playing it, and all other learners do similarly. And thence arose the sophistical quibble, that one who does not possess a science will be doing that which is the object of the science; for he who is learning it does not possess it. [35] But since, of that which is coming to be, some part must have come to be, and, of that which, in general, is changing, some part must have changed (this is shown in the treatise on **1050ᵃ** movement[3]), he who is learning must, it would seem, possess some part of the science. But *here* too, then, it is clear that actuality is in this sense also, viz. in order of generation and of time, prior to potency.

But (3) it is also prior in substantiality; firstly, (*a*) because the things that are posterior in becoming are prior in form and in sub- [5] stantiality (e.g. man is prior to boy and human being to seed; for the one already has its form, and the other has not), and because everything that comes to be moves towards a principle, i.e. an end (for that for the sake of which a thing is, is its principle, and the becoming is for the sake of the end), and the actuality is the end, and it is for the sake of [10] this that the potency is acquired. For animals do not see in order that they may have sight, but they have sight that they may see. And similarly men have the art of building that they may build, and theoretical science that they may theorize; but they do not theorize that they may have theoretical science, except those who are learning by practice; and these do not theorize except in a limited sense, or [15] because they have no need to theorize. Further, matter exists in a potential state, just

[2] Cf. vii. 7, 8.   [3] Cf. *Physics*, vi. 6.

because it may come to its form; and when it exists *actually,* then it is in its form. And the same holds good in all cases, even those in which the end is a movement. And so, as teachers think they have achieved their end when they have exhibited the pupil at work, nature does likewise. For if this is not the case, [20] we shall have Pauson's Hermes over again, since it will be hard to say about the knowledge, as about the figure in the picture, whether it is within or without. For the action is the end, and the actuality is the action. And so even the *word* 'actuality' is derived from 'action', and points to the complete reality.

And while in some cases the exercise is the ultimate thing (e.g. in sight the ultimate thing [25] is seeing, and no other product besides this results from sight), but from some things a product follows (e.g. from the art of building there results a house as well as the act of building), yet none the less the act is in the former case the end and in the latter more of an end than the potency is. For the act of building is realized in the thing that is being built, and comes to be, and is, at the same time as the house.

[30] Where, then, the result is something apart from the exercise, the actuality is in the thing that is being made, e.g. the act of building is in the thing that is being built and that of weaving in the thing that is being woven, and similarly in all other cases, and in general the movement is in the thing that is being moved; but where there is no product apart [35] from the actuality, the actuality is present in the agents, e.g. the act of seeing is in the seeing subject and that of theorizing in the theorizing subject and the life is in the soul 1050ᵇ (and therefore well-being also; for it is a certain kind of life).

Obviously, therefore, the substance or form is actuality. According to this argument, then, it is obvious that actuality is prior in substantial being to potency; and as we have said,[1] one actuality always precedes another in time right [5] back to the actuality of the eternal prime mover.

But (*b*) actuality is prior in a stricter sense also; for eternal things are prior in substance to perishable things, and no eternal thing exists potentially. The reason is this. Every potency is at one and the same time a potency of the opposite; for, while that which is not capable [10] of being present in a subject cannot be present, everything that is capable of being may possibly not be actual. That, then, which is capable of being may either be or not be; the same thing, then, is capable both of being and of not being. And that which is capable of not being may possibly not be; and that which may possibly not be is perishable, either in the full sense, or in the precise sense in which it is [15] said that it possibly may not be, i.e. in respect either of place or of quantity or quality; 'in the full sense' means 'in respect of substance'. Nothing, then, which is in the full sense imperishable is in the full sense potentially existent (though there is nothing to prevent its being so in some respect, e.g. potentially of a certain quality or in a certain place); all imperishable things, then, exist actually. Nor can anything which is of *necessity* exist potentially; yet these things are primary; for if these did not exist, nothing would exist. Nor [20] does eternal movement, if there be such, exist potentially; and, if there is an eternal *mobile,* it is not in motion in virtue of a potentiality, except in respect of 'whence' and 'whither' (there is nothing to prevent its having matter which makes it capable of movement in various directions). And so the sun and the stars and the whole heaven are ever active, and there is no fear that they may sometime stand still, as the natural philosophers fear they may. Nor do they tire in this activity; for movement [25] is not for them, as it is for perishable things, connected with the potentiality for opposites, so that the continuity of the movement should be laborious; for it is that kind of substance which is matter and potency, not actuality, that causes this.

Imperishable things are imitated by those that are involved in change, e.g. earth and fire. For these also are ever active; for they have their movement of themselves and in them- [30] selves. But the other potencies, according to our previous discussion,[2] are all potencies for opposites; for that which can move another in this way can also move it not in this way, i.e. if it acts according to a rational formula; and the same *non-rational* potencies will produce opposite results by their presence or absence.

[35] If, then, there are any entities or substances such as the dialecticians say the Ideas are, there must be something much more scientific than science-itself and something more 1051ᵃ mobile than movement-itself; for these will be more of the nature of actualities, while

---
[1] 1049ᵇ 17-29.
[2] Cf. ᵇ 8-12.

science-itself and movement-itself are potencies for these.

Obviously, then, actuality is prior both to potency and to every principle of change.

9

That the actuality is also better and more valuable than the good potency is evident from the following argument. Everything of which we [5] say that it can do something, is alike capable of contraries, e.g. that of which we say that it can be well is the same as that which can be ill, and has both potencies at once; for the same potency is a potency of health and illness, of rest and motion, of building and throwing down, of being built and being [10] thrown down. The capacity for contraries, then, is present at the same time; but contraries cannot be present at the same time, and the actualities also cannot be present at the same time, e.g. health and illness. Therefore, while the good must be one of them, the capacity is both alike, or neither; the actuality, then, [15] is better. Also in the case of bad things the end or actuality must be worse than the potency; for that which 'can' is both contraries alike. Clearly, then, the bad does not exist apart from bad things; for the bad is in its nature posterior to the potency. And therefore we may also say that in the things which are from the [20] beginning, i.e. in eternal things, there is nothing bad, nothing defective, nothing perverted (for perversion is something bad).

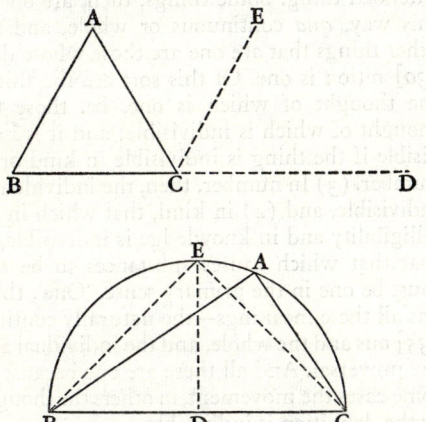

It is by an activity also that geometrical constructions are discovered; for we find them by dividing. If the figures had been already divided, the constructions would have been obvious; but as it is they are present only potentially. Why are the angles of the triangle equal to two right angles? Because the angles about one point are equal to two right angles. If, then, [25] the line parallel to the side had been already drawn upwards, the reason would have been evident to any one as soon as he saw the figure. Why is the angle in a semicircle in all cases a right angle? If three lines are equal—the two which form the base, and the perpendicular from the centre—the conclusion is evident at a glance to one who knows the former proposition. Obviously, therefore, the potentially existing constructions are discovered by [30] being brought to actuality; the reason is that the geometer's thinking is an actuality; so that the potency proceeds from an actuality; and therefore it is by making constructions that people come to know them (though the single actuality is later in generation than the corresponding potency).

10

The terms 'being' and 'non-being' are employed [35] firstly with reference to the categories, and secondly with reference to the potency or actuality of these or their non-potency or non-1051ᵇ actuality, and thirdly in the sense of true and false. This depends, on the side of the objects, on their being combined or separated, so that he who thinks the separated to be separated and the combined to be combined has the truth, while he whose thought is in a [5] state contrary to that of the objects is in error. This being so, when is what is called truth or falsity present, and when is it not? We must consider what we mean by these terms. It is not because we think truly that you are pale, that you *are* pale, but because you are pale we who say this have the truth. If, then, some things are always combined and cannot be [10] separated, and others are always separated and cannot be combined, while others are capable either of combination or of separation, 'being' is being combined and one, and 'not being' is being not combined but more than one. Regarding contingent facts, then, the same opinion or the same statement comes to be false and true, and it is possible for it to be at one time [15] correct and at another erroneous; but regarding things that cannot be otherwise opinions are not at one time true and at another false, but the same opinions are always true or always false.

But with regard to *incomposites,* what is being or not being, and truth or falsity? A thing of this sort is not composite, so as to 'be' when it is compounded, and not to 'be' if it is sep-[20] arated, like 'that the wood is white' or 'that the diagonal is incommensurable'; nor will truth and falsity be still present in the same way as in the previous cases. In fact, as truth is not the same in these cases, so also being is not the same; but (*a*) truth or falsity is as follows—contact and assertion are truth (asser-[25] tion not being the same as affirmation), and ignorance is non-contact. For it is not possible to be in *error* regarding the question what a thing is, save in an accidental sense; and the same holds good regarding non-composite substances (for it is not possible to be in error about them). And they all exist actually, not potentially; for otherwise they would have come to be and ceased to be; but, as it is, being itself does not come to be (nor cease to be); for if it had done so it would have had to [30] come out of something. About the things, then, which are essences and actualities, it is not possible to be in error, but only to know them or not to know them. But we do inquire what they are, viz. whether they are of such and such a nature or not.

(*b*) As regards the '*being*' that answers to truth and the 'non-being' that answers to falsity, in one case there is truth if the subject and the attribute are really combined, and fal-[35] sity if they are not combined; in the other case, if the object is existent it exists in a particular way, and if it does not exist in this way 1052ª it does not exist at all. And truth means knowing these objects, and falsity does not exist, nor error, but only ignorance—and not an ignorance which is like blindness; for blindness is akin to a total absence of the faculty of thinking.

It is evident also that about unchangeable [5] things there can be no error in respect of time, if we assume them to be unchangeable. E.g. if we suppose that the triangle does not change, we shall not suppose that at one time its angles are equal to two right angles while at another time they are not (for that would imply change). It is possible, however, to suppose that one member of such a class has a certain attribute and another has not; e.g. while we *may* suppose that no even number is prime, we *may* suppose that some are and some are not. But regarding a numerically single number not even this form of error is possible; for we can-[10] not in this case suppose that one instance has an attribute and another has not, but whether our judgement be true or false, it is implied that the fact is eternal.

BOOK X

I

[15] WE have said previously, in our distinction of the various meanings of words,[1] that 'one' has several meanings; the things that are directly and of their own nature and not accidentally called one may be summarized under four heads, though the word is used in more senses. (1) There is the continuous, either in general, or especially that which is continuous by nature and not by contact nor by being tied [20] together; and of these, that has more unity and is prior, whose movement is more indivisible and simpler. (2) That which is a whole and has a certain shape and form is *one* in a still higher degree; and especially if a thing is of this sort by nature, and not by force like the things which are unified by glue or nails or by being tied together, i.e. if it has in [25] itself the cause of its continuity. A thing is of this sort because its movement is one and indivisible in place and time; so that evidently if a thing has by nature a principle of movement that is of the first kind (i.e. local movement) and the first in that kind (i.e. circular movement), this is in the primary sense one extended thing. Some things, then, are one in this way, *qua* continuous or whole, and the other things that are one are those whose defi-[30] nition is one. Of this sort are the things the thought of which is one, i.e. those the thought of which is indivisible; and it is indivisible if the thing is indivisible in kind or in number. (3) In number, then, the individual is indivisible, and (4) in kind, that which in intelligibility and in knowledge is indivisible, so that that which causes substances to be one must be one in the primary sense. 'One', then, has all these meanings—the naturally continu-[35] ous and the whole, and the individual and the universal. And all these are one because in some cases the movement, in others the thought or the definition is indivisible.

1052ᵇ But it must be observed that the questions, what sort of things are said to be one, and what it is to be one and what is the definition of it, should not be assumed to be the same. 'One' has all these meanings, and each of the [5] things to which one of these kinds of unity

[1] v. 6.

belongs will be one; but 'to be one' will sometimes mean being one of these things, and sometimes being something else which is even nearer to the meaning of the *word* 'one' while these other things approximate to its *application*. This is also true of 'element' or 'cause', if one had both to specify the things of which it is predicable and to render the definition of the [10] word. For in a sense fire is an element (and doubtless also 'the indefinite' or something else of the sort is by its own nature the element), but in a sense it is not; for it is not the same thing to be fire and to be an element, but while as a particular thing with a nature of its own fire is an element, the name 'element' means that it has this attribute, that there is something which is made of it as a primary [15] constituent. And so with 'cause' and 'one' and all such terms. For this reason, too, 'to be one' means 'to be indivisible, being essentially a "this" and capable of being isolated either in place, or in form or thought'; or perhaps 'to be whole and indivisible'; but it means especially 'to be the first measure of a kind', and most strictly of quantity; for it is from this that it has been extended to the other categories. For [20] measure is that by which quantity is known; and quantity *qua* quantity is known either by a 'one' or by a number, and all number is known by a 'one'. Therefore all quantity *qua* quantity is known by the one, and that by which quantities are primarily known is the one itself; and so the one is the starting-point of number *qua* number. And hence in the other classes too 'measure' means that by which each [25] is first known, and the measure of each is a unit—in length, in breadth, in depth, in weight, in speed. (The words 'weight' and 'speed' are common to both contraries; for each of them has two meanings—'weight' means both that which has any amount of gravity and that which has an excess of gravity, and 'speed' both that which has any amount of movement and that which has an excess of movement; for [30] even the slow has a certain speed and the comparatively light a certain weight.)

In all these, then, the measure and starting-point is something one and indivisible, since even in lines we treat as indivisible the line a foot long. For everywhere we seek as the measure something one and indivisible; and this is [35] that which is simple either in quality or in quantity. Now where it is thought impossible to take away or to add, there the measure is exact (hence that of number is most exact; for we **1053ᵃ** posit the unit as indivisible in every respect); but in all other cases we imitate this sort of measure. For in the case of a furlong or a talent or of anything comparatively large any addition or subtraction might more easily escape our notice than in the case of something [5] smaller; so that the first thing from which, as far as our perception goes, nothing can be subtracted, all men make the measure, whether of liquids or of solids, whether of weight or of size; and they think they know the quantity when they know it by means of this measure. And indeed they know movement too by the simple movement and the quickest; for this [10] occupies least time. And so in astronomy a 'one' of this sort is the starting-point and measure (for they assume the movement of the heavens to be uniform and the quickest, and judge the others by reference to it), and in music the quarter-tone (because it is the least interval), and in speech the letter. And all these are ones in this sense—not that 'one' is something predicable in the same sense of all of these, but in the sense we have mentioned.

But the measure is not always one in number—sometimes there are several; e.g. the quar- [15] ter-tones (not to the ear, but as determined by the ratios) are two, and the articulate sounds by which we measure are more than one, and the diagonal of the square and its side are measured by two quantities, and all spatial magnitudes reveal similar varieties of unit. Thus, then, the one is the measure of all things, because we come to know the elements in the substance by dividing the things either in respect of quantity or in respect of kind. And the [20] one is indivisible just because the first of each class of things is indivisible. But it is not in the same way that every 'one' is indivisible e.g. a foot and a unit; the latter is indivisible in every respect, while the former must be placed among things which are undivided to perception, as has been said already[1]—only to perception, for doubtless every continuous thing is divisible.

The measure is always homogeneous with [25] the thing measured; the measure of spatial magnitudes is a spatial magnitude, and in particular that of length is a length, that of breadth a breadth, that of articulate sound an articulate sound, that of weight a weight, that of units a unit. (For we must state the matter so, and not say that the measure of numbers is a number; we ought indeed to say this if we were to use the corresponding form of words, but the claim does not really correspond—it is

[1] Cf. 1052ᵇ 33, 1053ᵃ 5.

[30] as if one claimed that the measure of units is units, and not a unit; number is a plurality of units.)

Knowledge, also, and perception, we call the measure of things for the same reason, because we come to know something by them—while as a matter of fact they are measured rather than measure other things. But it is with us as if some one else measured us and we came to know how big we are by seeing that he applied the cubit-measure to such and such a fraction [35] of us. But Protagoras says 'man is the measure of all things',[1] as if he had said 'the man who knows' or 'the man who perceives'; 1053ᵇ and these because they have respectively knowledge and perception, which we say are the measures of objects. Such thinkers are saying nothing, then, while they appear to be saying something remarkable.

Evidently, then, unity in the strictest sense, if [5] we define it according to the meaning of the word, is a measure, and most properly of quantity, and secondly of quality. And some things will be one if they are indivisible in quantity, and others if they are indivisible in quality; and so that which is one is indivisible, either absolutely or *qua* one.

2

With regard to the substance and nature of the [10] one we must ask in which of two ways it exists. This is the very question that we reviewed[2] in our discussion of problems, viz. what the one is and how we must conceive of it, whether we must take the one itself as being a substance (as both the Pythagoreans say in earlier and Plato in later times), or there is, rather, an underlying nature and the one should be described more intelligibly and more in the manner of the physical philosophers, of [15] whom one says the one is love, another says it is air, and another the indefinite.

If, then, no universal can be a substance, as has been said[3] in our discussion of substance and being, and if being itself cannot be a substance in the sense of a one apart from the many (for it is common to the many), but is only a predicate, clearly unity also cannot be a [20] substance; for being and unity are the most universal of all predicates. Therefore, on the one hand, genera are not certain entities and substances separable from other things; and on the other hand the one cannot be a genus, for the same reasons for which being and substance cannot be genera.

Further, the position must be similar in all the kinds of unity. Now 'unity' has just as many meanings as 'being'; so that since in the [25] sphere of qualities the one is something definite—some particular kind of thing—and similarly in the sphere of quantities, clearly we must in every category ask what the one is, as we must ask what the existent is, since it is not enough to say that its nature is just to be one or existent. But in colours the one is a colour, e.g. white, and then the other colours are observed to be produced out of this and black, and black [30] is the privation of white, as darkness of light. Therefore if all existent things were colours, existent things would have been a number, indeed, but of what? Clearly of colours; and the 'one' would have been a particular 'one', i.e. white. And similarly if all existing things were tunes, they would have been a number, [35] but a number of quarter-tones, and their essence would not have been number; and the one would have been something whose substance was not to be one but to be the quarter-1054ᵃ tone. And similarly if all existent things had been articulate sounds, they would have been a number of letters, and the one would have been a vowel. And if all existent things were rectilinear figures, they would have been a number of figures, and the one would have been the triangle. And the same argument applies to all other classes. Since, therefore, while [5] there are numbers and a one both in affections and in qualities and in quantities and in movement, in all cases the number is a number of particular things and the one is one something, and its substance is not just to be one, the same must be true of substances also; for it is true of all cases alike.

[10] That the one, then, in every class is a definite thing, and in no case is its nature just this, unity, is evident; but as in colours the one-itself which we must seek is one colour, so too in substance the one-itself is one substance. That in a sense unity means the same as being is clear from the facts that its meanings correspond to the categories one to one, and it is not com- [15] prised within any category (e.g. it is comprised neither in 'what a thing is' nor in quality, but is related to them just as being is); that in 'one man' nothing more is predicated than in 'man' (just as being is nothing apart from substance or quality or quantity); and that to be one is just to be a particular thing.

---

[1] Fr. 1. [2] III. 1001ᵃ 4-ᵇ25. [3] VII. 13.

3

[20] The one and the many are opposed in several ways, of which one is the opposition of the one and plurality as indivisible and divisible; for that which is either divided or divisible is called a plurality, and that which is indivisible or not divided is called one. Now since opposition is of four kinds, and one of these two terms is privative in meaning, they must be contra- [25] ries, and neither contradictory nor correlative in meaning. And the one derives its name and its explanation from its contrary, the indivisible from the divisible, because plurality and the divisible is more perceptible than the indivisible, so that in definition plurality is prior to the indivisible, because of the conditions of perception.

[30] To the one belong, as we indicated graphically in our distinction of the contraries,[1] the same and the like and the equal, and to plurality belong the other and the unlike and the unequal. 'The same' has several meanings; (1) we sometimes mean 'the same numerically'; again, (2) we call a thing the same if it is one both in definition and in number, e.g. you are one with yourself both in form and in matter; [35] and again, (3) if the definition of its primary essence is one; e.g. equal straight lines are the same, and so are equal and equal-angled quadrilaterals; there are many such, but in these equality constitutes unity.

Things are like if, not being absolutely the same, nor without difference in respect of their concrete substance, they are the same in form; [5] e.g. the larger square is like the smaller, and unequal straight lines are like; they are like, but not absolutely the same. Other things are like, if, having the same form, and being things in which difference of degree is possible, they have no difference of degree. Other things, if they have a quality that is in form one and [10] the same—e.g. whiteness—in a greater or less degree, are called like because their form is one. Other things are called like if the qualities they have in common are more numerous than those in which they differ—either the qualities in general or the prominent qualities; e.g. tin is like silver, *qua* white, and gold is like fire, *qua* yellow and red.

Evidently, then, 'other' and 'unlike' also have several meanings. And the other in one sense is the opposite of the same (so that everything is [15] either the same as or other than everything else). In another sense things are other unless both their matter and their definition are one (so that you are other than your neighbour). The other in the third sense is exemplified in the objects of mathematics. 'Other or the same' can therefore be predicated of everything with regard to everything else—but only if the things are one and existent, for 'other' is not the *contradictory* of 'the same'; which is [20] why it is not predicated of non-existent things (while 'not the same' *is* so predicated). It *is* predicated of all *existing* things; for everything that is existent and one is by its very nature either one or not one with anything else.

The other, then, and the same are thus opposed. But difference is not the same as otherness. For the other and that which it is other than need not be other in some definite respect (for everything that is existent is either other [25] or the same), but that which is different is different from some particular thing in some particular respect, so that there must be something identical whereby they differ. And this identical thing is genus or species; for everything that differs differs either in genus or in species, in genus if the things have not their matter in common and are not generated out of each other (i.e. if they belong to different figures of predication), and in species if they have the same genus ('genus' meaning that [30] identical thing which is essentially predicated of both the different things).

Contraries are different, and contrariety is a kind of difference. That we are right in this supposition is shown by induction. For all of these too are seen to be different; they are not [35] merely other, but some are other in genus, and others are in the same line of predication, and therefore in the same genus, and the same in genus. We have distinguished[2] elsewhere what sort of things are the same or other in genus.

4

Since things which differ may differ from one another more or less, there is also a greatest difference, and this I call contrariety. That con- [5] trariety is the greatest difference is made clear by induction. For things which differ in *genus* have no way to one another, but are too far distant and are not comparable; and for things that differ in *species* the extremes from which generation takes place are the contraries, and the distance between extremes—and

---
[1] Cf. IV, 1004ª 2. [2] v. 9.

therefore that between the contraries—is the greatest.

[10] But surely that which is greatest in each class is complete. For that is greatest which cannot be exceeded, and that is complete beyond which nothing can be found. For the complete difference marks the end of a series (just as the other things which are called complete are so called because they have attained an end), and beyond the end there is nothing; [15] for in everything it is the extreme and includes all else, and therefore there is nothing beyond the end, and the complete needs nothing further. From this, then, it is clear that contrariety is complete difference; and as contraries are so called in several senses, their modes of completeness will answer to the various modes of contrariety which attach to the contraries.

This being so, it is clear that one thing can- [20] not have more than one contrary (for neither can there be anything more extreme than the extreme, nor can there be more than two extremes for the one interval), and, to put the matter generally, this is clear if contrariety is a difference, and if difference, and therefore also the complete difference, must be between two things.

And the other commonly accepted definitions of contraries are also necessarily true. For not only is (1) the complete difference the [25] greatest difference (for we can get no difference beyond it of things differing either in genus or in species; for it has been shown[1] that there is *no* 'difference' between anything and the things outside its *genus*, and among the things which differ in *species* the complete difference is the greatest); but also (2) the things in the same genus which differ most are contrary (for the complete difference is the greatest difference between species of the same genus); and (3) the things in the same receptive [30] material which differ most are contrary (for the matter is the same for contraries); and (4) of the things which fall under the same faculty the most different are contrary (for one science deals with one class of things, and in these the complete difference is the greatest).

The primary contrariety is that between positive state and privation—not every privation, however (for 'privation' has several meanings), but that which is complete. And the other con- [35] traries must be called so with reference to these, some because they possess these, others because they produce or tend to produce them,

[1] Cf. ⁿ 6.

others because they are acquisitions or losses of these or of other contraries. Now if the kinds of opposition are contradiction and privation and contrariety and relation, and of these the first is contradiction, and contradiction admits of no intermediate, while contraries admit of one, clearly contradiction and contrariety are not the same. But privation is a kind of contradiction; for what suffers privation, either in general or in some determinate way, is either that which is quite incapable of [5] having some attribute or that which, being of such a nature as to have it, has it not; here we have already a variety of meanings, which have been distinguished[2] elsewhere. Privation, therefore, is a contradiction or incapacity which is determinate or taken along with the receptive material. This is the reason why, while contradiction does not admit of an intermediate, privation sometimes does; for everything [10] is equal or not equal, but not everything is equal or unequal, or if it is, it is only within the sphere of that which is receptive of equality. If, then, the comings-to-be which happen to the matter start from the contraries, and proceed either from the form and the possession of the form or from a privation of the form or shape, clearly all contrariety must be privation, but presumably not all privation is contrariety [15] (the reason being that that which has suffered privation may have suffered it in several ways); for it is only the *extremes* from which changes proceed that are contraries.

And this is obvious also by induction. For every contrariety involves, as one of its terms, a privation, but not all cases are alike; inequality is the privation of equality and unlikeness of likeness, and on the other hand vice is the [20] privation of virtue. But the cases differ in a way already described;[3] in one case we mean simply that the thing has suffered privation, in another case that it has done so either at a certain time or in a certain part (e.g. at a certain age or in the dominant part), or throughout. This is why in some cases there is a mean (there are men who are neither good nor bad), and in others there is not (a number must be either [25] odd or even). Further, some contraries have their subject defined, others have not.—Therefore it is evident that one of the contraries is always privative; but it is enough if this is true of the first—i.e. the generic—contraries, e.g. the one and the many; for the others can be reduced to these.

[2] v. 22.
[3] 1055ᵇ 4-6.

5

[30] Since one thing has one contrary, we might raise the question how the one is opposed to the many, and the equal to the great and the small. For if we used the word 'whether' only in an antithesis such as 'whether it is white or black', or 'whether it is white or not white' (we do not ask 'whether it is a man or white'), unless we are proceeding on a prior [35] assumption and asking something such as 'whether it was Cleon or Socrates that came' —but this is not a *necessary* disjunction in any class of things; yet even this is an extension from the case of opposites; for opposites alone cannot be present together; and we assume this incompatibility here too in asking which of the 1056ᵃ two came; for if they might both have come, the question would have been absurd; but if they might, even so this falls just as much into an antithesis, that of the 'one or many', i.e. 'whether both came or one of the two':—if, then, the question 'whether' is always concerned with opposites, and we can ask 'whether it is greater or less or equal', what is the op- [5] position of the equal to the other two? It is not contrary either to one alone or to both; for why should it be contrary to the greater rather than to the less? Further, the equal is contrary to the *unequal*. Therefore if it is contrary to the greater and the less, it will be contrary to more things than one. But if the unequal means the same as both the greater and the less together, the equal *will* be opposite to [10] both (and the difficulty supports those who say the unequal is a 'two'), but it follows that one thing is contrary to two others, which is impossible. Again, the equal is evidently intermediate between the great and the small, but no contrariety is either observed to be intermediate, or, from its definition, can be so; for it would not be complete if it were intermediate between any two things, but rather it always has something intermediate between its own terms.

[15] It remains, then, that it is opposed either as negation or as privation. It cannot be the negation or privation of one of the two; for why of the great rather than of the small? It is, then, the privative negation of both. This is why 'whether' is said with reference to both, not to one of the two (e.g. 'whether it is greater or equal' or 'whether it is equal or less'); there are [20] always three cases. But it is not a *necessary* privation; for not everything which is not greater or less is equal, but only the things which are of such a nature as to have these attributes.

The equal, then, is that which is neither great nor small but is naturally fitted to be either great or small; and it is opposed to both as a privative negation (and therefore is also intermediate). And that which is neither good [25] nor bad is opposed to both, but has no name; for each of these has several meanings and the recipient subject is not one; but that which is neither white nor black has more claim to unity. Yet even this has not one name, though the colours of which this negation is privatively predicated are in a way limited; for they must be either grey or yellow or some- [30] thing else of the kind. Therefore it is an incorrect criticism that is passed by those who think that all such phrases are used in the same way, so that that which is neither a shoe nor a hand would be intermediate between a shoe and a hand, since that which is neither good nor bad is intermediate between the good and the bad—as if there must be an intermediate in all cases. But this does not necessarily follow. [35] For the one phrase is a joint denial of opposites between which there is an intermediate and a certain natural interval; but between the 1056ᵇ other two there is no 'difference'; for the things, the denials of which are combined, belong to different classes, so that the substratum is not one.

6

We might raise similar questions about the one and the many. For if the many are absolutely opposed to the one, certain impossible results [5] follow. One will then be few, whether few be treated here as singular or plural; for the many are opposed also to the few. Further, two will be many, since the double is multiple and 'double' derives its meaning from 'two'; therefore one will be few; for what is that in comparison with which two are many, except one, which must therefore be few? For there is [10] nothing fewer. Further, if the much and the little are in plurality what the long and the short are in length, and whatever is much is also many, and the many are much (unless, indeed, there is a difference in the case of an easily-bounded continuum), the little (or few) will be a plurality. Therefore one is a plurality *if* it is few; and this it must be, if two are many. But perhaps, while the 'many' are in a sense [15] said to be also 'much', it is with a difference; e.g. water is much but not many. But 'many' is applied to the things that are divisible; in the one sense it means a plurality which is excessive either absolutely or relatively (while 'few' is similarly a plurality which is deficient), and in another sense it means number, in which sense alone it is opposed to the one. [20] For we say 'one or many', just as if one were to say 'one and ones' or 'white thing and white things', or to compare the things that have been measured with the measure. It is in this sense also that multiples are so called. For each number is said to be many because it consists of ones and because each number is measurable by one; and it is 'many' as that which is opposed to one, not to the few. In *this* sense, [25] then, even two is many—not, however, in the sense of a plurality which is excessive either relatively or absolutely; it is the *first* plurality. But *without qualification* two is few; for it is first plurality which is deficient (for this reason Anaxagoras was not right in leaving the subject with the statement[1] that 'all things were together, boundless both in plurality and in smallness'—where for 'and in smallness' he [30] should have said 'and in fewness'; for they could not have been boundless in fewness), since it is not one, as some say, but two, that make a few.

The one is opposed then to the many in numbers as measure to thing measurable; and these are opposed as are the relatives which are not from their very nature relatives. We have distinguished[2] elsewhere the two senses in which [35] relatives are so called:—(1) as contraries; (2) as knowledge to thing known, a term being called relative because another is relative to 1057ª it. There is nothing to prevent one from being fewer than something, e.g. than two; for if one is fewer, it is not therefore few. Plurality is as it were the class to which number belongs; for number is plurality measurable by one, and one and number are in a sense opposed, not as contrary, but as we have said some relative [5] terms are opposed; for inasmuch as one is measure and the other measurable, they are opposed. This is why not everything that is one is a number; i.e. if the thing is indivisible it is not a number. But though knowledge is similarly spoken of as relative to the knowable, the relation does not work out similarly; for while knowledge might be thought to be the measure, and the knowable the thing measured, the [10] fact is that all knowledge is knowable, but not all that is knowable is knowledge, because in a sense knowledge is measured by the knowable.—Plurality is contrary neither to the few

[1] Fr. 1. [2] v, 1021ª 26-30.

(the *many* being contrary to this as excessive plurality to plurality exceeded), nor to the one in every sense; but in the one sense these are contrary, as has been said, because the former is divisible and the latter indivisible, while in [15] another sense they are relative as knowledge is to knowable, if plurality is number and the one is a measure.

7

Since contraries admit of an intermediate and in some cases have it, intermediates must be composed of the contraries. For (1) all inter- [20] mediates are in the same genus as the things between which they stand. For we call those things intermediates, into which that which changes must change first; e.g. if we were to pass from the highest string to the lowest by the smallest intervals, we should come sooner to the intermediate notes, and in colours if we were to pass from white to black, we [25] should come sooner to crimson and grey than to black; and similarly in all other cases. But to change from one genus to another genus is not possible except in an incidental way, as from colour to figure. Intermediates, then, must be in the same genus both as one another and as the things they stand between.

[30] But (2) all intermediates stand between opposites of some kind; for only between these can change take place in virtue of their own nature (so that an intermediate is impossible between things which are not opposite; for then there would be change which was not from one opposite towards the other). Of opposites, contradictories admit of no middle term; for this [35] is what contradiction is—an opposition, one or other side of which must attach to anything whatever, i.e. which has no intermediate. Of other opposites, some are relative, others privative, others contrary. Of relative terms, those which are not contrary have no intermediate; the reason is that they are not in the same genus. For what intermediate could there be between knowledge and knowable? But 1057ᵇ between great and small there *is* one.

(3) If intermediates are in the same genus, as has been shown, and stand between contraries, they must be composed of these contraries. For either there will be a genus including the contraries or there will be none. And if (*a*) there is to be a genus in such a way that it is [5] something prior to the contraries, the differentiae which constituted the contrary species-of-a-genus will be contraries prior to the species; for species are composed of the genus

and the differentiae. (E.g. if white and black are contraries, and one is a piercing colour and the other a compressing colour, these differentiae—'piercing' and 'compressing'—are prior; [10] so that these are prior contraries of one another.) But, again, the species which differ contrariwise are the more truly contrary species. And the other species, i.e. the intermediates, must be composed of their genus and their differentiae. (E.g. all colours which are between white and black must be said to be composed of the genus, i.e. colour, and certain dif- [15] ferentiae. But these differentiae will not be the primary contraries; otherwise every colour would be either white or black. They are different, then, from the primary contraries; and therefore they will be between the primary contraries; the primary differentiae are 'piercing' and 'compressing'.)

Therefore it is (b) with regard to these contraries which do not fall within a genus that we must first ask of what their intermediates [20] are composed. (For things which *are* in the same genus must be composed of terms in which the genus is not an element, or else be themselves incomposite.) Now contraries do not involve one another in their composition, and are therefore first principles; but the intermediates are either all incomposite, or none of them. But there is something compounded out of the contraries, so that there can be a change from a contrary to it sooner than to the other [25] contrary; for it will have less of the quality in question than the one contrary and more than the other. This also, then, will come between the contraries. All the other intermediates also, therefore, are *composite;* for that which has more of a quality than one thing and less than another is compounded somehow out of the things than which it is said to have more and less respectively of the quality. And since there are no other things prior to the contraries [30] and homogeneous with the intermediates, all intermediates must be compounded *out of the contraries.* Therefore also all the inferior classes, both the contraries and their intermediates, will be compounded out of the primary contraries. Clearly, then, intermediates are (1) all in the same genus and (2) intermediate between contraries, and (3) all compounded out of the contraries.

8

[35] That which is other in species is other than something in something, and this must belong to both; e.g. if it is an animal other in species, both are animals. The things, then, which are other in species must be in the same genus. For by genus I mean that one identical thing which is predicated of both and is differentiated in no merely accidental way, whether 1058ª conceived as matter or otherwise. For not only must the common nature attach to the different things, e.g. not only must both be animals, but this very animality must also be different for each (e.g. in the one case equinity, in the other humanity), and so this common nature is specifically different for each from what it is for the other. One, then, will be in [5] virtue of its own nature one sort of animal, and the other another, e.g. one a horse and the other a man. This difference, then, must be an otherness of the genus. For I give the name of 'difference in the genus' to an otherness which makes the genus itself other.

This, then, will be a contrariety (as can be shown also by induction). For all things are [10] divided by opposites, and it has been proved that contraries are in the same genus[1]. For contrariety was seen[2] to be complete difference; and all difference in species is a difference from something *in something;* so that this is the same for both and is their genus. (Hence also all contraries which are different in species and not in genus are in the same line of predi- [15] cation, and other than one another in the highest degree—for the difference is complete—, and cannot be present along with one another.) The difference, then, is a contrariety.

This, then, is what it is to be 'other in species'—to have a contrariety, being in the same genus and being indivisible (and those things are the same in species which have no contrariety, being indivisible); we say 'being indivisible', for in the process of division contrarieties [20] arise in the intermediate stages before we come to the indivisibles. Evidently, therefore, with reference to that which is called the genus, none of the species-of-a-genus is either the same as it or other than it in species (and this is fitting; for the matter is indicated by negation, and the genus is the matter of that of which it is called the genus, not in the sense in which we speak of the genus or family of the Heraclidae, but in that in which the genus is an element in a thing's nature), nor is it so with reference to [25] things which are not in the same genus, but it will differ in *genus* from them, and in species from things in the same genus. For a thing's difference from that from which it dif-

---

[1] Chapter 4.   [2] 1055ª 16.

fers in species must be a contrariety; and this belongs only to things in the same genus.

9

One might raise the question, why woman does not differ from man in species, when fe-[30] male and male are contrary and their difference is a contrariety; and why a female and a male animal are not different in species, though this difference belongs to animal in virtue of its own nature, and not as paleness or darkness does; both 'female' and 'male' belong to it *qua* animal. This question is almost the same as the other, why one contrariety makes [35] things different in species and another does not, e.g. 'with feet' and 'with wings' do, but paleness and darkness do not. Perhaps it is because the former are modifications peculiar to the genus, and the latter are less so. And since one element is definition and one is mat-1058b ter, contrarieties which are in the definition make a difference in species, but those which are in the thing taken as including its matter do not make one. And so paleness in a man, or darkness, does not make one, nor is there a difference in species between the pale man and the dark man, not even if each of [5] them be denoted by one word. For man is here being considered on his material side, and matter does not create a difference; for it does not make individual men species of man, though the flesh and the bones of which this man and that man consist are other. The concrete thing is other, but not other in species, because in the definition there is no contrariety. This is the ultimate indivisible kind. Callias is [10] definition + *matter;* the pale man, then, is so also, because it is the individual Callias that is pale; man, then, is pale only incidentally. Neither do a brazen and a wooden circle, then, differ in species; and if a brazen triangle and a wooden circle differ in species, it is not because of the matter, but because there is a contrariety [15] in the definition. But does the matter not make things other in species, when it is other in a certain way, or is there a sense in which it does? For why is this horse other than this man in species, although their matter is included with their definitions? Doubtless because there is a contrariety in the *definition.* For while there is a contrariety also between pale man and dark horse, and it is a contrariety in spe-[20] cies, it does not depend on the paleness of the one and the darkness of the other, since even if both had been pale, yet they would have been other in species. But male and female, while they are modifications peculiar to 'animal', are so not in virtue of its essence but in the matter, i.e. the body. This is why the same seed becomes female or male by being acted on in a certain way. We have stated, [25] then, what it is to be other in species, and why some things differ in species and others do not.

10

Since contraries are other in form, and the perishable and the imperishable are contraries (for privation is a determinate incapacity), the perishable and the imperishable must be different in kind.

Now so far we have spoken of the general terms themselves, so that it might be thought [30] not to be necessary that every imperishable thing should be different from every perishable thing in form, just as not every pale thing is different in form from every dark thing. For the same thing can be both, and even at the same time if it is a universal (e.g. man can be both pale and dark), and if it is an individual it can still be both; for the same man [35] can be, though not at the same time, pale and dark. Yet pale is contrary to dark.

But while some contraries belong to certain things by accident (e.g. both those now mentioned and many others), others cannot, and among these are 'perishable' and 'imperish-1059a able'. For nothing is by accident perishable. For what is accidental is capable of not being present, but perishableness is one of the attributes that belong of necesstiy to the things to which they belong; or else one and the same [5] thing may be perishable and imperishable, if perishableness is capable of not belonging to it. Perishableness then must either be the essence or be present in the essence of each perishable thing. The same account holds good for imperishableness also; for both are attributes which are present of necessity. The characteristics, then, in respect of which and in direct consequence of which one thing is perishable and another imperishable, are opposite, so that the things must be different in kind.
[10] Evidently, then, there cannot be Forms such as some maintain, for then one man would be perishable and another imperishable. Yet the Forms are said to be the same in form with the individuals and not merely to have the same name; but things which differ in kind are farther apart than those which differ in form.

BOOK XI

1

That Wisdom is a science of first principles is evident from the introductory chapters,[1] in which we have raised objections to the statements of others about the first principles; but [20] one might ask the question whether Wisdom is to be conceived as one science or as several. If as one, it may be objected that one science always deals with contraries, but the first principles are not contrary. If it is *not* one, what sort of sciences are those with which it is to be identified?

Further, is it the business of one science, or of more than one, to examine the first principles of demonstration? If of one, why of this rather [25] than of any other? If of more, what sort of sciences must these be said to be?

Further, does Wisdom investigate all substances or not? If not all, it is hard to say which; but if, being one, it investigates them all, it is doubtful how the same science can embrace several subject-matters.

Further, does it deal with substances only or also with their attributes? If in the case of *attri-*[30] *butes* demonstration is possible, in that of *substances* it is not. But if the two sciences are different, what is each of them and which is Wisdom? If we think of it as demonstrative, the science of the attributes is Wisdom, but if as dealing with what is primary, the science of substances claims the title.

But again the science we are looking for must not be supposed to deal with the causes which have been mentioned in the *Physics*.[2] [35] For (A) it does not deal with the final cause (for that is the nature of the good, and this is found in the field of action and movement; and it is the first mover—for that is the nature of the end—but in the case of things unmovable there is nothing that moved them first), and (B) in general it is hard to say whether perchance the science we are now looking for deals with perceptible substances or not with them, but with certain others. If 1059[b] with others, it must deal either with the Forms or with the objects of mathematics. Now (*a*) evidently the Forms do not exist. (But it is hard to say, even if one suppose them to exist, why in the world the same is not true of the other things of which there are Forms, as of [5] the objects of mathematics. I mean that these thinkers place the objects of mathematics between the Forms and perceptible things, as a kind of third set of things apart both from the Forms and from the things in this world; but there is not a third man or horse besides the ideal and the individuals. If on the other hand it is not as they say, with what sort of things must the mathematician be supposed to deal? [10] Certainly not with the things in this world; for none of these is the sort of thing which the mathematical sciences demand.) Nor (*b*) does the science which we are now seeking treat of the objects of mathematics; for none of them can exist separately. But again it does not deal with perceptible substances; for they are perishable.

[15] In general one might raise the question, to what kind of science it belongs to discuss the difficulties about the matter of the objects of mathematics. Neither to physics (because the whole inquiry of the physicist is about the things that have in themselves a principle of movement and rest), nor yet to the science which inquires into demonstration and science; for *this* is just the subject which *it* investigates. [20] It remains then that it is the philosophy which we have set before ourselves that treats of those subjects.

One might discuss the question whether the science we are seeking should be said to deal with the principles which are by some called elements; all men suppose these to be present in composite things. But it might be thought [25] that the science we seek should treat rather of universals; for every definition and every science is of universals and not of *infimae species,* so that as far as this goes it would deal with the highest genera. These would turn out to be being and unity; for these might most of all be supposed to contain all things that are, and to be most like principles because they are [30] first by nature; for if they perish all other things are destroyed with them; for everything *is* and is one. But inasmuch as, if one is to suppose them to be genera, they must be predicable of their differentiae, and no genus is predicable of any of its differentiae, in this way it would seem that we should not make them genera nor principles. Further, if the simpler is more of a principle than the less simple, and [35] the ultimate members of the genus are simpler than the genera (for they are indivisible, but the genera are divided into many and

---

[1] Cf. I. 3-10.   [2] *Physics,* II. 3.

differing species), the species might seem to be the principles, rather than the genera. But inasmuch as the species are involved in the destruction of the genera, the genera are more like principles; for that which involves another in its destruction is a principle of it. These and others of the kind are the subjects that involve difficulties.

2

Further, must we suppose something apart from individual things, or is it these that the science we are seeking treats of? But these are [5] infinite in number. Yet the things that are apart from the individuals are genera or species; but the science we now seek treats of neither of these. The reason why this is impossible has been stated.[1] Indeed, it is in general hard to say whether one must assume that there is a separable substance besides the sensible substances (i.e. the substances in this world), or that these are the real things and Wisdom is [10] concerned with them. For we seem to seek another kind of substance, and this is our problem, i.e. to see if there is something which can exist apart by itself and belongs to no sensible thing.—Further, if there is another substance apart from and corresponding to sensible substances, which kinds of sensible substance must be supposed to have this corresponding to [15] them? Why should one suppose men or horses to have it, more than either the other animals or even all lifeless things? On the other hand to set up other and eternal substances equal in number to the sensible and perishable substances would seem to fall beyond the bounds of probability.—But if the principle we now seek is not separable from corporeal things, what has a better claim to the name [20] than matter? This, however, does not exist in actuality, but exists in potency. And it would seem rather that the form or shape is a more important principle than this; but the form is perishable, so that there is no eternal substance at all which can exist apart and independent. But this is paradoxical; for such a principle and substance seems to exist and is [25] sought by nearly all the most refined thinkers as something that exists; for how is there to be order unless there is something eternal and independent and permanent?

Further, if there is a substance or principle of such a nature as that which we are now seeking, and if this is one for all things, and the same for eternal and for perishable things, it is

[1] 1059[b] 24-38.

hard to say why in the world, if there is the [30] same principle, some of the things that fall under the principle are eternal, and others are not eternal; this is paradoxical. But if there is one principle of perishable and another of eternal things, we shall be in a like difficulty if the principle of perishable things, as well as that of eternal, is eternal; for why, if the principle is eternal, are not the things that fall under the principle also eternal? But if it is perishable another principle is involved to account for it, [35] and another to account for that, and this will go on to infinity.

If on the other hand we are to set up what are thought to be the most unchangeable principles, being and unity, firstly, if each of these does not indicate a 'this' or substance, how will they be separable and independent? Yet we expect the eternal and primary principles to be so. But if each of them does signify a 'this' or substance, all things that are are substances; [5] for being is predicated of all things (and unity also of some); but that all things that are are substance is false. Further, how can they be right who say that the first principle is unity and this is substance, and generate number as the first product from unity and from matter, [10] and assert that number is substance? How are we to think of 'two', and each of the other numbers composed of units, as one? On this point neither do they say anything nor is it easy to say anything. But if we are to suppose lines or what comes after these (I mean the primary surfaces) to be principles, these at least are not separable substances, but sections and divisions —the former of surfaces, the latter of bodies (while points are sections and divisions of [15] lines); and further they are limits of these same things; and all these are in other things and none is separable. Further, how are we to suppose that there is a substance of unity and the point? Every substance comes into being by a gradual process, but a point does not; for the point is a division.

[20] A further difficulty is raised by the fact that all knowledge is of universals and of the 'such', but substance is not a universal, but is rather a 'this'—a separable thing, so that if there is knowledge about the first principles, the question arises, how are we to suppose the first principle to be substance?

Further, is there anything apart from the concrete thing (by which I mean the matter and that which is joined with it), or not? If [25] not, we are met by the objection that all things that *are* in matter are perishable. But if there *is* something, it must be the form or shape. Now it is hard to determine in which cases this exists apart and in which it does not; for in some cases the form is evidently not separable, e.g. in the case of a house.

Further, are the principles the same in kind or in number? If they are one in number, all [30] things will be the same.

3

Since the science of the philosopher treats of being *qua* being universally and not in respect of a part of it, and 'being' has many senses and is not used in one only, it follows that if the word is used equivocally and in virtue of nothing common to its various uses, being does not fall under one science (for the meanings of an equivocal term do not form one genus); but if [35] the word is used in virtue of something common, being will fall under one science. The term seems to be used in the way we have mentioned, like 'medical' and 'healthy'. For each of these also we use in many senses. Terms are 1061ᵃ used in this way by virtue of some kind of reference, in the one case to medical science, in the other to health, in others to something else, but in each case to one identical concept. For a discussion and a knife are called medical because the former proceeds from medical sci- [5] ence, and the latter is useful to it. And a thing is called healthy in a similar way; one thing because it is indicative of health, another because it is productive of it. And the same is true in the other cases. Everything that is, then, is said to 'be' in this same way; each thing that is is said to 'be' because it is a modification of being *qua* being or a permanent or a transient state or a movement of it, or something else of [10] the sort. And since everything that is may be referred to something single and common, each of the contrarieties also may be referred to the first differences and contrarieties of being, whether the first differences of being are plurality and unity, or likeness and unlikeness, or some other differences; let these be taken as al- [15] ready discussed. It makes no difference whether that which is be referred to being or to unity. For even if they are not the same but different, at least they are convertible; for that which is one is also somehow being, and that which is being is one.

But since every pair of contraries falls to be examined by one and the same science, and in each pair one term is the privative of the other [20] —though one might regarding some contraries raise the question, how they can be pri- vately related, viz. those which have an intermediate, e.g. unjust and just—in all such cases one must maintain that the privation is not of the whole definition, but of the *infima species*. E.g. if the just man is 'by virtue of some per- [25] manent disposition obedient to the laws',[1] the unjust man will not in every case have the whole definition denied of him, but may be merely 'in some respect deficient in obedience to the laws', and in this respect the privation will attach to him; and similarly in all other cases.

As the mathematician investigates abstractions (for before beginning his investigation he [30] strips off all the sensible qualities, e.g. weight and lightness, hardness and its contrary, and also heat and cold and the other sensible contrarieties, and leaves only the quantitative and continuous, sometimes in one, sometimes in two, sometimes in three dimensions, [35] and the attributes of these qua quantitative and continuous, and does not consider them in any other respect, and examines the relative positions of some and the attributes of 1061ᵇ these, and the commensurabilities and incommensurabilities of others, and the ratios of others; but yet we posit one and the same science of all these things—geometry),—the same is true with regard to being. For the at- [5] tributes of this in so far as it is being, and the contrarieties in it *qua* being, it is the business of no other science than philosophy to investigate; for to physics one would assign the study of things not *qua* being, but rather *qua* sharing in movement; while dialectic and sophistic deal with the attributes of things that are, but not of things *qua* being, and not with [10] being itself in so far as it is being; therefore it remains that it is the philosopher who studies the things we have named, in so far as they are being. Since all that is is said to 'be' in virtue of something single and common, though the term has many meanings, and contraries are in the same case (for they are referred to the first contrarieties and differences of being), and things of this sort can fall un- [15] der one science, the difficulty we stated at the beginning[2] appears to be solved,—I mean the question how there can be a single science of things which are many and different in genus.

4

Since even the mathematician uses the common axioms only in a special application, it

---

[1] Cf. Plato, *Def.* 411 E. [2] 1059ᵃ 20-23.

must be the business of first philosophy to examine the principles of mathematics also. That when equals are taken from equals the remain-[20]ders are equal, is common to all quantities, but mathematics studies a part of its proper matter which it has detached, e.g. lines or angles or numbers or some other kind of quantity—not, however, *qua* being but in so far as [25] each of them is continuous in one or two or three dimensions; but philosophy does not inquire about particular subjects in so far as each of them has some attribute or other, but speculates about being, in so far as each particular thing *is*.—Physics is in the same position as mathematics; for physics studies the attributes and the principles of the things that [30] are, *qua* moving and not *qua* being (whereas the primary science, we have said, deals with these, only in so far as the underlying subjects are existent, and not in virtue of any other character); and so both physics and mathematics must be classed as *parts* of Wisdom.

5

There is a principle in things, about which we [35] cannot be deceived, but must always, on the contrary recognize the truth,—viz. that the same thing cannot at one and the same time **1062ᵃ** and not be, or admit any other similar pair of opposites. About such matters there is no proof in the full sense, though there is proof *ad hominem*. For it is not possible to infer this truth itself from a more certain principle, yet this is *necessary* if there is to be completed [5] proof of it in the full sense. But he who wants to prove to the asserter of opposites that he is wrong must get from him an admission which shall *be* identical with the principle that the same thing cannot be and not be at one and the same time, but shall not *seem* to be identical; for thus alone can his thesis be demon-[10]strated to the man who asserts that opposite statements can be truly made about the same subject. Those, then, who are to join in argument with one another must to some extent understand one another; for if this does not happen how are they to join in argument with one another? Therefore every word must be intelligible and indicate something, and not [15] many things but only one; and if it signifies more than one thing, it must be made plain to which of these the word is being applied. He, then, who says 'this is and is not' denies what he affirms, so that what the word signifies, he says it does not signify; and this is impossible. Therefore if 'this is' signifies something, one cannot truly assert its contradictory.

Further, if the word signifies something and [20] this is asserted truly, this connexion must be necessary; and it is not possible that that which necessarily is should ever not be; it is not possible therefore to make the opposed affirmations and negations truly of the same subject. Further, if the affirmation is no more true than the negation, he who says 'man' will be no more right than he who says 'not-man'. It [25] would seem also that in saying the man is not a horse one would be either more or not less right than in saying he is not a man, so that one will also be right in saying that the same person *is* a horse; for it was assumed to be possible to make opposite statements equally truly. It follows then that the same person is a man and a horse, or any other animal.

[30] While, then, there is no proof of these things in the full sense, there is a proof which may suffice against one who will make these suppositions. And perhaps if one had questioned Heraclitus himself in this way one might have forced him to confess that opposite statements can never be true of the same subjects. But, as it is, he adopted this opinion with-[35]out understanding what his statement involves. But in any case if what is said by him is true, not even this itself will be true—viz. that **1062ᵇ** the same thing can at one and the same time both be and not be. For as, when the statements are separated, the affirmation is no more true than the negation, in the same way—the combined and complex statement being like a [5] single affirmation—the whole taken as an affirmation will be no more true than the negation. Further, if it is not possible to affirm anything truly, this itself will be false—the assertion that there is no true affirmation. But if a true affirmation exists, this appears to refute [10] what is said by those who raise such objections and utterly destroy rational discourse.

6

The saying of Protagoras is like the views we have mentioned; he said that man is the measure of all things, meaning simply that that which seems to each man also assuredly is. If [15] this is so, it follows that the same thing both is and is not, and is bad and good, and that the contents of all other opposite statements are true, because often a particular thing appears beautiful to some and the contrary of beautiful to others, and that which appears to [20] each man is the measure. This difficulty may be solved by considering the source of this opinion. It seems to have arisen in some cases from the doctrine of the natural philosophers, and in others from the fact that all men have not the same views about the same things, but a particular thing appears pleasant to some and the contrary of pleasant to others.

That nothing comes to be out of that which [25] is not, but everything out of that which is, is a dogma common to nearly all the natural philosophers. Since, then, white cannot come to be if the perfectly white and in no respect not-white existed before, that which becomes white must come from that which is not white; so that it must come to be out of that which is not (so they argue), unless the same [30] thing was at the beginning white and not-white. But it is not hard to solve this difficulty; for we have said in our works on physics[1] in what sense things that come to be come to be from that which is not, and in what sense from that which is.

But to attend equally to the opinions and the fancies of disputing parties is childish; for clearly one of them must be mistaken. And [35] this is evident from what happens in respect of sensation; for the same thing never appears sweet to some and the contrary of 1063ª sweet to others, unless in the one case the sense-organ which discriminates the aforesaid flavours has been perverted and injured. And if this is so the one party must be taken to be the measure, and the other must not. And [5] I say the same of good and bad, and beautiful and ugly, and all other such qualities. For to maintain the view we are opposing is just like maintaining that the things that appear to people who put their finger under their eye and make the object appear two instead of one must be two (because they appear to be of that number) and again one (for to those who do not interfere with their eye the one object appears one).

[10] In general, it is absurd to make the fact that the things of this earth are observed to change and never to remain in the same state, the basis of our judgement about the truth. For in pursuing the truth one must start from the things that are always in the same state and [15] suffer no change. Such are the heavenly bodies; for these do not appear to be now of one nature and again of another, but are manifestly always the same and share in no change.

Further, if there is movement, there is also something moved, and everything is moved out of something and into something; it follows that that which is moved must first be in that out of which it is to be moved, and then [20] not be in it, and move into the other and come to be in it, and that the contradictory statements are not true at the same time, as these thinkers assert they are.

And if the things of this earth continuously flow and move in respect of quantity—if one were to suppose this, although it is not true— why should they not endure in respect of *quality*? For the assertion of contradictory statements about the same thing seems to have [25] arisen largely from the belief that the quantity of bodies does not endure, which, our opponents hold, justifies them in saying that the same thing both is and is not four cubits long. But essence depends on quality, and this is of determinate nature, though quantity is of indeterminate.

Further, when the doctor orders people to [30] take some particular food, why do they take it? In what respect is 'this is bread' truer than 'this is not bread'? And so it would make no difference whether one ate or not. But as a matter of fact they take the food which is ordered, assuming that they know the truth about it and that it is bread. Yet they should not, if there were no fixed constant nature in sensible things, but all natures moved and flowed for ever.

[35] Again, if we are always changing and never remain the same, what wonder is it if to us, as to the sick, things never appear the same? (For to them also, because they are not in the same condition as when they were well, sensible qualities do not appear alike; yet, for all that, the sensible things themselves need not share in any change, though they produce different, and not identical, sensations in the sick. And the same must [5] surely happen to the healthy if the aforesaid[2] change takes place.) But if we do not change but remain the same, there will be something that endures.

As for those to whom the difficulties mentioned are suggested by *reasoning,* it is not easy to solve the difficulties to their satisfaction, unless they will posit something and no longer [10] demand a reason for it; for it is only thus that all reasoning and all proof is accomplished; if they posit nothing, they destroy discussion and all reasoning. Therefore with such men there is no reasoning. But as for those who are

---

[1] *Physics,* I. 7-9; *On Generation and Corruption,* I, 317ᵇ 14-319ᵇ 5.

[2] Cf. 1063ª 35.

perplexed by the traditional difficulties, it is easy to meet them and to dissipate the causes of their perplexity. This is evident from what has been said.[1]

[15] It is manifest, therefore, from these arguments that contradictory statements cannot be truly made about the same subject at one time, nor can contrary statements, because every contrariety depends on privation. This is evident if we reduce the definitions of contraries to their principle.

Similarly, no intermediate between contraries can be predicated of one and the same subject, of which one of the contraries is predi- [20] cated. If the subject is white we shall be wrong in saying it is neither black nor white, for then it follows that it is and is not white; for the second of the two terms we have put together is true of it, and this is the contradictory of white.

We could not be right, then, in accepting the [25] views either of Heraclitus or of Anaxagoras. If we were, it would follow that contraries would be predicated of the same subject; for when Anaxagoras says that in everything there is a part of everything, he says nothing is sweet any more than it is bitter, and so with any other pair of contraries, since in everything everything is present not potentially only, but [30] actually and separately. And similarly all statements cannot be false nor all true, both because of many other difficulties which might be adduced as arising from this position, and because if all are false it will not be true to say even this, and if all are true it will not be false [35] to say all are false.

7

Every science seeks certain principles and 1064ª causes for each of its objects—e.g. medicine and gymnastics and each of the other sciences, whether productive or mathematical. For each of these marks off a certain class of things for itself and busies itself about this as about something existing and real,—not however *qua* real; the science that does *this* is another distinct from these. Of the sciences [5] mentioned each gets somehow the 'what' in some class of things and tries to prove the other truths, with more or less precision. Some get the 'what' through perception, others by hypothesis; so that it is clear from an induction of this sort that there is no *demonstration* of the substance or 'what'.

[10] There is a science of nature, and evidently

[1] In 1062b 20–1063b 7.

it must be different both from practical and from productive science. For in the case of productive science the principle of movement is in the producer and not in the product, and is either an art or some other faculty. And similarly in practical science the movement is not in the thing done, but rather in the doers. [15] But the science of the natural philosopher deals with the things that have *in themselves* a principle of movement. It is clear from these facts, then, that natural science must be neither practical nor productive, but theoretical (for it must fall into some one of these classes). And since each of the sciences must somehow know [20] the 'what' and use this as a principle, we must not fail to observe how the natural philosopher should define things and how he should state the definition of the essence—whether as akin to 'snub' or rather to 'concave'. For of these the definition of 'snub' includes the matter of the thing, but that of 'concave' is [25] independent of the matter; for snubness is found in a nose, so that we look for its definition without eliminating the nose, for what is snub is a concave nose. Evidently then the definition of flesh also and of the eye and of the other parts must always be stated without eliminating the matter.

Since there is a science of being *qua* being and capable of existing apart, we must consider whether this is to be regarded as the same as physics or rather as different. Physics deals [30] with the things that have a principle of movement in themselves; mathematics is theoretical, and *is* a science that deals with things that are at rest, but its subjects cannot exist apart. Therefore about that which can exist apart and is unmovable there is a science different from both of these, if there *is* a substance of this nature (I mean separable and un- [35] movable), as we shall try to prove there is. And if there is such a kind of thing in the world, here must surely be the divine, and this must be the first and most dominant principle. 1064b Evidently, then, there are three kinds of theoretical sciences—physics, mathematics, theology. The class of theoretical sciences is the best, and of these themselves the last named is best; for it deals with the highest of existing [5] things, and each science is called better or worse in virtue of its proper object.

One might raise the question whether the science of being *qua* being is to be regarded as universal or not. Each of the mathematical sciences deals with some one determinate class of things, but universal mathematics applies alike to all. Now if natural substances are the first of [*10*] existing things, physics must be the first of sciences; but if there is another entity and substance, separable and unmovable, the knowledge of it must be different and prior to physics and universal because it is prior.

8

[*15*] Since 'being' in general has several senses, of which one is 'being by accident', we must consider first that which 'is' in this sense. Evidently none of the traditional sciences busies itself about the accidental. For neither does architecture consider what will happen to those who are to use the house (e.g. whether they [*20*] will have a painful life in it or not), nor does weaving, or shoemaking, or the confectioner's art, do the like; but each of these sciences considers only what is peculiar to it, i.e. its proper end. And as for the argument that 'when he who is musical becomes lettered he will be both at once, not having been both be- [*25*] fore; and that which is, not always having been, must have come to be; therefore he must have at once become musical and lettered',— this none of the recognized sciences considers, but only sophistic; for this alone busies itself about the accidental, so that Plato is not far wrong when he says[1] that the sophist spends his time on non-being.

[*30*] That a science of the accidental is not even possible will be evident if we try to see what the accidental really is. We say that everything either is always and of necessity (necessity not in the sense of violence, but that which we ap- [*35*] peal to in demonstrations), or is for the most part, or is neither for the most part, nor always and of necessity, but merely as it chances; e.g. there might be cold in the dog-days, but this occurs neither always and of ne- 1065ᵃ cessity, nor for the most part, though it might happen sometimes. The accidental, then, is what occurs, but not always nor of necessity, nor for the most part. Now we have said what the accidental is, and it is obvious why there is no science of such a thing; for all science is of that which is always or for the most part, but [*5*] the accidental is in neither of these classes.

Evidently there are not causes and principles of the accidental, of the same kind as there are of the essential; for if there were, everything would be of necessity. If A is when B is, and B is when C is, and if C exists not by chance [*10*] but of necessity, that also of which C was cause will exist of necessity, down to the last

[1] Cf. *Sophist*, 254.

causatum as it is called (but this was supposed to be accidental). Therefore all things will be of necessity, and chance and the possibility of a thing's either occurring or not occurring are removed entirely from the range of events. And if the cause be supposed not to exist but to be coming to be, the same results will follow; [*15*] everything will occur of necessity. For to-morrow's eclipse will occur if A occurs, and A if B occurs, and B if C occurs; and in this way if we subtract time from the limited time between now and to-morrow we shall come sometime to the already existing condition. [*20*] Therefore since this exists, everything after this will occur of necessity, so that all things occur of necessity.

As to that which 'is' in the sense of being true or of being by accident, the *former* depends on a combination in thought and is an affection of thought (which is the reason why it is the principles, not of that which 'is' in this sense, but of that which is outside and can exist apart, that are sought); and the *latter* is not necessary but indeterminate (I mean the [*25*] accidental); and of such a thing the causes are unordered and indefinite.

Adaptation to an end is found in events that happen by nature or as the result of thought. It is 'luck' when one of these events happens by accident. For as a thing may exist, so it may be a cause, either by its own nature or by acci- [*30*] dent. Luck is an accidental cause at work in such events adapted to an end as are usually effected in accordance with purpose. And so luck and thought are concerned with the same sphere; for purpose cannot exist without thought. The causes from which lucky results might happen are indeterminate; and so luck is obscure to human calculation and is a cause by accident, but in the unqualified sense a cause [*35*] of nothing. It is good or bad luck when 1065ᵇ the result is good or evil; and prosperity or misfortune when the scale of the results is large.

Since nothing accidental is prior to the essential, neither are accidental causes prior. If, then, luck or spontaneity is a cause of the material universe, reason and nature are causes before it.

9

[*5*] Some things are only actually, some potentially, some potentially and actually, what they are, viz. in one case a particular reality, in another, characterized by a particular quantity, or the like. There is no movement apart from

things; for change is always according to the categories of being, and there is nothing common to these and in no one category. But each of the categories belongs to all its subjects in [10] either of two ways (e.g. 'this-ness'—for one kind of it is 'positive form', and the other is 'privation'; and as regards quality one kind is 'white' and the other 'black', and as regards quantity one kind is 'complete' and the other 'incomplete', and as regards spatial movement one is 'upwards' and the other 'downwards', or one thing is 'light' and another 'heavy'); so that there are as many kinds of movement and change as of being. There being a distinction [15] in each class of things between the potential and the completely real, I call the actuality of the potential as such, movement. That what we say is true, is plain from the following facts. When the 'buildable', in so far as it is what we mean by 'buildable', exists actually, it is being built, and this is the process of building. Similarly with learning, healing, walking, leaping, ageing, ripening. Movement takes [20] place when the complete reality itself exists, and neither earlier nor later. The complete reality, then, of that which exists potentially, when it is completely real and actual, not *qua* itself, but *qua* movable, is movement. By *qua* I mean this: bronze is potentially a statue; but yet it is not the complete reality of bronze *qua* [25] bronze that is movement. For it is not the same thing to be bronze and to be a certain potency. If it were absolutely the same in its definition, the complete reality of bronze would have been a movement. But it is not the same. (This is evident in the case of contraries; for to be capable of being well and to be capable of being ill are not the same—for if they were, being well and being ill would have been the [30] same—it is that which underlies and is healthy or diseased, whether it is moisture or blood, that is one and the same.) And since it is not the same, as colour and the visible are not the same, it is the complete reality of the potential, and *as potential,* that is movement. That it is this, and that movement takes place when [35] the complete reality itself exists, and neither earlier nor later, is evident. For each thing is capable of being sometimes actual, sometimes not, e.g. the buildable *qua* buildable; and the actuality of the buildable *qua* buildable is building. For the actuality is either this—the act of building—or the house. But when the *house* exists, it is no longer buildable; the buildable is what *is being* built. The actual- [5] ity, then, must be the *act of building,* and this is a movement. And the same account applies to all other movements.

That what we have said is right is evident from what all others say about movement, and from the fact that it is not easy to define it otherwise. For firstly one cannot put it in any [10] other class. This is evident from what people say. Some call it otherness and inequality and the unreal; none of these, however, is necessarily moved, and further, change is not either to these or from these any more than from their opposites. The reason why people put movement in these classes is that it is thought to be something indefinite, and the principles in one of the two 'columns of con- [15] traries' are indefinite because they are privative, for none of them is either a 'this' or a 'such' or in any of the other categories. And the reason why movement is thought to be indefinite is that it cannot be classed either with the potency of things or with their actuality; for neither that which is capable of being of a certain quantity, nor that which is actually of a certain quantity, is of necessity moved, and [20] movement is thought to be an actuality, but incomplete; the reason is that the potential, whose actuality it is, is incomplete. And therefore it is hard to grasp what movement is; for it must be classed either under privation or under potency or under absolute actuality, but evidently none of these is possible. Therefore [25] what remains is that it must be what we said—both actuality and the actuality we have described—which is hard to detect but capable of existing.

And evidently movement is in the movable; for it is the complete realization of this by that which is capable of causing movement. And the actuality of that which is capable of causing movement is no other than that of the movable. For it must be the complete reality of both. For while a thing is capable of causing movement because it *can* do this, it is a mover [30] because it is *active;* but it is on the movable that it is capable of acting, so that the actuality of both is one, just as there is the same interval from one to two as from two to one, and as the steep ascent and the steep descent are one, but the being of them is not one; the case of the mover and the moved is similar.

10

[35] The infinite is either that which is incapable of being traversed because it is not its nature to be traversed (this corresponds to the sense in which the voice is 'invisible'), or that

which admits only of incomplete traverse or scarcely admits of traverse, or that which, though it naturally admits of traverse, is not traversed or limited; further, a thing may be infinite in respect of addition or of subtraction, 1066[b] or both. The infinite cannot be a separate, independent thing. For if it is neither a spatial magnitude nor a plurality, but infinity itself is its substance and not an accident of it, it will be indivisible; for the divisible is either magnitude or plurality. But if indivisible, it is [5] not infinite, except as the voice is invisible; but people do not mean this, nor are we examining this sort of infinite, but the infinite as untraversable. Further, how can an infinite exist by itself, unless number and magnitude also exist by themselves,—since infinity is an attribute of these? Further, if the infinite is an accident of something else, it cannot be *qua* [10] infinite an element in things, as the invisible is not an element in speech, though the voice is invisible. And evidently the infinite cannot exist actually. For then any part of it that might be taken would be infinite (for 'to be infinite' and 'the infinite' are the same, if the infinite is substance and not predicated of a subject). Therefore it is either indivisible, or if it is partible, it is divisible into infinites; but [15] the same thing cannot be many infinites (as a part of air is air, so a part of the infinite would be infinite, if the infinite is substance and a principle). Therefore it must be impartible and indivisible. But the actually infinite cannot be indivisible; for it must be of a certain quantity. Therefore infinity belongs to its subject incidentally. But if so, then (as we have [20] said[1]) it cannot be it that is a principle, but that of which it is an accident—the air or the even number.

This inquiry is universal; but that the infinite is not *among sensible things,* is evident from the following argument. If the definition of a body is 'that which is bounded by planes', there cannot be an infinite body either [25] sensible or intelligible; nor a separate and infinite number, for number or that which has a number is numerable. Concretely, the truth is evident from the following argument. The infinite can neither be composite nor simple. For (*a*) it cannot be a composite body, since the elements are limited in multitude. For the contraries must be equal and no *one* of them must be infinite; for if one of the two bodies [30] falls at all short of the other in potency, the finite will be destroyed by the infinite.

[1] l. 9.

And that *each* should be infinite is impossible. For body is that which has extension in all directions, and the infinite is the boundlessly extended, so that if the infinite is a body it will be infinite in every direction. Nor (*b*) can the infinite body be one and simple—neither, [35] as some say, something apart from the elements, from which they generate these (for there is no such body apart from the elements; for everything can be resolved into that of which it consists, but no such product of analy-1067[a] sis is observed except the simple bodies), nor fire nor any other of the elements. For apart from the question how any of them could be infinite, the All, even if it is finite, cannot either be or become any one of them, as [5] Heraclitus says all things sometime become fire. The same argument applies to this as to the One which the natural philosophers posit *besides* the elements. For everything changes from contrary to contrary, e.g. from hot to cold.

Further, a sensible body is somewhere, and whole and part have the same proper place, e.g. the whole earth and part of the earth. Therefore if (*a*) the infinite body is homogeneous, it will be unmovable or it will be [10] always moving. But this is impossible; for why should it rather rest, or move, down, up, or anywhere, rather than anywhere else? E.g. if there were a clod which were part of an infinite body, where will this move or rest? The proper place of the body which is homogeneous with it is infinite. Will the clod occupy the whole place, then? And how? ⟨This is impossible.⟩ What then is its rest or its movement? It will either rest everywhere, and then [15] it cannot move; or it will move everywhere, and then it cannot be still. But (*b*) if the All has unlike parts, the proper places of the parts are unlike also, and, firstly, the body of the All is not one except by contact, and, secondly, the parts will be either finite or infinite in variety of kind. *Finite* they cannot be; for then those of one kind will be infinite in quantity and those of another will not (if the All is infinite), e.g. fire or water would be infinite, but such an infinite element would be destruction to the contrary elements. But if the parts are *in*-[20] *finite* and simple, their places also are infinite and there will be an infinite number of elements; and if this is impossible, and the places are finite, the All also must be limited.

In general, there cannot be an infinite body and also a proper place for bodies, if every sensible body has either weight or lightness. [25] For it must move either towards the middle or upwards, and the infinite—either the whole or the half of it—cannot do either; for how will you divide it? Or how will part of the infinite be down and part up, or part extreme and part middle? Further, every sensible body is in a place, and there are six kinds of place, [30] but these cannot exist in an infinite body. In general, if there cannot be an infinite place, there cannot be an infinite body; ⟨and there cannot be an infinite place,⟩ for that which is in a place is somewhere, and this means either up or down or in one of the other directions, and each of these is a limit.

The infinite is not the same in the sense that it is a single thing whether exhibited in distance or in movement or in time, but the posterior among these is called infinite in virtue [35] of its relation to the prior; i.e. a movement is called infinite in virtue of the distance covered by the spatial movement or alteration or growth, and a time is called infinite because of the movement which occupies it.

11

1067ᵇ Of things which change, some change in an accidental sense, like that in which 'the musical' may be said to walk, and others are said, without qualification, to change, because something in them changes, i.e. the things that change in parts; the body becomes healthy, because the eye does. But there is something which is by its own nature moved directly, and [5] this is the essentially movable. The same distinction is found in the case of the mover; for it causes movement either in an accidental sense or in respect of a part of itself or essentially. There is something that directly causes movement; and there is something that is moved, also the time in which it is moved, and that from which and that into which it is moved. But the forms and the affections and the place, which are the terminals of the move- [10] ment of moving things, are unmovable, e.g. knowledge or heat; it is not heat that is a movement, but heating. Change which is not accidental is found not in all things, but between contraries, and their intermediates, and between contradictories. We may convince ourselves of this by induction.
[15] That which changes changes either from positive into positive, or from negative into negative, or from positive into negative, or from negative into positive. (By positive I mean that which is expressed by an affirmative term.) Therefore there must be three changes; [20] for that from negative into negative is not change, because (since the terms are neither contraries nor contradictories) there is no opposition. The change from the negative into the positive which is its contradictory is generation—absolute change absolute generation, and partial change partial generation; and the change from positive to negative is destruction —absolute change absolute destruction, and [25] partial change partial destruction. If, then, 'that which is not' has several senses, and movement can attach neither to that which implies putting together or separating, nor to that which implies potency and is opposed to that which is in the full sense (true, the not-white or not-good *can* be moved *incidentally*, for the not-white might be a man; but that which is not a particular thing at all can in [30] no wise be moved), that which is not cannot be moved (and if this is so, generation cannot be movement; for that which is not *is* generated; for even if we admit to the full that its generation is accidental, yet it is true to say that 'not-being' is predicable of that which is generated absolutely). Similarly *rest* cannot belong to that which is not. These consequences, [35] then, turn out to be awkward, and also this, that everything that is moved is in a place, but that which is not is not in a place; for then it would be somewhere. Nor is destruction movement; for the contrary of movement is movement or rest, but the contrary of 1068ᵃ destruction is generation. Since every movement is a change, and the kinds of change are the three named above,[1] and of these those in the way of generation and destruction are not movements, and these are the changes from a thing to its contradictory, it follows that only the change from positive into posi- [5] tive is movement. And the positives are either contrary or intermediate (for even privation must be regarded as contrary), and are expressed by an affirmative term, e.g. 'naked' or 'toothless' or 'black'.

12

If the categories are classified as substance, quality, place, acting or being acted on, relation, quantity, there must be three kinds of movement—of quality, of quantity, of place. [10] There is no movement in respect of substance (because there is nothing contrary to substance), nor of relation (for it is possible that if one of two things in relation changes, the relative term which was true of the other thing ceases to be true, though this other does

[1] In 1067ᵇ 19.

not change at all,—so that their movement is accidental), nor of agent and patient, or mover and moved, because there is no movement of [15] movement nor generation of generation, nor, in general, change of change. For there *might* be movement of movement in two senses; (1) movement might be the subject moved, as a man is moved because he changes from pale to dark,—so that on this showing movement, too, may be either heated or cooled or change its place or increase. But this is impossible; for change is not a subject. Or (2) [20] some other subject might change from change into some other form of existence (e.g. a man from disease into health). But this also is not possible except incidentally. For every movement is change from something into [25] something. (And so are generation and destruction; only, these are changes into things opposed in certain ways while the other, movement, is into things opposed in another way.) A thing changes, then, at the same time from health into illness, and from this change itself into another. Clearly, then, if it has become ill, it will have changed into whatever may be the other change concerned (though it *may* be at rest), and, further, into a determinate change each time; and that new change will be from [30] something definite into some other definite thing; therefore it will be the opposite change, that of growing well. We answer that this happens only incidentally; e.g. there is a change from the process of recollection to that of forgetting, only because *that to which the process attaches* is changing, now into a state of knowledge, now into one of ignorance.

Further, the process will go on to infinity, if there is to be change of change and coming to be of coming to be. What is true of the later, [35] then, must be true of the earlier; e.g. if the simple coming to be was once coming to be, that which comes to be something was also once coming to be; therefore that which simply comes to be something was not yet in existence, but something which was coming to be coming to be something was already in existence. And this was once coming to be, so that at that time it was not yet coming to be something else. Now since of an infinite number of terms there is not a first, the first in this series will not exist, and therefore no following term will exist. Nothing, then, can either come [5] to be or move or change. Further, that which is capable of a movement is also capable of the contrary movement and rest, and that which comes to be also ceases to be. Therefore that which is coming to be is ceasing to be when it has come to be coming to be; for it cannot cease to be as soon as it is coming to be coming to be, nor after it has come to be; for [10] that which is ceasing to be must *be*. Further, there must be a matter underlying that which comes to be and changes. What will this be, then,—what is it that becomes movement or becoming, as body or soul is that which suffers alteration? And, again, what is it that they move into? For it must be the movement or becoming of something from something into something. How, then, can this condition be fulfilled? There can be no learning of learning, and therefore no becoming of becoming. [15] Since there is not movement either of substance or of relation or of activity and passivity, it remains that movement is in respect of quality and quantity and place; for each of these admits of contrariety. By quality I mean not that which is in the substance (for even the differentia is a quality), but the passive quality, in virtue of which a thing is said to be acted on or to be incapable of being acted on. [20] The immobile is either that which is wholly incapable of being moved, or that which is moved with difficulty in a long time or begins slowly, or that which is of a nature to be moved and can be moved but is not moved when and where and as it would naturally be moved. This alone among immobiles I describe as being at rest; for rest is contrary to [25] movement, so that it must be a privation in that which is *receptive of movement*.

Things which are in one proximate place are *together in place,* and things which are in different places are *apart:* things whose extremes are together *touch:* that at which a changing thing, if it changes continuously according to its nature, naturally arrives before it arrives at the extreme into which it is chang- [30] ing, is *between*. That which is most distant in a straight line is *contrary in place*. That is *successive* which is after the beginning (the order being determined by position or form or in some other way) and has nothing of the same class between it and that which it succeeds, e.g. lines in the case of a line, units in that of a unit, or a house in that of a house. (There is nothing to prevent a thing of some *other* class from being between.) For the suc- [35] cessive succeeds something and is something later; 'one' does not succeed 'two', nor the first day of the month the second. That which, being successive, touches, is *contiguous*. (Since all change is between opposites, and these are either contraries or contradictories, and there is no middle term for contradictories, clearly that which is *between* is between contraries.) The *continuous* is a [5] species of the contiguous. I call two things continuous when the limits of each, with which they touch and by which they are kept together, become one and the same, so that plainly the continuous is found in the things out of which a unity naturally arises in virtue of their contact. And plainly the successive is the first of these concepts (for the successive does not necessarily touch, but that which [10] touches is successive; and if a thing is continuous, it touches, but if it touches, it is not necessarily continuous; and in things in which there is no touching, there is no organic unity); therefore a point is not the same as a unit; for contact belongs to points, but not to units, which have only succession; and there is something between two of the former, but not between two of the latter.

BOOK XII

1

THE subject of our inquiry is substance; for the principles and the causes we are seeking are those of substances. For if the universe is of the nature of a whole, substance is its first [20] part; and if it coheres merely by virtue of serial succession, on this view also substance is first, and is succeeded by quality, and then by quantity. At the same time these latter are not even being in the full sense, but are qualities and movements of it,—or else even the not-white and the not-straight would be being; at least we say even these *are*, e.g. 'there is a not-white'. Further, none of the categories other [25] than substance can exist apart. And the early philosophers also in practice testify to the primacy of substance; for it was of substance that they sought the principles and elements and causes. The thinkers of the present day tend to rank universals as substances (for genera are universals, and these they tend to describe as principles and substances, owing to the abstract nature of their inquiry); but the thinkers of old ranked particular things as substances, e.g. fire and earth, not what is common to both, body.

[30] There are three kinds of substance—one that is sensible (of which one subdivision is eternal and another is perishable; the latter is recognized by all men, and includes e.g. plants and animals), of which we must grasp the elements, whether one or many; and another that is immovable, and this certain thinkers assert to be capable of existing apart, some di-[35] viding it into two, others identifying the Forms and the objects of mathematics, and others positing, of these two, only the objects of mathematics. The former two kinds of substance are the subject of physics **1069^b** (for they imply movement); but the third kind belongs to another science, if there is no principle common to it and to the other kinds.

2

Sensible substance is changeable. Now if change proceeds from opposites or from intermediates, and not from all opposites (for the voice is not-white ⟨, but it does not therefore [5] change to white⟩), but from the contrary, there must be something underlying which changes into the contrary state; for the *contraries* do not change. Further, something persists, but the contrary does not persist; there is, then, some third thing besides the contraries, viz. the matter. Now since changes are of four kinds—either in respect of the 'what' or of the quality or of the quantity or of the [10] place, and change in respect of 'thisness' is simple generation and destruction, and change in quantity is increase and diminution, and change in respect of an affection is alteration, and change of place is motion, changes will be from given states into those contrary to them in these several respects. The matter, [15] then, which changes must be capable of both states. And since that which 'is' has two senses, we must say that everything changes from that which is potentially to that which is actually, e.g. from potentially white to actually white, and similarly in the case of increase and diminution. Therefore not only can a thing come to be, incidentally, out of that which is not, but also all things come to be out of that [20] which is, but is potentially, and is not actually. And this is the 'One' of Anaxagoras; for instead of 'all things were together'[1]—and the 'Mixture' of Empedocles and Anaximander and the account given by Democritus—it is better to say 'all things were together potentially but not actually'. Therefore these thinkers seem to have had some notion of matter.

[1] Anaxagoras, fr. 1.

Now all things that change have matter, but [25] different matter; and of eternal things those which are not generable but are movable in space have matter—not matter for generation, however, but for motion from one place to another.

One might raise the question from what sort of non-being generation proceeds; for 'non-being' has three senses. If, then, one form of non-being exists potentially, still it is not by virtue of a potentiality for any and every thing, but different things come from different things; [30] nor is it satisfactory to say that 'all things were together'; for they differ in their matter, since otherwise why did an infinity of things come to be, and not one thing? For 'reason' is one, so that if matter also were one, that must have come to be in actuality which the matter was in potency. The causes and the principles, then, are three, two being the pair of contraries of which one is definition and form and the other is privation, and the third being the matter.

3

[35] Note, next, that neither the matter nor the form comes to be—and I mean the last matter and form. For everything that changes is something and is changed by something and into 1070ª something. That by which it is changed is the immediate mover; that which is changed, the matter; that into which it is changed, the form. The process, then, will go on to infinity, if not only the bronze comes to be round but also the round or the bronze comes to be; therefore there must be a stop.

Note, next, that each substance comes into [5] being out of something that shares its name. (Natural objects and other things both rank as substances.) For things come into being either by art or by nature or by luck or by spontaneity. Now art is a principle of movement in something other than the thing moved, nature is a principle in the thing itself (for man begets man), and the other causes are privations of these two.

There are three kinds of substance—the mat- [10] ter, which is a 'this' in appearance (for all things that are characterized by contact and not by organic unity are matter and sub- [19] stratum, e.g. fire, flesh, head; for these are all matter, and the last matter is the matter of that which is in the full sense substance); [11] the nature, which is a 'this' or positive state towards which movement takes place; and again, thirdly, the particular substance which is composed of these two, e.g. Socrates or Callias. Now in some cases the 'this' does not exist apart from the composite substance, e.g. the form of house does not so exist, unless [15] the art of building exists apart (nor is there generation and destruction of these forms, but it is in another way that the house apart from its matter, and health, and all ideals of art, exist and do not exist); but if the 'this' exists apart from the concrete thing, it is only in the case of natural objects. And so Plato was not far wrong when he said that there are as many Forms as there are kinds of natural object (if there *are* Forms distinct from the things of this earth). The moving [21] causes exist as things preceding the effects, but causes in the sense of definitions are simultaneous with their effects. For when a man is healthy, then health also exists; and the shape of a bronze sphere exists at the same time as the bronze sphere. (But we must ex- [25] amine whether any form also survives afterwards. For in some cases there is nothing to prevent this; e.g. the soul may be of this sort—not all soul but the reason; for presumably it is impossible that *all* soul should survive.) Evidently then there is no necessity, on this ground at least, for the existence of the Ideas. For man is begotten by man, a given man by an individual father; and similarly in [30] the arts; for the medical art is the formal cause of health.

4

The causes and the principles of different things are in a sense different, but in a sense, if one speaks universally and analogically, they are the same for all. For one might raise the question whether the principles and elements are different or the same for substances and for relative terms, and similarly in the case of [35] each of the categories. But it would be paradoxical if they were the same for all. For then from the same elements will proceed rela- 1070ᵇ tive terms and substances. What then will this common element be? For (1) (*a*) there is nothing common to and distinct from substance and the other categories, viz. those which are predicated; but an element is prior to the things of which it is an element. But again (*b*) substance is not an element in relative terms, nor is any of these an element in substance. Further, (2) how can all things have [5] the same elements? For none of the elements can be the same as that which is composed of elements, e.g. *b* or *a* cannot be the same as *ba*. (None, therefore, of the intelligibles, e.g.

being or unity, is an element; for these are predicable of each of the compounds as well.) None of the elements, then, will be either a substance or a relative term; but it must be one or other. All things, then, have not the same elements.

[10] Or, as we are wont to put it, in a sense they have and in a sense they have not; e.g. perhaps the elements of perceptible bodies are, as *form,* the hot, and in another sense the cold, which is the *privation;* and, as *matter,* that which directly and of itself potentially has these attributes; and substances comprise both these and the things composed of these, of which these are the principles, or any unity which is produced out of the hot and the cold, e.g. flesh [15] or bone; for the product must be different from the elements. These things then have the same elements and principles (though specifically different things have specifically different elements); but *all* things have not the same elements in this sense, but only analogically; i.e. one might say that there are three principles—the form, the privation, and the mat-[20] ter. But each of these is different for each class; e.g. in colour they are white, black, and surface, and in day and night they are light, darkness, and air.

Since not only the elements present in a thing are causes, but also something external, i.e. the moving cause, clearly while 'principle' and 'element' are different both are causes, and 'principle' is divided into these two kinds; and that which acts as producing movement or rest is a principle and a substance. Therefore [25] analogically there are three elements, and four causes and principles; but the elements are different in different things, and the proximate moving cause is different for different things. Health, disease, body; the moving cause is the medical art. Form, disorder of a particular kind, bricks; the moving cause is the [30] building art. And since the moving cause in the case of natural things is—for man, for instance, man, and in the products of thought the form or its contrary, there will be in a sense three causes, while in a sense there are four. For the medical art is in some sense health, and the building art is the form of the house, and man begets man; further, besides these there is that which as first of all things [35] moves all things.

5

Some things can exist apart and some cannot, 1071ᵃ and it is the former that are substances. And therefore all things have the same causes, because, without substances, modifications and movements do not exist. Further, these causes will probably be soul and body, or reason and desire and body.

And in yet another way, analogically iden-[5] tical things are principles, i.e. actuality and potency; but these also are not only different for different things but also apply in different ways to them. For in some cases the same thing exists at one time actually and at another potentially, e.g. wine or flesh or man does so. (And these too fall under the above-named causes. For the form exists actually, if it can exist apart, and so does the complex of form and matter, and the privation, e.g. darkness or [10] disease; but the matter exists potentially; for this is that which can become qualified either by the form or by the privation.) But the distinction of actuality and potentiality applies in another way to cases where the matter of cause and of effect is not the same, in some of which cases the form is not the same but different; e.g. the cause of man is (1) the elements in man (viz. fire and earth as matter, and the peculiar form), and further (2) something else outside, i.e. the father, and (3) be-[15] sides these the sun and its oblique course, which are neither matter nor form nor privation of man nor of the same species with him, but moving causes.

Further, one must observe that some causes can be expressed in universal terms, and some cannot. The proximate principles of all things are the 'this' which is proximate in actuality, and another which is proximate in potentiality. The universal causes, then, of which we spoke [20] do not *exist.* For it is the individual that is the originative principle of the individuals. For while man is the originative principle of man universally, there *is* no universal man, but Peleus is the originative principle of Achilles, and your father of you, and this particular *b* of this particular *ba,* though *b* in general is the originative principle of *ba* taken without qualification.

Further, if the causes of substances are the causes of all things, yet different things have different causes and elements, as was said[1]; the [25] causes of things that are not in the same class, e.g. of colours and sounds, of substances and quantities, are different except in an analogical sense; and those of things in the same species are different, not in species, but in the sense that the causes of different individuals

[1] In 1070ᵇ 17.

are different, your matter and form and moving cause being different from mine, while in their universal definition they are the same. [30] And if we inquire what are the principles or elements of substances and relations and qualities—whether they are the same or different—clearly when the names of the causes are used in several senses the causes of each are the same, but when the senses are distinguishd the causes are not the same but different, except that in the following senses the causes of all are the same. They are (1) the same or analogous in this sense, that matter, form, privation, and the moving cause are common to all things; and (2) the causes of substances may be treated as causes of all things in this sense, that when substances are removed [35] all things are removed; further, (3) that which is first in respect of complete reality is the cause of all things. But in another sense there are different first causes, viz. all the contraries which are neither generic nor ambiguous terms; and, further, the matters of different **1071ᵇ** things are different. We have stated, then, what are the principles of sensible things and how many they are, and in what sense they are the same and in what sense different.

6

Since there were three kinds of substance, two of them physical and one unmovable, regarding the latter we must assert that it is necessary that there should be an eternal unmovable [5] substance. For substances are the first of existing things, and if they are all destructible, all things are destructible. But it is impossible that movement should either have come into being or cease to be (for it must always have existed), or that time should. For there could not be a before and an after if time did not exist. Movement also is continuous, then, in the sense in which time is; for time is either the same thing as movement or an attribute of [10] movement. And there is no continuous movement except movement in place, and of this only that which is circular is continuous.

But if there is something which is capable of moving things or acting on them, but is not actually doing so, there will not necessarily be movement; for that which has a potency need not exercise it. Nothing, then, is gained even if we suppose eternal substances, as the be- [15] lievers in the Forms do, unless there is to be in them some principle which can cause change; nay, even this is not enough, nor is another substance besides the Forms enough; for if it is not to *act*, there will be no movement. Further even if it acts, this will not be enough, if its essence is potency; for there will not be *eternal* movement, since that which is potentially may possibly not be. There must, [20] then, be such a principle, whose very essence is actuality. Further, then, these substances must be without matter; for they must be eternal, if *anything* is eternal. Therefore they must be actuality.

Yet there is a difficulty; for it is thought that everything that acts is able to act, but that not everything that is able to act acts, so that [25] the potency is prior. But if this is so, nothing that is need be; for it is possible for all things to be capable of existing but not yet to exist.

Yet if we follow the theologians who generate the world from night, or the natural philosophers who say that 'all things were together',[1] the same impossible result ensues. For how will there be movement, if there is no actually existing cause? Wood will surely not move itself—the carpenter's art must act on it; [30] nor will the menstrual blood nor the earth set themselves in motion, but the seeds must act on the earth and the *semen* on the menstrual blood.

This is why some suppose eternal actuality —e.g. Leucippus and Plato[2]; for they say there is always movement. But why and what this movement is they do not say, nor, if the world moves in this way or that, do they tell us the cause of its doing so. Now nothing is moved at random, but there must always be something present to move it; e.g. as a matter of fact a [35] thing moves in one way by nature, and in another by force or through the influence of reason or something else. (Further, what sort of movement is primary? This makes a vast difference.) But again for Plato, at least, it is not permissible to name here that which he **1072ᵃ** sometimes supposes to be the source of movement—that which moves itself;[3] for the soul is later, and coeval with the heavens, according to his account.[4] To suppose potency prior to actuality, then, is in a sense right, and in a sense not; and we have specified these senses.[5] That actuality is prior is testified by [5] Anaxagoras (for his 'reason' is actuality) and by Empedocles in his doctrine of love and strife, and by those who say that there is always movement, e.g. Leucippus. Therefore

---

[1] Anaxagoras, fr. 1.   [2] Cf. *Timaeus*, 30.
[3] Cf. *Phaedrus*, 245; *Laws*, 894.
[4] Cf. *Timaeus*, 34.   [5] Cf. 1071ᵇ 22-26.

chaos or night did not exist for an infinite time, but the same things have always existed (either passing through a cycle of changes or obeying some other law), since actuality is prior to potency. If, then, there is a constant cycle, something must always remain, acting in the [10] same way. And if there is to be generation and destruction, there must be something else which is always acting in different ways. This must, then, act in one way in virtue of itself, and in another in virtue of something else— either of a third agent, therefore, or of the first. Now it must be in virtue of the first. For otherwise this again causes the motion both of the second agent and of the third. Therefore it is [15] better to say 'the first'. For it was the cause of eternal uniformity; and something else is the cause of variety, and evidently both together are the cause of eternal variety. This, accordingly, is the character which the motions actually exhibit. What need then is there to seek for other principles?

7

Since (1) this is a possible account of the matter, and (2) if it were not true, the world would have proceeded out of night and 'all things together'[1] and out of non-being, these [20] difficulties may be taken as solved. There is, then, something which is always moved with an unceasing motion, which is motion in a circle; and this is plain not in theory only but in fact. Therefore the first heaven must be eternal. There is therefore also something which moves it. And since that which moves and is moved is intermediate, there is something which moves without being moved, be-[25]ing eternal, substance, and actuality. And the object of desire and the object of thought move in this way; they move without being moved. The primary objects of desire and of thought are the same. For the apparent good is the object of appetite, and the real good is the primary object of rational wish. But desire is consequent on opinion rather than opinion on desire; for the thinking is the starting-point. [30] And thought is moved by the object of thought, and one of the two columns of opposites is in itself the object of thought; and in this, substance is first, and in substance, that which is simple and exists actually. (The one and the simple are not the same; for 'one' means a measure, but 'simple' means that the thing itself has a certain nature.) But the beautiful, also, and that which is in itself desirable

[1] Anaxagoras, fr. 1.

[35] are in the same column; and the first in any class is always best, or analogous to the best.

1072ᵇ That a final cause may exist among unchangeable entities is shown by the distinction of its meanings. For the final cause is (*a*) some being for whose good an action is done, and (*b*) something at which the action aims; and of these the latter exists among unchangeable entities though the former does not. The final cause, then, produces motion as being loved, but all other things move by being moved. Now if something is moved it is capable of being otherwise than as it is. Therefore [5] if its actuality is the primary form of spatial motion, then in so far as it is subject to change, in *this* respect it is capable of being otherwise,—in place, even if not in substance. But since there is something which moves while itself unmoved, existing actually, this can in no way be otherwise than as it is. For motion in space is the first of the kinds of change, and motion in a circle the first kind of spatial motion; and this the first mover pro-[10]duces. The first mover, then, exists of necessity; and in so far as it exists by necessity, its mode of being is good, and it is in this sense a first principle. For the necessary has all these senses—that which is necessary perforce because it is contrary to the natural impulse, that without which the good is impossible, and that which cannot be otherwise but can exist only in a single way.

On such a principle, then, depend the heavens and the world of nature. And it is a life such as the best which we enjoy, and enjoy for [15] but a short time (for it is ever in this state, which we cannot be), since its actuality is also pleasure. (And for this reason are waking, perception, and thinking most pleasant, and hopes and memories are so on account of these.) And thinking in itself deals with that which is best in itself, and that which is thinking in the fullest sense with that which is best in the fullest sense. And thought thinks on itself because it shares the nature of the object [20] of thought; for it becomes an object of thought in coming into contact with and thinking its objects, so that thought and object of thought are the same. For that which is *capable* of receiving the object of thought, i.e. the essence, is thought. But it is *active* when it *possesses* this object. Therefore the possession rather than the receptivity is the divine element which thought seems to contain, and the act of contemplation is what is most pleasant and best. If, then, God is always in that good state in which we sometimes are, this compels [25] our wonder; and if in a better this compels it yet more. And God *is* in a better state. And life also belongs to God; for the actuality of thought is life, and God is that actuality; and God's self-dependent actuality is life most good and eternal. We say therefore that God is a living being, eternal, most good, so that life and duration continuous and eternal belong to God; for this *is* God.

[30] Those who suppose, as the Pythagoreans and Speusippus do, that supreme beauty and goodness are not present in the beginning, because the beginnings both of plants and of animals are *causes,* but beauty and completeness [35] are in the *effects* of these, are wrong in their opinion. For the seed comes from other individuals which are prior and complete, and the first thing is not seed but the complete being; e.g. we must say that before the seed there is a man,—not the man produced from the seed, but another from whom the seed comes.

It is clear then from what has been said that there is a substance which is eternal and unmovable and separate from sensible things. It [5] has been shown also that this substance cannot have any magnitude, but is without parts and indivisible (for it produces movement through infinite time, but nothing finite has infinite power; and, while every magnitude is either infinite or finite, it cannot, for [10] the above reason, have finite magnitude, and it cannot have infinite magnitude because there is no infinite magnitude at all). But it has also been shown that it is impassive and unalterable; for all the other changes are posterior to change of place.

8

It is clear, then, why these things are as they are. But we must not ignore the question whether we have to suppose one such substance or more than one, and if the latter, how many; [15] we must also mention, regarding the opinions expressed by others, that they have said nothing about the number of the substances that can even be clearly stated. For the theory of Ideas has no special discussion of the subject; for those who speak of Ideas say the Ideas are numbers, and they speak of numbers now as unlimited, now as limited by the number [20] 10; but as for the reason why there should be just so many numbers, nothing is said with any demonstrative exactness. We however must discuss the subject, starting from the presuppositions and distinctions we have mentioned. The first principle or primary being is not movable either in itself or accident-[25] ally, but produces the primary eternal and single movement. But since that which is moved must be moved by something, and the first mover must be in itself unmovable, and eternal movement must be produced by something eternal and a single movement by a single thing, and since we see that besides the simple spatial movement of the universe, which [30] we say the first and unmovable substance produces, there are other spatial movements—those of the planets—which are eternal (for a body which moves in a circle is eternal and unresting; we have proved these points in the physical treatises[1]), each of *these* movements also must be caused by a substance both unmovable in itself and eternal. For the nature of the stars is eternal just because it is a certain [35] kind of substance, and the mover is eternal and prior to the moved, and that which is prior to a substance must be a substance. Evidently, then, there must be substances which are of the same number as the movements of the stars, and in their nature eternal, and in themselves unmovable, and without magnitude, for the reason before mentioned.[2]

That the movers are substances, then, and that one of these is first and another second according to the same order as the movements of the stars, is evident. But in the number of the movements we reach a problem which must be treated from the standpoint of that one of the mathematical sciences which is most akin to philosophy—viz. of astronomy; [5] for this science speculates about substance which is perceptible but eternal, but the other mathematical sciences, i.e. arithmetic and geometry, treat of no substance. That the movements are more numerous than the bodies that are moved is evident to those who have given even moderate attention to the matter; for each [10] of the planets has more than one movement. But as to the actual number of these movements, we now—to give some notion of the subject—quote what some of the mathematicians say, that our thought may have some definite number to grasp; but, for the rest, we must partly investigate for ourselves, [15] partly learn from other investigators, and if those who study this subject form an opinion

---

[1] Cf. *Physics,* VIII. 8, 9; *On the Heavens,* I. 2, II. 3-8.
[2] Cf. ll. 5-11.

contrary to what we have now stated, we must esteem both parties indeed, but follow the more accurate.

Eudoxus supposed that the motion of the sun or of the moon involves, in either case, three spheres, of which the first is the sphere of the fixed stars, and the second moves in the [20] circle which runs along the middle of the zodiac, and the third in the circle which is inclined across the breadth of the zodiac; but the circle in which the moon moves is inclined at a greater angle than that in which the sun moves. And the motion of the planets involves, in each case, four spheres, and of these also the first and second are the same as the first two [25] mentioned above (for the sphere of the fixed stars is that which moves all the other spheres, and that which is placed beneath this and has its movement in the circle which bisects the zodiac is common to all), but the *poles* of the third sphere of each planet are in the circle which bisects the zodiac, and the motion of the fourth sphere is in the circle which is inclined at an angle to the equator of the [30] third sphere; and the poles of the third sphere are different for each of the other planets, but those of Venus and Mercury are the same.

Callippus made the position of the spheres the same as Eudoxus did, but while he assigned the same number as Eudoxus did to [35] Jupiter and to Saturn, he thought two more spheres should be added to the sun and two to the moon, if one is to explain the observed facts; and one more to each of the other planets.

But it is necessary, if all the spheres combined are to explain the observed facts, that for each of the planets there should be other spheres (one fewer than those hitherto assigned) which counteract those already mentioned and bring back to the same position the outermost sphere of the star which in each case is situated below the star in question; for only [5] thus can all the forces at work produce the observed motion of the planets. Since, then, the spheres involved in the movement of the planets themselves are—eight for Saturn and Jupiter and twenty-five for the others, and of these only those involved in the movement of the lowest-situated planet need not be counteracted, the spheres which counteract those of the outermost two planets will be six in number, and the spheres which counteract those of the [10] next four planets will be sixteen; therefore the number of all the spheres—both those which move the planets and those which counteract these—will be fifty-five. And if one were not to add to the moon and to the sun the movements we mentioned,[1] the whole set of spheres will be forty-seven in number.

Let this, then, be taken as the number of the [15] spheres, so that the unmovable substances and principles also may probably be taken as just so many; the assertion of *necessity* must be left to more powerful thinkers. But if there can be no spatial movement which does not conduce to the moving of a star, and if further every being and every substance which is immune from change and in virtue of itself has attained to the best must be considered an end, [20] there can be no other being apart from these we have named, but this must be the number of the substances. For if there are others, they will cause change as being a final cause of movement; but there cannot *be* other movements besides those mentioned. And it is reasonable to infer this from a consideration of the bodies that are moved; for if everything [25] that moves is for the sake of that which is moved, and every movement belongs to something that is moved, no movement can be for the sake of itself or of another movement, but all the movements must be for the sake of the stars. For if there is to be a movement for the sake of a movement, this latter also will have to be for the sake of something else; so that since there cannot be an infinite regress, [30] the end of every movement will be one of the divine bodies which move through the heaven.

(Evidently there is but one heaven. For if there are many heavens as there are many men, the moving principles, of which each heaven will have one, will be one in form but in *number* many. But all things that are many in number have matter; for one and the same definition, e.g. that of man, applies to many [35] things, while Socrates is one. But the primary essence has not matter; for it is complete reality. So the unmovable first mover is one both in definition and in number; so too, therefore, is that which is moved always and continuously; therefore there is one heaven alone.)

Our forefathers in the most remote ages have handed down to their posterity a tradition, in the form of a myth, that these bodies are gods, and that the divine encloses the whole of nature. The rest of the tradition has been added later in mythical form with a view to the persuasion of the multitude and to its legal

---

[1] In 1073^b 35, 38–1074^a 4.

[5] and utilitarian expediency; they say these gods are in the form of men or like some of the other animals, and they say other things consequent on and similar to these which we have mentioned. But if one were to separate the first point from these additions and take it alone—that they thought the first substances [10] to be gods, one must regard this as an inspired utterance, and reflect that, while probably each art and each science has often been developed as far as possible and has again perished, these opinions, with others, have been preserved until the present like relics of the ancient treasure. Only thus far, then, is the opinion of our ancestors and of our earliest predecessors clear to us.

9

[15] The nature of the divine thought involves certain problems; for while thought is held to be the most divine of things observed by us, the question how it must be situated in order to have that character involves difficulties. For if it thinks of nothing, what is there here of dignity? It is just like one who sleeps. And if it thinks, but this depends on something else, then (since that which is its substance is not the act of thinking, but a potency) it cannot be [20] the best substance; for it is through thinking that its value belongs to it. Further, whether its substance is the faculty of thought or the act of thinking, what does it think of? Either of itself or of something else; and if of something else, either of the same thing always or of something different. Does it matter, then, or not, whether it thinks of the good or of any [25] chance thing? Are there not some things about which it is incredible that it should think? Evidently, then, it thinks of that which is most divine and precious, and it does not change; for change would be change for the worse, and this would be already a movement. First, then, if 'thought' is not the act of thinking but a potency, it would be reasonable to suppose that the continuity of its thinking is wearisome to it. Secondly, there would evidently be something else more precious than [30] thought, viz. that which is thought of. For both thinking and the act of thought will belong even to one who thinks of the worst thing in the world, so that if this ought to be avoided (and it ought, for there are even some things which it is better not to see than to see), the act of thinking cannot be the best of things. Therefore it must be of itself that the divine thought thinks (since it is the most excellent of things), and its thinking is a thinking on thinking.

[35] But evidently knowledge and perception and opinion and understanding have always something else as their object, and themselves only by the way. Further, if thinking and being thought of are different, in respect of which does goodness belong to thought? For to *be* an act of thinking and to *be* an object of thought are not the same thing. We answer 1075ᵃ that in some cases the knowledge is the object. In the productive sciences it is the substance or essence of the object, matter omitted, and in the theoretical sciences the definition or the act of thinking is the object. Since, then, thought and the object of thought are not different in the case of things that have not matter, the divine thought and its object will be the same, i.e. the thinking will be one with the object of its thought.

[5] A further question is left—whether the object of the divine thought is composite; for if it were, thought would change in passing from part to part of the whole. We answer that everything which has not matter is indivisible —as human thought, or rather the thought of composite beings, is in a certain period of time (for it does not possess the good at this moment or at that, but its best, being something *dif-* [10] *ferent* from it, is attained only in a whole period of time), so throughout eternity is the thought which has *itself* for its object.

10

We must consider also in which of two ways the nature of the universe contains the good and the highest good, whether as something separate and by itself, or as the order of the parts. Probably in both ways, as an army does; for its good is found both in its order and in [15] its leader, and more in the latter; for he does not depend on the order but it depends on him. And all things are ordered together somehow, but not all alike,—both fishes and fowls and plants; and the world is not such that one thing has nothing to do with another, but they are connected. For all are ordered together to one end, but it is as in a house, where the free- [20] men are least at liberty to act at random, but all things or most things are already ordained for them, while the slaves and the animals do little for the common good, and for the most part live at random; for this is the sort of principle that constitutes the nature of each. I mean, for instance, that all must at least come to be dissolved into their elements, and there are other functions similarly in which all share for the good of the whole.

[25] We must not fail to observe how many impossible or paradoxical results confront those who hold different views from our own, and what are the views of the subtler thinkers, and which views are attended by fewest difficulties. All make all things out of contraries. But neither 'all things' nor 'out of contraries' is right; nor do these thinkers tell us how all the things in which the contraries are present [30] can be made out of the contraries; for contraries are not affected by one another. Now for us this difficulty is solved naturally by the fact that there is a third element. These thinkers however make one of the two contraries matter; this is done for instance by those who make the unequal matter for the equal, or the many matter for the one. But this also is refuted in the same way; for the one matter which underlies any pair of contraries is contrary to nothing. Further, all things, except the one, will, on the view we are criticiz-[35] ing, partake of evil; for the bad itself is one of the two elements. But the other school does not treat the good and the bad even as principles; yet in all things the good is in the highest degree a principle. The school we first mentioned is right in saying that it is a principle, but *how* the good is a principle they do not say—whether as end or as mover or as form.

1075[b] Empedocles also has a paradoxical view; for he identifies the good with love, but this is a principle both as mover (for it brings things together) and as matter (for it is part of the mixture). Now even if it happens that [5] the same thing is a principle both as matter and as mover, still the being, at least, of the two is not the same. In which respect then is love a principle? It is paradoxical also that strife should be imperishable; the nature of his 'evil' is just strife.

Anaxagoras makes the good a motive principle; for his 'reason' moves things. But it moves them for an end, which must be something other than it, except according to *our* way of stating the case; for, on our view, the [10] medical art is in a sense health. It is paradoxical also not to suppose a contrary to the good, i.e. to reason. But all who speak of the contraries make no use of the contraries, unless we bring their views into shape. And why some things are perishable and others imperishable, no one tells us; for they make all existing things out of the same principles. Further, [15] some make existing things out of the non-existent; and others to avoid the necessity of this make all things one.

Further, why should there always be becoming, and what is the cause of becoming?—this no one tells us. And those who suppose two principles must suppose another, a superior principle, and so must those who believe in the Forms; for why did things come to participate, or why do they participate, in the [20] Forms? And all other thinkers are confronted by the necessary consequence that there is something contrary to Wisdom, i.e. to the highest knowledge; but *we* are not. For there is nothing contrary to that which is primary; for all contraries have matter, and things that have matter exist only potentially; and the ignorance which is contrary to any knowledge leads to an object contrary to the object of the knowledge; but what is primary has no contrary.

[25] Again, if besides sensible things no others exist, there will be no first principle, no order, no becoming, no heavenly bodies, but each principle will have a principle before it, as in the accounts of the theologians and all the natural philosophers. But if the Forms or the numbers are to exist, they will be causes of nothing; or if not that, at least not of movement. Further, how is extension, i.e. a *continuum,* to be produced out of unextended parts? For number will not, either as mover or as form, pro-[30] duce a *continuum.* But again there cannot be any *contrary* that is also essentially a productive or moving principle; for it would be possible for it not to be. Or at least its action would be posterior to its potency. The world, then, would not be eternal. But it is; one of these premisses, then, must be denied. And we have said how this must be done. Further, in virtue of what the numbers, or the soul and [35] the body, or in general the form and the thing, are one—of this no one tells us anything; nor can any one tell, unless he says, as we do, that the mover makes them one. And those who say mathematical number is first and go on to generate one kind of substance after an-**1076**[a] other and give different principles for each, make the substance of the universe a mere series of episodes (for one substance has no influence on another by its existence or non-existence), and they give us many governing principles; but the world refuses to be governed badly.

'The rule of many is not good; one ruler let there be.'[1]

---

[1] Cf. *Iliad,* II. 204.

BOOK XIII

1

We have stated what is the substance of sensible things, dealing in the treatise on physics[1] with matter, and later[2] with the substance [10] which has actual existence. Now since our inquiry is whether there is or is not besides the sensible substances any which is immovable and eternal, and, if there is, what it is, we must first consider what is said by others, so that, if there is anything which they say wrongly, we may not be liable to the same objections, while, if there is any opinion common to them and us, we shall have no private grievance [15] against ourselves on that account; for one must be content to state some points better than one's predecessors, and others no worse.

Two opinions are held on this subject; it is said that the objects of mathematics—i.e. numbers and lines and the like—are substances, and again that the Ideas are substances. And since (1) some recognize these as two different [20] classes—the Ideas and the mathematical numbers, and (2) some recognize both as having one nature, while (3) some others say that the mathematical substances are the only substances, we must consider first the objects of mathematics, not qualifying them by any other characteristic—not asking, for instance, whether they are in fact Ideas or not, or whether they are the principles and substances [25] of existing things or not, but only whether as objects of mathematics they exist or not, and if they exist, how they exist. Then after this we must separately consider the Ideas themselves in a general way, and only as far as the accepted mode of treatment demands; for most of the points have been repeatedly made even by the discussions outside our school, and, further, the greater part of our account must [30] finish by throwing light on that inquiry, viz. when we examine[3] whether the substances and the principles of existing things are numbers and Ideas; for after the discussion of the Ideas this remains as a third inquiry.

If the objects of mathematics exist, they must exist either in sensible objects, as some say, or [35] separate from sensible objects (and this also is said by some); or if they exist in neither of these ways, either they do not exist, or they exist only in some special sense. So that the subject of our discussion will be not whether they exist but how they exist.

2

That it is impossible for mathematical objects to exist *in* sensible things, and at the same time that the doctrine in question is an artificial one, has been said already in our discussion of difficulties[4]; we have pointed out that it is impossible for two solids to be in the same place, and also that according to the same argument the other powers and characteristics also should exist in sensible things and none of them separately. This we have said already. But, further, it is obvious that on this theory it is impossible for any body whatever to be divided; [5] for it would have to be divided at a plane, and the plane at a line, and the line at a point, so that if the point cannot be divided, neither can the line, and if the line cannot, neither can the plane nor the solid. What difference, then, does it make whether sensible things are such indivisible entities, or, without [10] being so themselves, have indivisible entities in them? The result will be the same; if the sensible entities are divided the others will be divided too, or else not even the sensible entities can be divided.

But, again, it is not possible that such entities should exist *separately*. For if besides the sensible solids there are to be other solids which are separate from them and prior to the sensible solids, it is plain that besides the planes also [15] there must be other and separate planes and points and lines; for consistency requires this. But if these exist, again besides the planes and lines and points of the mathematical solid there must be others which are separate. (For incomposites are prior to compounds; and if there are, prior to the sensible bodies, bodies [20] which are not sensible, by the same argument the planes which exist by themselves must be prior to those which are in the motionless solids. Therefore these will be planes and lines other than those that exist along with the mathematical solids to which these thinkers assign separate existence; for the latter exist along with the mathematical solids, while the others are prior to the mathematical solids.) [25] Again, therefore, there will be, belonging to these planes, lines, and prior to them there will have to be, by the same argument, other

---

[1] *Physics*, I. [2] *Metaphysics*, VII, VIII, IX.
[3] Cf. chapters 6-9. [4] Cf. III. 998ᵃ 7-19.

lines and points; and prior to these points in the prior lines there will have to be other points, though there will be no others prior to these. Now (1) the accumulation becomes absurd; for we find ourselves with one set of [30] solids apart from the sensible solids; three sets of planes apart from the sensible planes—those which exist apart from the sensible planes, and those in the mathematical solids, and those which exist apart from those in the mathematical solids; four sets of lines, and five sets of points. With which of these, then, will the mathematical sciences deal? Certainly not with the planes and lines and points in the [35] motionless solid; for science always deals with what is prior. And (2) the same account will apply also to numbers; for there will be a different set of units apart from each set of points, and also apart from each set of realities, from the objects of sense and again from those of thought; so that there will be various classes of mathematical numbers.

Again, how is it possible to solve the questions which we have already enumerated in our discussion of difficulties[1]? For the objects of 1077ᵃ astronomy will exist apart from sensible things just as the objects of geometry will; but how is it possible that a heaven and its parts—or anything else which has movement—should exist apart? Similarly also the objects of optics and of harmonics will exist apart; for [5] there will be both voice and sight besides the sensible or individual voices and sights. Therefore it is plain that the other senses as well, and the other objects of sense, will exist apart; for why should one set of them do so and another not? And if this is so, there will also be animals existing apart, since there will be senses.

Again, there are certain mathematical theo-[10]rems that are universal, extending beyond these substances. Here then we shall have another intermediate substance separate both from the Ideas and from the intermediates,—a substance which is neither number nor points nor spatial magnitude nor time. And if this is impossible, plainly it is also impossible that the *former* entities should exist separate from sensible things.

And, in general, conclusion contrary alike [15] to the truth and to the usual views follow, if one is to suppose the objects of mathematics to exist thus as separate entities. For because they exist thus they must be prior to sensible spatial magnitudes, but in truth they must be posterior; for the incomplete spatial magnitude is in the order of generation prior, but in the order of substance posterior, as the lifeless is to the living.

[20] Again, by virtue of what, and when, will mathematical magnitudes be one? For things in our perceptible world are one in virtue of soul, or of a part of soul, or of something else that is reasonable enough; when these are not present, the thing is a plurality, and splits up into parts. But in the case of the subjects of mathematics, which are divisible and are quantities, what is the cause of their being one and holding together?

Again, the modes of generation of the objects of mathematics show that we are right. For the dimension first generated is length, [25] then comes breadth, lastly depth, and the process is complete. If, then, that which is posterior in the order of generation is prior in the order of substantiality, the solid will be prior to the plane and the line. And in *this* way also it is both more complete and more whole, because it can become animate. How, on the other hand, could a line or a plane be animate? [30] The supposition passes the power of our senses.

Again, the solid is a sort of substance; for it already has in a sense completeness. But how can lines be substances? Neither as a form or shape, as the soul perhaps is, nor as matter, like the solid; for we have no experience of anything that can be put together out of lines [35] or planes or points, while if these had been a sort of material substance, we should have observed things which could be put together out of them.

1077ᵇ Grant, then, that they are prior in definition. Still not all things that are prior in definition are also prior in substantiality. For those things are prior in substantiality which when separated from other things surpass them in the power of independent existence, but things are prior in definition to those whose definitions are compounded out of their definitions; and these two properties are not co-[5]extensive. For if attributes do not exist apart from the substances (e.g. a 'mobile' or a 'pale'), pale is prior to the pale man in definition, but not in substantiality. For it cannot exist separately, but is always along with the concrete thing; and by the concrete thing I mean the pale man. Therefore it is plain that neither is the result of abstraction prior nor that which is produced by adding determinants [10] posterior; for it is by adding a determi-

---
[1] III. 997ᵇ 12-34.

nant to pale that we speak of the pale man.

It has, then, been sufficiently pointed out that the objects of mathematics are not substances in a higher degree than bodies are, and that they are not prior to sensibles in being, but only in definition, and that they cannot exist somewhere apart. But since it was not possible [15] for them to exist *in* sensibles either, it is plain that they either do not exist at all or exist in a special sense and therefore do not 'exist' without qualification. For 'exist' has many senses.

3

For just as the universal propositions of mathematics deal not with objects which exist separately, apart from extended magnitudes and from numbers, but with magnitudes and numbers, not however *qua* such as to have magni-[20] tude or to be divisible, clearly it is possible that there should also be both propositions and demonstrations about sensible magnitudes, not however *qua* sensible but *qua* possessed of certain definite qualities. For as there are many propositions about things merely considered as [25] in motion, apart from what each such thing is and from their accidents, and as it is not therefore necessary that there should be either a mobile separate from sensibles, or a distinct mobile entity in the sensibles, so too in the case of mobiles there will be propositions and sciences, which treat them however not *qua* mobile but only *qua* bodies, or again only *qua* [30] planes, or only *qua* lines, or *qua* divisibles, or *qua* indivisibles having position, or only *qua* indivisibles. Thus since it is true to say without qualification that not only things which are separable but also things which are inseparable exist (for instance, that mobiles exist), it is true also to say without qualification that the objects of mathematics exist, and with the character ascribed to them by mathematicians. And as it is true to say of the other sciences too, without qualification, that they deal with such and such a subject—not with [35] what is accidental to it (e.g. not with the pale, if the healthy thing is pale, and the science has the healthy as its subject), but with that which is the subject of each science—with 1078ᵃ the healthy if it treats its object *qua* healthy, with man if *qua* man:—so too is it with geometry; if its subjects happen to be sensible, though it does not treat them *qua* sensible, the mathematical sciences will not for that reason be sciences of sensibles—nor, on the [5] other hand, of other things separate from sensibles. Many properties attach to things in virtue of their own nature as possessed of each such character; e.g. there are attributes peculiar to the animal *qua* female or *qua* male (yet there is no 'female' nor 'male' separate from animals); so that there are also attributes which belong to things merely as lengths or as planes. And in proportion as we are dealing with things which are prior in definition and sim-[10] pler, our knowledge has more accuracy, i.e. simplicity. Therefore a science which abstracts from spatial magnitude is more precise than one which takes it into account; and a science is most precise if it abstracts from movement, but if it takes account of movement, it is most precise if it deals with the primary movement, for this is the simplest; and of this again uniform movement is the simplest form.

The same account may be given of har-[15] monics and optics; for neither considers its objects *qua* sight or *qua* voice, but *qua* lines and numbers; but the latter are attributes proper to the former. And mechanics too proceeds in the same way. Therefore if we suppose attributes separated from their fellow-attributes and make any inquiry concerning them as such, we shall not for this reason be in error, any more than when one draws a line on the ground and calls it a foot long when it [20] is not; for the error is not included in the premisses.

Each question will be best investigated in this way—by setting up by an act of separation what is not separate, as the arithmetician and the geometer do. For a man *qua* man is one indivisible thing; and the arithmetician supposed one indivisible thing, and then considered whether any attribute belongs to a man *qua* indivisible. But the geometer treats him neither [25] *qua* man nor *qua* indivisible, but as a solid. For evidently the properties which would have belonged to him even if perchance he had not been indivisible, can belong to him even apart from these attributes. Thus, then, geometers speak correctly; they talk about existing [30] things, and their subjects do exist; for being has two forms—it exists not only in complete reality but also materially.

Now since the good and the beautiful are different (for the former always implies conduct as its subject, while the beautiful is found also in motionless things), those who assert that the mathematical sciences say nothing of the beautiful or the good are in error. For these [35] sciences say and prove a great deal about them; if they do not expressly mention them, but prove attributes which are their results or their definitions, it is not true to say that they tell us nothing about them. The chief forms of beauty are order and symmetry and definiteness, which the mathematical sciences demonstrate in a special degree. And since these (e.g. order and definiteness) are obviously causes of many things, evidently these sciences must treat this sort of causative principle also (i.e. the beautiful) as in some sense [5] a cause. But we shall speak more plainly elsewhere about these matters.

4

So much then for the objects of mathematics; we have said that they exist and in what sense they exist, and in what sense they are prior and in what sense not prior. Now, regarding the Ideas, we must first examine the ideal [10] theory itself, not connecting it in any way with the nature of numbers, but treating it in the form in which it was originally understood by those who first maintained the existence of the Ideas. The supporters of the ideal theory were led to it because on the question about the truth of things they accepted the Heraclitean sayings which describe all sensible [15] things as ever passing away, so that if knowledge or thought is to have an object, there must be some other and permanent entities, apart from those which are sensible; for there could be no knowledge of things which were in a state of flux. But when Socrates was occupying himself with the excellences of character, and in connexion with them became the first to raise the problem of universal definition (for of the physicists Democritus only [20] touched on the subject to a small extent, and defined, after a fashion, the hot and the cold; while the Pythagoreans had before this treated of a few things, whose definitions— e.g. those of opportunity, justice, or marriage —they connected with numbers; but it was natural that Socrates should be seeking the essence, for he was seeking to syllogize, and 'what a thing is' is the starting-point of syllo- [25] gisms; for there was as yet none of the dialectical power which enables people even without knowledge of the essence to speculate about contraries and inquire whether the same science deals with contraries; for two things may be fairly ascribed to Socrates—inductive arguments and universal definition, both of which are concerned with the starting-point [30] of science):—but Socrates did not make the universals or the definitions exist apart: *they,* however, gave them separate existence, and this was the kind of thing they called Ideas. Therefore it followed for them, almost by the same argument, that there must be Ideas of all things that are spoken of universally, and it was almost as if a man wished to count certain things, and while they were few [35] thought he would not be able to count them, but made more of them and then counted them; for the Forms are, one may say, more numerous than the particular sensible things, yet it was in seeking the causes of these that they proceeded from them to the Forms. For to each thing there answers an entity which has the same name and exists apart from the substances, and so also in the case of all other groups there is a one over many, whether these be of this world or eternal.

Again, of the ways in which it is proved [5] that the Forms exist, none is convincing; for from some no inference necessarily follows, and from some arise Forms even of things of which they think there are no Forms. For according to the arguments from the sciences there will be Forms of all things of which there are sciences, and according to the argument of the 'one over many' there will be [10] Forms even of negations, and according to the argument that thought has an object when the individual object has perished, there will be Forms of perishable things; for we have an image of these. Again, of the most accurate arguments, some lead to Ideas of relations, of which they say there is no independent class, and others introduce the 'third man'.

And in general the arguments for the Forms destroy things for whose existence the believers in Forms are more zealous than for the exist- [15] ence of the Ideas; for it follows that not the dyad but number is first, and that prior to number is the relative, and that this is prior to the absolute—besides all the other points on which certain people, by following out the opinions held about the Forms, came into conflict with the principles of the theory.

Again, according to the assumption on [20] which the belief in the Ideas rests, there will be Forms not only of substances but also of many other things; for the concept is single not only in the case of substances, but also in that of non-substances, and there are sciences of other things than substance; and a thousand other such difficulties confront them. But according to the necessities of the case and the [25] opinions about the Forms, if they can be shared in there must be Ideas of substances only. For they are not shared in incidentally, but each Form must be shared in as something not predicated of a subject. (By 'being shared in incidentally' I mean that if a thing shares in 'double itself', it shares also in 'eternal', but incidentally; for 'the double' happens to be [30] eternal.) Therefore the Forms will be substance. But the same names indicate substance in this and in the ideal world (or what will be the meaning of saying that there is something apart from the particulars—the one over many?). And if the Ideas and the things that share in them have the same form, there will be something common: for why should '2' be one and the same in the perish- [35] able 2's, or in the 2's which are many but eternal, and not the same in the '2 itself' as in the individual 2? But if they have not the same form, they will have only the name in common, and it is as if one were to call both Callias and a piece of wood a 'man', without observing any community between them.

But if we are to suppose that in other respects the common definitions apply to the Forms, e.g. that 'plane figure' and the other [5] parts of the definition apply to the circle-itself, but 'what really is' has to be added, we must inquire whether this is not absolutely meaningless. For to what is this to be added? To 'centre' or to 'plane' or to all the parts of the definition? For all the elements in the essence are Ideas, e.g. 'animal' and 'two-footed'. [10] Further, there must be some Ideal answering to 'plane' above, some nature which will be present in all the Forms as their genus.

5

Above all one might discuss the question what in the world the Forms contribute to sensible things, either to those that are eternal or to those that come into being and cease to be; for they cause neither movement nor any change [15] in them. But again they help in no wise either towards the knowledge of other things (for they are not even the substance of these, else they would have been in them), or towards their being, if they are not *in* the individuals which share in them; though if they were, they might be thought to be causes, as white causes whiteness in a white object by entering [20] into its composition. But this argument, which was used first by Anaxagoras, and later by Eudoxus in his discussion of difficulties and by certain others, is very easily upset; for it is easy to collect many and insuperable objections to such a view.

But, further, all other things cannot come [25] from the Forms in any of the usual senses of 'from'. And to say that they are patterns and the other things share in them is to use empty words and poetical metaphors. For what is it that works, looking to the Ideas? And any thing can both be and come into being without being copied from something else, so that, whether Socrates exists or not, a man like Soc- [30] rates might come to be. And evidently this might be so even if Socrates were eternal. And there will be several patterns of the same thing, and therefore several Forms; e.g. 'animal' and 'two-footed', and also 'man-himself', will be Forms of man. Again, the Forms are patterns not only of sensible things, but of Forms themselves also; i.e. the genus is the pattern of the various forms-of-a-genus; therefore the same thing will be pattern and copy. [35] Again, it would seem impossible that substance and that whose substance it is should exist apart; how, therefore, could the Ideas, being the substances of things, exist apart?

In the *Phaedo*[1] the case is stated in this way —that the Forms are causes both of being and of becoming. Yet though the Forms exist, still things do not come into being, unless there is something to originate movement; and many other things come into being (e.g. a house or a [5] ring) of which they say there are no Forms. Clearly therefore even the things of which they say there are Ideas can both be and come into being owing to such causes as produce the things just mentioned, and not owing to the Forms. But regarding the Ideas it is possible, both in this way and by more abstract and [10] accurate arguments, to collect many objections like those we have considered.

6

Since we have discussed these points, it is well to consider again the results regarding numbers which confront those who say that numbers are separable substances and first causes [15] of things. If number is an entity and its substance is nothing other than just number, as some say, it follows that either (1) there is a first in it and a second, each being different in species,—and either (*a*) this is true of the units without exception, and any unit is inas- [20] sociable with any unit, or (*b*) they are all without exception successive, and any of them

[1] 100.

are associable with any, as they say is the case with mathematical number; for in mathematical number no one unit is in any way different from another. Or (c) some units must be associable and some not; e.g. suppose that 2 is first after 1, and then comes 3 and then the rest [25] of the number series, and the units in each number are associable, e.g. those in the first 2 are associable with one another, and those in the first 3 with one another, and so with the other numbers; but the units in the '2-itself' are inassociable with those in the '3-itself'; and similarly in the case of the other [30] successive numbers. And so while mathematical number is counted thus—after 1, 2 (which consists of another 1 besides the former 1), and 3 (which consists of another 1 besides these two), and the other numbers similarly, ideal number is counted thus—after 1, a distinct 2 which does not include the first 1, and a 3 which does not include the 2, and the rest of the number series similarly. Or (2) one kind [35] of number must be like the first that was named,[1] one like that which the mathematicians speak of, and that which we have named last[2] must be a third kind.

Again, these kinds of numbers must either 1080[b] be separable from things, or not separable but in objects of perception (not however in the way which we first considered,[3] but in the sense that objects of perception consists of numbers which are present in them)—either one kind and not another, or all of them.

[5] These are of necessity the only ways in which the numbers can exist. And of those who say that the 1 is the beginning and substance and element of all things, and that number is formed from the 1 and something else, almost every one has described number in one of these ways; only no one has said *all* the units are inassociable. And this has happened reason- [10] ably enough; for there can be no way besides those mentioned. Some say both kinds of number exist, that which has a before and after being identical with the Ideas, and mathematical number being different from the Ideas and from sensible things, and both being separable from sensible things; and others say [15] mathematical number alone exists, as the first of realities, separate from sensible things. And the Pythagoreans, also, believe in one kind of number—the mathematical; only they say it is not separate but sensible substances are formed out of it. For they construct the whole universe out of numbers—only not numbers consisting of abstract units; they suppose the [20] units to have spatial magnitude. But how the first 1 was constructed so as to have magnitude, they seem unable to say.

Another thinker says the first kind of number, that of the Forms, alone exists, and some say mathematical number is identical with this.

The case of lines, planes, and solids is similar. For some think that those which are the objects of mathematics are different from those [25] which come after the Ideas; and of those who express themselves otherwise some speak of the objects of mathematics and in a mathematical way—viz. those who do not make the Ideas numbers nor say that Ideas exist; and others speak of the objects of mathematics, but not mathematically; for they say that neither is every spatial magnitude divisible into magni- [30] tudes, nor do any two units taken at random make 2. All who say the 1 is an element and principle of things suppose numbers to consist of abstract units, except the Pythagoreans; but *they* suppose the numbers to have magnitude, as has been said before.[4] It is clear from this statement, then, in how many ways numbers may be described, and that all the [35] ways have been mentioned; and all these views are impossible, but some perhaps more than others.

7

First, then, let us inquire if the units are associ- 1081[a] able or inassociable, and if inassociable, in which of the two ways we distinguished. For it is possible that any unity is inassociable with any, and it is possible that those in the '2-itself' are inassociable with those in the '3-itself', and, generally, that those in each ideal number are inassociable with those in other [5] ideal numbers. Now (1) if all units are associable and without difference, we get mathematical number—only one kind of number, and the Ideas cannot be the numbers. For what sort of number will man-himself or animal-itself or any other Form be? There is one Idea of each thing, e.g. one of man-himself and [10] another one of animal-itself; but the similar and undifferentiated numbers are infinitely many, so that any particular 3 is no more man-himself than any other 3. But if the Ideas are not numbers, neither can they exist at all. For from what principles will the Ideas come? [15] It is number that comes from the 1 and the indefinite dyad, and the principles or elements are said to be principles and elements of

---

[1] ll. 15-20.   [2] ll. 23-35.   [3] Cf. 1076[a] 38-[b] 11.   [4] l. 19.

number, and the Ideas cannot be ranked as either prior or posterior to the numbers.

But (2) if the units are inassociable, and inassociable in the sense that any is inassociable with any other, number of this sort cannot be mathematical number; for mathematical num- [20] ber consists of undifferentiated units, and the truths proved of it suit this character. Nor can it be ideal number. For 2 will not proceed immediately from 1 and the indefinite dyad, and be followed by the successive numbers, as they say '2, 3, 4'—for the units in the ideal 2 are generated at the same time, whether, as the first holder of the theory said, from unequals (coming into being when these were [25] equalized) or in some other way—since, if one unit is to be prior to the other, it will be prior also to the 2 composed of these; for when there is one thing prior and another posterior, the resultant of these will be prior to one and posterior to the other.

[30] Again, since the 1-itself is first, and then there is a particular 1 which is first among the others and next after the 1-itself, and again a third which is next after the second and next but one after the first 1,—so the units must be prior to the numbers after which they are named when we count them; e.g. there will be a third unit in 2 before 3 exists, and a fourth and a fifth in 3 before the numbers 4 and 5 [35] exist.—Now none of these thinkers has said the units are inassociable in this way, but according to their principles it is reasonable that they should be so even in this way, though 1081[b] in truth it is impossible. For it is reasonable both that the units should have priority and posteriority if there is a first unit or first 1, and also that the 2's should if there is a first 2; for after the first it is reasonable and [5] necessary that there should be a second, and if a second, a third, and so with the others successively. (And to say both things at the same time, that a *unit* is first and another unit is second after the ideal 1, and that a 2 is first after it, is impossible.) But they make a first unit or 1, but not also a second and a third, and a first 2, but not also a second and a third. [10] Clearly, also, it is not possible, if all the units are inassociable, that there should be a 2-itself and a 3-itself; and so with the other numbers. For whether the units are undifferentiated or different each from each, number must be counted by addition, e.g. 2 by adding [15] another 1 to the one, 3 by adding another 1 to the two, and 4 similarly. This being so, numbers cannot be generated as they generate them, from the 2 and the 1; for 2 becomes part [20] of 3, and 3 of 4, and the same happens in the case of the succeeding numbers, but *they* say 4 came from the first 2 and the indefinite 2,—which makes it two 2's *other* than the 2-itself; if not, the 2-itself will be a part of 4 and one other 2 will be added. And similarly 2 [25] will consist of the 1-itself and another 1; but if this is so, the other element cannot be an indefinite 2; for it generates one unit, not, as the indefinite 2 does, a definite 2.

Again, besides the 3-itself and the 2-itself how can there be other 3's and 2's? And how do they consist of prior and posterior units? [30] All this is absurd and fictitious, and there cannot be a first 2 and then a 3-itself. Yet there must, if the 1 and the indefinite dyad are to be the elements. But if the results are impossible, it is also impossible that these are the generating principles.

If the units, then, are differentiated, each from each, these results and others similar to [35] these follow of necessity. But (3) if those in different numbers are differentiated, but those in the same number are alone undifferentiated from one another, even so the difficulties that follow are no less. E.g. in the 10-itself there are ten units, and the 10 is composed both of them and of two 5's. But since the 10-itself is not any chance number nor composed of any chance 5's—or, for that matter, units—the units in this 10 must differ. For [5] if they do not differ, neither will the 5's of which the 10 consists differ; but since these differ, the units also will differ. But if they differ, will there be no other 5's in the 10 but only these two, or will there be others? If there are not, this is paradoxical; and if there are, what [10] sort of 10 will consist of them? For there is no other 10 in *the* 10 but itself. But it is actually *necessary* on their view that the 4 should not consist of any chance 2's; for the indefinite 2, as they say, received the definite 2 and made two 2's; for its nature was to double what it received.

[15] Again, as to the 2 being an entity apart from its two units, and the 3 an entity apart from its three units, how is this possible? Either by one's sharing in the other, as 'pale man' is different from 'pale' and 'man' (for it shares in these), or when one is a differentia of the other, as 'man' is different from 'animal' and 'two-footed'.

[20] Again, some things are one by contact, some by intermixture, some by position; none of which can belong to the units of which the 2

or the 3 consists; but as two men are not a unity apart from both, so must it be with the units. And their being indivisible will make [25] no difference to them; for points too are indivisible, but yet a pair of them is nothing apart from the two.

But this consequence also we must not forget, that it follows that there are prior and posterior 2's, and similarly with the other numbers. For let the 2's in the 4 be simultaneous; [30] yet these are prior to those in the 8, and as the 2 generated them, they generated the 4's in the 8-itself. Therefore if the first 2 is an Idea, these 2's also will be Ideas of some kind. And the same account applies to the units; [35] for the units in the first 2 generate the four in 4, so that all the units come to be Ideas and an Idea will be composed of Ideas. Clearly therefore those things also of which these happen to be the Ideas will be composite, e.g. one might say that animals are composed of animals, if there are Ideas of them.

1082[b] In general, to differentiate the units in any way is an absurdity and a fiction; and by a fiction I mean a forced statement made to suit a hypothesis. For neither in quantity nor in [5] quality do we see unit differing from unit, and number must be either equal or unequal—all number but especially that which consists of abstract units—so that if one number is neither greater nor less than another, it is equal to it; but things that are equal and in no wise differentiated we take to be the same when we are speaking of numbers. If not, not even the 2's in the 10-itself will be undifferentiated, [10] though they are equal; for what reason will the man who alleges that they are not differentiated be able to give?

Again, if every unit + another unit makes two, a unit from the 2-itself and one from the 3-itself will make a 2. Now (α) this will consist of differentiated units; and (β) will it be prior to the 3 or posterior? It rather seems that [15] it must be prior; for one of the units is simultaneous with the 3, and the other is simultaneous with the 2. And we, for our part, suppose that in general 1 and 1, whether the things are equal or unequal, is 2, e.g. the good and the bad, or a man and a horse; but those who hold these views say that not even two *units* are 2.

[20] If the number of the 3-itself is not greater than that of the 2, this is surprising; and if it *is* greater, clearly there is also a number in it equal to the 2, so that *this* is not different from the 2-itself. But this is not possible, if there is a first and a second number.

Nor will the Ideas be numbers. For in this particular point they are right who claim that the units must be different, if there are to be [25] Ideas; as has been said before.[1] For the Form is unique; but if the units are not different, the 2's and the 3's also will not be different. This is also the reason why they must say that when we count thus—'1, 2'—we do not proceed by adding to the given number; for if we [30] do, neither will the numbers be generated from the indefinite dyad, nor can a number be an Idea; for then one Idea will be in another, and all Forms will be parts of one Form. And so with a view to their hypothesis their statements are right, but as a whole they are wrong; for their view is very destructive, since they will [35] admit that *this* question itself affords some difficulty—whether, when we count and say '1, 2, 3,' we count by addition or by separate portions. But we do both; and so it is absurd to reason back from this problem to so great a difference of essence.

8

1083[a] First of all it is well to determine what is the differentia of a number—and of a unit, if it has a differentia. Units must differ either in quantity or in quality; and neither of these seems to be possible. But number *qua* number differs in quantity. And if the units also did differ in quantity, number would differ from [5] number, though equal in number of units. Again, are the first units greater or smaller, and do the later ones increase or diminish? All these are irrational suppositions. But neither can they differ in *quality*. For no attribute can [10] attach to them; for even to numbers quality is said to belong *after* quantity. Again, quality could not come to them either from the 1 or the dyad; for the former has no quality, and the latter gives *quantity;* for this entity is what makes things to be many. If the facts are [15] really otherwise, they should state this quite at the beginning and determine if possible, regarding the differentia of the unit, why it must exist, and, failing this, what differentia they mean.

Evidently then, if the Ideas are numbers, the units cannot all be associable, nor can they be [20] inassociable in either of the two ways. But neither is the way in which some others speak about numbers correct. These are those

---
[1] 1081[a] 5-17.

who do not think there are Ideas, either without qualification or as identified with certain numbers, but think the objects of mathematics exist and the numbers are the first of existing things, and the 1-itself is the starting-point of them. It is paradoxical that there should be a 1 which is first of 1's, as *they* say, but not a 2 [25] which is first of 2's, nor a 3 of 3's; for the same reasoning applies to all. If, then, the facts with regard to number are so, and one supposes mathematical number alone to exist, the 1 is not the starting-point (for this sort of 1 [30] must differ from the other units; and if this is so, there must also be a 2 which is first of 2's, and similarly with the other successive numbers). But if the 1 is the starting-point, the truth about the numbers must rather be what Plato used to say, and there must be a first 2 and 3, and the numbers must not be associable [35] with one another. But if on the other hand one supposes this, many impossible results, as we have said,[1] follow. But either this or the other *must* be the case, so that if neither is, number cannot exist separately.

1083[b] It is evident, also, from this that the third version is the worst,—the view ideal and mathematical number is the same. For two mistakes must then meet in the one opinion. [5] (1) Mathematical number cannot be of this sort, but the holder of this view has to spin it out by making suppositions peculiar to himself. And (2) he must also admit all the consequences that confront those who speak of number in the sense of 'Forms'.

The Pythagorean version in one way affords fewer difficulties than those before named, but in another way has others peculiar to itself. [10] For not thinking of number as capable of existing separately removes many of the impossible consequences; but that bodies should be composed of numbers, and that this should be mathematical number, is impossible. For it is not true to speak of indivisible spatial magnitudes; and however much there might be magnitudes of this sort, units at least have not [15] magnitude; and how can a magnitude be composed of indivisibles? But arithmetical number, at least, consists of units, while these thinkers identify number with real things; at any rate they apply their propositions to bodies as if they consisted of those numbers.

If, then, it is necessary, if number is a self-[20] subsistent real thing, that it should exist in one of these ways which have been mentioned,[2] and if it cannot exist in any of these,

[1] Cf. 1080[b] 37–1083[a] 17. [2] 1080[a] 15–[b] 36.

evidently number has no such nature as those who make it separable set up for it.

Again, does each unit come from the great and the small, equalized, or one from the small, another from the great? (*a*) If the latter, [25] neither does each thing contain all the elements, nor are the units without difference; for in one there is the great and in another the small, which is contrary in its nature to the great. Again, how is it with the units in the 3-itself? One of them is an odd unit. But perhaps it is for this reason that they give 1-itself the middle place in odd numbers. (*b*) But if [30] each of the two units consists of both the great and the small, equalized, how will the 2, which is a single thing, consist of the great and the small? Or how will it differ from the unit? Again, the unit is prior to the 2; for when it is destroyed the 2 is destroyed. It must, then, be the Idea of an Idea since it is prior to an Idea, [35] and it must have come into being before it. From what, then? Not from the indefinite dyad, for *its* function was to double.

Again, number must be either infinite or finite; for these thinkers think of number as capable of existing separately, so that it is not 1084[a] possible that neither of those alternatives should be true. Clearly it cannot be *infinite;* for infinite number is neither odd nor even, but the generation of numbers is always the generation either of an odd or of an even number; in one way, when 1 operates on an even number, an odd number is produced; in [5] another way, when 2 operates, the numbers got from 1 by doubling are produced; in another way, when the odd numbers operate, the other even numbers are produced. Again, if every Idea is an Idea of something, and the numbers are Ideas, infinite number itself will be an Idea of something, either of some sensible thing or of something else. Yet this is not possible in view of their thesis any more than it is reasonable in itself, at least if they arrange the Ideas as they do.

[10] But if number is *finite,* how far does it go? With regard to this not only the fact but the reason should be stated. But if number goes only up to 10, as some say, firstly the Forms will soon run short; e.g. if 3 is man-himself, what number will be the horse-itself? The series [15] of the numbers which are the several things-themselves goes up to 10. It must, then, be one of the numbers within these limits; for it is these that are substances and Ideas. Yet they will run short; for the various forms of animal will outnumber them. At the same time it

is clear that if in this way *the* 3 is man-himself, the other 3's are so also (for those in identical [20] numbers are similar), so that there will be an infinite number of men; if each 3 is an Idea, each of the numbers will be man-himself, and if not, they will at least be men. And if the smaller number is part of the greater (being number of such a sort that the units in the same number are associable), then if the 4-itself is an Idea of something, e.g. of 'horse' or of 'white', man will be a part of horse, if man is [25] 2. It is paradoxical also that there should be an Idea of 10, but not of 11, nor of the succeeding numbers. Again, there both are and come to be certain things of which there are no Forms; why, then, are there not Forms of them also? We infer that the Forms are not causes. Again, it is paradoxical if the number-series up to 10 is more of a real thing and a [30] Form than 10 itself. There is no generation of the former as one thing, and there is of the latter. But they try to work on the assumption that the series of numbers up to 10 is a complete series. At least they generate the derivatives—e.g. the void, proportion, the odd, and the others of this kind—within the decade. For some things, e.g. movement and rest, good and bad, they assign to the originative prin-[35] ciples, and the others to the numbers. This is why they identify the odd with 1; for if the odd implied 3, how would 5 be odd? Again, spatial magnitudes and all such things are explained without going beyond a definite num-1084[b] ber; e.g. the first, the indivisible, line, then the 2, &c.; these entities also extend only up to 10.

Again, if number can exist separately, one might ask which is prior—1, or 3 or 2? Inasmuch as the number is composite, 1 is prior, but inasmuch as the universal and the form is [5] prior, the number is prior; for each of the units is part of the number as its matter, and the number acts as form. And in a sense the right angle is prior to the acute, because it is determinate and in virtue of its definition; but in a sense the acute is prior, because it is a part and the right angle is divided into acute angles. [10] As matter, then, the acute angle and the element and the unit are prior, but in respect of the form and of the substance as expressed in the definition, the right angle, and the whole consisting of the matter and the form, are prior; for the concrete thing is nearer to the form and to what is expressed in the definition, though in generation it is later. How then is 1 the starting-point? Because it is not divisible, they say; but both the universal, and the particular or the element, are indivisible. But [15] they are starting-points in different ways, one in definition and the other in time. In which way, then, is 1 the starting-point? As has been said, the right angle is thought to be prior to the acute, and the acute to the right, and each is one. Accordingly they make 1 the starting-point in both ways. But this is impossible. For the universal is one as form or substance, while the element is one as a part or as [20] matter. For each of the two is in a sense one—in *truth* each of the two units exists potentially (at least if the number is a unity and not like a heap, i.e. if different numbers consist of differentiated units, as they say), but not in complete reality; and the cause of the *error* they fell into is that they were conducting their inquiry at the same time from the standpoint of mathematics and from that of [25] universal definitions, so that (1) from the former standpoint they treated unity, their first principle, as a point; for the unit is a point without position. They put things together out of the smallest parts, as some others also have done. Therefore the unit becomes the matter of numbers and at the same time prior to 2; and again posterior, 2 being treated as a [30] whole, a unity, and a form. But (2) because they were seeking the universal they treated the unity which can be predicated of a number, as in this sense also a part of the number. But these characteristics cannot belong at the same time to the same thing.

If the 1-itself must be unitary (for it differs in nothing from other 1's except that it is the starting-point), and the 2 is divisible but the unit is not, the unit must be liker the 1-itself [35] than the 2 is. But if the unit is liker it, *it* must be liker to the unit than to the 2; therefore each of the units in 2 must be prior to the 2. But they deny this; at least they generate 1085[a] the 2 first. Again, if the 2-itself is a unity and the 3-itself is one also, both form a 2. From what, then, is this 2 produced?

9

Since there is not contact in numbers, but succession, viz. between the units between which there is nothing, e.g. between those in 2 or in [5] 3, one might ask whether these succeed the 1-itself or not, and whether, of the terms that succeed it, 2 or either of the units in 2 is prior.

Similar difficulties occur with regard to the classes of things posterior to number,—the line, the plane, and the solid. For some construct these out of the species of the 'great and small'; [10] e.g. lines from the 'long and short', planes from the 'broad and narrow', masses from the 'deep and shallow'; which are species of the 'great and small'. And the originative principle of such things which answers to the 1 different thinkers describe in different ways. And in [15] these also the impossibilities, the fictions, and the contradictions of all probability are seen to be innumerable. For (i) the geometrical classes are severed from one another, unless the principles of these are implied in one another in such a way that the 'broad and narrow' is also 'long and short' (but if this is so, the plane will be line and the solid a plane; again, how will angles and figures and such [20] things be explained?). And (ii) the same happens as in regard to number; for 'long and short', &c., are attributes of magnitude, but magnitude does not *consist* of these, any more than the line consists of 'straight and curved', or solids of 'smooth and rough'.

(All these views share a difficulty which occurs with regard to species-of-a-genus, when one posits the universals, viz. whether it is [25] animal-itself or something other than animal-itself that is in the particular animal. True, if the universal is not separable from sensible things, this will present no difficulty; but if the 1 and the numbers *are* separable, as those who express these views say, it is not easy to solve the difficulty, if one may apply the words 'not easy' to the impossible. For when we apprehend the unity in 2, or in gen- [30] eral in a number, do we apprehend a thing-itself or something else?).

Some, then, generate spatial magnitudes from matter of this sort, others from the point —and the point is thought by them to be not 1 but something like 1—and from other matter like plurality, but not identical with it; about [35] which principles none the less the same difficulties occur. For if the matter is one, line and plane and solid will be the same; for from the same elements will come one and the same 1085[b] thing. But if the matters are more than one, and there is one for the line and a second for the plane and another for the solid, they either are implied in one another or not, so that the same results will follow even so; for either the plane will not contain a line or it will *be* a line.

Again, how number can consist of the one [5] and plurality, they make no attempt to explain; but however they express themselves, the same objections arise as confront those who construct number out of the one and the indefinite dyad. For the one view generates number from the universally predicated plurality, and not from a particular plurality; and the other generates it from a particular plurality, but the first; for 2 is said to be a 'first plurality'. [10] Therefore there is practically no difference, but the same difficulties will follow,— is it intermixture or position or blending or generation? and so on. Above all one might press the question 'if each unit is one, what does it come from?' Certainly each is not the one-itself. It must, then, come from the one-itself and plurality, or a part of plurality. To [15] say that the unit is a plurality is impossible, for it is indivisible; and to generate it from a part of plurality involves many other objections; for (α) each of the parts must be indivisible (or it will be a plurality and the unit will be divisible) and the elements will [20] not be the one and *plurality;* for the single units do not come from plurality and the one. Again, (β) the holder of this view does nothing but presuppose another number; for his plurality of indivisibles is a number. Again, we must inquire, in view of this theory also, whether the number is infinite or finite. For there was at first, as it seems, a plurality that [25] was itself finite, from which and from the one comes the finite number of units. And there is another plurality that is plurality-itself and infinite plurality; which sort of plurality, then, is the element which co-operates with the one? One might inquire similarly about the point, i.e. the element out of which they make spatial magnitudes. For surely this is not the one and only point; at any rate, then, let them say out of what each of the other [30] points is formed. Certainly not of some *distance* + the point-itself. Nor again can there be indivisible parts of a distance, as the elements out of which the units are said to be made are indivisible parts of plurality; for number consists of indivisibles, but spatial magnitudes do not.

All these objections, then, and others of the [35] sort make it evident that number and spatial magnitudes cannot exist apart from things. Again, the discord about numbers be- 1086[a] tween the various versions is a sign that it is the incorrectness of the alleged facts themselves that brings confusion into the theories. For those who make the objects of mathematics alone exist apart from sensible things, seeing the difficulty about the Forms and their [5] fictitiousness, abandoned ideal number and posited mathematical. But those who wished to make the Forms at the same time also numbers, but did not see, if one assumed these principles, how mathematical number was to exist apart from ideal, made ideal and mathematical number the same—in *words,* since in *fact* [10] mathematical number has been destroyed; for they state hypotheses peculiar to themselves and not those of mathematics. And he who first supposed that the Forms exist and that the Forms are numbers and that the objects of mathematics exist, naturally separated the two. Therefore it turns out that all of them are right in some respect, but on the whole not right. And they themselves confirm this, for their statements [15] do not agree but conflict. The cause is that their hypotheses and their principles are false. And it is hard to make a good case out of bad materials, according to Epicharmus[1]: 'as soon as 'tis said, 'tis seen to be wrong.'

But regarding numbers the questions we have raised and the conclusions we have reached are sufficient (for while he who is already convinced might be further convinced [20] by a longer discussion, one not yet convinced would not come any nearer to conviction); regarding the first principles and the first causes and elements, the views expressed by those who discuss only sensible substance have been partly stated in our works on nature,[2] and partly do not belong to the present inquiry; but the views of those who assert that [25] there are other substances besides the sensible must be considered next after those we have been mentioning. Since, then, some say that the Ideas and the numbers are such substances, and that the elements of these are elements and principles of real things, we must inquire regarding these what they say and in what sense they say it.

Those who posit numbers only, and these [30] mathematical, must be considered later; but as regards those who believe in the Ideas one might survey at the same time their way of thinking and the difficulty into which they fall. For they at the same time make the Ideas universal and again treat them as separable and as individuals. That this is not possible has [35] been argued before.[3] The reason why those who described their substances as universal combined these two characteristics in one thing, is that they did not make substances identical with sensible things. They thought that the particulars in the sensible world were 1086[b] in a state of flux and none of them remained, but that the universal was apart from these and something different. And Socrates gave the impulse to this theory, as we said in our earlier discussion,[4] by reason of his definitions, but he did not *separate* universals from individuals; and in this he thought rightly, in [5] not separating them. This is plain from the results; for without the universal it is not possible to get knowledge, but the separation is the cause of the objections that arise with regard to the Ideas. His successors, however, treating it as necessary, if there are to be any substances besides the sensible and transient substances, that they must be separable, had no others, but gave separate existence to these universally [10] predicated substances, so that it followed that universals and individuals were almost the same sort of thing. This in itself, then, would be one difficulty in the view we have mentioned.

10

Let us now mention a point which presents a certain difficulty both to those who believe in the Ideas and to those who do not, and which [15] was stated before, at the beginning, among the problems. If we do not suppose substances to be separate, and in the way in which individual things are said to be separate, we shall destroy substance in the sense in which we understand 'substance'; but if we conceive substances to be separable, how are we to conceive their elements and their principles? [20] If they are individual and not universal, (*a*) real things will be just of the same number as the elements, and (*b*) the elements will not be knowable. For (*a*) let the syllables in speech be substances, and their elements elements of substances; then there must be only one *ba* and [25] one of each of the syllables, since they are not universal and the same in form but each is one in number and a 'this' and not a kind possessed of a common name (and again they suppose that the 'just what a thing is' is in each case one). And if the syllables are unique, so too are the parts of which they consist; there will not, then, be more *a*'s than one, nor more [30] than one of any of the other elements, on the same principle on which an identical syllable cannot exist in the plural number. But if this is so, there will not be other things existing besides the elements, but only the elements.

---

[1] Fr. 14, Diels, *Vorsokratiker.*
[2] *Physics,* I. 4-6; *On the Heavens,* III. 3-4; *On Generation and Corruption,* I. 1.
[3] III. 1003[a] 7-17.
[4] 1078[b] 17-30.

(b) Again, the elements will not be even knowable; for they are not universal, and knowledge is of universals. This is clear from demonstrations and from definitions; for we do not conclude that this triangle has its angles equal [35] to two right angles, unless every triangle has its angles equal to two right angles, nor that this man is an animal, unless every man is an animal.

But if the principles *are* universal, either the 1087ª substances composed of them are also universal, or non-substance will be prior to substance; for the universal is not a substance, but the element or principle is universal, and the element or principle is prior to the things of which it is the principle or element.

[5] All these difficulties follow naturally, when they make the Ideas out of elements and at the same time claim that apart from the substances which have the same form there are Ideas, a single separate entity. But if, e.g. in the case of the elements of speech, the *a*'s and the *b*'s may quite well be many and there need be no *a*-itself and *b*-itself besides the many, there may be, so far as this goes, an infinite number of [10] similar syllables. The statement that all knowledge is universal, so that the principles of things must also be universal and not separate substances, presents indeed, of all the points we have mentioned, the greatest difficulty, but yet the statement is in a sense true, although in a [15] sense it is not. For knowledge, like the verb 'to know', means two things, of which one is potential and one actual. The potency, being, as matter, universal and indefinite, deals with the universal and indefinite; but the actuality, being definite, deals with a definite object,—being a 'this', it deals with a 'this'. But *per accidens* sight sees universal colour, because this individual colour which it sees is colour; [20] and this individual *a* which the grammarian investigates is an *a*. For if the principles must be universal, what is derived from them must also be universal, as in demonstrations; and if this is so, there will be nothing capable of separate existence—i.e. no substance. But evidently in a sense knowledge is universal, [25] and in a sense it is not.

BOOK XIV

1

REGARDING this kind of substance, what we have said must be taken as sufficient. All philosophers make the first principles contraries: [30] as in natural things, so also in the case of unchangeable substances. But since there cannot be anything prior to the first principle of all things, the principle cannot be the principle and yet be an attribute of something else. To suggest this is like saying that the white is a first principle, not *qua* anything else but *qua* white, but yet that it is predicable of a subject, [35] i.e. that its being white presupposes its being something else; this is absurd, for then that subject will be prior. But all things which are generated from their contraries involve an underlying subject; a subject, then, must be present in the case of contraries, if anywhere. 1087ᵇ All contraries, then, are always predicable of a subject, and none can exist apart, but just as appearances suggest that there is nothing contrary to substance, argument confirms this. No contrary, then, is the first principle of all things in the full sense; the first principle is something different.

But these thinkers make one of the con-[5] traries matter, some making the unequal—which they take to be the essence of plurality —matter for the One, and others making plurality matter for the One. (The former generate numbers out of the dyad of the unequal, i.e. of the great and small, and the other thinker we have referred to generates them out of plurality, while according to both it is generated *by* the essence of the One.) For even the philosopher who says the unequal and the One are [10] the elements, and the unequal is a dyad composed of the great and small, treats the unequal, or the great and the small, as being one, and does not draw the distinction that they are one in definition, but not in number. But they do not describe rightly even the principles which they call elements, for some name the great and the small with the One and treat [15] these three as elements of numbers, two being matter, one the form; while others name the many and few, because the great and the small are more appropriate in their nature to magnitude than to number; and others name rather the universal character common to these —'that which exceeds and that which is exceeded'. None of these varieties of opinion makes any difference to speak of, in view of some of the consequences; they affect only the [20] abstract objections, which these thinkers take care to avoid because the demonstrations they themselves offer are abstract,—with this exception, that if the exceeding and the exceeded are the principles, and not the great and the small, consistency requires that number should come from the elements before 2 does; for number is more universal than 2, as the exceeding and the exceeded are more uni-[25] versal than the great and the small. But as it is, they say one of these things but do not say the other. Others oppose the different and the other to the One, and others oppose plurality to the One. But if, as they claim, things consist of contraries, and to the One either there is nothing contrary, or if there is to be anything it is plurality, and the unequal is contrary to the equal, and the different to the same, [30] and the other to the thing itself, those who oppose the One to plurality have most claim to plausibility, but even their view is inadequate, for the One would on their view be a few; for plurality is opposed to fewness, and the many to the few.

'The one' evidently means a measure. And in every case there is some underlying thing with [35] a distinct nature of its own, e.g. in the scale a quarter-tone, in spatial magnitude a finger or a foot or something of the sort, in rhythms a beat or a syllable; and similarly in 1088^a gravity it is a definite weight; and in the same way in all cases, in qualities a quality, in quantities a quantity (and the measure is indivisible, in the former case in kind, and in the latter to the sense); which implies that the one is not in itself the substance of anything. And this is reasonable; for 'the one' means the [5] measure of some plurality, and 'number' means a measured plurality and a plurality of measures. (Thus it is natural that one is not a number; for the measure is not measures, but both the measure and the one are starting-points.) The measure must always be some identical thing predicable of all the things it measures, e.g. if the things are horses, the measure is 'horse', and if they are men, 'man'. If [10] they are a man, a horse, and a god, the measure is perhaps 'living being', and the number of them will be a number of living beings. If the things are 'man' and 'pale' and 'walking', these will scarcely have a number, because all belong to a subject which is one and the same in number, yet the number of these will be a number of 'kinds' or of some such term.

[15] Those who treat the unequal as one thing, and the dyad as an indefinite compound of great and small, say what is very far from being probable or possible. For (a) these are modifications and accidents, rather than substrata, of numbers and magnitudes—the many and few of number, and the great and small of magnitude—like even and odd, smooth and [20] rough, straight and curved. Again, (b) apart from this mistake, the great and the small, and so on, must be relative to something; but what is relative is least of all things a kind of entity or substance, and is posterior to quality and quantity; and the relative is an accident [25] of quantity, as was said, not its matter, since something with a distinct nature of its own must serve as matter both to the relative in general and to its parts and kinds. For there is nothing either great or small, many or few, or, in general, relative to something else, which without having a nature of its own is many or few, great or small, or relative to something else. A sign that the relative is least of all a [30] substance and a real thing is the fact that it alone has no proper generation or destruction or movement, as in respect of quantity there is increase and diminution, in respect of quality alteration, in respect of place locomotion, in respect of substance simple generation and destruction. In respect of relation there is no proper change; for, without changing, a thing will be now greater and now less or [35] equal, if that with which it is compared 1088^b has changed in quantity. And (c) the matter of each thing, and therefore of substance, must be that which is potentially of the nature in question; but the relative is neither potentially nor actually substance. It is strange, then, or rather impossible, to make not-substance an element in, and prior to, substance; for all the categories are posterior to substance. Again, (d) elements are not predicated of the things of which they are elements, but many [5] and few are predicated both apart and together of number, and long and short of the line, and both broad and narrow apply to the plane. If there is a plurality, then, of which the one term, viz. few, is always predicated, e.g. 2 (which cannot be many, for if it were many, 1 would be few), there must be also one which is [10] absolutely many, e.g. 10 is many (if there is no number which is greater than 10), or 10,000. How then, in view of this, can number consist of few and many? Either both ought to be predicated of it, or neither; but in fact only the one *or* the other is predicated.

2

We must inquire generally, whether eternal [15] things can consist of elements. If they do, they will have matter; for everything that consists of elements is composite. Since, then, even if a thing exists for ever, out of that of which it consists it would necessarily also, if it *had* come into being, have come into being, and since everything comes to be what it comes to be out of that which is it potentially (for it could not have come to be out of that which had not this capacity, nor could it consist of such elements), and since the potential can be [20] either actual or not,—this being so, however everlasting number or anything else that has matter is, it must be capable of not existing, just as that which is any number of years old is as capable of not existing as that which is a day old; if this is capable of not existing, so is that which has lasted for a time so long that it has no limit. They cannot, then, be eternal, since that which is capable of not existing is not eternal, as we had occasion to show in [25] another context.[1] If that which we are now saying is true universally—that no substance is eternal unless it is actuality—and if the elements are matter that underlies substance, no eternal substance can have elements present in it, of which it consists.

There are some who describe the element which acts with the One as an indefinite dyad, and object to 'the unequal', reasonably enough, [30] because of the ensuing difficulties; but they have got rid only of those objections which inevitably arise from the treatment of the unequal, i.e. the relative, as an element; those which arise apart from this opinion must confront even these thinkers, whether it is ideal number, or mathematical, that they construct out of those elements.

[35] There are many causes which led them off **1089ᵃ** into these explanations, and especially the fact that they framed the difficulty in an obsolete form. For they thought that all things that are would be one (viz. Being itself), if one did not join issue with and refute the saying of Parmenides:[2]

'For never will this be proved, that things that are not are.'

They thought it necessary to prove that that [5] which is not is; for only thus—of that which is *and something else*—could the things that are be composed, if they are many.

But, first, if 'being' has many senses (for it means sometimes substance, sometimes that it is of a certain quality, sometimes that it is of a certain quantity, and at other times the other categories), what sort of 'one', then, are all the things that are, if non-being is to be supposed [10] not to be? Is it the substances that are one, or the affections and similarly the other categories as well, or all together—so that the 'this' and the 'such' and the 'so much' and the other categories that indicate each some one class of being will all be one? But it is strange, or rather impossible, that the coming into play of a single thing should bring it about that part of that which is is a 'this', part a 'such', part a 'so much', part a 'here'.

[15] Secondly, of what sort of non-being and being do the things that are consist? For 'non-being' also has many senses, since 'being' has; and 'not being a man' means not being a certain substance, 'not being straight' not being of a certain quality, 'not being three cubits long' not being of a certain quantity. What sort of being and non-being, then, by their union pluralize the things that are? This [20] thinker[3] means by the non-being the union of which with being pluralizes the things that are, the false and the character of falsity. This is also why it used to be said that we must assume something that is false, as geometers assume the line which is not a foot long to be a foot long. But this cannot be so. For neither do geometers assume anything false (for the enunciation is extraneous to the inference), nor is it [25] non-being in this sense that the things that are are generated from or resolved into. But since 'non-being' taken in its various cases has as many senses as there are categories, and besides this the false is said not to be, and so is the potential, it is from this that generation proceeds, man from that which is not man but [30] potentially man, and white from that which is not white but potentially white, and this whether it is some one thing that is generated or many.

The question evidently is, how being, in the sense of 'the *substances*', is many; for the things that are generated are numbers and lines and bodies. Now it is strange to inquire how being in the sense of the 'what' is many, [35] and not how either qualities or quantities are many. For surely the indefinite dyad or 'the great and the small' is not a reason why there should be two kinds of white or many **1089ᵇ** colours or flavours or shapes; for then these also would be numbers and units. But if they *had* attacked these other categories, they would have seen the cause of the plurality in substances also; for the same thing or some-

---

[1] Cf. ix, 1050ᵇ 7 ff.; *On the Heavens*, I. 12.
[2] Fr. 7.
[3] Plato; cf. *Sophist*, 237, 240.

thing analogous is the cause. This aberration is the reason also why in seeking the opposite [5] of being and the one, from which with being and the one the things that are proceed, they posited the relative term (i.e. the unequal), which is neither the contrary nor the contradictory of these, and is one kind of being as 'what' and quality also are.

They should have asked this question also, how relative terms are many and not one. But as it is, they inquire how there are many units [10] besides the first 1, but do not go on to inquire how there are many unequals besides *the* unequal. Yet they use them and speak of great and small, many and few (from which proceed numbers), long and short (from which proceeds the line), broad and narrow (from which proceeds the plane), deep and shallow (from which proceed solids); and they speak of yet more kinds of relative term. What is the reason, then, why there is a plurality of these?

[15] It is necessary, then, as we say, to presuppose for each thing that which is it potentially; and the holder of these views further declared what that is which is potentially a 'this' and a substance but is not in itself being —viz. that it is the relative (as if he had said 'the qualitative'), which is neither potentially [20] the one or being, nor the negation of the one nor of being, but one among beings. And it was much *more* necessary, as we said,[1] if he was inquiring how beings are many, not to inquire about those in the same category—how there are many substances or many qualities— but how beings as a whole are many; for some are substances, some modifications, some relations. In the categories other than substance there is yet another problem involved in the [25] existence of plurality. Since they are not separable from substances, qualities and quantities are many just because their substratum becomes and is many; yet there *ought* to be a matter for each category; only it cannot be separable from substances. But in the case of 'thises', it is possible to explain how the 'this' is many things, unless a this is to be treated [30] as both a 'this' and a general character. The difficulty arising from the facts about substances is rather this, how there are actually many substances and not one.

But further, if the 'this' and the quantitative are not the same, we are not told how and why the things that are are many, but how quantities are many. For all 'number' means a

[1] a 34.

[35] quantity, and so does the 'unit', unless it means a measure or the quantitatively indivisible. If, then, the quantitative and the 'what' are different, we are not told whence or how the 'what' is many; but if any one says they are the same, he has to face many inconsistencies.

One might fix one's attention also on the question, regarding the numbers, what justifies the belief that they exist. To the believer in Ideas they provide some sort of cause for ex- [5] isting things, since each number is an Idea, and the Idea is to other things somehow or other the cause of their being; for let this supposition be granted them. But as for him who does not hold this view because he sees the inherent objections to the Ideas (so that it is not for *this* reason that he posits numbers), but who posits *mathematical* number, why must [10] we believe his statement that such number exists, and of what use is such number to other things? Neither does he who says it exists maintain that it is the cause of anything (he rather says it is a thing existing by itself), nor is it observed to be the cause of anything; for the theorems of arithmeticians will all be [15] found true even of sensible things, as was said before.[2]

3

As for those, then, who suppose the Ideas to exist and to be numbers, by their assumption— in virtue of the method of setting out each term apart from its instances—of the unity of each general term they try at least to explain somehow why number must exist. Since their reasons, however, are neither conclusive nor in themselves possible, one must not, for these reasons at least, assert the existence of number. [20] Again, the Pythagoreans, because they saw many attributes of numbers belonging to sensible bodies, supposed real things to be numbers—not separable numbers, however, but numbers of which real things consist. But why? Because the attributes of numbers are present in a musical scale and in the heavens and in [25] many other things. Those, however, who say that mathematical number alone exists cannot according to their hypotheses say anything of this sort, but it used to be urged that these sensible things could not be the subject of the sciences. But we maintain that they are, as we said before.[3] And it is evident that the objects of mathematics do not exist apart; for

[2] Cf. XIII. 3, esp. 1077 b 17-22.
[3] Cf. XIII. 3.

if they existed apart their attributes would not [30] have been present in bodies. Now the Pythagoreans in this point are open to no objection; but in that they construct natural bodies out of numbers, things that have lightness and weight out of things that have not weight or lightness, they seem to speak of another heaven and other bodies, not of the sensi-[35] ble. But those who make number separable assume that it both exists and is separable because the axioms would not be true of sensible things, while the statements of mathematics *are* true and 'greet the soul'; and similarly with the spatial magnitudes of mathematics. It is **1090^b** evident, then, both that the rival theory will say the contrary of this, and that the difficulty we raised just now,[1] why if numbers are in no way present in sensible things their attributes are present in sensible things, has to be solved by those who hold these views.

[5] There are some who, because the point is the limit and extreme of the line, the line of the plane, and the plane of the solid, think there must be real things of this sort. We must therefore examine this argument too, and see whether it is not remarkably weak. For (i) extremes are not substances, but rather all these [10] things are limits. For even walking, and movement in general, has a limit, so that on their theory this will be a 'this' and a substance. But that is absurd. Not but what (ii) even if they are substances, they will all be the substances of the sensible things in this world; for it is to these that the argument applied. Why then should they be capable of existing apart?

Again, if we are not too easily satisfied, we may, regarding all number and the objects of mathematics, press this difficulty, that they con-[15] tribute nothing to one another, the prior to the posterior; for if number did not exist, none the less spatial magnitudes would exist for those who maintain the existence of the objects of mathematics only, and if spatial magnitudes did not exist, soul and sensible bodies would exist. But the observed facts show that nature [20] is not a series of episodes, like a bad tragedy. As for the believers in the Ideas, this difficulty misses them; for they construct spatial magnitudes out of matter and number, lines out of the number 2, planes doubtless out of 3, solids out of 4,—or they use other numbers, which makes no difference. But will these magnitudes be Ideas, or what is their manner of [25] existence, and what do they contribute to

[1] ^{a}29.

things? These contribute nothing, as the objects of mathematics contribute nothing. But not even is any theorem true of them, unless we want to change the objects of mathematics and invent doctrines of our own. But it is not [30] hard to assume any random hypotheses and spin out a long string of conclusions. These thinkers, then, are wrong in this way, in wanting to unite the objects of mathematics with the Ideas. And those who first posited two kinds of number, that of the Forms and that which is mathematical, neither have said nor can say how mathematical number is to exist and of what it is to consist. For they place it [35] between ideal and sensible number. If (i) it consists of the great and small, it will be the same as the other—ideal—number (he makes spatial magnitudes out of some other small and great). And if (ii) he names some **1091^a** other element, he will be making his elements rather many. And if the principle of each of the two kinds of number is a 1, unity will be something common to these, and we must inquire how the one is these *many* things, while at the same time *number,* according to him, cannot be generated except from one *and an indefinite dyad.*

[5] All this is absurd, and conflicts both with itself and with the probabilities, and we seem to see in it Simonides' 'long rigmarole'[2]; for the long rigmarole comes into play, like those of slaves, when men have nothing sound to say. And the very elements—the great and the small—seem to cry out against the violence [10] that is done to them; for they cannot in any way generate numbers other than those got from 1 by doubling.

It is strange also to attribute generation to things that are eternal, or rather this is one of the things that are impossible. There need be no doubt whether the Pythagoreans attribute [15] generation to them or not; for they say plainly that when the one had been constructed, whether out of planes or of surface or of seed or of elements which they cannot express, immediately the nearest part of the unlimited began to be constrained and limited by the limit. But since they are constructing a world and wish to speak the language of natural science, it is fair to make some examination of their physical theories, but to let them [20] off from the present inquiry; for we are investigating the principles at work in *unchangeable* things, so that it is numbers of *this* kind whose genesis we must study.

[2] Simonides Ceïus, Fr. 189. Bergk.

4

These thinkers say there is no generation of the odd number, which evidently implies that there *is* generation of the even; and some present the even as produced first from unequals —the great and the small—when these are [25] equalized. The inequality, then, must belong to them *before* they are equalized. If they had always been equalized, they would not have been unequal before; for there is nothing before that which is always. Therefore evidently they are not giving their account of the generation of numbers merely to assist contemplation of their nature.

A difficulty, and a reproach to any one who [30] finds it *no* difficulty, are contained in the question how the elements and the principles are related to the good and the beautiful; the difficulty is this, whether any of the elements is such a thing as we mean by the good itself and the best, or this is not so, but these are later in origin than the elements. The theologians seem to agree with some thinkers of the pres- [35] ent day, who answer the question in the negative, and say that both the good and the beautiful appear in the nature of things only when that nature has made some progress. (This they do to avoid a real objection which confronts those who say, as some do, that the 1091^b one is a first principle. The objection arises not from their ascribing goodness to the first principle as an attribute, but from their making the one a principle—and a principle in the sense of an element—and generating number from the one.) The old poets agree with this inasmuch as they say that not those who [5] are first in time, e.g. Night and Heaven or Chaos or Ocean, reign and rule, but Zeus. These poets, however, are led to speak thus only because they think of the rulers of the world as *changing;* for those of them who combine the two characters in that they do not use mythical language throughout, e.g. Pherecydes [10] and some others, make the original generating agent the Best, and so do the Magi, and some of the later sages also, e.g. both Empedocles and Anaxagoras, of whom one made love an element, and the other made reason a principle. Of those who maintain the existence of the *unchangeable* substances some say the One itself is the good itself; but they thought its substance lay mainly in its unity.

[15] This, then, is the problem,—which of the two ways of speaking is right. It would be strange if to that which is primary and eternal and most self-sufficient this very quality—self-sufficiency and self-maintenance—belongs primarily in some other way than *as a good*. But indeed it can be for no other reason indestructible or self-sufficient than because its nature is good. Therefore to say that the first [20] principle is good is probably correct; but that this principle should be the One or, if not that, at least an element, and an element of numbers, is impossible. Powerful objections arise, to avoid which some have given up the theory (viz. those who agree that the One is a first principle and element, but only of *mathematical* number). For on this view all the units [25] become identical with species of good, and there is a great profusion of goods. Again, if the Forms are numbers, all the Forms are identical with species of good. But let a man assume Ideas of anything he pleases. If these are Ideas only of goods, the Ideas will not be substances; but if the Ideas are also Ideas of substances, all animals and plants and all individuals that share in Ideas will be good.

[30] These absurdities follow, and it also follows that the contrary element, whether it is plurality or the unequal, i.e. the great and small, is the bad-itself. (Hence one thinker avoided attaching the good to the One, because it would necessarily follow, since generation is from contraries, that badness is the fundamental nature of plurality; while others [35] say inequality is the nature of the bad.) It follows, then, that all things partake of the bad except one—the One itself, and that numbers partake of it in a more undiluted form than 1092^a spatial magnitudes, and that the bad is the space in which the good is realized, and that it partakes in and desires that which tends to destroy it; for contrary tends to destroy contrary. And if, as we were saying, the matter is that which is potentially each thing, e.g. that of actual fire is that which is potentially fire, the bad will be just the potentially good.

[5] All these objections, then, follow, partly because they make every principle an element, partly because they make contraries principles, partly because they make the One a principle, partly because they treat the numbers as the first substances, and as capable of existing apart, and as Forms.

5

If, then, it is equally impossible not to put the good among the first principles and to put it among them in this way, evidently the prin- [10] ciples are not being correctly described, nor are the first substances. Nor does any one conceive the matter correctly if he compares the principles of the universe to that of animals and plants, on the ground that the more complete always comes from the indefinite and incomplete—which is what leads this thinker to say that this is also true of the first principles of reality, so that the One itself is not even an [15] existing thing. This is incorrect, for even in this world of animals and plants the principles from which these come are complete; for it is a man that produces a man, and the seed is not first.

It is out of place, also, to generate place simultaneously with the mathematical solids (for place is peculiar to the individual things, and hence they are separate in place; but mathe-[20] matical objects are nowhere), and to say that they must be somewhere, but not say what kind of thing their place is.

Those who say that existing things come from elements and that the first of existing things are the numbers, should have first distinguished the senses in which one thing comes from another, and then said in which sense number comes from its first principles.

By intermixture? But (1) not everything is [25] capable of intermixture, and (2) that which is produced by it is different from its elements, and on this view the one will not remain separate or a distinct entity; but they want it to be so.

By juxtaposition, like a syllable? But then (1) the elements must have position; and (2) he who thinks of number will be able to think of the unity and the plurality apart; number then will be this—a unit *and* plurality, or the one *and* the unequal.

Again, coming from certain things means in one sense that these are still to be found in the product, and in another that they are not; in [30] which sense does number come from these elements? Only things that are generated can come from elements which are present in them. Does number come, then, from its elements as from seed? But nothing can be excreted from that which is indivisible. Does it come from its contrary, its contrary not persisting? But all things that come in this way come also from something else which does per-[35] sist. Since, then, one thinker places the 1 as contrary to plurality, and another places it **1092ᵇ** as contrary to the unequal, treating the 1 as equal, number must be being treated as coming from contraries. There is, then, something else that persists, from which and from one contrary the compound is or has come to be. Again, why in the world do the other things that come from contraries, or that have contraries, perish (even when all of the contrary is used to produce them), while number [5] does not? Nothing is said about this. Yet whether present or not present in the compound the contrary destroys it, e.g. 'strife' destroys the 'mixture'[1] (yet it *should* not; for it is not to that that it is contrary).

Once more, it has not been determined at all in which way numbers are the causes of substances and of being—whether (1) as boundaries (as points are of spatial magnitudes). [10] This is how Eurytus decided what was the number of what (e.g. one of man and another of horse), viz. by imitating the figures of living things with pebbles, as some people bring numbers into the forms of triangle and square. Or (2) is it because harmony is a ratio [15] of numbers, and so is man and everything else? But how are the attributes—white and sweet and hot—numbers? Evidently it is not the numbers that are the essence or the causes of the form; for the ratio is the essence, while the number is the matter. E.g. the essence of flesh or bone is number only in this way, 'three parts of fire and two of earth'.[2] And a number, whatever number it is, is always a number of certain things, either of parts of fire or earth or of units; but the es-[20] sence is that there is so much of one thing to so much of another in the mixture; and this is no longer a number but a ratio of mixture of numbers, whether these are corporeal or of any other kind.

Number, then, whether it be number in general or the number which consists of abstract units, is neither the cause as agent, nor the matter, nor the ratio and form of things. Nor, of [25] course, is it the final cause.

6

One might also raise the question what the good is that things get from numbers because their composition is expressible by a number, either by one which is easily calculable or by an odd number. For in fact honey-water is no more wholesome if it is mixed in the proportion of three times three, but it would do more good if it were in no particular ratio but well diluted than if it were numerically expressible [30] but strong. Again, the ratios of mixtures are expressed by the *adding* of numbers, not

---

[1] Cf. Empedocles, Fr. 17.
[2] Cf. Empedocles, Fr. 96.

by mere numbers; e.g. it is 'three parts to two', not 'three times two'. For in any multiplication the genus of the things multiplied must be the same; therefore the product 1×2×3 must be measurable by 1, and 4×5×6 by 4, and therefore all products into which the same factor enters [35] must be measurable by that factor. The number of fire, then, cannot be 2×5×3×6, and at the same time that of water 2×3.

1093ª If all things must share in number, it must follow that many things are the same, and the same number must belong to one thing and to another. Is number the cause, then, and does the thing exist because of its number, or is this not certain? E.g. the motions of the sun [5] have a number, and again those of the moon,—yes, and the life and prime of each animal. Why, then, should not some of these numbers be squares, some cubes, and some equal, others double? There is no reason why they should not, and indeed they must move within these limits, since all things were assumed to share in number. And it was assumed that things that differed might fall under the [10] same number. Therefore if the same number had belonged to certain things, these would have been the same as one another, since they would have had the same form of number; e.g. sun and moon would have been the same. But why need these numbers be causes? There are seven vowels, the scale consists of seven strings, the Pleiades are seven, at seven animals lose their teeth (at least some do, though some [15] do not), and the champions who fought against Thebes were seven. Is it then because the number is the kind of number it is, that the champions were seven or the Pleiad consists of seven stars? Surely the champions were seven because there were seven gates or for some other reason, and the Pleiad we count as seven, as we count the Bear as twelve, while other peoples count more stars in both. Nay, [20] they even say that Ξ, Ψ, and Z are concords and that because there are three concords, the double consonants also are three. They quite neglect the fact that there might be a thousand such letters; for one symbol might be assigned to ΓΡ. But if they say that each of these three is equal to two of the other letters, and no other is so, and if the cause is that there are three parts of the mouth and one letter is in each applied to sigma, it is for this reason that there are only three, not because [25] the concords are three; since as a matter of fact the concords are more than three, but of double consonants there cannot be more.

These people are like the old-fashioned Homeric scholars, who see small resemblances but neglect great ones. Some say that there are many such cases, e.g. that the middle strings [30] are represented by nine and eight, and that the epic verse has seventeen syllables, which is equal in number to the two strings, and that the scansion is, in the right half of 1093ᵇ the line nine syllables, and in the left eight. And they say that the distance in the letters from alpha to omega is equal to that from the lowest note of the flute to the highest, and that the number of this note is equal to [5] that of the whole choir of heaven. It may be suspected that no one could find difficulty either in stating such analogies or in finding them in eternal things, since they can be found even in perishable things.

But the lauded characteristics of numbers, and the contraries of these, and generally the mathematical relations, as some describe them, making them causes of nature, seem, when we [10] inspect them in *this* way, to vanish; for none of them is a cause in any of the senses that have been distinguished in reference to the first principles.[1] In a sense, however, they make it plain that goodness belongs to numbers, and that the odd, the straight, the square, the potencies of certain numbers, are in the column of the beautiful. For the seasons and a particular kind of number go together; and [15] the other agreements that they collect from the theorems of mathematics all have this meaning. Hence they are like coincidences. For they are accidents, but the things that agree are all appropriate to one another, and one by analogy. For in each category of being an analogous term is found—as the straight is [20] in length, so is the level in surface, perhaps the odd in number, and the white in colour.

Again, it is not the *ideal* numbers that are the causes of musical phenomena and the like (for equal ideal numbers differ from one another in form; for even the units do); so that we need not assume Ideas for this reason at least.

These, then, are the results of the theory, and [25] yet more might be brought together. The fact that our opponnts have much trouble with the generation of numbers and can in no way make a system of them, seems to indicate that the objects of mathematics are not separable from sensible things, as some say, and that they are not the first principles.

[1] Cf. v. 1, 2.

ON THE SOUL

CONTENTS: ON THE SOUL

BOOK I

CHAP.		BERLIN NOS.
1.	The dignity, usefulness, and difficulty of Psychology	402^a 1
2.	The opinions of early thinkers about the soul	403^b 20
3.	Refutation of the view which assigns movement to the soul	405^b 32
4.	The soul not a harmony (407^b 27–408^a 34)	407^b 27
	The soul not moved with non-local movement (408^a 34–408^b 29)	
	The soul not a self-moving number (408^b 30–5. 409^b 18)	
5.	The soul not composed of elements (409^b 19–411^a 7)	409^a 31
	The soul not present in all things (411^a 7–23)	
	The unity of the soul (411^a 24–411^b 30)	

BOOK II

1.	First definition of soul	412^a 1
2.	Second definition of soul	413^a 11
3.	The faculties of the soul	414^a 27
4.	The nutritive faculty	415^a 14
5.	Sense-perception	416^b 32
6.	The different kinds of sensible object	418^a 6
7.	Sight and its object	418^a 26
8.	Hearing and its object	419^b 3
9.	Smell and its object	421^a 6
10.	Taste and its object	422^a 8
11.	Touch and its object	422^b 17
12.	General characteristics of the external senses	424^a 16

BOOK III

1–2.	The number of the external senses (424^b 20–2. 426^b 7)	424^b 20
2.	Common sense (426^b 8–427^a 16)	425^b 11
3.	Thinking, perceiving, and imagining distinguished (427^a 17–427^b 26) Imagination (427^b 27–429^a 9)	427^a 16
4.	Passive mind	429^a 10
5.	Active mind	430^a 10
6.	The double operation of mind	430^a 26
7.	The practical mind, and the difference between it and the contemplative	431^a 1
8.	Comparison of mind with sense and with imagination	431^b 20
9.	Problems about the motive faculty	432^a 15
10.	The cause of the movement of living things	433^a 8
11.	(Continued)	433^b 31
12.	The mutual relations of the faculties of soul, and their fitness for the conditions of life	434^a 23
13.	(Continued)	435^a 11

ON THE SOUL

BOOK I

I

402ª HOLDING as we do that, while knowledge of any kind is a thing to be honoured and prized, one kind of it may, either by reason of its greater exactness or of a higher dignity and greater wonderfulness in its objects, be more honourable and precious than another, on both accounts we should naturally be led to place in the front rank the study of the soul. The knowledge of the soul admittedly contributes [5] greatly to the advance of truth in general, and, above all, to our understanding of Nature, for the soul is in some sense the principle of animal life. Our aim is to grasp and understand, first its essential nature, and secondly its properties; of these some are taught to be affections proper to the soul itself, while others are considered to attach to the animal owing to the presence within it of soul.

[10] To attain any assured knowledge about the soul is one of the most difficult things in the world. As the form of question which here presents itself, viz. the question 'What is it?', recurs in other fields, it might be supposed that there was some single method of inquiry applicable to all objects whose essential nature [15] we are endeavouring to ascertain (as there is for derived properties the single method of demonstration); in that case what we should have to seek for would be this unique method. But if there is no such single and general method for solving the question of essence, our task becomes still more difficult; in the case of each different subject we shall have to determine the appropriate process of investigation. If to this there be a clear answer, e.g. that the process is demonstration or division, or [20] some other known method, difficulties and hesitations still beset us—with what facts shall we begin the inquiry? For the facts which form the starting-points in different subjects must be different, as e.g. in the case of numbers and surfaces.

NOTE: The bold face numbers and letters are approximate indications of the pages and columns of the standard Berlin Greek text; the bracketed numbers, of the lines in the Greek text; they are here assigned as they are assigned in the Oxford translation.

First, no doubt, it is necessary to determine in which of the *summa genera* soul lies, what it *is;* is it 'a this-somewhat,' a substance, or is it a quale or a quantum, or some other of the remaining kinds of predicates which we have [25] distinguished? Further, does soul belong to the class of potential existents, or is it not rather an actuality? Our answer to this question is of the greatest importance.

402ᵇ We must consider also whether soul is divisible or is without parts, and whether it is everywhere homogeneous or not; and if not homogeneous, whether its various forms are different specifically or generically: up to the present time those who have discussed and investigated soul seem to have confined them- [5] selves to the human soul. We must be careful not to ignore the question whether soul can be defined in a single unambiguous formula, as is the case with animal, or whether we must not give a separate formula for each sort of it, as we do for horse, dog, man, god (in the latter case the 'universal' animal—and so too every other 'common predicate'—being treated either as nothing at all or as a later product). Further, if what exists is not a plurality of souls, but a plurality of parts of one soul, which ought we to investigate first, the whole soul or [10] its parts? (It is also a difficult problem to decide which of these parts are in nature distinct from one another.) Again, which ought we to investigate first, these parts or their functions, mind or thinking, the faculty or the act of sensation, and so on? If the investigation of the functions precedes that of the parts, the further question suggests itself: ought we not before either to consider the correlative objects, [15] e.g. of sense or thought? It seems not only useful for the discovery of the causes of the derived properties of substances to be acquainted with the essential nature of those substances (as in mathematics it is useful for the understanding of the property of the equality of the [20] interior angles of a triangle to two right angles to know the essential nature of the straight and the curved or of the line and the plane) but also conversely, for the knowledge of the essential nature of a substance is largely promoted by an acquaintance with its properties: for, when we are able to give an account conformable to experience of all or most of the properties of a substance, we shall be in the most favourable position to say something worth saying about the essential nature of that [25] subject; in all demonstration a definition of the essence is required as a starting-point, so that definitions which do not enable us to discover the derived properties, or which fail to facilitate even a conjecture about them, must obviously, one and all, be dialectical and futile.

A further problem presented by the affections of soul is this: are they all affections of the complex of body and soul, or is there any one among them peculiar to the soul by itself? To determine this is indispensable but difficult. If [5] we consider the majority of them, there seems to be no case in which the soul can act or be acted upon without involving the body; e.g. anger, courage, appetite, and sensation generally. Thinking seems the most probable exception; but if this too proves to be a form of imagination or to be impossible without imagination, it too requires a body as a condition of [10] its existence. If there is any way of acting or being acted upon proper to soul, soul will be capable of separate existence; if there is none, its separate existence is impossible. In the latter case, it will be like what is straight, which has many properties arising from the straightness in it, e.g. that of touching a bronze sphere at a point, though straightness divorced from the other constituents of the straight thing cannot touch it in this way; it cannot be so divorced at [15] all, since it is always found in a body. It therefore seems that all the affections of soul involve a body—passion, gentleness, fear, pity, courage, joy, loving, and hating; in all these there is a concurrent affection of the body. In support of this we may point to the fact that, while sometimes on the occasion of violent and striking occurrences there is no excite- [20] ment or fear felt, on others faint and feeble stimulations produce these emotions, viz. when the body is already in a state of tension resembling its condition when we are angry. Here is a still clearer case: in the absence of any external cause of terror we find ourselves experiencing the feelings of a man in terror. From all this it is obvious that the affections of soul are enmattered formulable essences.

[25] Consequently their definitions ought to correspond, e.g. anger should be defined as a certain mode of movement of such and such a body (or part or faculty of a body) by this or that cause and for this or that end. That is precisely why the study of the soul must fall within the science of Nature, at least so far as in its affections it manifests this double character. Hence a physicist would define an affection of [30] soul differently from a dialectician; the latter would define e.g. anger as the appetite for returning pain for pain, or something like that, while the former would define it as a boiling of the blood or warm substance surrounding the heart. The latter assigns the material conditions, the former the form or formulable essence; for what he states is the formulable essence of the fact, though for its actual existence there must be embodiment of it in a material such as is described by the other. Thus the essence of a house is assigned in such a formula as 'a shelter against destruction by [5] wind, rain, and heat'; the physicist would describe it as 'stones, bricks, and timbers'; but there is a third possible description which would say that it was that form in that material with that purpose or end. Which, then, among these is entitled to be regarded as the genuine physicist? The one who confines himself to the material, or the one who restricts himself to the formulable essence alone? Is it not rather the one who combines both in a single formula? If this is so, how are we to characterize the other two? Must we not say that there is no type of thinker who concerns himself with those qualities or attributes of the material which are in fact inseparable from the material, and without attempting even in [10] thought to separate them? The physicist is he who concerns himself with all the properties active and passive of bodies or materials thus or thus defined; attributes not considered as being of this character he leaves to others, in certain cases it may be to a specialist, e.g. a carpenter or a physician, in others (*a*) where they are inseparable in fact, but are separable from any particular kind of body by an effort of ab- [15] straction, to the mathematician, (*b*) where they are separate both in fact and in thought from body altogether, to the First Philosopher or metaphysician. But we must return from this digression, and repeat that the affections of soul are inseparable from the material substratum of animal life, to which we have seen that such affections, e.g. passion and fear, attach, and have not the same mode of being as a line or a plane.

2

[20] For our study of soul it is necessary, while formulating the problems of which in our further advance we are to find the solutions, to call into council the views of those of our predecessors who have declared any opinion on this subject, in order that we may profit by whatever is sound in their suggestions and avoid their errors.

The starting-point of our inquiry is an exposition of those characteristics which have chiefly been held to belong to soul in its very [25] nature. Two characteristic marks have above all others been recognized as distinguishing that which has soul in it from that which has not—movement and sensation. It may be said that these two are what our predecessors have fixed upon as characteristic of soul.

Some say that what originates movement is both pre-eminently and primarily soul; believing that what is not itself moved cannot origi- [30] nate movement in another, they arrived at the view that soul belongs to the class of things in movement. This is what led Democritus to say that soul is a sort of fire or hot substance; his 'forms' or atoms are infinite in number; those which are spherical he calls fire and soul, and compares them to the motes in the air which we see in shafts of light coming through windows; the mixture of seeds of all sorts he calls the elements of the whole of [5] Nature (Leucippus gives a similar account); the spherical atoms are identified with soul because atoms of that shape are most adapted to permeate everywhere, and to set all the others moving by being themselves in movement. This implies the view that soul is identical with what produces movement in animals. That is why, further, they regard res- [10] piration as the characteristic mark of life; as the environment compresses the bodies of animals, and tends to extrude those atoms which impart movement to them, because they themselves are never at rest, there must be a reinforcement of these by similar atoms coming in from without in the act of respiration; for they prevent the extrusion of those which are already within by counteracting the compressing and consolidating force of the environment; and animals continue to live only [15] so long as they are able to maintain this resistance.

The doctrine of the Pythagoreans seems to rest upon the same ideas; some of them declared the motes in air, others what moved them, to be soul. These motes were referred to because they are seen always in movement, even in a complete calm.

[20] The same tendency is shown by those who define soul as that which moves itself; all seem to hold the view that movement is what is closest to the nature of soul, and that while all else is moved by soul, it alone moves itself. This belief arises from their never seeing anything originating movement which is not first itself moved.

[25] Similarly also Anaxagoras (and whoever agrees with him in saying that mind set the whole in movement) declares the moving cause of things to be soul. His position must, however, be distinguished from that of Democritus. Democritus roundly identifies soul and mind, for he identifies what appears with what is true—that is why he commends Homer for the phrase 'Hector lay with thought [30] distraught'[1]; he does not employ mind as a special faculty dealing with truth, but identifies soul and mind. What Anaxagoras says about them is more obscure; in many places he tells us that the cause of beauty and order is mind, elsewhere that it is soul; it is found, he says, in all animals, great and small, [5] high and low, but mind (in the sense of intelligence) appears not to belong alike to all animals, and indeed not even to all human beings.

All those, then, who had special regard to the fact that what has soul in it is moved, adopted the view that soul is to be identified with what is eminently originative of movement. All, on the other hand, who looked to the fact that what has soul in it knows or perceives what is, identify soul with the principle or principles [10] of Nature, according as they admit several such principles or one only. Thus Empedocles declares that it is formed out of all his elements, each of them also being soul; his words are:

For 'tis by Earth we see Earth, by Water Water,
By Ether Ether divine, by Fire destructive Fire,
[15] *By Love Love, and Hate by cruel Hate.*[2]

In the same way Plato in the *Timaeus*[3] fashions the soul out of his elements; for like, he holds, is known by like, and things are formed out of the principles or elements, so that soul

---
[1] *Iliad*, XXIII. 698.   [2] Fr. 109, Diels.   [3] 35 ff.

must be so too. Similarly also in his lectures 'On Philosophy' it was set forth that the [20] Animal-itself is compounded of the Idea itself of the One together with the primary length, breadth, and depth, everything else, the objects of its perception, being similarly constituted. Again he puts his view in yet other terms: Mind is the monad, science or knowledge the dyad (because it goes undeviatingly from one point to another), opinion the number of the plane, sensation the number of the solid; the numbers are by him expressly identified with the Forms themselves or principles, and are formed out of the elements; now [25] things are apprehended either by mind or science or opinion or sensation, and these same numbers are the Forms of things.

Some thinkers, accepting both premises, viz. that the soul is both originative of movement and cognitive, have compounded it of both and declared the soul to be a self-moving number.

[30] As to the nature and number of the first principles opinions differ. The difference is greatest between those who regard them as corporeal and those who regard them as incorporeal, 405ᵃ and from both dissent those who make a blend and draw their principles from both sources. The number of principles is also in dispute; some admit one only, others assert several. There is a consequent diversity in their several accounts of soul; they assume, naturally enough, that what is in its own nature originative of movement must be among what is [5] primordial. That has led some to regard it as fire, for fire is the subtlest of the elements and nearest to incorporeality; further, in the most primary sense, fire both is moved and originates movement in all the others.

Democritus has expressed himself more ingeniously than the rest on the grounds for ascribing each of these two characters to soul; soul and mind are, he says, one and the same [10] thing, and this thing must be one of the primary and indivisible bodies, and its power of originating movement must be due to its fineness of grain and the shape of its atoms; he says that of all the shapes the spherical is the most mobile, and that this is the shape of the particles of both fire and mind.

Anaxagoras, as we said above,[1] seems to distinguish between soul and mind, but in practice he treats them as a single substance, except [15] that it is mind that he specially posits as the principle of all things; at any rate what he

[1] 40ᵇ 1-6.

says is that mind alone of all that is is simple, unmixed, and pure. He assigns both characteristics, knowing and origination of movement, to the same principle, when he says that it was mind that set the whole in movement.

Thales, too, to judge from what is recorded about him, seems to have held soul to be a motive [20] force, since he said that the magnet has a soul in it because it moves the iron.

Diogenes (and others) held the soul to be air because he believed air to be finest in grain and a first principle; therein lay the grounds of the soul's powers of knowing and originating movement. As the primordial principle from which all other things are derived, it is cognitive; as finest in grain, it has the power to originate movement.

[25] Heraclitus too says that the first principle—the 'warm exhalation' of which, according to him, everything else is composed—is soul; further, that this exhalation is most incorporeal and in ceaseless flux; that what is in movement requires that what knows it should be in movement; and that all that is has its being essentially in movement (herein agreeing with the majority).

Alcmaeon also seems to have held a similar [30] view about soul; he says that it is immortal because it resembles 'the immortals,' and that this immortality belongs to it in virtue of its ceaseless movement; for all the 'things divine,' moon, sun, the planets, and the whole heavens, are in perpetual movement.

405ᵇ Of more superficial writers, some, e.g. Hippo, have pronounced it to be water; they seem to have argued from the fact that the seed of all animals is fluid, for Hippo tries to refute those who say that the soul is blood, on the ground that the seed, which is the primordial soul, is not blood.

[5] Another group (Critias, for example) did hold it to be blood; they take perception to be the most characteristic attribute of soul, and hold that perceptiveness is due to the nature of blood.

Each of the elements has thus found its partisan, except earth—earth has found no supporter unless we count as such those who have [10] declared soul to be, or to be compounded of, *all* the elements. All, then, it may be said, characterize the soul by three marks, Movement, Sensation, Incorporeality, and each of these is traced back to the first principles. That is why (with one exception) all those who define the soul by its power of knowing make it either an element or constructed out of the elements. The language they all use is similar; [15] like, they say, is known by like; as the soul knows everything, they construct it out of all the principles. Hence all those who admit but one cause or element, make the soul also one (e.g. fire or air), while those who admit a multiplicity of principles make the soul also multiple. The exception is Anaxagoras; he [20] alone says that mind is impassible and has nothing in common with anything else. But, if this is so, how or in virtue of what cause can it know? That Anaxagoras has not explained, nor can any answer be inferred from his words. All who acknowledge pairs of opposites among their principles, construct the soul also out of these contraries, while those who admit as principles only one contrary of each pair, [25] e.g. either hot or cold, likewise make the soul some one of these. That is why, also, they allow themselves to be guided by the names; those who identify soul with the hot argue that ζῆν (to live) is derived from ζεῖν (to boil), while those who identify it with the cold say that soul (ψυχή) is so called from the process of respiration and refrigeration (κατάψυξις). [30] Such are the traditional opinions concerning soul, together with the grounds on which they are maintained.

3

We must begin our examination with movement; for doubtless, not only is it false that the essence of soul is correctly described by those who say that it is what moves (or is capable of moving) itself, but it is an impossibility that movement should be even an attribute of it.

We have already[1] pointed out that there is no necessity that what originates movement should itself be moved. There are two senses in which anything may be moved—either (*a*) indirectly, owing to something other than itself, [5] or (*b*) directly, owing to itself. Things are 'indirectly moved' which are moved as being contained in something which is moved, e.g. sailors in a ship, for they are moved in a different sense from that in which the ship is moved; the ship is 'directly moved', they are 'indirectly moved', because they are in a moving vessel. This is clear if we consider their limbs; the movement proper to the legs (and so to man) is walking, and in this case the sailors [10] are not walking. Recognizing the double sense of 'being moved', what we have to consider now is whether the soul is 'directly

[1] *Physics*, VIII. 5, especially 257ᵃ 31-258ᵇ 9.

moved' and participates in such direct movement.

There are four species of movement—locomotion, alteration, diminution, growth; consequently if the soul is moved, it must be moved with one or several or all of these species of movement. Now if its movement is not [15] incidental, there must be a movement natural to it, and, if so, as all the species enumerated involve place, place must be natural to it. But if the essence of soul be to move itself, its being moved cannot be incidental to it, as it is to what is white or three cubits long; they too can be moved, but only incidentally—what is moved is that of which 'white' and 'three cubits long' are the attributes, the body in [20] which they inhere; hence *they* have no place: but if the soul naturally partakes in movement, it follows that it must have a place.

Further, if there be a movement natural to the soul, there must be a counter-movement unnatural to it, and conversely. The same applies to rest as well as to movement; for the *terminus ad quem* of a thing's natural move- [25] ment is the place of its natural rest, and similarly the *terminus ad quem* of its enforced movement is the place of its enforced rest. But what meaning can be attached to enforced movements or rests of the soul, it is difficult even to imagine.

Further, if the natural movement of the soul be upward, the soul must be fire; if downward, it must be earth; for upward and downward movements are the definitory characteristics of these bodies. The same reasoning applies to the intermediate movements, *termini,* and bodies. [30] Further, since the soul is observed to originate movement in the body, it is reasonable to suppose that it transmits to the body the movements by which it itself is moved, and so, reversing the order, we may infer from the movements of the body back to similar movements of the soul. Now the body is moved from place to place with movements of locomotion. Hence it would follow that the soul too must in accordance with the body change either its place as a whole or the relative places of its parts. This carries with it the possibility that the soul might even quit its body and re-enter it, and with this would be involved the possibility of a resurrection of ani- [5] mals from the dead. But, it may be contended, the soul can be moved indirectly by something else; for an animal can be pushed out of its course. Yes, but that to whose *essence* belongs the power of being moved by itself,

cannot be moved by something else except incidentally, just as what is good by or in itself cannot owe its goodness to something external to it or to some end to which it is a means.
[10] If the soul *is* moved, the most probable view is that what moves it is sensible things.

We must note also that, if the soul moves itself, it must be the mover itself that is moved, so that it follows that if movement is in every case a displacement of that which is in movement, in that respect in which it is said to be moved, the movement of the soul must be a departure from its essential nature, at least if its self-movement is essential to it, not incidental.
[15] Some go so far as to hold that the movements which the soul imparts to the body in which it is are the same in kind as those with which it itself is moved. An example of this is Democritus, who uses language like that of the comic dramatist Philippus, who accounts for the movements that Daedalus imparted to his wooden Aphrodite by saying that he poured quicksilver into it; similarly Democritus says [20] that the spherical atoms which according to him constitute soul, owing to their own ceaseless movements draw the whole body after them and so produce its movements. We must urge the question whether it is these very same atoms which produce rest also—how they could do so, it is difficult and even impossible to say. And, in general, we may object that it is not in this way that the soul appears [25] to originate movement in animals—it is through intention or process of thinking.

It is in the same fashion that the *Timaeus*[1] also tries to give a physical account of how the soul moves its body; the soul, it is there said, is in movement, and so owing to their mutual implication moves the body also. After compounding the soul-substance out of the elements and dividing it in accordance with the harmonic numbers, in order that it may pos- [30] sess a connate sensibility for 'harmony' and that the whole may move in movements well attuned, the Demiurge bent the straight line into a circle; this single circle he divided into two circles united at two common points; 407ª one of these he subdivided into seven circles. All this implies that the movements of the soul are identified with the local movements of the heavens.

Now, in the first place, it is a mistake to say that the soul is a spatial magnitude. It is evident that Plato means the soul of the whole to be like the sort of soul which is called mind— [5] not like the sensitive or the desiderative soul, for the movements of neither of these are circular. Now mind is one and continuous in the sense in which the process of thinking is so, and thinking is identical with the thoughts which are its parts; these have a serial unity like that of number, not a unity like that of a spatial magnitude. Hence mind cannot have that kind of unity either; mind is either without parts or is continuous in some other way than that which characterizes a spatial magnitude. How, indeed, if it were a spatial magni- [10] tude, could mind possibly think? Will it think with any one indifferently of its parts? In this case, the 'part' must be understood either in the sense of a spatial magnitude or in the sense of a point (if a point *can* be called a part of a spatial magnitude). If we accept the latter alternative, the points being infinite in number, obviously the mind can never exhaustively traverse them; if the former, the mind must think the same thing over and over again, indeed an infinite number of times (whereas [15] it is manifestly possible to think a thing once only). If contact of any part whatsoever of itself with the object is all that is required, why need mind move in a circle, or indeed possess magnitude at all? On the other hand, if contact with the whole circle is necessary, what meaning can be given to the contact of the parts? Further, how could what has no parts think what has parts, or what has parts think what has none? We must identify the circle referred to with mind; for it is mind whose [20] movement is thinking, and it is the circle whose movement is revolution, so that if thinking is a movement of revolution, the circle which has this characteristic movement must be mind.

If the circular movement is eternal, there must be something which mind is always thinking—what *can* this be? For all practical processes of thinking have limits—they all go on for the sake of something outside the process, and all theoretical processes come to a close in the same way as the phrases in speech which express processes and results of think- [25] ing. Every such linguistic phrase is either definitory or demonstrative. Demonstration has both a starting-point and may be said to end in a conclusion or inferred result; even if the process never reaches final completion, at any rate it never returns upon itself again to its starting-point, it goes on assuming a fresh middle term or a fresh extreme, and moves straight

---
[1] 35 ff.

forward, but circular movement returns to its [30] starting-point. Definitions, too, are closed groups of terms.

Further, if the same revolution is repeated, mind must repeatedly think the same object.

Further, thinking has more resemblance to a coming to rest or arrest than to a movement; the same may be said of inferring.

It might also be urged that what is difficult and enforced is incompatible with blessedness; 407ᵇ if the movement of the soul is not of its essence, movement of the soul must be contrary to its nature. It must also be painful for the soul to be inextricably bound up with the body; nay more, if, as is frequently said and widely accepted, it is better for mind not to be embodied, the union must be for it undesirable.

[5] Further, the cause of the revolution of the heavens is left obscure. It is not the essence of soul which is the cause of this circular movement—that movement is only incidental to soul—nor is, *a fortiori*, the body its cause. Again, it is not even asserted that it is better that soul should be so moved; and yet the reason for which God caused the soul to move in [10] a circle can only have been that movement was better for it than rest, and movement of this kind better than any other. But since this sort of consideration is more appropriate to another field of speculation, let us dismiss it for the present.

The view we have just been examining, in company with most theories about the soul, involves the following absurdity: they all join [15] the soul to a body, or place it in a body, without adding any specification of the reason of their union, or of the bodily conditions required for it. Yet such explanation can scarcely be omitted; for some community of nature is presupposed by the fact that the one acts and the other is acted upon, the one moves and the other is moved; interaction always implies a *special* nature in the two interagents. All, how- [20] ever, that these thinkers do is to describe the specific characteristics of the soul; they do not try to determine anything about the body which is to contain it, as if it were possible, as in the Pythagorean myths, that any soul could be clothed upon with any body—an absurd view, for each body seems to have a form and shape of its own. It is as absurd as to say that the art of carpentry could embody itself in [25] flutes; each art must use its tools, each soul its body.

4

There is yet another theory about soul, which has commended itself to many as no less probable than any of those we have hitherto mentioned, and has rendered public account [30] of itself in the court of popular discussion. Its supporters say that the soul is a kind of harmony, for (*a*) harmony is a blend or composition of contraries, and (*b*) the body is compounded out of contraries. Harmony, however, is a certain proportion or composition of the constituents blended, and soul can be neither the one nor the other of these. Further, the power of originating movement cannot belong to a harmony, while almost all concur in regarding this as a principal attribute of soul. 408ᵃ It is more appropriate to call health (or generally one of the good states of the body) a harmony than to predicate it of the soul. The absurdity becomes most apparent when we try to attribute the active and passive affections of the soul to a harmony; the necessary readjustment of their conceptions is difficult. Further, [5] in using the word 'harmony' we have one or other of two cases in our mind; the most proper sense is in relation to spatial magnitudes which have motion and position, where harmony means the disposition and cohesion of their parts in such a manner as to prevent the introduction into the whole of anything homogeneous with it, and the secondary sense, derived from the former, is that in which it means the ratio between the constituents so blended; in neither of these senses is it plausi- [10] ble to predicate it of soul. That soul is a harmony in the sense of the mode of composition of the parts of the body is a view easily refutable; for there are many composite parts and those variously compounded; of what bodily part is mind or the sensitive or the appetitive faculty the mode of composition? And what *is* the mode of composition which constitutes each of them? It is equally absurd to identify the soul with the ratio of the mixture; [15] for the mixture which makes flesh has a different ratio between the elements from that which makes bone. The consequence of this view will therefore be that distributed throughout the whole body there will be many souls, since every one of the bodily parts is a different mixture of the elements, and the ratio of mixture is in each case a harmony, i.e. a soul.

From Empedocles at any rate we might demand an answer to the following question—

for he says that each of the parts of the body is what it is in virtue of a ratio between the [20] elements: is the soul identical with this ratio, or is it not rather something over and above this which is formed in the parts? Is love the cause of any and every mixture, or only of those that are in the right ratio? Is love this ratio itself, or is love something over and above this? Such are the problems raised by this account. But, on the other hand, if the soul is different from the mixture, why does it [25] disappear at one and the same moment with that relation between the elements which constitutes flesh or the other parts of the animal body? Further, if the soul is not identical with the ratio of mixture, and it is consequently not the case that each of the parts has a soul, what is that which perishes when the soul quits the body?

That the soul cannot either be a harmony, or be moved in a circle, is clear from what we [30] have said. Yet that it can be moved incidentally is, as we said above,[1] possible, and even that in a sense it can move itself, i.e. in the sense that *the vehicle* in which it is can be moved, and moved by it; in no other sense can the soul be moved in space.

More legitimate doubts might remain as to its movement in view of the following facts. 408[b] We speak of the soul as being pained or pleased, being bold or fearful, being angry, perceiving, thinking. All these are regarded as modes of movement, and hence it might be inferred that the soul is moved. This, however, does not necessarily follow. We may admit to [5] the full that being pained or pleased, or thinking, are movements (each of them a 'being moved'), and that the movement is originated by the soul. For example we may regard anger or fear as such and such movements of the heart, and thinking as such and such another movement of that organ, or of some other; these modifications may arise either from changes of place in certain parts or from quali- [10] tative alterations (the special nature of the parts and the special modes of their changes being for our present purpose irrelevant). Yet to say that it is *the soul* which is angry is as inexact as it would be to say that it is the soul that weaves webs or builds houses. It is doubtless better to avoid saying that the soul pities or learns or thinks and rather to say that it is the man who does this with his soul. [15] What we mean is not that the movement is in the soul, but that sometimes it terminates

---
[1] 406[a] 30 ff., [b]5-8.

in the soul and sometimes starts from it, sensation e.g. coming from without inwards, and reminiscence starting from the soul and terminating with the movements, actual or residual, in the sense organs.

The case of mind is different; it seems to be an independent substance implanted within the soul and to be incapable of being destroyed. If it could be destroyed at all, it would be under the blunting influence of old age. [20] What really happens in respect of mind in old age is, however, exactly parallel to what happens in the case of the sense organs; if the old man could recover the proper kind of eye, he would see just as well as the young man. The incapacity of old age is due to an affection not of the soul but of its vehicle, as occurs in drunkenness or disease. Thus it is that in old age the activity of mind or intellectual apprehension declines only through the decay of some other inward part; mind itself is impas- [25] sible. Thinking, loving, and hating are affections not of mind, but of that which has mind, so far as it has it. That is why, when this vehicle decays, memory and love cease; they were activities not of mind, but of the composite which has perished; mind is, no doubt, something more divine and impassible. That [30] the soul cannot be moved is therefore clear from what we have said, and if it cannot be moved at all, manifestly it cannot be moved by itself.

Of all the opinions we have enumerated, by far the most unreasonable is that which declares the soul to be a self-moving number; it involves in the first place all the impossibilities which follow from regarding the soul as moved, and in the second special absurdities which follow from calling it a number. How 409[a] are we to imagine a unit being moved? By what agency? What sort of movement can be attributed to what is without parts or internal differences? If the unit is both originative of movement and itself capable of being moved, it must contain difference.

Further, since they say a moving line generates a surface and a moving point a line, [5] the movements of the psychic units must be lines (for a point is a unit having position, and the number of the soul is, of course, somewhere and has position).

Again, if from a number a number or a unit is subtracted, the remainder is another number; but plants and many animals when divided continue to live, and each segment is thought to retain the same kind of soul.

[10] It must be all the same whether we speak of units or corpuscles; for if the spherical atoms of Democritus became points, nothing being retained but their being a quantum, there must remain in each a moving and a moved part, just as there is in what is continuous; what happens has nothing to do with the size of the atoms, it depends solely upon their [15] being a quantum. That is why there must be something to originate movement in the units. If in the animal what originates movement is the soul, so also must it be in the case of the number, so that not the mover and the moved together, but the mover only, will be the soul. But how is it possible for one of the units to fulfil this function of originating movement? There must be *some* difference be-[20] tween such a unit and all the other units, and what difference can there be between one placed unit and another except a difference of position? If then, on the other hand, these psychic units within the body are different from the points *of* the body, there will be two sets of units both occupying the same place; for each unit will occupy a point. And yet, if there can be two, why cannot there be an infinite number? For if things can occupy an indivisible place, they must themselves be indivisible. [25] If, on the other hand, the points of the body are identical with the units whose number is the soul, or if the number of the points in the body is the soul, why have not all bodies souls? For all bodies contain points or an infinity of points.

Further, how is it possible for these points to be isolated or separated from their bodies, [30] seeing that lines cannot be resolved into points?

5

The result is, as we have said,[1] that this view, while on the one side identical with that of those who maintain that soul is a subtle kind of body, is on the other entangled in the absurdity peculiar to Democritus' way of describing the manner in which movement is 409^b originated by soul. For if the soul is present throughout the whole percipient body, there must, if the soul be a kind of body, be two bodies in the same place; and for those who call it a number, there must be many [5] points at one point, or every body must have a soul, unless the soul be a different sort of number—other, that is, than the sum of the points existing in a body. Another consequence that follows is that the animal must be moved by its number precisely in the way that Democritus explained its being moved by his spherical psychic atoms. What difference does it make whether we speak of small spheres or of large units, or, quite simply, of units in [10] movement? One way or another, the movements of the animal must be due to their movements. Hence those who combine movement and number in the same subject lay themselves open to these and many other similar absurdities. It is impossible not only that these characters should give the definition of soul—it is impossible that they should even be attributes of it. The point is clear if the [15] attempt be made to start from this as the account of soul and explain from it the affections and actions of the soul, e.g. reasoning, sensation, pleasure, pain, &c. For, to repeat what we have said earlier,[2] movement and number do not facilitate even conjecture about the derivative properties of soul.

Such are the three ways in which soul has traditionally been defined; one group of thinkers declared it to be that which is most orig-[20] inative of movement because it moves itself, another group to be the subtlest and most nearly incorporeal of all kinds of body. We have now sufficiently set forth the difficulties and inconsistencies to which these theories are exposed. It remains now to examine the doctrine that soul is composed of the elements.

The reason assigned for this doctrine is that thus the soul may perceive or come to know everything that is, but the theory necessarily [25] involves itself in many impossibilities. Its upholders assume that like is known only by like, and imagine that by declaring the soul to be composed of the elements they succeed in identifying the soul with all the things it is capable of apprehending. But the elements are not the only things it knows; there are many others, or, more exactly, an infinite number of others, formed out of the elements. Let us admit [30] that the soul knows or perceives the elements out of which each of these composites is made up; but by what means will it know or perceive the composite whole, e.g. what God, man, flesh, bone (or any other compound) is? For each *is*, not merely the elements of which it is composed, but those elements combined in a determinate mode or ratio, as Empedocles himself says of bone,

[1] 408^b 33 ff.

[2] 402^b 25-403^a 2.

The kindly Earth in its broad-bosomed moulds[1]
[5] Won of clear Water two parts out of eight
And four of Fire; and so white bones were formed.

Nothing, therefore, will be gained by the presence of the elements in the soul, unless there be also present there the various formulae of proportion and the various compositions in accordance with them. Each element will indeed know its fellow outside, but there will be no knowledge of bone or man, unless they too are present in the constitution of the soul. [10] The impossibility of this needs no pointing out; for who would suggest that stone or man could enter into the constitution of the soul? The same applies to 'the good' and 'the not-good', and so on.

Further, the word 'is' has many meanings: it may be used of a 'this' or substance, or of a quantum, or of a quale, or of any other of the kinds of predicates we have distinguished. [15] Does the soul consist of all of these or not? It does not appear that all have common elements. Is the soul formed out of those elements alone which enter into substances? If so, how will it be able to know each of the other kinds of thing? Will it be said that each kind of thing has elements or principles of its own, and that the soul is formed out of the whole of [20] these? In that case, the soul must be a quantum *and* a quale *and* a substance. But all that can be made out of the elements of a quantum is a quantum, not a substance. These (and others like them) are the consequences of the view that the soul is composed of all the elements.

It is absurd, also, to say both (*a*) that like is not capable of being affected by like, and (*b*) that like is perceived or known by like, for [25] perceiving, and also both thinking and knowing, are, on their own assumption, ways of being affected or moved.

There are many puzzles and difficulties raised by saying, as Empedocles does, that each set of things is known by means of its corporeal elements and by reference to something in soul which is like them, and addition- [30] al testimony is furnished by this new consideration; for all the parts of the animal body which consist wholly of earth such as bones, 410ᵇ sinews, and hair seem to be wholly insensitive and consequently not perceptive even of objects earthy like themselves, as they ought to have been.

[1] Fr. 96, Diels.

Further, each of the principles will have far more ignorance than knowledge, for though each of them will know one thing, there will be many of which it will be ignorant. Empedocles at any rate must conclude that his God [5] is the least intelligent of all beings, for of him alone is it true that there is one thing, Strife, which he does not know, while there is nothing which mortal beings do not know, for there is nothing which does not enter into their composition.

In general, we may ask, Why has not everything a soul, since everything either is an element, or is formed out of one or several or all of the elements? Each must certainly know one or several or all.

[10] The problem might also be raised, What is that which unifies the elements into a soul? The elements correspond, it would appear, to the matter; what unites them, whatever it is, is the supremely important factor. But it is impossible that there should be something superior to, and dominant over, the soul (and *a fortiori* over the mind); it is reasonable to hold that mind is by nature most primordial [15] and dominant, while their statement is that it is the elements which are first of all that is.

All, both those who assert that the soul, because of its knowledge or perception of what is, is compounded out of the elements, and those who assert that it is of all things the most originative of movement, fail to take into consideration all kinds of soul. In fact (1) not all beings that perceive can originate movement; there appear to be certain animals which are [20] stationary, and yet local movement is the only one, so it seems, which the soul originates in animals. And (2) the same objection holds against all those who construct mind and the perceptive faculty out of the elements; for it appears that plants live, and yet are not endowed with locomotion or perception, while a large number of animals are without discourse of reason. Even if these points were waived and mind admitted to be a part of the [25] soul (and so too the perceptive faculty), still, even so, there would be kinds and parts of soul of which they had failed to give any account.

The same objection lies against the view expressed in the 'Orphic' poems: there it is said that the soul comes in from the whole when breathing takes place, being borne in upon the [30] winds. Now this cannot take place in the case of plants, nor indeed in the case of certain classes of animal, for not all classes of 411ᵃ animal breathe. This fact has escaped the notice of the holders of this view.

If we must construct the soul out of the elements, there is no necessity to suppose that *all* the elements enter into its construction; one element in each pair of contraries will suffice to enable it to know both that ele- [5] ment itself and its contrary. By means of the straight line we know both itself and the curved—the carpenter's rule enables us to test both—but what is curved does not enable us to distinguish either itself or the straight.

Certain thinkers say that soul is intermingled in the whole universe, and it is perhaps for that reason that Thales came to the opinion that all things are full of gods. This presents some difficulties: Why does the soul [10] when it resides in air or fire not form an animal, while it does so when it resides in mixtures of the elements, and that although it is held to be of higher quality when contained in the former? (One might add the question, why the soul in air is maintained to be higher and more immortal than that in animals.) Both possible ways of replying to the former question lead to absurdity or paradox; for it [15] is beyond paradox to say that fire or air is an animal, and it is absurd to refuse the name of animal to what has soul in it. The opinion that the elements have soul in them seems to have arisen from the doctrine that a whole must be homogeneous with its parts. If it is true that animals become animate by drawing into themselves a portion of what surrounds them, the partisans of this view are bound to say that the soul of the Whole too is [20] homogeneous with all its parts. If the air sucked in is homogeneous, but soul heterogeneous, clearly while some part of soul will exist in the inbreathed air, some other part will not. The soul must either be homogeneous, or such that there are some parts of the Whole in which it is not to be found.

From what has been said it is now clear that knowing as an attribute of soul cannot be ex- [25] plained by soul's being composed of the elements, and that it is neither sound nor true to speak of soul as moved. But since (*a*) knowing, perceiving, opining, and further (*b*) desiring, wishing, and generally all other modes of appetition, belong to soul, and (*c*) the local [30] movements of animals, and (*d*) growth, maturity, and decay are produced by the soul, we must ask whether each of these is an attribute of the soul as a whole, i.e. whether it is with the whole soul we think, perceive, move ourselves, act or are acted upon, or whether each of them requires a different part of the soul? So too with regard to life. Does it depend on one of the parts of soul? Or is it dependent on more than one? Or on all? Or has it some quite other cause?

[5] Some hold that the soul is divisible, and that one part thinks, another desires. If, then, its nature admits of its being divided, what can it be that holds the parts together? Surely not the body; on the contrary it seems rather to be the soul that holds the body together; at any rate when the soul departs the body disintegrates and decays. If, then, there is something else which makes the soul one, this unifying agency would have the best right to the [10] name of soul, and we shall have to repeat for it the question: Is *it* one or multipartite? If it is one, why not at once admit that 'the soul' is one? If it has parts, once more the question must be put: What holds *its* parts together, and so *ad infinitum*?

The question might also be raised about the parts of the soul: What is the separate rôle of each in relation to the body? For, if the whole [15] soul holds together the whole body, we should expect each part of the soul to hold together a part of the body. But this seems an impossibility; it is difficult even to imagine what sort of bodily part mind will hold together, or how it will do this.

It is a fact of observation that plants and cer- [20] tain insects go on living when divided into segments; this means that each of the segments has a soul in it identical in species, though not numerically identical in the different segments, for both of the segments for a time possess the power of sensation and local movement. That this does not last is not surprising, for they no longer possess the organs necessary for self-maintenance. But, all the same, in each of the bodily parts there are pres- [25] ent all the parts of soul, and the souls so present are homogeneous with one another and with the whole; this means that the several parts of the soul are indisseverable from one another, although the whole soul is divisible. It seems also that the principle found in plants is also a kind of soul; for this is the only principle which is common to both animals and plants; and this exists in isolation from the principle of sensation, though there [30] is nothing which has the latter without the former.

BOOK II

1

412[a] Let the foregoing suffice as our account of the views concerning the soul which have been handed on by our predecessors; let us now dismiss them and make as it were a completely fresh start, endeavouring to give a pre- [5] cise answer to the question, What is soul? i.e. to formulate the most general possible definition of it.

We are in the habit of recognizing, as one determinate kind of what is, substance, and that in several senses, (a) in the sense of matter or that which in itself is not 'a this', and (b) in the sense of form or essence, which is that precisely in virtue of which a thing is called 'a this', and thirdly (c) in the sense of that which is compounded of both (a) and [10] (b). Now matter is potentiality, form actuality; of the latter there are two grades related to one another as e.g. knowledge to the exercise of knowledge.

Among substances are by general consent reckoned bodies and especially natural bodies; for they are the principles of all other bodies. Of natural bodies some have life in them, others not; by life we mean self-nutrition and [15] growth (with its correlative decay). It follows that every natural body which has life in it is a substance in the sense of a composite.

But since it is also a *body* of such and such a kind, viz. having life, the *body* cannot be soul; the body is the subject or matter, not what is attributed to it. Hence the soul must be a sub- [20] stance in the sense of the form of a natural body having life potentially within it. But substance is actuality, and thus soul is the actuality of a body as above characterized. Now the word actuality has two senses corresponding respectively to the possession of knowledge and the actual exercise of knowledge. It is obvious that the soul is actuality in the first sense, viz. that of knowledge as possessed, for both [25] sleeping and waking presuppose the existence of soul, and of these waking corresponds to actual knowing, sleeping to knowledge possessed but not employed, and, in the history of the individual, knowledge comes before its employment or exercise.

That is why the soul is the first grade of actuality of a natural body having life potentially in it. The body so described is a body 412[b] which is organized. The parts of plants in spite of their extreme simplicity are 'organs'; e.g. the leaf serves to shelter the pericarp, the pericarp to shelter the fruit, while the roots of plants are analogous to the mouth of animals, both serving for the absorption of food. If, then, we have to give a general formula applicable [5] to all kinds of soul, we must describe it as the first grade of actuality of a natural organized body. That is why we can wholly dismiss as unnecessary the question whether the soul and the body are one: it is as meaningless as to ask whether the wax and the shape given to it by the stamp are one, or generally the matter of a thing and that of which it is the matter. Unity has many senses (as many as 'is' has), but the most proper and fundamental sense of both is the relation of an actuality to that of which it is the actuality. [10] We have now given an answer to the question, What is soul?—an answer which applies to it in its full extent. It is substance in the sense which corresponds to the definitive formula of a thing's essence. That means that it is 'the essential whatness' of a body of the character just assigned. Suppose that what is literally an 'organ', like an axe, were a *natural* body, its 'essential whatness', would have been its essence, and so its soul; if this disappeared from it, it would have ceased to be an axe, ex- [15] cept in name. As it is, it is just an axe; it wants the character which is required to make its whatness or formulable essence a soul; for that, it would have had to be a *natural* body of a particular kind, viz. one having *in itself* the power of setting itself in movement and arresting itself. Next, apply this doctrine in the case of the 'parts' of the living body. Suppose that the eye were an animal—sight would have been its soul, for sight is the substance or essence of the eye which corresponds [20] to the formula, the eye being merely the matter of seeing; when seeing is removed the eye is no longer an eye, except in name—it is no more a real eye than the eye of a statue or of a painted figure. We must now extend our consideration from the 'parts' to the whole living body; for what the departmental sense is to the bodily part which is its organ, that the whole faculty of sense is to the whole sensitive body as such.

[25] We must not understand by that which is 'potentially capable of living' what has lost the soul it had, but only what still retains it;

but seeds and fruits are bodies which possess the qualification. Consequently, while waking is actuality in a sense corresponding to the cutting and the seeing, the soul is actuality in the sense corresponding to the power of sight and the power in the tool; the body corresponds to what exists in potentiality; as the pupil *plus* the power of sight constitutes the eye, so the soul *plus* the body constitutes the animal.

From this it indubitably follows that the soul is inseparable from its body, or at any rate that certain parts of it are (if it has parts)— [5] for the actuality of some of them is nothing but the actualities of their bodily parts. Yet some may be separable because they are not the actualities of any body at all. Further, we have no light on the problem whether the soul may not be the actuality of its body in the sense in which the sailor is the actuality of the ship.

This must suffice as our sketch or outline [10] determination of the nature of soul.

2

Since what is clear or logically more evident emerges from what in itself is confused but more observable by us, we must reconsider our results from this point of view. For it is not enough for a definitive formula to express as [15] most now do the mere fact; it must include and exhibit the ground also. At present definitions are given in a form analogous to the conclusion of a syllogism; e.g. What is squaring? The construction of an equilateral rectangle equal to a given oblong rectangle. Such a definition is in form equivalent to a conclusion. One that tells us that squaring is the discovery of a line which is a mean proportional between the two unequal sides of the given rectangle discloses the ground of what is defined.

[20] We resume our inquiry from a fresh starting-point by calling attention to the fact that what has soul in it differs from what has not, in that the former displays life. Now this word has more than one sense, and provided any one alone of these is found in a thing we say that thing is living. Living, that is, may mean thinking or perception or local movement and rest, or movement in the sense of [25] nutrition, decay and growth. Hence we think of plants also as living, for they are observed to possess in themselves an originative power through which they increase or decrease in all spatial directions; they grow up *and* down, and everything that grows increases its bulk alike in both directions or indeed in all, [30] and continues to live so long as it can absorb nutriment.

This power of self-nutrition can be isolated from the other powers mentioned, but not they from it—in mortal beings at least. The fact is obvious in plants; for it is the only psychic power they possess.

413ᵇ This is the originative power the possession of which leads us to speak of things as *living* at all, but it is the possession of sensation that leads us for the first time to speak of living things as animals; for even those beings which possess no power of local movement but do possess the power of sensation we call animals and not merely living things.

The primary form of sense is touch, which [5] belongs to all animals. Just as the power of self-nutrition can be isolated from touch and sensation generally, so touch can be isolated from all other forms of sense. (By the power of self-nutrition we mean that departmental power of the soul which is common to plants and animals: all animals whatsoever are observed to have the sense of touch.) What the [10] explanation of these two facts is, we must discuss later.[1] At present we must confine ourselves to saying that soul is the source of these phenomena and is characterized by them, viz. by the powers of self-nutrition, sensation, thinking, and motivity.

Is each of these a soul or a part of a soul? And if a part, a part in what sense? A part merely distinguishable by definition or a part [15] distinct in local situation as well? In the case of certain of these powers, the answers to these questions are easy, in the case of others we are puzzled what to say. Just as in the case of plants which when divided are observed to continue to live though removed to a distance from one another (thus showing that in *their* case the soul of each individual plant before division was actually one, potentially many), so we notice a similar result in other varieties [20] of soul, i.e. in insects which have been cut in two; each of the segments possesses both sensation and local movement; and if sensation, necessarily also imagination and appetition; for, where there is sensation, there is also pleasure and pain, and, where these, necessarily also desire.

We have no evidence as yet about mind or [25] the power to think; it seems to be a widely different kind of soul, differing as what is

---
[1] III. 12, esp. 434ᵃ 22-30, ᵇ10 ff.

eternal from what is perishable; it alone is capable of existence in isolation from all other psychic powers. All the other parts of soul, it is evident from what we have said, are, in spite of certain statements to the contrary, incapable of separate existence though, of course, distinguishable by definition. If opining is distinct [30] from perceiving, to be capable of opining and to be capable of perceiving must be distinct, and so with all the other forms of living above enumerated. Further, some animals possess all these parts of soul, some certain of them only, others one only (this is what enables us to classify animals); the cause must 414ª be considered later.[1] A similar arrangement is found also within the field of the senses; some classes of animals have all the senses, some only certain of them, others only one, the most indispensable, touch.

Since the expression 'that whereby we live [5] and perceive' has two meanings, just like the expression 'that whereby we know'—that may mean either (*a*) knowledge or (*b*) the soul, for we can speak of knowing *by* or *with* either, and similarly that whereby we are in health may be either (*a*) health or (*b*) the body or some part of the body; and since of the two terms thus contrasted knowledge or health is the name of a form, essence, or ratio, or if we so express it an actuality of a recipient [10] matter—knowledge of what is capable of knowing, health of what is capable of being made healthy (for the operation of that which is capable of originating change terminates and has its seat in what is changed or altered); further, since it is the soul by or with which primarily we live, perceive, and think:—it follows that the soul must be a ratio or formulable essence, not a matter or subject. For, as we said,[2] the word substance has three meanings— [15] form, matter, and the complex of both— and of these three what is called matter is potentiality, what is called form actuality. Since then the complex here is the living thing, the body cannot be the actuality of the soul; it is the soul which is the actuality of a certain kind of body. Hence the rightness of the view that the soul cannot be without a body, while it can- [20] not *be* a body; it is not a body but something relative to a body. That is why it is *in* a body, and a body of a definite kind. It was a mistake, therefore, to do as former thinkers did, merely to fit it into a body without adding a definite specification of the kind or character [25] of that body. Reflection confirms the ob-

served fact; the actuality of any given thing can only be realized in what is already potentially that thing, i.e. in a matter of its own appropriate to it. From all this it follows that soul is an actuality or formulable essence of something that possesses a potentiality of being besouled.

3

Of the psychic powers above enumerated[3] some kinds of living things, as we have said,[4] possess all, some less than all, others one only. [30] Those we have mentioned are the nutritive, the appetitive, the sensory, the locomotive, and the power of thinking. Plants have none but the first, the nutritive, while another order of living things has this *plus* the sensory. 414ᵇ If any order of living things has the sensory, it must also have the appetitive; for appetite is the genus of which desire, passion, and wish are the species; now all animals have one sense at least, viz. touch, and whatever has a sense has the capacity for pleasure and pain and therefore has pleasant and painful objects present to it, and wherever these are present, [5] there is desire, for desire is just appetition of what is pleasant. Further, all animals have the sense for food (for touch is the sense for food); the food of all living things consists of what is dry, moist, hot, cold, and these are the qualities apprehended by touch; all other sensible qualities are apprehended by touch only [10] indirectly. Sounds, colours, and odours contribute nothing to nutriment; flavours fall within the field of tangible qualities. Hunger and thirst are forms of desire, hunger a desire for what is dry and hot, thirst a desire for what is cold and moist; flavour is a sort of seasoning added to both. We must later[5] clear up these [15] points, but at present it may be enough to say that all animals that possess the sense of touch have also appetition. The case of imagination is obscure; we must examine it later.[6] Certain kinds of animals possess in addition the power of locomotion, and still another order of animate beings, i.e. man and possibly another order like man or superior to him, the [20] power of thinking, i.e. mind. It is now evident that a single definition can be given of soul only in the same sense as one can be given of figure. For, as in that case there is no figure distinguishable and apart from triangle, &c.,

---

[1] III. 12, 13.   [2] 412ª 7.

[3] 413ª 23-5, ᵇ11-13, 21-4.   [4] 413ᵇ 32-414ª 1.
[5] Chapter 11, III. 12 (434ᵇ 18-21); *Sense and the Sensible*, 4.
[6] III. 3, 11 (433ᵇ 31-434ª 7).

so here there is no soul apart from the forms of soul just enumerated. It is true that a highly general definition can be given for figure which will fit all figures without expressing the peculiar nature of any figure. So here in the case of soul and its specific forms. Hence [25] it is absurd in this and similar cases to demand an absolutely general definition which will fail to express the peculiar nature of anything that *is,* or again, omitting this, to look for separate definitions corresponding to each *infima species*. The cases of figure and soul are exactly parallel; for the particulars subsumed under the common name in both cases —figures and living beings—constitute a se-[30] ries, each successive term of which potentially contains its predecessor, e.g. the square the triangle, the sensory power the self-nutritive. Hence we must ask in the case of each order of living things, What is its soul, i.e. What is the soul of plant, animal, man? Why the terms are related in this serial way must form 415ª the subject of later examination.¹ But the facts are that the power of perception is never found apart from the power of self-nutrition, while—in plants—the latter is found isolated from the former. Again, no sense is found apart from that of touch, while touch *is* found [5] by itself; many animals have neither sight, hearing, nor smell. Again, among living things that possess sense some have the power of locomotion, some not. Lastly, certain living beings —a small minority—possess calculation and thought, for (among mortal beings) those which possess calculation have all the other [10] powers above mentioned, while the converse does not hold—indeed some live by imagination alone, while others have not even imagination. The mind that knows with immediate intuition presents a different problem.

It is evident that the way to give the most adequate definition of soul is to seek in the case of *each* of its forms for the most appropriate definition.

4

It is necessary for the student of these forms of soul first to find a definition of each, ex-[15] pressive of what it is, and then to investigate its derivative properties, &c. But if we are to express what each is, viz. what the thinking power is, or the perceptive, or the nutritive, we must go farther back and first give an account of thinking or perceiving, for in the or-

¹ III. 12, 13.

der of investigation the question of what an agent does precedes the question, what enables [20] it to do what it does. If this is correct, we must on the same ground go yet another step farther back and have some clear view of the objects of each; thus we must *start* with these objects, e.g. with food, with what is perceptible, or with what is intelligible.

It follows that first of all we must treat of nutrition and reproduction, for the nutritive soul is found along with all the others and is the most primitive and widely distributed power of soul, being indeed that one in virtue [25] of which all are said to have life. The acts in which it manifests itself are reproduction and the use of food—reproduction, I say, because for any living thing that has reached its normal development and which is unmutilated, and whose mode of generation is not spontaneous, the most natural act is the production of another like itself, an animal producing an animal, a plant a plant, in order that, as far as its nature allows, it may partake in the eternal 415ᵇ and divine. That is the goal towards which all things strive, that for the sake of which they do whatsoever their nature renders possible. The phrase 'for the sake of which' is ambiguous; it may mean either (*a*) the end to achieve which, or (*b*) the being in whose interest, the act is done. Since then no living thing is able to partake in what is eternal and divine by uninterrupted continuance (for nothing perishable can for ever remain one and [5] the same), it tries to achieve that end in the only way possible to it, and success is possible in varying degrees; so it remains not indeed as the self-same individual but continues its existence in something *like* itself—not numerically but specifically one.

The soul is the cause or source of the living body. The terms cause and source have many senses. But the soul is the cause of its body alike in all three senses which we explicitly [10] recognize. It is (*a*) the source or origin of movement, it is (*b*) the end, it is (*c*) the essence of the whole living body.

That it is the last, is clear; for in everything the essence is identical with the ground of its being, and here, in the case of living things, their being is to live, and of their being and their living the soul in them is the cause or source. Further, the actuality of whatever is potential is identical with its formulable essence.

[15] It is manifest that the soul is also the final cause of its body. For Nature, like mind,

always does whatever it does for the sake of something, which something is its end. To that something corresponds in the case of animals the soul and in this it follows the order of nature; all natural bodies are organs of the soul. This is true of those that enter into the constitution of plants as well as of those which enter into that of animals. This shows that that [20] for the sake of which they are is soul. We must here recall the two senses of 'that for the sake of which', viz. (a) the end to achieve which, and (b) the being in whose interest, anything is or is done.

We must maintain, further, that the soul is also the cause of the living body as the original source of local movement. The power of locomotion is not found, however, in all living things. But change of quality and change of quantity are also due to the soul. Sensation is held to be a qualitative alteration, and nothing except what has soul in it is capable of sensa- [25] tion. The same holds of the quantitative changes which constitute growth and decay; nothing grows or decays naturally except what feeds itself, and nothing feeds itself except what has a share of soul in it.

Empedocles is wrong in adding that growth in plants is to be explained, the downward rooting by the natural tendency of earth to 416ª travel downwards, and the upward branching by the similar natural tendency of fire to travel upwards. For he misinterprets up and down; up and down are not for all things what they are for the whole Cosmos: if we are to distinguish and identify organs according [5] to their *functions,* the roots of plants are analogous to the head in animals. Further, we must ask what is the force that holds together the earth and the fire which tend to travel in contrary directions; if there is no counteracting force, they will be torn asunder; if there is, this must be the soul and the cause of nutrition and growth. By some the element of fire is held to be *the* cause of nutrition and growth, [10] for it alone of the primary bodies or elements is observed to feed and increase *itself.* Hence the suggestion that in both plants and animals it is it which is the operative force. A concurrent cause in a sense it certainly is, but [15] not the principal cause, that is rather the soul; for while the growth of fire goes on without limit so long as there is a supply of fuel, in the case of all complex wholes formed in the course of nature there is a limit or ratio which determines their size and increase, and limit and ratio are marks of soul but not of fire, and belong to the side of formulable essence rather than that of matter.

Nutrition and reproduction are due to one and the same psychic power. It is necessary first to give precision to our account of food, [20] for it is by this function of absorbing food that this psychic power is distinguished from all the others. The current view is that what serves as food to a living thing is what is contrary to it—not that in every pair of contraries each is food to the other: to be food a contrary must not only be transformable into the other and vice versa, it must also in so doing increase the bulk of the other. Many a contrary is transformed into its other and vice versa, where neither is even a quantum and so cannot increase in bulk, e.g. an invalid into a [25] healthy subject. It is clear that not even those contraries which satisfy both the conditions mentioned above are food to one another in precisely the same sense; water may be said to feed fire, but not fire water. Where the members of the pair are elementary bodies only one of the contraries, it would appear, can be said to feed the other. But there is a difficulty here. One set of thinkers assert that like [30] is fed, as well as increased in amount, by like. Another set, as we have said, maintain the very reverse, viz. that what feeds and what is fed are contrary to one another; like, they argue, is incapable of being affected by like; but food is changed in the process of digestion, and change is always *to* what is opposite or to [35] what is intermediate. Further, food is 416ᵇ acted upon by what is nourished by it, not the other way round, as timber is worked by a carpenter and not conversely; there is a change in the carpenter but it is merely a change from not-working to working. In answering this problem it makes all the difference whether we mean by 'the food' the 'finished' or the 'raw' product. If we use the word food of both, viz. of the completely undigested and the completely digested matter, we can [5] justify both the rival accounts of it; taking food in the sense of undigested matter, it is the contrary of what is fed by it, taking it as digested it is like what is fed by it. Consequently it is clear that in a certain sense we may say that both parties are right, both wrong.

Since nothing except what is alive can be fed, what is fed is the besouled body and just because it has soul in it. Hence food is essen- [10] tially related to what has soul in it. Food has a power which is other than the power to increase the bulk of what is fed by it; so far forth as what has soul in it is a quantum, food may increase its quantity, but it is only so far as what has soul in it is a 'this-somewhat' or substance that food acts *as* food; in that case it maintains the being of what is fed, and that continues to be what it is so long as the process [15] of nutrition continues. Further, it is the agent in generation, i.e. not the generation of the individual fed but the reproduction of another like it; the substance of the individual fed is already in existence; the existence of no substance is a self-generation but only a self-maintenance.

Hence the psychic power which we are now studying may be described as that which tends to maintain whatever has this power in it of continuing such as it was, and food helps it to do its work. That is why, if deprived of food, it must cease to be.

[20] The process of nutrition involves three factors, (*a*) what is fed, (*b*) that wherewith it is fed, (*c*) what does the feeding; of these (*c*) is the first soul, (*a*) the body which has that soul in it, (*b*) the food. But since it is right to call things after the ends they realize, and the end of this soul is to generate another being like that in which it is, the first soul ought to [25] be named the reproductive soul. The expression (*b*) 'wherewith it is fed' is ambiguous just as is the expression 'wherewith the ship is steered'; that may mean either (i) the hand or (ii) the rudder, i.e. either (i) what is moved and sets in movement, or (ii) what is merely moved. We can apply this analogy here if we recall that all food must be capable of being digested, and that what produces digestion is warmth; that is why everything that has soul in it possesses warmth.

[30] We have now given an outline account of the nature of food; further details must be given in the appropriate place.

5

Having made these distinctions let us now speak of sensation in the widest sense. Sensation depends, as we have said,[1] on a process of movement or affection from without, for it is held to be some sort of change of quality. Now [35] some thinkers assert that like is affected only by like; in what sense this is possible and 417ª in what sense impossible, we have explained in our general discussion of acting and being acted upon.[2]

[1] 415ᵇ 24, cf. 410ª 25.
[2] *On Generation and Corruption*, 323ᵇ 18ff.

Here arises a problem: why do we not perceive the senses themselves as well as the external objects of sense, or why without the stimulation of external objects do they not produce sensation, seeing that they contain in [5] themselves fire, earth, and all the other elements, which are the direct or indirect objects of sense? It is clear that what is sensitive is so only potentially, not actually. The power of sense is parallel to what is combustible, for that never ignites itself spontaneously, but requires an agent which has the power of starting ignition; otherwise it could have set itself on fire, and would not have needed actual fire to set it ablaze.

In reply we must recall that we use the word [10] 'perceive' in two ways, for we say (*a*) that what has the power to hear or see, 'sees' or 'hears', even though it is at the moment asleep, and also (*b*) that what is actually seeing or hearing, 'sees' or 'hears'. Hence 'sense' too must have two meanings, sense potential, and sense actual. Similarly 'to be a sentient' means either (*a*) to have a certain power or (*b*) to manifest a certain activity. To begin with, for [15] a time, let us speak as if there were no difference between (i) being moved or affected, and (ii) being active, for movement is a kind of activity—an imperfect kind, as has elsewhere been explained.[3] Everything that is acted upon or moved is acted upon by an agent which is actually at work. Hence it is that in one sense, as has already been stated,[4] what [20] acts and what is acted upon are like, in another unlike, i.e. prior to and during the change the two factors are unlike, after it like.

But we must now distinguish not only *between* what is potential and what is actual but also different senses in which things can be said to be potential or actual; up to now we have been speaking as if each of these phrases had only one sense. We can speak of something as 'a knower' either (*a*) as when we say that man is a knower, meaning that man falls within the class of beings that know or have [25] knowledge, or (*b*) as when we are speaking of a man who possesses a knowledge of grammar; each of these is so called as having in him a certain potentiality, but there is a difference between their respective potentialities, the one (*a*) being a potential knower, because his kind or matter is such and such, the other (*b*), because he can in the absence of any external counteracting cause realize his knowl-

[3] *Physics*, 201ᵇ 31, 257ᵇ 8. [4] 416ª 29-ᵇ9.

edge in actual knowing at will. This implies a third meaning of 'a knower' (c), one who is already realizing his knowledge—he is a knower in actuality and in the most proper [30] sense is knowing, e.g. this A. Both the former are potential knowers, who realize their respective potentialities, the one (a) by change of quality, i.e. repeated transitions from one state to its opposite under instruction, the other (b) by the transition from the 417ᵇ inactive possession of sense or grammar to their active exercise. The two kinds of transition are distinct.

Also the expression 'to be acted upon' has more than one meaning; it may mean either (a) the extinction of one of two contraries by the other, or (b) the maintenance of what is potential by the agency of what is actual and already like what is acted upon, with such likeness as is compatible with one's being actual [5] and the other potential. For what possesses knowledge becomes an actual knower by a transition which is either not an alteration of it at all (being in reality a development into its true self or actuality) or at least an alteration in a quite different sense from the usual meaning.

Hence it is wrong to speak of a wise man as being 'altered' when he uses his wisdom, just as it would be absurd to speak of a builder as being altered when he is using his skill in building a house. [10] What in the case of knowing or understanding leads from potentiality to actuality ought not to be called teaching but something else. That which starting with the power to know learns or acquires knowledge through the agency of one who actually knows and has the power of teaching either (a) ought not to be said 'to be acted upon' at all or (b) we [15] must recognize two senses of alteration, viz. (i) the substitution of one quality for another, the first being the contrary of the second, or (ii) the development of an existent quality from potentiality in the direction of fixity or nature.

In the case of what is to possess sense, the first transition is due to the action of the male parent and takes place before birth so that at birth the living thing is, in respect of sensation, at the stage which corresponds to the *possession* of knowledge. Actual sensation corresponds to the stage of the exercise of knowledge. But between the two cases compared [20] there is a difference; the objects that excite the sensory powers to activity, the seen, the heard, &c., are outside. The ground of this difference is that what actual sensation apprehends is individuals, while what knowledge apprehends is universals, and these are in a sense within the soul. That is why a man can exercise his knowledge when he wishes, but his sensation does not depend upon himself— [25] a sensible object must be there. A similar statement must be made about our *knowledge* of what is sensible—on the same ground, viz. that the sensible objects are individual and external.

A later more appropriate occasion may be found¹ thoroughly to clear up all this. At pres- [30] ent it must be enough to recognize the distinctions already drawn; a thing may be said to be potential in either of two senses, (a) in the sense in which we might say of a boy that he may become a general or (b) in the sense in which we might say the same of an adult, and there are two corresponding senses 418ᵃ of the term 'a potential sentient'. There are no separate names for the two stages of potentiality; we have pointed out that they are different and how they are different. We cannot help using the incorrect terms 'being acted upon or altered' of the two transitions involved. As we have said,² what has the power of sensation is potentially like what the perceived object is actually; that is, while at the beginning of the process of its being acted upon the two interacting factors are dissimilar, [5] at the end the one acted upon is assimilated to the other and is identical in quality with it.

6

In dealing with each of the senses we shall have first to speak of the objects which are perceptible by each. The term 'object of sense' covers three kinds of objects, two kinds of which are, in our language, directly perceptible, while the remaining one is only incidentally perceptible. Of the first two kinds one (a) consists of what is perceptible by a single sense, [10] the other (b) of what is perceptible by any and all of the senses. I call by the name of special object of this or that sense that which cannot be perceived by any other sense than that one and in respect of which no error is possible; in this sense colour is the special object of sight, sound of hearing, flavour of taste. Touch, indeed, discriminates more than one set of different qualities. Each sense has one [15] kind of object which it discerns, and nev-

¹ III. 4, 5.   ² 417ᵃ 12-20.

er errs in reporting that what is before it is colour or sound (though it may err as to what it is that is coloured or where that is, or what it is that is sounding or where that is.) Such objects are what we propose to call the special objects of this or that sense.

'Common sensibles' are movement, rest, number, figure, magnitude; these are not peculiar to any one sense, but are common to all. There are at any rate certain kinds of movement which are perceptible both by touch and by sight.
[20] We speak of an incidental object of sense where e.g. the white object which we see is the son of Diares; here because 'being the son of Diares' is incidental to the directly visible white patch we speak of the son of Diares as being (incidentally) perceived or seen by us. Because this is only incidentally an object of sense, it in no way as such affects the senses. Of the two former kinds, both of which are in their own nature perceptible by sense, the first kind—that of special objects of the several senses—constitute *the* objects of sense in the [25] strictest sense of the term and it is to them that in the nature of things the structure of each several sense is adapted.

7

The object of sight is the visible, and what is visible is (*a*) colour and (*b*) a certain kind of object which can be described in words but which has no single name; what we mean by (*b*) will be abundantly clear as we proceed. Whatever is visible is colour and colour is what lies upon what is in its own nature visi-[30]ble; 'in its own nature' here means not that visibility is involved in the definition of what thus underlies colour, but that that substratum contains in itself the cause of visibility. Every colour has in it the power to set in movement what is actually transparent; that 418ᵇ power constitutes its very nature. That is why it is not visible except with the help of light; it is only in light that the colour of a thing is seen. Hence our first task is to explain what light is.

Now there clearly is something which is transparent, and by 'transparent' I mean what [5] is visible, and yet not visible in itself, but rather owing its visibility to the colour *of something else;* of this character are air, water, and many solid bodies. Neither air nor water is transparent because it is air or water; they are transparent because each of them has contained in it a certain substance which is the same in both and is also found in the eternal body which constitutes the uppermost shell of the physical Cosmos. Of this substance light is the activity—the activity of what is transparent so far forth as it has in it the determi-[10]nate power of becoming transparent; where this power is present, there is also the potentiality of the contrary, viz. darkness. Light is as it were the proper colour of what is transparent, and exists whenever the potentially transparent is excited to actuality by the influence of fire or something resembling 'the uppermost body'; for fire too contains something which is one and the same with the substance in question.

We have now explained what the transparent is and what light is; light is neither fire nor any kind whatsoever of body nor an efflux [15] from any kind of body (if it were, it would again itself be a kind of body)—it is the presence of fire or something resembling fire in what is transparent. It is certainly not a body, for two bodies cannot be present in the same place. The opposite of light is darkness; darkness is the absence from what is transparent of the corresponding positive state above characterized; clearly therefore, light is just the presence of that.

[20] Empedocles (and with him all others who used the same forms of expression) was wrong in speaking of light as 'travelling' or being at a given moment between the earth and its envelope, its movement being unobservable by us; that view is contrary both to the clear evidence of argument and to the observed facts; if the distance traversed were [25] short, the movement might have been unobservable, but where the distance is from extreme East to extreme West, the draught upon our powers of belief is too great.

What is capable of taking on colour is what in itself is colourless, as what can take on sound is what is soundless; what is colourless includes (*a*) what is transparent and (*b*) what is invisible or scarcely visible, i.e. what is [30] 'dark'. The latter (*b*) is the same as what is transparent, when it is potentially, not of course when it is actually transparent; it is the same substance which is now darkness, now light.
419ᵃ Not everything that is visible depends upon light for its visibility. This is only true of the 'proper' colour of things. Some objects of sight which in light are invisible, in darkness stimulate the sense; that is, things that appear fiery or shining. This class of objects has no

simple common name, but instances of it are [5] fungi, flesh, heads, scales, and eyes of fish. In none of these is what is seen their own 'proper' colour. Why we see these at all is another question. At present what is obvious is that what is seen in light is always colour. That is why without the help of light colour remains invisible. Its being colour at all means [10] precisely its having in it the power to set in movement what is already actually transparent, and, as we have seen, the actuality of what is transparent is just light.

The following experiment makes the necessity of a medium clear. If what has colour is placed in immediate contact with the eye, it cannot be seen. Colour sets in movement not the sense organ but what is transparent, e.g. the air, and that, extending continuously from [15] the object to the organ, sets the latter in movement. Democritus misrepresents the facts when he expresses the opinion that if the interspace were empty one could distinctly see an ant on the vault of the sky; that is an impossibility. Seeing is due to an affection or change of what has the perceptive faculty, and it cannot be affected by the seen colour itself; it remains that it must be affected by what comes between. Hence it is indispensable that there [20] be *something* in between—if there were nothing, so far from seeing with greater distinctness, we should see nothing at all.

We have now explained the cause why colour cannot be seen otherwise than in light. Fire on the other hand is seen both in darkness and in light; this double possibility follows necessarily from our theory, for it is just fire that makes what is potentially transparent actually transparent.

[25] The same account holds also of sound and smell; if the object of either of these senses is in immediate contact with the organ no sensation is produced. In both cases the object sets in movement only what lies between, and this in turn sets the organ in movement: if what sounds or smells is brought into immediate contact with the organ, no sensation will be [30] produced. The same, in spite of all appearances, applies also to touch and taste; why there is this apparent difference will be clear later.[1] What comes between in the case of sounds is air; the corresponding medium in the case of smell has no name. But, corresponding to what is transparent in the case of colour, there is a quality found both in air and water, which serves as a medium for what has

[1] 422[b] 34 ff.

[35] smell—I say 'in water' because animals that live in water as well as those that live on land seem to possess the sense of smell, and 'in air' because man and all other land animals that breathe, perceive smells only when they breathe air in. The explanation of this too will be given later.[2]

8

Now let us, to begin with, make certain distinctions about sound and hearing.

[5] Sound may mean either of two things—(*a*) actual, and (*b*) potential, sound. There are certain things which, as we say, 'have no sound', e.g. sponges or wool, others which have, e.g. bronze and in general all things which are smooth and solid—the latter are said to have a sound because they can make a sound, i.e. can generate actual sound between themselves and the organ of hearing.

Actual sound requires for its occurrence (i, ii) two such bodies and (iii) a space be-[10] tween them; for it is generated by an impact. Hence it is impossible for one body only to generate a sound—there must be a body impinging and a body impinged upon; what sounds does so by striking against something else, and this is impossible without a movement from place to place.

As we have said, not all bodies can by impact on one another produce sound; impact on wool makes no sound, while the impact on [15] bronze or any body which is smooth and hollow does. Bronze gives out a sound when struck because it is smooth; bodies which are hollow owing to reflection repeat the original impact over and over again, the body originally set in movement being unable to escape from the concavity.

Further, we must remark that sound is heard both in air and in water, though less distinctly in the latter. Yet neither air nor water is the principal cause of sound. What is re-[20] quired for the production of sound is an impact of two solids against one another and against the air. The latter condition is satisfied when the air impinged upon does not retreat before the blow, i.e. is not dissipated by it.

That is why it must be struck with a sudden sharp blow, if it is to sound—the movement of the whip must outrun the dispersion of the air, just as one might get in a stroke at a heap or whirl of sand as it was traveling rapidly past.

[25] An echo occurs, when, a mass of air hav-

[2] 421[b] 13-422[a] 6.

ing been unified, bounded, and prevented from dissipation by the containing walls of a vessel, the air originally struck by the impinging body and set in movement by it rebounds from this mass of air like a ball from a wall. It is probable that in all generation of sound echo takes place, though it is frequently only indistinctly heard. What happens here must be analogous to what happens in the case of light; light is *always* reflected—otherwise it would [30] not be diffused and outside what was directly illuminated by the sun there would be blank darkness; but this reflected light is not always strong enough, as it *is* when it is reflected from water, bronze, and other smooth bodies, to cast a shadow, which is the distinguishing mark by which we recognize light.

It is rightly said that an empty space plays the chief part in the production of hearing, for what people mean by 'the vacuum' is the air, which is what causes hearing, when that air is set in movement as one continuous mass; but [35] owing to its friability it emits no sound, being dissipated by impinging upon any surface which is not smooth. When the surface on which it impinges is quite smooth, what is produced by the original impact is a united mass, a result due to the smoothness of the surface with which the air is in contact at the other end.

What has the power of producing sound is what has the power of setting in movement a single mass of air which is continuous from the impinging body up to the organ of hearing. The organ of hearing is physically united with air, and because it is *in* air, the air inside [5] is moved concurrently with the air outside. Hence animals do not hear with all parts of their bodies, nor do all parts admit of the entrance of air; for even the part which can be moved and can sound has not air everywhere in it. Air in itself is, owing to its friability, quite soundless; only when its dissipation is prevented is its movement sound. The air in the ear is built into a chamber just to prevent this dissipating movement, in order that the [10] animal may accurately apprehend all varieties of the movements of the air outside. That is why we hear also in water, viz. because the water cannot get into the air chamber or even, owing to the spirals, into the outer ear. If this does happen, hearing ceases, as it also does if the tympanic membrane is damaged, just as sight ceases if the membrane covering the pupil is damaged. It is also a test of [15] deafness whether the ear does or does not reverberate like a horn; the air inside the ear has always a movement of its own, but the sound we hear is always the sounding of something else, not of the organ itself. That is why we say that we hear with what is empty and echoes, viz. because what we hear with is a chamber which contains a bounded mass of air.

Which is it that 'sounds', the striking body or the struck? Is not the answer 'it is both, but [20] each in a different way'? Sound is a movement of what can rebound from a smooth surface when struck against it. As we have explained[1] not everything sounds when it strikes or is struck, e.g. if one needle is struck against another, neither emits any sound. In order, [25] therefore, that sound may be generated, what is struck must be smooth, to enable the air to rebound and be shaken off from it in one piece.

The distinctions between different sounding bodies show themselves only in actual sound; as without the help of light colours remain invisible, so without the help of actual sound the distinctions between acute and grave sounds remain inaudible. Acute and grave are here metaphors, transferred from their proper sphere, viz. that of touch, where they mean [30] respectively (*a*) what moves the sense much in a short time, (*b*) what moves the sense little in a long time. Not that what is sharp really moves fast, and what is grave, slowly, but that the difference in the qualities of the one and the other movement is due to their respective speeds. There seems to be a sort of parallelism between what is acute or grave to hearing and what is sharp or blunt to touch; what is sharp as it were stabs, while what is blunt pushes, the one producing its effect in a short, the other in a long time, so that the one is quick, the other slow.

[5] Let the foregoing suffice as an analysis of sound. Voice is a kind of sound characteristic of what has soul in it; nothing that is without soul utters voice, it being only by a metaphor that we speak of the voice of the flute or the lyre or generally of what (being without soul) possesses the power of producing a succession of notes which differ in length and pitch and timbre. The metaphor is based on the fact that all these differences are found also in voice. Many animals are voiceless, e.g. all non-sanguineous animals and among sanguineous ani-[10] mals fish. This is just what we should expect, since voice is a certain movement of air. The fish, like those in the Achelous, which are

---
[1] 419[b] 6, 13.

said to have voice, really make the sounds with their gills or some similar organ. Voice is the sound made by an animal, and that with a special organ. As we saw, everything that makes a sound does so by the impact of something (*a*) [15] against something else, (*b*) across a space, (*c*) filled with air; hence it is only to be expected that no animals utter voice except those which take in air. Once air is inbreathed, Nature uses it for two different purposes, as the tongue is used both for tasting and for articulating; in that case of the two functions tasting is necessary for the animal's existence (hence it is found more widely distributed), while articulate speech is a luxury subserving its possessor's well-being; similarly in the former case [20] Nature employs the breath both as an indispensable means to the regulation of the inner temperature of the living body and also as the matter of articulate voice, in the interests of its possessor's well-being. Why its former use is indispensable must be discussed elsewhere.[1]

The organ of respiration is the windpipe, and the organ to which this is related as means to end is the lungs. The latter is the part of the body by which the temperature of land [25] animals is raised above that of all others. But what primarily requires the air drawn in by respiration is not only this but the region surrounding the heart. That is why when animals breathe the air must penetrate inwards.

Voice then is the impact of the inbreathed air against the 'windpipe', and the agent that produces the impact is the soul resident in these parts of the body. Not every sound, as we [30] said, made by an animal is voice (even with the tongue we may merely make a sound which is not voice, or without the tongue as in coughing); what produces the impact must have soul in it and must be accompanied by an act of imagination, for voice is a sound *with a meaning*, and is not *merely* the result of any impact of the breath as in coughing; in voice the breath in the windpipe is used as an instrument to knock with against the walls of the 421ª windpipe. This is confirmed by our inability to speak when we are breathing either out or in—we can only do so by holding our breath; we make the movements with the breath so checked. It is clear also why fish are voiceless; they have no windpipe. And they have no windpipe because they do not breathe [5] or take in air. Why they do not is a question belonging to another inquiry.[2]

9

Smell and its object are much less easy to determine than what we have hitherto discussed; the distinguishing characteristic of the object of smell is less obvious than those of sound or colour. The ground of this is that our power of smell is less discriminating and in general [10] inferior to that of many species of animals; men have a poor sense of smell and our apprehension of its proper objects is inseparably bound up with and so confused by pleasure and pain, which shows that in us the organ is inaccurate. It is probable that there is a parallel failure in the perception of colour by animals that have hard eyes: probably they discriminate differences of colour only by the presence or absence of what excites fear, and [15] that it is thus that human beings distinguish smells. It seems that there is an analogy between smell and taste, and that the species of tastes run parallel to those of smells—the only difference being that our sense of taste is more discriminating than our sense of smell, because the former is a modification of touch, which reaches in man the maximum of discriminative accuracy. While in respect of all [20] the other senses we fall below many species of animals, in respect of touch we far excel all other species in exactness of discrimination. That is why man is the most intelligent of all animals. This is confirmed by the fact that it is to differences in the organ of touch and to nothing else that the differences between man and man in respect of natural endowment are due; men whose flesh is hard are ill-endowed [25] by nature, men whose flesh is soft, well-endowed.

As flavours may be divided into (*a*) sweet, (*b*) bitter, so with smells. In some things the flavour and the smell have the same quality, i.e. both are sweet or both bitter, in others they diverge. Similarly a smell, like a flavour, may [30] be pungent, astringent, acid, or succulent. But, as we said, because smells are much less easy to discriminate than flavours, the names of these varieties are applied to smells only 421ᵇ metaphorically; for example 'sweet' is extended from the taste to the smell of saffron or honey, 'pungent' to that of thyme, and so on.

In the same sense in which hearing has for

---

[1] *On Breathing*, 478ª 28; *On the Parts of Animals*, 642ª 31-ᵇ4.

[2] Cf. *On Breathing*, 474ᵇ 25-9, 476ª 6-15; *On the Parts of Animals*, 669ª 2-5.

its object both the audible and the inaudible, [5] sight both the visible and the invisible, smell has for its object both the odorous and the inodorous. 'Inodorous' may be either (*a*) what has no smell at all, or (*b*) what has a small or feeble smell. The same ambiguity lurks in the word 'tasteless'.

Smelling, like the operation of the senses previously examined, takes place through a medium, i.e. through air or water—I add wa-[10] ter, because water-animals too (both sanguineous and non-sanguineous) seem to smell just as much as land-animals; at any rate some of them make directly for their food from a distance if it has any scent. That is why the following facts constitute a problem for us. All animals smell in the same way, but man smells only when he inhales; if he exhales or holds his breath, he ceases to smell, no difference being [15] made whether the odorous object is distant or near, or even placed inside the nose and actually on the wall of the nostril; it is a disability common to all the senses not to perceive what is in immediate contact with the organ of sense, but our failure to apprehend what is odorous without the help of inhalation is peculiar (the fact is obvious on making the experiment). Now since bloodless animals do [20] not breathe, they must, it might be argued, have some novel sense not reckoned among the usual five. Our reply must be that this is impossible, since it is scent that is perceived; a sense that apprehends what is odorous and what has a good or bad odour cannot be anything but smell. Further, they are observed to be deleteriously effected by the same strong odours as man is, e.g. bitumen, sulphur, [25] and the like. These animals must be able to smell without being able to breathe. The probable explanation is that in man the organ of smell has a certain superiority over that in all other animals just as his eyes have over those of hard-eyed animals. Man's eyes have in the eyelids a kind of shelter or envelope, which must be shifted or drawn back in order [30] that we may see, while hardeyed animals have nothing of the kind, but at once see whatever presents itself in the transparent medium. Similarly in certain species of animals the organ of smell is like the eye of hard-eyed animals, uncurtained, while in others which take in air it probably has a curtain over it, which is drawn back in inhalation, owing to the dilating of the veins or pores. That explains also why such animals cannot smell un-[5] der water; to smell they must first inhale, and that they cannot do under water.

Smells come from what is dry as flavours from what is moist. Consequently the organ of smell is potentially dry.

10

What can be tasted is always something that can be touched, and just for that reason it cannot be perceived *through* an interposed foreign body, for touch means the absence of any in-[10] tervening body. Further, the flavoured and tasteable body is suspended in a liquid matter, and this is tangible. Hence, if we lived in water, we should perceive a sweet object introduced into the water, but the water would not be the medium *through* which we perceived; our perception would be due to the solution of the sweet substance in what we imbibed, just as if it were mixed with some drink. There is no parallel here to the perception of colour, which is due neither to any blending of anything with anything, nor to any efflux of anything from anything. In the [15] case of taste, there is nothing corresponding to the medium in the case of the senses previously discussed; but as the object of sight is colour, so the object of taste is flavour. But nothing excites a perception of flavour without the help of liquid; what acts upon the sense of taste must be either actually or potentially liquid like what is saline; it must be both (*a*) itself easily dissolved, and (*b*) capable of dis-[20] solving along with itself the tongue. Taste apprehends both (*a*) what has taste and (*b*) what has no taste, if we mean by (*b*) what has only a slight or feeble flavour or what tends to destroy the sense of taste. In this it is exactly parallel to sight, which apprehends both what is visible and what is invisible (for darkness is invisible and yet is discriminated by sight; so is, in a different way, what is overbrilliant), and to hearing, which apprehends both sound and silence, of which the one is [25] audible and the other inaudible, and also over-loud sound. This corresponds in the case of hearing to over-bright light in the case of sight. As a faint sound is 'inaudible', so in a sense is a loud or violent sound. The word 'invisible' and similar privative terms cover not only (*a*) what is simply without some power, but also (*b*) what is adapted by nature to have it but has not it or has it only in a very low degree, as when we say that a species of swallow is 'footless' or that a variety of fruit is 'stoneless'. So too taste has as its object both [30] what can be tasted and the tasteless—the latter in the sense of what has little flavour or a bad flavour or one destructive of taste. The difference between what is tasteless and what is not seems to rest ultimately on that between what is drinkable and what is undrinkable— both are tasteable, but the latter is bad and tends to destroy taste, while the former is the normal stimulus of taste. What is drinkable is the common object of both touch and taste.

422[b] Since what can be tasted is liquid, the organ for its perception cannot be either (a) actually liquid or (b) incapable of becoming liquid. Tasting means a being affected by what can be tasted as such; hence the organ of taste must be liquefied, and so to start with must be non-liquid but capable of liquefaction without loss of its distinctive nature. This is [5] confirmed by the fact that the tongue cannot taste either when it is too dry or when it is too moist; in the latter case what occurs is due to a contact with the pre-existent moisture in the tongue itself, when after a foretaste of some strong flavour we try to taste another flavour; it is in this way that sick persons find everything they taste bitter, viz. because, when they taste, their tongues are overflowing with bitter moisture.

[10] The species of flavour are, as in the case of colour, (a) simple, i.e. the two contraries, the sweet and the bitter, (b) secondary, viz. (i) on the side of the sweet, the succulent, (ii) on the side of the bitter, the saline, (iii) between these come the pungent, the harsh, the astringent, and the acid; these pretty well exhaust the varieties of flavour. It follows that [15] what has the power of tasting is what is potentially of that kind, and that what is tasteable is what has the power of making it actually what it itself already is.

11

Whatever can be said of what is tangible, can be said of touch, and vice versa; if touch is not a single sense but a group of senses, there must be several kinds of what is tangible. It is a problem whether touch is a single sense or a [20] group of senses. It is also a problem, what is the organ of touch; is it or is it not the flesh (including what in certain animals is homologous with flesh)? On the second view, flesh is 'the medium' of touch, the real organ being situated farther inward. The problem arises because the field of each sense is according to the accepted view determined as the range between a single pair of contraries, white and black for sight, acute and grave for [25] hearing, bitter and sweet for taste; but in the field of what is tangible we find several such pairs, hot cold, dry moist, hard soft, &c. This problem finds a partial solution, when it is recalled that in the case of the other senses more than one pair of contraries are to be met with, e.g. in sound not only acute and grave [30] but loud and soft, smooth and rough, &c.; there are similar contrasts in the field of colour. Nevertheless we are unable clearly to detect in the case of touch what the single subject is which underlies the contrasted qualities and corresponds to sound in the case of hearing.

To the question whether the organ of touch lies inward or not (i.e. whether we need look any farther than the flesh), no indication in 423[a] favour of the second answer can be drawn from the fact that if the object comes into contact with the flesh it is at once perceived. For even under present conditions if the experiment is made of making a web and stretching it tight over the flesh, as soon as this web is touched the sensation is reported in the same manner as before, yet it is clear that the organ is not in this membrane. If the mem- [5] brane could be *grown* on to the flesh, the report would travel still quicker. The flesh plays in touch very much the same part as would be played in the other senses by an airenvelope growing round our body; had we such an envelope attached to us we should have supposed that it was by a single organ that we perceived sounds, colours, and smells, and we should have taken sight, hearing, and [10] smell to be a single sense. But as it is, because that through which the different movements are transmitted is not naturally attached to our bodies, the difference of the various sense-organs is too plain to miss. But in the case of touch the obscurity remains.

There must be such a naturally attached 'medium' as flesh, for no living body could be constructed of air or water; it must be something solid. Consequently it must be composed of earth along with these, which is just what flesh and its analogue in animals which have no true flesh tend to be. Hence of neces- [15] sity the medium through which are transmitted the manifoldly contrasted tactual qualities must be a body naturally attached to the organism. That they are manifold is clear when we consider touching with the tongue; we apprehend at the tongue all tangible qualities as well as flavour. Suppose all the rest of our flesh was, like the tongue, sensitive to flavour, we should have identified the sense of [20] taste and the sense of touch; what saves us from this identification is the fact that touch and taste are not always found together in the same part of the body. The following problem might be raised. Let us assume that every body has depth, i.e. has three dimensions, and that if two bodies have a third body between them they cannot be in contact with one another; let us remember that what is liquid is a body [25] and must be or contain water, and that if two bodies touch one another under water, their touching surfaces cannot be dry, but must have water between, viz. the water which wets their bounding surfaces; from all this it follows that in water two bodies cannot be in contact with one another. The same holds of two bodies in air—air being to bodies in air precisely what water is to bodies in wa- [30] ter—but the facts are not so evident to our observation, because we live in air, just as animals that live in water would not notice that the things which touch one another in 423[b] water have wet surfaces. The problem, then, is: does the perception of all objects of sense take place in the same way, or does it not, e.g. taste and touch requiring contact (as they are commonly thought to do), while all other senses perceive over a distance? The distinction is unsound; we perceive what is hard [5] or soft, as well as the objects of hearing, sight, and smell, through a 'medium', only that the latter are perceived over a *greater* distance than the former; that is why the facts escape our notice. For we do perceive everything through a medium; but in these cases the fact escapes us. Yet, to repeat what we said before, if the medium for touch were a membrane separating us from the object without our observing its existence, we should be relatively to [10] it in the same condition as we are now to air or water in which we are immersed; in their case we fancy we can touch objects, nothing coming in between us and them. But there remains this difference between what can be touched and what can be seen or can sound; in the latter two cases we perceive because the medium produces a certain effect upon us, whereas in the perception of objects of touch we are affected not *by* but *along with* the me- [15] dium; it is as if a man were struck through his shield, where the shock is not first given to the shield and passed on to the man, but the concussion of both is simultaneous.

In general, flesh and the tongue are related to the real organs of touch and taste, as air and water are to those of sight, hearing, and smell. [20] Hence in neither the one case nor the other can there be any perception of an object if it is placed immediately upon the organ, e.g. if a white object is placed on the surface of the eye. This again shows that what has the power of perceiving the tangible is seated inside. Only so would there be a complete analogy with all the other senses. In their case if you place the object on the *organ* it is not per- [25] ceived, here if you place it on the flesh it *is* perceived; therefore flesh is not the organ but the *medium* of touch.

What can be touched are distinctive qualities of body *as* body; by such differences I mean those which characterize the elements, viz, hot cold, dry moist, of which we have [30] spoken earlier in our treatise on the elements.[1] The organ for the perception of these is that of touch—that part of the body in which primarily the sense of touch resides. This is that part which is potentially such as its object is actually: for all sense-perception is a process of being so affected; so that that which makes 424[a] something such as it itself actually is makes the other such because the other is already potentially such. That is why when an object of touch is equally hot and cold or hard and soft we cannot perceive; what we perceive must have a degree of the sensible quality lying beyond the neutral point. This implies that the sense itself is a 'mean' between any two opposite qualities which determine the field of [5] that sense. It is to this that it owes its power of discerning the objects in that field. What is 'in the middle' is fitted to discern; relatively to either extreme it can put itself in the place of the other. As what is to perceive *both* white and black must, to begin with, be actually neither but potentially either (and so with all the other sense-organs), so the organ of touch must be neither hot nor cold.

[10] Further, as in a sense sight had for its object both what was visible and what was invisible (and there was a parallel truth about all the other senses discussed),[2] so touch has for its object both what is tangible and what is intangible. Here by 'intangible' is meant (*a*) what like air possesses some quality of tangible things in a very slight degree and (*b*) what possesses it in an excessive degree, as destructive things do.

[1] *On Generation and Corruption,* II. 2, 3.
[2] 421[b] 3-6, 422[a] 29.

[15] We have now given an outline account of each of the several senses.

12

The following results applying to any and every sense may now be formulated.

(A) By a 'sense' is meant what has the power of receiving into itself the sensible forms of things without the matter. This must be conceived of as taking place in the way in which a piece of wax takes on the impress of a signet-[20] ring without the iron or gold; we say that what produces the impression is a signet of bronze or gold, but its particular metallic constitution makes no difference: in a similar way the sense is affected by what is coloured or flavoured or sounding, but it is indifferent what in each case the *substance* is; what alone matters is what *quality* it has, i.e. in what *ratio* its constituents are combined.

(B) By 'an organ of sense' is meant that in which ultimately such a power is seated.

[25] The sense and its organ are the same in fact, but their essence is not the same. What perceives is, of course, a spatial magnitude, but we must not admit that either the having the power to perceive or the sense itself is a magnitude; what they are is a certain ratio or power *in* a magnitude. This enables us to explain why objects of sense which possess one of two opposite sensible qualities in a degree largely in excess of the other opposite destroy the or-[30] gans of sense; if the movement set up by an object is too strong for the organ, the equipoise of contrary qualities in the organ, which just *is* its sensory power, is disturbed; it is precisely as concord and tone are destroyed by too violently twanging the strings of a lyre. This explains also why plants cannot perceive, in spite of their having a portion of soul in them and obviously being affected by tangible objects themselves; for undoubtedly their temperature can be lowered or raised. The explanation is that they have no mean of contrary qualities, and so no principle in them capable of taking on the forms of sensible objects without their matter; in the case of plants the affection is an affection by form-and-matter together. The problem might be raised: Can what cannot smell be said to be affected by [5] smells or what cannot see by colours, and so on? It might be said that a smell is just what can be smelt, and if it produces any effect it can only be so as to make something smell it, and it might be argued that what cannot smell cannot be affected by smells and further that what can smell can be affected by it only in so far as it has in it the power to smell (similarly with the proper objects of all the other senses). Indeed that this *is* so is made quite evident as [10] follows. Light or darkness, sounds and smells leave *bodies* quite unaffected; what does affect bodies is not these but the bodies which are their vehicles, e.g. what splits the trunk of a tree is not the sound of the thunder but the air which accompanies thunder. Yes, but, it may be objected, bodies are affected by what is tangible and by flavours. If not, by what are things that are without soul affected, i.e. altered in quality? Must we not, then, admit that the objects of the other senses also may affect them? Is not the true account this, that all bodies *are* capable of being affected by smells [15] and sounds, but that some on being acted upon, having no boundaries of their own, disintegrate, as in the instance of air, which does become odorous, showing that *some* effect is produced on it by what is odorous? But smelling is more than such an affection by what is odorous—*what* more? Is not the answer that, while the air owing to the momentary duration of the action upon it of what is odorous does itself become perceptible to the sense of smell, smelling is an *observing* of the result produced?

BOOK III

1

[20] THAT there is no sixth sense in addition to the five enumerated—sight, hearing, smell, taste, touch—may be established by the following considerations:

If we have actually sensation of everything of which touch can give us sensation (for all [25] the qualities of the tangible *qua* tangible are perceived by us through touch); and if absence of a sense necessarily involves absence of a sense-organ; and if (1) all objects that we perceive by immediate contact with them are perceptible by touch, which sense we actually possess, and (2) all objects that we perceive through media, i.e. without immediate contact, [30] are perceptible by or through the simple elements, e.g. air and water (and this is so arranged that (*a*) if more than one kind of sensible object is perceivable through a single medium, the possessor of a sense-organ homogeneous with that medium has the power of perceiving both kinds of objects; for example, if the sense-organ is made of air, and air is a medium both for sound and for colour; and that (*b*) if more than one medium can transmit 425ª the same kind of sensible objects, as e.g. water as well as air can transmit colour, both being transparent, then the possessor of either alone will be able to perceive the kind of objects transmissible through both); and if of the simple elements two only, air and water, go to form sense-organs (for the pupil is made of water, the organ of hearing is made of air, and the organ of smell of one or other of these [5] two, while fire is found either in none or in all—warmth being an essential condition of all sensibility—and earth either in none or, if anywhere, specially mingled with the components of the organ of touch; wherefore it would remain that there can be no sense-organ formed of anything except water and air); and if these sense-organs are actually found in certain animals;—then all the possible senses are [10] possessed by those animals that are not imperfect or mutilated (for even the mole is observed to have eyes beneath its skin); so that, if there is no fifth element and no property other than those which belong to the four elements of our world, no sense can be wanting to such animals.

Further, there cannot be a special sense-[15] organ for the common sensibles either, i.e. the objects which we perceive incidentally through this or that special sense, e.g. movement, rest, figure, magnitude, number, unity; for all these we perceive by movement, e.g. magnitude by movement, and therefore also figure (for figure is a species of magnitude), what is at rest by the absence of movement: number is perceived by the negation of continuity, and by the special sensibles; for each sense perceives one class of sensible objects. So [20] that it is clearly impossible that there should be a special sense for any one of the common sensibles, e.g. movement; for, if that were so, our perception of it would be exactly parallel to our present perception of what is sweet by vision. *That* is so because we have a sense for each of the two qualities, in virtue of which when they happen to meet in one sensible object we are aware of both contemporaneously. If it were not like this our per-[25] ception of the common qualities would always be incidental, i.e. as is the perception of Cleon's son, where we perceive him not as Cleon's son but as white, and the white thing which we really perceive happens to be Cleon's son.

But in the case of the common sensibles there is already in us a general sensibility which enables us to perceive them directly; there is therefore no special sense required for their perception: if there were, our perception of them would have been exactly like what has been above[1] described.

[30] The senses perceive each other's special objects incidentally; not because the percipient sense is this or that special sense, but because all form a unity: this incidental perception takes place whenever sense is directed at one and the same moment to two disparate qualities in one and the same object, e.g. to the bitterness and the yellowness of bile, the assertion of the identity of both cannot be the act of either of the senses; hence the illusion of sense, e.g. the belief that if a thing is yellow it is bile.

It might be asked why we have more senses [5] than one. Is it to prevent a failure to apprehend the common sensibles, e.g. movement, magnitude, and number, which go along with the special sensibles? Had we no sense but sight, and that sense no object but white, they would have tended to escape our notice and everything would have merged for us into an indistinguishable identity because of the concomitance of colour and magnitude. As it is, the fact that the common sensibles are given in the objects of more than one sense reveals [10] their distinction from each and all of the special sensibles.

2

Since it is through sense that we are aware that we are seeing or hearing, it must be either by sight that we are aware of seeing, or by some sense other than sight. But the sense that gives us this new sensation must perceive both sight and its object, viz. colour: so that either (1) there will be two senses both percipient of the same sensible object, or (2) the sense must [15] be percipient of itself. Further, even if the sense which perceives sight were different from sight, we must either fall into an infinite regress, or we must somewhere assume a sense which is aware of itself. If so, we ought to do this in the first case.

This presents a difficulty: if to perceive by sight is just to see, and what is seen is colour (or the coloured), then if we are to *see* that
[1] ll. 24–7.

which sees, that which sees originally must be [20] coloured. It is clear therefore that 'to perceive by sight' has more than one meaning; for even when we are not *seeing,* it is by sight that we discriminate darkness from light, though not in the same way as we distinguish one colour from another. Further, in a sense even that which sees *is* coloured; for in each case the sense-organ is capable of receiving the sensible object without its matter. That is why even [25] when the sensible objects are gone the sensings and imaginings continue to exist in the sense-organs.

The activity of the sensible object and that of the percipient sense is one and the same activity, and yet the distinction between their being remains. Take as illustration actual sound and actual hearing: a man may have hearing and yet not be hearing, and that which has a sound is not always sounding. But when that which can hear is actively hearing and [30] that which can sound is sounding, then the actual hearing and the actual sound are merged in one (these one might call respectively hearkening and sounding).

If it is true that the movement, both the acting and the being acted upon, is to be found in that which is acted upon, both the sound and the hearing so far as it is actual must be found in that which has the faculty of hearing; for it is in the passive factor that the actuality of the active or motive factor is realized; that [5] is why that which causes movement may be at rest. Now the actuality of that which can sound is just sound or sounding, and the actuality of that which can hear is hearing or hearkening; 'sound' and 'hearing' are both ambiguous. The same account applies to the other senses and their objects. For as the-acting-and-[10] being-acted-upon is to be found in the passive, not in the active factor, so also the actuality of the sensible object and that of the sensitive subject are both realized in the latter. But while in some cases each aspect of the total actuality has a distinct name, e.g. sounding and hearkening, in some one or other is nameless, e.g. the actuality of sight is called seeing, but the actuality of colour has no name: the actuality of the faculty of taste is called tasting, but the actuality of flavour has no name. Since the [15] actualities of the sensible object and of the sensitive faculty are *one* actuality in spite of the difference between their modes of being, actual hearing and actual sounding appear and disappear from existence at one and the same moment, and so actual savour and actual tasting, &c., while as potentialities one of them [20] may exist without the other. The earlier students of nature were mistaken in their view that without sight there was no white or black, without taste no savour. This statement of theirs is partly true, partly false: 'sense' and 'the sensible object' are ambiguous terms, i.e. may denote either potentialities or actualities: [25] the statement is true of the latter, false of the former. This ambiguity they wholly failed to notice.

If voice always implies a concord, and if the voice and the hearing of it are in one sense one and the same, and if concord always implies a ratio, hearing as well as what is heard must [30] be a ratio. That is why the excess of either the sharp or the flat destroys the hearing. (So also in the case of savours excess destroys the sense of taste, and in the case of colours excessive brightness or darkness destroys the sight, and in the case of smell excess of strength whether in the direction of sweetness or bitterness is destructive.) This shows that the sense is a ratio.

That is also why the objects of sense are (1) pleasant when the sensible extremes such as acid or sweet or salt being pure and unmixed are brought into the proper ratio; then they are [5] pleasant: and in general what is blended is more pleasant than the sharp or the flat alone; or, to touch, that which is capable of being either warmed or chilled: the sense and the ratio are identical: while (2) in excess the sensible extremes are painful or destructive.

Each sense then is relative to its particular group of sensible qualities: it is found in a sense-organ as such and discriminates the differences which exist within that group; e.g. [10] sight discriminates white and black, taste sweet and bitter, and so in all cases. Since we also discriminate white from sweet, and indeed each sensible quality from every other, with what do we perceive that they are different? It must be by sense; for what is before us is [15] sensible objects. (Hence it is also obvious that the flesh cannot be the ultimate sense-organ: if it were, the discriminating power could not do its work without immediate contact with the object.)

Therefore (1) discrimination between white and sweet cannot be effected by two agencies which remain separate; both the qualities discriminated must be present to something that is one and single. On any other supposition even if I perceived sweet and you perceived [20] white, the difference between them would be apparent. What says that two things are different must be one; for sweet is different from white. Therefore what asserts this difference must be self-identical, and as what asserts, so also what thinks or perceives. That it is not possible by means of two agencies which remain separate to discriminate two objects which are separate, is therefore obvious; and that (2) it is not possible to do this in separate movements of time may be seen if we look at it as follows. For as what asserts the difference between the good and the bad is one and the [25] same, so also the time at which it asserts the one to be different and the other to be different is not accidental to the assertion (as it is for instance when I now assert a difference but do not assert that there is now a difference); it asserts thus—both now and that the objects are different now; the objects therefore must be present at one and the same moment. Both the discriminating power and the time of its exercise must be one and undivided.

But, it may be objected, it is impossible that [30] what is self-identical should be moved in one and the same time with contrary movements in so far as it is undivided, and in an undivided moment of time. For if what is sweet be the quality perceived, it moves the sense or thought in this determinate way, 427ᵃ while what is bitter moves it in a contrary way, and what is white in a different way. Is it the case then that what discriminates, though both numerically one and indivisible, is at the same time divided in its being? In one sense, it is what is divided that perceives two separate objects at once, but in another sense it does so *qua* undivided; for it is divisible in its being, but spatially and numerically undivided. [5] But is not this impossible? For while it is true that what is self-identical and undivided may be both contraries at once *potentially,* it cannot be self-identical in its being—it must lose its unity by being put into activity. It is not possible to be at once white and black, and therefore it must also be impossible for a thing to be affected at one and the same moment by the forms of both, assuming it to be the case that sensation and thinking are properly so described.
[10] The answer is that just as what is called a 'point' is, as being at once one and two, properly said to be divisible, so here, that which discriminates is *qua* undivided one, and active in a single moment of time, while so far forth as it is divisible it twice over uses the same dot at one and the same time. So far forth then as it takes the limit as two, it discriminates two separate objects with what in a sense is divided: while so far as it takes it as one, it does so with what is one and occupies in its activity a single moment of time.

About the principle in virtue of which we [15] say that animals are percipient, let this discussion suffice.

3

There are two distinctive peculiarities by reference to which we characterize the soul— (1) local movement and (2) thinking, discriminating, and perceiving. Thinking both speculative and practical is regarded as akin to [20] a form of perceiving; for in the one as well as the other the soul discriminates and is cognizant of something which *is*. Indeed the ancients go so far as to identify thinking and perceiving; e.g. Empedocles says[1] 'For 'tis in respect of what is present that man's wit is increased', and again[2] 'Whence it befalls them from time to time to think diverse thoughts', [25] and Homer's phrase[3] 'For suchlike is man's mind' means the same. They all look upon thinking as a bodily process like perceiving, and hold that like is *known* as well as *perceived* by like, as I explained at the beginning of our discussion.[4] Yet they ought at the same time to have accounted for error also; for 427ᵇ it is more intimately connected with animal existence and the soul continues longer in the state of error than in that of truth. They cannot escape the dilemma: either (1) whatever seems is true (and there are some who accept this) or (2) error is contact with the unlike; for that is the opposite of the knowing of like by like.
[5] But it is a received principle that error as well as knowledge in respect to contraries is one and the same.

That perceiving and practical thinking are not identical is therefore obvious; for the former is universal in the animal world, the latter is found in only a small division of it. Further, speculative thinking is also distinct from perceiving—I mean that in which we find rightness and wrongness—rightness in pru- [10] dence, knowledge, true opinion, wrongness in their opposites; for perception of the special objects of sense is always free from error, and is found in all animals, while it is possible to think falsely as well as truly, and thought is found only where there is discourse

---

[1] Fr. 106.   [2] Fr. 108.
[3] *Odyssey,* XVIII. 136.   [4] 404ᵇ 8-18.

of reason as well as sensibility. For imagination is different from either perceiving or dis- [15] cursive thinking, though it is not found without sensation, or judgement without it. That this activity is not the same kind of thinking as judgement is obvious. For imagining lies within our own power whenever we wish (e.g. we can call up a picture, as in the practice of mnemonics by the use of mental im- [20] ages), but in forming opinions we are not free: we cannot escape the alternative of falsehood or truth. Further, when we think something to be fearful or threatening, emotion is immediately produced, and so too with what is encouraging; but when we merely imagine we remain as unaffected as persons who are looking at a painting of some dreadful or encouraging scene. Again within the field [25] of judgement itself we find varieties— knowledge, opinion, prudence, and their opposites; of the differences between these I must speak elsewhere.

Thinking is different from perceiving and is held to be in part imagination, in part judgement: we must therefore first mark off the sphere of imagination and then speak of judge- 428ª ment. If then imagination is that in virtue of which an image arises for us, excluding metaphorical uses of the term, is it a single faculty or disposition relative to images, in virtue of which we discriminate and are either in error or not? The faculties in virtue of which we do this are sense, opinion, science, intelligence.
[5] That imagination is not sense is clear from the following considerations: Sense is either a faculty or an activity, e.g. sight or seeing: imagination takes place in the absence of both, as e.g. in dreams. (2) Again, sense is always present, imagination not. If actual imagination and actual sensation were the same, imagination would be found in all the brutes: this is [10] held not to be the case; e.g. it is not found in ants or bees or grubs. (3) Again, sensations are always true, imaginations are for the most part false. (4) Once more, even in ordinary speech, we do not, when sense functions precisely with regard to its object, say that we imagine it to be a man, but rather when there is some failure of accuracy in its exercise. And [15] (5), as we were saying before,[1] visions appear to us even when our eyes are shut. Neither is imagination *any* of the things that are never in error: e.g. knowledge or intelligence; for imagination may be false.

[1] ll. 7-8.

It remains therefore to see if it is opinion, for opinion may be either true or false.
[20] But opinion involves belief (for without belief in what we opine we cannot have an opinion), and in the brutes though we often find imagination we never find belief. Further, every opinion is accompanied by belief, belief by conviction, and conviction by discourse of reason: while there are some of the brutes in which we find imagination, without discourse of reason. It is clear then that imagi- [25] nation cannot, again, be (1) opinion *plus* sensation, or (2) opinion mediated by sensation, or (3) a blend of opinion and sensation; this is impossible both for these reasons and because the content of the supposed opinion cannot be different from that of the sensation (I mean that imagination must be the blending of the perception of white with the opinion that it is white: it could scarcely be a blend [30] of the opinion that it is good with the perception that it is white): to imagine is there- 428ᵇ fore (on this view) identical with the thinking of exactly the same as what one in the strictest sense perceives. But what we imagine is sometimes false though our contemporaneous judgement about it is true; e.g. we imagine the sun to be a foot in diameter though we are convinced that it is larger than the inhabited part of the earth, and the following dilemma presents itself. Either (*a*) while the fact has not changed and the [5] observer has neither forgotten nor lost belief in the true opinion which he had, that opinion has disappeared, or (*b*) if he retains it then his opinion is at once true and false. A true opinion, however, becomes false only when the fact alters without being noticed.

Imagination is therefore neither any one of the states enumerated, nor compounded out of them.
[10] But since when one thing has been set in motion another thing may be moved by it, and imagination is held to be a movement and to be impossible without sensation, i.e. to occur in beings that are percipient and to have for its content what can be perceived, and since movement may be produced by actual sensation and that movement is necessarily similar in character to the sensation itself, this movement must be (1) necessarily (*a*) incapable of [15] existing apart from sensation, (*b*) incapable of existing except when we perceive, (2) such that in virtue of its possession that in which it is found may present various phe-

nomena both active and passive, and (3) such that it may be either true or false.

The reason of the last characteristic is as follows. Perception (1) of the special objects of sense is never in error or admits the least possible amount of falsehood. (2) That of the concomitance of the objects concomitant with the sensible qualities comes next: in this case [20] certainly we may be deceived; for while the perception that there is white before us cannot be false, the perception that what is white is this or that may be false. (3) Third comes the perception of the universal attributes which accompany the concomitant objects to which the special sensibles attach (I mean e.g. of movement and magnitude); it is in respect of these that the greatest amount of sense-illusion is possible.

[25] The motion which is due to the activity of sense in these three modes of its exercise will differ from the activity of sense; (1) the first kind of derived motion is free from error while the sensation is present; (2) and (3) the others may be erroneous whether it is present or absent, especially when the object of per-[30] ception is far off. If then imagination presents no other features than those enumerated and is what we have described, then imagination must be a movement resulting from an actual exercise of a power of sense.

As sight is the most highly developed sense, the name φαντασία (imagination) has been formed from φάος (light) because it is not possible to see without light.

And because imaginations remain in the organs of sense and resemble sensations, ani-[5] mals in their actions are largely guided by them, some (i.e. the brutes) because of the non-existence in them of mind, others (i.e. men) because of the temporary eclipse in them of mind by feeling or disease or sleep.

About imagination, what it is and why it exists, let so much suffice.

4

[10] Turning now to the part of the soul with which the soul knows and thinks (whether this is separable from the others in definition only, or spatially as well) we have to inquire (1) what differentiates this part, and (2) how thinking can take place.

If thinking is like perceiving, it must be either a process in which the soul is acted upon by what is capable of being thought, or a process different from but analogous to that. The [15] thinking part of the soul must therefore be, while impassible, capable of receiving the form of an object; that is, must be potentially identical in character with its object without being the object. Mind must be related to what is thinkable, as sense is to what is sensible.

Therefore, since everything is a possible object of thought, mind in order, as Anaxagoras says, to dominate, that is, to know, must be [20] pure from all admixture; for the co-presence of what is alien to its nature is a hindrance and a block: it follows that it too, like the sensitive part, can have no nature of its own, other than that of having a certain capacity. Thus that in the soul which is called mind (by mind I mean that whereby the soul thinks and judges) is, before it thinks, not actually any real thing. For this reason it cannot reasonably be regarded as blended with the body: [25] if so, it would acquire some quality, e.g. warmth or cold, or even have an organ like the sensitive faculty: as it is, it has none. It was a good idea to call the soul 'the place of forms', though (1) this description holds only of the intellective soul, and (2) even this is the forms only potentially, not actually.

Observation of the sense-organs and their employment reveals a distinction between the [30] impassibility of the sensitive and that of the intellective faculty. After strong stimulation of a sense we are less able to exercise it than before, as e.g. in the case of a loud sound we cannot hear easily immediately after, or in the case of a bright colour or a powerful odour we cannot see or smell, but in the case of mind thought about an object that is highly intelligible renders it more and not less able afterwards to think objects that are less intelligible: the reason is that while the faculty of sensation is dependent upon the body, mind is separable from it.

[5] Once the mind has become each set of its possible objects, as a man of science has, when this phrase is used of one who is actually a man of science (this happens when he is now able to exercise the power on his own initiative), its condition is still one of potentiality, but in a different sense from the potentiality which preceded the acquisition of knowledge by learning or discovery: the mind too is then able to think *itself*.

[10] Since we can distinguish between a spatial magnitude and what it is to be such, and between water and what it is to be water, and so in many other cases (though not in all; for in certain cases the thing and its form are identical), flesh and what it is to be flesh are

discriminated either by different faculties, or by the same faculty in two different states: for flesh necessarily involves matter and is like what is snub-nosed, a *this* in a *this*. Now it is by means of the sensitive faculty that we discriminate the hot and the cold, i.e. the factors [15] which combined in a certain ratio constitute flesh: the essential character of flesh is apprehended by something different either wholly separate from the sensitive faculty or related to it as a bent line to the same line when it has been straightened out.

Again in the case of abstract objects what is straight is analogous to what is snub-nosed; for it necessarily implies a continuum as its matter: its constitutive essence is different, if we may distinguish between straightness and what is straight: let us take it to be two-ness. [20] It must be apprehended, therefore, by a different power or by the same power in a different state. To sum up, in so far as the realities it knows are capable of being separated from their matter, so it is also with the powers of mind.

The problem might be suggested: if thinking is a passive affection, then if mind is simple and impassible and has nothing in common with anything else, as Anaxagoras says, [25] how can it come to think at all? For interaction between two factors is held to require a precedent community of nature between the factors. Again it might be asked, is mind a possible object of thought to itself? For if mind is thinkable *per se* and what is thinkable is in kind one and the same, then either (*a*) mind will belong to everything, or (*b*) mind will contain some element common to it with all other realities which makes them all thinkable.

(1) Have not we already disposed of the difficulty about interaction involving a common [30] element, when we said[1] that mind is in a sense potentially whatever is thinkable, though actually it is nothing until it has thought? What it thinks must be in it just as 430ª characters may be said to be on a writing-tablet on which as yet nothing actually stands written: this is exactly what happens with mind.

(2) Mind is itself thinkable in exactly the same way as its objects are. For (*a*) in the case of objects which involve no matter, what thinks and what is thought are identical; for speculative knowledge and its object are identical. (Why mind is not always thinking we [5] must consider later.)[2] (*b*) In the case of those which contain matter each of the objects of thought is only potentially present. It follows that while *they* will not have mind in them (for mind is a potentiality of them only in so far as they are capable of being disengaged from matter) mind may yet be thinkable.

5

[10] Since in every class of things, as in nature as a whole, we find two factors involved, (1) a matter which is potentially all the particulars included in the class, (2) a cause which is productive in the sense that it makes them all (the latter standing to the former, as e.g. an art to its material), these distinct elements must likewise be found within the soul.

And in fact mind as we have described it[3] is what it is by virtue of becoming all things, [15] while there is another which is what it is by virtue of making all things: this is a sort of positive state like light; for in a sense light makes potential colours into actual colours.

Mind in this sense of it is separable, impassible, unmixed, since it is in its essential nature activity (for always the active is superior to the passive factor, the originating force to the matter which it forms).

[20] Actual knowledge is identical with its object: in the individual, potential knowledge is in time prior to actual knowledge, but in the universe as a whole it is not prior even in time. Mind is not at one time knowing and at another not. When mind is set free from its present conditions it appears as just what it is and nothing more: this alone is immortal and eternal (we do not, however, remember its former activity because, while mind in this sense is impassible, mind as passive is destructible), [25] and without it nothing thinks.

6

The thinking then of the simple objects of thought is found in those cases where falsehood is impossible: where the alternative of true or false applies, there we always find a putting together of objects of thought in a quasi-unity. As Empedocles said that 'where heads of many a creature sprouted without necks'[4] they afterwards by Love's power were [30] combined, so here too objects of thought which were given separate are combined, e.g. 'incommensurate' and 'diagonal': if the combination be of objects past or future the combination of thought includes in its content the

---

[1] ª15-24. [2] Chapter 5. [3] In chapter 4. [4] Fr. 57.

430ᵇ date. For falsehood always involves a synthesis; for even if you assert that what is white is not white you have included not-white in a synthesis. It is possible also to call all these cases division as well as combination. However that may be, there is not only the true or false assertion that Cleon is white but also the true or false assertion that he *was* or [5] *will be* white. In each and every case that which unifies is mind.

Since the word 'simple' has two senses, i.e. may mean either (*a*) 'not capable of being divided' or (*b*) 'not actually divided', there is nothing to prevent mind from knowing what is undivided, e.g. when it apprehends a length (which is actually undivided) and that in an undivided time; for the time is divided or undivided in the same manner as the line. It is [10] not possible, then, to tell what part of the line it was apprehending in each half of the time: the object has no actual parts until it has been divided: if in thought you think each half separately, then by the same act you divide the time also, the half-lines becoming as it were new wholes of length. But if you think it as a whole consisting of these two possible parts, then also you think it in a time which corresponds to both parts together. (But what is [15] not quantitatively but qualitatively simple is thought in a simple time and by a simple act of the soul.)

But that which mind thinks and the time in which it thinks are in this case divisible only incidentally and not as such. For in them too there is something indivisible (though, it may be, not isolable) which gives unity to the time and the whole of length; and this is found equally in every continuum whether temporal or spatial.

[20] Points and similar instances of things that divide, themselves being indivisible, are realized in consciousness in the same manner as privations.

A similar account may be given of all other cases, e.g. how evil or black is cognized; they are cognized, in a sense, by means of their contraries. That which cognizes must have an element of potentiality in its being, and one of the contraries must be in it. But if there is anything that has no contrary, then it knows it- [25] self and is actually and possesses independent existence.

Assertion is the saying of something concerning something, e.g. affirmation, and is in every case either true or false: this is not always the case with mind: the thinking of the definition in the sense of the constitutive essence is never in error nor is it the assertion of something concerning something, but, just as while the seeing of the special object of sight can never be in error, the belief that the white object seen is a man may be mistaken, so too [30] in the case of objects which are without matter.

7

431ᵃ Actual knowledge is identical with its object: potential knowledge in the individual is in time prior to actual knowledge but in the universe it has no priority even in time; for all things that come into being arise from what actually is. In the case of sense clearly the sensitive faculty already was potentially what the [5] object makes it to be actually; the faculty is not affected or altered. This must therefore be a different kind from movement; for movement is, as we saw,[1] an activity of what is imperfect, activity in the unqualified sense, i.e. that of what has been perfected, is different from movement.

To perceive then is like bare asserting or knowing; but when the object is pleasant or painful, the soul makes a quasi-affirmation or negation, and pursues or avoids the object. To [10] feel pleasure or pain is to act with the sensitive mean towards what is good or bad as such. Both avoidance and appetite when actual are identical with this: the faculty of appetite and avoidance are not different, either from one another or from the faculty of sense-perception; but their being *is* different.

To the thinking soul images serve as if they [15] were contents of perception (and when it asserts or denies them to be good or bad it avoids or pursues them). That is why the soul never thinks without an image. The process is like that in which the air modifies the pupil in this or that way and the pupil transmits the modification to some third thing (and similarly in hearing), while the ultimate point of arrival is one, a single mean, with different manners of being.

[20] With what part of itself the soul discriminates sweet from hot I have explained before[2] and must now describe again as follows: That with which it does so is a sort of unity, but in the way just mentioned, i.e. as a connecting term. And the two faculties it connects, being one by analogy and numerically, are each to each as the qualities discerned are to one another (for what difference does it make wheth-

[1] Cf. 417ᵇ 2-16.   [2] 426ᵇ 12-427ᵃ 14.

er we raise the problem of discrimination between disparates or between contraries, e.g. [25] white and black?). Let then C be to D as A is to B: it follows *alternando* that $C : A :: D : B$. If then C and D belong to one subject, the case will be the same with them as with A and B; A and B form a single identity with different modes of being; so too will the former pair. The same reasoning holds if A be sweet and B white.

The faculty of thinking then thinks the forms in the images, and as in the former case what is to be pursued or avoided is marked out for it, so where there is no sensation and it is engaged upon the images it is moved to pursuit or avoidance. E.g. perceiving by sense that the beacon is fire, it recognizes in virtue of the general faculty of sense that it signifies an enemy, because it sees it moving; but sometimes by means of the images or thoughts which are within the soul, just as if it were seeing, it calculates and deliberates what is to come by reference to what is present; and when it makes a pronouncement, as in the case of sensation it pronounces the object to be pleasant or painful, in this case it avoids or pursues; and so generally in cases of action.

[10] That too which involves no action, i.e. that which is true or false, is in the same province with what is good or bad: yet they differ in this, that the one set imply and the other do not a reference to a particular person.

The so-called abstract objects the mind thinks just as, if one had thought of the snub-nosed not as snub-nosed but as hollow, one would have thought of an actuality without [15] the flesh in which it is embodied: it is thus that the mind when it is thinking the objects of Mathematics thinks as separate elements which do not exist separate. In every case the mind which is actively thinking is the objects which it thinks. Whether it is possible for it while not existing separate from spatial conditions to think anything that is separate, or not, we must consider later.

8

[20] Let us now summarize our results about soul, and repeat that the soul is in a way all existing things; for existing things are either sensible or thinkable, and knowledge is in a way what is knowable, and sensation is in a way what is sensible: in *what* way we must inquire.

Knowledge and sensation are divided to correspond with the realities, potential knowledge [25] and sensation answering to potentialities, actual knowledge and sensation to actualities. Within the soul the faculties of knowledge and sensation are *potentially* these objects, the one what is knowable, the other what is sensible. They must be either the things themselves or their forms. The former alternative is of course impossible: it is not the stone which is present in the soul but its form.

It follows that the soul is analogous to the hand; for as the hand is a tool of tools, so the mind is the form of forms and sense the form of sensible things.

Since according to common agreement there is nothing outside and separate in existence from sensible spatial magnitudes, the objects of thought are in the sensible forms, viz. both [5] the abstract objects and all the states and affections of sensible things. Hence (1) no one can learn or understand anything in the absence of sense, and (2) when the mind is actively aware of anything it is necessarily aware of it along with an image; for images are like sensuous contents except in that they contain no matter.

Imagination is different from assertion and [10] denial; for what is true or false involves a synthesis of concepts. In what will the primary concepts differ from images? Must we not say that neither these nor even our other concepts are images, though they necessarily involve them?

9

[15] The soul of animals is characterized by two faculties, (*a*) the faculty of discrimination which is the work of thought and sense, and (*b*) the faculty of originating local movement. Sense and mind we have now sufficiently examined. Let us next consider what it is in the soul which originates movement. Is it a single part of the soul separate either spatially or in [20] definition? Or is it the soul as a whole? If it is a part, is that part different from those usually distinguished or already mentioned by us, or is it one of them? The problem at once presents itself, in what sense we are to speak of parts of the soul, or how many we should distinguish. For in a sense there is an infinity of parts: it is not enough to distinguish, with [25] some thinkers,[1] the calculative, the passionate, and the desiderative, or with others the rational and the irrational; for if we take the dividing lines followed by these thinkers we shall find parts far more distinctly separat-

[1] Plato, *Republic*, 435-41.

ed from one another than these, namely those we have just mentioned: (1) the nutritive, which belongs both to plants and to all ani- [30] mals, and (2) the sensitive, which cannot easily be classed as either irrational or rational; further (3) the imaginative, which is, 432^b in its being, different from all, while it is very hard to say with which of the others it is the same or not the same, supposing we determine to posit *separate* parts in the soul; and lastly (4) the appetitive, which would seem to be distinct both in definition and in power from all hitherto enumerated.

[5] It is absurd to break up the last-mentioned faculty: as these thinkers do, for wish is found in the calculative part and desire and passion in the irrational; and if the soul is tripartite appetite will be found in all three parts. Turning our attention to the present object of discussion, let us ask what that is which originates local movement of the animal.

The movement of growth and decay, being found in all living things, must be attributed to [10] the faculty of reproduction and nutrition, which is common to all: inspiration and expiration, sleep and waking, we must consider later:[1] these too present much difficulty: at present we must consider local movement, asking what it is that originates forward movement in the animal.

[15] That it is not the nutritive faculty is obvious; for this kind of movement is always for an end and is accompanied either by imagination or by appetite; for no animal moves except by compulsion unless it has an impulse towards or away from an object. Further, if it were the nutritive faculty, even plants would have been capable of originating such movement and would have possessed the organs necessary to carry it out. Similarly it cannot be the sensitive faculty either; for there are many animals which have sensibility but remain fast and immovable throughout their [20] lives.

If then Nature never makes anything without a purpose and never leaves out what is necessary (except in the case of mutilated or imperfect growths; and that here we have neither mutilation nor imperfection may be argued from the facts that such animals (*a*) can reproduce their species and (*b*) rise to completeness of nature and decay to an end), it [25] follows that, had they been capable of originating forward movement, they would have possessed the organs necessary for that

[1] Cf. *On Breathing, On Sleep and Sleeplessness.*

purpose. Further, neither can the calculative faculty or what is called 'mind' be the cause of such movement; for mind as speculative never thinks what is practicable, it never says anything about an object to be avoided or pursued, while this movement is always in something which is avoiding or pursuing an object. [30] No, not even when it is aware of such an object does it at once enjoin pursuit or avoidance of it; e.g. the mind often thinks of something terrifying or pleasant without enjoining the emotion of fear. It is the heart that is moved (or in the case of a pleasant object some other 433^a part). Further, even when the mind does command and thought bids us pursue or avoid something, sometimes no movement is produced; we act in accordance with desire, as in the case of moral weakness. And, generally, we observe that the possessor of medical knowledge is not necessarily healing, which shows that something else is required to produce action in accordance with knowledge; the knowl- [5] edge alone is not the cause. Lastly, appetite too is incompetent to account fully for movement; for those who successfully resist temptation have appetite and desire and yet follow mind and refuse to enact that for which they have appetite.

10

These two at all events appear to be sources of movement: appetite and mind (if one may venture to regard imagination as a kind of [10] thinking; for many men follow their imaginations contrary to knowledge, and in all animals other than man there is no thinking or calculation but only imagination).

Both of these then are capable of originating local movement, mind and appetite: (1) mind, that is, which calculates means to an end, i.e. mind practical (it differs from mind specula- [15] tive in the character of its end); while (2) appetite is in every form of it relative to an end: for that which is the object of appetite is the stimulant of mind practical; and that which is last in the process of thinking is the beginning of the action. It follows that there is a justification for regarding these two as the sources of movement, i.e. appetite and practical thought; for the object of appetite starts a movement and as a result of that thought gives rise to movement, the object of appetite being [20] to it a source of stimulation. So too when imagination originates movement, it necessarily involves appetite.

That which moves therefore is a single faculty and the faculty of appetite; for if there had been two sources of movement—mind and appetite—they would have produced movement in virtue of some common character. As it is, mind is never found producing movement without appetite (for wish is a form of appetite; and when movement is produced according to calculation it is also according to [25] wish), but appetite can originate movement contrary to calculation, for desire is a form of appetite. Now mind is always right, but appetite and imagination may be either right or wrong. That is why, though in any case it is the object of appetite which originates movement, this object may be either the real or the apparent good. To produce movement the object must be more than this: it must be good that can be brought into being by action; and only what can be otherwise than as it is [30] can thus be brought into being. That then such a power in the soul as has been described, i.e. that called appetite, originates movement is clear. Those who distinguish 433b parts in the soul, if they distinguish and divide in accordance with differences of power, find themselves with a very large number of parts, a nutritive, a sensitive, an intellective, a deliberative, and now an appetitive part; for these are more different from one another than the faculties of desire and passion.

[5] Since appetites run counter to one another, which happens when a principle of reason and a desire are contrary and is possible only in beings with a sense of time (for while mind bids us hold back because of what is future, desire is influenced by what is just at hand: a pleasant object which is just at hand presents itself as both pleasant and good, without condition in either case, because of want of foresight into [10] what is farther away in time), it follows that while that which originates movement must be specifically one, viz. the faculty of appetite as such (or rather farthest back of all the object of that faculty; for it is it that itself remaining unmoved originates the movement by being apprehended in thought or imagination), the things that originate movement are numerically many.

All movement involves three factors, (1) that which originates the movement, (2) that by means of which it originates it, and (3) that which is moved. The expression 'that which originates the movement' is ambiguous: it may mean either (*a*) something which itself is unmoved or (*b*) that which at once moves [15] and is moved. Here that which moves without itself being moved is the realizable good, that which at once moves and is moved is the faculty of appetite (for that which is influenced by appetite so far as it is actually so influenced is set in movement, and appetite in the sense of actual appetite *is* a kind of movement), while that which is in motion is the animal. The instrument which appetite employs to produce movement is no longer psy- [20] chical but bodily: hence the examination of it falls within the province of the functions common to body and soul. To state the matter summarily at present, that which is the instrument in the production of movement is to be found where a beginning and an end coincide as e.g. in a ball and socket joint; for there the convex and the concave sides are respectively an end and a beginning (that is why while the one remains at rest, the other is moved): they are separate in definition but not separable [25] spatially. For everything is moved by pushing and pulling. Hence just as in the case of a wheel, so here there must be a point which remains at rest, and from that point the movement must originate.

To sum up, then, and repeat what I have said, inasmuch as an animal is capable of appetite it is capable of self-movement; it is not capable of appetite without possessing imagination; and all imagination is either (1) calculative or (2) sensitive. In the latter all ani- [30] mals, and not only man, partake.

11

We must consider also in the case of imperfect animals, sc. those which have no sense but touch, what it is that in them originates movement. Can they have imagination or not? or desire? Clearly they have feelings of pleasure and pain, and if they have these they must have desire. But how can they have imagination? Must not we say that, as their movements are indefinite, they have imagination and desire, but indefinitely?

[5] Sensitive imagination, as we have said,[1] is found in all animals, deliberative imagination only in those that are calculative: for whether this or that shall be enacted is already a task requiring calculation; and there must be a single standard to measure by, for that is pursued which is *greater*. It follows that what acts in this way must be able to make a unity out of several images.

[10] This is the reason why imagination is held not to involve opinion, in that it does not

[1] 433b 29.

involve opinion based on inference, though opinion involves imagination. Hence appetite contains no deliberative element. Sometimes it overpowers wish and sets it in movement: at times wish acts thus upon appetite, like one sphere imparting its movement to another, or appetite acts thus upon appetite, i.e. in the condition of moral weakness (though by *nature* the higher faculty is *always* more authoritative and gives rise to movement). Thus *three* [15] modes of movement are possible.

The faculty of knowing is never moved but remains at rest. Since the one premiss or judgement is universal and the other deals with the particular (for the first tells us that such and such a kind of man should do such and such a kind of act, and the second that *this* is an act of the kind meant, and I a person of the type intended), it is the latter opinion that really [20] originates movement, not the universal; or rather it is both, but the one does so while it remains in a state more like rest, while the other partakes in movement.

12

The nutritive soul then must be possessed by everything that is alive, and every such thing is endowed with soul from its birth to its death. For what has been born must grow, reach maturity, and decay—all of which are impossible without nutrition. Therefore the [25] nutritive faculty must be found in everything that grows and decays.

But sensation need not be found in all things that live. For it is impossible for touch to belong either (1) to those whose body is uncompounded or (2) to those which are incapable of taking in the forms without their matter.

[30] But animals must be endowed with sensation, since Nature does nothing in vain. For all things that exist by Nature are means to an end, or will be concomitants of means to an end. Every body capable of forward movement would, if unendowed with sensation, perish and fail to reach its end, which is the aim of Nature; for how could it obtain nutriment? Stationary living things, it is true, have as their nutriment that from which they have arisen; but it is not possible that a body which is not stationary but produced by generation should have a soul and a discerning mind without also having sensation. (Nor yet even if it were not produced by generation. Why should it not have sensation? Because it were [5] better so either for the body or for the soul? But clearly it would not be better for either: the absence of sensation will not enable the one to think better or the other to exist better.) Therefore no body which is not stationary has soul without sensation.

But if a body *has* sensation, it must be either simple or compound. And simple it cannot be; [10] for then it could not have touch, which is indispensable. This is clear from what follows. An animal is a body with soul in it: every body is tangible, i.e. perceptible by touch; hence necessarily, if an animal is to survive, its body [15] must have tactual sensation. All the other senses, e.g. smell, sight, hearing, apprehend through media; but where there is immediate contact the animal, if it has no sensation, will be unable to avoid some things and take others, and so will find it impossible to survive. That is why taste also is a sort of touch; it is relative to nutriment, which is just tangible body; whereas sound, colour, and odour are innutritious, and further neither grow nor de- [20] cay. Hence it is that taste also must be a sort of touch, because it is the sense for what is tangible and nutritious.

Both these senses, then, are indispensable to the animal, and it is clear that without touch it is impossible for an animal to be. All the other senses subserve well-being and for that very reason belong not to any and every kind [25] of animal, but only to some, e.g. those capable of forward movement must have them; for, if they are to survive, they must perceive not only by immediate contact but also at a distance from the object. This will be possible if they can perceive through a medium, the medium being affected and moved by the perceptible object, and the animal by the [30] medium. Just as that which produces local movement causes a change extending to a certain point, and that which gave an impulse causes another to produce a new impulse so that the movement traverses a medium— the first mover impelling without being impelled, the last moved being impelled without impelling, while the medium (or media, for there are many) is both—so is it also in the case of alteration, except that the agent produces it without the patient's changing its place. Thus if an object is dipped into wax, the movement goes on until submersion has taken place, and in stone it goes no distance at all, while in water the disturbance goes far beyond the object dipped: in air the disturbance is propagated farthest of all, the air acting and being acted upon, so long as it maintains an unbroken unity. That is why in the case of re-[5] flection it is better, instead of saying that the sight issues from the eye and is reflected, to say that the air, so long as it remains one, is affected by the shape and colour. On a smooth surface the air possesses unity; hence it is that it in turn sets the sight in motion, just as if the impression on the wax were transmitted as [10] far as the wax extends.

13

It is clear that the body of an animal cannot be simple, i.e. consist of one element such as fire or air. For without touch it is impossible to have any other sense; for every body that has soul in it must, as we have said,[1] be capable of touch. All the other elements with the excep-[15] tion of earth can constitute organs of sense, but all of them bring about perception only through something else, viz. through the media. Touch takes place by direct contact with its objects, whence also its name. All the other organs of sense, no doubt, perceive by contact, only the contact is mediate: touch alone perceives by immediate contact. Consequently no animal body can consist of these other elements.
[20] Nor can it consist solely of earth. For touch is as it were a mean between all tangible qualities, and its organ is capable of receiving not only all the specific qualities which characterize earth, but also the hot and the cold and all other tangible qualities whatsoever. That [25] is why we have no sensation by means of bones, hair, &c., because they consist of earth. So too plants, because they consist of earth, have no sensation. Without touch there can be no other sense, and the organ of touch cannot consist of earth or of any other single element.

[1] 434^b 10-24.

It is evident, therefore, that the loss of this one sense alone must bring about the death of [5] an animal. For as on the one hand nothing which is not an animal can have this sense, so on the other it is the only one which is indispensably necessary to what is an animal. This explains, further, the following difference between the other senses and touch. In the case of all the others excess of intensity in the qualities which they apprehend, i.e. excess of intensity in colour, sound, and smell, destroys not [10] the animal but only the organs of the sense (except incidentally, as when the sound is accompanied by an impact or shock, or where through the objects of sight or of smell certain other things are set in motion, which destroy by contact); flavour also destroys only in so far as it is at the same time tangible. But excess of intensity in tangible qualities, e.g. [15] heat, cold, or hardness, destroys the animal itself. As in the case of every sensible quality excess destroys the organ, so here what is tangible destroys touch, which is the essential mark of life; for it has been shown that without touch it is impossible for an animal to be. That is why excess in intensity of tangible qualities destroys not merely the organ, but the animal itself, because this is the only sense which it must have.

All the other senses are necessary to animals, [20] as we have said,[2] not for their being, but for their well-being. Such, e.g. is sight, which, since it lives in air or water, or generally in what is pellucid, it must have in order to see, and taste because of what is pleasant or painful to it, in order that it may perceive these qualities in its nutriment and so may desire to be set in motion, and hearing that it may have [25] communication made to it, and a tongue that it may communicate with its fellows.

[2] 434^b 24.

SHORT PHYSICAL TREATISES

CONTENTS: SHORT PHYSICAL TREATISES

ON SENSE AND THE SENSIBLE

CHAP.		BERLIN NOS.
1.	Source of sensation. Sensations as means of preservation. Effect of sensation on intelligence	436^a 1
2.	Characteristics of bodily organs of sensation as connected with the four elements	437^a 17
3.	Natures of sensible objects: Theories of colour	439^a 6
4.	Theories of savours	440^b 26
5.	Theories of odours	442^b 27
6.	Divisibility and movement of sensible qualities. Simultaneous perception of one object by many. Affection of parts of the medium	445^b 3
7.	Reactions to simultaneous sensory stimuli. Magnitudes and divisibility of perceptible objects	447^a 13

ON MEMORY AND REMINISCENCE

| 1. | Objects of memory. Definition of nature and faculty of memory | 449^b 1 |
| 2. | Definition, manner, and causes of recollection | 451^a 19 |

ON SLEEP AND SLEEPLESSNESS

1.	Nature and effects of sleeping and waking	453^b 12
2.	Reason and need of sleeping and waking	455^a 3
3.	Processes and causes of sleeping and waking	456^a 30

ON DREAMS

1.	Faculty of the soul to which dreams pertain	458^b 1
2.	Nature of perceptions in a dream	459^a 23
3.	Nature of the dream itself	460^b 28

ON PROPHESYING BY DREAMS

| 1. | Dreams as tokens, coincidences, causes of future events | 462^b 12 |
| 2. | Consummation of dreams. Mentality of dreamers and interpreters of dreams | 463^b 11 |

ON LONGEVITY AND THE SHORTNESS OF LIFE

1.	Introductory	464^b 19
2.	Dissolution of the soul	465^a 12
3.	Perishability of opposites. State of transition of all things. Reaction to environment	465^b 1
4.	Longevity as immunity from decay	466^a 1
5.	Reasons for longevity in animals	466^a 17
6.	Reasons for longevity in plants and insects	467^a 6

ON YOUTH AND OLD AGE, ON LIFE AND DEATH, ON BREATHING

1.	The organ of sensation, or source of nutritive soul	467^b 10
2.	The position of the source of nutritive soul. The unity and divisibility of animals and plants	468^a 12
3.	The genesis of plants. The growth of animals. The position of the organ of perception	468^b 16
4.	Life and the maintenance of heat	469^a 23
5.	The two manners of death. The need for refrigeration	469^b 21
6.	The need for refrigeration of animals and plants	470^a 20

ON BREATHING

7.	(1) Comparative need for breathing in animals	470^b 6
8.	(2) Comparative need for breathing in fishes	470^b 28
9.	(3) (Continued)	471^a 20
10.	(4) Connexion between breathing and life	471^b 30
11.	(5) Hot and cold air in breathing	472^b 7
12.	(6) Connexion between nutrition and breathing	473^a 3
13.	(7) Connexion between breathing and the flux of blood	473^a 15
14.	(8) The need for refrigeration of body heat	474^a 25
15.	(9) (Continued)	474^b 25
16.	(10) The organs of breathing	475^b 15
17.	(11) (Continued)	476^a 16
18.	(12) (Continued)	476^b 13
19.	(13) The higher nature of man	477^a 12
20.	(14) The character of substances and their necessary environment	477^a 32
21.	(15) The necessary degree of refrigeration	478^a 11
22.	(16) The relative position and movement of heart and lungs in fishes and animals	478^a 26

ON LIFE AND DEATH I

23. (17) The single cause of death 478^b 21
24. (18) Account and reason of generation, life, and death 479^a 28
25. (19) The change of natural environment. The cause of motion of gills and lungs 479^b 8

ON LIFE AND DEATH II

26. (20) Nature of motion of the heart 479^b 16
27. (21) Nature of motion of the lungs 480^a 16

On Sense and the Sensible

I

436ª HAVING now definitely considered the soul, by itself, and its several faculties, we must next make a survey of animals and all living things, in order to ascertain what functions are peculiar, and what functions are common, to [5] them. What has been already determined respecting the soul [sc. by itself] must be assumed throughout. The remaining parts [sc. the attributes of soul and body conjointly] of our subject must be now dealt with, and we may begin with those that come first.

The most important attributes of animals, whether common to all or peculiar to some, are, manifestly, attributes of soul and body in conjunction, e.g. *sensation, memory, passion, appetite* and *desire* in general, and, in addition *pleasure* and *pain*. For these may, in fact, be [10] said to belong to all animals. But there are, besides these, certain other attributes, of which some are common to all living things, while others are peculiar to certain species of animals. The most important of these may be summed up in four pairs, viz. *waking* and *sleeping, youth* and *old age, inhalation* and *exhalation, life* and *death*. We must endeav-[15] our to arrive at a scientific conception of these, determining their respective natures, and the causes of their occurrence.

But it behoves the Physical Philosopher to obtain also a clear view of the first principles of *health* and *disease*, inasmuch as neither health nor disease can exist in lifeless things. Indeed [20] we may say of most physical inquirers, and of those physicians who study their art philosophically, that while the former complete their works with a disquisition **436ᵇ** on medicine, the latter usually base their medical theories on principles derived from Physics.

That all the attributes above enumerated belong to soul and body in conjunction, is obvious; for they all either imply sensation as a concomitant, or have it as their medium. Some [5] are either affections or states of sensation, others, means of defending and safe-guarding it, while others, again, involve its destruction or negation. Now it is clear, alike by reasoning and observation, that sensation is generated in the soul through the medium of the body.

We have already, in our treatise *On the Soul,* explained the nature of sensation and the act of perceiving by sense, and the reason why [10] this affection belongs to animals. Sensation must, indeed, be attributed to all animals as such, for by its presence or absence we distinguish essentially between what is and what is not an animal.

But coming now to the special senses severally, we may say that touch and taste necessarily appertain to all animals, touch, for the reason given in *On the Soul,*[1] and taste, be-[15] cause of nutrition. It is by taste that one distinguishes in food the pleasant from the unpleasant, so as to flee from the latter and pursue the former: and savour in general is an affection of nutrient matter.

The senses which operate through external media, viz. *smelling, hearing, seeing,* are found in all animals which possess the faculty of locomotion. To all that possess them they are a means of preservation; their final cause [20] being that such creatures may, guided by *antecedent* perception, both pursue their food, and shun things that are bad or destructive. **437ª** But in animals which have also intelligence they serve for the attainment of a higher perfection. They bring in tidings of many distinctive qualities of things, from which the knowledge of truth, speculative and practical, is generated in the soul.

Of the two last mentioned, seeing, regarded as a supply for the primary wants of life, and in its direct effects, is the superior sense; but [5] for developing intelligence, and in its indirect consequences, hearing takes the precedence. The faculty of seeing, thanks to the fact that all bodies are coloured, brings tidings of multitudes of distinctive qualities of all sorts; whence it is through this sense especially that we perceive the common sensibles, viz. *figure, magnitude, motion, number:* while hearing

---
[1] Cf. *On the Soul,* 434ᵇ 10-24.

announces only the distinctive qualities of [10] sound, and, to some few animals, those also of voice. Indirectly, however, it is hearing that contributes most to the growth of intelligence. For rational discourse is a cause of instruction in virtue of its being audible, which it is, not directly, but indirectly; since it is [15] composed of words, and each word is a thought-symbol. Accordingly, of persons destitute from birth of either sense, the blind are more intelligent than the deaf and dumb.

2

Of the distinctive potency of each of the faculties of sense enough has been said already.

But as to the nature of the sensory organs, or parts of the body in which each of the senses is naturally implanted, inquirers now usually [20] take as their guide the fundamental elements of bodies. Not, however, finding it easy to coordinate five senses with four elements, they are at a loss respecting the fifth sense. But they hold the organ of sight to consist of fire, being prompted to this view by a certain sensory affection of whose true cause they are ignorant. This is that, when the eye is pressed or moved, fire appears to flash from it. This [25] naturally takes place in darkness, or when the eyelids are closed, for then, too, darkness is produced.

This theory, however, solves one question only to raise another; for, unless on the hypothesis that a person who is in his full senses can see an object of vision without being aware of it, the eye must on this theory see itself. But then why does the above affection not occur also when the eye is at rest? The true explana- [30] tion of this affection, which will contain the answer to our question, and account for the current notion that the eye consists of fire, must be determined in the following way:—

Things which are smooth have the natural property of shining in darkness, without, however, producing light. Now, the part of the 437[b] eye called 'the black', i.e. its central part, is manifestly smooth. The phenomenon of the flash occurs only when the eye is moved, because only then could it possibly occur that the same one object should become as it were two. The rapidity of the movement has the effect of making that which sees and that which is seen [5] seem different from one another. Hence the phenomenon does not occur unless the motion is rapid and takes place in darkness. For it is in the dark that that which is smooth, e.g. the heads of certain fishes, and the sepia of the cuttle-fish, naturally shines, and, when the movement of the eye is slow, it is impossible that that which sees and that which is seen should appear to be simultaneously two and one. But, in fact, the eye sees itself in the above [10] phenomenon merely as it does so in ordinary optical reflexion.

If the visual organ proper really were fire, which is the doctrine of Empedocles, a doctrine taught also in the *Timaeus*,[1] and if vision were the result of light issuing from the eye as from a lantern, why should the eye not have had the power of seeing even in the dark? It is totally idle to say, as the *Timaeus* does, that [15] the visual ray coming forth in the darkness is quenched. What is the meaning of this 'quenching' of light? That which, like a fire of coals or an ordinary flame, is hot and dry is, indeed, quenched by the moist or cold; but heat and dryness are evidently not attributes of light. Or if they are attributes of it, but belong to it in a degree so slight as to be imper- [20] ceptible to us, we should have expected that in the daytime the light of the sun should be quenched when rain falls, and that darkness should prevail in frosty weather. Flame, for example, and ignited bodies are subject to such extinction, but experience shows that nothing of this sort happens to the sunlight.

Empedocles at times seems to hold that vision is to be explained as above stated by light [25] issuing forth from the eye, e.g. in the following passage:—

As when one who purposes going abroad prepares a lantern,
A gleam of fire blazing through the stormy night,
Adjusting thereto, to screen it from all sorts of winds, transparent sides,
Which scatter the breath of the winds as they blow,
[30] *While, out through them leaping, the fire, i.e. all the more subtle part of this,*
Shines along his threshold with incessant beams:
438[a] *So [Divine love] embedded the round "lens", [viz.] the primaeval fire fenced within the membranes,*
In [its own] delicate tissues;
And these fended off the deep surrounding flood,
While leaping forth the fire, i.e. all its more subtile part—.

Sometimes he accounts for vision thus, but at other times he explains it by emanations from the visible objects.

[1] 45.

[5] Democritus, on the other hand, is right in his opinion that the eye is of water; not, however, when he goes on to explain seeing as mere mirroring. The mirroring that takes place in an eye is due to the fact that the eye is smooth, and it really has its seat not in the eye which *is seen,* but in that which *sees*. For the case is merely one of reflexion. But it would seem that even in his time there was no [10] scientific knowledge of the general subject of the formation of images and the phenomena of reflexion. It is strange too, that it never occurred to him to ask why, if his theory be true, the eye alone sees, while none of the other things in which images are reflected do so.

True, then, the visual organ proper is composed of water, yet vision appertains to it not because it is so composed, but because it is translucent—a property common alike to wa- [15] ter and to air. But water is more easily confined and more easily condensed than air; wherefore it is that the pupil, i.e. the eye proper, consists of water. That it does so is proved by facts of actual experience. The substance which flows from eyes when decomposing is seen to be water, and this in undeveloped embryos is remarkably cold and glistening. In [20] sanguineous animals the white of the eye is fat and oily, in order that the moisture of the eye may be proof against freezing. Wherefore the eye is of all parts of the body the least sensitive to cold: no one ever feels cold in the part sheltered by the eyelids. The eyes of bloodless animals are covered with a hard scale which gives them similar protection.

[25] It is, to state the matter generally, an irrational notion that the eye should see in virtue of something issuing from it; that the visual ray should extend itself all the way to the stars, or else go out merely to a certain point, and there coalesce, as some say, with rays which proceed from the object. It would be better to suppose this coalescence to take place in the fundament of the eye itself. But even this would be mere trifling. For what is meant [30] by the 'coalescence' of light with light? Or how is it possible? Coalescence does not occur between any two things taken at random. And how could the light within the 438ᵇ eye coalesce with that outside it? For the environing membrane comes between them.

That without light vision is impossible has been stated elsewhere;[1] but, whether the medi-

um between the eye and its objects is air or light, vision is caused by a process through this medium.

[5] Accordingly, that the inner part of the eye consists of water is easily intelligible, water being translucent.

Now, as vision outwardly is impossible without [extra-organic] light, so also it is impossible inwardly [without light within the organ]. There must, therefore, be some translucent medium within the eye, and, as this is not air, it must be water. The soul or its perceptive part is not situated at the external surface of the eye, but obviously somewhere within: whence [10] the necessity of the interior of the eye being translucent, i.e. capable of admitting light. And that it is so is plain from actual occurrences. It is matter of experience that soldiers wounded in battle by a sword slash on the temple, so inflicted as to sever the passages of [i.e. inward from] the eye, feel a sudden onset of darkness, as if a lamp had gone out; because what is called the pupil, i.e. the translucent, [15] which is a sort of inner lamp, is then cut off [from its connexion with the soul].

Hence, if the facts be at all as here stated, it is clear that—if one should explain the nature of the sensory organs in this way, i.e. by correlating each of them with one of the four elements,—we must conceive that the part of the eye immediately concerned in vision consists of water, that the part immediately concerned [20] in the perception of sound consists of air, and that the sense of smell consists of fire. ⟨I say the *sense* of smell, not the *organ*.⟩ For the organ of smell is only potentially that which the sense of smell, as realized, is actually; since the object of sense is what causes the actualization of each sense, so that it (the sense) must ⟨at the instant of actualization⟩ be ⟨actually⟩ that which before ⟨the moment of actualization⟩ it was potentially. Now, odour is a smoke-like evaporation, and smoke-like evaporation arises from fire. This also [25] helps us to understand why the olfactory organ has its proper seat in the environment of the brain, for cold matter is potentially hot. In the same way must the genesis of the eye be explained. Its structure is an offshoot from the brain, because the latter is the moistest and coldest of all the bodily parts.

[30] The organ of touch proper consists of 439ᵃ earth, and the faculty of taste is a particular form of touch. This explains why the sensory organ of both touch and taste is closely related to the heart. For the heart, as being the

---

[1] Cf. *On the Soul,* 418ᵇ 1 sqq.

hottest of all the bodily parts, is the counterpoise of the brain.

This then is the way in which the character-[5] istics of the bodily organs of sense must be determined.

3

Of the sensibles corresponding to each sensory organ, viz. colour, sound, odour, savour, touch, we have treated in *On the Soul*[1] in general terms, having there determined what their function is, and what is implied in their becoming actualized in relation to their respec-[10] tive organs. We must next consider what account we are to give of any one of them; what, for example, we should say *colour* is, or *sound,* or *odour,* or *savour;* and so also respecting [the object of] *touch*. We begin with *colour.*

Now, each of them may be spoken of from two points of view, i.e. either as actual or as potential. We have in *On the Soul*[2] explained in what sense the colour, or sound, regarded as actualized [for sensation], is the same as, and [15] in what sense it is different from, the correlative sensation, the actual seeing or hearing. The point of our present discussion is, therefore, to determine what each sensible object must be in itself, in order to be perceived as it is in actual consciousness.

We have[3] already in *On the Soul* stated of Light that it is the colour of the Translucent, [being so related to it] incidentally; for whenever a fiery element is in a translucent medium [20] its presence there is Light; while the privation of it is Darkness. But the 'Translucent', as we call it, is not something peculiar to air, or water, or any other of the bodies usually called translucent, but is a common 'nature' and power, capable of no separate existence of its own, but residing in these, and subsisting likewise in all other bodies in a greater or less [25] degree. As the bodies in which it subsists must have some extreme bounding surface, so too must this. Here, then, we may say that Light is a 'nature' inhering in the Translucent when the latter is without determinate boundary. But it is manifest that, when the Translucent is in determinate bodies, its bounding extreme must be something real; and that colour is just this 'something' we are plainly taught by facts—colour being actually either

[1] Cf. *On the Soul,* 418ª 26 sqq., 419ᵇ 5 sqq., 421ª 7 sqq., 422ª 8 sqq., 422ᵇ 17 sqq., for Aristotle's treatment of these sensibles respectively.
[2] *On the Soul,* 425ᵇ 25-426ᵇ 8.
[3] *On the Soul,* 418ª 26 sqq.

[30] *at* the external limit, or being *itself* that limit, in bodies. Hence it was that the Pythagoreans named the superficies of a body its 'hue', for 'hue', indeed, lies *at* the limit of the body; but the limit of the body is not a real thing; rather we must suppose that the same natural substance which, externally, is the vehicle of colour exists [as such a possible vehicle] also in the interior of the body.

439ᵇ Air and water, too [i.e. as well as determinately bounded bodies], are seen to possess colour; for their brightness is of the nature of colour. But the colour which air or sea presents, since the body in which it resides is not determinately bounded, is not the same when one approaches and views it close by as it is [5] when one regards it from a distance; whereas in determinate bodies the colour presented is definitely fixed, unless, indeed, when the atmospheric environment causes it to change. Hence it is clear that that in them which is susceptible of colour is in both cases the same. It is therefore the Translucent, according to the degree to which it subsists in bodies (and it does so in all more or less), that [10] causes them to partake of colour. But since the colour is at the extremity of the body, it must be at the extremity of the Translucent in the body. Whence it follows that we may define colour as the limit of the Translucent in determinately bounded body. For whether we consider the special class of bodies called translucent, as water and such others, or determinate bodies, which appear to possess a fixed colour of their own, it is at the exterior bounding surface that all alike exhibit their colour.

Now, that which when present in air produces light may be present also in the Translu-[15] cent which pervades determinate bodies; or again, it may not be present, but there may be a privation of it. Accordingly, as in the case of air the one condition is light, the other darkness, in the same way the colours White and Black are generated in determinate bodies.

We must now treat of the other colours, reviewing the several hypotheses invented to explain their genesis.

[20] (1.) It is conceivable that the White and the Black should be juxtaposed in quantities so minute that [a particle of] either separately would be invisible, though the joint product [of two particles, a black and a white] would be visible; and that they should thus have the other colours for resultants. Their product could, at all events, appear neither white nor black; and, as it must have some colour, and

can have neither of these, this colour must be [25] of a mixed character—in fact, a species of colour different from either. Such, then, is a possible way of conceiving the existence of a plurality of colours besides the White and Black; and we may suppose that [of this 'plurality'] many are the result of a [numerical] ratio; for the blacks and whites may be juxtaposed in the ratio of 3 to 2, or of 3 to 4, or in ratios expressible by other numbers; while some may be juxtaposed according to no nu- [30] merically expressible ratio, but according to some relation of excess or defect in which the blacks and whites involved would be incommensurable quantities; and, accordingly, we may regard all these colours [viz. all those based on numerical ratios] as analogous to the sounds that enter into music, and suppose that those involving simple numerical ratios, like the concords in music, may be those generally regarded as most agreeable; as, for example, purple, crimson, and some few such colours, their fewness being due to the same causes 440ᵃ which render the concords few. The other compound colours may be those which are not based on numbers. Or it may be that, while all colours whatever [except black and white] are based on numbers, some are regular in this respect, others irregular; and that the latter [though now supposed to be all based on numbers], whenever they are not pure, owe this character to a corresponding impurity in [the arrangement of] their nu- [5] merical ratios. This then is one conceivable hypothesis to explain the genesis of intermediate colours.

(2.) Another is that the Black and White appear the one through the medium of the other, giving an effect like that sometimes produced by painters overlaying a less vivid upon a more vivid colour, as when they desire to [10] represent an object appearing under water or enveloped in a haze, and like that produced by the sun, which in itself appears white, but takes a crimson hue when beheld through a fog or a cloud of smoke. On this hypothesis, too, a variety of colours may be conceived to arise in the same way as that already described; for between those at the surface and those underneath a definite ratio might sometimes exist; in other cases they might stand in no determinate ratio. To [introduce a theory of colour which would set all these hypotheses [15] aside, and] say with the ancients that colours are emanations, and that the visibility of objects is due to such a cause, is absurd. For they must, in any case, explain sense-perception through Touch; so that it were better to say at once that visual perception is due to a process set up by the perceived object in the medium between this object and the sensory organ; due, that is, to contact [with the medium affected], not to emanations.

[20] If we accept the hypothesis of juxtaposition, we must assume not only invisible magnitude, but also imperceptible time, in order that the succession in the arrival of the stimulatory movements may be unperceived, and that the compound colour seen may appear to be one, owing to its successive parts seeming to present themselves at once. On the hypothesis of superposition, however, no such assumption is needful: the stimulatory process produced in the medium by the upper colour, when this is itself unaffected, will be different [25] in kind from that produced by it when affected by the underlying colour. Hence it presents itself as a different colour, i.e. as one which is neither white nor black. So that, if it is impossible to suppose any magnitude to be invisible, and we must assume that there is some distance from which every magnitude is visible, this superposition theory, too [i.e. as well as No. 3 *infra*], might pass as a real theory of colour-mixture. Indeed, in the previous case also there is no reason why, to persons at a distance from the juxtaposed blacks and whites, some one colour should not appear to [30] present itself as a blend of both. [But it would not be so on a nearer view], for it will be shown, in a discussion to be undertaken later on, that there is no magnitude absolutely invisible.

(3.) There is a mixture of bodies, however, not merely such as some suppose, i.e. by juxta- 440ᵇ position of their minimal parts, which, owing to [the weakness of our] sense, are imperceptible by us, but a mixture by which they [i.e. the 'matter' of which they consist] are wholly blent together by interpenetration, as we have described it in the treatise on Mixture,[1] where we dealt with this subject generally in its most comprehensive aspect. For, on the supposition we are criticizing, the only [5] totals capable of being mixed are those which are divisible into minimal parts, [e.g. genera into individuals] as men, horses, or the [various kinds of] seeds. For of mankind as a whole the individual man is such a least part; of horses [as an aggregate], the individual horse. Hence by the juxtaposition of these we

[1] Cf. 328ᵃ 5 sqq.

obtain a mixed total, consisting [like a troop of cavalry] of both together; but we do not say that by such a process any individual man has been mixed with any individual horse. Not [10] in this way, but by complete interpenetration [of their matter], must we conceive those things to be mixed which are not divisible into minima; and it is in the case of these that natural mixture exhibits itself in its most perfect form. We have explained already in our discourse 'On Mixture' how such mixture is possible. This being the true nature of mixture, it is plain that when bodies are mixed their colours also are necessarily mixed at the same [15] time; and [it is no less plain] that this is the real cause determining the existence of a plurality of colours—not superposition or juxtaposition. For when bodies are thus mixed, their resultant colour presents itself as one and the same at all distances alike; not varying as it is seen nearer or farther away.

Colours will thus, too [as well as on the former hypotheses], be many in number on account of the fact that the ingredients may be [20] combined with one another in a multitude of ratios; some will be based on determinate numerical ratios, while others again will have as their basis a relation of quantitative excess or defect not expressible in integers. And all else that was said in reference to the colours, considered as juxtaposed or superposed, may be said of them likewise when regarded as mixed in the way just described.

Why colours, as well as savours and sounds, consist of species determinate [in themselves] and not infinite [in number] is a question [25] which we shall discuss hereafter.[1]

4

We have now explained what colour is, and the reason why there are many colours; while before, in our work *On the Soul*,[2] we explained the nature of sound and voice. We have next to speak of Odour and Savour, both of which are almost the same physical affection, although they each have their being in [30] different things. Savours, as a class, display their nature more clearly to us than Odours, the cause of which is that the olfactory sense of man is inferior in acuteness to that of the lower animals, and is, when compared with our other senses, the least perfect of all. Man's sense of Touch, on the contrary, excels that of all other animals in fineness, and Taste is a modification of Touch.

Now the natural substance water *per se* tends to be tasteless. But [since without water tasting is impossible] either (*a*) we must suppose that water contains in itself [uniformly diffused through it] the various kinds of savour, already formed, though in amounts so [5] small as to be imperceptible, which is the doctrine of Empedocles; or (*b*) the water must be a sort of matter, qualified, as it were, to produce germs of savours of all kinds, so that all kinds of savour are generated from the water, though different kinds from its different parts, or else (*c*) the water is in itself quite undifferentiated in respect of savour [whether developed or undeveloped], but some agent, such for example as one might conceive Heat or the Sun to be, is the efficient cause of savour.

[10] (*a*) Of these three hypotheses, the falsity of that held by Empedocles is only too evident. For we see that when pericarpal fruits are plucked [from the tree] and exposed in the sun, or subjected to the action of fire, their sapid juices are changed by the heat, which shows that their qualities are not due to their drawing anything from the water in the ground, but to a change which they undergo within the pericarp itself; and we see, moreover, that these juices, when extracted and al- [15] lowed to lie, instead of sweet become by lapse of time harsh or bitter, or acquire savours of any and every sort; and that, again, by the process of boiling or fermentation they are made to assume almost all kinds of new savours.

(*b*) It is likewise impossible that water should be a material qualified to generate all kinds of Savour germs [so that different savours should arise out of different parts of the water]; for we see different kinds of taste generated from the same water, having it as their nutriment.

[20] (*c*) It remains, therefore, to suppose that the water is changed by passively receiving some affection from an external agent. Now, it is manifest that water does not contract the quality of sapidity from the agency of Heat alone. For water is of all liquids the thinnest, thinner even than oil itself, though oil, owing [25] to its viscosity, is more ductile than water, the latter being uncohesive in its particles; whence water is more difficult than oil to hold in the hand without spilling. But since perfectly pure water does not, when subjected to the action of Heat, show any tendency to acquire

---

[1] Chapter 6, 445[b] 21-29, 446[a] 16-20.
[2] *On the Soul*, 419[b] 5 sqq. (sound), and 420[b] 5 sqq. (voice).

consistency, we must infer that some other agency than heat is the cause of sapidity. For all savours [i.e. sapid liquors] exhibit a comparative consistency. Heat is, however, a co-agent in the matter.

441^b Now the sapid juices found in pericarpal fruits evidently exist also in the earth. Hence many of the old natural philosophers assert that water has qualities like those of the earth through which it flows, a fact especially manifest in the case of saline springs, for salt is a form of earth. Hence also when liquids are [5] filtered through ashes, a bitter substance, the taste they yield is bitter. There are many wells, too, of which some are bitter, others acid, while others exhibit other tastes of all kinds.

As was to be anticipated, therefore, it is in the vegetable kingdom that tastes occur in richest variety. For, like all things else, the Moist, by nature's law, is affected only by its contrary; and this contrary is the Dry. Thus we [10] see why the Moist is affected by Fire, which as a natural substance, is dry. Heat is, however, the essential property of Fire, as Dryness is of Earth, according to what has been said in our treatise[1] on the elements. Fire and Earth, therefore, taken absolutely as such, have no natural power to affect, or be affected by, one another; nor have any other pair of sub-[15]stances. Any two things can affect, or be affected by, one another only so far as contrariety to the other resides in either of them.

As, therefore, persons washing Colours or Savours in a liquid cause the water in which they wash to acquire such a quality [as that of the colour or savour], so nature, too, by washing the Dry and Earthy in the Moist, and by filtering the latter, that is, moving it on by the agency of heat through the dry and earthy, imparts to it a certain quality. This affection, [20] wrought by the aforesaid Dry in the Moist, capable of transforming the sense of Taste from potentiality to actuality, is Savour. Savour brings into actual exercise the perceptive faculty which pre-existed only in potency. The activity of sense-perception in general is analogous, not to the process of acquiring knowledge, but to that of exercising knowledge already acquired.

That Savours, either as a quality or as the [25] privation of a quality, belong not to every form of the Dry but to the Nutrient, we shall see by considering that neither the Dry without the Moist, nor the Moist without the Dry,

is nutrient. For no single element, but only composite substance, constitutes nutriment for animals. Now, among the perceptible elements of the food which animals assimilate, the tangible are the efficient causes of growth and decay; it is *qua* hot or cold that the food assim-[30]ilated causes these; for the heat or cold is the direct cause of growth or decay. It is *qua* 442^a gustable, however, that the assimilated food supplies nutrition. For all organisms are nourished by the Sweet [i.e. the 'gustable' proper], either by itself or in combination with other savours. Of this we must speak with more precise detail in our work on Generation:[2] for the present we need touch upon it only so far as our subject here requires. Heat causes growth, and fits the food-stuff for ali-[5]mentation; it attracts [into the organic system] that which is light [viz. the sweet], while the salt and bitter it rejects because of their heaviness. In fact, whatever effects external heat produces in external bodies, the same are produced by their internal heat in animal and vegetable organisms. Hence it is [i.e. by the agency of heat as described] that nourishment is effected by the sweet. The other savours are introduced into and blended in [10] food [naturally] on a principle analogous to that on which the saline or the acid is used artificially, i.e. for seasoning. These latter are used because they counteract the tendency of the sweet to be too nutrient, and to float on the stomach.

As the intermediate colours arise from the mixture of white and black, so the intermediate savours arise from the Sweet and Bitter; and these savours, too, severally involve either a definite ratio, or else an indefinite relation of degree, between their components, [15] either having certain integral numbers at the basis of their mixture, and, consequently, of their stimulative effect, or else being mixed in proportions not arithmetically expressible. The tastes which give pleasure in their combination are those which have their components joined in a definite ratio.

The sweet taste alone is Rich, [therefore the latter may be regarded as a variety of the former], while [so far as both imply privation of the Sweet] the Saline is fairly identical with the Bitter. Between the extremes of sweet and bitter come the Harsh, the Pungent, the Astringent, and the Acid. Savours and Colours, it will be observed, contain respectively about the same number of species. For

---

[1] Cf. *On Generation and Corruption*, 328^b 33 sqq.

[2] *On Generation of Animals*, 762^b 12 sqq.

[20] there are seven species of each, if, as is reasonable, we regard Dun [or Grey] as a variety of Black (for the alternative is that Yellow should be classed with White, as Rich with Sweet); while [the irreducible colours, viz.] Crimson, Violet, leek-Green, and deep Blue, come between White and Black, and from these all others are derived by mix-[25] ture.

Again, as Black is a privation of White in the Translucent, so Saline or Bitter is a privation of Sweet in the Nutrient Moist. This explains why the ash of all burnt things is bitter; for the potable [sc. the sweet] moisture has been exuded from them.

[30] Democritus and most of the natural philosophers who treat of sense-perception **442^b** proceed quite irrationally, for they represent all objects of sense as objects of Touch. Yet, if this is really so, it clearly follows that each of the other senses is a mode of Touch; but one can see at a glance that this is impossible.

Again, they treat the percepts common to all senses as proper to one. For [the qualities [5] by which they explain taste, viz.] Magnitude and Figure, Roughness and Smoothness, and, moreover, the Sharpness and Bluntness found in solid bodies, are percepts common to all the senses, or if not to all, at least to Sight and Touch. This explains why it is that the senses are liable to err regarding them, while no such error arises respecting their proper sensibles; e.g. the sense of Seeing is not deceived as to Colour, nor is that of Hearing as to Sound.

[10] On the other hand, they reduce the proper to common sensibles, as Democritus does with White and Black; for he asserts that the latter is [a mode of the] rough, and the former [a mode of the] smooth, while he reduces Savours to the atomic figures. Yet surely no one sense, or, if any, the sense of Sight rather than any other, can discern the common sensibles. But if we suppose that the sense of Taste is better able to do so, then—since to dis-[15] cern the smallest objects in each kind is what marks the acutest sense—Taste should have been the sense which best perceived the common sensibles generally, and showed the most perfect power of discerning figures in general.

Again, all the sensibles involve contrariety; e.g. in Colour White is contrary to Black, and in Savours Bitter is contrary to Sweet; but no [20] one figure is reckoned as contrary to any other figure. Else, to which of the possible polygonal figures [to which Democritus reduces Bitter] is the spherical figure [to which he reduces Sweet] contrary?

Again, since figures are infinite in number, savours also should be infinite; [the possible rejoinder—'that they are so, only that some are not perceived'—cannot be sustained] for why should one savour be perceived, and another not?

This completes our discussion of the object of Taste, i.e. Savour; for the other affections of [25] Savours are examined in their proper place in connection with the natural history of Plants.

5

Our conception of the nature of Odours must be analogous to that of Savours; inasmuch as the Sapid Dry effects in air and water alike, but in a different province of sense, precisely what the Dry effects in the Moist of water only. We customarily predicate Translucency of [30] both air and water in common; but it is not *qua* translucent that either is a vehicle of **443^a** odour, but *qua* possessed of a power of washing or rinsing [and so imbibing] the Sapid Dryness.

For the object of Smell exists not in air only: it also exists in water. This is proved by the case of fishes and testacea, which are seen to [5] possess the faculty of smell, although water contains no air (for whenever air is generated within water it rises to the surface), and these creatures do not respire. Hence, if one were to assume that air and water are both moist, it would follow that Odour is the natural substance consisting of the Sapid Dry diffused in the Moist, and whatever is of this kind would be an object of Smell.

That the property of odorousness is based upon the Sapid may be seen by comparing the things which possess with those which do not [10] possess odour. The elements, viz. Fire, Air, Earth, Water, are inodorous, because both the dry and the moist among them are without sapidity, unless some added ingredient produces it. This explains why sea-water possesses odour, for [unlike 'elemental' water] it contains savour and dryness. Salt, too, is more odorous than natron, as the oil which [15] exudes from the former proves, for natron is allied to ['elemental'] earth more nearly than salt. Again, a stone is inodorous, just because it is tasteless, while, on the contrary, wood is odorous, because it is sapid. The kinds of wood, too, which contain more ['elemental'] water are less odorous than others. Moreover, to take the case of metals, gold is inodorous because it is without taste, but bronze and iron are odorous; and when the [sapid] moisture has been burnt out of them, their slag is, in all cases, less odorous [than the metals themselves]. Silver and tin are more odorous than the one class of metals, less so than the other, inasmuch as they are watery [to a [20] greater degree than the former, to a less degree than the latter].

Some writers look upon Fumid exhalation, which is a compound of Earth and Air, as the essence of Odour. [Indeed all are inclined to rush to this theory of Odour.] Heraclitus implied his adherence to it when he declared that if all existing things were turned into Smoke, the nose would be the organ to discern them with. All writers incline to refer odour to this cause [sc. exhalation of some [25] sort], but some regard it as aqueous, others as fumid, exhalation; while others, again, hold it to be either. Aqueous exhalation is merely a form of moisture, but fumid exhalation is, as already remarked, composed of Air and Earth. The former when condensed turns into water; the latter, in a particular species of earth. Now, it is unlikely that odour is [30] either of these. For vaporous exhalation consists of mere water [which, being tasteless, is inodorous]; and fumid exhalation cannot occur in water at all, though, as has been before stated, aquatic creatures also have the sense of smell.

443ᵇ Again, the exhalation theory of odour is analogous to the theory of emanations. If, therefore, the latter is untenable, so, too, is the former.

It is clearly conceivable that the Moist, whether in air (for air, too, is essentially moist) or in water, should imbibe the influ-[5] ence of, and have effects wrought in it by, the Sapid Dryness. Moreover, if the Dry produces in moist media, i.e. water and air, an effect as of something washed out in them, it is manifest that odours must be something analogous to savours. Nay, indeed, this analogy is, in some instances, a fact [registered in language]; for odours as well as savours are spoken of as *pungent, sweet, harsh, astringent,* [10] *rich* [= 'savoury']; and one might regard fetid smells as analogous to bitter tastes; which explains why the former are offensive to inhalation as the latter are to deglutition. It is clear, therefore, that Odour is in both water and air what Savour is in water alone. This explains why coldness and freezing [15] render Savours dull, and abolish odours altogether; for cooling and freezing tend to annul the kinetic heat which helps to fabricate sapidity.

There are two species of the Odorous. For the statement of certain writers that the odorous is not divisible into species is false; it is so divisible. We must here define the sense in which these species are to be admitted or denied.

One class of odours, then, is that which runs parallel, as has been observed, to savours: to [20] odours of this class their pleasantness or unpleasantness belongs incidentally. For owing to the fact that Savours are qualities of nutrient matter, the odours connected with these [e.g. those of a certain food] are agreeable as long as animals have an appetite for the food, but they are not agreeable to them when sated and no longer in want of it; nor are they agreeable, either, to those animals that do not like the food itself which yields the odours. Hence, [25] as we observed, these odours are pleasant or unpleasant incidentally, and the same reasoning explains why it is that they are perceptible to all animals in common.

The other class of odours consists of those agreeable in their essential nature, e.g. those of flowers. For these do not in any degree stimulate animals to food, nor do they contribute in any way to appetite; their effect upon it, if any, is rather the opposite. For the verse [30] of Strattis ridiculing Euripides—

Use not perfumery to flavour soup,
contains a truth.

Those who nowadays introduce such flavours into beverages deforce our sense of plea-**444ᵃ** sure by habituating us to them, until, from two distinct kinds of sensations combined, pleasure arises as it might from one simple kind.

Of this species of odour man alone is sensible; the other, viz. that correlated with Tastes, is, as has been said before, perceptible also to [5] the lower animals. And odours of the latter sort, since their pleasureableness depends upon taste, are divided into as many species as there are different tastes; but we cannot go on to say this of the former kind of odour, since its nature is agreeable or disagreeable *per se*. The reason why the perception of such odours is peculiar to man is found in the character-[10] istic state of man's brain. For his brain is naturally cold, and the blood which it contains in its vessels is thin and pure but easily cooled (whence it happens that the exhalation arising from food, being cooled by the coldness of this region, produces unhealthy rheums); therefore it is that odours of such a species have been generated for human beings, as a [15] safeguard to health. This is their sole function, and that they perform it is evident. For food, whether dry or moist, though sweet to taste, is often unwholesome; whereas the odour arising from what is fragrant, that odour which is pleasant in its own right, is, so to say, always beneficial to persons in any state of bodily health whatever.

For this reason, too, the perception of odour [in general] is effected through respiration, [20] not in all animals, but in man and certain other sanguineous animals, e.g. quadrupeds, and all that participate freely in the natural substance air; because when odours, on account of the lightness of the heat in them, mount to the brain, the health of this region is thereby promoted. For odour, as a power, is naturally heat-giving. Thus Nature has em-[25] ployed respiration for two purposes: primarily for the relief thereby brought to the thorax, secondarily for the inhalation of odour. For while an animal is inhaling, odour moves in through its nostrils, as it were 'from a side-entrance.'

But the perception of the second class of odours above described [does not belong to all animals, but] is confined to human beings, [30] because man's brain is, in proportion to his whole bulk, larger and moister than the brain of any other animal. This is the reason of the further fact that man alone, so to speak, among animals perceives and takes pleasure in the odours of flowers and such things. For the heat and stimulation set up by these odours are commensurate with the excess of **444[b]** moisture and coldness in his cerebral region. On all the other animals which have lungs, Nature has bestowed their due perception of one of the two kinds of odour [i.e. that connected with nutrition] through the act of respiration, guarding against the needless creation of two organs of sense; for in the fact that they respire the other animals have already sufficient provision for their perception of the one species of odour only, as human [5] beings have for their perception of both.

But that creatures which do not respire have the olfactory sense is evident. For fishes, and all insects as a class, have, thanks to the species of odour correlated with nutrition, a keen olfactory sense of their proper food from a [10] distance, even when they are very far away from it; such is the case with bees, and also with the class of small ants, which some denominate knîpes. Among marine animals, too, the murex and many other similar animals have an acute perception of their food by its odour.

It is not equally certain what the organ is whereby they so perceive. This question, of [15] the organ whereby they perceive odour, may well cause a difficulty, if we assume that smelling takes place in animals only while respiring (for that this is the fact is manifest in all the animals which do respire), whereas none of those just mentioned respires, and yet they have the sense of smell—unless, indeed, they have some other sense not included in the ordinary five. This supposition is, however, [20] impossible. For any sense which perceives odour is a sense of smell, and this they do perceive, though probably not in the same way as creatures which respire, but when the latter are respiring the current of breath removes something that is laid like a lid upon the organ proper (which explains why they do not perceive odours when not respiring); while in creatures which do not respire this is always off: just as some animals have eye-[25] lids on their eyes, and when these are not raised they cannot see, whereas hard-eyed animals have no lids, and consequently do not need, besides eyes, an agency to raise the lids, but see straightway [without intermission] from the actual moment at which it is first possible for them to do so [i.e. from the moment when an object first comes within their field of vision].

Consistently with what has been said above, not one of the lower animals shows repugnance to the odour of things which are es-[30] sentially ill-smelling, unless one of the latter is positively pernicious. They are destroyed, however, by these things, just as human beings are; i.e. as human beings get headaches from, and are often asphyxiated by, the fumes of charcoal, so the lower animals perish from the strong fumes of brimstone and bituminous substances; and it is owing to **445[a]** experience of such effects that they shun these. For the disagreeable odour in itself they care nothing whatever (though the odours of many plants are essentially disagreeable), unless, indeed, it has some effect upon the taste of their food.

[5] The senses making up an odd number,

and an odd number having always a middle unit, the *sense* of smell occupies in itself as it were a middle position between the tactual senses, i.e. Touch and Taste, and those which perceive through a medium, i.e. Sight and Hearing. Hence the *object* of smell, too, is an affection of nutrient substances (which fall within the class of Tangibles), and is also an [10] affection of the audible and the visible; whence it is that creatures have the sense of smell both in air and water. Accordingly, the object of smell is something common to both of these provinces, i.e. it appertains both to the tangible on the one hand, and on the other to the audible and translucent. Hence the propriety of the figure by which it has been described by us as an immersion or washing of dryness in the Moist and Fluid. Such then [15] must be our account of the sense in which one is or is not entitled to speak of the odorous as having *species*.

The theory held by certain of the Pythagoreans, that some animals are nourished by odours alone, is unsound. For, in the first place, we see that food must be composite, since the bodies nourished by it are not simple. This explains why waste matter is secreted from food, either within the organisms, or, as [20] in plants, outside them. But since even water by itself alone, that is, when unmixed, will not suffice for food—for anything which is to form a consistency must be corporeal—, it is still much less conceivable that air should be so corporealized [and thus fitted to be food]. But, besides this, we see that all animals have a receptacle for food, from which, when it has entered, the body absorbs it. Now, the organ [25] which perceives odour is in the head, and odour enters with the inhalation of the breath; so that it goes to the respiratory region. It is plain, therefore, that odour, *qua* odour, does not contribute to nutrition; that, however, it is serviceable to health is equally plain, as well by immediate perception as from the arguments above employed; so that odour is in re-[30] lation to general health what savour is in the province of nutrition and in relation to the bodies nourished.

445ᵇ This then must conclude our discussion of the several organs of sense-perception.

6

One might ask: if every body is infinitely di-[5] visible, are its sensible qualities—Colour, Savour, Odour, Sound, Weight, Cold or Heat, [Heaviness or] Lightness, Hardness or Softness—also infinitely divisible? Or, is this impossible?

[One might well ask this question], because each of them is productive of sense-perception, since, in fact, all derive their name [of 'sensible qualities'] from the very circumstance of their being *able* to stimulate this. Hence, [if this is so] both our perception of them should likewise be divisible to infinity, and every part [10] of a body [however small] should be a perceptible magnitude. For it is impossible, e.g. to see a thing which is white but not of a certain magnitude.

Since if it were not so, [if its sensible qualities were not divisible, *pari passu* with body], we might conceive a body existing but having no colour, or weight, or any such quality; accordingly not perceptible at all. For these qualities are the objects of sense-perception. On this supposition, every perceptible object should be regarded as composed not of perceptible [but of imperceptible] parts. Yet it [15] must [be really composed of perceptible parts], since assuredly it does not consist of mathematical [and therefore purely abstract and non-sensible] quantities. Again, by what faculty should we discern and cognize these [hypothetical real things without sensible qualities]? Is it by Reason? But they are not objects of Reason; nor does reason apprehend objects in space, except when it acts in conjunction with sense-perception. At the same time, if this be the case [that there are magnitudes, physically real, but without sensible quality], it seems to tell in favour of the atomistic hypothesis; for thus, indeed, [by accepting this hypothesis], the question [with which this chapter begins] might be solved [negatively]. But it is impossible [to accept this hy-[20] pothesis]. Our views on the subject of atoms are to be found in our treatise on Movement.[1]

The solution of these questions will bring with it also the answer to the question why the species of Colour, Taste, Sound, and other sensible qualities are limited. For in all classes of things lying between extremes the intermediates must be limited. But contraries are extremes, and every object of sense-perception in-[25] volves contrariety: e.g. in Colour, White x Black; in Savour, Sweet x Bitter, and in all the other sensibles also the contraries are extremes. Now, that which is continuous is divisible into an infinite number of unequal parts, but into a finite number of equal parts, while that

[1] See *Physics*, VI, 1-2 (231ᵃ 21-232ᵃ 25).

which is not *per se* continuous is divisible into species which are finite in number. Since then, the several sensible qualities of things are to be [30] reckoned as species, while continuity always subsists in these, we must take account of the difference between the Potential and the Actual. It is owing to this difference that we do 446ᵃ not [actually] see its ten-thousandth part in a grain of millet, although sight has embraced the whole grain within its scope; and it is owing to this, too, that the sound contained in a quarter-tone escapes notice, and yet one hears the whole strain, inasmuch as it is a continuum; but the interval between the extreme sounds [that bound the quarter-tone] escapes the ear [being only potentially audible, not actually]. So, in the case of other objects of sense, extremely small constituents are unnoticed; [5] because they are only potentially not actually [perceptible, e.g.] visible, unless when they have been parted from the wholes. So the foot-length too exists potentially in the two-foot length, but actually only when it has been separated from the whole. But objective increments so small as those above might well, if separated from their totals, [instead of achieving 'actual' existence] be dissolved in their environments, like a drop of sapid moisture poured out into the sea. But even if this were not so [sc. with the objective magnitude], still, [10] since the [subjective] increment of sense-perception is not perceptible in itself, nor capable of separate existence (since it exists only potentially in the more distinctly perceivable whole of sense-perception), so neither will it be possible to perceive [actually] its correlatively small object [sc. its quantum of πάθημα or sensible quality] when separated from the object-total. But yet this [small object] is to be considered as perceptible: for it is both potentially so already [i.e. even when alone], and destined to be actually so when it has become [15] part of an aggregate. Thus, therefore, we have shown that some magnitudes and their sensible qualities escape notice, and the reason why they do so, as well as the manner in which they are still perceptible or not perceptible in such cases. Accordingly then, when these [minutely subdivided] sensibles have once again become *aggregated* in a whole in such a manner, relatively to one another, as to be perceptible actually, and not merely because they are in the whole, but even apart from it, it follows necessarily [from what has been already stated[1]] that their sensible qualities,

[1] Sc. in 445ᵇ 25-29.

[20] whether colours or tastes or sounds, are limited in number.

One might ask:—do the objects of sense-perception, or the movements proceeding from them ([since movements there are,] in whichever of the two ways [viz. by emanations or by stimulatory κίνησις] sense-perception takes place), when these are actualized for perception, always arrive first at a spatial middle point [between the sense-organ and its object], as Odour evidently does, and also Sound? For he who is nearer [to the odorous object] perceives the Odour sooner [than he [25] who is farther away], and the Sound of a stroke reaches us some time after it has been struck. Is it thus also with an object seen, and with Light? Empedocles, for example, says that the Light from the Sun arrives first in the intervening space before it comes to the eye, or reaches the Earth. This might plausibly seem to be the case. For whatever is moved [in space], is moved from one place to another; hence there must be a corresponding interval [30] of time also in which it is moved from the one place to the other. But any given time is divisible into parts; so that we should assume a time when the sun's ray was not as yet seen, but was still travelling in the middle space.

Now, even if it be true that the acts of 'hearing' and 'having heard', and, generally, those of 'perceiving' and 'having perceived', form co-instantaneous wholes, in other words, that acts of sense-perception do not involve a process of becoming, but have their being none the [5] less without involving such a process; yet, just as, [in the case of sound], though the stroke which causes the Sound has been already struck, the Sound is not yet at the ear (and that this last is a fact is further proved by the transformation which the letters [viz. the consonants as heard] undergo [in the case of words spoken from a distance], implying that the local movement [involved in Sound] takes place in the space between [us and the speaker]; for the reason why [persons addressed from a distance] do not succeed in catching the sense of what is said is evidently that the air [sound wave] in moving towards them has its form changed) [granting this, then, the question arises]: is the same also true in the case of Colour and Light? For certainly [10] it is not true that the beholder sees, and the object is seen, in virtue of some merely abstract relationship between them, such as that between equals. For if it were so, there would be no need [as there is] that either [the beholder or the thing beheld] should occupy some particular place; since to the equalization of things their being near to, or far from, one another makes no difference.

Now this [travelling through successive positions in the medium] may with good reason take place as regards Sound and Odour, for [15] these, like [their media] Air and Water, are continuous, but the movement of both is divided into parts. This too is the ground of the fact that the object which the person first in order of proximity hears or smells is the same as that which each subsequent person perceives, while yet it is not the same.

Some, indeed, raise a question also on these very points; they declare it impossible that one person should hear, or see, or smell, the same object as another, urging the impossibility of [20] several persons in different places hearing or smelling [the same object], for the one same thing would [thus] be divided from itself. The answer is that, in perceiving the object which first set up the motion—e.g. a bell, or frankincense, or fire—all perceive an object numerically one and the same; while, of course, in the special object perceived they perceive an object numerically different for each, though specifically the same for all; and this, accordingly, explains how it is that many persons together see, or smell, or hear [the same object]. These things [the odour or sound [25] proper] are not bodies, but an affection or process of some kind (otherwise this [viz. simultaneous perception of the one object by many] would not have been, as it is, a fact of experience), though, on the other hand, they each imply a body [as their cause].

But [though sound and odour may travel,] with regard to Light the case is different. For Light has its *raison d'être* in the being [not *becoming*] of something, but it is not a movement. And in general, even in qualitative change the case is different from what it is in local movement [both being different species [30] of κίνησις]. Local movements, of course, arrive first at a point midway before reaching their goal (and Sound, it is currently believed, is a movement of something locally moved), 447ᵃ but we cannot go on to assert this [arrival at a point midway] in like manner of things which undergo qualitative change. For this kind of change may conceivably take place in a thing all at once, without one half of it being changed before the other; e.g. it is conceivable that water should be frozen simultaneously in every part. But still, for all that, if the body which is heated or frozen is extensive, each part of it successively is affected by the part contiguous, while the part first changed in [5] quality is so changed by the cause itself which originates the change, and thus the change throughout the whole need not take place coinstantaneously and all at once. Tasting would have been as smelling now is, if we lived in a liquid medium, and perceived [the sapid object] at a distance, before touching it.

Naturally, then, the parts of media between [10] a sensory organ and its object are not all affected at once—except in the case of Light [illumination], for the reason[1] above stated, and also in the case of seeing, for the same reason; for Light is an efficient cause of seeing.

7

Another question respecting sense-perception is as follows: assuming, as is natural, that of two [simultaneous] sensory stimuli the stronger always tends to extrude the weaker [from consciousness], is it conceivable or not that one should be able to discern two objects coinstantaneously in the same individual time? [15] The above assumption explains why persons do not perceive what is brought before their eyes, if they are at the time deep in thought, or in a fright, or listening to some loud noise. This assumption, then, must be made, and also the following: that it is easier to discern each object of sense when in its simple form than when an ingredient in a mixture; easier, for example, to discern wine when neat than when blended, and so also honey, and [in other provinces] a colour, or to discern the *nêtê* by itself alone, than [when [20] sounded with the *hypatê*] in the octave; the reason being that component elements tend to efface [the distinctive characteristics of] one another. Such is the effect [on one another] of all ingredients of which, when compounded, some one thing is formed.

If, then, the greater stimulus tends to expel the less, it necessarily follows that, when they concur, this greater should itself too be less distinctly perceptible than if it were alone, since the less by blending with it has removed some of its individuality, according to our assumption that simple objects are in all cases more distinctly perceptible.

[25] Now, if the two stimuli are equal but heterogeneous, no perception of either will ensue; they will alike efface one another's character-

---
[1] That is, the reason given 446ᵇ 27.

istics. But in such a case the perception of either stimulus in its simple form is impossible. Hence either there will then be no sense-perception at all, or there will be a perception compounded of both and differing from either. The latter is what actually seems to result from ingredients blended together, whatever may be the compound in which they are so mixed.

Since, then, from some concurrent [sensory stimuli] a resultant object is produced, while from others no such resultant is produced, and [30] of the latter sort are those things which belong to different sense provinces (for only those things are capable of mixture whose extremes are contraries, and no one compound can be formed from, e.g. White and Sharp, except indirectly, i.e. not as a concord is formed of Sharp and Grave); there follows logically the impossibility of discerning such concurrent stimuli coinstantaneously. For we must suppose that the stimuli, when equal, [5] tend alike to efface one another, since no one [form of stimulus] results from them; while, if they are unequal, the stronger alone is distinctly perceptible.

Again, the soul would be more likely to perceive coinstantaneously, with one and the same sensory act, two things in the same sensory province, such as the Grave and the Sharp in sound; for the sensory stimulation in this one province is more likely to be unitemporal than that involving two different provinces, as Sight [10] and Hearing. But it is impossible to perceive two objects coinstantaneously in the same sensory act unless they have been mixed, [when, however, they are no longer two], for their amalgamation involves their becoming one, and the sensory act related to one object is itself one, and such act, when one, is, of course, coinstantaneous with itself. Hence, when things are mixed we of necessity perceive them coinstantaneously: for we perceive them by a perception actually one. For an object numerically one means that which is perceived by a perception actually one, whereas an object specifically one means that which is [15] perceived by a sensory act potentially one [i.e. by an ἐνέργεια of the same sensuous faculty]. If then the actualized perception is one, it will declare its data to be one object; they must, therefore, have been mixed. Accordingly, when they have not been mixed, the actualized perceptions which perceive them will be two; but [if so, their perception must be successive not coinstantaneous, for] in one and the same faculty the perception actualized at any single moment is necessarily one, only one stimulation or exertion of a single faculty being possible at a single instant, and in the case supposed here the faculty is one. It follows, therefore, that we cannot conceive the possi- [20] bility of perceiving two distinct objects coinstantaneously with one and the same sense.

But if it be thus impossible to perceive coinstantaneously two objects in the same province of sense *if they are really two*, manifestly it is still less conceivable that we should perceive coinstantaneously objects in two different sensory provinces, as White and Sweet. For it appears that when the Soul predicates numerical [25] unity it does so in virtue of nothing else than such coinstantaneous perception [of one object, in one instant, by one ἐνέργεια]: while it predicates specific unity in virtue of [the unity of] the discriminating faculty of sense together with [the unity of] the mode in which this operates. What I mean, for example, is this; the same sense no doubt discerns White and Black, [which are hence generically one] though specifically different from one another, and so, too, a faculty of sense self-identical, but different from the former, discerns Sweet and Bitter; but while both these faculties differ from one another [and each from itself] in their modes of discerning either of their respective contraries, yet in perceiving [30] the co-ordinates in each province they proceed in manners analogous to one another; for instance, as Taste perceives Sweet, so Sight perceives White; and as the latter perceives Black, so the former perceives Bitter.

Again, if the stimuli of sense derived from Contraries are themselves Contrary, and if Contraries cannot be conceived as subsisting together in the same individual subject, and if Contraries, e.g. Sweet and Bitter, come under one and the same sense-faculty, we must con- [5] clude that it is impossible to discern them coinstantaneously. It is likewise clearly impossible so to discern such homogeneous sensibles as are not [indeed] Contrary, [but are yet of different species]. For these are, [in the sphere of colour, for instance], classed some with White, others with Black, and so it is, likewise, in the other provinces of sense; for example, of savours, some are classed with Sweet, and others with Bitter. Nor can one discern the components in compounds coinstantaneously (for [10] these are ratios of Contraries, as e.g. the Octave or the Fifth); unless, indeed, on condition of perceiving them as one. For thus, and not otherwise, the ratios of the extreme sounds are compounded into one ratio; since we should have together the ratio, on the one hand, of Many to Few or of Odd to Even, on the other, that of Few to Many or of Even to Odd [and these, to be perceived together, must be unified].

If, then, the sensibles denominated co-ordinates though in different provinces of sense [15] (e.g. I call Sweet and White co-ordinates though in different provinces) stand yet more aloof, and differ more, from one another than do any sensibles in the same province; while Sweet differs from White even more than Black does from White, it is still less conceivable that one should discern them [viz. sensibles in different sensory provinces whether co-ordinates or not] coinstantaneously than sensibles which are in the same province. Therefore, if coinstantaneous perception of the latter be impossible, that of the former is *a fortiori* impossible.

[20] Some of the writers who treat of concords assert that the sounds combined in these do not reach us simultaneously, but only appear to do so, their real successiveness being unnoticed whenever the time it involves is [so small as to be] imperceptible. Is this true or not? One might perhaps, following this up, go so far as to say that even the current opinion that one sees and hears coinstantaneously is due merely to the fact that the intervals of time [between the really successive perceptions of sight and hearing] escape observation. But this can scarcely be true, nor is it conceivable that any [25] portion of time should be [absolutely] imperceptible, or that any should be absolutely unnoticeable; the truth being that it is possible to perceive every instant of time. [This is so]; because, if it is inconceivable that a person should, while perceiving himself or aught else in a continuous time, be at any instant unaware of his own existence; while, obviously, the assumption, that there is in the time-continuum a time so small as to be absolutely imperceptible, carries the implication that a person would, during such time, be unaware of his own existence, as well as of his seeing and perceiving; [this assumption must be false].

Again, if there is any magnitude, whether time or thing, absolutely imperceptible owing [30] to its smallness, it follows that there would not be either a thing which one perceives, or a time in which one perceives it, unless in the sense that in some part of the given time he sees some part of the given 448^b thing. For [let there be a line $\alpha\beta$, divided into two parts at γ, and let this line represent a whole object and a corresponding whole time. Now,] if one sees the whole line, and perceives it during a time which forms one and the same continuum, only in the sense that he does so in some portion of this time, let us [5] suppose the part $\gamma\beta$, representing a time in which by supposition he was perceiving nothing, cut off from the whole. Well, then, he perceives *in* a certain part [viz. in the remainder] of the time, or perceives *a part* [viz. the remainder] of the line, after the fashion in which one sees the whole earth by seeing some given part of it, or walks in a year by walking in some given part of the year. But [by hypothesis] in the part $\beta\gamma$ he perceives nothing: therefore, in fact, he is said to perceive the whole object and during the whole time simply because he perceives [some part of the object] in some part of the time $\alpha\beta$. But the same argument holds also in the case of $\alpha\gamma$ [the re-[10] mainder, regarded in its turn as a whole]; for it will be found [on this theory of vacant times and imperceptible magnitudes] that one always perceives only in some part of a given whole time, and perceives only some part of a whole magnitude, and that it is impossible to perceive any [really] whole [object in a really whole time; a conclusion which is absurd, as it would logically annihilate the perception of both Objects and Time].

Therefore we must conclude that all magnitudes are perceptible, but their actual dimensions do not present themselves immediately in their presentation as objects. One sees the sun, or a four-cubit rod at a distance, as a magnitude, but their exact dimensions are not given in their visual presentation: nay, at times an object of sight appears indivisible, but [vision, like other special senses, is fallible respecting 'common sensibles', e.g. magnitude, and] nothing that one sees is really indivisible. The [15] reason of this has been previously explained.[1] It is clear then, from the above arguments, that no portion of time is imperceptible.

But we must here return to the question proposed above for discussion, whether it is possible or impossible to perceive several objects coinstantaneously; by 'coinstantaneously' I mean perceiving the several objects in a time one and indivisible relatively to one another, i.e. indivisible in a sense consistent with its being all a continuum.

[20] First, then, is it conceivable that one

[1] Viz. in the passage 445^b 2-446^b 20.

should perceive the different things coinstantaneously, but each with a different part of the Soul? Or [must we object] that, in the first place, to begin with the objects of one and the same sense, e.g. Sight, if we assume it [the Soul *qua* exercising Sight] to perceive one colour with one part, and another colour with a different part, it will have a plurality of parts the same in species, [as they must be,] since the objects which it thus perceives fall with-[25] in the same genus?

Should any one [to illustrate how the Soul might have in it two different parts specifically identical, each directed to a set of αἰσθητά the same in genus with that to which the other is directed] urge that, as there are two eyes, so there may be in the Soul something analogous, [the reply is] that of the eyes, doubtless, some one organ is formed, and hence their actualization in perception is one; but if this is so in the Soul, then, in so far as what is formed of both [i.e. of any two specifically identical parts as assumed] is one, the true perceiving subject also will be one, [and the contradictory of the above hypothesis (of different parts of Soul remaining engaged in simultaneous perception with one sense) is what emerges from the analogy]; while if the two parts of Soul remain separate, the analogy of the eyes will fail, [for of these some one is really formed].

Furthermore, [on the supposition of the need of different parts of Soul, co-operating in [30] each sense, to discern different objects coinstantaneously], the senses will be each at the same time one and many, as if we should say that they were each a set of diverse sciences; for neither will an 'activity' exist without its proper faculty, nor without activity will there be sensation.

449ª But if the Soul does not, in the way suggested [i.e. with different parts of itself acting simultaneously], perceive in one and the same individual time sensibles of the same sense, *a fortiori* it is not thus that it perceives sensibles of different senses. For it is, as already stated, more conceivable that it should perceive a plurality of the former together in this way than a plurality of heterogeneous objects.

[5] If then, as is the fact, the Soul with one part perceives Sweet, with another, White, either that which results from these is some one part, or else there is no such one resultant. But there must be such an one, inasmuch as the general faculty of sense-perception is one. What one object, then, does that one faculty [when perceiving an object, e.g. as both White and Sweet] perceive? [None]; for assuredly no one object arises by composition of these [heterogeneous objects, such as White and Sweet]. We must conclude, therefore, that there is, as has been stated before, some one faculty in the soul with which the latter per-[10] ceives all its percepts, though it perceives each different genus of sensibles through a different organ.

May we not, then, conceive this faculty which perceives White and Sweet to be one *qua* indivisible [sc. *qua* combining its different simultaneous objects] in its actualization, but different, when it has become divisible [sc. *qua* distinguishing its different simultaneous objects] in its actualization?

Or is what occurs in the case of the perceiving Soul conceivably analogous to what holds true in that of the things themselves? For the [15] same numerically one thing is white and sweet, and has many other qualities, [while its numerical oneness is not thereby prejudiced] if the fact is not that the qualities are really separable in the object from one another, but that the *being* of each quality is different [from that of every other]. In the same way therefore we must assume also, in the case of the Soul, that the faculty of perception in general is in itself numerically one and the same, but different [differentiated] in its *being;* different, that is to say, in genus as regards some of its objects, in species as regards others. Hence too, we may conclude that one can perceive [numerically different objects] coinstantaneously with a faculty which is numerically [20] one and the same, but not the same in its relationship [sc. according as the objects to which it is directed are not the same].

That every sensible object is a magnitude, and that nothing which it is possible to perceive is indivisible, may be thus shown. The distance whence an object could not be seen is indeterminate, but that whence it is visible is determinate. We may say the same of the objects of Smelling and Hearing, and of all sensibles not discerned by actual contact. Now, there is, in the interval of distance, some ex-[25] treme place, the last from which the object is invisible, and the first from which it is visible. This place, beyond which if the object be one cannot perceive it, while if the object be on the hither side one must perceive it, is, I presume, itself necessarily indivisible. Therefore, if any sensible object be indivisible, such object, if set in the said extreme place whence imperceptibility ends and perceptibility begins, will have to be both visible and invisible [30] at the same time; but this is impossible.

This concludes our survey of the characteristics of the organs of Sense-perception and their objects, whether regarded in general or in relation to each organ. Of the remaining subjects, we must first consider that of memory and remembering.

On Memory and Reminiscence

I

449ᵇ We have, in the next place, to treat of Memory and Remembering, considering its nature, its cause, and the part of the soul to [5] which this experience, as well as that of Recollecting, belongs. For the persons who possess a retentive memory are not identical with those who excel in power of recollection; indeed, as a rule, slow people have a good memory, whereas those who are quick-witted and clever are better at recollecting.

We must first form a true conception of the [10] objects of memory, a point on which mistakes are often made. Now to remember the future is not possible, but this is an object of opinion or expectation (and indeed there might be actually a science of expectation, like that of divination, in which some believe); nor is there memory of the present, but only sense-perception. For by the latter we know not the future, nor the past, but the present only. But [15] memory relates to the past. No one would say that he remembers the present, when it is present, e.g. a given white object at the moment when he sees it; nor would one say that he remembers an object of scientific contemplation at the moment when he is actually contemplating it, and has it full before his mind; —of the former he would say only that he perceives it, of the latter only that he knows it. But when one has scientific knowledge, or perception, apart from the actualizations of the [20] faculty concerned, he thus 'remembers' [that the angles of a triangle are together equal to two right angles]; as to the former, that he learned it, or thought it out for himself, as to the latter, that he heard, or saw, it, or had some such sensible experience of it. For whenever one exercises the faculty of remembering, he must say within himself, 'I formerly heard (or otherwise perceived) this,' or 'I formerly had this thought'.

Memory is, therefore, neither Perception nor Conception, but a state or affection of one [25] of these, conditioned by lapse of time. As already observed, there is no such thing as memory of the present while present, for the present is object only of perception, and the future, of expectation, but the object of memory is the past. All memory, therefore, implies a time elapsed; consequently only those animals which perceive time remember, and the organ whereby they perceive time is also that whereby they remember.

[30] The subject of 'presentation' has been already considered in our work *On the Soul*.[1] Without a presentation intellectual activity is **450ᵃ** impossible. For there is in such activity an incidental affection identical with one also incidental in geometrical demonstrations. For in the latter case, though we do not for the purpose of the proof make any use of the fact that the quantity in the triangle [for example, which we have drawn] is determinate, we nevertheless draw it determinate in quantity. So likewise when one exerts the intellect [e.g. on the subject of first principles], although the [5] object may not be quantitative, one envisages it as quantitative, though he thinks it in abstraction from quantity; while, on the other hand, if the object of the intellect is essentially of the class of things that are quantitative, but indeterminate, one envisages it as if it had determinate quantity, though subsequently, in thinking it, he abstracts from its determinateness. Why we cannot exercise the intellect on any object absolutely apart from the continuous, or apply it even to non-temporal things unless in connexion with time, is [10] another question. Now, one must cognize magnitude and motion by means of the same faculty by which one cognizes time [i.e. by that which is also the faculty of memory], and the presentation [involved in such cognition] is an affection of the *sensus communis;* whence this follows, viz. that the cognition of these objects [magnitude, motion, time] is effected by the [said *sensus communis,* i.e. the] primary faculty of perception. Accordingly, memory [not merely of sensible, but] even of intellectual objects involves a presentation: hence we may conclude that it belongs to the faculty of intelligence only incidentally, while directly and essentially it belongs to the primary faculty of sense-perception.

[15] Hence not only human beings and the beings which possess opinion or intelligence, but also certain other animals, possess memory.

[1] Cf. 427ᵇ 29 sqq.

If memory were a function of [pure] intellect, it would not have been as it is an attribute of many of the lower animals, but probably, in that case, no mortal beings would have had memory; since, even as the case stands, it is not an attribute of them all, just because all have not the faculty of perceiving time. Whenever one actually remembers having seen or heard, [20] or learned, something, he includes in this act (as we have already observed) the consciousness of 'formerly'; and the distinction of 'former' and 'latter' is a distinction in time.

Accordingly if asked, of which among the parts of the soul memory is a function, we reply: manifestly of that part to which 'presentation' appertains; and all objects capable of being presented [viz. $αἰσθητά$] are immediately and properly objects of memory, while those [viz. $νοητά$] which necessarily involve [25] [but *only* involve] presentation are objects of memory incidentally.

One might ask how it is possible that though the affection [the presentation] alone is present, and the [related] fact absent, the latter— that which is not present—is remembered. [This question arises], because it is clear that we must conceive that which is generated through sense-perception in the sentient soul, and in the part of the body which is its seat,— viz. that affection the state whereof we call memory—to be some such thing as a picture. [30] The process of movement [sensory stimulation] involved in the act of perception stamps in, as it were, a sort of impression of the percept, just as persons do who make an **450b** impression with a seal. This explains why, in those who are strongly moved owing to passion, or time of life, no mnemonic impression is formed; just as no impression would be formed if the movement of the seal were to impinge on running water; while there are others in whom, owing to the re- [5] ceiving surface being frayed, as happens to [the stucco on] old [chamber] walls, or owing to the hardness of the receiving surface, the requisite impression is not implanted at all. Hence both very young and very old persons are defective in memory; they are in a state of flux, the former because of their growth, the latter, owing to their decay. In like manner, also, both those who are too quick [10] and those who are too slow have bad memories. The former are too soft, the latter too hard [in the texture of their receiving organs], so that in the case of the former the presented image [though imprinted] does not remain in the soul, while on the latter it is not imprinted at all.

But then, if this truly describes what happens in the genesis of memory, [the question stated above arises:] when one remembers, is it this impressed affection that he remembers, or is it the objective thing from which this was derived? If the former, it would follow that we remember nothing which is absent; if [15] the latter, how is it possible that, though perceiving directly only the impression, we remember that absent thing which we do not perceive? Granted that there is in us something like an impression or picture, why should the perception of the mere impression be memory of something else, instead of being related to this impression alone? For when one actually remembers, this impression is what he contemplates, and this is what he perceives. How then does he remember what is not present? One might as well suppose it possible also to see or hear that which is not present. In re- [20] ply, we suggest that this very thing is quite conceivable, nay, actually occurs in experience. A picture painted on a panel is at once a picture and a likeness: that is, while one and the same, it is both of these, although the 'being' of both is not the same, and one may contemplate it either as a picture, or as a likeness. Just in the same way we have to conceive that the mnemonic presentation within [25] us is something which by itself is merely an object of contemplation, while, in relation to something else, it is also a presentation of that other thing. In so far as it is regarded in itself, it is only an object of contemplation, or a presentation; but when considered as relative to something else, e.g. as its likeness, it is also a mnemonic token. Hence, whenever the residual sensory process implied by it is actualized in consciousness, if the soul perceives this in so far as it is something absolute, it appears to occur as a mere thought or presentation; but if the soul perceives it *qua* related to something else, then,—just as when one contemplates the painting in the picture as being a likeness, and [30] without having [at the moment] seen the actual Koriskos, contemplates it as a likeness of Koriskos, and in that case the experience **451a** involved in this contemplation of it [as relative] is different from what one has when he contemplates it simply as a painted figure— [so in the case of memory we have the analogous difference, for], of the objects in the soul, the one [the unrelated object] presents itself simply as a thought, but the other [the related object], just because, as in the painting, it is a likeness, presents itself as a mnemonic token.

We can now understand why it is that sometimes, when we have such processes, based on some former act of perception, occurring in the soul, we do not know whether this really implies our having had perceptions corresponding to them, and we doubt whether the case is or is not one of memory. But occasionally it happens that [while thus doubting] we get a sudden idea and recollect that we heard or saw something formerly. This [occurrence of the 'sudden idea'] happens whenever, from contemplating a mental object as absolute, one changes his point of view, and regards it as relative to something else.

The opposite [sc. to the case of those who at first do not recognize their phantasms as mnemonic] also occurs, as happened in the cases of Antipheron of Oreus and others suffering [10] from mental derangement; for they were accustomed to speak of their mere phantasms as facts of their past experience, and as if remembering them. This takes place whenever one contemplates what is not a likeness as if it were a likeness.

Mnemonic exercises aim at preserving one's memory of something by repeatedly reminding him of it; which implies nothing else [on the learner's part] than the frequent contemplation of something [viz. the 'mnemonic', whatever it may be] as a likeness, and not as out of relation.

[15] As regards the question, therefore, what memory or remembering is, it has now been shown that it is the state of a presentation, related as a *likeness* to that of which it is a presentation; and as to the question of which of the faculties within us memory is a function, [it has been shown] that it is a function of the primary faculty of sense-perception, i.e. of that faculty whereby we perceive time.

2

Next comes the subject of Recollection, in [20] dealing with which we must assume as fundamental the truths elicited above in our introductory discussions. For recollection is not the 'recovery' or 'acquisition' of memory; since at the instant when one at first learns [a fact of science] or experiences [a particular fact of sense], he does not thereby 'recover' a memory, inasmuch as none has preceded, nor does he acquire one *ab initio*. It is only at the instant when the aforesaid state or affection [of the αἴσθησις or ὑπόληψις; see 449^b 24] is implanted in the soul that memory exists, and [25] therefore memory is not itself implanted concurrently with the continuous implantation of the [original] sensory experience.

Further: at the very individual and concluding instant when first [the sensory experience or scientific knowledge] has been completely implanted, there is then already established in the person affected the [sensory] affection, or the scientific knowledge (if one ought to apply the term 'scientific knowledge' to the [mnemonic] state or affection; and indeed one may well remember, in the 'incidental' sense, some of the things [i.e. τὰ καθόλου] which are properly objects of scientific knowledge); but to remember, strictly and properly [30] speaking, is an activity which will not be immanent until the original experience has undergone lapse of time. For one remembers now what one saw or otherwise experienced formerly; the moment of the original experience and the moment of the memory of it are never identical.

Again, [even when time has elapsed, and one can be said really to have acquired memory, this is not necessarily recollection, for 451^b firstly] it is obviously possible, without any present act of recollection, to remember as a continued consequence of the original perception or other experience; whereas when [after an interval of obliviscence] one recovers some scientific knowledge which he had before, or some perception, or some other experience, the state of which we above declared to be memory, it is then, and then only, that this recovery may amount to a recollection of any of the things aforesaid. But, [though, as [5] observed above, remembering does not necessarily imply recollecting], recollecting always implies remembering, and actualized memory follows [upon the successful act of recollecting].

But secondly, even the assertion that recollection is the reinstatement in consciousness of something which was there before but had disappeared requires qualification. This assertion may be true, but it may also be false; for the same person may twice learn [from some teacher], or twice discover [i.e. excogitate], the same fact. Accordingly, the act of recollecting ought [in its definition] to be distinguished from these acts; i.e. recollecting must imply in those who recollect the presence of some spring over and above that from which they originally learn.

[*10*] Acts of recollection, as they occur in experience, are due to the fact that one movement has by nature another that succeeds it in regular order.

If this order be necessary, whenever a subject experiences the former of two movements thus connected, it will [invariably], experience the latter; if, however, the order be not necessary, but customary, only in the majority of cases will the subject experience the latter of the two movements. But it is a fact that there are some movements, by a single experience of which persons take the impress of custom more deeply than they do by experiencing [*15*] others many times; hence upon seeing some things but once we remember them better than others which we may have been frequently.

Whenever, therefore, we are recollecting, we are experiencing certain of the antecedent movements until finally we experience the one after which customarily comes that which we seek. This explains why we hunt up the series [of κινήσεις], having started in thought either from a present intuition or some other, and from something either similar, or contrary, to [*20*] what we seek, or else from that which is contiguous with it. Such is the empirical ground of the process of recollection; for the mnemonic movements involved in these starting-points are in some cases identical, in others, again, simultaneous, with those of the idea we seek, while in others they comprise a portion of them, so that the remnant which one experienced after that portion [and which still requires to be excited in memory] is comparatively small.

Thus, then, it is that persons seek to recollect, and thus, too, it is that they recollect even without the effort of seeking to do so, viz. when the movement implied in recollection [*25*] has supervened on some other which is its condition. For, as a rule, it is when antecedent movements of the classes here described have first been excited, that the particular movement implied in recollection follows. We need not examine a series of which the beginning and end lie far apart, in order to see how [by recollection] we remember; one in which they lie near one another will serve equally well. For it is clear that the method is in each case the same, that is, one hunts up the objective series, without any previous search or previous recollection. For [there is, besides the natural order, viz. the order of the πράγματα, or events of the primary experience, also a customary order, and] by the effect of custom the mnemonic movements tend to succeed one another in a certain order. Accordingly, therefore, [*30*] when one wishes to recollect, this is what he will do: he will try to obtain a beginning of movement whose sequel shall be the movement which he desires to reawaken. This explains why attempts at recollection succeed soonest and best when they start from a beginning [of some objective series]. For, in order of succession, the mnemonic movements are to one another as the objective facts [from which they are derived]. Accordingly, things arranged in a fixed order, like the successive demonstrations in geometry, are easy to remember [or recollect], while badly arranged subjects are remembered with difficulty.

Recollecting differs also in this respect from relearning, that one who recollects will be able, [*5*] somehow, to move, solely by his own effort, to the term next after the starting-point. When one cannot do this of himself, but only by external assistance, he no longer remembers [i.e. he has totally forgotten, and therefore of course cannot recollect]. It often happens that, though a person cannot recollect at the moment, yet by seeking he can do so, and discovers what he seeks. This he succeeds in doing by setting up many movements, until finally he excites one of a kind which will have for its sequel the fact he wishes to recollect. [*10*] For remembering [which is the *condicio sine qua non* of recollecting] is the existence, potentially, in the mind of a movement capable of stimulating it to the desired movement, and this, as has been said, in such a way that the person should be moved [prompted to recollection] from within himself, i.e. in consequence of movements wholly contained within himself.

But one must get hold of a starting-point. This explains why it is that persons are supposed to recollect sometimes by starting from mnemonic *loci*. The cause is that they pass [*15*] swiftly in thought from one point to another, e.g. from milk to white, from white to mist, and thence to moist, from which one remembers Autumn [the 'season of mists'], if this be the season he is trying to recollect.

It seems true in general that the middle point also among all things is a good mnemonic starting-point from which to reach any of them. For if one does not recollect before, he will do so when he has come to this, or, if not, nothing can help him; as, e.g. if one were to have in mind the numerical series denoted by

[20] the symbols A, B, Γ, Δ, E, Z, I, H, Θ. For, if he does not remember what he wants at E, then at E he remembers Θ; because from E movement in either direction is possible, to Δ or to Z. But, if it is not for one of these that he is searching, he will remember [what he *is* searching for] when he has come to Γ if he is searching for H or I. But if [it is] not [for H or I that he is searching, but for one of the terms that remain], he will remember by going to A, and so in all cases [in which one starts from a middle point]. The [25] cause of one's sometimes recollecting and sometimes not, though starting from the same point, is, that from the same starting-point a movement can be made in several directions, as, for instance, from Γ to I or to Δ. If, then, the mind has not [when starting from E] moved in an old path [i.e. one in which it moved when first having the objective experience, and that, therefore, in which un-'ethized' φύσις would have it again move], it tends to move to the more customary; for [the mind having, by chance or otherwise, *missed* moving in the 'old' way] Custom now assumes the rôle of Nature. Hence the rapidity with which we recollect what we frequently think about. For as regular sequence of events is in accordance with nature, so, too, regular sequence is observed in the actualization of κινήσεις [in consciousness], and here frequency tends to [30] produce [the regularity of] nature. And since in the realm of nature occurrences take place which are even contrary to nature, or fortuitous, the same happens *a fortiori* in the sphere swayed by custom, since in this sphere natural law is not similarly established. Hence it is that [from the same starting-point] the mind receives an impulse to move sometimes in the required direction, and at other times otherwise, [doing the latter] particularly when something else somehow deflects the mind from the right direction and attracts it to itself. This last consideration explains too [5] how it happens that, when we want to remember a name, we remember one somewhat like it, indeed, but blunder in reference to [i.e. in pronouncing] the one we intended.

Thus, then, recollection takes place.

But the point of capital importance is that [for the purpose of recollection] one should cognize, determinately or indeterminately, the time-relation [of that which he wishes to recollect]. There is,—let it be taken as a fact,— something by which one distinguishes a greater and a smaller time; and it is reasonable to think that one does this in a way analogous to that in which one discerns [spatial] magni- [10] tudes. For it is not by the mind's reaching out towards them, as some say a visual ray from the eye does [in seeing], that one thinks of large things at a distance in space (for even if they are not there, one may similarly think them); but one does so by a proportionate mental movement. For there are in the mind the like figures and movements [i.e. 'like' to those of objects and events]. Therefore, when one thinks the greater objects, in what will his thinking those differ from his thinking the smaller? [In nothing,] because all the internal though smaller are as it were proportional to the external. Now, as we may assume within [15] a person something proportional to the forms [of distant magnitudes], so, too, we may doubtless assume also something else proportional to their distances. As, therefore, if one has [psychically] the movement in AB, BE, he constructs in thought [i.e. knows objectively] ΓΔ, since AΓ and ΓΔ bear equal ratios respectively [to AB and BE], [so he who recollects also proceeds]. Why then does he construct ΓΔ rather than ZH? Is it not because as AΓ is to AB, so is Θ to I? These move- [20] ments therefore [sc. in AB, BE, and in Θ]: I] he has simultaneously. But if he wishes to construct to thought ZH, he has in mind

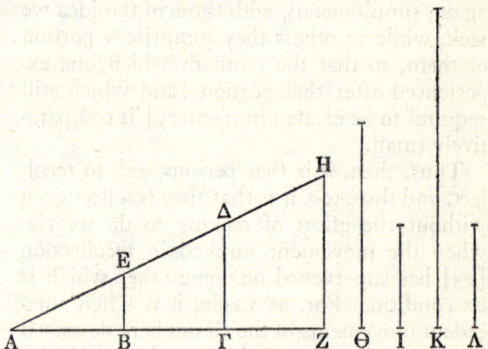

BE in like manner as before [when constructing ΓΔ], but now, instead of [the movements of the ratio] Θ: I, he has in mind [those of the ratio] K: Λ; for K: Λ:: ZA: BA.

When, therefore, the 'movement' corresponding to the object and that corresponding to its time concur, then one actually remembers. If one supposes [himself to move in these different but concurrent ways] without really doing so, he supposes himself to remember.

[25] For one may be mistaken, and think that he remembers when he really does not. But it is not possible, conversely, that when one actually remembers he should not suppose himself to remember, but should remember unconsciously. For remembering, as we have conceived it, essentially implies consciousness of itself. If, however, the movement corresponding to the objective fact takes place without that corresponding to the time, or, if the latter takes place without the former, one does not remember.

[30] The movement answering to the time is of two kinds. Sometimes in remembering a fact one has no determinate time-notion of it, 453a no such notion as that e.g. he did something or other on the day before yesterday; while in other cases he has a determinate notion of the time. Still, even though one does not remember with actual determination of the time, he genuinely remembers, none the less. Persons are wont to say that they remember [something], but yet do not know when [it occurred, as happens] whenever they do not know determinately the exact length of time implied in the 'when'.

[5] It has been already stated that those who have a good memory are not identical with those who are quick at recollecting. But the act of recollecting differs from that of remembering, not only chronologically, but also in this, that many also of the other animals [as well as man] have memory, but, of all that we are acquainted with, none, we venture to say, except man, shares in the faculty of recollection. The cause of this is that recollection is, as it were, [10] a mode of inference. For he who endeavours to recollect *infers* that he formerly saw, or heard, or had some such experience, and the process [by which he succeeds in recollecting] is, as it were, a sort of investigation. But to investigate in this way belongs naturally to those animals alone which are also endowed with the faculty of deliberation; [which proves what was said above], for deliberation is a form of inference.

[15] That the affection is corporeal, i.e. that recollection is a searching for an 'image' in a corporeal substrate, is proved by the fact that in some persons, when, despite the most strenuous application of thought, they have been unable to recollect, it [viz. the ἀνάμνησις = the effort at recollection] excites a feeling of discomfort, which, even though they abandon the effort at recollection, persists in them none the less; and especially in persons of melancholic temperament. For these are most powerfully moved by presentations. The reason why the [20] effort of recollection is not under the control of their will is that, as those who throw a stone cannot stop it at their will when thrown, so he who tries to recollect and 'hunts' [after an idea] sets up a process in a material part, [that] in which resides the affection. Those who have moisture around that part which is the centre of sense-perception suffer most discomfort of this kind. For when once the moisture has been set in motion it is not easily [25] brought to rest, until the idea which was sought for has again presented itself, and thus the movement has found a straight course. For a similar reason bursts of anger or fits of terror, when once they have excited such motions, are not at once allayed, even though the angry or terrified persons [by efforts of will] set up counter motions, but the passions continue to move them on, in the same direction as at first, in opposition to such counter motions. The affection resembles also that in the case of words, tunes, or sayings, whenever one of them has become inveterate on the lips. People give them up and resolve to avoid them; yet again and [30] again they find themselves humming the forbidden air, or using the prohibited word.

453b Those whose upper parts are abnormally large, as is the case with dwarfs, have abnormally weak memory, as compared with their opposites, because of the great weight which they have resting upon the organ of perception, and because their mnemonic movements are, from the very first, not able to keep [5] true to a course, but are dispersed, and because, in the effort at recollection, these movements do not easily find a direct onward path. Infants and very old persons have bad memories, owing to the amount of movement going on within them; for the latter are in process of rapid decay, the former in process of vigorous growth; and we may add that children, until considerably advanced in years, are dwarf-like in their bodily structure. Such then is our theory as regards memory and remembering—their nature, and the particular organ of the [10] soul by which animals remember; also as regards recollection, its formal definition, and the manner and causes of its performance.

On Sleep and Sleeplessness

I

WITH regard to sleep and waking, we must consider what they are: whether they are peculiar to soul or to body, or common to both; and if common, to what part of soul or body they appertain: further, from what cause it arises that they are attributes of animals, and [15] whether all animals share in them both, or some partake of the one only, others of the other only, or some partake of neither and some of both.

Further, in addition to these questions, we must also inquire what the dream is, and from what cause sleepers sometimes dream, and sometimes do not; or whether the truth is that sleepers always dream but do not always remember [20] (their dream); and if this occurs, what its explanation is.

Again, [we must inquire] whether it is possible or not to foresee the future (in dreams), and if it be possible, in what manner; further, whether, supposing it possible, it extends only to things to be accomplished by the agency of Man, or to those also of which the cause lies in supra-human agency, and which result from the workings of Nature, or of Spontaneity.

[25] First, then, this much is clear, that waking and sleep appertain to the same part of an animal, inasmuch as they are opposites, and sleep is evidently a privation of waking. For contraries, in natural as well as in all other matters, are seen always to present themselves in the same subject, and to be affections of the [30] same: examples are—health and sickness, beauty and ugliness, strength and weakness, sight and blindness, hearing and deafness. This is also clear from the following considera-454a tions. The criterion by which we know the waking person to be awake is identical with that by which we know the sleeper to be asleep; for we assume that one who is exercising sense-perception is awake, and that every one who is awake perceives either some external movement or else some movement in his own consciousness. If waking, then, consists in [5] nothing else than the exercise of sense-perception, the inference is clear, that the organ, in virtue of which animals perceive, is that by which they wake, when they are awake, or sleep, when they are asleep.

But since the exercise of sense-perception does not belong to soul or body exclusively, then (since the subject of actuality is in every case identical with that of potentiality, and what is called sense-perception, as actuality, is a movement of the soul through the body) it is [10] clear that its affection is not an affection of soul exclusively, and that a soulless body has not the potentiality of perception. [Thus sleep and waking are not attributes of pure intelligence, on the one hand, or of inanimate bodies, on the other.]

Now, whereas we have already elsewhere distinguished what are called the parts of the soul, and whereas the nutrient is, in all living bodies, capable of existing without the other parts, while none of the others can exist without the nutrient; it is clear that sleep and wak- [15] ing are not affections of such living things as partake only of growth and decay, e.g. not of plants, because these have not the faculty of sense-perception, whether or not this be capable of separate existence; in its potentiality, indeed, and in its relationships, it *is* separable.

Likewise it is clear that [of those which either sleep or wake] there is no animal which is always awake or always asleep, but that both [20] these affections belong [alternately] to the same animals. For if there be an animal not endued with sense-perception, it is impossible that this should either sleep or wake; since both these are affections of the activity of the primary faculty of sense-perception. But it is equally impossible also that either of these two affections should perpetually attach itself to the same animal, e.g. that some species of [25] animal should be always asleep or always awake, without intermission; for all organs which have a natural function must lose power when they work beyond the natural time-limit of their working period; for instance, the eyes [must lose power] from [too-long continued] seeing, and must give it up; and so it is with the hand and every other member [30] which has a function. Now, if sense-perception is the function of a special organ, this also, if it continues perceiving beyond the appointed time-limit of its continuous working period, will lose its power, and will do its work no longer. Accordingly, if the waking period is determined by this fact, that in it 454ᵇ sense-perception is free; if in the case of some contraries one of the two must be present, while in the case of others this is not necessary; if waking is the contrary of sleeping, and one of these two must be present to every animal: it must follow that the state of sleeping is necessary. Finally, if such affection is Sleep, and this is a state of powerlessness aris- [5] ing from excess of waking, and excess of waking is in its origin sometimes morbid, sometimes not, so that the powerlessness or dissolution of activity will be so or not; it is inevitable that every creature which wakes must also be capable of sleeping, since it is impossible that it should continue actualizing its powers perpetually.

So, also, it is impossible for any animal to continue always sleeping. For sleep is an affec- [10] tion of the organ of sense-perception—a sort of tie or inhibition of function imposed on it, so that every creature that sleeps must needs have the organ of sense-perception. Now, that alone which is capable of sense-perception in actuality has the faculty of sense-perception; but to realize this faculty, in the proper and unqualified sense, is impossible while one is asleep. All sleep, therefore, must be susceptible of awakening. Accordingly, almost all other [15] animals are clearly observed to partake in sleep, whether they are aquatic, aerial, or terrestrial, since fishes of all kinds, and molluscs, as well as all others which have eyes, have been seen sleeping. 'Hard-eyed' creatures and insects manifestly assume the posture of sleep; but the sleep of all such creatures is of brief duration, so that often it might well baffle [20] one's observation to decide whether they sleep or not. Of testaceous animals, on the contrary, no direct sensible evidence is as yet forthcoming to determine whether they sleep, but if the above reasoning be convincing to any one, he who follows it will admit this [viz. that they do so.]

That, therefore, all animals sleep may be gathered from these considerations. For an animal is defined as such by its possessing sense- [25] perception; and we assert that sleep is, in a certain way, an inhibition of function, or, as it were, a tie, imposed on sense-perception, while its loosening or remission constitutes the being awake. But no plant can partake in either of these affections, for without sense-perception there is neither sleeping nor waking. But creatures which have sense-perception have like- [30] wise the feeling of pain and pleasure, while those which have these have appetite as well; but plants have none of these affections. A mark of this is that the nutrient part does its 455ᵃ own work better when (the animal) is asleep than when it is awake. Nutrition and growth are then especially promoted, a fact which implies that creatures do not need sense-perception to assist these processes.

2

We must now proceed to inquire into the cause why one sleeps and wakes, and into the particular nature of the sense-perception, or sense-perceptions, if there be several, on which [5] these affections depend. Since, then, some animals possess all the modes of sense-perception, and some not all, not, for example, sight, while all possess touch and taste, except such animals as are imperfectly developed, a class of which we have already treated in our work on the soul; and since an animal when asleep is unable to exercise, in the simple sense, any [10] particular sensory faculty whatever, it follows that in the state called sleep the same affection must extend to all the special senses; because, if it attaches itself to one of them but not to another, then an animal while asleep may perceive with the latter; but this is impossible.

Now, since every sense has something peculiar, and also something common; peculiar, as, e.g. seeing is to the sense of sight, hearing [15] to the auditory sense, and so on with the other senses severally; while all are accompanied by a common power, in virtue whereof a person perceives *that* he sees or hears (for, assuredly, it is not by the special sense of sight that one sees that he sees; and it is not by mere taste, or sight, or both together that one discerns, and has the faculty of discerning, that sweet things are different from white things, but by a faculty connected in common with all the organs of sense; for there is one sensory [20] function, and the controlling sensory faculty is one, though differing as a faculty of perception in relation to each genus of sensibles, e.g. sound or colour); and since this [common sensory activity] subsists in association chiefly with the faculty of touch (for this [touch] can exist apart from all the other organs of sense, but none of them can exist apart from it—a subject of which we have treated in [25] our speculations concerning the Soul); it is therefore evident that waking and sleeping are an affection of this [common and controlling organ of sense-perception]. This explains why they belong to all animals, for touch [with which this common organ is chiefly connected], alone, [is common] to all [animals].

For if sleeping were caused by the *special* senses having each and all undergone some affection, it would be strange that these senses, for which it is neither necessary nor in a manner possible to realize their powers simultan-[30] eously, should necessarily all go idle and become motionless simultaneously. For the contrary experience, viz. that they should not go to rest altogether, would have been more reasonably anticipated. But, according to the explanation just given, all is quite clear regarding those also. For, when the sense organ which controls all the others, and to which all the others are tributary, has been in some way 455b affected, that these others should be all affected at the same time is inevitable, whereas, if one of the tributaries becomes powerless, that the controlling organ should also become powerless need in no wise follow.

It is indeed evident from many considerations that sleep does not consist in the mere fact that the special senses do not function or that one does not employ them; and that it does not consist merely in an inability to exer-[5] cise the sense-perceptions; for such is what happens in cases of swooning. A swoon means just such impotence of perception, and certain other cases of unconsciousness also are of this nature. Moreover, persons who have the blood-vessels in the neck compressed become insensible. But sleep supervenes when such incapacity of exercise has neither arisen in some casual organ of sense, nor from some chance cause, but [10] when, as has been just stated, it has its seat in the primary organ with which one perceives objects in general. For when this has become powerless all the other sensory organs also must lack power to perceive; but when one of them has become powerless, it is not necessary for this also to lose its power.

We must next state the cause to which it is due, and its quality as an affection. Now, since there are several types of cause (for we [15] assign equally the 'final', the 'efficient', the 'material', and the 'formal' as causes), in the first place, then, as we assert that Nature operates for the sake of an end, and that this end is a *good;* and that to every creature which is endowed by nature with the power to move, but cannot with pleasure to itself move always and continuously, rest is necessary and benefi-[20] cial; and since, taught by experience, men apply to sleep this metaphorical term, calling it a 'rest' [from the strain of movement implied in sense-perception]: we conclude that its end is the conservation of animals. But the waking state is for an animal its highest end, since the exercise of sense-perception or of thought is the highest end for all beings to which either of these appertains; inasmuch as these are best, and the highest end is what is [25] best: whence it follows that sleep belongs of necessity to each animal. I use the term 'necessity' in its conditional sense, meaning that if an animal is to exist and have its own proper nature, it must have certain endowments; and, if these are to belong to it, certain others likewise must belong to it [as their condition].

The next question to be discussed is that of the kind of movement or action, taking place within their bodies, from which the affection [30] of waking or sleeping arises in animals. Now, we must assume that the causes of this affection in all other animals are identical with, or analogous to, those which operate in sanguineous animals; and that the causes operating in sanguineous animals generally are identical with those operating in man. Hence we must consider the entire subject in the light of these instances [afforded by sanguineous 456a animals, especially man]. Now, it has been definitely settled already in another work that sense-perception in animals originates in the same part of the organism in which movement originates. This locus of origination is one of three determinate loci, viz. that which lies midway between the head and the abdomen. This is sanguineous animals is the region of the heart; for all sanguineous animals have [5] a heart; and from this it is that both motion and the controlling sense-perception originate. Now, as regards movement, it is obvious that that of breathing and of the cooling process generally takes its rise there; and it is with a view to the conservation of the [due amount of] heat in this part that nature has formed as she has both the animals which respire, and those which cool themselves by moisture. Of [10] this [cooling process] *per se* we shall treat hereafter. In bloodless animals, and insects, and such as do not respire, the 'connatural spirit' is seen alternately puffed up and subsiding in the part which is in them analogous [to the region of the heart in sanguineous animals]. This is clearly observable in the holoptera [insects with undivided wings] as wasps and bees; also in flies and such creatures. And since [15] to move anything, or do anything, is impossible without strength, and holding the breath produces strength—in creatures which inhale, the holding of that breath which comes from without, but, in creatures which do not respire, of that which is connatural (which explains why winged insects of the class holoptera, when they move, are perceived to make a humming noise, due to the friction of the connatural spirit colliding with the diaphragm); [20] and since movement is, in every animal, attended with some sense-perception, either internal or external, in the primary organ of sense, [we conclude] accordingly that if sleeping and waking are affections of this organ, the place in which, or the organ in which, [25] sleep and waking originate, is self-evident [being that in which movement and sense-perception originate, viz. the heart].

Some persons move in their sleep, and perform many acts like waking acts, but not without a phantasm or an exercise of sense-perception; for a dream is in a certain way a sense-impression. But of them we have to speak later on. Why it is that persons when aroused remember their dreams, but do not remember these acts which are like waking acts, has been already explained in the work 'Of Problems'.

3

[30] The point for consideration next in order to the preceding is:—What are the processes in which the affection of waking and sleeping originates, and whence do they arise? Now, since it is when it has sense-perception that an animal must first *take* food and receive growth, and in all cases food in its ultimate [35] form is, in sanguineous animals, the natural substance blood, or, in bloodless animals, that which is analogous to this; and since the veins are the place of the blood, while the origin of these is the heart—an assertion which is proved by anatomy—it is manifest that, when the external nutriment enters the parts fitted for its reception, the evaporation arising from it enters into the veins, and there, undergoing a change, is converted into blood, [5] and makes its way to their source [the heart]. We have treated of all this when discussing the subject of nutrition, but must here recapitulate what was there said, in order that we may obtain a scientific view of the beginnings of the process, and come to know what exactly happens to the primary organ of sense-perception to account for the occurrence of waking and sleep. For sleep, as has been [10] shown, is not any given impotence of the perceptive faculty; for unconsciousness, a certain form of asphyxia, and swooning, all produce such impotence. Moreover it is an established fact that some persons in a profound trance have still had the imaginative faculty in play. This last point, indeed, gives rise to a difficulty; for if it is conceivable that one who had swooned should in this state fall asleep, the phantasm also which then presented itself to his mind might be regarded as a dream. [15] Persons, too, who have fallen into a deep trance, and have come to be regarded as dead, say many things while in this condition. The same view, however, is to be taken of all these cases, [i.e. that they are not cases of sleeping or dreaming].

As we observed above, sleep is not co-extensive with any and every impotence of the perceptive faculty, but this affection is one which arises from the evaporation attendant upon the [20] process of nutrition. The matter evaporated must be driven onwards to a certain point, then turn back, and change its current to and fro, like a tide-race in a narrow strait. Now, in every animal the hot naturally tends to move [and carry other things] upwards, but when it has reached the parts above [becoming cool],[1] it turns back again, and moves downwards in a mass. This explains why fits of drowsiness are especially apt to come on after meals; for the matter, both the liquid and the [25] corporeal, which is borne upwards in a mass, is then of considerable quantity. When, therefore, this comes to a stand it weighs a person down and causes him to nod, but when it has actually sunk downwards, and by its return has repulsed the hot, sleep comes on, and the animal so affected is presently asleep. A confirmation of this appears from considering [30] the things which induce sleep; they all, whether potable or edible, for instance poppy, mandragora, wine, darnel, produce a heaviness in the head; and persons borne down [by sleepiness] and nodding [drowsily] all seem affected in this way, i.e. they are unable to lift up the head or the eye-lids. And it is after meals especially that sleep comes on like this, for the evaporation from the foods eaten is then copious. It also follows certain forms of fatigue; for fatigue operates as a solvent, and [35] the dissolved matter acts, if not cold, like food prior to digestion. Moreover, some kinds of illness have this same effect; those

---

[1] See 457b 30.

arising from moist and hot secretions, as happens with fever-patients and in cases of lethargy. Extreme youth also has this effect; infants, for example, sleep a great deal, because of the food being all borne upwards—a mark [5] whereof appears in the disproportionately large size of the upper parts compared with the lower during infancy, which is due to the fact that growth predominates in the direction of the former. Hence also they are subject to epileptic seizures; for sleep is like epilepsy, and, [10] in a sense, actually is a seizure of this sort. Accordingly, the beginning of this malady takes place with many during sleep, and their subsequent habitual seizures occur in sleep, not in waking hours. For when the spirit [evaporation] moves upwards in a volume, on its return downwards it distends the veins, and forcibly compresses the passage through which respiration is effected. This explains why wines are not good for infants or for wet nurses (for [15] it makes no difference, doubtless, whether the infants themselves, or their nurses, drink them), but such persons should drink them [if at all] diluted with water and in small quantity. For wine is spirituous, and of all wines the dark more so than any other. The upper parts, in infants, are so filled with nutriment that within five months [after birth] they do not even turn the neck [sc. to raise the head]; for in them, as in persons deeply intoxicated, [20] there is ever a large quantity of moisture ascending. It is reasonable, too, to think that this affection is the cause of the embryo's remaining at rest in the womb at first. Also, as a general rule, persons whose veins are inconspicuous, as well as those who are dwarf-like, or have abnormally large heads, are addicted to sleep. For in the former the veins are narrow, so that it is not easy for the moisture to flow down through them; while in the case of dwarfs and those whose heads are abnormally [25] large, the impetus of the evaporation upwards is excessive. Those [on the contrary] whose veins are large are, thanks to the easy flow through the veins, not addicted to sleep, unless, indeed, they labour under some other affection which counteracts [this easy flow]. Nor are the 'atrabilious' addicted to sleep, for in them the inward region is cooled so that the quantity of evaporation in their case is not great. For this reason they have large appetites, though spare and lean; for their bodily [30] condition is as if they derived no benefit from what they eat. The dark bile, too, being itself naturally cold, cools also the nutrient tract, and the other parts wheresoever such secretion [bile] is potentially present [i.e. tends to be formed].

457^b Hence it is plain from what has been said that sleep is a sort of concentration, or natural recoil, of the hot matter inwards [towards its centre], due to the cause above mentioned. Hence restless movement is a marked feature in the case of a person when drowsy. But where it [the heat in the upper and outer parts] begins to fail, he grows cool, and owing to this cooling process his eye-lids droop. Accordingly [5] [in sleep] the upper and outward parts are cool, but the inward and lower, i.e. the parts at the feet and in the interior of the body, are hot.

Yet one might found a difficulty on the facts that sleep is most oppressive in its onset after meals, and that wine, and other such things, though they possess heating properties, are productive of sleep, for it is not probable that sleep should be a process of cooling while the [10] things that cause sleeping are themselves hot. Is the explanation of this, then, to be found in the fact that, as the stomach when empty is hot, while replenishment cools it by the movement it occasions, so the passages and tracts in the head are cooled as the 'evaporation' ascends thither? Or, as those who have hot water [15] poured on them feel a sudden shiver of cold, just so in the case before us, may it be that, when the hot substance ascends, the cold rallying to meet it cools [the aforesaid parts], deprives their native heat of all its power, and compels it to retire? Moreover, when much food is taken, which [i.e. the nutrient evaporation from which] the hot substance carries upwards, this latter, like a fire when fresh logs are laid upon it, is itself cooled, until the food has been digested.

[20] For, as has been observed elsewhere,[1] sleep comes on when the corporeal element [in the 'evaporation'] is conveyed upwards by the hot, along the veins, to the head. But when that which has been thus carried up can no longer ascend, but is too great in quantity [to do so], it forces the hot back again and flows downwards. Hence it is that men sink down [as they do in sleep] when the heat which tends to keep them erect (man alone, among [25] animals, being naturally erect) is withdrawn; and this, when it befalls them, causes unconsciousness, and afterwards phantasy.

Or are the solutions thus proposed barely conceivable accounts of the refrigeration

---
[1] *On the Parts of Animals*, II, 653^a 10.

which takes place, while, as a matter of fact, the region of the brain is, as stated elsewhere, the main determinant of the matter? For the [30] brain, or in creatures without a brain that which corresponds to it, is of all parts of the body the coolest. Therefore, as moisture turned into vapour by the sun's heat is, when it has ascended to the upper regions, cooled by the coldness of the latter, and becoming condensed, is carried downwards, and turned into 458ᵃ water once more; just so the excrementitious evaporation, when carried up by the heat to the region of the brain, is condensed into a 'phlegm' (which explains why catarrhs are seen to proceed from the head); while that evaporation which is nutrient and not un- [5] wholesome, becoming condensed, descends and cools the hot. The tenuity or narrowness of the veins about the brain itself contributes to its being kept cool, and to its not readily admitting the evaporation. This, then, is a sufficient explanation of the cooling which takes place, despite the fact that the evaporation is exceedingly hot.

[10] A person awakes from sleep when digestion is completed: when the heat, which had been previously forced together in large quantity within a small compass from out the surrounding part, has once more prevailed, and when a separation has been effected between the more corporeal and the purer blood. The finest and purest blood is that contained in the head, while the thickest and most turbid is that in the lower parts. The source of all the [15] blood is, as has been stated both here and elsewhere, the heart. Now of the chambers in the heart the central communicates with each of the two others. Each of the latter again acts as receiver from each, respectively, of the two vessels, called the 'great' and the 'aorta'. It is in the central chamber that the [above-men- [20] tioned] separation takes place. To go into these matters in detail would, however, be more properly the business of a different treatise from the present. Owing to the fact that the blood formed after the assimilation of food is especially in need of separation, sleep [then especially] occurs [and lasts] until the purest part of this blood has been separated off into the upper parts of the body, and the most turbid into the lower parts. When this has taken place animals awake from sleep, being released from the heaviness consequent on taking food. [25] We have now stated the *cause* of sleeping, viz. that it consists in the recoil by the corporeal element, upborne by the connatural heat, in a mass upon the primary sense-organ; we have also stated *what* sleep is, having shown that it is a seizure of the primary sense-organ, rendering it unable to actualize its powers; [30] arising of necessity (for it is impossible for an animal to exist if the conditions which render it an animal be not fulfilled), i.e. for the sake of its conservation; since remission of movement tends to the conservation of animals.

On Dreams

I

458[b] We must, in the next place, investigate the subject of the dream, and first inquire to which of the faculties of the soul it presents itself, i.e. whether the affection is one which pertains to the faculty of intelligence or to that of sense-perception; for these are the only faculties within us by which we acquire knowledge.

If, then, the exercise of the faculty of sight is actual seeing, that of the auditory faculty, hearing, and, in general that of the faculty of sense-perception, perceiving; and if there are [5] some perceptions common to the senses, such as figure, magnitude, motion, &c., while there are others, as colour, sound, taste, peculiar [each to its own sense]; and further, if all creatures, when the eyes are closed in sleep, are unable to see, and the analogous statement is true of the other senses, so that manifestly we perceive nothing when asleep; we may conclude that it is not by sense-perception we perceive a dream.

But neither is it by opinion that we do so. [10] For [in dreams] we not only assert, e.g. that some object approaching is a man or a horse [which would be an exercise of opinion], but that the object is white or beautiful, points on which opinion without sense-perception asserts nothing either truly or falsely. It is, however, a fact that the soul makes such assertions in sleep. We seem to see equally well that the approaching figure is a man, and that it is [15] white. [In dreams], too, we think something else, over and above the dream presentation, just as we do in waking moments when we perceive something; for we often also reason about that which we perceive. So, too, in sleep we sometimes have thoughts other than the mere phantasms immediately before our minds. This would be manifest to any one who should attend and try, immediately on arising from sleep, to remember [his dreaming [20] experiences]. There are cases of persons who have seen such dreams, those, for example, who believe themselves to be mentally arranging a given list of subjects according to the mnemonic rule. They frequently find themselves engaged in something else besides the dream, viz. in setting a phantasm which they envisage into its mnemonic position. Hence it is plain that not every 'phantasm' in sleep is [25] a mere dream-image, and that the further thinking which we perform then is due to an excercise of the faculty of opinion.

So much at least is plain on all these points, viz. that the faculty by which, in waking hours, we are subject to illusion when affected by disease, is identical with that which produces illusory effects in sleep. So, even when persons are in excellent health, and know the facts of the case perfectly well, the sun, nevertheless, appears to them to be only a foot wide. Now, whether the presentative faculty of the [30] soul be identical with, or different from, the faculty of sense-perception, in either case the illusion does not occur without our actually seeing or [otherwise] perceiving something. Even to see wrongly or to hear wrongly can happen only to one who sees or hears something real, though not exactly what he supposes. But we have assumed that in sleep one **459**[a] neither sees, nor hears, nor exercises any sense whatever. Perhaps we may regard it as true that the dreamer sees nothing, yet as false that his faculty of sense-perception is unaffected, the fact being that the sense of seeing and the other senses may possibly be then in a certain way affected, while each of these affections, as duly as when he is awake, gives its impulse in a certain manner to his [primary] [5] faculty of sense, though not in precisely the same manner as when he is awake. Sometimes, too, opinion says [to dreamers] just as to those who are awake, that the object seen is an illusion; at other times it is inhibited, and becomes a mere follower of the phantasm.

It is plain therefore that this affection, which we name 'dreaming', is no mere exercise of opinion or intelligence, but yet is not an af- [10] fection of the faculty of perception in the simple sense. If it were the latter it would be possible [when asleep] to hear and see in the simple sense.

How then, and in what manner, it takes place, is what we have to examine. Let us assume, what is indeed clear enough, that the affection [of dreaming] pertains to sense-perception as surely as sleep itself does. For sleep does not pertain to one organ in animals and dreaming to another; both pertain to the same organ.

[15] But since we have, in our work *On the Soul*,[1] treated of presentation, and the faculty of presentation is identical with that of sense-perception, though the essential notion of a faculty of presentation is different from that of a faculty of sense-perception; and since presentation is the movement set up by a sensory faculty when actually discharging its function, while a dream appears to be a presentation [20] (for a presentation which occurs in sleep —whether simply or in some particular way —is what we call a dream): it manifestly follows that dreaming is an activity of the faculty of sense-perception, but belongs to this faculty *qua* presentative.

2

We can best obtain a scientific view of the nature of the dream and the manner in which it originates by regarding it in the light of the [25] circumstances attending sleep. The objects of sense-perception corresponding to each sensory organ produce sense-perception in us, and the affection due to their operation is present in the organs of sense not only when the perceptions are actualized, but even when they have departed.

What happens in these cases may be compared with what happens in the case of projectiles moving in space. For in the case of these the movement continues even when that [30] which set up the movement is no longer in contact [with the things that are moved]. For that which set them in motion moves a certain portion of air, and this, in turn, being moved excites motion in another portion; and so, accordingly, it is in this way that [the bodies], whether in air or in liquids, continue moving, until they come to a standstill.

459[b] This we must likewise assume to happen in the case of qualitative change; for that part which [for example] has been heated by something hot, heats [in turn] the part next to it, and this propagates the affection continuously onwards until the process has come round to its point of origination. This must also happen [5] in the organ wherein the exercise of sense-perception takes place, since sense-perception, as realized in actual perceiving, is a mode of qualitative change. This explains why the affection continues in the sensory organs, both in their deeper and in their more superficial parts, not merely while they are actually engaged in perceiving, but even after they have ceased to do so. That they do this, indeed, is obvious in cases where we continue for some time engaged in a particular form of perception, for then, when we shift the scene of our perceptive activity, the previous affection remains; for instance, when we have turned our gaze from sunlight into darkness. For the result of this is that one sees nothing, owing to the [10] motion excited by the light still subsisting in our eyes. Also, when we have looked steadily for a long while at one colour, e.g. at white or green, that to which we next transfer our gaze appears to be of the same colour. Again if, after having looked at the sun or some other brilliant object, we close the eyes, then, if we [15] watch carefully, it appears in a right line with the direction of vision (whatever this may be), at first in its own colour; then it changes to crimson, next to purple, until it becomes black and disappears. And also when persons turn away from looking at objects in motion, e.g. rivers, and especially those which flow very rapidly, they find that the visual [20] stimulations still present themselves, for the things really at rest are then seen moving; persons become very deaf after hearing loud noises, and after smelling very strong odours their power of smelling is impaired; and similarly in other cases. These phenomena manifestly take place in the way above described.

That the sensory organs are acutely sensitive to even a slight qualitative difference [in their objects] is shown by what happens in the case [25] of mirrors; a subject to which, even taking it independently, one might devote close consideration and inquiry. At the same time it becomes plain from them that as the eye [in seeing] is affected [by the object seen], so also it produces a certain effect upon it. 'If a woman chances during her menstrual period to look into a highly polished mirror, the surface [30] of it will grow cloudy with a blood-coloured haze. It is very hard to remove this stain from a new mirror, but easier to remove from an older mirror. As we have said before, the cause of this lies in the fact that in the act of sight there occurs not only a passion in the sense organ acted on by the polished surface, but the organ, as an agent, also produces an action, as is proper to a brilliant object. For sight is the property of an organ possessing brilliance and colour. The eyes, therefore, have their [5] proper action as have other parts of the

[1] 427[b] 27–429[a] 9.

body. Because it is natural to the eye to be filled with blood-vessels, a woman's eyes, during the period of menstrual flux and inflammation, will undergo a change, although her husband will not note this since his seed is of the same nature as that of his wife. The surrounding atmosphere, through which operates the action [10] of sight, and which surrounds the mirror also, will undergo a change of the same sort that occurred shortly before in the woman's eyes, and hence the surface of the mirror is likewise affected. And as in the case of a garment, the cleaner it is the more quickly it is soiled, so the same holds true in the case of the mirror. For anything that is clean will show quite clearly a stain that it chances to receive, and the cleanest object shows up even the slightest stain. A bronze mirror, because of its shininess, is especially sensitive to any sort of [15] contact (the movement of the surrounding air acts upon it like a rubbing or pressing or wiping); on that account, therefore, what is clean will show up clearly the slightest touch on its surface. It is hard to cleanse smudges off new mirrors because the stain penetrates deep- [20] ly and is suffused to all parts; it penetrates deeply because the mirror is not a dense medium, and is suffused widely because of the smoothness of the object. On the other hand, in the case of old mirrors, stains do not remain because they do not penetrate deeply, but only smudge the surface.'

From this therefore it is plain that stimulatory motion is set up even by slight differences, and that sense-perception is quick to respond to it; and further that the organ which per- [25] ceives colour is not only affected by its object, but also reacts upon it. Further evidence to the same point is afforded by what takes place in wines, and in the manufacture of unguents. For both oil, when prepared, and wine become rapidly infected by the odours of the [30] things near them; they not only acquire the odours of the things thrown into or mixed with them, but also those of the things which are placed, or which grow, near the vessels containing them.

In order to answer our original question, let 460^b us now, therefore, assume one proposition, which is clear from what precedes, viz. that even when the external object of perception has departed, the impressions it has made persist, and are themselves objects of perception; and [let us assume], besides, that we are easily deceived respecting the operations of sense-perception when we are excited by emotions, and different persons according to their different emotions; for example, the coward [5] when excited by fear, the amorous person by amorous desire; so that, with but little resemblance to go upon, the former thinks he sees his foes approaching, the latter, that he sees the object of his desire; and the more deeply one is under the influence of the emotion, the less similarity is required to give rise to these illusory impressions. Thus too, both in fits of anger, and also in all states of appetite, [10] all men become easily deceived, and more so the more their emotions are excited. This is the reason too why persons in the delirium of fever sometimes think they see animals on their chamber walls, an illusion arising from the faint resemblance to animals of the markings thereon when put together in patterns; and this sometimes corresponds with the emotional states of the sufferers, in such a way that, if the latter be not very ill, they know well enough that it is an illusion; but if the illness [15] is more severe they actually move according to the appearances. The cause of these occurrences is that the faculty in virtue of which the controlling sense judges is not identical with that in virtue of which presentations come before the mind. A proof of this is, that the sun presents itself as only a foot in diameter, though often something else gainsays the [20] presentation. Again, when the fingers are crossed, the one object [placed between them] is felt [by the touch] as two; but yet we deny that it is two; for sight is more authoritative than touch. Yet, if touch stood alone, we should actually have pronounced the one object to be two. The ground of such false judgements is that any appearances whatever present themselves, not only when its object stimulates a sense, but also when the sense by itself alone is stimulated, provided only it be stimu- [25] lated in the same manner as it is by the object. For example, to persons sailing past the land seems to move, when it is really the eye that is being moved by something else [the moving ship].

3

From this it is manifest that the stimulatory movements based upon sensory impressions, whether the latter are derived from external objects or from causes within the body, present [30] themselves not only when persons are awake, but also then, when this affection which is called sleep has come upon them, with even greater impressiveness. For by day, while the senses and the intellect are working together, they (i.e. such movements) are extruded from consciousness or obscured, just as a smaller is beside a larger fire, or as small beside great pains or pleasures, though, as soon as the latter have ceased, even those which are trifling emerge into notice. But by night [i.e. in sleep] owing to the inaction of the particular senses, and their powerlessness to realize themselves, [5] which arises from the reflux of the hot from the exterior parts to the interior, they [i.e. the above 'movements'] are borne in to the head quarters of sense-perception, and there display themselves as the disturbance (of waking life) subsides. We must suppose that, like the little eddies which are being ever formed in rivers, so the sensory movements are each a continuous process, often remaining [10] like what they were when first started, but often, too, broken into other forms by collisions with obstacles. This [last mentioned point], moreover, gives the reason why no dreams occur in sleep immediately after meals, or to sleepers who are extremely young, e.g. to infants. The internal movement in such cases is excessive, owing to the heat generated from the food. Hence, just as in a liquid, if one [15] vehemently disturbs it, sometimes no reflected image appears, while at other times one appears, indeed, but utterly distorted, so as to seem quite unlike its original; while, when once the motion has ceased, the reflected images are clear and plain; in the same manner during sleep the phantasms, or residuary movements, which are based upon the sensory impressions, become sometimes quite obliter- [20] ated by the above described motion when too violent; while at other times the sights are indeed seen, but confused and weird, and the dreams [which then appear] are unhealthy, like those of persons who are atrabilious, or feverish, or intoxicated with wine. For all such affections, being spirituous, cause much commotion and disturbance. In sanguineous animals, in [25] proportion as the blood becomes calm, and as its purer are separated from its less pure elements, the fact that the movement, based on impressions derived from each of the organs of sense, is preserved in its integrity, renders the dreams healthy, causes a [clear] image to present itself, and makes the dreamer think, owing to the effects borne in from the organ of sight, that he actually sees, and owing to those which come from the organ of hearing, that he [30] really hears; and so on with those also which proceed from the other sensory organs. For it is owing to the fact that the movement which reaches the primary organ of sense comes from them, that one even when awake believes himself to see, or hear, or otherwise perceive; just as it is from a belief that the organ of sight is being stimulated, though in reality not so stimulated, that we sometimes erroneously declare ourselves to see, or that, from the fact that touch announces two movements, we think that the one object is two. For, as a rule, the governing sense affirms the report of each particular sense, unless another particular sense, more authoritative, makes a contra- [5] dictory report. In every case an appearance presents itself, but what appears does not in every case seem real, unless when the deciding faculty is inhibited, or does not move with its proper motion. Moreover, as we said that different men are subject to illusions, each according to the different emotion present in him, so it is that the sleeper, owing to sleep, and to the movements then going on in his sensory organs, as well as to the other facts of the sensory [10] process, [is liable to illusion], so that the dream presentation, though but little like it, appears as some actual given thing. For when one is asleep, in proportion as most of the blood sinks inwards to its fountain [the heart], the internal [sensory] movements, some potential, others actual accompany it inwards. They are so related [in general] that, if anything move the blood, some one sensory movement will emerge from it, while if this perishes [15] another will take its place; while to one another also they are related in the same way as the artificial frogs in water which severally rise [in fixed succession] to the surface in the order in which the salt [which keeps them down] becomes dissolved. The residuary movements are like these: they are within the soul potentially, but actualize themselves only when the impediment to their doing so has been relaxed; and according as they are thus set free, they begin to move in the blood which remains in the sensory organs, and which is now but scanty, while they possess verisimilitude after the manner of cloud-shapes, which [20] in their rapid metamorphoses one compares now to human beings and a moment afterwards to centaurs. Each of them is however, as has been said, the remnant of a sensory impression taken when sense was actualizing itself; and when this, the true impression, has departed, its remnant is still immanent, and it is correct to say of it, that though not actually Koriskos, it is like Koriskos. For when the per-

[25] son was actually perceiving, his controlling and judging sensory faculty did not call it Koriskos, but, prompted by this [impression], called the genuine person yonder Koriskos. Accordingly, this sensory impulse, which, when actually perceiving, it [the controlling faculty] so describes (unless completely inhibited by the blood), it now [in dreams], when quasi-perceiving, receives from the movements persisting in the sense-organs, and mistakes it —an impulse that is merely like the true [objective] impression—for the true impression itself, while the effect of sleep is so great that it [30] causes this mistake to pass unnoticed. Accordingly, just as if a finger be inserted beneath the eyeball without being observed, one object will not only present two visual images, 462ᵃ but will create an opinion of its being two objects; while if it [the finger] be observed, the presentation will be the same, but the same opinion will not be formed of it; exactly so it is in states of sleep: if the sleeper perceives that he is asleep, and is conscious of the sleeping state during which the perception comes before his mind, it presents itself still, [5] but something within him speaks to this effect: 'the image of Koriskos presents itself, but the real Koriskos is not present'; for often, when one is asleep, there is something in consciousness which declares that what then presents itself is but a dream. If, however, he is not aware of being asleep, there is nothing which will contradict the testimony of the bare presentation.

That what we here urge is true, i.e. that there are such presentative movements in the sensory organs, any one may convince himself, [10] if he attends to and tries to remember the affections we experience when sinking into slumber or when being awakened. He will sometimes, in the moment of awakening, surprise the images which present themselves to him in sleep, and find that they are really but movements lurking in the organs of sense. And indeed some very young persons, if it is dark, though looking with wide open eyes, see multitudes of phantom figures moving before them, so that they often cover up their heads in terror.

[15] From all this, then, the conclusion to be drawn is, that the dream is a sort of presentation, and, more particularly, one which occurs in sleep; since the phantoms just mentioned are not dreams, nor is any other a dream which presents itself when the sense-perceptions are in a state of freedom. Nor is every presentation which occurs in sleep necessarily a dream. For in the first place, some persons [when [20] asleep] actually, in a certain way, perceive sounds, light, savour, and contact; feebly, however, and, as it were, remotely. For there have been cases in which persons while asleep, but with the eyes partly open, saw faintly in their sleep (as they supposed) the light of a lamp, and afterwards, on being awakened, straightway recognized it as the actual light of a real lamp; while, in other cases, persons who faintly heard the crowing of cocks or the bark- [25] ing of dogs identified these clearly with the real sounds as soon as they awoke. Some persons, too, return answers to questions put to them in sleep. For it is quite possible that, of waking or sleeping, while the one is present in the ordinary sense, the other also should be present in a certain way. But none of these occurrences should be called a dream. Nor should the true thoughts, as distinct from the mere presentations, which occur in sleep [be called dreams]. The dream proper is a presentation [30] based on the movement of sense impressions, when such presentation occurs during sleep, taking sleep in the strict sense of the term.

There are cases of persons who in their whole lives have never had a dream, while others dream when considerably advanced in years, having never dreamed before. The cause of their not having dreams appears somewhat like that which operates in the case of infants, and [that which operates] immediately after meals. It is intelligible enough that no [5] dream-presentation should occur to persons whose natural constitution is such that in them copious evaporation is borne upwards, which, when borne back downwards, causes a large quantity of motion. But it is not surprising that, as age advances, a dream should at length appear to them. Indeed, it is inevitable [10] that, as a change is wrought in them in proportion to age or emotional experience, this reversal [from non-dreaming to dreaming] should occur also.

On Prophesying by Dreams

I

As to the divination which takes place in sleep, and is said to be based on dreams, we cannot lightly either dismiss it with contempt or give it implicit confidence. The fact that all persons, or many, suppose dreams to possess a special significance, tends to inspire us with be- [15] lief in it [such divination], as founded on the testimony of experience; and indeed that divination in dreams should, as regards some subjects, be genuine, is not incredible, for it has a show of reason; from which one might form a like opinion also respecting all other dreams. Yet the fact of our seeing no probable cause to account for such divination tends to inspire us [20] with distrust. For, in addition to its further unreasonableness, it is absurd to combine the idea that the sender of such dreams should be God with the fact that those to whom he sends them are not the best and wisest, but merely commonplace persons. If, however, we abstract from the causality of God, none of the other causes assigned appears probable. For that certain persons should have foresight in dreams concerning things destined to take place at the Pillars of Hercules, or on the [25] banks of the Borysthenes, seems to be something to discover the explanation of which surpasses the wit of man. Well then, the dreams in question must be regarded either as *causes*, or as *tokens*, of the events, or else as *coincidences*; either as all, or some, of these, or as one only. I use the word 'cause' in the sense in which the moon is [the cause] of an eclipse of the sun, or in which fatigue is [a cause] of fe- [30] ver; 'token' [in the sense in which] the entrance of a star [into the shadow] is a token of the eclipse, or [in which] roughness of the tongue [is a token] of fever; while by 'coincidence' I mean, for example, the occurrence of an eclipse of the sun while some one is taking a walk; for the walking is neither a token nor 463ᵃ a cause of the eclipse, nor the eclipse [a cause or token] of the walking. For this reason no coincidence takes place according to a universal or general rule. Are we then to say that some dreams are causes, others tokens, e.g. of events taking place in the bodily organism? At all events, even scientific physicians tell us [5] that one should pay diligent attention to dreams, and to hold this view is reasonable also for those who are not practitioners, but speculative philosophers. For the movements which occur in the daytime [within the body] are, unless very great and violent, lost sight of in contrast with the waking movements, which [10] are more impressive. In sleep the opposite takes place, for then even trifling movements seem considerable. This is plain in what often happens during sleep; for example, dreamers fancy that they are affected by thunder and lightning, when in fact there are only faint ringings in their ears; or that they are enjoying honey or other sweet savours, when only a tiny drop of phlegm is flowing down [15] [the oesophagus]; or that they are walking through fire, and feeling intense heat, when there is only a slight warmth affecting certain parts of the body. When they are awakened, these things appear to them in this their true character. But since the beginnings of all events are small, so, it is clear, are those also of the diseases or other affections about to occur [20] in our bodies. In conclusion, it is manifest that these beginnings must be more evident in sleeping than in waking moments.

Nay, indeed, it is not improbable that some of the presentations which come before the mind in sleep may even be causes of the actions cognate to each of them. For as when we are about to act [in waking hours], or are engaged in any course of action, or have already performed certain actions, we often find our- [25] selves concerned with these actions, or performing them, in a vivid dream; the cause whereof is that the dream-movement has had a way paved for it from the original movements set up in the daytime; exactly so, but conversely, it must happen that the movements set up first in sleep should also prove to be starting-points of actions to be performed in the daytime, since the recurrence by day of the thought of these actions also has had its way [30] paved for it in the images before the mind at night. Thus then it is quite conceivable that some dreams may be tokens and causes [of future events].

Most [so-called prophetic] dreams are, how- 463ᵇ ever, to be classed as mere coincidences, especially all such as are extravagant, and those in the fulfilment of which the dreamers have no initiative, such as in the case of a sea-fight, or of things taking place far away. As regards these it is natural that the fact should stand as it does whenever a person, on mentioning [5] something, finds the very thing mentioned come to pass. Why, indeed, should this not happen also in sleep? The probability is, rather, that many such things should happen. As, then, one's mentioning a particular person is neither token nor cause of this person's presenting himself, so, in the parallel instance, the dream is, to him who has seen it, neither token nor cause of its [so-called] fulfilment, but a mere coincidence. Hence the fact that many dreams have no 'fulfilment', for coincidences [10] do not occur according to any universal or general law.

2

On the whole, forasmuch as certain of the lower animals also dream, it may be concluded that dreams are not sent by God, nor are they designed for this purpose [to reveal the future]. They have a divine aspect, however, for Nature [their cause] is divinely planned, [15] though not itself divine. A special proof [of their not being sent by God] is this: the power of foreseeing the future and of having vivid dreams is found in persons of inferior type, which implies that God does not send their dreams; but merely that all those whose physical temperament is, as it were, garrulous and excitable, see sights of all descriptions; for, inasmuch as they experience many movements of every kind, they just chance to have visions resembling objective facts, their luck in these [20] matters being merely like that of persons who play at even and odd. For the principle which is expressed in the gambler's maxim: 'If you make many throws your luck must change,' holds good in their case also.

That many dreams have no fulfilment is not strange, for it is so too with many bodily symptoms and weather-signs, e.g. those of [25] rain or wind. For if another movement occurs more influential than that from which, while [the event to which it pointed was] still future, the given token was derived, the event [to which such token pointed] does not take place. So, of the things which ought to be accomplished by human agency, many, though well-planned, are by the operation of other principles more powerful [than man's agency] brought to nought. For, speaking generally, that which *was* about to happen is not in every case what now *is happening;* nor is that which *shall* hereafter *be* identical with that which *is* now *going to* be. Still, however, we must hold [30] that the beginnings from which, as we said, no consummation follows, are *real* beginnings, and these constitute natural tokens of certain events, even though the events do not come to pass.

As for [prophetic] dreams which involve not such beginnings [sc. of future events] as we have here described, but such as are extravagant in times, or places, or magnitudes; or **464ᵃ** those involving beginnings which are not extravagant in any of these respects, while yet the persons who see the dream hold not in their own hands the beginnings [of the event to which it points]: unless the foresight which such dreams give is the result of pure coincidence, the following would be a better explanation of it than that proposed by Democritus, [5] who alleges 'images' and 'emanations' as its cause. As, when something has caused motion in water or air, this [the portion moved] moves another [portion of water or air], and, though the cause has ceased to operate, such motion propagates itself to a certain point, though there the prime movement is not present; just so it may well be that a movement and a consequent sense-perception should reach [10] sleeping souls from the objects from which Democritus represents 'images' and 'emanations' as coming; that such movements, in whatever way they arrive, should be more perceptible at night [than by day], because when proceeding thus in the daytime they are more liable to dissolution (since at night the air is less disturbed, there being then less [15] wind); and that they shall be perceived within the body owing to sleep, since persons are more sensitive even to slight sensory movements when asleep than when awake. It is these movements then that cause 'presentations', as a result of which sleepers foresee the future even relatively to such events as those referred[1] to above. These considerations also [20] explain why this experience befalls commonplace persons and not the most intelligent. For it would have regularly occurred both in the daytime and to the wise had it been God who sent it; but, as we have explained the matter, it is quite natural that commonplace persons should be those who have foresight [in dreams]. For the mind of such persons is not given to thinking, but, as it were, derelict, or

[1] I.e. those referred to 464ᵃ 1-4.

totally vacant, and, when once set moving, is borne passively on in the direction taken by that which moves it. With regard to the fact [25] that some persons who are liable to derangement have this foresight, its explanation is that their normal mental movements do not impede [the alien movements], but are beaten off by the latter. Therefore it is that they have an especially keen perception of the alien movements.

That certain persons in particular should have vivid dreams, e.g. that familiar friends should thus have foresight in a special degree respecting one another, is due to the fact that such friends are most solicitous on one another's behalf. For as acquaintances in particular [30] recognize and perceive one another a long way off, so also they do as regards the sensory movements respecting one another; for sensory movements which refer to persons familiarly known are themselves more familiar. Atrabilious persons, owing to their impetuosity, are, when they, as it were, shoot from a distance, expert at hitting; while, owing to their mutability, the series of movements deploys quickly before their minds. For even as the insane recite, or con over in thought, the poems of Philaegides, e.g. the Aphrodite, whose parts succeed in order of similitude, just so do they [the 'atrabilious'] go on and on stringing sensory movements together. Moreover, owing to their aforesaid impetuosity, one movement [5] within them is not liable to be knocked out of its course by some other movement.

The most skilful interpreter of dreams is he who has the faculty of observing resemblances. Any one may interpret dreams which are vivid and plain. But, speaking of 'resemblances', I mean that dream presentations are analogous to the forms reflected in water, as indeed we have already stated. In the latter case, if the [10] motion in the water be great, the reflexion has no resemblance to its original, nor do the forms resemble the real objects. Skilful, indeed, would he be in interpreting such reflexions who could rapidly discern, and at a glance comprehend, the scattered and distorted fragments of such forms, so as to perceive that one of them represents a man, or a horse, [15] or anything whatever. Accordingly, in the other case also, in a similar way, some such thing as this [blurred image] is all that a dream amounts to; for the internal movement effaces the clearness of the dream.

The questions, therefore, which we proposed as to the nature of sleep and the dream, and the cause to which each of them is due, and also as to divination as a result of dreams, in every form of it, have now been discussed.

On Longevity and Shortness of Life

1

THE reasons for some animals being long-lived and others short-lived, and, in a word, [20] the causes of the length and brevity of life call for investigation.

The necessary beginning to our inquiry is a statement of the difficulties about these points. For it is not clear whether in animals and plants universally it is a single or diverse cause that makes some to be long-lived, others [25] short-lived. Plants too have in some cases a long life, while in others it lasts but for a year.

Further, in a natural structure are longevity and a sound constitution coincident, or is shortness of life independent of unhealthiness? Perhaps in the case of certain maladies a diseased state of the body and shortness of life are [30] interchangeable, while in the case of others ill-health is perfectly compatible with long life.

Of sleep and waking we have already treated; about life and death we shall speak later on, and likewise about health and disease, in so far as it belongs to the science of nature to 465ª do so. But at present we have to investigate the causes of some creatures being long-lived, and others short-lived. We find this distinction affecting not only entire genera opposed as wholes to one another, but applying also to contrasted sets of individuals within the same species. As an instance of the difference [5] applying to the genus I give man and horse (for mankind has a longer life than the horse), while within the species there is the difference between man and man; for of men also some are long-lived, others short-lived, differing from each other in respect of the different regions in which they dwell. Races inhabiting warm [10] countries have longer life, those living in a cold climate live a shorter time. Likewise there are similar differences among individuals occupying the same locality.

2

In order to find premisses for our argument, we must answer the question, What is that which, in natural objects, makes them easily destroyed, or the reverse? Since fire and water, [15] and whatsoever is akin thereto, do not possess identical powers they are reciprocal causes of generation and decay. Hence it is natural to infer that everything else arising from them and composed of them should share in the same nature, in all cases where things are not, like a house, a composite unity formed by the synthesis of many things.

In other matters a different account must be given; for in many things their mode of dissolution is something peculiar to themselves, e.g. [20] in knowledge and health and disease. These pass away even though the medium in which they are found is not destroyed but continues to exist; for example, take the termination of ignorance, which is recollection or learning, while knowledge passes away into forgetfulness, or error. But accidentally the disintegration of a natural object is accompanied by the destruction of the non-physical re- [25] ality; for, when the animal dies, the health or knowledge resident in it passes away too. Hence from these considerations we may draw a conclusion about the soul too; for, if the inherence of soul in body is not a matter of nature but like that of knowledge in the soul, there would be another mode of dissolution pertaining to it besides that which occurs [30] when the body is destroyed. But since evidently it does not admit of this dual dissolution, the soul must stand in a different case in respect of its union with the body.

3

465ᵇ Perhaps one might reasonably raise the question whether there is any place where what is corruptible becomes incorruptible, as fire does in the upper regions where it meets with no opposite. Opposites destroy each other, and hence accidentally, by their destruction, [5] whatsoever is attributed to them is destroyed. But no opposite in a real substance is accidentally destroyed, because real substance is not predicated of any subject. Hence a thing which has no opposite, or which is situated where it has no opposite, cannot be destroyed. For what will that be which can destroy it, if destruction comes only through contraries, but [10] no contrary to it exists either absolutely or in the particular place where it is? But perhaps this is in one sense true, in another sense not true, for it is impossible that anything containing matter should not have in any sense an opposite. Heat and straightness can be present in every part of a thing, but it is impossible that the thing should be nothing but hot or white or straight; for, if that were so, attributes would have an independent existence. [15] Hence if, in all cases, whenever the active and the passive exist together, the one acts and the other is acted on, it is impossible that no change should occur. Further, this is so if a waste product is an opposite, and waste must always be produced; for opposition is always the source of change, and *refuse* is what remains of the previous opposite. But, after expelling everything of a nature actually opposed, would an object in this case also be im-[20] perishable? No, it would be destroyed by the environment.

If then that is so, what we have said sufficiently accounts for the change; but, if not, we must assume that something of actually opposite character is in the changing object, and refuse is produced.

Hence accidentally a lesser flame is consumed by a greater one, for the nutriment, to [25] wit the smoke, which the former takes a long period to expend, is used up by the big flame quickly.

Hence [too] all things are at all times in a state of transition and are coming into being and passing away. The environment acts on them either favourably or antagonistically, and, owing to this, things that change their situation become more or less enduring than their nature warrants, but never are they eternal when they contain contrary qualities; for [30] their matter is an immediate source of contrariety, so that if it involves locality they show change of situation, if quantity, increase and diminution, while if it involves qualitative affection we find alteration of character.

4

466ᵃ We find that a superior immunity from decay attaches neither to the largest animals (the horse has shorter life than man) nor to those that are small (for most insects live but for a year). Nor are plants as a whole less liable to perish than animals (many plants are annuals), nor have sanguineous animals the pre-eminence (for the bee is longer-lived than [5] certain sanguineous animals). Neither is it the bloodless animals that live longest (for molluscs live only a year, though bloodless), nor terrestrial organisms (there are both plants and terrestrial animals of which a single year is the period), nor the occupants of the sea (for there we find the crustaceans and the molluscs, which are short-lived).

Speaking generally, the longest-lived things occur among the plants, e.g. the date-palm. [10] Next in order we find them among the sanguineous animals rather than among the bloodless, and among those with feet rather than among the denizens of the water. Hence, taking these two characters together, the longest-lived animals fall among sanguineous animals which have feet, e.g. man and elephant. As a matter of fact also it is a general rule that [15] the larger live longer than the smaller, for the other long-lived animals too happen to be of a large size, as are also those I have mentioned.

5

The following considerations may enable us to understand the reasons for all these facts. We must remember that an animal is by na-[20] ture humid and warm, and to live is to be of such a constitution, while old age is dry and cold, and so is a corpse. This is plain to observation. But the material constituting the bodies of all things consists of the following—the hot and the cold, the dry and the moist. Hence when they age they must become dry, and therefore the fluid in them requires to be not easily dried up. Thus we explain why fat things are not liable to decay. The reason is that they contain air; now air relatively to the [25] other elements is fire, and fire never becomes corrupted.

Again the humid element in animals must not be small in quantity, for a small quantity is easily dried up. This is why both plants and animals that are large are, as a general rule, longer-lived than the rest, as was said before; it is to be expected that the larger should contain more moisture. But it is not merely this that makes them longer lived; for the cause is [30] twofold, to wit, the quality as well as the quantity of the fluid. Hence the moisture must be not only great in amount but also warm, in order to be neither easily congealed nor easily dried up.

It is for this reason also that man lives longer than some animals which are larger; for animals live longer though there is a deficiency in 466ᵇ the amount of their moisture, if the ratio of its qualitative superiority exceeds that of its quantitative deficiency.

In some creatures the warm element is their fatty substance, which prevents at once desiccation and congelation; but in others it assumes a different flavour. Further, that which is designed to be not easily destroyed should [5] not yield waste products. Anything of such a nature causes death either by disease or naturally, for the potency of the waste product works adversely and destroys now the entire constitution, now a particular member.

This is why salacious animals and those abounding in seed age quickly; the seed is a residue, and further, by being lost, it produces dryness. Hence the mule lives longer than either the horse or the ass from which it sprang, [10] and females live longer than males if the males are salacious. Accordingly cock-sparrows have a shorter life than the females. Again males subject to great toil are short-lived and age more quickly owing to the labour; toil produces dryness and old age is dry. But by natural constitution and as a general [15] rule males live longer than females, and the reason is that the male is an animal with more warmth than the female.

The same kind of animals are longer-lived in warm than in cold climates for the same reason, on account of which they are of larger size. The size of animals of cold constitution [20] illustrates this particularly well, and hence snakes and lizards and scaly reptiles are of great size in warm localities, as also are testacea in the Red Sea: the warm humidity there is the cause equally of their augmented size and of their life. But in cold countries the humidity in animals is more of a watery nature, and hence is readily congealed. Consequently it [25] happens that animals with little or no blood are in northerly regions either entirely absent (both the land animals with feet and the water creatures whose home is the sea) or, when they do occur, they are smaller and have shorter life; for the frost prevents growth.

Both plants and animals perish if not fed, for in that case they consume themselves; just [30] as a large flame consumes and burns up a small one by using up its nutriment, so the natural warmth which is the primary cause of digestion consumes the material in which it is located.

Water animals have a shorter life than terrestrial creatures, not strictly because they are 467ª humid, but because they are watery, and watery moisture is easily destroyed, since it is cold and readily congealed. For the same reason bloodless animals perish readily unless protected by great size, for there is neither fatness nor sweetness about them. In animals fat [5] is sweet, and hence bees are longer-lived than other animals of larger size.

6

It is amongst the plants that we find the longest life—more than among the animals, for, in the first place, they are less watery and hence less easily frozen. Further they have an oiliness and a viscosity which makes them retain their moisture in a form not easily dried up, even though they are dry and earthy.
[10] But we must discover the reason why trees are of an enduring constitution, for it is peculiar to them and is not found in any animals except the insects.

Plants continually renew themselves and hence last for a long time. New shoots continually come and the others grow old, and with the roots the same thing happens. But both processes do not occur together. Rather it happens that at one time the trunk and the [15] branches alone die and new ones grow up beside them, and it is only when this has taken place that the fresh roots spring from the surviving part. Thus it continues, one part dying and the other growing, and hence also it lives a long time.

There is a similarity, as has been already said, between plants and insects, for they live, though divided, and two or more may be de- [20] rived from a single one. Insects, however, though managing to live, are not able to do so long, for they do not possess organs; nor can the principle resident in each of the separated parts create organs. In the case of a plant, however, it can do so; every part of a plant contains potentially both root and stem. Hence it is from this source that issues that continued [25] growth when one part is renewed and the other grows old; it is practically a case of longevity. The taking of slips furnishes a similar instance, for we might say that, in a way, when we take a slip the same thing happens; the shoot cut off is part of the plant. Thus in taking slips this perpetuation of life occurs though their connexion with the plant is severed, but in the former case it is the continuity that is operative. The reason is that the life [30] principle potentially belonging to them is present in every part.

Identical phenomena are found both in plants and in animals. For in animals the males are, in general, the longer-lived. They have their upper parts larger than the lower (the male is more of the dwarf type of build than the female), and it is in the upper part that warmth resides, in the lower cold. In plants also those with great heads are longer-lived, and such are those that are not annual but of the tree-type, for the roots are the head and upper part of a plant, and among the annuals growth occurs in the direction of their lower parts and the fruit.

These matters however will be specially in- [5] vestigated in the work *On Plants*. But this is our account of the reasons for the duration of life and for short life in animals. It remains for us to discuss youth and age, and life and death. To come to a definite understanding about these matters would complete our course of study on animals.

• • •

On Youth and Old Age, On Life and Death, On Breathing

1

[10] We must now treat of youth and old age and life and death. We must probably also at the same time state the causes of respiration as well, since in some cases living and the reverse depend on this.

We have elsewhere given a precise account of the soul, and while it is clear that its essential reality cannot be corporeal, yet manifestly [15] it must exist in some bodily part which must be one of those possessing control over the members. Let us for the present set aside the other divisions or faculties of the soul (whichever of the two be the correct name). But as to being what is called an animal and a living thing, we find that in all beings endowed with both characteristics (viz. being an animal [20] and being alive) there must be a single identical part in virtue of which they live and are called animals; for an animal *qua* animal cannot avoid being alive. But a thing need not, though alive, be animal, for plants live without having sensation, and it is by sensation that [25] we distinguish animal from what is not animal.

This organ, then, must be numerically one and the same and yet possess multiple and disparate aspects, for being animal and living are not identical. Since then the organs of special sensation have one common organ in which the senses when functioning must meet, and [30] this must be situated midway between what is called before and behind (we call 'before' the direction from which sensation comes, 'behind' the opposite), further, since in all living things the body is divided into upper and lower (they all have upper and lower parts, so that this is true of plants as well), clearly the nutritive principle must be situated midway 468ª between these regions. That part where food enters we call upper, considering it by itself and not relatively to the surrounding universe, while downward is that part by which the primary excrement is discharged.

[5] Plants are the reverse of animals in this respect. To man in particular among the animals, on account of his erect stature, belongs the characteristic of having his upper parts pointing upwards in the sense in which that applies to the universe, while in the others these are in an intermediate position. But in plants, owing to their being stationary and drawing their sustenance from the ground, the upper part must always be down; for there is a correspondence between the roots in a [10] plant and what is called the mouth in animals, by means of which they take in their food, whether the source of supply be the earth or each other's bodies.

2

All perfectly formed animals are to be divided into three parts, one that by which food is taken in, one that by which excrement is dis-[15] charged, and the third the region intermediate between them. In the largest animals this latter is called the chest and in the others something corresponding; in some also it is more distinctly marked off than in others. All those also that are capable of progression have additional members subservient to this purpose, by means of which they bear the whole trunk, to wit legs and feet and whatever parts [20] are possessed of the same powers. Now it is evident both by observation and by inference that the source of the nutritive soul is in the midst of the three parts. For many animals, when either part—the head or the receptacle [25] of the food—is cut off, retain life in that member to which the middle remains attached. This can be seen to occur in many insects, e.g. wasps and bees, and many animals also besides insects can, though divided, continue to live by means of the part connected with nutrition.

While this member is indeed in actuality single, yet potentially it is multiple, for these animals have a constitution similar to that of [30] plants; plants when cut into sections continue to live, and a number of trees can be derived from one single source. A separate account will be given of the reason why some plants cannot live when divided, while others 468ᵇ can be propagated by the taking of slips. In this respect, however, plants and insects are alike.

714

It is true that the nutritive soul, in beings possessing it, while actually single must be potentially plural. And so it is too with the principle of sensation, for evidently the divided [5] segments of these animals have sensation. They are unable, however, to preserve their constitution, as plants can, not possessing the organs on which the continuance of life depends, for some lack the means for seizing, others for receiving their food; or again they may be destitute of other organs as well.

Divisible animals are like a number of animals grown together, but animals of superior [10] construction behave differently because their constitution is a unity of the highest possible kind. Hence some of the organs on division display slight sensitiveness because they retain some psychical susceptibility; the animals continue to move after the vitals have [15] been abstracted: tortoises, for example, do so even after the heart has been removed.

3

The same phenomenon is evident both in plants and in animals, and in plants we note it both in their propagation by seed and in grafts and cuttings. Genesis from seeds always starts from the middle. All seeds are bivalvular, and [20] the place of junction is situated at the point of attachment (to the plant), an intermediate part belonging to both halves. It is from this part that both root and stem of growing things emerge; the starting-point is in a central position between them. In the case of grafts and cuttings this is particularly true of the buds; for the bud is in a way the starting-point of the branch, but at the same time it is [25] in a central position. Hence it is either this that is cut off, or into this that the new shoot is inserted, when we wish either a new branch or a new root to spring from it; which proves that the point of origin in growth is intermediate between stem and root.

Likewise in sanguineous animals the heart is the first organ developed; this is evident from what has been observed in those cases where observation of their growth is possible. [30] Hence in bloodless animals also what corresponds to the heart must develop first. We have already asserted in our treatise on *The Parts of Animals*[1] that it is from the heart 469ª that the veins issue, and that in sanguineous animals the blood is the final nutriment from which the members are formed. Hence it is clear that there is one function in nutrition

[1] Cf. *On the Parts of Animals*, III, 665ᵇ 15.

which the mouth has the faculty of performing, and a different one appertaining to the stomach. But it is the heart that has supreme control, exercising an additional and completing function. Hence in sanguineous animals [5] the source both of the sensitive and of the nutritive soul must be in the heart, for the functons relative to nutrition exercised by the other parts are ancillary to the activity of the heart. It is the part of the dominating organ to achieve the final result, as of the physician's efforts to be directed towards health, and not to be occupied with subordinate offices.

[10] Certainly, however, all saguineous animals have the supreme organ of the sense-faculties in the heart, for it is here that we must look for the common sensorium belonging to all the sense-organs. These in two cases, taste and touch, can be clearly seen to extend to the heart, and hence the others also must [15] lead to it, for in it the other organs may possibly initiate changes, whereas with the upper region of the body taste and touch have no connexion. Apart from these considerations, if the life is always located in this part, evidently the principle of sensation must be situated there too, for it is *qua* animal that an animal is said to be a living thing, and it is called animal because endowed with sensation. [20] Elsewhere in other works[2] we have stated the reasons why some of the sense-organs are, as is evident, connected with the heart, while others are situated in the head. (It is this fact that causes some people to think that it is in virtue of the brain that the function of perception belongs to animals.)

4

Thus if, on the one hand, we look to the observed facts, what we have said makes it clear that the source of the sensitive soul, together with that connected with growth and nutri- [25] tion, is situated in this organ and in the central one of the three divisions of the body. But it follows by deduction also; for we see that in every case, when several results are open to her, Nature always brings to pass the best. Now if both principles are located in the [30] midst of the substance, the two parts of the body, viz. that which elaborates and that which receives the nutriment in its final form will best perform their appropriate function; for the soul will then be close to each, and the central situation which it will, as such, occupy is the position of a dominating power.

[2] *Ibid.*, II, 656ᵇ 5.

469[b] Further, that which employs an instrument and the instrument it employs must be distinct (and must be spatially diverse too, if possible, as in capacity), just as the flute and that which plays it—the hand—are diverse. Thus if animal is defined by the possession of sensitive soul, this soul must in the sanguin-[5] eous animals be in the heart, and, in the bloodless ones, in the corresponding part of their body. But in animals all the members and the whole body possess some connate warmth of constitution, and hence when alive they are observed to be warm, but when dead and deprived of life they are the opposite. In-[10] deed, the source of this warmth must be in the heart in sanguineous animals, and in the case of bloodless animals in the corresponding organ, for, though all parts of the body by means of their natural heat elaborate and concoct the nutriment, the governing organ takes the chief share in this process. Hence, though the other members become cold, life remains; but when the warmth here is quenched, death always ensues, because the source of heat in all the other members de-[15] pends on this, and the soul is, as it were, set aglow with fire in this part, which in sanguineous animals is the heart and in the bloodless order the analogous member. Hence, of necessity, life must be coincident with the maintenance of heat, and what we call death [20] is its destruction.

5

However, it is to be noticed that there are two ways in which fire ceases to exist; it may go out either by exhaustion or by extinction. That which is self-caused we call exhaustion, that due to its opposites extinction. [The former is that due to old age, the latter to violence.] But either of these ways in which fire ceases to be may be brought about by the same cause, for, when there is a deficiency of nutri-[25] ment and the warmth can obtain no maintenance, the fire fails; and the reason is that the opposite, checking digestion, prevents the fire from being fed. But in other cases the result is exhaustion,—when the heat accumulates excessively owing to lack of respiration and of refrigeration. For in this case what happens is that the heat, accumulating in great quantity, quickly uses up its nutriment and [30] consumes it all before more is sent up by evaporation. Hence not only is a smaller fire readily put out by a large one, but of itself the candle flame is consumed when inserted in a 470[a] large blaze, just as is the case with any other combustible. The reason is that the nutriment in the flame is seized by the larger one before fresh fuel can be added, for fire is ever coming into being and rushing just like a river, but so speedily as to elude observation.

[5] Clearly therefore, if the bodily heat must be conserved (as is necessary if life is to continue), there must be some way of cooling the heat resident in the source of warmth. Take as an illustration what occurs when coals are confined in a brazier. If they are kept covered up continuously by the so-called 'choker', they are [10] quickly extinguished, but, if the lid is in rapid alternation lifted up and put on again they remain glowing for a long time. Banking up a fire also keeps it in, for the ashes, being porous, do not prevent the passage of air, and again they enable it to resist extinction by the surrounding air by means of the supply of heat which it possesses. However, we have stated [15] in *The Problems* the reasons why these operations, namely banking up and covering up a fire, have the opposite effects (in the one case the fire goes out, in the other it continues alive for a considerable time).

6

[20] Everything living has soul, and it, as we have said, cannot exist without the presence of heat in the constitution. In plants the natural heat is sufficiently well kept alive by the aid which their nutriment and the surrounding air supply. For the food has a cooling effect [as it enters, just as it has in man] when first it is taken in, whereas abstinence from food pro-[25] duces heat and thirst. The air, if it be motionless, becomes hot, but by the entry of food a motion is set up which lasts until digestion is completed and so cools it. If the surrounding air is excessively cold owing to the time of year, there being severe frost, plants shrivel, or if, in the extreme heats of summer the moisture drawn from the ground cannot [30] produce its cooling effect, the heat comes to an end by exhaustion. Trees suffering at such seasons are said to be blighted or starstricken. Hence the practice of laying beneath the roots stones of certain species or water in pots, for the purpose of cooling the roots of the plants.

470[b] Some animals pass their life in the water, others in the air, and therefore these media furnish the source and means of refrigeration, water in the one case, air in the other. We must proceed—and it will require further application on our part—to give an account of [5] the way and manner in which this refrigeration occurs.

(Chapter 1 of that part which deals specially with Breathing)

7

A few of the previous physical philosophers have spoken of respiration. The reason, however, why it exists in animals they have either not declared or, when they have, their statements are not correct and show a comparative lack of acquaintance with the facts. Moreover they assert that all animals respire—which is [10] untrue. Hence these points must first claim our attention, in order that we may not be thought to make unsubstantiated charges against authors no longer alive.

First then, it is evident that all animals with lungs breathe, but in some cases breathing animals have a bloodless and spongy lung, and then there is less need for respiration. These [15] animals can remain under water for a time, which relatively to their bodily strength, is considerable. All oviparous animals, e.g. the frog-tribe, have a spongy lung. Also hemydes and tortoises can remain for a long time immersed [20] in water; for their lung, containing little blood, has not much heat. Hence, when once it is inflated, it itself, by means of its motion, produces a cooling effect and enables the animal to remain immersed for a long time. Suffocation, however, always ensues if the animal is forced to hold its breath for too long a time, for none of this class take in water in the way fishes do. On the other hand, animals which have the lung charged [25] with blood have greater need of respiration on account of the amount of their heat, while none at all of the others which do not possess lungs breathe.

8 (2)

Democritus of Abdera and certain others who have treated of respiration, while saying nothing definite about the lungless animals, [30] nevertheless seem to speak as if all breathed. But Anaxagoras and Diogenes both maintain that all breathe, and state the manner in which fishes and oysters respire. Anaxagoras says that when fishes discharge water through their gills, air is formed in the mouth, 471ᵃ for there can be no vacuum, and that it is by drawing in this that they respire. Diogenes' statement is that, when they discharge water through their gills, they suck the air out of the water surrounding the mouth by means of the vacuum formed in the mouth, for he believes there is air in the water.

[5] But these theories are untenable. Firstly, they state only what is the common element in both operations and so leave out the half of the matter. For what goes by the name of respiration consists, on the one hand, of inhalation, and, on the other, of the exhalation of breath; but, about the latter they say nothing, nor do they describe how such animals emit their breath. Indeed, explanation is for them [10] impossible for, when the creatures respire, they must discharge their breath by the same passage as that by which they draw it in, and this must happen in alternation. Hence, as a result, they must take the water into their mouth at the same time as they breathe out. But the air and the water must meet and obstruct each other. Further, when they discharge the water they must emit their breath [15] by the mouth or the gills, and the result will be that they will breathe in and breathe out at the same time, for it is at that moment that respiration is said to occur. But it is impossible that they should do both at the same time. Hence, if respiring creatures must both exhale and inhale the air, and if none of these animals can breathe out, evidently none can respire at all.

9 (3)

[20] Further, the assertion that they draw in air out of the mouth or out of the water by means of the mouth is an impossibility, for, not having a lung, they have no windpipe; rather the stomach is closely juxtaposed to the mouth, so that they must do the sucking with the stomach. But in that case the other animals would do so also, which is not the truth; and the water-animals also would be seen to do it [25] when out of the water, whereas quite evidently they do not. Further, in all animals that respire and draw breath there is to be observed a certain motion in the part of the body which draws in the air, but in the fishes this does not occur. Fishes do not appear to move any of the parts in the region of the stomach, except the gills alone, and these move both when they are in the water and when [30] they are thrown on to dry land and gasp. 471ᵇ Moreover, always when respiring animals are killed by being suffocated in water, bubbles are formed of the air which is forcibly discharged, as happens, e.g. when one

forces a tortoise or a frog or any other animal of a similar class to stay beneath water. But with fishes this result never occurs, in whatsoever way we try to obtain it, since they do [5] not contain air drawn from an external source. Again, the manner of respiration said to exist in them might occur in the case of men also when they are under water. For if fishes draw in air out of the surrounding water by means of their mouth why should not men too and other animals do so also; they should also, in the same way as fishes, draw in air out of [10] the mouth. If in the former case it were possible, so also should it be in the latter. But, since in the one it is not so, neither does it occur in the other. Furthermore, why do fishes, if they respire, die in the air and gasp (as can be seen) as in suffocation? It is not want of food that produces this effect upon them, and [15] the reason given by Diogenes is foolish, for he says that in air they take in too much air and hence die, but in the water they take in a moderate amount. But that should be a possible occurrence with land animals also; as facts are, however, no land animal seems to be suffocated by excessive respiration. Again, if all animals breathe, insects must do so also. [20] But many of them seem to live though divided not merely into two, but into several parts, e.g. the class called Scolopendra. But how can they, when thus divided, breathe, and what is the organ they employ? The main reason why these writers have not given a good account of these facts is that they have no acquaintance with the internal organs, and that [25] they did not accept the doctrine that there is a final cause for whatever Nature does. If they had asked for what purpose respiration exists in animals, and had considered this with reference to the organs, e.g. the gills and the lungs, they would have discovered the reason more speedily.

10 (4)

[30] Democritus, however, does teach that in the breathing animals there is a certain result produced by respiration; he asserts that it prevents the soul from being extruded from the 472a body. Nevertheless, he by no means asserts that it is for this purpose that Nature so contrives it, for he, like the other physical philosophers, altogether fails to attain to any such explanation. His statement is that the soul and the hot element are identical, being the primary forms among the spherical particles. Hence, [5] when these are being crushed together by the surrounding atmosphere thrusting them out, respiration, according to his account, comes in to succour them. For in the air there are many of those particles which he calls mind and soul. Hence, when we breathe and the air enters, these enter along with it, and by their action cancel the pressure, thus preventing the expulsion of the soul which resides in the animal.

[10] This explains why life and death are bound up with the taking in and letting out of the breath; for death occurs when the compression by the surrounding air gains the upper hand, and, the animal being unable to respire, the air from outside can no longer enter and counteract the compression. Death is the departure of those forms owing to the expulsive pressure exerted by the surrounding air. Death, however, occurs not by haphazard but, when natural, owing to old age, and, when unnatural, to violence.

But the reason for this and why all must die Democritus has by no means made clear. And yet, since evidently death occurs at one time of life and not at another, he should have said [20] whether the cause is external or internal. Neither does he assign the cause of the beginning of respiration, nor say whether it is internal or external. Indeed, it is not the case that the external mind superintends the reinforcement; rather the origin of breathing and of the respiratory motion must be within: it is not due to pressure from around. It is absurd also that what surrounds should compress and at the same time by entering dilate. This then is [25] practically his theory, and how he puts it.

But if we must consider that our previous account is true, and that respiration does not occur in every animal, we must deem that this explains death not universally, but only in respiring animals. Yet neither is it a good account of these even, as may clearly be [30] seen from the facts and phenomena of which we all have experience. For in hot weather we grow warmer, and, having more need of respiration, we always breathe faster. But, when the air around is cold and contracts and solidifies the body, retardation of the breathing results. Yet this was just the time when the external air should enter and annul the expulsive movement, whereas it is the opposite that occurs. For when the breath is not let out and the heat accumulates too much then we need to respire, and to respire we must draw in the breath. When hot, people breathe rapidly, because they must do so in order to cool themselves, just when the theory of Democritus would make them add fire to fire.

11 (5)

The theory found in the *Timaeus,* of the passing round of the breath by pushing, by no means determines how, in the case of the animals other than land-animals, their heat is preserved, and whether it is due to the same or a different cause. For if respiration occurs only in land-animals we should be told what is the [10] reason of that. Likewise, if it is found in others also, but in a different form, this form of respiration, if they all can breathe, must also be described.

Further, the method of explaining involves a fiction. It is said that when the hot air issues from the mouth it pushes the surrounding air, which being carried on enters the very place [15] whence the internal warmth issued, through the interstices of the porous flesh; and this reciprocal replacement is due to the fact that a vacuum cannot exist. But when it has become hot the air passes out again by the same route, and pushes back inwards through the mouth the air that had been discharged in a warm condition. It is said that it is this action which goes on continuously when the breath is taken in and let out.
[20] But according to this way of thinking it will follow that we breathe out before we breathe in. But the opposite is the case, as evidence shows, for though these two functions go on in alternation, yet the last act when life comes to a close is the letting out of the breath, and hence its admission must have been the beginning of the process.

Once more, those who give this kind of explanation by no means state the final cause of the presence in animals of this function (to [25] wit the admission and emission of the breath), but treat it as though it were a contingent accompaniment of life. Yet it evidently has control over life and death, for it results synchronously that when respiring animals are unable to breathe they perish. Again, it is absurd [30] that the passage of the hot air out through the mouth and back again should be quite perceptible, while we were not able to detect the thoracic influx and the return outwards once more of the heated breath. It is also nonsense that respiration should consist in the entrance of heat, for the evidence is to the contrary effect; what is breathed out is hot, and [35] what is breathed in is cold. When it is hot we pant in breathing, for, because what enters 473ª does not adequately perform its cooling function, we have as a consequence to draw the breath frequently.

12 (6)

It is certain, however, that we must not entertain the notion that it is for purposes of nutrition that respiration is designed, and believe that the internal fire is fed by the breath; [5] respiration, as it were, adding fuel to the fire, while the feeding of the flame results in the outward passage of the breath. To combat this doctrine I shall repeat what I said in opposition to the previous theories. This, or something analogous to it, should occur in the other animals also (on this theory), for all possess [10] vital heat. Further, how are we to describe this fictitious process of the generation of heat from the breath? Observation shows rather that it is a product of the food. A consequence also of this theory is that the nutriment would enter and the refuse be discharged by the same channel, but this does not appear to occur in the other instances.

13 (7)

[15] Empedocles also gives an account of respiration without, however, making clear what its purpose is, or whether or not it is universal in animals. Also when dealing with respiration by means of the nostrils he imgaines he is dealing with what is the primary kind of respiration. Even the breath which passes through the nostrils passes through the windpipe out [20] of the chest as well, and without the latter the nostrils cannot act. Again, when animals are bereft of respiration through the nostrils, no detrimental result ensues, but, when prevented from breathing through the windpipe, they die. Nature employs respiration through the nostrils as a secondary function in [25] certain animals in order to enable them to smell. But the reason why it exists in some only is that though almost all animals are endowed with the sense of smell, the sense-organ is not the same in all.

A more precise account has been given about 473ᵇ this elsewhere.[1] Empedocles, however, explains the passage inwards and outwards of the breath, by the theory that there are certain blood-vessels, which, while containing blood, are not filled by it, but have passages leading to the outer air, the calibre of which is fine in

---

[1] Cf. *On the Soul,* III, 421ª 10; *Sense and the Sensible,* chapter 5, 443ª 4, 444ᵇ 7-15; *History of Animals,* IV, 534ᵇ 16; *On the Parts of Animals,* II, 659ᵇ 15.

contrast to the size of the solid particles, but [5] large relatively to those in the air. Hence, since it is the nature of the blood to move upwards and downwards, when it moves down the air rushes in and inspiration occurs; when the blood rises, the air is forced out and the outward motion of the breath results. He compares this process to what occurs in a clepsydra.

> Thus all things outwards breathe and in;—
> their flesh has tubes
> [10] Bloodless, that stretch towards the body's
> outmost edge,
> Which, at their mouths, full many frequent
> channels pierce,
> Cleaving the extreme nostrils through; thus,
> while the gore
> Lies hid, for air is cut a thoroughfare most
> plain.
> And thence, whenever shrinks away the tender blood,
> [15] Enters the blustering wind with swelling
> billow wild.
> But when the blood leaps up, backward it
> breathes. As when
> With water-clock of polished bronze a maiden
> sporting,
> Sets on her comely hand the narrow of the tube
> And dips it in the frail-formed water's silvery
> sheen;
> [20] Not then the flood the vessel enters, but
> the air,
> Pressing within on the dense orifices, checks it,
> Until she frees the crowded stream. But then
> indeed
> Upon the air's escape runs in the water meet.
> So also when within the vessel's deeps the water
> [25] Remains, the opening by the hand of
> flesh being closed,
> The outer air that entrance craves restrains the
> flood
> At the gates of the sounding narrow, upon the
> surface pressing,
> Until the maid withdraws her hand. But
> then in contrariwise
> Once more the air comes in and water meet
> flows out.
> Thus to the subtle blood, surging throughout
> the limbs,
> Whene'er it shrinks away into the far recesses
> Admits a stream of air rushing with swelling
> wave,
> [5] But, when it backward leaps, in like bulk
> air flows out.

This then is what he says of respiration. But, as we said, all animals that evidently respire do so by means of the windpipe, when they breathe either through the mouth or through the nostrils. Hence, if it is of this kind of res- [10] piration that he is talking, we must ask how it tallies with the explanation given. But the facts seem to be quite opposed. The chest is raised in the manner of a forge-bellows when the breath is drawn in—it is quite reasonable that it should be heat which raises up and that the blood should occupy the hot region—but it collapses and sinks down, like the bellows once [15] more, when the breath is let out. The difference is that in a bellows it is not by the same channel that the air is taken in and let out, but in breathing it is.

But, if Empedocles is accounting only for respiration through the nostrils, he is much in error, for that does not involve the nostrils alone, but passes by the channel beside the [20] uvula where the extremity of the roof of the mouth is, some of the air going this way through the apertures of the nostrils and some through the mouth, both when it enters and when it passes out. Such then is the nature and magnitude of the difficulties besetting the theories of other writers concerning respiration.

14 (8)

[25] We have already stated that life and the presence of soul involve a certain heat. Not even the digesting process to which is due the nutrition of animals occurs apart from soul and warmth, for it is to fire that in all cases elaboration is due. It is for this reason, precisely, that the primary nutritive soul also must [30] be located in that part of the body and in that division of this region which is the immediate vehicle of this principle. The region in question is intermediate between that where food enters and that where excrement is discharged. In bloodless animals it has no name, but in the sanguineous class this organ is called the heart. The blood constitutes the nutriment from which the organs of the animal are directly formed. Likewise the blood- [5] vessels must have the same originating source, since the one exists for the other's behoof—as a vessel or receptacle for it. In sanguineous animals the heart is the starting-point of the veins; they do not traverse it, but are found to stretch out from it, as dissections enable us to see.

[10] Now the other psychical faculties cannot exist apart from the power of nutrition (the reason has already been stated in the treatise

On the Soul),[1] and this depends on the natural fire, by the union with which Nature has set it aglow. But fire, as we have already stated, is destroyed in two ways, either by extinction or by exhaustion. It suffers extinction from its [15] opposites. Hence it can be extinguished by the surrounding cold both when in mass and (though more speedily) when scattered. Now this way of perishing is due to violence equally in living and in lifeless objects, for the division of an animal by instruments and consequent congelation by excess of cold cause death. But exhaustion is due to excess of heat; [20] for, if there is too much heat close at hand and the thing burning does not have a fresh supply of fuel added to it, it goes out by exhaustion, not by the action of cold. Hence, if it is going to continue it must be cooled, for cold is a preventive against this form of extinction.

15 (9)

[25] Some animals occupy the water, others live on land, and, that being so, in the case of those which are very small and bloodless the refrigeration due to the surrounding water or air is sufficient to prevent destruction from this cause. Having little heat, they require little [30] cold to combat it. Hence too such animals are almost all short-lived, for, being small, they have less scope for deflection towards either extreme. But some insects are longer-lived 475a (though bloodless, like all the others), and these have a deep indentation beneath the waist, in order to secure cooling through the membrane, which there is thinner. They are warmer animals and hence require more refrigeration, and such are bees (some of which [5] live as long as seven years) and all that make a humming noise, like wasps, cockchafers, and crickets. They make a sound as if of panting by means of air, for, in the middle section itself, the air which exists internally and is involved in their construction, causing a rising and falling movement, produces friction against the membrane. The way in which they [10] move this region is like the motion due to the lungs in animals that breathe the outer air, or to the gills in fishes. What occurs is comparable to the suffocation of a respiring animal by holding its mouth, for then the lung causes a heaving motion of this kind. In the case of these animals this internal motion is not sufficient for refrigeration, but in insects it is. It is [15] by friction against the membrane that

[1] *On the Soul*, I, 411b 18; II, 413b 1.

they produce the humming sound, as we said, in the way that children do by blowing through the holes of a reed covered by a fine membrane. It is thus that the singing crickets too produce their song; they possess greater warmth and are indented at the waist, but the songless variety have no fissure there.

[20] Animals also which are sanguineous and possess a lung, though that contains little blood and is spongy, can in some cases, owing to the latter fact, live a long time without breathing; for the lung, containing little blood or fluid, can rise a long way: its own motion can for a long time produce sufficient refrigeration. But [25] at last it ceases to suffice, and the animal dies of suffocation if it does not respire—as we have already said. For of exhaustion that kind which is destruction due to lack of refrigeration is called suffocation, and whatsoever is thus destroyed is said to be suffocated.

We have already stated that among animals insects do not respire, and the fact is open to [30] observation in the case of even small creatures like flies and bees, for they can swim about in a fluid for a long time if it is not too 475b hot or too cold. Yet animals with little strength tend to breathe more frequently. These, however, die of what is called suffocation when the stomach becomes filled and the heat in the central segment is destroyed. This explains also why they revive after being among ashes for a time.

[5] Again among water-animals those that are bloodless remain alive longer in air than those that have blood and admit the sea-water, as, for example, fishes. Since it is a small quantity of heat they possess, the air is for a long time adequate for the purposes of refrigeration in [10] such animals as the crustacea and the polyps. It does not however suffice, owing to their want of heat, to keep them finally in life, for most fishes also live though among earth, yet in a motionless state, and are to be found by digging. For all animals that have no lung at all or have a bloodless one require less refrigeration.

16 (10)

[15] Concerning the bloodless animals we have declared that in some cases it is the surrounding air, in others fluid, that aids the maintenance of life. But in the case of animals possessing blood and heart, all which have a lung admit the air and produce the cooling effect by breathing in and out. All animals have [20] a lung that are viviparous and are so in-

ternally, not externally merely (the Selachia are viviparous, but not internally), and of the oviparous class those that have wings, e.g. birds, and those with scales, e.g. tortoises, lizards, and snakes. The former class have a lung charged with blood, but in the most part of the latter it is spongy. Hence they employ res-[25] piration more sparingly as already said. The function is found also in all that frequent and pass their life in the water, e.g. the class of water-snakes and frogs and crocodiles and hemydes, both sea- and land-tortoises, and seals.

All these and similar animals both bring [30] forth on land and sleep on shore or, when they do so in the water, keep the head 476ᵃ above the surface in order to respire. But all with gills produce refrigeration by taking in water; the Selachia and all other footless animals have gills. Fish are footless, and the limbs they have get their name (πτερύγιον) [5] from their similarity to wings (πτέρυξ). But of those with feet one only, so far as observed, has gills. It is called the tadpole.

No animal yet has been seen to possess both lungs and gills, and the reason for this is that the lung is designed for the purpose of refrigeration by means of the air (it seems to have derived its name (πνεύμων) from its function [10] as a receptacle of the breath (πνεῦμα)), while gills are relevant to refrigeration by water. Now for one purpose one organ is adapted and one single means of refrigeration is sufficient in every case. Hence, since we see that Nature does nothing in vain, and if there were two organs one would be purposeless, this is [15] the reason why some animals have gills, others lungs, but none possess both.

17 (11)

Every animal in order to exist requires nutriment, in order to prevent itself from dying, refrigeration; and so Nature employs the same organ for both purposes. For, as in some cases the tongue serves both for discerning tastes [20] and for speech, so in animals with lungs the mouth is employed both in working up the food and in the passage of the breath outwards and inwards. In lungless and non-respiring animals it is employed in working up the food, while in those of them that require refrigeration it is the gills that are created for this purpose.

[25] We shall state further on how it is that these organs have the faculty of producing refrigeration. But to prevent their food from impeding these operations there is a similar contrivance in the respiring animals and in those that admit water. At the moment of respiration they do not take in food, for otherwise [30] suffocation results owing to the food, whether liquid or dry, slipping in through the windpipe and lying on the lung. The windpipe is situated before the oesophagus, through which food passes into what is called the stomach, but in quadrupeds which are sanguineous there is, as it were, a lid over the windpipe—the epiglottis. In birds and oviparous quadrupeds this covering is absent, but its office is discharged by a contraction of the windpipe. The latter class contract the windpipe when swallowing their food; the former close down the epiglottis. When the food has passed, the epiglottis is in the one case raised, and in the other the windpipe is expanded, and the air enters to effect refrigeration. In animals with [5] gills the water is first discharged through them and then the food passes in through the mouth; they have no windpipe and hence can take no harm from liquid lodging in this organ, only from its entering the stomach. For these reasons the expulsion of water and the [10] seizing of their food is rapid, and their teeth are sharp and in almost all cases arranged in a saw-like fashion, for they are debarred from chewing their food.

18 (12)

Among water-animals the cetaceans may give rise to some perplexity, though they too can be rationally explained.

[15] Examples of such animals are dolphins and whales, and all others that have a blow-hole. They have no feet, yet possess a lung though admitting the sea-water. The reason for possessing a lung is that which we have now stated [refrigeration]; the admission of water is not for the purpose of refrigeration. That is effected by respiration, for they have a lung. [20] Hence they sleep with their head out of the water, and dolphins, at any rate, snore. Further, if they are entangled in nets they soon die of suffocation owing to lack of respiration, and hence they can be seen to come to the surface owing to the necessity of breathing. But, since they have to feed in the water, they must [25] admit it, and it is in order to discharge this that they all have a blow-hole; after admitting the water they expel it through the blow-hole as the fishes do through the gills. The position of the blow-hole is an indication of this, for it leads to none of the organs which

are charged with blood; but it lies before the brain and thence discharges water.

[30] It is for the very same reason that molluscs and crustaceans admit water— I mean such animals as Carabi and Carcini. For none of these is refrigeration a necessity, for in every case they have little heat and are bloodless, and hence are sufficiently cooled by the surrounding water. But in feeding they admit water, and hence must expel it in order to prevent its being swallowed simultaneously with the food. Thus crustaceans, like the Carcini and Carabi, discharge water through the folds beside their shaggy parts, while cuttlefish and the polyps employ for this purpose the hollow above the head. There is, however, a [5] more precise account of these in the *History of Animals*.[1]

Thus it has been explained that the cause of the admission of the water is refrigeration, and [10] the fact that animals constituted for a life in water must feed in it.

19 (13)

An account must next be given of refrigeration and the manner in which it occurs in respiring animals and those possessed of gills. We have already said that all animals with lungs respire. The reason why some creatures have [15] this organ, and why those having it need respiration, is that the higher animals have a greater proportion of heat, for at the same time they must have been assigned a higher soul and they have a higher nature than plants. Hence too those with most blood and most warmth in the lung are of greater size, and [20] that animal in which the blood in the lung is purest and most plentiful is the most erect, namely man; and the reason why he alone has his upper part directed to the upper part of the universe is that he possesses such a lung. Hence this organ as much as any other must be assigned to the essence of the animal both in man and in other cases.

[25] This then is the purpose of refrigeration. As for the constraining and efficient cause, we must believe that it created animals like this, just as it created many others also not of this constitution. For some have a greater proportion of earth in their composition, like plants, and others, e.g. aquatic animals, contain a larger amount of water; while winged and terrestrial animals have an excess of air and fire [30] respectively. It is always in the region

[1] Cf. *History of Animals*, II. 2; IV. 1-3.

proper to the element preponderating in the scheme of their constitution that things exist.

20 (14)

Empedocles is then in error when he says that those animals which have the most warmth and fire live in the water to counterbalance the excess of heat in their constitution, in order that, since they are deficient in cold and fluid, they may be kept in life by the contrary character of the region they occupy; for water has less heat than air. But it is wholly [5] absurd that the water-animals should in every case originate on dry land, and afterwards change their place of abode to the water; for they are almost all footless. He, however, when describing their original structure says that, though originating on dry land, they have abandoned it and migrated to the water. But again it is evident that they are not warm- [10] er than land-animals, for in some cases they have no blood at all, in others little.

The question, however, as to what sorts of animals should be called warm and what cold, has in each special case received consideration. Though in one respect there is reason in the explanation which Empedocles aims at establishing, yet his account is not correct. Excess in [15] a bodily state is cured by a situation or season of opposite character, but the constitution is best maintained by an environment akin to it. There is a difference between the material of which any animal is constituted and the states and dispositions of that material. For example, if nature were to constitute a thing of wax or of ice, she would not preserve it by [20] putting it in a hot place, for the opposing quality would quickly destroy it, seeing that heat dissolves that which cold congeals. Again, a thing composed of salt or nitre would not be taken and placed in water, for fluid dissolves that of which the consistency is due to the hot and the dry.

Hence if the fluid and the dry supply the material for all bodies, it is reasonable that things the composition of which is due to the fluid and the cold should have liquid for their [25] medium [and, if they are cold, they will exist in the cold], while that which is due to the dry will be found in the dry. Thus trees grow not in water but on dry land. But the same theory would relegate them to the water, on account of their excess of dryness, just as it does the things that are excessively fiery. They would migrate thither not on account of its cold but owing to its fluidity.

[30] Thus the natural character of the material of objects is of the same nature as the region in which they exist; the liquid is found in 478ᵃ liquid, the dry on land, the warm in air. With regard, however, to states of body, a cold situation has, on the other hand, a beneficial effect on excess of heat, and a warm environment on excess of cold, for the region reduces to a mean the excess in the bodily condition. The regions appropriate to each material and the revolutions of the seasons which all expe- [5] rience supply the means which must be sought in order to correct such excesses; but, while states of the body can be opposed in character to the environment, the material of which it is composed can never be so. This, then, is a sufficient explanation of why it is not owing to the heat in their constitution that some animals are aquatic, others terrestrial, as Empedocles maintains, and of why some pos- [10] sess lungs and others do not.

21 (15)

The explanation of the admission of air and respiration in those animals in which a lung is found, and especially in those in which it is full of blood, is to be found in the fact that it is of a spongy nature and full of tubes, and that it is the most fully charged with blood of all the visceral organs. All animals with a full- [15] blooded lung require rapid refrigeration because there is little scope for deviation from the normal amount of their vital fire; the air also must penetrate all through it on account of the large quantity of blood and heat it contains. But both these operations can be easily performed by air, for, being of a subtle nature, it penetrates everywhere and that rapidly, and so performs its cooling function; but water has [20] the opposite characteristics.

The reason why animals with a full-blooded lung respire most is hence manifest; the more heat there is, the greater is the need for refrigeration, and at the same time breath can easily [25] pass to the source of heat in the heart.

22 (16)

In order to understand the way in which the heart is connected with the lung by means of passages, we must consult both dissections and the account in the *History of Animals*.[1] The universal cause of the need which the animal has for refrigeration, is the union of the soul with fire that takes place in the heart. Respira- [30] tion is the means of effecting refrigera-

[1] *History of Animals*, I. 17; III, 2-3.

tion, of which those animals make use that possess a lung as well as a heart. But when they, as for example the fishes, which on account of their aquatic nature have no lung, possess the latter organ without the former, the cooling is effected through the gills by means of water. For ocular evidence as to how the [35] heart is situated relatively to the gills we must employ dissections, and for precise details 478ᵇ we must refer to Natural History.[2] As a summarizing statement, however, and for present purposes, the following is the account of the matter.

It might appear that the heart has not the same position in terrestrial animals and in fishes, but the position really is identical, for the apex of the heart is in the direction in [5] which they incline their heads. But it is towards the mouth in fishes that the apex of the heart points, seeing that they do not incline their heads in the same direction as land-animals do. Now from the extremity of the heart a tube of a sinewy, arterial character runs to the centre where the gills all join. This then [10] is the largest of those ducts, but on either side of the heart others also issue and run to the extremity of each gill, and by means of the ceaseless flow of water through the gills, effect the cooling which passes to the heart.

In similar fashion as the fish move their gills, respiring animals with rapid action raise and let fall the chest according as the breath is ad- [15] mitted or expelled. If air is limited in amount and unchanged they are suffocated, for either medium, owing to contact with the blood, rapidly becomes hot. The heat of the blood counteracts the refrigeration and, when respiring animals can no longer move the lung [20] or aquatic animals their gills, whether owing to disease or old age, their death ensues.

(On Life and Death I)

23 (17)

To be born and to die are common to all animals, but there are specifically diverse ways in which these phenomena occur; of destruction there are different types, though yet something is common to them all. There is violent death [25] and again natural death, and the former occurs when the cause of death is external, the latter when it is internal, and involved from the beginning in the constitution of the organ, and not an affection derived from a foreign

[2] *Ibid.*, II, 507ᵇ 3.

source. In the case of plants the name given to this is withering, in animals senility. Death and decay pertain to all things that are not imperfectly developed; to the imperfect also they [30] may be ascribed in nearly the same but not an identical sense. Under the imperfect I class eggs and seeds of plants as they are before the root appears.

It is always to some lack of heat that death is due, and in perfect creatures the cause is its failure in the organ containing the source of the creature's essential nature. This member is situate, as has been said, at the junction of the upper and lower parts; in plants it is intermediate between the root and the stem, in san- [35] guineous animals it is the heart, and in those that are bloodless the corresponding part 479a of their body. But some of these animals have potentially many sources of life, though in actuality they possess only one. This is why some insects live when divided, and why, even among sanguineous animals, all whose vitality is not intense live for a long time after the heart has been removed. Tortoises, for exam- [5] ple, do so and make movements with their feet, so long as the shell is left, a fact to be explained by the natural inferiority of their constitution, as it is in insects also.

The source of life is lost to its possessors when the heat with which it is bound up is no longer tempered by cooling, for, as I have [10] often remarked, it is consumed by itself. Hence when, owing to lapse of time, the lung in the one class and the gills in the other get dried up, these organs become hard and earthy and incapable of movement, and cannot be expanded or contracted. Finally things come to a climax, and the fire goes out from exhaustion.

[15] Hence a small disturbance will speedily cause death in old age. Little heat remains, for the most of it has been breathed away in the long period of life preceding, and hence any increase of strain on the organ quickly causes extinction. It is just as though the heart contained a tiny feeble flame which the slightest [20] movement puts out. Hence in old age death is painless, for no violent disturbance is required to cause death, and there is an entire absence of feeling when the soul's connexion is severed. All diseases which harden the lung by forming tumours or waste residues, or by excess of morbid heat, as happens in fevers, [25] accelerate the breathing owing to the inability of the lung to move far either upwards or downwards. Finally, when motion is no longer possible, the breath is given out and death ensues.

24 (18)

Generation is the initial participation, mediated by warm substance, in the nutritive soul, and life is the maintenance of this participa- [30] tion. Youth is the period of the growth of the primary organ of refrigeration, old age of its decay, while the intervening time is the prime of life.

A violent death or dissolution consists in the extinction or exhaustion of the vital heat (for either of these may cause dissolution), while 479b natural death is the exhaustion of the heat owing to lapse of time, and occurring at the end of life. In plants this is to wither, in animals to die. Death, in old age, is the exhaustion due to inability on the part of the organ, owing to old age, to produce refrigeration. [5] This then is our account of generation and life and death, and the reason for their occurrence in animals.

25 (19)

It is hence also clear why respiring animals are suffocated in water and fishes in air. For it [10] is by water in the latter class, by air in the former that refrigeration is effected, and either of these means of performing the function is removed by a change of environment.

There is also to be explained in either case the cause of the motion of the gills and of the lungs, the rise and fall of which effects the admission and expulsion of the breath or of wa- [15] ter. The following, moreover, is the manner of the constitution of the organ.

... (On Life and Death II)

26 (20)

In connexion with the heart there are three phenomena, which, though apparently of the same nature, are really not so, namely palpitation, pulsation, and respiration.

Palpitation is the rushing together of the hot substance in the heart owing to the chilling in- [20] fluence of residual or waste products. It occurs, for example, in the ailment known as 'spasms' and in other diseases. It occurs also in fear, for when one is afraid the upper parts become cold, and the hot substance, fleeing away, by its concentration in the heart produces pal- [25] pitation. It is crushed into so small a space that sometimes life is extinguished, and the animals die of the fright and morbid disturbance.

The beating of the heart, which, as can be seen, goes on continuously, is similar to the throbbing of an abscess. That, however, is accompanied by pain, because the change produced in the blood is unnatural, and it goes on until the matter formed by concoction is discharged. There is a similarity between this phenomenon and that of boiling; for boiling is due to the volatilization of fluid by heat and the expansion consequent on increase of bulk. But in an abscess, if there is no evaporation through the walls, the process terminates in suppuration due to the thickening of the liquid, while in boiling it ends in the escape of the fluid out of the containing vessel.

In the heart the beating is produced by the heat expanding the fluid, of which the food furnishes a constant supply. It occurs when the fluid rises to the outer wall of the heart, and it goes on continuously; for there is a constant flow of the fluid that goes to constitute the blood, it being in the heart that the blood receives its primary elaboration. That this is so we can perceive in the initial stages of generation, for the heart can be seen to contain blood before the veins become distinct. This explains why pulsation in youth exceeds that in older people, for in the young the formation of vapour is more abundant.

All the veins pulse, and do so simultaneously with each other, owing to their connexion with the heart. The heart always beats, and hence they also beat continuously and simultaneously with each other and with it.

Palpitation, then, is the recoil of the heart against the compression due to cold; and pulsation is the volatilization of the heated fluid.

27 (21)

Respiration takes place when the hot substance which is the seat of the nutritive principle increases. For it, like the rest of the body, requires nutrition, and more so than the members, for it is through it that they are nourished. But when it increases it necessarily causes the organ to rise. This organ we must take to be constructed like the bellows in a smithy, for both heart and lungs conform pretty well to this shape. Such a structure must be double, for the nutritive principle must be situated in the centre of the natural force.

Thus on increase of bulk expansion results, which necessarily causes the surrounding parts to rise. Now this can be seen to occur when people respire; they raise their chest because the motive principle of the organ described resident within the chest causes an identical expansion of this organ. When it dilates the outer air must rush in as into a bellows, and, being cold, by its chilling influence reduces by extinction the excess of the fire. But, as the increase of bulk causes the organ to dilate, so diminution causes contraction, and when it collapses the air which entered must pass out again. When it enters the air is cold, but on issuing it is warm owing to its contact with the heat resident in this organ, and this is specially the case in those animals that possess a full-blooded lung. The numerous canal-like ducts in the lung, into which it passes, have each a blood-vessel lying alongside, so that the whole lung is thought to be full of blood. The inward passage of the air is called respiration, the outward expiration, and this double movement goes on continuously just so long as the animal lives and keeps this organ in continuous motion; it is for this reason that life is bound up with the passage of the breath outwards and inwards.

It is in the same way that the motion of the gills in fishes takes place. When the hot substance in the blood throughout the members rises, the gills rise too, and let the water pass through, but when it is chilled and retreats through its channels to the heart, they contract and eject the water. Continually as the heat in the heart rises, continually on being chilled it returns thither again. Hence, as in respiring animals life and death are bound up with respiration, so in the other animals class they depend on the admission of water.

Our discussion of life and death and kindred topics is now practically complete. But health and disease also claim the attention of the scientist, and not merely of the physician, in so far as an account of their causes is concerned. The extent to which these two differ and investigate diverse provinces must not escape us, since facts show that their inquiries are, to a certain extent, at least conterminous. For physicians of culture and refinement make some mention of natural science, and claim to derive their principles from it, while the most accomplished investigators into nature generally push their studies so far as to conclude with an account of medical principles.